Trapezoid: A four-sided figure with one pair of parallel sides

Area: $A = \frac{1}{2}h(b_1 + b_2)$

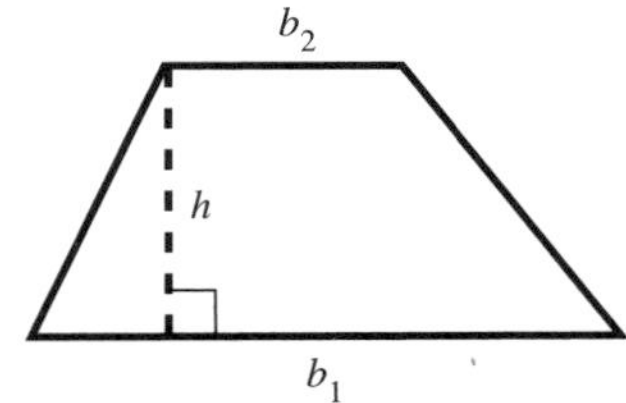

Parallelogram: A four-sided figure with opposite sides parallel

Area: $A = bh$

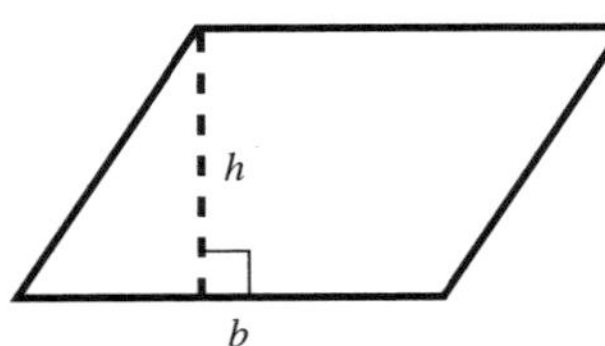

Rectangle: A four-sided figure with four right angles

Area: $A = LW$

Perimeter: $P = 2L + 2W$

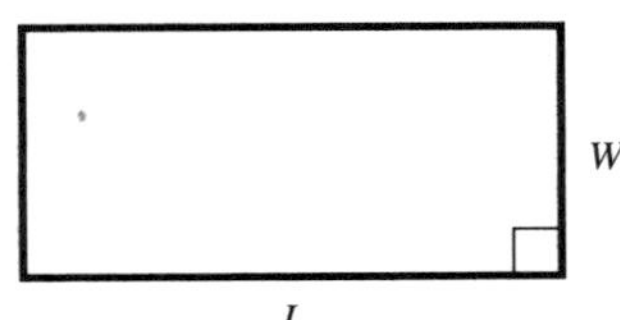

Rhombus: A four-sided figure with four equal sides

Perimeter: $P = 4a$

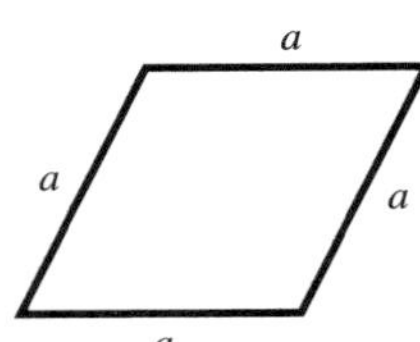

Square: A four-sided figure with four equal sides and four right angles

Area: $A = s^2$

Perimeter: $P = 4s$

s

Circle

Area: $A = \pi r^2$

Circumference: $C = 2\pi r$

Diameter: $d = 2r$

Value of pi: $\pi \approx 3.14$

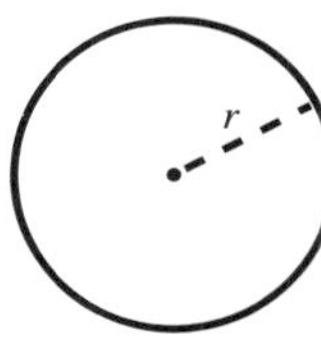

Sphere

Volume: $V = \frac{4}{3}\pi r^3$

Surface Area: $S = 4\pi r^2$

Right Circular Cone

Volume: $V = \frac{1}{3}\pi r^2 h$

Lateral Surface Area: $S = \pi r\sqrt{r^2 +}$.

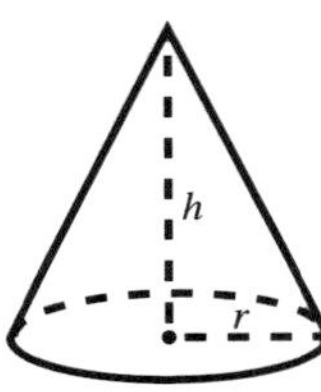

Right Circular Cylinder

Volume: $V = \pi r^2 h$

Lateral Surface Area: $S = 2\pi rh$

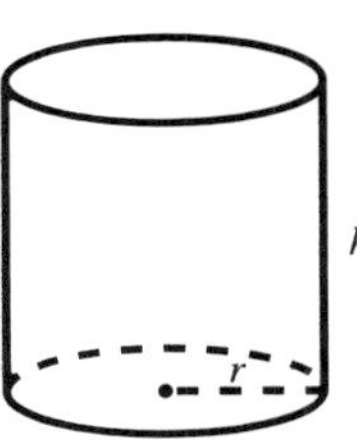

Rectangular Solid

Volume: $V = LWH$

Surface Area:
$A = 2LW + 2WH + 2LH$

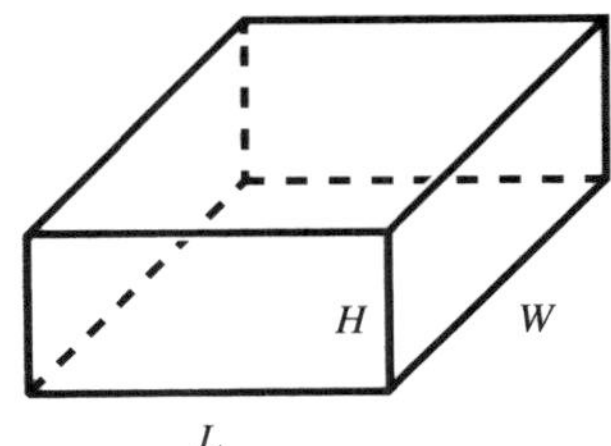

Elementary Algebra

sixth edition

Mark Dugopolski
Southeastern Louisiana University

McGraw-Hill Higher Education

Boston Burr Ridge, IL Dubuque, IA New York San Francisco St. Louis
Bangkok Bogotá Caracas Kuala Lumpur Lisbon London Madrid Mexico City
Milan Montreal New Delhi Santiago Seoul Singapore Sydney Taipei Toronto

The McGraw·Hill Companies

ELEMENTARY ALGEBRA, SIXTH EDITION

This book is printed on acid-free paper.

1 2 3 4 5 6 7 8 9 0 VNH/VNH 0 9 8

ISBN 978–0–07–353350–6
MHID 0–07–353350–5

ISBN 978–0–07–334076–0 (Annotated Instructor's Edition)
MHID 0–07–334076–6

Editorial Director: *Stewart K. Mattson*
Senior Sponsoring Editor: *Richard Kolasa*
Senior Developmental Editor: *Michelle L. Flomenhoft*
Marketing Manager: *Torie Anderson*
Senior Project Manager: *Vicki Krug*
Lead Production Supervisor: *Sandy Ludovissy*
Lead Media Project Manager: *Stacy A. Patch*
Designer: *John Joran*
Interior Designer: *Asylum Studios*
(USE) Cover Image: © *iStockphoto/Giovanni Rinaldi*
Lead Photo Research Coordinator: *Carrie K. Burger*
Supplement Producer: *Melissa M. Leick*
Compositor: *ICC Macmillan Inc.*
Typeface: *10.5/12 Times Roman*
Printer: *Von Hoffmann Press*

Photo Credits:
Page 75: © Vol. 141/Corbis; p. 82: © Reuters/Corbis; p. 151: © George Disario/Corbis; p. 195 (bottom): © Ann M. Job/AP/Wide World Photos; p. 235 (middle): © Gary Conner/PhotoEdit; p. 240: © Michael Keller/Corbis; p. 257: © Richard T. Nowitz/Corbis; p. 297: © DV169/Digital Vision; p. 558: © DV49/Digital Vision. All other photos © PhotoDisc/Getty.

Library of Congress Cataloging-in-Publication Data

Dugopolski, Mark.
Elementary algebra / Mark Dugopolski. — 6th ed.
p. cm.
Includes index.
ISBN 978–0–07–353350–6 — ISBN 0–07–353350–5 (hard copy : acid-free paper) 1. Algebra—Textbooks. I. Title.
QA152.3.D839 2009
512.9—dc22

2007028859

www.mhhe.com

In loving memory of my parents,
Walter and Anne Dugopolski

About the Author

Mark Dugopolski was born and raised in Menominee, Michigan. He received a degree in mathematics education from Michigan State University and then taught high school mathematics in the Chicago area. While teaching high school, he received a master's degree in mathematics from Northern Illinois University. He then entered a doctoral program in mathematics at the University of Illinois in Champaign, where he earned his doctorate in topology in 1977. He was then appointed to the faculty at Southeastern Louisiana University, where he taught for 25 years. He is now professor emeritus of mathematics at SLU. He is a member of MAA and AMATYC. He has written many articles and numerous mathematics textbooks. He has a wife and two daughters. When he is not working, he enjoys gardening, hiking, bicycling, jogging, tennis, fishing, and motorcycling.

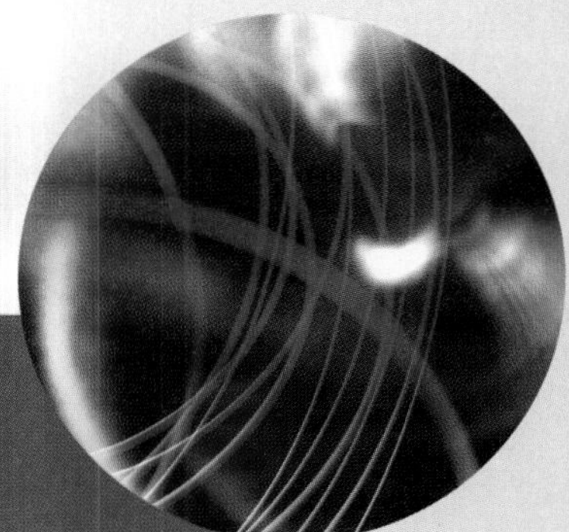

Contents

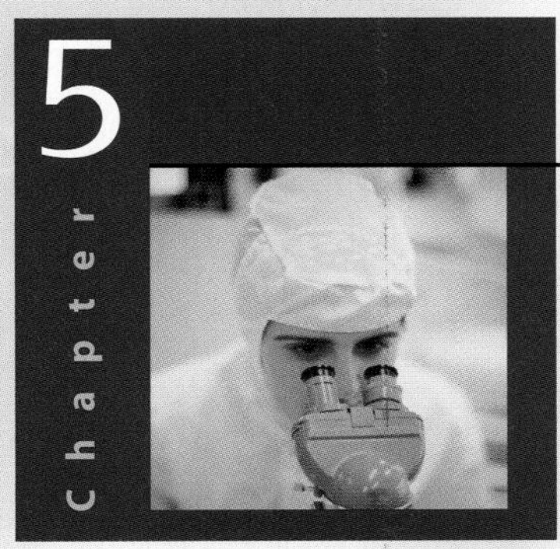

Exponents and Polynomials 297

Factoring 361

Rational Expressions 419

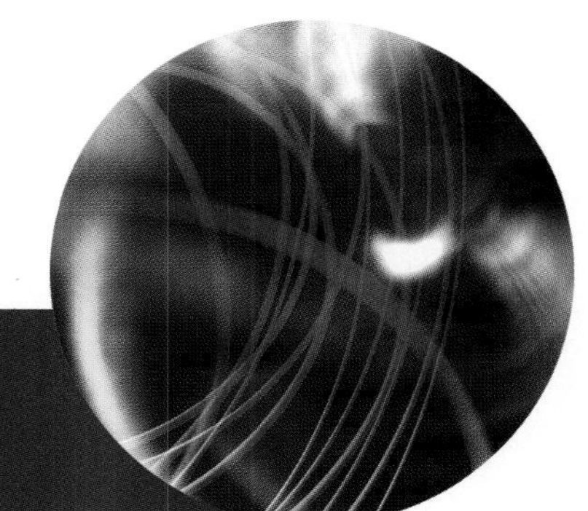

Preface

FROM THE AUTHOR

I would like to thank the many students and faculty that have used my books over the years. You have provided me with excellent feedback that has assisted me in writing a better, more student-focused book in each edition. Your comments are always taken seriously, and I have adjusted my focus on each revision to satisfy your needs.

In this edition, subsection heads are now in the end-of-section exercise sets, and section heads are now in the Chapter Review exercises. Additionally, I have maintained both the high quality and quantity of exercises and applications for which the series is known.

Understandable Explanations

I originally undertook the task of writing my own book for the elementary algebra course so I could explain mathematical concepts to students in language they would understand. Most books claim to do this, but my experience with a variety of texts had proven otherwise. What students and faculty will find in my book are **short, precise explanations** of terms and concepts that are written in **understandable language.** For example, when I introduce the Commutative Property of Addition, I make the concrete analogy that "the price of a hamburger plus a Coke is the same as the price of a Coke plus a hamburger," a mathematical fact in their daily lives that students can readily grasp. Math doesn't need to remain a mystery to students, and students reading my book will find other analogies like this one that connect abstractions to everyday experiences.

Detailed Examples Keyed to Exercises

My experience as a teacher has taught me two things about examples: they need to be detailed, and they need to help students do their homework. As a result, users of my book will find abundant examples with every step carefully laid out and explained where necessary so that students can follow along in class if the instructor is demonstrating an example on the board. Students will also be able to read them on their own later when they're ready to do the exercise sets. I have also included a **double cross-referencing** system between my examples and exercise sets so that no matter which one students start with, they'll see the connection to the other. All examples in this edition refer to specific exercises by ending with a phrase such as "Now do

Exercises 11–18" so that students will have the opportunity for immediate practice of that concept. If students work an exercise and find they are stumped on how to finish it, they'll see that for that group of exercises they're directed to a specific example to follow as a model. Either way, students will find my book's examples give them the guidance they need to succeed in the course.

Varied Exercises and Applications

A third goal of mine in writing this book was to give students **more variety** in the kinds of exercises they perform than I found in other books. Students won't find an intimidating page of endless drills in my book, but instead will see exercises in manageable groups with specific goals. They will also be able to augment their math proficiency using different formats (true/false, written response, multiple choice) and different methods (discussion, collaboration, calculators). Not only is there an abundance of skill-building exercises, I have also researched a wide variety of **realistic applications** using **real data** so that those "dreaded word problems" will be seen as a useful and practical extension of what students have learned. Finally, every chapter ends with **critical thinking exercises** that go beyond numerical computation and call on students to employ their intuitive problem-solving skills to find the answers to mathematical puzzles in **fun and innovative** ways. With all of these resources to choose from, I am sure that instructors will be comfortable adapting my book to fit their course, and that students will appreciate having a text written for their level and to stimulate their interest.

Listening to Student and Instructor Concerns

McGraw-Hill has given me a wonderful resource for making my textbook more responsive to the immediate concerns of students and faculty. In addition to sending my manuscript out for review by instructors at many different colleges, several times a year McGraw-Hill holds symposia and focus groups with math instructors where the emphasis is *not* on selling products but instead on the **publisher listening** to the needs of faculty and their students. These encounters have provided me with a wealth of ideas on how to improve my chapter organization, make the page layout of my books more readable, and fine-tune exercises in every chapter. Consequently, students and faculty will feel comfortable using my book because it incorporates their specific suggestions and anticipates their needs. These events have particularly helped me in the shaping of the Sixth Edition.

Improvements in the Sixth Edition

- Subsection heads are now in the end-of-section exercise sets, and section heads are now in the Chapter Review Exercises.
- References to page numbers on which Strategy Boxes are located have been inserted into the direction lines for the exercises when appropriate.
- Study tips have been removed from the margins to give the pages a better look. Two study tips now precede each exercise set.
- In **Chapter 1,** unit conversion by the cancellation of units method has been moved to Section 1.2 Fractions. There is a new strategy for finding the LCD, and an improved explanation of subtracting signed numbers. We provided a new example on finding net worth, and improved our explanation on division of signed numbers. Based on reviews, we improved our coverage of order of

operations, and included a new applied example in Section 1.5. Finally, we provided new examples on simplifying algebraic expressions and removing parentheses.

- In **Chapter 3,** points used for graphing lines are now identified on the graph. We improved the graphics in Section 3.2 for slope. There is an improved explanation of why the same slope gives parallel lines and on the relationship of the slopes for perpendicular lines, with new figures. We improved the discussion on the meaning of slope. There is a new boxed summary of how to graph depending on the form of the equation in Section 3.3, as well as a new summary on how to find the slope of a line depending on what is given. Section 3.5 on variation has been rearranged in a more logical order. The number of exercises in the Chapter Review increased by 28. There are many other new exercises as well as lots of minor tweaking to the text, examples, and exercises.
- In **Chapter 4,** we improved the discussion on types of systems of linear equations and added a new figure to make it clear. We included a new example for solving independent equations by graphing. For each method, the systems are now discussed consistently in the order independent, dependent, and inconsistent. We added a new example on identifying the type of system. We included more graphing calculator exercises. There is a new strategy for solving a system by substitution, as well as a new box for recognizing dependent and inconsistent systems. We improved the strategy for solving by addition. We also improved examples for solving by addition. We improved the discussion on graphing linear inequalities. We added a new strategy for the test point method. We included a new graphical summary of equations and inequalities in Section 4.4. We also improved the discussion on graphing systems of inequalities with new graphs to illustrate intersections, as well as added new graphs to show why a system of inequalities can have no solution. We included a new application on systems of inequalities. There are new exercises in the Chapter Review on picking the method for solving a system. Eighteen new exercises were added to the Making Connections Chapters 1–4.
- **Chapter 5** now starts with rules for positive exponents in Section 5.1 and then introduces negative exponents and scientific notation in Section 5.2. Previously, negative exponents were at the end of the chapter and the rules for exponents were discussed when needed for the polynomials. The compound amount and present value formulas are also presented in Sections 5.1 and 5.2. Function notation is used for evaluating polynomials in Section 5.3. A new example and a new caution were added for multiplying monomials in Section 5.4.
- In **Chapter 6,** Section 6.5 now emphasizes the general strategy for factoring polynomials with two new examples and 38 new exercises.

Acknowledgments

I would like to extend my appreciation to the people at McGraw-Hill for their whole-hearted support in producing the new editions of my books. My thanks go to Rich Kolasa, Senior Sponsoring Editor, for making the revision process work like a well-oiled machine; to Michelle Flomenhoft, Senior Developmental Editor, for her advice on shaping the new editions; to Torie Anderson, Marketing Manager, for getting the book in front of instructors; to Vicki Krug, Senior Project Manager, for expertly overseeing the many details of the production process along with Sandy Ludovissy, Lead Production Supervisor; to John Joran, Designer, for the wonderful design of my texts;

to Carrie Burger, Lead Photo Research Coordinator, for her aid in picking out excellent photos; to Melissa Leick, Supplements Producer, for producing top-notch print supplements; and to Amber Bettcher, Media Technology Producer, and Stacy Patch, Lead Media Project Manager, for shepherding the development of high-quality media supplements that accompany my textbook. To all of them, my many thanks for their efforts to make my books bestsellers when there are many good books for faculty to choose from. I sincerely appreciate the efforts of the reviewers who made many helpful suggestions to improve my series of books. I specifically want to thank the Board of Advisors who contributed feedback throughout the process.

Board of Advisors

Rebecca Berg, *Bowie State University*

Don Gabriel, *Cuyahoga Community College–West Parma*

Laura Kalbaugh, *Wake Tech University*

S. Maheshwari, *William Paterson University*

Manuscript Reviewers

Laura Adkins, *Missouri Southern State University*

Kent Aeschliman, *Oakland Community College*

Marie Aratari, *Oakland Community College*

Lynn Beckett-Lemus, *El Camino College*

Ellen Brook Kopelovich, *Cuyahoga Community College*

Eleanor Browne, *Richland College*

Debra Bryant, *Sacramento City College*

Kirby Bunas, *Santa Rosa Junior College*

Jan Butler, *CCC Online*

Laurie Carman, *Arkansas Tech University*

Amy Cupit, *Copiah-Lincoln Community College*

Manju Dargar, *Dickinson State University*

Alain D'Amour, *Southern Connecticut State University*

Emmett Dennis, *Southern Connecticut State University*

Patricia Ellington, *University of Texas–Arlington*

Rhoderick Fleming, *Wake Tech University*

Mary Foster, *Southern University A&M College*

Monica Geist, *Front Range Community College–Westminster*

Marcella Jones, *Minneapolis Community and Technical College*

Patrick Kimani, *Morrisville State College*

Susan Knights, *Boise State University*

Julianne Labbiento, *Lehigh Carbon Community College*

Linda Laine, *Honolulu Community College*

Geza Laszlo, *Tillamook Bay Community College*

Kathryn Lavelle, *Westchester Community College*
Tam LeDuc, *Houston Community College Northeast*
Joseph Magnotta, *Cuyahoga Community College–Metro*
Jason Malozzi, *Lehigh Carbon Community College*
Mikal McDowell, *Cedar Valley College*
Marianne Morea, *The College at Old Westbury, State University of New York*
Bette Nelson, *Alvin Community College*
John Pflughoeft, *Northwest Michigan College*
Debra Pharo, *Northwest Michigan College*
Brenda Reed, *Lincoln University*
Nancy Ressler, *Oakton Community College*
Ned Schillow, *Lehigh Carbon Community College*
Jennifer Siegel, *Tallahassee Community College*
Frances Smith, *Oakland Community College*
Kelly Stady, *Cuyahoga Community College–West*
Jason Teichman, *Northwest Michigan College*
Debra Van Sickle, *Sacramento Community College*
Karen Villarreal, *Louisiana State University–Alexandria*
Joel D. Williams, *Houston Community College South*
Kathy Willis, *Southern New Hampshire University*
Rebecca Wong, *West Valley College*

AMATYC Focus Group Participants
Rich Basich, *Lakeland Community College*
Mary Kay Best, *Coastal Bend College*
Rebecca Hubiak, *Tidewater Community College*
Paul W. Jones II, *University of Cincinnati*
William A. Kincaid, *Wilmington College*
Carlotte Newsom, *Tidewater Community College*
Nan Strebeck, *Navarro College*
Dave Stumpf, *Lakeland Community College*
Amy Young, *Navarro College*

I also want to express my sincere appreciation to my wife, Cheryl, for her invaluable patience and support.

Mark Dugopolski
Ponchatoula, Louisiana

A COMMITMENT TO ACCURACY

You have a right to expect an accurate textbook, and McGraw-Hill invests considerable time and effort to make sure that we deliver one. Listed below are the many steps we take to make sure this happens.

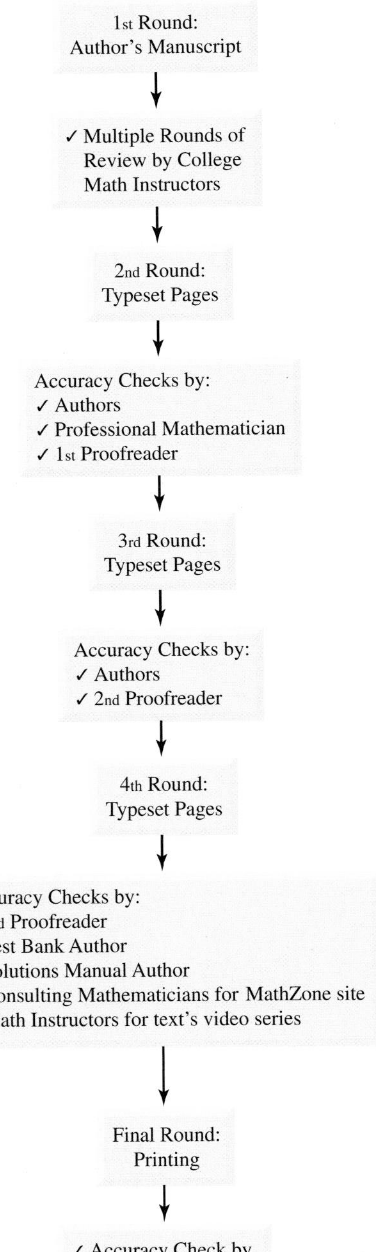

OUR ACCURACY VERIFICATION PROCESS

First Round

Step 1: Numerous **college math instructors** review the manuscript and report on any errors that they may find, and the authors make these corrections in their final manuscript.

Second Round

Step 2: Once the manuscript has been typeset, the **authors** check their manuscript against the first page proofs to ensure that all illustrations, graphs, examples, exercises, solutions, and answers have been correctly laid out on the pages, and that all notation is correctly used.

Step 3: An outside, **professional mathematician** works through every example and exercise in the page proofs to verify the accuracy of the answers.

Step 4: A **proofreader** adds a triple layer of accuracy assurance in the first pages by hunting for errors, then a second, corrected round of page proofs is produced.

Third Round

Step 5: The **author team** reviews the second round of page proofs for two reasons: 1) to make certain that any previous corrections were properly made, and 2) to look for any errors they might have missed on the first round.

Step 6: A **second proofreader** is added to the project to examine the new round of page proofs to double check the author team's work and to lend a fresh, critical eye to the book before the third round of paging.

Fourth Round

Step 7: A **third proofreader** inspects the third round of page proofs to verify that all previous corrections have been properly made and that there are no new or remaining errors.

Step 8: Meanwhile, in partnership with **independent mathematicians,** the text accuracy is verified from a variety of fresh perspectives:

- The **test bank author** checks for consistency and accuracy as they prepare the computerized test item file.
- The **solutions manual author** works every single exercise and verifies their answers, reporting any errors to the publisher.
- A **consulting group of mathematicians,** who write material for the text's MathZone site, notifies the publisher of any errors they encounter in the page proofs.
- A video production company employing **expert math instructors** for the text's videos will alert the publisher of any errors they might find in the page proofs.

Final Round

Step 9: The **project manager,** who has overseen the book from the beginning, performs a **fourth proofread** of the textbook during the printing process, providing a final accuracy review.

⇒ What results is a mathematics textbook that is as accurate and error-free as is humanly possible, and our authors and publishing staff are confident that our many layers of quality assurance have produced textbooks that are the leaders of the industry for their integrity and correctness.

Guided Tour

Features and Supplements

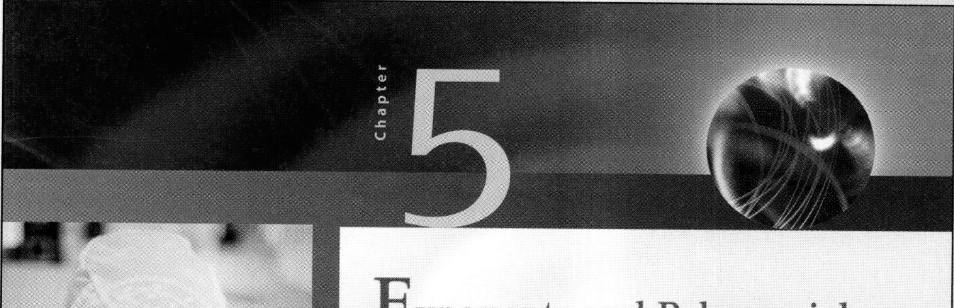

Chapter Opener

Each chapter opener features a real-world situation that can be modeled using mathematics. The application then refers students to a specific exercise in the chapter's exercise sets.

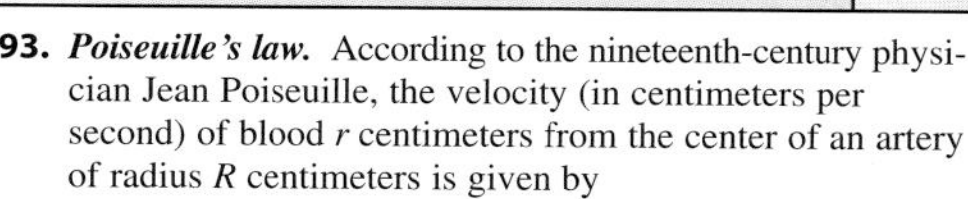

93. ***Poiseuille's law.*** According to the nineteenth-century physician Jean Poiseuille, the velocity (in centimeters per second) of blood r centimeters from the center of an artery of radius R centimeters is given by

$$v = k(R - r)(R + r),$$

where k is a constant. Rewrite the formula using a special product rule.

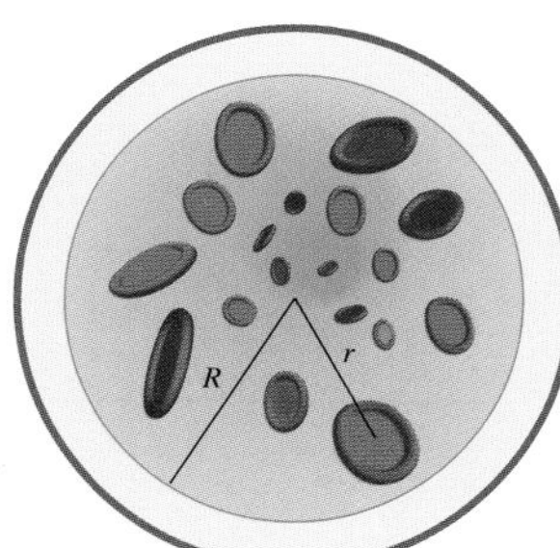

Figure for Exercise 93

Exponents and Polynomials

The nineteenth-century physician and physicist Jean Louis Marie Poiseuille (1799–1869) is given credit for discovering a formula associated with the circulation of blood through arteries. Poiseuille's law, as it is known, can be used to determine the velocity of blood in an artery at a given distance from the center of the artery. The formula states that the flow of blood in an artery is faster toward the center of the blood vessel and is slower toward the outside. Blood flow can also be affected by a person's blood pressure, the length of the blood vessel, and the viscosity of the blood itself.

In later years, Poiseuille's continued interest in blood circulation led him to experiments to show that blood pressure rises and falls when a person exhales and inhales. In modern medicine, physicians can use Poiseuille's law to determine how much the radius of a blocked blood vessel must be widened to create a healthy flow of blood.

In this chapter, you will study polynomials, the fundamental expressions of algebra. Polynomials are to algebra what integers are to arithmetic. We use polynomials to represent quantities in general, such as perimeter, area, revenue, and the volume of blood flowing through an artery.

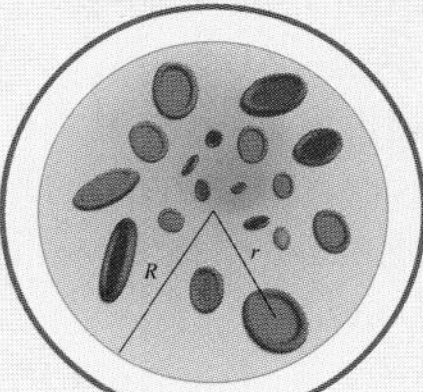

In Exercise 93 of Section 5.6, you will see Poiseuille's law represented by a polynomial.

In This Section

The In This Section listing gives a preview of the topics to be covered in the section. These subsections have now been numbered for easier reference. In addition, these subsections are listed in the relevant places in the end-of-section exercises.

5.1 The Rules of Exponents

In This Section

⟨1⟩ The Product Rule for Exponents
⟨2⟩ Zero Exponent
⟨3⟩ The Quotient Rule for Exponents
⟨4⟩ The Power of a Power Rule
⟨5⟩ The Power of a Product Rule
⟨6⟩ The Power of a Quotient Rule
⟨7⟩ The Amount Formula

We defined exponential expressions with positive integral exponents in Chapter 1. In this section, we will review that definition and then learn the rules for positive integral exponents.

⟨1⟩ The Product Rule for Exponents

Exponents were defined in Chapter 1 as a simple way of expressing repeated multiplication. For example,

$$x^1 = x, \quad y^2 = y \cdot y, \quad 5^3 = 5 \cdot 5 \cdot 5, \quad \text{and} \quad a^4 = a \cdot a \cdot a \cdot a.$$

To find the product of the exponential expressions x^3 and x^5 we could simply count the number of times x appears in the product:

$$x^3 \cdot x^5 = \underbrace{\overbrace{(x \cdot x \cdot x)}^{3\text{ factors}}\overbrace{(x \cdot x \cdot x \cdot x \cdot x)}^{5\text{ factors}}}_{8\text{ factors}} = x^8$$

Instead of counting to find that x occurs 8 times it is easier to add 3 and 5 to get 8. This example illustrates the **product rule for exponents.**

Product Rule for Exponents

If a is any real number, and m and n are positive integers, then

$$a^m \cdot a^n = a^{m+n}.$$

Examples

Examples refer directly to exercises, and those exercises in turn refer back to that example. This **double cross-referencing** helps students connect examples to exercises no matter which one they start with.

EXAMPLE 4 **Higher powers of a binomial**

Expand each binomial.

a) $(x + 4)^3$ **b)** $(y - 2)^4$

Solution

a)
$$\begin{aligned}(x + 4)^3 &= (x + 4)^2(x + 4)\\ &= (x^2 + 8x + 16)(x + 4) && \text{Square of a sum}\\ &= (x^2 + 8x + 16)x + (x^2 + 8x + 16)4 && \text{Distributive property}\\ &= x^3 + 8x^2 + 16x + 4x^2 + 32x + 64\\ &= x^3 + 12x^2 + 48x + 64\end{aligned}$$

b)
$$\begin{aligned}(y - 2)^4 &= (y - 2)^2(y - 2)^2\\ &= (y^2 - 4y + 4)(y^2 - 4y + 4)\\ &= (y^2 - 4y + 4)(y^2) + (y^2 - 4y + 4)(-4y) + (y^2 - 4y + 4)(4)\\ &= y^4 - 4y^3 + 4y^2 - 4y^3 + 16y^2 - 16y + 4y^2 - 16y + 16\\ &= y^4 - 8y^3 + 24y^2 - 32y + 16\end{aligned}$$

Now do Exercises 49–56

Expand each binomial. See Example 4.

49. $(x + 1)^3$
50. $(y - 1)^3$
VIDEO **51.** $(2a - 3)^3$
52. $(3w - 1)^3$
53. $(a - 3)^4$
54. $(2b + 1)^4$
55. $(a + b)^4$
56. $(2a - 3b)^4$

Math at Work

The Math at Work feature appears in each chapter to reinforce the book's theme of real applications in the everyday world of work.

Math *at Work* **Aerospace Engineering**

Aircraft design is a delicate balance between weight and strength. Saving 1 pound of weight could save the plane's operators $5000 over 20 years. Mathematics is used to calculate the strength of each of a plane's parts and to predict when the material making up a part will fail. If calculations show that one kind of metal isn't strong enough, designers usually have to choose another material or change the design.

As an example, consider an aluminum stringer with a circular cross section. The stringer is used inside the wing of an airplane as shown in the accompanying figure. The aluminum rod has a diameter of 20 mm and will support a load of 5×10^4 Newtons (N). The maximum stress on aluminum is 1×10^8 Pascals (Pa), where 1 Pa = 1 N/m^2. To calculate the stress S on the rod we use S = (load)/(cross sectional area). Note that we must divide the diameter by 2 to get the radius and convert square millimeters to square meters:

Stringer

$$S = \frac{L}{\pi r^2} = \frac{5 \times 10^4 \text{ N}}{\pi(10 \text{ mm})^2} \cdot \left(\frac{1000 \text{ mm}}{1 \text{ m}}\right)^2 \approx 1.6 \times 10^8 \text{ Pa}$$

Since the stress is 1.6×10^8 Pa and the maximum stress on aluminum is 1×10^8 Pa, the aluminum rod is not strong enough. The design must be changed. The diameter of the aluminum rod could be increased or stronger/lighter metal such as titanium could be used.

Strategy Boxes

The strategy boxes provide a handy reference for students to use when they review key concepts and techniques to prepare for tests and homework. They are now directly referenced in the end-of-section exercises where appropriate.

Solution

a) Because the exponent is positive, move the decimal point six places to the right:

$$7.02 \times 10^6 = 7020000. = 7{,}020{,}000$$

b) Because the exponent is negative, move the decimal point five places to the left:

$$8.13 \times 10^{-5} = 0.0000813$$

Now do Exercises 65–72

To convert a positive number to scientific notation, we just reverse the strategy for converting from scientific notation.

Strategy for Converting to Scientific Notation

1. Count the number of places (n) that the decimal must be moved so that it will follow the first nonzero digit of the number.
2. If the original number was larger than 10, use 10^n.
3. If the original number was smaller than 1, use 10^{-n}.

Remember that the scientific notation for a number larger than 10 will have a positive power of 10 and the scientific notation for a number between 0 and 1 will have a negative power of 10.

Margin Notes

Margin notes include **Helpful Hints,** which give advice on the topic they're adjacent to; **Calculator Close-Ups,** which provide advice on using calculators to verify students' work; and **Teaching Tips,** which are especially helpful in programs with new instructors who are looking for alternate ways to explain and reinforce material.

‹ Helpful Hint ›

The exponent rules in this section apply to expressions that involve only multiplication and division. This is not too surprising since exponents, multiplication, and division are closely related.

‹ Teaching Tip ›

Many students have trouble converting 24×10^{14} to scientific notation. Be sure they write $2.4 \times 10^1 \times 10^{14}$ and then add exponents.

‹ Calculator Close-Up ›

With a calculator's built-in scientific notation, some parentheses can be omitted as shown below. Writing out the powers of 10 can lead to errors.

```
4E5/8E-2
                5E6
4*10^5/8*10^-2
                5E2
```

Try these computations with your calculator.

Exercises

Section exercises are preceded by true/false **Warm-Ups,** which can be used as quizzes or for class discussion.

Warm-Ups

True or false? Explain your answer.

1. $10^{-2} = \frac{1}{100}$

2. $\left(-\frac{1}{5}\right)^{-1} = 5$

3. $3^{-2} \cdot 2^{-1} = 6^{-3}$

4. $\frac{3^{-2}}{3^{-1}} = \frac{1}{3}$

Study Tips have been moved to the beginning of each exercise set to both open up the margins, as well as place them where students are most apt to need them. **MathZone** is referenced at the beginning of each exercise set to remind the reader of other available resources. Next come **Reading and Writing** exercises that can be used for class discussion and to verify students' conceptual understanding. Exercise sets supply a generous and varied amount of drill and realistic **applications** so students can put into practice the skills they have developed.

Boost your grade at mathzone.com!
> Practice Problems
> NetTutor
> Self-Tests
> e-Professors
> Videos

5.2 Exercises

‹ Study Tips ›

- Studying in an environment similar to the one in which you will be tested can increase your chances of recalling information.
- If possible, do some studying in the classroom where you will be taking the test.

Reading and Writing *After reading this section, write out the answers to these questions. Use complete sentences.*

1. What does a negative exponent mean?

2. What is the proper order for evaluating the operations indicated by a negative exponent?

3. For what exponents is the product rule valid?

4. How do you convert a number from scientific notation to standard notation?

5. How do you convert a number from standard notation to scientific notation?

6. Which number are not usually written in scientific notation?

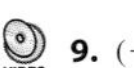

9. $(-2)^{-4}$ **10.** $(-3)^{-4}$

11. -4^{-2} **12.** -2^{-4}

13. -3^{-3} **14.** -5^{-3}

15. $\frac{5^{-2}}{10^{-2}}$ **16.** $\frac{3^{-4}}{6^{-2}}$

Simplify. See Example 2.

17. $6^{-1} + 6^{-1}$ **18.** $2^{-1} + 4^{-1}$

19. $\frac{10}{5^{-3}}$ **20.** $\frac{1}{25 \cdot 10^{-4}}$

21. $\frac{3a^{-3}}{b^{-9}}$ **22.** $\frac{6x^{-5}}{5y^{-1}}$

23. $\left(\frac{1}{b}\right)^{-7}$ **24.** $\left(\frac{1}{y}\right)^{-4}$

Getting More Involved concludes the exercise set with **Discussion, Writing, Exploration,** and **Cooperative Learning** activities for well-rounded practice in the skills for that section.

initial velocity for a ball that has traveled 370 feet.

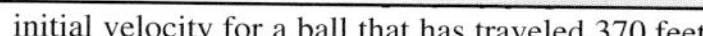

Figure for Exercise 102

Getting More Involved

105. ***Writing***

Explain why the square of the sum of two numbers is different from the sum of the squares of two numbers.

106. ***Cooperative learning***

The sum of the integers from 1 through n is $\frac{n(n+1)}{2}$. The sum of the squares of the integers from 1 through n is $\frac{n(n+1)(2n+1)}{6}$. The sum of the cubes of the integers from 1 through n is $\frac{n^2(n+1)^2}{4}$. Use the appropriate expressions to find the following values.

98. $(200)^4(0.0005)^3$

99. $\dfrac{(4000)(90{,}000)}{0.00000012}$

100. $\dfrac{(30{,}000)(80{,}000)}{(0.000006)(0.002)}$

Perform the following computations with the aid of a calculator. Write answers in scientific notation. Round to three decimal places.

101. $(6.3 \times 10^6)(1.45 \times 10^{-4})$

102. $(8.35 \times 10^9)(4.5 \times 10^3)$

103. $(5.36 \times 10^{-4}) + (3.55 \times 10^{-5})$

104. $(8.79 \times 10^8) + (6.48 \times 10^9)$

Getting More Involved

115. ***Exploration***

a) If $w^{-3} < 0$, then what can you say about w?
b) If $(-5)^m < 0$, then what can you say about m?
c) What restriction must be placed on w and m so that $w^m < 0$?

116. ***Discussion***

Which of the following expressions is not equal to -1? Explain your answer.

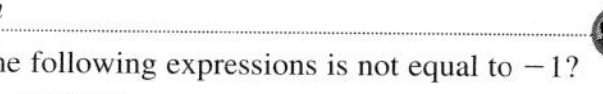

a) -1^{-1} b) -1^{-2} c) $(-1^{-1})^{-1}$
d) $(-1)^{-1}$ e) $(-1)^{-2}$

Calculator Exercises
Optional calculator exercises provide students with the opportunity to use scientific or graphing calculators to solve various problems.

Video Exercises
A video icon indicates an exercise that has a video walking students through how to solve it.

57. $(2z^2 - 3z) - (3z^2 - 5z)$ **58.** $(z^2 - 4z) - (5z^2 - 3z)$

59. $(w^5 - w^3) - (-w^4 + w^2)$
60. $(w^6 - w^3) - (-w^2 + w)$
61. $(t^2 - 3t + 4) - (t^2 - 5t - 9)$
62. $(t^2 - 6t + 7) - (5t^2 - 3t - 2)$
63. $(9 - 3y - y^2) - (2 + 5y - y^2)$
VIDEO **64.** $(4 - 5y + y^3) - (2 - 3y + y^2)$
65. $(3.55x - 879) - (26.4x - 455.8)$
66. $(345.56x - 347.4) - (56.6x + 433)$

Add or subtract the polynomials as indicated. See Examples 5 and 6.

67. Add:
$3a - 4$
$\underline{a + 6}$

68. Add:
$2w - 8$
$\underline{w + 3}$

69. Subtract:
$3x + 11$
$\underline{-(5x + 7)}$

70. Subtract:
$4x + 3$
$\underline{-(2x + 9)}$

71. Add:
$a - b$
$\underline{a + b}$

72. Add:
$s - 6$
$\underline{s - 1}$

73. Subtract:
$-3m + 1$
$\underline{-(2m - 6)}$

74. Subtract:
$-5n + 2$
$\underline{-(3n - 4)}$

87. $(-x^2 - 5x + 4) + (6x^2 - 8x + 9) - (3x^2 - 7x + 1)$

88. $(-8x^2 + 5x - 12) + (-3x^2 - 9x + 18)$
$- (-3x^2 + 9x - 4)$

89. $(-6z^4 - 3z^3 + 7z^2) - (5z^3 + 3z^2 - 2) + (z^4 - z^2 + 5)$

90. $(-v^3 - v^2 - 1) - (v^4 - v^2 - v - 1) + (v^3 - 3v^2 + 6)$

⟨5⟩ Applications

Solve each problem. See Example 8.

91. ***Water pumps.*** Walter uses the polynomials $R(x) = 400x$ and $C(x) = 120x + 800$ to estimate his monthly revenue and cost in dollars for producing x water pumps per month.
a) Write a polynomial $P(x)$ for his monthly profit.

b) Find the monthly profit for $x = 50$.

92. ***Manufacturing costs.*** Ace manufacturing has determined that the cost of labor for producing x transmissions is $L(x) = 0.3x^2 + 400x + 550$ dollars, while the cost of materials is $M(x) = 0.1x^2 + 50x + 800$ dollars.
a) Write a polynomial $T(x)$ that represents the total cost of materials and labor for producing x transmissions.
b) Evaluate the total cost polynomial for $x = 500$.
c) Find the cost of labor for 500 transmissions and the cost of materials for 500 transmissions.

Wrap-Up
The extensive and varied review in the chapter Wrap-Up will help students prepare for tests. First comes the **Summary** with key terms and concepts illustrated by examples, then **Enriching Your Mathematical Word Power** enables students to test their recall of new terminology in a multiple-choice format.

Chapter 5 Wrap-Up

Summary

The Rules of Exponents		Examples
The following rules hold for any integers m and n, and nonzero real numbers a and b.		
Zero exponent	$a^0 = 1$	$(-3)^0 = 1, \quad -3^0 = -1$
Product rule for exponents	$a^m \cdot a^n = a^{m+n}$	$a^2 \cdot a^3 = a^5, \quad b^{-5} \cdot b^3 = b^{-2}$
Quotient rule for exponents	$\frac{a^m}{a^n} = a^{m-n}$	$x^8 \div x^2 = x^6, \quad \frac{y^{-3}}{y^{-7}} = y^4$

Enriching Your Mathematical Word Power

For each mathematical term, choose the correct meaning.

1. **integral exponent**
   a. an exponent that is an integer
   b. a positive exponent
   c. a rational exponent
   d. a fractional exponent
2. **scientific notation**
   a. the notation of rational exponents
   b. the notation of algebra
   c. a sum of four or more numbers
   d. a single term or a finite sum of terms
5. **degree of a polynomial**
   a. the number of terms in a polynomial
   b. the highest degree of any of the terms of a polynomial
   c. the value of a polynomial when $x = 0$
   d. the largest coefficient of any of the terms of a polynomial

Next come **Review Exercises,** which are first linked back to the section of the chapter that they review, and then the exercises are mixed without section references in the **Miscellaneous** section.

Review Exercises

5.1 The Rules of Exponents
Simplify each expression. Assume all variables represent nonzero real numbers.

1. $-5^0 + 3^0$ **2.** $-4^0 - 3^0$
3. $-3a^3 \cdot 2a^4$ **4.** $2y^{10}(-3y^{20})$
5. $\frac{-10b^5c^9}{2b^5c^3}$ **6.** $\frac{-30k^3y^9}{15k^3y^2}$
7. $(b^5)^6$ **8.** $(y^5)^8$
9. $(-2x^3y^2)^3$ **10.** $(-3a^4b^6)^4$

Write each number in scientific notation.
33. 8,070,000 **34.** 90,000
35. 0.000709 **36.** 0.0000005

Perform each computation without a calculator. Write the answer in scientific notation.
37. $(5(2 \times 10^4))^3$
38. $(6(2 \times 10^{-3}))^2$
39. $\frac{(2 \times 10^{-9})(3 \times 10^7)}{5(6 \times 10^{-4})}$

115. $\frac{x^2}{x + 1}$
116. $\frac{-2x^2}{x - 3}$

Miscellaneous
Perform the indicated operations.
117. $(x + 3)(x + 7)$
118. $(k + 5)(k + 4)$
119. $(t - 3y)(t - 4y)$

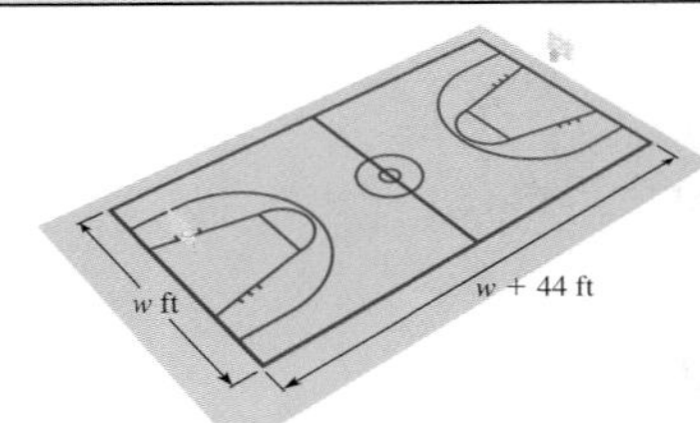

Figure for Exercise 145

Chapter Test
The test gives students additional practice to make sure they're ready for the real thing, with **all** answers provided at the back of the book and **all** solutions available in the Student's Solutions Manual.

Chapter 5 Test

Use the rules of exponents to simplify each expression. Write answers without negative exponents.

1. $-5x^3 \cdot 7x^5$
2. $3x^3y \cdot (2xy^4)^2$
3. $-4a^6b^5 \div (2a^5b)$
4. $3x^{-2} \cdot 5x^7$
5. $\left(\frac{-2a}{b^2}\right)^5$
6. $\frac{-6a^7b^6c^2}{-2a^3b^8c^2}$
7. $\frac{6t^{-7}}{2t^9}$
8. $\frac{w^{-6}}{w^{-4}}$
9. $(-3s^{-3}t^2)^{-2}$
10. $(-2x^{-6}y)^3$

Convert to scientific notation.

11. 5,433,000

26. $(3t^2 - 7)(3t^2 + 7)$
27. $(4x^2 - 3)(x^2 + 2)$
28. $(x - 2)(x + 3)(x - 4)$

Write each expression in the form

$$\textit{quotient} + \frac{\textit{remainder}}{\textit{divisor}}.$$

29. $\frac{2x}{x - 3}$
30. $\frac{x^2 - 3x + 5}{x + 2}$

The **Making Connections** feature following the Chapter Test is a cumulative review of all chapters up to and including the one just finished, helping to tie the course concepts together for students on a regular basis.

Making Connections | A Review of Chapters 1–5

Evaluate each arithmetic expression.

1. $-16 \div (-2)$
2. $-16 \div \left(-\frac{1}{2}\right)$
3. $(-5)^2 - 3(-5) + 1$
4. $-5^2 - 4(-5) + 3$
5. $2^{15} \div 2^{10}$
6. $2^6 - 2^5$
7. $-3^2 \cdot 4^2$
8. $(-3 \cdot 4)^2$
9. $\left(\frac{1}{2}\right)^3 + \frac{1}{2}$
10. $\left(\frac{2}{3}\right)^2 - \frac{1}{3}$
11. $(5 + 3)^2$
12. $5^2 + 3^2$
13. $3^{-1} + 2^{-1}$
14. $2^{-2} - 3^{-2}$
15. $(30 - 1)(30 + 1)$
16. $(30 - 1) \div (1 - 30)$

Perform the indicated operations.

17. $(x + 3)(x + 5)$
18. $x + 3(x + 5)$
19. $-5t^3v \cdot 3t^2v^6$
20. $(-10t^3v^2) \div (-2t^2v)$
21. $(x^2 + 8x + 15) + (x + 5)$
22. $(x^2 + 8x + 15) - (x + 5)$
23. $(x^2 + 8x + 15) \div (x + 5)$
24. $(x^2 + 8x + 15)(x + 5)$
25. $(-6y^3 + 8y^2) \div (-2y^2)$
26. $(18y^4 - 12y^3 + 3y^2) \div (3y^2)$

Solve each equation.

27. $2x + 1 = 0$
28. $x - 7 = 0$
29. $\frac{3}{4}x - 3 = \frac{1}{2}$
30. $\frac{x}{2} - \frac{3}{4} = \frac{1}{8}$
31. $2(x - 3) = 3(x - 2)$
32. $2(3x - 3) = 3(2x - 2)$

Solve.

33. Find the x-intercept for the line $y = 2x + 1$.
34. Find the y-intercept for the line $y = x - 7$.
35. Find the slope of the line $y = 2x + 1$.
36. Find the slope of the line that goes through (0, 0) and $\left(\frac{1}{2}, \frac{1}{3}\right)$.
37. If $y = \frac{3}{4}x - 3$ and y is $\frac{1}{2}$, then what is x?
38. Find y if $y = \frac{x}{2} - \frac{3}{4}$ and x is $\frac{1}{2}$.

Solve the problem.

39. ***Average cost.*** Pineapple Recording plans to spend \$100,000 to record a new CD by the Woozies and \$2.25 per CD to manufacture the disks. The polynomial $2.25n + 100{,}000$ represents the total cost in dollars for recording and manufacturing n disks. Find an expression that represents the average cost per disk by dividing the total cost by n. Find the average cost per disk for $n = 1000$, 100,000, and 1,000,000. What happens to the large initial investment of \$100,000 if the company sells one million CDs?

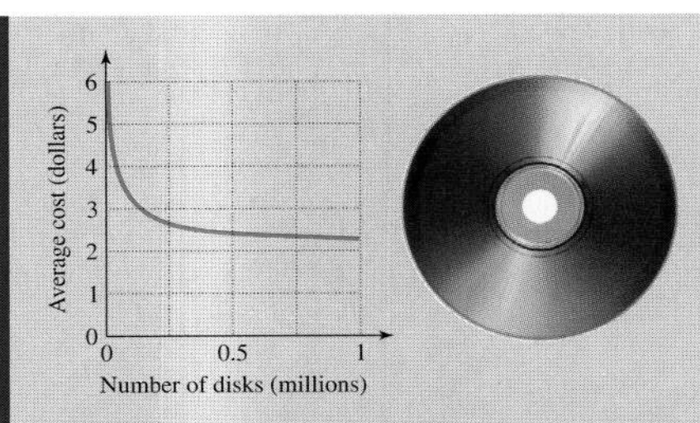

Figure for Exercise 39

Critical Thinking

The Critical Thinking section that concludes every chapter encourages students to think creatively to solve unique and intriguing problems and puzzles.

Critical Thinking | For Individual or Group Work | Chapter 5

These exercises can be solved by a variety of techniques, which may or may not require algebra. So be creative and think critically. Explain all answers. Answers are in the Instructor's Edition of this text.

1. ***Counting cubes.*** What is the total number of cubes that are in each of the following diagrams?

a)  

b) 

c) 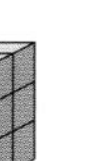

d) 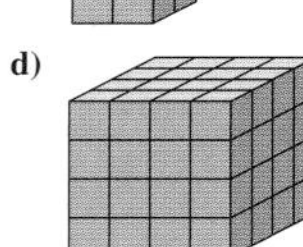

2. ***More cubes.*** Imagine a large cube that is made up of 125 small cubes like those in the previous exercise. What is the total number of cubes that could be found in this arrangement?

3. ***Timely coincidence.*** Starting at 8 A.M. determine the number of times in the next 24 hours for which the hour and minute hands on a clock coincide.

Photo for Exercise 3

4. ***Chess board.*** There are 64 squares on a square chess board. How many squares are neither diagonal squares nor edge squares?

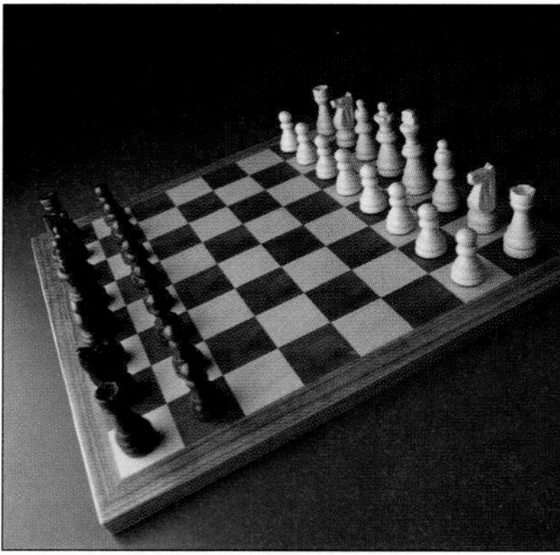

Photo for Exercise 4

5. ***Last digit.*** Find the last digit in 3^{9999}.

6. ***Reconciling remainders.*** Find a positive integer smaller than 500 that has a remainder of 3 when divided by 5, a remainder of 6 when divided by 9, and a remainder of 8 when divided by 11.

7. ***Exact sum.*** Find this sum exactly:

$$\frac{1}{2} + \frac{1}{2^2} + \frac{1}{2^3} + \frac{1}{2^4} + \cdots + \frac{1}{2^{19}}$$

8. ***Ten-digit number.*** Find a 10-digit number whose first digit is the number of 1's in the 10-digit number, whose second digit is the number of 2's in the 10-digit number, whose third digit is the number of 3's in the 10-digit number, and so on. The ninth digit must be the number of nines in the 10-digit number and the tenth digit must be the number of zeros in the 10-digit number.

SUPPLEMENTS

Multimedia Supplements

www.mathzone.com

McGraw-Hill's MathZone is a complete online tutorial and homework management system for mathematics and statistics, designed for greater ease of use than any other system available. Instructors have the flexibility to create and share courses and assignments with colleagues, adjunct faculty, and teaching assistants with only a few clicks of the mouse. All algorithmic exercises, online tutoring, and a variety of video and animations are directly tied to text-specific materials.

MathZone is completely customizable to suit individual instructor and student needs. Exercises can be easily edited, multimedia is assignable, importing additional content is easy, and instructors can even control the level of help available to students while doing their homework. Students have the added benefit of full access to the study tools to individually improve their success without having to be part of a MathZone course.

MathZone has automatic grading and reporting of easy-to-assign algorithmically generated problem types for homework, quizzes, and tests. Grades are readily accessible through a fully integrated grade book that can be exported in one click to Microsoft Excel, WebCT, or BlackBoard.

MathZone offers:

- Practice exercises, based on the text's end-of-section material, generated in an unlimited number of variations, for as much practice as needed to master a particular topic.
- Subtitled videos demonstrating text-specific exercises and reinforcing important concepts within a given topic.
- Net Tutor™ integrating online whiteboard technology with live personalized tutoring via the Internet.
- Assessment capabilities which provide students and instructors with the diagnostics to offer a detailed knowledge base through advanced reporting and remediation tools.
- Faculty with the ability to create and share courses and assignments with colleagues and adjuncts, or to build a course from one of the provided course libraries.
- An Assignment Builder that provides the ability to select algorithmically generated exercises from any McGraw-Hill math textbook, edit content, as well as assign a variety of MathZone material including an ALEKS Assessment.
- Accessibility from multiple operating systems and Internet browsers.

Instructors: To access MathZone, request registration information from your McGraw-Hill sales representative.

Computerized Test Bank (CTB) Online (Instructors Only)

Available through MathZone, this **computerized test bank,** utilizing Brownstone Diploma® algorithm-based testing software, enables users to create customized exams quickly. This user-friendly program enables instructors to search for questions by topic, format, or difficulty level; to edit existing questions or to add new ones; and to scramble questions and answer keys for multiple versions of the same test. Hundreds of text-specific open-ended and multiple-choice questions are included in the question bank. Sample chapter tests in Microsoft Word® and PDF formats are also provided.

Online Instructor's Solutions Manual (Instructors Only)

Available on MathZone, the Instructor's Solutions Manual provides comprehensive, **worked-out solutions** to all exercises in the text. The methods used to solve the problems in the manual are the same as those used to solve the examples in the textbook.

NetTutor

Available through MathZone, NetTutor is a revolutionary system that enables students to interact with a live tutor over the World Wide Web. NetTutor's Web-based, graphical chat capabilities enable students and tutors to use mathematical notation and even to draw graphs as they work through a problem together. Students can also submit questions and receive answers, browse previously answered questions, and view previous live-chat sessions. Tutors are familiar with the textbook's objectives and problem-solving styles.

Video Lectures on Digital Video Disk (DVD)

In the videos, qualified teachers work through selected exercises from the textbook, following the solution methodology employed in the text. The video series is available on DVD or online as an assignable element of MathZone. The DVDs are closed-captioned for the hearing impaired, subtitled in Spanish, and meet the Americans with Disabilities Act Standards for Accessible Design. Instructors may use them as resources in a learning center, for online courses, and/or to provide extra help for students who require extra practice.

www.ALEKS.com

ALEKS (**A**ssessment and **LE**arning in **K**nowledge **S**paces) is a dynamic online learning system for mathematics education, available over the Web 24/7. ALEKS assesses students, accurately determines their knowledge, and then guides them to the material that they are most ready to learn. With a variety of reports, Textbook Integration Plus, quizzes, and homework assignment capabilities, ALEKS offers flexibility and ease of use for instructors.

- ALEKS uses artificial intelligence to determine exactly what each student knows and is ready to learn. ALEKS remediates student gaps and provides highly efficient learning and improved learning outcomes.
- ALEKS is a comprehensive curriculum that aligns with syllabi or specified textbooks. Used in conjunction with a McGraw-Hill text, students also receive links to text-specific videos, multimedia tutorials, and textbook pages.
- Textbook Integration Plus enables ALEKS to be automatically aligned with syllabi or specified McGraw-Hill textbooks with instructor chosen dates, chapter goals, homework, and quizzes.
- ALEKS with AI-2 gives instructors increased control over the scope and sequence of student learning. Students using ALEKS demonstrate a steadily increasing mastery of the content of the course.
- ALEKS offers a dynamic classroom management system that enables instructors to monitor and direct student progress toward mastery of course objectives. See: www.aleks.com

Printed Supplements

Annotated Instructor's Edition (Instructors Only)

This ancillary contains answers to exercises in the text, including answers to all section exercises, all *Enriching Your Mathematical Word Powers, Review Exercises, Chapter Tests,* and *Making Connections.* These answers are printed in a special color for ease of use by the instructor and are located on the appropriate pages throughout the text.

Student's Solutions Manual

The Student's Solutions Manual provides comprehensive, **worked-out solutions** to all of the odd-numbered exercises. The steps shown in the solutions match the style of solved examples in the textbook.

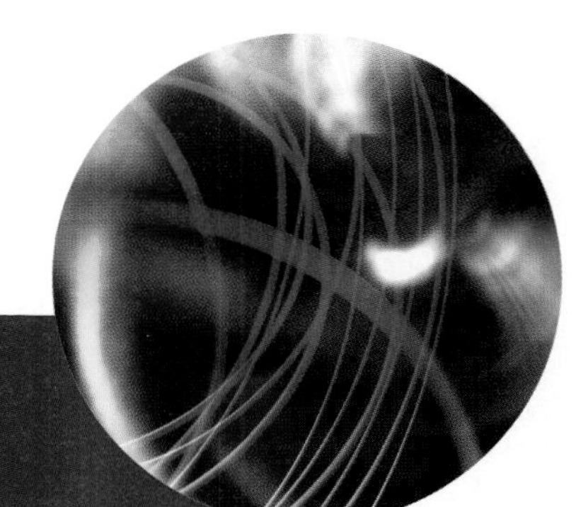

Applications Index

Biology/Health/Life Sciences

Business

Chemistry and Mixture Problems

Construction

Consumer Applications

Distance/Rate/Time

Environment

Geometry

Investment

Politics

School

Science

Sports

Statistics/Demographics

Chapter

Real Numbers and Their Properties

It has been said that baseball is the "great American pastime." All of us who have played the game or who have only been spectators believe we understand the game. But do we realize that a pitcher must aim for an invisible three-dimensional target that is about 20 inches wide by 23 inches high by 17 inches deep and that a pitcher must throw so that the batter has difficulty hitting the ball? A curve ball may deflect 14 inches to skim over the outside corner of the plate, or a knuckle ball can break 11 inches off center when it is 20 feet from the plate and then curve back over the center of the plate.

The batter is trying to hit a rotating ball that can travel up to 120 miles per hour and must make split-second decisions about shifting his weight, changing his stride, and swinging the bat. The size of the bat each batter uses depends on his strengths, and pitchers in turn try to capitalize on a batter's weaknesses.

Millions of baseball fans enjoy watching this game of strategy and numbers. Many watch their favorite teams at the local ballparks, while others cheer for the home team on television. Of course, baseball fans are always interested in which team is leading the division and the number of games that their favorite team is behind the leader. Finding the number of games behind for each team in the division involves both arithmetic and algebra. Algebra provides the formula for finding games behind, and arithmetic is used to do the computations.

In Exercise 101 of Section 1.6 we will find the number of games behind for each team in the American League East.

1.1 The Real Numbers

In This Section

The numbers that we use in algebra are called the real numbers. We start the discussion of the real numbers with some simpler sets of numbers.

⟨1⟩ The Integers

The most fundamental collection or **set** of numbers is the set of **counting numbers** or **natural numbers.** Of course, these are the numbers that we use for counting. The set of natural numbers is written in symbols as follows.

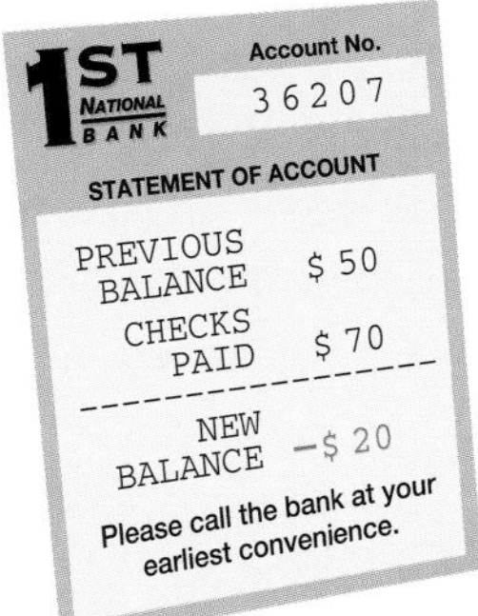

Figure 1.1

The Natural Numbers

$$\{1, 2, 3, \ldots\}$$

Braces, { }, are used to indicate a set of numbers. The three dots after 1, 2, and 3, which are read "and so on," mean that the pattern continues without end. There are infinitely many natural numbers.

The natural numbers, together with the number 0, are called the **whole numbers.** The set of whole numbers is written as follows.

The Whole Numbers

$$\{0, 1, 2, 3, \ldots\}$$

Although the whole numbers have many uses, they are not adequate for indicating losses or debts. A debt of \$20 can be expressed by the negative number -20 (negative twenty). See Fig. 1.1. When a thermometer reads 10 degrees below zero on a Fahrenheit scale, we say that the temperature is $-10°$F. See Fig. 1.2. The whole numbers together with the negatives of the counting numbers form the set of **integers.**

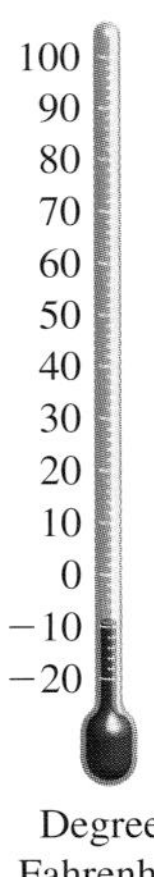

Figure 1.2

The Integers

$$\{\ldots, -3, -2, -1, 0, 1, 2, 3, \ldots\}$$

⟨2⟩ The Rational Numbers

In arithmetic, we discuss and perform operations with specific numbers. In algebra, we like to make more general statements about numbers. In making general statements, we often use letters to represent numbers. A letter that is used to represent a number is called a **variable** because its value may vary. For example, we might say that a and b are integers. This means that a and b could be any of the infinitely many possible integers. They could be different integers or they could even be the same integer. We will use variables to describe the next set of numbers.

The set of **rational numbers** consists of all possible ratios of the form $\frac{a}{b}$, where a and b are integers, except that b is not allowed to be 0. For example,

$$\frac{1}{2}, \quad \frac{-9}{8}, \quad \frac{6}{1}, \quad \frac{150}{-70}, \quad \frac{2}{4}, \quad \frac{-9}{-1}, \quad \text{and} \quad \frac{0}{2}$$

Helpful Hint

Rational numbers are used for ratios. For example, if 2 out of 5 students surveyed attend summer school, then the ratio of students who attend summer school to the total number surveyed is 2/5. Note that the ratio 2/5 does not tell how many were surveyed or how many attend summer school.

are rational numbers. These numbers are not all in their simplest forms. We usually write 6 instead of $\frac{6}{1}$, $\frac{1}{2}$ instead of $\frac{2}{4}$, and 0 instead of $\frac{0}{2}$. A ratio such as $\frac{5}{0}$ does not represent any number. So we say that it is **undefined.** Any integer is a rational number because it could be written with a denominator of 1 as we did with 6 or $\frac{6}{1}$. Don't be concerned about how to simplify all of these ratios now. You will learn how to simplify all of them when we study fractions and signed numbers later in this chapter.

We cannot make a nice list of rational numbers like we did for the natural numbers, the whole numbers, and the integers. So we write the set of rational numbers in symbols using **set-builder notation** as follows.

The Rational Numbers

$$\left\{\frac{a}{b}\,\middle|\, a \text{ and } b \text{ are integers, with } b \neq 0\right\}$$

The set of ↑ such that ↑ conditions ↑

We read this notation as "the set of all numbers of the form $\frac{a}{b}$, where a and b are integers, with b not equal to 0."

If you divide the denominator into the numerator, then you can convert a rational number to decimal form. As a decimal, every rational number either repeats indefinitely $\left(\frac{1}{3} = 0.\overline{3} = 0.333\ldots\right)$ or terminates $\left(\frac{1}{8} = 0.125\right)$. The line over the 3 indicates that it repeats forever. The part that repeats can have more digits than the display of your calculator. In this case you will have to divide by hand to do the conversion. For example, try converting $\frac{11}{17}$ to a repeating decimal.

⟨3⟩ The Number Line

The number line is a diagram that helps us visualize numbers and their relationships to each other. A number line is like the scale on the thermometer in Fig. 1.2. To construct a number line, we draw a straight line and label any convenient point with the number 0. Now we choose any convenient length and use it to locate other points. Points to the right of 0 correspond to the positive numbers, and points to the left of 0 correspond to the negative numbers. Zero is neither positive nor negative. The number line is shown in Fig. 1.3.

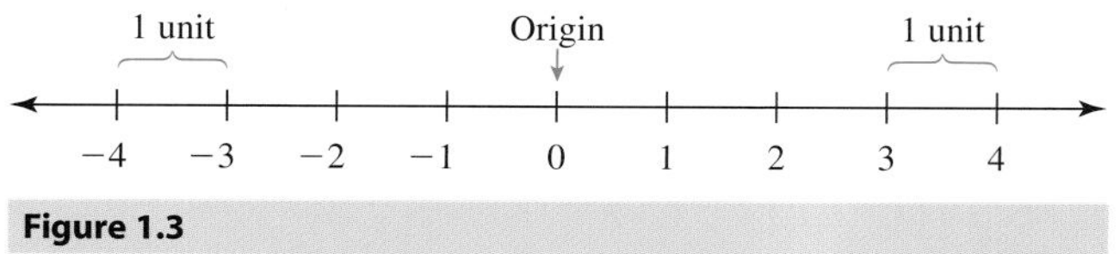

Figure 1.3

The numbers corresponding to the points on the line are called the **coordinates** of the points. The distance between two consecutive integers is called a **unit** and is the same for any two consecutive integers. The point with coordinate 0 is called the **origin.** The numbers on the number line increase in size from left to right. *When we compare the size of any two numbers, the larger number lies to the right of the smaller on the number line.* Zero is larger than any negative number and smaller than any positive number.

EXAMPLE 1

Comparing numbers on a number line

Determine which number is the larger in each given pair of numbers.

a) $-3, 2$ **b)** $0, -4$ **c)** $-2, -1$

Solution

a) The larger number is 2, because 2 lies to the right of -3 on the number line. In fact, any positive number is larger than any negative number.

b) The larger number is 0, because 0 lies to the right of -4 on the number line.

c) The larger number is -1, because -1 lies to the right of -2 on the number line.

Now do Exercises 7–18

The set of integers is illustrated or *graphed* in Fig. 1.4 by drawing a point for each integer. The three dots to the right and left below the number line and the blue arrows indicate that the numbers go on indefinitely in both directions.

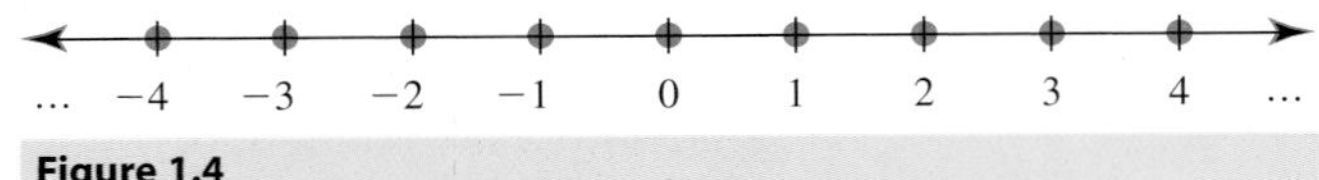

Figure 1.4

EXAMPLE 2

Graphing numbers on a number line

List the numbers described, and graph the numbers on a number line.

a) The whole numbers less than 4

b) The integers between 3 and 9

c) The integers greater than -3

Solution

a) The whole numbers less than 4 are 0, 1, 2, and 3. These numbers are shown in Fig. 1.5.

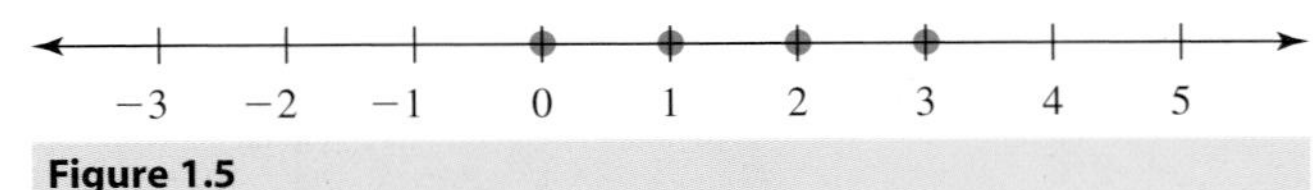

Figure 1.5

b) The integers between 3 and 9 are 4, 5, 6, 7, and 8. Note that 3 and 9 are not considered to be *between* 3 and 9. The graph is shown in Fig. 1.6.

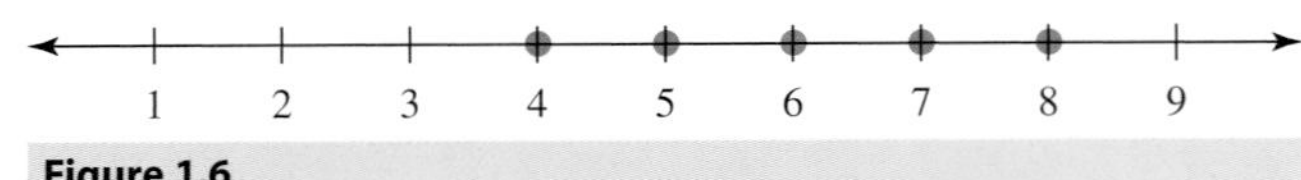

Figure 1.6

c) The integers greater than -3 are $-2, -1, 0, 1$, and so on. To indicate the continuing pattern, we use three dots on the graph shown in Fig. 1.7.

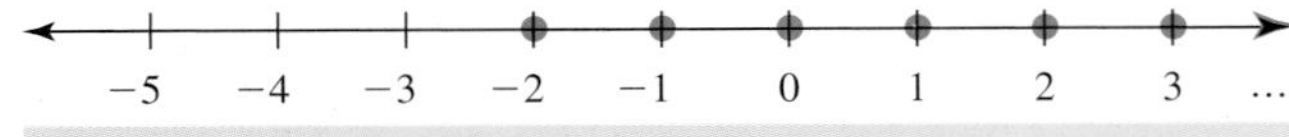

Figure 1.7

Now do Exercises 19–28

⟨4⟩ The Real Numbers

For every rational number there is a point on the number line. For example, the number $\frac{1}{2}$ corresponds to a point halfway between 0 and 1 on the number line, and $-\frac{5}{4}$ corresponds to a point one and one-quarter units to the left of 0, as shown in Fig. 1.8. Since there is a correspondence between numbers and points on the number line, the points are often referred to as numbers.

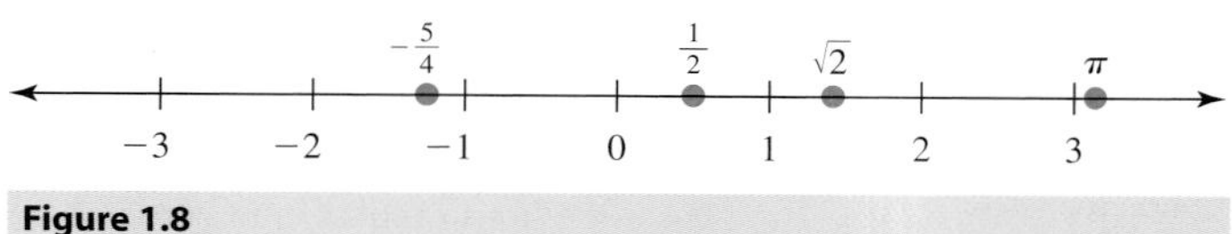

Figure 1.8

⟨ Calculator Close-Up ⟩

A calculator can give rational approximations for irrational numbers such as $\sqrt{2}$ and π.

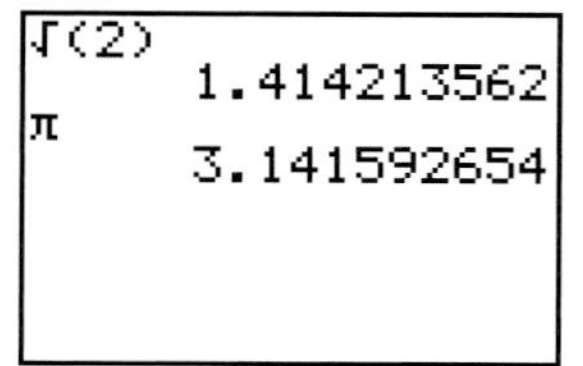

The calculator screens in this text may differ from the screen of the calculator model you use. If so, you may have to consult your manual to get the desired results.

The set of numbers that corresponds to *all* points on a number line is called the set of **real numbers** or R. A graph of the real numbers is shown on a number line by shading all points as in Fig. 1.9. All rational numbers are real numbers, but there are points on the number line that do not correspond to rational numbers. Those real numbers that are not rational are called **irrational.** An irrational number cannot be written as a ratio of integers. It can be shown that numbers such as $\sqrt{2}$ (the square root of 2) and π (Greek letter pi) are irrational. The number $\sqrt{2}$ is a number that can be multiplied by itself to obtain $2\,(\sqrt{2} \cdot \sqrt{2} = 2)$. The number π is the ratio of the circumference and diameter of any circle. Irrational numbers are not as easy to represent as rational numbers. That is why we use symbols such as $\sqrt{2}$, $\sqrt{3}$, and π for irrational numbers. When we perform computations with irrational numbers, we sometimes use rational approximations for them. For example, $\sqrt{2} \approx 1.414$ and $\pi \approx 3.14$. The symbol $\approx$ means "is approximately equal to." Note that not all square roots are irrational. For example, $\sqrt{9} = 3$, because $3 \cdot 3 = 9$. We will deal with irrational numbers in greater depth when we discuss roots in Chapter 8.

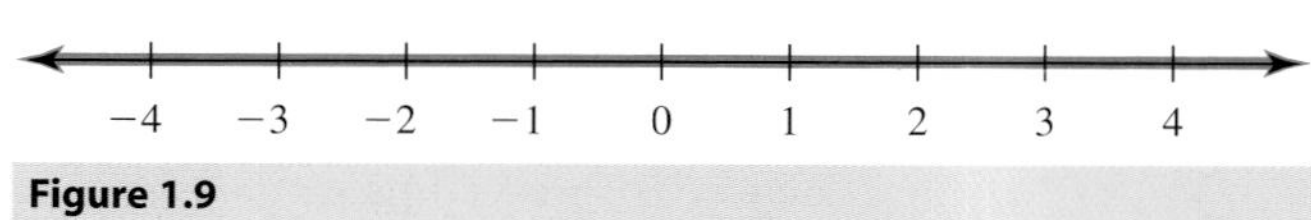

Figure 1.9

Figure 1.10 summarizes the sets of numbers that make up the real numbers, and shows the relationships between them.

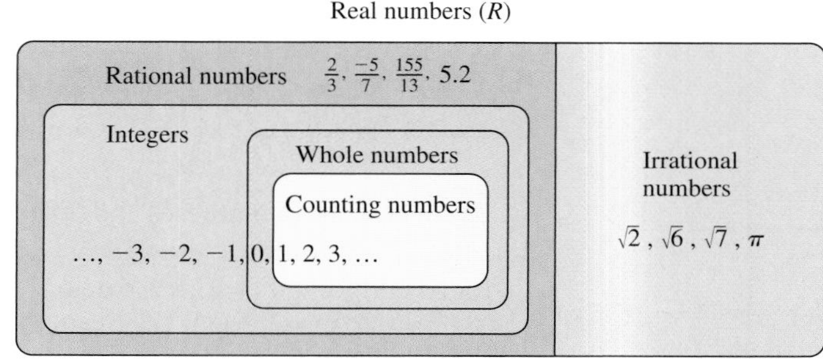

Figure 1.10

EXAMPLE 3

Types of numbers

Determine whether each statement is true or false.

a) Every rational number is an integer.

b) Every counting number is an integer.

c) Every irrational number is a real number.

‹ Teaching Tip ›

Remind students that in math every statement is either true or false. If there is one exception to a statement, then the statement is false. If the exception is noted in the statement, then the statement is true.

Solution

a) False. For example, $\frac{1}{2}$ is a rational number that is not an integer.

b) True, because the integers consist of the counting numbers, the negatives of the counting numbers, and zero.

c) True, because the rational numbers together with the irrational numbers form the real numbers.

Now do Exercises 29–40

‹5› Intervals of Real Numbers

Retailers often have a sale for a certain *interval* of time. Between 6 A.M. and 8 A.M. you get a 20% discount. A **bounded** or finite interval of real numbers is the set of real numbers that are between two real numbers, which are called the **endpoints** of the interval. The endpoints may or may not belong to an interval. **Interval notation** is used to represent intervals of real numbers. In interval notation, parentheses are used to indicate that the endpoints do not belong to the interval and brackets indicate that the endpoints do belong to the interval. The following box shows the four types of finite intervals for two real numbers a and b, where a is less than b.

Finite Intervals

Verbal Description	Interval Notation	Graph
The set of real numbers between a and b	(a, b)	(a ——— b)
The set of real numbers between a and b inclusive	$[a, b]$	[a ——— b]
The set of real numbers greater than a and less than or equal to b	$(a, b]$	(a ——— b]
The set of real numbers greater than or equal to a and less than b	$[a, b)$	[a ——— b)

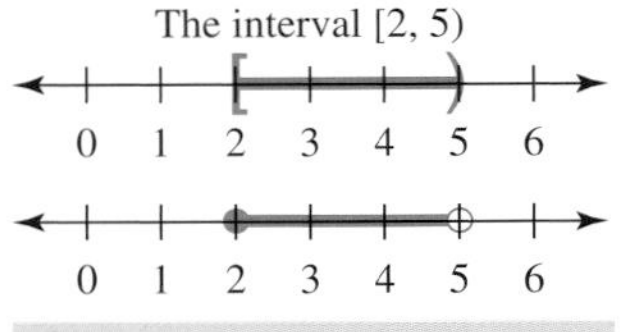

Figure 1.11

Note how the parentheses and brackets are used on the graph and in the interval notation. It is also common to draw the graph of an interval of real numbers using an open circle for an endpoint that does not belong to the interval and a closed circle for an endpoint that belongs to the interval. For example, see the graphs of the interval [2, 5) in Fig. 1.11. In this text, graphs of intervals will be drawn with parentheses and brackets so that they agree with interval notation.

EXAMPLE 4

Interval notation for finite intervals

Write the interval notation for each interval of real numbers and graph the interval.

a) The set of real numbers greater than 3 and less than or equal to 5
b) The set of real numbers between 0 and 4 inclusive
c) The set of real numbers greater than or equal to -1 and less than 4
d) The set of real numbers between -2 and -1

Solution

a) The set of real numbers greater than 3 and less than or equal to 5 is written in interval notation as $(3, 5]$ and graphed in Fig. 1.12.

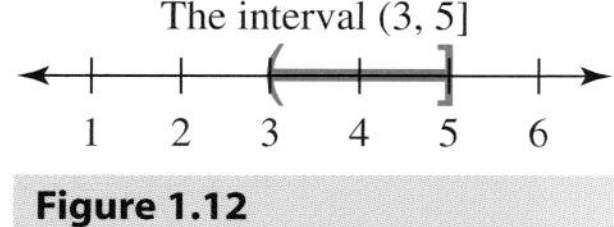

Figure 1.12

b) The set of real numbers between 0 and 4 inclusive is written in interval notation as $[0, 4]$ and graphed in Fig. 1.13.

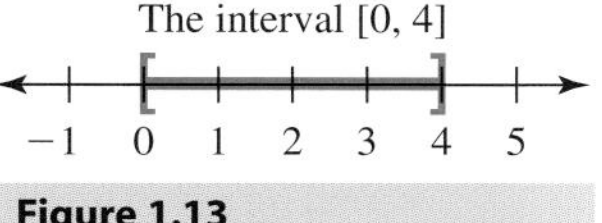

Figure 1.13

c) The set of real numbers greater than or equal to -1 and less than 4 is written in interval notation as $[-1, 4)$ and graphed in Fig. 1.14.

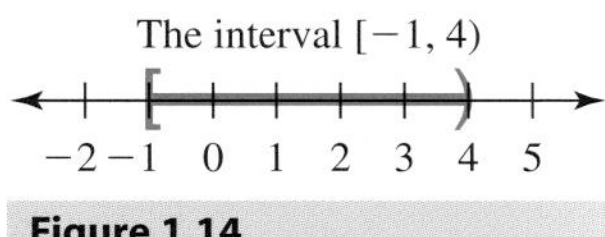

Figure 1.14

d) The set of real numbers between -2 and -1 is written in interval notation as $(-2, -1)$ and graphed in Fig. 1.15.

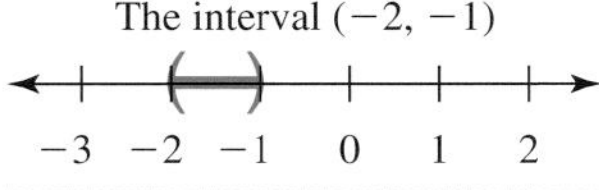

Figure 1.15

Now do Exercises 41–46

Some sales never end. After 8 A.M. all merchandise is 10% off. An **unbounded** or **infinite interval** of real numbers is missing at least one endpoint. It may extend infinitely far to the right or left on the number line. In this case the infinity symbol ∞ is used as an endpoint in the interval notation. Note that parentheses are always used next to ∞ or $-\infty$ in interval notation, because ∞ is not a number. It is just used to indicate that there is no end to the interval. The following box shows the five types of infinite intervals for a real number a.

Infinite Intervals

Verbal Description	Interval Notation	Graph
The set of real numbers greater than a	(a, ∞)	
The set of real numbers greater than or equal to a	$[a, \infty)$	
The set of real numbers less than a	$(-\infty, a)$	
The set of real numbers less than or equal to a	$(-\infty, a]$	
The set of all real numbers	$(-\infty, \infty)$	

EXAMPLE 5

Interval notation for infinite intervals

Write each interval of real numbers in interval notation and graph it.

a) The set of real numbers greater than or equal to 3

b) The set of real numbers less than -2

c) The set of real numbers greater than 2.5

Solution

a) The set of real numbers greater than or equal to 3 is written in interval notation as $[3, \infty)$ and graphed in Fig. 1.16.

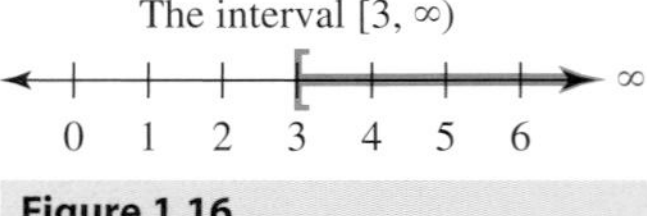

Figure 1.16

b) The set of real numbers less than -2 is written in interval notation as $(-\infty, -2)$ and graphed in Fig. 1.17.

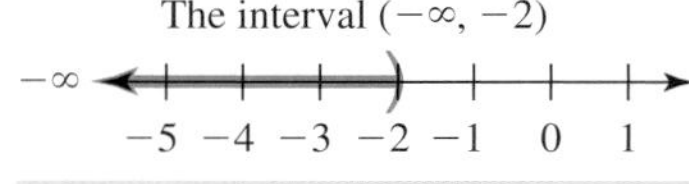

Figure 1.17

c) The set of real numbers greater than 2.5 is written in interval notation as $(2.5, \infty)$ and graphed in Fig. 1.18.

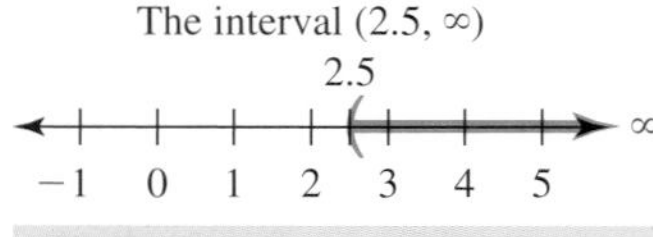

Figure 1.18

Now do Exercises 47–52

⟨6⟩ Absolute Value

The concept of absolute value will be used to define the basic operations with real numbers in Section 1.3. The **absolute value** of a number is the number's distance from 0 on the number line. For example, the numbers 5 and -5 are both five units away from 0 on the number line. So the absolute value of each of these numbers is 5. See Fig. 1.19. We write $|a|$ for "the absolute value of a." So

$$|5| = 5 \qquad \text{and} \qquad |-5| = 5.$$

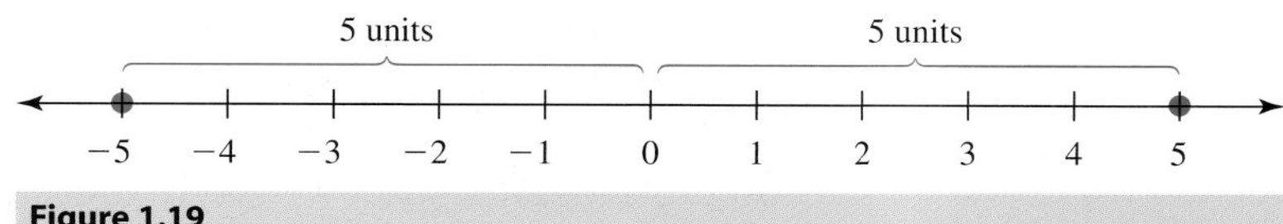

Figure 1.19

The notation $|a|$ represents distance, and distance is never negative. So $|a|$ is greater than or equal to zero for any real number a.

EXAMPLE 6 Finding absolute value

Evaluate.

a) $|3|$ **b)** $|-3|$

c) $|0|$ **d)** $\left|\frac{2}{3}\right|$

e) $|-0.39|$

Solution

a) $|3| = 3$ because 3 is three units away from 0.

b) $|-3| = 3$ because -3 is three units away from 0.

c) $|0| = 0$ because 0 is zero units away from 0.

d) $\left|\frac{2}{3}\right| = \frac{2}{3}$

e) $|-0.39| = 0.39$

Now do Exercises 53–60

Two numbers that are located on opposite sides of zero and have the same absolute value are called **opposites** of each other. The numbers 5 and -5 are opposites of each other. We say that the opposite of 5 is -5 and the opposite of -5 is 5. The symbol "$-$" is used to indicate "opposite" as well as "negative." When the negative sign is used before a number, it should be read as "negative." When it is used in front of parentheses or a variable, it should be read as "opposite." For example, $-(5) = -5$ means "the opposite of 5 is negative 5," and $-(-5) = 5$ means "the opposite of negative 5 is 5." Zero does not have an opposite in the same sense as nonzero numbers. Zero is its own opposite. We read $-(0) = 0$ as the "the opposite of zero is zero."

‹ Teaching Tip ›

Ask students whether $-(-(-(-(-(-(-5))))))$ is positive or negative. Ask them to write a rule for deciding.

In general, $-a$ means "the opposite of a." If a is positive, $-a$ is negative. If a is negative, $-a$ is positive. Opposites have the following property.

Opposite of an Opposite

For any real number a,

$$-(-a) = a.$$

Remember that we have defined $|a|$ to be the distance between 0 and a on the number line. Using opposites, we can give a symbolic definition of absolute value.

Absolute Value

$$|a| = \begin{cases} a & \text{if } a \text{ is positive or zero} \\ -a & \text{if } a \text{ is negative} \end{cases}$$

EXAMPLE 7

Using the symbolic definition of absolute value

Evaluate.

a) $|8|$ **b)** $|0|$ **c)** $|-8|$

Solution

a) From the definition, $|a| = a$ if a is positive. Since 8 is positive, we replace a with 8 to get $|8| = 8$.

b) From the definition, $|a| = a$ if a is zero. Replacing a with 0, we get $|0| = 0$.

c) From the definition, $|a| = -a$ if a is negative. Since -8 is negative, we replace a with -8 to get $|-8| = -(-8) = 8$.

Now do Exercises 61–66

Warm-Ups ▼

True or false? Explain your answer.

1. The natural numbers and the counting numbers are the same. True
2. The number 8,134,562,877,565 is a counting number. True
3. Zero is a counting number. False
4. Zero is not a rational number. False
5. The opposite of negative 3 is positive 3. True
6. The absolute value of 4 is -4. False
7. $-(-9) = 9$ True
8. The real number π is in the interval (3, 4). True
9. Negative 6 is greater than negative 3. False
10. Negative 5 is between 4 and 6. False

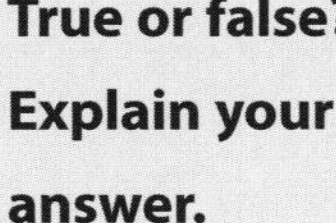

‹ Teaching Tip ›

The Warm-Ups can be done orally. Ask students to explain their answers.

MathZone

Boost your grade at mathzone.com!
- Practice Problems
- NetTutor
- Self-Tests
- e-Professors
- Videos

Exercises 1.1

‹ **Study Tips** ›

- Exercise sets are designed to increase gradually in difficulty. So start from the beginning and work lots of exercises.
- Find a group of students to work with outside of class. Explaining things to others improves your own understanding of the concepts.

Reading and Writing *After reading this section write out the answers to these questions. Use complete sentences.*

1. What are the integers?
The integers are the numbers in the set $\{\ldots, -3, -2, -1, 0, 1, 2, 3, \ldots\}$.

2. What are the rational numbers?
The rational numbers are numbers of the form $\frac{a}{b}$ where a and b are integers and $b \neq 0$.

3. What is the difference between a rational and an irrational number?
A rational number is a ratio of integers and an irrational number is not.

4. What is a number line?
A number line is a line on which there is a point corresponding to every real number.

5. How do you know that one number is larger than another?
The number a is larger than b if a lies to the right of b on the number line.

6. What is the ratio of the circumference and diameter of any circle?
The ratio of the circumference and diameter of any circle is the number π, which is approximately 3.14.

‹3› The Number Line

Determine which number is the larger in each given pair of numbers. See Example 1.

7. 0, 6   6
8. 7, 4   7
9. −3, 6   6
10. 7, −10   7
11. 0, −6   0
12. −8, 0   0
13. −3, −2   −2
14. −5, −8   −5
15. −12, −15   −12
16. −13, −7   −7
17. −2.9, −2.1   −2.1
18. 2.1, 2.9   2.9

List the numbers described and graph them on a number line. See Example 2.

19. The counting numbers smaller than 6

1, 2, 3, 4, 5

20. The natural numbers larger than 4

5, 6, 7, 8, 9, . . .

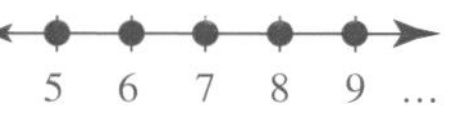

21. The whole numbers smaller than 5

0, 1, 2, 3, 4

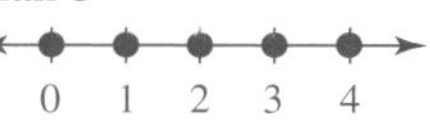

22. The integers between −3 and 3

−2, −1, 0, 1, 2

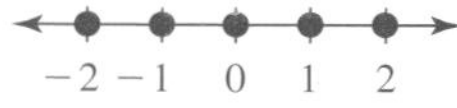

23. The whole numbers between −5 and 5

0, 1, 2, 3, 4

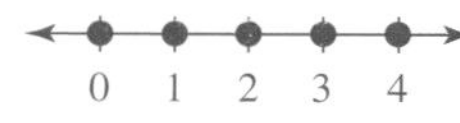

24. The integers smaller than −1

−2, −3, −4, −5, . . .

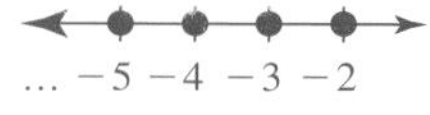

25. The counting numbers larger than −4

1, 2, 3, 4, 5, . . .

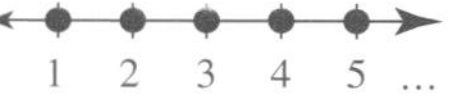

26. The natural numbers between −5 and 7

1, 2, 3, 4, 5, 6

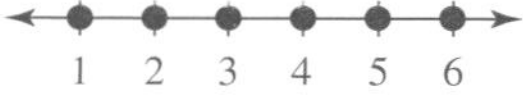

27. The integers larger than $\frac{1}{2}$

1, 2, 3, 4, 5, . . .

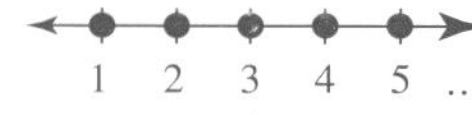

28. The whole numbers smaller than $\frac{7}{4}$

0, 1

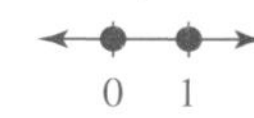

‹4› The Real Numbers

Determine whether each statement is true or false. Explain your answer. See Example 3.

29. Every integer is a rational number.   True
30. Every counting number is a whole number.   True
31. Zero is a counting number.   False
32. Every whole number is a counting number.   False
33. The ratio of the circumference and diameter of a circle is an irrational number.   True
34. Every rational number can be expressed as a ratio of integers.   True
35. Every whole number can be expressed as a ratio of integers.   True
36. Some of the rational numbers are integers.   True
37. Some of the integers are natural numbers.   True
38. There are infinitely many rational numbers.   True
39. Zero is an irrational number.   False
40. Every irrational number is a real number.   True

⟨5⟩ Intervals of Real Numbers

Write each interval of real numbers in interval notation and graph it. See Example 4.

41. The set of real numbers between 0 and 1

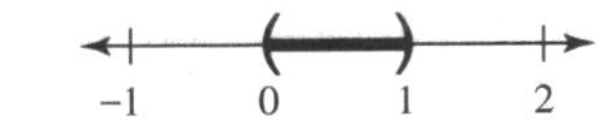

42. The set of real numbers between 2 and 6

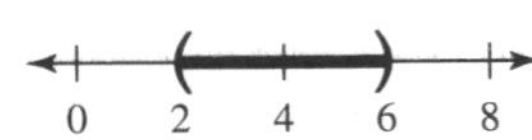

43. The set of real numbers between −2 and 2 inclusive

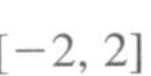

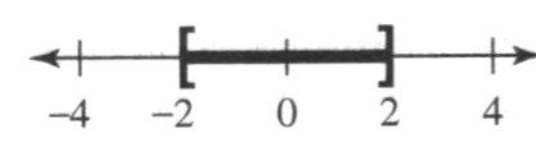

44. The set of real numbers between −3 and 4 inclusive

[−3, 4]

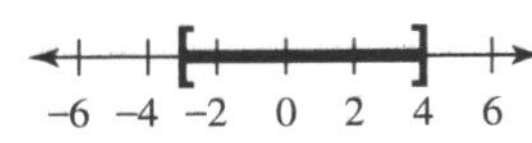

VIDEO **45.** The set of real numbers greater than 0 and less than or equal to 5

46. The set of real numbers greater than or equal to −1 and less than 6

[−1, 6)

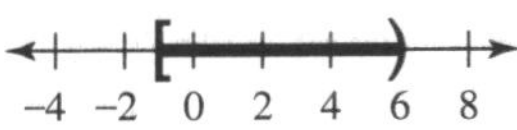

Write each interval of real numbers in interval notation and graph it. See Example 5.

47. The set of real numbers greater than 4

48. The set of real numbers greater than 2

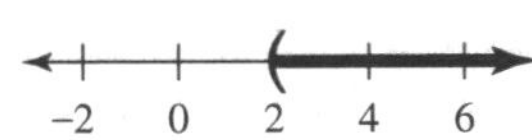

49. The set of real numbers less than or equal to −1

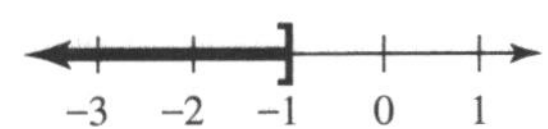

50. The set of real numbers less than or equal to −4

(−∞, −4]

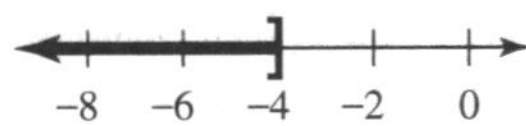

51. The set of real numbers greater than or equal to 0

[0, ∞)

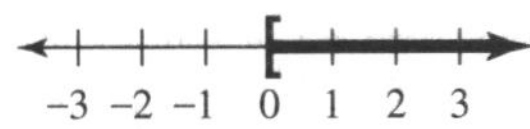

52. The set of real numbers greater than or equal to 6

[6, ∞)

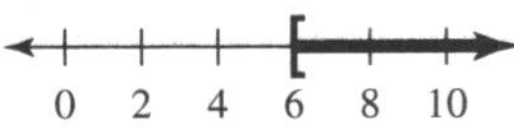

⟨6⟩ Absolute Value

Determine the values of the following. See Examples 6 and 7.

53. $|-6|$ 6 **54.** $|4|$ 4
55. $|0|$ 0 VIDEO **56.** $|2|$ 2
57. $|7|$ 7 **58.** $|-7|$ 7
59. $|-9|$ 9 **60.** $|-2|$ 2
61. $|-45|$ 45 **62.** $|-30|$ 30
63. $\left|\frac{3}{4}\right|$ $\frac{3}{4}$ **64.** $\left|-\frac{1}{2}\right|$ $\frac{1}{2}$
65. $|-5.09|$ 5.09 **66.** $|0.00987|$ 0.00987

Select the smaller number in each given pair of numbers.

67. −16, 9 −16 **68.** −12, −7 −12
69. $-\frac{5}{2}, -\frac{9}{4}$ $-\frac{5}{2}$ **70.** $\frac{5}{8}, \frac{6}{7}$ $\frac{5}{8}$
71. $|-3|$, 2 2 **72.** $|-6|$, 0 0
73. $|-4|$, 3 3 **74.** $|5|$, −4 −4

Which number in each given pair has the larger absolute value?

75. −5, −9 −9 **76.** −12, −8 −12
77. 16, −9 16 **78.** −12, 7 −12

Determine which number in each pair is closer to 0 on the number line.

79. −4, −5 −4 **80.** −8.1, 7.9 7.9
81. −2.01, −1.99 −1.99 **82.** 2.01, 1.99 1.99
83. −75, 74 74 **84.** −75, −74 −74

What is the distance on the number line between 0 and each of the following numbers?

85. 5.25 5.25 **86.** 4.2 4.2 **87.** −40 40
88. −33 33 **89.** $-\frac{1}{2}$ $\frac{1}{2}$ **90.** $-\frac{1}{3}$ $\frac{1}{3}$

Consider the following nine integers:

−4, −3, −2, −1, 0, 1, 2, 3, 4

91. Which of these integers has an absolute value equal to 3? −3 and 3
92. Which of these integers has an absolute value equal to 0? 0
93. Which of these integers has an absolute value greater than 2? −4, −3, 3, 4
94. Which of these integers has an absolute value greater than 1? −4, −3, −2, 2, 3, 4
95. Which of these integers has an absolute value less than 2? −1, 0, 1
96. Which of these integers has an absolute value less than 4? −3, −2, −1, 0, 1, 2, 3

Miscellaneous

Write the interval notation for the interval of real numbers shown in each graph.

97. 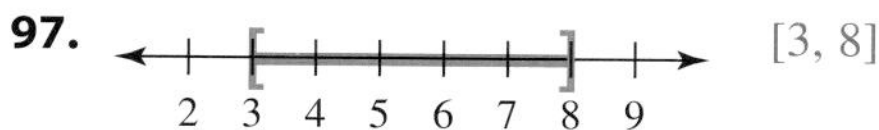 [3, 8]

98. [−4, 4]

99. (−30, −20]

100. [−40, −30)

101. [30, ∞)

102. (−∞, 20)

True or false? Explain your answer.

103. If we add the absolute values of −3 and −5, we get 8. True

104. If we multiply the absolute values of −2 and 5, we get 10. True

105. The absolute value of any negative number is greater than 0. True

106. The absolute value of any positive number is less than 0. False

107. The absolute value of −9 is larger than the absolute value of 6. True

108. The absolute value of 12 is larger than the absolute value of −11. True

Getting More Involved

109. ***Exploration***

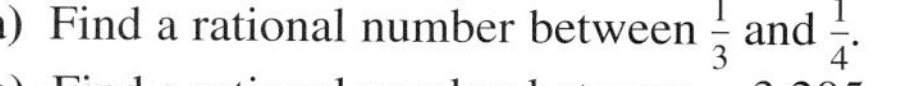

a) Find a rational number between $\frac{1}{3}$ and $\frac{1}{4}$.

b) Find a rational number between −3.205 and −3.114.

c) Find a rational number between $\frac{2}{3}$ and 0.6667.

d) Explain how to find a rational number between any two given rational numbers. Answers may vary.

a) $\frac{7}{24}$ b) −3.115 c) 0.66669

d) Add them and divide the result by 2.

110. ***Discussion***

Suppose that a is a negative real number. Determine whether each of the following is positive or negative, and explain your answer.

a) $-a$ **b)** $|-a|$ **c)** $-|a|$ **d)** $-(-a)$ **e)** $-|-a|$

If a is negative, then $-a$ and $|-a|$ are positive. The rest are negative.

111. ***Discussion***

Determine whether each number listed in the table below is a member of each set listed on the side of the table. For example, $\frac{1}{2}$ is a real number and a rational number. So check marks are placed in those two cells of the table.

	$\frac{1}{2}$	-2	π	$\sqrt{3}$	$\sqrt{9}$	6	0	$-\frac{7}{3}$
Real	✓	✓	✓	✓	✓	✓	✓	✓
Irrational			✓	✓				
Rational	✓	✓			✓	✓	✓	✓
Integer		✓			✓	✓	✓	
Whole					✓	✓	✓	
Counting					✓	✓		

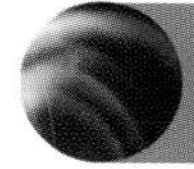

1.2 Fractions

In This Section

In this section and Sections 1.3 and 1.4 we will discuss operations performed with real numbers. We begin by reviewing operations with fractions. Note that this section on fractions is not an entire arithmetic course. We are simply reviewing selected fraction topics that will be used in this text.

⟨1⟩ Equivalent Fractions

A **fraction** is a rational number that is not an integer. The rational number $\frac{2}{3}$ is a fraction. If a pizza is cut into 3 equal pieces and you eat 2, you have eaten $\frac{2}{3}$ of the pizza. If the

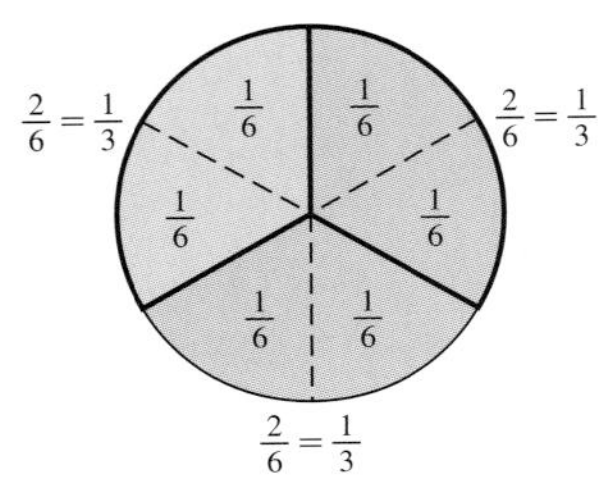

Figure 1.20

pizza is cut into 6 equal pieces and you eat 4, you have still eaten 2 out of every 3 pieces. So the fraction $\frac{4}{6}$ is considered **equal** or **equivalent** to $\frac{2}{3}$. See Fig. 1.20. Every fraction can be written in infinitely many equivalent forms. Consider the following equivalent forms of $\frac{2}{3}$:

$$\frac{2}{3} = \frac{4}{6} = \frac{6}{9} = \frac{8}{12} = \frac{10}{15} = \underbrace{\cdots}$$

The three dots mean "and so on."

Notice that each equivalent form of $\frac{2}{3}$ can be obtained by multiplying the numerator (top number) and denominator (bottom number) of $\frac{2}{3}$ by the same nonzero number. For example,

$$\frac{2}{3} = \frac{2 \cdot 5}{3 \cdot 5} = \frac{10}{15}.$$

The raised dot indicates multiplication.

‹ Teaching Tip ›

Insist that students use the methods shown here for building up and reducing fractions. These same methods will be used on rational expressions in Chapter 7.

Converting a fraction into an equivalent fraction with a larger denominator is called **building up** the fraction. As we have just seen, $\frac{2}{3}$ is built up to $\frac{10}{15}$ by multiplying its numerator and denominator by 5.

Building Up Fractions

If $b \neq 0$ and $c \neq 0$, then

$$\frac{a}{b} = \frac{a \cdot c}{b \cdot c}.$$

Multiplying the numerator and denominator of a fraction by a nonzero number changes the fraction's appearance but not its value.

EXAMPLE 1

Building up fractions

Build up each fraction so that it is equivalent to the fraction with the indicated denominator.

a) $\frac{3}{4} = \frac{?}{28}$ **b)** $\frac{5}{3} = \frac{?}{30}$

Solution

a) Because $4 \cdot 7 = 28$, we multiply both the numerator and denominator by 7:

$$\frac{3}{4} = \frac{3 \cdot 7}{4 \cdot 7} = \frac{21}{28}$$

b) Because $3 \cdot 10 = 30$, we multiply both the numerator and denominator by 10:

$$\frac{5}{3} = \frac{5 \cdot 10}{3 \cdot 10} = \frac{50}{30}$$

Now do Exercises 7–18

The method for building up fractions shown in Example 1 will be used again on rational expressions in Chapter 7. So it is good to use this method and show the details. The same goes for the method of reducing fractions that is coming next.

Converting a fraction to an equivalent fraction with a smaller denominator is called **reducing** the fraction. For example, to reduce $\frac{10}{15}$, we *factor* 10 as $2 \cdot 5$ and 15 as $3 \cdot 5$, and then divide out the *common factor* 5:

$$\frac{10}{15} = \frac{2 \cdot \cancel{5}}{3 \cdot \cancel{5}} = \frac{2}{3}$$

The fraction $\frac{2}{3}$ cannot be reduced further because the numerator 2 and the denominator 3 have no factors (other than 1) in common. So we say that $\frac{2}{3}$ is in **lowest terms.**

Reducing Fractions

If $b \neq 0$ and $c \neq 0$, then

$$\frac{a \cdot c}{b \cdot c} = \frac{a}{b}.$$

CAUTION Reducing a fraction changes its appearance, but not its value. The fraction $\frac{2}{3}$ is *not* smaller than $\frac{10}{15}$.

EXAMPLE 2

Reducing fractions

Reduce each fraction to lowest terms.

a) $\frac{15}{24}$ **b)** $\frac{42}{30}$ **c)** $\frac{13}{26}$ **d)** $\frac{35}{7}$

Solution

For each fraction, factor the numerator and denominator and then divide by the common factor:

a) $\frac{15}{24} = \frac{3 \cdot 5}{3 \cdot 8} = \frac{5}{8}$

b) $\frac{42}{30} = \frac{7 \cdot \cancel{6}}{5 \cdot \cancel{6}} = \frac{7}{5}$

c) $\frac{13}{26} = \frac{1 \cdot \cancel{13}}{2 \cdot \cancel{13}} = \frac{1}{2}$ The number 1 in the numerator is essential.

d) $\frac{35}{7} = \frac{5 \cdot \cancel{7}}{1 \cdot \cancel{7}} = \frac{5}{1} = 5$

Now do Exercises 19–34

‹ Calculator Close-Up ›

To reduce a fraction to lowest terms using a graphing calculator, display the fraction and use the fraction feature.

```
15/24▸Frac
             5/8
42/30▸Frac
             7/5
123456/222222▸Fr
ac
     .5555525556
```

If the fraction is too complicated, the calculator will return a decimal equivalent instead of reducing it.

Strategy for Obtaining Equivalent Fractions

Equivalent fractions can be obtained by multiplying or dividing the numerator and denominator by the same nonzero number.

‹2› Multiplying Fractions

Suppose a pizza is cut into three equal pieces. If you eat $\frac{1}{2}$ of one piece, you have eaten $\frac{1}{6}$ of the pizza. See Fig. 1.21. You can obtain $\frac{1}{6}$ by multiplying $\frac{1}{2}$ and $\frac{1}{3}$:

$$\frac{1}{2} \cdot \frac{1}{3} = \frac{1 \cdot 1}{2 \cdot 3} = \frac{1}{6}$$

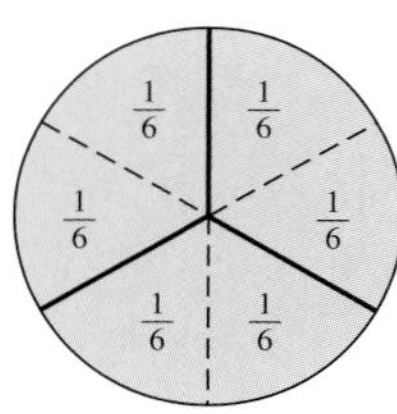

Figure 1.21

This example illustrates the definition of multiplication of fractions. To multiply two fractions, we multiply their numerators and multiply their denominators.

Multiplication of Fractions

If $b \neq 0$ and $d \neq 0$, then

$$\frac{a}{b} \cdot \frac{c}{d} = \frac{a \cdot c}{b \cdot d}.$$

We can multiply the numerators and the denominators and then reduce, as in Example 3(a) or we can reduce before multiplying as in Examples 3(b) and (c). It is usually simpler to reduce before multiplying.

EXAMPLE 3

Multiplying fractions

Find each product.

a) $\frac{2}{3} \cdot \frac{5}{8}$ **b)** $\frac{1}{3} \cdot \frac{3}{4}$ **c)** $\frac{4}{5} \cdot \frac{15}{22}$

Solution

a) First multiply the numerators and the denominators, and then reduce:

$$\frac{2}{3} \cdot \frac{5}{8} = \frac{10}{24}$$

$$= \frac{\not{2} \cdot 5}{\not{2} \cdot 12} \quad \text{Factor the numerator and denominator.}$$

$$= \frac{5}{12} \quad \text{Divide out the common factor 2.}$$

b) Reduce before multiplying:

$$\frac{1}{3} \cdot \frac{3}{4} = \frac{1}{\not{3}} \cdot \frac{\not{3}}{4} = \frac{1}{4}$$

c) Factor the numerators and denominators, and then divide out the common factors before multiplying:

$$\frac{4}{5} \cdot \frac{15}{22} = \frac{2 \cdot \not{2}}{\not{5}} \cdot \frac{3 \cdot \not{5}}{\not{2} \cdot 11} = \frac{6}{11}$$

Now do Exercises 35–46

‹ Teaching Tip ›

Keep on reminding students that canceling works only for multiplication in the numerator and denominator.

‹ Calculator Close-Up ›

A graphing calculator can multiply fractions and get fractional answers using the fraction feature.

```
2/3*5/8▸Frac
            5/12
1/3*3/4▸Frac
             1/4
4/5*15/22▸Frac
            6/11
```

Multiplication of fractions can help us better understand the idea of building up fractions. For example, we have already seen that multiplying $\frac{2}{3}$ by 5 in its numerator and denominator builds it up to $\frac{10}{15}$:

$$\frac{2}{3} = \frac{2 \cdot 5}{3 \cdot 5} = \frac{10}{15}$$

We can get this same result by multiplying $\frac{2}{3}$ by 1, using $\frac{5}{5}$ for 1:

$$\frac{2}{3} = \frac{2}{3} \cdot 1 = \frac{2}{3} \cdot \frac{5}{5} = \frac{10}{15}$$

So building up a fraction is equivalent to multiplying it by 1, which does not change its value.

⟨3⟩ Unit Conversion

Most measurements can be expressed in a variety of units. For example, distance could be in miles or kilometers. Converting from one unit of measurement to another can always be done by multiplying by a conversion factor expressed as a fraction. (Some common conversion factors can be found on the inside back cover of this text.) This method is called **cancellation of units,** because the units cancel just like the common factors cancel in multiplication of fractions.

EXAMPLE 4

Unit conversion

a) Convert 6 yards to feet.

b) Convert 12 miles to kilometers.

c) Convert 60 miles per hour to feet per second.

‹ Teaching Tip ›

Emphasize that the cancellation of units method is generally taught and used in the sciences and can be used on any conversions.

Solution

a) Because 3 feet = 1 yard, multiplying by $\frac{3 \text{ feet}}{1 \text{ yard}}$ is equivalent to multiplying by 1. Notice how yards cancels and the result is feet.

$$6 \text{ yd} = 6 \cancel{\text{yd}} \cdot \frac{3 \text{ ft}}{1 \cancel{\text{yd}}} = 18 \text{ ft}$$

b) There are two ways to convert 12 miles to kilometers using the conversion factors given on the inside back cover:

$$12 \text{ mi} = 12 \cancel{\text{mi}} \cdot \frac{1.609 \text{ km}}{1 \cancel{\text{mi}}} \approx 19.31 \text{ km}$$

$$12 \text{ mi} = 12 \cancel{\text{mi}} \cdot \frac{1 \text{ km}}{0.6214 \cancel{\text{mi}}} \approx 19.31 \text{ km}$$

Notice that in the second method we are also multiplying by a fraction that is equivalent to 1, but we actually divide 12 by 0.6214.

c) Convert 60 miles per hour to feet per second as follows:

$$60 \text{ mi/hr} = \frac{60 \cancel{\text{mi}}}{1 \cancel{\text{hr}}} \cdot \frac{5280 \text{ ft}}{1 \cancel{\text{mi}}} \cdot \frac{1 \cancel{\text{hr}}}{60 \cancel{\text{min}}} \cdot \frac{1 \cancel{\text{min}}}{60 \text{ sec}} = 88 \text{ ft/sec}$$

Now do Exercises 47–58

⟨4⟩ Dividing Fractions

Suppose that a pizza is cut into three pieces. If one piece is divided between two people $\left(\frac{1}{3} \div 2\right)$, then each of these two people gets $\frac{1}{6}$ of the pizza. Of course $\frac{1}{3}$ times $\frac{1}{2}$ is also $\frac{1}{6}$. So dividing by 2 is equivalent to multiplying by $\frac{1}{2}$. In symbols:

$$\frac{1}{3} \div 2 = \frac{1}{3} \div \frac{2}{1} = \frac{1}{3} \cdot \frac{1}{2} = \frac{1}{6}$$

The pizza example illustrates the general rule for dividing fractions.

Division of Fractions

If $b \neq 0$, $c \neq 0$, and $d \neq 0$, then

$$\frac{a}{b} \div \frac{c}{d} = \frac{a}{b} \cdot \frac{d}{c}.$$

In general if $m \div n = p$, then n is called the **divisor** and p (the result of the division) is called the **quotient** of m and n. We also refer to $m \div n$ and $\frac{m}{n}$ as the quotient of m and n. So in words, *to find the quotient of two fractions we invert the divisor and multiply.*

EXAMPLE 5 Dividing fractions

Find the indicated quotients.

a) $\frac{1}{3} \div \frac{7}{6}$ **b)** $\frac{2}{3} \div 5$ **c)** $\frac{3}{8} \div \frac{3}{2}$

Solution

In each case we invert the divisor (the number on the right) and multiply.

a) $\frac{1}{3} \div \frac{7}{6} = \frac{1}{3} \cdot \frac{6}{7}$ Invert the divisor.

$= \frac{1}{\cancel{3}} \cdot \frac{2 \cdot \cancel{3}}{7}$ Reduce.

$= \frac{2}{7}$ Multiply.

b) $\frac{2}{3} \div 5 = \frac{2}{3} \div \frac{5}{1} = \frac{2}{3} \cdot \frac{1}{5} = \frac{2}{15}$

c) $\frac{3}{8} \div \frac{3}{2} = \frac{3}{8} \cdot \frac{2}{3} = \frac{\cancel{3} \cdot 1}{4 \cdot \cancel{2}} \cdot \frac{\cancel{2}}{\cancel{3}} = \frac{1}{4}$

Now do Exercises 59–68

‹ Calculator Close-Up ›

When the divisor is a fraction on a graphing calculator, it must be in parentheses. A different result is obtained without using parentheses. Note that when the divisor is a whole number, parentheses are not necessary.

```
1/3/(7/6)▸Frac
             2/7
1/3/7/6▸Frac
           1/126
2/3/5▸Frac
            2/15
```

Try these computations on your calculator.

‹5› Adding and Subtracting Fractions

To understand addition and subtraction of fractions, again consider the pizza that is cut into six equal pieces as shown in Fig. 1.22. If you eat $\frac{3}{6}$ and your friend eats $\frac{2}{6}$, together you have eaten $\frac{5}{6}$ of the pizza. Similarly, if you remove $\frac{1}{6}$ from $\frac{6}{6}$ you have $\frac{5}{6}$ left. To add or subtract fractions with identical denominators, we add or subtract their numerators and write the result over the common denominator.

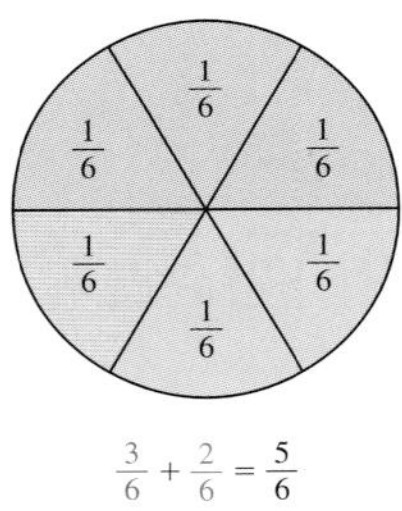

$\frac{3}{6} + \frac{2}{6} = \frac{5}{6}$

Figure 1.22

Addition and Subtraction of Fractions

If $b \neq 0$, then

$$\frac{a}{b} + \frac{c}{b} = \frac{a + c}{b} \quad \text{and} \quad \frac{a}{b} - \frac{c}{b} = \frac{a - c}{b}.$$

An **improper fraction** is a fraction in which the numerator is larger than the denominator. For example, $\frac{7}{6}$ is an improper fraction. A **mixed number** is a natural number plus a fraction, with the plus sign removed. For example, $1\frac{1}{6}$ $\left(\text{or } 1 + \frac{1}{6}\right)$ is a mixed number. Since $1 + \frac{1}{6} = \frac{6}{6} + \frac{1}{6} = \frac{7}{6}$, we have $1\frac{1}{6} = \frac{7}{6}$.

EXAMPLE 6 Adding and subtracting fractions

Perform the indicated operations.

a) $\frac{1}{7} + \frac{2}{7}$

b) $\frac{7}{10} - \frac{3}{10}$

Solution

a) $\frac{1}{7} + \frac{2}{7} = \frac{3}{7}$

b) $\frac{7}{10} - \frac{3}{10} = \frac{4}{10} = \frac{2 \cdot 2}{2 \cdot 5} = \frac{2}{5}$

Now do Exercises 69–72

‹ Helpful Hint ›

A good way to remember that you need common denominators for addition is to think of a simple example. If you own 1/3 share of a car wash and your spouse owns 1/3, then together you own 2/3 of the business.

CAUTION Do not add the denominators when adding fractions: $\frac{1}{7} + \frac{2}{7} \neq \frac{3}{14}$.

To add or subtract fractions with different denominators, we must convert them to equivalent fractions with the same denominator and then add or subtract. For example, to add $\frac{1}{2}$ and $\frac{1}{3}$, we build up each fraction to a denominator of 6. See Fig. 1.23. Since $\frac{1}{2} = \frac{3}{6}$ and $\frac{1}{3} = \frac{2}{6}$, we have

$$\frac{1}{2} + \frac{1}{3} = \frac{3}{6} + \frac{2}{6} = \frac{5}{6}.$$

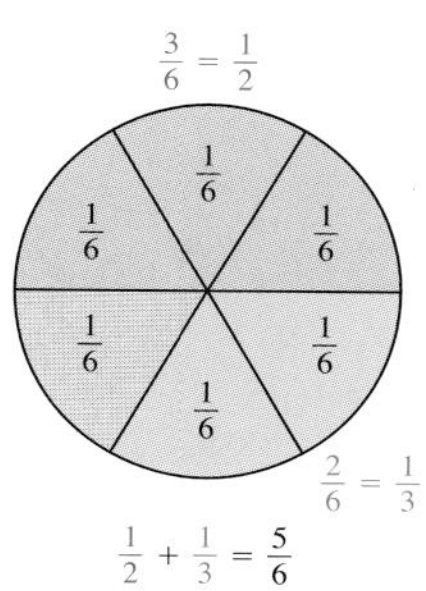

Figure 1.23

The smallest number that is a multiple of the denominators of two or more fractions is called the **least common denominator (LCD).** So 6 is the LCD for $\frac{1}{2}$ and $\frac{1}{3}$. Note that we obtained the LCD 6 by examining Fig. 1.23. We must have a more systematic way.

The procedure for finding the LCD is based on factors. For example, to find the LCD for the denominators 6 and 9, factor 6 and 9 as $6 = 2 \cdot 3$ and $9 = 3 \cdot 3$. To obtain a multiple of both 6 and 9 the number must have two 3's as factors and one 2. So the LCD for 6 and 9 is $2 \cdot 3 \cdot 3$ or 18. If any number is omitted from $2 \cdot 3 \cdot 3$, we will not have a multiple of both 6 and 9. So each factor found in either 6 or 9 appears in the LCD the maximum number of times that it appears in either 6 or 9. The general strategy follows.

‹ Helpful Hint ›

The *least* common denominator is *greater than* or equal to all of the denominators, because they must all divide into the LCD.

Strategy for Finding the LCD

1. Factor each denominator completely.
2. Determine the maximum number of times each distinct factor occurs in any denominator.
3. The LCD is the product of all of the distinct factors, where each factor is used the maximum number of times from step 2.

Note that a **prime number** is a number 2 or larger that has no factors other than itself and 1. If a denominator is prime (such as 2, 3, 5, 7, 11) then we do not factor it. A number is **factored completely** when it is written as a product of prime numbers.

EXAMPLE 7

Adding and subtracting fractions

Perform the indicated operations.

a) $\frac{3}{4} + \frac{1}{6}$

b) $\frac{1}{3} - \frac{1}{12}$

c) $\frac{7}{12} + \frac{5}{18}$

d) $2\frac{1}{3} + \frac{5}{9}$

Solution

a) First factor the denominators as $4 = 2 \cdot 2$ and $6 = 2 \cdot 3$. Since 2 occurs twice in 4 and once in 6, it appears twice in the LCD. Since 3 appears once in 6 and not at all in 4, it appears once in the LCD. So the LCD is $2 \cdot 2 \cdot 3$ or 12. Now build up each denominator to 12:

$$\frac{3}{4} + \frac{1}{6} = \frac{3 \cdot 3}{4 \cdot 3} + \frac{1 \cdot 2}{6 \cdot 2} \quad \text{Build up each denominator to 12.}$$

$$= \frac{9}{12} + \frac{2}{12} \quad \text{Simplify.}$$

$$= \frac{11}{12} \quad \text{Add.}$$

b) The denominators are 12 and 3. Factor 12 as $12 = 2 \cdot 6 = 2 \cdot 2 \cdot 3$. Since 3 is a prime number we do not factor it. Since 2 occurs twice in 12 and not at all in 3, it appears twice in the LCD. Since 3 occurs once in 3 and once in 12, 3 appears once in the LCD. The LCD is $2 \cdot 2 \cdot 3$ or 12. So we must build up $\frac{1}{3}$ to have a denominator of 12:

$$\frac{1}{3} - \frac{1}{12} = \frac{1 \cdot 4}{3 \cdot 4} - \frac{1}{12} \quad \text{Build up the first fraction to the LCD.}$$

$$= \frac{4}{12} - \frac{1}{12} \quad \text{Simplify.}$$

$$= \frac{3}{12} \quad \text{Subtract.}$$

$$= \frac{1}{4} \quad \text{Reduce to lowest terms.}$$

c) Since $12 = 2 \cdot 6 = 2 \cdot 2 \cdot 3$ and $18 = 2 \cdot 9 = 2 \cdot 3 \cdot 3$, the factor 2 appears twice in the LCD and the factor 3 appears twice in the LCD. So the LCD is $2 \cdot 2 \cdot 3 \cdot 3$ or 36:

$$\frac{7}{12} + \frac{5}{18} = \frac{7 \cdot 3}{12 \cdot 3} + \frac{5 \cdot 2}{18 \cdot 2} \quad \text{Build up each denominator to 36.}$$

$$= \frac{21}{36} + \frac{10}{36} \quad \text{Simplify.}$$

$$= \frac{31}{36} \quad \text{Add.}$$

d) To perform addition with the mixed number $2\frac{1}{3}$, first convert it into an improper fraction: $2\frac{1}{3} = 2 + \frac{1}{3} = \frac{6}{3} + \frac{1}{3} = \frac{7}{3}$.

‹ Teaching Tip ›

Emphasize the method for adding and subtracting fractions. Encourage students to write the details as shown in Example 7.

‹ Calculator Close-Up ›

You can check these results with a graphing calculator. Note how a graphing calculator handles mixed numbers.

```
1/3-1/12▸Frac
              1/4
7/12+5/18▸Frac
            31/36
(2+1/3)+5/9▸Frac
             26/9
```

$$2\frac{1}{3} + \frac{5}{9} = \frac{7}{3} + \frac{5}{9}$$ Write $2\frac{1}{3}$ as an improper fraction.

$$= \frac{7 \cdot 3}{3 \cdot 3} + \frac{5}{9}$$ The LCD is 9.

$$= \frac{21}{9} + \frac{5}{9}$$ Simplify.

$$= \frac{26}{9}$$ Add.

Note that $\frac{1}{3} + \frac{5}{9} = \frac{3}{9} + \frac{5}{9} = \frac{8}{9}$. Then add on the 2 to get $2\frac{8}{9}$, which is the same as $\frac{26}{9}$.

Now do Exercises 73–84

‹ Helpful Hint ›

Recall the *place value* for decimal numbers:

tenths, hundredths, thousandths, ten thousandths
0.2635

So $0.2635 = \frac{2635}{10{,}000}$.

‹6› Fractions, Decimals, and Percents

In the decimal number system, fractions with a denominator of 10, 100, 1000, and so on are written as decimal numbers. For example,

$$\frac{3}{10} = 0.3, \quad \frac{25}{100} = 0.25, \quad \text{and} \quad \frac{5}{1000} = 0.005.$$

Fractions with a denominator of 100 are often written as percents. Think of the percent symbol (%) as representing the denominator of 100. For example,

$$\frac{25}{100} = 25\%, \quad \frac{5}{100} = 5\%, \quad \text{and} \quad \frac{300}{100} = 300\%.$$

Example 8 illustrates further how to convert from any one of the forms (fraction, decimal, percent) to the others.

EXAMPLE 8

‹ Teaching Tip ›

Work some examples like $6\frac{3}{4}\%$, $3\frac{1}{3}\%$, and 5.24%.

‹ Calculator Close-Up ›

A calculator can convert fractions to decimals and decimals to fractions. The calculator shown here converts the terminating decimal 0.333333333333 into 1/3 even though 1/3 is a repeating decimal with infinitely many threes after the decimal point.

```
1/3
      .3333333333
.333▸Frac
         333/1000
.333333333333▸Fr
ac
              1/3
```

Changing forms

Convert each given fraction, decimal, or percent into its other two forms.

a) $\frac{1}{5}$ **b)** 6% **c)** 0.1

Solution

a) $\frac{1}{5} = \frac{1 \cdot 20}{5 \cdot 20} = \frac{20}{100} = 20\%$ and $\frac{1}{5} = \frac{1 \cdot 2}{5 \cdot 2} = \frac{2}{10} = 0.2$

So $\frac{1}{5} = 0.2 = 20\%$. Note that a fraction can also be converted to a decimal by dividing the denominator into the numerator with long division.

b) $6\% = \frac{6}{100} = 0.06$ and $\frac{6}{100} = \frac{2 \cdot 3}{2 \cdot 50} = \frac{3}{50}$

So $6\% = 0.06 = \frac{3}{50}$.

c) $0.1 = \frac{1}{10} = \frac{1 \cdot 10}{10 \cdot 10} = \frac{10}{100} = 10\%$

So $0.1 = \frac{1}{10} = 10\%$.

Now do Exercises 85–96

⟨7⟩ Applications

The dimensions for lumber used in construction are usually given in fractions. For example, a two-by-four (2×4) stud used in framing walls is actually $1\frac{1}{2}$ in. by $3\frac{1}{2}$ in. by $92\frac{5}{8}$ in. A two-by-twelve (2×12) floor joist with a width of $1\frac{1}{2}$ in. and height of $11\frac{1}{2}$ in. comes in various lengths, usually 8, 10, 12, 14, and 16 feet. In Example 9 we find the height of a wall.

EXAMPLE 9

Framing a two-story house

In framing a two-story house, a carpenter uses a 2×4 shoe, a wall stud, two 2×4 plates, then 2×12 floor joists, and a $\frac{3}{4}$-in. plywood floor, before starting the second level. Use the dimensions in Fig. 1.24 to find the total height of the framing shown.

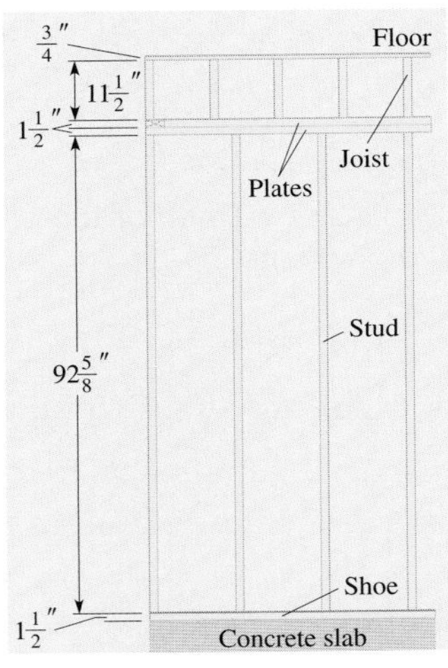

Figure 1.24

Solution

We can find the total height using multiplication and addition:

$$3 \cdot 1\frac{1}{2} + 92\frac{5}{8} + 11\frac{1}{2} + \frac{3}{4} = 4\frac{1}{2} + 92\frac{5}{8} + 11\frac{1}{2} + \frac{3}{4}$$
$$= 4\frac{4}{8} + 92\frac{5}{8} + 11\frac{4}{8} + \frac{6}{8}$$
$$= 107\frac{19}{8}$$
$$= 107 + \frac{16}{8} + \frac{3}{8} = 107 + 2 + \frac{3}{8} = 109\frac{3}{8}$$

The total height of the framing shown is $109\frac{3}{8}$ in.

Now do Exercises 121–124

Warm-Ups ▼

True or false? Explain your answer.

1. Every fraction is equal to infinitely many equivalent fractions. True
2. The fraction $\frac{8}{12}$ is equivalent to the fraction $\frac{4}{6}$. True
3. The fraction $\frac{8}{12}$ reduced to lowest terms is $\frac{4}{6}$. False
4. $\frac{1}{2} \cdot \frac{2}{3} = \frac{1}{3}$ True
5. $\frac{1}{2} \cdot \frac{3}{5} = \frac{3}{10}$ True
6. $\frac{1}{2} \cdot \frac{6}{5} = \frac{6}{10}$ True
7. $\frac{1}{2} \div 3 = \frac{1}{6}$ True
8. $5 \div \frac{1}{2} = 10$ True
9. $\frac{1}{2} + \frac{1}{4} = \frac{2}{6}$ False
10. $2 - \frac{1}{2} = \frac{3}{2}$ True

Exercises 1.2

‹ Study Tips ›

- Get to know your fellow students. If you are an online student, ask your instructor how you can communicate with other online students.
- Set your goals, make plans, and schedule your time. Before you know it, you will have the discipline that is necessary for success.

Reading and Writing *After reading this section write out the answers to these questions. Use complete sentences.*

1. What are equivalent fractions?
If two fractions are identical when reduced to lowest terms, then they are equivalent fractions.

2. How can you find all fractions that are equivalent to a given fraction?
Reduce the fraction to lowest terms and then multiply the numerator and denominator by every counting number.

3. What does it mean to reduce a fraction to lowest terms?
To reduce a fraction to lowest terms means to find an equivalent fraction that has no factor common to the numerator and denominator.

4. For which operations with fractions are you required to have common denominators? Why?
Common denominators are required for addition and subtraction, because it makes sense to add $\frac{1}{3}$ of a pie and $\frac{1}{3}$ of a pie and get $\frac{2}{3}$ of a pie.

5. How do you convert a fraction to a decimal?
Convert a fraction to a decimal by dividing the denominator into the numerator.

6. How do you convert a percent to a fraction?
Convert a percent to a fraction by dividing by 100 and dropping the percent symbol, as in $4\% = \frac{4}{100}$.

‹1› Equivalent Fractions

Build up each fraction or whole number so that it is equivalent to the fraction with the indicated denominator. See Example 1.

7. $\frac{3}{4} = \frac{?}{8}$ $\frac{6}{8}$ **8.** $\frac{5}{7} = \frac{?}{21}$ $\frac{15}{21}$ **9.** $\frac{8}{3} = \frac{?}{12}$ $\frac{32}{12}$

VIDEO **10.** $\frac{7}{2} = \frac{?}{8}$ $\frac{28}{8}$ **11.** $5 = \frac{?}{2}$ $\frac{10}{2}$ **12.** $9 = \frac{?}{3}$ $\frac{27}{3}$

13. $\frac{3}{4} = \frac{?}{100}$ $\frac{75}{100}$ **14.** $\frac{1}{2} = \frac{?}{100}$ $\frac{50}{100}$ **15.** $\frac{3}{10} = \frac{?}{100}$ $\frac{30}{100}$

16. $\frac{2}{5} = \frac{?}{100}$ $\frac{40}{100}$ **17.** $\frac{5}{3} = \frac{?}{42}$ $\frac{70}{42}$ **18.** $\frac{5}{7} = \frac{?}{98}$ $\frac{70}{98}$

Reduce each fraction to lowest terms. See Example 2.

19. $\frac{3}{6}$ $\frac{1}{2}$ **20.** $\frac{2}{10}$ $\frac{1}{5}$ **21.** $\frac{12}{18}$ $\frac{2}{3}$ VIDEO **22.** $\frac{30}{40}$ $\frac{3}{4}$

23. $\frac{15}{5}$ 3 **24.** $\frac{39}{13}$ 3 **25.** $\frac{50}{100}$ $\frac{1}{2}$ **26.** $\frac{5}{1000}$ $\frac{1}{200}$

27. $\frac{200}{100}$ 2 **28.** $\frac{125}{100}$ $\frac{5}{4}$ **29.** $\frac{18}{48}$ $\frac{3}{8}$ **30.** $\frac{34}{102}$ $\frac{1}{3}$

31. $\frac{26}{42}$ $\frac{13}{21}$ **32.** $\frac{70}{112}$ $\frac{5}{8}$ **33.** $\frac{84}{91}$ $\frac{12}{13}$ **34.** $\frac{121}{132}$ $\frac{11}{12}$

‹2› Multiplying Fractions

Find each product. See Example 3.

35. $\frac{2}{3} \cdot \frac{5}{9}$ $\frac{10}{27}$ **36.** $\frac{1}{8} \cdot \frac{1}{8}$ $\frac{1}{64}$ **37.** $\frac{1}{3} \cdot 15$ 5

38. $\frac{1}{4} \cdot 16$ 4 **39.** $\frac{3}{4} \cdot \frac{14}{15}$ $\frac{7}{10}$ **40.** $\frac{5}{8} \cdot \frac{12}{35}$ $\frac{3}{14}$

VIDEO **41.** $\frac{2}{5} \cdot \frac{35}{26}$ $\frac{7}{13}$ **42.** $\frac{3}{10} \cdot \frac{20}{21}$ $\frac{2}{7}$ **43.** $\frac{1}{2} \cdot \frac{6}{5}$ $\frac{3}{5}$

44. $\frac{1}{2} \cdot \frac{3}{5}$ $\frac{3}{10}$ **45.** $\frac{1}{2} \cdot \frac{1}{3}$ $\frac{1}{6}$ **46.** $\frac{3}{16} \cdot \frac{1}{7}$ $\frac{3}{112}$

‹3› Unit Conversion

Perform the indicated unit conversions. See Example 4. Round approximate answers to the nearest hundredth. Answers can vary slightly depending on the conversion factors used.

47. Convert 96 feet to inches. 1152 in.
48. Convert 33 yards to feet. 99 ft
49. Convert 14.22 miles to kilometers. 22.88 km
50. Convert 33.6 kilometers to miles. 20.88 mi
51. Convert 13.5 centimeters to inches. 5.31 in.
52. Convert 42.1 inches to centimeters. 106.93 cm
53. Convert 14.2 ounces to grams. 402.57 g
54. Convert 233 grams to ounces. 8.22 oz
55. Convert 40 miles per hour to feet per second. 58.67 ft/sec
56. Convert 200 feet per second to miles per hour. 136.36 mi/hr
57. Convert 500 feet per second to kilometers per hour. 548.53 km/hr
58. Convert 230 yards per second to miles per minute. 7.84 mi/min

⟨4⟩ Dividing Fractions

Find each quotient. See Example 5.

59. $\frac{3}{4} \div \frac{1}{4}$ 3

60. $\frac{2}{3} \div \frac{1}{2}$ $\frac{4}{3}$

61. $\frac{1}{3} \div 5$ $\frac{1}{15}$

62. $\frac{3}{5} \div 3$ $\frac{1}{5}$

63. $5 \div \frac{5}{4}$ 4

64. $8 \div \frac{2}{3}$ 12

65. $\frac{6}{10} \div \frac{3}{4}$ $\frac{4}{5}$

VIDEO **66.** $\frac{2}{3} \div \frac{10}{21}$ $\frac{7}{5}$

67. $\frac{3}{16} \div \frac{5}{2}$ $\frac{3}{40}$

68. $\frac{1}{8} \div \frac{5}{16}$ $\frac{2}{5}$

⟨5⟩ Adding and Subtracting Fractions

Find each sum or difference.

See Examples 6 and 7.

See Strategy for Finding the LCD box on page 19.

69. $\frac{1}{4} + \frac{1}{4}$ $\frac{1}{2}$

70. $\frac{1}{10} + \frac{1}{10}$ $\frac{1}{5}$

71. $\frac{5}{12} - \frac{1}{12}$ $\frac{1}{3}$

72. $\frac{17}{14} - \frac{5}{14}$ $\frac{6}{7}$

73. $\frac{1}{2} - \frac{1}{4}$ $\frac{1}{4}$

74. $\frac{1}{3} + \frac{1}{6}$ $\frac{1}{2}$

75. $\frac{1}{3} + \frac{1}{4}$ $\frac{7}{12}$

76. $\frac{1}{2} + \frac{3}{5}$ $\frac{11}{10}$

77. $\frac{3}{4} - \frac{2}{3}$ $\frac{1}{12}$

78. $\frac{4}{5} - \frac{3}{4}$ $\frac{1}{20}$

VIDEO **79.** $\frac{1}{6} + \frac{5}{8}$ $\frac{19}{24}$

80. $\frac{3}{4} + \frac{1}{6}$ $\frac{11}{12}$

81. $\frac{5}{24} - \frac{1}{18}$ $\frac{11}{72}$

82. $\frac{3}{16} - \frac{1}{20}$ $\frac{11}{80}$

83. $3\frac{5}{6} + \frac{5}{16}$ $\frac{199}{48}$

84. $5\frac{3}{8} - \frac{15}{16}$ $\frac{71}{16}$

⟨6⟩ Fractions, Decimals, and Percents

Convert each given fraction, decimal, or percent into its other two forms. See Example 8.

85. $\frac{3}{5}$ 60%, 0.6

86. $\frac{19}{20}$ 95%, 0.95

87. 9% $\frac{9}{100}$, 0.09

88. 60% 0.6, $\frac{3}{5}$

89. 0.08 8%, $\frac{2}{25}$

90. 0.4 40%, $\frac{2}{5}$

91. $\frac{3}{4}$ 0.75, 75%

92. $\frac{5}{8}$ 0.625, 62.5%

93. 2% $\frac{1}{50}$, 0.02

94. 120% $\frac{6}{5}$, 1.2

95. 0.01 $\frac{1}{100}$, 1%

96. 0.005 $\frac{1}{200}$, 0.5%

Perform the indicated operations.

97. $\frac{3}{8} \div \frac{1}{8}$ 3

98. $\frac{7}{8} \div \frac{3}{14}$ $\frac{49}{12}$

99. $\frac{3}{4} \cdot \frac{28}{21}$ 1

100. $\frac{5}{16} \cdot \frac{3}{10}$ $\frac{3}{32}$

101. $\frac{7}{12} + \frac{5}{32}$ $\frac{71}{96}$

102. $\frac{2}{15} + \frac{8}{21}$ $\frac{18}{35}$

103. $\frac{5}{24} - \frac{1}{15}$ $\frac{17}{120}$

104. $\frac{9}{16} - \frac{1}{12}$ $\frac{23}{48}$

105. $3\frac{1}{8} + \frac{15}{16}$ $\frac{65}{16}$

106. $5\frac{1}{4} - \frac{9}{16}$ $\frac{75}{16}$

107. $7\frac{2}{3} \cdot 2\frac{1}{4}$ $\frac{69}{4}$

108. $6\frac{1}{2} \div \frac{7}{2}$ $\frac{13}{7}$

109. $\frac{1}{2} + \frac{1}{3} + \frac{1}{4}$ $\frac{13}{12}$

110. $\frac{1}{2} + \frac{1}{3} - \frac{1}{6}$ $\frac{2}{3}$

111. $\frac{1}{2} \cdot \frac{1}{2} \cdot \frac{1}{2}$ $\frac{1}{8}$

112. $\frac{2}{3} \cdot \frac{2}{3} \cdot \frac{2}{3}$ $\frac{8}{27}$

Fill in the blank so that each equation is correct.

113. $\frac{1}{4} + \underline{\frac{3}{8}} = \frac{5}{8}$

114. $\frac{1}{3} + \underline{\frac{1}{9}} = \frac{4}{9}$

115. $\frac{5}{16} - \underline{\frac{3}{16}} = \frac{1}{8}$

116. $\frac{3}{5} - \underline{\frac{1}{2}} = \frac{1}{10}$

117. $\frac{4}{9} \cdot \underline{\frac{2}{3}} = \frac{8}{27}$

118. $\frac{3}{8} \cdot \underline{2} = \frac{3}{4}$

119. $\frac{2}{3} \div \underline{\frac{1}{2}} = \frac{4}{3}$

120. $\frac{1}{15} \div \underline{\frac{1}{3}} = \frac{1}{5}$

⟨7⟩ Applications

Solve each problem. See Example 9.

121. ***Planned giving.*** Marie's will specifies that one-sixth of her estate will go to Tulane University and one-thirty-second will go to the Humane Society. What is the total portion of her estate that will go to these two organizations? $\frac{19}{96}$

122. ***Diversification.*** Helen has $\frac{1}{5}$ of her portfolio in U.S. stocks, $\frac{1}{8}$ of her portfolio in European stocks, and $\frac{1}{10}$ of her portfolio in Japanese stocks. The remainder is invested in municipal bonds. What fraction of her portfolio is invested in municipal bonds? What percent is invested in municipal bonds? $\frac{23}{40}$, 57.5%

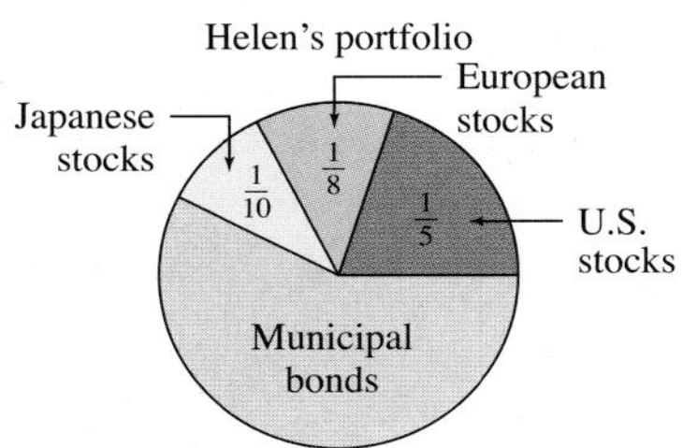

Figure for Exercise 122

123. ***Concrete patio.*** A contractor plans to pour a concrete rectangular patio.

a) Use the table to find the approximate volume of concrete in cubic yards for a 9 ft by 12 ft patio that is 4 inches thick. 1.3 yd^3

b) Find the exact volume of concrete in cubic feet and cubic yards for a patio that is $12\frac{1}{2}$ feet long, $8\frac{3}{4}$ feet wide, and 4 inches thick. $36\frac{11}{24}$ ft^3 or $1\frac{227}{648}$ yd^3

Concrete required for 4 in. thick patio

L (ft)	W (ft)	V (yd^3)
16	14	2.8
14	10	1.7
12	9	1.3
10	8	1.0

Figure for Exercise 123

124. ***Bundle of studs.*** A lumber yard receives 2 × 4 studs in a bundle that contains 25 rows (or layers) of studs with 20 studs in each row. A 2 × 4 stud is actually $1\frac{1}{2}$ in. by $3\frac{1}{2}$ in. by $92\frac{5}{8}$ in. Find the cross-sectional area of a bundle in square inches. Find the volume of a bundle in cubic feet. (The formula $V = LWH$ gives the volume of a rectangular solid.) Round approximate answers to the nearest tenth. 2625 in.^{2}, 140.7 ft^3

Getting More Involved

125. ***Writing*** 

Find an example of a real-life situation in which it is necessary to add two fractions.

126. ***Cooperative learning*** 

Write a step-by-step procedure for adding two fractions with different denominators. Give your procedure to a classmate to try out on some addition problems. Refine your procedure as necessary.

127. ***Fraction puzzle.*** A wheat farmer in Manitoba left his L-shaped farm (shown in the diagram) to his four daughters. Divide the property into four pieces so that each piece is exactly the same size and shape.
Each daughter gets 3 km^2 ÷ 4 or a $\frac{3}{4}$-km^2 piece of the farm. Divide the farm into 12 equal squares. Give each daughter an L-shaped piece consisting of 3 of those 12 squares.

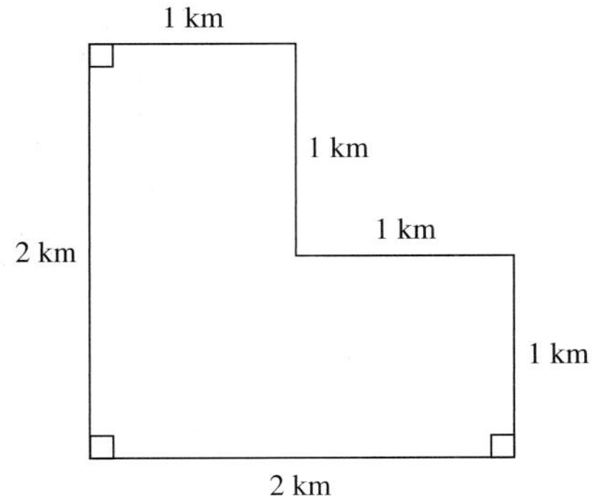

Figure for Exercise 127

Math *at Work* Stock Price Analysis

Stock market analysts use mathematics daily to evaluate the potential success of a stock based on its financial statements and its current performance. Each analyst has a philosophy of investing. If an analyst is working for a mutual fund that specializes in retirement investing for clients with a lengthy time horizon, the analyst may recommend higher-risk stocks. If the client base is older and has a shorter time horizon, the analyst may recommend more secure investments.

There are hundreds of ratios and formulas that a stock market analyst uses to estimate the value of a stock. Two popular ones are the capital asset pricing model (CAPM) and the price/earnings ratio (P/E). The CAPM is used to assess the price of a stock in relation to general movements in the stock market whereas the P/E ratio is used to compare the price of one stock to others in the same industry.

Using CAPM a stock's price P is determined by $P = A + BM$, where A is the stock's variance, B is the stock's fluctuation in relation to the market, and M is the market level. For example, a stock trading at \$10.50 on the New York Stock Exchange has a variance of 3.24 and fluctuation of 0.001058 using the Dow Jones Industrial Average. If the Dow is at 13,125, then $P = 3.24 + 0.001058(13{,}125) \approx 17.13$. So the stock is worth \$17.13 and is a good buy at \$10.50. If the company has earned \$1.53 per share, then $\text{P/E} = 10.50/1.53 \approx 6.9$. If other stocks in the same industry have higher P/E ratios, then this stock is a good buy.

Since there are hundreds of ways to analyze a stock and all analysts have access to the same data, the analysts must decide which data are most important. The analyst must also look beyond data and formulas to determine whether to buy a stock.

1.3 Addition and Subtraction of Real Numbers

In This Section

⟨1⟩ Addition of Two Negative Numbers
⟨2⟩ Addition of Numbers with Unlike Signs
⟨3⟩ Subtraction of Signed Numbers
⟨4⟩ Applications

In arithmetic we add and subtract only positive numbers and zero. In Section 1.1 we introduced the concept of absolute value of a number. Now we will use absolute value to extend the operations of addition and subtraction to the real numbers. We will work only with rational numbers in this chapter. You will learn to perform operations with irrational numbers in Chapter 8.

⟨1⟩ Addition of Two Negative Numbers

A good way to understand positive and negative numbers is to *think of the positive numbers as assets and the negative numbers as debts.* For this illustration we can think of assets simply as cash. For example, if you have \$3 and \$5 in cash, then your total cash is \$8. You get the total by adding two positive numbers.

Think of debts as unpaid bills such as the electric bill or the phone bill. If you have debts of \$70 and \$80, then your total debt is \$150. You can get the total debt by adding negative numbers:

$$\underset{\$70\text{ debt}}{\underset{\uparrow}{(-70)}} \quad \underset{\text{plus}}{\underset{\uparrow}{+}} \quad \underset{\$80\text{ debt}}{\underset{\uparrow}{(-80)}} \quad = \quad \underset{\$150\text{ debt}}{\underset{\uparrow}{-150}}$$

‹ Teaching Tip ›

Addition of signed numbers can also be illustrated on the number line, but students seem to understand money better. Note how we need absolute value to write a precise rule for addition.

We think of this addition as adding the absolute values of -70 and -80 ($70 + 80 = 150$), and then putting a negative sign on that result to get -150. These examples illustrate the following rule.

Sum of Two Numbers with Like Signs

To find the sum of two numbers with the same sign, add their absolute values. The sum has the same sign as the given numbers.

EXAMPLE 1

Adding numbers with like signs

Perform the indicated operations.

a) $23 + 56$

b) $(-12) + (-9)$

c) $(-3.5) + (-6.28)$

d) $\left(-\frac{1}{2}\right) + \left(-\frac{1}{4}\right)$

Solution

a) The sum of two positive numbers is a positive number: $23 + 56 = 79$.

b) The absolute values of -12 and -9 are 12 and 9, and $12 + 9 = 21$. So

$$(-12) + (-9) = -21.$$

c) Add the absolute values of -3.5 and -6.28, and put a negative sign on the sum. Remember to line up the decimal points when adding decimal numbers:

$$\begin{array}{r} 3.50 \\ \underline{6.28} \\ 9.78 \end{array}$$

So $(-3.5) + (-6.28) = -9.78$.

d) $\left(-\frac{1}{2}\right) + \left(-\frac{1}{4}\right) = \left(-\frac{2}{4}\right) + \left(-\frac{1}{4}\right) = -\frac{3}{4}$

Now do Exercises 7–16

‹2› Addition of Numbers with Unlike Signs

If you have a debt of \$5 and have only \$5 in cash, then your debts equal your assets (in absolute value), and your net worth is \$0. **Net worth** is the total of debts and assets. Symbolically,

$$\underset{\text{\$5 debt}}{\underset{\uparrow}{-5}} \quad + \quad \underset{\text{\$5 cash}}{\underset{\uparrow}{5}} \quad = \quad \underset{\text{Net worth}}{\underset{\uparrow}{0.}}$$

For any number a, a and its opposite, $-a$, have a sum of zero. For this reason, a and $-a$ are called **additive inverses** of each other. Note that the words "negative," "opposite," and "additive inverse" are often used interchangeably.

Additive Inverse Property

For any number a,

$$a + (-a) = 0 \quad \text{and} \quad (-a) + a = 0.$$

EXAMPLE 2

Finding the sum of additive inverses

Evaluate.

a) $34 + (-34)$ **b)** $-\frac{1}{4} + \frac{1}{4}$ **c)** $2.97 + (-2.97)$

Solution

a) $34 + (-34) = 0$

b) $-\frac{1}{4} + \frac{1}{4} = 0$

c) $2.97 + (-2.97) = 0$

Now do Exercises 17–20

‹ Helpful Hint ›

We use the illustrations with debts and assets to make the rules for adding signed numbers understandable. However, in the end the carefully written rules tell us exactly how to perform operations with signed numbers, and we must obey the rules.

To understand the sum of a positive and a negative number that are not additive inverses of each other, consider the following situation. If you have a debt of \$6 and \$10 in cash, you may have \$10 in hand, but your net worth is only \$4. Your assets exceed your debts (in absolute value), and you have a positive net worth. In symbols,

$$-6 + 10 = 4.$$

Note that to get 4, we actually subtract 6 from 10.

If you have a debt of \$7 but have only \$5 in cash, then your debts exceed your assets (in absolute value). You have a negative net worth of $-\$2$. In symbols,

$$-7 + 5 = -2.$$

Note that to get the 2 in the answer, we subtract 5 from 7.

‹ Teaching Tip ›

Note how we need absolute value to state precise rules for adding.

As you can see from these examples, the sum of a positive number and a negative number (with different absolute values) may be either positive or negative. These examples help us to understand the rule for adding numbers with unlike signs and different absolute values.

Sum of Two Numbers with Unlike Signs (and Different Absolute Values)

To find the sum of two numbers with unlike signs (and different absolute values), subtract their absolute values.

- The answer is positive if the number with the larger absolute value is positive.
- The answer is negative if the number with the larger absolute value is negative.

EXAMPLE 3

Adding numbers with unlike signs

Evaluate.

a) $-5 + 13$ **b)** $6 + (-7)$ **c)** $-6.4 + 2.1$

d) $-5 + 0.09$ **e)** $\left(-\frac{1}{3}\right) + \left(\frac{1}{2}\right)$ **f)** $\frac{3}{8} + \left(-\frac{5}{6}\right)$

‹ Calculator Close-Up ›

Your calculator can add signed numbers. Most calculators have a key for subtraction and a different key for the negative sign.

```
-5+13
                 8
-5+.09
             -4.91
3/8+-5/6▸Frac
            -11/24
```

You should do the exercises in this section by hand and then check with a calculator.

Solution

a) The absolute values of -5 and 13 are 5 and 13. Subtract them to get 8. Since the number with the larger absolute value is 13 and it is positive, the result is positive:

$$-5 + 13 = 8$$

b) The absolute values of 6 and -7 are 6 and 7. Subtract them to get 1. Since -7 has the larger absolute value, the result is negative:

$$6 + (-7) = -1$$

c) Line up the decimal points and subtract 2.1 from 6.4.

$$\begin{array}{r} 6.4 \\ -2.1 \\ \hline 4.3 \end{array}$$

Since 6.4 is larger than 2.1, and 6.4 has a negative sign, the sign of the answer is negative. So $-6.4 + 2.1 = -4.3$.

d) Line up the decimal points and subtract 0.09 from 5.00.

$$\begin{array}{r} 5.00 \\ -0.09 \\ \hline 4.91 \end{array}$$

Since 5.00 is larger than 0.09, and 5.00 has the negative sign, the sign of the answer is negative. So $-5 + 0.09 = -4.91$.

e) $\left(-\frac{1}{3}\right) + \left(\frac{1}{2}\right) = \left(-\frac{2}{6}\right) + \left(\frac{3}{6}\right) = \frac{1}{6}$

f) $\frac{3}{8} + \left(-\frac{5}{6}\right) = \frac{9}{24} + \left(-\frac{20}{24}\right) = -\frac{11}{24}$

Now do Exercises 21–30

‹3› Subtraction of Signed Numbers

Each subtraction problem with signed numbers is solved by doing an equivalent addition problem. So before attempting subtraction of signed numbers be sure that you understand addition of signed numbers.

We can think of subtraction as removing debts or assets, and addition as receiving debts or assets. Removing a debt means the debt is forgiven. If you owe your mother \$20 and she tells you to forget it, then that debt is removed, your net worth has gone up by \$20. Paying off a debt is not the same. Paying off a debt does not affect your net worth. If you lose your wallet, which contains \$50, then that asset is removed. When your electric bill arrives, you have received a debt. When you get your paycheck you have received an asset.

How does removing debts or assets affect your net worth? Suppose that your net worth is \$100. Losing \$30 or receiving a phone bill for \$30 has the same effect. Your net worth goes down to \$70.

$$\underset{\text{Remove}}{100 \;-\;} \underset{\text{Cash}}{30} = \underset{\text{Receive}}{100 \;+\;} \underset{\text{Debt}}{(-30)}$$

Removing an asset (cash) is equivalent to receiving a debt.

‹ Teaching Tip ›

Point out that even with whole numbers, we learn addition before subtraction.

Suppose you have \$15 but owe a friend \$5. Your net worth is only \$10. If the debt of \$5 is canceled or forgiven, your net worth will go up to \$15, the same as if you received \$5 in cash. In symbols,

$$\underset{\text{Remove}}{10 \;-\;} \underset{\text{Debt}}{(-5)} = \underset{\text{Receive}}{10 \;+\;} \underset{\text{Cash}}{5.}$$

Removing a debt is equivalent to receiving cash.

Notice that each subtraction problem is equivalent to an addition problem in which we add the opposite of what we want to subtract. In other words, *subtracting a number is the same as adding its opposite.*

Subtraction of Real Numbers

For any real numbers a and b,

$$a - b = a + (-b).$$

EXAMPLE 4

Subtracting signed numbers

Perform each subtraction.

a) $-5 - 3$

b) $5 - (-3)$

c) $-5 - (-3)$

d) $\frac{1}{2} - \left(-\frac{1}{4}\right)$

e) $-3.6 - (-5)$

f) $0.02 - 8$

Solution

To do *any* subtraction, we can change it to addition of the opposite.

a) $-5 - 3 = -5 + (-3) = -8$

b) $5 - (-3) = 5 + (3) = 8$

c) $-5 - (-3) = -5 + 3 = -2$

d) $\frac{1}{2} - \left(-\frac{1}{4}\right) = \frac{2}{4} + \frac{1}{4} = \frac{3}{4}$

e) $-3.6 - (-5) = -3.6 + 5 = 1.4$

f) $0.02 - 8 = 0.02 + (-8) = -7.98$

Now do Exercises 31–58

⟨4⟩ Applications

EXAMPLE 5

Net worth

A couple has \$18,000 in credit card debt, \$2000 in their checking account, and \$6000 in a 401(k). The mortgage balance on their \$180,000 house is \$170,000. Their two cars are worth a total of \$19,000, but the loan balances on them total \$23,000. Find their net worth.

Solution

Net worth is the total of all debts and assets. To find it, subtract the debts from the assets:

$$2000 + 6000 + 180{,}000 + 19{,}000 - 18{,}000 - 170{,}000 - 23{,}000 = -4000$$

The net worth is $-\$4000$.

Now do Exercises 105–108

Warm-Ups ▼

True or false? Explain your answer.

1. $-9 + 8 = -1$ True
2. $(-2) + (-4) = -6$ True
3. $0 - 7 = -7$ True
4. $5 - (-2) = 3$ False
5. $-5 - (-2) = -7$ False
6. The additive inverse of -3 is 0. False
7. If b is a negative number, then $-b$ is a positive number. True
8. The sum of a positive number and a negative number is a negative number. False
9. The result of a subtracted from b is the same as b plus the opposite of a. True
10. If a and b are negative numbers, then $a - b$ is a negative number. False

1.3 Exercises

MathZone

Boost your grade at mathzone.com!
- Practice Problems
- NetTutor
- Self-Tests
- e-Professors
- Videos

‹ Study Tips ›

- Note how the exercises are keyed to the examples and the examples are keyed to the exercises. If you get stuck on an exercise study the corresponding example.
- The keys to success are desire and discipline. You must want success and you must discipline yourself to do what it takes to get success.

Reading and Writing *After reading this section write out the answers to these questions. Use complete sentences.*

1. What operations did we study in this section?
   We studied addition and subtraction of signed numbers.
2. How do you find the sum of two numbers with the same sign?
   The sum of two numbers with the same sign is found by adding their absolute values. The sum is negative if the two numbers are negative.
3. When can we say that two numbers are additive inverses of each other?
   Two numbers are additive inverses of each other if their sum is zero.
4. What is the sum of two numbers with opposite signs and the same absolute value?
   The sum of two numbers with opposite signs and the same absolute value is zero.
5. How do we find the sum of two numbers with unlike signs?
   To find the sum of two numbers with unlike signs, subtract their absolute values. The answer is given the sign of the number with the larger absolute value.
6. What is the relationship between subtraction and addition?
   Subtraction is defined in terms of addition as $a - b = a + (-b)$.

‹1› Addition of Two Negative Numbers

Perform the indicated operation. See Example 1.

7. $3 + 10$ 13

8. $81 + 19$ 100

9. $(-3) + (-10)$ -13

10. $(-81) + (-19)$ -100

11. $-3 + (-5)$ -8

12. $-7 + (-2)$ -9

13. $-0.25 + (-0.9)$ -1.15

14. $-0.8 + (-2.35)$ -3.15

15. $\left(-\frac{1}{3}\right) + \left(-\frac{1}{6}\right)$ $-\frac{1}{2}$

16. $\frac{2}{3} + \frac{1}{12}$ $\frac{3}{4}$

‹2› Addition of Numbers with Unlike Signs

Evaluate. See Examples 2 and 3.

17. $-8 + 8$ 0

18. $20 + (-20)$ 0

19. $-\frac{17}{50} + \frac{17}{50}$ 0

20. $\frac{12}{13} + \left(-\frac{12}{13}\right)$ 0

21. $-7 + 9$ 2

22. $10 + (-30)$ -20 (VIDEO)

23. $7 + (-13)$ -6

24. $-8 + 20$ 12 (VIDEO)

25. $8.6 + (-3)$ 5.6

26. $-9.5 + 12$ 2.5

27. $3.9 + (-6.8)$ -2.9

28. $-5.24 + 8.19$ 2.95

29. $\frac{1}{4} + \left(-\frac{1}{2}\right)$ $-\frac{1}{4}$

30. $-\frac{2}{3} + 2$ $\frac{4}{3}$

‹3› Subtraction of Signed Numbers

Fill in the parentheses to make each statement correct. See Example 4.

31. $8 - 2 = 8 + (?)$ $8 + (-2)$

32. $3.5 - 1.2 = 3.5 + (?)$ $3.5 + (-1.2)$

33. $4 - 12 = 4 + (?)$ $4 + (-12)$

34. $\frac{1}{2} - \frac{5}{6} = \frac{1}{2} + (?)$ $\frac{1}{2} + \left(-\frac{5}{6}\right)$

35. $-3 - (-8) = -3 + (?)$ $-3 + 8$

36. $-9 - (-2.3) = -9 + (?)$ $-9 + (2.3)$

37. $8.3 - (-1.5) = 8.3 + (?)$ $8.3 + (1.5)$

38. $10 - (-6) = 10 + (?)$ $10 + (6)$

Perform the indicated operation. See Example 4.

39. $6 - 10$ -4

40. $3 - 19$ -16

41. $-3 - 7$ -10

42. $-3 - 12$ -15

43. $5 - (-6)$ 11

44. $5 - (-9)$ 14

45. $-6 - 5$ -11

46. $-3 - 6$ -9

47. $\frac{1}{4} - \frac{1}{2}$ $-\frac{1}{4}$

48. $\frac{2}{5} - \frac{2}{3}$ $-\frac{4}{15}$

49. $\frac{1}{2} - \left(-\frac{1}{4}\right)$ $\frac{3}{4}$

50. $\frac{2}{3} - \left(-\frac{1}{6}\right)$ $\frac{5}{6}$

51. $10 - 3$ 7

52. $13 - 3$ 10

53. $1 - 0.07$ 0.93

54. $0.03 - 1$ -0.97

55. $7.3 - (-2)$ 9.3

56. $-5.1 - 0.15$ -5.25

57. $-0.03 - 5$ -5.03

58. $0.7 - (-0.3)$ 1

Miscellaneous

Perform the indicated operations. Do not use a calculator.

59. $-5 + 8$ 3

60. $-6 + 10$ 4

61. $-6 + (-3)$ -9

62. $(-13) + (-12)$ -25

63. $-80 - 40$ -120

64. $44 - (-15)$ 59

65. $61 - (-17)$ 78

66. $-19 - 13$ -32

67. $(-12) + (-15)$ -27

68. $-12 + 12$ 0

69. $13 + (-20)$ -7

70. $15 + (-39)$ -24

71. $-102 - 99$ -201

72. $-94 - (-77)$ -17

73. $-161 - 161$ -322

74. $-19 - 88$ -107

75. $-16 + 0.03$ -15.97

76. $0.59 + (-3.4)$ -2.81

77. $0.08 - 3$ -2.92

78. $1.8 - 9$ -7.2

79. $-3.7 + (-0.03)$ -3.73

80. $0.9 + (-1)$ -0.1

81. $-2.3 - (-6)$ 3.7

82. $-7.08 - (-9)$ 1.92

83. $\frac{3}{4} + \left(-\frac{3}{5}\right)$ $\frac{3}{20}$

84. $-\frac{1}{3} + \frac{3}{5}$ $\frac{4}{15}$

85. $-\frac{1}{12} - \left(-\frac{3}{8}\right)$ $\frac{7}{24}$

86. $-\frac{1}{17} - \left(-\frac{1}{17}\right)$ 0

Fill in the parentheses so that each equation is correct.

87. $-5 + (13) = 8$

88. $-9 + (31) = 22$

89. $12 + (-10) = 2$

90. $13 + (-17) = -4$

91. $10 - (14) = -4$

92. $14 - (22) = -8$

93. $6 - (-4) = 10$

94. $3 - (-12) = 15$

95. $-4 - (-3) = -1$

96. $-11 - (-13) = 2$

Use a calculator to perform the indicated operations.

97. $45.87 + (-49.36)$ -3.49

98. $-0.357 + (-3.465)$ -3.822

99. $0.6578 + (-1)$ -0.3422

100. $-2.347 + (-3.5)$ -5.847

101. $-3.45 - 45.39$ -48.84

102. $9.8 - 9.974$ -0.174

103. $-5.79 - 3.06$ -8.85

104. $0 - (-4.537)$ 4.537

‹4› Applications

Solve each problem. See Example 5.

105. ***Overdrawn.*** Willard opened his checking account with a deposit of \$97.86. He then wrote checks and had other charges as shown in his account register. Find his current balance. $-\$8.85$

Deposit		97.86
Wal-Mart	27.89	
Kmart	42.32	
ATM cash	25.00	
Service charge	3.50	
Check printing	8.00	

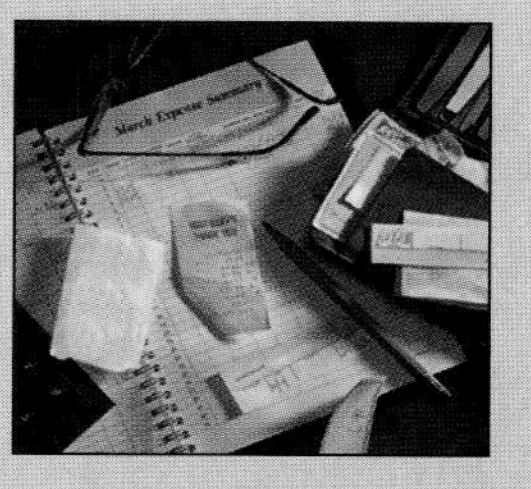

Figure for Exercise 105

106. ***Net worth.*** Melanie's house is worth \$125,000, but she still owes \$78,422 on her mortgage. She has \$21,236 in a savings account and has \$9477 in credit card debt. She owes \$6131 to the credit union and figures that her cars and other household items are worth a total of \$15,000. What is Melanie's net worth? \$67,206

107. ***Falling temperatures.*** At noon the temperature in Montreal was 5°C. By midnight the mercury had fallen 12°. What was the temperature at midnight? -7°C

108. ***Bitter cold.*** The overnight low temperature in Milwaukee was -13°F for Monday night. The temperature went up 20° during the day on Tuesday and then fell 15° to reach Tuesday night's overnight low temperature.

a) What was the overnight low Tuesday night? -8°F

b) Judging from the accompanying graph, was the average low for the week above or below 0°F? Below zero

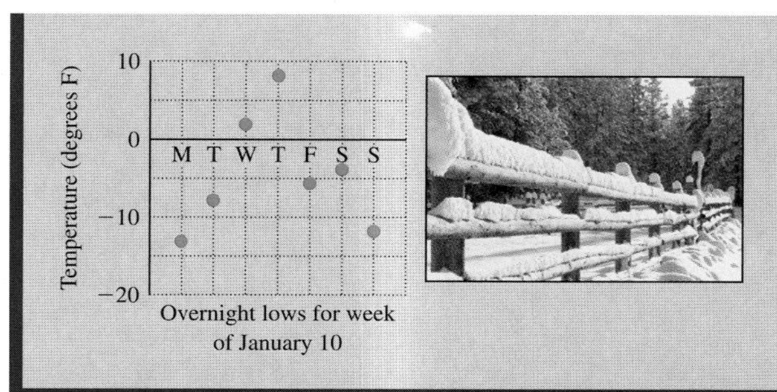

Figure for Exercise 108

Getting More Involved

109. *Writing*

What does absolute value have to do with adding signed numbers? Can you add signed numbers without using absolute value?

When adding signed numbers, we add or subtract only positive numbers which are the absolute values of the original numbers. We then determine the appropriate sign for the answer.

110. *Discussion*

Why do we learn addition of signed numbers before subtraction?

Subtraction is defined as addition of the opposite, $a - b = a + (-b)$.

111. *Discussion*

Aimee and Joni are traveling south in separate cars on Interstate 5 near Stockton. While they are speaking to each other on cellular telephones, Aimee gives her location as mile marker x and Joni gives her location as mile marker y. Which of the following expressions gives the distance between them? Explain your answer.

a) $y - x$ **b)** $x - y$
c) $|x - y|$ **d)** $|y - x|$
e) $|x| + |y|$

The distance between x and y is given by either $|x - y|$ or $|y - x|$.

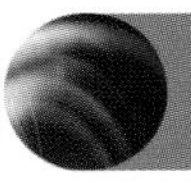

1.4 Multiplication and Division of Real Numbers

In This Section

- ⟨1⟩ Multiplication of Real Numbers
- ⟨2⟩ Division of Real Numbers
- ⟨3⟩ Division by Zero

In this section, we will complete the study of the four basic operations with real numbers.

⟨1⟩ Multiplication of Real Numbers

The result of multiplying two numbers is referred to as the **product** of the numbers. The numbers multiplied are called **factors.** In algebra we use a raised dot between the factors to indicate multiplication, or we place symbols next to one another to indicate multiplication. Thus $a \cdot b$ or ab are both referred to as the product of a and b. When multiplying numbers, we may enclose them in parentheses to make the meaning clear. To write 5 times 3, we may write it as $5 \cdot 3$, $5(3)$, $(5)3$, or $(5)(3)$. In multiplying a number and a variable, no sign is used between them. Thus, $5x$ is used to represent the product of 5 and x.

Multiplication is just a short way to do repeated additions. Adding together five 3's gives

$$3 + 3 + 3 + 3 + 3 = 15.$$

So we have the multiplication fact $5 \cdot 3 = 15$. Adding together five -3's gives

$$(-3) + (-3) + (-3) + (-3) + (-3) = -15.$$

So we should have $5(-3) = -15$. Receiving five debts of \$3 each is the same as a \$15 debt. If you have five debts of \$3 each and they are forgiven, then you have gained \$15. So we should have $(-5)(-3) = 15$.

These examples illustrate the rule for multiplying signed numbers.

⟨ Helpful Hint ⟩

The product of two numbers with like signs is positive, but the product of three numbers with like signs can be positive or negative. For example,

$$2 \cdot 2 \cdot 2 = 8$$

and

$$(-2)(-2)(-2) = -8.$$

Product of Signed Numbers

To find the product of two nonzero real numbers, multiply their absolute values.

- The product is *positive* if the numbers have *like* signs.
- The product is *negative* if the numbers have *unlike* signs.

EXAMPLE 1

Multiplying signed numbers

Evaluate each product.

a) $(-2)(-3)$ **b)** $3(-6)$ **c)** $-5 \cdot 10$

d) $\left(-\frac{1}{3}\right)\left(-\frac{1}{2}\right)$ **e)** $(-0.02)(0.08)$ **f)** $(-300)(-0.06)$

Solution

a) First find the product of the absolute values:

$$|-2| \cdot |-3| = 2 \cdot 3 = 6$$

Because -2 and -3 have the same sign, we get $(-2)(-3) = 6$.

b) First find the product of the absolute values:

$$|3| \cdot |-6| = 3 \cdot 6 = 18$$

Because 3 and -6 have unlike signs, we get $3(-6) = -18$.

c) $-5 \cdot 10 = -50$ Unlike signs, negative result

d) $\left(-\frac{1}{3}\right)\left(-\frac{1}{2}\right) = \frac{1}{6}$ Like signs, positive result

e) When multiplying decimals, we total the number of decimal places in the factors to get the number of decimal places in the product. Thus,

$$(-0.02)(0.08) = -0.0016.$$

f) $(-300)(-0.06) = 18$ Like signs, positive result

Now do Exercises 7–18

‹ Calculator Close-Up ›

Try finding the products in Example 1 with your calculator.

```
(-2)(-3)
                6
3(-6)
              -18
-5*10
              -50
```

‹2› Division of Real Numbers

We say that $10 \div 2 = 5$ because $5 \cdot 2 = 10$. This example illustrates how division is defined in terms of multiplication.

‹ Teaching Tip ›

Point out to students that you have to learn multiplication before you can divide. Ask them to recall another pair of operations that are related in this manner.

Division of Real Numbers

If a, b, and c are any real numbers with $b \neq 0$, then

$$a \div b = c \quad \text{provided that} \quad c \cdot b = a.$$

Using the definition of division, we can make the following table:

Positive quotient	$10 \div 2 = 5$	because $5 \cdot 2 = 10$
	$-10 \div (-2) = 5$	because $5(-2) = -10$
Negative quotient	$10 \div (-2) = -5$	because $-5(-2) = 10$
	$-10 \div 2 = -5$	because $-5 \cdot 2 = -10$

Notice that in this table, the quotient for two numbers with the same sign is positive and the quotient for two numbers with opposite signs is negative. These examples illustrate the rule for dividing signed numbers. The rule for dividing signed numbers is similar to that for multiplying signed numbers because of the definition of division.

Division of Signed Numbers

To find the quotient of two nonzero real numbers, divide their absolute values.

- The quotient is *positive* if the two numbers have *like* signs.
- The quotient is *negative* if the two numbers have *unlike* signs.

Zero divided by any nonzero real number is zero.

EXAMPLE 2

Dividing signed numbers

Evaluate.

a) $(-8) \div (-4)$ **b)** $(-8) \div 8$ **c)** $8 \div (-4)$

d) $-4 \div \frac{1}{3}$ **e)** $-2.5 \div 0.05$ **f)** $0 \div (-6)$

Solution

a) $(-8) \div (-4) = \frac{-8}{-4} = 2$ Same sign, positive result

b) $(-8) \div 8 = \frac{-8}{8} = -1$ Unlike signs, negative result

c) $8 \div (-4) = \frac{8}{-4} = -2$ Unlike signs, negative result

d) $-4 \div \frac{1}{3} = -4 \cdot \frac{3}{1}$ Invert and multiply.

$= -4 \cdot 3$

$= -12$

e) $-2.5 \div 0.05 = \frac{-2.5}{0.05}$ Write in fraction form.

$= \frac{-2.5 \cdot 100}{0.05 \cdot 100}$ Multiply by 100 to eliminate the decimals.

$= \frac{-250}{5}$ Simplify.

$= -50$ Divide.

f) $0 \div (-6) = \frac{0}{-6} = 0$ Zero divided by a nonzero number is zero.

Now do Exercises 19–32

‹ Helpful Hint ›

Do not use negative numbers in long division. To find $-378 \div 7$, divide 378 by 7:

```
   54
7)378
  35
   28
   28
    0
```

Since a negative divided by a positive is negative

$-378 \div 7 = -54.$

Division can also be indicated by a fraction bar. For example,

$$24 \div 6 = \frac{24}{6} = 4.$$

If signed numbers occur in a fraction, we use the rules for dividing signed numbers. For example,

$$\frac{-9}{3} = -3, \quad \frac{9}{-3} = -3, \quad \frac{-1}{2} = \frac{1}{-2} = -\frac{1}{2}, \quad \text{and} \quad \frac{-4}{-2} = 2.$$

Note that if one negative sign appears in a fraction, the fraction has the same value whether the negative sign is in the numerator, in the denominator, or in front of the fraction. If the numerator and denominator of a fraction are both negative, then the fraction has a positive value.

‹ Teaching Tip ›

Students often confuse 0/8 and 8/0. Ask them how they will remember the difference.

‹3› Division by Zero

Why do we exclude division by zero from the definition of division? If we write $10 \div 0 = c$, we need to find a number c such that $c \cdot 0 = 10$. This is impossible. If we write $0 \div 0 = c$, we need to find a number c such that $c \cdot 0 = 0$. In fact, $c \cdot 0 = 0$ is true for any value of c. Having $0 \div 0$ equal to any number would be confusing in doing computations. Thus, $a \div b$ is defined only for $b \neq 0$. Quotients such as

$$8 \div 0, \quad 0 \div 0, \quad \frac{8}{0}, \quad \text{and} \quad \frac{0}{0}$$

are said to be **undefined.**

EXAMPLE 3

Division involving zero

Evaluate. If the operation is undefined say so.

a) $0 \div 1$ **b)** $\frac{3}{4} \div 0$

c) $\frac{-12}{0}$ **d)** $\frac{0}{-9}$

Solution

a) The result of 0 divided by a nonzero number is zero. So $0 \div 1 = 0$.

b) Since division by zero is not allowed, $\frac{3}{4} \div 0$ is an undefined operation.

c) Since division by zero is not allowed, $\frac{-12}{0}$ is undefined.

d) The result of 0 divided by a nonzero number is zero. So $\frac{0}{-9} = 0$.

Now do Exercises 33–40

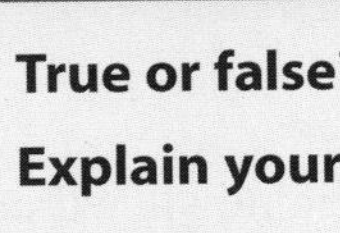

Warm-Ups ▼

True or false? Explain your answer.

1. The product of 7 and y is written as $7y$. True
2. The product of -2 and 5 is 10. False
3. The quotient of x and 3 can be written as $x \div 3$ or $\frac{x}{3}$. True
4. $0 \div 6$ is undefined. False
5. $(-9) \div (-3) = 3$ True
6. $6 \div (-2) = -3$ True
7. $\left(-\frac{1}{2}\right)\left(-\frac{1}{2}\right) = \frac{1}{4}$ True
8. $(-0.2)(0.2) = -0.4$ False
9. $\left(-\frac{1}{2}\right) \div \left(-\frac{1}{2}\right) = 1$ True
10. $\frac{0}{0} = 0$ False

1.4 Exercises

Boost your grade at mathzone.com!

- Practice Problems
- NetTutor
- Self-Tests
- e-Professors
- Videos

‹ Study Tips ›

- If you don't know how to get started on the exercises, go back to the examples. Read the solution in the text, then cover it with a piece of paper and see if you can solve the example.
- If you need help, don't hesitate to get it. If you don't straighten out problems in a timely manner, you can get hopelessly lost.

Reading and Writing *After reading this section write out the answers to these questions. Use complete sentences.*

1. What operations did we study in this section?
We learned to multiply and divide signed numbers.
2. What is a product?
A product is the result of multiplication. The product of a and b is ab. The product of 2 and 4 is 8.
3. How do you find the product of two signed numbers?
To find the product of signed numbers, multiply their absolute values and then affix a negative sign if the two original numbers have opposite signs.
4. What is the relationship between division and multiplication?
Division is defined in terms of multiplication as $a \div b = c$ provided $c \cdot b = a$ and $b \neq 0$.
5. How do you find the quotient of nonzero real numbers?
To find the quotient of nonzero numbers divide their absolute values and then affix a negative sign if the two original numbers have opposite signs.
6. Why is division by zero undefined?
Division by zero is undefined because it cannot be made consistent with the definition of division: $a \div b = c$ provided $c \cdot b = a$.

‹1› Multiplication of Real Numbers

Evaluate. See Example 1.

7. $-3 \cdot 9$ -27
8. $6(-4)$ -24
9. $(-12)(-11)$ 132
10. $(-9)(-15)$ 135
11. $-\frac{3}{4} \cdot \frac{4}{9}$ $-\frac{1}{3}$
12. $\left(-\frac{2}{3}\right)\left(-\frac{6}{7}\right)$ $\frac{4}{7}$
13. $0.5(-0.6)$ -0.3
14. $(-0.3)(0.3)$ -0.09
15. $(-12)(-12)$ 144
16. $(-11)(-11)$ 121
17. $-3 \cdot 0$ 0
18. $0(-7)$ 0

⟨2⟩ Division of Real Numbers

Evaluate. See Example 2.

19. $8 \div (-8)$ -1

20. $-6 \div 2$ -3

21. $(-90) \div (-30)$ 3

22. $(-20) \div (-40)$ $\frac{1}{2}$

23. $\frac{44}{-66}$ $-\frac{2}{3}$

24. $\frac{-33}{-36}$ $\frac{11}{12}$

25. $\left(-\frac{2}{3}\right) \div \left(-\frac{4}{5}\right)$ $\frac{5}{6}$

26. $-\frac{1}{3} \div \frac{4}{9}$ $-\frac{3}{4}$

27. $0 \div \left(-\frac{1}{3}\right)$ 0

28. $0 \div 43.568$ 0

29. $40 \div (-0.5)$ -80

30. $3 \div (-0.1)$ -30

31. $-0.5 \div (-2)$ 0.25

32. $-0.75 \div (-0.5)$ 1.5

⟨3⟩ Division by Zero

Evaluate. If the operation is undefined say so. See Example 3.

33. $0 \div 125$ 0

34. $0 \div (-99)$ 0

35. $\frac{-125}{0}$ Undefined

36. $\frac{3.5}{0}$ Undefined

37. $\frac{1}{2} \div 0$ Undefined

38. $0.236 \div 0$ Undefined

39. $\frac{0}{2}$ 0

40. $\frac{0}{-5}$ 0

Miscellaneous

Perform the indicated operations.

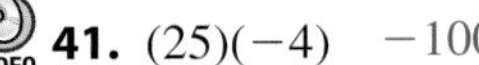

41. $(25)(-4)$ -100

42. $(5)(-4)$ -20

43. $(-3)(-9)$ 27

44. $(-51) \div (-3)$ 17

45. $-9 \div 3$ -3

46. $86 \div (-2)$ -43

47. $20 \div (-5)$ -4

48. $(-8)(-6)$ 48

49. $(-6)(5)$ -30

50. $(-18) \div 3$ -6

51. $(-57) \div (-3)$ 19

52. $(-30)(4)$ -120

53. $(0.6)(-0.3)$ -0.18

54. $(-0.2)(-0.5)$ 0.1

55. $(-0.03)(-10)$ 0.3

56. $(0.05)(-1.5)$ -0.075

57. $(-0.6) \div (0.1)$ -6

58. $8 \div (-0.5)$ -16

59. $(-0.6) \div (-0.4)$ 1.5

60. $(-63) \div (-0.9)$ 70

61. $-\frac{12}{5}\left(-\frac{55}{6}\right)$ 22

62. $-\frac{9}{10} \cdot \frac{4}{3}$ $-\frac{6}{5}$

63. $-2\frac{3}{4} \div 8\frac{1}{4}$ $-\frac{1}{3}$

64. $-9\frac{1}{2} \div \left(-3\frac{1}{6}\right)$ 3

Use a calculator to perform the indicated operations. Round approximate answers to two decimal places.

65. $(0.45)(-365)$ -164.25

66. $8.5 \div (-0.15)$ -56.67

67. $(-52) \div (-0.034)$ 1529.41

68. $(-4.8)(5.6)$ -26.88

Fill in the parentheses so that each equation is correct.

69. $-5 \cdot (-12) = 60$

70. $-9 \cdot (-6) = 54$

71. $12 \cdot (-8) = -96$

72. $11 \cdot (-4) = -44$

73. $24 \div (-6) = -4$

74. $51 \div (-3) = -17$

75. $-36 \div (-1) = 36$

76. $-48 \div (-8) = 6$

77. $-40 \div (5) = -8$

78. $-13 \div (13) = -1$

Perform the indicated operations. Use a calculator to check.

79. $(-4)(-4)$ 16

80. $-4 - 4$ -8

81. $-4 + (-4)$ -8

82. $-4 \div (-4)$ 1

83. $-4 + 4$ 0

84. $-4 \cdot 4$ -16

85. $-4 - (-4)$ 0

86. $0 \div (-4)$ 0

87. $0.1 - 4$ -3.9

88. $(0.1)(-4)$ -0.4

VIDEO **89.** $(-4) \div (0.1)$ -40

90. $-0.1 - 4$ -4.1

91. $(-0.1)(-4)$ 0.4

92. $-0.1 + 4$ 3.9

93. $|-0.4|$ 0.4

94. $|0.4|$ 0.4

95. $\frac{-0.06}{0.3}$ -0.2

96. $\frac{2}{-0.04}$ -50

97. $\frac{3}{-0.4}$ -7.5

98. $\frac{-1.2}{-0.03}$ 40

99. $-\frac{1}{5} + \frac{1}{6}$ $-\frac{1}{30}$

100. $-\frac{3}{5} - \frac{1}{4}$ $-\frac{17}{20}$

101. $\left(-\frac{3}{4}\right)\left(\frac{2}{15}\right)$ $-\frac{1}{10}$

102. $-1 \div \left(-\frac{1}{4}\right)$ 4

Use a calculator to perform the indicated operations. Round approximate answers to three decimal places.

103. $\frac{45.37}{6}$ 7.562

104. $(-345) \div (28)$ -12.321

105. $(-4.3)(-4.5)$ 19.35

106. $\frac{-12.34}{-3}$ 4.113

107. $\frac{0}{6.345}$ 0

108. $0 \div (34.51)$ 0

109. $199.4 \div 0$ Undefined

110. $\frac{23.44}{0}$ Undefined

Applications

111. ***Big loss.*** Ford Motor Company's profit for 2006 was $-\$12.7$ billion. Find the rate in dollars per minute (to the nearest dollar) at which Ford was "making" money in 2006. $-\$24{,}163$/min

112. ***Negative divided by a positive.*** As of January 2007, the national debt was \$8.686 trillion dollars and the U.S. population was 300.814 million people. Find the amount of the debt per person to the nearest dollar. \$28,875/person

Getting More Involved

113. *Discussion*

If you divide $0 among five people, how much does each person get? If you divide $5 among zero people, how much does each person get? What do these questions illustrate?

114. *Discussion*

What is the difference between the non-negative numbers and the positive numbers?

115. *Writing*

Why do we learn multiplication of signed numbers before division?

116. *Writing*

Try to rewrite the rules for multiplying and dividing signed numbers without using the idea of absolute value. Are your rewritten rules clearer than the original rules?

1.5 Exponential Expressions and the Order of Operations

In This Section

⟨1⟩ Arithmetic Expressions
⟨2⟩ Exponential Expressions
⟨3⟩ The Order of Operations
⟨4⟩ Applications

In Sections 1.3 and 1.4, you learned how to perform operations with a pair of real numbers to obtain a third real number. In this section, you will learn to evaluate expressions involving several numbers and operations.

⟨1⟩ Arithmetic Expressions

The result of writing numbers in a meaningful combination with the ordinary operations of arithmetic is called an **arithmetic expression** or simply an **expression.** Consider the expressions

$$(3 + 2) \cdot 5 \qquad \text{and} \qquad 3 + (2 \cdot 5).$$

The parentheses are used as **grouping symbols** and indicate which operation to perform first. Because of the parentheses, these expressions have different values:

$$(3 + 2) \cdot 5 = 5 \cdot 5 = 25$$
$$3 + (2 \cdot 5) = 3 + 10 = 13$$

Absolute value symbols and fraction bars are also used as grouping symbols. The numerator and denominator of a fraction are treated as if each is in parentheses.

EXAMPLE 1

Using grouping symbols

Evaluate each expression.

a) $(3 - 6)(3 + 6)$ **b)** $|3 - 4| - |5 - 9|$ **c)** $\dfrac{4 - (-8)}{5 - 9}$

Solution

a) $(3 - 6)(3 + 6) = (-3)(9)$ Evaluate within parentheses first.

$= -27$ Multiply.

‹ Calculator Close-Up ›

One advantage of a graphing calculator is that you can enter an entire expression on its display and then evaluate it. If your calculator does not allow built-up form for fractions, then you must use parentheses around the numerator and denominator as shown here.

```
(3-6)(3+6)
                -27
abs(3-4)-abs(5-9
)
                 -3
(4--8)/(5-9)
                 -3
```

b) $|3-4|-|5-9| = |-1|-|-4|$ Evaluate within absolute value symbols.

$= 1 - 4$ Find the absolute values.

$= -3$ Subtract.

c) $\dfrac{4-(-8)}{5-9} = \dfrac{12}{-4}$ Evaluate the numerator and denominator.

$= -3$ Divide.

Now do Exercises 7–18

‹2› Exponential Expressions

An arithmetic expression with repeated multiplication can be written by using exponents. For example,

$$2 \cdot 2 \cdot 2 = 2^3 \quad \text{and} \quad 5 \cdot 5 = 5^2.$$

The 3 in 2^3 is the number of times that 2 occurs in the product $2 \cdot 2 \cdot 2$, while the 2 in 5^2 is the number of times that 5 occurs in $5 \cdot 5$. We read 2^3 as "2 cubed" or "2 to the third power." We read 5^2 as "5 squared" or "5 to the second power." In general, an expression of the form a^n is called an **exponential expression** and is defined as follows.

Exponential Expression

For any counting number n,

$$a^n = \underbrace{a \cdot a \cdot a \cdot \ldots \cdot a}_{n \text{ factors}}.$$

We call a the **base** and n the **exponent.**

The expression a^n is read "a to the nth power." If the exponent is 1, it is usually omitted. For example, $9^1 = 9$.

EXAMPLE 2

Using exponential notation

Write each product as an exponential expression.

a) $6 \cdot 6 \cdot 6 \cdot 6 \cdot 6$ **b)** $(-3)(-3)(-3)(-3)$ **c)** $\dfrac{3}{2} \cdot \dfrac{3}{2} \cdot \dfrac{3}{2}$

Solution

a) $6 \cdot 6 \cdot 6 \cdot 6 \cdot 6 = 6^5$

b) $(-3)(-3)(-3)(-3) = (-3)^4$

c) $\dfrac{3}{2} \cdot \dfrac{3}{2} \cdot \dfrac{3}{2} = \left(\dfrac{3}{2}\right)^3$

Now do Exercises 19–26

EXAMPLE 3

Writing an exponential expression as a product

Write each exponential expression as a product without exponents.

a) y^6 **b)** $(-2)^4$ **c)** $\left(\frac{5}{4}\right)^3$ **d)** $(-0.1)^2$

Solution

a) $y^6 = y \cdot y \cdot y \cdot y \cdot y \cdot y$

b) $(-2)^4 = (-2)(-2)(-2)(-2)$

c) $\left(\frac{5}{4}\right)^3 = \frac{5}{4} \cdot \frac{5}{4} \cdot \frac{5}{4}$

d) $(-0.1)^2 = (-0.1)(-0.1)$

Now do Exercises 27–32

To evaluate an exponential expression, write the base as many times as indicated by the exponent, then multiply the factors from left to right.

EXAMPLE 4

Evaluating exponential expressions

Evaluate.

a) 3^3 **b)** $(-2)^3$ **c)** $\left(\frac{2}{3}\right)^4$ **d)** $(0.4)^2$

Solution

a) $3^3 = 3 \cdot 3 \cdot 3 = 9 \cdot 3 = 27$

b) $(-2)^3 = (-2)(-2)(-2)$
$= 4(-2)$
$= -8$

c) $\left(\frac{2}{3}\right)^4 = \frac{2}{3} \cdot \frac{2}{3} \cdot \frac{2}{3} \cdot \frac{2}{3}$
$= \frac{4}{9} \cdot \frac{2}{3} \cdot \frac{2}{3}$
$= \frac{8}{27} \cdot \frac{2}{3}$
$= \frac{16}{81}$

d) $(0.4)^2 = (0.4)(0.4) = 0.16$

Now do Exercises 33–48

‹ Calculator Close-Up ›

You can use the power key for any power. Most calculators also have an x^2 key that gives the second power. Note that parentheses must be used when raising a fraction to a power.

```
(-2)^3
                -8
(2/3)^4▸Frac
             16/81
.4²
               .16
```

CAUTION Note that $3^3 \neq 9$. We do not multiply the exponent and the base when evaluating an exponential expression.

‹ Teaching Tip ›

Remind students not to multiply by the exponent: $(-2)^4 \neq -2 \cdot 4$.

Be especially careful with exponential expressions involving negative numbers. An exponential expression with a negative base is written with parentheses around the base as in $(-2)^4$:

$$(-2)^4 = (-2)(-2)(-2)(-2) = 16$$

To evaluate $-(2^4)$, use the base 2 as a factor four times, then find the opposite:

$$-(2^4) = -(2 \cdot 2 \cdot 2 \cdot 2) = -(16) = -16$$

We often omit the parentheses in $-(2^4)$ and simply write -2^4. So

$$-2^4 = -(2^4) = -16.$$

To evaluate $-(-2)^4$, use the base -2 as a factor four times, then find the opposite:

$$-(-2)^4 = -(16) = -16$$

EXAMPLE 5

Evaluating exponential expressions involving negative numbers

Evaluate.

a) $(-10)^4$ **b)** -10^4

c) $-(-0.5)^2$ **d)** $-(5 - 8)^2$

Solution

a) $(-10)^4 = (-10)(-10)(-10)(-10)$ Use -10 as a factor four times.
$= 10{,}000$

b) $-10^4 = -(10^4)$ Rewrite using parentheses.
$= -(10{,}000)$ Find 10^4.
$= -10{,}000$ Then find the opposite of 10,000.

c) $-(-0.5)^2 = -(-0.5)(-0.5)$ Use -0.5 as a factor two times.
$= -(0.25)$
$= -0.25$

d) $-(5 - 8)^2 = -(-3)^2$ Evaluate within parentheses first.
$= -(9)$ Square -3 to get 9.
$= -9$ Take the opposite of 9 to get -9.

Now do Exercises 49–56

CAUTION Be careful with -10^4 and $(-10)^4$. It is tempting to evaluate these two the same. However, we have agreed that $-10^4 = -(10^4)$, where the exponent is applied only to positive 10. The negative sign is handled last. So $-10^4 = -10{,}000$, a negative number. Likewise, $-1^2 = -1$, $-2^2 = -4$, and $-3^4 = -81$.

⟨3⟩ The Order of Operations

When we evaluate expressions, operations within grouping symbols are always performed first. For example,

$$(3 + 2) \cdot 5 = (5) \cdot 5 = 25 \quad \text{and} \quad (2 \cdot 3)^2 = 6^2 = 36.$$

To make expressions look simpler, we often omit some or all parentheses. In this case, we must agree on the order in which to perform the operations. We agree to do multiplication before addition and exponential expressions before multiplication. So

$$3 + 2 \cdot 5 = 3 + 10 = 13 \quad \text{and} \quad 2 \cdot 3^2 = 2 \cdot 9 = 18.$$

⟨ Helpful Hint ⟩

"Please Excuse My Dear Aunt Sally" (PEMDAS) is often used as a memory aid for the order of operations. Do Parentheses, Exponents, Multiplication and Division, then Addition and Subtraction. Multiplication and division have equal priority. The same goes for addition and subtraction.

We state the complete **order of operations** in the following box.

Order of Operations

1. Evaluate expressions within grouping symbols first. Parentheses and brackets are grouping symbols. Absolute value bars and fraction bars indicate grouping and an operation.
2. Evaluate each exponential expression (in order from left to right).
3. Perform multiplication and division (in order from left to right).
4. Perform addition and subtraction (in order from left to right).

Multiplication and division have equal priority in the order of operations. If both appear in an expression, they are performed in order from left to right. The same holds for addition and subtraction. For example,

$$8 \div 4 \cdot 3 = 2 \cdot 3 = 6 \quad \text{and} \quad 9 - 3 + 5 = 6 + 5 = 11.$$

EXAMPLE 6

Using the order of operations

Evaluate each expression.

a) $2^3 \cdot 3^2$ **b)** $2 \cdot 5 - 3 \cdot 4 + 4^2$ **c)** $2 \cdot 3 \cdot 4 - 3^3 + \frac{8}{2}$

Solution

a) $2^3 \cdot 3^2 = 8 \cdot 9$ Evaluate exponential expressions before multiplying.
$= 72$

b) $2 \cdot 5 - 3 \cdot 4 + 4^2 = 2 \cdot 5 - 3 \cdot 4 + 16$ Exponential expressions first
$= 10 - 12 + 16$ Multiplication second
$= 14$ Addition and subtraction from left to right

c) $2 \cdot 3 \cdot 4 - 3^3 + \frac{8}{2} = 2 \cdot 3 \cdot 4 - 27 + \frac{8}{2}$ Exponential expressions first
$= 24 - 27 + 4$ Multiplication and division second
$= 1$ Addition and subtraction from left to right

Now do Exercises 57–72

‹ Calculator Close-Up ›

Most calculators follow the same order of operations shown here. Evaluate these expressions with your calculator.

```
2^3*3²
                72
2*5-3*4+4²
                14
2*3*4-3^3+8/2
                 1
```

When grouping symbols are used, we perform operations within grouping symbols first. The order of operations is followed within the grouping symbols.

EXAMPLE 7

Grouping symbols and the order of operations

Evaluate.

a) $3 - 2(7 - 2^3)$ **b)** $3 - |7 - 3 \cdot 4|$ **c)** $\dfrac{9 - 5 + 8}{-5^2 - 3(-7)}$

Solution

a) $3 - 2(7 - 2^3) = 3 - 2(7 - 8)$ Evaluate within parentheses first.
$= 3 - 2(-1)$
$= 3 - (-2)$ Multiply.
$= 5$ Subtract.

‹ Teaching Tip ›

Some students think that the first operation to perform is "parentheses." Parentheses are grouping symbols, not an operation. Point out the difference. Absolute value bars, fraction bars, and radicals are used for grouping and an operation.

b) $3 - |7 - 3 \cdot 4| = 3 - |7 - 12|$ Evaluate within the absolute value symbols first.

$= 3 - |-5|$

$= 3 - 5$ Evaluate the absolute value.

$= -2$ Subtract.

c) $\dfrac{9 - 5 + 8}{-5^2 - 3(-7)} = \dfrac{12}{-25 + 21} = \dfrac{12}{-4} = -3$ Numerator and denominator are treated as if in parentheses.

Now do Exercises 73–86

When grouping symbols occur within grouping symbols, we evaluate within the innermost grouping symbols first and then work outward. In this case, brackets [ ] can be used as grouping symbols along with parentheses to make the grouping clear.

EXAMPLE 8

Grouping within grouping

Evaluate each expression.

a) $6 - 4[5 - (7 - 9)]$

b) $-2|3 - (9 - 5)| - |-3|$

‹ Teaching Tip ›

Remind students to be neat and organized. Show steps like the examples.

‹ Calculator Close-Up ›

Graphing calculators can handle grouping symbols within grouping symbols. Since parentheses must occur in pairs, you should have the same number of left parentheses as right parentheses. You might notice other grouping symbols on your calculator, but they may or may not be used for grouping. See your manual.

```
6-4(5-(7-9))
                -22
-2abs(3-(9-5))-a
bs(-3)
                 -5
```

Solution

a) $6 - 4[5 - (7 - 9)] = 6 - 4[5 - (-2)]$ Innermost parentheses first

$= 6 - 4[7]$ Next evaluate within the brackets.

$= 6 - 28$ Multiply.

$= -22$ Subtract.

b) $-2|3 - (9 - 5)| - |-3| = -2|3 - 4| - |-3|$ Innermost grouping first

$= -2|-1| - |-3|$ Evaluate within the first absolute value.

$= -2 \cdot 1 - 3$ Evaluate absolute values.

$= -2 - 3$ Multiply.

$= -5$ Subtract.

Now do Exercises 87–94

‹4› Applications

EXAMPLE 9

Doubling your bet

A strategy among gamblers is to double your bet and bet again after a loss. The only problem with this strategy is that you might run out of money before you get a win. A gambler loses \$100 and employs this strategy. He keeps losing, six times in a row. His seventh bet will be $100 \cdot 2^6$ dollars.

a) Find the amount of the seventh bet.

b) Find the total amount lost on the first six bets.

Solution

a) By the order of operations, $100 \cdot 2^6 = 100 \cdot 64 = 6400$. So the seventh bet is \$6400.

b) Now find the total of the first six losses:

$$\begin{aligned}100 + 100 \cdot 2 + 100 \cdot 2^2 + 100 \cdot 2^3 + 100 \cdot 2^4 + 100 \cdot 2^5 \\ = 100 + 200 + 400 + 800 + 1600 + 3200 \\ = 6300\end{aligned}$$

So the gambler has lost a total of \$6300 on the first six bets.

Now do Exercises 127-130

Warm-Ups ▼

True or false? Explain your answer.

1. $(-3)^2 = -6$ False

2. $5 - 3 \cdot 2 = 4$ False

3. $(5 - 3)2 = 4$ True

4. $|5 - 6| = |5| - |6|$ False

5. $5 + 6 \cdot 2 = (5 + 6) \cdot 2$ False

6. $(2 + 3)^2 = 2^2 + 3^2$ False

7. $5 - 3^3 = 8$ False

8. $(5 - 3)^3 = 8$ True

9. $6 - \frac{6}{2} = \frac{0}{2}$ False

10. $\frac{6 - 6}{2} = 0$ True

1.5 Exercises

‹ Study Tips ›

- Take notes in class. Write down everything that you can. As soon as possible after class, rewrite your notes. Fill in details and make corrections.
- If your instructor takes the time to work an example, it is a good bet that your instructor expects you to understand the concepts involved.

Reading and Writing *After reading this section write out the answers to these questions. Use complete sentences.*

1. What is an arithmetic expression?
An arithmetic expression is the result of writing numbers in a meaningful combination with the ordinary operations of arithmetic.

2. What is the purpose of grouping symbols?
The purpose of grouping symbols is to indicate the order in which to perform operations.

3. What is an exponential expression?
An exponential expression is an expression of the form a^n.

4. What is the difference between -3^6 and $(-3)^6$?
The value of -3^6 is negative while the value of $(-3)^6$ is positive.

5. What is the purpose of the order of operations?
The order of operations tells us the order in which to perform operations when grouping symbols are omitted.

6. What were the different types of grouping symbols used in this section?
Grouping symbols used in this section were parentheses, absolute value bars, and the fraction bar.

⟨1⟩ Arithmetic Expressions

Evaluate each expression. See Example 1.

7. $(4 - 3)(5 - 9)$ -4
8. $(5 - 7)(-2 - 3)$ 10
9. $|3 + 4| - |-2 - 4|$ 1
10. $|-4 + 9| + |-3 - 5|$ 13
11. $\frac{7 - (-9)}{3 - 5}$ -8
12. $\frac{-8 + 2}{-1 - 1}$ 3
13. $(-6 + 5)(7)$ -7
14. $-6 + (5 \cdot 7)$ 29
15. $(-3 - 7) - 6$ -16
16. $-3 - (7 - 6)$ -4
17. $-16 \div (8 \div 2)$ -4
18. $(-16 \div 8) \div 2$ -1

⟨2⟩ Exponential Expressions

Write each product as an exponential expression. See Example 2.

19. $4 \cdot 4 \cdot 4 \cdot 4$ 4^4
20. $1 \cdot 1 \cdot 1 \cdot 1 \cdot 1$ 1^5
21. $(-5)(-5)(-5)(-5)$ $(-5)^4$
22. $(-7)(-7)(-7)$ $(-7)^3$
23. $(-y)(-y)(-y)$ $(-y)^3$
24. $x \cdot x \cdot x \cdot x \cdot x$ x^5
25. $\frac{3}{7} \cdot \frac{3}{7} \cdot \frac{3}{7} \cdot \frac{3}{7} \cdot \frac{3}{7}$ $\left(\frac{3}{7}\right)^5$
26. $\frac{y}{2} \cdot \frac{y}{2} \cdot \frac{y}{2} \cdot \frac{y}{2}$ $\left(\frac{y}{2}\right)^4$

Write each exponential expression as a product without exponents. See Example 3.

27. 5^3 $5 \cdot 5 \cdot 5$
28. $(-8)^4$ $(-8)(-8)(-8)(-8)$
29. b^2 $b \cdot b$
30. $(-a)^5$ $(-a)(-a)(-a)(-a)(-a)$
31. $\left(-\frac{1}{2}\right)^5$ $\left(-\frac{1}{2}\right)\left(-\frac{1}{2}\right)\left(-\frac{1}{2}\right)\left(-\frac{1}{2}\right)\left(-\frac{1}{2}\right)$
32. $\left(-\frac{13}{12}\right)^3$ $\left(-\frac{13}{12}\right)\left(-\frac{13}{12}\right)\left(-\frac{13}{12}\right)$

Evaluate each exponential expression. See Examples 4 and 5.

33. 3^4 81
34. 5^3 125
35. 0^9 0
36. 0^{12} 0
VIDEO **37.** $(-5)^4$ 625
38. $(-2)^5$ -32
39. $(-6)^3$ -216
40. $(-12)^2$ 144
41. $(10)^5$ $100{,}000$
42. $(-10)^6$ $1{,}000{,}000$
43. $(-0.1)^3$ -0.001
44. $(-0.2)^2$ 0.04
45. $\left(\frac{1}{2}\right)^3$ $\frac{1}{8}$
46. $\left(\frac{2}{3}\right)^3$ $\frac{8}{27}$
47. $\left(-\frac{1}{2}\right)^2$ $\frac{1}{4}$
48. $\left(-\frac{2}{3}\right)^2$ $\frac{4}{9}$
49. -8^2 -64
VIDEO **50.** -7^2 -49
51. -8^4 -4096
52. -7^4 -2401
53. $-(7 - 10)^3$ 27
54. $-(6 - 9)^4$ -81
55. $(-2^2) - (3^2)$ -13
56. $(-3^4) - (-5^2)$ -56

⟨3⟩ The Order of Operations

Evaluate each expression. See Example 6.

57. $20 \div 2 \cdot 5$ 50
58. $30 \div 6 \cdot 5$ 25
59. $11 - 6 + 5$ 10
60. $8 - 2 + 4$ 10
61. $3^2 \cdot 2^2$ 36
62. $5 \cdot 10^2$ 500
63. $-3 \cdot 2 + 4 \cdot 6$ 18
64. $-5 \cdot 4 - 8 \cdot 3$ -44
65. $(-3)^3 + 2^3$ -19
66. $3^2 - 5(-1)^3$ 14
67. $-21 + 36 \div 3^2$ -17
68. $-18 - 9^2 \div 3^3$ -21
69. $-3 \cdot 2^3 - 5 \cdot 2^2$ -44
70. $2 \cdot 5 - 3^2 + 4 \cdot 0$ 1
71. $\frac{-8}{2} + 2 \cdot 3 \cdot 5 - 2^3$ 18
72. $-4 \cdot 2 \cdot 6 - \frac{12}{3} + 3^3$ -25

Evaluate each expression. See Example 7.

73. $(-3 + 4^2)(-6)$ -78
74. $-3 \cdot (2^3 + 4) \cdot 5$ -180
75. $(-3 \cdot 2 + 6)^3$ 0
76. $5 - 2(-3 + 2)^3$ 7
77. $2 - 5(3 - 4 \cdot 2)$ 27
78. $(3 - 7)(4 - 6 \cdot 2)$ 32
79. $3 - 2 \cdot |5 - 6|$ 1
80. $3 - |6 - 7 \cdot 3|$ -12
81. $(3^2 - 5) \cdot |3 \cdot 2 - 8|$ 8
82. $|4 - 6 \cdot 3| + |6 - 9|$ 17
VIDEO **83.** $\frac{3 - 4 \cdot 6}{7 - 10}$ 7
84. $\frac{6 - (-8)^2}{-3 - (-1)}$ 29
85. $\frac{7 - 9 - 3^2}{9 - 7 - 3}$ 11
86. $\frac{3^2 - 2 \cdot 4}{-30 + 2 \cdot 4^2}$ $\frac{1}{2}$

Evaluate each expression. See Example 8.

87. $3 + 4[9 - 6(2 - 5)]$ 111
VIDEO **88.** $9 + 3[5 - (3 - 6)^2]$ -3
89. $6^2 - [(2 + 3)^2 - 10]$ 21
90. $3[(2 - 3)^2 + (6 - 4)^2]$ 15
91. $4 - 5 \cdot |3 - (3^2 - 7)|$ -1
92. $2 + 3 \cdot |4 - (7^2 - 6^2)|$ 29
93. $-2|3 - (7 - 3)| - |-9|$ -11
94. $[3 - (2 - 4)][3 + |2 - 4|]$ 25

Evaluate each expression. Use a calculator to check.

95. $1 + 2^3$ 9
96. $(1 + 2)^3$ 27
97. $(-2)^2 - 4(-1)(3)$ 16
98. $(-2)^2 - 4(-2)(-3)$ -20
99. $4^2 - 4(1)(-3)$ 28
100. $3^2 - 4(-2)(3)$ 33
101. $(-11)^2 - 4(5)(0)$ 121
102. $(-12)^2 - 4(3)(0)$ 144
VIDEO **103.** $-5^2 - 3 \cdot 4^2$ -73
104. $-6^2 - 5(-3)^2$ -81
105. $[3 + 2(-4)]^2$ 25
106. $[6 - 2(-3)]^2$ 144
107. $|-1| - |-1|$ 0
108. $4 - |1 - 7|$ -2
109. $\frac{4 - (-4)}{-2 - 2}$ -2
110. $\frac{3 - (-7)}{3 - 5}$ -5
111. $3(-1)^2 - 5(-1) + 4$ 12
112. $-2(1)^2 - 5(1) - 6$ -13
113. $5 - 2^2 + 3^4$ 82
114. $5 + (-2)^2 - 3^2$ 0

115. $-2 \cdot |9 - 6^2|$ -54 **116.** $8 - 3|5 - 4^2 + 1|$ -22

117. $-3^2 - 5[4 - 2(4 - 9)]$ -79

118. $-2[(3 - 4)^3 - 5] + 7$ 19

119. $1 - 5|5 - (9 + 1)|$ -24

120. $|6 - 3 \cdot 7| + |7 - (5 - 2)|$ 19

Use a calculator to evaluate each expression. Round approximate answers to four decimal places.

121. $3.2^2 - 4(3.6)(-2.2)$ 41.92

122. $(-4.5)^2 - 4(-2.8)(-4.6)$ -31.27

123. $(5.63)^3 - [4.7 - (-3.3)^2]$ 184.643547

124. $9.8^3 - [1.2 - (4.4 - 9.6)^2]$ 967.032

125. $\dfrac{3.44 - (-8.32)}{6.89 - 5.43}$ 8.0548

126. $\dfrac{-4.56 - 3.22}{3.44 - (-6.26)}$ -0.8021

⟨4⟩ Applications

Solve each problem. See Example 9.

127. ***Gambler's ruin.*** A gambler bets \$5 and loses. He doubles his bet and loses again. He continues this pattern, losing eight times in a row. His ninth bet will be $5 \cdot 2^8$ dollars.

a) Calculate the amount of the ninth bet. \$1280

b) What is the total amount lost on the first eight bets? \$1275

128. ***Big profits.*** Big Bulldog Motorcycles showed a profit of \$50,000 in its first year of operation. The company plans to double the profit each year for the next 9 years.

a) What will be the amount of the profit in the tenth year? \$25.6 million

b) What will be the total amount of profit for the first 10 years of business? \$51.15 million

129. ***Population of the United States.*** In 2006 the population of the United States was 300.2 million (U.S. Census Bureau, www.census.gov). If the population continues to grow at an annual rate of 1.05%, then the population in the year 2020 will be $300.2(1.0105)^{14}$ million.

a) Evaluate the expression to find the predicted population in 2020 to the nearest tenth of a million people. 347.5 million

b) Use the accompanying graph to estimate the year in which the population will reach 400 million people. 2033

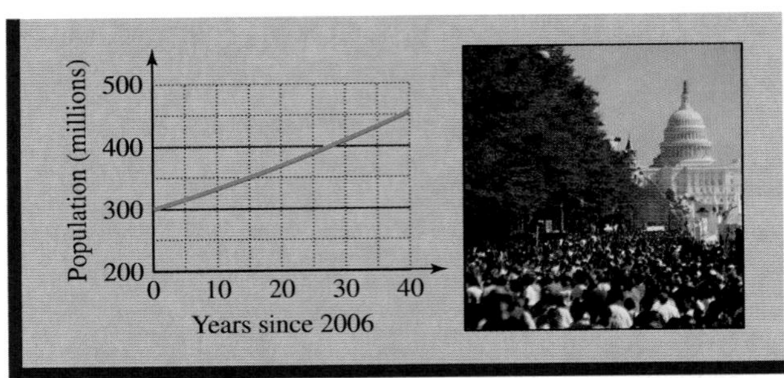

Figure for Exercise 129

130. ***Population of Mexico.*** In 2006 the population of Mexico was 107.4 million. If Mexico's population continues to grow at an annual rate of 1.43%, then the population in 2020 will be $107.4(1.0143)^{14}$ million.

a) Find the predicted population in 2020 to the nearest tenth of a million people. 131.0 million

b) Use the result of Exercise 129 to determine whether the United States or Mexico will have the greater increase in population between 2006 and 2020. United States

Getting More Involved

131. ***Discussion***

How do the expressions $(-5)^3$, $-(5^3)$, -5^3, $-(-5)^3$, and $-1 \cdot 5^3$ differ?
$(-5)^3 = -(5^3) = -5^3 = -1 \cdot 5^3$ and $-(-5)^3 = 5^3$

132. ***Discussion***

How do the expressions $(-4)^4$, $-(4^4)$, -4^4, $-(-4)^4$, and $-1 \cdot 4^4$ differ?
$-(4^4) = -4^4 = -(-4)^4 = -1 \cdot 4^4$ and $(-4)^4 = 4^4$

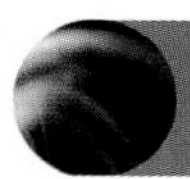

1.6 Algebraic Expressions

In This Section

In Section 1.5, you studied arithmetic expressions. In this section, you will study expressions that are more general—expressions that involve variables.

⟨1⟩ Identifying Algebraic Expressions

Variables (or letters) are used to represent numbers. With variables we can express ideas better than we can with numbers alone. For example, we know that $3 + 3 = 2(3)$, $4 + 4 = 2(4)$, $5 + 5 = 2(5)$, and so on. But using the variable x we can say that $x + x = 2x$ is true for any real number x.

The result of combining numbers and variables with the ordinary operations of arithmetic (in some meaningful way) is called an **algebraic expression** or simply an **expression.** Some examples of algebraic expressions are

$$x + x, \quad 2x, \quad \pi r^2, \quad b^2 - 4ac, \quad \text{and} \quad \frac{a - b}{c - d}.$$

⟨ Teaching Tip ⟩

Note that we are concentrating on only a few nouns here. We will do more translating of verbal expressions into algebraic expressions in Section 2.5.

Expressions are often named by the last operation to be performed in the expression. For example, the expression $x + 2$ is a **sum** because the only operation in the expression is addition. The expression $a - bc$ is referred to as a **difference** because subtraction is the last operation to be performed. The expression $3(x - 4)$ is a **product,** while $\frac{3}{x - 4}$ is a **quotient.** The expression $(a + b)^2$ is a **square** because the addition is performed before the square is found.

EXAMPLE 1

Naming expressions

Identify each expression as either a sum, difference, product, quotient, or square.

a) $3(x + 2)$

b) $b^2 - 4ac$

c) $\dfrac{a - b}{c - d}$

d) $(a - b)^2$

⟨ Helpful Hint ⟩

Sum, difference, product, and quotient are nouns. They are used as names for expressions. Add, subtract, multiply, and divide are verbs. They indicate an action to perform.

Solution

a) In $3(x + 2)$ we add before we multiply. So this expression is a product.

b) By the order of operations the last operation to perform in $b^2 - 4ac$ is subtraction. So this expression is a difference.

c) The last operation to perform in this expression is division. So this expression is a quotient.

d) In $(a - b)^2$ we subtract before we square. This expression is a square.

Now do Exercises 7–18

⟨2⟩ Translating Algebraic Expressions

Algebra is useful because it can be used to solve problems. Since problems are often communicated verbally, we must be able to translate verbal expressions into algebraic expressions and translate algebraic expressions into verbal expressions. Consider the following examples of verbal expressions and their corresponding algebraic expressions.

‹ Teaching Tip ›

We emphasize the names of the common algebraic expressions now so that phrases like "the sum of two squares" make sense in factoring. You must know the order of operations to name expressions.

Verbal Expressions and Corresponding Algebraic Expressions

Verbal Expression	Algebraic Expression
The sum of $5x$ and 3	$5x + 3$
The product of 5 and $x + 3$	$5(x + 3)$
The sum of 8 and $\frac{x}{3}$	$8 + \frac{x}{3}$
The quotient of $8 + x$ and 3	$\frac{8 + x}{3}$, $(8 + x)/3$, or $(8 + x) \div 3$
The difference of 3 and x^2	$3 - x^2$
The square of $3 - x$	$(3 - x)^2$

Note that the word "difference" must be used carefully. To be consistent, we say that the difference between a and b is $a - b$. So the difference between 10 and 12 is $10 - 12$ or -2. However, outside of a textbook most people would say that the difference in age between a 10-year-old and a 12-year-old is 2, not -2. Users of the English language do not follow precise rules like we follow in mathematics. Of course, in mathematics we must make our mathematics and our English sentences perfectly clear. So we try to avoid using "difference" in an ambiguous or vague manner. (We will study verbal and algebraic expressions further in Section 2.5.)

Example 2 shows how the terms sum, difference, product, quotient, and square are used to describe expressions.

EXAMPLE 2

Algebraic expressions to verbal expressions

Translate each algebraic expression into a verbal expression. Use the word sum, difference, product, quotient, or square.

a) $\frac{3}{x}$ **b)** $2y + 1$ **c)** $3x - 2$ **d)** $(a - b)(a + b)$ **e)** $(a + b)^2$

Solution

a) The quotient of 3 and x

b) The sum of $2y$ and 1

c) The difference of $3x$ and 2

d) The product of $a - b$ and $a + b$

e) The square of the sum $a + b$

Now do Exercises 19–28

EXAMPLE 3

Verbal expressions to algebraic expressions

Translate each verbal expression into an algebraic expression.

a) The quotient of $a + b$ and 5

b) The difference of x^2 and y^2

c) The product of π and r^2

d) The square of the difference $x - y$

Solution

a) $\frac{a + b}{5}$, $(a + b) \div 5$, or $(a + b)/5$

b) $x^2 - y^2$

c) πr^2

d) $(x - y)^2$

Now do Exercises 29–44

‹3› Evaluating Algebraic Expressions

The value of an algebraic expression depends on the values given to the variables. For example, the value of $x - 2y$ when $x = -2$ and $y = -3$ is found by replacing x and y by -2 and -3, respectively:

$$x - 2y = -2 - 2(-3) = -2 - (-6) = 4$$

If $x = 1$ and $y = 2$, the value of $x - 2y$ is found by replacing x by 1 and y by 2, respectively:

$$x - 2y = 1 - 2(2) = 1 - 4 = -3$$

Note that we use the order of operations when evaluating an algebraic expression.

EXAMPLE 4

Evaluating algebraic expressions

Evaluate each expression using $a = 3$, $b = -2$, and $c = -4$.

a) $2a + b - c$ **b)** $(a - b)(a + b)$ **c)** $b^2 - 4ac$ **d)** $\frac{-a^2 - b^2}{c - b}$

Solution

a)
$$\begin{aligned} 2a + b - c &= 2(3) + (-2) - (-4) && \text{Replace } a \text{ by 3, } b \text{ by } -2\text{, and } c \text{ by } -4. \\ &= 6 - 2 + 4 && \text{Multiply and remove parentheses.} \\ &= 8 && \text{Addition and subtraction last} \end{aligned}$$

b)
$$\begin{aligned} (a - b)(a + b) &= [3 - (-2)][3 + (-2)] && \text{Replace.} \\ &= [5][1] && \text{Simplify within the brackets.} \\ &= 5 && \text{Multiply.} \end{aligned}$$

c)
$$\begin{aligned} b^2 - 4ac &= (-2)^2 - 4(3)(-4) && \text{Replace.} \\ &= 4 - (-48) && \text{Square } -2\text{, and then multiply before subtracting.} \\ &= 52 && \text{Subtract.} \end{aligned}$$

d) $$\frac{-a^2 - b^2}{c - b} = \frac{-3^2 - (-2)^2}{-4 - (-2)} = \frac{-9 - 4}{-2} = \frac{13}{2}$$

Now do Exercises 45–68

‹ Teaching Tip ›

Note that the expressions that we are evaluating here are the same kinds of expressions that we will use later in the text.

Mathematical notation is readily available in scientific word processors. However, on Internet pages or in email, multiplication is often written with a star (*), fractions are written with a slash (/), and exponents with a caret (^). For example, $\frac{x + y}{2x^3}$ is written as (x + y)/(2*x^3). If the numerator or denominator contain more than one symbol it is best to enclose them in parentheses to avoid confusion. An expression such as $1/2x$ is confusing. If your class evaluates it for $x = 4$, some students will probably assume that it is $1/(2x)$ and get $1/8$, and some will assume that it is $(1/2)x$ and get 2.

⟨4⟩ Equations

An **equation** is a statement of equality of two expressions. For example,

$$11 - 5 = 6, \qquad x + 3 = 9, \qquad 2x + 5 = 13, \qquad \text{and} \qquad \frac{x}{2} - 4 = 1$$

are equations. In an equation involving a variable, any number that gives a true statement when we replace the variable by the number is said to **satisfy** the equation and is called a **solution** or **root** to the equation. For example, 6 is a solution to $x + 3 = 9$ because $6 + 3 = 9$ is true. Because $5 + 3 = 9$ is false, 5 is not a solution to the equation $x + 3 = 9$. We have **solved** an equation when we have found all solutions to the equation. You will learn how to solve certain equations in Chapter 2.

EXAMPLE 5

Satisfying an equation

Determine whether the given number is a solution to the equation following it.

a) $6,\ 3x - 7 = 9$ **b)** $-3,\ \dfrac{2x - 4}{5} = -2$ **c)** $-5,\ -x - 2 = 3(x + 6)$

Solution

a) Replace x by 6 in the equation $3x - 7 = 9$:

$$3(6) - 7 = 9$$
$$18 - 7 = 9$$
$$11 = 9 \quad \text{False}$$

The number 6 is not a solution to the equation $3x - 7 = 9$.

b) Replace x by -3 in the equation $\dfrac{2x - 4}{5} = -2$:

$$\frac{2(-3) - 4}{5} = -2$$
$$\frac{-10}{5} = -2$$
$$-2 = -2 \quad \text{True}$$

The number -3 is a solution to the equation.

c) Replace x by -5 in $-x - 2 = 3(x + 6)$:

$$-(-5) - 2 = 3(-5 + 6)$$
$$5 - 2 = 3(1)$$
$$3 = 3 \quad \text{True}$$

The number -5 is a solution to the equation $-x - 2 = 3(x + 6)$.

Now do Exercises 69–82

Just as we translated verbal expressions into algebraic expressions, we can translate verbal sentences into algebraic equations. In an algebraic equation we use the equality symbol (=). Equality is indicated in words by phrases such as "is equal to," "is the same as," or simply "is."

EXAMPLE 6

Writing equations

Translate each sentence into an equation.

a) The sum of x and 7 is 12.

b) The product of 4 and x is the same as the sum of y and 5.

c) The quotient of $x + 3$ and 5 is equal to -1.

‹ Teaching Tip ›

Note how important it is to know the meaning of sum, difference, product, and quotient.

Solution

a) $x + 7 = 12$ **b)** $4x = y + 5$ **c)** $\frac{x + 3}{5} = -1$

Now do Exercises 83–90

‹5› Applications

Algebraic expressions are used to describe or **model** real-life situations. We can evaluate an algebraic expression for many values of a variable to get a collection of data. A graph (picture) of this data can give us useful information. For example, a forensic scientist can use a graph to estimate the length of a person's femur from the person's height.

EXAMPLE 7

Reading a graph

A forensic scientist uses the expression $69.1 + 2.2F$ as an estimate of the height in centimeters of a male with a femur of length F centimeters (National Space Biomedical Research Institute, www.nsbri.org).

a) If the femur of a male skeleton measures 50.6 cm, then what was the person's height?

b) Use the graph shown in Fig. 1.25 to estimate the length of a femur for a person who is 150 cm tall.

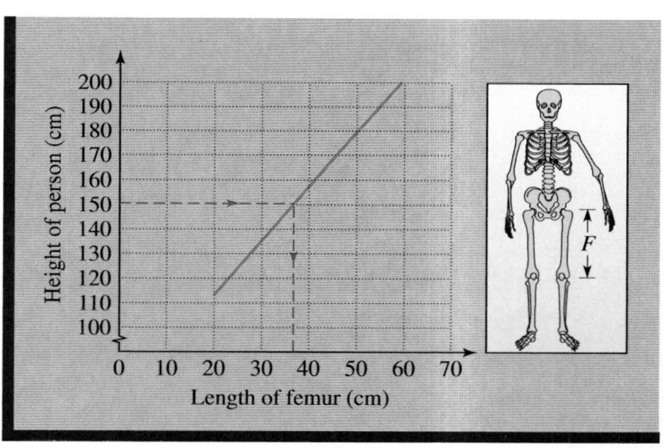

Figure 1.25

Solution

a) To find the height of the person, we use $F = 50.6$ in the expression $69.1 + 2.2F$:

$$69.1 + 2.2(50.6) \approx 180.4$$

So the person was approximately 180.4 cm tall.

b) To find the length of a femur for a person who is 150 cm tall, first locate 150 cm on the height scale of the graph in Fig. 1.25. Now draw a horizontal line to the graph and then a vertical line down to the length scale. So the length of a femur for a person who is 150 cm tall is approximately 36 cm.

Now do Exercises 99–104

Warm-Ups ▼

True or false? Explain your answer.

1. The expression $2x + 3y$ is referred to as a sum. True
2. The expression $5(y - 9)$ is a difference. False
3. The expression $2(x + 3y)$ is a product. True
4. The expression $\frac{x}{2} + \frac{y}{3}$ is a quotient. False
5. The expression $(a - b)(a + b)$ is a product of a sum and a difference. True
6. If x is -2, then the value of $2x + 4$ is 8. False
7. If $a = -3$, then $a^3 - 5 = 22$. False
8. The number 5 is a solution to the equation $2x - 3 = 13$. False
9. The product of $x + 3$ and 5 is $(x + 3)5$. True
10. The expression $2(x + 7)$ should be read as "the sum of 2 times x plus 7." False

1.6 Exercises

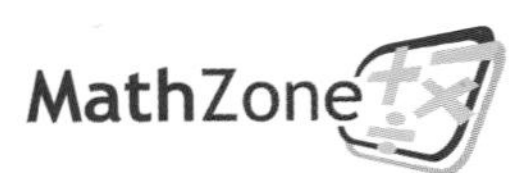

Boost your grade at mathzone.com!
- Practice Problems
- NetTutor
- Self-Tests
- e-Professors
- Videos

‹ Study Tips ›

- The review exercises at the end of this chapter are keyed to the sections in this chapter. If you have trouble with the review exercises, go back and study the corresponding section.
- Work the sample test at the end of this chapter to see if you are ready for your instructor's chapter test. Your instructor might not ask the same questions, but you will get a good idea of your test readiness.

Reading and Writing *After reading this section write out the answers to these questions. Use complete sentences.*

1. What is an algebraic expression?
An algebraic expression is the result of combining numbers and variables with the operations of arithmetic in some meaningful way.
2. What is the difference between an algebraic expression and an arithmetic expression?
An arithmetic expression involves only numbers.
3. How can you tell whether an algebraic expression should be referred to as a sum, difference, product, quotient, or square?
An algebraic expression is named according to the last operation to be performed.
4. How do you evaluate an algebraic expression?
An algebraic expression is evaluated by replacing the variables with numbers and evaluating the resulting arithmetic expression.
5. What is an equation?
An equation is a sentence that expresses equality between two algebraic expressions.
6. What is a solution to an equation?
If an equation is true when the variable is replaced by a number, then that number is a solution to the equation.

‹1› Identifying Algebraic Expressions

Identify each expression as a sum, difference, product, quotient, square, or cube. See Example 1.

7. $a^3 - 1$ Difference

8. $b(b - 1)$ Product

9. $(w - 1)^3$ Cube

10. $m^2 + n^2$ Sum

11. $3x + 5y$ Sum

12. $\frac{a - b}{b - a}$ Quotient

13. $\frac{u}{v} - \frac{v}{u}$ Difference

14. $(s - t)^2$ Square

15. $3(x + 5y)$ Product **16.** $a - \frac{a}{2}$ Difference

17. $\left(\frac{2}{z}\right)^2$ Square **18.** $(2q - p)^3$ Cube

⟨2⟩ Translating Algebraic Expressions

Use the term sum, difference, product, quotient, square, or cube to translate each algebraic expression into a verbal expression. See Example 2.

19. $x^2 - a^2$ The difference of x^2 and a^2

20. $a^3 + b^3$ The sum of a^3 and b^3

21. $(x - a)^2$ The square of $x - a$

22. $(a + b)^3$ The cube of $a + b$

23. $\frac{x - 4}{2}$ The quotient of $x - 4$ and 2

24. $2(x - 3)$ The product of 2 and $x - 3$

25. $\frac{x}{2} - 4$ The difference of $\frac{x}{2}$ and 4

26. $2x - 3$ The difference of $2x$ and 3

27. $(ab)^3$ The cube of ab

28. a^3b^3 The product of a^3 and b^3

Translate each verbal expression into an algebraic expression. Do not simplify. See Example 3.

29. The sum of 8 and y $8 + y$

30. The sum of $8x$ and $3y$ $8x + 3y$

31. The product of $5x$ and z $5xz$

32. The product of $x + 9$ and $x + 12$ $(x + 9)(x + 12)$

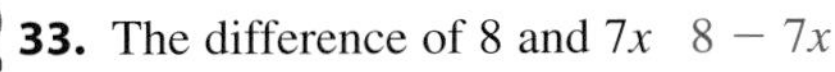

33. The difference of 8 and $7x$ $8 - 7x$

34. The difference of a^3 and b^3 $a^3 - b^3$

35. The quotient of 6 and $x + 4$ $\frac{6}{x + 4}$

36. The quotient of $x - 7$ and $7 - x$ $\frac{x - 7}{7 - x}$

37. The square of $a + b$ $(a + b)^2$

38. The cube of $x - y$ $(x - y)^3$

39. The sum of the cube of x and the square of y $x^3 + y^2$

40. The quotient of the square of a and the cube of b $\frac{a^2}{b^3}$

41. The product of 5 and the square of m $5m^2$

42. The difference of the square of m and the square of n $m^2 - n^2$

43. The square of the sum of s and t $(s + t)^2$

44. The cube of the difference of a and b $(a - b)^3$

⟨3⟩ Evaluating Algebraic Expressions

Evaluate each expression using $a = -1$, $b = 2$, and $c = -3$. See Example 4.

45. $-(a - b)$ 3 **46.** $b - a$ 3

47. $-b^2 + 7$ 3 **48.** $-c^2 - b^2$ -13

49. $c^2 - 2c + 1$ 16 **50.** $b^2 - 2b + 4$ 4

51. $a^3 - b^3$ -9 **52.** $b^3 - c^3$ 35

53. $(a - b)(a + b)$ -3 **54.** $(a - c)(a + c)$ -8

VIDEO **55.** $b^2 - 4ac$ -8 **56.** $a^2 - 4bc$ 25

57. $\frac{a - c}{a - b}$ $-\frac{2}{3}$ **58.** $\frac{b - c}{b + a}$ 5

59. $\frac{2}{a} + \frac{6}{b} - \frac{9}{c}$ 4 **60.** $\frac{c}{a} + \frac{6}{b} - \frac{b}{a}$ 8

61. $a \div |-a|$ -1 **62.** $|a| \div a$ -1

63. $|b| - |a|$ 1 **64.** $|c| + |b|$ 5

65. $-|-a - c|$ -4 **66.** $-|-a - b|$ -1

67. $(3 - |a - b|)^2$ 0 **68.** $(|b + c| - 2)^3$ -1

⟨4⟩ Equations

Determine whether the given number is a solution to the equation following it. See Example 5.

69. $2, 3x + 7 = 13$ Yes

VIDEO **70.** $-1, -3x + 7 = 10$ Yes

71. $-2, \frac{3x - 4}{2} = 5$ No

72. $-3, \frac{-2x + 9}{3} = 5$ Yes

73. $-2, -x + 4 = 6$ Yes

74. $-9, -x + 3 = 12$ Yes

75. $4, 3x - 7 = x + 1$ Yes

VIDEO **76.** $5, 3x - 7 = 2x + 1$ No

77. $3, -2(x - 1) = 2 - 2x$ Yes

78. $-8, x - 9 = -(9 - x)$ Yes

79. $8, \frac{x}{x - 8} = 0$ No **80.** $3, \frac{x - 3}{x + 3} = 0$ Yes

81. $-6, \frac{x + 6}{x + 6} = 1$ No **82.** $9, \frac{9}{x - 9} = 0$ No

Translate each sentence into an equation. See Example 6.

83. The sum of $5x$ and $3x$ is $8x$. $5x + 3x = 8x$

84. The sum of $\frac{y}{2}$ and 3 is 7. $\frac{y}{2} + 3 = 7$

85. The product of 3 and $x + 2$ is equal to 12. $3(x + 2) = 12$

86. The product of -6 and $7y$ is equal to 13. $-6(7y) = 13$

87. The quotient of x and 3 is the same as the product of x and 5. $\frac{x}{3} = 5x$

88. The quotient of $x + 3$ and $5y$ is the same as the product of x and y. $\frac{x+3}{5y} = xy$

89. The square of the sum of a and b is equal to 9. $(a + b)^2 = 9$

90. The sum of the squares of a and b is equal to the square of c. $a^2 + b^2 = c^2$

Miscellaneous

Fill in the tables with the appropriate values for the given expressions.

91.

x	$2x - 3$
-2	-7
-1	-5
0	-3
1	-1
2	1

92.

x	$-\frac{1}{2}x + 4$
-4	6
-2	5
0	4
2	3
4	2

93.

a	a^2	a^3	a^4
2	4	8	16
$\frac{1}{2}$	$\frac{1}{4}$	$\frac{1}{8}$	$\frac{1}{16}$
10	100	1000	10,000
0.1	0.01	0.001	0.0001

94.

b	$\frac{1}{b}$	$\frac{1}{b^2}$	$\frac{1}{b^3}$
3	$\frac{1}{3}$	$\frac{1}{9}$	$\frac{1}{27}$
$\frac{1}{3}$	3	9	27
10	0.1	0.01	0.001
0.1	10	100	1000

Use a calculator to find the value of $b^2 - 4ac$ for each of the following choices of a, b, and c.

95. $a = 4.2$, $b = 6.7$, $c = 1.8$ 14.65

96. $a = -3.5$, $b = 9.1$, $c = 3.6$ 133.21

97. $a = -1.2$, $b = 3.2$, $c = 5.6$ 37.12

98. $a = 2.4$, $b = -8.5$, $c = -5.8$ 127.93

⟨5⟩ Applications

Solve each problem. See Example 7.

99. ***Forensics.*** A forensic scientist uses the expression $81.7 + 2.4T$ to estimate the height in centimeters of a male with a tibia of length T centimeters. If a male skeleton has a tibia of length 36.5 cm, then what was the height of the person? Use the accompanying graph to estimate the length of a tibia for a male with a height of 180 cm. 169.3 cm, 41 cm

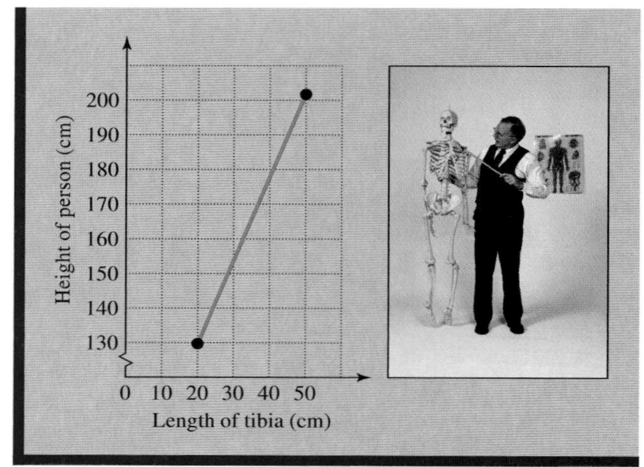

Figure for Exercise 99

100. ***Forensics.*** A forensic scientist uses the expression $72.6 + 2.5T$ to estimate the height in centimeters of a female with a tibia of length T centimeters. If a female skeleton has a tibia of length 32.4 cm, then what was the height of the person? Find the length of your tibia in centimeters, and use the expression from this exercise or the previous exercise to estimate your height. 153.6 cm

101. ***Games behind.*** In baseball a team's standing is measured by its percentage of wins and by the number of games it

	W	L	Pct	GB
Boston	50	29	0.633	—
NY Yankees	46	33	0.582	?
Toronto	46	35	0.568	?
Baltimore	38	45	0.458	?
Tampa Bay	35	47	0.427	?

Table for Exercise 101

is behind the leading team in its division. The expression

$$\frac{(X - x) + (y - Y)}{2}$$

gives the number of games behind for a team with x wins and y losses, where the division leader has X wins and Y losses. The table shown gives the won-lost records for the American League East on July 3, 2006 (www.espn.com). Fill in the column for the games behind (GB). 4, 5, 14, 16.5

102. ***Fly ball.*** The approximate distance in feet that a baseball travels when hit at an angle of 45° is given by the expression

$$\frac{(v_0)^2}{32}$$

where v_0 is the initial velocity in feet per second. If Barry Bonds of the Giants hits a ball at a 45° angle with an initial velocity of 120 feet per second, then how far will the ball travel? Use the accompanying graph to estimate the initial velocity for a ball that has traveled 370 feet. 450 feet, 109 feet per second

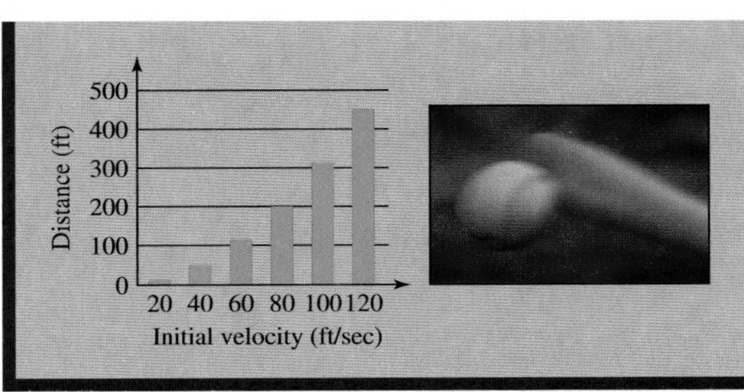

Figure for Exercise 102

103. ***Football field.*** The expression $2L + 2W$ gives the perimeter of a rectangle with length L and width W. What is the perimeter of a football field with length 100 yards and width 160 feet? 920 feet

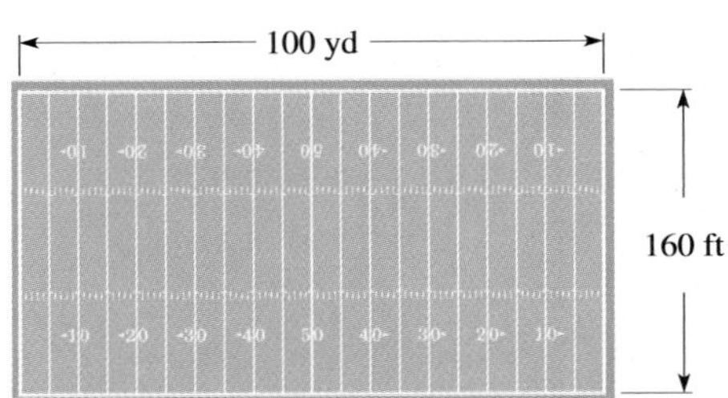

Figure for Exercise 103

104. ***Crop circles.*** The expression πr^2 gives the area of a circle with radius r. How many square meters of wheat were destroyed when an alien ship made a crop circle of diameter 25 meters in the wheat field at the Southwind Ranch? Round to the nearest tenth. Find π on your calculator. 490.9 m^2

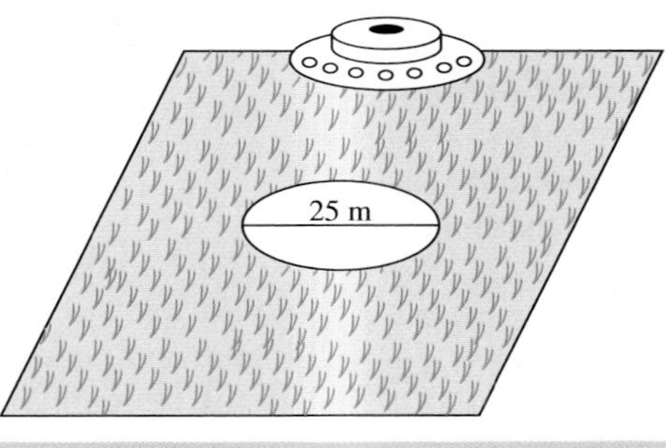

Figure for Exercise 104

Getting More Involved

105. ***Writing***

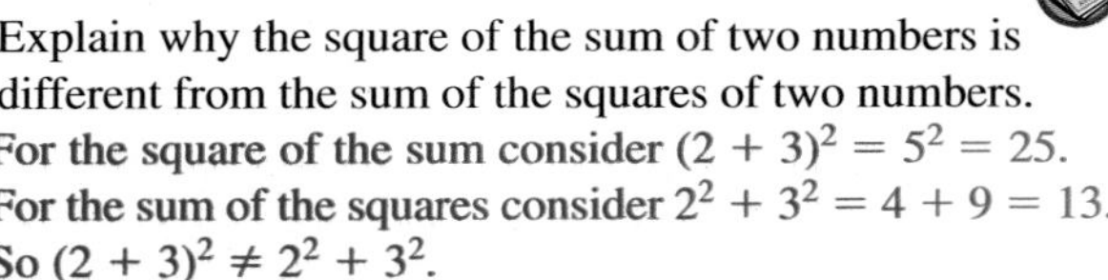

Explain why the square of the sum of two numbers is different from the sum of the squares of two numbers. For the square of the sum consider $(2 + 3)^2 = 5^2 = 25$. For the sum of the squares consider $2^2 + 3^2 = 4 + 9 = 13$. So $(2 + 3)^2 \neq 2^2 + 3^2$.

106. ***Cooperative learning***

The sum of the integers from 1 through n is $\frac{n(n + 1)}{2}$. The sum of the squares of the integers from 1 through n is $\frac{n(n + 1)(2n + 1)}{6}$. The sum of the cubes of the integers from 1 through n is $\frac{n^2(n + 1)^2}{4}$. Use the appropriate expressions to find the following values.

a) The sum of the integers from 1 through 30. 465

b) The sum of the squares of the integers from 1 through 30. 9455

c) The sum of the cubes of the integers from 1 through 30. 216,225

d) The square of the sum of the integers from 1 through 30. 216,225

e) The cube of the sum of the integers from 1 through 30. 100,544,625

1.7 Properties of the Real Numbers

In This Section

Everyone knows that the price of a hamburger plus the price of a Coke is the same as the price of a Coke plus the price of a hamburger. But do you know that this example illustrates the commutative property of addition? The properties of the real numbers are commonly used by anyone who performs the operations of arithmetic. In algebra we must have a thorough understanding of these properties.

⟨1⟩ The Commutative Properties

We get the same result whether we evaluate $3 + 5$ or $5 + 3$. This example illustrates the commutative property of addition. The fact that $4 \cdot 6$ and $6 \cdot 4$ are equal illustrates the commutative property of multiplication.

⟨ Teaching Tip ⟩

Discuss whether some real-life operations are commutative. For example, putting on your socks and putting on your shoes.

Commutative Property of Addition

For any real numbers a and b,

$$a + b = b + a.$$

Commutative Property of Multiplication

For any real numbers a and b,

$$ab = ba.$$

EXAMPLE 1

The commutative property of addition

Use the commutative property of addition to rewrite each expression.

a) $2 + (-10)$ **b)** $8 + x^2$ **c)** $2y - 4x$

⟨ Teaching Tip ⟩

Ask students to explain each property in their own words.

Solution

a) $2 + (-10) = -10 + 2$

b) $8 + x^2 = x^2 + 8$

c) $2y - 4x = 2y + (-4x) = -4x + 2y$

Now do Exercises 7–12

EXAMPLE 2

The commutative property of multiplication

Use the commutative property of multiplication to rewrite each expression.

a) $n \cdot 3$ **b)** $(x + 2) \cdot 3$ **c)** $5 - yx$

Solution

a) $n \cdot 3 = 3 \cdot n = 3n$ **b)** $(x + 2) \cdot 3 = 3(x + 2)$

c) $5 - yx = 5 - xy$

Now do Exercises 13–18

Addition and multiplication are commutative operations, but what about subtraction and division? Since $5 - 3 = 2$ and $3 - 5 = -2$, subtraction is not commutative. To see that division is not commutative, try dividing \$8 among 4 people and \$4 among 8 people.

‹2› The Associative Properties

Consider the computation of $2 + 3 + 6$. Using the order of operations, we add 2 and 3 to get 5 and then add 5 and 6 to get 11. If we add 3 and 6 first to get 9 and then add 2 and 9, we also get 11. So

$$(2 + 3) + 6 = 2 + (3 + 6).$$

We get the same result for either order of addition. This property is called the **associative property of addition.** The commutative and associative properties of addition are the reason that a hamburger, a Coke, and French fries cost the same as French fries, a hamburger, and a Coke.

We also have an **associative property of multiplication.** Consider the following two ways to find the product of 2, 3, and 4:

$$(2 \cdot 3)4 = 6 \cdot 4 = 24$$
$$2(3 \cdot 4) = 2 \cdot 12 = 24$$

We get the same result for either arrangement.

‹ Helpful Hint ›

In arithmetic we would probably write $(2 + 3) + 7 = 12$ without thinking about the associative property. In algebra, we need the associative property to understand that

$$(x + 3) + 7 = x + (3 + 7)$$
$$= x + 10.$$

Associative Property of Addition

For any real numbers a, b, and c,

$$(a + b) + c = a + (b + c).$$

Associative Property of Multiplication

For any real numbers a, b, and c,

$$(ab)c = a(bc).$$

EXAMPLE 3

Using the properties of multiplication

Use the commutative and associative properties of multiplication and exponential notation to rewrite each product.

a) $(3x)(x)$ **b)** $(xy)(5yx)$

Solution

a) $(3x)(x) = 3(x \cdot x) = 3x^2$

b) The commutative and associative properties of multiplication allow us to rearrange the multiplication in any order. We generally write numbers before variables, and we usually write variables in alphabetical order:

$$(xy)(5yx) = 5xxyy = 5x^2y^2$$

Now do Exercises 19–24

Consider the expression

$$3 - 9 + 7 - 5 - 8 + 4 - 13.$$

According to the accepted order of operations, we could evaluate this by computing from left to right. However, using the definition of subtraction, we can rewrite this expression as addition:

$$3 + (-9) + 7 + (-5) + (-8) + 4 + (-13)$$

The commutative and associative properties of addition allow us to add these numbers in any order we choose. It is usually faster to add the positive numbers, add the negative numbers, and then combine those two totals:

$$3 + 7 + 4 + (-9) + (-5) + (-8) + (-13) = 14 + (-35) = -21$$

Note that by performing the operations in this manner, we must subtract only once. There is no need to rewrite this expression as we have done here. We can sum the positive numbers and the negative numbers from the original expression and then combine their totals.

EXAMPLE 4

Using the properties of addition

Evaluate.

a) $3 - 7 + 9 - 5$ **b)** $4 - 5 - 9 + 6 - 2 + 4 - 8$

Solution

a) First add the positive numbers and the negative numbers:

$$3 - 7 + 9 - 5 = 12 + (-12)$$
$$= 0$$

b) $4 - 5 - 9 + 6 - 2 + 4 - 8 = 14 + (-24)$
$= -10$

Now do Exercises 25–32

‹ Teaching Tip ›

Emphasize that knowing the properties of the real numbers will help students use the real numbers. How many things do you know about your car that help you use it?

It is certainly not essential that we evaluate the expressions of Example 4 as shown. We get the same answer by adding and subtracting from left to right. However, in algebra, just getting the answer is not always the most important point. Learning new methods often increases understanding.

Even though addition is associative, subtraction is not an associative operation. For example, $(8 - 4) - 3 = 1$ and $8 - (4 - 3) = 7$. So

$$(8 - 4) - 3 \neq 8 - (4 - 3).$$

We can also use a numerical example to show that division is not associative. For instance, $(16 \div 4) \div 2 = 2$ and $16 \div (4 \div 2) = 8$. So

$$(16 \div 4) \div 2 \neq 16 \div (4 \div 2).$$

‹3› The Distributive Property

If four men and five women pay \$3 each for a movie, there are two ways to find the total amount spent:

$$3(4 + 5) = 3 \cdot 9 = 27$$
$$3 \cdot 4 + 3 \cdot 5 = 12 + 15 = 27$$

‹ Helpful Hint ›

To visualize the distributive property, we can determine the number of circles shown here in two ways:

o o o o   o o o o o
o o o o   o o o o o
o o o o   o o o o o

There are $3 \cdot 9$ or 27 circles, or there are $3 \cdot 4$ circles in the first group and $3 \cdot 5$ circles in the second group for a total of 27 circles.

Since we get \$27 either way, we can write

$$3(4 + 5) = 3 \cdot 4 + 3 \cdot 5.$$

We say that the multiplication by 3 is *distributed* over the addition. This example illustrates the **distributive property.**

Consider the following expressions involving multiplication and subtraction:

$$5(6 - 4) = 5 \cdot 2 = 10$$
$$5 \cdot 6 - 5 \cdot 4 = 30 - 20 = 10$$

Since both expressions have the same value, we can write

$$5(6 - 4) = 5 \cdot 6 - 5 \cdot 4.$$

Multiplication by 5 is distributed over each number in the parentheses. This example illustrates that multiplication distributes over subtraction.

‹ Teaching Tip ›

Since subtraction is defined in terms of addition, it is not really necessary to state the second distributive property.

Distributive Property

For any real numbers a, b, and c,

$$a(b + c) = ab + ac \quad \text{and} \quad a(b - c) = ab - ac.$$

We can use the distributive property to remove parentheses. If we start with $4(x + 3)$ and write

$$4(x + 3) = 4x + 4 \cdot 3 = 4x + 12,$$

we are using it to multiply 4 and $x + 3$ or to remove the parentheses. We wrote the product $4(x + 3)$ as the sum $4x + 12$.

EXAMPLE 5

Writing a product as a sum or difference

Use the distributive property to remove the parentheses.

a) $a(3 - b)$ **b)** $-3(x - 2)$

Solution

a) $a(3 - b) = a3 - ab$ Distributive property
$= 3a - ab$ $a3 = 3a$

b) $-3(x - 2) = -3x - (-3)(2)$ Distributive property
$= -3x - (-6)$ $(-3)(2) = -6$
$= -3x + 6$ Simplify.

Now do Exercises 33–44

When we write a number or an expression as a product, we are **factoring.** If we start with $3x + 15$ and write

$$3x + 15 = 3x + 3 \cdot 5 = 3(x + 5),$$

we are using the distributive property to factor $3x + 15$. We factored out the common factor 3.

EXAMPLE 6

Writing a sum or difference as a product

Use the distributive property to factor each expression.

a) $7x - 21$ **b)** $5a + 5$

Solution

a) $7x - 21 = 7x - 7 \cdot 3$ Write 21 as $7 \cdot 3$.

$= 7(x - 3)$ Distributive property

b) $5a + 5 = 5a + 5 \cdot 1$ Write 5 as $5 \cdot 1$.

$= 5(a + 1)$ Factor out the common factor 5.

Now do Exercises 45–56

‹4› The Identity Properties

The numbers 0 and 1 have special properties. Multiplication of a number by 1 does not change the number, and addition of 0 to a number does not change the number. That is why 1 is called the **multiplicative identity** and 0 is called the **additive identity.**

Additive Identity Property

For any real number a,

$$a + 0 = 0 + a = a.$$

Multiplicative Identity Property

For any real number a,

$$a \cdot 1 = 1 \cdot a = a.$$

‹ Teaching Tip ›

In the identity properties 0 and 1 are used in the operations. In the inverse properties 0 and 1 are the results of the operations.

‹5› The Inverse Properties

The idea of additive inverses was introduced in Section 1.3. Every real number a has an **additive inverse** or **opposite,** $-a$, such that $a + (-a) = 0$. Every nonzero real number a also has a **multiplicative inverse** or **reciprocal,** written $\frac{1}{a}$, such that $a \cdot \frac{1}{a} = 1$. Note that the sum of additive inverses is the additive identity and that the product of multiplicative inverses is the multiplicative identity.

Additive Inverse Property

For any real number a, there is a unique number $-a$ such that

$$a + (-a) = 0.$$

Multiplicative Inverse Property

For any nonzero real number a, there is a unique number $\frac{1}{a}$ such that

$$a \cdot \frac{1}{a} = 1.$$

We are already familiar with multiplicative inverses for rational numbers. For example, the multiplicative inverse of $\frac{2}{3}$ is $\frac{3}{2}$ because

$$\frac{2}{3} \cdot \frac{3}{2} = \frac{6}{6} = 1.$$

EXAMPLE 7

Multiplicative inverses

Find the multiplicative inverse of each number.

a) 5 **b)** 0.3 **c)** $-\frac{3}{4}$ **d)** 1.7

‹ Calculator Close-Up ›

You can find multiplicative inverses with a calculator as shown here.

```
1/.3▸Frac
                10/3
1/(-3/4)▸Frac
                -4/3
1/1.7▸Frac
               10/17
```

When the divisor is a fraction, it must be in parentheses.

Solution

a) The multiplicative inverse of 5 is $\frac{1}{5}$ because

$$5 \cdot \frac{1}{5} = 1.$$

b) To find the reciprocal of 0.3, we first write 0.3 as a ratio of integers:

$$0.3 = \frac{3}{10}$$

The multiplicative inverse of 0.3 is $\frac{10}{3}$ because

$$\frac{3}{10} \cdot \frac{10}{3} = 1.$$

c) The reciprocal of $-\frac{3}{4}$ is $-\frac{4}{3}$ because

$$\left(-\frac{3}{4}\right)\left(-\frac{4}{3}\right) = 1.$$

d) First convert 1.7 to a ratio of integers:

$$1.7 = 1\frac{7}{10} = \frac{17}{10}$$

The multiplicative inverse is $\frac{10}{17}$.

Now do Exercises 57–68

‹6› Identifying the Properties

Zero has a property that no other number has. Multiplication involving zero always results in zero.

Multiplication Property of Zero

For any real number a,

$$0 \cdot a = 0 \quad \text{and} \quad a \cdot 0 = 0.$$

EXAMPLE 8

Identifying the properties

Name the property that justifies each equation.

a) $5 \cdot 7 = 7 \cdot 5$

b) $4 \cdot \frac{1}{4} = 1$

c) $1 \cdot 864 = 864$

d) $6 + (5 + x) = (6 + 5) + x$

e) $3x + 5x = (3 + 5)x$

f) $6 + (x + 5) = 6 + (5 + x)$

g) $\pi x^2 + \pi y^2 = \pi(x^2 + y^2)$

h) $325 + 0 = 325$

i) $-3 + 3 = 0$

j) $455 \cdot 0 = 0$

Solution

a) Commutative property of multiplication
b) Multiplicative inverse property
c) Multiplicative identity property
d) Associative property of addition
e) Distributive property
f) Commutative property of addition
g) Distributive property
h) Additive identity property
i) Additive inverse property
j) Multiplication property of 0

Now do Exercises 69–88

Warm-Ups ▼

True or false? Explain your answer.

1. $24 \div (4 \div 2) = (24 \div 4) \div 2$ False
2. $1 \div 2 = 2 \div 1$ False
3. $6 - 5 = -5 + 6$ True
4. $9 - (4 - 3) = (9 - 4) - 3$ False
5. Multiplication is a commutative operation. True
6. $5x + 5 = 5(x + 1)$ for any value of x. True
7. The multiplicative inverse of 0.02 is 50. True
8. $-3(x - 2) = -3x + 6$ for any value of x. True
9. $3x + 2x = (3 + 2)x$ for any value of x. True
10. The additive inverse of 0 is 0. True

1.7 Exercises

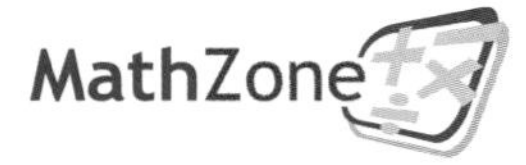

‹ Study Tips ›

- Don't stay up all night cramming for a test. Prepare for a test well in advance and get a good night's sleep before a test.
- Do your homework on a regular basis so that there is no need to cram.

Reading and Writing *After reading this section write out the answers to these questions. Use complete sentences.*

1. What is the difference between the commutative property of addition and the associative property of addition?
The commutative property says that $a + b = b + a$ and the associative property says that $(a + b) + c = a + (b + c)$.
2. Which property involves two different operations?
The distributive property involves multiplication and addition.
3. What is factoring?
Factoring is the process of writing an expression or number as a product.
4. Which two numbers play a prominent role in the properties studied here?
The number 0 is the additive identity and the number 1 is the multiplicative identity.
5. What is the purpose of studying the properties of real numbers?
The properties help us to understand the operations and how they are related to each other.
6. What is the distributive property?
The distributive property says that $a(b + c) = ab + ac$.

⟨1⟩ The Commutative Properties

Use the commutative property of addition to rewrite each expression. See Example 1.

7. $9 + r$ $r + 9$
8. $t + 6$ $6 + t$
9. $3(2 + x)$ $3(x + 2)$
10. $P(1 + rt)$ $P(rt + 1)$
11. $4 - 5x$ $-5x + 4$
12. $b - 2a$ $-2a + b$

Use the commutative property of multiplication to rewrite each expression. See Example 2.

13. $x \cdot 6$ $6x$
14. $y \cdot (-9)$ $-9y$
15. $(x - 4)(-2)$ $-2(x - 4)$
16. $a(b + c)$ $(b + c)a$
17. $4 - y \cdot 8$ $4 - 8y$
18. $z \cdot 9 - 2$ $9z - 2$

⟨2⟩ The Associative Properties

Use the commutative and associative properties of multiplication and exponential notation to rewrite each product. See Example 3.

19. $(4w)(w)$ $4w^2$
20. $(y)(2y)$ $2y^2$
21. $3a(ba)$ $3a^2b$
22. $(x \cdot x)(7x)$ $7x^3$
23. $(x)(9x)(xz)$ $9x^3z$
24. $y(y \cdot 5)(wy)$ $5y^3w$

Evaluate by finding first the sum of the positive numbers and then the sum of the negative numbers. See Example 4.

25. $8 - 4 + 3 - 10$ -3
26. $-3 + 5 - 12 + 10$ 0
27. $8 - 10 + 7 - 8 - 7$ -10
28. $6 - 11 + 7 - 9 + 13 - 2$ 4
29. $-4 - 11 + 7 - 8 + 15 - 20$ -21
30. $-8 + 13 - 9 - 15 + 7 - 22 + 5$ -29
31. $-3.2 + 2.4 - 2.8 + 5.8 - 1.6$ 0.6
32. $5.4 - 5.1 + 6.6 - 2.3 + 9.1$ 13.7

⟨3⟩ The Distributive Property

Use the distributive property to remove the parentheses. See Example 5.

33. $3(x - 5)$ $3x - 15$
34. $4(b - 1)$ $4b - 4$
35. $a(2 + t)$ $2a + at$
36. $b(a + w)$ $ab + bw$
37. $-3(w - 6)$ $-3w + 18$
VIDEO **38.** $-3(m - 5)$ $-3m + 15$
39. $-4(5 - y)$ $-20 + 4y$
40. $-3(6 - p)$ $-18 + 3p$
41. $-1(a - 7)$ $-a + 7$
42. $-1(c - 8)$ $-c + 8$
43. $-1(t + 4)$ $-t - 4$
44. $-1(x + 7)$ $-x - 7$

Use the distributive property to factor each expression. See Example 6.

45. $2m + 12$ $2(m + 6)$
46. $3y + 6$ $3(y + 2)$
47. $4x - 4$ $4(x - 1)$
48. $6y + 6$ $6(y + 1)$
49. $4y - 16$ $4(y - 4)$
VIDEO **50.** $5x + 15$ $5(x + 3)$
51. $4a + 8$ $4(a + 2)$
52. $7a - 35$ $7(a - 5)$
53. $x + xy$ $x(1 + y)$
54. $a - ab$ $a(1 - b)$
55. $6a - 2b$ $2(3a - b)$
56. $8a + 2c$ $2(4a + c)$

⟨5⟩ The Inverse Properties

Find the multiplicative inverse (reciprocal) of each number. See Example 7.

57. $\frac{1}{2}$ 2
58. $\frac{1}{3}$ 3
59. -5 $-\frac{1}{5}$
60. -6 $-\frac{1}{6}$
61. 7 $\frac{1}{7}$
VIDEO **62.** 8 $\frac{1}{8}$
63. 1 1
64. -1 -1
65. -0.25 -4
66. 0.75 $\frac{4}{3}$
67. 2.5 $\frac{2}{5}$
68. 3.5 $\frac{2}{7}$

⟨6⟩ Identifying the Properties

Name the property that justifies each equation. See Example 8.

69. $3 \cdot x = x \cdot 3$ Commutative property of multiplication
70. $x + 5 = 5 + x$ Commutative property of addition
71. $2(x - 3) = 2x - 6$ Distributive property
72. $a(bc) = (ab)c$ Associative property of multiplication
73. $-3(xy) = (-3x)y$ Associative property of multiplication
74. $3(x + 1) = 3x + 3$ Distributive property
VIDEO **75.** $4 + (-4) = 0$ Additive inverse property
76. $1.3 + 9 = 9 + 1.3$ Commutative property of addition
VIDEO **77.** $x^2 \cdot 5 = 5x^2$ Commutative property of multiplication
78. $0 \cdot \pi = 0$ Multiplication property of 0
79. $1 \cdot 3y = 3y$ Multiplicative identity property
80. $(0.1)(10) = 1$ Multiplicative inverse property
81. $2a + 5a = (2 + 5)a$ Distributive property
82. $3 + 0 = 3$ Additive identity property
83. $-7 + 7 = 0$ Additive inverse property
84. $1 \cdot b = b$ Multiplicative identity property
85. $(2346)0 = 0$ Multiplication property of 0
86. $4x + 4 = 4(x + 1)$ Distributive property
87. $ay + y = y(a + 1)$ Distributive property
88. $ab + bc = b(a + c)$ Distributive property

Complete each equation, using the property named.

89. $a + y =$ ____, commutative property of addition $y + a$
90. $6x + 6 =$ ____, distributive property $6(x + 1)$
91. $5(aw) =$ ____, associative property of multiplication $(5a)w$
92. $x + 3 =$ ____, commutative property of addition $3 + x$

93. $\frac{1}{2}x + \frac{1}{2} =$ _____, distributive property $\frac{1}{2}(x + 1)$

94. $-3(x - 7) =$ _____, distributive property $-3x + 21$

95. $6x + 15 =$ _____, distributive property $3(2x + 5)$

96. $(x + 6) + 1 =$ _____, associative property of addition $x + (6 + 1)$

97. $4(0.25) =$ _____, multiplicative inverse property 1

98. $-1(5 - y) =$ _____, distributive property $-5 + y$

99. $0 = 96($_____$)$, multiplication property of zero 0

100. $3 \cdot ($_____$) = 3$, multiplicative identity property 1

101. $0.33($_____$) = 1$, multiplicative inverse property $\frac{100}{33}$

102. $-8(1) =$ _____, multiplicative identity property -8

Getting More Involved

103. ***Writing***

The perimeter of a rectangle is the sum of twice the length and twice the width. Write in words another way to find the perimeter that illustrates the distributive property.
The perimeter is twice the sum of the length and width.

104. ***Discussion***

Eldrid bought a loaf of bread for $1.69 and a gallon of milk for $2.29. Using a tax rate of 5%, he correctly figured that the tax on the bread would be 8 cents and the tax on the milk would be 11 cents, for a total of $4.17. However, at the cash register he was correctly charged $4.18. How could this happen? Which property of the real numbers is in question in this case?
Due to rounding off, the tax on each item separately does not equal the tax on the total. It looks like the distributive property fails.

105. ***Exploration***

Determine whether each of the following pairs of tasks are "commutative." That is, does the order in which they are performed produce the same result?

a) Put on your coat; put on your hat. Commutative
b) Put on your shirt; put on your coat. Not commutative

Find another pair of "commutative" tasks and another pair of "noncommutative" tasks.

1.8 Using the Properties to Simplify Expressions

In This Section

- ⟨1⟩ Using the Properties in Computation
- ⟨2⟩ Combining Like Terms
- ⟨3⟩ Products and Quotients
- ⟨4⟩ Removing Parentheses
- ⟨5⟩ Applications

The properties of the real numbers can be helpful when we are doing computations. In this section we will see how the properties can be applied in arithmetic and algebra.

⟨1⟩ Using the Properties in Computation

The properties of the real numbers can often be used to simplify computations. For example, to find the product of 26 and 200, we can write

$$\begin{aligned}(26)(200) &= (26)(2 \cdot 100)\\ &= (26 \cdot 2)(100)\\ &= 52 \cdot 100\\ &= 5200.\end{aligned}$$

It is the associative property that allows us to multiply 26 by 2 to get 52, then multiply 52 by 100 to get 5200.

EXAMPLE 1

Using the properties

Use the appropriate property to aid you in evaluating each expression.

a) $347 + 35 + 65$ **b)** $3 \cdot 435 \cdot \frac{1}{3}$ **c)** $6 \cdot 28 + 4 \cdot 28$

Solution

a) Notice that the sum of 35 and 65 is 100. So apply the associative property as follows:

$$347 + (35 + 65) = 347 + 100$$
$$= 447$$

b) Use the commutative and associative properties to rearrange this product. We can then do the multiplication quickly:

$$3 \cdot 435 \cdot \frac{1}{3} = 435\left(3 \cdot \frac{1}{3}\right) \quad \text{Commutative and associative properties}$$
$$= 435 \cdot 1 \quad \text{Multiplicative inverse property}$$
$$= 435 \quad \text{Multiplicative identity property}$$

c) Use the distributive property to rewrite this expression.

$$6 \cdot 28 + 4 \cdot 28 = (6 + 4)28$$
$$= 10 \cdot 28$$
$$= 280$$

Now do Exercises 7–22

⟨2⟩ Combining Like Terms

An expression containing a number or the product of a number and one or more variables raised to powers is called a **term.** For example,

$$-3, \quad 5x, \quad -3x^2y, \quad a, \quad \text{and} \quad -abc$$

are terms. The number preceding the variables in a term is called the **coefficient.** In the term $5x$, the coefficient of x is 5. In the term $-3x^2y$ the coefficient of x^2y is -3. In the term a, the coefficient of a is 1 because $a = 1 \cdot a$. In the term $-abc$ the coefficient of abc is -1 because $-abc = -1 \cdot abc$. If two terms contain the same variables with the same exponents, they are called **like terms.** For example, $3x^2$ and $-5x^2$ are like terms, but $3x^2$ and $-5x^3$ are not like terms.

Using the distributive property on an expression involving the sum of like terms allows us to combine the like terms as shown in Example 2.

EXAMPLE 2

Combining like terms

Use the distributive property to perform the indicated operations.

a) $3x + 5x$ **b)** $-5xy - (-4xy)$

‹ Teaching Tip ›

Having students read the expression $-5xy - (-4xy)$ will help them understand the difference between minus and negative.

Solution

a) $3x + 5x = (3 + 5)x$ Distributive property

$= 8x$ Add the coefficients.

Because the distributive property is valid for any real numbers, we have $3x + 5x = 8x$ no matter what number is used for x.

b) Since the distributive property is valid also for subtraction, $ab - ac = a(b - c)$, we can remove xy from the two terms.

$-5xy - (-4xy) = [-5 - (-4)]xy$ Distributive property

$= -1xy$ $\quad -5 - (-4) = -5 + 4 = -1$

$= -xy$ Multiplying by -1 is the same as taking the opposite.

Now do Exercises 23–28

Of course, we do not want to write out all of the steps shown in Example 2 every time we combine like terms. We can combine like terms as easily as we can add or subtract their coefficients.

EXAMPLE 3

Combining like terms

Perform the indicated operations.

a) $w + 2w$ **b)** $-3a + (-7a)$ **c)** $-9x + 5x$

d) $7xy - (-12xy)$ **e)** $2x^2 + 4x^2$ **f)** $\frac{1}{2}x - \frac{1}{4}x$

Solution

a) $w + 2w = 1w + 2w = 3w$

b) $-3a + (-7a) = -10a$

c) $-9x + 5x = -4x$

d) $7xy - (-12xy) = 19xy$

e) $2x^2 + 4x^2 = 6x^2$

f) $\frac{1}{2}x - \frac{1}{4}x = \left(\frac{1}{2} - \frac{1}{4}\right)x = \frac{1}{4}x$

Now do Exercises 29–42

CAUTION There are no like terms in expressions such as

$$2 + 5x, \quad 3xy + 5y, \quad 3w + 5a, \quad \text{and} \quad 3z^2 + 5z.$$

The terms in these expressions cannot be combined.

‹3› Products and Quotients

To **simplify** an expression means to perform operations, combine like terms, and get an equivalent expression that looks simpler. However, *simplify* is *not* a precisely defined term. An expression that uses fewer symbols is usually considered simpler, but we should not be too picky with this idea. Simplifying $2x + 3x$ we get $5x$, but we would not say that $\frac{x}{2}$ is simpler than $\frac{1}{2}x$. Some would say that $2ax + 2ay$ is simpler than $2a(x + y)$ because the parentheses have been removed. However, there are seven symbols in each expression, and five operations indicated in $2ax + 2ay$ with only three in $2a(x + y)$. If you are asked to write $2a(x + y)$ as a sum or to remove the parentheses rather than to simplify it, then the answer is clearly $2ax + 2ay$.

In Example 4 we use the associative property of multiplication to simplify some products.

EXAMPLE 4

Finding products

Simplify.

a) $3(5x)$ **b)** $2\left(\frac{x}{2}\right)$

c) $(4x)(6x)$ **d)** $(-2a)(4b)$

‹ **Teaching Tip** ›

Emphasize that $\frac{1}{2}x$ and $\frac{x}{2}$ are equivalent.

Solution

a) $3(5x) = (3 \cdot 5)x$ Associative property of multiplication

$= (15)x$ Multiply.

$= 15x$ Remove unnecessary parentheses.

b) $2\left(\frac{x}{2}\right) = 2\left(\frac{1}{2} \cdot x\right)$ Multiplying by $\frac{1}{2}$ is the same as dividing by 2.

$= \left(2 \cdot \frac{1}{2}\right)x$ Associative property of multiplication

$= 1 \cdot x$ Multiplicative inverse property

$= x$ Multiplicative identity property

c) $(4x)(6x) = 4 \cdot 6 \cdot x \cdot x$ Commutative and associative properties

$= 24x^2$ Definition of exponent

d) $(-2a)(4b) = -2 \cdot 4 \cdot a \cdot b = -8ab$

Now do Exercises 43–52

Note that $\frac{x}{2}$ is equivalent to $\frac{1}{2} \cdot x$ in Example 4(b) because division is defined as multiplication by the reciprocal of the divisor. In general, $\frac{x}{b}$ is equivalent to $\frac{1}{b} \cdot x$.

CAUTION Be careful with expressions such as $3(5x)$ and $3(5 + x)$. In $3(5x)$, we multiply 5 by 3 to get $3(5x) = 15x$. In $3(5 + x)$, both 5 and x are multiplied by the 3 to get $3(5 + x) = 15 + 3x$.

In Example 4 we showed how the properties are used to simplify products. However, in practice we usually do not write out any steps for these problems—we can write just the answer.

EXAMPLE 5

Finding products quickly

Find each product.

a) $(-3)(4x)$ **b)** $(-4a)(-7a)$ **c)** $(-3a)\left(\frac{b}{3}\right)$ **d)** $6 \cdot \frac{x}{2}$

Solution

a) $-12x$ **b)** $28a^2$ **c)** $-ab$ **d)** $3x$

Now do Exercises 53–58

In Section 1.2 we found the quotient of two numbers by inverting the divisor and then multiplying. Since $a \div b = a \cdot \frac{1}{b}$, any quotient can be written as a product.

EXAMPLE 6

Simplifying quotients

Simplify.

a) $\frac{10x}{5}$ **b)** $\frac{4x + 8}{2}$

Solution

a) Since dividing by 5 is equivalent to multiplying by $\frac{1}{5}$, we have

$$\frac{10x}{5} = \frac{1}{5}(10x) = \left(\frac{1}{5} \cdot 10\right)x = (2)x = 2x.$$

Note that you can simply divide 10 by 5 to get 2.

b) Since dividing by 2 is equivalent to multiplying by $\frac{1}{2}$, we have

$$\frac{4x + 8}{2} = \frac{1}{2}(4x + 8)$$

$$= \frac{1}{2} \cdot 4x + \frac{1}{2} \cdot 8 \quad \text{Distributive property}$$

$$= 2x + 4.$$

Note that both 4 and 8 are divided by 2. So we could have written

$$\frac{4x + 8}{2} = \frac{4x}{2} + \frac{8}{2} = 2x + 4 \text{ or } \frac{4x + 8}{2} = \frac{\cancel{2}(2x + 4)}{\cancel{2}} = 2x + 4.$$

Now do Exercises 59–70

CAUTION It is not correct to divide only one term in the numerator by the denominator. For example,

$$\frac{4 + 7}{2} \neq 2 + 7$$

because $\frac{4 + 7}{2} = \frac{11}{2}$ and $2 + 7 = 9$.

‹ Calculator Close-Up ›

A negative sign in front of parentheses changes the sign of every term inside the parentheses.

```
-(5-3)
                -2
-1(5-3)
                -2
-5+3
                -2
```

‹4› Removing Parentheses

In Section 1.7 we used the distributive property to multiply a sum or difference by -1 and remove the parentheses. For example,

$$-1(a + 5) = -a - 5 \quad \text{and} \quad -1(-x - 2) = x + 2.$$

If -1 is replaced with a negative sign the parentheses are removed in the same manner because multiplying a number by -1 is equivalent to finding its opposite. So

$$-(a + 5) = -1(a + 5) = -a - 5 \quad \text{and} \quad -(-x - 2) = -1(-x - 2) = x + 2.$$

If a subtraction sign precedes the parentheses it is removed in the same manner also, because subtraction is defined as addition of the opposite. So

$$3a - (a + 5) = 3a - a - 5 = 2a - 5 \quad \text{and} \quad 5x - (-x - 2) = 5x + x + 2 = 6x + 2.$$

If parentheses are preceded by a negative sign or a subtraction symbol, the signs of all terms within the parentheses are changed when the parentheses are removed.

EXAMPLE 7

Removing parentheses with opposites and subtraction

Remove the parentheses and combine the like terms.

a) $-(x - 4) + 5x - 1$ **b)** $-(-5 - y) + 2y - 6$

c) $10 - (x + 3)$ **d)** $3x - 6 - (2x - 4)$

Solution

The procedure is the same for each part: change the signs of each term in parentheses and then combine like terms.

a) $-(x - 4) + 5x - 1 = -x + 4 + 5x - 1$
$= 4x + 3$

b) $-(-5 - y) + 2y - 6 = 5 + y + 2y - 6$
$= 3y - 1$

c) $10 - (x + 3) = 10 - x - 3$
$= -x + 7$

d) $3x - 6 - (2x - 4) = 3x - 6 - 2x + 4$
$= x - 2$

Now do Exercises 71–86

Some parentheses are used for emphasis or clarity and are unnecessary. They can be removed without changing anything. For example,

$$(2x + 3) + (x - 4) = 2x + 3 + x - 4 = 3x - 1.$$

In Example 8, we simplify more algebraic expressions, some of which contain unnecessary parentheses.

EXAMPLE 8

Simplifying algebraic expressions

Simplify each expression.

a) $(-2x + 3) + (5x - 7)$ **b)** $(-3x + 6x) + 5(4 - 2x)$

c) $-2x(3x - 7) - 3(x - 6)$ **d)** $x - 0.02(x + 500)$

Solution

a) $(-2x + 3) + (5x - 7) = -2x + 3 + 5x - 7$ Remove unnecessary parentheses.
$= 3x - 4$ Combine like terms.

b) $(-3x + 6x) + 5(4 - 2x) = -3x + 6x + 20 - 10x$ Distributive property
$= -7x + 20$ Combine like terms.

c) $-2x(3x - 7) - 3(x - 6) = -6x^2 + 14x - 3x + 18$ Distributive property

$= -6x^2 + 11x + 18$ Combine like terms.

d) $x - 0.02(x + 500) = 1x - 0.02x - 10$ Distributive property

$= 0.98x - 10$ Combine like terms.

Now do Exercises 87–104

⟨5⟩ Applications

EXAMPLE 9

Perimeter of a rectangle

Find an algebraic expression for the perimeter of the rectangle shown here and then find the perimeter if $x = 15$ inches.

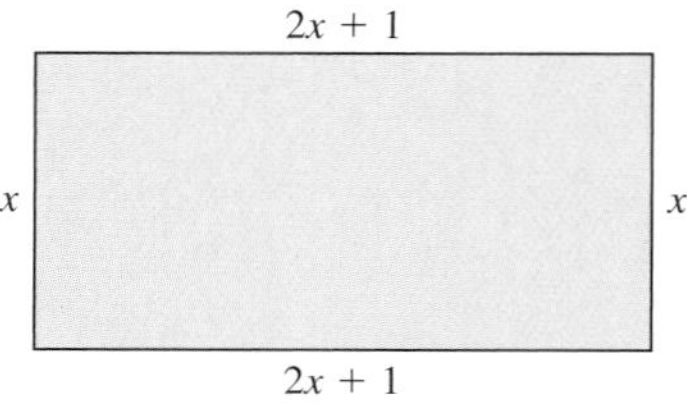

Solution

The perimeter of any figure is the sum of the lengths of its sides:

$$2(x) + 2(2x + 1) = 2x + 4x + 2$$
$$= 6x + 2$$

So $6x + 2$ is an algebraic expression for the perimeter. If $x = 15$ inches, then the perimeter is $6(15) + 2$ or 92 inches.

Now do Exercises 121–124

Warm-Ups ▼

True or false? Explain your answer.

A statement involving variables should be marked true only if it is true for all values of the variable.

1. $3(x + 6) = 3x + 18$ True

2. $-3x + 9 = -3(x + 9)$ False

3. $-1(x - 4) = -x + 4$ True

4. $3a + 4a = 7a$ True

5. $(3a)(4a) = 12a$ False

6. $3(5 \cdot 2) = 15 \cdot 6$ False

7. $x + x = x^2$ False

8. $x \cdot x = 2x$ False

9. $3 + 2x = 5x$ False

10. $-(5x - 2) = -5x + 2$ True

Study Tips

- When you get a test back don't simply file it in your notebook. Rework all of the problems that you missed.
- Being a full-time student is a full-time job. A successful student spends 2 to 4 hours studying outside of class for every hour spent in the classroom.

Reading and Writing *After reading this section write out the answers to these questions. Use complete sentences.*

1. What are like terms?
   Like terms are terms with the same variables and exponents.
2. What is the coefficient of a term?
   The coefficient of a term is the number preceding the variable.
3. What can you do to like terms that you cannot do to unlike terms?
   We can add or subtract like terms.
4. What operations can you perform with unlike terms?
   Unlike terms can be multiplied and divided.
5. What is the difference between a positive sign preceding a set of parentheses and a negative sign preceding a set of parentheses?
   If a negative sign precedes a set of parentheses, then signs for all terms in the parentheses are changed when the parentheses are removed.
6. What happens when a number is multiplied by -1?
   Multiplying a number by -1 changes the sign of the number.

⟨1⟩ Using the Properties in Computation

Use the appropriate properties to evaluate the expressions. See Example 1.

7. $35(200)$ 7000

8. $15(300)$ 4500

9. $\frac{4}{3}(0.75)$ 1

10. $5(0.2)$ 1

11. $256 + 78 + 22$ 356

12. $12 + 88 + 376$ 476

13. $35 \cdot 3 + 35 \cdot 7$ 350

14. $98 \cdot 478 + 2 \cdot 478$ 47,800

15. $18 \cdot 4 \cdot 2 \cdot \frac{1}{4}$ 36

16. $19 \cdot 3 \cdot 2 \cdot \frac{1}{3}$ 38

17. $(120)(300)$ 36,000

18. $150 \cdot 200$ 30,000

19. $12 \cdot 375(-6 + 6)$ 0

20. $354^2(-2 \cdot 4 + 8)$ 0

21. $78 + 6 + 8 + 4 + 2$ 98

22. $-47 + 12 - 6 - 12 + 6$ -47

⟨2⟩ Combining Like Terms

Combine like terms where possible. See Examples 2 and 3.

23. $5w + 6w$ $11w$

24. $4a + 10a$ $14a$ (VIDEO)

25. $4x - x$ $3x$

26. $a - 6a$ $-5a$

27. $2x - (-3x)$ $5x$

28. $2b - (-5b)$ $7b$

29. $-3a - (-2a)$ $-a$

30. $-10m - (-6m)$ $-4m$

31. $-a - a$ $-2a$

32. $a - a$ 0

33. $10 - 6t$ $10 - 6t$

34. $9 - 4w$ $9 - 4w$

35. $3x^2 + 5x^2$ $8x^2$

36. $3r^2 + 4r^2$ $7r^2$

37. $-4x + 2x^2$ $-4x + 2x^2$

38. $6w^2 - w$ $6w^2 - w$

39. $5mw^2 - 12mw^2$ $-7mw^2$

40. $4ab^2 - 19ab^2$ $-15ab^2$

41. $\frac{1}{3}a + \frac{1}{2}a$ $\frac{5}{6}a$

42. $\frac{3}{5}b - b$ $-\frac{2}{5}b$

⟨3⟩ Products and Quotients

Simplify the following products or quotients. See Examples 4–6.

43. $3(4h)$ $12h$

44. $2(5h)$ $10h$

45. $6b(-3)$ $-18b$

46. $-3m(-1)$ $3m$

47. $(-3m)(3m)$ $-9m^2$

48. $(2x)(-2x)$ $-4x^2$

49. $(-3d)(-4d)$ $12d^2$

50. $(-5t)(-2t)$ $10t^2$

51. $(-y)(-y)$ y^2

52. $y(-y)$ $-y^2$

53. $-3a(5b)$ $-15ab$

54. $-7w(3r)$ $-21rw$ (VIDEO)

55. $-3a(2 + b)$ $-6a - 3ab$

56. $-2x(3 + y)$ $-6x - 2xy$

57. $-k(1 - k)$ $-k + k^2$

58. $-t(t - 1)$ $-t^2 + t$

59. $\frac{3y}{3}$ y

60. $\frac{-9t}{9}$ $-t$

61. $\frac{-15y}{5}$ $-3y$

62. $\frac{-12b}{2}$ $-6b$

63. $2\left(\frac{y}{2}\right)$ y

64. $6\left(\frac{m}{3}\right)$ $2m$

65. $8y\left(\frac{y}{4}\right)$ $2y^2$

66. $10\left(\frac{2a}{5}\right)$ $4a$

67. $\frac{6a - 3}{3}$ $2a - 1$

VIDEO **68.** $\frac{-8x + 6}{2}$ $-4x + 3$

69. $\frac{-9x + 6}{-3}$ $3x - 2$

70. $\frac{10 - 5x}{-5}$ $-2 + x$

⟨4⟩ Removing Parentheses

Simplify each expression by removing the parentheses and combining like terms. See Example 7.

71. $-(5x + 1) + 7x$ $2x - 1$

72. $-(7a + 3) + 8a$ $a - 3$

73. $-(-c + 4) + 5c - 9$ $6c - 13$

74. $-(-y + 4) + 9 + 4y$ $5y + 5$

75. $-(7b - 2) - 1$ $-7b + 1$

76. $-(a - 1) - 9$ $-a - 8$

77. $-(-w - 4) - 8 + w$ $2w - 4$

78. $-(-y - 3) - 9y - 1$ $-8y + 2$

79. $x - (3x - 1)$ $-2x + 1$

80. $4x - (2x - 5)$ $2x + 5$

81. $5 - (y - 3)$ $8 - y$

82. $8 - (m - 6)$ $-m + 14$

83. $2m + 3 - (m + 9)$ $m - 6$

84. $7 - 8t - (2t + 6)$ $-10t + 1$

85. $-3 - (-w + 2)$ $w - 5$

VIDEO **86.** $-5x - (-2x + 9)$ $-3x - 9$

Simplify the following expressions by combining like terms. See Example 8.

87. $3x + 5x + 6 + 9$ $8x + 15$

88. $2x + 6x + 7 + 15$ $8x + 22$

89. $(-2x + 3) + (7x - 4)$ $5x - 1$

90. $(-3x + 12) + (5x - 9)$ $2x + 3$

91. $3a - 7 - (5a - 6)$ $-2a - 1$

92. $4m - 5 - (m - 2)$ $3m - 3$

93. $2(a - 4) - 3(-2 - a)$ $5a - 2$

VIDEO **94.** $2(w + 6) - 3(-w - 5)$ $5w + 27$

95. $3x(2x - 3) + 5(2x - 3)$ $6x^2 + x - 15$

96. $2a(a - 5) + 4(a - 5)$ $2a^2 - 6a - 20$

97. $-b(2b - 1) - 4(2b - 1)$ $-2b^2 - 7b + 4$

98. $-2c(c - 8) - 3(c - 8)$ $-2c^2 + 13c + 24$

99. $-5m + 6(m - 3) + 2m$ $3m - 18$

100. $-3a + 2(a - 5) + 7a$ $6a - 10$

101. $5 - 3(x + 2) - 6$ $-3x - 7$

102. $7 + 2(k - 3) - k + 6$ $k + 7$

103. $x - 0.05(x + 10)$ $0.95x - 0.5$

104. $x - 0.02(x + 300)$ $0.98x - 6$

Simplify each expression.

105. $3x - (4 - x)$ $4x - 4$

106. $2 + 8x - 11x$ $2 - 3x$

107. $y - 5 - (-y - 9)$ $2y + 4$

108. $a - (b - c - a)$ $2a - b + c$

109. $7 - (8 - 2y - m)$ $2y + m - 1$

110. $x - 8 - (-3 - x)$ $2x - 5$

111. $\frac{1}{2}(10 - 2x) + \frac{1}{3}(3x - 6)$ 3

112. $\frac{1}{2}(x - 20) - \frac{1}{5}(x + 15)$ $\frac{3}{10}x - 13$

113. $\frac{1}{2}(3a + 1) - \frac{1}{3}(a - 5)$ $\frac{7}{6}a + \frac{13}{6}$

114. $\frac{1}{4}(6b + 2) - \frac{2}{3}(3b - 2)$ $-\frac{1}{2}b + \frac{11}{6}$

115. $0.2(x + 3) - 0.05(x + 20)$ $0.15x - 0.4$

116. $0.08x + 0.12(x + 100)$ $0.2x + 12$

117. $2k + 1 - 3(5k - 6) - k + 4$ $-14k + 23$

118. $2w - 3 + 3(w - 4) - 5(w - 6)$ 15

119. $-3m - 3[2m - 3(m + 5)]$ 45

120. $6h + 4[2h - 3(h - 9) - (h - 1)]$ $-2h + 112$

⟨5⟩ Applications

Solve each problem. See Example 9.

121. ***Perimeter of a corral.*** The perimeter of a rectangular corral that has width x feet and length $x + 40$ feet is $2(x) + 2(x + 40)$. Simplify the expression for the perimeter. Find the perimeter if $x = 30$ feet.
$4x + 80$, 200 feet

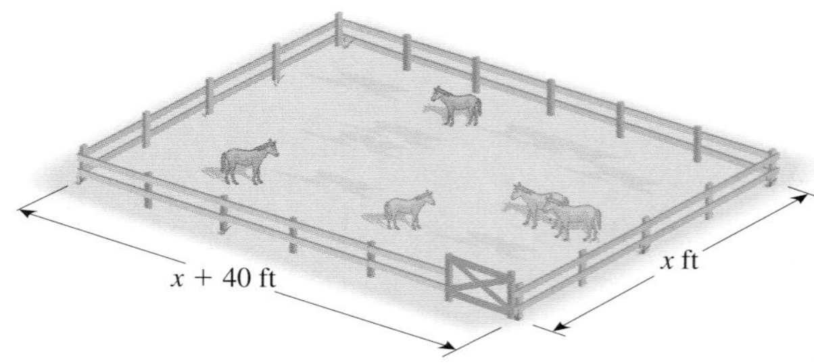

Figure for Exercise 121

122. ***Perimeter of a mirror.*** The perimeter of a rectangular mirror that has a width of x inches and a length of $x + 16$ inches is $2(x) + 2(x + 16)$ inches. Simplify the expression for the perimeter. Find the perimeter if $x = 14$ inches. $4x + 32$, 88 inches

123. ***Married filing jointly.*** The value of the expression

$$8440 + 0.25(x - 61{,}300)$$

is the 2006 federal income tax for a married couple filing jointly with a taxable income of x dollars, where x is over \$61,300 but not over \$123,700 (Internal Revenue Service, www.irs.gov).

a) Simplify the expression. $0.25x - 6885$

b) Use the expression to find the amount of tax for a couple with a taxable income of \$80,000. \$13,115

c) Use the accompanying graph to estimate the 2006 federal income tax for a couple with a taxable income of \$200,000 \$46,000

d) Use the accompanying graph to estimate the taxable income for a couple who paid \$80,000 in federal income tax. \$303,000

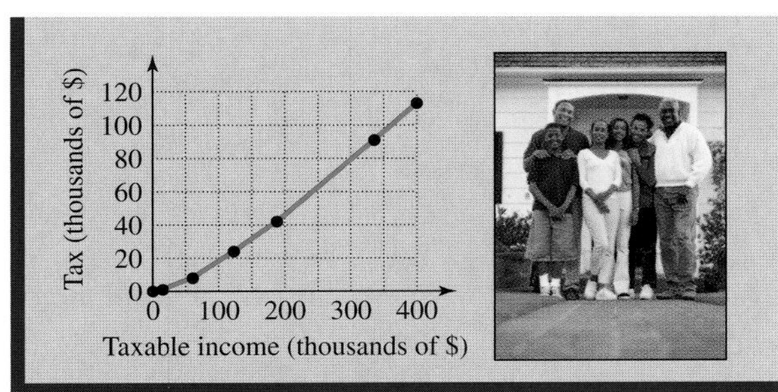

Figure for Exercise 123

124. ***Marriage penalty eliminated.*** The value of the expression

$$4220 + 0.25(x - 30{,}650)$$

is the 2006 federal income tax for a single taxpayer with taxable income of x dollars, where x is over \$30,650 but not over \$74,200.

a) Simplify the expression. $0.25x - 3442.5$

b) Find the amount of tax for a single taxpayer with taxable income of \$40,000. \$6557.50

c) Who pays more, a married couple with a joint taxable income of \$80,000 or two single taxpayers with taxable incomes of \$40,000 each? See Exercise 123. Both pay same tax.

Getting More Involved

125. ***Discussion***

What is wrong with the way in which each of the following expressions is simplified?

a) $4(2 + x) = 8 + x$ $4(2 + x) = 8 + 4x$

b) $4(2x) = 8 \cdot 4x = 32x$ $4(2x) = (4 \cdot 2)x = 8x$

c) $\dfrac{4 + x}{2} = 2 + x$ $\dfrac{4 + x}{2} = \dfrac{1}{2}(4 + x) = 2 + \dfrac{1}{2}x$

d) $5 - (x - 3) = 5 - x - 3 = 2 - x$
$5 - (x - 3) = 5 - x + 3 = 8 - x$

126. ***Discussion***

An instructor asked his class to evaluate the expression $1/2x$ for $x = 5$. Some students got 0.1; others got 2.5. Which answer is correct and why?
If $x = 5$, then $1/2 \cdot 5 = \frac{1}{2} \cdot 5 = 2.5$ because we do division and multiplication from left to right.

Wrap-Up

Summary

The Real Numbers		**Examples**
Counting or natural numbers	$\{1, 2, 3, \ldots\}$	
Whole numbers	$\{0, 1, 2, 3, \ldots\}$	
Integers	$\{\ldots, -3, -2, -1, 0, 1, 2, 3, \ldots\}$	
Rational numbers	$\left\{\frac{a}{b} \,\middle|\, a \text{ and } b \text{ are integers with } b \neq 0\right\}$	$\frac{3}{2}$, 5, -6, 0
Irrational numbers	$\{x \mid x \text{ is a real number that is not rational}\}$	$\sqrt{2}$, $\sqrt{3}$, π
Real numbers	The set of real numbers consists of all rational numbers together with all irrational numbers.	
Intervals of real numbers	If a is less than b, then the set of real numbers between a and b is written as (a, b). The set of real numbers between a and b inclusive is written as $[a, b]$.	The notation (1, 9) represents the real numbers between 1 and 9. The notation [1, 9] represents the real numbers between 1 and 9 inclusive.

Fractions		**Examples**
Reducing fractions	$\frac{a \cdot c}{b \cdot c} = \frac{a}{b}$	$\frac{4}{6} = \frac{2 \cdot 2}{2 \cdot 3} = \frac{2}{3}$
Building up fractions	$\frac{a}{b} = \frac{a \cdot c}{b \cdot c}$	$\frac{3}{8} = \frac{3 \cdot 5}{8 \cdot 5} = \frac{15}{40}$
Multiplying fractions	$\frac{a}{b} \cdot \frac{c}{d} = \frac{ac}{bd}$	$\frac{2}{3} \cdot \frac{4}{5} = \frac{8}{15}$
Dividing fractions	$\frac{a}{b} \div \frac{c}{d} = \frac{a}{b} \cdot \frac{d}{c}$	$\frac{2}{3} \div \frac{4}{5} = \frac{2}{3} \cdot \frac{5}{4} = \frac{10}{12} = \frac{5}{6}$
Adding or subtracting fractions	$\frac{a}{b} + \frac{c}{b} = \frac{a + c}{b}$ $\frac{a}{b} - \frac{c}{b} = \frac{a - c}{b}$	$\frac{1}{5} + \frac{2}{5} = \frac{3}{5}$ $\frac{3}{5} - \frac{2}{5} = \frac{1}{5}$

Least common denominator	The smallest number that is a multiple of all denominators.	$\frac{1}{4} + \frac{1}{6} = \frac{3}{12} + \frac{2}{12} = \frac{5}{12}$

Operations with Real Numbers		**Examples**
Absolute value	$\lvert a \rvert = \begin{cases} a & \text{if } a \text{ is positive or zero} \\ -a & \text{if } a \text{ is negative} \end{cases}$	$\lvert 3 \rvert = 3, \lvert 0 \rvert = 0$ $\lvert -3 \rvert = 3$
Sum of two numbers with like signs	Add their absolute values. The sum has the same sign as the given numbers.	$-3 + (-4) = -7$
Sum of two numbers with unlike signs (and different absolute values)	Subtract the absolute values of the numbers. The answer is positive if the number with the larger absolute value is positive. The answer is negative if the number with the larger absolute value is negative.	$-4 + 7 = 3$ $-7 + 4 = -3$
Sum of opposites	The sum of any number and its opposite is 0.	$-6 + 6 = 0$
Subtraction of signed numbers	$a - b = a + (-b)$ Subtract any number by adding its opposite.	$3 - 5 = 3 + (-5) = -2$ $4 - (-3) = 4 + 3 = 7$
Product or quotient	Like signs $\leftrightarrow$ Positive result Unlike signs $\leftrightarrow$ Negative result	$(-3)(-2) = 6$ $(-8) \div 2 = -4$
Definition of exponents	For any counting number n, $a^n = \underbrace{a \cdot a \cdot a \cdot \ldots \cdot a}_{n \text{ factors}}.$	$2^3 = 2 \cdot 2 \cdot 2 = 8$ $(-5)^2 = 25$ $-5^2 = -(5^2) = -25$
Order of operations	No parentheses or absolute value present: 1. Exponential expressions 2. Multiplication and division 3. Addition and subtraction With parentheses or absolute value: First evaluate within each set of parentheses or absolute value, using the order of operations.	 $5 + 2^3 = 13$ $2 + 3 \cdot 5 = 17$ $4 + 5 \cdot 3^2 = 49$ $(2 + 3)(5 - 7) = -10$ $2 + 3 \lvert 2 - 5 \rvert = 11$

Properties of the Real Numbers		**Examples**
	For any real numbers a, b, and c	
Commutative property of Addition Multiplication	 $a + b = b + a$ $a \cdot b = b \cdot a$	 $5 + 7 = 7 + 5$ $6 \cdot 3 = 3 \cdot 6$

Associative property of Addition Multiplication	 $a + (b + c) = (a + b) + c$ $a \cdot (b \cdot c) = (a \cdot b) \cdot c$	 $1 + (2 + 3) = (1 + 2) + 3$ $2(3 \cdot 4) = (2 \cdot 3)4$
Distributive properties	$a(b + c) = ab + ac$ $a(b - c) = ab - ac$	$2(3 + x) = 6 + 2x$ $-2(x - 5) = -2x + 10$
Additive identity property	$a + 0 = a$ and $0 + a = a$ Zero is the additive identity.	$5 + 0 = 0 + 5 = 5$
Multiplicative identity property	$1 \cdot a = a$ and $a \cdot 1 = a$ One is the multiplicative identity.	$7 \cdot 1 = 1 \cdot 7 = 7$
Additive inverse property	For any real number a, there is a number $-a$ (additive inverse or opposite) such that $a + (-a) = 0$ and $-a + a = 0$.	$3 + (-3) = 0$ $-3 + 3 = 0$
Multiplicative inverse property	For any nonzero real number a there is a number $\frac{1}{a}$ (multiplicative inverse or reciprocal) such that $a \cdot \frac{1}{a} = 1$ and $\frac{1}{a} \cdot a = 1.$	$3 \cdot \frac{1}{3} = 1$ $\frac{1}{3} \cdot 3 = 1$
Multiplication property of 0	$a \cdot 0 = 0$ and $0 \cdot a = 0$	$5 \cdot 0 = 0$ $0(-7) = 0$

Enriching Your Mathematical Word Power

For each mathematical term, choose the correct meaning.

1. like terms
- a. terms that are identical
- b. the terms of a sum
- c. terms that have the same variables with the same exponents
- d. terms with the same variables c

2. equivalent fractions
- a. identical fractions
- b. fractions that represent the same number
- c. fractions with the same denominator
- d. fractions with the same numerator b

3. variable
- a. a letter that is used to represent some numbers
- b. the letter x
- c. an equation with a letter in it
- d. not the same a

4. reducing
- a. less than
- b. losing weight
- c. making equivalent
- d. dividing out common factors d

5. lowest terms
- a. numerator is smaller than the denominator
- b. no common factors
- c. the best interest rate
- d. when the numerator is 1 b

6. additive inverse
- a. the number -1
- b. the number 0
- c. the opposite of addition
- d. opposite d

7. order of operations
a. the order in which operations are to be performed in the absence of grouping symbols
b. the order in which the operations were invented
c. the order in which operations are written
d. a list of operations in alphabetical order a

8. least common denominator
a. the smallest divisor of all denominators
b. the denominator that appears the least
c. the smallest identical denominator
d. the least common multiple of the denominators d

9. absolute value
a. definite value
b. positive number
c. distance from 0 on the number line
d. the opposite of a number c

10. natural numbers
a. the counting numbers
b. numbers that are not irrational
c. the nonnegative numbers
d. numbers that we find in nature a

Review Exercises

1.1 The Real Numbers

Which of the numbers $-\sqrt{5}, -2, 0, 1, 2, 3.14, \pi$, *and* 10 *are*

1. whole numbers? 0, 1, 2, 10

2. natural numbers? 1, 2, 10

3. integers? $-2, 0, 1, 2, 10$

4. rational numbers? $-2, 0, 1, 2, 3.14, 10$

5. irrational numbers? $-\sqrt{5}, \pi$

6. real numbers? All of them

True or false? Explain your answer.

7. Every whole number is a rational number. True

8. Zero is not a rational number. False

9. The counting numbers between -4 and 4 are $-3, -2, -1, 0, 1, 2$, and 3. False

10. There are infinitely many integers. True

11. The set of counting numbers smaller than the national debt is infinite. False

12. The decimal number 0.25 is a rational number. True

13. Every integer greater than -1 is a whole number. True

14. Zero is the only number that is neither rational nor irrational. False

Graph each set of numbers.

15. The set of integers between -3 and 3

−3 −2 −1 0 1 2 3

16. The set of natural numbers between -3 and 3

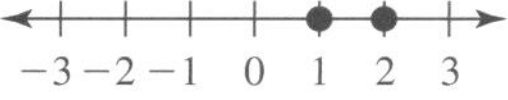

17. The set of real numbers between -1 and 4

−2 −1 0 1 2 3 4 5

18. The set of real numbers between -2 and 3 inclusive

−3 −2 −1 0 1 2 3 4

Write the interval notation for each interval of real numbers.

19. The set of real numbers between 4 and 6 inclusive $[4, 6]$

20. The set of real numbers greater than 2 and less than 5 $(2, 5)$

21. The set of real numbers greater than or equal to -30 $[-30, \infty)$

22. The set of real numbers less than 50 $(-\infty, 50)$

1.2 Fractions

Perform the indicated operations.

23. $\frac{1}{3} + \frac{3}{8}$ $\frac{17}{24}$

24. $\frac{2}{3} - \frac{1}{4}$ $\frac{5}{12}$

25. $\frac{3}{5} \cdot 10$ 6

26. $\frac{3}{5} \div 10$ $\frac{3}{50}$

27. $\frac{2}{5} \cdot \frac{15}{14}$ $\frac{3}{7}$

28. $7 \div \frac{1}{2}$ 14

29. $4 + \frac{2}{3}$ $\frac{14}{3}$

30. $\frac{7}{12} - \frac{1}{4}$ $\frac{1}{3}$

31. $\frac{1}{2} + \frac{1}{3} + \frac{1}{4}$ $\frac{13}{12}$

32. $\frac{3}{4} \div 9$ $\frac{1}{12}$

1.3 Addition and Subtraction of Real Numbers

Evaluate.

33. $-5 + 7$ 2

34. $-9 + (-4)$ -13

35. $35 - 48$ -13

36. $-3 - 9$ -12

37. $-12 + 5$ -7

38. $-12 - 5$ -17

39. $-12 - (-5)$ -7

40. $-9 - (-9)$ 0

41. $-0.05 + 12$ 11.95

42. $-0.03 + (-2)$ -2.03

43. $-0.1 - (-0.05)$ -0.05

44. $-0.3 + 0.3$ 0

45. $\frac{1}{3} - \frac{1}{2}$ $-\frac{1}{6}$

46. $-\frac{2}{3} + \frac{1}{4}$ $-\frac{5}{12}$

47. $-\frac{1}{3} + \left(-\frac{2}{5}\right)$ $-\frac{11}{15}$

48. $\frac{1}{3} - \left(-\frac{1}{4}\right)$ $\frac{7}{12}$

1.4 Multiplication and Division of Real Numbers

Evaluate.

49. $(-3)(5)$ -15

50. $(-9)(-4)$ 36

51. $(-8) \div (-2)$ 4

52. $50 \div (-5)$ -10

53. $\frac{-20}{-4}$ 5

54. $\frac{30}{-5}$ -6

55. $\left(-\frac{1}{2}\right)\left(-\frac{1}{3}\right)$ $\frac{1}{6}$

56. $8 \div \left(-\frac{1}{3}\right)$ -24

57. $-0.09 \div 0.3$ -0.3

58. $4.2 \div (-0.3)$ -14

59. $(0.3)(-0.8)$ -0.24

60. $0 \div (-0.0538)$ 0

61. $(-5)(-0.2)$ 1

62. $\frac{1}{2}(-12)$ -6

1.5 Exponential Expressions and the Order of Operations

Evaluate.

63. $3 + 7(9)$ 66

64. $(3 + 7)9$ 90

65. $(3 + 4)^2$ 49

66. $3 + 4^2$ 19

67. $3 + 2 \cdot |5 - 6 \cdot 4|$ 41

68. $3 - (8 - 9)$ 4

69. $(3 - 7) - (4 - 9)$ 1

70. $3 - 7 - 4 - 9$ -17

71. $-2 - 4(2 - 3 \cdot 5)$ 50

72. $3^2 - 7 + 5^2$ 27

73. $3^2 - (7 + 5)^2$ -135

74. $|4 - 6 \cdot 3| - |7 - 9|$ 12

75. $\frac{-3 - 5}{2 - (-2)}$ -2

76. $\frac{1 - 9}{4 - 6}$ 4

77. $\frac{6 + 3}{3} - 5 \cdot 4 + 1$ -16

78. $\frac{2 \cdot 4 + 4}{3} - 3(1 - 2)$ 7

1.6 Algebraic Expressions

Let $a = -1$, $b = -2$, and $c = 3$. Find the value of each algebraic expression.

79. $b^2 - 4ac$ 16

80. $a^2 - 4b$ 9

81. $(c - b)(c + b)$ 5

82. $(a + b)(a - b)$ -3

83. $a^2 + 2ab + b^2$ 9

84. $a^2 - 2ab + b^2$ 1

85. $a^3 - b^3$ 7

86. $a^3 + b^3$ -9

87. $\frac{b + c}{a + b}$ $-\frac{1}{3}$

88. $\frac{b - c}{2b - a}$ $\frac{5}{3}$

89. $|a - b|$ 1

90. $|b - a|$ 1

91. $(a + b)c$ -9

92. $ac + bc$ -9

Determine whether the given number is a solution to the equation following it.

93. 4, $3x - 2 = 10$ Yes

94. 1, $5(x + 3) = 20$ Yes

95. -6, $\frac{3x}{2} = 9$ No

96. -30, $\frac{x}{3} - 4 = 6$ No

97. 15, $\frac{x + 3}{2} = 9$ Yes

98. 1, $\frac{12}{2x + 1} = 4$ Yes

99. 4, $-x - 3 = 1$ No

100. 7, $-x + 1 = 6$ No

1.7 Properties of the Real Numbers

Name the property that justifies each statement.

101. $a(x + y) = ax + ay$ Distributive property

102. $3(4y) = (3 \cdot 4)y$ Associative property of multiplication

103. $(0.001)(1000) = 1$ Multiplicative inverse property

104. $xy = yx$ Commutative property of multiplication

105. $0 + y = y$ Additive identity property

106. $325 \cdot 1 = 325$ Multiplicative identity property

107. $3 + (2 + x) = (3 + 2) + x$ Associative property of addition

108. $2x - 6 = 2(x - 3)$ Distributive property

109. $5 \cdot 200 = 200 \cdot 5$ Commutative property of multiplication

110. $3 + (x + 2) = (x + 2) + 3$ Commutative property of addition

111. $-50 + 50 = 0$ Additive inverse property

112. $43 \cdot 59 \cdot 82 \cdot 0 = 0$ Multiplication property of 0

113. $12 \cdot 1 = 12$ Multiplicative identity property

114. $3x + 1 = 1 + 3x$ Commutative property of addition

1.8 Using the Properties to Simplify Expressions

Simplify by combining like terms.

115. $3a + 7 - (4a - 5)$ $-a + 12$

116. $2m + 6 - (m - 2)$ $m + 8$

117. $2a(3a - 5) + 4a$ $6a^2 - 6a$

118. $3a(a - 5) + 5a(a + 2)$ $8a^2 - 5a$

119. $3(t - 2) - 5(3t - 9)$ $-12t + 39$

120. $2(m + 3) - 3(3 - m)$ $5m - 3$

121. $0.1(a + 0.3) - (a + 0.6)$ $-0.9a - 0.57$

122. $0.1(x + 0.3) - (x - 0.9)$ $-0.9x + 0.93$

123. $0.05(x - 20) - 0.1(x + 30)$ $-0.05x - 4$

124. $0.02(x - 100) + 0.2(x - 50)$ $0.22x - 12$

125. $5 - 3x(-5x - 2) + 12x^2$ $27x^2 + 6x + 5$

126. $7 - 2x(3x - 7) - x^2$ $-7x^2 + 14x + 7$

127. $-(a - 2) - 2 - a$ $-2a$

128. $-(w - y) - 3(y - w)$ $-2y + 2w$

129. $x(x + 1) + 3(x - 1)$ $x^2 + 4x - 3$

130. $y(y - 2) + 3(y + 1)$ $y^2 + y + 3$

Miscellaneous

Evaluate each expression. Use a calculator to check.

131. $752(-13) + 752(13)$ 0

132. $75 - (-13)$ 88

133. $|15 - 23|$ 8

134. $4^2 - 6^2$ -20

135. $-6^2 + 3(5)$ -21

136. $(0.03)(-200)$ -6

137. $\frac{2}{5} + \frac{1}{10}$ $\frac{1}{2}$

138. $\frac{2 + 1}{5 + 10}$ $\frac{1}{5}$

139. $(0.05) \div (-0.1)$ -0.5

140. $(4 - 9)^2 + (2 \cdot 3 - 1)^2$ 50

141. $2\left(-\frac{1}{2}\right)^2 + \left(-\frac{1}{2}\right) - 1$ -1

142. $\left(-\frac{6}{7}\right)\left(\frac{21}{26}\right)$ $-\frac{9}{13}$

Simplify each expression if possible.

143. $\frac{2x + 4}{2}$ $x + 2$

144. $4(2x)$ $8x$

145. $4 + 2x$ $4 + 2x$

146. $4(2 + x)$ $8 + 4x$

147. $4 \cdot \frac{x}{2}$ $2x$

148. $4 - (x - 2)$ $-x + 6$

149. $-4(x - 2)$ $-4x + 8$

150. $(4x)(2x)$ $8x^2$

151. $4x + 2x$ $6x$

152. $2 + (x + 4)$ $x + 6$

153. $4 \cdot \frac{x}{4}$ x

154. $4 \cdot \frac{3x}{2}$ $6x$

155. $2 \cdot x \cdot 4$ $8x$

156. $4 - 2(2 - x)$ $2x$

157. $2(x - 4) - x(x - 4)$ $-x^2 + 6x - 8$

158. $-x(2 - x) - 2(2 - x)$ $x^2 - 4$

159. $\frac{1}{2}(x - 4) - \frac{1}{4}(x - 2)$ $\frac{1}{4}x - \frac{3}{2}$

160. $\frac{1}{4}(x + 2) - \frac{1}{2}(x - 4)$ $-\frac{1}{4}x + \frac{5}{2}$

Fill in the tables with the appropriate values for the given expressions.

161.

x	$-\frac{1}{3}x + 1$
-6	3
-3	2
0	1
3	0
6	-1

162.

x	$\frac{1}{2}x + 3$
-4	1
-2	2
0	3
2	4
4	5

163.

a	a^2	a^3	a^4
5	25	125	625
−4	16	−64	256

164.

b	$\frac{1}{b}$	$\frac{1}{b^2}$	$\frac{1}{b^3}$
−3	$-\frac{1}{3}$	$\frac{1}{9}$	$-\frac{1}{27}$
$-\frac{1}{2}$	−2	4	−8

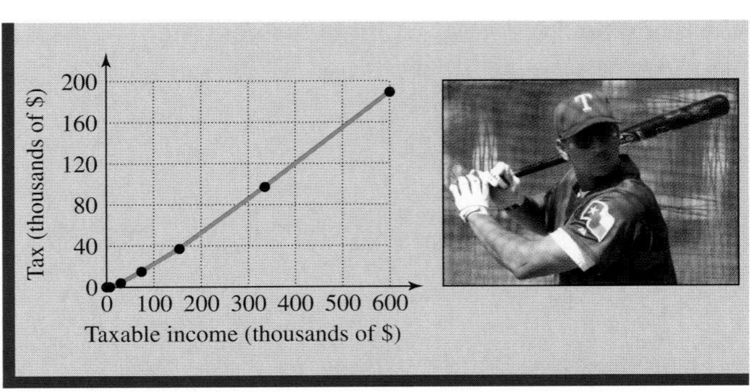

Figure for Exercise 165

Applications

Solve each problem.

165. ***High-income bracket.*** The expression

$$97{,}653 + 0.35(x - 336{,}550)$$

represents the amount for the 2006 federal income tax in dollars for a single taxpayer with x dollars of taxable income, where x is over \$336,550.

a) Simplify the expression. $0.35x - 20{,}139.5$

b) Use the graph in the accompanying figure to estimate the amount of tax for a single taxpayer with a taxable income of \$500,000. Approximately \$150,000

c) Find the amount of tax for MLB player Alex Rodriguez for 2006. At \$25,680,727 he was the highest paid baseball player that year. \$8,968,115

166. ***Married filing jointly.*** The expression

$$24{,}040 + 0.28(x - 123{,}700)$$

represents the amount for the 2006 federal income tax in dollars for a married couple with x dollars of taxable income, where x is over \$123,700 but not over \$188,450.

a) Simplify the expression. $0.28x - 10{,}596$

b) Find the amount of tax for Mr. and Mrs. Smith who teach at a college and have a taxable income of \$130,341. \$25,899

Chapter 1 Test

Which of the numbers $-3, -\sqrt{3}, -\frac{1}{4}, 0, \sqrt{5}, \pi,$ *and* 8 *are*

1. whole numbers? 0, 8

2. integers? −3, 0, 8

3. rational numbers? $-3, -\frac{1}{4}, 0, 8$

4. irrational numbers? $-\sqrt{3}, \sqrt{5}, \pi$

Evaluate each expression.

5. $6 + 3(-9)$ −21

6. $(-2)^2 - 4(-2)(-1)$ −4

7. $\dfrac{-3^2 - 9}{3 - 5}$ 9

8. $-5 + 6 - 12 + 4$ −7

9. $0.05 - 1$ −0.95

10. $(5 - 9)(5 + 9)$ −56

11. $(878 + 89) + 11$ 978

12. $6 + |3 - 5(2)|$ 13

13. $8 - 3|7 - 10|$ −1

14. $(839 + 974)[3(-4) + 12]$ 0

15. $974(7) + 974(3)$ 9740

16. $-\frac{2}{3} + \frac{3}{8}$ $-\frac{7}{24}$

17. $(-0.05)(400)$ −20

18. $\left(-\frac{3}{4}\right)\left(\frac{2}{9}\right)$ $-\frac{1}{6}$

19. $13 \div \left(-\frac{1}{3}\right)$ −39

Graph each set of numbers.

20. The set of whole numbers less than 5

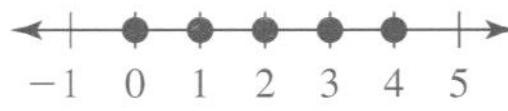

21. The set of real numbers less than or equal to 4

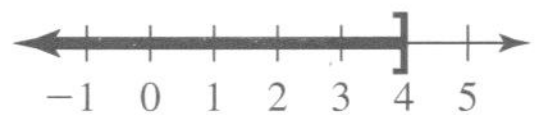

Write the interval notation for each interval of real numbers.

22. The real numbers greater than 2 $(2, \infty)$

23. The real numbers greater than or equal to 3 and less than 9 $[3, 9)$

Identify the property that justifies each equation.

24. $2(x + 7) = 2x + 14$ Distributive property

25. $48 \cdot 1000 = 1000 \cdot 48$ Commutative property of multiplication

26. $2 + (6 + x) = (2 + 6) + x$ Associative property of addition

27. $-348 + 348 = 0$ Additive inverse property

28. $1 \cdot (-6) = -6$ Multiplicative identity property

29. $0 \cdot 388 = 0$ Multiplication property of 0

Use the distributive property to write each sum or difference as a product.

30. $3x + 30$ $3(x + 10)$

31. $7w - 7$ $7(w - 1)$

Simplify each expression.

32. $6 + 4x + 2x$ $6x + 6$

33. $6 + 4(x - 2)$ $4x - 2$

34. $5x - (3 - 2x)$ $7x - 3$

35. $x + 10 - 0.1(x + 25)$ $0.9x + 7.5$

36. $2a(4a - 5) - 3a(-2a - 5)$ $14a^2 + 5a$

37. $\frac{6x + 12}{6}$ $x + 2$

38. $8 \cdot \frac{t}{2}$ $4t$

39. $(-9xy)(-6xy)$ $54x^2y^2$

40. $\frac{1}{2}(3x + 2) - \frac{1}{4}(3x - 2)$ $\frac{3}{4}x + \frac{3}{2}$

Evaluate each expression if $a = -2$, $b = 3$, and $c = 4$.

41. $b^2 - 4ac$ 41

42. $\frac{a - b}{b - c}$ 5

43. $(a - c)(a + c)$ -12

Determine whether the given number is a solution to the equation following it.

44. -2, $3x - 4 = 2$ No

45. 13, $\frac{x + 3}{8} = 2$ Yes

46. -3, $-x + 5 = 8$ Yes

Solve each problem.

47. A forensic scientist uses the expression $80.405 + 3.660R - 0.06(A - 30)$ to estimate the height in centimeters for a male with a radius (bone in the forearm) of length R centimeters and age A in years, where A is over 30. Simplify the expression. Use the expression to estimate the height of an 80-year-old male with a radius of length 25 cm. $3.66R - 0.06A + 82.205$, 168.905 cm

Critical **Thinking** | For Individual or Group Work | Chapter 1

These exercises can be solved by a variety of techniques, which may or may not require algebra. So be creative and think critically. Explain all answers. Answers are in the Instructor's Edition of this text.

1. ***Dividing evenly.*** Suppose that you have a three-ounce glass, a five-ounce glass, and an eight-ounce glass, as shown in the accompanying figure. The two smaller glasses are empty, but the largest glass contains eight ounces of milk. How can you divide the milk into two equal parts by using only these three glasses as measuring devices?

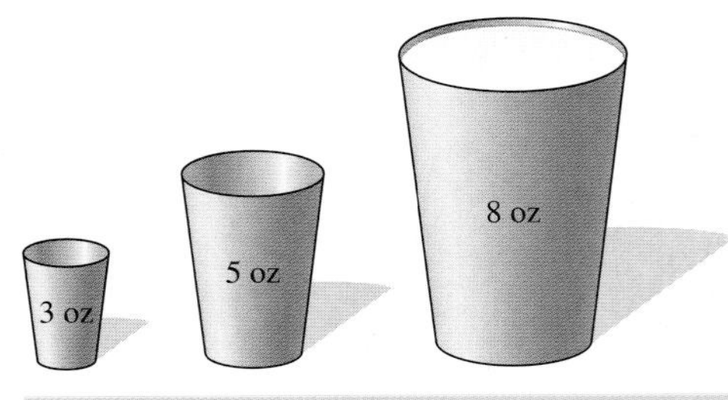

Figure for Exercise 1

2. ***Totaling one hundred.*** Start with the sequence of digits 123456789. Place any number of plus or minus signs between the digits in the sequence so that the value of the resulting expression is 100. For example, we could write

$$123 - 45 + 6 + 78 - 9,$$

but the value is not 100.

3. ***More hundreds.*** We can easily find an expression whose value is 6 using only 2's. For example, $2^2 + 2 = 6$. Find an expression whose value is 100 using only 3's. Only 4's, and so on.

4. ***Forming triangles.*** It is possible to draw three straight lines through a capital M to form nine nonoverlapping triangles. Try it.

5. ***The right time.*** Starting at 12 noon determine the number of times in the next 24 hours for which the hour and minute hands on a clock form a right angle.

Photo for Exercise 5

6. ***Perfect power.*** One is the smallest positive integer that is a perfect square, a perfect cube, and a perfect fifth power. What is the next larger positive integer that is a perfect square, a perfect cube, and a perfect fifth power?

7. ***Summing the digits.*** The sum of all of the digits that are used in writing the integers from 29 through 32 is

$$2 + 9 + 3 + 0 + 3 + 1 + 3 + 2$$

or 23. Find the sum of all of the digits that are used in writing the integers from 1 through 1000 without using a calculator.

8. ***Integral rectangles.*** Find all rectangles whose sides are integers and the numerical value for the area is equal to the numerical value for the perimeter.

1. If (0, 0, 8) is the original amount of milk in the 3, 5, and 8 ounce glasses, then pour as follows: (0, 0, 8), (3, 0, 5), (3, 3, 2), (1, 5, 2), (1, 0, 7), (0, 1, 7), (3, 1, 4), (0, 4, 4) **2.** $12 + 3 - 4 + 5 + 67 + 8 + 9 = 100$ or $123 + 4 - 5 + 67 - 89 = 100$ **3.** $3 \cdot 33 + 3/3 = 100$, $4 \cdot 4 \cdot 4 + 4 \cdot 4 + 4 \cdot 4 + 4 = 100$, $5 \cdot 5 \cdot 5 - 5 \cdot 5 = 100$ **4.** **5.** 44 **6.** 2^{30} or 1,073,741,824 **7.** 13,501 **8.** 3 by 6 and 4 by 4

Chapter 2

Linear Equations and Inequalities in One Variable

Some ancient peoples chewed on leaves to cure their headaches. Thousands of years ago, the Egyptians used honey, salt, cedar oil, and sycamore bark to cure illnesses. Currently, some of the indigenous people of North America use black birch as a pain reliever.

Today, we are grateful for modern medicine and the seemingly simple cures for illnesses. From our own experiences we know that just the right amount of a drug can work wonders but too much of a drug can do great harm. Even though physicians often prescribe the same drug for children and adults, the amount given must be tailored to the individual. The portion of a drug given to children is usually reduced on the basis of factors such as the weight and height of the child. Likewise, older adults frequently need a lower dosage of medication than what would be prescribed for a younger, more active person.

Various algebraic formulas have been developed for determining the proper dosage for a child and an older adult.

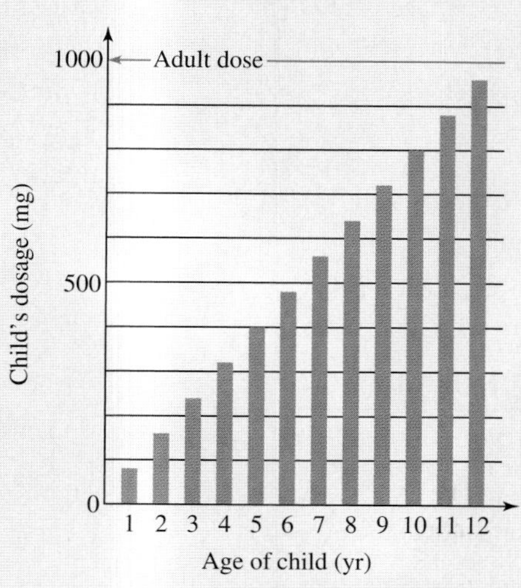

In Exercises 97 and 98 of Section 2.4 you will see two formulas that are used to determine a child's dosage by using the adult dosage and the child's age.

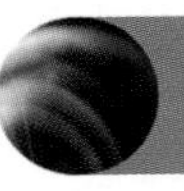

2.1 The Addition and Multiplication Properties of Equality

In This Section

In Section 1.6, an **equation** was defined as a statement that two expressions are equal. A **solution** to an equation is a number that can be used in place of the variable to make the equation a true statement. The **solution set** is the set of all solutions to an equation. Equations with the same solution set are **equivalent equations.** To **solve** an equation means to find all solutions to the equation. In this section you will learn systematic procedures for solving equations.

⟨1⟩ The Addition Property of Equality

If two workers have equal salaries and each gets a \$1000 raise, then they will have equal salaries after the raise. If two people are the same age now, then in 5 years they will still be the same age. If you add the same number to two equal quantities, the results will be equal. This idea is called the *addition property of equality:*

The Addition Property of Equality

Adding the same number to both sides of an equation does not change the solution to the equation. In symbols, $a = b$ and

$$a + c = b + c$$

are equivalent equations.

Consider the equation $x = 5$. The only possible number that could be used in place of x to get a true statement is 5, because $5 = 5$ is true. So the solution set is $\{5\}$. We say that x in $x = 5$ is **isolated** because it occurs only once in the equation and it is by itself. The variable in $x - 3 = -7$ is not isolated. In Example 1, we solve $x - 3 = -7$ by using the addition property of equality to isolate the variable.

EXAMPLE 1

Adding the same number to both sides

Solve $x - 3 = -7$.

Solution

Because 3 is subtracted from x in $x - 3 = -7$, adding 3 to each side of the equation will isolate x:

$$x - 3 = -7$$
$$x - 3 + 3 = -7 + 3 \quad \text{Add 3 to each side.}$$
$$x + 0 = -4 \quad \text{Simplify each side.}$$
$$x = -4 \quad \text{Zero is the additive identity.}$$

Since -4 satisfies the last equation, it should also satisfy the original equation because all of the previous equations are equivalent. Check that -4 satisfies the original equation by replacing x by -4:

$$x - 3 = -7 \quad \text{Original equation}$$
$$-4 - 3 = -7 \quad \text{Replace } x \text{ by } -4.$$
$$-7 = -7 \quad \text{Simplify.}$$

Since $-4 - 3 = -7$ is correct, $\{-4\}$ is the solution set to the equation.

Now do Exercises 7–14

⟨ Helpful Hint ⟩

Think of an equation like a balance scale. To keep the scale in balance, what you add to one side you must also add to the other side.

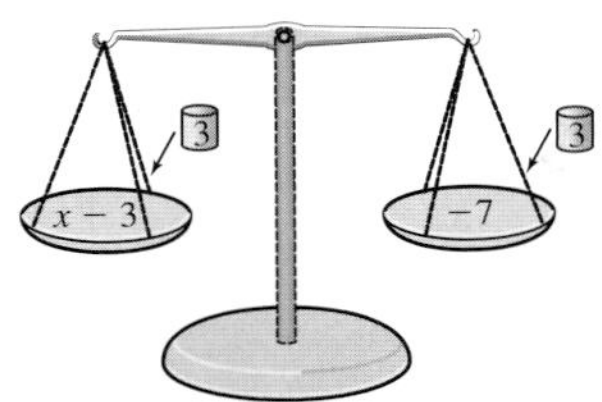

Note that enclosing the solutions to an equation in braces is not absolutely necessary. It is simply a formal way of stating the answer. At times we may simply state that the solution to the equation is -4.

The equations that we work with in this section and Sections 2.2 and 2.3 are called linear equations. The name comes from the fact that similar equations in two variables that we will study in Chapter 3 have graphs that are straight lines.

Linear Equation

A **linear equation in one variable** x is an equation that can be written in the form

$$ax = b$$

where a and b are real numbers and $a \neq 0$.

An equation such as $2x = 3$ is a linear equation. We also refer to equations such as

$$x + 8 = 0, \quad 2x + 5 = 9 - 5x, \quad \text{and} \quad 3 + 5(x - 1) = -7 + x$$

as linear equations, because these equations could be written in the form $ax = b$ using the properties of equality.

In Example 1, we used addition to isolate the variable on the left-hand side of the equation. Once the variable is isolated, we can determine the solution to the equation. Because subtraction is defined in terms of addition, we can also use subtraction to isolate the variable.

EXAMPLE 2

Subtracting the same number from both sides

Solve $9 + x = -2$.

‹ **Teaching Tip** ›

Remind students that -9 is the additive inverse of 9 and that we will be using the properties from Chapter 1 in this chapter.

Solution

We can remove the 9 from the left side by adding -9 to each side or by subtracting 9 from each side of the equation:

$$9 + x = -2$$
$$9 + x - 9 = -2 - 9 \quad \text{Subtract 9 from each side.}$$
$$x = -11 \quad \text{Simplify each side.}$$

Check that -11 satisfies the original equation by replacing x by -11:

$$9 + x = -2 \quad \text{Original equation}$$
$$9 + (-11) = -2 \quad \text{Replace } x \text{ by } -11.$$

Since $9 + (-11) = -2$ is correct, $\{-11\}$ is the solution set to the equation.

Now do Exercises 15–24

Our goal in solving equations is to isolate the variable. In Examples 1 and 2, the variable was isolated on the left side of the equation. In Example 3, we isolate the variable on the right side of the equation.

EXAMPLE 3

Isolating the variable on the right side

Solve $\frac{1}{2} = -\frac{1}{4} + y$.

Solution

We can remove $-\frac{1}{4}$ from the right side by adding $\frac{1}{4}$ to both sides of the equation:

$$\frac{1}{2} = -\frac{1}{4} + y$$

$$\frac{1}{2} + \frac{1}{4} = -\frac{1}{4} + y + \frac{1}{4} \quad \text{Add } \tfrac{1}{4} \text{ to each side.}$$

$$\frac{3}{4} = y \quad \frac{1}{2} + \frac{1}{4} = \frac{2}{4} + \frac{1}{4} = \frac{3}{4}$$

Check that $\frac{3}{4}$ satisfies the original equation by replacing y by $\frac{3}{4}$:

$$\frac{1}{2} = -\frac{1}{4} + y \quad \text{Original equation}$$

$$\frac{1}{2} = -\frac{1}{4} + \frac{3}{4} \quad \text{Replace } y \text{ by } \tfrac{3}{4}.$$

$$\frac{1}{2} = \frac{2}{4} \quad \text{Simplify.}$$

Since $\frac{1}{2} = \frac{2}{4}$ is correct, $\left\{\frac{3}{4}\right\}$ is the solution set to the equation.

Now do Exercises 25–32

⟨2⟩ The Multiplication Property of Equality

To isolate a variable that is involved in a product or a quotient, we need the multiplication property of equality.

The Multiplication Property of Equality

Multiplying both sides of an equation by the same nonzero number does not change the solution to the equation. In symbols, for $c \neq 0$, $a = b$ and

$$ac = bc$$

are equivalent equations.

We specified that $c \neq 0$ in the multiplication property of equality because multiplying by 0 can change the solution to an equation. For example, $x = 4$ is satisfied only by 4, but $0 \cdot x = 0 \cdot 4$ is true for any real number x.

In Example 4, we use the multiplication property of equality to solve an equation.

EXAMPLE 4

Multiplying both sides by the same number

Solve $\frac{z}{2} = 6$.

Solution

We isolate the variable z by multiplying each side of the equation by 2.

$$\frac{z}{2} = 6 \quad \text{Original equation}$$

$$2 \cdot \frac{z}{2} = 2 \cdot 6 \quad \text{Multiply each side by 2.}$$

$$1 \cdot z = 12 \quad \text{Because } 2 \cdot \frac{z}{2} = 2 \cdot \frac{1}{2}z = 1z$$

$$z = 12 \quad \text{Multiplicative identity}$$

Because $\frac{12}{2} = 6$, $\{12\}$ is the solution set to the equation.

Now do Exercises 33–40

‹ Teaching Tip ›

Point out how we are using the multiplicative inverse and multiplicative identity properties here.

Because dividing by a number is the same as multiplying by its reciprocal, the multiplication property of equality allows us to divide each side of the equation by any nonzero number.

EXAMPLE 5

Dividing both sides by the same number

Solve $-5w = 30$.

Solution

Since w is multiplied by -5, we can isolate w by dividing by -5:

$$-5w = 30 \quad \text{Original equation}$$

$$\frac{-5w}{-5} = \frac{30}{-5} \quad \text{Divide each side by } -5.$$

$$1 \cdot w = -6 \quad \text{Because } \frac{-5}{-5} = 1$$

$$w = -6 \quad \text{Multiplicative identity}$$

We could also solve this equation by multiplying each side by $-\frac{1}{5}$:

$$-\frac{1}{5} \cdot -5w = -\frac{1}{5} \cdot 30$$

$$1 \cdot w = -6$$

$$w = -6$$

Because $-5(-6) = 30$, $\{-6\}$ is the solution set to the equation.

Now do Exercises 41–50

In Example 6, the coefficient of the variable is a fraction. We could divide each side by the coefficient as we did in Example 5, but it is easier to multiply each side by the reciprocal of the coefficient.

EXAMPLE 6

Multiplying by the reciprocal

Solve $\frac{4}{5}p = 40$.

Solution

Multiply each side by $\frac{5}{4}$, the reciprocal of $\frac{4}{5}$, to isolate p on the left side.

$$\frac{4}{5}p = 40$$

$$\frac{5}{4} \cdot \frac{4}{5}p = \frac{5}{4} \cdot 40 \quad \text{Multiply each side by } \tfrac{5}{4}.$$

$$1 \cdot p = 50 \quad \text{Multiplicative inverses}$$

$$p = 50 \quad \text{Multiplicative identity}$$

Because $\frac{4}{5} \cdot 50 = 40$, we can be sure that the solution set is $\{50\}$.

Now do Exercises 51–58

‹ Helpful Hint ›

You could solve this equation by multiplying each side by 5 to get $4p = 200$, and then dividing each side by 4 to get $p = 50$.

If the coefficient of the variable is an integer, we usually divide each side by that integer, as we did in solving $-5w = 30$ in Example 5. Of course, we could also solve that equation by multiplying each side by $-\frac{1}{5}$. If the coefficient of the variable is a fraction, we usually multiply each side by the reciprocal of the fraction as we did in solving $\frac{4}{5}p = 40$ in Example 6. Of course, we could also solve that equation by dividing each side by $\frac{4}{5}$. If $-x$ appears in an equation, we can multiply by -1 to get x or divide by -1 to get x, because $-1(-x) = x$ and $\frac{-x}{-1} = x$.

EXAMPLE 7

Multiplying or dividing by −1

Solve $-h = 12$.

Solution

This equation can be solved by multiplying each side by -1 or dividing each side by -1. We show both methods here. First replace $-h$ with $-1 \cdot h$:

Multiplying by −1

$$-h = 12$$

$$-1(-1 \cdot h) = -1 \cdot 12$$

$$h = -12$$

Dividing by −1

$$-h = 12$$

$$\frac{-1 \cdot h}{-1} = \frac{12}{-1}$$

$$h = -12$$

Since $-(-12) = 12$, the solution set is $\{-12\}$.

Now do Exercises 59–66

‹3› Variables on Both Sides

In Example 8, the variable occurs on both sides of the equation. Because the variable represents a real number, we can still isolate the variable by using the addition property of equality. Note that it does not matter whether the variable ends up on the right side or the left side.

EXAMPLE 8

Subtracting an algebraic expression from both sides

Solve $-9 + 6y = 7y$.

Solution

The expression $6y$ can be removed from the left side of the equation by subtracting $6y$ from both sides.

$$\begin{aligned} -9 + 6y &= 7y \\ -9 + 6y - 6y &= 7y - 6y \quad \text{Subtract } 6y \text{ from each side.} \\ -9 &= y \quad \text{Simplify each side.} \end{aligned}$$

Check by replacing y by -9 in the original equation:

$$\begin{aligned} -9 + 6(-9) &= 7(-9) \\ -63 &= -63 \end{aligned}$$

The solution set to the equation is $\{-9\}$.

Now do Exercises 67–74

‹ Helpful Hint ›

It does not matter whether the variable ends up on the left or right side of the equation. Whether we get $y = -9$ or $-9 = y$ we can still conclude that the solution is -9.

‹4› Applications

In Example 9, we use the multiplication property of equality in an applied situation.

EXAMPLE 9

Comparing populations

In the 2000 census, Georgia had $\frac{2}{3}$ as many people as Illinois (U.S. Bureau of Census, www.census.gov). If the population of Georgia was 8 million, then what was the population of Illinois?

Solution

If p represents the population of Illinois, then $\frac{2}{3}p$ represents the population of Georgia. Since the population of Georgia was 8 million we can write the equation $\frac{2}{3}p = 8$. To find p, solve the equation:

$$\begin{aligned} \frac{2}{3}p &= 8 \\ \frac{3}{2} \cdot \frac{2}{3}p &= \frac{3}{2} \cdot 8 \quad \text{Multiply each side by } \tfrac{3}{2}. \\ p &= 12 \quad \text{Simplify.} \end{aligned}$$

So the population of Illinois was 12 million in 2000.

Now do Exercises 95–100

‹ Teaching Tip ›

We are doing a few simple word problems here to build student confidence with word problems.

Warm-Ups

True or false? Explain your answer.

1. The solution to $x - 5 = 5$ is 10. True
2. The equation $\frac{x}{2} = 4$ is equivalent to the equation $x = 8$. True
3. To solve $\frac{3}{4}y = 12$, we should multiply each side by $\frac{3}{4}$. False
4. The equation $\frac{x}{7} = 4$ is equivalent to $\frac{1}{7}x = 4$. True
5. Multiplying each side of an equation by any real number will result in an equation that is equivalent to the original equation. False
6. To isolate t in $2t = 7 + t$, subtract t from each side. True
7. To solve $\frac{2r}{3} = 30$, we should multiply each side by $\frac{3}{2}$. True
8. Adding any real number to both sides of an equation will result in an equation that is equivalent to the original equation. True
9. The equation $5x = 0$ is equivalent to $x = 0$. True
10. The solution to $2x - 3 = x + 1$ is 4. True

2.1 Exercises

Boost your grade at mathzone.com!
- Practice Problems
- NetTutor
- Self-Tests
- e-Professors
- Videos

‹ Study Tips ›

- Get to know your classmates whether you are an online student or in a classroom.
- Talk about what you are learning. Verbalizing ideas helps you get them straight in your mind.

Reading and Writing *After reading this section, write out the answers to these questions. Use complete sentences.*

1. What does the addition property of equality say?
The addition property of equality says that adding the same number to each side of an equation does not change the solution to the equation.

2. What are equivalent equations?
Equivalent equations are equations that have the same solution set.

3. What is the multiplication property of equality?
The multiplication property of equality says that multiplying both sides of an equation by the same nonzero number does not change the solution to the equation.

4. What is a linear equation in one variable?
A linear equation in one variable is an equation of the form $ax = b$ where $a \neq 0$.

5. How can you tell if your solution to an equation is correct?
Replace the variable in the equation with your solution. If the resulting statement is correct, then the solution is correct.

6. To obtain an equivalent equation, what are you not allowed to do to both sides of the equation?
In solving equations, you are not allowed to multiply or divide both sides by 0.

‹1› The Addition Property of Equality

Solve each equation. Show your work and check your answer. See Example 1.

7. $x - 6 = -5$ $\{1\}$

8. $x - 7 = -2$ $\{5\}$

9. $-13 + x = -4$ $\{9\}$

10. $-8 + x = -12$ $\{-4\}$

11. $y - \frac{1}{2} = \frac{1}{2}$ $\{1\}$

12. $y - \frac{1}{4} = \frac{1}{2}$ $\left\{\frac{3}{4}\right\}$

13. $w - \frac{1}{3} = \frac{1}{3}$ $\left\{\frac{2}{3}\right\}$

14. $w - \frac{1}{3} = \frac{1}{2}$ $\left\{\frac{5}{6}\right\}$

Solve each equation. Show your work and check your answer. See Example 2.

15. $x + 3 = -6$ $\{-9\}$

VIDEO **16.** $x + 4 = -3$ $\{-7\}$

17. $12 + x = -7$ $\{-19\}$

18. $19 + x = -11$ $\{-30\}$

19. $t + \frac{1}{2} = \frac{3}{4}$ $\left\{\frac{1}{4}\right\}$

20. $t + \frac{1}{3} = 1$ $\left\{\frac{2}{3}\right\}$

21. $\frac{1}{19} + m = \frac{1}{19}$ $\{0\}$

22. $\frac{1}{3} + n = \frac{1}{2}$ $\left\{\frac{1}{6}\right\}$

23. $a + 0.05 = 6$ $\{5.95\}$

24. $b + 4 = -0.7$ $\{-4.7\}$

Solve each equation. Show your work and check your answer. See Example 3.

25. $2 = x + 7$ $\{-5\}$

26. $3 = x + 5$ $\{-2\}$

27. $-13 = y - 9$ $\{-4\}$

28. $-14 = z - 12$ $\{-2\}$

29. $0.5 = -2.5 + x$ $\{3\}$

30. $0.6 = -1.2 + x$ $\{1.8\}$

31. $\frac{1}{8} = -\frac{1}{8} + r$ $\left\{\frac{1}{4}\right\}$

32. $\frac{1}{6} = -\frac{1}{6} + h$ $\left\{\frac{1}{3}\right\}$

⟨2⟩ The Multiplication Property of Equality

Solve each equation. Show your work and check your answer. See Example 4.

33. $\frac{x}{2} = -4$ $\{-8\}$

34. $\frac{x}{3} = -6$ $\{-18\}$

35. $0.03 = \frac{y}{60}$ $\{1.8\}$

36. $0.05 = \frac{y}{80}$ $\{4\}$

37. $\frac{a}{2} = \frac{1}{3}$ $\left\{\frac{2}{3}\right\}$

38. $\frac{b}{2} = \frac{1}{5}$ $\left\{\frac{2}{5}\right\}$

39. $\frac{1}{6} = \frac{c}{3}$ $\left\{\frac{1}{2}\right\}$

40. $\frac{1}{12} = \frac{d}{3}$ $\left\{\frac{1}{4}\right\}$

Solve each equation. Show your work and check your answer. See Example 5.

41. $-3x = 15$ $\{-5\}$

42. $-5x = -20$ $\{4\}$

43. $20 = 4y$ $\{5\}$

VIDEO **44.** $18 = -3a$ $\{-6\}$

45. $2w = 2.5$ $\{1.25\}$

46. $-2x = -5.6$ $\{2.8\}$

47. $5 = 20x$ $\left\{\frac{1}{4}\right\}$

48. $-3 = 27d$ $\left\{-\frac{1}{9}\right\}$

49. $5x = \frac{3}{4}$ $\left\{\frac{3}{20}\right\}$

50. $3x = -\frac{2}{3}$ $\left\{-\frac{2}{9}\right\}$

Solve each equation. Show your work and check your answer. See Example 6.

51. $\frac{3}{2}x = -3$ $\{-2\}$

52. $\frac{2}{3}x = -8$ $\{-12\}$

53. $90 = \frac{3y}{4}$ $\{120\}$

54. $14 = \frac{7y}{8}$ $\{16\}$

55. $-\frac{3}{5}w = -\frac{1}{3}$ $\left\{\frac{5}{9}\right\}$

VIDEO **56.** $-\frac{5}{2}t = -\frac{3}{5}$ $\left\{\frac{6}{25}\right\}$

57. $\frac{2}{3} = -\frac{4x}{3}$ $\left\{-\frac{1}{2}\right\}$

58. $\frac{1}{14} = -\frac{6p}{7}$ $\left\{-\frac{1}{12}\right\}$

Solve each equation. Show your work and check your answer. See Example 7.

59. $-x = 8$ $\{-8\}$

VIDEO **60.** $-x = 4$ $\{-4\}$

61. $-y = -\frac{1}{3}$ $\left\{\frac{1}{3}\right\}$

62. $-y = -\frac{7}{8}$ $\left\{\frac{7}{8}\right\}$

63. $3.4 = -z$ $\{-3.4\}$

64. $4.9 = -t$ $\{-4.9\}$

65. $-k = -99$ $\{99\}$

66. $-m = -17$ $\{17\}$

⟨3⟩ Variables on Both Sides

Solve each equation. Show your work and check your answer. See Example 8.

67. $4x = 3x - 7$ $\{-7\}$

VIDEO **68.** $3x = 2x + 9$ $\{9\}$

69. $9 - 6y = -5y$ $\{9\}$

70. $12 - 18w = -17w$ $\{12\}$

71. $-6x = 8 - 7x$ $\{8\}$

72. $-3x = -6 - 4x$ $\{-6\}$

73. $\frac{1}{2}c = 5 - \frac{1}{2}c$ $\{5\}$

74. $-\frac{1}{2}h = 13 - \frac{3}{2}h$ $\{13\}$

Miscellaneous

Use the appropriate property of equality to solve each equation.

75. $12 = x + 17$ $\{-5\}$

76. $-3 = x + 6$ $\{-9\}$

77. $\frac{3}{4}y = -6$ $\{-8\}$

78. $\frac{5}{9}z = -10$ $\{-18\}$

79. $-3.2 + x = -1.2$ $\{2\}$

80. $t - 3.8 = -2.9$ $\{0.9\}$

81. $2a = \frac{1}{3}$ $\left\{\frac{1}{6}\right\}$

82. $-3w = \frac{1}{2}$ $\left\{-\frac{1}{6}\right\}$

83. $-9m = 3$ $\left\{-\frac{1}{3}\right\}$

84. $-4h = -2$ $\left\{\frac{1}{2}\right\}$

85. $-b = -44$ $\{44\}$

86. $-r = 55$ $\{-55\}$

87. $\frac{2}{3}x = \frac{1}{2}$ $\left\{\frac{3}{4}\right\}$

88. $\frac{3}{4}x = \frac{1}{3}$ $\left\{\frac{4}{9}\right\}$

89. $-5x = 7 - 6x$ $\{7\}$

90. $-\frac{1}{2} + 3y = 4y$ $\left\{-\frac{1}{2}\right\}$

91. $\frac{5a}{7} = -10$ $\{-14\}$

92. $\frac{7r}{12} = -14$ $\{-24\}$

93. $\frac{1}{2}v = -\frac{1}{2}v + \frac{3}{8}$ $\left\{\frac{3}{8}\right\}$

94. $\frac{1}{3}s + \frac{7}{9} = \frac{4}{3}s$ $\left\{\frac{7}{9}\right\}$

⟨4⟩ Applications

Solve each problem by writing and solving an equation. See Example 9.

95. ***Births to teenagers.*** In 2000 there were 48.5 births per 1000 females 15 to 19 years of age (National Center for

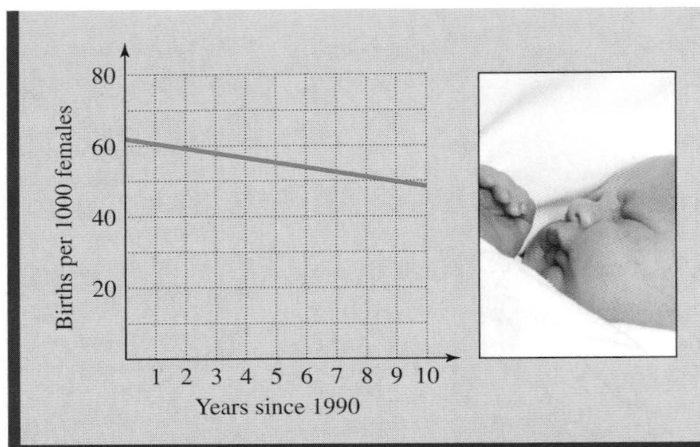

Figure for Exercise 95

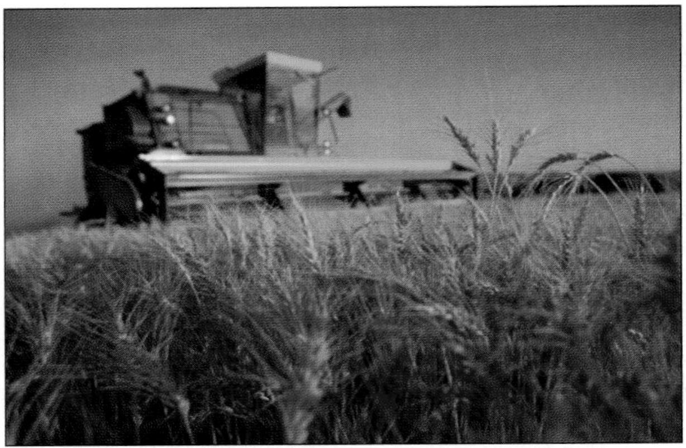

Photo for Exercise 96

Health Statistics, www.cdc.gov/nchs). This birth rate is $\frac{4}{5}$ of the birth rate for teenagers in 1991.

a) Write an equation and solve it to find the birth rate for teenagers in 1991.
$\frac{4}{5}x = 48.5$, 60.6 births per 1000 females

b) Use the accompanying graph to estimate the birth rate to teenagers in 1996. 54 births per 1000 females

96. ***World grain demand.*** Freeport McMoRan projects that in 2010 world grain supply will be 1.8 trillion metric tons and the supply will be only $\frac{3}{4}$ of world grain demand. What will world grain demand be in 2010?
2.4 trillion metric tons

97. ***Advancers and decliners.*** On Thursday, $\frac{2}{3}$ of the stocks traded on the New York Stock Exchange advanced in price. If 1918 stocks advanced, then how many stocks were traded on that day? 2877 stocks

98. ***Births in the United States.*** In 2000, one-third of all births in the United States were to unmarried women (National Center for Health Statistics, www.cdc.gov/nchs). If there were 1,352,938 births to unmarried women, then how many births were there in 2000?
4,058,814 births

99. ***College students.*** At Springfield College 40% of the students are male. If there are 1200 males, then how many students are there at the college?
3000 students

100. ***Credit card revenue.*** Seventy percent of the annual revenue for a credit card company comes from interest and penalties. If the amount for interest and penalties was $210 million, then what was the annual revenue?
$300 million

2.2 Solving General Linear Equations

In This Section

- ⟨1⟩ Equations of the Form $ax + b = 0$
- ⟨2⟩ Equations of the Form $ax + b = cx + d$
- ⟨3⟩ Equations with Parentheses
- ⟨4⟩ Applications

All of the equations that we solved in Section 2.1 required only a single application of a property of equality. In this section you will solve equations that require more than one application of a property of equality.

⟨1⟩ Equations of the Form $ax + b = 0$

To solve an equation of the form $ax + b = 0$ we might need to apply both the addition property of equality and the multiplication property of equality.

EXAMPLE 1

Using the addition and multiplication properties of equality

Solve $3r - 5 = 0$.

Solution

To isolate r, first add 5 to each side, then divide each side by 3.

$$3r - 5 = 0 \quad \text{Original equation}$$

$$3r - 5 + 5 = 0 + 5 \quad \text{Add 5 to each side.}$$

$$3r = 5 \quad \text{Combine like terms.}$$

$$\frac{3r}{3} = \frac{5}{3} \quad \text{Divide each side by 3.}$$

$$r = \frac{5}{3} \quad \text{Simplify.}$$

Checking $\frac{5}{3}$ in the original equation gives

$$3 \cdot \frac{5}{3} - 5 = 5 - 5 = 0.$$

So $\left\{\frac{5}{3}\right\}$ is the solution set to the equation.

Now do Exercises 5–10

‹ Helpful Hint ›

If we divide each side by 3 first, we must divide each term on the left side by 3 to get $r - \frac{5}{3} = 0$. Then add $\frac{5}{3}$ to each side to get $r = \frac{5}{3}$. Although we get the correct answer, we usually save division to the last step so that fractions do not appear until necessary.

CAUTION In solving $ax + b = 0$, we usually use the addition property of equality first and the multiplication property last. Note that this is the reverse of the order of operations (multiplication before addition), because we are undoing the operations that are done in the expression $ax + b$.

EXAMPLE 2

Using the addition and multiplication properties of equality

Solve $-\frac{2}{3}x + 8 = 0$.

Solution

To isolate x, first subtract 8 from each side, then multiply each side by $-\frac{3}{2}$.

$$-\frac{2}{3}x + 8 = 0 \quad \text{Original equation}$$

$$-\frac{2}{3}x + 8 - 8 = 0 - 8 \quad \text{Subtract 8 from each side.}$$

$$-\frac{2}{3}x = -8 \quad \text{Combine like terms.}$$

$$-\frac{3}{2}\left(-\frac{2}{3}x\right) = -\frac{3}{2}(-8) \quad \text{Multiply each side by } -\tfrac{3}{2}.$$

$$x = 12 \quad \text{Simplify.}$$

Checking 12 in the original equation gives

$$-\frac{2}{3}(12) + 8 = -8 + 8 = 0.$$

So $\{12\}$ is the solution set to the equation.

Now do Exercises 11–18

‹ Teaching Tip ›

Remind students that being neat and organized will help eliminate errors.

‹2› Equations of the Form $ax + b = cx + d$

In solving equations, our goal is to isolate the variable. We use the addition property of equality to eliminate unwanted terms. Note that it does not matter whether the variable ends up on the right or left side. For some equations, we will perform fewer steps if we isolate the variable on the right side.

EXAMPLE 3

Isolating the variable on the right side

Solve $3w - 8 = 7w$.

Solution

To eliminate the $3w$ from the left side, we can subtract $3w$ from both sides.

$$3w - 8 = 7w \quad \text{Original equation}$$
$$3w - 8 - 3w = 7w - 3w \quad \text{Subtract } 3w \text{ from each side.}$$
$$-8 = 4w \quad \text{Simplify each side.}$$
$$-\frac{8}{4} = \frac{4w}{4} \quad \text{Divide each side by 4.}$$
$$-2 = w \quad \text{Simplify.}$$

To check, replace w with -2 in the original equation:

$$3w - 8 = 7w \quad \text{Original equation}$$
$$3(-2) - 8 = 7(-2)$$
$$-14 = -14$$

Since -2 satisfies the original equation, the solution set is $\{-2\}$.

Now do Exercises 19–26

You should solve the equation in Example 3 by isolating the variable on the left side to see that it takes more steps. In Example 4, it is simplest to isolate the variable on the left side.

EXAMPLE 4

Isolating the variable on the left side

Solve $\frac{1}{2}b - 8 = 12$.

Solution

To eliminate the 8 from the left side, we add 8 to each side.

$$\frac{1}{2}b - 8 = 12 \quad \text{Original equation}$$
$$\frac{1}{2}b - 8 + 8 = 12 + 8 \quad \text{Add 8 to each side.}$$
$$\frac{1}{2}b = 20 \quad \text{Simplify each side.}$$
$$2 \cdot \frac{1}{2}b = 2 \cdot 20 \quad \text{Multiply each side by 2.}$$
$$b = 40 \quad \text{Simplify.}$$

‹ Teaching Tip ›

Point out that to isolate b we undo the operations on the left side in reverse of the order of operations. You put on your shirt and coat, but you take off your coat and then your shirt.

To check, replace b with 40 in the original equation:

$$\frac{1}{2}b - 8 = 12 \quad \text{Original equation}$$

$$\frac{1}{2}(40) - 8 = 12$$

$$12 = 12$$

Since 40 satisfies the original equation, the solution set is $\{40\}$.

Now do Exercises 27–34

In Example 5, both sides of the equation contain two terms.

EXAMPLE 5

Solving $ax + b = cx + d$

Solve $2m - 4 = 4m - 10$.

Solution

First, we decide to isolate the variable on the left side. So we must eliminate the 4 from the left side and eliminate $4m$ from the right side:

$$2m - 4 = 4m - 10$$

$$2m - 4 + 4 = 4m - 10 + 4 \quad \text{Add 4 to each side.}$$

$$2m = 4m - 6 \quad \text{Simplify each side.}$$

$$2m - 4m = 4m - 6 - 4m \quad \text{Subtract } 4m \text{ from each side.}$$

$$-2m = -6 \quad \text{Simplify each side.}$$

$$\frac{-2m}{-2} = \frac{-6}{-2} \quad \text{Divide each side by } -2.$$

$$m = 3 \quad \text{Simplify.}$$

To check, replace m by 3 in the original equation:

$$2m - 4 = 4m - 10 \quad \text{Original equation}$$

$$2 \cdot 3 - 4 = 4 \cdot 3 - 10$$

$$2 = 2$$

Since 3 satisfies the original equation, the solution set is $\{3\}$.

Now do Exercises 35–42

⟨3⟩ Equations with Parentheses

Equations that contain parentheses or like terms on the same side should be simplified as much as possible before applying any properties of equality.

EXAMPLE 6 Simplifying before using properties of equality

Solve $2(q - 3) + 5q = 8(q - 1)$.

Solution

First remove parentheses and combine like terms on each side of the equation.

$$2(q - 3) + 5q = 8(q - 1) \quad \text{Original equation}$$
$$2q - 6 + 5q = 8q - 8 \quad \text{Distributive property}$$
$$7q - 6 = 8q - 8 \quad \text{Combine like terms.}$$
$$7q - 6 + 6 = 8q - 8 + 6 \quad \text{Add 6 to each side.}$$
$$7q = 8q - 2 \quad \text{Combine like terms.}$$
$$7q - 8q = 8q - 2 - 8q \quad \text{Subtract } 8q \text{ from each side.}$$
$$-q = -2$$
$$-1(-q) = -1(-2) \quad \text{Multiply each side by } -1.$$
$$q = 2 \quad \text{Simplify.}$$

To check, we replace q by 2 in the original equation and simplify:

$$2(q - 3) + 5q = 8(q - 1) \quad \text{Original equation}$$
$$2(2 - 3) + 5(2) = 8(2 - 1) \quad \text{Replace } q \text{ by 2.}$$
$$2(-1) + 10 = 8(1)$$
$$8 = 8$$

Because both sides have the same value, the solution set is $\{2\}$.

Now do Exercises 43–50

‹ Calculator Close-Up ›

You can check an equation by entering the equation on the home screen as shown here. The equal sign is in the TEST menu.

When you press ENTER, the calculator returns the number 1 if the equation is true or 0 if the equation is false. Since the calculator shows a 1, we can be sure that 2 is the solution.

```
2(2-3)+5(2)=8(2-
1)
               1
```

Linear equations can vary greatly in appearance, but there is a strategy that you can use for solving any of them. The following strategy summarizes the techniques that we have been using in the examples. Keep it in mind when you are solving linear equations.

Strategy for Solving Equations

1. Remove parentheses by using the distributive property and then combine like terms to simplify each side as much as possible.
2. Use the addition property of equality to get like terms from opposite sides onto the same side so that they can be combined.
3. The multiplication property of equality is generally used last.
4. Check that the solution satisfies the original equation.

⟨4⟩ Applications

Linear equations occur in business situations where there is a fixed cost and a per item cost. A mail-order company might charge \$3 plus \$2 per CD for shipping and handling. A lawyer might charge \$300 plus \$65 per hour for handling your lawsuit. AT&T might charge 5 cents per minute plus \$2.95 for long distance calls. Example 7 illustrates the kind of problem that can be solved in this situation.

EXAMPLE 7

Long-distance charges

With AT&T's One Rate plan you are charged 5 cents per minute plus \$2.95 for long-distance service for one month. If a long-distance bill is \$4.80, then what is the number of minutes used?

‹ Teaching Tip ›

We are again doing a few simple word problems to build student confidence.

Solution

Let x represent the number of minutes of calls in the month. At \$0.05 per minute, the cost for x minutes is the product $0.05x$ dollars. Since there is a fixed cost of \$2.95, an expression for the total cost is $0.05x + 2.95$ dollars. Since the total cost is \$4.80, we have $0.05x + 2.95 = 4.80$. Solve this equation to find x.

$$0.05x + 2.95 = 4.80$$

$$0.05x + 2.95 - 2.95 = 4.80 - 2.95 \quad \text{Subtract 2.95 from each side.}$$

$$0.05x = 1.85 \quad \text{Simplify.}$$

$$\frac{0.05x}{0.05} = \frac{1.85}{0.05} \quad \text{Divide each side by 0.05.}$$

$$x = 37 \quad \text{Simplify.}$$

So the bill is for 37 minutes.

Now do Exercises 91–98

Warm-Ups ▼

True or false? Explain your answer.

1. The solution to $4x - 3 = 3x$ is 3. True
2. The equation $2x + 7 = 8$ is equivalent to $2x = 1$. True
3. To solve $3x - 5 = 8x + 7$, you should add 5 to each side and subtract $8x$ from each side. True
4. To solve $5 - 4x = 9 + 7x$, you should subtract 9 from each side and then subtract $7x$ from each side. False
5. Multiplying each side of an equation by the same nonzero real number will result in an equation that is equivalent to the original equation. True
6. To isolate y in $3y - 7 = 6$, divide each side by 3 and then add 7 to each side. False
7. To solve $\frac{3w}{4} = 300$, we should multiply each side by $\frac{4}{3}$. True
8. The equation $-n = 9$ is equivalent to $n = -9$. True
9. The equation $-y = -7$ is equivalent to $y = 7$. True
10. The solution to $7x = 5x$ is 0. True

2.2 Exercises

Boost your grade at mathzone.com!
- Practice Problems
- NetTutor
- Self-Tests
- e-Professors
- Videos

‹ Study Tips ›

- Don't simply work exercises to get answers. Keep reminding yourself of what you are actually doing.
- Look for the big picture. Where have we come from? Where are we going next? When will the picture be complete?

Reading and Writing *After reading this section, write out the answers to these questions. Use complete sentences.*

1. What properties of equality do you apply to solve $ax + b = 0$?
We can solve $ax + b = 0$ with the addition property and the multiplication property of equality.

2. Which property of equality is usually applied last?
The multiplication property of equality is usually applied last.

3. What property of equality is used to solve $-x = 8$?
Use the multiplication property of equality to solve $-x = 8$.

4. What is usually the first step in solving a linear equation involving parentheses?
If an equation involves parentheses, then we first remove the parentheses.

‹1› Equations of the Form $ax + b = 0$

Solve each equation. Show your work and check your answer. See Examples 1 and 2.

5. $5a - 10 = 0$ $\{2\}$
6. $8y + 24 = 0$ $\{-3\}$
7. $-3y - 6 = 0$ $\{-2\}$
8. $-9w - 54 = 0$ $\{-6\}$
9. $3x - 2 = 0$ $\left\{\frac{2}{3}\right\}$
10. $5y + 1 = 0$ $\left\{-\frac{1}{5}\right\}$
11. $\frac{1}{2}w - 3 = 0$ $\{6\}$
12. (VIDEO) $\frac{3}{8}t + 6 = 0$ $\{-16\}$
13. $-\frac{2}{3}x + 8 = 0$ $\{12\}$
14. $-\frac{1}{7}z - 5 = 0$ $\{-35\}$
15. $-m + \frac{1}{2} = 0$ $\left\{\frac{1}{2}\right\}$
16. $-y - \frac{3}{4} = 0$ $\left\{-\frac{3}{4}\right\}$
17. $3p + \frac{1}{2} = 0$ $\left\{-\frac{1}{6}\right\}$
18. $9z - \frac{1}{4} = 0$ $\left\{\frac{1}{36}\right\}$

‹2› Equations of the Form $ax + b = cx + d$

Solve each equation. See Examples 3 and 4.

19. $6x - 8 = 4x$ $\{4\}$
20. $9y + 14 = 2y$ $\{-2\}$
21. $4z = 5 - 2z$ $\left\{\frac{5}{6}\right\}$
22. $3t = t - 3$ $\left\{-\frac{3}{2}\right\}$
23. $4a - 9 = 7$ $\{4\}$
24. $7r + 5 = 47$ $\{6\}$
25. $9 = -6 - 3b$ $\{-5\}$
26. $13 = 3 - 10s$ $\{-1\}$
27. $\frac{1}{2}w - 4 = 13$ $\{34\}$
28. $\frac{1}{3}q + 13 = -5$ $\{-54\}$
29. $6 - \frac{1}{3}d = \frac{1}{3}d$ $\{9\}$
30. $9 - \frac{1}{2}a = \frac{1}{4}a$ $\{12\}$
31. $2w - 0.4 = 2$ $\{1.2\}$
32. $10h - 1.3 = 6$ $\{0.73\}$
33. $x = 3.3 - 0.1x$ $\{3\}$
34. (VIDEO) $y = 2.4 - 0.2y$ $\{2\}$

Solve each equation. See Example 5.

35. $3x - 3 = x + 5$ $\{4\}$
36. $9y - 1 = 6y + 5$ $\{2\}$
37. $4 - 7d = 13 - 4d$ $\{-3\}$
38. $y - 9 = 12 - 6y$ $\{3\}$
39. $c + \frac{1}{2} = 3c - \frac{1}{2}$ $\left\{\frac{1}{2}\right\}$
40. $x - \frac{1}{4} = \frac{1}{2} - x$ $\left\{\frac{3}{8}\right\}$
41. $\frac{2}{3}a - 5 = \frac{1}{3}a + 5$ $\{30\}$
42. $\frac{1}{2}t - 3 = \frac{1}{4}t - 9$ $\{-24\}$

‹3› Equations with Parentheses

Solve each equation. See Example 6.

43. $5(a - 1) + 3 = 28$ $\{6\}$
44. (VIDEO) $2(w + 4) - 1 = 1$ $\{-3\}$
45. $2 - 3(q - 1) = 10 - (q + 1)$ $\{-2\}$
46. $-2(y - 6) = 3(7 - y) - 5$ $\{4\}$
47. $2(x - 1) + 3x = 6x - 20$ $\{18\}$
48. (VIDEO) $3 - (r - 1) = 2(r + 1) - r$ $\{1\}$
49. $2\left(y - \frac{1}{2}\right) = 4\left(y - \frac{1}{4}\right) + y$ $\{0\}$
50. $\frac{1}{2}(4m - 6) = \frac{2}{3}(6m - 9) + 3$ $\{0\}$

Miscellaneous

Solve each equation.

Show your work and check your answer.

See the Strategy for Solving Equations box on page 98.

51. $2x = \frac{1}{3}$ $\left\{\frac{1}{6}\right\}$
52. $3x = \frac{6}{11}$ $\left\{\frac{2}{11}\right\}$
53. $5t = -2 + 4t$ $\{-2\}$
54. $8y = 6 + 7y$ $\{6\}$
55. $3x - 7 = 0$ $\left\{\frac{7}{3}\right\}$
56. $5x + 4 = 0$ $\left\{-\frac{4}{5}\right\}$
57. $-x + 6 = 5$ $\{1\}$
58. $-x - 2 = 9$ $\{-11\}$
59. $-9 - a = -3$ $\{-6\}$
60. $4 - r = 6$ $\{-2\}$
61. $2q + 5 = q - 7$ $\{-12\}$
62. $3z - 6 = 2z - 7$ $\{-1\}$
63. $-3x + 1 = 5 - 2x$ $\{-4\}$
64. $5 - 2x = 6 - x$ $\{-1\}$
65. $-12 - 5x = -4x + 1$ $\{-13\}$
66. $-3x - 4 = -2x + 8$ $\{-12\}$

67. $3x + 0.3 = 2 + 2x$ $\{1.7\}$

68. $2y - 0.05 = y + 1$ $\{1.05\}$

69. $k - 0.6 = 0.2k + 1$ $\{2\}$

70. $2.3h + 6 = 1.8h - 1$ $\{-14\}$

71. $0.2x - 4 = 0.6 - 0.8x$ $\{4.6\}$

72. $0.3x = 1 - 0.7x$ $\{1\}$

73. $-3(k - 6) = 2 - k$ $\{8\}$

74. $-2(h - 5) = 3 - h$ $\{7\}$

75. $2(p + 1) - p = 36$ $\{34\}$

76. $3(q + 1) - q = 23$ $\{10\}$

77. $7 - 3(5 - u) = 5(u - 4)$ $\{6\}$

78. $v - 4(4 - v) = -2(2v - 1)$ $\{2\}$

79. $4(x + 3) = 12$ $\{0\}$

80. $5(x - 3) = -15$ $\{0\}$

81. $\frac{w}{5} - 4 = -6$ $\{-10\}$

82. $\frac{q}{2} + 13 = -22$ $\{-70\}$

83. $\frac{2}{3}y - 5 = 7$ $\{18\}$

84. $\frac{3}{4}u - 9 = -6$ $\{4\}$

85. $4 - \frac{2n}{5} = 12$ $\{-20\}$

86. $9 - \frac{2m}{7} = 19$ $\{-35\}$

87. $-\frac{1}{3}p - \frac{1}{2} = \frac{1}{2}$ $\{-3\}$

88. $-\frac{3}{4}z - \frac{2}{3} = \frac{1}{3}$ $\left\{-\frac{4}{3}\right\}$

89. $3.5x - 23.7 = -38.75$ $\{-4.3\}$

90. $3(x - 0.87) - 2x = 4.98$ $\{7.59\}$

‹4› Applications

Solve each problem. See Example 7.

91. ***The practice.*** A lawyer charges \$300 plus \$65 per hour for a divorce. If the total charge for Bill's divorce was \$1405, then for what number of hours did the lawyer work on the case? 17 hr

92. ***The plumber.*** Tamika paid \$165 to her plumber for a service call. If her plumber charges \$45 plus \$40 per hour for a service call, then for how many hours did the plumber work? 3 hr

93. ***Celsius temperature.*** If the air temperature in Quebec is 68° Fahrenheit, then the solution to the equation $\frac{9}{5}C + 32 = 68$ gives the Celsius temperature of the air. Find the Celsius temperature. 20°C

94. ***Fahrenheit temperature.*** Water boils at 212°F.

a) Use the accompanying graph to determine the Celsius temperature at which water boils. 100°C

b) Find the Fahrenheit temperature of hot tap water at 70°C by solving the equation

$$70 = \frac{5}{9}(F - 32).$$ 158°F

95. ***Rectangular patio.*** If the rectangular patio in the accompanying figure has a length that is 3 feet longer than its width and a perimeter of 42 feet, then the width can be found by solving the equation $2x + 2(x + 3) = 42$. What is the width? 9 ft

Figure for Exercise 94

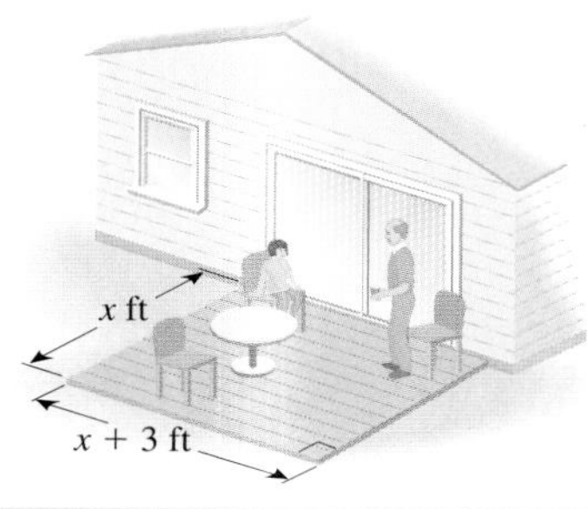

Figure for Exercise 95

96. ***Perimeter of a triangle.*** The perimeter of the triangle shown in the accompanying figure is 12 meters. Determine the values of x, $x + 1$, and $x + 2$ by solving the equation

$$x + (x + 1) + (x + 2) = 12.$$

3 m, 4 m, 5 m

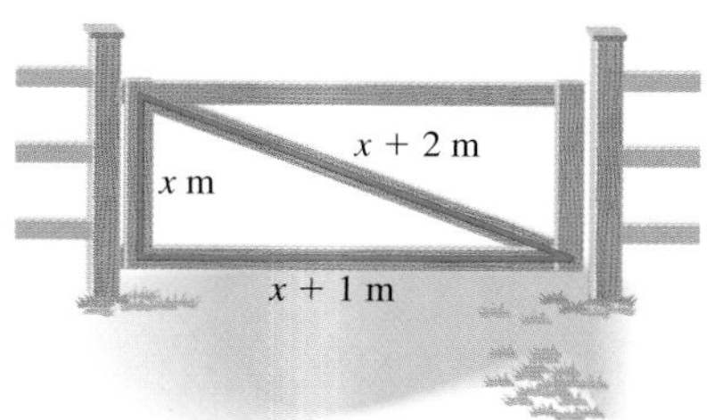

Figure for Exercise 96

97. ***Cost of a car.*** Jane paid 9% sales tax and a \$150 title and license fee when she bought her new Saturn for a total of \$16,009.50. If x represents the price of the car, then x satisfies $x + 0.09x + 150 = 16{,}009.50$. Find the price of the car by solving the equation. \$14,550

98. ***Cost of labor.*** An electrician charged Eunice \$29.96 for a service call plus \$39.96 per hour for a total of \$169.82 for installing her electric dryer. If n represents the number of hours for labor, then n satisfies

$$39.96n + 29.96 = 169.82.$$

Find n by solving this equation. 3.5 hrs

2.3 More Equations

In This Section

In this section we will solve more equations of the type that we solved in Sections 2.1 and 2.2. However, some equations in this section will contain fractions or decimal numbers. Some equations will have infinitely many solutions and some will have no solution.

⟨1⟩ Equations Involving Fractions

We solved some equations involving fractions in Sections 2.1 and 2.2. Here, we will solve equations with fractions by eliminating all fractions in the first step. All of the fractions will be eliminated if we multiply each side by the least common denominator.

EXAMPLE 1

Multiplying by the least common denominator

Solve $\frac{y}{2} - 1 = \frac{y}{3} + 1$.

Solution

The least common denominator (LCD) for the denominators 2 and 3 is 6. Since both 2 and 3 divide into 6 evenly, multiplying each side by 6 will eliminate the fractions:

$$6\left(\frac{y}{2} - 1\right) = 6\left(\frac{y}{3} + 1\right) \quad \text{Multiply each side by 6.}$$

$$6 \cdot \frac{y}{2} - 6 \cdot 1 = 6 \cdot \frac{y}{3} + 6 \cdot 1 \quad \text{Distributive property}$$

$$3y - 6 = 2y + 6 \quad \text{Simplify: } 6 \cdot \tfrac{y}{2} = 3y$$

$$3y = 2y + 12 \quad \text{Add 6 to each side.}$$

$$y = 12 \quad \text{Subtract } 2y \text{ from each side.}$$

Check 12 in the original equation:

$$\frac{12}{2} - 1 = \frac{12}{3} + 1$$

$$5 = 5$$

Since 12 satisfies the original equation, the solution set is $\{12\}$.

Now do Exercises 7–24

⟨ Helpful Hint ⟩

Note that the fractions in Example 1 will be eliminated if you multiply each side of the equation by any number divisible by both 2 and 3. For example, multiplying by 24 yields

$$12y - 24 = 8y + 24$$
$$4y = 48$$
$$y = 12.$$

CAUTION You can multiply each side of the equation in Example 1 by 6 to clear the fractions and get an equivalent equation, but multiplying an expression by a number to clear the fraction is not allowed. For example, multiplying the expression $\frac{1}{6}x + \frac{2}{3}$ by 6 to simplify it will change its value when x is replaced with a number.

⟨2⟩ Equations Involving Decimals

When an equation involves decimal numbers, we can work with the decimal numbers or we can eliminate all of the decimal numbers by multiplying both sides by 10, or 100, or 1000, and so on. Multiplying a decimal number by 10 moves the decimal point one place to the right. Multiplying by 100 moves the decimal point two places to the right, and so on.

EXAMPLE 2

An equation involving decimals

Solve $0.3p + 8.04 = 12.6$.

Solution

The largest number of decimal places appearing in the decimal numbers of the equation is two (in the number 8.04). Therefore we multiply each side of the equation by 100 because multiplying by 100 moves decimal points two places to the right:

$0.3p + 8.04 = 12.6$	Original equation
$100(0.3p + 8.04) = 100(12.6)$	Multiplication property of equality
$100(0.3p) + 100(8.04) = 100(12.6)$	Distributive property
$30p + 804 = 1260$	
$30p + 804 - 804 = 1260 - 804$	Subtract 804 from each side.
$30p = 456$	
$\frac{30p}{30} = \frac{456}{30}$	Divide each side by 30.
$p = 15.2$	

You can use a calculator to check that

$$0.3(15.2) + 8.04 = 12.6.$$

The solution set is $\{15.2\}$.

Now do Exercises 25–34

‹ Helpful Hint ›

After you have used one of the properties of equality on each side of an equation, be sure to simplify all expressions as much as possible before using another property of equality.

EXAMPLE 3

Another equation with decimals

Solve $0.5x + 0.4(x + 20) = 13.4$.

Solution

First use the distributive property to remove the parentheses:

$0.5x + 0.4(x + 20) = 13.4$	Original equation
$0.5x + 0.4x + 8 = 13.4$	Distributive property
$10(0.5x + 0.4x + 8) = 10(13.4)$	Multiply each side by 10.
$5x + 4x + 80 = 134$	Simplify.
$9x + 80 = 134$	Combine like terms.
$9x + 80 - 80 = 134 - 80$	Subtract 80 from each side.
$9x = 54$	Simplify.
$x = 6$	Divide each side by 9.

‹ Teaching Tip ›

Ask students to solve this equation without multiplying by 10 to eliminate the decimals.

Check 6 in the original equation:

$$0.5(6) + 0.4(6 + 20) = 13.4 \quad \text{Replace } x \text{ by 6.}$$
$$3 + 0.4(26) = 13.4$$
$$3 + 10.4 = 13.4$$

Since both sides of the equation have the same value, the solution set is $\{6\}$.

Now do Exercises 35–38

CAUTION If you multiply each side by 10 in Example 3 before using the distributive property, be careful how you handle the terms in parentheses:

$$10 \cdot 0.5x + 10 \cdot 0.4(x + 20) = 10 \cdot 13.4$$
$$5x + 4(x + 20) = 134$$

It is not correct to multiply 0.4 by 10 *and also* to multiply $x + 20$ by 10.

⟨3⟩ Simplifying the Process

It is very important to develop the skill of solving equations in a systematic way, writing down every step as we have been doing. As you become more skilled at solving equations, you will probably want to simplify the process a bit. One way to simplify the process is by writing only the result of performing an operation on each side. Another way is to isolate the variable on the side where the variable has the larger coefficient, when the variable occurs on both sides. We use these ideas in Example 4 and in future examples in this text.

EXAMPLE 4

Simplifying the process

Solve each equation.

a) $2a - 3 = 0$ **b)** $2k + 5 = 3k + 1$

Solution

a) Add 3 to each side, then divide each side by 2:

$$2a - 3 = 0$$
$$2a = 3 \quad \text{Add 3 to each side.}$$
$$a = \frac{3}{2} \quad \text{Divide each side by 2.}$$

Check that $\frac{3}{2}$ satisfies the original equation. The solution set is $\left\{\frac{3}{2}\right\}$.

b) For this equation we can get a single k on the right by subtracting $2k$ from each side. (If we subtract $3k$ from each side, we get $-k$, and then we need another step.)

$$2k + 5 = 3k + 1$$
$$5 = k + 1 \quad \text{Subtract } 2k \text{ from each side.}$$
$$4 = k \quad \text{Subtract 1 from each side.}$$

Check that 4 satisfies the original equation. The solution set is $\{4\}$.

Now do Exercises 39–54

‹ Teaching Tip ›

Ask students to give some examples of identities.

‹4› Identities, Conditional Equations, and Inconsistent Equations

It is easy to find equations that are satisfied by any real number that we choose as a replacement for the variable. For example, the equations

$$x \div 2 = \frac{1}{2}x, \qquad x + x = 2x, \qquad \text{and} \qquad x + 1 = x + 1$$

are satisfied by all real numbers. The equation

$$\frac{5}{x} = \frac{5}{x}$$

is satisfied by any real number except 0 because division by 0 is undefined.

All of these equations are called *identities*. Remember that the solution set for an identity is not always the entire set of real numbers. There might be some exclusions because of undefined expressions.

Identity

An equation that is satisfied by every real number for which both sides are defined is called an **identity.**

We cannot recognize that the equation in Example 5 is an identity until we have simplified each side.

EXAMPLE 5

Solving an identity

Solve $7 - 5(x - 6) + 4 = 3 - 2(x - 5) - 3x + 28$.

Solution

We first use the distributive property to remove the parentheses:

$$7 - 5(x - 6) + 4 = 3 - 2(x - 5) - 3x + 28$$
$$7 - 5x + 30 + 4 = 3 - 2x + 10 - 3x + 28$$
$$41 - 5x = 41 - 5x \qquad \text{Combine like terms.}$$

This last equation is true for any value of x because the two sides are identical. So the solution set to the original equation is the set of all real numbers or R.

Now do Exercises 55–56

CAUTION If you get an equation in which both sides are identical, as in Example 5, there is no need to continue to simplify the equation. If you do continue, you will eventually get $0 = 0$, from which you can still conclude that the equation is an identity.

The statement $2x + 4 = 10$ is true only on condition that we choose $x = 3$. The equation $x^2 = 4$ is satisfied only if we choose $x = 2$ or $x = -2$. These equations are called conditional equations.

Conditional Equation

A **conditional equation** is an equation that is satisfied by at least one real number but is not an identity.

Every equation that we solved in Sections 2.1 and 2.2 is a conditional equation.

‹ Teaching Tip ›

Ask students for some examples of inconsistent equations.

It is easy to find equations that are false no matter what number we use to replace the variable. Consider the equation

$$x = x + 1.$$

If we replace x by 3, we get $3 = 3 + 1$, which is false. If we replace x by 4, we get $4 = 4 + 1$, which is also false. Clearly, there is no number that will satisfy $x = x + 1$. Other examples of equations with no solutions include

$$x = x - 2, \qquad x - x = 5, \qquad \text{and} \qquad 0 \cdot x + 6 = 7.$$

Inconsistent Equation

An equation that has no solution is called an **inconsistent equation.**

The solution set to an inconsistent equation has no members. The set with no members is called the **empty set** and it is denoted by the symbol $\emptyset$.

EXAMPLE 6

Solving an inconsistent equation

Solve $2 - 3(x - 4) = 4(x - 7) - 7x$.

Solution

Use the distributive property to remove the parentheses:

$2 - 3(x - 4) = 4(x - 7) - 7x$	The original equation
$2 - 3x + 12 = 4x - 28 - 7x$	Distributive property
$14 - 3x = -28 - 3x$	Combine like terms on each side.
$14 - 3x + 3x = -28 - 3x + 3x$	Add $3x$ to each side.
$14 = -28$	Simplify.

The last equation is not true for any x. So the solution set to the original equation is the empty set, $\emptyset$. The equation is inconsistent.

Now do Exercises 57–74

Keep the following points in mind when solving equations.

Recognizing Identities and Inconsistent Equations

If you are solving an equation and you get

1. an equation in which both sides are identical, the original equation is an identity.
2. an equation that is false, the original equation is an inconsistent equation.

The solution set to an identity is the set of all real numbers for which both sides of the equation are defined. The solution set to an inconsistent equation is the empty set, $\varnothing$.

⟨5⟩ Applications

EXAMPLE 7

Discount

Olivia got a 6% discount when she bought a new XBOX. If she paid \$399.50 and x is the original price, then x satisfies the equation $x - 0.06x = 399.50$. Solve the equation to find the original price.

Solution

We could multiply each side by 100, but in this case, it might be easier to just work with the decimals:

$$x - 0.06x = 399.50$$

$$0.94x = 399.50 \qquad 1.00 - 0.06 = 0.94$$

$$x = \frac{399.50}{0.94} = 425 \qquad \text{Divide each side by 0.94.}$$

Check that $425 - 0.06(425) = 399.50$. The original price was \$425.

Now do Exercises 93–96

Warm-Ups ▼

True or false? Explain your answer.

1. To solve $\frac{1}{2}x - \frac{1}{3} = x + \frac{1}{6}$ multiply each side by 6. True
2. The equation $\frac{1}{2}x - \frac{1}{3} = x + \frac{1}{6}$ is equivalent to $3x - 2 = 6x + 1$. True
3. The equation $0.2x + 0.03x = 8$ is equivalent to $20x + 3x = 8$. False
4. The solution set to $3h + 8 = 0$ is $\left\{\frac{8}{3}\right\}$. False
5. The equation $5a + 3 = 0$ is an inconsistent equation. False
6. The equation $2t = t$ is a conditional equation. True
7. The equation $w - 0.1w = 0.9w$ is an identity. True
8. All real numbers satisfy the equation $1 \div x = \frac{1}{x}$. False
9. The equation $\frac{x}{x} = 1$ is an identity. True
10. The equation $x - x = 99$ has no solution. True

2.3 Exercises

‹ Study Tips ›

- What's on the final exam? If your instructor thinks a problem is important enough for a test or quiz, it is probably important enough for the final exam. You should be thinking of the final exam all semester.
- Write all of the test and quiz questions on note cards, one to a card. To prepare for the final, shuffle the cards and try to answer the questions in a random order.

Reading and Writing *After reading this section, write out the answers to these questions. Use complete sentences.*

1. What is the usual first step when solving an equation involving fractions?
If an equation involves fractions we usually multiply each side by the LCD of all of the fractions.

2. What is a good first step for solving an equation involving decimals?
If an equation involves decimals we usually multiply each side by a power of 10 to eliminate all decimals.

3. What is an identity?
An identity is an equation that is satisfied by all numbers for which both sides are defined.

4. What is a conditional equation?
A conditional equation has at least one solution but is not an identity.

5. What is an inconsistent equation?
An inconsistent equation has no solutions.

6. What is the solution set to an inconsistent equation?
The solution set to an inconsistent equation is the empty set, $\varnothing$.

‹1› Equations Involving Fractions

Solve each equation by first eliminating the fractions. See Example 1.

7. $\frac{x}{4} - \frac{3}{10} = 0$ $\left\{\frac{6}{5}\right\}$

8. $\frac{x}{15} + \frac{1}{6} = 0$ $\left\{-\frac{5}{2}\right\}$

9. $3x - \frac{1}{6} = \frac{1}{2}$ $\left\{\frac{2}{9}\right\}$

10. $5x + \frac{1}{2} = \frac{3}{4}$ $\left\{\frac{1}{20}\right\}$

11. $\frac{x}{2} + 3 = x - \frac{1}{2}$ $\{7\}$

12. $13 - \frac{x}{2} = x - \frac{1}{2}$ $\{9\}$

13. $\frac{x}{2} + \frac{x}{3} = 20$ $\{24\}$

14. $\frac{x}{2} - \frac{x}{3} = 5$ $\{30\}$

15. $\frac{w}{2} + \frac{w}{4} = 12$ $\{16\}$

16. $\frac{a}{4} - \frac{a}{2} = -5$ $\{20\}$

17. $\frac{3z}{2} - \frac{2z}{3} = -10$ $\{-12\}$

18. $\frac{3m}{4} + \frac{m}{2} = -5$ $\{-4\}$

19. $\frac{1}{3}p - 5 = \frac{1}{4}p$ $\{60\}$

20. $\frac{1}{2}q - 6 = \frac{1}{5}q$ $\{20\}$

21. $\frac{1}{6}v + 1 = \frac{1}{4}v - 1$ $\{24\}$

22. $\frac{1}{15}k + 5 = \frac{1}{6}k - 10$ $\{150\}$

23. $\frac{1}{2}x + \frac{1}{3} = \frac{1}{4}x$ $\left\{-\frac{4}{3}\right\}$

24. $\frac{1}{3}x - \frac{2}{5}x = \frac{5}{6}$ $\left\{-\frac{25}{2}\right\}$

‹2› Equations Involving Decimals

Solve each equation by first eliminating the decimal numbers. See Examples 2 and 3.

25. $x - 0.2x = 72$ $\{90\}$

26. $x - 0.1x = 63$ $\{70\}$

27. $0.3x + 1.2 = 0.5x$ $\{6\}$

28. $0.4x - 1.6 = 0.6x$ $\{-8\}$

29. $0.02x - 1.56 = 0.8x$ $\{-2\}$

VIDEO **30.** $0.6x + 10.4 = 0.08x$ $\{-20\}$

31. $0.1a - 0.3 = 0.2a - 8.3$ $\{80\}$

32. $0.5b + 3.4 = 0.2b + 12.4$ $\{30\}$

33. $0.05r + 0.4r = 27$ $\{60\}$

34. $0.08t + 28.3 = 0.5t - 9.5$ $\{90\}$

35. $0.05y + 0.03(y + 50) = 17.5$ $\{200\}$

36. $0.07y + 0.08(y - 100) = 44.5$ $\{350\}$

37. $0.1x + 0.05(x - 300) = 105$ $\{800\}$

38. $0.2x - 0.05(x - 100) = 35$ $\{200\}$

‹3› Simplifying the Process

Solve each equation. If you feel proficient enough, try simplifying the process, as described in Example 4.

39. $2x - 9 = 0$ $\left\{\frac{9}{2}\right\}$

40. $3x + 7 = 0$ $\left\{-\frac{7}{3}\right\}$

41. $-2x + 6 = 0$ $\{3\}$

42. $-3x - 12 = 0$ $\{-4\}$

43. $\frac{z}{5} + 1 = 6$ $\{25\}$

44. $\frac{s}{2} + 2 = 5$ $\{6\}$

45. $\frac{c}{2} - 3 = -4$ $\{-2\}$

46. $\frac{b}{3} - 4 = -7$ $\{-9\}$

47. $3 = t + 6$ $\{-3\}$

48. $-5 = y - 9$ $\{4\}$

49. $5 + 2q = 3q$ {5}

50. $-4 - 5p = -4p$ {−4}

51. $8x - 1 = 9 + 9x$ {−10}

52. $4x - 2 = -8 + 5x$ {6}

53. $-3x + 1 = -1 - 2x$ {2}

54. $-6x + 3 = -7 - 5x$ {10}

⟨4⟩ Identities, Conditional Equations, and Inconsistent Equations

Solve each equation. Identify each as a conditional equation, an inconsistent equation, or an identity.

See Examples 5 and 6.

See Recognizing Identities and Inconsistent Equations on page 107.

55. $x + x = 2x$ All real numbers, identity

VIDEO **56.** $2x - x = x$ All real numbers, identity

57. $a - 1 = a + 1$ ∅, inconsistent

58. $r + 7 = r$ ∅, inconsistent

59. $3y + 4y = 12y$ {0}, conditional

VIDEO **60.** $9t - 8t = 7$ {7}, conditional

61. $-4 + 3(w - 1) = w + 2(w - 2) - 1$ ∅, inconsistent

62. $4 - 5(w + 2) = 2(w - 1) - 7w - 4$
All real numbers, identity

VIDEO **63.** $3(m + 1) = 3(m + 3)$ ∅, inconsistent

64. $5(m - 1) - 6(m + 3) = 4 - m$ ∅, inconsistent

65. $x + x = 2$ {1}, conditional

66. $3x - 5 = 0$ $\left\{\frac{5}{3}\right\}$, conditional

67. $2 - 3(5 - x) = 3x$ ∅, inconsistent

68. $3 - 3(5 - x) = 0$ {4}, conditional

69. $(3 - 3)(5 - z) = 0$ All real numbers, identity

70. $(2 \cdot 4 - 8)p = 0$ All real numbers, identity

71. $\frac{0}{x} = 0$ All nonzero real numbers, identity

72. $\frac{2x}{2} = x$ All real numbers, identity

73. $x \cdot x = x^2$ All real numbers, identity

74. $\frac{2x}{2x} = 1$ All nonzero real numbers, identity

Miscellaneous

Solve each equation.

75. $3x - 5 = 2x - 9$ {−4}

76. $5x - 9 = x - 4$ $\left\{\frac{5}{4}\right\}$

77. $x + 2(x + 4) = 3(x + 3) - 1$ R

78. $u + 3(u - 4) = 4(u - 5)$ ∅

79. $23 - 5(3 - n) = -4(n - 2) + 9n$ R

80. $-3 - 4(t - 5) = -2(t + 3) + 11$ {6}

81. $0.05x + 30 = 0.4x - 5$ {100}

82. $x - 0.08x = 460$ {500}

83. $-\frac{2}{3}a + 1 = 2$ $\left\{-\frac{3}{2}\right\}$

84. $-\frac{3}{4}t = \frac{1}{2}$ $\left\{-\frac{2}{3}\right\}$

85. $\frac{y}{2} + \frac{y}{6} = 20$ {30}

86. $\frac{3w}{5} - 1 = \frac{w}{2} + 1$ {20}

87. $0.09x - 0.2(x + 4) = -1.46$ {6}

88. $0.08x + 0.5(x + 100) = 73.2$ {40}

89. $436x - 789 = -571$ {0.5}

90. $0.08x + 4533 = 10x + 69$ {450}

91. $\frac{x}{344} + 235 = 292$ {19,608}

92. $34(x - 98) = \frac{x}{2} + 475$ {113.642}

⟨5⟩ Applications

Solve each problem. See Example 7.

93. ***Sales commission.*** Danielle sold her house through an agent who charged 8% of the selling price. After the commission was paid, Danielle received \$117,760. If x is the selling price, then x satisfies

$$x - 0.08x = 117{,}760.$$

Solve this equation to find the selling price. \$128,000

94. ***Raising rabbits.*** Before Roland sold two female rabbits, half of his rabbits were female. After the sale, only one-third of his rabbits were female. If x represents his original number of rabbits, then

$$\frac{1}{2}x - 2 = \frac{1}{3}(x - 2).$$

Solve this equation to find the number of rabbits that he had before the sale. 8 rabbits

95. ***Eavesdropping.*** Reginald overheard his boss complaining that his federal income tax for 2006 was \$60,531.

a) Use the accompanying graph to estimate his boss's taxable income for 2006. \$240,000

b) Find his boss's exact taxable income for 2006 by solving the equation

$$42{,}170 + 0.33(x - 188{,}450) = 60{,}531.$$

\$244,089

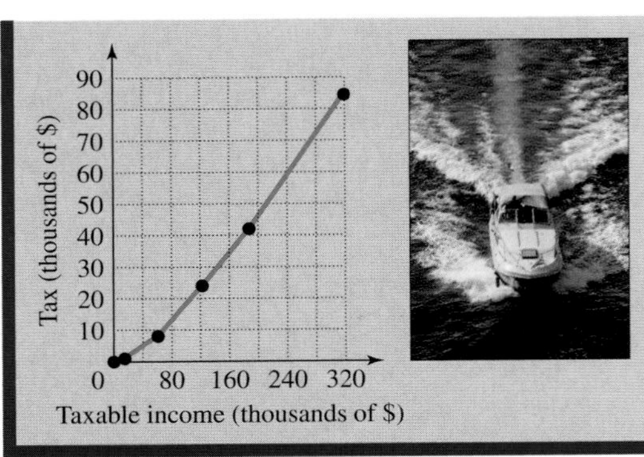

Figure for Exercise 95

96. ***Federal taxes.*** According to Bruce Harrell, CPA, the federal income tax for a class C corporation is found by solving a linear equation. The reason for the equation is that the amount x of federal tax is deducted before the state tax is figured, and the amount of state tax is deducted before the federal tax is figured. To find the amount of federal tax for a corporation with a taxable income of \$200,000, for which the federal tax rate is 25% and the state tax rate is 10%, Bruce must solve

$$x = 0.25[200{,}000 - 0.10(200{,}000 - x)].$$

Solve the equation for Bruce. \$46,154

2.4 Formulas

In This Section

In this section, you will learn to rewrite formulas using the same properties of equality that we used to solve equations. You will also learn how to find the value of one of the variables in a formula when we know the value of all of the others.

⟨1⟩ Solving for a Variable

Most drivers know the relationship between distance, rate, and time. For example, if you drive 70 mph for 3 hours, then you will travel 210 miles. At 60 mph a 300-mile trip will take 5 hours. If a 400-mile trip took 8 hours, then you averaged 50 mph. The relationship between distance D, rate R, and time T is expressed by the formula

$$D = R \cdot T.$$

A **formula** or **literal equation** is an equation involving two or more variables.

To find the time for a 300-mile trip at 60 mph, you are using the formula in the form $T = \frac{D}{R}$. The process of rewriting a formula for one variable in terms of the others is called **solving for a certain variable.** To solve for a certain variable, we use the same techniques that we use in solving equations.

EXAMPLE 1

Solving for a certain variable

Solve the formula $D = RT$ for T.

Solution

Since T is multiplied by R, dividing each side of the equation by R will isolate T:

$$D = RT \quad \text{Original formula}$$

$$\frac{D}{R} = \frac{R \cdot T}{R} \quad \text{Divide each side by } R.$$

$$\frac{D}{R} = T \quad \text{Divide out (or cancel) the common factor } R.$$

$$T = \frac{D}{R} \quad \text{It is customary to write the single variable on the left.}$$

Now do Exercises 7–18

The formula $C = \frac{5}{9}(F - 32)$ is used to find the Celsius temperature for a given Fahrenheit temperature. If we solve this formula for F, then we have a formula for finding Fahrenheit temperature for a given Celsius temperature.

EXAMPLE 2

Solving for a certain variable

Solve the formula $C = \frac{5}{9}(F - 32)$ for F.

Solution

We could apply the distributive property to the right side of the equation, but it is simpler to proceed as follows:

$$C = \frac{5}{9}(F - 32)$$

$$\frac{9}{5}C = \frac{9}{5} \cdot \frac{5}{9}(F - 32) \quad \text{Multiply each side by } \tfrac{9}{5}\text{, the reciprocal of } \tfrac{5}{9}.$$

$$\frac{9}{5}C = F - 32 \quad \text{Simplify.}$$

$$\frac{9}{5}C + 32 = F - 32 + 32 \quad \text{Add 32 to each side.}$$

$$\frac{9}{5}C + 32 = F \quad \text{Simplify.}$$

The formula is usually written as $F = \frac{9}{5}C + 32$.

Now do Exercises 19–24

‹ Teaching Tip ›

Ask students to solve this equation by using the distributive property first.

When solving for a variable that appears more than once in the equation, we must combine the terms to obtain a single occurrence of the variable. *When a formula has been solved for a certain variable, that variable will not occur on both sides of the equation.*

EXAMPLE 3

Solving for a variable that appears on both sides

Solve $5x - b = 3x + d$ for x.

Solution

First get all terms involving x onto one side and all other terms onto the other side:

$$5x - b = 3x + d \quad \text{Original formula}$$

$$5x - 3x - b = d \quad \text{Subtract } 3x \text{ from each side.}$$

$$5x - 3x = b + d \quad \text{Add } b \text{ to each side.}$$

$$2x = b + d \quad \text{Combine like terms.}$$

$$x = \frac{b + d}{2} \quad \text{Divide each side by 2.}$$

The formula solved for x is $x = \frac{b + d}{2}$.

Now do Exercises 25–32

In Chapter 3, it will be necessary to solve an equation involving x and y for y.

EXAMPLE 4

‹ Helpful Hint ›

If we simply wanted to solve $x + 2y = 6$ for y, we could have written

$$y = \frac{6 - x}{2} \text{ or } y = \frac{-x + 6}{2}.$$

However, in Example 4 we requested the form $y = mx + b$. This form is a popular form that we will study in detail in Chapter 3.

Solving for y

Solve $x + 2y = 6$ for y. Write the answer in the form $y = mx + b$, where m and b are real numbers.

Solution

$x + 2y = 6$ Original equation

$2y = 6 - x$ Subtract x from each side.

$\frac{1}{2} \cdot 2y = \frac{1}{2}(6 - x)$ Multiply each side by $\frac{1}{2}$.

$y = 3 - \frac{1}{2}x$ Distributive property

$y = -\frac{1}{2}x + 3$ Rearrange to get $y = mx + b$ form.

Now do Exercises 33–42

Notice that in Example 4 we multiplied each side of the equation by $\frac{1}{2}$, and so we multiplied each term on the right-hand side by $\frac{1}{2}$. Instead of multiplying by $\frac{1}{2}$, we could have divided each side of the equation by 2. We would then divide each term on the right side by 2. This idea is illustrated in Example 5.

EXAMPLE 5

‹ Teaching Tip ›

Remind students that if plus is written in a general form such as $y = mx + b$, then we also allow minus, and vice versa.

Solving for y

Solve $2x - 3y = 9$ for y. Write the answer in the form $y = mx + b$, where m and b are real numbers. (When we study lines in Chapter 3 you will see that $y = mx + b$ is the slope-intercept form of the equation of a line.)

Solution

$2x - 3y = 9$ Original equation

$-3y = -2x + 9$ Subtract $2x$ from each side.

$\frac{-3y}{-3} = \frac{-2x + 9}{-3}$ Divide each side by -3.

$y = \frac{-2x}{-3} + \frac{9}{-3}$ By the distributive property, each term is divided by -3.

$y = \frac{2}{3}x - 3$ Simplify.

Now do Exercises 43–54

Even though we wrote $y = \frac{2}{3}x - 3$ in Example 5, the equation is still considered to be in the form $y = mx + b$ because we could have written $y = \frac{2}{3}x + (-3)$.

⟨2⟩ Finding the Value of a Variable

In many situations, we know the values of all variables in a formula except one. We use the formula to determine the unknown value.

EXAMPLE 6 Finding the value of a variable in a formula

If $2x - 3y = 9$, find y when $x = 6$.

Solution

Method 1: First solve the equation for y. Because we have already solved this equation for y in Example 5 we will not repeat that process in this example. We have

$$y = \frac{2}{3}x - 3.$$

Now replace x by 6 in this equation:

$$y = \frac{2}{3}(6) - 3$$

$$= 4 - 3 = 1$$

So when $x = 6$, we have $y = 1$.

Method 2: First replace x by 6 in the original equation, then solve for y:

$$2x - 3y = 9 \quad \text{Original equation}$$

$$2 \cdot 6 - 3y = 9 \quad \text{Replace } x \text{ by 6.}$$

$$12 - 3y = 9 \quad \text{Simplify.}$$

$$-3y = -3 \quad \text{Subtract 12 from each side.}$$

$$y = 1 \quad \text{Divide each side by } -3.$$

So when $x = 6$, we have $y = 1$.

Now do Exercises 55–64

It usually does not matter which method from Example 6 is used. However, if you want many y-values, it is best to have the equation solved for y. For example, completing the y-column in the following table is straightforward if you have the equation solved for y:

x	y
0	
3	
6	

$$y = \frac{2}{3}x - 3$$

$$y = \frac{2}{3}(0) - 3 = -3$$

$$y = \frac{2}{3}(3) - 3 = -1$$

$$y = \frac{2}{3}(6) - 3 = 1$$

x	y
0	−3
3	−1
6	1

⟨3⟩ Applications

Example 7 involves the simple interest formula $I = Prt$, where I is the amount of interest, P is the principal or the amount invested, r is the annual interest rate, and t is the time in years. The interest rate is usually expressed as a percent. When using a rate in computations, you must convert it to a decimal number.

EXAMPLE 7

Finding the simple interest rate

The principal is \$400 and the time is 2 years. Find the simple interest rate for each of the following amounts of interest: \$120, \$60, \$30.

‹ Helpful Hint ›

All interest computation is based on simple interest. However, depositors do not like to wait 2 years to get interest as in Example 7. More often the time is $\frac{1}{12}$ year or $\frac{1}{365}$ year. Simple interest computed every month is said to be compounded monthly. Simple interest computed every day is said to be compounded daily.

Solution

First solve the formula $I = Prt$ for r:

$$Prt = I \quad \text{Simple interest formula}$$

$$\frac{Prt}{Pt} = \frac{I}{Pt} \quad \text{Divide each side by } Pt.$$

$$r = \frac{I}{Pt} \quad \text{Simplify.}$$

Now insert the values for P, t, and the three amounts of interest:

$$r = \frac{120}{400 \cdot 2} = 0.15 = 15\% \quad \text{Move the decimal point two places to the left.}$$

$$r = \frac{60}{400 \cdot 2} = 0.075 = 7.5\%$$

$$r = \frac{30}{400 \cdot 2} = 0.0375 = 3.75\%$$

If the amount of interest is \$120, \$60, or \$30, then the simple interest rate is 15%, 7.5%, or 3.75%, respectively.

Now do Exercises 73–76

In solving a geometric problem, it is always helpful to draw a diagram, as we do in Example 8.

EXAMPLE 8

Using a geometric formula

The perimeter of a rectangle is 36 feet. If the width is 6 feet, then what is the length?

‹ Teaching Tip ›

Many students confuse area and perimeter. It is also very useful to know that length plus width is half the perimeter.

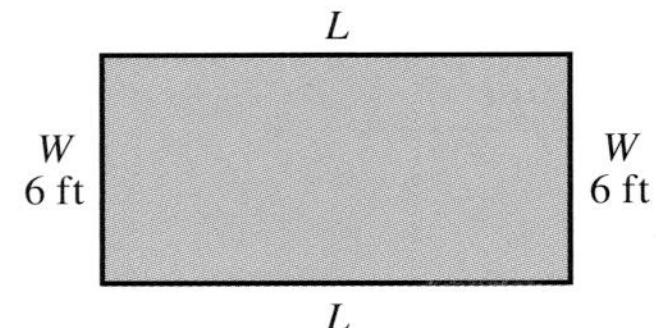

Figure 2.1

Solution

First, put the given information on a diagram as shown in Fig. 2.1. Substitute the given values into the formula for the perimeter of a rectangle found inside the front cover of this book, and then solve for L. (We could solve for L first and then insert the given values.)

$$P = 2L + 2W \quad \text{Perimeter of a rectangle}$$

$$36 = 2L + 2 \cdot 6 \quad \text{Substitute 36 for } P \text{ and 6 for } W.$$

$$36 = 2L + 12 \quad \text{Simplify.}$$

$$24 = 2L \quad \text{Subtract 12 from each side.}$$

$$12 = L \quad \text{Divide each side by 2.}$$

Check: If $L = 12$ and $W = 6$, then $P = 2(12) + 2(6) = 36$ feet. So we can be certain that the length is 12 feet.

Now do Exercises 77–80

If L is the list price or original price of an item and r is the rate of discount, then the amount of discount is rL, the product of the rate and the list price. The sale price S is the list price minus the amount of discount. So $S = L - rL$. The rate of discount is generally expressed as a percent. In computations, rates must be written as decimals or fractions.

EXAMPLE 9

Finding the original price

What was the original price of a stereo that sold for \$560 after a 20% discount?

Solution

Express 20% as the decimal 0.20 or 0.2 and use the formula $S = L - rL$:

$$\text{Selling price} = \text{list price} - \text{amount of discount}$$

$$560 = L - 0.2L$$

$$10(560) = 10(L - 0.2L) \quad \text{Multiply each side by 10.}$$

$$5600 = 10L - 2L \quad \text{Remove the parentheses.}$$

$$5600 = 8L \quad \text{Combine like terms.}$$

$$\frac{5600}{8} = \frac{8L}{8} \quad \text{Divide each side by 8.}$$

$$700 = L$$

Since 20% of \$700 is \$140 and \$700 − \$140 = \$560, we can be sure that the original price was \$700. Note that if the discount is 20%, then the selling price is 80% of the list price. So we could have started with the equation $560 = 0.80L$.

Now do Exercises 81–86

Warm-Ups ▼

True or false? Explain your answer.

1. If we solve $D = R \cdot T$ for T, we get $T \cdot R = D$. False
2. If we solve $a - b = 3a - m$ for a, we get $a = 3a - m + b$. False
3. Solving $A = LW$ for L, we get $L = \frac{W}{A}$. False
4. Solving $D = RT$ for R, we get $R = \frac{d}{t}$. False
5. The perimeter of a rectangle is the product of its length and width. False
6. The volume of a shoe box is the product of its length, width, and height. True
7. The sum of the length and width of a rectangle is one-half of its perimeter. True
8. Solving $y - x = 5$ for y gives us $y = x + 5$. True
9. If $x = -1$ and $y = -3x + 6$, then $y = 3$. False
10. The circumference of a circle is the product of its diameter and the number π. True

2.4 Exercises

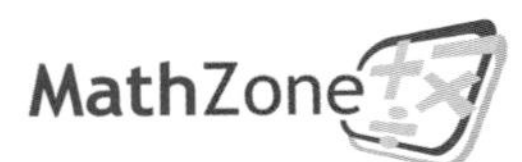

Boost your grade at mathzone.com!
- Practice Problems
- NetTutor
- Self-Tests
- e-Professors
- Videos

‹ Study Tips ›

- When studying for an exam, start by working the exercises in the Chapter Review. They are grouped by section so that you can go back and review any topics that you have trouble with.
- Never leave an exam early. Most papers turned in early contain careless errors that could be found and corrected. Every point counts.

Reading and Writing *After reading this section, write out the answers to these questions. Use complete sentences.*

1. What is a formula?
A formula is an equation with two or more variables.

2. What is a literal equation?
A literal equation is a formula.

3. What does it mean to solve a formula for a certain variable?
To solve for a variable means to find an equivalent equation in which the variable is isolated.

4. How do you solve a formula for a variable that appears on both sides?
If the variable appears on both sides, then get all terms with the variable onto the same side. Then combine like terms to get one occurrence of the variable.

5. What are the two methods shown for finding the value of a variable in a formula?
To find the value of a variable in a formula, we can solve for the variable and then insert values for the other variables, or insert values for the other variables and then solve for the variable.

6. What formula expresses the perimeter of a rectangle in terms of its length and width? The formula for the perimeter of a rectangle is $P = 2L + 2W$.

‹1› Solving for a Variable

Solve each formula for the specified variable. See Examples 1 and 2.

7. $D = RT$ for R $\quad R = \frac{D}{T}$

8. $A = LW$ for W $\quad W = \frac{A}{L}$

9. $C = \pi D$ for D $\quad D = \frac{C}{\pi}$

10. $F = ma$ for a $\quad a = \frac{F}{m}$

11. $I = Prt$ for P $\quad P = \frac{I}{rt}$

VIDEO **12.** $I = Prt$ for t $\quad t = \frac{I}{Pr}$

13. $F = \frac{9}{5}C + 32$ for C $\quad C = \frac{5}{9}(F - 32)$

14. $y = \frac{3}{4}x - 7$ for x $\quad x = \frac{4y + 28}{3}$

15. $A = \frac{1}{2}bh$ for h $\quad h = \frac{2A}{b}$

16. $A = \frac{1}{2}bh$ for b $\quad b = \frac{2A}{h}$

17. $P = 2L + 2W$ for L $\quad L = \frac{P - 2W}{2}$

VIDEO **18.** $P = 2L + 2W$ for W $\quad W = \frac{P - 2L}{2}$

19. $A = \frac{1}{2}(a + b)$ for a $\quad a = 2A - b$

20. $A = \frac{1}{2}(a + b)$ for b $\quad b = 2A - a$

21. $S = P + Prt$ for r $\quad r = \frac{S - P}{Pt}$

22. $S = P + Prt$ for t $\quad t = \frac{S - P}{Pr}$

23. $A = \frac{1}{2}h(a + b)$ for a $\quad a = \frac{2A - bh}{h}$

24. $A = \frac{1}{2}h(a + b)$ for b $\quad b = \frac{2A - ah}{h}$

Solve each equation for x. See Example 3.

25. $5x + a = 3x + b$ $\quad x = \frac{b - a}{2}$

26. $2c - x = 4x + c - 5b$ $\quad x = \frac{c + 5b}{5}$

27. $4(a + x) - 3(x - a) = 0$ $\quad x = -7a$

28. $-2(x - b) - (5a - x) = a + b$ $\quad x = b - 6a$

29. $3x - 2(a - 3) = 4x - 6 - a$ $\quad x = 12 - a$

30. $2(x - 3w) = -3(x + w)$ $\quad x = \frac{3w}{5}$

31. $3x + 2ab = 4x - 5ab$ $\quad x = 7ab$

32. $x - a = -x + a + 4b$ $\quad x = a + 2b$

Solve each equation for y. See Examples 4 and 5.

33. $x + y = -9$ $\quad y = -x - 9$

34. $3x + y = -5$ $\quad y = -3x - 5$

35. $x + y - 6 = 0$ $\quad y = -x + 6$

36. $4x + y - 2 = 0$ $\quad y = -4x + 2$

37. $2x - y = 2$ $\quad y = 2x - 2$

38. $x - y = -3$ $\quad y = x + 3$

39. $3x - y + 4 = 0$ $\quad y = 3x + 4$

40. $-2x - y + 5 = 0$ $\quad y = -2x + 5$

41. $x + 2y = 4$ $\quad y = -\frac{1}{2}x + 2$

VIDEO **42.** $3x + 2y = 6$ $\quad y = -\frac{3}{2}x + 3$

43. $2x - 2y = 1$ $\quad y = x - \frac{1}{2}$

44. $3x - 2y = -6$ $y = \frac{3}{2}x + 3$

45. $y + 2 = 3(x - 4)$ $y = 3x - 14$

46. $y - 3 = -3(x - 1)$ $y = -3x + 6$

47. $y - 1 = \frac{1}{2}(x - 2)$ $y = \frac{1}{2}x$

48. $y - 4 = -\frac{2}{3}(x - 9)$ $y = -\frac{2}{3}x + 10$

49. $\frac{1}{2}x - \frac{1}{3}y = -2$ $y = \frac{3}{2}x + 6$

50. $\frac{x}{2} + \frac{y}{4} = \frac{1}{2}$ $y = -2x + 2$

51. $y - 2 = \frac{3}{2}(x + 3)$ $y = \frac{3}{2}x + \frac{13}{2}$

52. $y + 4 = \frac{2}{3}(x - 2)$ $y = \frac{2}{3}x - \frac{16}{3}$

53. $y - \frac{1}{2} = -\frac{1}{4}\left(x - \frac{1}{2}\right)$ $y = -\frac{1}{4}x + \frac{5}{8}$

54. $y + \frac{1}{2} = -\frac{1}{3}\left(x + \frac{1}{2}\right)$ $y = -\frac{1}{3}x - \frac{2}{3}$

‹2› Finding the Value of a Variable

For each equation that follows, find y given that x = 2. See Example 6.

55. $y = 3x - 4$ 2

56. $y = -2x + 5$ 1

57. $3x - 2y = -8$ 7

58. $4x + 6y = 8$ 0

59. $\frac{3x}{2} - \frac{5y}{3} = 6$ $-\frac{9}{5}$

60. $\frac{2y}{5} - \frac{3x}{4} = \frac{1}{2}$ 5

61. $y - 3 = \frac{1}{2}(x - 6)$ 1

62. $y - 6 = -\frac{3}{4}(x - 2)$ 6

63. $y - 4.3 = 0.45(x - 8.6)$ 1.33

64. $y + 33.7 = 0.78(x - 45.6)$ -67.708

Fill in the tables using the given formulas.

65. $y = -3x + 30$

x	y
−10	60
0	30
10	0
20	−30
30	−60

66. $y = 4x - 20$

x	y
−10	−60
−5	−40
0	−20
5	0
10	20

67. $F = \frac{9}{5}C + 32$

C	F
−10	14
−5	23
0	32
40	104
100	212

68. $C = \frac{5}{9}(F - 32)$

F	C
−40	−40
14	−10
32	0
59	15
86	30

69. $T = \frac{400}{R}$

R (mph)	T (hr)
10	40
20	20
40	10
80	5
100	4

70. $R = \frac{100}{T}$

T (hr)	R (mph)
1	100
5	20
20	5
50	2
100	1

71. $S = \frac{n(n+1)}{2}$

n	S
1	1
2	3
3	6
4	10
5	15

72. $S = \frac{n(n+1)(2n+1)}{6}$

n	S
1	1
2	5
3	14
4	30
5	55

‹3› Applications

Solve each of the following problems. Some geometric formulas that may be helpful can be found inside the front cover of this text. See Examples 7–9.

73. ***Finding the rate.*** A loan of $5000 is made for 3 years. Find the interest rate for simple interest amounts of $600, $700, and $800.   4%, $4\frac{2}{3}$%, $5\frac{1}{3}$%

74. ***Finding the rate.*** A loan of $1000 is made for 7 years. Find the interest rate for simple interest amounts of $420, $455, and $472.50.   6%, 6.5%, 6.75%

75. ***Finding the time.*** Kathy paid $500 in simple interest on a loan of $2500. If the annual interest rate was 5%, then what was the time?   4 years

76. ***Finding the time.*** Robert paid $240 in simple interest on a loan of $1000. If the annual interest rate was 8%, then what was the time?   3 years

77. ***Finding the length.*** The area of a rectangle is 28 square yards. Find the length if the width is 2 yards, 3 yards, or 4 yards.   14 yards, $9\frac{1}{3}$ yards, 7 yards

78. ***Finding the width.*** The area of a rectangle is 60 square feet. Find the width if the length is 10 feet, 16 feet, or 18 feet.   6 feet, 3.75 feet, $3\frac{1}{3}$ feet

79. ***Finding the length.*** If it takes 600 feet of wire fencing to fence a rectangular feed lot that has a width of 75 feet, then what is the length of the lot?   225 feet

80. ***Finding the depth.*** If it takes 500 feet of fencing to enclose a rectangular lot that is 104 feet wide, then how deep is the lot?   146 feet

81. ***Finding MSRP.*** What was the manufacturer's suggested retail price (MSRP) for a Lexus SC 430 that sold for \$54,450 after a 10% discount? \$60,500

82. ***Finding MSRP.*** What was the MSRP for a Hummer H1 that sold for \$107,272 after an 8% discount? \$116,600

83. ***Finding the original price.*** Find the original price if there is a 15% discount and the sale price is \$255. \$300

84. ***Finding the list price.*** Find the list price if there is a 12% discount and the sale price is \$4400. \$5000

85. ***Rate of discount.*** Find the rate of discount if the discount is \$40 and the original price is \$200. 20%

86. ***Rate of discount.*** Find the rate of discount if the discount is \$20 and the original price is \$250. 8%

87. ***Width of a football field.*** The perimeter of a football field in the NFL, excluding the end zones, is 920 feet. How wide is the field? 160 feet

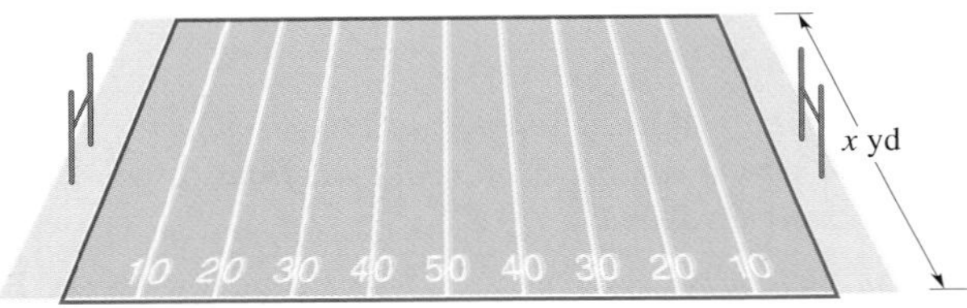

Figure for Exercise 87

88. ***Perimeter of a frame.*** If a picture frame is 16 inches by 20 inches, then what is its perimeter? 72 inches

89. ***Volume of a box.*** A rectangular box measures 2 feet wide, 3 feet long, and 4 feet deep. What is its volume? 24 cubic feet

90. ***Volume of a refrigerator.*** The volume of a rectangular refrigerator is 20 cubic feet. If the top measures 2 feet by 2.5 feet, then what is the height? 4 feet

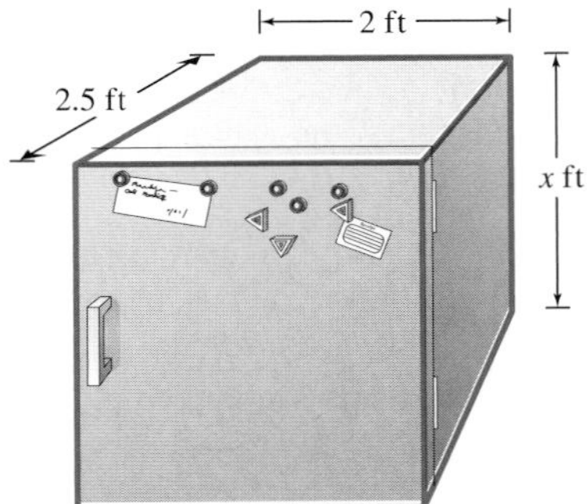

Figure for Exercise 90

91. ***Radius of a pizza.*** If the circumference of a pizza is 8π inches, then what is the radius? 4 inches

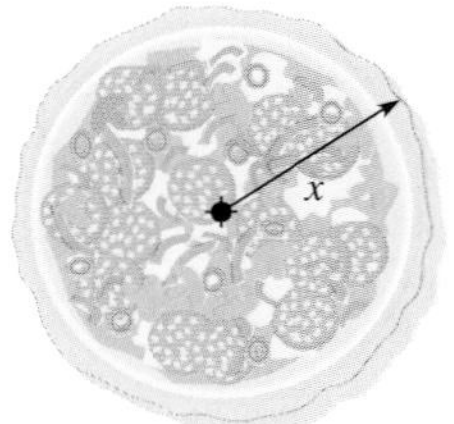

Figure for Exercise 91

92. ***Diameter of a circle.*** If the circumference of a circle is 4π meters, then what is the diameter? 4 meters

93. ***Height of a banner.*** If a banner in the shape of a triangle has an area of 16 square feet with a base of 4 feet, then what is the height of the banner? 8 feet

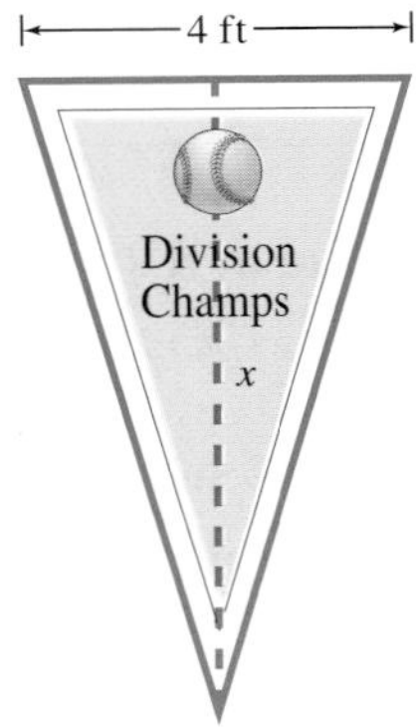

Figure for Exercise 93

94. ***Length of a leg.*** If a right triangle has an area of 14 square meters and one leg is 4 meters in length, then what is the length of the other leg? 7 meters

95. ***Length of the base.*** A trapezoid with height 20 inches and lower base 8 inches has an area of 200 square inches. What is the length of its upper base? 12 inches

96. ***Height of a trapezoid.*** The end of a flower box forms the shape of a trapezoid. The area of the trapezoid is 300 square

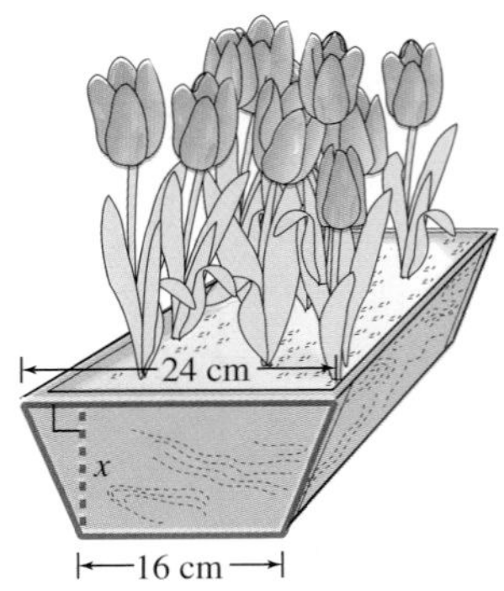

Figure for Exercise 96

centimeters. The bases are 16 centimeters and 24 centimeters in length. Find the height. 15 centimeters

97. ***Fried's rule.*** Doctors often prescribe the same drugs for children as they do for adults. The formula $d = 0.08aD$ (Fried's rule) is used to calculate the child's dosage d, where a is the child's age and D is the adult dosage. If a doctor prescribes 1000 milligrams of acetaminophen for an adult, then how many milligrams would the doctor prescribe for an eight-year-old child? Use the bar graph to determine the age at which a child would get the same dosage as an adult. 640 milligrams, age 13

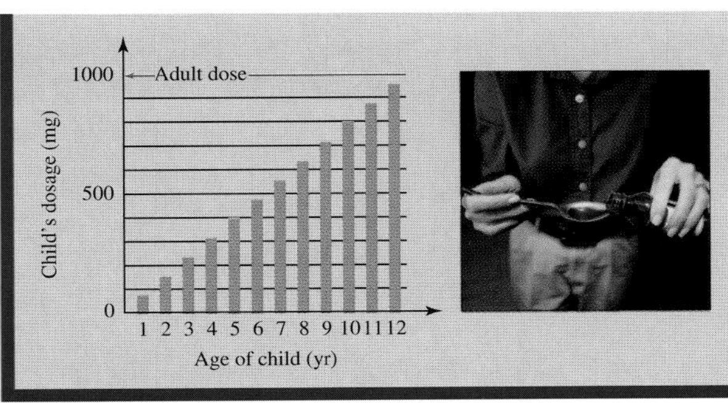

Figure for Exercise 97

98. ***Cowling's rule.*** Cowling's rule is another method for determining the dosage of a drug to prescribe to a child. For this rule, the formula

$$d = \frac{D(a + 1)}{24}$$

gives the child's dosage d, where D is the adult dosage and a is the age of the child in years. If the adult dosage of a drug is 600 milligrams and a doctor uses this formula to determine that a child's dosage is 200 milligrams, then how old is the child? Age 7

99. ***Administering vancomycin.*** A patient is to receive 750 mg of the antibiotic vancomycin. However, vancomycin comes in a solution containing 1 gram (available dose) of vancomycin per 5 milliliters (quantity) of solution. Use the formula

$$\text{Amount} = \frac{\text{desired dose}}{\text{available dose}} \times \text{quantity}$$

to find the amount of this solution that should be administered to the patient. 3.75 milliliters

100. ***International communications.*** The global investment in telecom infrastructure since 1990 can be modeled by the formula

$$I = 7.5t + 115,$$

where I is in billions of dollars and t is the number of years since 1990 (*Fortune,* www.fortune.com).

a) Use the formula to find the global investment in 2000. $190 billion

b) Use the accompanying graph to estimate the year in which the global investment will reach $250 billion. 2008

c) Use the formula to find the year in which the global investment will reach $250 billion. 2008

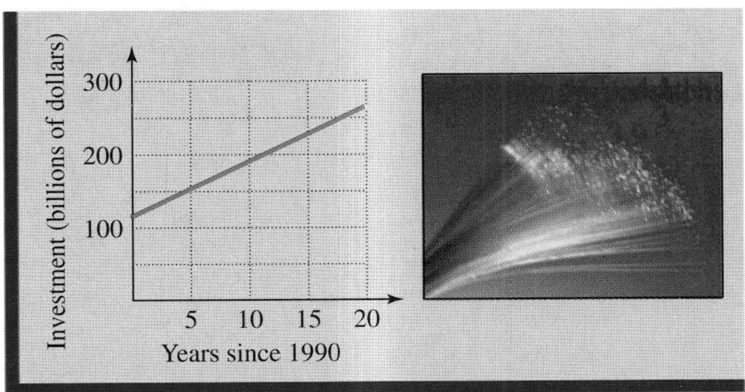

Figure for Exercise 100

101. ***The 2.4-meter rule.*** A 2.4-meter sailboat is a one-person boat that is about 13 feet in length, has a displacement of about 550 pounds, and a sail area of about 81 square feet. To compete in the 2.4-meter class, a boat must satisfy the formula

$$2.4 = \frac{L + 2D - F\sqrt{S}}{2.37},$$

where L = length, F = freeboard, D = girth, and S = sail area. Solve the formula for L. $L = F\sqrt{S} - 2D + 5.688$

Photo for Exercise 101

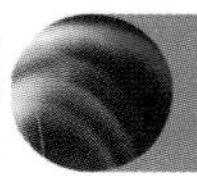

2.5 Translating Verbal Expressions into Algebraic Expressions

In This Section

You translated some verbal expressions into algebraic expressions in Section 1.6; in this section you will study translating in more detail.

⟨1⟩ Writing Algebraic Expressions

The following box contains a list of some frequently occurring verbal expressions and their equivalent algebraic expressions.

⟨ Teaching Tip ⟩

Note that, in common usage, difference can mean subtract in either order. A difference in ages is always given as a positive number no matter who is mentioned first.

Translating Words into Algebra

	Verbal Phrase	Algebraic Expression
Addition:	The sum of a number and 8	$x + 8$
	Five is added to a number	$x + 5$
	Two more than a number	$x + 2$
	A number increased by 3	$x + 3$
Subtraction:	Four is subtracted from a number	$x - 4$
	Three less than a number	$x - 3$
	The difference between 7 and a number	$7 - x$
	A number decreased by 2	$x - 2$
Multiplication:	The product of 5 and a number	$5x$
	Twice a number	$2x$
	One-half of a number	$\frac{1}{2}x$
	Five percent of a number	$0.05x$
Division:	The ratio of a number to 6	$\frac{x}{6}$
	The quotient of 5 and a number	$\frac{5}{x}$
	Three divided by some number	$\frac{3}{x}$

EXAMPLE 1

Writing algebraic expressions

Translate each verbal expression into an algebraic expression.

a) The sum of a number and 9

b) Eighty percent of a number

c) A number divided by 4

d) The result of a number subtracted from 5

e) Three less than a number

Solution

a) If x is the number, then the sum of x and 9 is $x + 9$.

b) If w is the number, then eighty percent of the number is $0.80w$.

c) If y is the number, then the number divided by 4 is $\frac{y}{4}$.

d) If z is the number, then the result of subtracting z from 5 is $5 - z$.

e) If a is the number, then 3 less than a is $a - 3$.

Now do Exercises 7–18

‹ Helpful Hint ›

We know that x and $10 - x$ have a sum of 10 for any value of x. We can easily check that fact by adding:

$$x + 10 - x = 10$$

In general it is not true that x and $x - 10$ have a sum of 10, because

$$x + x - 10 = 2x - 10.$$

For what value of x is the sum of x and $x - 10$ equal to 10?

‹2› Pairs of Numbers

There is often more than one unknown quantity in a problem, but a relationship between the unknown quantities is given. For example, if one unknown number is 5 more than another unknown number, we can use x to represent the smaller one and $x + 5$ to represent the larger one. If we use x to represent the larger unknown number, then $x - 5$ represents the smaller. Either way is correct.

If two numbers differ by 5, then one of them is 5 more than the other. So x and $x + 5$ can also be used to represent two numbers that differ by 5. Likewise, x and $x - 5$ could represent two numbers that differ by 5.

How would you represent two numbers that have a sum of 10? If one of the numbers is 2, the other is certainly $10 - 2$, or 8. Thus, if x is one of the numbers, then $10 - x$ is the other. The expressions

$$x \quad \text{and} \quad 10 - x$$

have a sum of 10 for any value of x.

EXAMPLE 2

Algebraic expressions for pairs of numbers

Write algebraic expressions for each pair of numbers.

a) Two numbers that differ by 12

b) Two numbers with a sum of -8

Solution

a) The expressions x and $x - 12$ represent two numbers that differ by 12. We can check by subtracting:

$$x - (x - 12) = x - x + 12 = 12$$

Of course, x and $x + 12$ also differ by 12 because $x + 12 - x = 12$.

b) The expressions x and $-8 - x$ have a sum of -8. We can check by addition:

$$x + (-8 - x) = x - 8 - x = -8$$

Now do Exercises 19–28

Pairs of numbers occur in geometry in discussing measures of angles. You will need the following facts about degree measures of angles.

‹ Teaching Tip ›

Some students might not be familiar with degree measures. You might have to review this topic.

Degree Measures of Angles

Two angles are called **complementary** if the sum of their degree measures is 90°.

Two angles are called **supplementary** if the sum of their degree measures is 180°.

The sum of the degree measures of the three angles of any triangle is 180°.

For complementary angles, we use x and $90 - x$ for their degree measures. For supplementary angles, we use x and $180 - x$. Complementary angles that share a common side form a right angle. Supplementary angles that share a common side form a straight angle or straight line.

EXAMPLE 3

Degree measures

Write algebraic expressions for each pair of angles shown.

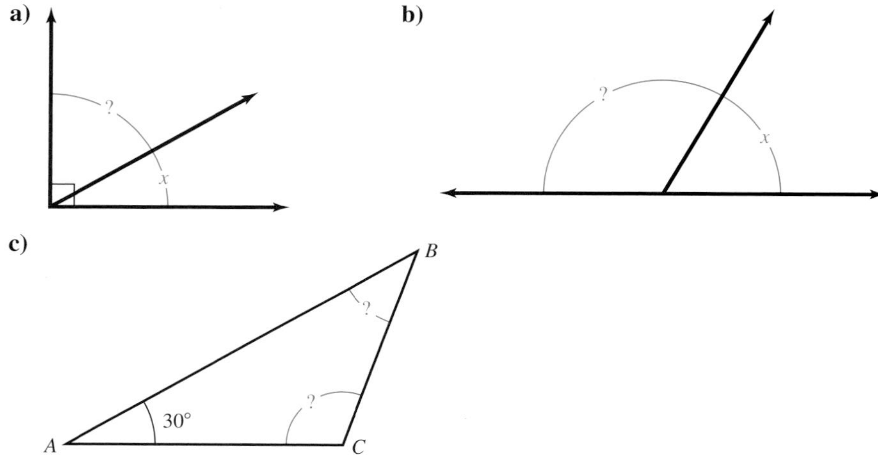

Solution

a) Since the angles shown are complementary, we can use x to represent the degree measure of the smaller angle and $90 - x$ to represent the degree measure of the larger angle.

b) Since the angles shown are supplementary, we can use x to represent the degree measure of the smaller angle and $180 - x$ to represent the degree measure of the larger angle.

c) If we let x represent the degree measure of angle B, then $180 - x - 30$, or $150 - x$, represents the degree measure of angle C.

Now do Exercises 29–32

‹3› Consecutive Integers

Note that each integer is one larger than the previous integer. For example, if $x = 5$, then $x + 1 = 6$ and $x + 2 = 7$. So if x is an integer, then x, $x + 1$, and $x + 2$ represent three consecutive integers. Each even (or odd) integer is two larger than the previous even (or odd) integer. For example, if $x = 6$, then $x + 2 = 8$, and $x + 4 = 10$. If $x = 7$, then $x + 2 = 9$, and $x + 4 = 11$. So x, $x + 2$, and $x + 4$ represent three consecutive even integers if x is even and three consecutive odd integers if x is odd.

CAUTION The expressions x, $x + 1$, and $x + 3$ do not represent three consecutive odd integers no matter what x represents.

EXAMPLE 4

Expressions for integers

Write algebraic expressions for the following unknown integers.

a) Two consecutive integers, the smallest of which is w.

b) Three consecutive even integers, the smallest of which is z.

c) Four consecutive odd integers, the smallest of which is y.

‹ Teaching Tip ›

Integer problems are relatively easy and should build student confidence.

Solution

a) Each integer is 1 larger than the preceding integer. So if w represents the smallest of two consecutive integers, then w and $w + 1$ represent the integers.

b) Each even integer is 2 larger than the preceding even integer. So if z represents the smallest of three consecutive even integers, then z, $z + 2$, and $z + 4$ represent the three consecutive even integers.

c) Each odd integer is 2 larger than the preceding odd integer. So if y represents the smallest of four consecutive odd integers, then y, $y + 2$, $y + 4$, and $y + 6$ represent the four consecutive odd integers.

Now do Exercises 33–40

The following box contains a summary of some common verbal phrases and algebraic expressions for pairs of numbers.

Summary of Algebraic Expressions for Pairs of Numbers

Verbal Phrase	Algebraic Expressions
Two numbers that differ by 5	x and $x + 5$
Two numbers with a sum of 6	x and $6 - x$
Two consecutive integers	x and $x + 1$
Two consecutive even integers	x and $x + 2$
Two consecutive odd integers	x and $x + 2$
Complementary angles	x and $90 - x$
Supplementary angles	x and $180 - x$

‹4› Using Formulas

In writing expressions for unknown quantities, we often use standard formulas such as those given inside the front cover of this book.

EXAMPLE 5

Writing algebraic expressions using standard formulas

Find an algebraic expression for

a) the distance if the rate is 30 miles per hour and the time is T hours.

b) the discount if the rate is 40% and the original price is p dollars.

Solution

a) Using the formula $D = RT$, we have $D = 30T$. So $30T$ is an expression that represents the distance in miles.

b) Since the discount is the rate times the original price, an algebraic expression for the discount is $0.40p$ dollars.

Now do Exercises 41–64

⟨5⟩ Writing Equations

To solve a problem using algebra, we describe or **model** the problem with an equation. In this section we write the equations only, and in Section 2.6 we write and solve them. Sometimes we must write an equation from the information given in the problem and sometimes we use a standard model to get the equation. Some standard models are shown in the following box.

Uniform Motion Model

Distance = Rate · Time $\quad D = R \cdot T$

Percentage Models

What number is 5% of 40? $\quad x = 0.05 \cdot 40$
Ten is what percent of 80? $\quad 10 = x \cdot 80$
Twenty is 4% of what number? $\quad 20 = 0.04 \cdot x$

Selling Price and Discount Model

Discount = Rate of discount · Original price $\quad d = r \cdot L$
Selling Price = Original price − Discount $\quad S = L - r \cdot L$

Real Estate Commission Model

Commission = Rate of commission · Selling price
Amount for owner = Selling price − Commission

Geometric Models for Perimeter

Perimeter of any figure = the sum of the lengths of the sides
Rectangle: $P = 2L + 2W$ $\quad$ Square: $P = 4s$

Geometric Models for Area

Rectangle: $A = LW$ $\quad$ Square: $A = s^2$
Parallelogram: $A = bh$ $\quad$ Triangle: $A = \frac{1}{2}bh$
More geometric formulas can be found inside the front cover of this text.

EXAMPLE 6

Writing equations

Identify the variable and write an equation that describes each situation.

a) Find two numbers that have a sum of 14 and a product of 45.

b) A coat is on sale for 25% off the list price. If the sale price is \$87, then what is the list price?

c) What percent of 8 is 2?

d) The value of x dimes and $x - 3$ quarters is \$2.05.

‹ Helpful Hint ›

At this point we are simply learning to write equations that model certain situations. Don't worry about solving these equations now. In Section 2.6 we will solve problems by writing an equation and solving it.

Solution

a) Let x = one of the numbers and $14 - x$ = the other number. Since their product is 45, we have

$$x(14 - x) = 45.$$

b) Let x = the list price and $0.25x$ = the amount of discount. We can write an equation expressing the fact that the selling price is the list price minus the discount:

$$\text{List price} - \text{discount} = \text{selling price}$$
$$x - 0.25x = 87$$

c) If we let x represent the percentage, then the equation is $x \cdot 8 = 2$, or $8x = 2$.

d) The value of x dimes at 10 cents each is $10x$ cents. The value of $x - 3$ quarters at 25 cents each is $25(x - 3)$ cents. We can write an equation expressing the fact that the total value of the coins is 205 cents:

$$\text{Value of dimes} + \text{value of quarters} = \text{total value}$$
$$10x + 25(x - 3) = 205$$

Now do Exercises 65–90

CAUTION The value of the coins in Example 6(d) is either 205 cents or 2.05 dollars. If the total value is expressed in dollars, then all of the values must be expressed in dollars. So we could also write the equation as

$$0.10x + 0.25(x - 3) = 2.05.$$

Warm-Ups 

True or false? Explain your answer.

1. For any value of x, the numbers x and $x + 6$ differ by 6. True
2. For any value of a, a and $10 - a$ have a sum of 10. True
3. If Jack ran at x miles per hour for 3 hours, he ran $3x$ miles. True
4. If Jill ran at x miles per hour for 10 miles, she ran for $10x$ hours. False
5. If the realtor gets 6% of the selling price and the house sells for x dollars, the owner gets $x - 0.06x$ dollars. True
6. If the owner got \$50,000 and the realtor got 10% of the selling price, the house sold for \$55,000. False
7. Three consecutive odd integers can be represented by x, $x + 1$, and $x + 3$. False
8. The value in cents of n nickels and d dimes is $0.05n + 0.10d$. False
9. If the sales tax rate is 5% and x represents the price of the goods purchased, then the total bill is $1.05x$. True
10. If the length of a rectangle is 4 feet more than the width w, then the perimeter is $w + (w + 4)$ feet. False

Exercises

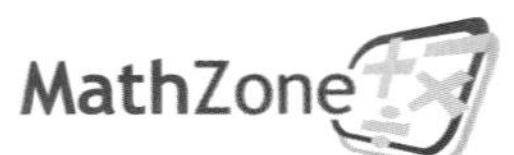

Boost your grade at mathzone.com!

- Practice Problems
- NetTutor
- Self-Tests
- e-Professors
- Videos

‹ Study Tips ›

- Almost everything that we do in algebra can be redone by another method or checked. So don't close your mind to a new method or checking. The answers will not always be in the back of the book.
- When you take a test, work the problems that are easiest for you first. This will build your confidence. Make sure that you do not forget to answer a question.

Reading and Writing *After reading this section, write out the answers to these questions. Use complete sentences.*

1. What are the different ways of verbally expressing the operation of addition? To express addition we use words such as plus, sum, increased by, and more than.

2. How can you algebraically express two numbers using only one variable? We can algebraically express two numbers using one variable provided the numbers are related in some known way.

3. What are complementary angles? Complementary angles have degree measures with a sum of 90°.

4. What are supplementary angles? Supplementary angles have degree measures with a sum of 180°.

5. What is the relationship between distance, rate, and time? Distance is the product of rate and time.

6. What is the difference between expressing consecutive even integers and consecutive odd integers algebraically? If x is an even integer, then x and $x + 2$ represent consecutive even integers. If x is an odd integer, then x and $x + 2$ represent consecutive odd integers.

‹1› Writing Algebraic Expressions

Translate each verbal expression into an algebraic expression. See Example 1.

See Translating Words into Algebra box on page 120.

7. The sum of a number and 3 $x + 3$

8. Two more than a number $x + 2$

9. Three less than a number $x - 3$

10. Four subtracted from a number $x - 4$

11. The product of a number and 5 $5x$

12. Five divided by some number $\frac{5}{x}$

13. Ten percent of a number $0.1x$

14. Eight percent of a number $0.08x$

15. The ratio of a number and 3 $\frac{x}{3}$

16. The quotient of 12 and a number $\frac{12}{x}$

17. One-third of a number $\frac{1}{3}x$

18. Three-fourths of a number $\frac{3}{4}x$

‹2› Pairs of Numbers

Write algebraic expressions for each pair of numbers. See Example 2.

19. Two numbers with a difference of 15 x and $x + 15$

20. Two numbers that differ by 9 x and $x + 9$

21. Two numbers with a sum of 6 x and $6 - x$

22. Two numbers with a sum of 5 x and $5 - x$

VIDEO **23.** Two numbers such that one is 3 larger than the other x and $x + 3$

24. Two numbers such that one is 8 smaller than the other x and $x + 8$

25. Two numbers such that one is 5% of the other x and $0.05x$

26. Two numbers such that one is 40% of the other x and $0.4x$

27. Two numbers such that one is 30% more than the other x and $1.30x$

28. Two numbers such that one is 20% smaller than the other x and $0.80x$

Each of the following figures shows a pair of angles. Write algebraic expressions for the degree measures of each pair of angles. See Example 3.

29.

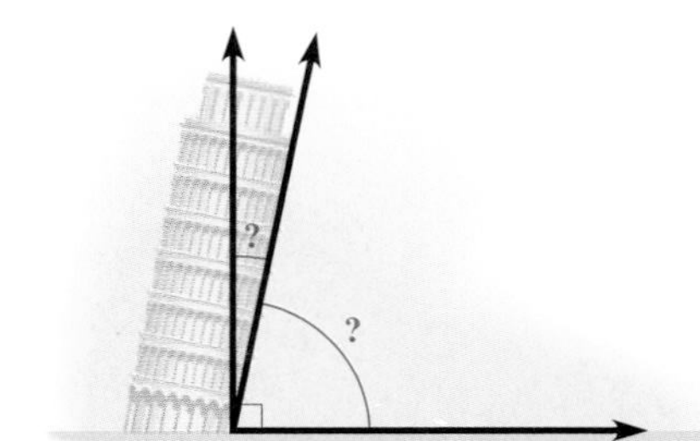

Figure for Exercise 29

x and $90 - x$

30.

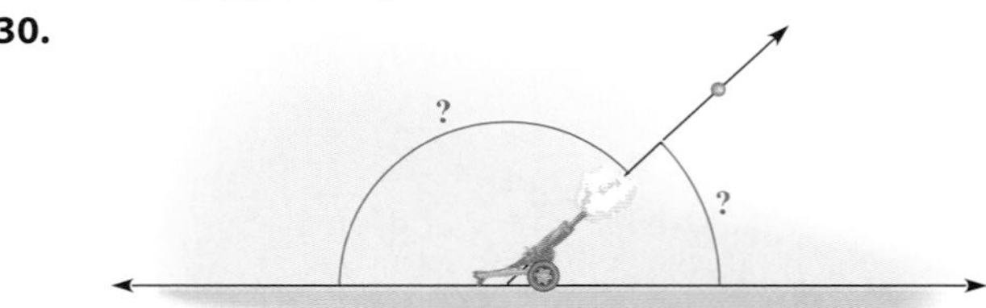

Figure for Exercise 30

x and $180 - x$

31.

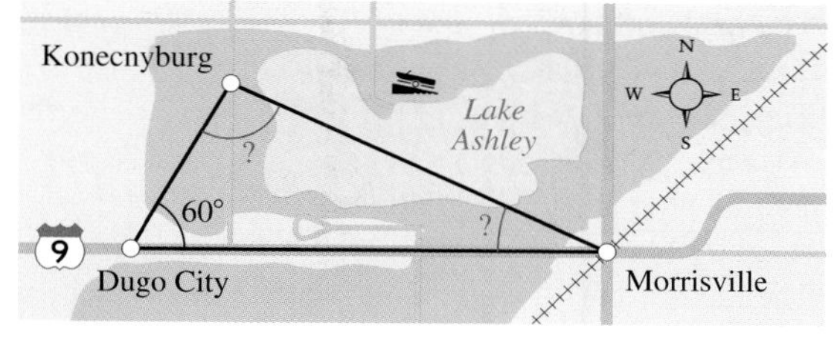

Figure for Exercise 31

x and $120 - x$

32.

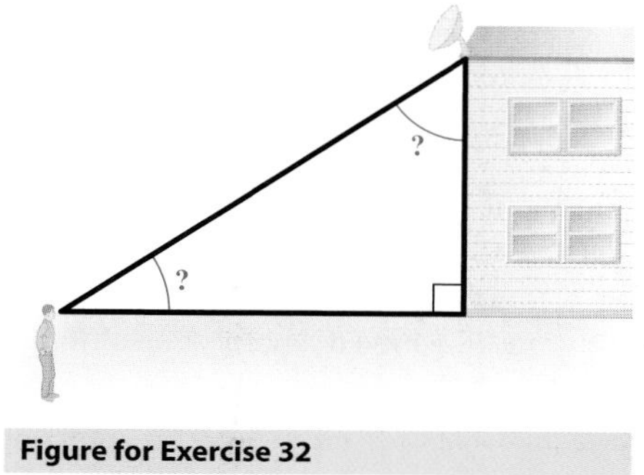

Figure for Exercise 32

x and $90 - x$

⟨3⟩ Consecutive Integers

Write algebraic expressions for the following unknown integers. See Example 4.

33. Two consecutive even integers, the smallest of which is n n and $n + 2$, where n is an even integer

34. Two consecutive odd integers, the smallest of which is x x and $x + 2$, where x is an odd integer

VIDEO **35.** Two consecutive integers x and $x + 1$, where x is an integer

36. Three consecutive even integers x, $x + 2$, and $x + 4$, where x is an even integer

37. Three consecutive odd integers x, $x + 2$, and $x + 4$, where x is an odd integer

38. Three consecutive integers x, $x + 1$, and $x + 2$, where x is an integer

39. Four consecutive even integers x, $x + 2$, $x + 4$, and $x + 6$, where x is an even integer

40. Four consecutive odd integers x, $x + 2$, $x + 4$, and $x + 6$, where x is an odd integer

⟨4⟩ Using Formulas

Find an algebraic expression for the quantity in italics using the given information. See Example 5.

41. The *distance,* given that the rate is x miles per hour and the time is 3 hours $3x$ miles

42. The *distance,* given that the rate is $x + 10$ miles per hour and the time is 5 hours $5x + 50$ miles

43. The *discount,* given that the rate is 25% and the original price is q dollars $0.25q$ dollars

44. The *discount,* given that the rate is 10% and the original price is t yen $0.10t$ yen

VIDEO **45.** The *time,* given that the distance is x miles and the rate is 20 miles per hour $\frac{x}{20}$ hour

46. The *time,* given that the distance is 300 kilometers and the rate is $x + 30$ kilometers per hour $\frac{300}{x + 30}$ hour

47. The *rate,* given that the distance is $x - 100$ meters and the time is 12 seconds $\frac{x - 100}{12}$ meters per second

48. The *rate,* given that the distance is 200 feet and the time is $x + 3$ seconds $\frac{200}{x + 3}$ feet per second

49. The *area* of a rectangle with length x meters and width 5 meters $5x$ square meters

50. The *area* of a rectangle with sides b yards and $b - 6$ yards $b(b - 6)$ square yards

51. The *perimeter* of a rectangle with length $w + 3$ inches and width w inches $2w + 2(w + 3)$ inches

52. The *perimeter* of a rectangle with length r centimeters and width $r - 1$ centimeters $2r + 2(r - 1)$ centimeters

53. The *width* of a rectangle with perimeter 300 feet and length x feet $150 - x$ feet

54. The *length* of a rectangle with area 200 square feet and width w feet $\frac{200}{w}$ feet

VIDEO **55.** The *length* of a rectangle, given that its width is x feet and its length is 1 foot longer than twice the width $2x + 1$ feet

56. The *length* of a rectangle, given that its width is w feet and its length is 3 feet shorter than twice the width $2w - 3$ feet

57. The *area* of a rectangle, given that the width is x meters and the length is 5 meters longer than the width $x(x + 5)$ square meters

58. The *perimeter* of a rectangle, given that the length is x yards and the width is 10 yards shorter $2(x) + 2(x - 10)$ yards

59. The *simple interest,* given that the principal is $x + 1000$, the rate is 18%, and the time is 1 year $0.18(x + 1000)$

60. The *simple interest,* given that the principal is $3x$, the rate is 6%, and the time is 1 year $0.06(3x)$

61. The *price per pound* of peaches, given that x pounds sold for \$16.50 $\frac{16.50}{x}$ dollars per pound

62. The *rate per hour* of a mechanic who gets \$480 for working x hours $\frac{480}{x}$ dollars per hour

63. The *degree measure* of an angle, given that its complementary angle has measure x degrees $90 - x$ degrees

64. The *degree measure* of an angle, given that its supplementary angle has measure x degrees $180 - x$ degrees

⟨5⟩ Writing Equations

Identify the variable and write an equation that describes each situation. Do not solve the equation. See Example 6.

65. Two numbers differ by 5 and have a product of 8.
x is the smaller number, $x(x + 5) = 8$

66. Two numbers differ by 6 and have a product of -9.
x is the smaller number, $x(x + 6) = -9$

67. Herman's house sold for x dollars. The real estate agent received 7% of the selling price and Herman received $84,532.
x is the selling price, $x - 0.07x = 84{,}532$

68. Gwen sold her car on consignment for x dollars. The saleswoman's commission was 10% of the selling price and Gwen received $6570.
x is the selling price, $x - 0.10x = 6570$

69. What percent of 500 is 100?
x is the percent, $500x = 100$

70. What percent of 40 is 120?
x is the percent, $40x = 120$

71. The value of x nickels and $x + 2$ dimes is $3.80.
x is the number of nickels, $0.05x + 0.10(x + 2) = 3.80$

VIDEO **72.** The value of d dimes and $d - 3$ quarters is $6.75.
d is the number of dimes, $0.10d + 0.25(d - 3) = 6.75$

73. The sum of a number and 5 is 13.
x is the number, $x + 5 = 13$

74. Twelve subtracted from a number is -6.
x is the number, $x - 12 = -6$

75. The sum of three consecutive integers is 42.
x is the smallest integer, $x + (x + 1) + (x + 2) = 42$

76. The sum of three consecutive odd integers is 27.
x is the smallest odd integer, $x + x + 2 + x + 4 = 27$

77. The product of two consecutive integers is 182.
x is the smaller integer, $x(x + 1) = 182$

78. The product of two consecutive even integers is 168.
x is the smaller even integer, $x(x + 2) = 168$

79. Twelve percent of Harriet's income is $3000.
x is Harriet's income, $0.12x = 3000$

80. If 9% of the members buy tickets, then we will sell 252 tickets to this group.
x is the number of members, $0.09x = 252$

81. Thirteen is 5% of what number?
x is the number, $0.05x = 13$

82. Three hundred is 8% of what number?
x is the number, $0.08x = 300$

83. The length of a rectangle is 5 feet longer than the width, and the area is 126 square feet.
x is the width, $x(x + 5) = 126$

84. The length of a rectangle is 1 yard shorter than twice the width, and the perimeter is 298 yards.
x is the width, $2x + 2(2x - 1) = 298$

85. The value of n nickels and $n - 1$ dimes is 95 cents.
n is the number of nickels, $5n + 10(n - 1) = 95$

86. The value of q quarters, $q + 1$ dimes, and $2q$ nickels is 90 cents.
q is the number of quarters, $25q + 10(q + 1) + 5(2q) = 90$

87. The measure of an angle is 38° smaller than the measure of its supplementary angle.
x is the measure of the larger angle, $x + x - 38 = 180$

88. The measure of an angle is 16° larger than the measure of its complementary angle.
x is the measure of the smaller angle, $x + x + 16 = 90$

89. ***Target heart rate.*** For a cardiovascular workout, fitness experts recommend that you reach your target heart rate and stay at that rate for at least 20 minutes (HealthStatus, www.healthstatus.com). To find your target heart rate, find the sum of your age and your resting heart rate, then subtract that sum from 220. Find 60% of that result and add it to your resting heart rate.

a) Write an equation with variable r expressing the fact that the target heart rate for 30-year-old Bob is 144.

b) Judging from the accompanying graph, does the target heart rate for a 30-year-old increase or decrease as the resting heart rate increases?

a) $r + 0.6(220 - (30 + r)) = 144$, where r is the resting heart rate
b) Target heart rate increases as resting heart rate increases.

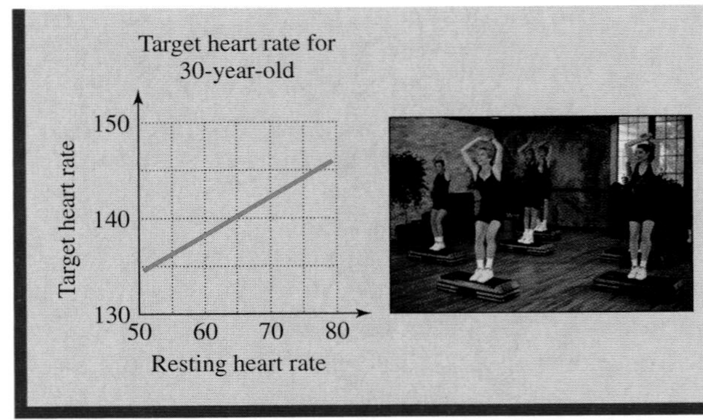

Figure for Exercise 89

90. ***Adjusting the saddle.*** The saddle height on a bicycle should be 109% of the rider's inside leg measurement L (www.harriscyclery.com). See the figure. Write an equation expressing the fact that the saddle height for Brenda is 36 in.
$1.09L = 36$, where L is the inside leg measurement

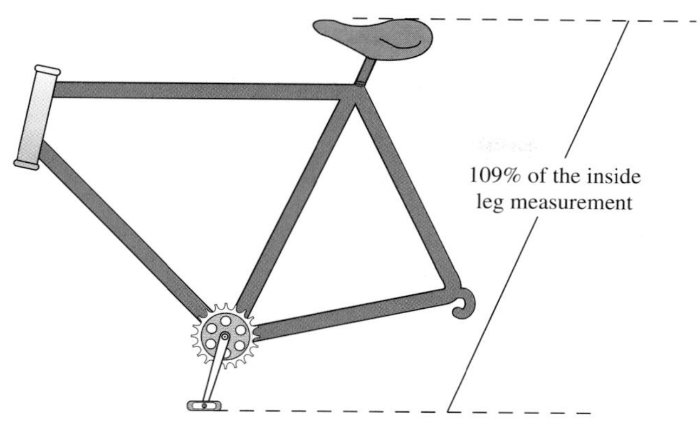

Figure for Exercise 90

Miscellaneous

Translate each verbal expression into an algebraic expression. Do not simplify.

91. The sum of 6 and x $6 + x$

92. w less than 12 $12 - w$

93. m increased by 9 $m + 9$

94. q decreased by 5 $q - 5$

95. t multiplied by 11 $11t$

96. 10 less than the square of y $y^2 - 10$

97. 5 times the difference between x and 2 $5(x - 2)$

98. The sum of two-thirds of k and 1 $\frac{2}{3}k + 1$

99. m decreased by the product of 3 and m $m - 3m$

100. 7 increased by the quotient of x and 2 $7 + \frac{x}{2}$

101. The ratio of 8 more than h and h $\frac{h + 8}{h}$

102. The product of 5 and the total of r and 3 $5(r + 3)$

103. 5 divided by the difference between y and 9 $\frac{5}{y - 9}$

104. The product of n and the sum of n and 6 $n(n + 6)$

105. The quotient of 8 less than w and twice w $\frac{w - 8}{2w}$

106. 3 more than one-third of the square of b $\frac{1}{3}b^2 + 3$

107. 9 less than the product of v and -3 $-3v - 9$

108. The total of 4 times the cube of t and the square of b $4t^3 + b^2$

109. x decreased by the quotient of x and 7 $x - \frac{x}{7}$

110. Five-eighths of the sum of y and 3 $\frac{5}{8}(y + 3)$

111. The difference between the square of m and the total of m and 7 $m^2 - (m + 7)$

112. The product of 13 and the total of t and 6 $13(t + 6)$

113. x increased by the difference between 9 times x and 8 $x + (9x - 8)$

114. The quotient of twice y and 8 $\frac{2y}{8}$

115. 9 less than the product of 13 and n $13n - 9$

116. The product of s and 5 more than s $s(s + 5)$

117. 6 increased by one-third of the sum of x and 2 $6 + \frac{1}{3}(x + 2)$

118. x decreased by the difference between $5x$ and 9 $x - (5x - 9)$

119. The sum of x divided by 2 and x $\frac{x}{2} + x$

120. Twice the sum of 6 times n and 5 $2(6n + 5)$

Given that the area of each figure is 24 square feet, use the dimensions shown to write an equation expressing this fact. Do not solve the equation.

121.

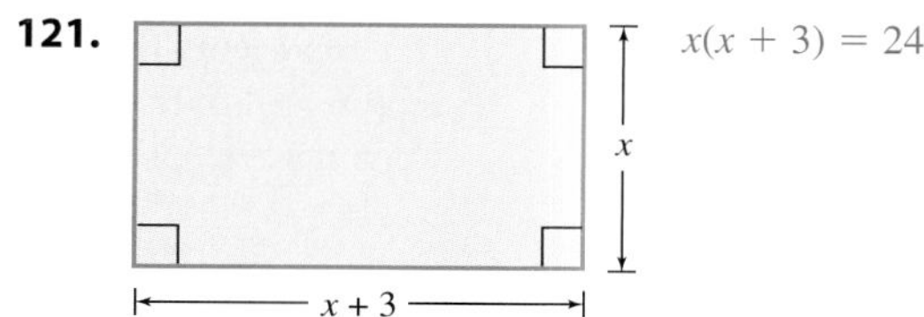

$x(x + 3) = 24$

122. $h + 2$, $h + 2$

$(h + 2)(h + 2) = 24$

123. $w - 4$, w

$w(w - 4) = 24$

124. $y - 2$, y

$\frac{1}{2}y(y - 2) = 24$

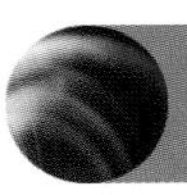

2.6 Number, Geometric, and Uniform Motion Applications

In This Section

In this section, we apply the ideas of Section 2.5 to solving problems. Many of the problems can be solved by using arithmetic only and not algebra. However, remember that we are not just trying to find the answer, we are trying to learn how to apply algebra. So even if the answer is obvious to you, set the problem up and solve it by using algebra as shown in the examples.

⟨1⟩ Number Problems

Algebra is often applied to problems involving time, rate, distance, interest, or discount. **Number problems** do not involve any physical situation. In number problems we simply find some numbers that satisfy some given conditions. Number problems can provide good practice for solving more complex problems.

EXAMPLE 1

A consecutive integer problem

The sum of three consecutive integers is 48. Find the integers.

Solution

If x represents the smallest of the three consecutive integers, then x, $x + 1$, and $x + 2$ represent the three consecutive integers. Since the sum of x, $x + 1$, and $x + 2$ is 48, we write that fact as an equation and solve it:

$$x + (x + 1) + (x + 2) = 48$$

$$3x + 3 = 48 \quad \text{Combine like terms.}$$

$$3x = 45 \quad \text{Subtract 3 from each side.}$$

$$x = 15 \quad \text{Divide each side by 3.}$$

$$x + 1 = 16 \quad \text{If } x \text{ is 15, then } x + 1 \text{ is 16 and } x + 2 \text{ is 17.}$$

$$x + 2 = 17$$

Because $15 + 16 + 17 = 48$, the three consecutive integers that have a sum of 48 are 15, 16, and 17.

Now do Exercises 7–14

⟨ Helpful Hint ⟩

Making a guess can be a good way to get familiar with the problem. For example, let's guess that the answers to Example 1 are 20, 21, and 22. Since $20 + 21 + 22 = 63$, these are not the correct numbers. But now we realize that we should use x, $x + 1$, and $x + 2$ and that the equation should be

$$x + x + 1 + x + 2 = 48.$$

⟨2⟩ General Strategy for Solving Verbal Problems

You should use the following steps as a guide for solving problems.

Strategy for Solving Problems

1. Read the problem as many times as necessary. Guessing the answer and checking it will help you understand the problem.
2. If possible, draw a diagram to illustrate the problem.
3. Choose a variable and *write* what it represents.
4. Write algebraic expressions for any other unknowns in terms of that variable.
5. Write an equation that describes the situation.

⟨ Teaching Tip ⟩

Use guessing to familiarize only when students are having a lot of trouble getting started. To make a guess and check it you must understand the problem.

6. Solve the equation.
7. Answer the original question.
8. Check your answer in the original problem (not the equation).

〈3〉 Geometric Problems

For geometric problems, always draw the figure and label it. Common geometric formulas are given in Section 2.5 and inside the front cover of this text. The **perimeter** of any figure is the sum of the lengths of all of the sides of the figure. The perimeter for a square is given by $P = 4s$, for a rectangle $P = 2L + 2W$, and for a triangle $P = a + b + c$. You can use these formulas or simply remember that the sum of the lengths of all sides is the perimeter.

EXAMPLE 2

A perimeter problem

The length of a rectangular piece of property is 1 foot less than twice the width. If the perimeter is 748 feet, find the length and width.

Solution

Let $x =$ the width. Since the length is 1 foot less than twice the width, $2x - 1 =$ the length. Draw a diagram as in Fig. 2.2. We know that $2L + 2W = P$ is the formula for perimeter of a rectangle. Substituting $2x - 1$ for L and x for W in this formula yields an equation in x:

$$2L + 2W = P$$

$$2(2x - 1) + 2(x) = 748 \quad \text{Replace } L \text{ by } 2x - 1 \text{ and } W \text{ by } x.$$

$$4x - 2 + 2x = 748 \quad \text{Remove the parentheses.}$$

$$6x - 2 = 748 \quad \text{Combine like terms.}$$

$$6x = 750 \quad \text{Add 2 to each side.}$$

$$x = 125 \quad \text{Divide each side by 6.}$$

If $x = 125$, then $2x - 1 = 2(125) - 1 = 249$. Check by computing the perimeter:

$$P = 2L + 2W = 2(249) + 2(125) = 748$$

So the width is 125 feet and the length is 249 feet.

Now do Exercises 15–20

‹ Helpful Hint ›

To get familiar with the problem, guess that the width is 50 ft. Then the length is $2 \cdot 50 - 1$ or 99. The perimeter would be

$$2(50) + 2(99) = 298,$$

which is too small. But now we realize that we should let x be the width, $2x - 1$ be the length, and we should solve

$$2x + 2(2x - 1) = 748.$$

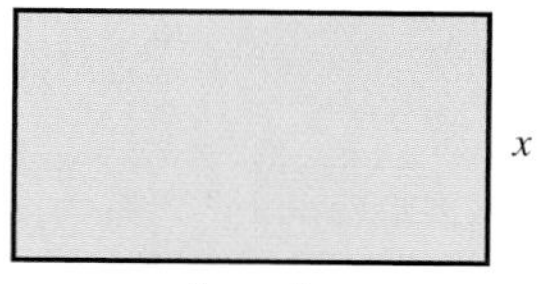

Figure 2.2

Example 3 involves the degree measures of angles. For this problem, the figure is given.

EXAMPLE 3

Complementary angles

In Fig. 2.3 on the next page, the angle formed by the guy wire and the ground is 3.5 times as large as the angle formed by the guy wire and the antenna. Find the degree measure of each of these angles.

Solution

Let $x =$ the degree measure of the smaller angle, and let $3.5x =$ the degree measure of the larger angle. Since the antenna meets the ground at a 90° angle, the sum of the degree

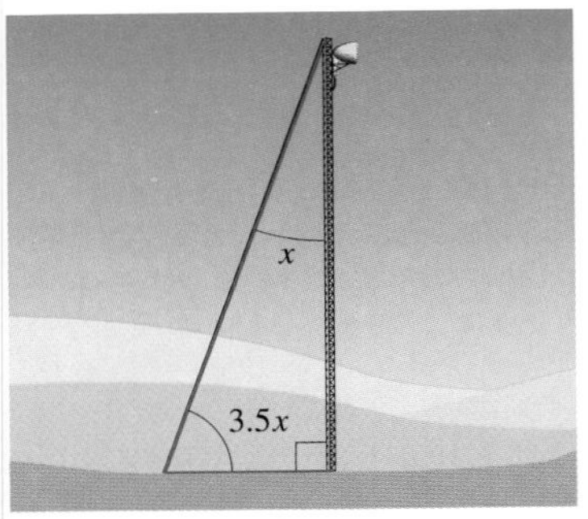

Figure 2.3

measures of the other two angles of the right triangle is 90°. (They are complementary angles.) So we have the following equation:

$$x + 3.5x = 90$$
$$4.5x = 90 \quad \text{Combine like terms.}$$
$$x = 20 \quad \text{Divide each side by 4.5.}$$
$$3.5x = 70 \quad \text{Find the other angle.}$$

Check: 70° is 3.5 · 20° and 20° + 70° = 90°. So the smaller angle is 20°, and the larger angle is 70°.

Now do Exercises 21–22

‹4› Uniform Motion Problems

Problems involving motion at a constant rate are called **uniform motion problems.** In uniform motion problems, we often use an average rate when the actual rate is not constant. For example, you can drive all day and average 50 miles per hour, but you are not driving at a constant 50 miles per hour.

EXAMPLE 4

Finding the rate

Bridgette drove her car for 2 hours on an icy road. When the road cleared up, she increased her speed by 35 miles per hour and drove 3 more hours, completing her 255-mile trip. How fast did she travel on the icy road?

‹ Helpful Hint ›

To get familiar with the problem, guess that she traveled 20 mph on the icy road and 55 mph (20 + 35) on the clear road. Her total distance would be

$$20 \cdot 2 + 55 \cdot 3 = 205 \text{ mi.}$$

Of course this is not correct, but now you are familiar with the problem.

Solution

It is helpful to draw a diagram and then make a table to classify the given information. Remember that $D = RT$.

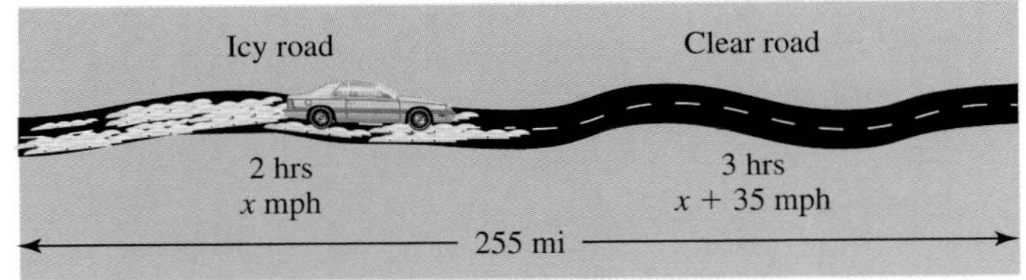

	Rate	Time	Distance
Icy road	$x \frac{\text{mi}}{\text{hr}}$	2 hr	$2x$ mi
Clear road	$x + 35 \frac{\text{mi}}{\text{hr}}$	3 hr	$3(x + 35)$ mi

The equation expresses the fact that her total distance traveled was 255 miles:

$$\text{Icy road distance} + \text{clear road distance} = \text{total distance}$$

$$2x + 3(x + 35) = 255$$
$$2x + 3x + 105 = 255$$
$$5x + 105 = 255$$
$$5x = 150$$
$$x = 30$$
$$x + 35 = 65$$

If she drove at 30 miles per hour for 2 hours on the icy road, she went 60 miles. If she drove at 65 miles per hour for 3 hours on the clear road, she went 195 miles. Since $60 + 195 = 255$, we can be sure that her speed on the icy road was 30 mph.

Now do Exercises 23–26

In the next uniform motion problem we find the time.

EXAMPLE 5

Finding the time

Pierce drove from Allentown to Baker, averaging 55 miles per hour. His journey back to Allentown using the same route took 3 hours longer because he averaged only 40 miles per hour. How long did it take him to drive from Allentown to Baker? What is the distance between Allentown and Baker?

Solution

Draw a diagram and then make a table to classify the given information. Remember that $D = RT$.

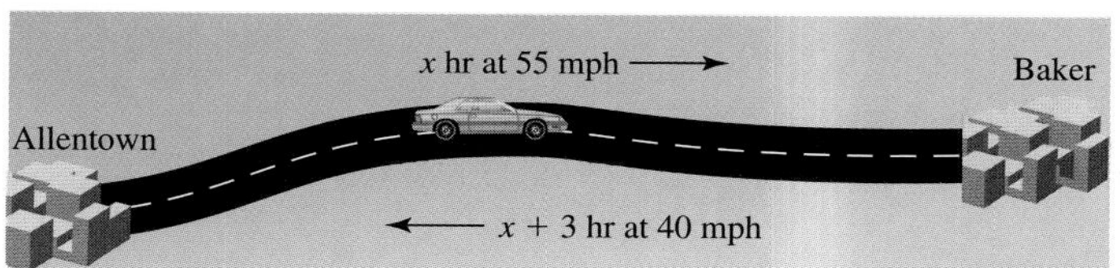

	Rate	Time	Distance
Going	$55 \frac{\text{mi}}{\text{hr}}$	x hr	$55x$ mi
Returning	$40 \frac{\text{mi}}{\text{hr}}$	$x + 3$ hr	$40(x + 3)$ mi

We can write an equation expressing the fact that the distance either way is the same:

$$\text{Distance going} = \text{distance returning}$$
$$55x = 40(x + 3)$$
$$55x = 40x + 120$$
$$15x = 120$$
$$x = 8$$

The trip from Allentown to Baker took 8 hours. The distance between Allentown and Baker is $55 \cdot 8$, or 440 miles.

Now do Exercises 27–28

Warm-Ups 

True or false? Explain your answer.

1. The first step in solving a word problem is to write the equation. False
2. You should always write down what the variable represents. True
3. Diagrams and tables are used as aids in solving problems. True
4. To represent two consecutive odd integers, we use x and $x + 1$. False
5. If $5x$ is 2 miles more than $3(x + 20)$, then $5x + 2 = 3(x + 20)$. False
6. We can represent two numbers with a sum of 6 by x and $6 - x$. True
7. Two numbers that differ by 7 can be represented by x and $x + 7$. True
8. The degree measures of two complementary angles can be represented by x and $90 - x$. True
9. The degree measures of two supplementary angles can be represented by x and $x + 180$. False
10. If x is half as large as $x + 50$, then $2x = x + 50$. True

2.6 Exercises

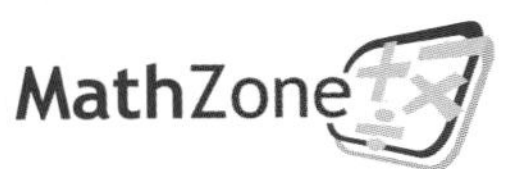

‹ Study Tips ›

- Make sure you know how your grade in this course is determined. How much weight is given to tests, homework, quizzes, and projects? Does your instructor give any extra credit?
- You should keep a record of all of your scores and compute your own final grade.

Reading and Writing *After reading this section, write out the answers to these questions. Use complete sentences.*

1. What types of problems are discussed in this section? In this section we studied number, geometric, and uniform motion problems.
2. Why do we solve number problems? We solve number problems to gain experience at problem solving.
3. What is uniform motion? Uniform motion is motion at a constant rate of speed.
4. What are supplementary angles? Supplementary angles are angles whose degree measures have a sum of 180°.
5. What are complementary angles? Complementary angles are angles whose degree measures have a sum of 90°.
6. What should you always do when solving a geometric problem? When solving a geometric problem draw a figure and label the sides.

‹1› Number Problems

Show a complete solution to each problem. See Example 1.

7. ***Consecutive integers.*** Find two consecutive integers whose sum is 79. 39, 40
8. ***Consecutive odd integers.*** Find two consecutive odd intergers whose sum is 56. 27, 29
9. VIDEO ***Consecutive integers.*** Find three consecutive integers whose sum is 141. 46, 47, 48
10. ***Consecutive even integers.*** Find three consecutive even integers whose sum is 114. 36, 38, 40
11. ***Consecutive odd integers.*** Two consecutive odd integers have a sum of 152. What are the integers? 75, 77
12. VIDEO ***Consecutive odd integers.*** Four consecutive odd integers have a sum of 120. What are the integers? 27, 29, 31, 33

13. ***Consecutive integers.*** Find four consecutive integers whose sum is 194. 47, 48, 49, 50

14. ***Consecutive even integers.*** Find four consecutive even integers whose sum is 340. 82, 84, 86, 88

⟨3⟩ Geometric Problems

Show a complete solution to each problem.

See Examples 2 and 3.

See the Strategy for Solving Problems box on page 130.

15. ***Olympic swimming.*** If an Olympic swimming pool is twice as long as it is wide and the perimeter is 150 meters, then what are the length and width? Length 50 meters, width 25 meters

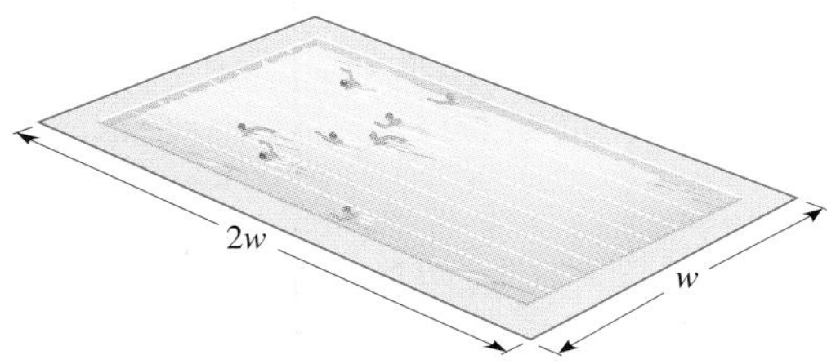

Figure for Exercise 15

VIDEO
16. ***Wimbledon tennis.*** If the perimeter of a tennis court is 228 feet and the length is 6 feet longer than twice the width, then what are the length and width? Length 78 feet, width 36 feet

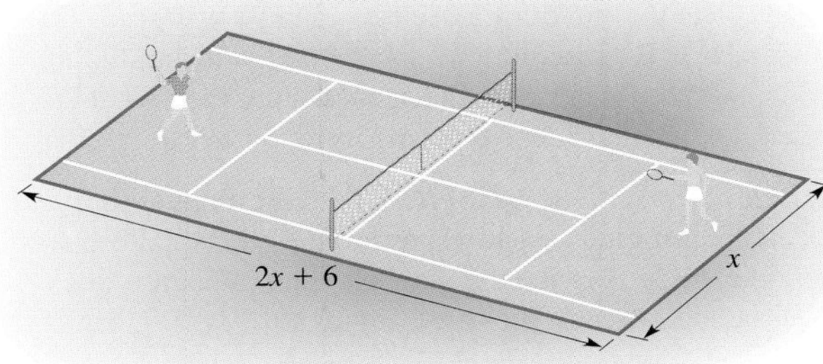

Figure for Exercise 16

17. ***Framed.*** Julia framed an oil painting that her uncle gave her. The painting was 4 inches longer than it was wide, and it took 176 inches of frame molding. What were the dimensions of the picture? Width 42 inches, length 46 inches

18. ***Industrial triangle.*** Geraldo drove his truck from Indianapolis to Chicago, then to St. Louis, and then back to Indianapolis. He observed that the second side of his triangular route was 81 miles short of being twice as long as the first side and that the third side was 61 miles longer than the first side. If he traveled a total of 720 miles, then how long is each side of this triangular route? 185 miles, 289 miles, 246 miles

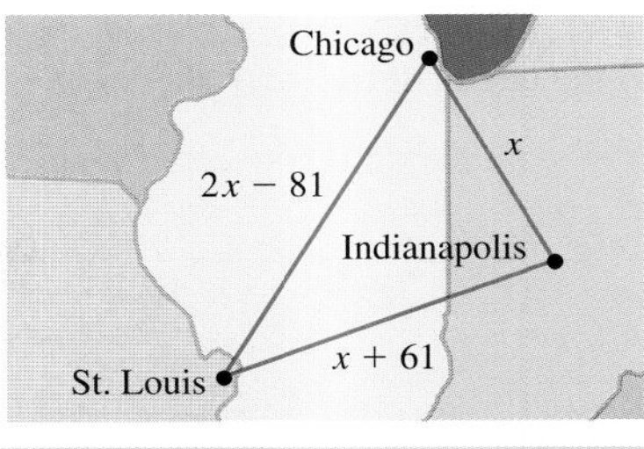

Figure for Exercise 18

VIDEO
19. ***Triangular banner.*** A banner in the shape of an isosceles triangle has a base that is 5 inches shorter than either of the equal sides. If the perimeter of the banner is 34 inches, then what is the length of the equal sides? 13 inches

20. ***Border paper.*** Dr. Good's waiting room is 8 feet longer than it is wide. When Vincent wallpapered Dr. Good's waiting room, he used 88 feet of border paper. What are the dimensions of Dr. Good's waiting room? 18 feet by 26 feet

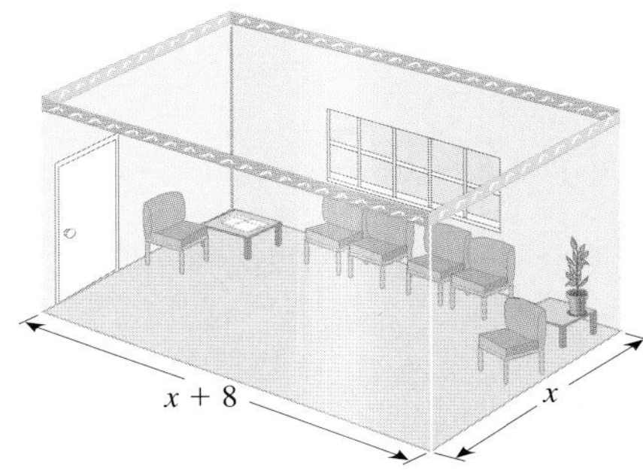

Figure for Exercise 20

21. ***Roof truss design.*** An engineer is designing a roof truss as shown in the accompanying figure. Find the degree measure of the angle marked w. 35°

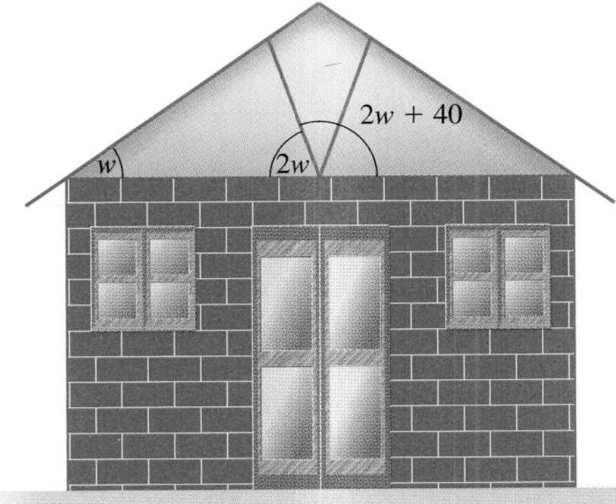

Figure for Exercise 21

22. ***Another truss.*** Another truss is shown in the accompanying figure. Find the degree measure of the angle marked z. 24°

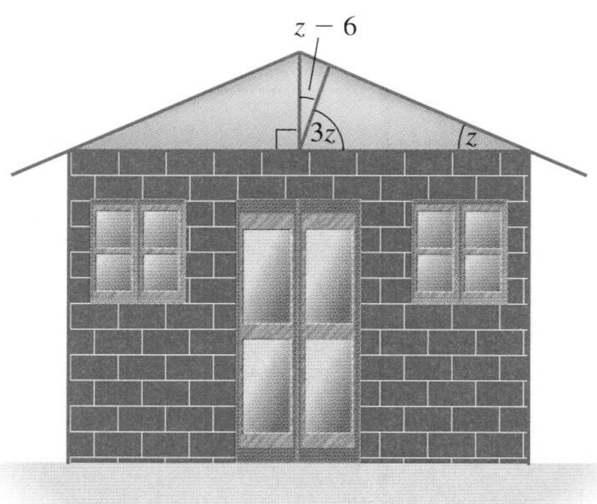

Figure for Exercise 22

‹4› Uniform Motion Problems

Show a complete solution to each problem. See Examples 4 and 5.

23. ***Highway miles.*** Bret drove for 4 hours on the freeway, then decreased his speed by 20 miles per hour and drove for 5 more hours on a country road. If his total trip was 485 miles, then what was his speed on the freeway? 65 miles per hour

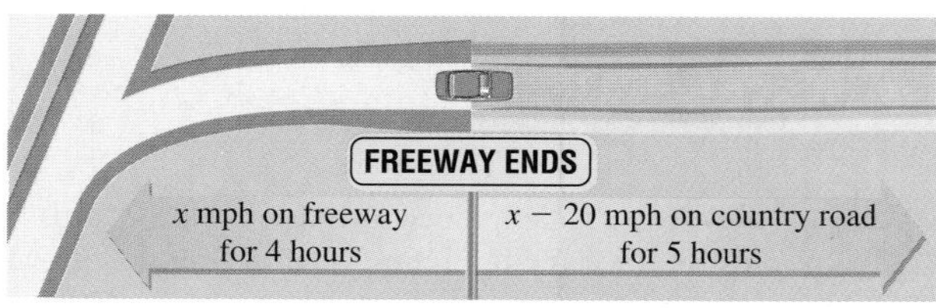

Figure for Exercise 23

24. ***Walking and running.*** On Saturday morning, Lynn walked for 2 hours and then ran for 30 minutes. If she ran twice as fast as she walked and she covered 12 miles altogether, then how fast did she walk? 4 miles per hour

VIDEO 25. ***Driving all night.*** Kathryn drove her rig 5 hours before dawn and 6 hours after dawn. If her average speed was 5 miles per hour more in the dark and she covered 630 miles altogether, then what was her speed after dawn? 55 miles per hour

26. ***Commuting to work.*** On Monday, Roger drove to work in 45 minutes. On Tuesday he averaged 12 miles per hour more, and it took him 9 minutes less to get to work. How far does he travel to work? 36 miles

27. ***Head winds.*** A jet flew at an average speed of 640 mph from Los Angeles to Chicago. Because of head winds the jet averaged only 512 mph on the return trip, and the return trip took 48 minutes longer. How many hours was the flight from Chicago to Los Angeles? How far is it from Chicago to Los Angeles? 4 hours, 2048 miles

28. ***Ride the Peaks.*** Penny's bicycle trip from Colorado Springs to Pikes Peak took 1.5 hours longer than the return trip to Colorado Springs. If she averaged 6 mph on the way to Pikes Peak and 15 mph for the return trip, then how long was the ride from Colorado Springs to Pikes Peak? 2.5 hours

Miscellaneous

Solve each problem.

29. ***Perimeter of a frame.*** The perimeter of a rectangular frame is 64 in. If the width of the frame is 8 in. less than the length, then what are the length and width of the frame? Length 20 inches, width 12 inches

30. ***Perimeter of a box.*** The width of a rectangular box is 20% of the length. If the perimeter is 192 cm, then what are the length and width of the box? Length 80 cm, width 16 cm

31. ***Isosceles triangle.*** An isosceles triangle has two equal sides. If the shortest side of an isosceles triangle is 2 ft less than one of the equal sides and the perimeter is 13 ft, then what are the lengths of the sides? 5 ft, 5 ft, 3 ft

32. ***Scalene triangle.*** A scalene triangle has three unequal sides. The perimeter of a scalene triangle is 144 m. If the first side is twice as long as the second side and the third side is 24 m longer than the second side, then what are the measures of the sides? 60 m, 30 m, 54 m

33. ***Angles of a scalene triangle.*** The largest angle in a scalene triangle is six times as large as the smallest. If the middle angle is twice the smallest, then what are the degree measures of the three angles? 20°, 40°, 120°

34. ***Angles of a right triangle.*** If one of the acute angles in a right triangle is 38°, then what are the degree measures of all three angles? 38°, 52°, 90°

35. ***Angles of an isosceles triangle.*** One of the equal angles in an isosceles triangle is four times as large as the smallest angle in the triangle. What are the degree measures of the three angles? 20°, 80°, 80°

36. ***Angles of an isosceles triangle.*** The measure of one of the equal angles in an isosceles triangle is 10° larger than twice the smallest angle in the triangle. What are the degree measures of the three angles? 32°, 74°, 74°

37. ***Super Bowl score.*** The 1977 Super Bowl was played in the Rose Bowl in Pasadena. In that football game the Oakland Raiders scored 18 more points than the Minnesota

Vikings. If the total number of points scored was 46, then what was the final score for the game?
Raiders 32, Vikings 14

38. ***Top payrolls.*** Payrolls for the three highest paid baseball teams (the Yankees, Red Sox, and Angels) for 2006 totaled $418 million (www.usatoday.com). If the team payroll for the Yankees was $75 million greater than the payroll for the Red Sox and the payroll for the Red Sox was $17 million greater than the payroll for the Angels, then what was the 2006 payroll for each team?
Yankees $195 million, Red Rox $120 million, Angels $103 million

39. ***Idabel to Lawton.*** Before lunch, Sally drove from Idabel to Ardmore, averaging 50 mph. After lunch she continued on to Lawton, averaging 53 mph. If her driving time after lunch was 1 hour less than her driving time before lunch and the total trip was 256 miles, then how many hours did she drive before lunch? How far is it from Ardmore to Lawton? 3 hours, 106 miles

40. ***Norfolk to Chadron.*** On Monday, Chuck drove from Norfolk to Valentine, averaging 47 mph. On Tuesday, he continued on to Chadron, averaging 69 mph. His driving time on Monday was 2 hours longer than his driving time on Tuesday. If the total distance from Norfolk to Chadron is 326 miles, then how many hours did he drive on Monday? How far is it from Valentine to Chadron?
4 hours, 138 miles

41. ***Golden oldies.*** Joan Crawford, John Wayne, and James Stewart were born in consecutive years (*Doubleday Almanac*). Joan Crawford was the oldest of the three, and James Stewart was the youngest. In 1950, after all three had their birthdays, the sum of their ages was 129. In what years were they born?
Crawford 1906, Wayne 1907, Stewart 1908

42. ***Leading men.*** Bob Hope was born 2 years after Clark Gable and 2 years before Henry Fonda (*Doubleday Almanac*). In 1951, after all three of them had their birthdays, the sum of their ages was 144. In what years were they born? Hope 1903, Gable 1901, Fonda 1905

43. ***Trimming a garage door.*** A carpenter used 30 ft of molding in three pieces to trim a garage door. If the long piece was 2 ft longer than twice the length of each shorter piece, then how long was each piece? 7 ft, 7 ft, 16 ft

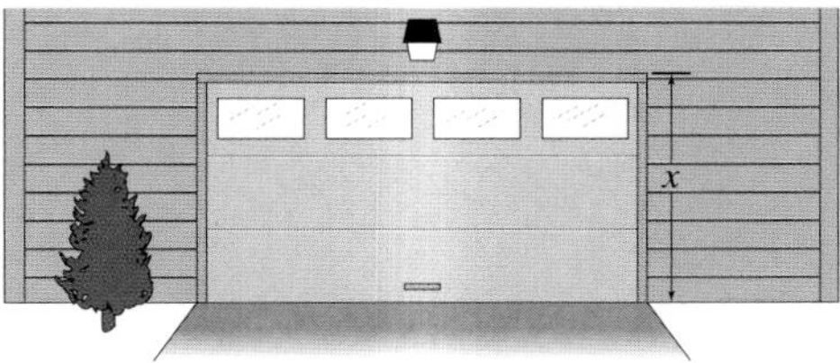

Figure for Exercise 43

44. ***Fencing dog pens.*** Clint is constructing two adjacent rectangular dog pens. Each pen will be three times as long as it is wide, and the pens will share a common long side. If Clint has 65 ft of fencing, what are the dimensions of each pen? 5 ft by 15 ft

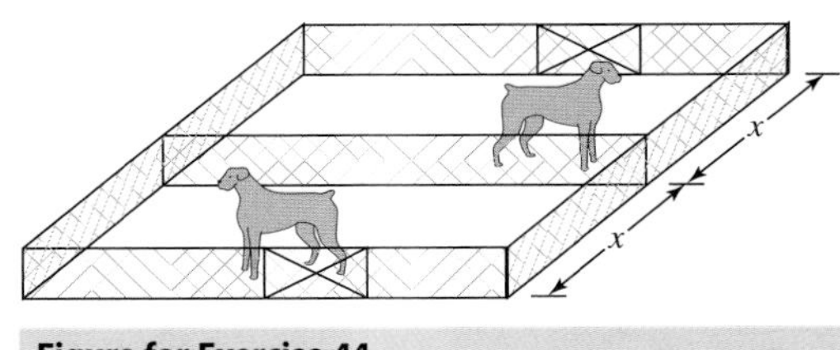

Figure for Exercise 44

2.7 Discount, Investment, and Mixture Applications

In This Section

In this section, we continue our study of applications of algebra. The problems in this section involve percents.

⟨1⟩ Discount Problems

When an item is sold at a discount, the amount of the discount is usually described as being a percentage of the original price. The percentage is called the **rate of discount.** Multiplying the rate of discount and the original price gives the amount of the discount.

EXAMPLE 1

Finding the original price

Ralph got a 12% discount when he bought his new 2007 Corvette Coupe. If the amount of his discount was \$6606, then what was the original price of the Corvette?

Solution

Let x represent the original price. The discount is found by multiplying the 12% rate of discount and the original price:

$$\text{Rate of discount} \cdot \text{original price} = \text{amount of discount}$$

$$0.12x = 6606$$

$$x = \frac{6606}{0.12} \quad \text{Divide each side by 0.12.}$$

$$x = 55{,}050$$

To check, find 12% of \$55,050. Since $0.12 \cdot 55{,}050 = 6606$, the original price of the Corvette was \$55,050.

Now do Exercises 7–8

EXAMPLE 2

Finding the original price

When Susan bought her new car, she also got a discount of 12%. She paid \$17,600 for her car. What was the original price of Susan's car?

Solution

Let x represent the original price for Susan's car. The amount of discount is 12% of x, or $0.12x$. We can write an equation expressing the fact that the original price minus the discount is the price Susan paid.

$$\text{Original price} - \text{discount} = \text{sale price}$$

$$x - 0.12x = 17{,}600$$

$$0.88x = 17{,}600 \quad 1.00x - 0.12x = 0.88x$$

$$x = \frac{17{,}600}{0.88} \quad \text{Divide each side by 0.88.}$$

$$x = 20{,}000$$

Check: 12% of \$20,000 is \$2400, and \$20,000 − \$2400 = \$17,600. The original price of Susan's car was \$20,000.

Now do Exercises 9–10

‹ Helpful Hint ›

To get familiar with the problem, guess that the original price was \$30,000. Then her discount is 0.12(30,000) or \$3600. The price she paid would be 30,000 − 3600 or \$26,400, which is incorrect.

‹2› Commission Problems

A salesperson's commission for making a sale is often a percentage of the selling price. **Commission problems** are very similar to other problems involving percents. The commission is found by multiplying the rate of commission and the selling price.

EXAMPLE 3

Real estate commission

Sarah is selling her house through a real estate agent whose commission rate is 7%. What should the selling price be so that Sarah can get the \$83,700 she needs to pay off the mortgage?

‹ Teaching Tip ›

Students often have trouble with $x - 0.07x$. You might need to do more examples of this idea.

Solution

Let x be the selling price. The commission is 7% of x (not 7% of \$83,700). Sarah receives the selling price less the sales commission:

$$\text{Selling price} - \text{commission} = \text{Sarah's share}$$

$$x - 0.07x = 83{,}700$$

$$0.93x = 83{,}700 \quad 1.00x - 0.07x = 0.93x$$

$$x = \frac{83{,}700}{0.93}$$

$$x = 90{,}000$$

Check: 7% of \$90,000 is \$6300, and \$90,000 − \$6300 = \$83,700. So the house should sell for \$90,000.

Now do Exercises 11–14

‹3› Investment Problems

The interest on an investment is a percentage of the investment, just as the sales commission is a percentage of the sale amount. However, in **investment problems** we must often account for more than one investment at different rates. So it is a good idea to make a table, as in Example 4.

EXAMPLE 4

Diversified investing

Ruth Ann invested some money in a certificate of deposit with an annual yield of 9%. She invested twice as much in a mutual fund with an annual yield of 10%. Her interest from the two investments at the end of the year was \$232. How much was invested at each rate?

‹ Helpful Hint ›

To get familiar with the problem, guess that she invested \$1000 at 9% and \$2000 at 10%. Then her earnings in 1 year would be

$$0.09(1000) + 0.10(2000)$$

or \$290, which is close but incorrect.

Solution

When there are many unknown quantities, it is often helpful to identify them in a table. Since the time is 1 year, the amount of interest is the product of the interest rate and the amount invested.

	Interest Rate	**Amount Invested**	**Interest for 1 Year**
CD	9%	x	$0.09x$
Mutual fund	10%	$2x$	$0.10(2x)$

Since the total interest from the investments was \$232, we can write the following equation:

$$\text{CD interest} + \text{mutual fund interest} = \text{total interest}$$

$$0.09x + 0.10(2x) = 232$$

$$0.09x + 0.20x = 232$$

$$0.29x = 232$$

$$x = \frac{232}{0.29}$$

$$x = 800$$

$$2x = 1600$$

To check, we find the total interest:

$$0.09(800) + 0.10(1600) = 72 + 160$$

$$= 232$$

So Ruth Ann invested \$800 at 9% and \$1600 at 10%.

Now do Exercises 15–18

‹4› Mixture Problems

Mixture problems are concerned with the result of mixing two quantities, each of which contains another substance. Notice how similar the following mixture problem is to the last investment problem.

EXAMPLE 5

Mixing milk

How many gallons of milk containing 4% butterfat must be mixed with 80 gallons of 1% milk to obtain 2% milk?

‹ Helpful Hint ›

To get familiar with the problem, guess that we need 100 gal of 4% milk. Mixing that with 80 gal of 1% milk would produce 180 gal of 2% milk. Now the two milks separately have

$$0.04(100) + 0.01(80)$$

or 4.8 gal of fat. Together the amount of fat is 0.02(180) or 3.6 gal. Since these amounts are not equal, our guess is incorrect.

Solution

It is helpful to draw a diagram and then make a table to classify the given information.

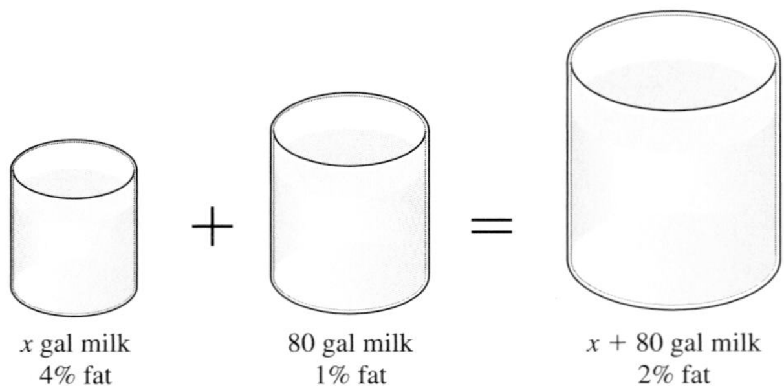

	Percentage of Fat	Amount of Milk	Amount of Fat
4% milk	4%	x	$0.04x$
1% milk	1%	80	$0.01(80)$
2% milk	2%	$x + 80$	$0.02(x + 80)$

The equation expresses the fact that the total fat from the first two types of milk is the same as the fat in the mixture:

$$\begin{aligned}
\text{Fat in 4\% milk} + \text{fat in 1\% milk} &= \text{fat in 2\% milk} \\
0.04x + 0.01(80) &= 0.02(x + 80) \\
0.04x + 0.8 &= 0.02x + 1.6 && \text{Simplify.} \\
100(0.04x + 0.8) &= 100(0.02x + 1.6) && \text{Multiply each side by 100.} \\
4x + 80 &= 2x + 160 && \text{Distributive property} \\
2x + 80 &= 160 && \text{Subtract } 2x \text{ from each side.} \\
2x &= 80 && \text{Subtract 80 from each side.} \\
x &= 40 && \text{Divide each side by 2.}
\end{aligned}$$

To check, calculate the total fat:

$$2\% \text{ of 120 gallons} = 0.02(120) = 2.4 \text{ gallons of fat}$$
$$0.04(40) + 0.01(80) = 1.6 + 0.8 = 2.4 \text{ gallons of fat}$$

So we mix 40 gallons of 4% milk with 80 gallons of 1% milk to get 120 gallons of 2% milk.

Now do Exercises 19–22

In mixture problems, the solutions might contain fat, alcohol, salt, or some other substance. We always assume that the substance neither appears nor disappears in the process. For example, if there are 3 grams of salt in one glass of water and 2 grams in another, then there are exactly 5 grams in a mixture of the two.

Warm-Ups ▼

True or false? Explain your answer.

1. If Jim gets a 12% commission for selling a \$1000 Wonder Vac, then his commission is \$120. True
2. If Bob earns a 5% commission on an \$80,000 motorhome sale, then Bob earns \$400. False
3. If Sue gets a 20% discount on a TV with a list price of x dollars, then Sue pays $0.8x$ dollars. True
4. If you get a 6% discount on a car that has an MSRP of x dollars, then your discount is $0.6x$ dollars. False
5. If the original price is w and the discount is 8%, then the selling price is $w - 0.08w$. True
6. If x is the selling price and the commission is 8% of the selling price, then the commission is $0.08x$. True
7. If you need \$40,000 for your house and the agent gets 10% of the selling price, then the agent gets \$4000, and the house sells for \$44,000. False
8. If you mix 10 liters of a 20% acid solution with x liters of a 30% acid solution, then the total amount of acid is $2 + 0.3x$ liters. True
9. A 10% acid solution mixed with a 14% acid solution results in a 24% acid solution. False
10. If a TV costs x dollars and sales tax is 5%, then the total bill is $1.05x$ dollars. True

2.7 Exercises

‹ Study Tips ›

- Find out what kinds of help are available for commuting students, online students, and on-campus students.
- Sometimes a minor issue can be resolved very quickly and you can get back on the path to success.

Reading and Writing *After reading this section, write out the answers to these questions. Use complete sentences.*

1. What types of problems are discussed in this section? We studied discount, investment, and mixture problems in this section.

2. What is the difference between discount and rate of discount? The rate of discount is a percentage and the discount is the actual amount that the price is reduced.

3. What is the relationship between discount, original price, rate of discount, and sale price? The product of the rate and the original price gives the amount of discount. The original price minus the discount is the sale price.

4. What do mixture problems and investment problems have in common? Both mixture problems and investment problems involve rates.

5. Why do we make a table when solving certain problems. A table helps us to organize the information given in a problem.

6. What is the relationship between amount of interest, amount invested, and interest rate? The product of the interest rate and the amount invested gives the amount of interest.

‹1› Discount Problems

Show a complete solution to each problem. See Examples 1 and 2.

VIDEO

7. ***Close-out sale.*** At a 25% off sale, Jose saved \$80 on a 19-inch Panasonic TV. What was the original price of the television. \$320

8. ***Nice tent.*** A 12% discount on a Walrus tent saved Melanie \$75. What was the original price of the tent? \$625

9. ***Circuit city.*** After getting a 20% discount, Robert paid \$320 for a Pioneer CD player for his car. What was the original price of the CD player? \$400

10. ***Chrysler Sebring.*** After getting a 15% discount on the price of a new Chrysler Sebring convertible, Helen paid \$27,000. What was the original price of the convertible to the nearest dollar? \$31,765

‹2› Commission Problems

Show a complete solution to each problem. See Example 3.

11. ***Selling price of a home.*** Kirk wants to get \$115,000 for his house. The real estate agent gets a commission equal to 8% of the selling price for selling the house. What should the selling price be? \$125,000

Photo for Exercise 11

12. ***Horse trading.*** Gene is selling his palomino at an auction. The auctioneer's commission is 10% of the selling price. If Gene still owes \$810 on the horse, then what must the horse sell for so that Gene can pay off his loan? \$900

13. ***Sales tax collection.*** Merilee sells tomatoes at a roadside stand. Her total receipts including the 7% sales tax were \$462.24. What amount of sales tax did she collect? \$30.24

14. ***Toyota Corolla.*** Gwen bought a new Toyota Corolla. The selling price plus the 8% state sales tax was \$15,714. What was the selling price? \$14,550

‹3› Investment Problems

Show a complete solution to each problem. See Example 4.

15. ***Wise investments.*** Wiley invested some money in the Berger 100 Fund and \$3000 more than that amount in the Berger 101 Fund. For the year he was in the fund, the 100 Fund paid 18% simple interest and the 101 Fund paid 15% simple interest. If the income from the two investments totaled \$3750 for 1 year, then how much did he invest in each fund? 100 Fund \$10,000, 101 Fund \$13,000

VIDEO **16.** ***Loan shark.*** Becky lent her brother some money at 8% simple interest, and she lent her sister twice as much at twice the interest rate. If she received a total of 20 cents interest, then how much did she lend to each of them? Brother \$0.50, sister \$1.00

17. ***Investing in bonds.*** David split his \$25,000 inheritance between Fidelity Short-Term Bond Fund with an annual yield of 5% and T. Rowe Price Tax-Free Short-Intermediate Fund with an annual yield of 4%. If his total income for

1 year on the two investments was \$1140, then how much did he invest in each fund? Fidelity \$14,000, Price \$11,000

18. ***High-risk funds.*** Of the \$50,000 that Natasha pocketed on her last real estate deal, \$20,000 went to charity. She invested part of the remainder in Dreyfus New Leaders Fund with an annual yield of 16% and the rest in Templeton Growth Fund with an annual yield of 25%. If she made \$6060 on these investments in 1 year, then how much did she invest in each fund? Dreyfus \$16,000, Templeton \$14,000

⟨4⟩ Mixture Problems

Show a complete solution to each problem. See Example 5.

19. ***Mixing milk.*** How many gallons of milk containing 1% butterfat must be mixed with 30 gallons of milk containing 3% butterfat to obtain a mixture containing 2% butterfat? 30 gallons

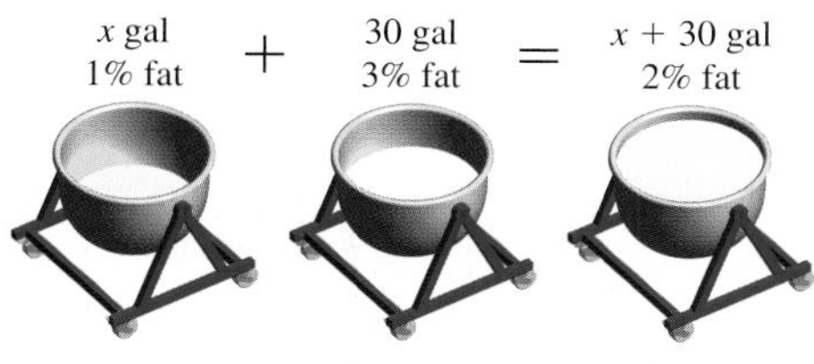

Figure for Exercise 19

20. ***Acid solutions.*** How many gallons of a 5% acid solution should be mixed with 30 gallons of a 10% acid solution to obtain a mixture that is 8% acid? 20 gallons

VIDEO

21. ***Alcohol solutions.*** Gus has on hand a 5% alcohol solution and a 20% alcohol solution. He needs 30 liters of a 10% alcohol solution. How many liters of each solution should he mix together to obtain the 30 liters?
20 liters of 5% alcohol, 10 liters of 20% alcohol

22. ***Adjusting antifreeze.*** Angela needs 20 quarts of 50% antifreeze solution in her radiator. She plans to obtain this by mixing some pure antifreeze with an appropriate amount of a 40% antifreeze solution. How many quarts of each should she use?
$\frac{10}{3}$ quarts of pure antifreeze, $\frac{50}{3}$ quarts of 40% solution

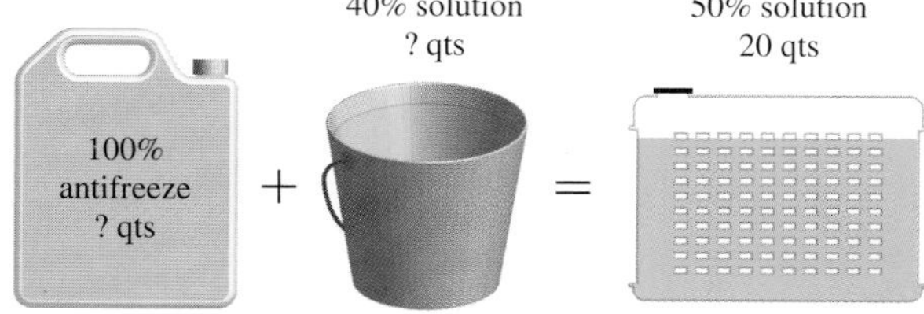

Figure for Exercise 22

Miscellaneous

Solve each problem.

23. ***Registered voters.*** If 60% of the registered voters of Lancaster County voted in the November election and 33,420 votes were cast, then how many registered voters are there in Lancaster County? 55,700

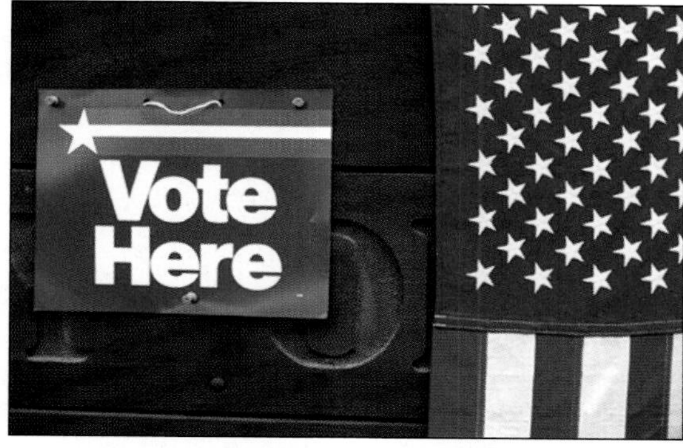

Photo for Exercise 23

24. ***Tough on crime.*** In a random sample of voters, 594 respondents said that they favored passage of a \$33 billion crime bill. If the number in favor of the crime bill was 45% of the number of voters in the sample, then how many voters were in the sample? 1320 voters

25. ***Ford Taurus.*** At an 8% sales tax rate, the sales tax on Peter's new Ford Taurus was \$1200. What was the price of the car? \$15,000

26. ***Taxpayer blues.*** Last year, Faye paid 24% of her income to taxes. If she paid \$9600 in taxes, then what was her income? \$40,000

27. ***Making a profit.*** A retail store buys shirts for \$8 and sells them for \$14. What percent increase is this? 75%

28. ***Monitoring AIDS.*** If 28 new AIDS cases were reported in Landon County this year and 35 new cases were reported last year, then what percent decrease in new cases is this? 20%

29. ***High school integration.*** Wilson High School has 400 students, of whom 20% are African American. The school board plans to merge Wilson High with Jefferson High. This one school will then have a student population that is 44% African American. If Jefferson currently has a student population that is 60% African American, then how many students are at Jefferson? 600 students

30. ***Junior high integration.*** The school board plans to merge two junior high schools into one school of 800 students in which 40% of the students will be Caucasian. One of the schools currently has 58% Caucasian students; the other has only 10% Caucasian students. How many students are in each of the two schools? 500 students in the 58% school, 300 students in the 10% school

31. ***Hospital capacity.*** When Memorial Hospital is filled to capacity, it has 18 more people in semiprivate rooms (two patients to a room) than in private rooms. The room rates are \$200 per day for a private room and \$150 per day for a semiprivate room. If the total receipts for rooms is

$17,400 per day when all are full, then how many rooms of each type does the hospital have? 42 private rooms, 30 semiprivate rooms

32. ***Public relations.*** Memorial Hospital is planning an advertising campaign. It costs the hospital $3000 each time a television ad is aired and $2000 each time a radio ad is aired. The administrator wants to air 60 more television ads than radio ads. If the total cost of airing the ads is $580,000, then how many ads of each type will be aired? 140 TV ads, 80 radio ads

33. ***Mixed nuts.*** Cashews sell for $4.80 per pound, and pistachios sell for $6.40 per pound. How many pounds of pistachios should be mixed with 20 pounds of cashews to get a mixture that sells for $5.40 per pound? 12 pounds

34. ***Premium blend.*** Premium coffee sells for $6.00 per pound, and regular coffee sells for $4.00 per pound. How many pounds of each type of coffee should be blended to obtain 100 pounds of a blend that sells for $4.64 per pound? 32 pounds of premium, 68 pounds of regular

35. ***Nickels and dimes.*** Candice paid her library fine with 10 coins consisting of nickels and dimes. If the fine was $0.80, then how many of each type of coin did she use? 4 nickels, 6 dimes

36. ***Dimes and quarters.*** Jeremy paid for his breakfast with 36 coins consisting of dimes and quarters. If the bill was $4.50, then how many of each type of coin did he use? 30 dimes, 6 quarters

37. ***Cooking oil.*** Crisco Canola Oil is 7% saturated fat. Crisco blends corn oil that is 14% saturated fat with Crisco Canola Oil to get Crisco Canola and Corn Oil, which is 11% saturated fat. How many gallons of corn oil must Crisco mix with 600 gallons of Crisco Canola Oil to get Crisco Canola and Corn Oil? 800 gallons

38. ***Chocolate ripple.*** The Delicious Chocolate Shop makes a dark chocolate that is 35% fat and a white chocolate that is 48% fat. How many kilograms of dark chocolate should be mixed with 50 kilograms of white chocolate to make a ripple blend that is 40% fat? 80 kilograms

39. ***Hawaiian Punch.*** Hawaiian Punch is 10% fruit juice. How much water would you have to add to one gallon of Hawaiian Punch to get a drink that is 6% fruit juice? $\frac{2}{3}$ gallon

40. ***Diluting wine.*** A restaurant manager has 2 liters of white wine that is 12% alcohol. How many liters of white grape juice should he add to get a drink that is 10% alcohol? $\frac{2}{5}$ liter

41. ***Bargain hunting.*** A smart shopper bought 5 pairs of shorts and 8 tops for a total of $108. If the price of a pair of shorts was twice the price of a top, then what was the price of each type of clothing? Shorts $12, tops $6

42. ***VCRs and CDs.*** The manager of a stereo shop placed an order for $10,710 worth of VCRs at $120 each and CD players at $150 each. If the number of VCRs she ordered was three times the number of CD players, then how many of each did she order? 21 CD players, 63 VCRs

2.8 Inequalities

In This Section

- ⟨1⟩ Inequalities
- ⟨2⟩ Graphing Inequalities
- ⟨3⟩ Graphing Compound Inequalities
- ⟨4⟩ Checking Inequalities
- ⟨5⟩ Writing Inequalities

⟨ Helpful Hint ⟩

A good way to learn inequality symbols is to notice that the inequality symbol always points at the smaller number. This observation will help you read an inequality such as $-2 < x$. Reading right to left, we say that x is greater than -2. It is usually easier to understand an inequality if you read the variable first.

In Chapter 1, we defined inequality in terms of the number line. One number is greater than another number if it lies to the right of the other number on the number line. In this section, you will study inequality in greater depth.

⟨1⟩ Inequalities

The symbols used to express inequality and their meanings are given in the following box.

Inequality Symbols

Symbol	Meaning
$<$	Is less than
$\le$	Is less than or equal to
$>$	Is greater than
$\ge$	Is greater than or equal to

The statement $a < b$ means that a is to the left of b on the number line as shown in Fig. 2.4. The statement $c > d$ means that c is to the right of d on the number line, as shown in Fig. 2.5. Of course, $a < b$ has the same meaning as $b > a$. The statement $a \le b$ means that either a is to the left of b or a corresponds to the same point as b on the number line. The statement $a \le b$ has the same meaning as the statement $b \ge a$.

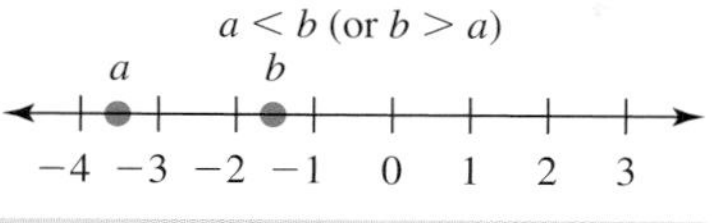

Figure 2.4

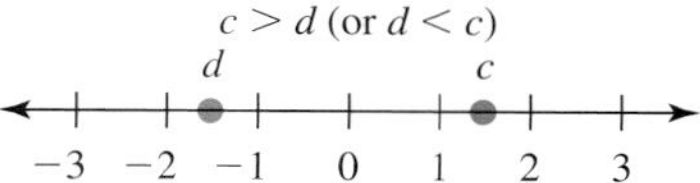

Figure 2.5

EXAMPLE 1

Verifying inequalities

Determine whether each of the following statements is correct.

a) $3 < 4$ **b)** $-1 < -2$ **c)** $-2 \le 0$

d) $0 \ge 0$ **e)** $2(-3) + 8 > 9$ **f)** $(-2)(-5) \le 10$

‹ Calculator Close-Up ›

A graphing calculator can determine whether an inequality is correct. Use the inequality symbols from the TEST menu to enter the inequality.

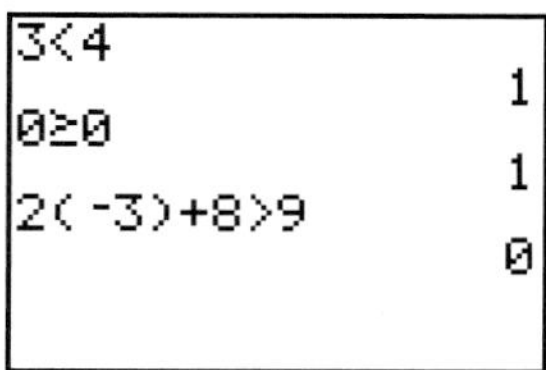

When ENTER is pressed, the calculator returns a 1 if the inequality is correct or a 0 if the inequality is incorrect.

Solution

a) Locate 3 and 4 on the number line shown in Fig. 2.6. Because 3 is to the left of 4 on the number line, $3 < 4$ is correct.

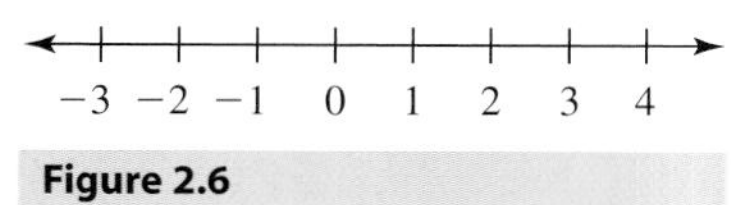

Figure 2.6

b) Locate -1 and -2 on the number line shown in Fig. 2.6. Because -1 is to the right of -2, on the number line, $-1 < -2$ is not correct.

c) Because -2 is to the left of 0 on the number line, $-2 \le 0$ is correct.

d) Because 0 is equal to 0, $0 \ge 0$ is correct.

e) Simplify the left side of the inequality to get $2 > 9$, which is not correct.

f) Simplify the left side of the inequality to get $10 \le 10$, which is correct.

Now do Exercises 7–22

‹2› Graphing Inequalities

If a is a fixed real number, then any real number x located to the right of a on the number line satisfies $x > a$. The set of real numbers located to the right of a on the number line is the solution set to $x > a$. This solution set is written in set-builder notation as $\{x \mid x > a\}$, or more simply in interval notation as (a, ∞). We **graph the inequality** by graphing the solution set (a, ∞). Recall from Chapter 1 that a bracket means that an endpoint is included in an interval and a parenthesis means that an endpoint is not included in an interval. Remember also that ∞ is not a number. It simply indicates that there is no end to the interval.

EXAMPLE 2

Graphing inequalities

State the solution set to each inequality in interval notation and sketch its graph.

a) $x < 5$ **b)** $-2 < x$ **c)** $x \geq 10$

Solution

a) All real numbers less than 5 satisfy $x < 5$. The solution set is the interval $(-\infty, 5)$ and the graph of the solution set is shown in Fig. 2.7.

b) The inequality $-2 < x$ indicates that x is greater than -2. The solution set is the interval $(-2, \infty)$ and the graph of the inequality is shown in Fig. 2.8.

c) All real numbers greater than or equal to 10 satisfy $x \geq 10$. The solution set is the interval $[10, \infty)$ and the graph is shown in Fig. 2.9.

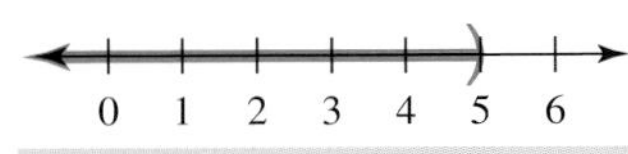

Figure 2.7

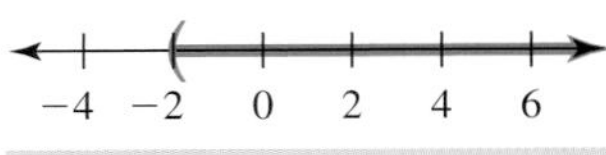

Figure 2.8

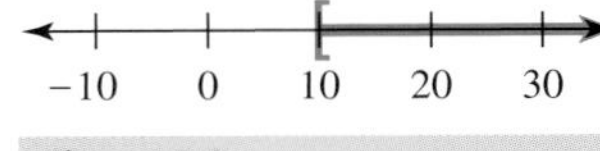

Figure 2.9

Now do Exercises 23–34

‹ Helpful Hint ›

A person in debt has a negative net worth. If Bob's net worth is $-\$8000$ and Mary's net worth is $-\$3000$, then Bob certainly has the greater debt, but we write

$$-8000 < -3000$$

because -8000 lies to the left of -3000 on the number line.

‹ Teaching Tip ›

The obvious inequality symbol $\neq$ is not mentioned here because we do not want to solve inequalities using it at this time.

‹3› Graphing Compound Inequalities

A statement involving more than one inequality is a **compound inequality.** We will study one type of compound inequality here and see other types in Section 8.1.

If a and b are real numbers and $a < b$, then the compound inequality

$$a < x < b$$

means that $a < x$ *and* $x < b$. Reading x first makes $a < x < b$ clearer:

"x is greater than a *and* x is less than b."

If x is greater than a and less than b, then x is between a and b. So the solution set to $a < x < b$ is the interval (a, b).

EXAMPLE 3

Graphing compound inequalities

State the solution set to each inequality in interval notation and sketch its graph.

a) $2 < x < 3$ **b)** $-2 \leq x < 1$

Solution

a) All real numbers between 2 and 3 satisfy $2 < x < 3$. The solution set is the interval $(2, 3)$ and the graph of the solution set is shown in Fig. 2.10.

b) The real numbers that satisfy $-2 \leq x < 1$ are between -2 and 1, including -2 but not including 1. So the solution set is the interval $[-2, 1)$ and the graph of this compound inequality is shown in Fig. 2.11.

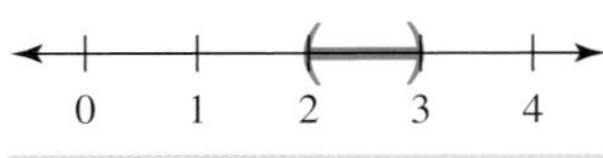

Figure 2.10

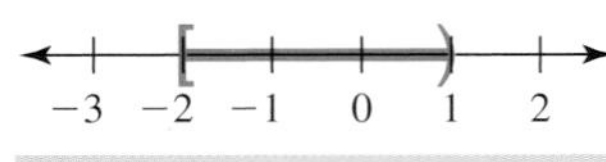

Figure 2.11

Now do Exercises 35–42

CAUTION We write $a < x < b$ only if $a < b$, and we write $a > x > b$ only if $a > b$. Similar rules hold for $\le$ and $\ge$. So $4 < x < 9$ and $-6 \ge x \ge -8$ are correct uses of this notation, but $5 < x < 2$ is not correct. Also, the inequalities should *not* point in opposite directions as in $5 < x > 7$.

⟨4⟩ Checking Inequalities

In Examples 2 and 3 we determined the solution sets to some inequalities. In Section 2.9, more complicated inequalities will be solved by using steps similar to those used for solving equations. In Example 4, we determine whether a given number satisfies an inequality of the type that we will be solving in Section 2.9.

EXAMPLE 4

Checking inequalities

Determine whether the given number satisfies the inequality following it.

a) $0,\ 2x - 3 \le -5$ **b)** $-4,\ x - 5 > 2x + 1$ **c)** $\frac{13}{3},\ 6 < 3x - 5 < 14$

Solution

a) Replace x by 0 in the inequality and simplify:

$$2x - 3 \le -5$$
$$2 \cdot 0 - 3 \le -5$$
$$-3 \le -5 \quad \text{Incorrect}$$

Since this last inequality is incorrect, 0 is not a solution to the inequality.

b) Replace x by -4 and simplify:

$$x - 5 > 2x + 1$$
$$-4 - 5 > 2(-4) + 1$$
$$-9 > -7 \quad \text{Incorrect}$$

Since this last inequality is incorrect, -4 is not a solution to the inequality.

c) Replace x by $\frac{13}{3}$ and simplify:

$$6 < 3x - 5 < 14$$
$$6 < 3 \cdot \frac{13}{3} - 5 < 14$$
$$6 < 13 - 5 < 14$$
$$6 < 8 < 14 \quad \text{Correct}$$

Since 8 is greater than 6 and less than 14, this inequality is correct. So $\frac{13}{3}$ satisfies the original inequality.

Now do Exercises 53–70

‹ Calculator Close-Up ›

To check 13/3 in

$$6 < 3x - 5 < 14$$

we check each part of the compound inequality separately.

```
6<3(13/3)-5
                1
3(13/3)-5<14
                1
```

Because both parts of the compound inequality are correct, 13/3 satisfies the compound inequality.

⟨5⟩ Writing Inequalities

Inequalities occur in applications, just as equations do. Certain verbal phrases indicate inequalities. For example, if you must be at least 18 years old to vote, then you can vote if you are 18 or older. The phrase "at least" means "greater than or equal to." If an elevator has a capacity of at most 20 people, then it can hold 20 people or fewer. The phrase "at most" means "less than or equal to."

EXAMPLE 5

Writing inequalities

Write an inequality that describes each situation.

a) Lois plans to spend at most \$500 on a washing machine including the 9% sales tax.

b) The length of a certain rectangle must be 4 meters longer than the width, and the perimeter must be at least 120 meters.

c) Fred made a 76 on the midterm exam. To get a B, the average of his midterm and his final exam must be between 80 and 90.

Solution

a) If x is the price of the washing machine, then $0.09x$ is the amount of sales tax. Since the total must be less than or equal to \$500, the inequality is

$$x + 0.09x \leq 500.$$

b) If W represents the width of the rectangle, then $W + 4$ represents the length. Since the perimeter $(2W + 2L)$ must be greater than or equal to 120, the inequality is

$$2(W) + 2(W + 4) \geq 120.$$

c) If we let x represent Fred's final exam score, then his average is $\frac{x + 76}{2}$. To indicate that the average is between 80 and 90, we use the compound inequality

$$80 < \frac{x + 76}{2} < 90.$$

Now do Exercises 79–91

‹ Teaching Tip ›

Students often have trouble with "at least" and "at most." Ask them to write a few sentences using these phrases and analyze them.

CAUTION In Example 5(b) you are given that L is 4 meters longer than W. So $L = W + 4$, and you can use $W + 4$ in place of L. If you knew only that L was longer than W, then you would know only that $L > W$.

Warm-Ups ▼

True or false? Explain your answer.

1. $-2 \leq -2$ True **2.** $-5 < 4 < 6$ True **3.** $-3 < 0 < -1$ False

4. The inequalities $7 < x$ and $x > 7$ have the same graph. True

5. The graph of $x < -3$ includes the point at -3. False

6. The number 5 satisfies the inequality $x > 2$. True

7. The number -3 is a solution to $-2 < x$. False

8. The number 4 satisfies the inequality $2x - 1 < 4$. False

9. The number 0 is a solution to the inequality $2x - 3 \leq 5x - 3$. True

10. The inequalities $2x - 1 < x$ and $x < 2x - 1$ have the same solutions. False

Exercises 2.8

‹ Study Tips ›

- Be careful not to spend too much time on a single problem when taking a test. If a problem seems to be taking too much time, you might be on the wrong track. Be sure to finish the test.
- Before you take a test on this chapter, work the test given in this book at the end of this chapter. This will give you a good idea of your test readiness.

Reading and Writing *After reading this section, write out the answers to these questions. Use complete sentences.*

1. What are the inequality symbols used in this section?
The inequality symbols are $<$, $\le$, $>$, and $\ge$.

2. What different looking inequality means the same as $a < b$?
The inequalities $a < b$ and $b > a$ have the same meaning.

3. How do you know when to use a bracket and when to use a parenthesis when graphing an inequality on a number line?
For $\le$ and $\ge$ use a bracket and for $<$ and $>$ use a parenthesis.

4. What is a compound inequality?
A compound inequality is a statement involving more than one inequality.

5. What is the meaning of the compound inequality $a < b < c$?
The compound inequality $a < b < c$ means $b > a$ and $b < c$, or b is between a and c.

6. What is the difference between "at most" and "at least?"
"At most" means less than or equal to and "at least" means greater than or equal to.

‹1› Inequalities

Determine whether each of the following statements is true. See Example 1.

7. $-5 < -8$ False

8. $-6 > -3$ False

9. $-3 < 5$ True

10. $-6 < 0$ True

11. $4 \le 4$ True

12. $-3 \ge -3$ True

13. $-6 > -5$ False

14. $-2 < -9$ False

15. $-4 \le -3$ True

16. $-5 \ge -10$ True

17. $(-3)(4) - 1 < 0 - 3$ True

18. $2(4) - 6 \le -3(5) + 1$ False

19. $-4(5) - 6 \ge 5(-6)$ True

20. $4(8) - 30 > 7(5) - 2(17)$ True

21. $7(4) - 12 \le 3(9) - 2$ True

22. $-3(4) + 12 \le 2(3) - 6$ True

‹2› Graphing Inequalities

State the solution set to each inequality in interval notation and sketch its graph. See Example 2.

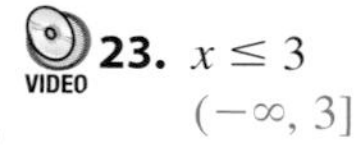

VIDEO **23.** $x \le 3$
$(-\infty, 3]$

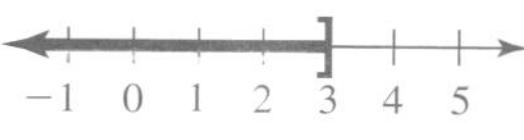

24. $x \le -7$
$(-\infty, -7]$

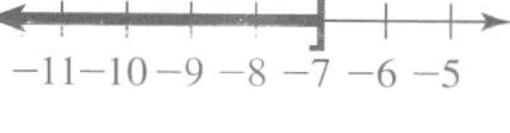

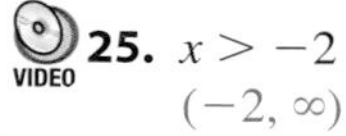

VIDEO **25.** $x > -2$
$(-2, \infty)$

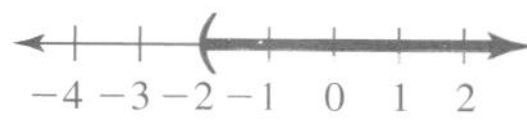

26. $x > 4$
$(4, \infty)$

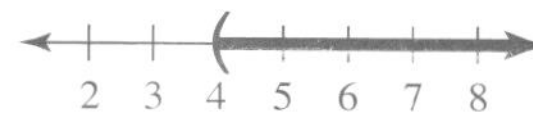

27. $-1 > x$
$(-\infty, -1)$

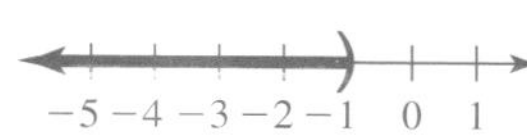

28. $0 > x$
$(-\infty, 0)$

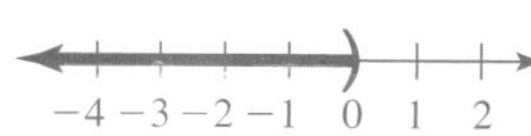

29. $-2 \le x$
$[-2, \infty)$

−4 −3 −2 −1 0 1 2

30. $-5 \ge x$
$(-\infty, -5]$

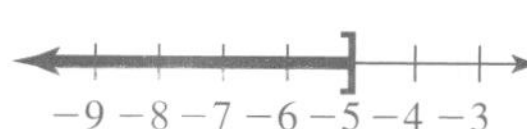

31. $x \ge \frac{1}{2}$

$\left[\frac{1}{2}, \infty\right)$

$\frac{1}{2}$
−1 0 1 2 3

32. $x \ge -\frac{2}{3}$

$\left[-\frac{2}{3}, \infty\right)$

$-\frac{2}{3}$
−3 −2 −1 0 1 2

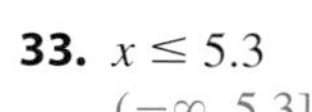

33. $x \le 5.3$
$(-\infty, 5.3]$

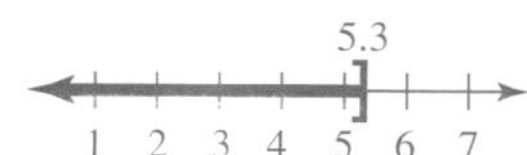

34. $x \le -3.4$
$(-\infty, -3.4]$

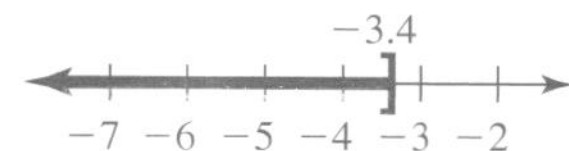

⟨3⟩ Graphing Compound Inequalities

State the solution set to each inequality in interval notation and sketch its graph. See Example 3.

35. $-3 < x < 1$
$(-3, 1)$
$-4\ -3\ -2\ -1\ 0\ 1\ 2$

36. $0 < x < 5$
$(0, 5)$
$0\ 1\ 2\ 3\ 4\ 5$

37. $3 \le x \le 7$
$[3, 7]$
$2\ 3\ 4\ 5\ 6\ 7\ 8$

38. $-3 \le x \le -1$
$[-3, -1]$
$-5\ -4\ -3\ -2\ -1\ 0\ 1$

39. $-5 \le x < 0$
$[-5, 0)$

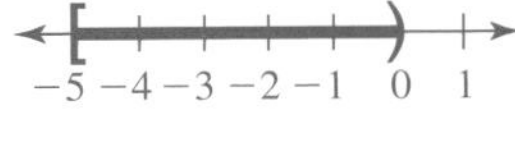

40. $-2 < x \le 2$
$(-2, 2]$
$-3\ -2\ -1\ 0\ 1\ 2\ 3$

41. $40 < x \le 100$
$(40, 100]$
$20\ 40\ 60\ 80\ 100\ 120$

42. $0 \le x < 600$
$[0, 600)$
$-200\ 0\ 200\ 400\ 600\ 800$

For each graph, write the corresponding inequality and the solution set to the inequality using interval notation.

43. $-3\ -2\ -1\ 0\ 1\ 2\ 3\ 4\ 5\ 6\ 7$ $x > 3, (3, \infty)$

44. $-4\ -3\ -2\ -1\ 0\ 1\ 2\ 3\ 4\ 5\ 6$ $x \le 4, (-\infty, 4]$

45. $-6\ -5\ -4\ -3\ -2\ -1\ 0\ 1\ 2\ 3\ 4$ $x \le 2, (-\infty, 2]$

46. $-5\ -4\ -3\ -2\ -1\ 0\ 1\ 2\ 3\ 4\ 5$ $0 < x \le 3, (0, 3]$

47. $-5\ -4\ -3\ -2\ -1\ 0\ 1\ 2\ 3\ 4\ 5$ $0 < x < 2, (0, 2)$

48. $-5\ -4\ -3\ -2\ -1\ 0\ 1\ 2\ 3\ 4\ 5$ $-1 \le x < 3, [-1, 3)$

49. $-6\ -4\ -2\ 0\ 2\ 4\ 6\ 8$ $-5 < x \le 7, (-5, 7]$

50. $-5\ -4\ -3\ -2\ -1\ 0\ 1\ 2\ 3\ 4\ 5$ $x < 4, (-\infty, 4)$

51. $-5\ -4\ -3\ -2\ -1\ 0\ 1\ 2\ 3\ 4\ 5$ $x > -4, (-4, \infty)$

52. $-5\ -4\ -3\ -2\ -1\ 0\ 1\ 2\ 3\ 4\ 5$ $0 < x \le 2, (0, 2]$

⟨4⟩ Checking Inequalities

Determine whether the given number satisfies the inequality following it. See Example 4.

53. $-9, -x > 3$ Yes
54. $5, -3 < -x$ No
55. $-2, 5 \le x$ No
56. $4, 4 \ge x$ Yes
57. $-6, 2x - 3 > -11$ No
58. $4, 3x - 5 < 7$ No
59. $3, -3x + 4 > -7$ Yes
60. $-4, -5x + 1 > -5$ Yes
61. $0, 3x - 7 \le 5x - 7$ Yes
62. $0, 2x + 6 \ge 4x - 9$ Yes
63. $2.5, -10x + 9 \le 3(x + 3)$ Yes
64. $1.5, 2x - 3 \le 4(x - 1)$ Yes
65. $-7, -5 < x < 9$ No
66. $-9, -6 \le x \le 40$ No
67. $-2, -3 \le 2x + 5 \le 9$ Yes
68. $-5, -3 < -3x - 7 \le 8$ Yes
69. $-3.4, -4.25x - 13.29 < 0.89$ No
70. $4.8, 3.25x - 14.78 \le 1.3$ Yes

For each inequality, determine which of the numbers -5.1, 0, and 5.1 satisfies the inequality.

71. $x > -5$ 0, 5.1
72. $x \le 0$ -5.1, 0
73. $5 < x$ 5.1
74. $-5 > x$ -5.1
75. $5 < x < 7$ 5.1
76. $5 < -x < 7$ -5.1
77. $-6 < -x < 6$ -5.1, 0, 5.1
78. $-5 \le x - 0.1 \le 5$ 5.1, 0

⟨5⟩ Writing Inequalities

Write an inequality to describe each situation. Do not solve. See Example 5.

79. ***Sales tax.*** At an 8% sales tax rate, Susan paid more than \$1500 sales tax when she purchased her new Camaro. Let p represent the price of the Camaro. $0.08p > 1500$

80. ***Internet shopping.*** Carlos paid less than \$1000 including \$40 for shipping and 9% sales tax when he bought his new computer. Let p represent the price of the computer. $p + 0.09p + 40 < 1000$

81. ***Fine dining.*** At Burger Brothers the price of a hamburger is twice the price of an order of French fries, and the price of a Coke is \$0.25 more than the price of the fries. Burger Brothers advertises that you can get a complete meal (burger, fries, and Coke) for under \$2.00. Let p represent the price of an order of fries. $p + 2p + p + 0.25 < 2.00$

82. ***Cats and dogs.*** Willow Creek Kennel boards only cats and dogs. One Friday night there were twice as many dogs as cats in the kennel and at least 30 animals spent the night there. Let d represent the number of dogs.
$d + \frac{1}{2}d \geq 30$

VIDEO **83.** ***Barely passing.*** Travis made 44 and 72 on the first two tests in algebra and has one test remaining. The average on the three tests must be at least 60 for Travis to pass the course. Let s represent his score on the last test.
$\frac{44 + 72 + s}{3} \geq 60$

84. ***Ace the course.*** Florence made 87 on her midterm exam in psychology. The average of her midterm and her final must be at least 90 to get an A in the course. Let s represent her score on the final. $\frac{87 + s}{2} \geq 90$

85. ***Coast to coast.*** On Howard's recent trip from Bangor to San Diego, he drove for 8 hours each day and traveled between 396 and 453 miles each day. Let R represent his average speed for each day. $396 < 8R < 453$

86. ***Mother's Day present.*** Bart and Betty are looking at color televisions that range in price from \$399.99 to \$579.99. Bart can afford more than Betty and has agreed to spend \$100 more than Betty when they purchase this gift for their mother. Let b represent Betty's portion of the gift.
$399.99 < b + b + 100 < 579.99$

87. ***Positioning a ladder.*** Write an inequality in the variable x for the degree measure of the angle at the base of the ladder shown in the figure, given that the angle at the base must be between 60° and 70°. $60 < 90 - x < 70$

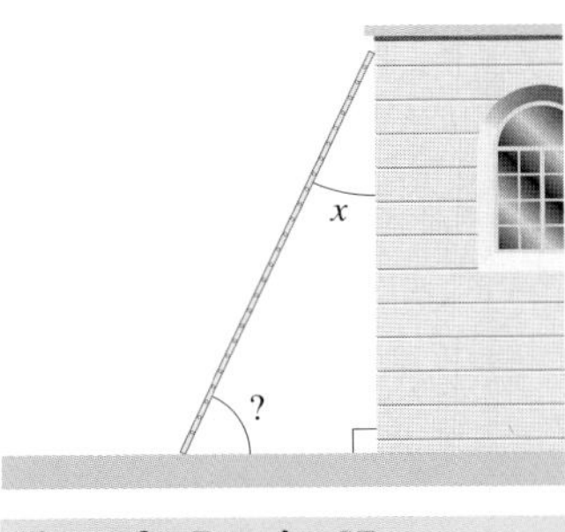

Figure for Exercise 87

88. ***Building a ski ramp.*** Write an inequality in the variable x for the degree measure of the smallest angle of the triangle shown in the figure, given that the degree measure of the smallest angle is at most 30°. $180 - x - (x + 8) \leq 30$

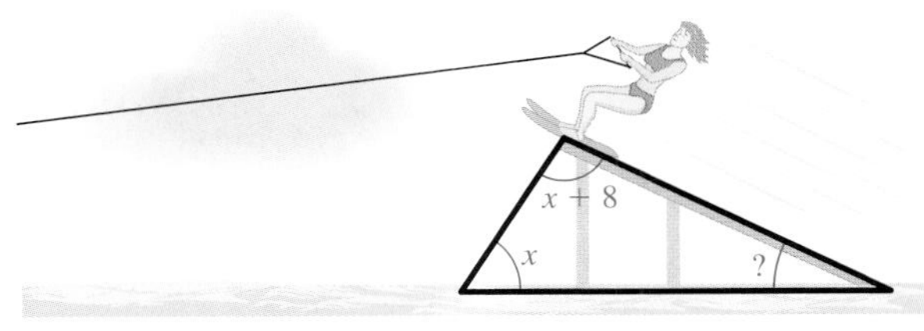

Figure for Exercise 88

89. ***Maximum girth.*** United Parcel Service defines the girth of a box as the sum of the length, twice the width, and twice the height. The maximum girth that UPS will ship is 130 in.

a) If a box has a length of 45 in. and a width of 30 in., then what inequality must be satisfied by the height?
$45 + 2(30) + 2h \leq 130$

b) The accompanying graph shows the girth of a box with a length of 45 in., a width of 30 in., and height of h in. Use the graph to estimate the maximum height that is allowed for this box. Approximately 12 in.

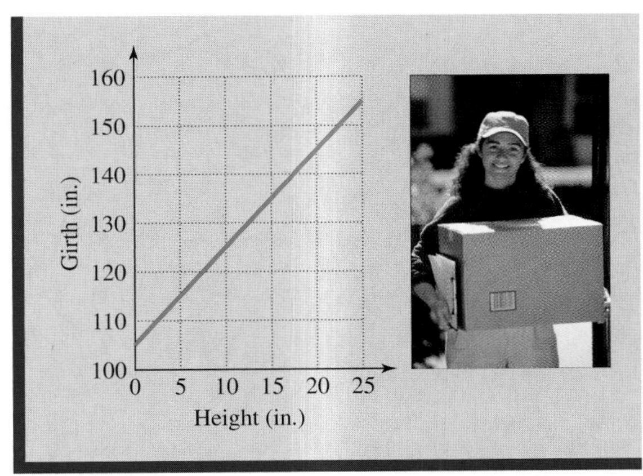

Figure for Exercise 89

90. ***Batting average.*** Near the end of the season a professional baseball player has 93 hits in 317 times at bat for an average of 93/317 or 0.293. He gets a \$1 million bonus if his season average is over 0.300. He estimates that he will bat 20 more times before the season ends. Let x represent the number of hits in the last 20 at bats of the season.

a) Write an inequality that must be satisfied for him to get the bonus. $\frac{93 + x}{337} > 0.300$

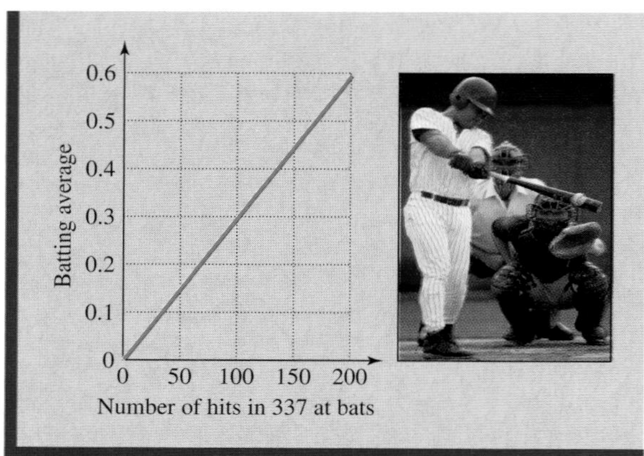

Figure for Exercise 90

b) Use the accompanying graph to estimate the number of hits in 337 at bats that will put his average over 0.300.
More than 100 hits

Solve.

91. ***Bicycle gear ratios.*** The gear ratio r for a bicycle is defined by the formula

$$r = \frac{Nw}{n},$$

where N is the number of teeth on the chainring (by the pedal), n is the number of teeth on the cog (by the wheel), and w is the wheel diameter in inches (*Cycling,* Burkett and Darst). The following chart gives uses for the various gear ratios.

Ratio	Use
$r > 90$	hard pedaling on level ground
$70 < r \le 90$	moderate effort on level ground
$50 < r \le 70$	mild hill climbing
$35 < r \le 50$	long hill climbing with load

A bicycle with a 27-inch diameter wheel has 50 teeth on the chainring and 17 teeth on the cog. Find the gear ratio and indicate what this gear ratio is good for.
79, moderate effort on level ground

Math *at Work* Body Mass Index

Medical professionals say that two-thirds of all Americans are overweight and excess weight has about the same effect on life expectancy as smoking. How can you tell if you are overweight or normal? Body mass index (BMI) can help you decide. To determine BMI divide your weight in kilograms by the square of your height in meters. Don't know your weight and height in the metric system? Then use the formula BMI $= 703W/H^2$, where W is your weight in pounds and H is your height in inches.

If $23 <$ BMI < 25, then you are probably not overweight. If BMI ≥ 26, then you are probably overweight and are statistically likely to have a lower life expectancy. According to the National Heart, Lung, and Blood Institute, you are overweight if $25 <$ BMI < 29.9 and obese if BMI ≥ 30. If your BMI is between 17 and 22, your life span might be longer than average. Men are usually happy with a BMI between 23 and 25 and women like to see their BMI between 20 and 22. However, BMI does not distinguish between muscle and fat and can wrongly suggest that a person with a short muscular build is overweight. Also, the BMI does not work well for children, because normal varies with age.

If you want to learn more about body mass index or don't want to do the calculations yourself, then check out any of the numerous websites that discuss BMI and even have online BMI calculators. Just do a search for body mass index.

2.9 Solving Inequalities and Applications

In This Section

To solve equations, we write a sequence of equivalent equations that ends in a very simple equation whose solution is obvious. In this section, you will learn that the procedure for solving inequalities is the same. However, the rules for performing operations on each side of an inequality are slightly different from the rules for equations.

⟨1⟩ Rules for Inequalities

Equivalent inequalities are inequalities that have exactly the same solutions. Inequalities such as $x > 3$ and $x + 2 > 5$ are equivalent because any number that is larger than 3 certainly satisfies $x + 2 > 5$ and any number that satisfies $x + 2 > 5$ must certainly be larger than 3.

We can get equivalent inequalities by performing operations on each side of an inequality just as we do for solving equations. If we start with the inequality $6 < 10$ and add 2 to each side, we get the true statement $8 < 12$. Examine the results of performing the same operation on each side of $6 < 10$.

⟨ Helpful Hint ⟩

You can think of an inequality like a seesaw that is out of balance.

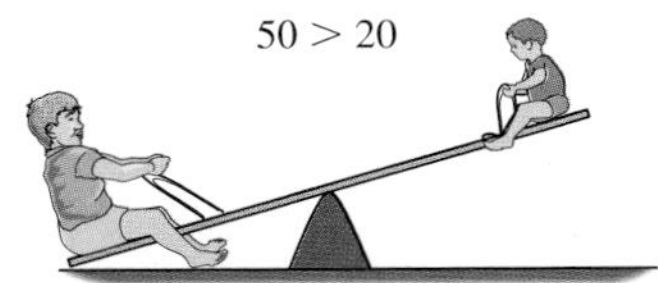

If the same weight is added to or subtracted from each side, it will remain in the same state of imbalance.

Perform these operations on each side:

	Add 2	Subtract 2	Multiply by 2	Divide by 2
Start with $6 < 10$	$8 < 12$	$4 < 8$	$12 < 20$	$3 < 5$

All of the resulting inequalities are correct. Now if we repeat these operations using -2, we get the following results.

Perform these operations on each side:

	Add -2	Subtract -2	Multiply by -2	Divide by -2
Start with $6 < 10$	$4 < 8$	$8 < 12$	$-12 > -20$	$-3 > -5$

Notice that the direction of the inequality symbol is the same for all of the results except the last two. When we multiplied each side by -2 and when we divided each side by -2, we had to reverse the inequality symbol to get a correct result. These tables illustrate the rules for solving inequalities.

Addition Property of Inequality

If we add the same number to each side of an inequality we get an equivalent inequality. If $a < b$, then $a + c < b + c$.

The addition property of inequality also enables us to subtract the same number from each side of an inequality because subtraction is defined in terms of addition.

Helpful Hint

Changing the signs of numbers changes their relative position on the number line. For example, 3 lies to the left of 5 on the number line, but -3 lies to the right of -5. So $3 < 5$, but $-3 > -5$. Since multiplying and dividing by a negative cause sign changes, these operations reverse the inequality.

Multiplication Property of Inequality

If we multiply each side of an inequality by the same *positive* number, we get an equivalent inequality. If $a < b$ and $c > 0$, then $ac < bc$. If we multiply each side of an inequality by the same *negative* number and *reverse the inequality symbol,* we get an equivalent inequality. If $a < b$ and $c < 0$, then $ac > bc$.

The multiplication property of inequality also enables us to divide each side of an inequality by a nonzero number because division is defined in terms of multiplication. So if we multiply or divide each side by a negative number, the inequality symbol is reversed.

EXAMPLE 1

Writing equivalent inequalities

Write the appropriate inequality symbol in the blank so that the two inequalities are equivalent.

a) $x + 3 > 9$, x ______ 6 **b)** $-2x \le 6$, x ______ -3

Solution

a) If we subtract 3 from each side of $x + 3 > 9$, we get the equivalent inequality $x > 6$.

b) If we divide each side of $-2x \le 6$ by -2, we get the equivalent inequality $x \ge -3$.

Now do Exercises 7–16

CAUTION We use the properties of inequality just as we use the properties of equality. However, when we multiply or divide each side by a negative number, we must reverse the inequality symbol.

⟨2⟩ Solving Inequalities

To solve inequalities, we use the properties of inequality to isolate x on one side.

EXAMPLE 2

Isolating the variable on the left side

Solve the inequality $4x - 5 > 19$. State the solution set using interval notation and sketch its graph.

Solution

$4x - 5 > 19$	Original inequality
$4x - 5 + 5 > 19 + 5$	Add 5 to each side.
$4x > 24$	Simplify.
$x > 6$	Divide each side by 4.

Since the last inequality is equivalent to the first, it has the same solution set as the first. So the solution set to $4x - 5 > 19$ is $(6, \infty)$. The graph is shown in Fig. 2.12.

1 2 3 4 5 6 7 8

Figure 2.12

Now do Exercises 17–18

‹ Calculator Close-Up ›

You can use the TABLE feature of a graphing calculator to numerically support the solution to the inequality $4x - 5 > 19$ in Example 2. Use the Y = key to enter the equation $y_1 = 4x - 5$.

```
Plot1 Plot2 Plot3
\Y1■4X-5
\Y2=
\Y3=
\Y4=
\Y5=
\Y6=
\Y7=
```

Next, use TBLSET to set the table so that the values of x start at 4.5 and the change in x is 0.5.

Finally, press TABLE to see lists of x-values and the corresponding y-values.

X	Y1
4.5	13
5	15
5.5	17
6	19
6.5	21
7	23
7.5	25
X=6	

Notice that when x is larger than 6, y_1 (or $4x - 5$) is larger than 19. The table verifies or supports the algebraic solution, but it should not replace the algebraic method.

Remember that $5 < x$ is equivalent to $x > 5$. So the variable can be isolated on the right side of an inequality as shown in Example 3.

EXAMPLE 3

Isolating the variable on the right side

Solve the inequality $5x - 2 \leq 7x - 5$. State the solution set using interval notation and sketch its graph.

Solution

$$5x - 2 \leq 7x - 5 \quad \text{Original inequality}$$

$$5x - 2 - 5x \leq 7x - 5 - 5x \quad \text{Subtract } 5x \text{ from each side.}$$

$$-2 \leq 2x - 5 \quad \text{Simplify.}$$

$$3 \leq 2x \quad \text{Add 5 to each side.}$$

$$\frac{3}{2} \leq x \quad \text{Divide each side by 2.}$$

Note that $\frac{3}{2} \leq x$ is equivalent to $x \geq \frac{3}{2}$. The solution set is the interval $\left[\frac{3}{2}, \infty\right)$ and the graph is shown in Fig. 2.13. Notice that $\frac{3}{2}$ is half way between 1 and 2 on the number line.

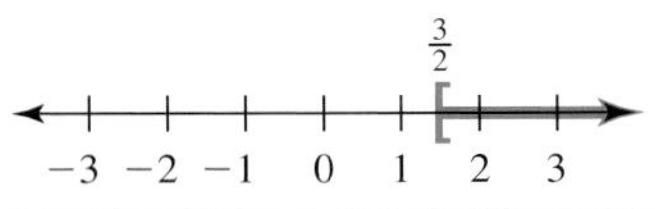

Figure 2.13

Now do Exercises 19–22

Rewriting $\frac{3}{2} \leq x$ as $x \geq \frac{3}{2}$ in Example 3 is not "reversing the inequality." Multiplying or dividing each side of $\frac{3}{2} \leq x$ by a negative number would reverse the inequality. For example, multiplying by -1 yields $-\frac{3}{2} \geq -x$. In Example 4, we divide each side of an inequality by a negative number and reverse the inequality symbol.

EXAMPLE 4

Reversing the inequality symbol

Solve $5 - 5x \le 1 + 2(5 - x)$. State the solution set in interval notation and sketch its graph.

Solution

$5 - 5x \le 1 + 2(5 - x)$	Original inequality
$5 - 5x \le 11 - 2x$	Simplify the right side.
$5 - 3x \le 11$	Add $2x$ to each side.
$-3x \le 6$	Subtract 5 from each side.
$x \ge -2$	Divide each side by -3, and reverse the inequality.

Figure 2.14

The solution set is the interval $[-2, \infty)$ and the graph is shown in Fig. 2.14.

Now do Exercises 23–44

We can use the rules for solving inequalities on the compound inequalities that we studied in Section 2.8.

EXAMPLE 5

Solving a compound inequality

Solve $-9 \le \frac{2x}{3} - 7 < 5$. State the solution set in interval notation and sketch its graph.

Solution

$-9 \le \frac{2x}{3} - 7 < 5$	Original inequality
$-9 + 7 \le \frac{2x}{3} - 7 + 7 < 5 + 7$	Add 7 to each part.
$-2 \le \frac{2x}{3} < 12$	Simplify.
$\frac{3}{2}(-2) \le \frac{3}{2} \cdot \frac{2x}{3} < \frac{3}{2} \cdot 12$	Multiply each part by $\frac{3}{2}$.
$-3 \le x < 18$	Simplify.

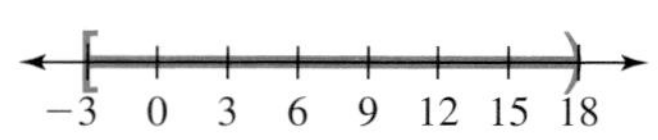

Figure 2.15

Since the last compound inequality is equivalent to the first, the solution set is $[-3, 18)$. The graph is shown in Fig. 2.15.

Now do Exercises 45–48

CAUTION There are many negative numbers in Example 5, but the inequality was not reversed, since we did not multiply or divide by a negative number. An inequality is reversed only if you multiply or divide by a negative number.

EXAMPLE 6

Reversing inequality symbols in a compound inequality

Solve $-3 \le 5 - x \le 5$. State the solution set in interval notation and sketch its graph.

Solution

$-3 \le 5 - x \le 5$	Original inequality
$-3 - 5 \le 5 - x - 5 \le 5 - 5$	Subtract 5 from each part.
$-8 \le -x \le 0$	Simplify.
$(-1)(-8) \ge (-1)(-x) \ge (-1)(0)$	Multiply each part by -1, reversing the inequality symbols.
$8 \ge x \ge 0$	

It is customary to write $8 \ge x \ge 0$ with the smallest number on the left:

$$0 \le x \le 8$$

Since the last compound inequality is equivalent to the first, the solution set is [0, 8]. The graph is shown in Fig. 2.16.

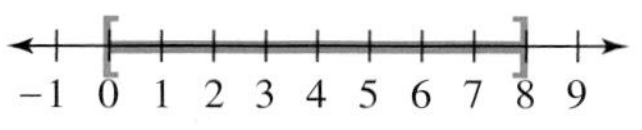

Figure 2.16

Now do Exercises 49–58

‹3› Applications

Example 7 shows how inequalities can be used in applications.

EXAMPLE 7

Averaging test scores

Mei Lin made a 76 on the midterm exam in history. To get a B, the average of her midterm and her final exam must be between 80 and 90. For what range of scores on the final exam will she get a B?

Solution

Let x represent the final exam score. Her average is then $\frac{x + 76}{2}$. The inequality expresses the fact that the average must be between 80 and 90:

$80 < \frac{x + 76}{2} < 90$	
$2(80) < 2\left(\frac{x + 76}{2}\right) < 2(90)$	Multiply each part by 2.
$160 < x + 76 < 180$	Simplify.
$160 - 76 < x + 76 - 76 < 180 - 76$	Subtract 76 from each part.
$84 < x < 104$	Simplify.

The last inequality indicates that Mei Lin's final exam score must be between 84 and 104.

Now do Exercises 65–80

‹ Helpful Hint ›

Remember that all inequality symbols in a compound inequality must point in the same direction. We usually have them all point to the left so that the numbers are increasing in size as you go from left to right in the inequality.

Warm-Ups 

True or false? Explain your answer.

1. The inequality $2x > 18$ is equivalent to $x > 9$. True
2. The inequality $x - 5 > 0$ is equivalent to $x < 5$. False
3. We can divide each side of an inequality by any real number. False
4. The inequality $-2x \leq 6$ is equivalent to $-x \leq 3$. True
5. The statement "x is at most 7" is written as $x < 7$. False
6. "The sum of x and $0.05x$ is at least 76" is written as $x + 0.05x \geq 76$. True
7. The statement "x is not more than 85" is written as $x < 85$. False
8. The inequality $-3 > x > -9$ is equivalent to $-9 < x < -3$. True
9. If x is the sale price of Glen's truck, the sales tax rate is 8%, and the title fee is \$50, then the total that he pays is $1.08x + 50$ dollars. True
10. If the selling price of the house, x, less the sales commission of 6% must be at least \$60,000, then $x - 0.06x \leq 60,000$. False

2.9 Exercises

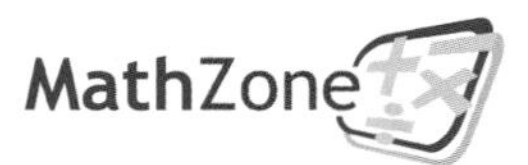

‹ Study Tips ›

- Do some review on a regular basis. The Making Connections exercises at the end of each chapter can be used to review, compare, and contrast different concepts that you have studied.
- No one covers every topic in this text. Be sure you know what you are responsible for.

Reading and Writing *After reading this section, write out the answers to these questions. Use complete sentences.*

1. What are equivalent inequalities? Equivalent inequalities are inequalities that have the same solutions.
2. What is the addition property of inequality? The addition property of inequality says that adding any real number to each side of an inequality produces an equivalent inequality.
3. What is the multiplication property of inequality? According to the multiplication property of inequality, the inequality symbol is reversed when multiplying (or dividing) by a negative number and not reversed when multiplying (or dividing) by a positive number.
4. What similarities are there between solving equations and solving inequalities? For equations or inequalities we try to isolate the variable. The properties of equality and inequality are similar.
5. How do we solve compound inequalities? We solve compound inequalities using the properties of inequality as we do for simple inequalities.
6. How do you know when to reverse the direction of an inequality symbol? The direction of the inequality symbol is reversed when we multiply or divide by a negative number.

‹1› Rules for Inequalities

Write the appropriate inequality symbol in the blank so that the two inequalities are equivalent. See Example 1.

7. $x + 7 > 0$
   $x \geq -7$
8. $x - 6 < 0$
   $x \leq 6$
9. $9 \leq 3w$
   $w \geq 3$
10. $10 \geq 5z$
    $z \leq 2$
11. $-x < 8$
    $x \geq -8$
12. $-x \geq -3$
    $x \leq 3$

13. $-4k < -4$
$k \geq 1$

14. $-9t > 27$
$t \leq -3$

15. $-\frac{1}{2}y \geq 4$
$y \leq -8$

16. $-\frac{1}{3}x \leq 4$
$x \geq -12$

⟨2⟩ Solving Inequalities

Solve each inequality. State the solution set in interval notation and sketch its graph. See Examples 2–4.

17. $x + 3 > 0$ $(-3, \infty)$

18. $x + 9 \leq -8$ $(-\infty, -17]$

19. $-3 < w - 1$ $(-2, \infty)$

20. $9 > w - 12$ $(-\infty, 21)$

21. $8 > 2b$ $(-\infty, 4)$

22. $35 < 7b$ $(5, \infty)$

23. $-8z \leq 4$ $\left[-\frac{1}{2}, \infty\right)$

24. $-4y \geq -10$ $\left(-\infty, \frac{5}{2}\right]$

VIDEO **25.** $3y - 2 < 7$ $(-\infty, 3)$

26. $2y - 5 > -9$ $(-2, \infty)$

27. $3 - 9z \leq 6$ $\left[-\frac{1}{3}, \infty\right)$

28. $5 - 6z \geq 13$ $\left(-\infty, -\frac{4}{3}\right]$

29. $6 > -r + 3$ $(-3, \infty)$

30. $6 \leq 12 - r$ $(-\infty, 6]$

31. $5 - 4p > -8 - 3p$ $(-\infty, 13)$

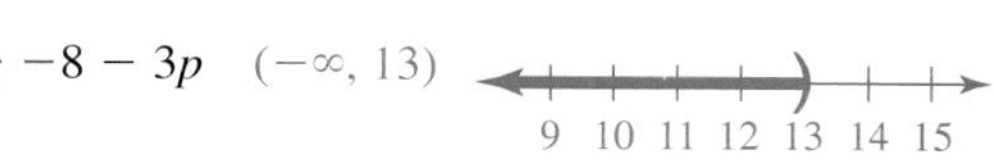

32. $7 - 9p > 11 - 8p$ $(-\infty, -4)$

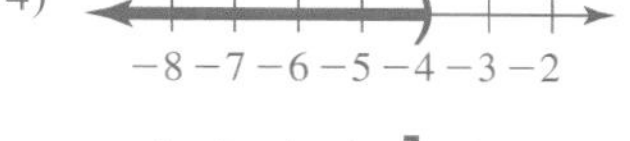

33. $-\frac{5}{6}q \geq -20$ $(-\infty, 24]$

VIDEO **34.** $-\frac{2}{3}q \geq -4$ $(-\infty, 6]$

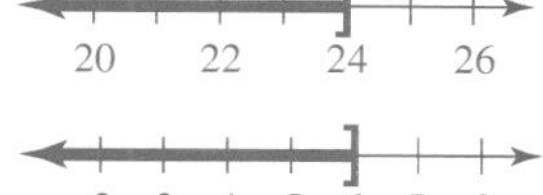

35. $1 - \frac{1}{4}t \geq \frac{1}{8}$ $\left(-\infty, \frac{7}{2}\right]$

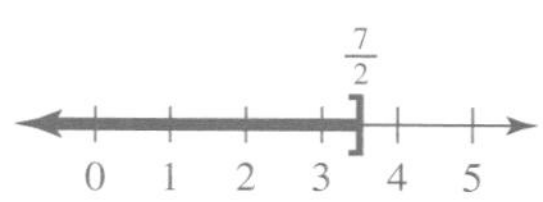

36. $\frac{1}{6} - \frac{1}{3}t > 0$ $\left(-\infty, \frac{1}{2}\right)$

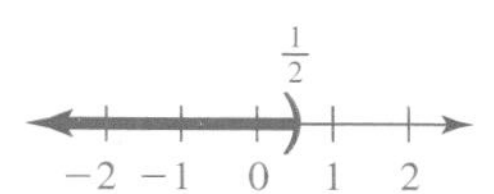

37. $0.1x + 0.35 > 0.2$
$(-1.5, \infty)$

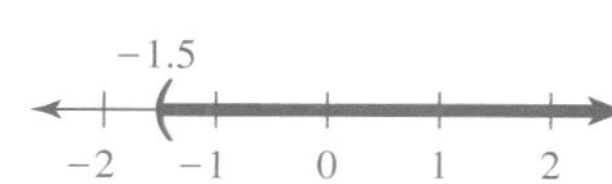

38. $1 - 0.02x \leq 0.6$ $[20, \infty)$

39. $2x + 5 < x - 6$ $(-\infty, -11)$

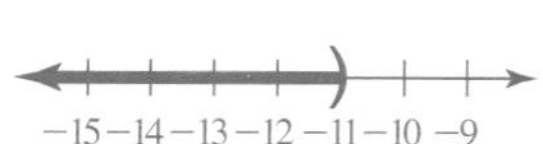

VIDEO **40.** $3x - 4 < 2x + 9$ $(-\infty, 13)$

41. $x - 4 < 2(x + 3)$ $(-10, \infty)$

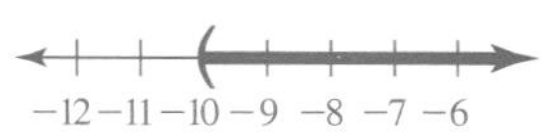

42. $2x + 3 < 3(x - 5)$ $(18, \infty)$

43. $0.52x - 35 < 0.45x + 8$
$(-\infty, 614.3)$

44. $8455(x - 3.4) > 4320$
$(3.91, \infty)$

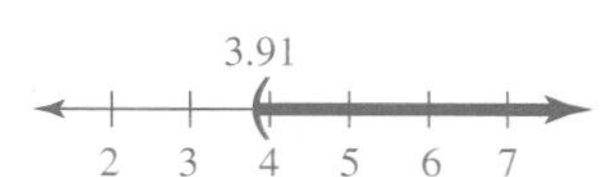

Solve each compound inequality. State the solution set in interval notation and sketch its graph. See Examples 5 and 6.

45. $5 < x - 3 < 7$ $(8, 10)$

46. $2 < x - 5 < 6$ $(7, 11)$

47. $3 < 2v + 1 < 10$ $\left(1, \frac{9}{2}\right)$

48. $-3 < 3v + 4 < 7$ $\left(-\frac{7}{3}, 1\right)$

49. $-4 \le 5 - k \le 7$ $[-2, 9]$

50. $2 \le 3 - k \le 8$ $[-5, 1]$

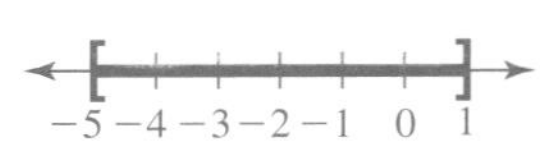

51. $-2 < 7 - 3y \le 22$ $[-5, 3)$

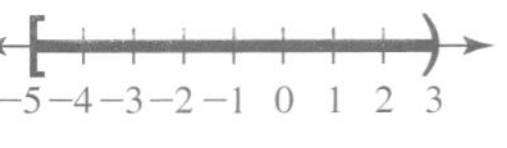

52. $-1 \le 1 - 2y < 3$ $(-1, 1]$

53. $5 < \frac{2u}{3} - 3 < 17$ $(12, 30)$

54. $-4 < \frac{3u}{4} - 1 < 11$ $(-4, 16)$

55. $-2 < \frac{4m - 4}{3} \le \frac{2}{3}$ $\left(-\frac{1}{2}, \frac{3}{2}\right]$

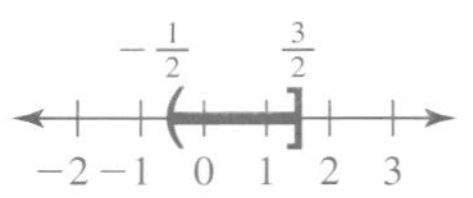

56. $0 \le \frac{3 - 2m}{2} < 9$ $\left(-\frac{15}{2}, \frac{3}{2}\right]$

57. $0.02 < 0.54 - 0.0048x < 0.05$
$(102.1, 108.3)$

58. $0.44 < \frac{34.55 - 22.3x}{124.5} < 0.76$
$(-2.69, -0.91)$

Solve each inequality. State the solution set in interval notation and sketch its graph.

59. $\frac{1}{2}x - 1 \le 4 - \frac{1}{3}x$ $(-\infty, 6]$

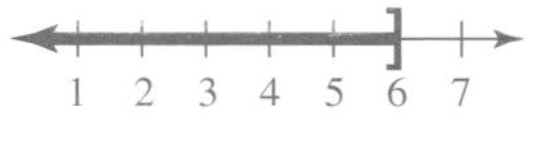

60. $\frac{y}{4} - \frac{5}{12} \ge \frac{y}{3} + \frac{1}{4}$ $(-\infty, -8]$

61. $\frac{1}{2}\left(x - \frac{1}{4}\right) > \frac{1}{4}\left(6x - \frac{1}{2}\right)$
$(-\infty, 0)$

62. $-\frac{1}{2}\left(z - \frac{2}{5}\right) < \frac{2}{3}\left(\frac{3}{4}z - \frac{6}{5}\right)$
$(1, \infty)$

63. $\frac{1}{3} < \frac{1}{4}x - \frac{1}{6} < \frac{7}{12}$
$(2, 3)$

64. $-\frac{3}{5} < \frac{1}{5} - \frac{2}{15}w < -\frac{1}{3}$ $(4, 6)$

⟨3⟩ Applications

Solve each of the following problems by using an inequality. See Example 7.

65. ***Boat storage.*** The length of a rectangular boat storage shed must be 4 meters more than the width, and the perimeter must be at least 120 meters. What is the range of values for the width? At least 28 meters

66. ***Fencing a garden.*** Elka is planning a rectangular garden that is to be twice as long as it is wide. If she can afford to buy at most 180 feet of fencing, then what are the possible values for the width? At most 30 feet

Photo for Exercise 66

67. ***Car shopping.*** Harold Ivan is shopping for a new car. In addition to the price of the car, there is a 5% sales tax and a \$144 title and license fee. If Harold Ivan decides that he will spend less than \$9970 total, then what is the price range for the car? Less than \$9358

68. ***Car selling.*** Ronald wants to sell his car through a broker who charges a commission of 10% of the selling price. Ronald still owes \$11,025 on the car. Ronald must get enough to at least pay off the loan. What is the range of the selling price? At least \$12,250

69. ***Microwave oven.*** Sherie is going to buy a microwave in a city with an 8% sales tax. She has at most \$594 to spend. In what price range should she look? At most \$550

70. ***Dining out.*** At Burger Brothers the price of a hamburger is twice the price of an order of French fries, and the price of a Coke is \$0.40 more than the price of the fries. Burger Brothers advertises that you can get a complete meal (burger, fries, and Coke) for under \$4.00. What is the price range of an order of fries? Less than 90 cents

71. ***Averaging test scores.*** Tilak made 44 and 72 on the first two tests in algebra and has one test remaining. For Tilak to pass the course, the average on the three tests must be at least 60. For what range of scores on his last test will Tilak pass the course? At least 64

72. ***Averaging income.*** Helen earned \$400 in January, \$450 in February, and \$380 in March. To pay all of her bills, she must average at least \$430 per month. For what income in April would her average for the 4 months be at least \$430? At least \$490

73. ***Going for a C.*** Professor Williams gives only a midterm exam and a final exam. The semester average is computed by taking $\frac{1}{3}$ of the midterm exam score plus $\frac{2}{3}$ of the final exam score. To get a C, Stacy must have a semester average between 70 and 79 inclusive. If Stacy scored only 48 on the midterm, then for what range of scores on the final exam will Stacy get a C? Between 81 and 94.5 inclusive

74. ***Different weights.*** Professor Williamson counts his midterm as $\frac{2}{3}$ of the grade and his final as $\frac{1}{3}$ of the grade. Wendy scored only 48 on the midterm. What range of scores on the final exam would put Wendy's average between 70 and 79 inclusive? Compare to the previous exercise. Between 114 and 141 inclusive

75. ***Average driving speed.*** On Halley's recent trip from Bangor to San Diego, she drove for 8 hours each day and traveled between 396 and 453 miles each day. In what range was her average speed for each day of the trip? Between 49.5 and 56.625 miles per hour

76. ***Driving time.*** On Halley's trip back to Bangor, she drove at an average speed of 55 mph every day and traveled between 330 and 495 miles per day. In what range was her daily driving time? Between 6 and 9 hours

77. ***Sailboat navigation.*** As the sloop sailed north along the coast, the captain sighted the lighthouse at points A and B as shown in the figure. If the degree measure of the angle at the lighthouse is less than 30°, then what are the possible values for x? Between 55° and 85°

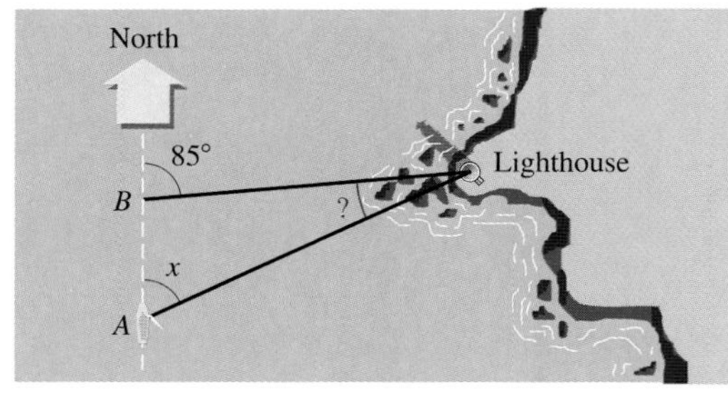

Figure for Exercise 77

78. ***Flight plan.*** A pilot started at point A and flew in the direction shown in the diagram for some time. At point B she made a 110° turn to end up at point C, due east of where she started. If the measure of angle C is less than 85°, then what are the possible values for x? Between 0° and 65°

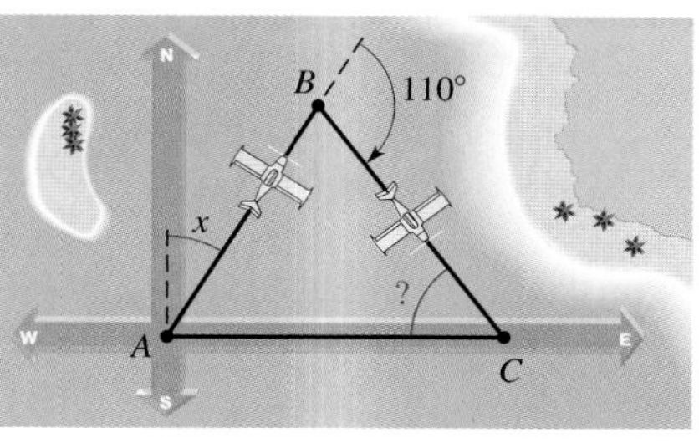

Figure for Exercise 78

79. ***Bicycle gear ratios.*** The gear ratio r for a bicycle is defined by the formula

$$r = \frac{Nw}{n},$$

where N is the number of teeth on the chainring (by the pedal), n is the number of teeth on the cog (by the wheel), and w is the wheel diameter in inches (www.sheldonbrown.com/gears).

a) If the wheel has a diameter of 27 in. and there are 12 teeth on the cog, then for what number of teeth on the chainring is the gear ratio between 60 and 80? Between 27 and 35 teeth inclusive

b) If a bicycle has 48 teeth on the chainring and 17 teeth on the cog, then for what diameter wheel is the gear ratio between 65 and 70? Between 23.02 in. and 24.79 in.

c) If a bicycle has a 26-in. diameter wheel and 40 teeth on the chainring, then for what number of teeth on the cog is the gear ratio less than 75? At least 14 teeth

80. ***Virtual demand.*** The weekly demand (the number bought by consumers) for the Acme Virtual Pet is given by the formula

$$d = 9000 - 60p$$

where p is the price each in dollars.

a) What is the demand when the price is \$30 each? 7200

b) In what price range will the demand be above 6000? Less than \$50

Chapter 2 Wrap-Up

Summary

Equations		**Examples**
Linear equation	An equation of the form $ax = b$ with $a \neq 0$	$3x = 7$
Identity	An equation that is satisfied by every number for which both sides are defined	$x + x = 2x$
Conditional equation	An equation that has at least one solution but is not an identity	$5x - 10 = 0$
Inconsistent equation	An equation that has no solution	$x = x + 1$
Equivalent equations	Equations that have exactly the same solutions	$2x + 1 = 5$ $2x = 4$
Properties of equality	If the same number is added to or subtracted from each side of an equation, the resulting equation is equivalent to the original equation.	$x - 5 = -9$ $x = -4$
	If each side of an equation is multiplied or divided by the same nonzero number, the resulting equation is equivalent to the original equation.	$9x = 27$ $x = 3$
Solving equations	1. Remove parentheses by using the distributive property and then combine like terms to simplify each side as much as possible. 2. Use the addition property of equality to get like terms from opposite sides onto the same side so that they may be combined. 3. The multiplication property of equality is generally used last. 4. Check that the solution satisfies the original equation.	$2(x - 3) = -7 + 3(x - 1)$ $2x - 6 = -10 + 3x$ $-x - 6 = -10$ $-x = -4$ $x = 4$ *Check:* $2(4 - 3) = -7 + 3(4 - 1)$ $2 = 2$

Applications

Steps in solving applied problems

1. Read the problem.
2. If possible, draw a diagram to illustrate the problem.
3. Choose a variable and write down what it represents.

4. Represent any other unknowns in terms of that variable.
5. Write an equation that describes the situation.
6. Solve the equation.
7. Answer the original question.
8. Check your answer by using it to solve the original problem (not the equation).

Inequalities		**Examples**
Properties of inequality	Addition, subtraction, multiplication, and division may be performed on each side of an inequality, just as we do in solving equations, with one exception. When multiplying or dividing by a negative number, the inequality symbol is reversed.	$-3x + 1 > 7$ $-3x > 6$ $x < -2$

Enriching Your Mathematical Word Power

For each mathematical term, choose the correct meaning.

1. linear equation
a. an equation in which the terms are in line
b. an equation of the form $ax = b$ where $a \neq 0$
c. the equation $a = b$
d. an equation of the form $a^2 + b^2 = c^2$ b

2. identity
a. an equation that is satisfied by all real numbers
b. an equation that is satisfied by every real number
c. an equation that is identical
d. an equation that is satisfied by every real number for which both sides are defined d

3. conditional equation
a. an equation that has at least one real solution
b. an equation that is correct
c. an equation that is satisfied by at least one real number but is not an identity
d. an equation that we are not sure how to solve c

4. inconsistent equation
a. an equation that is wrong
b. an equation that is only sometimes consistent
c. an equation that has no solution
d. an equation with two variables c

5. equivalent equations
a. equations that are identical
b. equations that are correct
c. equations that are equal
d. equations that have the same solution d

6. formula
a. an equation
b. a type of race car
c. a process
d. an equation involving two or more variables d

7. literal equation
a. a formula
b. an equation with words
c. a false equation
d. a fact a

8. complementary angles
a. angles that compliment each other
b. angles whose degree measures total 90°
c. angles whose degree measures total 180°
d. angles with the same vertex b

9. supplementary angles
a. angles with soft flexible sides
b. angles whose degree measures total 90°
c. angles whose degree measures total 180°
d. angles that form a square c

10. uniform motion
a. movement of an army
b. movement in a straight line
c. consistent motion
d. motion at a constant rate d

Review Exercises

2.1 The Addition and Multiplication Properties of Equality

Solve each equation and check your answer.

1. $x - 23 = 12$ $\{35\}$

2. $14 = 18 + y$ $\{-4\}$

3. $\frac{2}{3}u = -4$ $\{-6\}$

4. $-\frac{3}{8}r = 15$ $\{-40\}$

5. $-5y = 35$ $\{-7\}$

6. $-12 = 6h$ $\{-2\}$

7. $6m = 13 + 5m$ $\{13\}$

8. $19 - 3n = -2n$ $\{19\}$

2.2 Solving General Linear Equations

Solve each equation and check your answer.

9. $2x - 5 = 9$ $\{7\}$

10. $5x - 8 = 38$ $\left\{\frac{46}{5}\right\}$

11. $3p - 14 = -4p$ $\{2\}$

12. $36 - 9y = 3y$ $\{3\}$

13. $2z + 12 = 5z - 9$ $\{7\}$

14. $15 - 4w = 7 - 2w$ $\{4\}$

15. $2(h - 7) = -14$ $\{0\}$

16. $2(t - 7) = 0$ $\{7\}$

17. $3(w - 5) = 6(w + 2) - 3$ $\{-8\}$

18. $2(a - 4) + 4 = 5(9 - a)$ $\{7\}$

2.3 More Equations

Solve each equation. Identify each equation as a conditional equation, an inconsistent equation, or an identity.

19. $2(x - 7) - 5 = 5 - (3 - 2x)$ $\varnothing$, inconsistent

20. $2(x - 7) + 5 = -(9 - 2x)$ All real numbers, identity

21. $2(w - w) = 0$ All real numbers, identity

22. $2y - y = 0$ $\{0\}$, conditional

23. $\frac{3r}{3r} = 1$ All nonzero real numbers, identity

24. $\frac{3t}{3} = 1$ $\{1\}$, conditional

25. $\frac{1}{2}a - 5 = \frac{1}{3}a - 1$ $\{24\}$, conditional

26. $\frac{1}{2}b - \frac{1}{2} = \frac{1}{4}b$ $\{2\}$, conditional

27. $0.06q + 14 = 0.3q - 5.2$ $\{80\}$, conditional

28. $0.05(z + 20) = 0.1z - 0.5$ $\{30\}$, conditional

29. $0.05(x + 100) + 0.06x = 115$ $\{1000\}$, conditional

30. $0.06x + 0.08(x + 1) = 0.41$ $\left\{\frac{33}{14}\right\}$, conditional

Solve each equation.

31. $2x + \frac{1}{2} = 3x + \frac{1}{4}$ $\left\{\frac{1}{4}\right\}$

32. $5x - \frac{1}{3} = 6x - \frac{1}{2}$ $\left\{\frac{1}{6}\right\}$

33. $\frac{x}{2} - \frac{3}{4} = \frac{x}{6} + \frac{1}{8}$ $\left\{\frac{21}{8}\right\}$

34. $\frac{1}{3} - \frac{x}{5} = \frac{1}{2} - \frac{x}{10}$ $\left\{-\frac{5}{3}\right\}$

35. $\frac{5}{6}x = -\frac{2}{3}$ $\left\{-\frac{4}{5}\right\}$

36. $-\frac{2}{3}x = \frac{3}{4}$ $\left\{-\frac{9}{8}\right\}$

37. $-\frac{1}{2}(x - 10) = \frac{3}{4}x$ $\{4\}$

38. $-\frac{1}{3}(6x - 9) = 23$ $\{-10\}$

39. $3 - 4(x - 1) + 6 = -3(x + 2) - 5$ $\{24\}$

40. $6 - 5(1 - 2x) + 3 = -3(1 - 2x) - 1$ $\{-2\}$

41. $5 - 0.1(x - 30) = 18 + 0.05(x + 100)$ $\{-100\}$

42. $0.6(x - 50) = 18 - 0.3(40 - 10x)$ $\{-15\}$

2.4 Formulas

Solve each equation for x.

43. $ax + b = 0$

$x = -\frac{b}{a}$

44. $mx + e = t$

$x = \frac{t - e}{m}$

45. $ax - 2 = b$

$x = \frac{b + 2}{a}$

46. $b = 5 - x$

$x = 5 - b$

47. $LWx = V$

$x = \frac{V}{LW}$

48. $3xy = 6$

$x = \frac{2}{y}$

49. $2x - b = 5x$
$x = -\frac{b}{3}$

50. $t - 5x = 4x$
$x = \frac{t}{9}$

Solve each equation for y. Write the answer in the form $y = mx + b$, where m and b are real numbers.

51. $5x + 2y = 6$
$y = -\frac{5}{2}x + 3$

52. $5x - 3y + 9 = 0$
$y = \frac{5}{3}x + 3$

53. $y - 1 = -\frac{1}{2}(x - 6)$
$y = -\frac{1}{2}x + 4$

54. $y + 6 = \frac{1}{2}(x + 8)$
$y = \frac{1}{2}x - 2$

55. $\frac{1}{2}x + \frac{1}{4}y = 4$
$y = -2x + 16$

56. $-\frac{x}{3} + \frac{y}{2} = 1$
$y = \frac{2}{3}x + 2$

Find the value of y in each formula if $x = -3$.

57. $y = 3x - 4$ -13

58. $2x - 3y = -7$ $\frac{1}{3}$

59. $5xy = 6$ $-\frac{2}{5}$

60. $3xy - 2x = -12$ 2

61. $y - 3 = -2(x - 4)$ 17

62. $y + 1 = 2(x - 5)$ -17

Fill in the tables using the given formulas.

63. $y = -5x + 10$

x	y
−1	15
0	10
1	5
2	0
3	−5

64. $y = 2x - 4$

x	y
0	−4
1	−2
2	0
3	2
4	4

65. $y = \frac{2}{3}x - 1$

x	y
−3	−3
0	−1
3	1
6	3

66. $y = 10x + 100$

x	y
−20	−100
−10	0
0	100
10	200

2.5 Translating Verbal Expressions into Algebraic Expressions

Translate each verbal expression into an algebraic expression.

67. The sum of a number and 9
$x + 9$, where x is the number

68. The product of a number and 7
$7x$, where x is the number

69. Two numbers that differ by 8
x and $x + 8$, where x is the smaller number

70. Two numbers with a sum of 12
x and $12 - x$, where x is one number

71. Sixty-five percent of a number
$0.65x$, where x is the number

72. One half of a number
$\frac{1}{2}x$, where x is the number

Identify the variable, and write an equation that describes each situation. Do not solve the equation.

73. One side of a rectangle is 5 feet longer than the other, and the area is 98 square feet.
$x(x + 5) = 98$, where x is the width

74. One side of a rectangle is one foot longer than twice the other side, and the perimeter is 56 feet.
$2x + 2(2x + 1) = 56$, where x is the width

75. By driving 10 miles per hour slower than Jim, Barbara travels the same distance in 3 hours as Jim does in 2 hours.
$2x = 3(x - 10)$, where x is Jim's rate

76. Gladys and Ned drove 840 miles altogether, with Gladys averaging 5 miles per hour more in her 6 hours at the wheel than Ned did in his 5 hours at the wheel.
$6(x + 5) + 5x = 840$, where x is Ned's rate

77. The sum of three consecutive even integers is 90.
$x + x + 2 + x + 4 = 90$, where x is the smallest of the three even integers

78. The sum of two consecutive odd integers is 40.
$x + x + 2 = 40$, where x is the smaller of the two odd integers

79. The three angles of a triangle have degree measures of t, $2t$, and $t - 10$.
$t + 2t + t - 10 = 180$, where t is the degree measure of an angle

80. Two complementary angles have degree measures p and $3p - 6$.
$p + 3p - 6 = 90$, where p is the degree measure of an angle

2.6–7 Applications

Solve each problem.

81. ***Odd integers.*** If the sum of three consecutive odd integers is 237, then what are the integers?
77, 79, 81

82. ***Even integers.*** Find two consecutive even integers that have a sum of 450.
224, 226

83. ***Driving to the shore.*** Lawanda and Betty both drive the same distance to the shore. By driving 15 miles per hour faster than Betty, Lawanda can get there in 3 hours while Betty takes 4 hours. How fast does each of them drive?
Betty 45 mph, Lawanda 60 mph

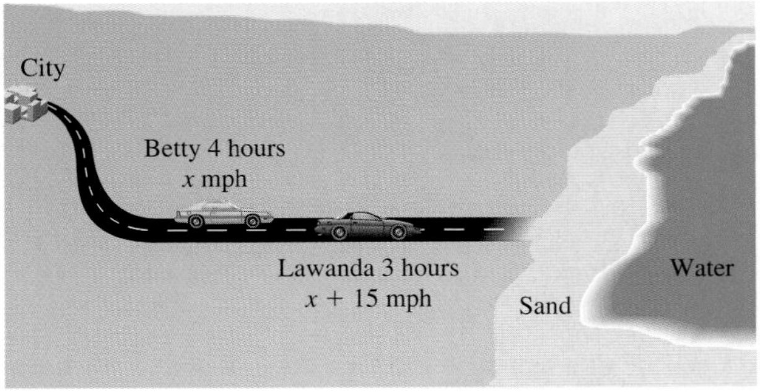

Figure for Exercise 83

84. ***Rectangular lot.*** The length of a rectangular lot is 50 feet more than the width. If the perimeter is 500 feet, then what are the length and width? Length 150 feet, width 100 feet

85. ***Combined savings.*** Wanda makes \$6000 more per year than her husband does. Wanda saves 10% of her income for retirement, and her husband saves 6%. If together they save \$5400 per year, then how much does each of them make per year? Wanda \$36,000, husband \$30,000

86. ***Layoffs looming.*** American Products plans to lay off 10% of its employees in its aerospace division and 15% of its employees in its agricultural division. If altogether 12% of the 3000 employees in these two divisions will be laid off, then how many employees are in each division?
Aerospace 1800, agriculture 1200

2.8 Inequalities

Determine whether the given number is a solution to the inequality following it.

87. 3, $-2x + 5 \le x - 6$ No

88. −2, $5 - x > 4x + 3$ Yes

89. −1, $-2 \le 6 + 4x < 0$ No

90. 0, $4x + 9 \ge 5(x - 3)$ Yes

For each graph write the corresponding inequality and the solution set to the inequality using interval notation.

91. 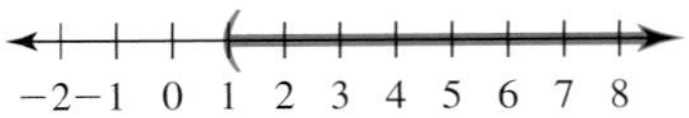

$x > 1$, $(1, \infty)$

92. 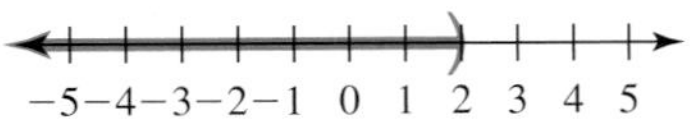

$x < 2$, $(-\infty, 2)$

93. 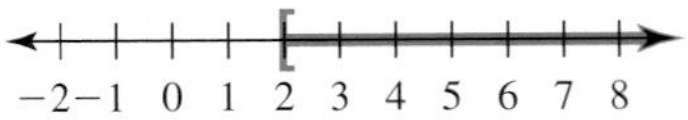

$x \ge 2$, $[2, \infty)$

94. 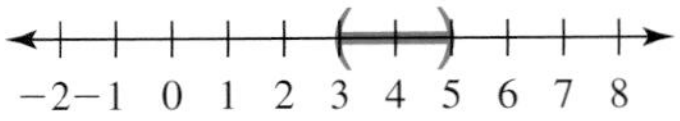

$3 < x < 5$, $(3, 5)$

95. 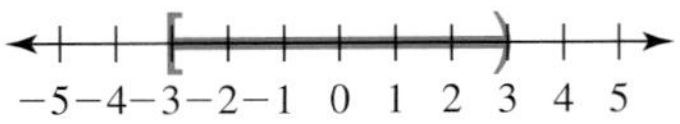

$-3 \le x < 3$, $[-3, 3)$

96. 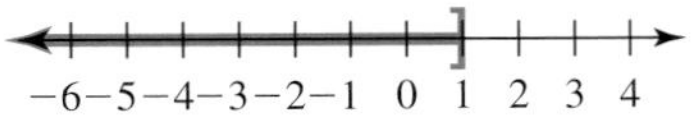

$x \le 1$, $(-\infty, 1]$

97. 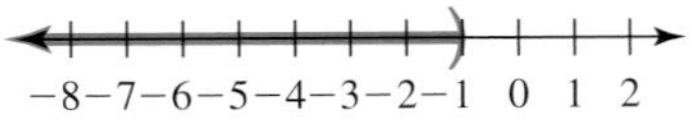

$x < -1$, $(-\infty, -1)$

98. 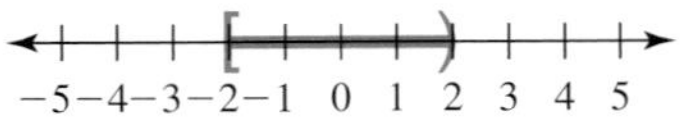

$-2 \le x < 2$, $[-2, 2)$

2.9 Solving Inequalities and Applications

Solve each inequality. State the solution set in interval notation and sketch its graph.

99. $x + 2 > 1$ $(-1, \infty)$

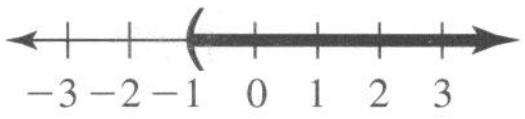

100. $x - 3 > 7$ $(10, \infty)$

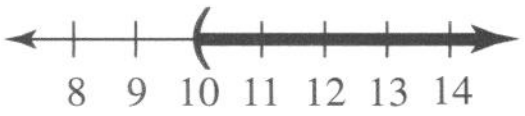

101. $3x - 5 < x + 1$ $(-\infty, 3)$

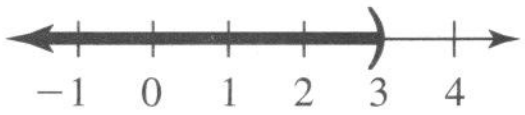

102. $5x - 5 > 9 - 2x$ $(2, \infty)$

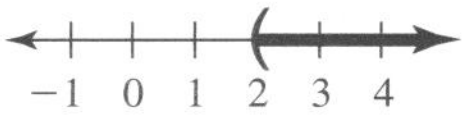

103. $-\frac{3}{4}x \geq 3$ $(-\infty, -4]$

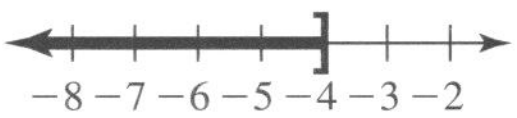

104. $-\frac{2}{3}x \leq 10$ $[-15, \infty)$

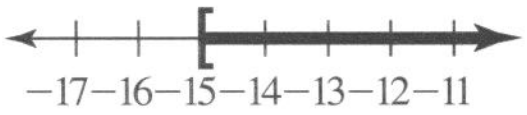

105. $3 - 2x < 11$ $(-4, \infty)$

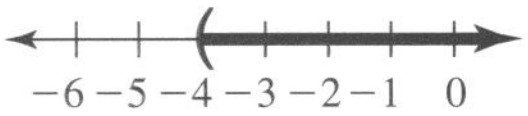

106. $5 - 3x > 35$ $(-\infty, -10)$

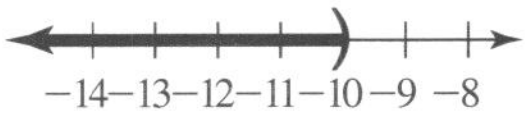

107. $-3 < 2x - 1 < 9$ $(-1, 5)$

108. $2 \leq 3x + 2 < 8$ $[0, 2)$

109. $0 \leq 1 - 2x < 5$ $\left(-2, \frac{1}{2}\right]$

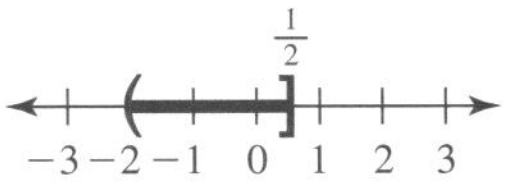

110. $-5 < 3 - 4x \leq 7$ $[-1, 2)$

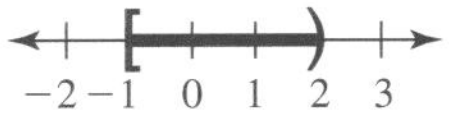

111. $-1 \leq \frac{2x - 3}{3} \leq 1$ $[0, 3]$

112. $-3 < \frac{4 - x}{2} < 2$ $(0, 10)$

113. $\frac{1}{3} < \frac{1}{3} + \frac{x}{2} < \frac{5}{6}$ $(0, 1)$

114. $-\frac{3}{8} \leq -\frac{1}{4}x + \frac{1}{8} < \frac{5}{8}$ $(-2, 2]$

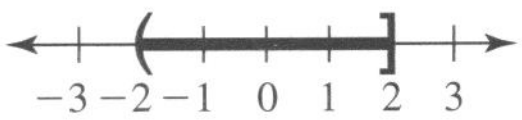

Miscellaneous

Use an equation, inequality, or formula to solve each problem.

115. ***Plasma TV discount.*** Nexus got a 14% discount when he bought a new plasma television. If the amount of the discount was \$392, then what was the original price of the television? \$2800

116. ***Laptop discount.*** Zeland got a 12% discount on a new laptop computer. If he paid \$1166 for the laptop, then what was the original price? \$1325

117. ***Rug commission.*** Caroline sold an antique rug through a broker who got 8% of the selling price as a commission. If Caroline got \$7820 for the rug after the broker's commission, then what was the selling price of the rug? \$8500

118. ***Buyer's premium.*** Brittany paid \$95,920 for a 1966 Mustang at a classic car auction where there is a 9% buyer's premium. This means that the buyer pays the bid price plus 9% of the bid price. What was the bid price? \$88,000

119. ***Long-term yields.*** The annual yield on a 30-year treasury bond is 5.375%. Use the simple interest formula to find the amount of interest earned during the first year on a \$10,000 bond. \$537.50

120. ***High interest rate.*** Eddie wrote a \$280 check to a check holding company, which gave him \$260 in cash. After two weeks the company will cash his \$280 check. Find the annual simple interest rate for this loan. Note that the time is a fraction of a year. 200%

121. ***Combined videos.*** The owners of ABC Video discovered that they had no movies in common with XYZ Video and bought XYZ's entire stock. Although XYZ had 200 titles, they had no children's movies, while 60% of ABC's titles were children's movies. If 40% of the movies in the combined stock are children's movies, then how many movies did ABC have before the merger? 400 movies

122. ***Living comfortably.*** Gary has figured that he needs to take home \$30,400 a year to live comfortably. If the government gets 24% of Gary's income, then what must his income be for him to live comfortably? \$40,000

123. ***Bracing a gate.*** The diagonal brace on a rectangular gate forms an angle with the horizontal side with degree measure x and an angle with the vertical side with degree measure $2x - 3$. Find x. 31°

124. ***Digging up the street.*** A contractor wants to install a pipeline connecting point A with point C on opposite sides of a road as shown in the figure on the next page. To save money, the contractor has decided to lay the pipe to point B and then under the road to point C. Find the measure of the angle marked x in the figure. 70°

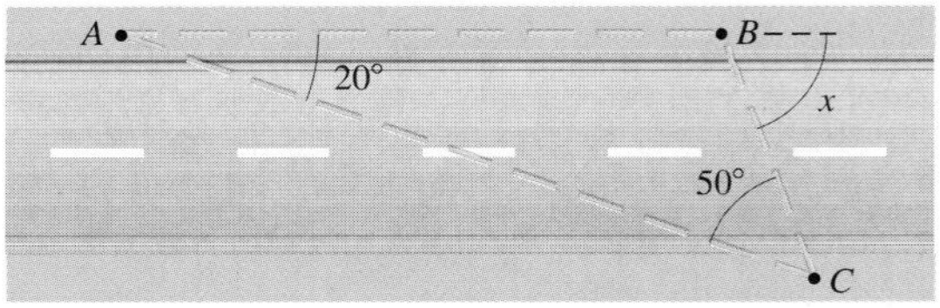

Figure for Exercise 124

125. ***Perimeter of a triangle.*** One side of a triangle is 1 foot longer than the shortest side, and the third side is twice as long as the shortest side. If the perimeter is less than 25 feet, then what is the range of the length of the shortest side? Less than 6 feet

126. ***Restricted hours.*** Alana makes \$5.80 per hour working in the library. To keep her job, she must make at least \$116 per week; but to keep her scholarship, she must not earn more than \$145 per week. What is the range of the number of hours per week that she may work? Between 20 and 25 hours per week inclusive

Chapter 2 Test

Solve each equation.

1. $-10x - 6 + 4x = -4x + 8$ $\{-7\}$

2. $5(2x - 3) = x + 3$ $\{2\}$

3. $-\frac{2}{3}x + 1 = 7$ $\{-9\}$

4. $x + 0.06x = 742$ $\{700\}$

5. $x - 0.03x = 0.97$ $\{1\}$

6. $6x - 7 = 0$ $\left\{\frac{7}{6}\right\}$

7. $\frac{1}{2}x - \frac{1}{3} = \frac{1}{4}x + \frac{1}{6}$ $\{2\}$

8. $2(x + 6) = 2x - 5$ $\emptyset$

9. $x + 7x = 8x$ All real numbers

Solve for the indicated variable.

10. $2x - 3y = 9$ for y

$y = \frac{2}{3}x - 3$

11. $m = aP - w$ for a

$a = \frac{m + w}{P}$

For each graph write the corresponding inequality and the solution set to the inequality using interval notation.

12.

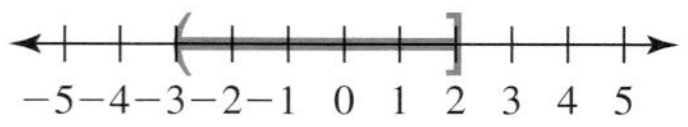

$-3 < x \le 2$, $(-3, 2]$

13.

$x > 1$, $(1, \infty)$

Solve each inequality. State the solution set in interval notation and sketch its graph.

14. $4 - 3(w - 5) < -2w$ $(19, \infty)$

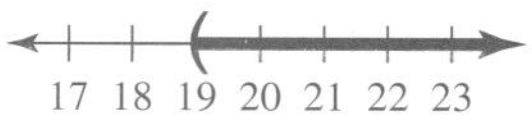

15. $1 < \frac{1 - 2x}{3} < 5$ $(-7, -1)$

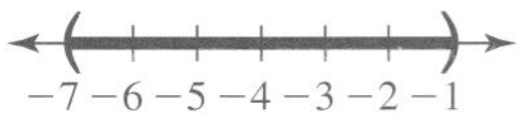

16. $1 < 3x - 2 < 7$ $(1, 3)$

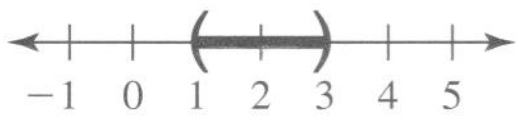

17. $-\frac{2}{3}y < 4$ $(-6, \infty)$

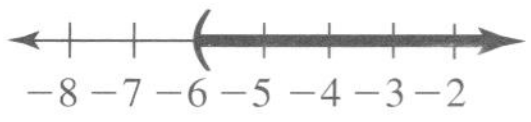

Write a complete solution to each problem.

18. The perimeter of a rectangle is 72 meters. If the width is 8 meters less than the length, then what is the width of the rectangle? 14 meters

19. If the area of a triangle is 54 square inches and the base is 12 inches, then what is the height? 9 in.

20. How many liters of a 20% alcohol solution should Maria mix with 50 liters of a 60% alcohol solution to obtain a 30% solution? 150 liters

21. Brandon gets a 40% discount on loose diamonds where he works. The cost of the setting is \$250. If he plans to spend at most \$1450, then what is the price range (list price) of the diamonds that he can afford? At most \$2000

22. If the degree measure of the smallest angle of a triangle is one-half of the degree measure of the second largest angle and one-third of the degree measure of the largest angle, then what is the degree measure of each angle? 30°, 60°, 90°

Making Connections | A Review of Chapters 1–2

Simplify each expression.

1. $3x + 5x$ $8x$

2. $3x \cdot 5x$ $15x^2$

3. $\dfrac{4x + 2}{2}$ $2x + 1$

4. $5 - 4(3 - x)$ $4x - 7$

5. $3x + 8 - 5(x - 1)$ $-2x + 13$

6. $(-6)^2 - 4(-3)2$ 60

7. $3^2 \cdot 2^3$ 72

8. $4(-7) - (-6)(3)$ -10

9. $-2x \cdot x \cdot x$ $-2x^3$

10. $(-1)(-1)(-1)(-1)(-1)$ -1

Perform the following operations.

11. $\dfrac{1}{2} + \dfrac{1}{6}$ $\dfrac{2}{3}$

12. $\dfrac{1}{2} - \dfrac{1}{3}$ $\dfrac{1}{6}$

13. $\dfrac{5}{3} \cdot \dfrac{1}{15}$ $\dfrac{1}{9}$

14. $\dfrac{2}{3} \cdot \dfrac{5}{6}$ $\dfrac{5}{9}$

15. $6 \cdot \left(\dfrac{5}{3} + \dfrac{1}{2}\right)$ 13

16. $15\left(\dfrac{2}{3} - \dfrac{2}{15}\right)$ 8

17. $4 \cdot \left(\dfrac{x}{2} + \dfrac{1}{4}\right)$ $2x + 1$

18. $12\left(\dfrac{5}{6}x - \dfrac{3}{4}\right)$ $10x - 9$

Find the solution set to each equation or inequality.

19. $x - \dfrac{1}{2} = \dfrac{1}{6}$ $\left\{\dfrac{2}{3}\right\}$

20. $x + \dfrac{1}{3} = \dfrac{1}{2}$ $\left\{\dfrac{1}{6}\right\}$

21. $x - \dfrac{1}{2} > \dfrac{1}{6}$ $\left(\dfrac{2}{3}, \infty\right)$

22. $x + \dfrac{1}{3} \le \dfrac{1}{2}$ $\left(-\infty, \dfrac{1}{6}\right]$

23. $\dfrac{3}{5}x = \dfrac{1}{15}$ $\left\{\dfrac{1}{9}\right\}$

24. $\dfrac{3}{2}x = \dfrac{5}{6}$ $\left\{\dfrac{5}{9}\right\}$

25. $-\dfrac{3}{5}x \le \dfrac{1}{15}$ $\left[-\dfrac{1}{9}, \infty\right)$

26. $-\dfrac{3}{2}x > \dfrac{5}{6}$ $\left(-\infty, -\dfrac{5}{9}\right)$

27. $\dfrac{5}{3}x + \dfrac{1}{2} = 1$ $\left\{\dfrac{3}{10}\right\}$

28. $\dfrac{2}{3}x - \dfrac{2}{15} = 2$ $\left\{\dfrac{16}{5}\right\}$

29. $\dfrac{x}{2} + \dfrac{1}{4} = \dfrac{1}{2}$ $\left\{\dfrac{1}{2}\right\}$

30. $\dfrac{5}{6}x - \dfrac{3}{4} = \dfrac{5}{12}$ $\left\{\dfrac{7}{5}\right\}$

31. $3x + 5x = 8$
$\{1\}$

32. $3x + 5x = 8x$
All real numbers

33. $3x + 5x = 7x$
$\{0\}$

34. $3x + 5 = 8$
$\{1\}$

35. $3x + 5x > 7x$
$(0, \infty)$

36. $3x + 5x > 8x$
$\varnothing$

37. $3x + 1 = 7$
$\{2\}$

38. $5 - 4(3 - x) = 1$
$\{2\}$

39. $3x + 8 = 5(x - 1)$
$\left\{\dfrac{13}{2}\right\}$

40. $x - 0.05x = 190$
$\{200\}$

Solve the problem.

41. ***Linear Depreciation.*** In computing income taxes, a company is allowed to depreciate a \$20,000 computer system over five years. Using *linear depreciation,* the value V of the computer system at any year t from 0 through 5 is given by

$$V = C - \frac{(C - S)}{5}t,$$

where C is the initial cost of the system and S is the scrap value of the system.

a) What is the value of the computer system after two years if its scrap value is \$4000?
\$13,600

b) If the value of the system after three years is claimed to be \$14,000, then what is the scrap value of the company's system?
\$10,000

c) If the accompanying graph models the depreciation of the system, then what is the scrap value of the system?
\$12,000

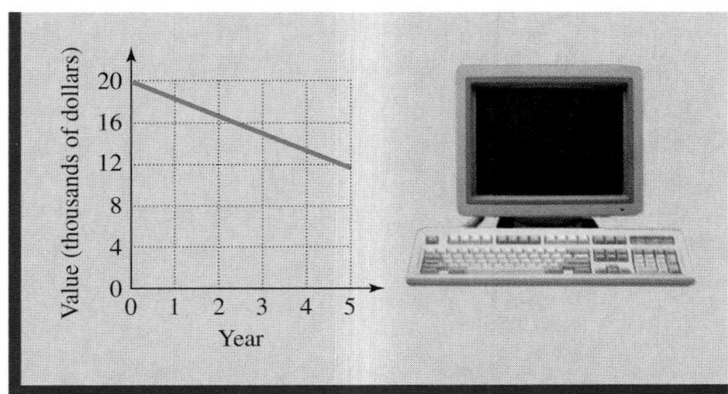

Figure for Exercise 41

Critical **Thinking** | For Individual or Group Work | Chapter 2

These exercises can be solved by a variety of techniques, which may or may not require algebra. So be creative and think critically. Explain all answers. Answers are in the Instructor's Edition of this text.

1. ***Visible squares.*** How many squares are visible in each of the following diagrams?

a) 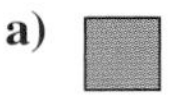

b) 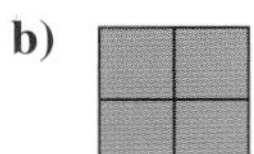

c) 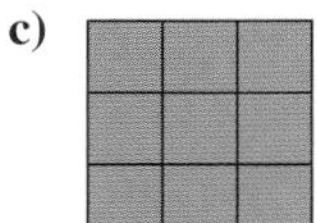

d) 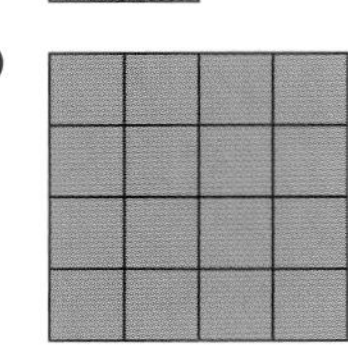

2. ***Baker's dilemma.*** A baker needs 8 cups of flour. He sends his apprentice to the flour bin with a scoop that holds 6 cups and a scoop that holds 11 cups. How can the apprentice measure 8 cups of flour with these scoops?

Photo for Exercise 2

3. ***Totaling one hundred.*** Start with the sequence of digits 987654321. Place any number of plus or minus signs between the digits in the sequence so that the value of the resulting expression is 100. For example,

$$98 + 7 - 6 - 5 + 4 + 3 - 2 + 1 = 100.$$

4. ***Four threes.*** Check out these equations:

$$\frac{3 \cdot 3}{3 \cdot 3} = 1, \frac{3}{3} + \frac{3}{3} = 2, (3 - 3)3 + 3 = 3.$$

Using exactly four 3's write arithmetic expressions whose values are 4, 5, 6, and so on. How far can you go?

5. ***Palindrome time.*** A palindrome is a sequence of words or numbers that reads the same forward or backward. For example, "A TOYOTA" is a palindrome and 14341 is a palindromic number. How many times per day does a digital clock display a palindromic number? Of course the answer depends on the format in which the digital clock displays the time. First, state precisely the type of digital clock display you are using, then count the palindromic numbers for that type of display.

6. ***Reversible products.*** Find the product of 32 and 46. Now reverse the digits and find the product of 23 and 64. The products are the same. Does this happen with any pair of two-digit numbers? Find two other pairs of two-digit numbers (with different digits) that have this property.

7. ***Running late.*** Alice, Bea, Carl, and Don all have an 8 o'clock class. Alice's watch is 8 minutes fast, but she thinks it is 4 minutes slow. Bea's watch is 8 minutes slow, but she thinks it is 8 minutes fast. Carl's watch is 4 minutes slow, but he thinks it is 8 minutes fast. Don's watch is 4 minutes fast, but he thinks it is 8 minutes slow. Each student leaves so they will get to class at exactly 8 o'clock. Each student assumes the correct time is what they think it is by their watch. Who is late to class and by how much?

8. ***Automorphic numbers.*** Automorphic numbers are integers whose squares end in the given integer. Since $1^2 = 1$ and $6^2 = 36$, both 1 and 6 are automorphic. Find the next four automorphic numbers.

1. a) 1 **b)** 5 **c)** 14 **d)** 30 **2.** The apprentice can fill a scoop, pour from one scoop to the other, or empty a scoop into the bin. Use the following sequence of amounts in the scoops: (0, 11), (6, 5), (0, 5), (5, 0), (5, 11), (6, 10), (0, 10), (6, 4), (0, 4), (4, 0), (4, 11), (6, 9), (0, 9), (6, 3), (0, 3), (3, 0), (3, 11), (6, 8), (0, 8). **3.** $9 + 8 + 76 + 5 - 4 + 3 + 2 + 1 = 100$ or $98 - 76 + 54 + 3 + 21 = 100$ **4.** $3 + 3^{3-3} = 4$, $3 + 3 - 3/3 = 5$, $3 + 3 + 3 - 3 = 6$ **5.** With hours from 1–12 (no leading zeros) and minutes from 00–59 (no seconds), there are 57 palindromic displays. **6.** 39 and 62, 64 and 69. **7.** Bea 16 minutes late, Carl 12 minutes late. **8.** 25, 76, 376, 625.

Chapter 3

Linear Equations in Two Variables and Their Graphs

If you pick up any package of food and read the label, you will find a long list that usually ends with some mysterious looking names. Many of these strange elements are food additives. A food additive is a substance or a mixture of substances other than basic foodstuffs that is present in food as a result of production, processing, storage, or packaging. They can be natural or synthetic and are categorized in many ways: preservatives, coloring agents, processing aids, and nutritional supplements, to name a few.

Food additives have been around since prehistoric humans discovered that salt would help to preserve meat. Today, food additives can include simple ingredients such as red color from Concord grape skins, calcium, or an enzyme. Throughout the centuries there have been lively discussions on what is healthy to eat. At the present time the food industry is working to develop foods that have less cholesterol, fats, and other unhealthy ingredients.

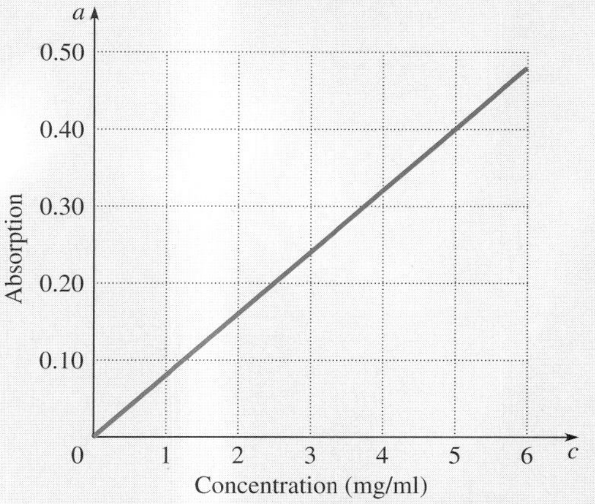

Although they frequently have different viewpoints, the food industry and the Food and Drug Administration (FDA) are working to provide consumers with information on a healthier diet. Recent developments such as the synthetically engineered tomato stirred great controversy, even though the FDA declared the tomato safe to eat.

In Exercise 93 of Section 3.4 you will see how a food chemist uses a linear equation in testing the concentration of an enzyme in a fruit juice.

3.1 Graphing Lines in the Coordinate Plane

In This Section

In Chapter 1 you learned to graph numbers on a number line. We also used number lines to illustrate the solution to inequalities in Chapter 2. In this section, you will learn to graph pairs of numbers in a coordinate system made up of a pair of number lines. We will use this coordinate system to illustrate the solution to equations and inequalities in two variables.

⟨1⟩ Ordered Pairs

The equation $y = 2x - 1$ is an equation in two variables. This equation is satisfied if we choose a value for x and a value for y that make it true. If we choose $x = 2$ and $y = 3$, then $y = 2x - 1$ becomes

$$\overset{\substack{y\\\downarrow}}{3} = 2(\overset{\substack{x\\\downarrow}}{2}) - 1$$
$$3 = 3.$$

⟨ Helpful Hint ⟩

In this chapter, you will be doing a lot of graphing. Using graph paper will help you understand the concepts and help you recognize errors. For your convenience, a page of graph paper can be found on page 238 of this text. Make as many copies of it as you wish.

Because the last statement is true, we say that the pair of numbers 2 and 3 **satisfies the equation** or is a **solution to the equation.** We use the **ordered pair** (2, 3) to represent $x = 2$ and $y = 3$. The format is to always write the value for x first and the value for y second. The numbers in an ordered pair are called **coordinates.** In the pair (2, 3) the first coordinate or x-coordinate is 2 and the second coordinate or y-coordinate is 3.

CAUTION The ordered pair (3, 2) does not satisfy $y = 2x - 1$, because for $x = 3$ and $y = 2$, we have

$$2 \neq 2(3) - 1.$$

The variable corresponding to the first coordinate of an ordered pair is called the **independent variable** and the variable corresponding to the second coordinate is called the **dependent variable.** The value for the first coordinate is selected arbitrarily and the value for the second coordinate is determined from the first coordinate by a rule such as $y = 2x - 1$. Of course, if the ordered pair must satisfy a simple equation, then we can find either coordinate when given the other coordinate.

EXAMPLE 1 Finding solutions to an equation

Each of the ordered pairs below is missing one coordinate. Complete each ordered pair so that it satisfies the equation $y = -3x + 4$.

a) (2,) **b)** (, −5) **c)** (0,)

Solution

a) The x-coordinate of (2,) is 2. Let $x = 2$ in the equation $y = -3x + 4$:

$$\begin{aligned} y &= -3 \cdot 2 + 4 \\ &= -6 + 4 \\ &= -2 \end{aligned}$$

The ordered pair (2, −2) satisfies the equation.

‹ Teaching Tip ›

Point out the connection between the x-coordinate and the solution to a linear equation. The skills learned in Chapter 2 will be needed here.

b) The y-coordinate of (, −5) is −5. Let $y = -5$ in the equation $y = -3x + 4$:

$$-5 = -3x + 4$$
$$-9 = -3x$$
$$3 = x$$

The ordered pair (3, −5) satisfies the equation.

c) Replace x by 0 in the equation $y = -3x + 4$:

$$y = -3 \cdot 0 + 4 = 4$$

So (0, 4) satisfies the equation.

Now do Exercises 7–22

‹2› The Rectangular Coordinate System

We use the **rectangular** (or **Cartesian**) **coordinate system** to get a visual image of ordered pairs of real numbers. The rectangular coordinate system consists of two number lines drawn at a right angle to one another, intersecting at zero on each number line, as shown in Fig. 3.1. The plane containing these number lines is called the **coordinate plane.** On the horizontal number line the positive numbers are to the right of zero, and on the vertical number line the positive numbers are above zero.

‹ Teaching Tip ›

Students do much better with graphing when they use graph paper. A page of blank grids that can be copied is provided on page 238 of this text. You will also find pages of graph paper in the Instructor's Solutions Manual and Student's Solutions Manual.

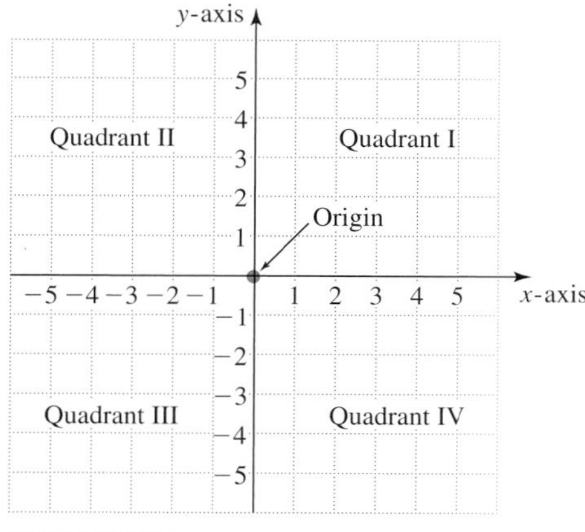

Figure 3.1

The horizontal number line is called the ***x*-axis,** and the vertical number line is called the ***y*-axis.** The point at which they intersect is called the **origin.** The two number lines divide the plane into four regions called **quadrants.** They are numbered as shown in Fig. 3.1. The quadrants do not include any points on the axes.

‹3› Plotting Points

Just as every real number corresponds to a point on the number line, *every pair of real numbers corresponds to a point in the rectangular coordinate system.* For example, the point corresponding to the pair (2, 3) is found by starting at the origin and moving two units to the right and then three units up. The point corresponding to the pair (−3, −2) is found by starting at the origin and moving three units to the left and then two units down. Both of these points are shown in Fig. 3.2.

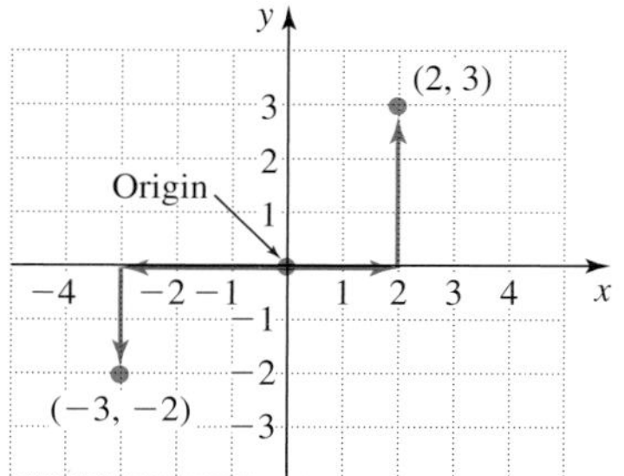

Figure 3.2

When we locate a point in the rectangular coordinate system, we are **plotting** or **graphing** the point. Because ordered pairs of numbers correspond to points in the coordinate plane, we frequently refer to an ordered pair as a point.

EXAMPLE 2

Plotting points

Plot the points (2, 5), (−1, 4), (−3, −4), and (3, −2).

Solution

To locate (2, 5), start at the origin, move two units to the right, and then move up five units. To locate (−1, 4), start at the origin, move one unit to the left, and then move up four units. All four points are shown in Fig. 3.3.

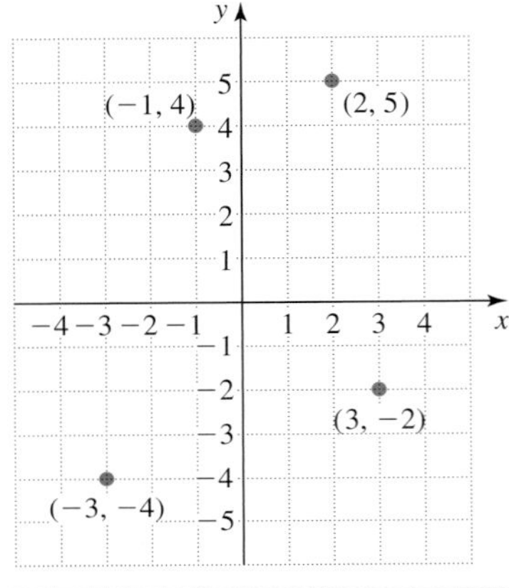

Figure 3.3

Now do Exercises 23–50

⟨4⟩ Graphing a Linear Equation in Two Variables

In Chapter 2 we defined a linear equation in one variable as an equation of the form $ax = b$, where $a \neq 0$. Every linear equation in one variable has a single real number in its solution set. The graph of the solution set is a single point on the number line. A linear equation in two variables is defined similarly.

Linear Equation in Two Variables

A **linear equation in two variables** is an equation of the form

$$Ax + By = C,$$

where A and B are not both zero.

Consider the linear equation $-2x + y = -1$. It is simple to find ordered pairs that satisfy the equation if it is solved for y as $y = 2x - 1$. Now if x is replaced by 4, we get $y = 2 \cdot 4 - 1 = 7$. So the ordered pair (4, 7) satisfies this equation. Since there are infinitely many real numbers that could be used for x, there are infinitely many ordered pairs in the solution set. To get a better understanding of the solution set to a linear equation we look at its graph. It can be proved that *the graph of the solution set is a straight line in the coordinate plane*. We will not prove this statement. Proving it requires a geometric definition of a straight line and is beyond the scope of this text. However, it is easy to graph the straight line by simply plotting a selection of points from the solution set and drawing a straight line through the points, as shown in Example 3.

EXAMPLE 3

Graphing an equation

Graph the equation $y = 2x - 1$ in the coordinate plane.

Solution

To find ordered pairs that satisfy $y = 2x - 1$, we arbitrarily select some x-coordinates and calculate the corresponding y-coordinates:

If $x = -3$, then $y = 2(-3) - 1 = -7$.
If $x = -2$, then $y = 2(-2) - 1 = -5$.
If $x = -1$, then $y = 2(-1) - 1 = -3$.
If $x = 0$, then $y = 2(0) - 1 = -1$.
If $x = 1$, then $y = 2(1) - 1 = 1$.
If $x = 2$, then $y = 2(2) - 1 = 3$.
If $x = 3$, then $y = 2(3) - 1 = 5$.

We can make a table for these results as follows:

x	-3	-2	-1	0	1	2	3
$y = 2x - 1$	-7	-5	-3	-1	1	3	5

The ordered pairs $(-3, -7)$, $(-2, -5)$, $(-1, -3)$, $(0, -1)$, $(1, 1)$, $(2, 3)$, and $(3, 5)$ are graphed in Fig. 3.4. Draw a straight line through these points, as shown in Fig. 3.5. The line in Fig. 3.5 is the graph of the solution set to $y = 2x - 1$. The arrows on the ends of the line indicate that it goes indefinitely in both directions.

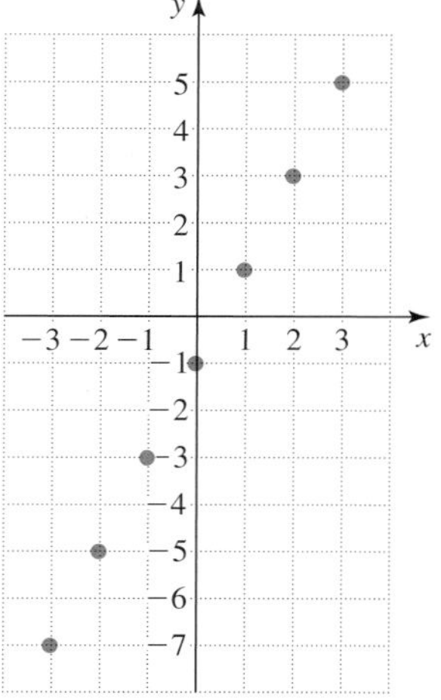

Figure 3.4

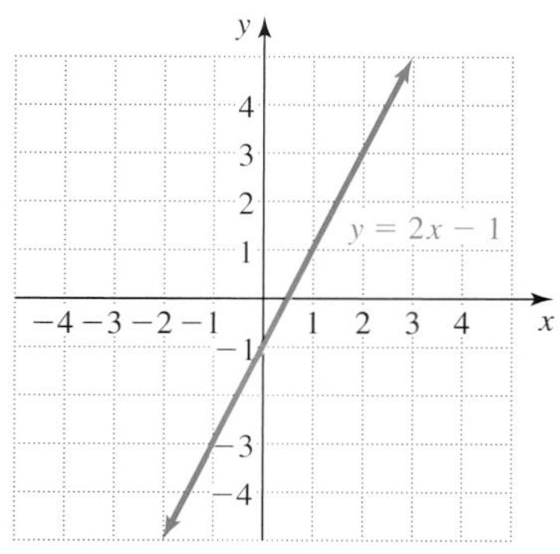

Figure 3.5

Now do Exercises 51–58

‹ Calculator Close-Up ›

You can make a table of values for x and y with a graphing calculator. Enter the equation $y = 2x - 1$ using $Y =$ and then press TABLE.

X	Y1
-3	-7
-2	-5
-1	-3
0	-1
1	1
2	3
3	5

X=0

A linear equation in two variables is an equation of the form $Ax + By = C$, where A and B are not both zero. Note that we can have $A = 0$ if $B \neq 0$, and we can have $B = 0$ with $A \neq 0$. So equations such as $x = 8$ and $y = 2$ are linear equations. Equations such as $x - y - 5 = 0$ and $y = 2x + 3$ are also called linear equations because they could be rewritten in the form $Ax + By = C$. Equations such as $y = 2x^2$ or $y = \frac{5}{x}$ are not linear equations.

EXAMPLE 4

Graphing an equation

Graph the equation $3x + y = 2$. Plot at least five points.

Solution

It is easier to make a table of ordered pairs if the equation is solved for y. So subtract $3x$ from each side to get $y = -3x + 2$. Now select some values for x and then calculate the corresponding y-coordinates:

$$\begin{aligned} &\text{If } x = -2, &&\text{then } y = -3(-2) + 2 = 8.\\ &\text{If } x = -1, &&\text{then } y = -3(-1) + 2 = 5.\\ &\text{If } x = 0, &&\text{then } y = -3(0) + 2 = 2.\\ &\text{If } x = 1, &&\text{then } y = -3(1) + 2 = -1.\\ &\text{If } x = 2, &&\text{then } y = -3(2) + 2 = -4. \end{aligned}$$

The following table shows these five ordered pairs:

x	-2	-1	0	1	2
$y = -3x + 2$	8	5	2	-1	-4

Plot $(-2, 8)$, $(-1, 5)$, $(0, 2)$, $(1, -1)$, and $(2, -4)$. Draw a line through them, as shown in Fig. 3.6.

Now do Exercises 59–62

‹ Teaching Tip ›

Ask students to identify the pattern in the table. Does the equation $y = -3x + 2$ have anything to do with this?

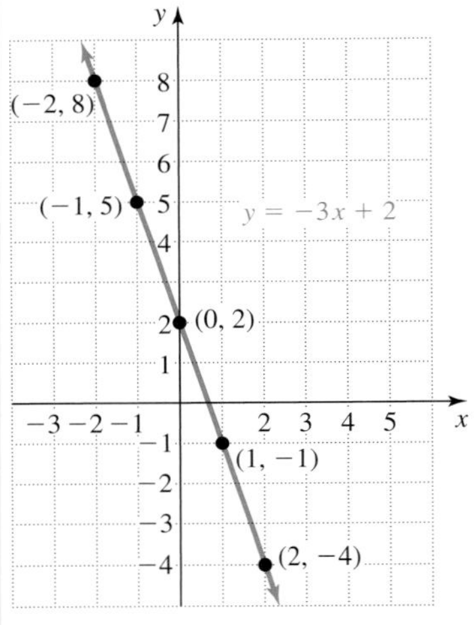

Figure 3.6

‹ Calculator Close-Up ›

To graph $y = -3x + 2$, enter the equation using the Y = key:

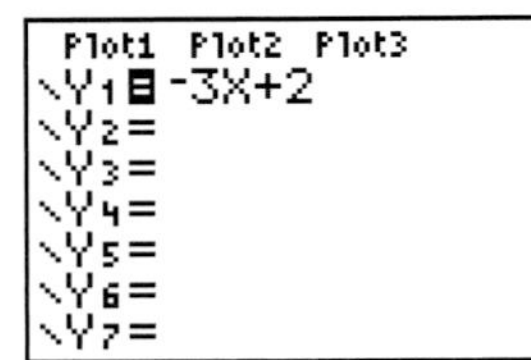

Next, set the viewing window (WINDOW) to get the desired view of the graph. Xmin and Xmax indicate the minimum and maximum x-values used for the graph; likewise for Ymin and Ymax. Xscl and Yscl (scale) give the distance between tick marks on the respective axes.

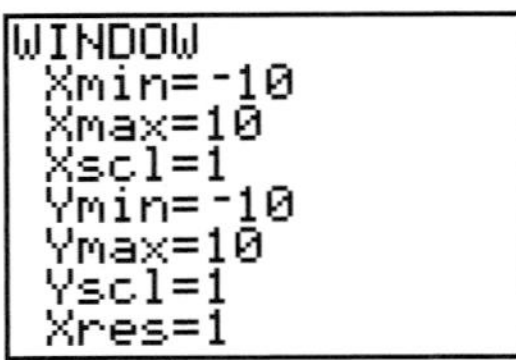

Press GRAPH to get the graph:

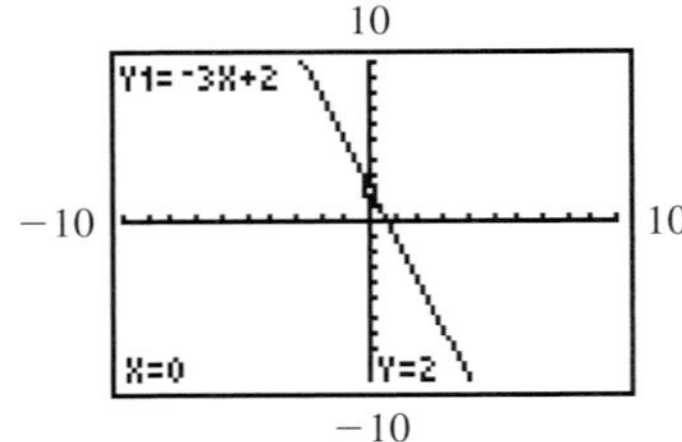

Even though the graph is not really "straight," it is consistent with the graph of $y = -3x + 2$ in Fig. 3.6.

EXAMPLE 5

Horizontal and vertical lines

Graph each linear equation.

a) $y = 4$ **b)** $x = 3$

Solution

a) The equation $y = 4$ is a simplification of $0 \cdot x + y = 4$. So if y is replaced with 4, then we can use any real number for x. For example, $(-1, 4)$ satisfies $0 \cdot x + y = 4$ because $0(-1) + 4 = 4$ is correct. The following table shows five ordered pairs that satisfy $y = 4$.

x	-2	-1	0	1	2
$y = 4$	4	4	4	4	4

Figure 3.7 shows a horizontal line through these points.

b) The equation $x = 3$ is a simplification of $x + 0 \cdot y = 3$. So if x is replaced with 3, then we can use any real number for y. For example, $(3, -2)$ satisfies $x + 0 \cdot y = 3$ because $3 + 0(-2) = 3$ is correct. The following table shows five ordered pairs that satisfy $x = 3$.

$x = 3$	3	3	3	3	3
y	-2	-1	0	1	2

Figure 3.8 shows a vertical line through these points.

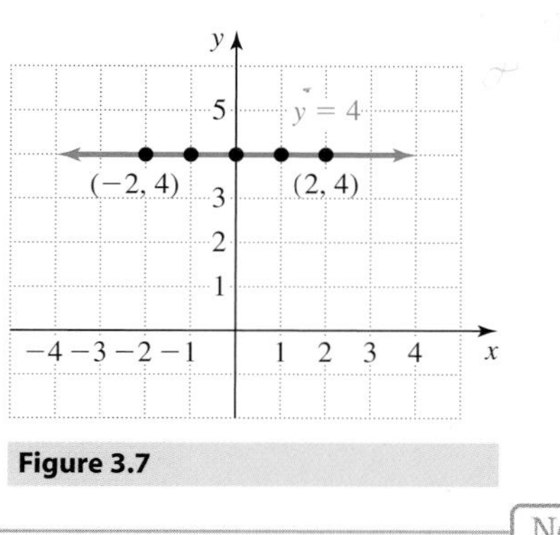

Figure 3.7

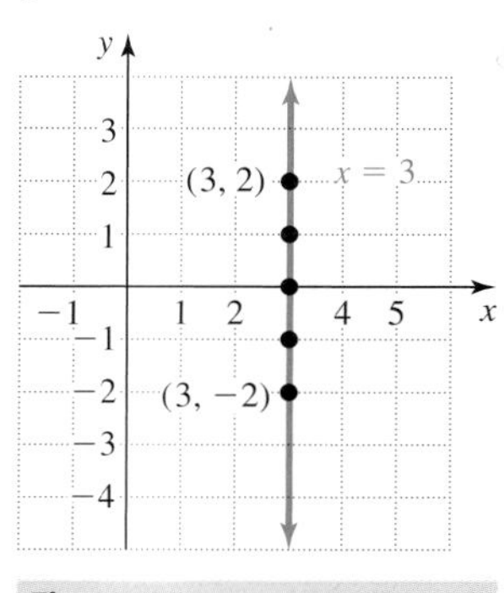

Figure 3.8

Now do Exercises 63–74

‹ Calculator Close-Up ›

You cannot graph the vertical line $x = 3$ on most graphing calculators. The only equations that can be graphed are ones in which y is written in terms of x.

CAUTION If $x = 3$ occurs in the context of equations in a single variable, then $x = 3$ has only one solution, 3. In the context of equations in two variables, $x = 3$ is assumed to be a simplified form of $x + 0 \cdot y = 3$, and it has infinitely many solutions (all of the ordered pairs on the line in Fig. 3.8).

All of the equations we have considered so far have involved single-digit numbers. If an equation involves large numbers, then we must change the scale on the x-axis, the y-axis, or both to accommodate the numbers involved. The change of scale is arbitrary, and the graph will look different for different scales.

EXAMPLE 6

Adjusting the scale

Graph the equation $y = 20x + 500$. Plot at least five points.

‹ Teaching Tip ›

Students often have trouble picking a scale other than 1, 2, 3. Remind them that they can find the intercepts first and then select a scale to accommodate the intercepts.

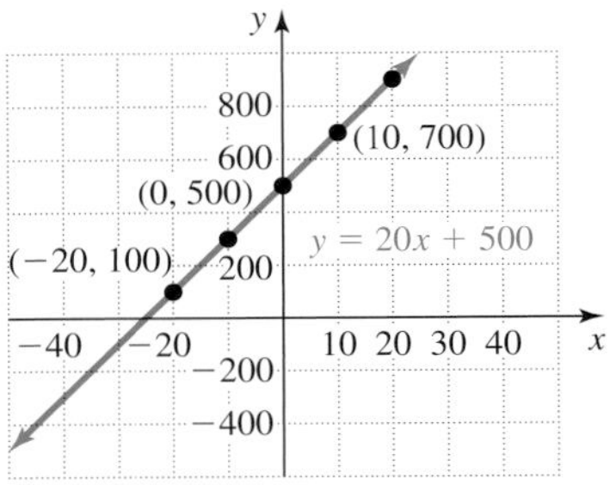

Figure 3.9

Solution

The following table shows five ordered pairs that satisfy the equation.

x	-20	-10	0	10	20
$y = 20x + 500$	100	300	500	700	900

To fit these points onto a graph, we change the scale on the x-axis to let each division represent 10 units and change the scale on the y-axis to let each division represent 200 units. The graph is shown in Fig. 3.9.

Now do Exercises 75–80

‹5› Graphing a Line Using Intercepts

We know that the graph of a linear equation is a straight line. Because it takes only two points to determine a line, we can graph a linear equation using only two points. The two points that are the easiest to locate are usually the points where the line crosses the axes. The point where the graph crosses the x-axis is the ***x*-intercept.** The y-coordinate of the x-intercept is zero. The point where the graph crosses the y-axis is the ***y*-intercept.** The x-coordinate of the y-intercept is zero.

EXAMPLE 7

Graphing a line using intercepts

Graph the equation $2x - 3y = 6$ by using the x- and y-intercepts.

‹ Helpful Hint ›

You can find the intercepts for $2x - 3y = 6$ using the *cover-up method.* Cover up $-3y$ with your pencil, then solve $2x = 6$ mentally to get $x = 3$ and an x-intercept of (3, 0). Now cover up $2x$ and solve $-3y = 6$ to get $y = -2$ and a y-intercept of $(0, -2)$.

Solution

To find the x-intercept, let $y = 0$ in the equation $2x - 3y = 6$:

$$2x - 3 \cdot 0 = 6$$
$$2x = 6$$
$$x = 3$$

The x-intercept is (3, 0). To find the y-intercept, let $x = 0$ in $2x - 3y = 6$:

$$2 \cdot 0 - 3y = 6$$
$$-3y = 6$$
$$y = -2$$

The y-intercept is $(0, -2)$. Locate the intercepts and draw a line through them, as shown in Fig. 3.10. To check, find one additional point that satisfies the equation, say (6, 2), and see whether the line goes through that point.

‹ Calculator Close-Up ›

To graph $2x - 3y = 6$ on a calculator you must solve for y. In this case, $y = (2/3)x - 2$.

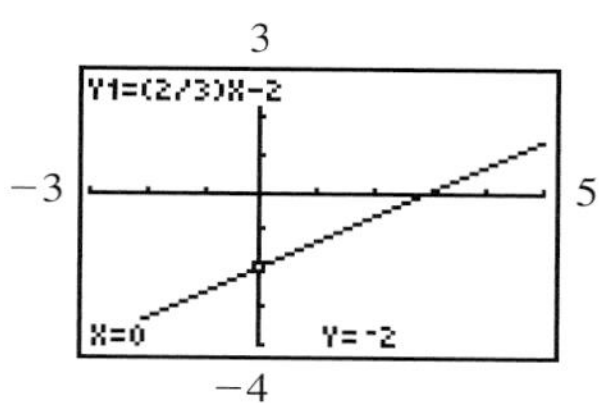

Since the calculator graph appears to be the same as the graph in Fig. 3.10, it supports the conclusion that Fig. 3.10 is correct.

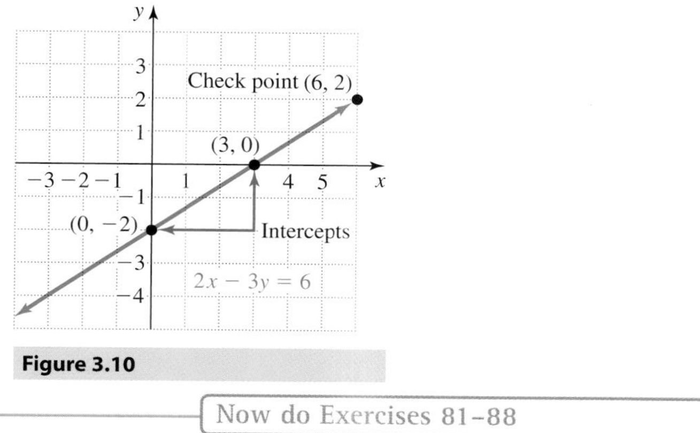

Figure 3.10

Now do Exercises 81–88

‹6› Applications

Linear equations occur in many real-life situations.

EXAMPLE 8

House plans

An architect uses the equation $C = 900 + 30x$ to determine the cost for drawing house plans, where x is the number of copies of the plan that the client receives.

a) What is the cost if the client gets eight copies?

b) Find the intercepts and interpret them.

c) Graph the linear equation.

d) What happens to the cost as x increases?

Solution

a) If $x = 8$, then $C = 900 + 30(8) = \$1140$.

b) If $x = 0$, then $C = 900 + 30(0) = \$900$. The C-intercept is (0, 900). The cost is \$900 for the labor involved in drawing the plans, even if you get no copies of the plan. If $C = 0$, then $900 + 30x = 0$ or $x = -30$. So the x-intercept is $(-30, 0)$, but in this situation, the x-intercept is meaningless. The number of plans can't be negative.

c) The graph goes through (0, 900) and (8, 1140), as shown in Fig. 3.11. Since negative values for x are meaningless, we draw the graph in the first quadrant only.

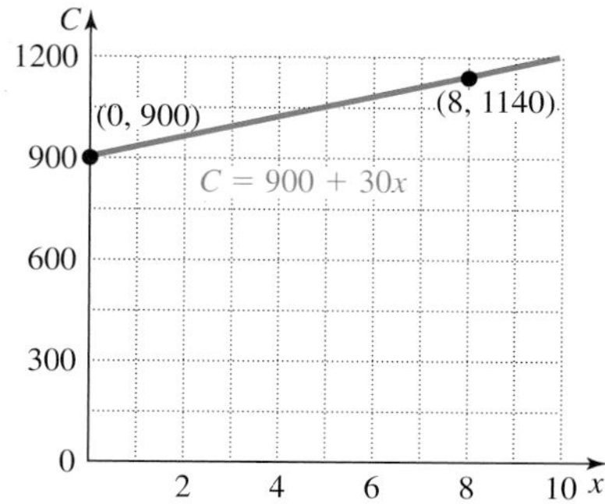

Figure 3.11

d) As x increases, the cost increases.

Now do Exercises 89–92

EXAMPLE 9

Ticket demand

The demand for tickets to see the Ice Gators play hockey can be modeled by the equation $d = 8000 - 100p$, where d is the number of tickets sold and p is the price per ticket in dollars.

a) How many tickets will be sold at \$20 per ticket?

b) Find the intercepts and interpret them.

‹ Teaching Tip ›

Point out how knowing the intercepts helps you determine the scale to use on the graph.

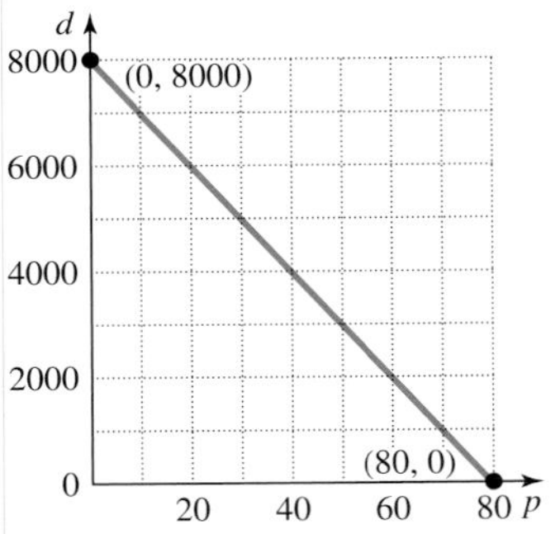

Figure 3.12

c) Graph the linear equation.

d) What happens to the demand as the price increases?

Solution

a) If tickets are \$20 each, then $d = 8000 - 100 \cdot 20 = 6000$. So at \$20 per ticket, the demand will be 6000 tickets.

b) Replace d with 0 in the equation $d = 8000 - 100p$ and solve for p:

$$0 = 8000 - 100p$$

$$100p = 8000 \quad \text{Add } 100p \text{ to each side.}$$

$$p = 80 \quad \text{Divide each side by 100.}$$

If $p = 0$, then $d = 8000 - 100 \cdot 0 = 8000$. So the intercepts are (0, 8000) and (80, 0). If the tickets are free, the demand will be 8000 tickets. At \$80 per ticket, no tickets will be sold.

c) Graph the line using the intercepts (0, 8000) and (80, 0) as shown in Fig. 3.12. The line is graphed in the first quadrant only, because negative values for demand or price are meaningless.

d) When the tickets are free, the demand is high. As the price increases, the demand goes down. At \$80 per ticket, there will be no demand.

Now do Exercises 93–96

Note that $d = 8000 - 100p$ is a *model* for the demand in Example 9. A model car has only some of the features of a real car, and the same is true here. For instance, the line in Fig. 3.12 contains infinitely many points. But there is really only a finite number of possibilities for price and demand, because we cannot sell a fraction of a ticket.

Warm-Ups 

True or false? Explain your answer.

1. The point (2, 4) satisfies the equation $2y - 3x = -8$. False
2. If (1, 5) satisfies an equation, then (5, 1) also satisfies the equation. False
3. The origin is in quadrant I. False
4. The point (4, 0) is on the y-axis. False
5. The graph of $x + 0 \cdot y = 9$ is the same as the graph of $x = 9$. True
6. The graph of $x = -5$ is a vertical line. True
7. The graph of $0 \cdot x + y = 6$ is a horizontal line. True
8. The y-intercept for the line $x + 2y = 5$ is (5, 0). False
9. The point (5, −3) is in quadrant II. False
10. The point (−349, 0) is on the x-axis. True

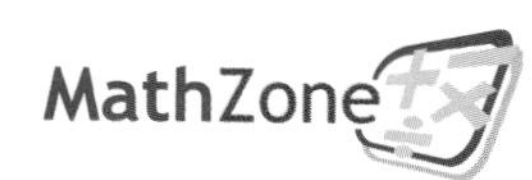

Study Tips

- It is a good idea to work with others, but don't be misled. Working a problem with help is not the same as working a problem on your own.
- Math is personal. Make sure that you can do it.

Reading and Writing *After reading this section, write out the answers to these questions. Use complete sentences.*

1. What is an ordered pair?
   An ordered pair is a pair of numbers in which there is a first number and a second number, usually written as (a, b).
2. What is the rectangular coordinate system?
   The rectangular coordinate system is a means of dividing up the plane with two number lines in order to picture all ordered pairs of real numbers.
3. What name is given to the point of intersection of the x-axis and the y-axis?
   The origin is the point of intersection of the x-axis and y-axis.
4. What is the graph of an equation?
   The graph of an equation is a picture of all ordered pairs that satisfy the equation drawn in the rectangular coordinate system.
5. What is a linear equation in two variables?
   A linear equation in two variables is an equation of the form $Ax + By = C$, where A and B are not both zero.
6. What are intercepts?
   Intercepts are the points at which a graph crosses the axes.

‹1› Ordered Pairs

Complete each ordered pair so that it satisfies the given equation. See Example 1.

7. $y = 3x + 9$: $(0,\ \ )$, $(\ \ , 24)$, $(2,\ \ )$
   $(0, 9)$, $(5, 24)$, $(2, 15)$

VIDEO

8. $y = 2x + 5$: $(8,\ \ )$, $(-1,\ \ )$, $(\ \ , -1)$
   $(8, 21)$, $(-1, 3)$, $(-3, -1)$
9. $y = -3x - 7$: $(0,\ \ )$, $\left(\frac{1}{3},\ \ \right)$, $(\ \ , -5)$
   $(0, -7)$, $\left(\frac{1}{3}, -8\right)$, $\left(-\frac{2}{3}, -5\right)$
10. $y = -5x - 3$: $(-1,\ \ )$, $\left(-\frac{1}{2},\ \ \right)$, $(\ \ , -2)$
    $(-1, 2)$, $\left(-\frac{1}{2}, -\frac{1}{2}\right)$, $\left(-\frac{1}{5}, -2\right)$
11. $y = 1.2x + 54.3$: $(0,\ \ )$, $(10,\ \ )$, $(\ \ , 54.9)$
    $(0, 54.3)$, $(10, 66.3)$, $(0.5, 54.9)$
12. $y = 1.8x + 22.6$: $(1,\ \ )$, $(-10,\ \ )$, $(\ \ , 22.6)$
    $(1, 24.4)$, $(-10, 4.6)$, $(0, 22.6)$
13. $2x - 3y = 6$: $(3,\ \ )$, $(\ \ , -2)$, $(12,\ \ )$
    $(3, 0)$, $(0, -2)$, $(12, 6)$
14. $3x + 5y = 0$: $(-5,\ \ )$, $(\ \ , -3)$, $(10,\ \ )$
    $(-5, 3)$, $(5, -3)$, $(10, -6)$
15. $0 \cdot y + x = 5$: $(\ \ , -3)$, $(\ \ , 5)$, $(\ \ , 0)$
    $(5, -3)$, $(5, 5)$, $(5, 0)$
16. $0 \cdot x + y = -6$: $(3,\ \ )$, $(-1,\ \ )$, $(4,\ \ )$
    $(3, -6)$, $(-1, -6)$, $(4, -6)$

Use the given equations to find the missing coordinates in the following tables.

17. $y = -2x + 5$

x	y
−2	9
0	5
2	1
4	−3
6	−7

18. $y = -x + 4$

x	y
−2	6
0	4
2	2
4	0
6	−2

19. $y = \frac{1}{3}x + 2$

x	y
−6	0
−3	1
0	2
3	3

20. $y = -\frac{1}{2}x + 1$

x	y
−2	2
−1	$\frac{3}{2}$
0	1
1	$\frac{1}{2}$

21. $y - 20x = 400$

x	y
−30	−200
−20	0
−10	200
0	400
10	600

22. $200x + y = 50$

x	y
$-\frac{1}{2}$	150
$-\frac{1}{4}$	100
0	50
$\frac{1}{4}$	0
$\frac{1}{2}$	−50

⟨3⟩ Plotting Points

Plot the points on a rectangular coordinate system. See Example 2.

23. $(1, 5)$ **24.** $(4, 3)$

25. $(-2, 1)$ VIDEO **26.** $(-3, 5)$

27. $\left(3, -\dfrac{1}{2}\right)$ **28.** $\left(2, -\dfrac{1}{3}\right)$

29. $(-2, -4)$ **30.** $(-3, -5)$

31. $(0, 3)$ **32.** $(0, -2)$

33. $(-3, 0)$ **34.** $(5, 0)$

35. $(\pi, 1)$ **36.** $(-2, \pi)$

37. $(1.4, 4)$ **38.** $(-3, 0.4)$

23–37 odd 24–38 even

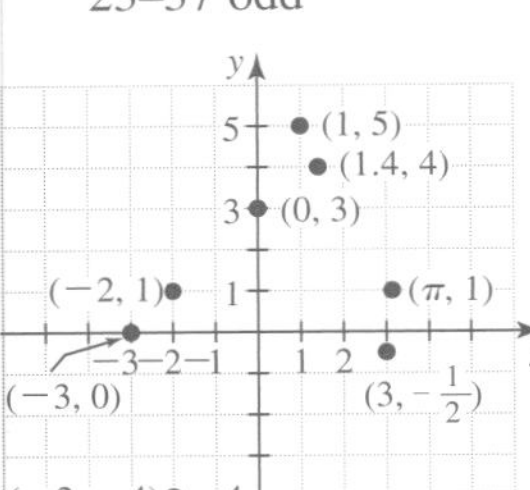

For each point, name the quadrant in which it lies or the axis on which it lies.

39. $(-3, 45)$ Quadrant II

40. $(-33, 47)$ Quadrant II

41. $(-3, 0)$ x-axis

42. $(0, -9)$ y-axis

43. $(-2.36, -5)$ Quadrant III

44. $(89.6, 0)$ x-axis

45. $(3.4, 8.8)$ Quadrant I

46. $(4.1, 44)$ Quadrant I

47. $\left(-\dfrac{1}{2}, 50\right)$ Quadrant II

48. $\left(-6, -\dfrac{1}{2}\right)$ Quadrant III

49. $(0, -99)$ y-axis

50. $(\pi, 0)$ x-axis

⟨4⟩ Graphing a Linear Equation in Two Variables

Graph each equation. Plot at least five points for each equation. Use graph paper. See Examples 3–5. If you have a graphing calculator, use it to check your graphs when possible.

51. $y = x + 1$

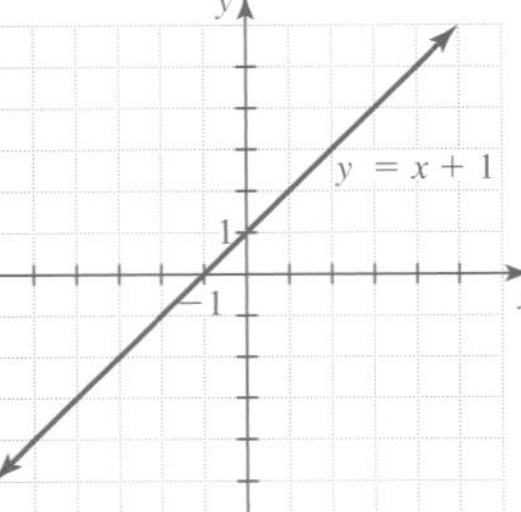

52. $y = x - 1$

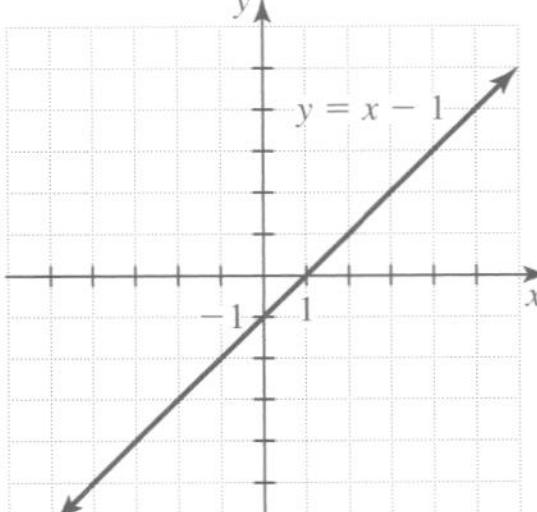

53. $y = 2x + 1$

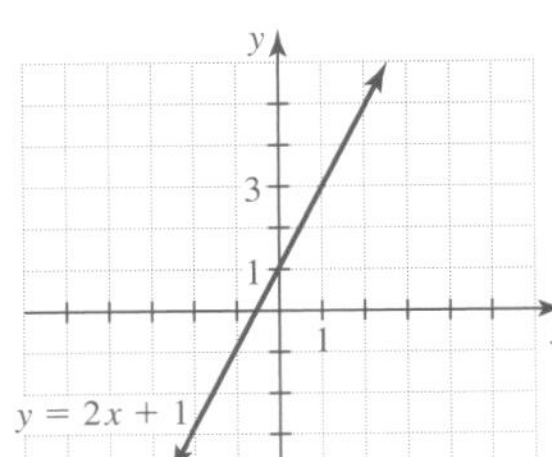

VIDEO **54.** $y = 3x - 1$

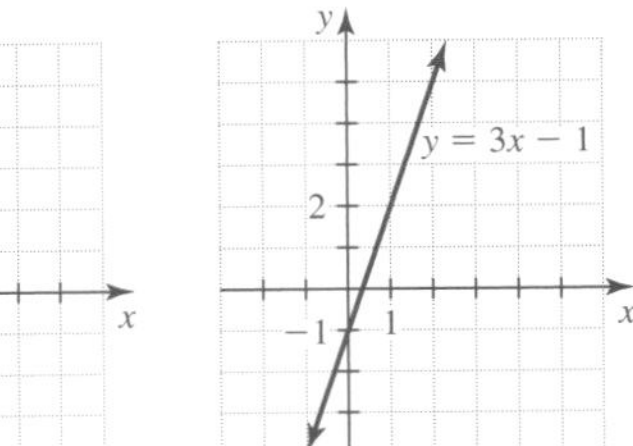

55. $y = 3x - 2$

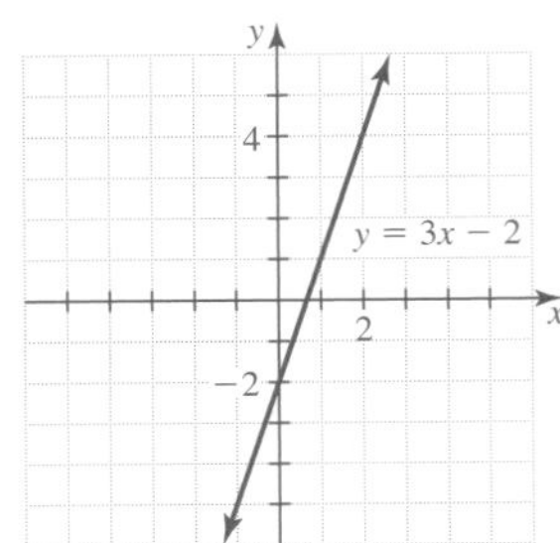

56. $y = 2x + 3$

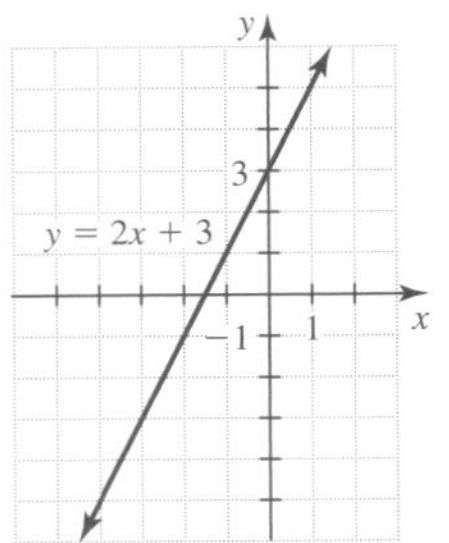

VIDEO **57.** $y = x$

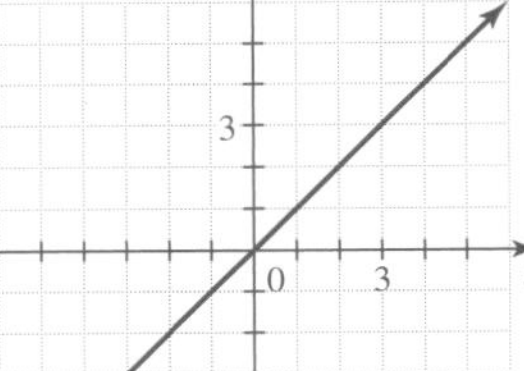

58. $y = -x$

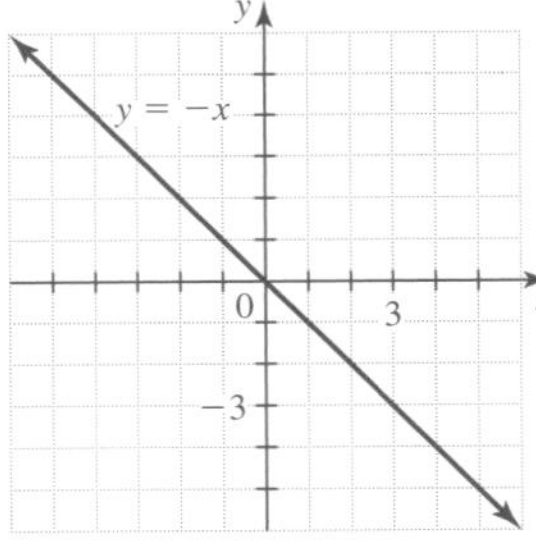

59. $y = 1 - x$

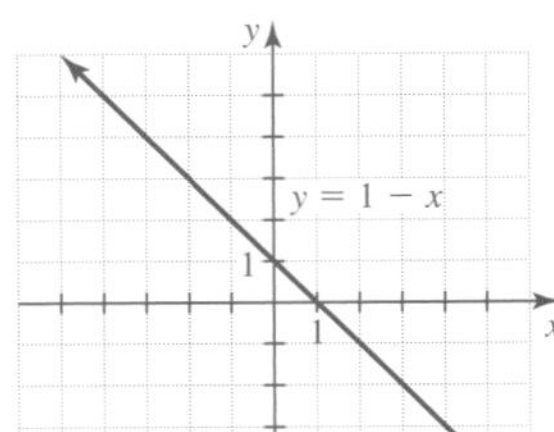

60. $y = 2 - x$

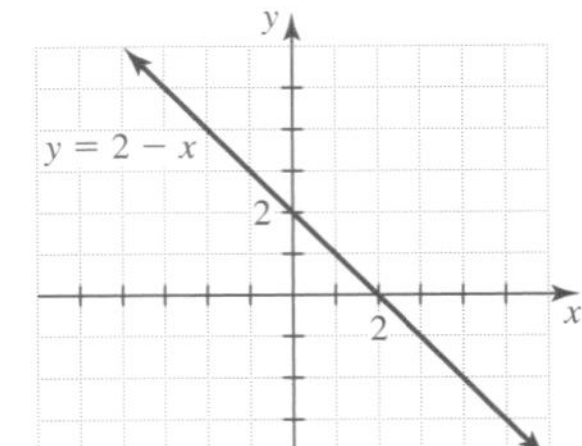

61. $y = -2x + 3$

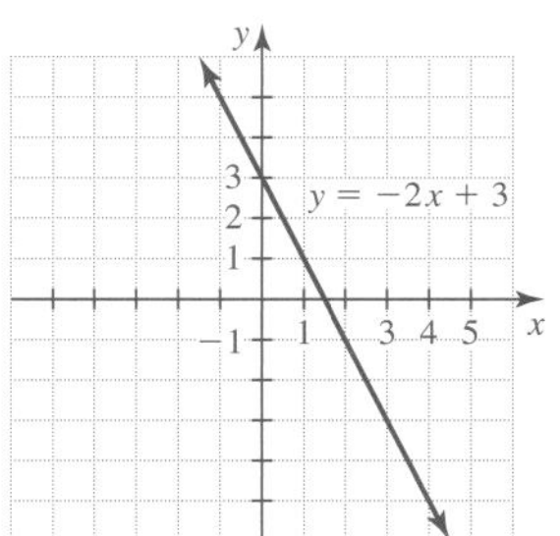

62. $y = -3x + 2$

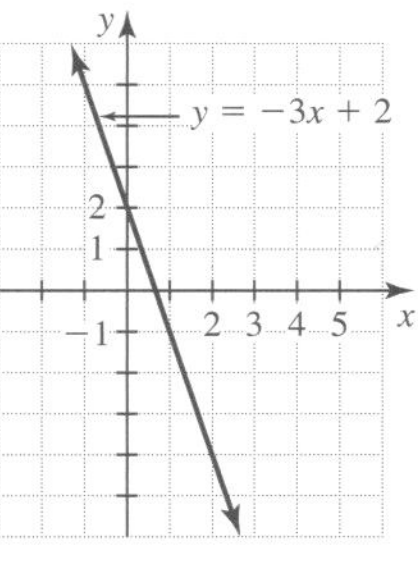

63. $y = -3$

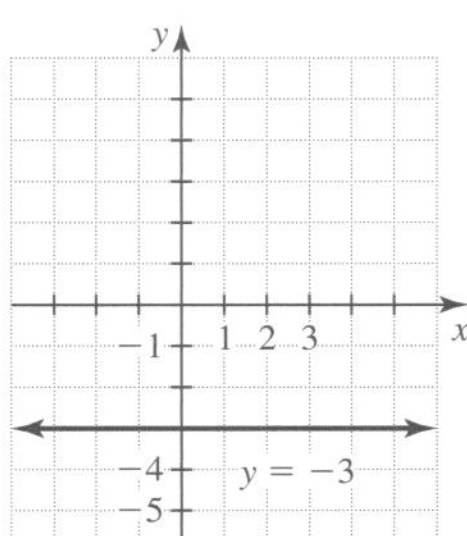

64. $y = 2$

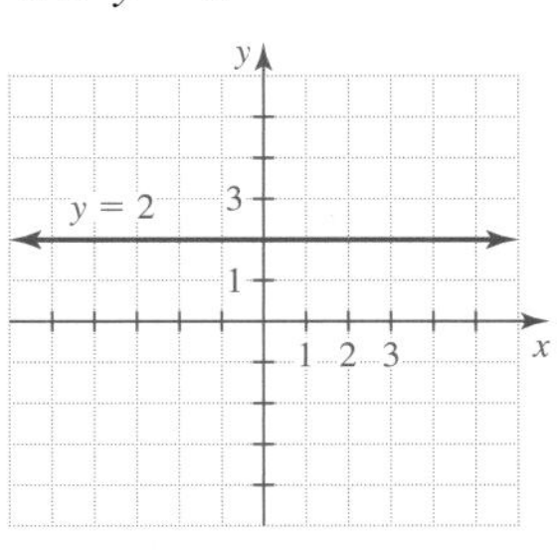

65. $x = 2$

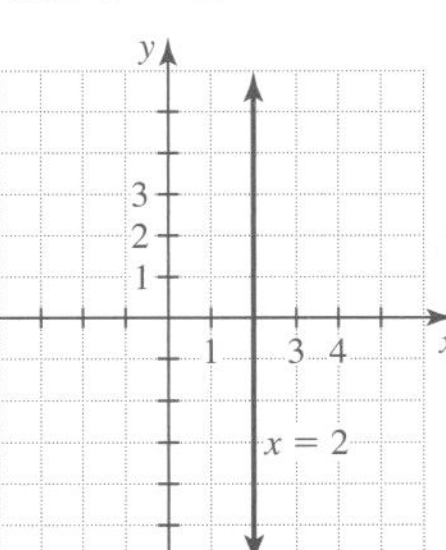

66. $x = -4$

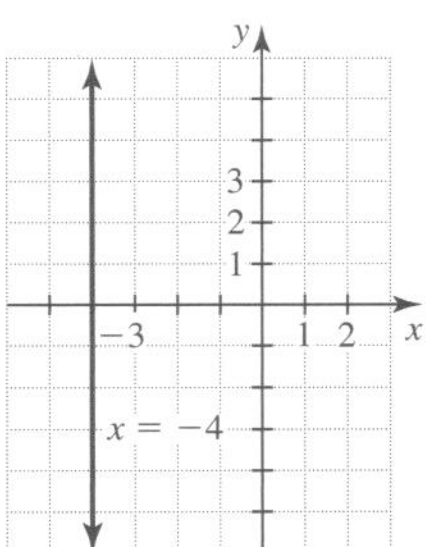

67. $2x + y = 5$

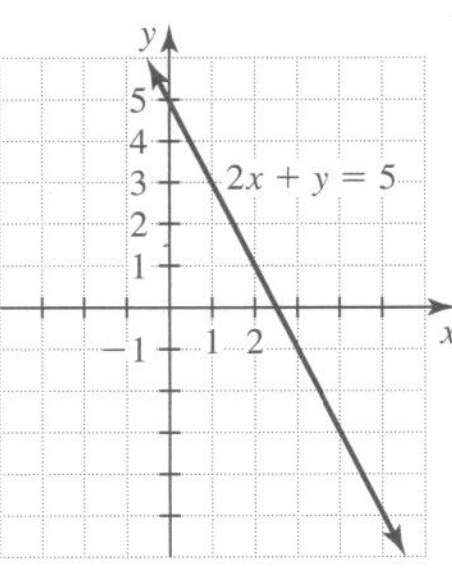

68. $3x + y = 5$

69. $x + 2y = 4$

70. $x - 2y = 6$

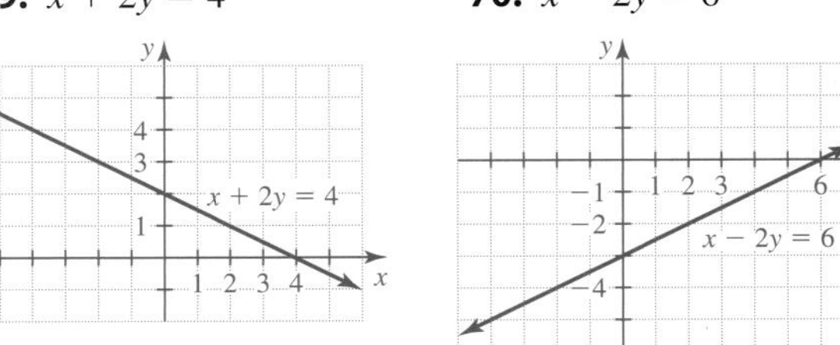

71. $x - 3y = 6$

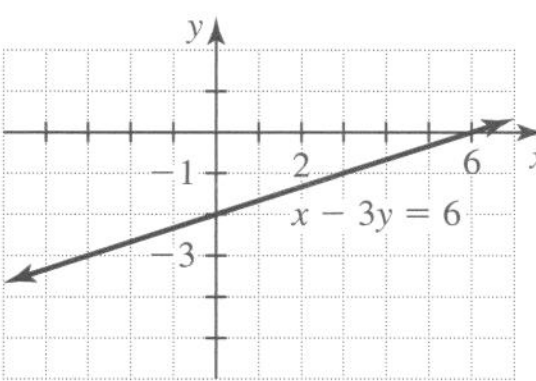

72. $x + 4y = 5$

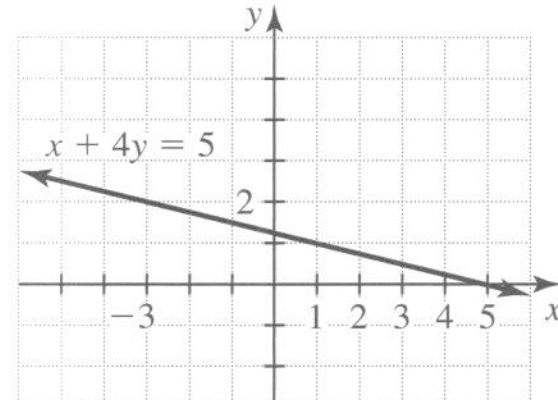

73. $y = 0.36x + 0.4$

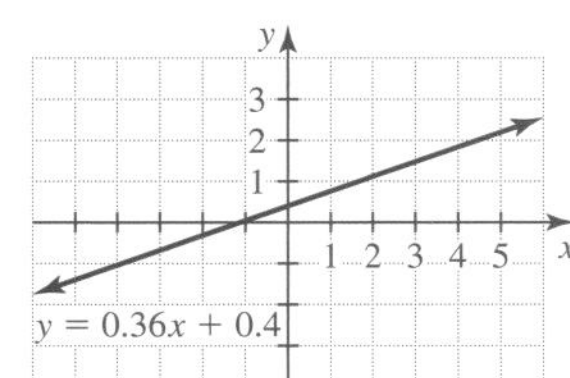

74. $y = 0.27x - 0.42$

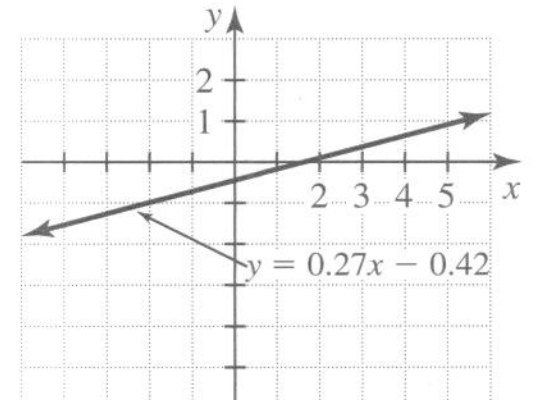

Graph each equation. Plot at least five points for each equation. Use graph paper. See Example 6. If you have a graphing calculator, use it to check your graphs.

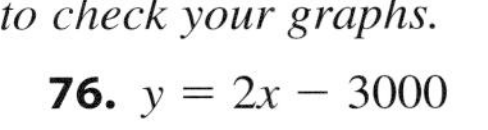
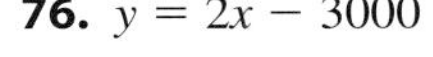

75. $y = x + 1200$

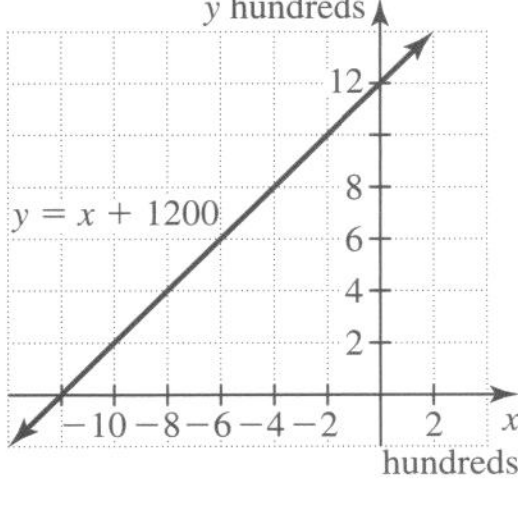

76. $y = 2x - 3000$

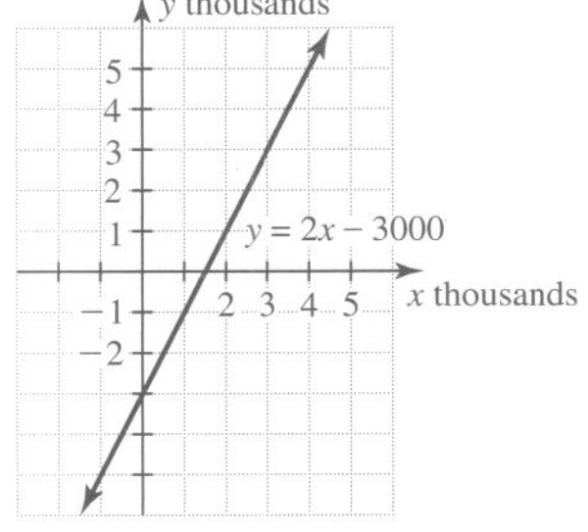

77. $y = 50x - 2000$

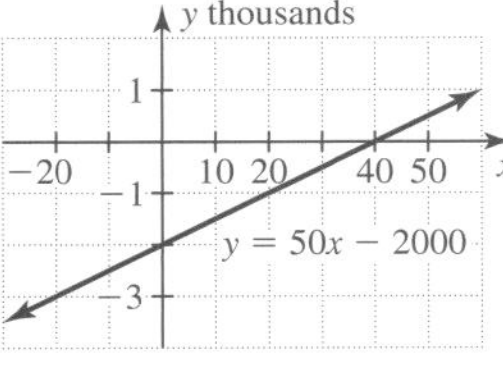

78. $y = -300x + 4500$

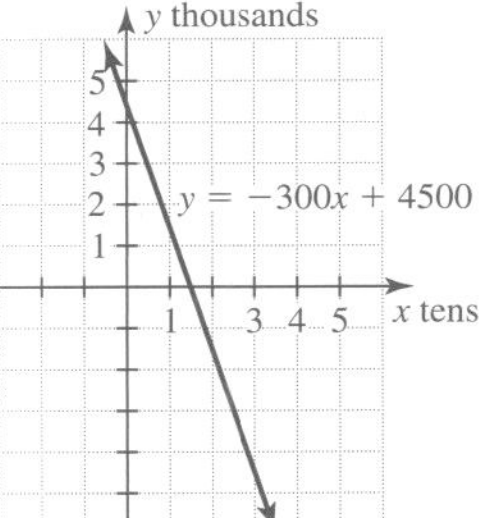

79. $y = -400x + 2000$

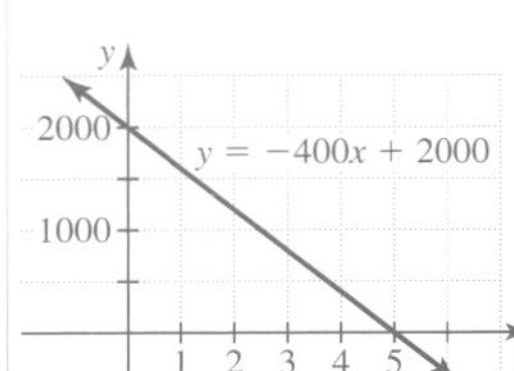

80. $y = 500x + 3$

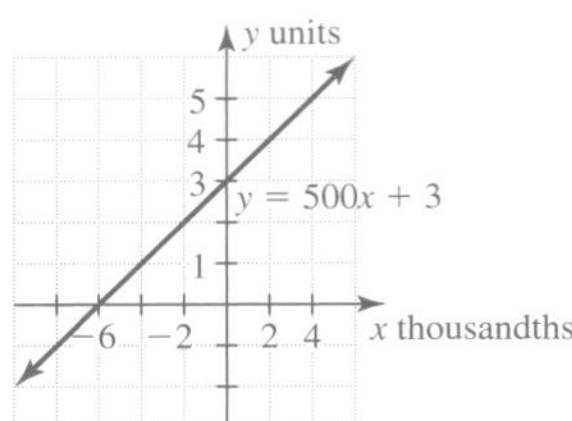

⟨5⟩ Graphing a Line Using Intercepts

For each equation, state the x-intercept and y-intercept. Then graph the equation using the intercepts and a third point. See Example 7.

81. $3x + 2y = 6$

(2, 0), (0, 3)

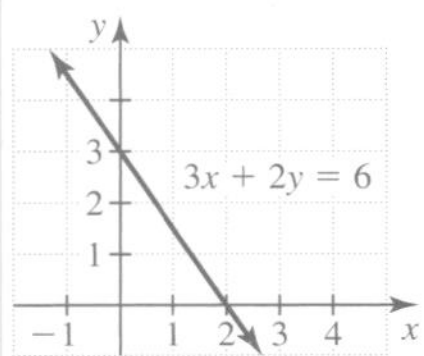

82. $2x + y = 6$

(3, 0), (0, 6)

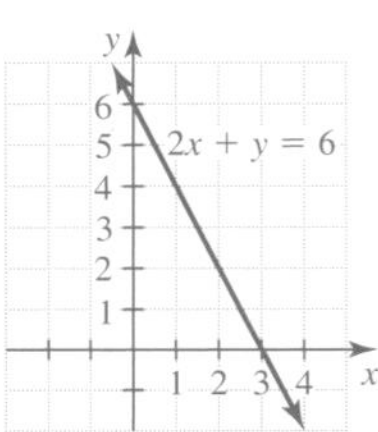

VIDEO **83.** $x - 4y = 4$

(4, 0), (0, −1)

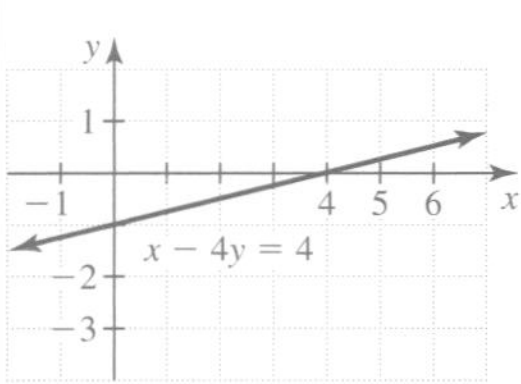

84. $-2x + y = 4$

(−2, 0), (0, 4)

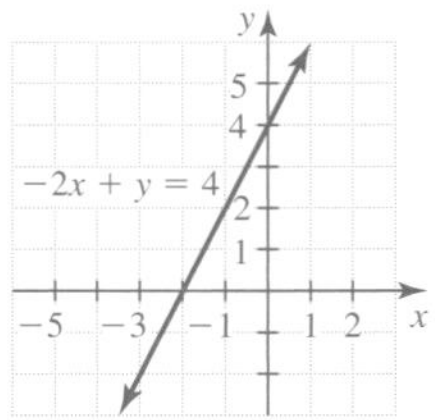

85. $y = \frac{3}{4}x - 9$

(12, 0), (0, −9)

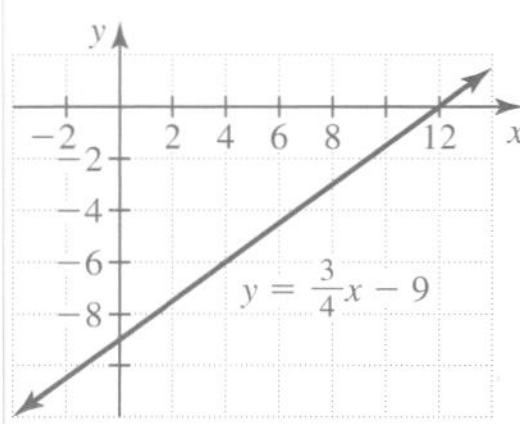

86. $y = -\frac{1}{2}x + 5$

(10, 0), (0, 5)

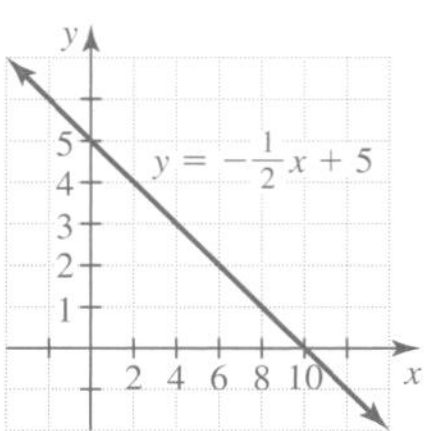

87. $\frac{1}{2}x + \frac{1}{4}y = 1$

(2, 0), (0, 4)

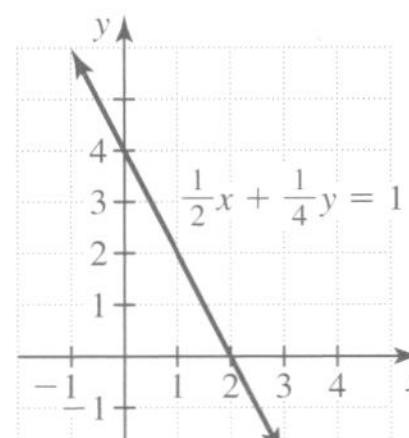

88. $\frac{1}{3}x - \frac{1}{2}y = 3$

(9, 0), (0, −6)

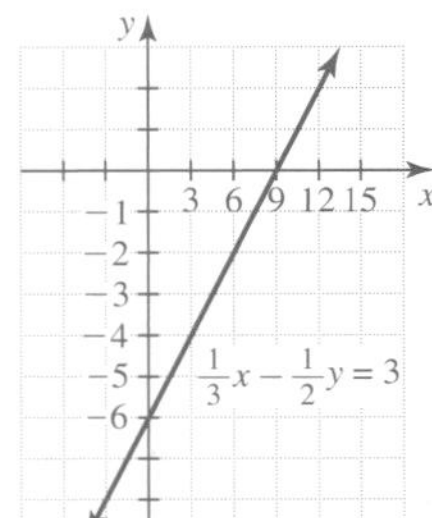

⟨6⟩ Applications

Solve each problem. See Examples 8 and 9.

89. ***Percentage of full benefit.*** The age at which you retire affects your Social Security benefits. The accompanying graph gives the percentage of full benefit for each age from 62 through 70, based on current legislation and retirement after the year 2005 (Source: Social Security Administration). What percentage of full benefit does a person receive if that person retires at age 63? At what age will a retiree receive the full benefit? For what ages do you receive more than the full benefit? 75%, 67, 68 and up

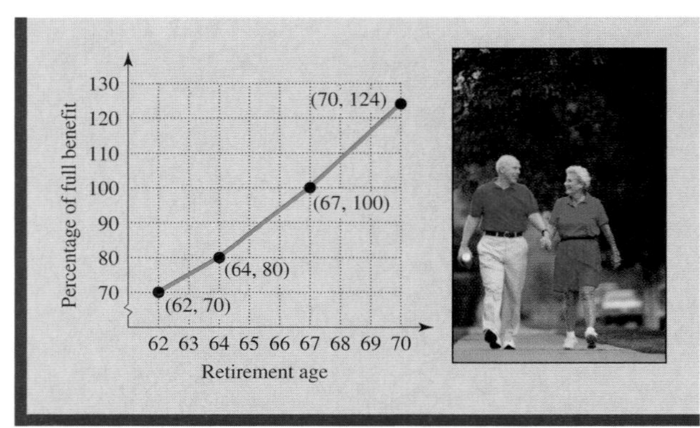

Figure for Exercise 89

90. ***Heel motion.*** When designing running shoes, Chris Edington studies the motion of a runner's foot. The following data gives the coordinates of the heel (in centimeters) at intervals of 0.05 millisecond during one cycle of level treadmill running at 3.8 meters per second (*Sagittal Plane Kinematics, Milliron and Cavanagh*):

$$(31.7, 5.7), (48.0, 5.7), (68.3, 5.8), (88.9, 6.9),$$
$$(107.2, 13.3), (119.4, 24.7), (127.2, 37.8),$$
$$(125.7, 52.0), (116.1, 60.2), (102.2, 59.5),$$
$$(88.7, 50.2), (73.9, 35.8), (52.6, 20.6),$$
$$(29.6, 10.7), (22.4, 5.9)$$

Graph these ordered pairs to see the heel motion.

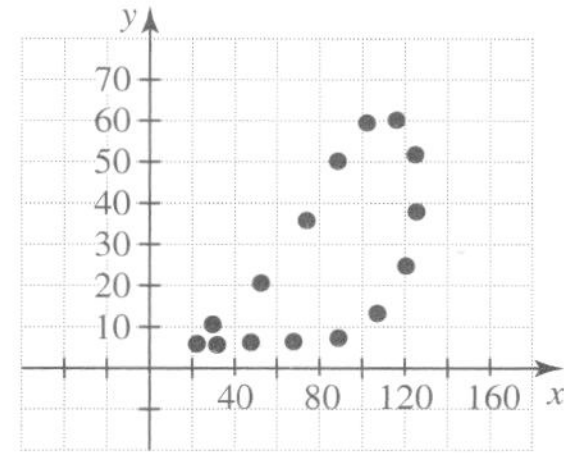

91. ***Medicaid spending.*** The cost in billions of dollars for federal Medicaid (health care for the poor) can be modeled by the equation

$$C = 3.2n + 65.3,$$

where n is the number of years since 1990 (Health Care Financing Administration, www.hcfa.gov).

a) What was the cost of federal Medicaid in 2000?
b) In what year will the cost reach \$150 billion?
c) Graph the equation for n ranging from 0 through 20.

a) \$97.3 billion **b)** 2016
c)

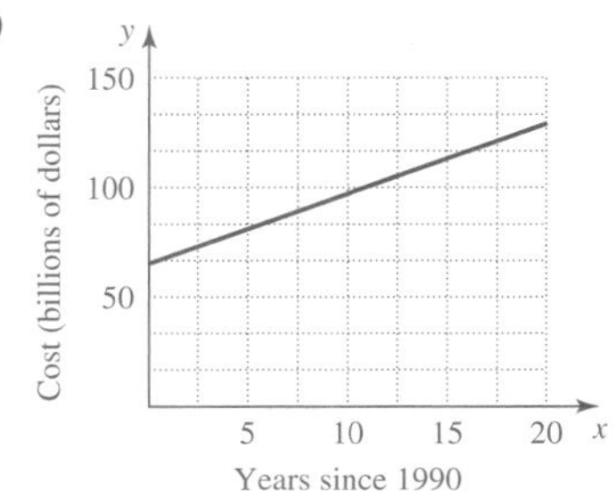

92. ***Dental services.*** The national cost C in billions of dollars for dental services can be modeled by the linear equation

$$C = 2.85n + 30.52,$$

where n is the number of years since 1990 (Health Care Financing Administration, www.hcfa.gov).

a) Find and interpret the C-intercept for the line.
b) Find and interpret the n-intercept for the line.
c) Graph the line for n ranging from 0 through 20.
d) If this trend continues, then in what year will the cost of dental services reach 100 billion?

a) (0, 30.52); The cost was \$30.52 billion in 1990.
b) (−10.71, 0); The cost was zero dollars in 1979.
c) **d)** 2014

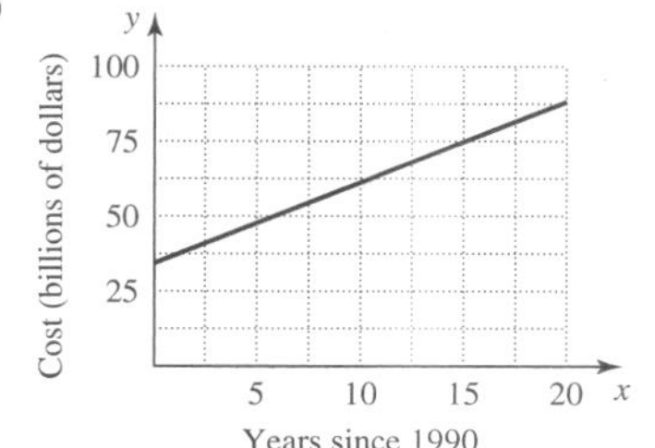

93. ***Hazards of depth.*** The accompanying table shows the depth below sea level and atmospheric pressure. The equation

$$A = 0.03d + 1$$

expresses the atmospheric pressure in terms of the depth d.

a) Find the atmospheric pressure at the depth where nitrogen narcosis begins. 4 atm
b) Find the maximum depth for intermediate divers. 130 ft
c) Graph the equation for d ranging from 0 to 250 feet.

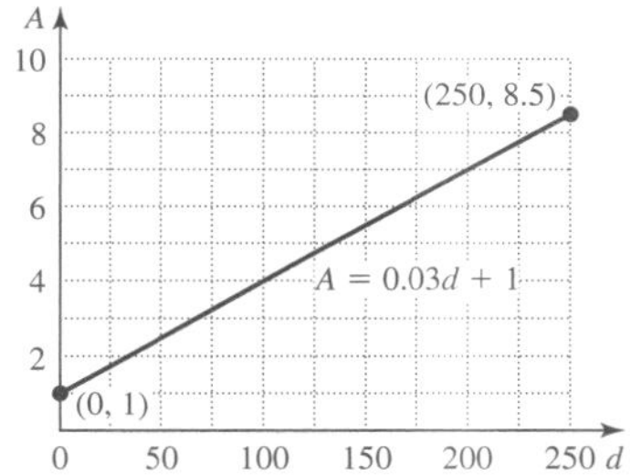

Depth (ft)	Atmospheric Pressure (atm)	Comments
21	1.63	Bends are a danger
60	2.8	Maximum for beginners
100		Nitrogen narcosis begins
	4.9	Maximum for intermediate
200	7.0	Severe nitrogen narcosis
250	8.5	Extremely dangerous depth

Figure for Exercise 93

94. ***Demand equation.*** Helen's Health Foods usually sells 400 cans of ProPac Muscle Punch per week when the price is \$5 per can. After experimenting with prices for some time, Helen has determined that the weekly demand can be found by using the equation

$$d = 600 - 40p,$$

where d is the number of cans and p is the price per can.

a) Will Helen sell more or less Muscle Punch if she raises her price from \$5? Less

b) What happens to her sales every time she raises her price by \$1? Goes down by 40 cans

c) Graph the equation.

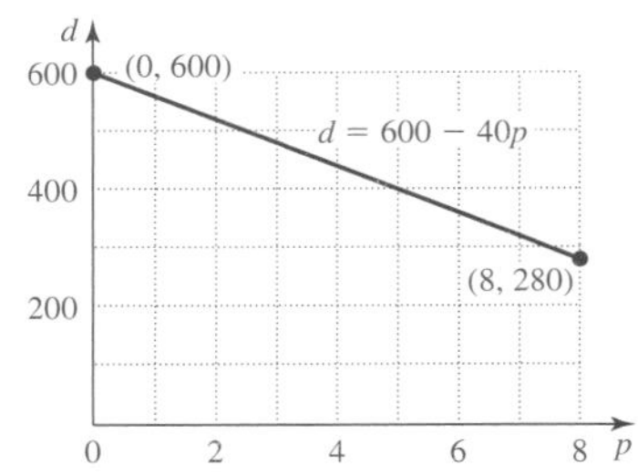

d) What is the maximum price that she can charge and still sell at least one can? \$14.97

95. ***Advertising blitz.*** Furniture City in Toronto had \$24,000 to spend on advertising a year-end clearance sale. A 30-second radio ad costs \$300, and a 30-second local television ad costs \$400. To model this situation, the advertising manager wrote the equation $300x + 400y = 24{,}000$. What do x and y represent? Graph the equation. How many solutions are there to the equation, given that the number of ads of each type must be a whole number?
x = the number of radio ads,
y = the number of TV ads, 21 solutions

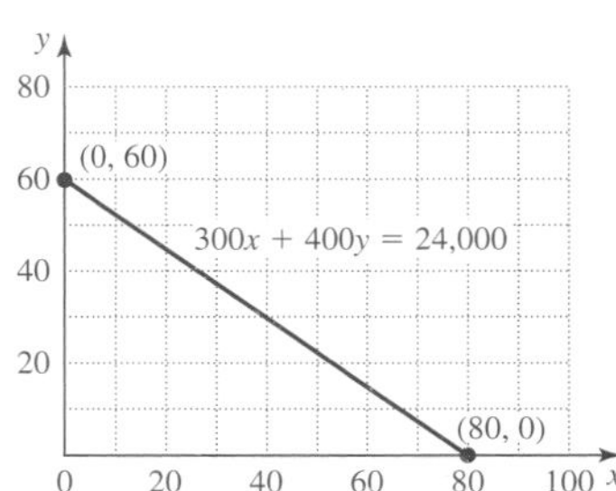

96. ***Material allocation.*** A tent maker had 4500 square yards of nylon tent material available. It takes 45 square yards of nylon to make an 8×10 tent and 50 square yards to make a 9×12 tent. To model this situation, the manager wrote the equation $45x + 50y = 4500$. What do x and y represent? Graph the equation. How many solutions are there to the equation, given that the number of tents of each type must be a whole number?
x = the number of 8×10 tents,
y = the number of 9×12 tents, 11 solutions

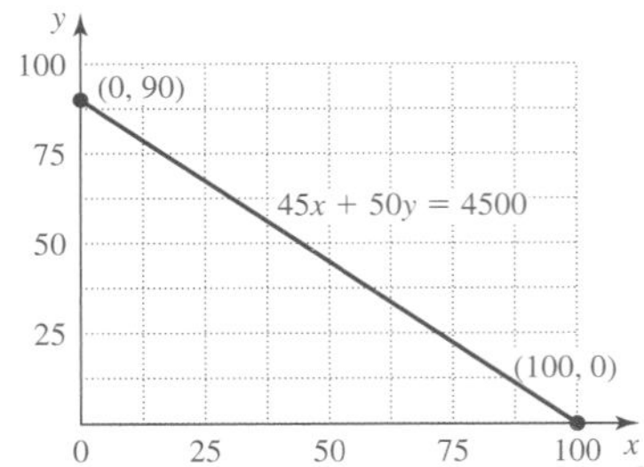

Graphing Calculator Exercises

Graph each straight line on your graphing calculator using a viewing window that shows both intercepts. Answers may vary.

97. $2x + 3y = 1200$

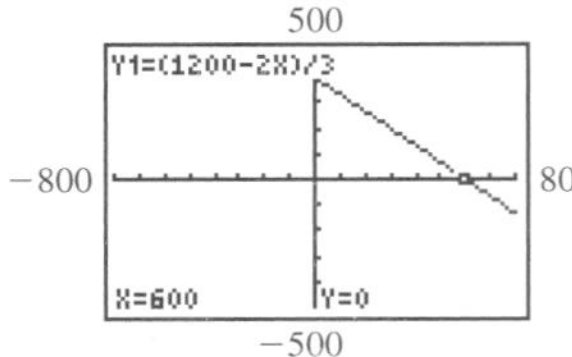

98. $3x - 700y = 2100$

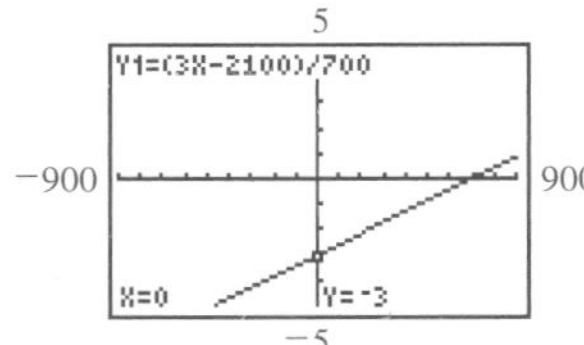

99. $200x - 300y = 6$

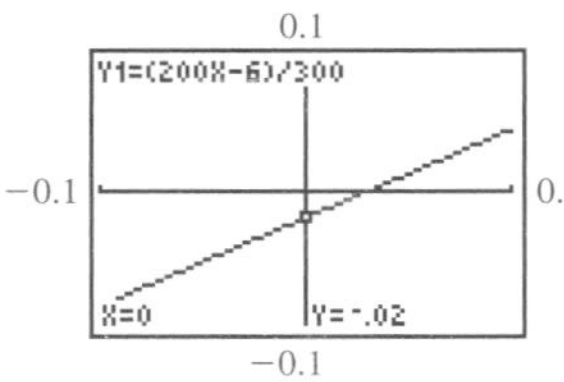

100. $300x + 5y = 20$

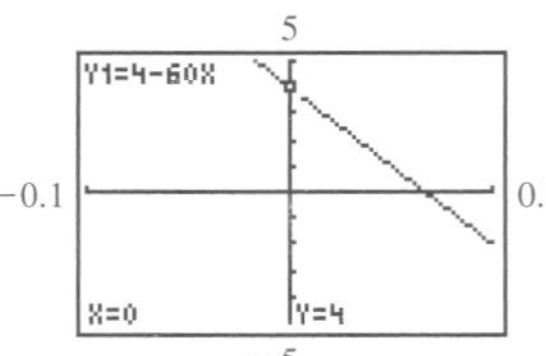

101. $y = 300x - 1$

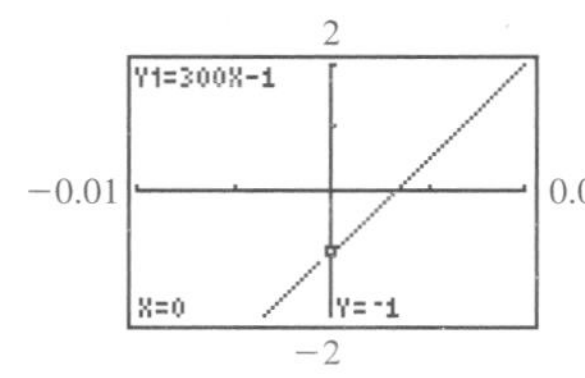

102. $y = 300x - 6000$

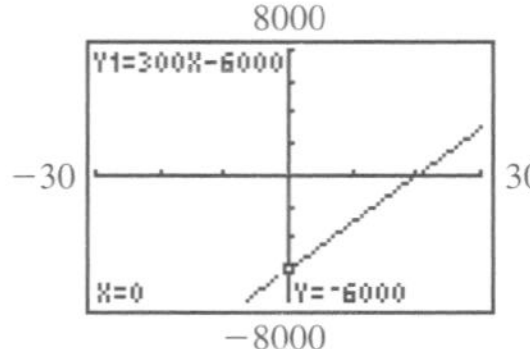

Math *at Work* Predicting the Future

No one knows what the future may bring, but everyone plans for and tries to predict the future. Stock market analysts predict the profits of companies, pollsters predict the outcomes of elections, and urban planners predict sizes of cities. These predictions of the future are often based on the trends of the past.

Consider the accompanying table, which shows the population of the United States in millions for each census year from 1950 through 2000. It certainly appears that the population is going up and it would be a safe bet to predict that the population in 2010 will be somewhat larger than 279 million. We get a different perspective if we look at the accompanying graph of the population data. Not only does the graph show an increasing population, it shows the population increasing in a linear manner. Now we can make a prediction based on the line that appears to fit the data. The equation of this line, the *regression line*, is $y = 2.47x - 4666$, where x is the year and y is the population. The equation of the regression line can be found with a computer or graphing calculator. Now if $x = 2010$, then $y = 2.47(2010) - 4666 \approx 299$. So we can predict 299 million people in 2010.

Year	Population (millions)
1950	152
1960	180
1970	204
1980	227
1990	249
2000	279

3.2 Slope

In This Section

- ⟨1⟩ Slope
- ⟨2⟩ Slope Using Coordinates
- ⟨3⟩ Graphing a Line Given a Point and Slope
- ⟨4⟩ Parallel Lines
- ⟨5⟩ Perpendicular Lines
- ⟨6⟩ Applications

In Section 3.1 you learned that the graph of a linear equation is a straight line. In this section, we will continue our study of lines in the coordinate plane.

⟨1⟩ Slope

If a highway rises 6 feet in a horizontal run of 100 feet, then the grade is $\frac{6}{100}$ or 6%. See Fig. 3.13. The grade is a measurement of the steepness of the road. A road with an 8% grade rises 8 feet in a horizontal run of 100 feet, and it is steeper than a road with a 6% grade. We use exactly the same idea to measure the steepness of a line in a coordinate system, but the measurement is called **slope** rather than grade. For the line in Fig. 3.14, the y-coordinate increases by 2 units and the x-coordinate increases by 3 units as you move from (1, 1) to (4, 3). So its slope is $\frac{2}{3}$.

In general, the change in y-coordinate is the **rise** and the change in x-coordinate is the **run.** The letter m is often used for slope.

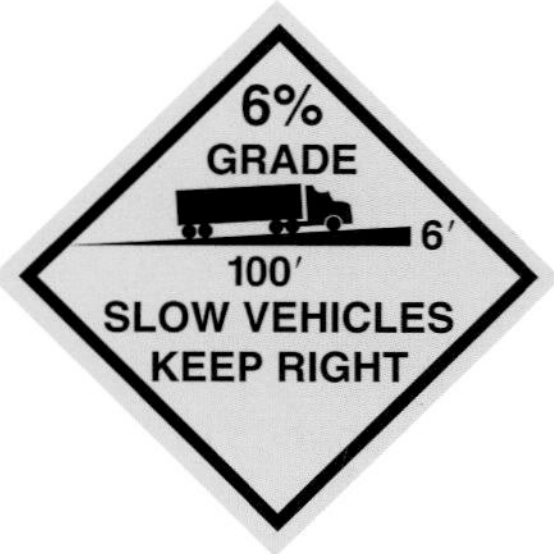

Figure 3.13

Slope

$$m = \text{slope} = \frac{\text{rise}}{\text{run}} = \frac{\text{change in } y\text{-coordinate}}{\text{change in } x\text{-coordinate}}$$

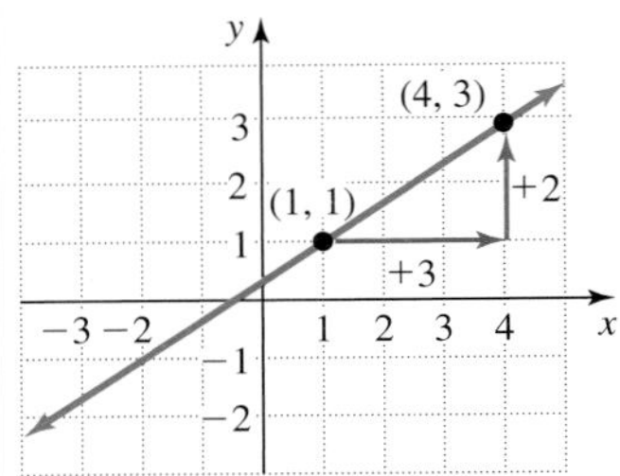

Figure 3.14

Signed numbers are not used to describe the grade of a road, but they are used for lines in a coordinate system. If the y-coordinate increases (moving upward) as you move from one point on the line to another, the rise is positive. If it decreases (moving downward), the rise is negative. The same goes for the run. If the x-coordinate increases (moving to the right), then the run is positive, and if it decreases (moving to the left), the run is negative. Using signed numbers for the rise and run causes the slope to be positive or negative, as shown in Example 1.

EXAMPLE 1

Finding the slope of a line

Find the slope of each blue line by going from point A to point B.

a)

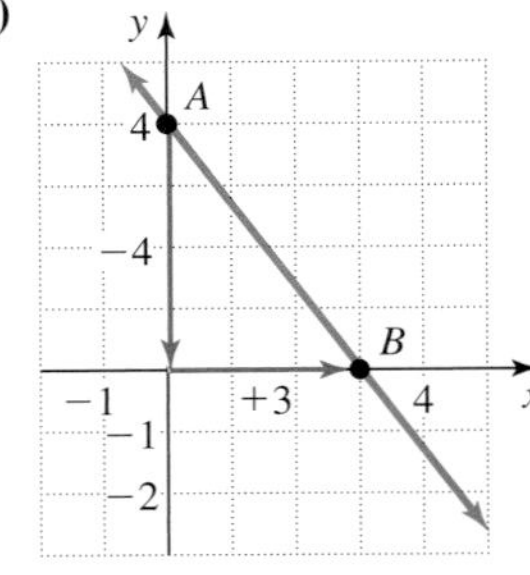

b)

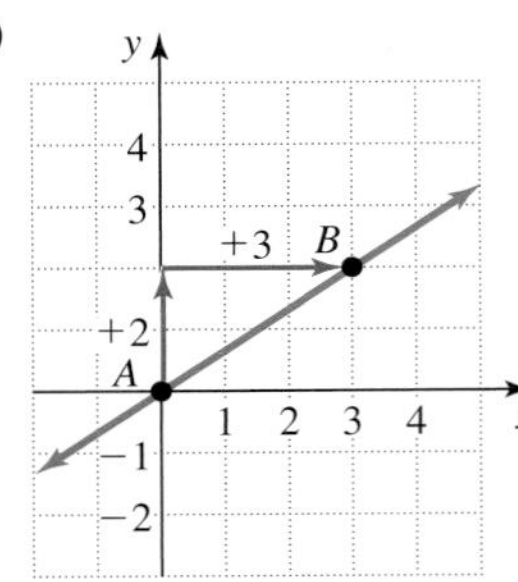

c)

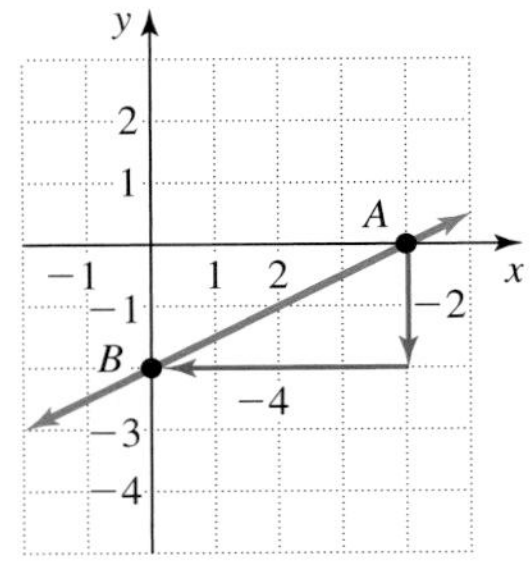

Solution

a) The coordinates of point A are $(0, 4)$, and the coordinates of point B are $(3, 0)$. Going from A to B, the change in y is -4, and the change in x is $+3$. So

$$m = \frac{-4}{3} = -\frac{4}{3}.$$

Note that it does not matter whether you move from A to B or from B to A. Moving from B to A, the y-coordinate increases by 4 units (rise $+4$) and the x-coordinate decreases by 3 units (run -3). So rise over run is $\frac{+4}{-3}$ or $-\frac{4}{3}$.

b) Going from A to B, the rise is 2, and the run is 3. So

$$m = \frac{2}{3}.$$

c) Going from A to B, the rise is -2, and the run is -4. So

$$m = \frac{-2}{-4} = \frac{1}{2}.$$

Now do Exercises 7–10

‹ Teaching Tip ›

Another example of slope is the pitch of a roof. A 5–12 pitch means a roof rises 5 feet in a run of 12 feet. Ask students to determine the pitch of the roof in the house in which they live.

CAUTION The change in y is always in the numerator, and the change in x is always in the denominator.

The ratio of rise to run is the ratio of the lengths of the two legs of any right triangle whose hypotenuse is on the line. As long as one leg is vertical and the other is horizontal, all such triangles for a certain line have the same shape. These triangles are similar triangles. The ratio of the length of the vertical side to the length of the horizontal side for any two such triangles is the same number. So we get the same value for the slope no matter which two points of the line are used to calculate it or in which order the points are used.

EXAMPLE 2

Finding slope

Find the slope of the line shown here using points A and B, points A and C, and points B and C.

Solution

Using A and B, we get

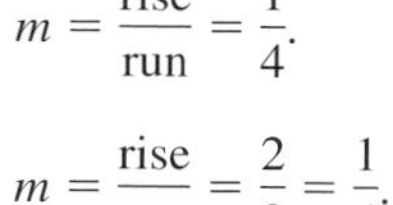

$$m = \frac{\text{rise}}{\text{run}} = \frac{1}{4}.$$

Using A and C, we get

$$m = \frac{\text{rise}}{\text{run}} = \frac{2}{8} = \frac{1}{4}.$$

Using B and C, we get

$$m = \frac{\text{rise}}{\text{run}} = \frac{1}{4}.$$

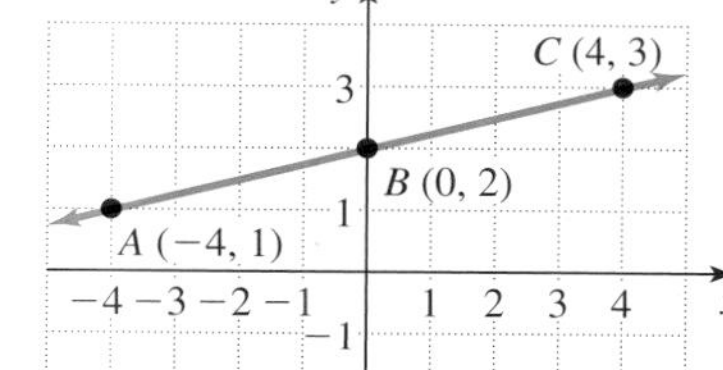

Now do Exercises 11–18

‹ Helpful Hint ›

It is good to think of what the slope represents when x and y are measured quantities rather than just numbers. For example, if the change in y is 50 miles and the change in x is 2 hours, then the slope is 25 mph (or 25 miles per 1 hour). So the slope is the amount of change in y for a change of one in x.

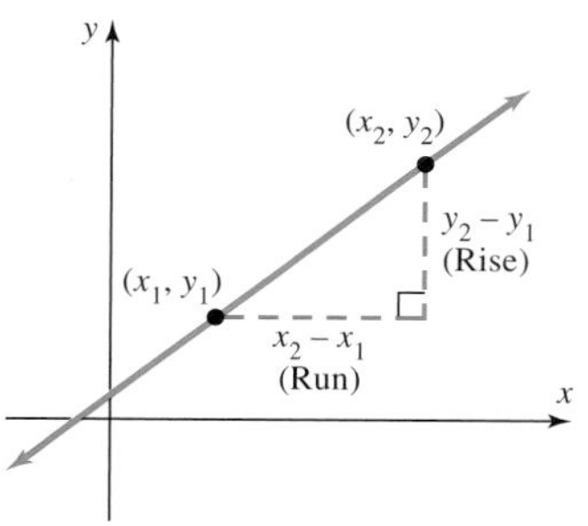

Figure 3.15

‹2› Slope Using Coordinates

One way to obtain the rise and run is from a graph. The rise and run can also be found by using the coordinates of two points on the line as shown in Fig. 3.15.

Coordinate Formula for Slope

The slope of the line containing the points (x_1, y_1) and (x_2, y_2) is given by

$$m = \frac{y_2 - y_1}{x_2 - x_1},$$

provided that $x_2 - x_1 \neq 0$.

The small lowered numbers following x and y in the slope formula are **subscripts.** We read x_1 as "x sub one" or simply "x one." We think of (x_1, y_1) as the x- and y-coordinates of the first point and (x_2, y_2) as the x- and y-coordinates of the second point.

EXAMPLE 3

Using coordinates to find slope

Find the slope of each of the following lines.

a) The line through (0, 5) and (6, 3)

b) The line through (−3, −4) and (−5, −2)

c) The line through (−4, 2) and the origin

Solution

a) If $(x_1, y_1) = (0, 5)$ and $(x_2, y_2) = (6, 3)$ then

$$m = \frac{y_2 - y_1}{x_2 - x_1}$$

$$= \frac{3 - 5}{6 - 0} = \frac{-2}{6} = -\frac{1}{3}.$$

If $(x_1, y_1) = (6, 3)$ and $(x_2, y_2) = (0, 5)$ then

$$m = \frac{y_2 - y_1}{x_2 - x_1}$$

$$= \frac{5 - 3}{0 - 6} = \frac{2}{-6} = -\frac{1}{3}.$$

Note that it does not matter which point is called (x_1, y_1) and which is called (x_2, y_2). In either case, the slope is $-\frac{1}{3}$.

b) Let $(x_1, y_1) = (-3, -4)$ and $(x_2, y_2) = (-5, -2)$:

$$m = \frac{y_2 - y_1}{x_2 - x_1}$$

$$= \frac{-2 - (-4)}{-5 - (-3)}$$

$$= \frac{2}{-2} = -1$$

c) Let $(x_1, y_1) = (0, 0)$ and $(x_2, y_2) = (-4, 2)$:

$$m = \frac{2 - 0}{-4 - 0} = \frac{2}{-4} = -\frac{1}{2}$$

Now do Exercises 19–32

‹ Teaching Tip ›

To get the numbers in the right positions in the slope formula, observe that the coordinates of each point are lined up vertically.

CAUTION Order matters. If you divide $y_2 - y_1$ by $x_1 - x_2$, your slope will have the wrong sign. However, you will get the correct slope regardless of which point is called (x_1, y_1) and which is called (x_2, y_2).

Because division by zero is undefined, slope is undefined if $x_2 - x_1 = 0$ or $x_2 = x_1$. The x-coordinates of two distinct points on a line are equal only if the points are on a vertical line. *So slope is undefined for vertical lines.* The concept of slope does not exist for a vertical line.

Any two points on a horizontal line have equal y-coordinates. So for points on a horizontal line we have $y_2 - y_1 = 0$. Since $y_2 - y_1$ is in the numerator of the slope formula, *the slope for any horizontal line is zero.* We never refer to a line as having "no slope," because in English no can mean zero or does not exist.

EXAMPLE 4

Slope for vertical and horizontal lines

Find the slope of the line through each pair of points.

a) $(2, 1)$ and $(2, -3)$

b) $(-2, 2)$ and $(4, 2)$

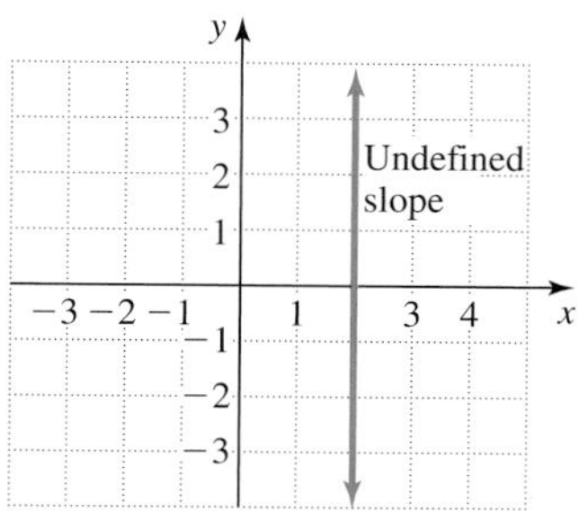

Figure 3.16

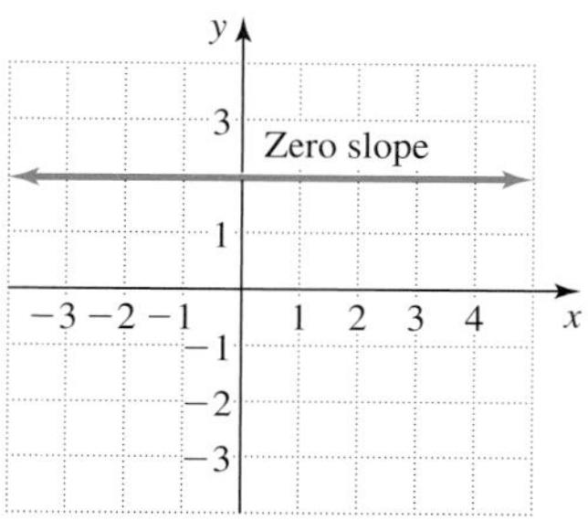

Figure 3.17

‹ Teaching Tip ›

Emphasize that slope is the amount of change in y for a unit change in x. Slope is the rate at which y is changing with respect to x.

Solution

a) The points (2, 1) and (2, −3) are on the vertical line shown in Fig. 3.16. Since slope is undefined for vertical lines, this line does not have a slope. Using the slope formula we get

$$m = \frac{-3 - 1}{2 - 2} = \frac{-4}{0}.$$

Since division by zero is undefined, we can again conclude that slope is undefined for the vertical line through the given points.

b) The points (−2, 2) and (4, 2) are on the horizontal line shown in Fig. 3.17. Using the slope formula we get

$$m = \frac{2 - 2}{-2 - 4} = \frac{0}{-6} = 0.$$

So the slope of the horizontal line through these points is 0.

Now do Exercises 33–38

Note that for a line with *positive slope,* the y-values increase as the x-values increase. For a line with *negative slope,* the y-values decrease as the x-values increase. See Fig. 3.18. As the absolute value of the slope increases, the line gets steeper.

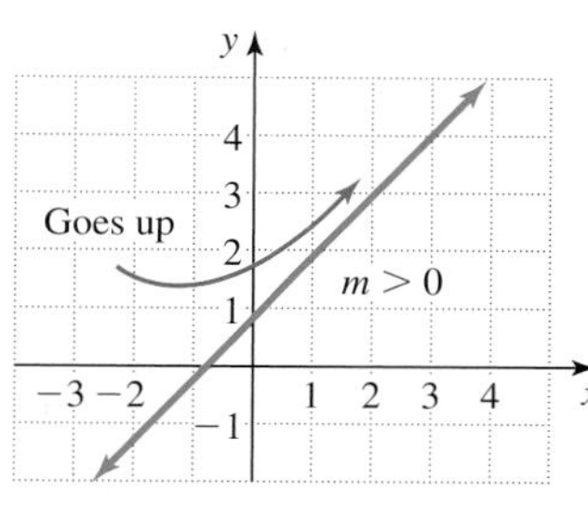

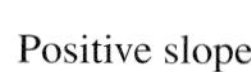

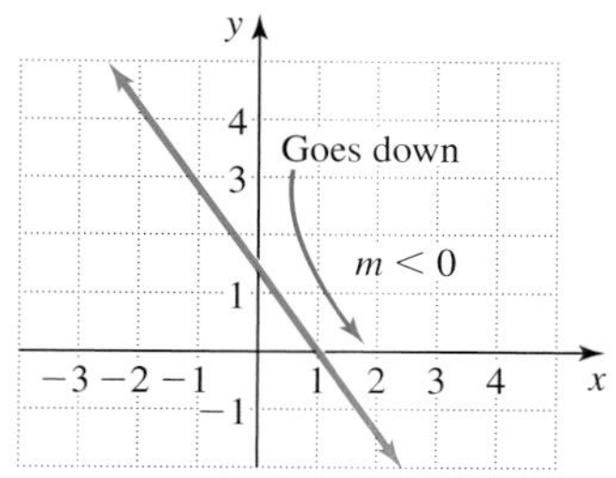

Figure 3.18

‹3› Graphing a Line Given a Point and Slope

To graph a line from its equation we usually make a table of ordered pairs and then draw a line through the points or we use the intercepts. In Example 5 we will graph a line using one point and the slope. From the slope we find additional points by using the rise and the run.

EXAMPLE 5 Graphing a line given a point and its slope

Graph each line.

a) The line through (2, 1) with slope $\frac{3}{4}$

b) The line through (−2, 4) with slope −3

‹ Teaching Tip ›

Remind students that a slope of $-3/1$ can be stepped off on the graph as a rise of -3 and a run of 1 or a run of -1 and a rise of 3, whichever is more convenient.

‹ Calculator Close-Up ›

When we graph a line we usually draw a graph that shows both intercepts, because they are important features of the graph. If the intercepts are not between -10 and 10, you will have to adjust the window to get a good graph. The viewing window that has x- and y-values ranging from a minimum of -10 to a maximum of 10 is called the *standard viewing window.*

Solution

a) First locate the point (2, 1). Because the slope is $\frac{3}{4}$, we can find another point on the line by going up three units and to the right four units to get the point (6, 4), as shown in Fig. 3.19. Now draw a line through (2, 1) and (6, 4). Since $\frac{3}{4} = \frac{-3}{-4}$ we could have obtained the second point by starting at (1, 2) and going down 3 units and to the left 4 units.

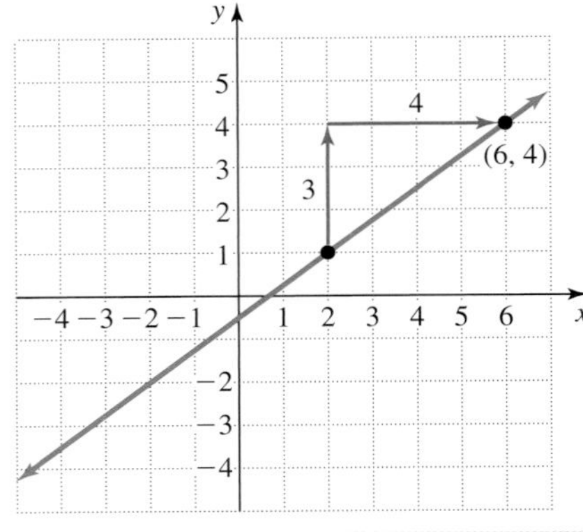

Figure 3.19

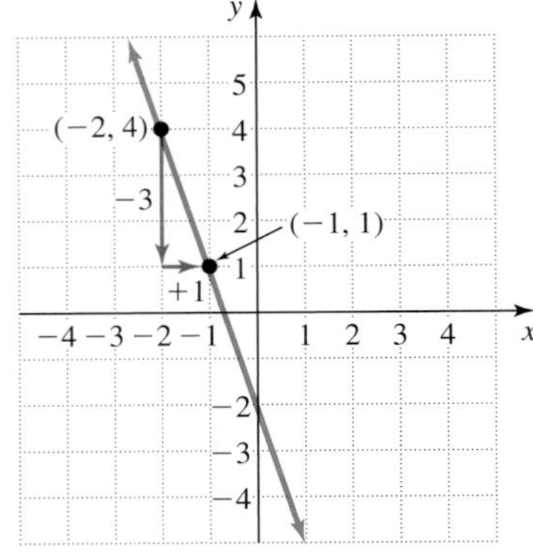

Figure 3.20

b) First locate the point $(-2, 4)$. Because the slope is -3, or $\frac{-3}{1}$, we can locate another point on the line by starting at $(-2, 4)$ and moving down three units and then one unit to the right to get the point $(-1, 1)$. Now draw a line through $(-2, 4)$ and $(-1, 1)$ as shown in Fig. 3.20. Since $\frac{-3}{1} = \frac{3}{-1}$ we could have obtained the second point by starting at $(-2, 4)$ and going up 3 units and to the left 1 unit.

Now do Exercises 39–44

‹4› Parallel Lines

Two lines in a coordinate plane that do not intersect are **parallel.** Consider the two lines with slope $\frac{1}{3}$ shown in Fig. 3.21. At the y-axis these lines are 4 units apart, measured vertically. A slope of $\frac{1}{3}$ means that you can forever rise 1 and run 3 to get to another point on the line. So the lines will always be 4 units apart vertically, and they will never intersect. This example illustrates the following fact.

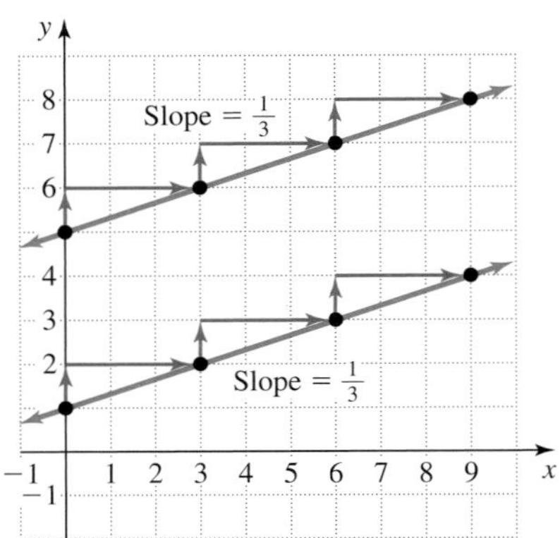

Figure 3.21

Parallel Lines

Two lines with slopes m_1 and m_2 are parallel if and only if $m_1 = m_2$.

For lines that have slope, the slopes can be used to determine whether the lines are parallel. The only lines that do not have slope are vertical lines. Of course, any two vertical lines are parallel.

EXAMPLE 6

Graphing parallel lines

Draw a line through the point $(-2, 1)$ with slope $\frac{1}{2}$ and a line through $(3, 0)$ with slope $\frac{1}{2}$.

Solution

Because slope is the ratio of rise to run, a slope of $\frac{1}{2}$ means that we can locate a second point of the line by starting at $(-2, 1)$ and going up one unit and to the right two units. For the line through $(3, 0)$ we start at $(3, 0)$ and go up one unit and to the right two units. See Fig. 3.22.

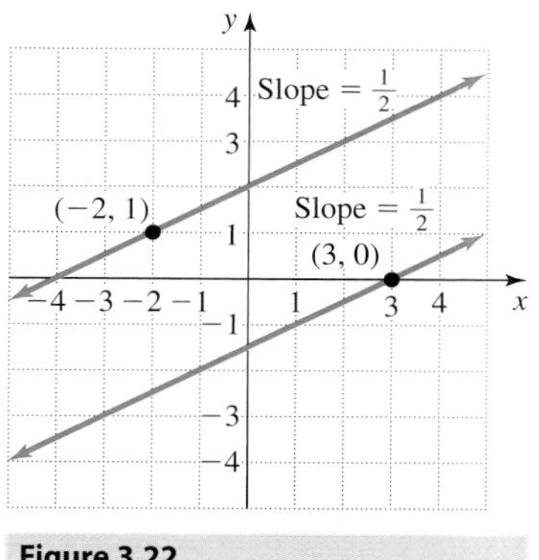

Figure 3.22

Now do Exercises 45–46

‹ Teaching Tip ›

Graphing with a point and a slope can be very inaccurate using only two points. Have students locate several points using slope before drawing the line.

‹ Teaching Tip ›

Using graph paper have students graph $y = -\frac{1}{2}x$ and then visually draw a perpendicular to $y = -\frac{1}{2}x$ through (0, 0). Now determine the slope of the perpendicular. The class average should be 2.

‹5› Perpendicular Lines

Figure 3.23 shows line l_1 with positive slope m_1. The rise m_1 and the run 1 are the sides of a right triangle. If l_1 and the triangle are rotated 90° clockwise, then l_1 will coincide with line l_2, and the slope of l_2 can be determined from the triangle in its new position. Starting at the point of intersection, the run for l_2 is m_1 and the rise is -1 (moving downward). So if m_2 is the slope of l_2, then $m_2 = -\frac{1}{m_1}$. *The slope of l_2 is the opposite of the reciprocal of the slope of l_1.* This result can be stated also as $m_1m_2 = -1$ or as follows.

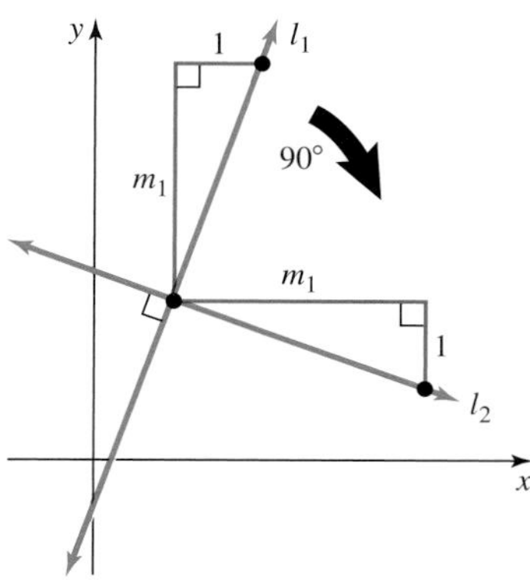

Figure 3.23

Perpendicular Lines

Two lines with slopes m_1 and m_2 are perpendicular if and only if

$$m_1 = -\frac{1}{m_2}.$$

Notice that we cannot compare slopes of horizontal and vertical lines to see if they are perpendicular because slope is undefined for vertical lines. However, you should just remember that any horizontal line is perpendicular to any vertical line and vice versa.

EXAMPLE 7

Graphing perpendicular lines

Draw two lines through the point $(-1, 2)$, one with slope $-\frac{1}{3}$ and the other with slope 3.

Solution

Because slope is the ratio of rise to run, a slope of $-\frac{1}{3}$ means that we can locate a second point on the line by starting at $(-1, 2)$ and going down one unit and to the right three units. For the line with slope 3, we start at $(-1, 2)$ and go up three units and to the right one unit. See Fig. 3.24.

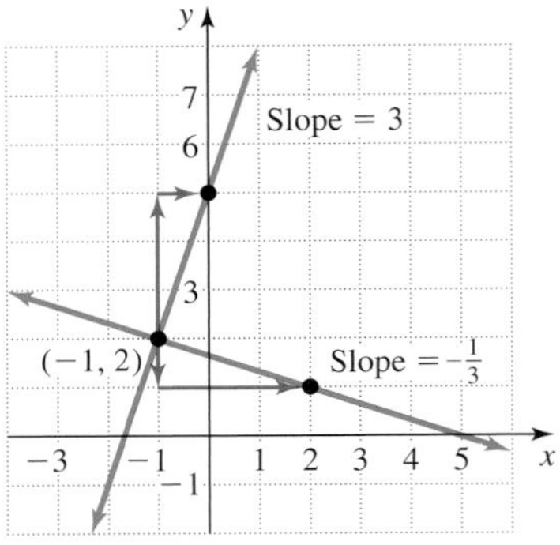

Figure 3.24

Now do Exercises 47–54

Helpful Hint

The relationship between the slopes of perpendicular lines can also be remembered as

$$m_1 \cdot m_2 = -1.$$

For example, lines with slopes -3 and $\frac{1}{3}$ are perpendicular because $-3 \cdot \frac{1}{3} = -1$.

EXAMPLE 8

Parallel, perpendicular, or neither

Determine whether the lines l_1 and l_2 are parallel, perpendicular, or neither.

a) l_1 goes through $(1, 2)$ and $(4, 8)$, l_2 goes through $(0, 3)$ and $(1, 5)$.

b) l_1 goes through $(-2, 5)$ and $(3, 7)$, l_2 goes through $(8, 4)$ and $(6, 9)$.

c) l_1 goes through $(0, 4)$ and $(-1, 6)$, l_2 goes through $(7, 7)$ and $(4, 4)$.

Solution

a) The slope of l_1 is $\frac{8 - 2}{4 - 1}$ or 2. The slope of l_2 is $\frac{5 - 3}{1 - 0}$ or 2. Since the slopes are equal, the lines are parallel.

b) The slope of l_1 is $\frac{7 - 5}{3 - (-2)}$ or $\frac{2}{5}$. The slope of l_2 is $\frac{4 - 9}{8 - 6}$ or $-\frac{5}{2}$. Since one slope is the opposite of the reciprocal of the slope of the other, the lines are perpendicular.

c) The slope of l_1 is $\frac{6 - 4}{-1 - 0}$ or -2. The slope of l_2 is $\frac{7 - 4}{7 - 4}$ or 1. Since $-2 \neq 1$ and $-2 \neq -\frac{1}{1}$, the lines are neither parallel nor perpendicular.

Now do Exercises 55–62

⟨6⟩ Applications

The slope of a line is the ratio of the rise and the run. If the rise is measured in dollars and the run in days, then the slope is measured in dollars per day (dollars/day). The slope is the amount of increase or decrease in dollars for *one* day. The slope of a line is the rate at which the dependent variable is increasing or decreasing. It is the amount of change in the dependent variable per a change of one unit in the independent variable. In some cases, the slope is a fraction, but whole numbers sound better for interpretation. For example, the birth rate at a hospital of $\frac{1}{3}$ birth/day might sound better stated as one birth per three days.

EXAMPLE 9

Interpreting slope as a rate of change

A car goes from 60 mph to 0 mph in 120 feet after applying the brakes.

a) Find and interpret the slope of the line shown here.

b) What is the velocity at a distance of 80 feet?

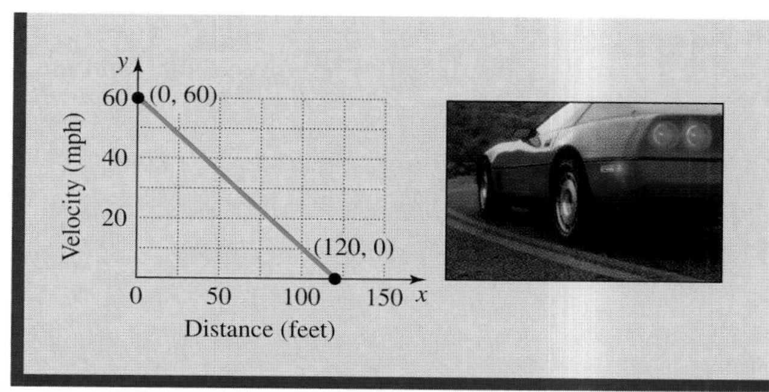

Solution

a) Find the slope of the line through (0, 60) and (120, 0):

$$m = \frac{60 - 0}{0 - 120} = -0.5$$

Because the vertical axis is miles per hour and the horizontal axis is feet, the slope is -0.5 mph/ft, which means the car is losing 0.5 mph of velocity for every foot it travels after the brakes are applied.

b) If the velocity is decreasing 0.5 mph for every foot the car travels, then in 80 feet the velocity goes down 0.5(80) or 40 mph. So the velocity at 80 feet is $60 - 40$ or 20 mph.

Now do Exercises 63–66

EXAMPLE 10

Finding points when given the slope

Assume that the base price of a new Jeep Wrangler is increasing \$300 per year. Find the data that is missing from the table.

Year (*x*)	Price (*y*)
2001	\$15,600
2002	
2003	
	\$18,300
	\$20,100

Solution

The price in 2002 is \$15,900 and in 2003 it is \$16,200 because the slope is \$300 per year. The rise in price from \$16,200 to \$18,300 is \$2100, which takes 7 years at \$300 per year. So in 2010 the price is \$18,300. The rise from \$18,300 to \$20,100 is \$1800, which takes 6 years at \$300 per year. So in 2016 the price is \$20,100.

Now do Exercises 67–68

Warm-Ups ▼

True or false? Explain your answer.

1. Slope is a measurement of the steepness of a line. True
2. Slope is rise divided by run. True
3. Every line in the coordinate plane has a slope. False
4. The line through the point (1, 1) and the origin has slope 1. True
5. Slope can never be negative. False
6. A line with slope 2 is perpendicular to any line with slope -2. False
7. The slope of the line through (0, 3) and (4, 0) is $\frac{3}{4}$. False
8. Two different lines cannot have the same slope. False
9. The line through (1, 3) and (−5, 3) has zero slope. True
10. Slope can have units such as feet per second. True

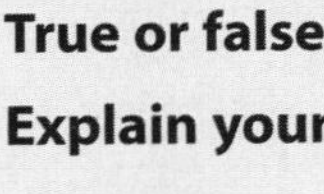

3.2 Exercises

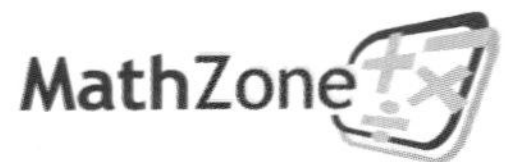

‹ Study Tips ›

- Don't expect to understand a topic the first time you see it. Learning mathematics takes time, patience, and repetition.
- Keep reading the text, asking questions, and working problems. Someone once said, "All math is easy once you understand it."

Reading and Writing *After reading this section, write out the answers to these questions. Use complete sentences.*

1. What is the slope of a line?
   The slope of a line is the ratio of its rise and run.
2. What is the difference between rise and run?
   Rise is the amount of vertical change and run is the amount of horizontal change.
3. For which lines is slope undefined?
   Slope is undefined for vertical lines.
4. Which lines have zero slope?
   Horizontal lines have zero slope.
5. What is the difference between lines with positive slope and lines with negative slope?
   Lines with positive slope are rising as you go from left to right, while lines with negative slope are falling as you go from left to right.
6. What is the relationship between the slopes of perpendicular lines?
   If m_1 and m_2 are slopes of perpendicular lines, then $m_1 = -\frac{1}{m_2}$.

⟨1⟩ Slope

In Exercises 7–18, find the slope of each line. See Examples 1 and 2.

7.

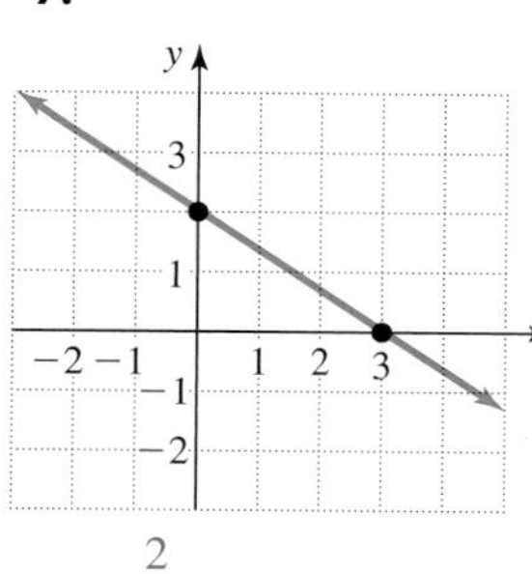

$-\frac{2}{3}$

8.

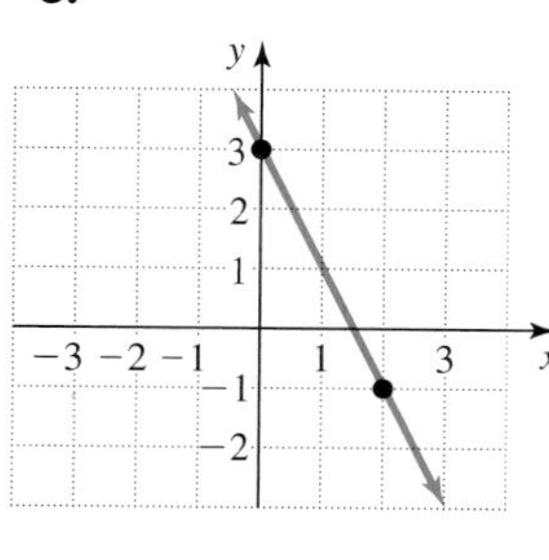

−2

9.

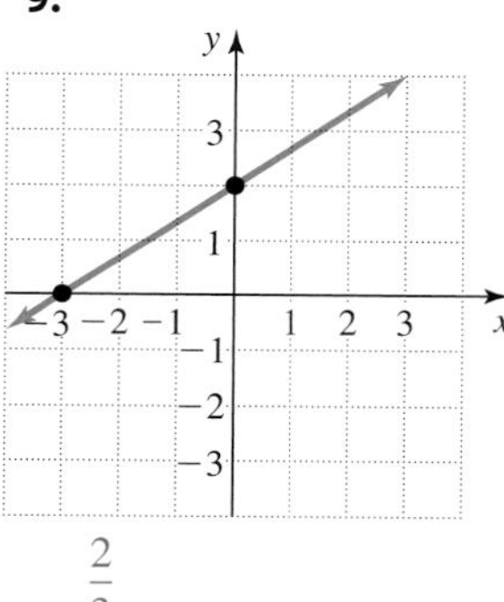

$\frac{2}{3}$

10.

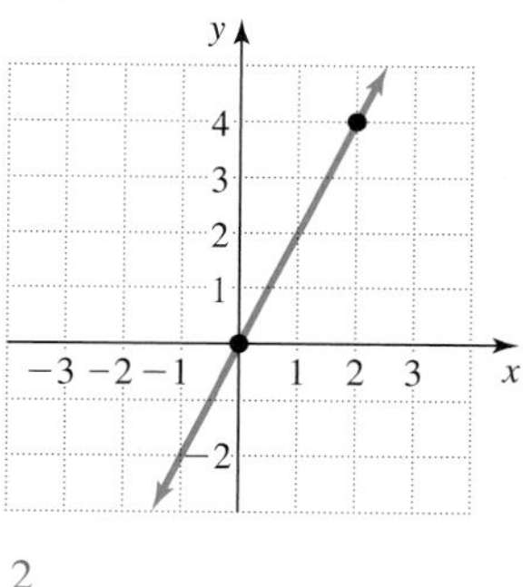

2

11.

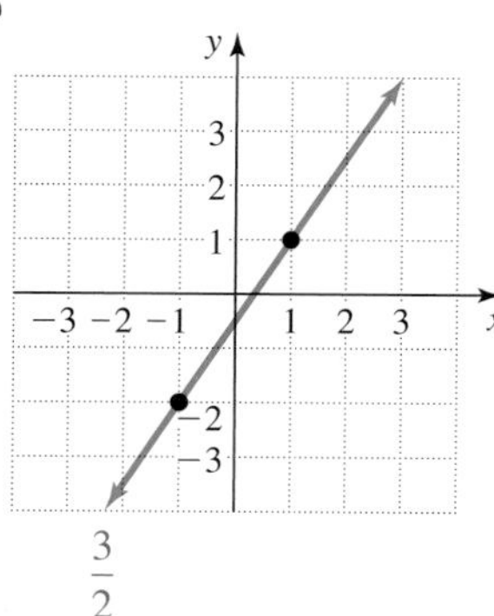

$\frac{3}{2}$

12.

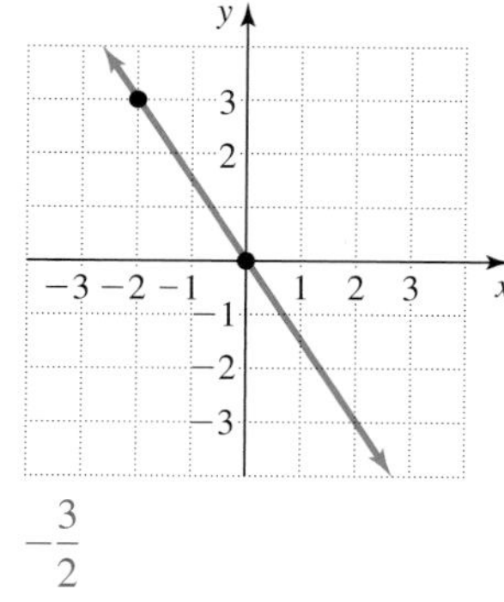

$-\frac{3}{2}$

13.

0

14.

0

15.

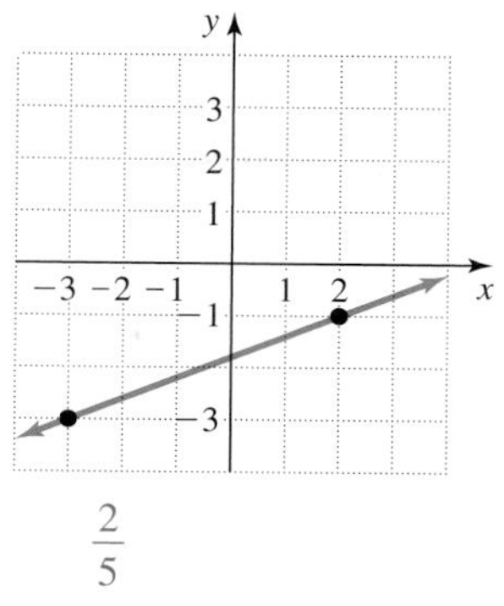

$\frac{2}{5}$

16.

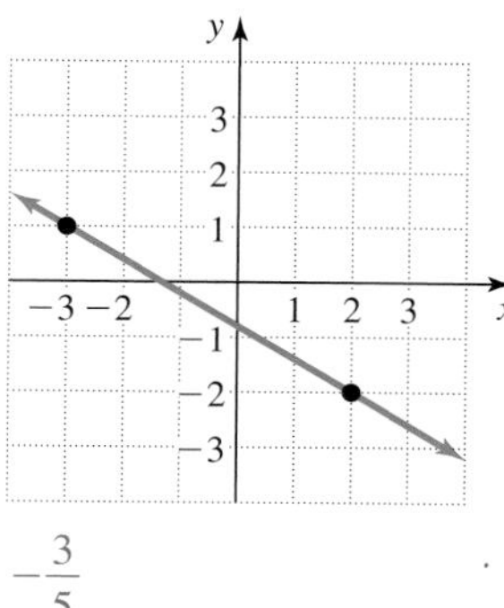

$-\frac{3}{5}$

17.

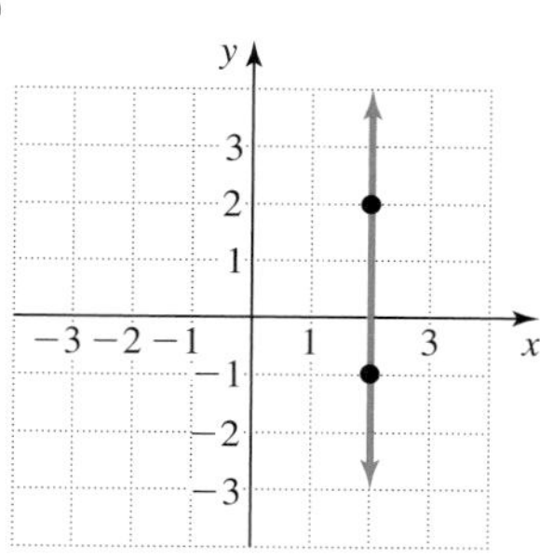

Undefined

18.

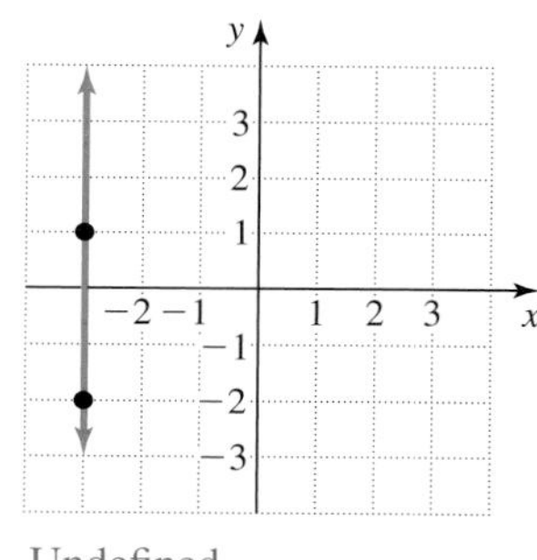

Undefined

⟨2⟩ Slope Using Coordinates

Find the slope of the line that goes through each pair of points. See Examples 3 and 4.

19. (1, 2), (3, 6) 2

20. (2, 7), (3, 10) 3

21. (2, 5), (6, 10) $\frac{5}{4}$

22. (5, 1), (8, 9) $\frac{8}{3}$

23. (2, 4), (5, −1) $-\frac{5}{3}$

24. (3, 1), (6, −2) −1

25. (−2, 4), (5, 9) $\frac{5}{7}$

26. (−1, 3), (3, 5) $\frac{1}{2}$

27. (−2, −3), (−5, 1) $-\frac{4}{3}$

28. (−6, −3), (−1, 1) $\frac{4}{5}$

29. (−3, 4), (3, −2) −1

30. (−1, 3), (5, −2) $-\frac{5}{6}$

31. $\left(\frac{1}{2}, 2\right), \left(-1, \frac{1}{2}\right)$ 1

32. $\left(\frac{1}{3}, 2\right), \left(-\frac{1}{3}, 1\right)$ $\frac{3}{2}$

33. (2, 3), (2, −9) Undefined

34. (−3, 6), (8, 6) 0

35. (−2, −5), (9, −5) 0

36. (4, −9), (4, 6) Undefined

37. (0.3, 0.9), (−0.1, −0.3) 3

38. (−0.1, 0.2), (0.5, 0.8) 1

⟨3⟩ Graphing a Line Given a Point and Slope

Graph the line with the given point and slope. See Example 5.

39. The line through (1, 1) with slope $\frac{2}{3}$

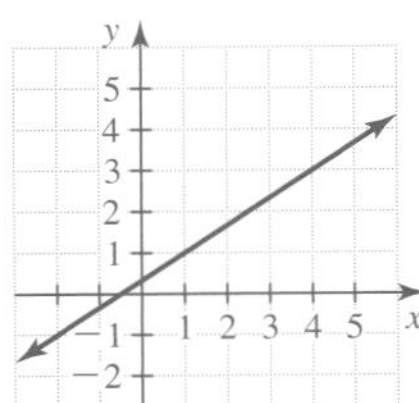

40. The line through (2, 3) with slope $\frac{1}{2}$

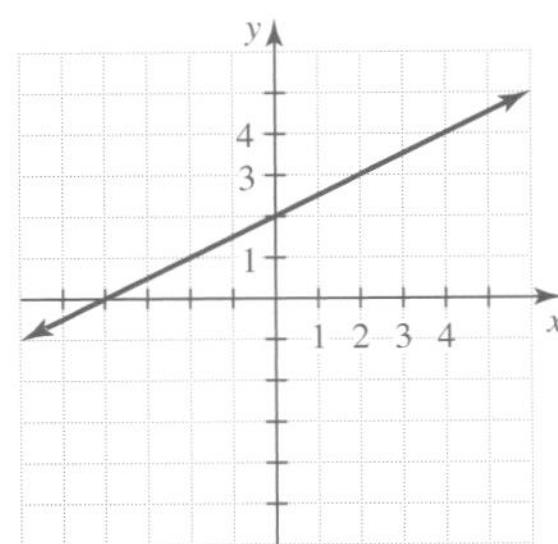

41. The line through $(-2, 3)$ with slope -2

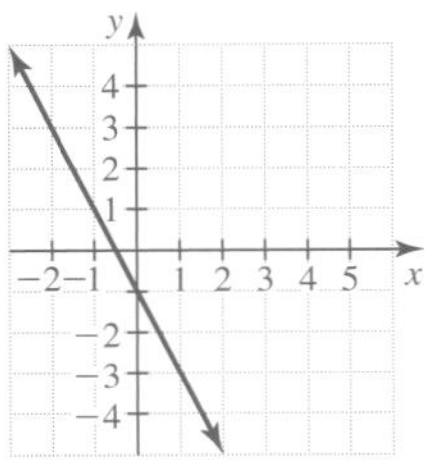

42. The line through $(-2, 5)$ with slope -1

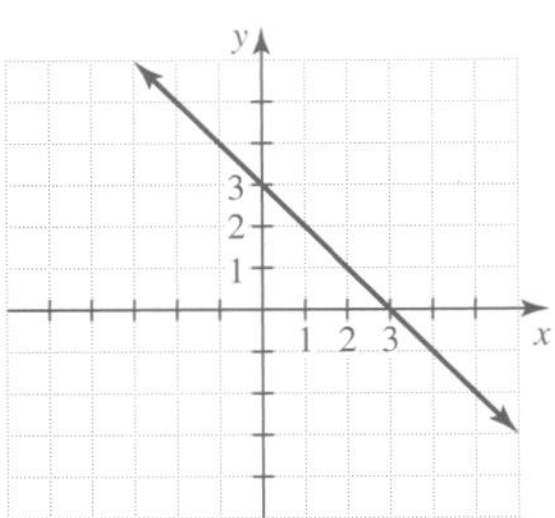

43. The line through (0, 0) with slope $-\frac{2}{5}$

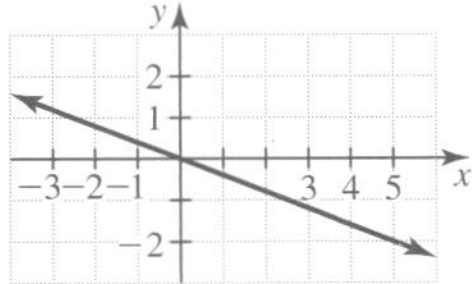

44. The line through $(-1, 4)$ with slope $-\frac{2}{3}$

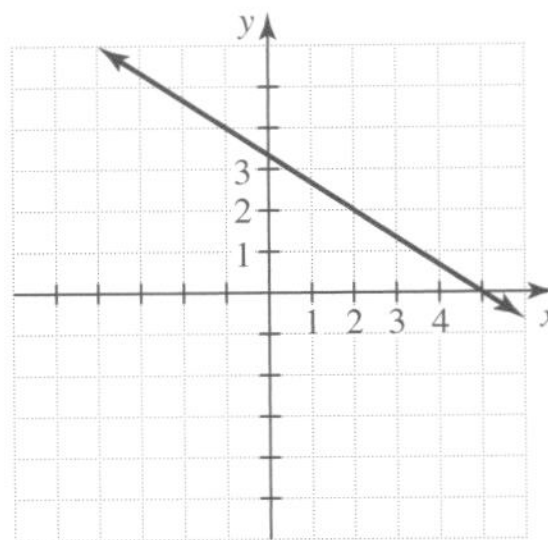

⟨4–5⟩ Parallel and Perpendicular Lines

Solve each problem. See Examples 6 and 7.

45. Draw line l_1 through $(1, -2)$ with slope $\frac{1}{2}$ and line l_2 through $(-1, 1)$ with slope $\frac{1}{2}$.

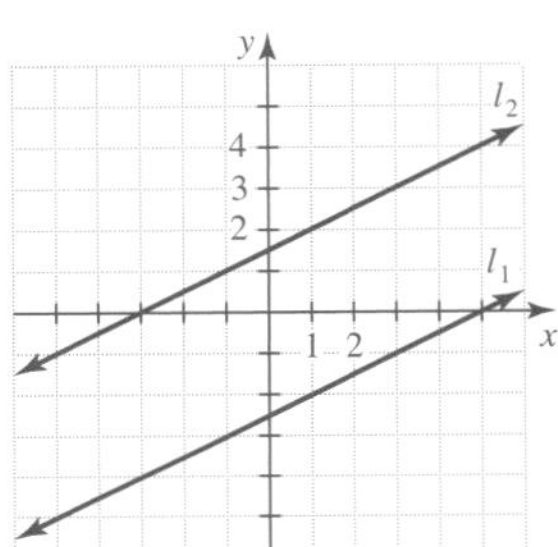

46. Draw line l_1 through (0, 3) with slope 1 and line l_2 through (0, 0) with slope 1.

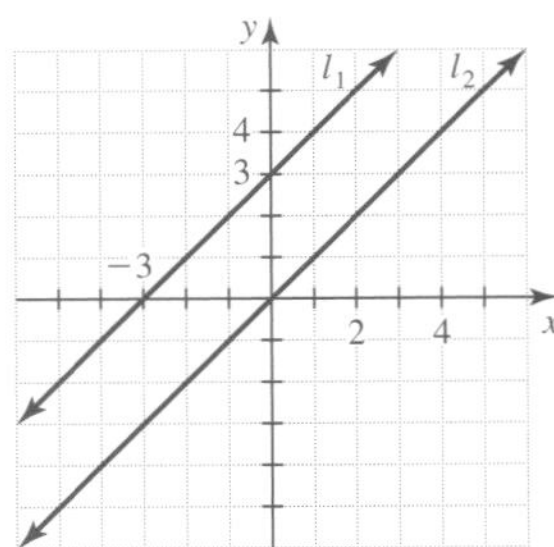

47. Draw l_1 through (1, 2) with slope $\frac{1}{2}$, and draw l_2 through (1, 2) with slope -2.

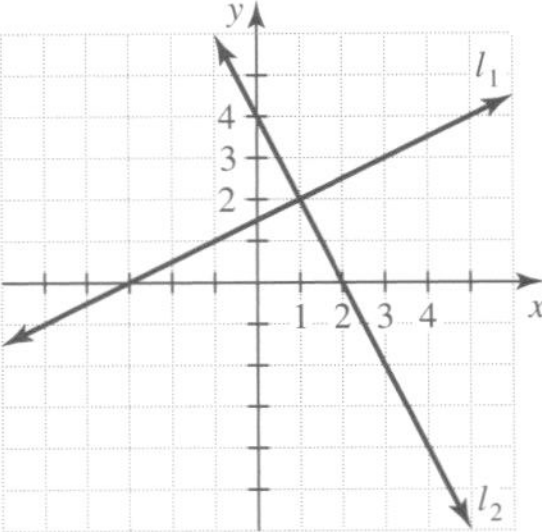

48. Draw l_1 through $(-2, 1)$ with slope $\frac{2}{3}$, and draw l_2 through $(-2, 1)$ with slope $-\frac{3}{2}$.

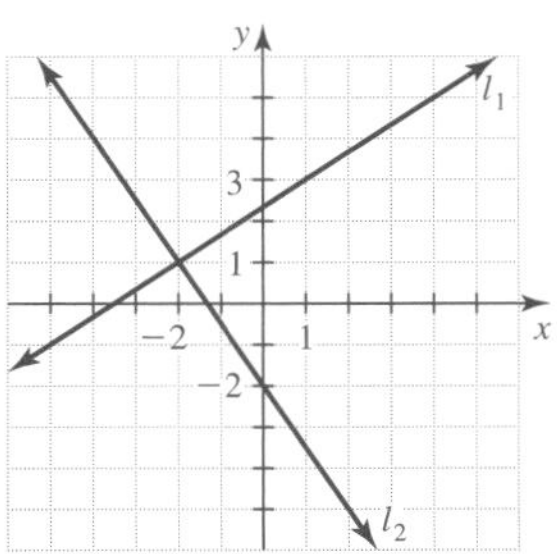

49. Draw any line l_1 with slope $\frac{3}{4}$. What is the slope of any line perpendicular to l_1? Draw any line l_2 perpendicular to l_1.

$-\frac{4}{3}$

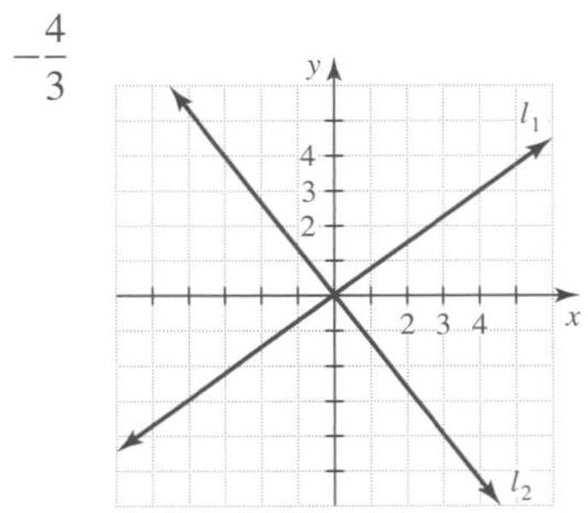

50. Draw any line l_1 with slope -1. What is the slope of any line perpendicular to l_1? Draw any line l_2 perpendicular to l_1.

1

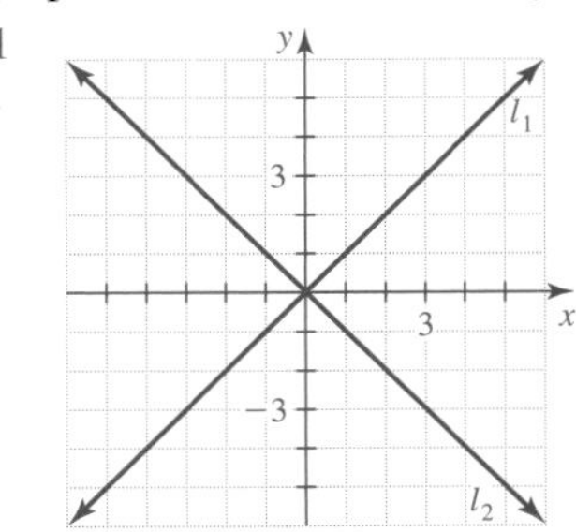

51. Draw l_1 through $(-2, -3)$ and $(4, 0)$. What is the slope of any line parallel to l_1? Draw l_2 through $(1, 2)$ so that it is parallel to l_1.

$\frac{1}{2}$

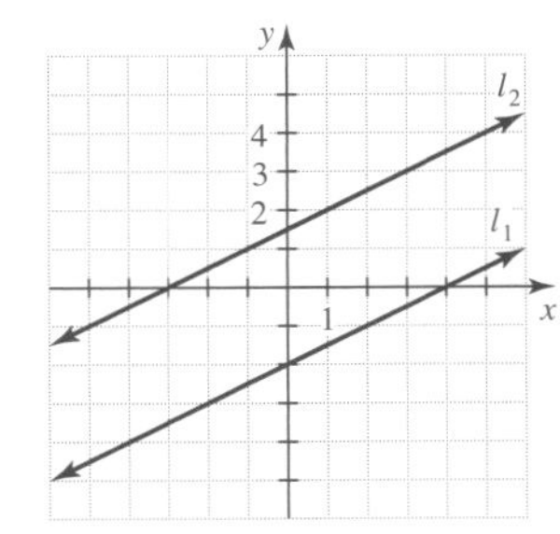

52. Draw l_1 through $(-4, 0)$ and $(0, 6)$. What is the slope of any line parallel to l_1? Draw l_2 through the origin and parallel to l_1.

$\frac{3}{2}$

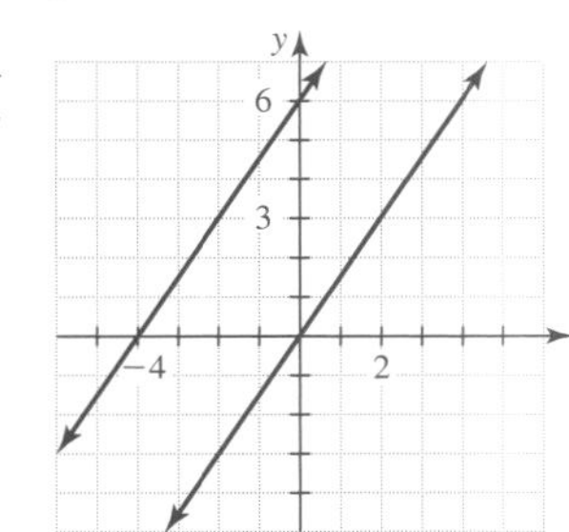

53. Draw l_1 through $(-2, 4)$ and $(3, -1)$. What is the slope of any line perpendicular to l_1? Draw l_2 through $(1, 3)$ so that it is perpendicular to l_1.

1

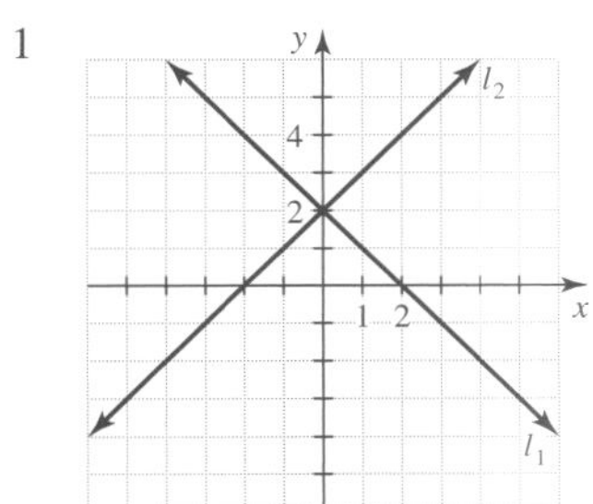

54. Draw l_1 through $(0, -3)$ and $(3, 0)$. What is the slope of any line perpendicular to l_1? Draw l_2 through the origin so that it is perpendicular to l_1.

-1

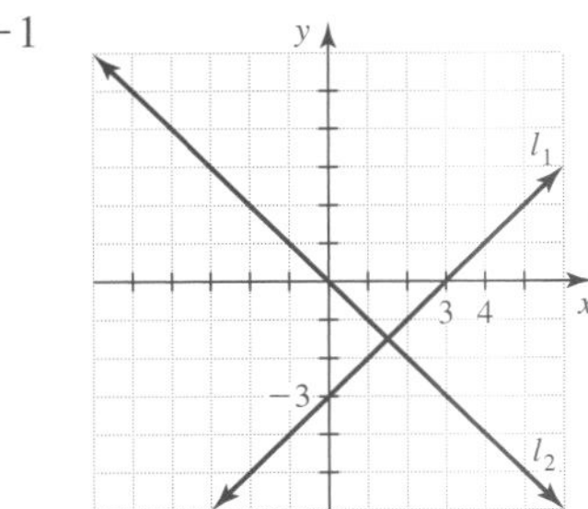

In each case, determine whether the lines l_1 and l_2 are parallel, perpendicular, or neither. See Example 8.

55. Line l_1 goes through $(3, 5)$ and $(4, 7)$. Line l_2 goes through $(11, 7)$ and $(12, 9)$. Parallel

56. Line l_1 goes through $(-2, -2)$ and $(2, 0)$. Line l_2 goes through $(-2, 5)$ and $(-1, 3)$. Perpendicular

57. Line l_1 goes through $(-1, 4)$ and $(2, 6)$. Line l_2 goes through $(2, -2)$ and $(4, 1)$. Neither

58. Line l_1 goes through $(-2, 5)$ and $(4, 7)$. Line l_2 goes through $(2, 4)$ and $(3, 1)$. Perpendicular

59. Line l_1 goes through $(-1, 4)$ and $(4, 6)$. Line l_2 goes through $(-7, 0)$ and $(3, 4)$. Parallel

60. Line l_1 goes through (1, 2) and (1, −1). Line l_2 goes through (4, 4) and (3, 3). Neither

61. Line l_1 goes through (3, 5) and (3, 6). Line l_2 goes through (−2, 4) and (−3, 4). Perpendicular

62. Line l_1 goes through (−3, 7) and (4, 7). Line l_2 goes through (−5, 1) and (−3, 1). Parallel

‹6› Applications

Solve each problem. See Examples 9 and 10.

63. ***Super cost.*** The average cost of a 30-second ad during the 1998 Super Bowl was \$1.3 million, and in 2006 it was \$2.8 million (www.adage.com).

a) Find the slope of the line through (1998, 1.3) and (2006, 2.8) and interpret your result.
Slope 0.1875; Cost is increasing about \$187,500 per year.

b) Use the slope to estimate the average cost of an ad in 2002. Is your estimate consistent with the accompanying graph? \$2.05 million; yes

c) Use the slope to predict the average cost in 2010.
\$3.55 million

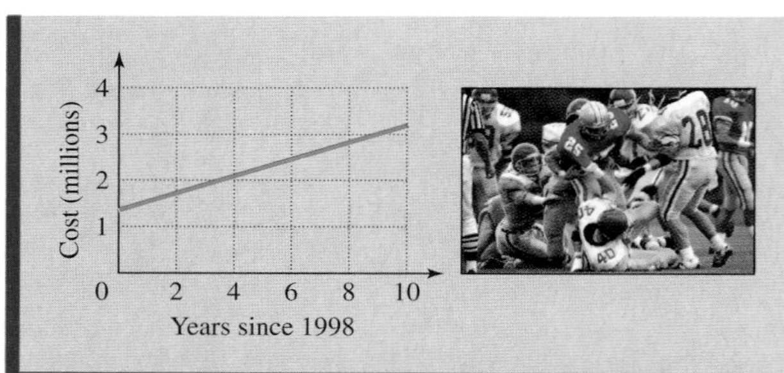

Figure for Exercise 63

64. ***Retirement pay.*** The annual Social Security benefit of a retiree depends on the age at the time of retirement. The accompanying graph gives the annual benefit for persons retiring at ages 62 through 70 in the year 2005 or later (Social Security Administration, www.ssa.gov). What is the annual benefit for a person who retires at age 64? At what retirement age does a person receive an annual benefit of \$11,600? Find the slope of each line segment on the graph, and interpret your results. Why do people who postpone retirement until 70 years of age get the highest benefit?
\$8000, 69, 500, 666.66, 800; The slopes are the yearly increases for each segment.

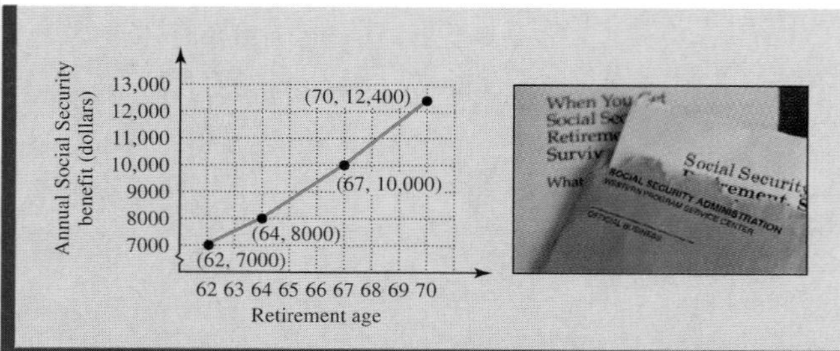

Figure for Exercise 64

65. ***Increasing training.*** The accompanying graph shows the percentage of U.S. workers receiving training by their employers. The percentage went from 5% in 1982 to 29% in 2006 (Department of Labor, www.dol.gov). Find the slope of this line. Interpret your result.
1 slope; The percentage increases 1% per year.

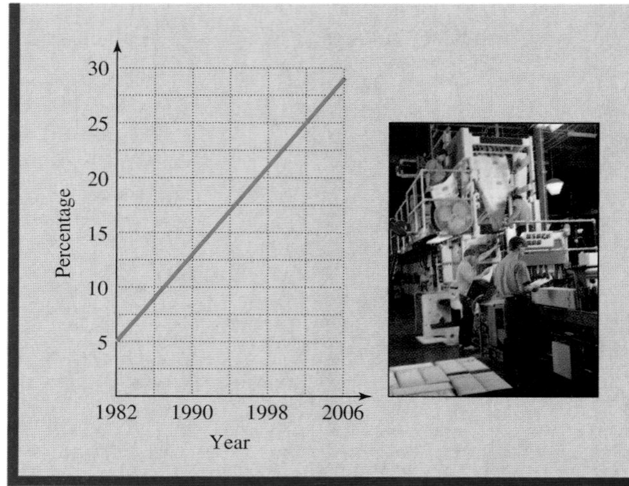

Figure for Exercise 65

66. ***Saving for retirement.*** Financial advisors at Fidelity Investments, Boston, use the accompanying table as a measure of whether a client is on the road to a comfortable retirement.

a) Graph these points and draw a line through them.

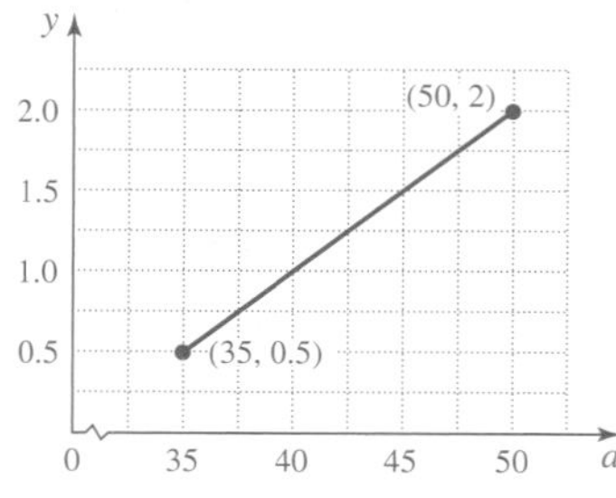

b) What is the slope of the line? 0.1

c) By what percentage of your salary should you be increasing your savings every year? 10%

Age (a)	Years of Salary Saved (y)
35	0.5
40	1.0
45	1.5
50	2.0

Figure for Exercise 66

67. ***Increasing salary.*** An elementary school teacher gets a raise of \$400 per year. Find the data that is missing from the accompanying table.

Year	Salary (dollars)
2000	28,100
2002	28,900
2003	29,300
2012	32,900
2015	34,100

68. ***Declining population.*** The population of Springfield is decreasing at a rate of 250 people per year. Find the data that is missing from the table.

Year	Population
2001	8400
2002	8150
2008	6650
2011	5900
2015	4900

Determine whether the points in each table lie on a straight line.

69. Yes

x	y
4	10
7	19
11	31
17	49

70. Yes

x	y
2	−4
4	−14
8	−34
13	−59

71. No

x	y
−2	7
0	3
3	−3
9	−16

72. No

x	y
−3	−12
0	2
2	10
6	26

3.3 Equations of Lines in Slope-Intercept Form

In This Section

- ⟨1⟩ Slope-Intercept Form
- ⟨2⟩ Standard Form
- ⟨3⟩ Using Slope-Intercept Form for Graphing
- ⟨4⟩ Writing the Equation for a Line
- ⟨5⟩ Applications

In Section 3.1 you learned that the graph of all solutions to a linear equation in two variables is a straight line. In this section, we start with a line or a description of a line and write an equation for the line. The equation of a line in any form is called a **linear equation in two variables.**

⟨1⟩ Slope-Intercept Form

Consider the line through (0, 1) with slope $\frac{2}{3}$ shown in Fig. 3.25. If we use the points (x, y) and (0, 1) in the slope formula, we get an equation that is satisfied by every point on the line:

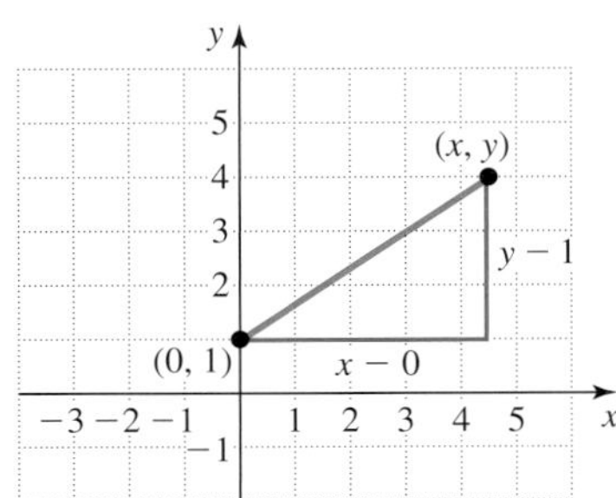

Figure 3.25

$$\frac{y_2 - y_1}{x_2 - x_1} = m \quad \text{Slope formula}$$

$$\frac{y - 1}{x - 0} = \frac{2}{3} \quad \text{Let } (x_1, y_1) = (0, 1) \text{ and } (x_2, y_2) = (x, y).$$

$$\frac{y - 1}{x} = \frac{2}{3}$$

Now solve the equation for y:

$$x \cdot \frac{y-1}{x} = \frac{2}{3} \cdot x \quad \text{Multiply each side by } x.$$

$$y - 1 = \frac{2}{3}x$$

$$y = \frac{2}{3}x + 1 \quad \text{Add 1 to each side.}$$

Because (0, 1) is on the y-axis, it is called the **y-intercept** of the line. Note how the slope $\frac{2}{3}$ and the y-coordinate of the y-intercept (0, 1) appear in $y = \frac{2}{3}x + 1$. For this reason, it is called the **slope-intercept form** of the equation of the line.

Slope-Intercept Form

The equation of the line with y-intercept $(0, b)$ and slope m is

$$y = mx + b.$$

EXAMPLE 1

Using slope-intercept form

Write the equation of each line in slope-intercept form.

a)

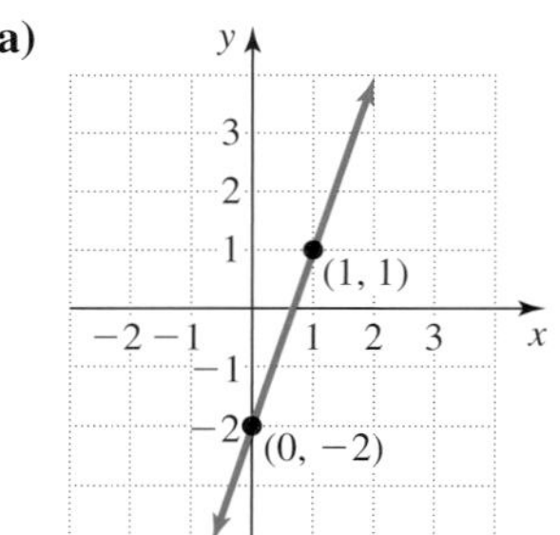

b)

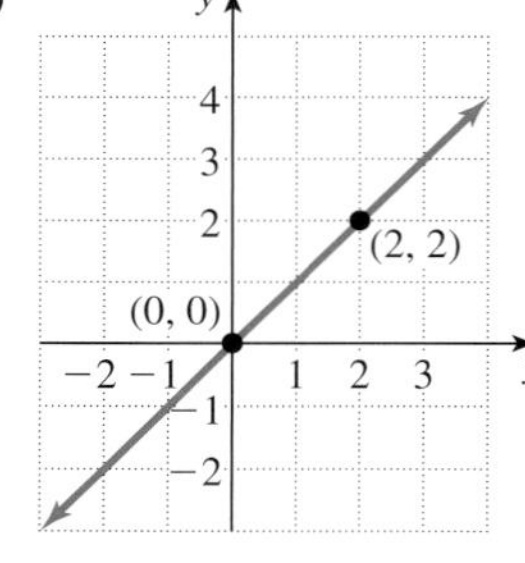

c)

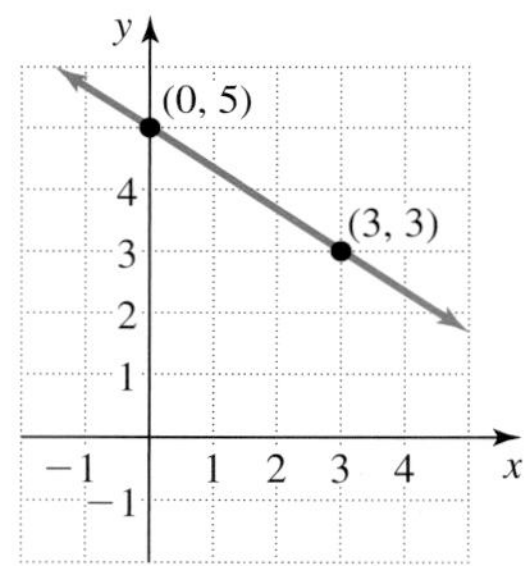

Solution

a) The y-intercept is $(0, -2)$, and the slope is 3. Use the form $y = mx + b$ with $b = -2$ and $m = 3$. The equation in slope-intercept form is

$$y = 3x - 2.$$

b) The y-intercept is (0, 0), and the slope is 1. So the equation is

$$y = x.$$

c) The y-intercept is (0, 5), and the slope is $-\frac{2}{3}$. So the equation is

$$y = -\frac{2}{3}x + 5.$$

Now do Exercises 7–18

The equation of a line may take many different forms. The easiest way to find the slope and y-intercept for a line is to rewrite the equation in slope-intercept form.

EXAMPLE 2

Finding slope and *y*-intercept

Determine the slope and y-intercept of the line $3x - 2y = 6$.

Solution

Solve for y to get slope-intercept form:

$$3x - 2y = 6$$
$$-2y = -3x + 6$$
$$y = \frac{3}{2}x - 3$$

The slope is $\frac{3}{2}$, and the y-intercept is $(0, -3)$.

Now do Exercises 19–38

‹ Teaching Tip ›

Remind students to write built-up fractions clearly and to use grouping symbols with slash fractions. Writing $y = (3/2)x - 3$ is correct, but $y = 3/2x - 3$ could be confusing.

‹2› Standard Form

In Section 3.1 we defined a linear equation in two variables as an equation of the form $Ax + By = C$, where A and B are not both zero. The form $Ax + By = C$ is called the **standard form** of the equation of a line. It includes vertical lines such as $x = 6$ and horizontal lines such as $y = 5$. *Every line has an equation in standard form.* Since slope is undefined for vertical lines, there is no equation in slope-intercept form for a vertical line. *Every nonvertical line has an equation in slope-intercept form.*

There is only one slope-intercept equation for a given line, but standard form is not unique. For example,

$$2x - 3y = 5, \quad 4x - 6y = 10, \quad x - \frac{3}{2}y = \frac{5}{2}, \quad \text{and} \quad -2x + 3y = -5$$

are all equations in standard form for the same line. When possible, we will write the standard form in which A is positive, and A, B, and C are integers with a greatest common factor of 1. So $2x - 3y = 5$ is the *preferred* standard form for this line.

In Example 2 we converted an equation in standard form to slope-intercept form. In Example 3, we convert an equation in slope-intercept form to standard form.

EXAMPLE 3

Converting to standard form

Write the equation of the line $y = \frac{2}{5}x + 3$ in standard form using only integers.

Solution

To get standard form, first subtract $\frac{2}{5}x$ from each side:

$$y = \frac{2}{5}x + 3$$
$$-\frac{2}{5}x + y = 3$$
$$-5\left(-\frac{2}{5}x + y\right) = -5 \cdot 3$$ Multiply each side by -5 to eliminate the fraction and get positive $2x$.
$$2x - 5y = -15$$

Now do Exercises 39–54

‹3› Using Slope-Intercept Form for Graphing

One way to graph a linear equation is to find several points that satisfy the equation and then draw a straight line through them. We can also graph a linear equation by using the *y*-intercept and the slope.

Strategy for Graphing a Line Using *y*-Intercept and Slope

1. Write the equation in slope-intercept form if necessary.
2. Plot the *y*-intercept.
3. Starting from the *y*-intercept, use the rise and run to locate a second point.
4. Draw a line through the two points.

EXAMPLE 4

Graphing a line using *y*-intercept and slope

Graph the line $2x - 3y = 3$.

Solution

First write the equation in slope-intercept form:

$$2x - 3y = 3$$
$$-3y = -2x + 3 \quad \text{Subtract } 2x \text{ from each side.}$$
$$y = \frac{2}{3}x - 1 \quad \text{Divide each side by } -3.$$

The slope is $\frac{2}{3}$, and the *y*-intercept is $(0, -1)$. A slope of $\frac{2}{3}$ means a rise of 2 and a run of 3. Start at $(0, -1)$ and go up two units and to the right three units to locate a second point on the line. Now draw a line through the two points. See Fig. 3.26 for the graph of $2x - 3y = 3$.

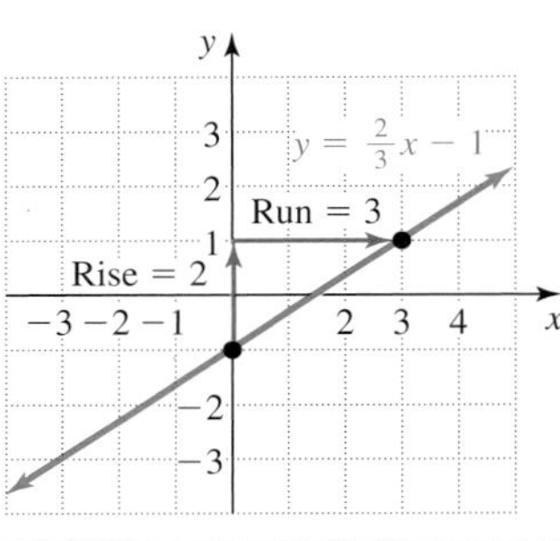

Figure 3.26

Now do Exercises 55–56

‹ Calculator Close-Up ›

To check Example 4, graph $y = (2/3)x - 1$ on a graphing calculator as follows:

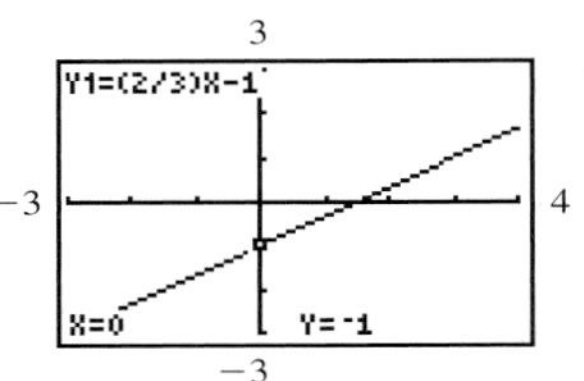

The calculator graph is consistent with the graph in Fig. 3.26.

CAUTION When using the slope to find a second point on the line, be sure to start at the *y*-intercept, not at the origin.

EXAMPLE 5

Graphing lines with *y*-intercept and slope

Graph each line.

a) $y = -3x + 4$ **b)** $2y - 5x = 0$

Solution

a) For $y = -3x + 4$ the slope is -3 and the *y*-intercept is $(0, 4)$. Because $-3 = \frac{-3}{1}$, the rise is -3 and the run is 1. First plot the *y*-intercept $(0, 4)$. To locate a second point on the line start at $(0, 4)$ and go down three units and to the right one unit. Draw a line through $(0, 4)$ and $(1, 1)$. See Fig. 3.27.

b) First solve the equation for *y*:

$$2y - 5x = 0$$
$$2y = 5x$$
$$y = \frac{5}{2}x$$

‹ Teaching Tip ›

Students often count off the slope from (0, 0) rather than from the *y*-intercept.

The slope is $\frac{5}{2}$ and the y-intercept is (0, 0). Using a rise of five and a run of two from the origin yields the point (2, 5). Draw a line through (0, 0) and (2, 5) as shown in Fig. 3.28.

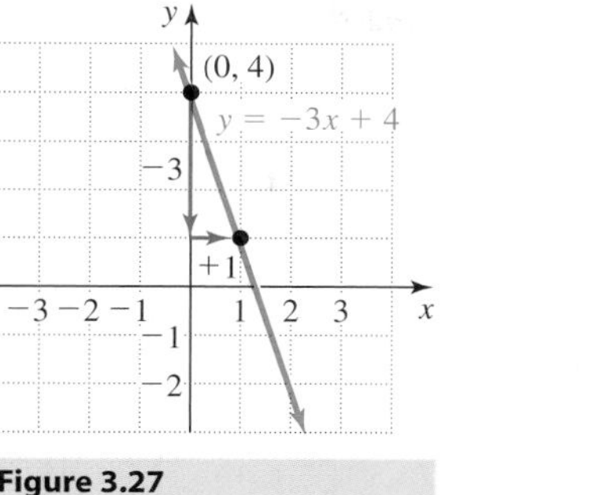

Figure 3.27

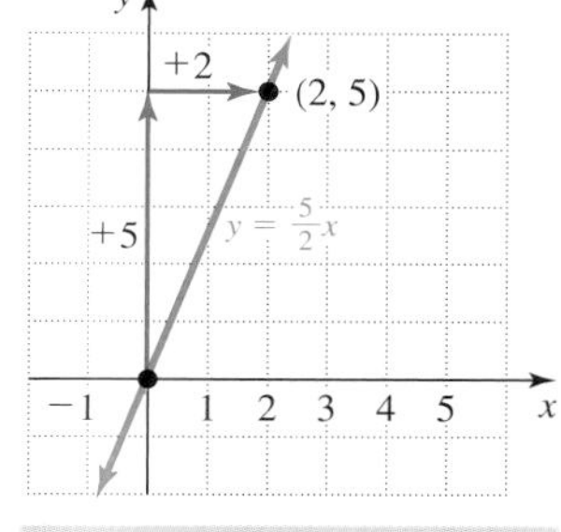

Figure 3.28

Now do Exercises 57–68

If your equation is in slope-intercept form, it is usually easiest to use the y-intercept and the slope to graph the line, as shown in Example 5. If your equation is in standard form, it is usually easiest to graph the line using the intercepts, as discussed in Section 3.1. These guidelines are summarized as follows.

The Method for Graphing Depends on the Form

Slope-intercept form $y = mx + b$	Start at the y-intercept $(0, b)$ and count off the rise and run. This works best if b is an integer and m is rational.
Standard form $Ax + By = C$	Find the x-intercept by setting $y = 0$. Find the y-intercept by setting $x = 0$. Find one additional point as check.

‹4› Writing the Equation for a Line

In Example 1 we wrote the equation of a line by finding its slope and y-intercept from a graph. In Example 6 we write the equation of a line from a description of the line.

EXAMPLE 6

Writing an equation

Write the equation in slope-intercept form for each line:

a) The line through (0, 3) that is parallel to the line $y = 2x - 1$

b) The line through (0, 4) that is perpendicular to the line $2x - 4y = 1$

Solution

a) The line $y = 2x - 1$ has slope 2 and any line parallel to it has slope 2. So the equation of the line with y-intercept (0, 3) and slope 2 is $y = 2x + 3$.

b) First find the slope of $2x - 4y = 1$:

$$2x - 4y = 1$$
$$-4y = -2x + 1$$
$$y = \frac{1}{2}x - \frac{1}{4}$$

So $2x - 4y = 1$ has slope $\frac{1}{2}$ and the slope of any line perpendicular to $2x - 4y = 1$ is the opposite of the reciprocal of $\frac{1}{2}$ or -2. The equation of the line through the y-intercept $(0, 4)$ with slope -2 is $y = -2x + 4$.

Now do Exercises 77–90

‹ Calculator Close-Up ›

If you use the same minimum and maximum window values for x and y, then the length of one unit on the x-axis is larger than on the y-axis because the screen is longer in the x-direction. In this case, perpendicular lines will not look perpendicular. The viewing window chosen here for the lines in Example 6 makes them look perpendicular.

Any viewing window proportional to this one will also produce approximately the same unit length on each axis. Some calculators have a square feature that automatically makes the unit length the same on both axes.

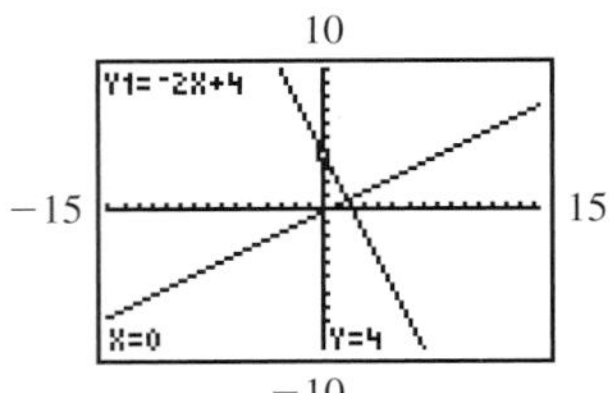

We have now seen four ways to find the slope of a line. These methods are summarized as follows:

Finding the Slope of a Line

1. Starting with a graph of a line, count the rise and run between two points and use $m = \frac{\text{rise}}{\text{run}}$.
2. Starting with the coordinates of two points on a line (x_1, y_1) and (x_2, y_2) use the formula $m = \frac{y_2 - y_1}{x_2 - x_1}$.
3. Starting with the equation of a line rewrite it in the form $y = mx + b$ if necessary. The slope is m, the coefficient of x.
4. If a line with unknown slope m_1 is parallel or perpendicular to a line with known slope m_2, then use $m_1 = m_2$ for parallel lines or $m_1 = -\frac{1}{m_2}$ for perpendicular lines.

‹5› Applications

In Example 7 we see that the slope-intercept and standard forms are both important in applications.

EXAMPLE 7

Changing forms

A landscaper has a total of \$800 to spend on bushes at \$20 each and trees at \$50 each. So if x is the number of bushes and y is the number of trees he can buy, then $20x + 50y = 800$. Write this equation in slope-intercept form. Find and interpret the y-intercept and the slope.

‹ **Teaching Tip** ›

This is a good example to show the importance of standard and slope-intercept form.

Solution

Write in slope-intercept form:

$$20x + 50y = 800$$
$$50y = -20x + 800$$
$$y = -\frac{2}{5}x + 16$$

The slope is $-\frac{2}{5}$ and the intercept is (0, 16). So he can get 16 trees if he buys no bushes and he loses $\frac{2}{5}$ of a tree for each additional bush that he purchases.

Now do Exercises 91–98

Warm-Ups ▼

True or false? Explain your answer.

1. There is only one line with y-intercept (0, 3) and slope $-\frac{4}{3}$. True
2. The equation of the line through (1, 2) with slope 3 is $y = 3x + 2$. False
3. The vertical line $x = -2$ has no y-intercept. True
4. The equation $x = 5$ has a graph that is a vertical line. True
5. The line $y = x - 3$ is perpendicular to the line $y = 5 - x$. True
6. The line $y = 2x - 3$ is parallel to the line $y = 4x - 3$. False
7. The line $2y = 3x - 8$ has a slope of 3. False
8. Every straight line in the coordinate plane has an equation in standard form. True
9. The line $x = 2$ is perpendicular to the line $y = 5$. True
10. The line $y = x$ has no y-intercept. False

Exercises 3.3

Boost your grade at mathzone.com!
> Practice Problems
> NetTutor
> Self-Tests
> e-Professors
> Videos

‹ **Study Tips** ›

- Finding out what happened in class and attending class are not the same. Attend every class and be attentive.
- Don't just take notes and let your mind wander. Use class time as a learning time.

Reading and Writing *After reading this section, write out the answers to these questions. Use complete sentences.*

1. What is the slope-intercept form for the equation of a line?
Slope-intercept form is $y = mx + b$.

2. How can you determine the slope and y-intercept from the slope-intercept form.
The slope is m and the y-intercept is $(0, b)$.

3. What is the standard form for the equation of a line?
The standard form is $Ax + By = C$.

4. How can you graph a line when the equation is in slope-intercept form?
From slope-intercept form, locate the intercept and a second point by counting the rise and run from the y-intercept.

5. What form is used in this section to write an equation of a line from a description of the line?
The slope-intercept form allows us to write the equation from the y-intercept and the slope.

6. What makes lines look perpendicular on a graph?
Lines with slopes m and $\frac{-1}{m}$ look perpendicular only if the same unit distance is used on both axes.

⟨1⟩ Slope-Intercept Form

Write an equation for each line. Use slope-intercept form if possible. See Example 1.

7.

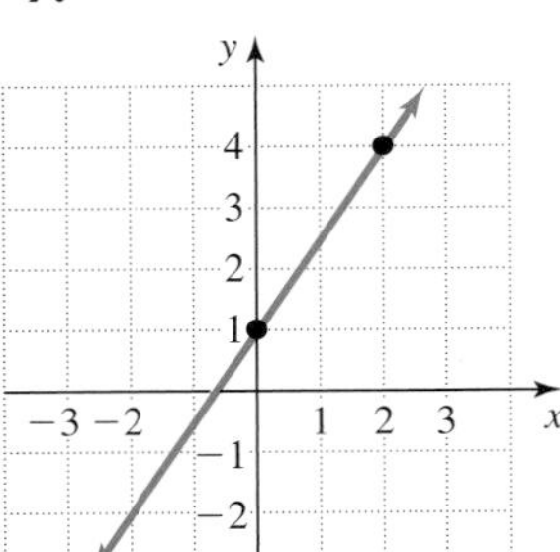

$y = \frac{3}{2}x + 1$

8.

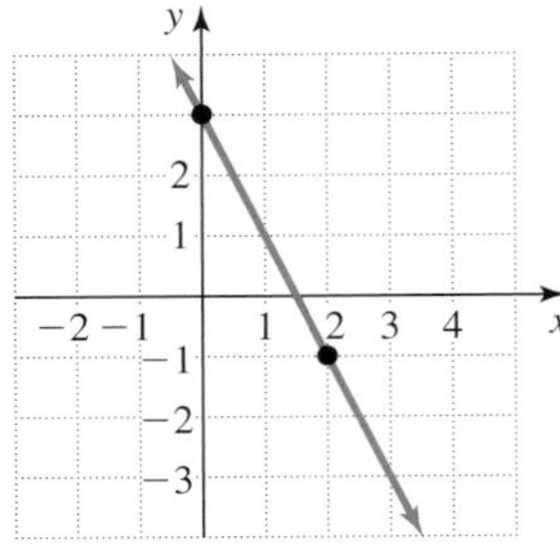

$y = -2x + 3$

9.

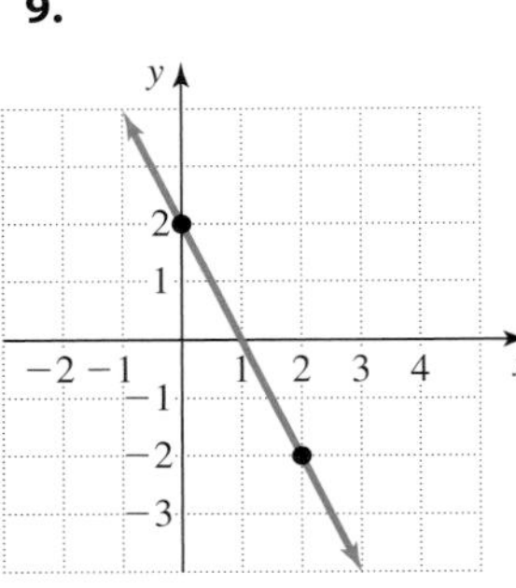

$y = -2x + 2$

10.

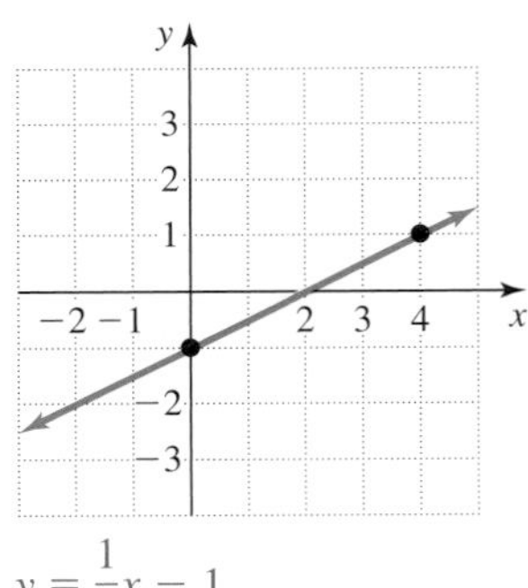

$y = \frac{1}{2}x - 1$

11.

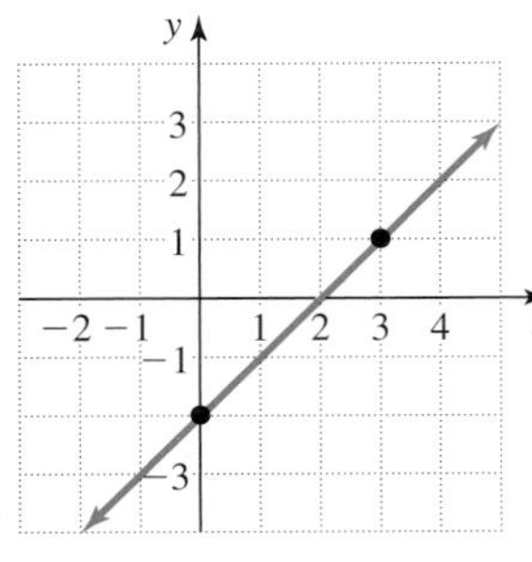

$y = x - 2$

12.

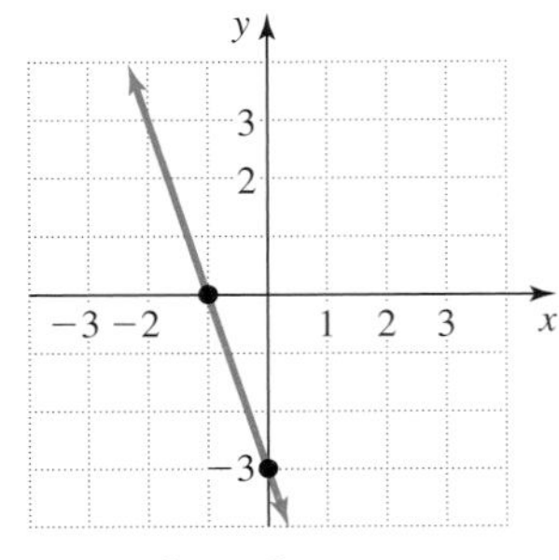

$y = -3x - 3$

13.

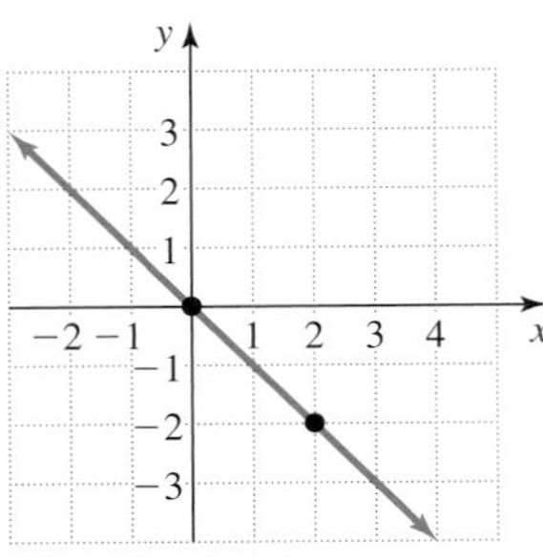

$y = -x$

14.

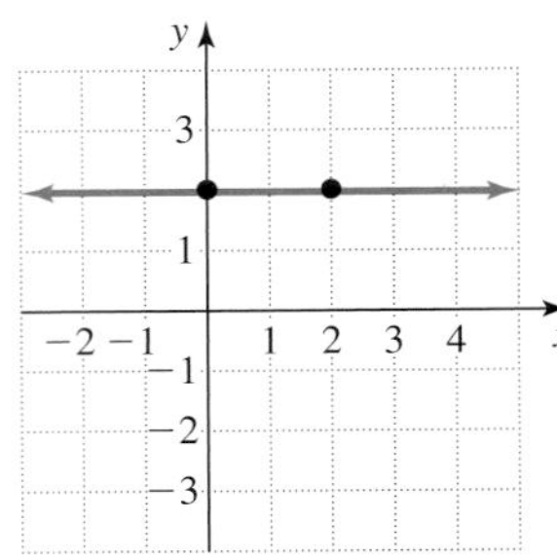

$y = 2$

15.

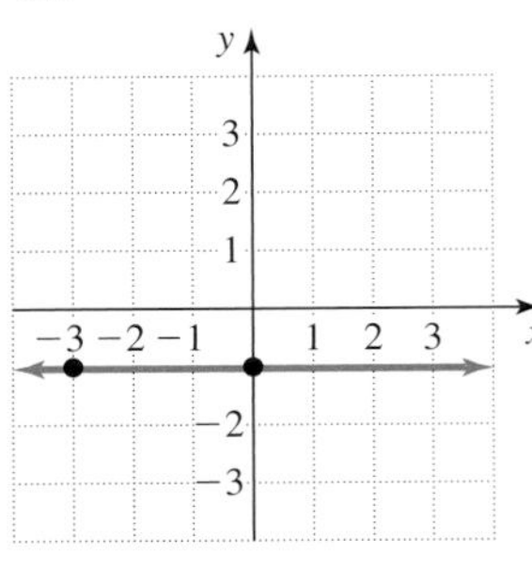

$y = -1$

16.

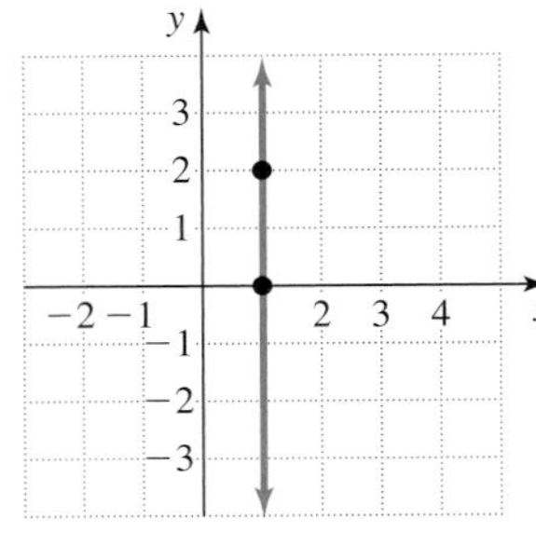

$x = 1$

17.

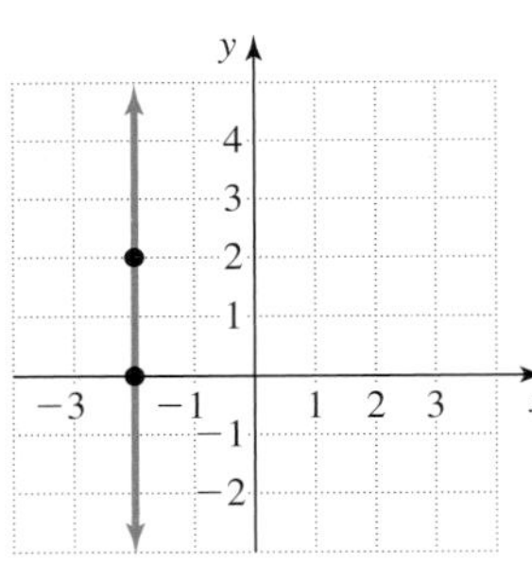

$x = -2$

18.

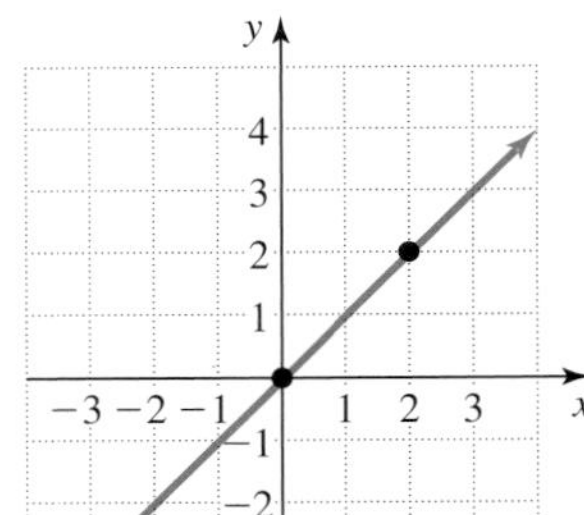

$y = x$

Find the slope and y-intercept for each line that has a slope and y-intercept. See Example 2.

19. $y = 3x - 9$
$3, (0, -9)$

20. $y = -5x + 4$
$-5, (0, 4)$

21. $y = -\frac{1}{2}x + 3$
$-\frac{1}{2}, (0, 3)$

22. $y = \frac{1}{4}x + 2$
$\frac{1}{4}, (0, 2)$

23. $y = 4$
$0, (0, 4)$

24. $y = -5$
$0, (0, -5)$

25. $y = x$
$1, (0, 0)$

26. $y = -x$
$-1, (0, 0)$

27. $y = -3x$ $-3, (0, 0)$

28. $y = 2x$ $2, (0, 0)$

29. $x + y = 5$ $-1, (0, 5)$

30. $x - y = 4$ $1, (0, -4)$

31. $x - 2y = 4$ $\frac{1}{2}, (0, -2)$

32. $x + 2y = 3$ $-\frac{1}{2}, \left(0, \frac{3}{2}\right)$

VIDEO **33.** $2x - 5y = 10$ $\frac{2}{5}, (0, -2)$

34. $2x + 3y = 9$ $-\frac{2}{3}, (0, 3)$

35. $2x - y + 3 = 0$
$2, (0, 3)$

36. $3x - 4y - 8 = 0$
$\frac{3}{4}, (0, -2)$

37. $x = -3$ Undefined slope, no y-intercept

38. $\frac{2}{3}x = 4$ Undefined slope, no y-intercept

⟨2⟩ Standard Form

Write each equation in standard form using only integers. See Example 3.

39. $y = -x + 2$ $x + y = 2$

40. $y = 3x - 5$ $3x - y = 5$

41. $y = \frac{1}{2}x + 3$
$x - 2y = -6$

42. $y = \frac{2}{3}x - 4$
$2x - 3y = 12$

43. $y = \frac{3}{2}x - \frac{1}{3}$
$9x - 6y = 2$

44. $y = \frac{4}{5}x + \frac{2}{3}$
$12x - 15y = -10$

45. $y = -\frac{3}{5}x + \frac{7}{10}$
$6x + 10y = 7$

VIDEO **46.** $y = -\frac{2}{3}x - \frac{5}{6}$
$4x + 6y = -5$

47. $\frac{3}{5}x + 6 = 0$
$x = -10$

48. $\frac{1}{2}x - 9 = 0$
$x = 18$

49. $\frac{3}{4}y = \frac{5}{2}$ $3y = 10$

50. $\frac{2}{3}y = \frac{1}{9}$ $6y = 1$

51. $\frac{x}{2} = \frac{3y}{5}$ $5x - 6y = 0$

52. $\frac{x}{8} = -\frac{4y}{5}$ $5x + 32y = 0$

53. $y = 0.02x + 0.5$
$x - 50y = -25$

54. $0.2x = 0.03y - 0.1$
$20x - 3y = -10$

⟨3⟩ Using Slope-Intercept Form for Graphing

Graph each line using its y-intercept and slope.

See Examples 4 and 5.

See the Strategy for Graphing a Line Using y-Intercept and Slope on page 204.

55. $y = 2x - 1$

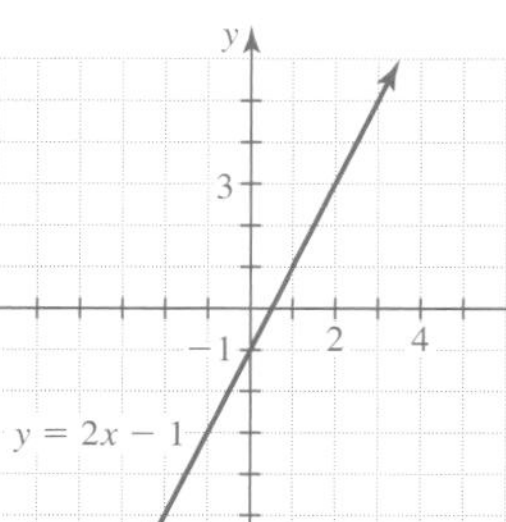

56. $y = 3x - 2$

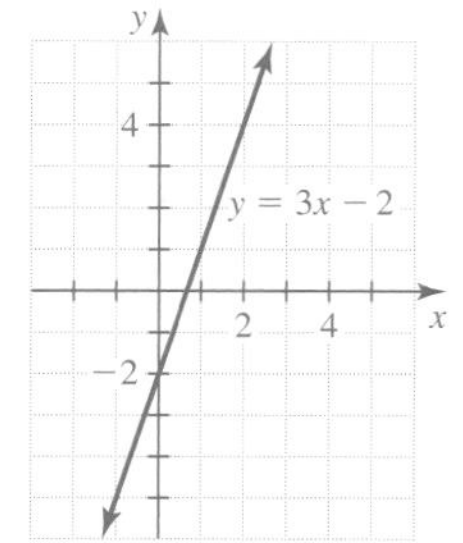

57. $y = -3x + 5$

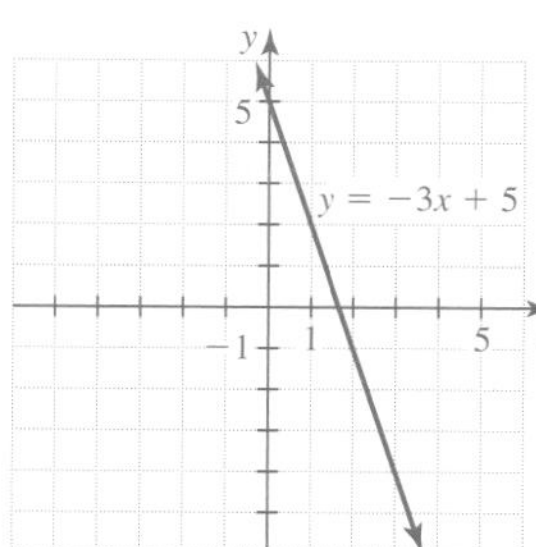

58. $y = -4x + 1$

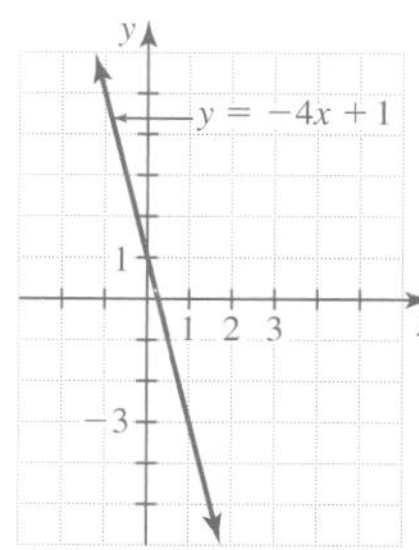

59. $y = \frac{3}{4}x - 2$

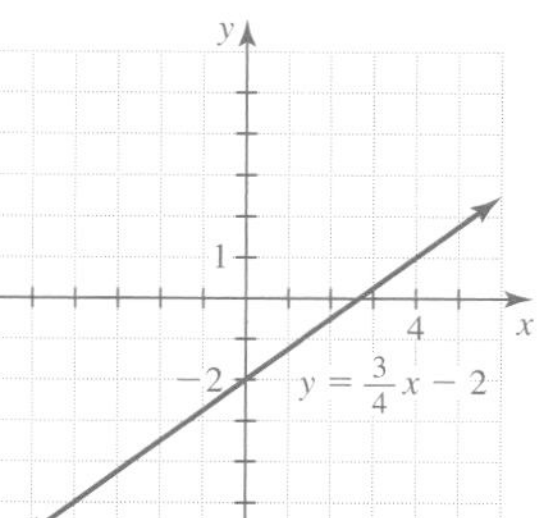

VIDEO **60.** $y = \frac{3}{2}x - 4$

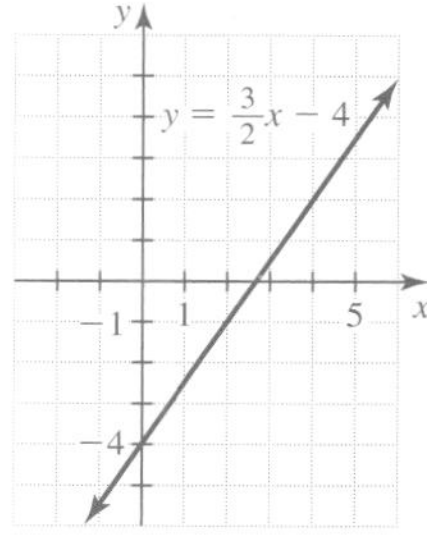

61. $2y + x = 0$

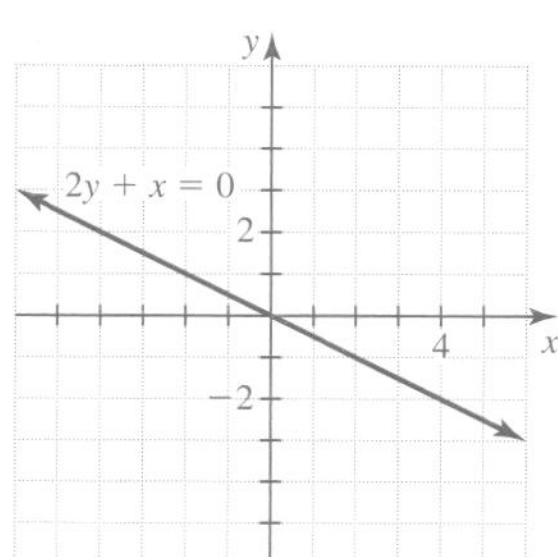

62. $2x + y = 0$

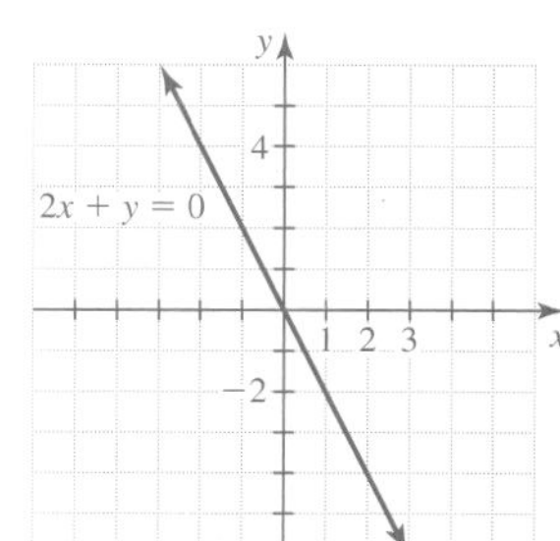

63. $3x - 2y = 10$

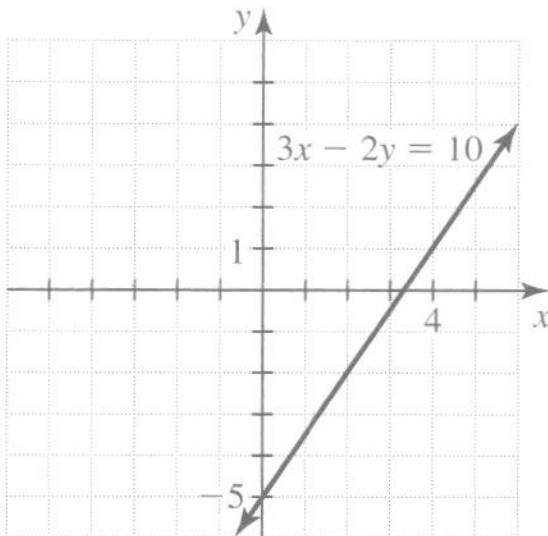

64. $4x + 3y = 9$

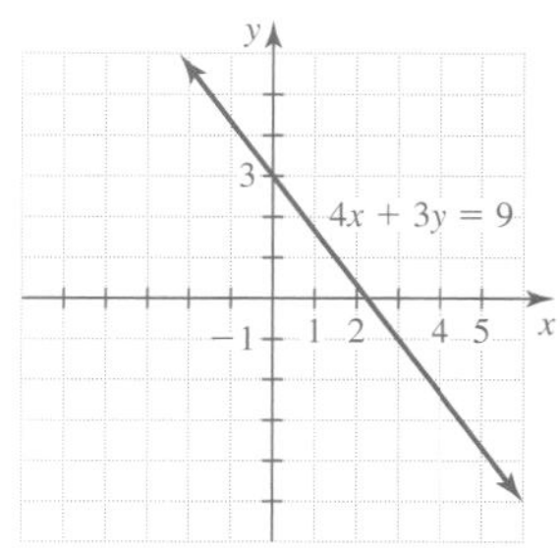

65. $4y + x = 8$

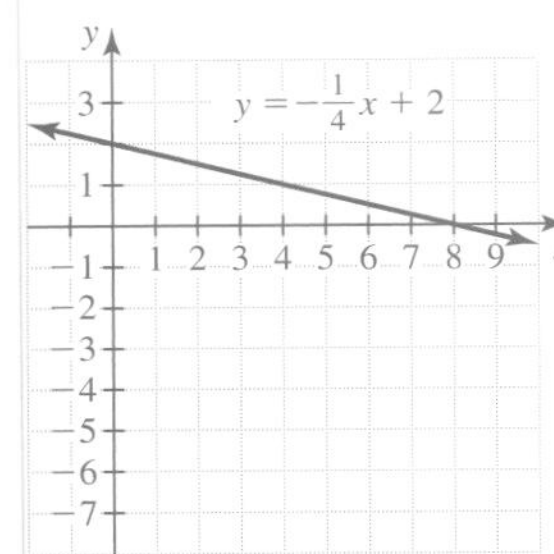

66. $y + 4x = 8$

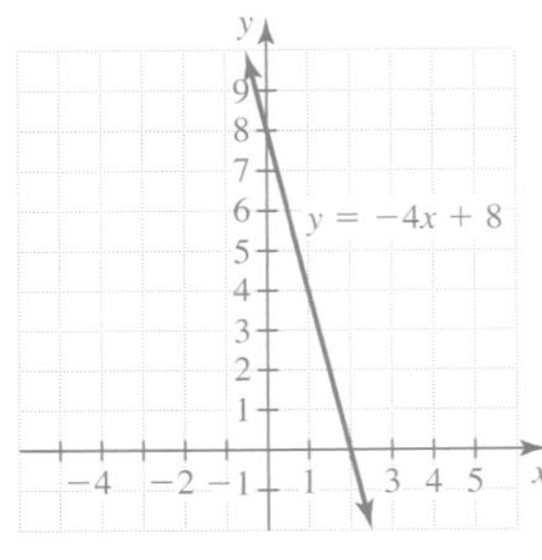

67. $y - 2 = 0$

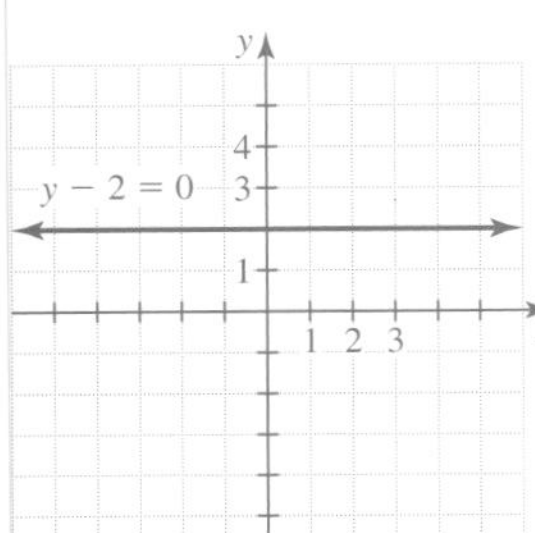

68. $y + 5 = 0$

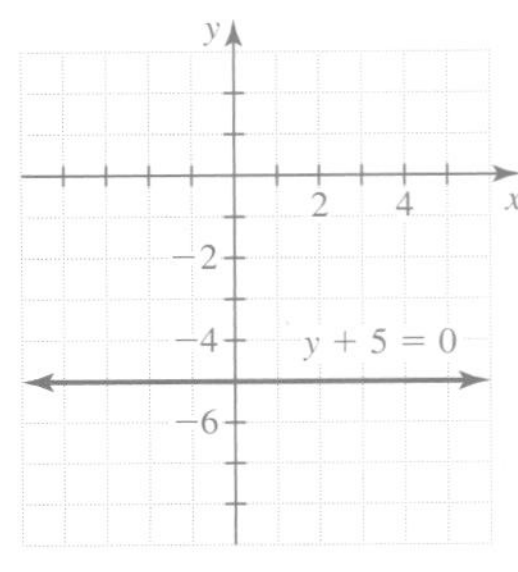

In each case determine whether the lines are parallel, perpendicular, or neither.

69. $y = 3x - 4$
$y = 3x - 9$
Parallel

70. $y = -5x + 7$
$y = \frac{1}{5}x - 6$
Perpendicular

71. $y = 2x - 1$
$y = -2x + 1$
Neither

72. $y = x + 7$
$y = -x + 2$
Perpendicular

73. $y = 3$
$y = -\frac{1}{3}$
Parallel

74. $y = 3x + 2$
$y = \frac{1}{3}x - 4$
Neither

75. $y = -4x + 1$
$y = \frac{1}{4}x - 5$
Perpendicular

76. $y = \frac{1}{3}x + \frac{1}{2}$
$y = \frac{1}{3}x - 2$
Parallel

⟨4⟩ Writing the Equation for a Line

Write an equation in slope-intercept form, if possible, for each line. See Example 6.

77. The line through $(0, -4)$ with slope $\frac{1}{2}$ $y = \frac{1}{2}x - 4$

78. The line through $(0, 4)$ with slope $-\frac{1}{2}$ $y = -\frac{1}{2}x + 4$

79. The line through $(0, 3)$ that is parallel to the line $y = 2x - 1$ $y = 2x + 3$

80. The line through $(0, -2)$ that is parallel to the line $y = -\frac{1}{3}x + 6$ $y = -\frac{1}{3}x - 2$

VIDEO **81.** The line through $(0, 6)$ that is perpendicular to the line $y = 3x - 5$ $y = -\frac{1}{3}x + 6$

82. The line through $(0, -1)$ that is perpendicular to the line $y = x$ $y = -x - 1$

83. The line with y-intercept $(0, 3)$ that is parallel to the line $2x + y = 5$ $y = -2x + 3$

84. The line through the origin that is parallel to the line $y - 3x = -3$ $y = 3x$

85. The line through $(2, 3)$ that runs parallel to the x-axis $y = 3$

86. The line through $(-3, 5)$ that runs parallel to the y-axis $x = -3$

87. The line through $(0, 4)$ that is perpendicular to $2x - 3y = 6$ $y = -\frac{3}{2}x + 4$

88. The line through $(0, -1)$ that is perpendicular to $2x - 5y = 10$ $y = -\frac{5}{2}x - 1$

89. The line through $(0, 4)$ and $(5, 0)$ $y = -\frac{4}{5}x + 4$

90. The line through $(0, -3)$ and $(4, 0)$ $y = \frac{3}{4}x - 3$

⟨5⟩ Applications

Solve each problem. See Example 7.

91. ***Labor cost.*** An appliance repair service uses the formula $C = 50n + 80$ to determine the labor cost for a service call, where C is the cost in dollars and n is the number of hours.

a) Find the cost of labor for $n = 0$, 1, and 2 hours.
\$80, \$130, \$180

b) Find the slope and C-intercept for the line $C = 50n + 80$.
50, (0, 80)

c) Interpret the slope and C-intercept.
There is an \$80 fixed cost, plus \$50 per hour.

92. ***Decreasing price.*** World Auto uses the formula $P = -3000n + 17{,}000$ to determine the wholesale price for a used Ford Focus, where P is the price in dollars and n is the age of the car in years.

a) Find the price for a Focus that is 1, 2, or 3 years old.
\$14,000, \$11,000, \$8,000

b) Find the slope and P-intercept for the line $P = -3000n + 17{,}000$. -3000, (0, 17,000)

c) Interpret the slope and P-intercept. The new price is \$17,000 and it decreases \$3000 per year.

93. ***Marginal cost.*** A manufacturer plans to spend \$150,000 on research and development for a new lawn mower and then \$200 to manufacture each mower. The formula $C = 200n + 150{,}000$ gives the cost in dollars of n mowers. What is the cost of 5000 mowers? What is the cost of 5001

mowers? By how much did the one extra lawn mower increase the cost? (The increase in cost is called the *marginal cost* of the 5001st lawn mower.)
\$1,150,000, \$1,150,200, \$200

94. *Marginal revenue.* A defense attorney charges her client \$4000 plus \$120 per hour. The formula $R = 120n + 4000$ gives her revenue in dollars for n hours of work. What is her revenue for 100 hours of work? What is her revenue for 101 hours of work? By how much did the one extra hour of work increase the revenue? (The increase in revenue is called the *marginal revenue* for the 101st hour.)
\$16,000, \$16,120, \$120

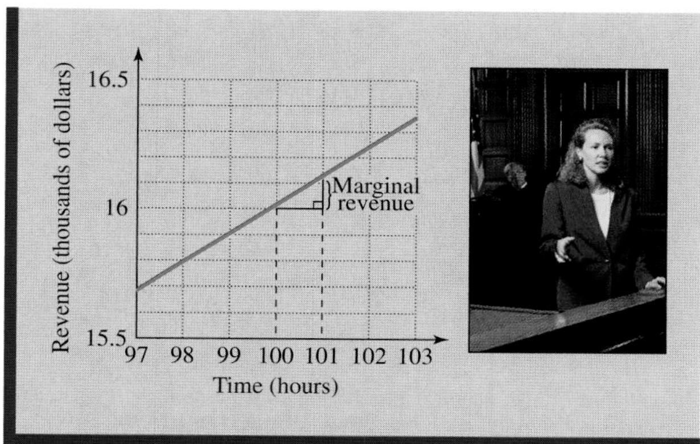

Figure for Exercise 94

95. *In-house training.* The accompanying graph shows the percentage of U.S. workers receiving training by their employers (Department of Labor, www.dol.gov). The percentage went from 5% in 1982 to 29% in 2006.

a) Find and interpret the slope of the line.
b) Write the equation of the line in slope-intercept form.
c) What is the meaning of the y-intercept?

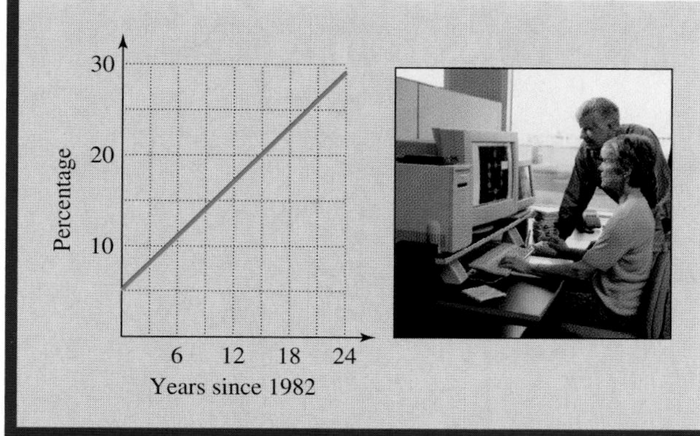

Figure for Exercise 95

d) Use your equation to predict the percentage that will be receiving training in 2010.

a) A slope of 1 means that the percentage of workers receiving training is going up 1% per year.
b) $y = x + 5$ where x is the number of years since 1982
c) The y-intercept (0, 5) means that 5% of the workers received training in 1982.
d) 33%

96. *Single women.* The percentage of women in the 20–24 age group who have never married went from 55% in 1970 to 73% in 2000 (Census Bureau, www.census.gov). Let 1970 be year 0 and 2000 be year 30.

a) Find and interpret the slope of the line through the points (0, 55) and (30, 73).
b) Find the equation of the line in part (a).
c) What is the meaning of the y-intercept?
d) Use the equation to predict the percentage in 2010.
e) If this trend continues, then in what year will the percentage of women in the 20–24 age group who have never married reach 100%?

a) A slope of 0.6 means that the percentage is increasing by 0.6% per year.
b) $y = 0.6x + 55$
c) The y-intercept (0, 55) means that in 1970 55% of the women between 20 and 24 had never been married.
d) 79%
e) 2045

97. *Pansies and snapdragons.* A nursery manager plans to spend \$100 on 6-packs of pansies at 50 cents per pack and snapdragons at 25 cents per pack. The equation $0.50x + 0.25y = 100$ can be used to model this situation.

a) What do x and y represent?
x = the number of packs of pansies, y = the number of packs of snapdragons
b) Graph the equation.

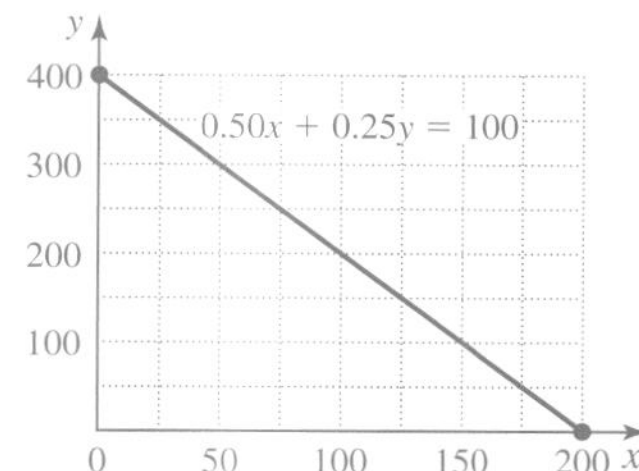

c) Write the equation in slope-intercept form.
$y = -2x + 400$
d) What is the slope of the line? -2
e) What does the slope tell you?
If the number of packs of pansies goes up by 1, then the number of packs of snapdragons goes down by 2.

98. *Pens and pencils.* A bookstore manager plans to spend \$60 on pens at 30 cents each and pencils at 10 cents each.

The equation $0.10x + 0.30y = 60$ can be used to model this situation.

a) What do x and y represent?
x = the number of pencils, y = the number of pens

b) Graph the equation.

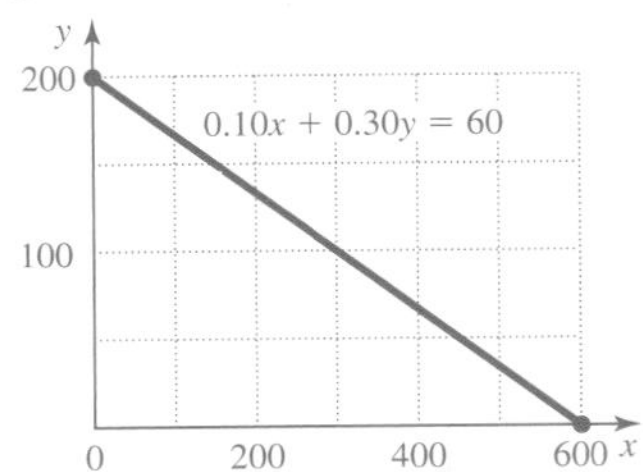

c) Write the equation in slope-intercept form.
$y = -\frac{1}{3}x + 200$

d) What is the slope of the line? $-\frac{1}{3}$

e) What does the slope tell you?
If the number of pencils increases by 3, then the number of pens goes down by 1.

Getting More Involved

Exploration

If $a \neq 0$ and $b \neq 0$, then $\frac{x}{a} + \frac{y}{b} = 1$ is called the double-intercept form for the equation of a line.

99. Find the x- and y-intercepts for $\frac{x}{2} + \frac{y}{3} = 1$. (2, 0), (0, 3)

100. Find the x- and y-intercepts for $\frac{x}{a} + \frac{y}{b} = 1$. $(a, 0)$, $(0, b)$

101. Write the equation of the line through (0, 5) and (9, 0) in double-intercept form. $\frac{x}{9} + \frac{y}{5} = 1$

102. Write the equation of the line through $\left(\frac{1}{2}, 0\right)$ and $\left(0, \frac{1}{3}\right)$ in standard form. $2x + 3y = 1$

Graphing Calculator Exercises

Graph each pair of straight lines on your graphing calculator using a viewing window that makes the lines look perpendicular. Answers may vary.

103. $y = 12x - 100$, $y = -\frac{1}{12}x + 50$

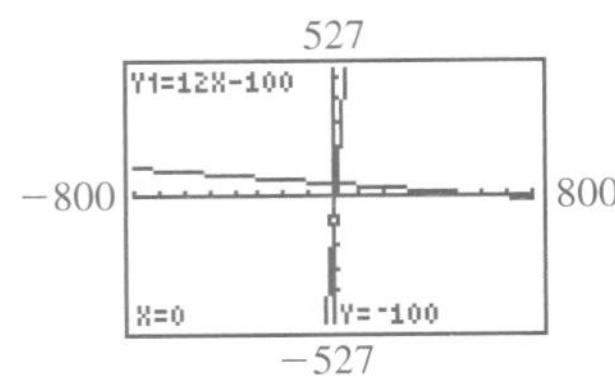

104. $2x - 3y = 300$, $3x + 2y = -60$

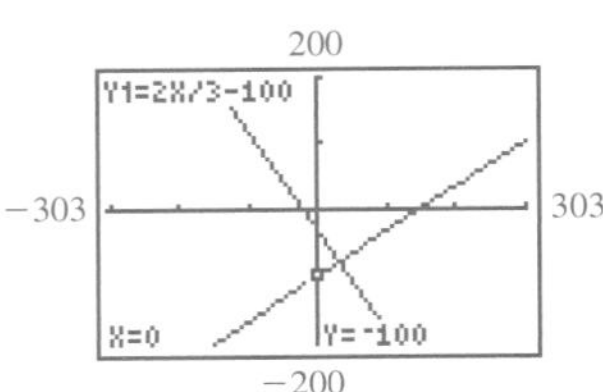

3.4 The Point-Slope Form

In This Section

In Section 3.3 we wrote the equation of a line given its slope and y-intercept. In this section, you will learn to write the equation of a line given the slope and *any* other point on the line.

⟨1⟩ Point-Slope Form

Consider a line through the point (4, 1) with slope $\frac{2}{3}$ as shown in Fig. 3.29. Because the slope can be found by using any two points on the line, we use (4, 1) and an arbitrary point (x, y) in the formula for slope:

$$\frac{y_2 - y_1}{x_2 - x_1} = m \qquad \text{Slope formula}$$

$$\frac{y - 1}{x - 4} = \frac{2}{3} \qquad \text{Let } m = \tfrac{2}{3},\ (x_1, y_1) = (4, 1), \text{ and } (x_2, y_2) = (x, y).$$

$$y - 1 = \frac{2}{3}(x - 4) \qquad \text{Multiply each side by } x - 4.$$

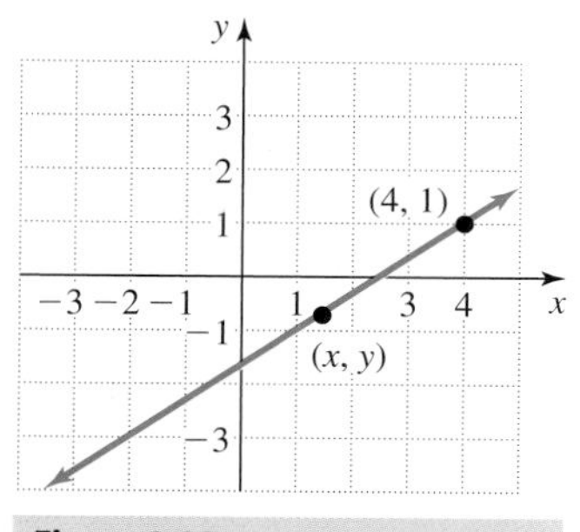

Figure 3.29

Note how the coordinates of the point (4, 1) and the slope $\frac{2}{3}$ appear in the above equation. We can use the same procedure to get the equation of any line given one point on the line and the slope. The resulting equation is called the **point-slope form** of the equation of the line.

Helpful Hint

If a point (x, y) is on a line with slope m through (x_1, y_1), then

$$\frac{y - y_1}{x - x_1} = m.$$

Multiplying each side of this equation by $x - x_1$ gives us the point-slope form.

Point-Slope Form

The equation of the line through the point (x_1, y_1) with slope m is

$$y - y_1 = m(x - x_1).$$

EXAMPLE 1

Writing an equation given a point and a slope

Find the equation of the line through $(-2, 3)$ with slope $\frac{1}{2}$, and write it in slope-intercept form.

Solution

Because we know a point and the slope, we can use the point-slope form:

$$y - y_1 = m(x - x_1) \quad \text{Point-slope form}$$

$$y - 3 = \frac{1}{2}[x - (-2)] \quad \text{Substitute } m = \tfrac{1}{2} \text{ and } (x_1, y_1) = (-2, 3).$$

$$y - 3 = \frac{1}{2}(x + 2) \quad \text{Simplify.}$$

$$y - 3 = \frac{1}{2}x + 1 \quad \text{Distributive property}$$

$$y = \frac{1}{2}x + 4 \quad \text{Slope-intercept form}$$

Alternate Solution

Replace m by $\frac{1}{2}$, x by -2, and y by 3 in the slope-intercept form:

$$y = mx + b \quad \text{Slope-intercept form}$$

$$3 = \frac{1}{2}(-2) + b \quad \text{Substitute } m = \tfrac{1}{2} \text{ and } (x, y) = (-2, 3).$$

$$3 = -1 + b \quad \text{Simplify.}$$

$$4 = b$$

Since $b = 4$, we can write $y = \frac{1}{2}x + 4$.

Now do Exercises 7–24

Teaching Tip

Have students practice some problems in class using both methods. Students usually resist knowing two methods.

The alternate solution to Example 1 is shown because many students have seen that method in the past. This does not mean that you should ignore the point-slope form. It is always good to know more than one method to accomplish a task. The good thing about using the point-slope form is that you immediately write down the equation and then you simplify it. In the alternate solution, the last thing you do is to write the equation.

The point-slope form can be used to find the equation of a line for *any* given point and slope. However, if the given point is the y-intercept, then it is simpler to use the slope-intercept form. Note that it is not necessary that the slope be given, because the slope can be found from any two points. So if we know two points on a line, then we can find the slope and use the slope with either one of the points in the point-slope form.

EXAMPLE 2

Writing an equation given two points

Find the equation of the line that contains the points $(-3, -2)$ and $(4, -1)$, and write it in standard form.

‹ Calculator Close-Up ›

Graph $y = (x + 3)/7 - 2$ to see that the line goes through $(-3, -2)$ and $(4, -1)$.

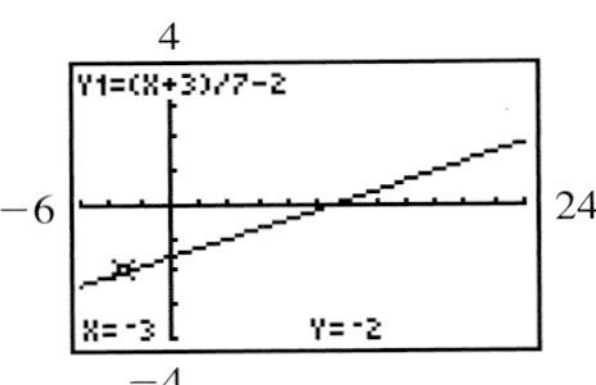

Note that the form of the equation does not matter on the calculator as long as it is solved for y.

Solution

First find the slope using the two given points:

$$m = \frac{-2 - (-1)}{-3 - 4} = \frac{-1}{-7} = \frac{1}{7}$$

Now use one of the points, say $(-3, -2)$, and slope $\frac{1}{7}$ in the point-slope form:

$$y - y_1 = m(x - x_1) \quad \text{Point-slope form}$$

$$y - (-2) = \frac{1}{7}[x - (-3)] \quad \text{Substitute.}$$

$$y + 2 = \frac{1}{7}(x + 3) \quad \text{Simplify.}$$

$$7(y + 2) = 7 \cdot \frac{1}{7}(x + 3) \quad \text{Multiply each side by 7.}$$

$$7y + 14 = x + 3$$

$$7y = x - 11 \quad \text{Subtract 14 from each side.}$$

$$-x + 7y = -11 \quad \text{Subtract } x \text{ from each side.}$$

$$x - 7y = 11 \quad \text{Multiply each side by } -1.$$

The equation in standard form is $x - 7y = 11$. Using the other given point, $(4, -1)$, would give the same final equation in standard form. Try it.

Now do Exercises 25–44

‹2› Parallel Lines

In Section 3.2 you learned that parallel lines have the same slope. We will use this fact in Example 3.

EXAMPLE 3

Using point-slope form with parallel lines

Find the equation of each line. Write the answer in slope-intercept form.

a) The line through $(2, -1)$ that is parallel to $y = -3x + 9$

b) The line through $(3, 4)$ that is parallel to $2x - 3y = 6$

Solution

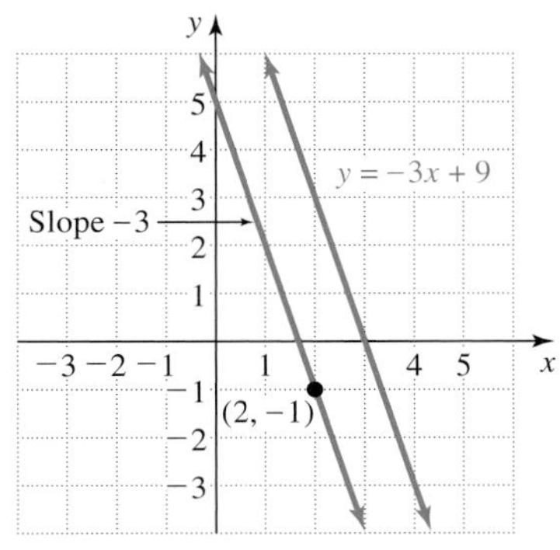

Figure 3.30

a) The slope of $y = -3x + 9$ and any line parallel to it is -3. See Fig. 3.30. Now use the point $(2, -1)$ and slope -3 in point-slope form:

$$y - y_1 = m(x - x_1) \quad \text{Point-slope form}$$
$$y - (-1) = -3(x - 2) \quad \text{Substitute.}$$
$$y + 1 = -3x + 6 \quad \text{Simplify.}$$
$$y = -3x + 5 \quad \text{Slope-intercept form}$$

Since $-1 = -3(2) + 5$ is correct, the line $y = -3x + 5$ goes through $(2, -1)$. It is certainly parallel to $y = -3x + 9$. So $y = -3x + 5$ is the desired equation.

b) Solve $2x - 3y = 6$ for y to determine its slope:

$$2x - 3y = 6$$
$$-3y = -2x + 6$$
$$y = \frac{2}{3}x - 2$$

So the slope of $2x - 3y = 6$ and any line parallel to it is $\frac{2}{3}$. Now use the point $(3, 4)$ and slope $\frac{2}{3}$ in the point-slope form:

$$y - y_1 = m(x - x_1) \quad \text{Point-slope form}$$
$$y - 4 = \frac{2}{3}(x - 3) \quad \text{Substitute.}$$
$$y - 4 = \frac{2}{3}x - 2 \quad \text{Simplify.}$$
$$y = \frac{2}{3}x + 2 \quad \text{Slope-intercept form}$$

Since $4 = \frac{2}{3}(3) + 2$ is correct, the line $y = \frac{2}{3}x + 2$ contains the point $(3, 4)$. Since $y = \frac{2}{3}x + 2$ and $y = \frac{2}{3}x - 2$ have the same slope, they are parallel. So the equation is $y = \frac{2}{3}x + 2$.

Now do Exercises 49–50

‹ Teaching Tip ›

Even though a graph is not required to solve this problem, it is a good idea for students to draw a graph showing both lines.

‹3› Perpendicular Lines

In Section 3.2 you learned that lines with slopes m and $-\frac{1}{m}$ (for $m \neq 0$) are perpendicular to each other. For example, the lines

$$y = -2x + 7 \qquad \text{and} \qquad y = \frac{1}{2}x - 8$$

are perpendicular to each other. In the next example we will write the equation of a line that is perpendicular to a given line and contains a given point.

EXAMPLE 4

Writing an equation given a point and a perpendicular line

Write the equation of the line that is perpendicular to $3x + 2y = 8$ and contains the point $(1, -3)$. Write the answer in slope-intercept form.

‹ Calculator Close-Up ›

Graph $y_1 = (2/3)x - 11/3$ and $y_2 = (-3/2)x + 4$ as shown:

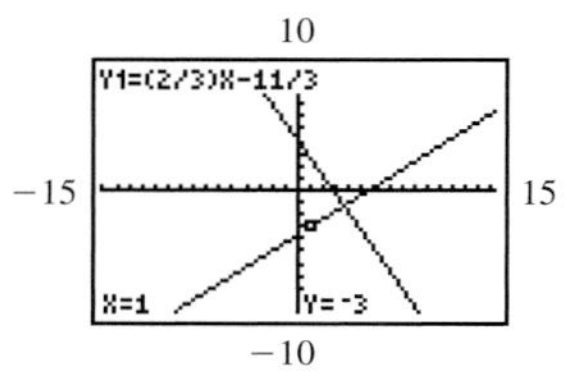

Because the lines look perpendicular and y_1 goes through $(1, -3)$, the graph supports the answer to Example 4.

Solution

First graph $3x + 2y = 8$ and a line through $(1, -3)$ that is perpendicular to $3x + 2y = 8$ as shown in Fig. 3.31. The right angle symbol is used in the figure to indicate that the lines are perpendicular. Now write $3x + 2y = 8$ in slope-intercept form to determine its slope:

$$3x + 2y = 8$$
$$2y = -3x + 8$$
$$y = -\frac{3}{2}x + 4 \quad \text{Slope-intercept form}$$

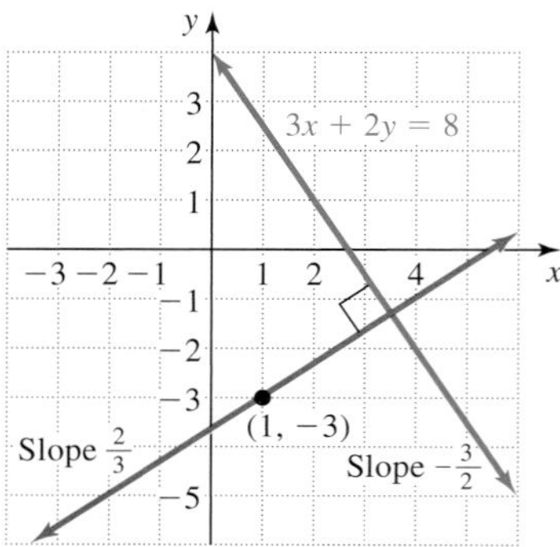

Figure 3.31

The slope of the given line is $-\frac{3}{2}$. The slope of any line perpendicular to it is $\frac{2}{3}$. Now we use the point-slope form with the point $(1, -3)$ and the slope $\frac{2}{3}$:

$$y - y_1 = m(x - x_1) \quad \text{Point-slope form}$$
$$y - (-3) = \frac{2}{3}(x - 1)$$
$$y + 3 = \frac{2}{3}x - \frac{2}{3}$$
$$y = \frac{2}{3}x - \frac{2}{3} - 3 \quad \text{Subtract 3 from each side.}$$
$$y = \frac{2}{3}x - \frac{11}{3} \quad \text{Slope-intercept form}$$

So $y = \frac{2}{3}x - \frac{11}{3}$ is the equation of the line that contains $(1, -3)$ and is perpendicular to $3x + 2y = 8$. Check that $(1, -3)$ satisfies $y = \frac{2}{3}x - \frac{11}{3}$.

Now do Exercises 51–60

‹4› Applications

We use the point-slope form to find the equation of a line given two points on the line. In Example 5, we use that same procedure to find a linear equation that relates two variables in an applied situation.

EXAMPLE 5

Writing a formula given two points

A contractor charges \$30 for installing 100 feet of pipe and \$120 for installing 500 feet of pipe. To determine the charge he uses a linear equation that gives the charge C in terms of the length L. Find the equation and find the charge for installing 240 feet of pipe.

‹ Teaching Tip ›

Students have trouble getting the right numbers on top in the slope formula here. Deciding what comes first and writing the ordered pairs (100, 30) and (500, 120) will clear this up. Of course, reversing everything will also give the correct answer.

Solution

Because C is determined from L, we let C take the place of the dependent variable y and let L take the place of the independent variable x. So the ordered pairs are in the form (L, C). We can use the slope formula to find the slope of the line through the two points (100, 30) and (500, 120) shown in Fig. 3.32.

$$m = \frac{120 - 30}{500 - 100} = \frac{90}{400} = \frac{9}{40}$$

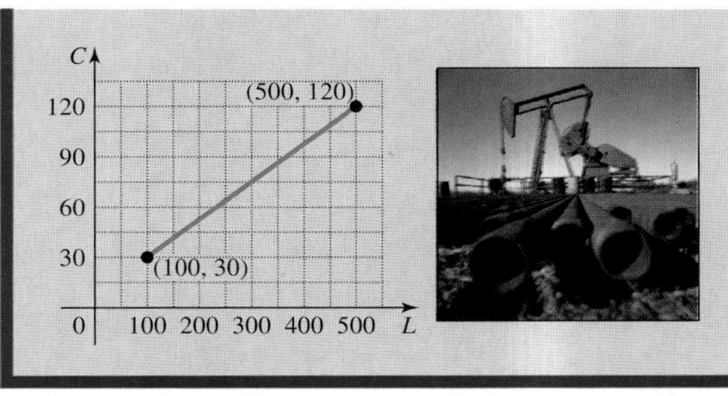

Figure 3.32

Now we use the point-slope form with the point (100, 30) and slope $\frac{9}{40}$:

$$y - y_1 = m(x - x_1)$$

$$C - 30 = \frac{9}{40}(L - 100)$$

$$C - 30 = \frac{9}{40}L - \frac{45}{2}$$

$$C = \frac{9}{40}L - \frac{45}{2} + 30$$

$$C = \frac{9}{40}L + \frac{15}{2}$$

Note that $C = \frac{9}{40}L + \frac{15}{2}$ means that the charge is $\frac{9}{40}$ dollars/foot plus a fixed charge of $\frac{15}{2}$ dollars (or \$7.50). We can now find C when $L = 240$:

$$C = \frac{9}{40} \cdot 240 + \frac{15}{2}$$

$$C = 54 + 7.5$$

$$C = 61.5$$

The charge for installing 240 feet of pipe is \$61.50.

Now do Exercises 79–94

Warm-Ups

True or false? Explain your answer.

1. The formula $y = m(x - x_1)$ is the point-slope form for a line. False
2. It is impossible to find the equation of a line through (2, 5) and (−3, 1). False
3. The point-slope form will not work for the line through (3, 4) and (3, 6). True
4. The equation of the line through the origin with slope 1 is $y = x$. True
5. The slope of the line $5x + y = 4$ is 5. False
6. The slope of any line perpendicular to the line $y = 4x - 3$ is $-\frac{1}{4}$. True
7. The slope of any line parallel to the line $x + y = 1$ is −1. True
8. The line $2x - y = -1$ goes through the point (−2, −3). True
9. The lines $2x + y = 4$ and $y = -2x + 7$ are parallel. True
10. The equation of the line through (0, 0) perpendicular to $y = x$ is $y = -x$. True

3.4 Exercises

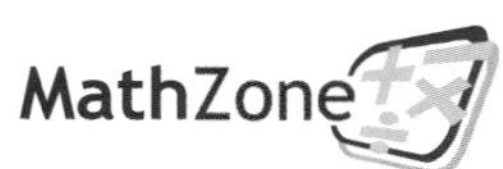

Boost your grade at mathzone.com!
- Practice Problems
- NetTutor
- Self-Tests
- e-Professors
- Videos

‹ Study Tips ›

- When taking a test, put a check mark beside every problem that you have answered and checked. Spend any extra time working on unchecked problems.
- Make sure that you don't forget to answer any of the questions on a test.

Reading and Writing *After reading this section, write out the answers to these questions. Use complete sentences.*

1. What is the point-slope form for the equation of a line?
   Point-slope form is $y - y_1 = m(x - x_1)$.
2. For what is the point-slope form used?
   If we know any point and the slope of a line we can use point-slope form to write the equation.
3. What is the procedure for finding the equation of a line when given two points on the line?
   If you know two points on a line, find the slope. Then use it along with either point in point-slope form to write the equation of the line.
4. How can you find the slope of a line when given the equation of the line?
   Rewrite any equation in slope-intercept form to find the slope of the line.
5. What is the relationship between the slopes of parallel lines?
   Nonvertical parallel lines have equal slopes.
6. What is the relationship between the slopes of perpendicular lines?
   If lines with slopes m_1 and m_2 are perpendicular, then $m_1 = -\frac{1}{m_2}$.

‹1› Point-Slope Form

Write each equation in slope-intercept form. See Example 1.

7. $x + y = 1$ $\quad y = -x + 1$
8. $x - y = 1$ $\quad y = x - 1$
9. $y - 1 = 5(x + 2)$ $\quad y = 5x + 11$
10. $y + 3 = -3(x - 6)$ $\quad y = -3x + 15$

11. $3x - 4y = 80$ $y = \frac{3}{4}x - 20$

12. $2x + 3y = 90$ $y = -\frac{2}{3}x + 30$

13. $y - \frac{1}{2} = \frac{2}{3}\left(x - \frac{1}{4}\right)$ $y = \frac{2}{3}x + \frac{1}{3}$

14. $y + \frac{2}{3} = -\frac{1}{2}\left(x - \frac{2}{5}\right)$ $y = -\frac{1}{2}x - \frac{7}{15}$

Find the equation of the line that goes through the given point and has the given slope. Write the answer in slope-intercept form. See Example 1.

15. (1, 2), 3
$y = 3x - 1$

16. (2, 5), 4
$y = 4x - 3$

VIDEO **17.** (2, 4), $\frac{1}{2}$
$y = \frac{1}{2}x + 3$

18. (4, 6), $\frac{1}{2}$
$y = \frac{1}{2}x + 4$

19. (2, 3), $\frac{1}{3}$
$y = \frac{1}{3}x + \frac{7}{3}$

20. (1, 4), $\frac{1}{4}$
$y = \frac{1}{4}x + \frac{15}{4}$

21. (−2, 5), $-\frac{1}{2}$
$y = -\frac{1}{2}x + 4$

22. (−3, 1), $-\frac{1}{3}$
$y = -\frac{1}{3}x$

23. (−1, −7), −6
$y = -6x - 13$

24. (−1, −5), −8
$y = -8x - 13$

Write each equation in standard form using only integers. See Example 2.

25. $y - 3 = 2(x - 5)$
$2x - y = 7$

26. $y + 2 = -3(x - 1)$
$3x + y = 1$

27. $y = \frac{1}{2}x - 3$
$x - 2y = 6$

28. $y = \frac{1}{3}x + 5$
$x - 3y = -15$

29. $y - 2 = \frac{2}{3}(x - 4)$
$2x - 3y = 2$

30. $y + 1 = \frac{3}{2}(x + 4)$
$3x - 2y = -10$

Find the equation of the line through each given pair of points. Write the answer in standard form using only integers. See Example 2.

31. (1, 3), (2, 5)
$2x - y = -1$

32. (2, 5), (3, 9)
$4x - y = 3$

33. (1, 1), (2, 2)
$x - y = 0$

34. (−1, 1), (1, −1)
$x + y = 0$

35. (1, 2), (5, 8)
$3x - 2y = -1$

VIDEO **36.** (3, 5), (8, 15)
$2x - y = 1$

37. (−2, −1), (3, −4)
$3x + 5y = -11$

38. (−1, −3), (2, −1)
$2x - 3y = 7$

39. (−2, 0), (0, 2)
$x - y = -2$

40. (0, 3), (5, 0)
$3x + 5y = 15$

41. (2, 4), (2, 6)
$x = 2$

42. (−3, 5), (−3, −1)
$x = -3$

43. (−3, 9), (3, 9)
$y = 9$

44. (2, 5), (4, 5)
$y = 5$

⟨2–3⟩ Parallel and Perpendicular Lines

The lines in each figure are perpendicular. Find the equation (in slope-intercept form) for the solid line.

45. $y = -x + 4$

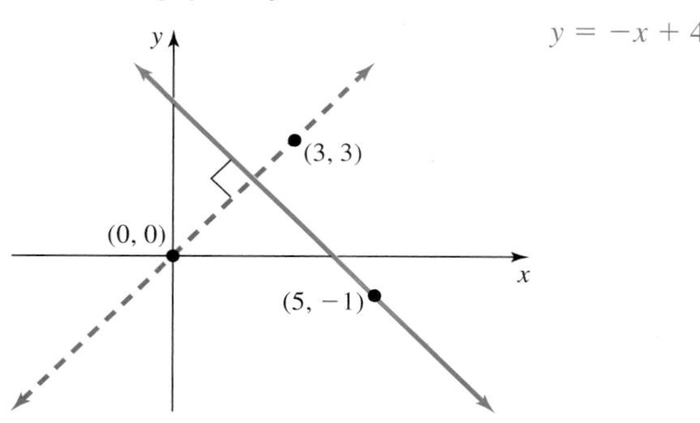

46. $y = -x - 4$

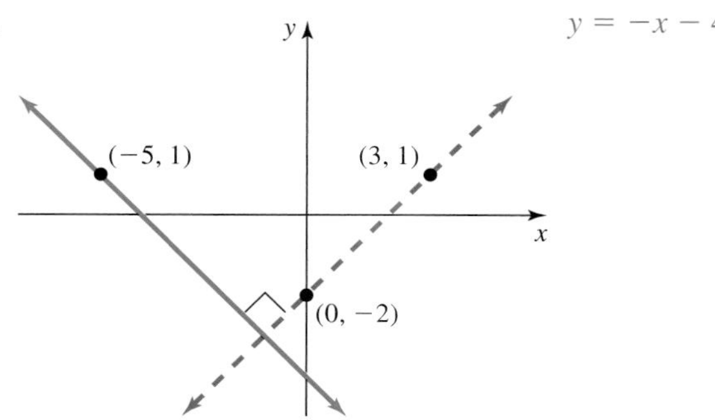

47. $y = \frac{5}{3}x - 1$

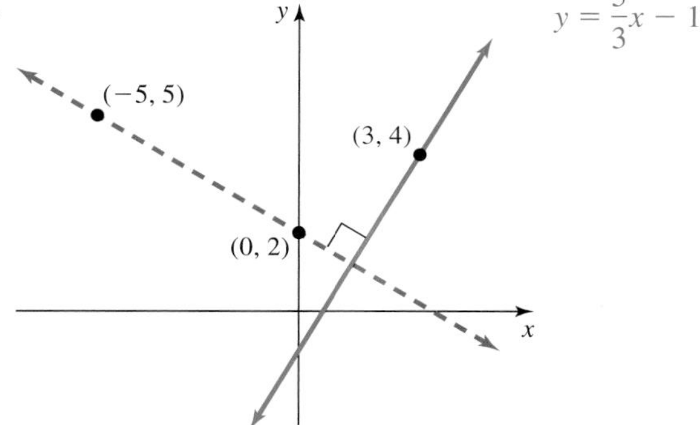

48.

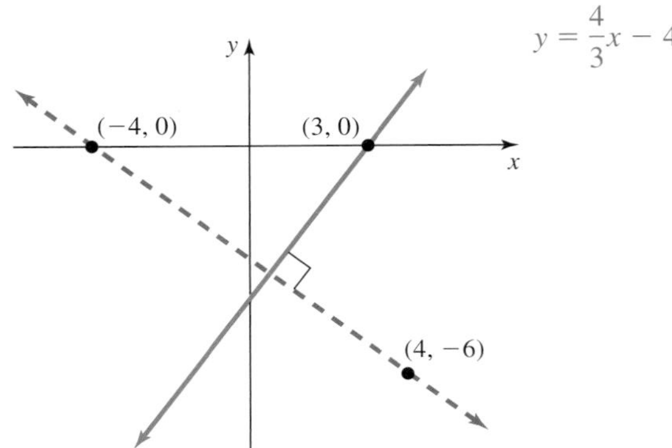

Find the equation of each line. Write each answer in slope-intercept form. See Examples 3 and 4.

VIDEO **49.** The line is parallel to $y = x - 9$ and goes through the point (7, 10). $y = x + 3$

50. The line is parallel to $y = -x + 5$ and goes through the point (−3, 6). $y = -x + 3$

51. The line contains the point (3, 4) and is perpendicular to $y = 3x - 1$. $y = -\frac{1}{3}x + 5$

52. The line contains the point (−2, 3) and is perpendicular to $y = 2x + 7$. $y = -\frac{1}{2}x + 2$

53. The line is perpendicular to $3x - 2y = 10$ and passes through the point (1, 1). $y = -\frac{2}{3}x + \frac{5}{3}$

54. The line is perpendicular to $x - 5y = 4$ and passes through the point (−1, 1). $y = -5x - 4$

55. The line is parallel to $2x + y = 8$ and contains the point (−1, −3). $y = -2x - 5$

56. The line is parallel to $-3x + 2y = 9$ and contains the point (−2, 1). $y = \frac{3}{2}x + 4$

57. The line goes through (−1, 2) and is perpendicular to $3x + y = 5$. $y = \frac{1}{3}x + \frac{7}{3}$

58. The line goes through (1, 2) and is perpendicular to $y = \frac{1}{2}x - 3$. $y = -2x + 4$

59. The line goes through (2, 3) and is parallel to $-2x + y = 6$. $y = 2x - 1$

60. The line goes through (1, 4) and is parallel to $x - 2y = 6$. $y = \frac{1}{2}x + \frac{7}{2}$

Miscellaneous

Find the equation of each line in the form $y = mx + b$ if possible.

61. The line through (3, 2) with slope 0 $y = 2$

VIDEO **62.** The line through (3, 2) with undefined slope $x = 3$

63. The line through (3, 2) and the origin $y = \frac{2}{3}x$

64. The line through the origin that is perpendicular to $y = \frac{2}{3}x$ $y = -\frac{3}{2}x$

65. The line through the origin that is parallel to the line through (5, 0) and (0, 5) $y = -x$

66. The line through the origin that is perpendicular to the line through (−3, 0) and (0, −3) $y = x$

67. The line through (−30, 50) that is perpendicular to the line $x = 400$ $y = 50$

68. The line through (20, −40) that is parallel to the line $y = 6000$ $y = -40$

69. The line through (−5, −1) that is perpendicular to the line through (0, 0) and (3, 5) $y = -\frac{3}{5}x - 4$

70. The line through (3, 1) that is parallel to the line through (−3, −2) and (0, 0) $y = \frac{2}{3}x - 1$

For each line described here choose the correct equation from (a) through (h).

71. The line through (1, 3) and (2, 5) e

72. The line through (1, 3) and (5, 2) a

73. The line through (1, 3) with no x-intercept f

74. The line through (1, 3) with no y-intercept b

75. The line through (1, 3) with x-intercept (5, 0) h

76. The line through (1, 3) with y-intercept (0, −5) d

77. The line through (1, 3) with slope −2 g

78. The line through (1, 3) with slope $\frac{1}{2}$ c

a) $x + 4y = 13$ **b)** $x = 1$
c) $x - 2y = -5$ **d)** $y = 8x - 5$
e) $y = 2x + 1$ **f)** $y = 3$
g) $2x + y = 5$ **h)** $3x + 4y = 15$

‹4› Applications

Solve each problem. See Example 5.

79. ***Automated tellers.*** ATM volume reached 10.6 billion transactions in 1996 and 14.2 billion transactions in 2000 as shown in the accompanying graph. If 1996 is year 0 and 2000 is year 4, then the line goes through the points (0, 10.6) and (4, 14.2).

a) Find and interpret the slope of the line.
b) Write the equation of the line in slope-intercept form.
c) Use your equation from part (b) to predict the number of transactions at automated teller machines in 2010.

a) Slope 0.9 means that the number of ATM transactions is increasing by 0.9 billion per year.
b) $y = 0.9x + 10.6$ c) 23.2 billion

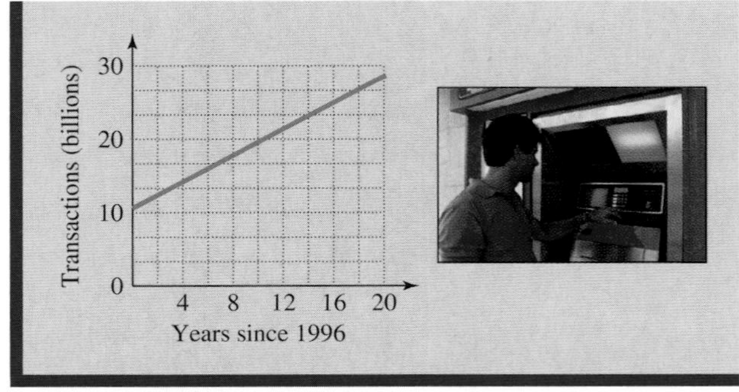

Figure for Exercise 79

80. ***Direct deposit.*** The percentage of workers receiving direct deposit of their paychecks went from 32% in 1994 to 60% in 2004 (www.directdeposit.com). Let 1994 be year 0 and 2004 be year 10.

a) Write the equation of the line through (0, 32) and (10, 60) to model the growth of direct deposit. $y = 2.8x + 32$

b) Use the accompanying graph to predict the year in which 100% of all workers will receive direct deposit of their paychecks. About 2018

c) Use the equation from part (a) to predict the year in which 100% of all workers will receive direct deposit. 2018

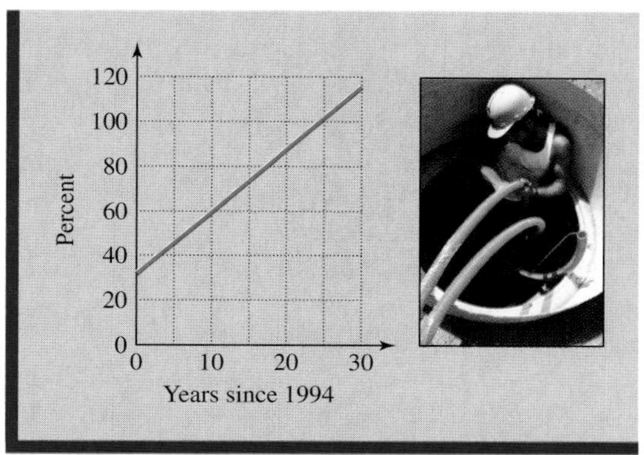

Figure for Exercise 80

81. ***Gross domestic product.*** The U.S. gross domestic product (GDP) per employed person increased from \$62.7 thousand in 1996 to \$71.6 thousand in 2002 (Bureau of Labor Statistics, www.bls.gov). Let 1996 be year 6 and 2002 be year 12.

a) Find the equation of the line through (6, 62.7) and (12, 71.6) to model the gross domestic product. $y = 1.5x + 53.8$

b) What do x and y represent in your equation? x = years since 1990, y = GDP in thousands of dollars

c) Use the equation to predict the GDP per employed person in 2010. \$83,800

d) Graph the equation.

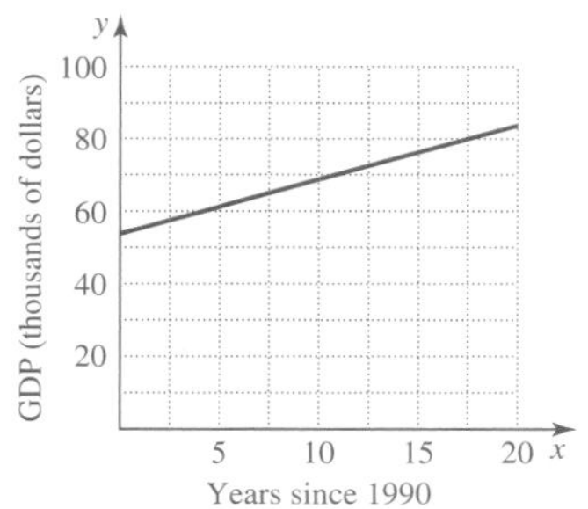

82. ***Age at first marriage.*** The median age at first marriage for females increased from 24.5 years in 1995 to 25.1 years in 2000 (U.S. Census Bureau, www.census.gov). Let 1995 be year 5 and 2000 be year 10.

a) Find the equation of the line through (5, 24.5) and (10, 25.1). $y = 0.12x + 23.9$

b) What do x and y represent in your equation? x = the number of years since 1990, y = median age at first marriage

c) Interpret the slope of this line. Median age increases 0.12 year each year or approximately 1 year in 8 years.

d) In what year will the median age be 30? 2041

e) Graph the equation.

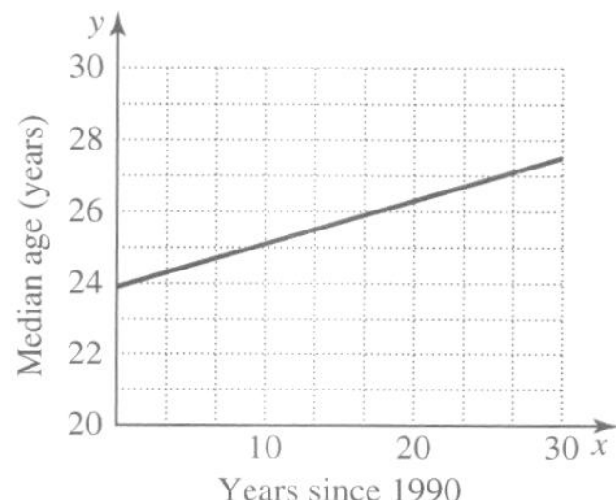

83. ***Plumbing charges.*** Pete the plumber worked 2 hours at Millie's house and charged her \$70. He then worked 4 hours at Rosalee's house and charged her \$110. To determine the amount he charges, Pete uses a linear equation that gives the charge C in terms of the number of hours worked n. Find the equation and find the charge for 7 hours at Fred's house. $C = 20n + 30$, \$170

84. ***Interior angles.*** The sum of the measures of the interior angles of a triangle is 180°. The sum of the measures of the interior angles of a square is 360°. Let S represent the sum of the measures of the interior angles of a polygon and n represent the number of sides of the polygon. There is a linear equation that gives S in terms of n. Find the equation and find the sum of the measures of the interior angles of the stop sign shown in the accompanying figure. $S = 180n - 360$, 1080°

Figure for Exercise 84

85. ***Shoe sizes.*** If a child's foot is 7.75 inches long, then the child wears a size 13 shoe. If a child's foot is 5.75 inches long, then the child wears a size 7 shoe. Let S represent the shoe size and L represent the length of the foot in inches. There is a linear equation that gives S in terms of L. Find the equation and find the shoe size for a child with a 6.25-inch foot. See the accompanying figure.
$S = 3L - \frac{41}{4}$, 8.5

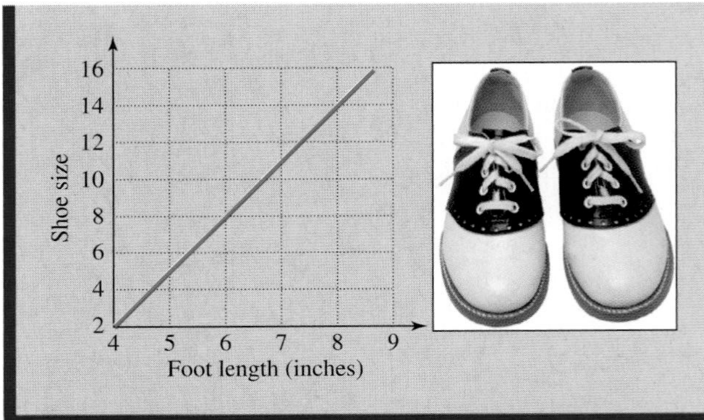

Figure for Exercise 85

86. ***Celsius to Fahrenheit.*** Water freezes at 0°C or 32°F and boils at 100°C or 212°F. There is a linear equation that expresses the number of degrees Fahrenheit (F) in terms of the number of degrees Celsius (C). Find the equation and find the Fahrenheit temperature when the Celsius temperature is 45°.
$F = \frac{9}{5}C + 32$, 113°F

87. ***Velocity of a projectile.*** A ball is thrown downward from the top of a tall building. Its velocity is 42 feet per second after 1 second and 74 feet per second after 2 seconds. There is a linear equation that expresses the velocity v in terms of the time t. Find the equation and find the velocity after 3.5 seconds. $v = 32t + 10$, 122 ft/sec

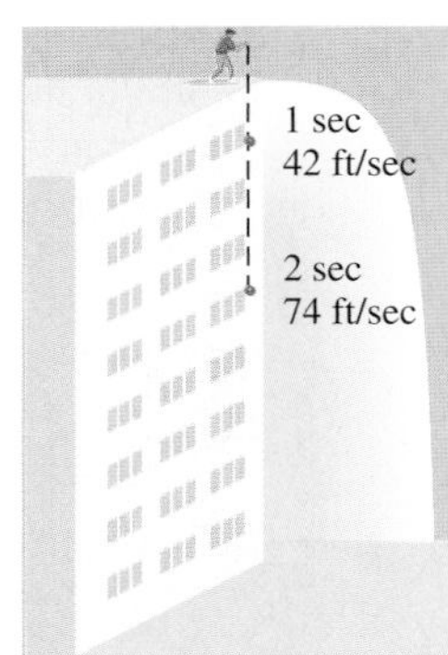

Figure for Exercise 87

88. ***Natural gas.*** The cost of 1000 cubic feet of natural gas is \$39 and the cost of 3000 cubic feet is \$99. There is a linear equation that expresses the cost C in terms of the number of cubic feet n. Find the equation and find the cost of 2400 cubic feet of natural gas. $C = 0.03n + 9$, \$81

89. ***Expansion joint.*** When the temperature is 90°F the width of an expansion joint on a bridge is 0.75 inch. When the temperature is 30°F the width is 1.25 inches. There is a linear equation that expresses the width w in terms of the temperature t.

a) Find the equation.
b) What is the width when the temperature is 80°F?
c) What is the temperature when the width is 1 inch?
a) $w = -\frac{1}{120}t + \frac{3}{2}$ **b)** $\frac{5}{6}$ inch **c)** 60°F

90. ***Perimeter of a rectangle.*** A rectangle has a fixed width and a variable length. Let P represent the perimeter and L represent the length. $P = 28$ inches when $L = 6.5$ inches and $P = 36$ inches when $L = 10.5$ inches. There is a linear equation that expresses P in terms of L.

a) Find the equation.
b) What is the perimeter when $L = 40$ inches?
c) What is the length when $P = 215$ inches?
d) What is the width of the rectangle?
a) $P = 2L + 15$ **b)** 95 in. **c)** 100 in. **d)** 7.5 in.

91. ***Stretching a spring.*** A weight of 3 pounds stretches a spring 1.8 inches beyond its natural length and weight of 5 pounds stretches the same spring 3 inches beyond its natural length. Let A represent the amount of stretch and w the weight. There is a linear equation that expresses A in terms of w. Find the equation and find the amount that the spring will stretch with a weight of 6 pounds.
$A = 0.6w$, 3.6 in.

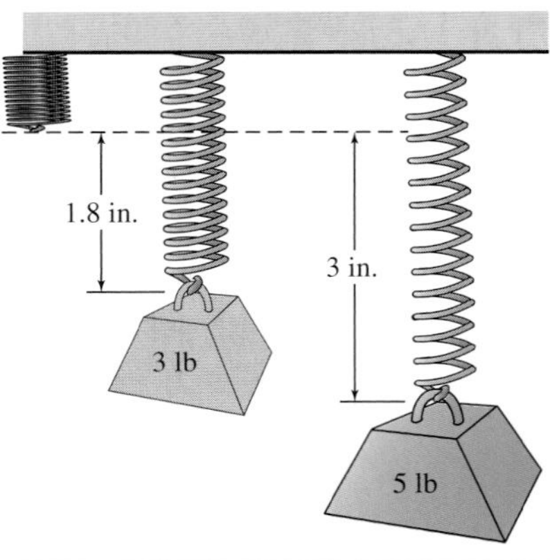

Figure for Exercise 91

92. ***Velocity of a bullet.*** A gun is fired straight upward. The bullet leaves the gun at 100 feet per second (time $t = 0$). After 2 seconds the velocity of the bullet is 36 feet per second. There is a linear equation that gives the velocity v in terms of the time t. Find the equation and find the velocity after 3 seconds. $v = -32t + 100$, 4 ft/sec

93. ***Enzyme concentration.*** The amount of light absorbed by a certain liquid depends on the concentration of an enzyme in the liquid. A concentration of 2 milligrams per milliliter (mg/ml) produces an absorption of 0.16 and a concentration of 5 mg/ml produces an absorption of 0.40. There is a linear equation that expresses the absorption a in terms of the concentration c.

a) Find the equation.
b) What is the absorption when the concentration is 3 mg/ml?
c) Use the accompanying graph to estimate the concentration when the absorption is 0.50.

a) $a = 0.08c$ **b)** 0.24 **c)** 6.25 mg/ml

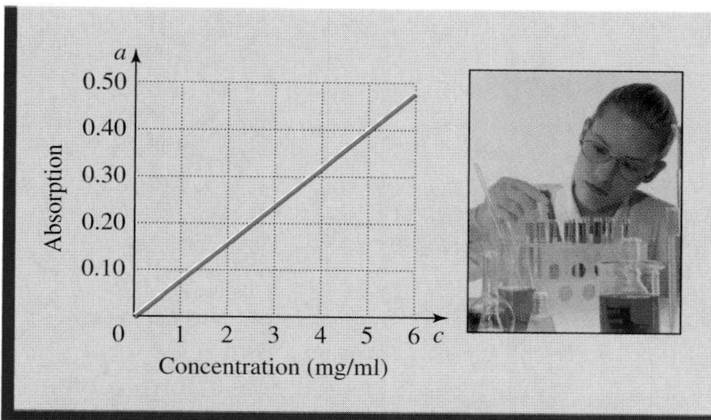

Figure for Exercise 93

94. ***Basal energy requirement.*** The basal energy requirement B is the number of calories that a person needs to maintain the life process. For a 28-year-old female with a height of 160 centimeters and a weight of 45 kilograms (kg), B is 1300 calories. If her weight increases to 50 kg, then B is 1365 calories. There is a linear equation that expresses B in terms of her weight w. Find the equation and find the basal energy requirement if her weight is 53.2 kg.
$B = 13w + 715$, 1406.6 calories

Getting More Involved

95. ***Exploration***

Each linear equation in the following table is given in standard form $Ax + By = C$. In each case identify A, B, and the slope of the line.

Equation	A	B	Slope
$2x + 3y = 9$	2	3	$-\frac{2}{3}$
$4x - 5y = 6$	4	-5	$\frac{4}{5}$
$\frac{1}{2}x + 3y = 1$	$\frac{1}{2}$	3	$-\frac{1}{6}$
$2x - \frac{1}{3}y = 7$	2	$-\frac{1}{3}$	6

96. ***Exploration***

Find a pattern in the table of Exercise 95 and write a formula for the slope of $Ax + By = C$, where $B \neq 0$.
$m = -\frac{A}{B}$

Graphing Calculator Exercises

97. Graph each equation on a graphing calculator. Choose a viewing window that includes both the x- and y-intercepts. Use the calculator output to help you draw the graph on paper.

a) $y = 20x - 300$
b) $y = -30x + 500$
c) $2x - 3y = 6000$

a)
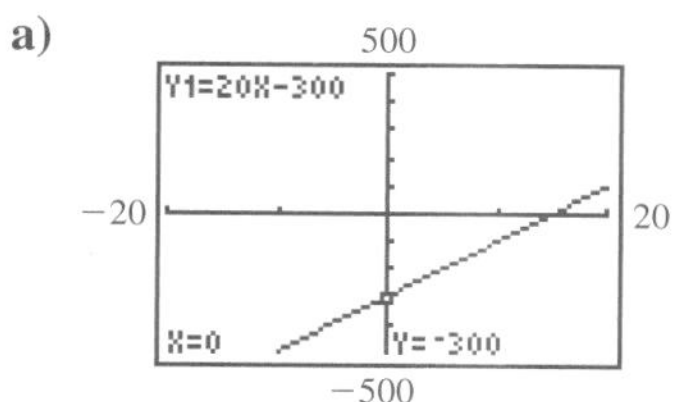

b)
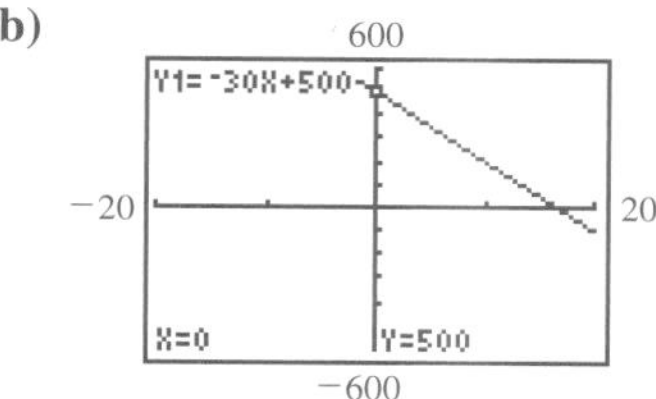

c)
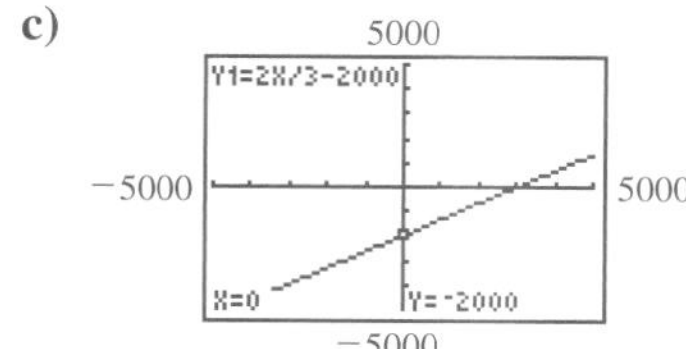

98. Graph $y = 2x + 1$ and $y = 1.99x - 1$ on a graphing calculator. Are these lines parallel? Explain your answer.
They look parallel, but they are not.

99. Graph $y = 0.5x + 0.8$ and $y = 0.5x + 0.7$ on a graphing calculator. Find a viewing window in which the two lines are separate.
$-1 \leq x \leq 1, -1 \leq y \leq 1$

100. Graph $y = 3x + 1$ and $y = -\frac{1}{3}x + 2$ on a graphing calculator. Do the lines look perpendicular? Explain.
They will look perpendicular in the right window.

3.5 Variation

In This Section

If $y = 5x$, then the value of y depends on the value of x. As x varies, so does y. Simple relationships like $y = 5x$ are customarily expressed in terms of variation. In this section, you will learn the language of variation and learn to write formulas from verbal descriptions.

⟨1⟩ Direct, Inverse, and Joint Variation

Suppose you average 60 miles per hour on the freeway. The distance D that you travel depends on the amount of time T that you travel. Using the formula $D = R \cdot T$, we can write

$$D = 60T.$$

Consider the possible values for T and D given in the following table.

T (hours)	1	2	3	4	5	6
D (miles)	60	120	180	240	300	360

The graph of $D = 60T$ is shown in Fig. 3.33. Note that as T gets larger, so does D. In this situation we say that *D varies directly with T*, or *D is directly proportional to T*. The constant rate of 60 miles per hour is called the **variation constant** or **proportionality constant.** Notice that $D = 60T$ is simply a linear equation. We are just introducing some new terms to express an old idea.

⟨ Teaching Tip ⟩

Note that in $y = 3x + 5$ there is something besides x (the constant 5) that is used to determine y, and so y does not vary directly with x.

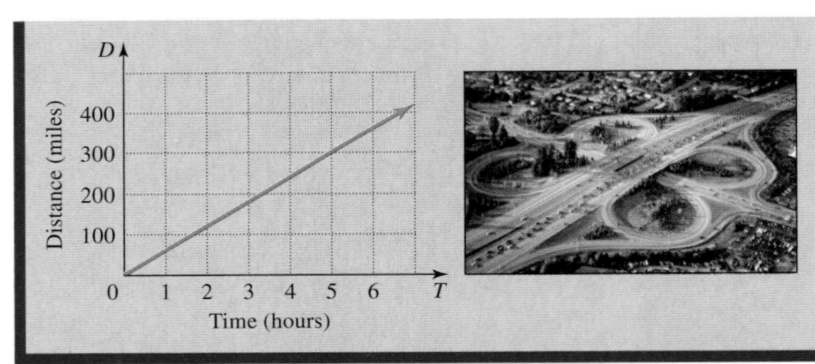

Figure 3.33

⟨ Teaching Tip ⟩

Ask students for examples of direct variation.

Direct Variation

The statement **"y varies directly as x"** or **"y is directly proportional to x"** means that

$$y = kx$$

for some constant k. The constant of variation k is a fixed nonzero real number.

CAUTION Direct variation refers only to equations of the form $y = kx$ (lines through the origin). We do *not* refer to $y = 3x + 5$ as a direct variation.

If you plan to make a 400-mile trip by car, the time it will take depends on your rate of speed. Using the formula $D = RT$, we can write

$$T = \frac{400}{R}.$$

Consider the possible values for R and T given in the following table:

‹ Teaching Tip ›

Having the students make some tables like this will improve their understanding of these concepts.

R (mph)	10	20	40	50	80	100
T (hours)	40	20	10	8	5	4

The graph of $T = \frac{400}{R}$ is shown in Fig. 3.34. As your rate increases, the time for the trip decreases. In this situation we say that the time is *inversely proportional* to the speed. Note that the graph of $T = \frac{400}{R}$ is not a straight line because $T = \frac{400}{R}$ is not a linear equation.

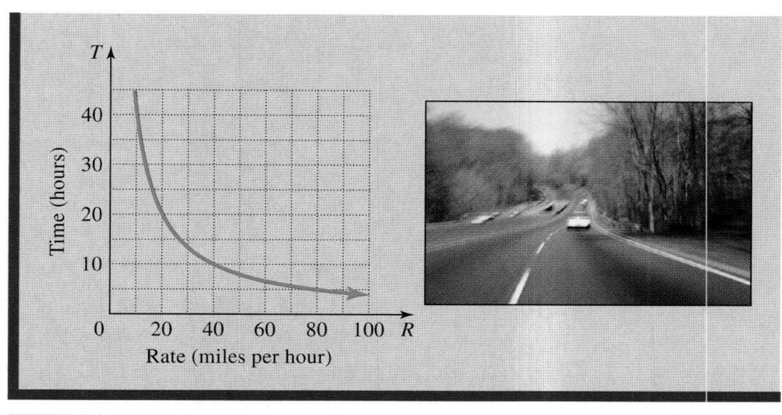

Figure 3.34

‹ Teaching Tip ›

Ask students for examples of inverse variation.

Inverse Variation

The statement **"y varies inversely as x"** or **"y is inversely proportional to x"** means that

$$y = \frac{k}{x}$$

for some nonzero constant of variation k.

CAUTION The constant of variation is usually positive because most physical examples involve positive quantities. However, the definitions of direct and inverse variation do not rule out a negative constant.

If the price of carpet is \$30 per square yard, then the cost C of carpeting a rectangular room depends on the width W (in yards) and the length L (in yards). As the width or length of the room increases, so does the cost. We can write the cost in terms of the two variables L and W:

$$C = 30LW$$

We say that C *varies jointly* as L and W.

Joint Variation

The statement "**y varies jointly as x and z**" or "**y is jointly proportional to x and z**" means that

$$y = kxz$$

for some nonzero constant of variation k.

EXAMPLE 1

Writing the formula

Write a formula that expresses the relationship described in each statement. Use k as the variation constant.

a) a varies directly as t.

b) c is inversely proportional to m.

c) q varies jointly as x and y.

Solution

a) Since a varies directly as t, we have $a = kt$.

b) Since c is inversely proportional to m, we have $c = \frac{k}{m}$.

c) Since q varies jointly as x and y, we have $q = kxy$.

Now do Exercises 5-14

⟨2⟩ Finding the Variation Constant

If we know the values of all variables in a variation statement, we can find the value of the constant and write a formula using the value of the constant rather than an unknown constant k.

EXAMPLE 2

Finding the variation constant

Find the variation constant and write a formula that expresses the relationship described in each statement.

a) a varies directly as x and $a = 10$ when $x = 2$.

b) w is inversely proportional to t, and $w = 10$ when $t = 5$.

c) m varies jointly as a and b, and $m = 24$ when $a = 2$ and $b = 3$.

Solution

a) Since a varies directly as x, we have $a = kx$. Since $a = 10$ when $x = 2$, we have $10 = k(2)$. Solve $2k = 10$ to get $k = 5$. So we can write the formula as $a = 5x$.

b) Since w is inversely proportional to t, we have $w = \frac{k}{t}$. Since $w = 10$ when $t = 5$, we have $10 = \frac{k}{5}$. Solve $\frac{k}{5} = 10$ to get $k = 50$. So we can write the formula $w = \frac{50}{t}$.

c) Since m varies jointly as a and b, we have $m = kab$. Since $m = 24$ when $a = 2$ and $b = 3$, we have $24 = k \cdot 2 \cdot 3$. Solve $6k = 24$ to get $k = 4$. So we can write the formula as $m = 4ab$.

Now do Exercises 15-24

‹3› Applications

Examples 3, 4, and 5 illustrate applications of the language of variation.

EXAMPLE 3

A direct variation problem

Your electric bill at Middle States Electric Co-op varies directly with the amount of electricity that you use. If the bill for 2800 kilowatts of electricity is \$196, then what is the bill for 4000 kilowatts of electricity?

‹ Helpful Hint ›

In any variation problem you must first determine the general form of the relationship. Because this problem involves direct variation, the general form is $y = kx$.

Solution

Because the amount A of the electric bill varies directly as the amount E of electricity used, we have

$$A = kE$$

for some constant k. Because 2800 kilowatts cost \$196, we have

$$196 = k \cdot 2800$$

or

$$0.07 = k.$$

So $A = 0.07E$. Now if $E = 4000$, we get

$$A = 0.07(4000) = 280.$$

The bill for 4000 kilowatts would be \$280.

Now do Exercises 25–26

EXAMPLE 4

An inverse variation problem

The volume of a gas in a cylinder is inversely proportional to the pressure on the gas. If the volume is 12 cubic centimeters when the pressure on the gas is 200 kilograms per square centimeter, then what is the volume when the pressure is 150 kilograms per square centimeter? See Fig. 3.35.

Figure 3.35

Solution

Because the volume V is inversely proportional to the pressure P, we have

$$V = \frac{k}{P}$$

for some constant k. Because $V = 12$ when $P = 200$, we can find k:

$$12 = \frac{k}{200}$$

$$200 \cdot 12 = 200 \cdot \frac{k}{200} \quad \text{Multiply each side by 200.}$$

$$2400 = k$$

Now to find V when $P = 150$, we can use the formula $V = \frac{2400}{P}$:

$$V = \frac{2400}{150} = 16$$

So the volume is 16 cubic centimeters when the pressure is 150 kilograms per square centimeter.

Now do Exercises 27–28

EXAMPLE 5

A joint variation problem

The cost of shipping a piece of machinery by truck varies jointly with the weight of the machinery and the distance that it is shipped. It costs \$3000 to ship a 2500-lb milling machine a distance of 600 miles. Find the cost for shipping a 1500-lb lathe a distance of 800 miles.

Solution

Because the cost C varies jointly with the weight w and the distance d, we have

$$C = kwd$$

where k is the constant of variation. To find k, we use $C = 3000$, $w = 2500$, and $d = 600$:

$$3000 = k \cdot 2500 \cdot 600$$

$$\frac{3000}{2500 \cdot 600} = k \quad \text{Divide each side by } 2500 \cdot 600.$$

$$0.002 = k$$

Now use $w = 1500$ and $d = 800$ in the formula $C = 0.002wd$:

$$C = 0.002 \cdot 1500 \cdot 800$$
$$= 2400$$

So the cost of shipping the lathe is \$2400.

Now do Exercises 29–30

‹ Helpful Hint ›

Because the variation in this problem is joint, we know the general form is $y = kxz$, where k is the constant of variation.

‹ Teaching Tip ›

Ask students for another example of joint variation in real life. Does the cost of a fill-up vary jointly with the size of the tank and the price per gallon? Do UPS shipping costs vary jointly with weight and distance?

CAUTION The variation words (directly, inversely, or jointly) are never used to indicate addition or subtraction. We use multiplication in the formula unless we see the word "inversely." We use division for inverse variation.

Warm-Ups ▼

True or false? Explain your answer.

1. If y varies directly as z, then $y = kz$ for some constant k. True
2. If a varies inversely as b, then $a = \frac{b}{k}$ for some constant k. False
3. If y varies directly as x and $y = 8$ when $x = 2$, then the variation constant is 4. True
4. If y varies inversely as x and $y = 8$ when $x = 2$, then the variation constant is $\frac{1}{4}$. False
5. If C varies jointly as h and t, then $C = ht$. False
6. The amount of sales tax on a new car varies directly with the purchase price of the car. True
7. If z varies inversely as w and $z = 10$ when $w = 2$, then $z = \frac{20}{w}$. True
8. The time that it takes to travel a fixed distance varies inversely with the rate. True
9. If m varies directly as w, then $m = w + k$ for some constant k. False
10. If y varies jointly as x and z, then $y = k(x + z)$ for some constant k. False

Exercises

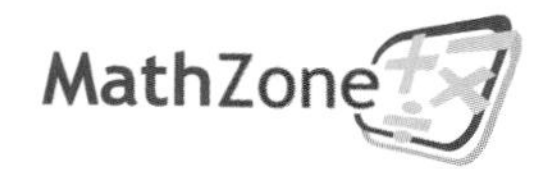

‹ Study Tips ›

- Get in a habit of checking your work. Don't look in the back of the book for the answer until after you have checked your work.
- You will not always have an answer section for your problems.

Reading and Writing *After reading this section, write out the answers to these questions. Use complete sentences.*

1. What does it mean to say that y varies directly as x?
If y varies directly as x, then there is a constant k such that $y = kx$.

2. What is a variation constant?
A variation constant is the constant k in the formulas $y = kx$ or $y = \frac{k}{x}$.

3. What does it mean to say that y is inversely proportional to x?
If y is inversely proportional to x, then there is a constant k such that $y = \frac{k}{x}$.

4. What does it mean to say that y varies jointly as x and z?
If y varies jointly as x and z, then there is a constant k such that $y = kxz$.

‹1› Direct, Inverse, and Joint Variation

Write a formula that expresses the relationship described by each statement. Use k for the constant in each case. See Example 1.

5. T varies directly as h. $T = kh$

6. m varies directly as p. $m = kp$

7. y varies inversely as r. $y = \frac{k}{r}$

8. u varies inversely as n. $u = \frac{k}{n}$

9. R is jointly proportional to t and s. $R = kts$

10. W varies jointly as u and v. $W = kuv$

11. i is directly proportional to b. $i = kb$

12. p is directly proportional to x. $p = kx$

13. A is jointly proportional to y and m. $A = kym$

14. t is inversely proportional to e. $t = \frac{k}{e}$

‹2› Finding the Variation Constant

Find the variation constant, and write a formula that expresses the indicated variation. See Example 2.

15. y varies directly as x, and $y = 5$ when $x = 3$. $y = \frac{5}{3}x$

16. m varies directly as w, and $m = \frac{1}{2}$ when $w = \frac{1}{4}$. $m = 2w$

17. A varies inversely as B, and $A = 3$ when $B = 2$. $A = \frac{6}{B}$

18. c varies inversely as d, and $c = 5$ when $d = 2$. $c = \frac{10}{d}$

19. m varies inversely as p, and $m = 22$ when $p = 9$. $m = \frac{198}{p}$

VIDEO **20.** s varies inversely as v, and $s = 3$ when $v = 4$. $s = \frac{12}{v}$

21. A varies jointly as t and u, and $A = 24$ when $t = 6$ and $u = 2$. $A = 2tu$

22. N varies jointly as p and q, and $N = 720$ when $p = 3$ and $q = 2$. $N = 120pq$

VIDEO **23.** T varies directly as u, and $T = 9$ when $u = 2$. $T = \frac{9}{2}u$

24. R varies directly as p, and $R = 30$ when $p = 6$. $R = 5p$

‹3› Applications

Solve each variation problem. See Examples 3–5.

25. Y varies directly as x, and $Y = 100$ when $x = 20$. Find Y when $x = 5$. 25

26. n varies directly as q, and $n = 39$ when $q = 3$. Find n when $q = 8$. 104

27. a varies inversely as b, and $a = 3$ when $b = 4$. Find a when $b = 12$. 1

28. y varies inversely as w, and $y = 9$ when $w = 2$. Find y when $w = 6$. 3

VIDEO **29.** P varies jointly as s and t, and $P = 56$ when $s = 2$ and $t = 4$. Find P when $s = 5$ and $t = 3$. 105

30. B varies jointly as u and v, and $B = 12$ when $u = 4$ and $v = 6$. Find B when $u = 5$ and $v = 8$. 20

31. ***Aluminum flatboat.*** The weight of an aluminum flatboat varies directly with the length of the boat. If a 12-foot boat weighs 86 pounds, then what is the weight of a 14-foot boat?
100.3 pounds

32. ***Christmas tree.*** The price of a Christmas tree varies directly with the height. If a 5-foot tree costs $20, then what is the price of a 6-foot tree?
$24

33. ***Sharing the work.*** The time it takes to erect the big circus tent varies inversely as the number of elephants working on the job. If it takes four elephants 75 minutes, then how long would it take six elephants?
50 minutes

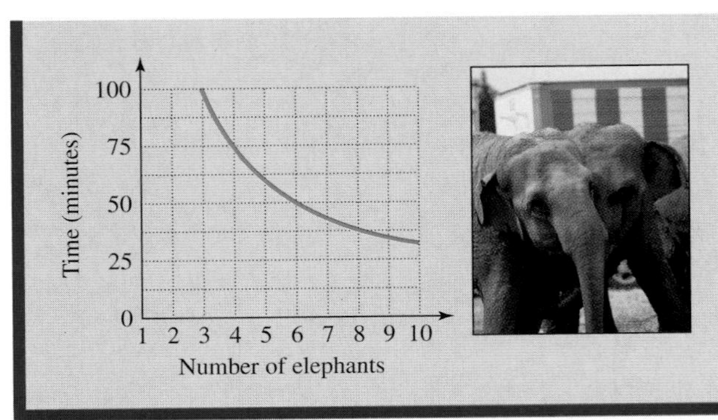

Figure for Exercise 33

34. ***Gas laws.*** The volume of a gas is inversely proportional to the pressure on the gas. If the volume is 6 cubic centimeters when the pressure on the gas is 8 kilograms per square centimeter, then what is the volume when the pressure is 12 kilograms per square centimeter?
4 cm^3

35. ***Steel tubing.*** The cost of steel tubing is jointly proportional to its length and diameter. If a 10-foot tube with a 1-inch diameter costs \$5.80, then what is the cost of a 15-foot tube with a 2-inch diameter?
\$17.40

36. ***Sales tax.*** The amount of sales tax varies jointly with the number of Cokes purchased and the price per Coke. If the sales tax on eight Cokes at 65 cents each is 26 cents, then what is the sales tax on six Cokes at 90 cents each?
27 cents

37. ***Approach speed.*** The approach speed of an airplane is directly proportional to its landing speed. If the approach speed for a Piper Cheyenne is 90 mph with a landing speed of 75 mph, then what is the landing speed for an airplane with an approach speed of 96 mph?
80 mph

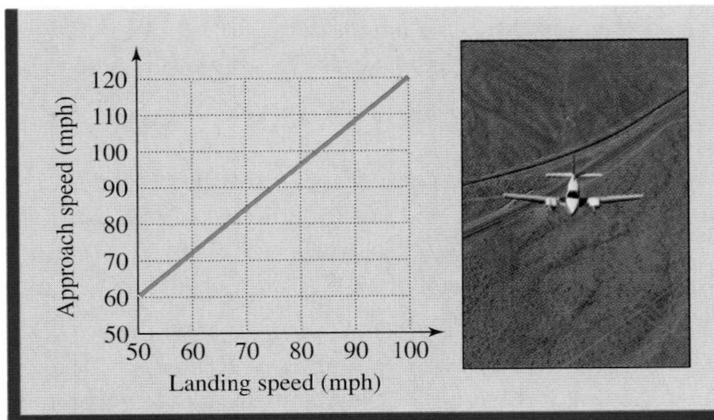

Figure for Exercise 37

38. ***Ideal waist size.*** According to Dr. Aaron R. Folsom of the University of Minnesota School of Public Health, your maximum ideal waist size is directly proportional to your hip size. For a woman with 40-inch hips, the maximum ideal waist size is 32 inches. What is the maximum ideal waist size for a woman with 35-inch hips?
28 inches

39. ***Sugar Pops.*** The number of days that it takes to eat a large box of Sugar Pops varies inversely with the size of the family. If a family of three eats a box in 7 days, then how many days does it take a family of seven?
3 days

40. ***Cost of CDs.*** The cost for manufacturing a CD varies inversely with the number of CDs made. If the cost is \$2.50 per CD when 10,000 are made, then what is the cost per CD when 100,000 are made?
\$0.25 per CD

41. ***Carpeting.*** The cost C of carpeting a rectangular living room with \$20 per square yard carpet varies jointly with the length L and the width W. Fill in the missing entries in the following table.

Length (yd)	Width (yd)	Cost (\$)
8	10	1600
10	12	2400
12	14	3360

42. ***Waterfront property.*** At \$50 per square foot, the price of a rectangular waterfront lot varies jointly with the length and width. Fill in the missing entries in the following table.

Length (ft)	Width (ft)	Cost (\$)
60	100	300,000
80	90	360,000
100	150	750,000

Miscellaneous

Use the given formula to fill in the missing entries in each table and determine whether b varies directly or inversely as a.

43. $b = \dfrac{300}{a}$

a	*b*
$\frac{1}{2}$	600
1	300
30	10
900	$\frac{1}{3}$

Inversely

44. $b = \dfrac{500}{a}$

a	*b*
$\frac{1}{5}$	2500
1	500
50	10
1500	$\frac{1}{3}$

Inversely

45. $b = \frac{3}{4}a$

a	*b*
$\frac{1}{3}$	$\frac{1}{4}$
8	6
12	9
20	15

Directly

46. $b = \frac{2}{3}a$

a	*b*
$\frac{1}{2}$	$\frac{1}{3}$
3	2
9	6
21	14

Directly

For each table, determine whether y varies directly or inversely as x and find a formula for y in terms of x.

47.

x	*y*
2	7
3	10.5
4	14
5	17.5

Directly, $y = 3.5x$

48.

x	*y*
10	5
15	7.5
20	10
25	12.5

Directly, $y = 0.5x$

49.

x	*y*
2	10
4	5
10	2
20	1

Inversely, $y = \frac{20}{x}$

50.

x	*y*
5	100
10	50
50	10
250	2

Inversely, $y = \frac{500}{x}$

Solve each problem.

51. ***Distance.*** With the cruise control set at 65 mph, the distance traveled varies directly with the time spent traveling. Fill in the missing entries in the following table.

Time (hours)	1	2	3	4
Distance (miles)	65	130	195	260

52. ***Cost.*** With gas selling for \$1.60 per gallon, the cost of filling your tank varies directly with the amount of gas that you pump. Fill in the missing entries in the following table.

Amount (gallons)	5	10	15	20
Cost (dollars)	8	16	24	32

53. ***Time.*** The time that it takes to complete a 400-mile trip varies inversely with your average speed. Fill in the missing entries in the following table.

Speed (mph)	20	40	50	200
Time (hours)	20	10	8	2

54. ***Amount.*** The amount of gasoline that you can buy for \$20 varies inversely with the price per gallon. Fill in the missing entries in the following table.

Price per gallon (dollars)	1	2	4	10
Amount (gallons)	20	10	5	2

Getting More Involved

55. ***Discussion***

If y varies directly as x, then the graph of the equation is a straight line. What is its slope? What is the y-intercept? If $y = 3x + 2$, then does y vary directly as x? Which straight lines correspond to direct variations?

k, (0, 0), no, $y = kx$

56. ***Writing***

Write a summary of the three types of variation. Include an example of each type that is not found in this text.

Wrap-Up

Summary

Slope of a Line		**Examples**
Slope	The slope of the line through (x_1, y_1) and (x_2, y_2) is given by $$m = \frac{y_2 - y_1}{x_2 - x_1}, \text{ provided that } x_2 - x_1 \neq 0.$$	(0, 1), (3, 5) $m = \frac{5-1}{3-0} = \frac{4}{3}$
	Slope is the ratio of the rise to the run for any two points on the line: $$m = \frac{\text{change in } y}{\text{change in } x} = \frac{\text{rise}}{\text{run}}$$	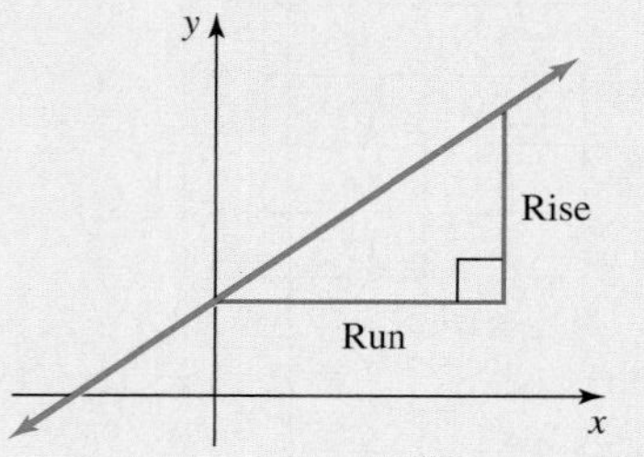
Types of slope	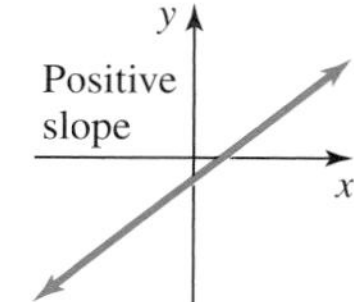 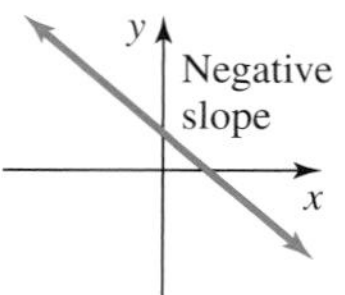 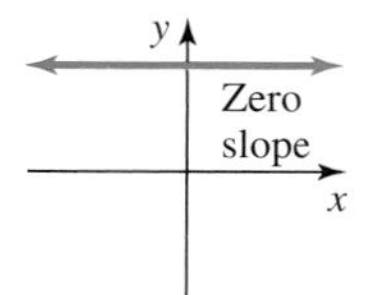 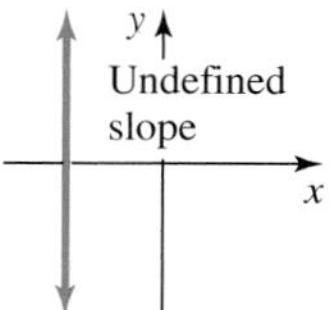	
Parallel lines	Nonvertical parallel lines have equal slopes. Two vertical lines are parallel.	The lines $y = 3x - 9$ and $y = 3x + 7$ are parallel lines.
Perpendicular lines	Lines with slopes m and $-\frac{1}{m}$ are perpendicular. Any vertical line is perpendicular to any horizontal line.	The lines $y = -5x + 7$ and $y = \frac{1}{5}x$ are perpendicular.

Equations of Lines		**Examples**
Slope-intercept form	The equation of the line with y-intercept $(0, b)$ and slope m is $y = mx + b$.	$y = 3x - 1$ has slope 3 and y-intercept $(0, -1)$.
Point-slope form	The equation of the line with slope m that contains the point (x_1, y_1) is $y - y_1 = m(x - x_1)$.	The line through $(2, -1)$ with slope -5 is $y + 1 = -5(x - 2)$.
Standard form	Every line has an equation of the form $Ax + By = C$, where A, B, and C are real numbers with A and B not both equal to zero.	$4x - 9y = 15$ $x = 5$ (vertical line) $y = -7$ (horizontal line)

Graphing a line using y-intercept and slope	1. Write the equation in slope-intercept form. 2. Plot the y-intercept. 3. Use the rise and run to locate a second point. 4. Draw a line through the two points.

Variation		**Examples**
Direct	If $y = kx$, then y varies directly as x.	$D = 50T$
Inverse	If $y = \frac{k}{x}$, then y varies inversely as x.	$R = \frac{400}{T}$
Joint	If $y = kxz$, then y varies jointly as x and z.	$V = 6LW$

Enriching Your Mathematical Word Power

For each mathematical term, choose the correct meaning.

1. graph of an equation
a. the Cartesian coordinate system
b. two number lines that intersect at a right angle
c. the x-axis and y-axis
d. an illustration in the coordinate plane that shows all ordered pairs that satisfy an equation d

2. x-coordinate
a. the first number in an ordered pair
b. the second number in an ordered pair
c. a point on the x-axis
d. a point where a graph crosses the x-axis a

3. y-intercept
a. the second number in an ordered pair
b. a point at which a graph intersects the y-axis
c. any point on the y-axis
d. the point where the y-axis intersects the x-axis b

4. coordinate plane
a. a matching plane
b. when the x-axis is coordinated with the y-axis
c. a plane with a rectangular coordinate system
d. a coordinated system for graphs c

5. slope
a. the change in x divided by the change in y
b. a measure of the steepness of a line
c. the run divided by the rise
d. the slope of a line b

6. slope-intercept form
a. $y = mx + b$
b. rise over run
c. the point at which a line crosses the y-axis
d. $y - y_1 = m(x - x_1)$ a

7. point-slope form
a. $Ax + By = C$
b. rise over run
c. $y - y_1 = m(x - x_1)$
d. the slope of a line at a single point c

8. independent variable
a. a rational constant
b. an irrational constant
c. the first variable of an ordered pair
d. the second variable of an ordered pair c

9. dependent variable
a. an irrational variable
b. a rational variable
c. the first variable of an ordered pair
d. the second variable of an ordered pair d

10. direct variation
a. $y = \pi$ b. $y = kx$
c. $y = k/x$ d. $y = kxz$ b

11. inverse variation
a. $y = \pi$ b. $y = kx$
c. $y = k/x$ d. $y = kxz$ c

12. joint variation
a. $y = \pi$ b. $y = kx$
c. $y = k/x$ d. $y = kxz$ d

Review Exercises

3.1 Graphing Lines in the Coordinate Plane

For each point, name the quadrant in which it lies or the axis on which it lies.

1. $(-2, 5)$ Quadrant II
2. $(-3, -5)$ Quadrant III
3. $(3, 0)$ x-axis
4. $(9, 10)$ Quadrant I
5. $(0, -6)$ y-axis
6. $(0, \pi)$ y-axis
7. $(1.414, -3)$ Quadrant IV
8. $(-4, 1.732)$ Quadrant II

Complete the given ordered pairs so that each ordered pair satisfies the given equation.

9. $y = 3x - 5$: (0,), (−3,), (4,)
$(0, -5), (-3, -14), (4, 7)$

10. $y = -2x + 1$: (9,), (3,), (−1,)
$(9, -17), (3, -5), (-1, 3)$

11. $2x - 3y = 8$: (0,), (3,), (−6,)
$\left(0, -\frac{8}{3}\right), \left(3, -\frac{2}{3}\right), \left(-6, -\frac{20}{3}\right)$

12. $x + 2y = 1$: (0,), (−2,), (2,)
$\left(0, \frac{1}{2}\right), \left(-2, \frac{3}{2}\right), \left(2, -\frac{1}{2}\right)$

Sketch the graph of each equation by finding three ordered pairs that satisfy each equation.

13. $y = -3x + 4$ **14.** $y = 2x - 6$

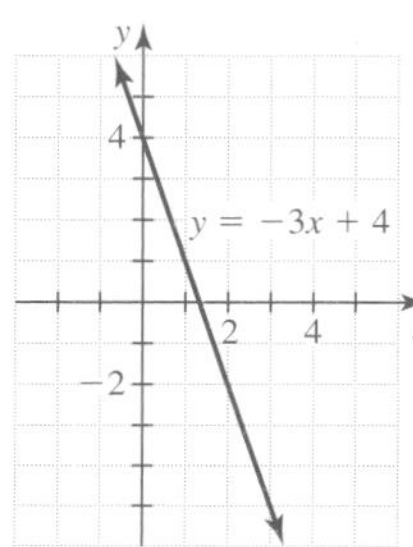

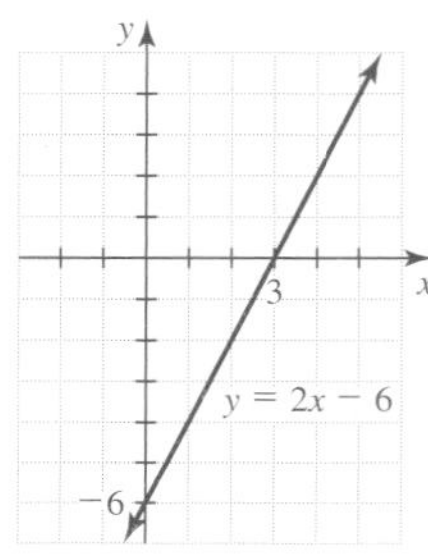

15. $x + y = 7$  **16.** $x - y = 4$

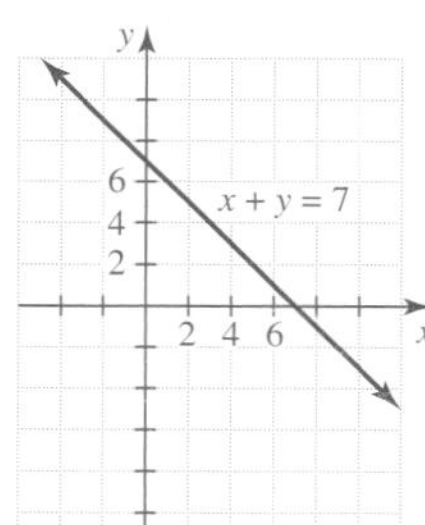

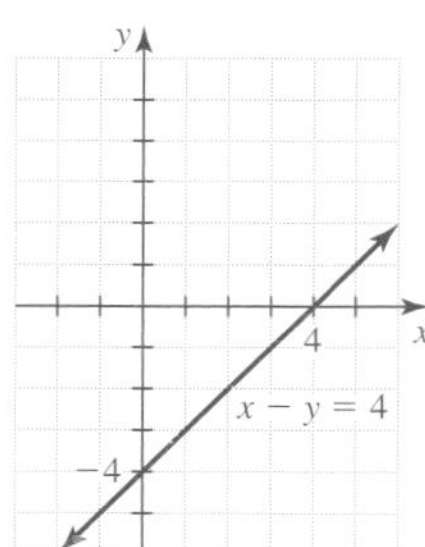

3.2 Slope

Determine the slope of the line that goes through each pair of points.

17. (0, 0) and (1, 1) 1

18. (−1, 1) and (2, −2) -1

19. (−2, −3) and (0, 0) $\frac{3}{2}$

20. (−1, −2) and (4, −1) $\frac{1}{5}$

21. (−4, −2) and (3, 1) $\frac{3}{7}$

22. (0, 4) and (5, 0) $-\frac{4}{5}$

3.3 Equations of Lines in Slope-Intercept Form

Find the slope and y-intercept for each line.

23. $y = 3x - 18$ $3, (0, -18)$

24. $y = -x + 5$ $-1, (0, 5)$

25. $2x - y = 3$ $2, (0, -3)$

26. $x - 2y = 1$ $\frac{1}{2}, \left(0, -\frac{1}{2}\right)$

27. $4x - 2y - 8 = 0$ $2, (0, -4)$

28. $3x + 5y + 10 = 0$ $-\frac{3}{5}, (0, -2)$

Sketch the graph of each equation.

29. $y = \frac{2}{3}x - 5$ 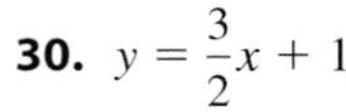 **30.** $y = \frac{3}{2}x + 1$

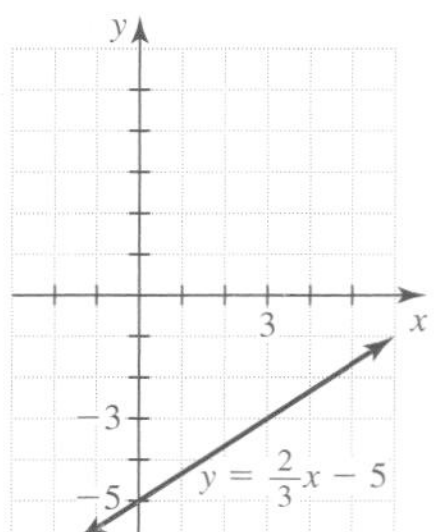

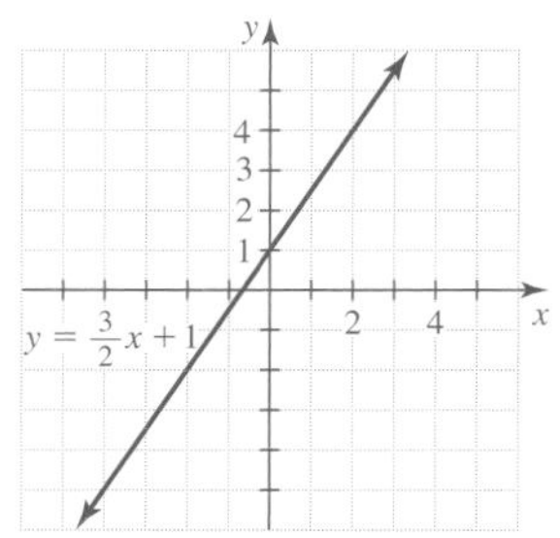

31. $2x + y = -6$ 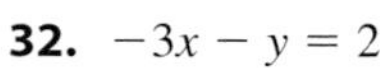 **32.** $-3x - y = 2$

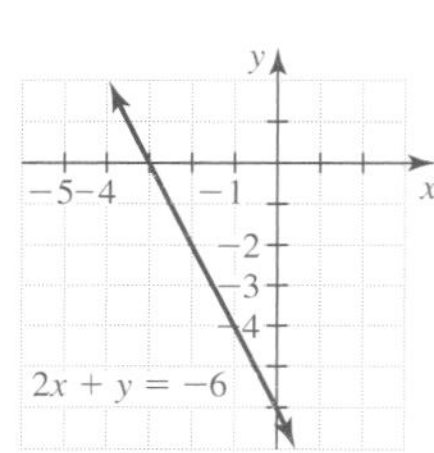

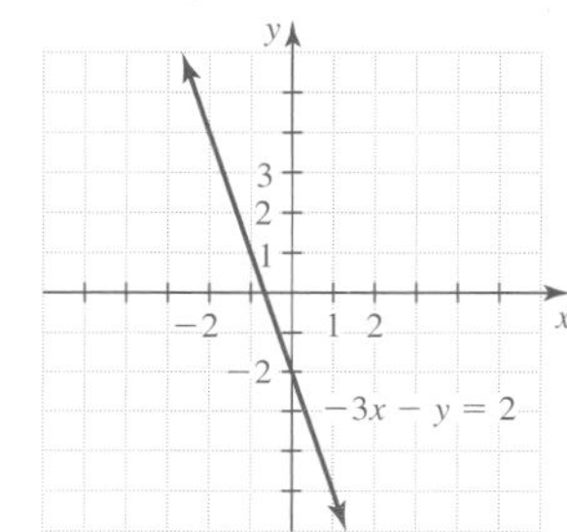

33. $y = -4$ 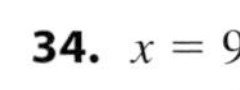 **34.** $x = 9$

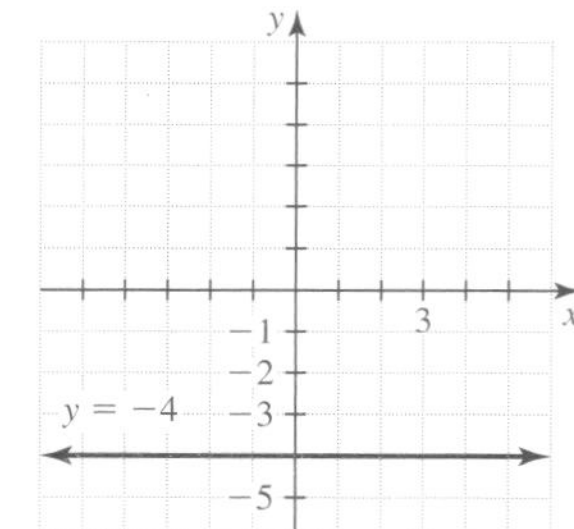

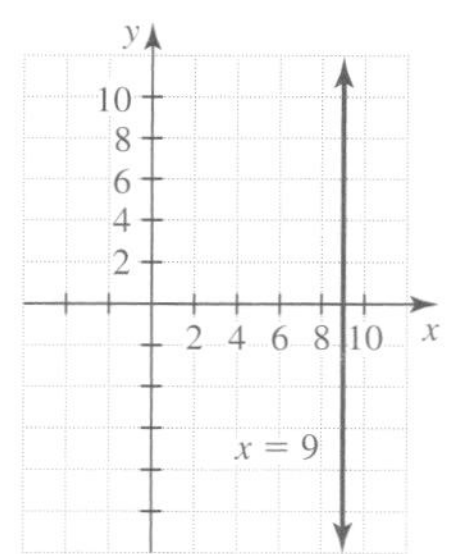

Determine the equation of each line. Write the answer in standard form using only integers as the coefficients.

35. The line through (0, 4) with slope $\frac{1}{3}$ $x - 3y = -12$

36. The line through (−2, 0) with slope $-\frac{3}{4}$ $3x + 4y = -6$

37. The line through the origin that is perpendicular to the line $y = 2x - 1$ $x + 2y = 0$

38. The line through (0, 9) that is parallel to the line $3x + 5y = 15$ $3x + 5y = 45$

39. The line through (3, 5) that is parallel to the x-axis $y = 5$

40. The line through (−2, 4) that is perpendicular to the x-axis $x = -2$

3.4 The Point-Slope Form

Write each equation in slope-intercept form.

41. $y - 3 = \frac{2}{3}(x + 6)$ $y = \frac{2}{3}x + 7$

42. $y + 2 = -6(x - 1)$ $y = -6x + 4$

43. $3x - 7y - 14 = 0$ $y = \frac{3}{7}x - 2$

44. $1 - x - y = 0$ $y = -x + 1$

45. $y - 5 = -\frac{3}{4}(x + 1)$ $y = -\frac{3}{4}x + \frac{17}{4}$

46. $y + 8 = -\frac{2}{5}(x - 2)$ $y = -\frac{2}{5}x - \frac{36}{5}$

Determine the equation of each line. Write the answer in slope-intercept form.

47. The line through $(-4, 7)$ with slope -2 $y = -2x - 1$

48. The line through $(9, 0)$ with slope $\frac{1}{2}$ $y = \frac{1}{2}x - \frac{9}{2}$

49. The line through the two points $(-2, 1)$ and $(3, 7)$ $y = \frac{6}{5}x + \frac{17}{5}$

50. The line through the two points $(4, 0)$ and $(-3, -5)$ $y = \frac{5}{7}x - \frac{20}{7}$

51. The line through $(3, -5)$ that is parallel to the line $y = 3x - 1$ $y = 3x - 14$

52. The line through $(4, 0)$ that is perpendicular to the line $x + y = 3$ $y = x - 4$

Solve each problem.

53. ***Rental charge.*** The charge for renting an air hammer for two days is \$113 and the charge for five days is \$209. The charge C is determined by the number of days n using a linear equation. Find the equation and find the charge for a four-day rental. $C = 32n + 49$, \$177

54. ***Time on a treadmill.*** After 2 minutes on a treadmill, Jenny has a heart rate of 82. After 3 minutes she has a heart rate of 86. Assume that there is a linear equation that gives her heart rate h in terms of time on the treadmill t. Find the equation and use it to predict her heart rate after 10 minutes on the treadmill. $h = 4t + 74$, 114

55. ***Probability of rain.*** If the probability p of rain is 90%, the probability q that it does not rain is 10%. If the probability of rain is 80%, then the probability that it does not rain is 20%. There is a linear equation that gives q in terms of p.

a) Find the equation.

b) Use the accompanying graph to determine the probability of rain if the probability that it does not rain is 0.

a) $q = 1 - p$ b) 1

56. ***Social Security benefits.*** If you earned an average of \$25,000 over your working life and you retire after 2005 at age 62, 63, or 64, then your annual Social Security benefit

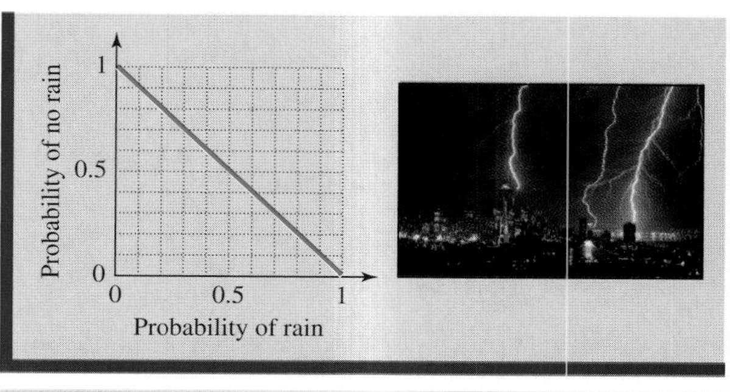

Figure for Exercise 55

will be \$7000, \$7500, or \$8000, respectively (Social Security Administration, www.ssa.gov). There is a linear equation that gives the annual benefit b in terms of age a for these three years. Find the equation. $b = 500a - 24{,}000$

57. ***Predicting freshmen GPA.*** A researcher who is studying the relationship between ACT score and grade point average for freshmen gathered the data shown in the accompanying table. Find the equation of the line in slope-intercept form that goes through these points. $y = 0.1x + 0.6$

ACT Score (x)	GPA (y)
4	1.0
14	2.0
24	3.0
34	4.0

Table for Exercise 57

58. ***Interest rates.*** A credit manager rates each applicant for a car loan on a scale of 1 through 5 and then determines the interest rate from the accompanying table. Find the equation of the line in slope-intercept form that goes through these points. $y = -4x + 28$

Credit Rating	Interest Rate (%)
1	24
2	20
3	16
4	12
5	8

Table for Exercise 58

3.5 Variation

Solve each variation problem.

59. Suppose y varies directly as w. If $y = 48$ when $w = 4$, then what is y when $w = 11$? 132

60. Suppose m varies directly as t. If $m = 13$ when $t = 2$, then what is m when $t = 6$? 39

61. If y varies inversely as v and $y = 8$ when $v = 6$, then what is y when $v = 24$? 2

62. If y varies inversely as r and $y = 9$ when $r = 3$, then what is y when $r = 9$? 3

63. Suppose y varies jointly as u and v, and $y = 72$ when $u = 3$ and $v = 4$. Find y when $u = 5$ and $v = 2$. 60

64. Suppose q varies jointly as s and t, and $q = 10$ when $s = 4$ and $t = 3$. Find q when $s = 25$ and $t = 6$. 125

65. ***Taxi fare.*** The cost of a taxi ride varies directly with the length of the ride in minutes. A 12-minute ride costs \$9.00.

a) Write the cost C in terms of the length T of the ride.
b) What is the cost of a 20-minute ride?
c) Is the cost increasing or decreasing as the length of the ride increases?

a) $C = 0.75T$ **b)** \$15 **c)** Increasing

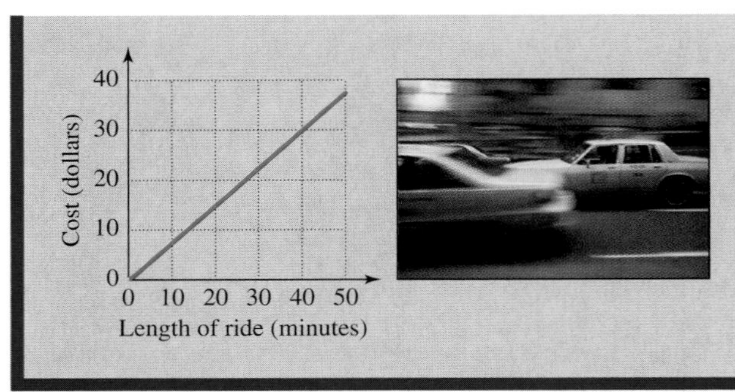

Figure for Exercise 65

66. ***Applying shingles.*** The number of hours that it takes to apply 296 bundles of shingles varies inversely with the number of roofers working on the job. Three workers can complete the job in 40 hours.

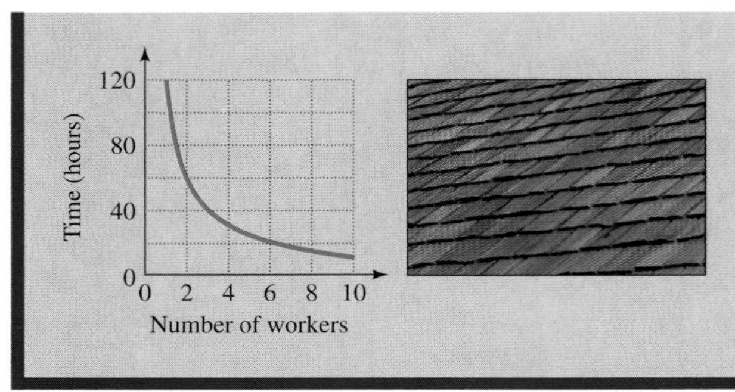

Figure for Exercise 66

a) Write the number of hours h in terms of the number n of roofers on the job.
b) How long would it take five roofers to complete the job?
c) Is the time to complete the job increasing or decreasing as the number of workers increases?

a) $h = \frac{120}{n}$ **b)** 24 hours **c)** Decreasing

Miscellaneous

Write each equation in slope-intercept form.

67. $x - y = 1$ $y = x - 1$

68. $x = 5 - y$ $y = -x + 5$

69. $2x + 4y = 16$ $y = -\frac{1}{2}x + 4$

70. $3x + 5y = 10$ $y = -\frac{3}{5}x + 2$

71. $y - 3 = 4(x - 2)$ $y = 4x - 5$

72. $y + 6 = -3(x - 1)$ $y = -3x - 3$

73. $\frac{1}{2}x - \frac{1}{3}y = 12$ $y = \frac{3}{2}x - 36$

74. $\frac{2}{3}x + \frac{3}{4}y = 18$ $y = -\frac{8}{9}x + 24$

Find the x- and y-intercepts for each line.

75. $x + y = 1$ $(1, 0), (0, 1)$

76. $x - y = 6$ $(6, 0), (0, -6)$

77. $3x + 4y = 12$ $(4, 0), (0, 3)$

78. $5x + 6y = 30$ $(6, 0), (0, 5)$

79. $y = 4x - 2$ $\left(\frac{1}{2}, 0\right), (0, -2)$

80. $y = -3x - 1$ $\left(-\frac{1}{3}, 0\right), (0, -1)$

81. $\frac{3}{2}x + \frac{1}{3}y = 6$ $(4, 0), (0, 18)$

82. $-\frac{2}{3}x + \frac{1}{4}y = 2$ $(-3, 0), (0, 8)$

Find the equation of each line in slope-intercept form.

83. The line through $(6, 0)$ with slope $\frac{1}{2}$ $y = \frac{1}{2}x - 3$

84. The line through $(-3, 0)$ with slope $\frac{2}{3}$ $y = \frac{2}{3}x + 2$

85. The line through $(2, 3)$ that is parallel to $y = 9$ $y = 3$

86. The line through $(4, -5)$ that is perpendicular to $x = 1$ $y = -5$

87. The line through $(-3, 0)$ and $(0, 9)$ $y = 3x + 9$

88. The line through $(4, 0)$ and $(0, -6)$ $y = \frac{3}{2}x - 6$

89. The line through $(1, 1)$ and $(-2, 2)$ $y = -\frac{1}{3}x + \frac{4}{3}$

90. The line through $(-5, -3)$ and $(1, 1)$ $y = \frac{2}{3}x + \frac{1}{3}$

91. The line through (0, 2) that is perpendicular to $y = \frac{1}{4}x$
$y = -4x + 2$

92. The line through (0, 5) that is perpendicular to $y = -2x$
$y = \frac{1}{2}x + 5$

93. The line through (1, 2) that is parallel to $3x - y = 0$
$y = 3x - 1$

94. The line through $(2, -11)$ that is parallel to $y + 3x = 1$
$y = -3x - 5$

Chapter 3 Test

For each point, name the quadrant in which it lies or the axis on which it lies.

1. $(-2, 7)$ Quadrant II

2. $(-\pi, 0)$ x-axis

3. $(3, -6)$ Quadrant IV

4. $(0, 1785)$ y-axis

Find the slope of the line through each pair of points.

5. (3, 3) and (4, 4) 1

6. $(-2, -3)$ and $(4, -8)$ $-\frac{5}{6}$

Find the slope of each line.

7. The line $y = 3x - 5$ 3

8. The line $y = 3$ 0

9. The line $x = 5$ Undefined

10. The line $2x - 3y = 4$ $\frac{2}{3}$

Write the equation of each line. Give the answer in slope-intercept form.

11. The line through (0, 3) with slope $-\frac{1}{2}$ $y = -\frac{1}{2}x + 3$

12. The line through $(-1, -2)$ with slope $\frac{3}{7}$ $y = \frac{3}{7}x - \frac{11}{7}$

Write the equation of each line. Give the answer in standard form using only integers as the coefficients.

13. The line through $(2, -3)$ that is perpendicular to the line $y = -3x + 12$ $x - 3y = 11$

14. The line through (3, 4) that is parallel to the line $5x + 3y = 9$
$5x + 3y = 27$

Sketch the graph of each equation.

15. $y = \frac{1}{2}x - 3$

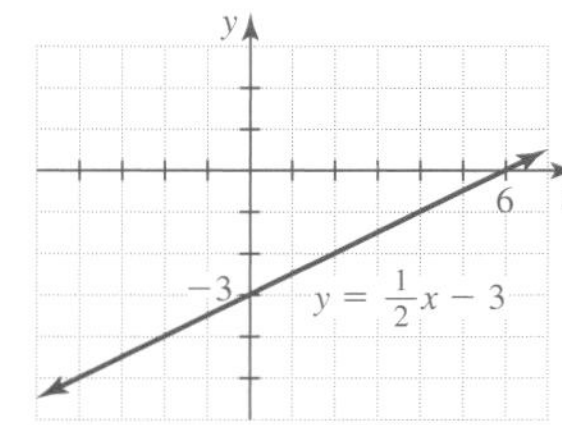

16. $2x - 3y = 6$

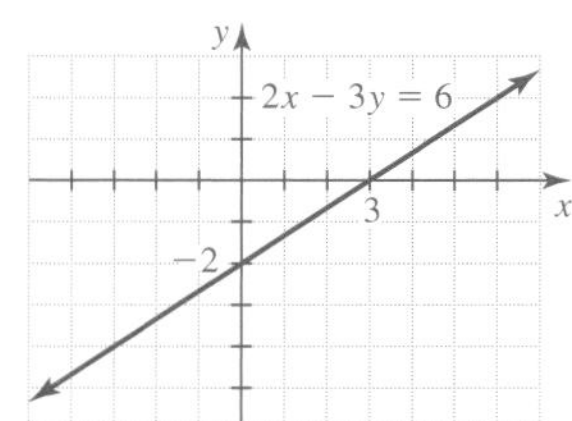

17. $y = 4$

18. $x = -2$

Solve each problem.

19. Julie's mail-order CD club charges a shipping and handling fee of \$2.50 plus \$0.75 per CD for each order shipped. Write the shipping and handling fee S in terms of the number n of CDs in the order. $S = 0.75n + 2.50$

20. A 10-ounce soft drink sells for 50 cents, and a 16-ounce soft drink sells for 68 cents. The price P is determined from the volume v of the cup by a linear equation.
a) Find the equation. $P = 3v + 20$
b) Find the price of a 20-ounce soft drink. 80 cents

21. The demand for tickets to a play can be modeled by the equation $d = 1000 - 20p$, where d is the number of tickets sold and p is the price per ticket in dollars.
a) How many tickets will be sold at \$10 per ticket? 800
b) Find the intercepts and interpret them.
(0, 1000), (50, 0); At \$0 per ticket 1000 tickets will be sold and at \$50 per ticket zero tickets will be sold.
c) Find and interpret the slope, including units.
−20 tickets/dollar; For every \$1 increase in price, 20 fewer tickets will be sold.

22. The price P for a watermelon varies directly with its weight w.
a) Write a formula for this variation. $P = kw$
b) If the price of a 30-pound watermelon is \$4.20, then what is the price of a 20-pound watermelon? \$2.80

23. The number n of days that Jerry spends on the road is inversely proportional to the amount A of his sales for the previous month.
a) Write a formula for this variation. $n = \frac{k}{A}$
b) Jerry spent 15 days on the road in February because his January sales amount was \$75,000. If his August sales amount is \$60,000, then how many days would he spend on the road in September? 18.75 days
c) Does his road time increase or decrease as his sales increase? Decreases

24. The cost C for installing ceramic floor tile in a rectangular room varies jointly with the length L and width W of the room.
a) Write a formula for this variation. $C = kLW$
b) The cost is \$400 for a room that is 8 feet by 10 feet. What is the cost for a room that is 11 feet by 14 feet?
\$770

Graph Paper

Use these grids for graphing. Make as many copies of this page as you need. If you have access to a computer, you can download this page from www.mhhe.com/dugopolski and print it.

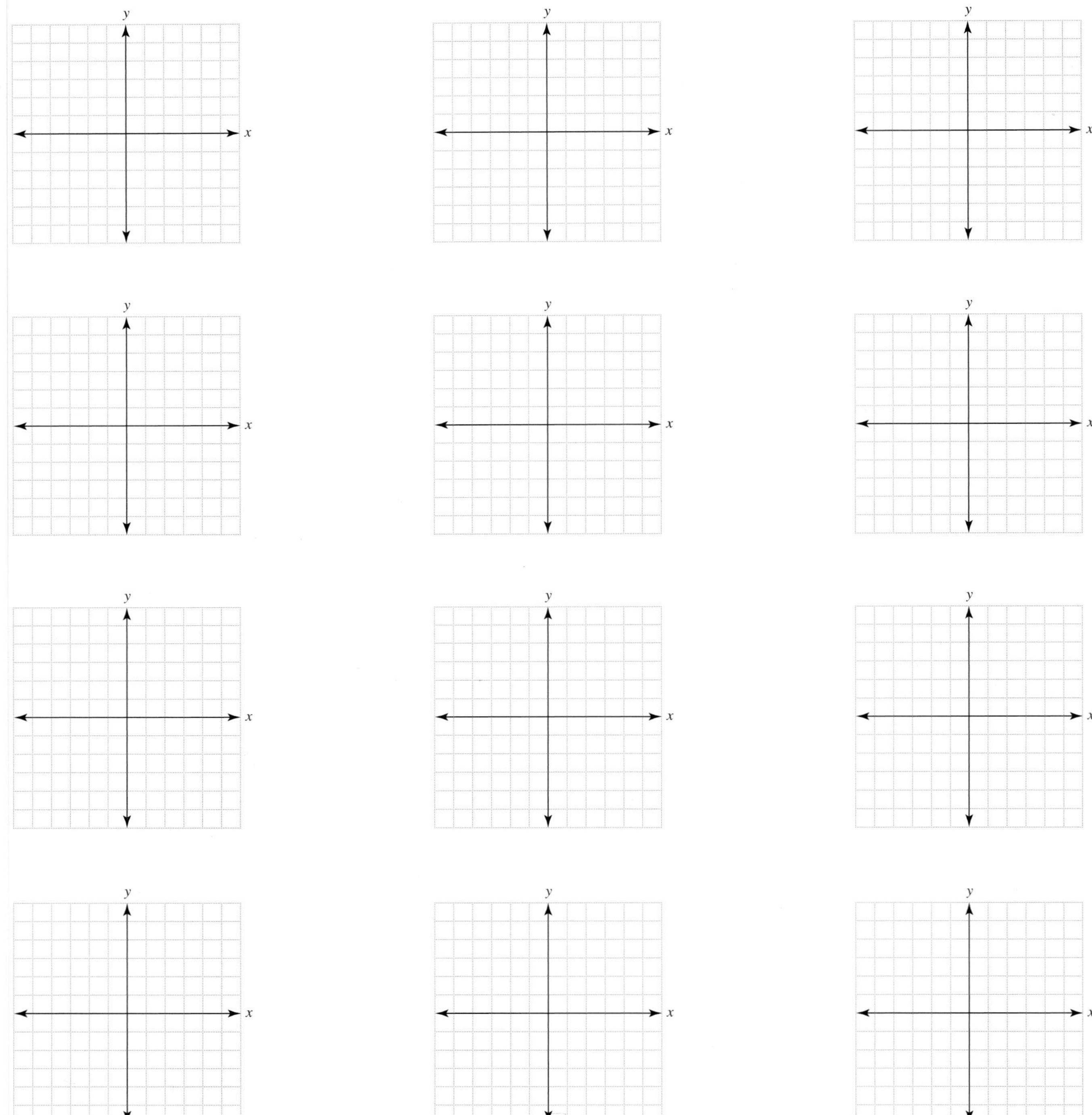

Making Connections | A Review of Chapters 1–3

Simplify each arithmetic expression.

1. $9 - 5 \cdot 2$ -1

2. $-4 \cdot 5 - 7 \cdot 2$ -34

3. $3^2 - 2^3$ 1

4. $3^2 \cdot 2^3$ 72

5. $(-4)^2 - 4(1)(5)$ -4

6. $-4^2 - 4 \cdot 3$ -28

7. $\dfrac{-5 - 9}{2 - (-2)}$ $-\dfrac{7}{2}$

8. $\dfrac{6 - 3.6}{6}$ 0.4

9. $\dfrac{1 - \frac{1}{2}}{4 - (-1)}$ $\dfrac{1}{10}$

10. $\dfrac{4 - (-6)}{1 - \frac{1}{3}}$ 15

Simplify the given expression or solve the given equation, whichever is appropriate.

11. $4x - (-9x)$ $13x$

12. $4(x - 9) - x$ $3x - 36$

13. $5(x - 3) + x = 0$ $\left\{\dfrac{5}{2}\right\}$

14. $5 - 2(x - 1) = x$ $\left\{\dfrac{7}{3}\right\}$

15. $\dfrac{1}{2} - \dfrac{1}{3}$ $\dfrac{1}{6}$

16. $\dfrac{1}{4} + \dfrac{1}{6}$ $\dfrac{5}{12}$

17. $\dfrac{1}{2}x - \dfrac{1}{3} = \dfrac{1}{4}x + \dfrac{1}{6}$ $\{2\}$

18. $\dfrac{2}{3}x + \dfrac{1}{5} = \dfrac{3}{5}x - \dfrac{1}{15}$ $\{-4\}$

19. $\dfrac{4x - 8}{2}$ $2x - 4$

20. $\dfrac{-5x - 10}{-5}$ $x + 2$

21. $\dfrac{6 - 2(x - 3)}{2} = 1$ $\{5\}$

22. $\dfrac{20 - 5(x - 5)}{5} = 6$ $\{3\}$

23. $-4(x - 9) - 4 = -4x$ $\varnothing$

24. $4(x - 6) = -4(6 - x)$ All real numbers

Solve each inequality. State the solution set using interval notation.

25. $2x - 3 > 6$ $(4.5, \infty)$

26. $5 - 3x < 7$ $\left(-\dfrac{2}{3}, \infty\right)$

27. $51 - 2x \le 3x + 1$ $[10, \infty)$

28. $4x - 80 \ge 60 - 3x$ $[20, \infty)$

29. $-1 < 4 - 2x \le 5$ $\left[-\dfrac{1}{2}, \dfrac{5}{2}\right)$

30. $1 - 2x \le x + 1 < 3 - 2x$ $\left[0, \dfrac{2}{3}\right)$

Solve each equation for y.

31. $3\pi y + 2 = t$ $y = \dfrac{t - 2}{3\pi}$

32. $x = \dfrac{y - b}{m}$ $y = mx + b$

33. $3x - 3y - 12 = 0$ $y = x - 4$

34. $2y - 3 = 9$ $y = 6$

35. $\dfrac{y}{2} - \dfrac{y}{4} = \dfrac{1}{5}$ $y = \dfrac{4}{5}$

36. $0.6y - 0.06y = 108$ $y = 200$

Solve.

37. ***Financial planning.*** Financial advisors at Fidelity Investments use the information in the accompanying graph as a guide for retirement investing.

a) What is the slope of the line segment for ages 35 through 50?

b) What is the slope of the line segment for ages 50 through 65?

c) If a 38-year-old man is making \$40,000 per year, then what percent of his income should he be saving?

d) If a 58-year-old woman has an annual salary of \$60,000, then how much should she have saved and how much should she be saving per year?

a) $\dfrac{2}{15}$ **b)** $\dfrac{1}{5}$ **c)** About 13% per year
d) \$276,000 saved, \$12,000 per year

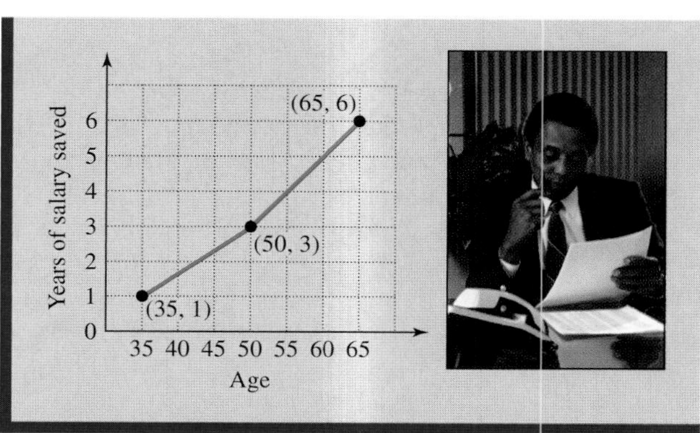

Figure for Exercise 37

Critical Thinking | For Individual or Group Work | Chapter 3

These exercises can be solved by a variety of techniques, which may or may not require algebra. So be creative and think critically. Explain all answers. Answers are in the Instructor's Edition of this text.

1. ***Share and share alike.*** A chocolate bar consists of two rows of small squares with four squares in each row as shown in (a) of the accompanying figure. You want to share it with your friends.

a) How many times must you break it to get it divided into 8 small squares?

b) If the bar has 3 rows of 5 squares in each row as shown in (b) of the accompanying figure, then how many breaks does it take to separate it into 15 small squares?

c) If the bar is divided into m rows with n small squares in each row, then how many breaks does it take to separate it into mn small squares?

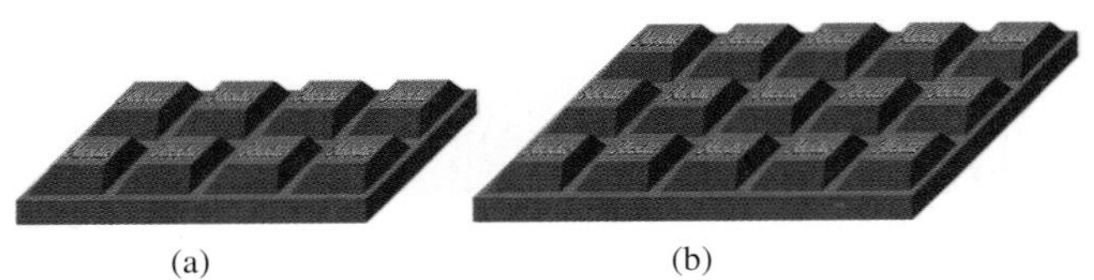

(a) (b)

Figure for Exercise 1

2. ***Straight time.*** Starting at 8 A.M. determine the number of times in the next 24 hours for which the hour and minute hands on a clock form a 180° angle.

3. ***Dividing days by months.*** For how many days of the year do you get a whole number when you divide the day number by the month number? For example, for December 24, the result of 24 divided by 12 is 2.

4. ***Crossword fanatic.*** Ms. Smith loves to work the crossword puzzle in her daily newspaper. To keep track of her efforts, she gives herself 2 points for every crossword puzzle that she completes correctly and deducts 3 points for every crossword puzzle that she fails to complete or completes incorrectly. For the month of June her total score was zero. How many puzzles did she solve correctly in June?

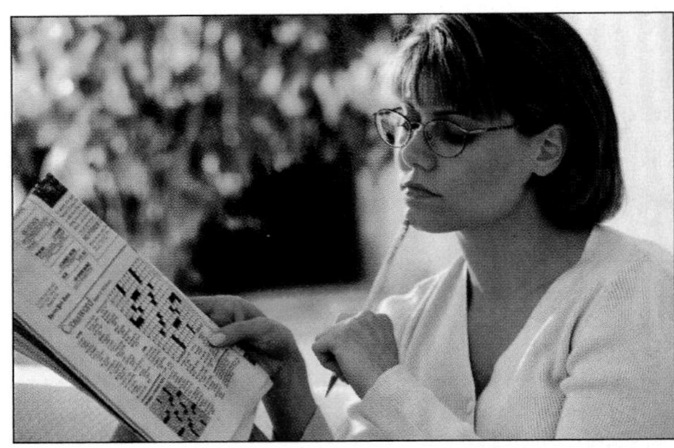

Photo for Exercise 4

5. ***Counting ones.*** If you write down the integers between 1 and 100 inclusive, then how many times will you write the number one?

6. ***Smallest sum.*** What is the smallest possible sum that can be obtained by adding five positive integers that have a product of 48?

7. ***Mind control.*** Each student in your class should think of an integer between 2 and 9 inclusive. Multiply your integer by 9. Think of the sum of the digits in your answer. Subtract 5 from your answer. Think of the letter in the alphabet that corresponds to the last answer. Think of a state that begins with that letter. Think of the second letter in the name of the state. Think of a large mammal that begins with that letter. Think of the color of that animal. What is the color that is on everyone's mind? Explain.

8. ***Four-digit numbers.*** How many four-digit whole numbers are there such that the thousands digit is odd, the hundreds digit is even, and all four digits are different? How many four-digit whole numbers are there such that the thousands digit is even, hundreds digit is odd, and all four digits are different?

1. a) 7 **b)** 14 **c)** $mn - 1$ **2.** 22 **3.** 90 **4.** 18 **5.** 21 **6.** 11 **7.** Fourth letter, Delaware, elephant, gray **8.** 1400, 1120

Chapter

Systems of Linear Equations and Inequalities

What determines the prices of the products that you buy? Why do prices of some products go down while the prices of others go up? Economists theorize that prices result from the collective decisions of consumers and producers. Ideally, the demand or quantity purchased by consumers depends only on the price, and price is a function of the supply. Theoretically, if the demand is greater than the supply, then prices rise and manufacturers produce more to meet the demand. As the supply of goods increases, the price comes down. The price at which the supply is equal to the demand is called the equilibrium price.

However, what happens in the real world does not always match the theory. Manufacturers cannot always control the supply, and factors other than price can affect a consumer's decision to buy. For example, droughts in Brazil decreased the supply of coffee and drove coffee prices up. Floods in California did the same to the prices of produce. With one of the most abundant wheat crops ever in 1994, cattle gained weight more quickly, increasing the supply of cattle ready for market. With supply going up, prices went down. Decreased demand for beef in Japan and Mexico drove the price of beef down further. With lower prices, consumers should be buying more beef, but increased competition from chicken and pork products, as well as health concerns, have kept consumer demand low.

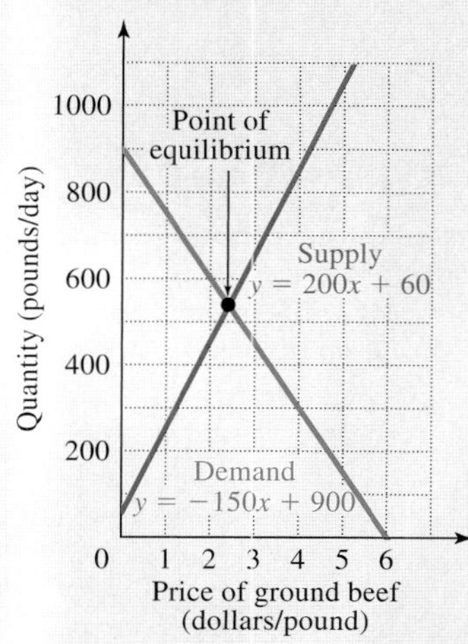

The two functions that govern supply and demand form a system of equations. In this chapter you will learn how to solve systems of equations.

In Exercise 57 of Section 4.2 you will see an example of supply and demand equations for ground beef.

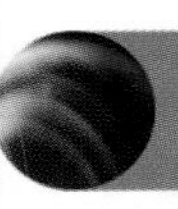

4.1 The Graphing Method

In This Section

You studied linear equations in two variables in Chapter 3. In this section, you will learn to solve systems of linear equations in two variables and use systems to solve problems.

⟨1⟩ Solving a System by Graphing

Consider the linear equation $y = 2x - 1$. The graph of this equation is a straight line, and every point on the line is a solution to the equation. Now consider a second linear equation, $x + y = 2$. The graph of this equation is also a straight line, and every point on the line is a solution to this equation. Taken together, the pair of equations

$$y = 2x - 1$$
$$x + y = 2$$

is called a **system of equations.** A point that satisfies both equations is called a **solution to the system.**

EXAMPLE 1

A solution to a system

Determine whether the point $(-1, 3)$ is a solution to each system of equations.

a) $3x - y = -6$
$x + 2y = 5$

b) $y = 2x - 1$
$x + y = 2$

Solution

a) If we let $x = -1$ and $y = 3$ in both equations of the system, we get the following equations:

$$3(-1) - 3 = -6 \quad \text{Correct}$$
$$-1 + 2(3) = 5 \quad \text{Correct}$$

Because both of these equations are correct, $(-1, 3)$ is a solution to the system.

b) If we let $x = -1$ and $y = 3$ in both equations of the system, we get the following equations:

$$3 = 2(-1) - 1 \quad \text{Incorrect}$$
$$-1 + 3 = 2 \quad \text{Correct}$$

Because the first equation is not satisfied by $(-1, 3)$, the point $(-1, 3)$ is not a solution to the system.

Now do Exercises 7–12

⟨ Calculator Close-Up ⟩

Solve both equations in Example 1(a) for y to get $y = 3x + 6$ and $y = (5 - x)/2$. The graphs show that $(-1, 3)$ is on both lines.

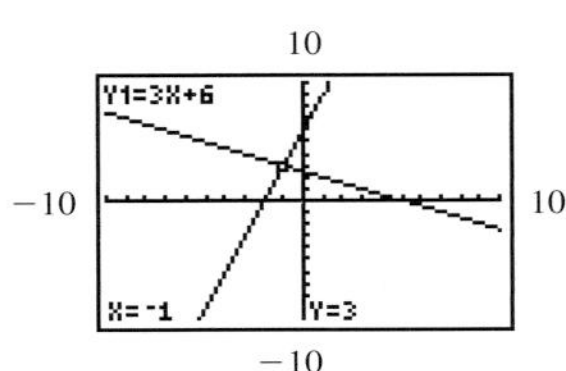

For Example 1(b), graph $y = 2x - 1$ and $y = 2 - x$ to see that $(-1, 3)$ is on one line but not the other.

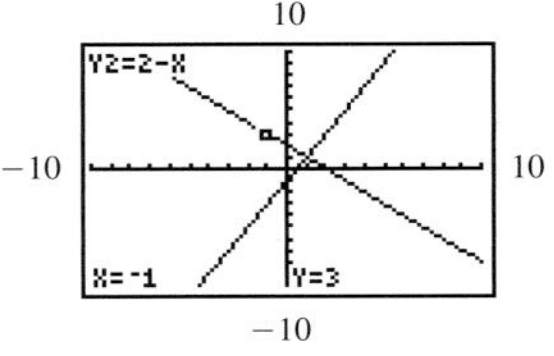

If we graph each equation of a system on the same coordinate plane, then we may be able to see the points that they have in common. Any point that is on both graphs is a solution to the system.

EXAMPLE 2

A system with exactly one solution

Solve the system by graphing:

$$y = 2x - 1$$
$$x + y = 2$$

Solution

We first write each equation in slope-intercept form:

$$y = 2x - 1$$
$$y = -x + 2$$

Use the y-intercept and the slope to draw the graphs as in Fig. 4.1. From the graph, it appears that these lines intersect at $(1, 1)$. To be certain, check that $(1, 1)$ satisfies both equations. Let $x = 1$ and $y = 1$ in the original equations:

$y = 2x - 1$	$x + y = 2$
$1 = 2(1) - 1$ Correct	$1 + 1 = 2$ Correct

Figure 4.1

Because these equations are both true, $(1, 1)$ is the solution to the system.

Now do Exercises 15–26

In Example 3, we graph the lines using the x- and y-intercepts.

EXAMPLE 3

A system with exactly one solution

Solve the system by graphing:

$$x - y = 6$$
$$2x + y = 6$$

Solution

We can graph these equations using their x- and y-intercepts. The intercepts for $x - y = 6$ are $(6, 0)$ and $(0, -6)$. The intercepts for $2x + y = 6$ are $(3, 0)$ and $(0, 6)$. Draw the graphs through the intercepts as shown in Fig. 4.2. The lines appear to cross at $(4, -2)$. To be certain, check $(4, -2)$ in both equations:

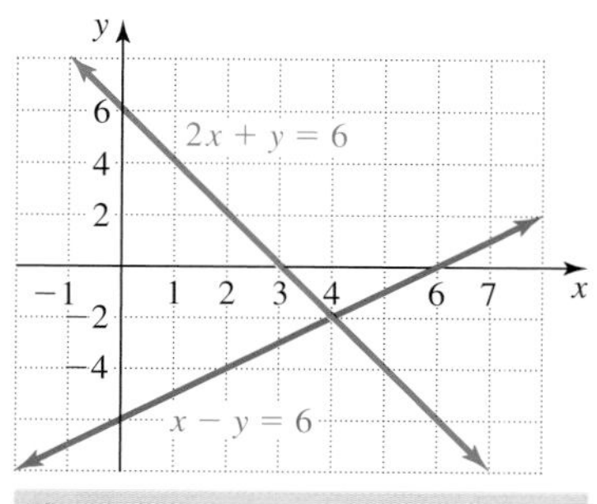

Figure 4.2

$x - y = 6$	$2x + y = 6$
$4 - (-2) = 6$ Correct	$2 \cdot 4 + (-2) = 6$ Correct

Because both of the equations are correct, $(4, -2)$ is the solution to the system.

Now do Exercises 27–30

EXAMPLE 4

A system with infinitely many solutions

Solve the system by graphing:

$$4x - 2y = 6$$
$$y - 2x = -3$$

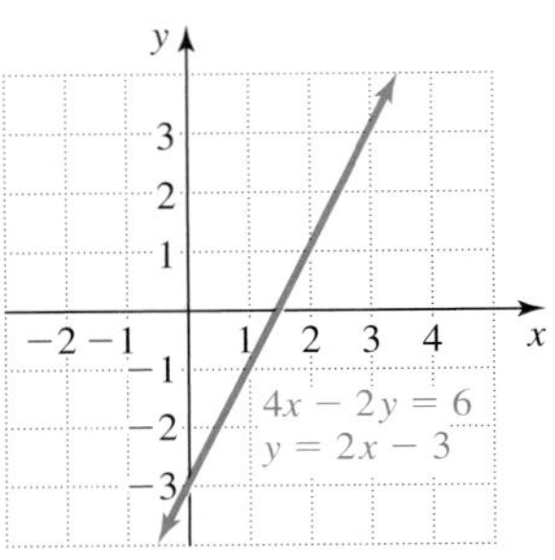

Figure 4.3

Solution

Rewrite both equations in slope-intercept form for easy graphing:

$$4x - 2y = 6 \qquad\qquad y - 2x = -3$$
$$-2y = -4x + 6 \qquad\qquad y = 2x - 3$$
$$y = 2x - 3$$

By writing the equations in slope-intercept form, we discover that they are identical. So the equations have the same graph, which is shown in Fig. 4.3. So any point on that line satisfies both of the equations and there are infinitely many solutions to the system. The solution set consists of all points on the line $y = 2x - 3$, which is written in set notation as

$$\{(x, y) \mid y = 2x - 3\}.$$

Now do Exercises 39–42

In Example 4 we read $\{(x, y) \mid y = 2x - 3\}$ as "the set of ordered pairs (x, y) such that $y = 2x - 3$." Note that we could have used $4x - 2y = 6$ or $y - 2x = -3$ in place of $y = 2x - 3$ in set notation since these three equations are equivalent. We usually choose the simplest equation for set notation.

EXAMPLE 5

A system with no solution

Solve the system by graphing:

$$3y = 2x - 6$$
$$2x - 3y = 3$$

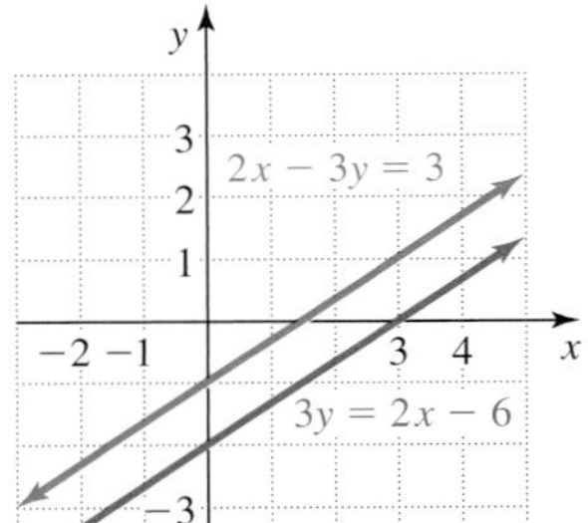

Figure 4.4

Solution

Write each equation in slope-intercept form to get the following system:

$$y = \frac{2}{3}x - 2$$

$$y = \frac{2}{3}x - 1$$

Each line has slope $\frac{2}{3}$, but they have different y-intercepts. Their graphs are shown in Fig. 4.4. Because these two lines have equal slopes, they are parallel. There is no point of intersection and no solution to the system.

Now do Exercises 43–46

‹2› Types of Systems

A system of equations that has at least one solution is **consistent** (Examples 2, 3, and 4). A system with no solutions is **inconsistent** (Example 5). There are two types of consistent systems. A consistent system with exactly one solution is **independent** (Examples 2 and 3) and a consistent system with infinitely many solutions is **dependent** (Example 4). These ideas are summarized in Fig. 4.5.

You can classify a system as independent, dependent, or inconsistent by examining the slope-intercept form of each equation, as shown in Example 6.

‹ Teaching Tip ›

To illustrate independence ask each student to secretly write down an equation in standard form. Collect them and see if the graphs of any two are parallel or coincident lines.

Consistent systems:

Independent
Exactly one solution

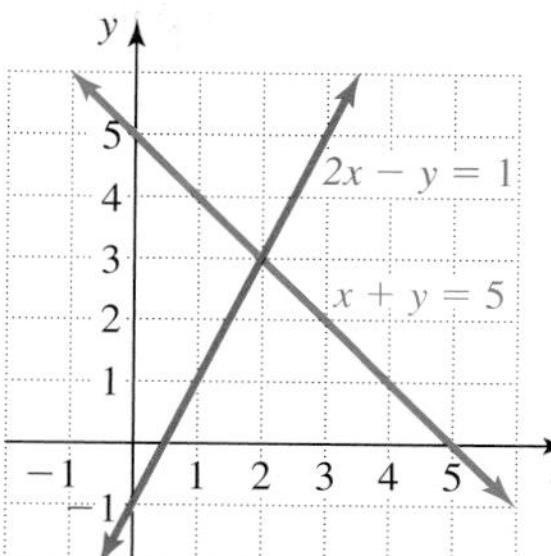

Dependent
Infinitely many solutions

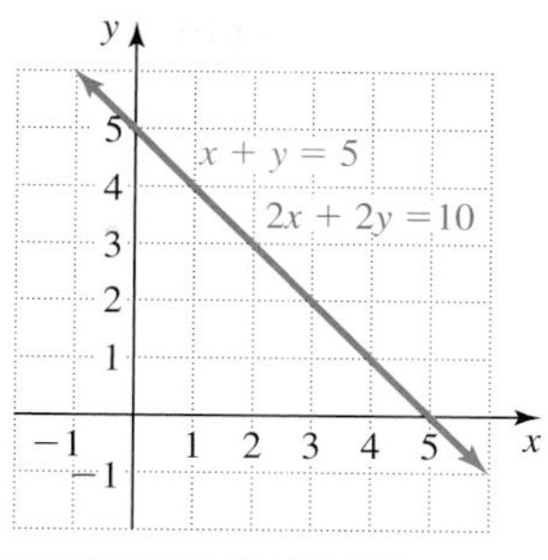

Inconsistent system:

No solution

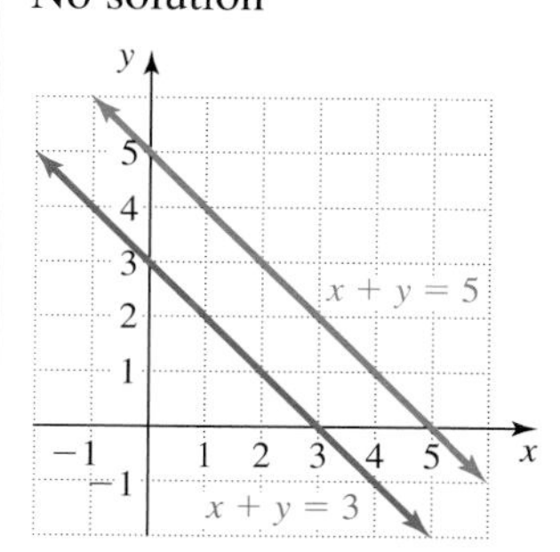

Figure 4.5

EXAMPLE 6

Types of systems

Determine whether each system is independent, dependent, or inconsistent.

a) $y = 3x - 5$
$y = 3x + 2$

b) $y = 2x + 3$
$y = -2x + 5$

c) $y = 5x - 1$
$2y - 10x = -2$

Solution

a) Since $y = 3x - 5$ and $y = 3x + 2$ have the same slope and different y-intercepts, the two lines are parallel. There is no point of intersection. The system is inconsistent.

b) Since $y = 2x + 3$ and $y = -2x + 5$ have different slopes, they are not parallel. These two lines intersect at a single point. The system is independent.

c) First rewrite the second equation in slope-intercept form:

$$\begin{aligned} 2y - 10x &= -2 \\ 2y &= 10x - 2 \\ y &= 5x - 1 \end{aligned}$$

Since the first equation is also $y = 5x - 1$, these are two different-looking equations for the same line. So every point on that line satisfies both equations. The system is dependent.

Now do Exercises 47–60

‹ Calculator Close-Up ›

With a graphing calculator, you can graph both equations of a system in a single viewing window. The TRACE feature can then be used to estimate the solution to an independent system. You could also use ZOOM to "blow up" the intersection and get more accuracy. Many calculators have an intersect feature, which can find a point of intersection. First graph $y_1 = 2x - 1$ and $y_2 = 2 - x$.

From the CALC menu choose intersect.

Verify the curves (or lines) that you want to intersect by pressing ENTER. After you make a guess as to the intersection by positioning the cursor or entering a number, the calculator will find the intersection.

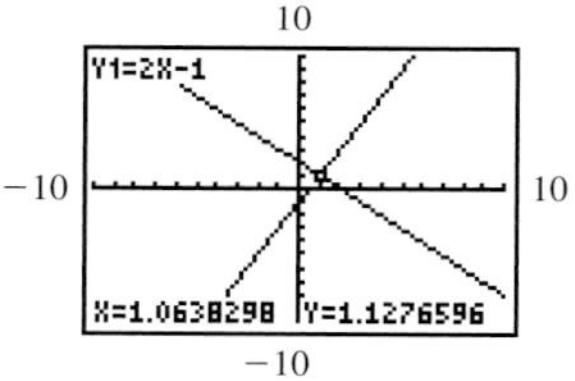


```
CALCULATE
1:value
2:zero
3:minimum
4:maximum
5:intersect
6:dy/dx
7:∫f(x)dx
```

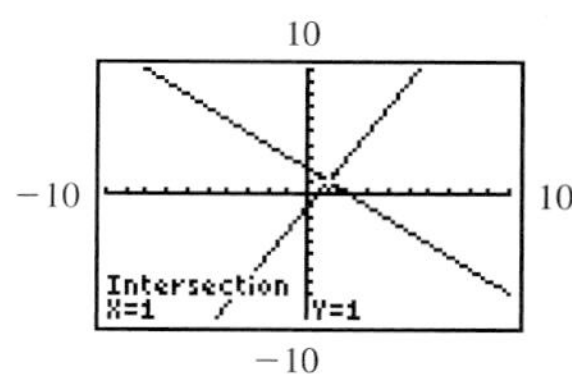

⟨3⟩ Applications

In a simple economic model, both supply and demand depend only on price. **Supply** is the quantity of an item that producers are willing to make or supply. **Demand** is the quantity consumers will purchase. As the price increases, producers increase the supply to take advantage of rising prices. However, as the price increases, consumer demand decreases. The **equilibrium price** is the price at which supply equals demand.

EXAMPLE 7 Supply and demand

Monthly demand for Greeny Babies (small toy frogs) is given by the equation $y = 8000 - 400x$, while monthly supply is given by the equation $y = 400x$, where x is the price in dollars. Graph the two equations and find the equilibrium price and the demand at the equilibrium price.

Solution

The graph of $y = 8000 - 400x$ goes through (0, 8000) and (20, 0). The graph of $y = 400x$ goes through (0, 0) and (20, 8000). The two lines cross at (10, 4000) as shown in Fig. 4.6. So the equilibrium price is \$10 and the monthly demand is 4000 Greeny Babies.

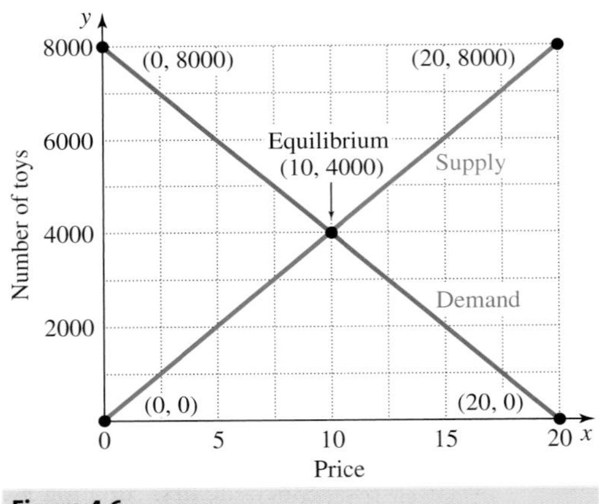

Figure 4.6

Now do Exercises 71–74

Warm-Ups ▼

True or false? Explain your answer.

The statements refer to the following systems:

a) $y = 2x - 5$
$y = -2x - 5$

b) $y = 3x - 4$
$y = 3x + 5$

c) $x + y = 9$
$y = 9 - x$

1. The ordered pair $(1, -3)$ satisfies the equation $y = 2x - 5$. True
2. The ordered pair $(1, -3)$ satisfies the equation $y = -2x - 5$. False
3. The ordered pair $(1, -3)$ is a solution to system (a). False
4. System (a) is inconsistent. False
5. System (b) has no solution. True

6. The equations of system (b) are inconsistent. True

7. System (c) is dependent. True

8. The set of ordered pairs that satisfy system (c) is $\{(x, y) \mid y = 9 - x\}$. True

9. Two distinct straight lines in the coordinate plane either are parallel or intersect each other in exactly one point. True

10. Any system of two linear equations can be solved by graphing. False

Exercises 4.1

Boost your grade at mathzone.com!
- Practice Problems
- NetTutor
- Self-Tests
- e-Professors
- Videos

‹ Study Tips ›

- Working problems 1 hour per day every day of the week is better than working problems for 7 hours on one day of the week. Spread out your study time. Avoid long study sessions.
- No two students learn in exactly the same way or at the same speed. Figure out what works for you.

Reading and Writing *After reading this section, write out the answers to these questions. Use complete sentences.*

1. What is a system of equations?
A system of equations is a pair of equations.

2. What is a solution to a system of equations?
A solution to a system is a point or ordered pair that satisfies both equations.

3. What method was used to solve a system of equations?
In this section systems of equations were solved by graphing.

4. What is an independent system?
An independent system is a system with exactly one solution.

5. What is a dependent system?
A dependent system is one that has infinitely many solutions.

6. What is an inconsistent system?
An inconsistent system is one that has no solution.

‹1› Solving a System by Graphing

Which of the given points is a solution to the given system? See Example 1.

7. $2x + y = 4$ $(6, 1), (3, -2), (2, 4)$
$x - y = 5$ $(3, -2)$

VIDEO **8.** $2x - 3y = -5$ $(-1, 1), (3, 4), (2, 3)$
$y = x + 1$ $(2, 3)$

9. $6x - 2y = 4$ $(0, -2), (2, 4), (3, 7)$
$y = 3x - 2$ All three

10. $y = -2x + 5$ $(9, -13), (-1, 7), (0, 5)$
$4x + 2y = 10$ All three

11. $2x - y = 3$ $(3, 3), (5, 7), (7, 11)$
$2x - y = 2$ None

12. $y = x + 5$ $(1, -2), (3, 0), (6, 3)$
$y = x - 3$ None

Use the given graph to find an ordered pair that satisfies each system of equations. Check that your answer satisfies both equations of each system.

13. $y = 3x + 9$
$2x + 3y = 5$

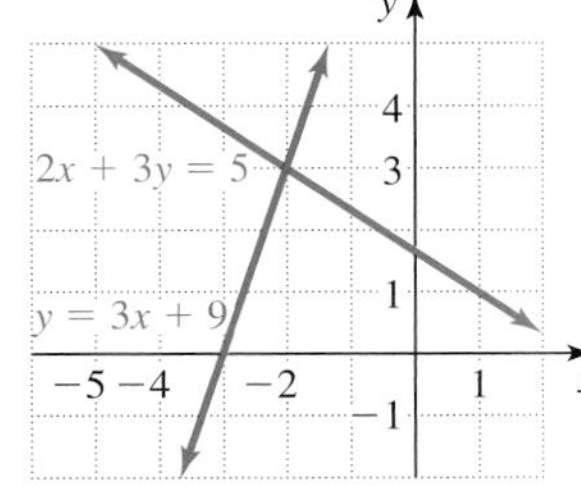

$(-2, 3)$

14. $x - 2y = 5$
$y = -\frac{2}{3}x + 1$

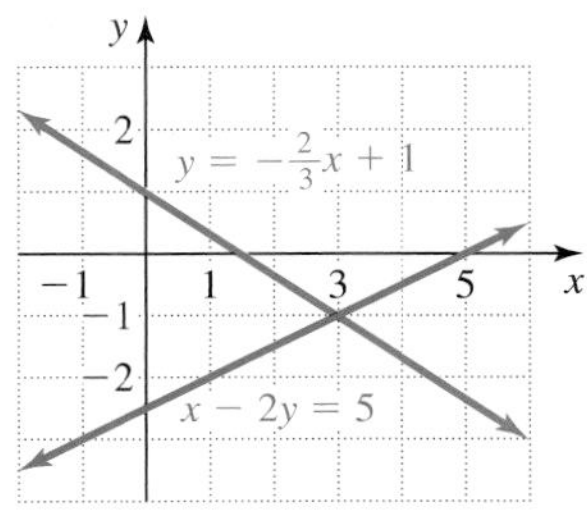

$(3, -1)$

Solve each system by graphing. See Examples 2 and 3.

15. $y = 2x$
$y = -x + 6$ (2, 4)

16. $y = 3x$
$y = -x + 4$ (1, 3)

17. $3x - y = 1$
$2y - 3x = 1$ (1, 2)

VIDEO **18.** $2x + y = 3$
$x + y = 1$ (2, −1)

19. $x - y = 5$
$x + y = -5$ (0, −5)

20. $y + 4x = 10$
$2x - y = 2$ (2, 2)

21. $2y + x = 4$
$2x - y = -7$ (−2, 3)

22. $2x + y = -1$
$x + y = -2$ (1, −3)

23. $y = x$
$x + y = 0$ (0, 0)

24. $x = 2y$
$0 = 9x - y$ (0, 0)

25. $y = 2x - 1$
$x - 2y = -4$ (2, 3)

26. $y = x - 1$
$2x - y = 0$ (−1, −2)

27. $x - y = 2$
$x + 3y = 6$ (3, 1)

28. $x - y = -1$
$3x - y = 3$ (2, 3)

29. $x - 2y = -8$
$3x - 2y = -12$ (−2, 3)

30. $x + 3y = 9$
$2x + 3y = 12$ (3, 2)

Solve each system by graphing both equations on a graphing calculator and using the intersection feature of the calculator to find the point of intersection.

31. $y = x + 5$
$y = 9 - x$ (2, 7)

32. $y = 2x + 1$
$y = 5 - 2x$ (1, 3)

33. $y = 3x - 18$
$y = 32 - 2x$ (10, 12)

34. $y = -x + 26$
$y = 2x - 34$ (20, 6)

35. $x + y = 12$
$3x + 2y = 14$ (−10, 22)

36. $x - y = -10$
$x - 4y = 20$ (−20, −10)

37. $x + 5y = -1$
$x - 5y = 2$
(0.5, −0.3)

38. $x + y = 0.6$
$2y + 3x = -0.5$
(−1.7, 2.3)

Solve each system by graphing. See Examples 4 and 5.

39. $x - y = 3$
$3x = 3y + 9$ $\{(x, y) \mid x - y = 3\}$

40. $2x + y = 3$
$6x - 9 = -3y$ $\{(x, y) \mid 2x + y = 3\}$

41. $4y - 2x = -16$
$x - 2y = 8$ $\{(x, y) \mid x - 2y = 8\}$

VIDEO **42.** $x - y = 0$
$5x = 5y$ $\{(x, y) \mid y = x\}$

43. $x - y = 3$
$3x = 3y + 12$ No solution

44. $2y = -3x + 6$
$2y = -3x - 2$ No solution

45. $x + y = 4$
$2y = -2x + 6$ No solution

46. $y = 3x - 5$
$y - 3x = 0$ No solution

‹2› Types of Systems

Determine whether each system is independent, dependent, or inconsistent. See Example 6.

47. $y = \frac{1}{2}x + 3$
$y = \frac{1}{2}x - 5$ Inconsistent

48. $y = -3x - 60$
$y = \frac{1}{3}x - 60$ Independent

49. $y = 4x + 3$
$y = 3 + 4x$ Dependent

50. $y = 5x - 4$
$y = 4 + 5x$ Inconsistent

51. $y = \frac{1}{2}x + 3$
$y = -3x - 1$ Independent

52. $y = -x - 1$
$y = -1 - x$ Dependent

53. $2x - 3y = 5$
$2x - 3y = 7$ Inconsistent

54. $x + y = 1$
$2x + 2y = 2$ Dependent

Use the following graphs to determine whether the systems in Exercises 55–60 are independent, dependent, or inconsistent.

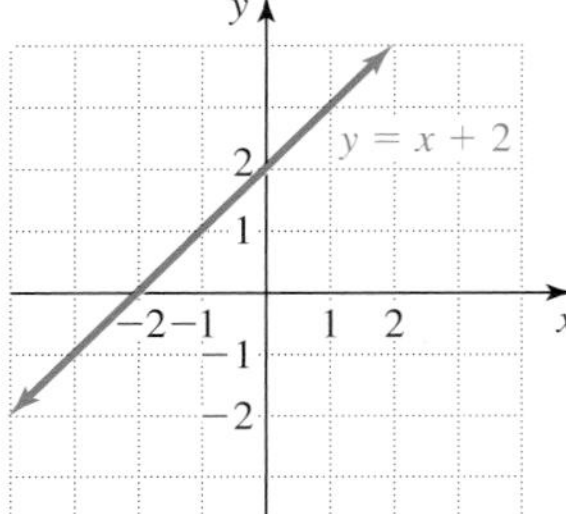

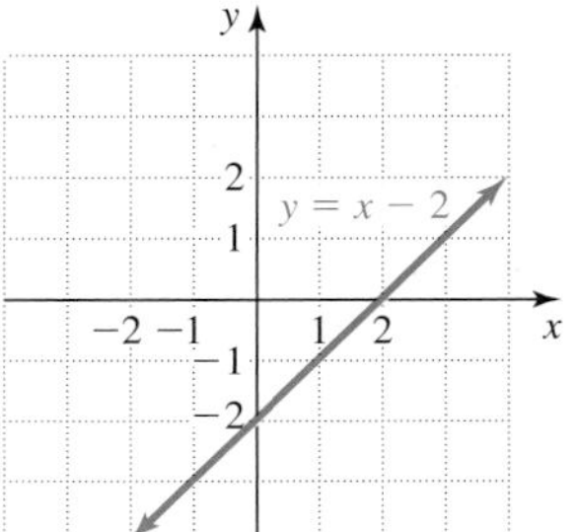

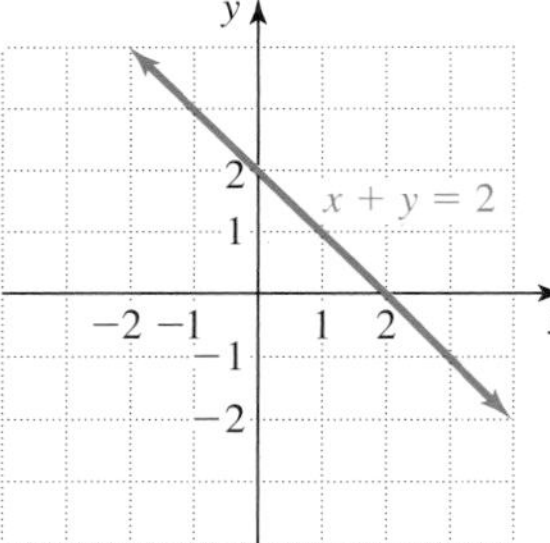

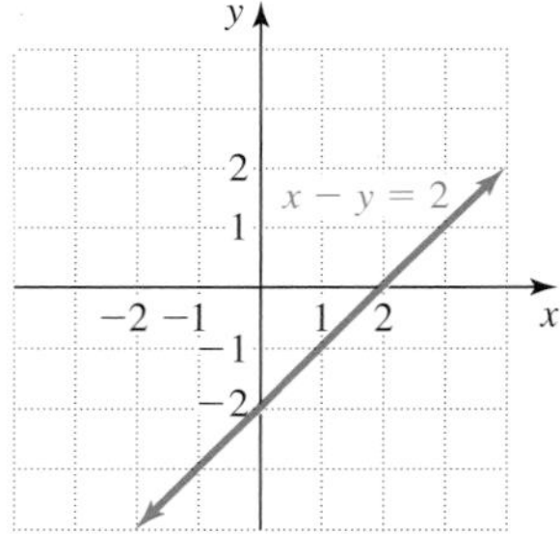

55. $y = x - 2$
$y = x + 2$ Inconsistent

56. $y = x - 2$
$x - y = 2$ Dependent

57. $y = x + 2$
$x + y = 2$ Independent

58. $y = x - 2$
$x + y = 2$ Independent

59. $y = x + 2$
$x - y = 2$ Inconsistent

60. $x - y = 2$
$x + y = 2$ Independent

Solve each system by graphing. Indicate whether each system is independent, dependent, or inconsistent. See Examples 2–6.

VIDEO **61.** $x - y = 3$
$3x = y + 5$ (1, −2), independent

62. $3x + 2y = 6$
$2x - y = 4$ (2, 0), independent

63. $x - y = 5$
$x - y = 8$ No solution, inconsistent

64. $y + 3x = 6$
$y - 5 = -3x$ No solution, inconsistent

65. $y = \frac{1}{3}x + 2$
$y = -\frac{1}{3}x$ $(-3, 1)$, independent

66. $y - 4x = 4$
$y + 4x = -4$ $(-1, 0)$, independent

67. $x - y = 1$
$-2y = -2x + 2$ $\{(x, y) \mid x - y = 1\}$, dependent

68. $x = \frac{1}{3}y$
$y = 3x$ $\{(x, y) \mid y = 3x\}$, dependent

69. $x - y = -1$
$y = \frac{1}{2}x - 1$ $(-4, -3)$, independent

70. $y = -3x + 1$
$2 - 2y = 6x$ $\{(x, y) \mid y = -3x + 1\}$, dependent

‹3› Applications

Solve each problem by using the graphing method. See Example 7.

71. ***Competing pizzas.*** Mamma's Pizza charges \$10 plus \$2 per topping for a deep dish pizza. Papa's Pizza charges \$5 plus \$3 per topping for a similar pizza. The equations $C = 2n + 10$ and $C = 3n + 5$ express the cost C at each restaurant in terms of the number of toppings n.

a) Solve this system of equations by examining the accompanying graph. (5, 20)

b) Interpret the solution.
For 5 toppings the cost is \$20 at both restaurants.

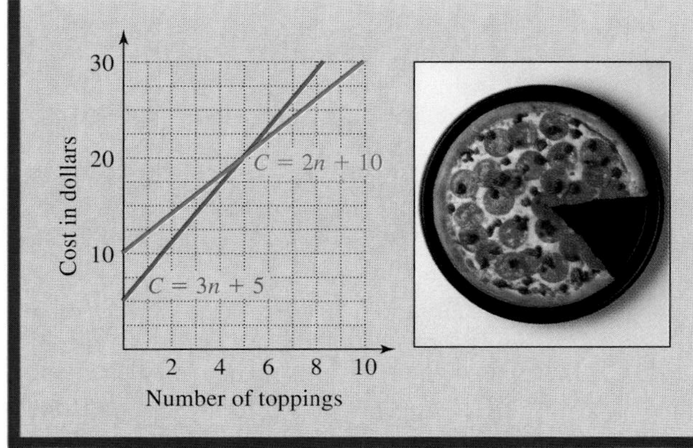

Figure for Exercise 71

72. ***Equilibrium price.*** A manufacturer plans to supply y units of its model 1020P CD player per month when the retail price is p dollars per player, where $y = 6p + 100$. Consumer studies show that consumer demand for the model 1020P is y units per month, where $y = -3p + 910$.

a) Fill in the missing entries in the following table.

Price	Supply	Demand
\$ 0	100	910
50	400	760
100	700	610
300	1900	10

b) Use the data in part (a) to graph both linear equations on the same coordinate system.

c) What is the price at which the supply is equal to the demand, the *equilibrium price?* \$90

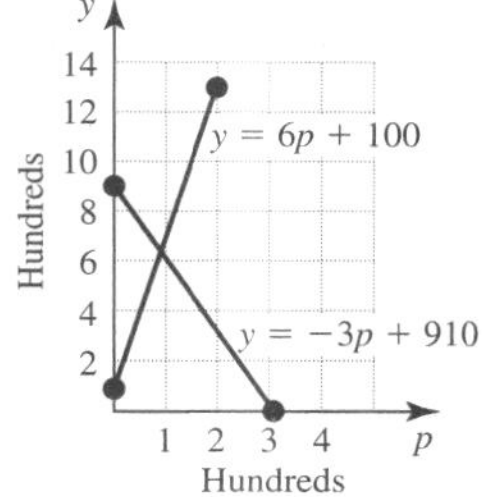

73. ***Cost of two copiers.*** An office manager figures the total cost in dollars for a certain used Xerox copier is given by $C = 800 + 0.05x$, where x is the number of copies made. She is also considering a used Panasonic copier for which the total cost is $C = 500 + 0.07x$.

a) Fill in the missing entries in the following table.

Number of Copies	Cost Xerox	Cost Panasonic
0	\$ 800	\$ 500
5000	1050	850
10,000	1300	1200
20,000	1800	1900

b) Use the data from part (a) to graph both equations on the same coordinate system.

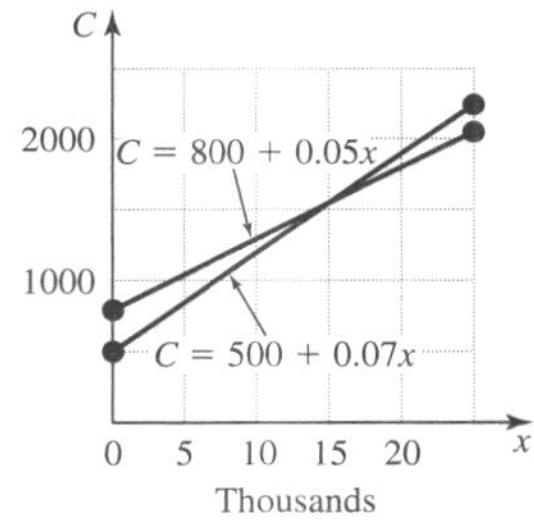

c) For what number of copies is the total cost the same for either copier?
15,000

d) If she plans to buy another copier before 10,000 copies are made, then which copier is cheaper?
Panasonic

74. ***Flat tax proposals.*** Representative Schneider has proposed a flat income tax of 15% on earnings in excess of \$10,000. Under his proposal the tax T for a person earning E dollars is given by $T = 0.15(E - 10{,}000)$. Representative Humphries has proposed that the income tax should be 20% on earnings in excess of \$20,000, or $T = 0.20(E - 20{,}000)$. Graph both linear equations on the same coordinate system. For what earnings would you pay the same amount of income tax under either plan? Under which plan does a rich person pay less income tax?
\$50,000, Schneider's plan

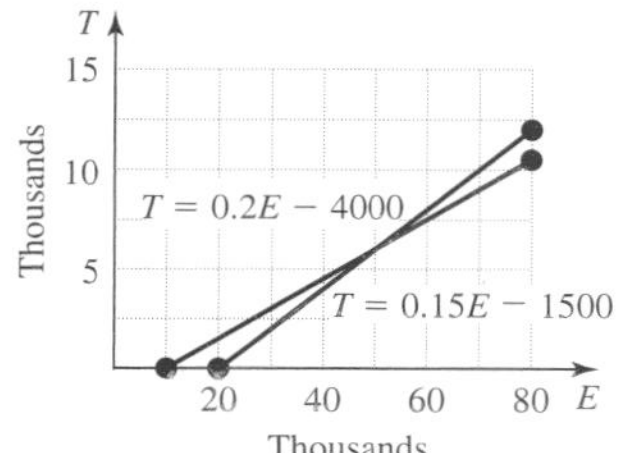

Getting More Involved

75. *Discussion*

If both $(-1, 3)$ and $(2, 7)$ satisfy a system of two linear equations, then what can you say about the system?
It is a dependent system.

76. *Cooperative learning*

Working in groups, write an independent system of two linear equations whose solution is $(3, 5)$. Each group should then give its system to another group to solve. $x + y = 8,\ x - y = -2$

77. *Cooperative learning*

Working in groups, write an inconsistent system of linear equations such that $(-2, 3)$ satisfies one equation and $(1, 4)$ satisfies the other. Each group should then give its system to another group to solve. $x + y = 1,\ x + y = 5$

78. *Cooperative learning*

Suppose that $2x + 3y = 6$ is one equation of a system. Find the second equation given that $(4, 8)$ satisfies the second equation and the system is inconsistent.
$2x + 3y = 32$

Graphing Calculator Exercises

Solve each system by graphing each pair of equations on a graphing calculator and using the calculator to estimate the point of intersection. Give the coordinates of the intersection to the nearest tenth.

79. $y = 2.5x - 6.2$

$y = -1.3x + 8.1$ $(3.8, 3.2)$

80. $y = 305x + 200$

$y = -201x - 999$ $(-2.4, -522.7)$

81. $2.2x - 3.1y = 3.4$

$5.4x + 6.2y = 7.3$ $(1.4, -0.1)$

82. $34x - 277y = 1$

$402x + 306y = 12{,}000$ $(27.3, 3.3)$

4.2 The Substitution Method

In This Section

⟨1⟩ Solving a System by Substitution
⟨2⟩ Dependent and Inconsistent Systems
⟨3⟩ Applications

Solving a system by graphing is certainly limited by the accuracy of the graph. If the lines intersect at a point whose coordinates are not integers, then it is difficult to identify the solution from a graph. In this section we introduce a method for solving systems of linear equations in two variables that does not depend on a graph and is totally accurate.

⟨1⟩ Solving a System by Substitution

To solve a system by **substitution** we replace a variable in one equation by an equivalent expression for that variable (obtained from the other equation). The result should be an equation in only one variable, which we can solve by the usual techniques.

EXAMPLE 1

Solving a system by substitution

Solve:

$$3x + 4y = 5$$
$$x = y - 1$$

Solution

Because the second equation states that $x = y - 1$, we can substitute $y - 1$ for x in the first equation:

$$\begin{aligned} 3x + 4y &= 5 \\ 3(y - 1) + 4y &= 5 \quad \text{Replace } x \text{ with } y - 1. \\ 3y - 3 + 4y &= 5 \quad \text{Simplify.} \\ 7y - 3 &= 5 \\ 7y &= 8 \\ y &= \frac{8}{7} \end{aligned}$$

Now use the value $y = \frac{8}{7}$ in one of the original equations to find x. The simplest one to use is $x = y - 1$:

$$x = \frac{8}{7} - 1$$
$$x = \frac{1}{7}$$

Check that $\left(\frac{1}{7}, \frac{8}{7}\right)$ satisfies both equations. The solution to the system is $\left(\frac{1}{7}, \frac{8}{7}\right)$.

Now do Exercises 7–14

‹ Calculator Close-Up ›

To check Example 1, graph

$$y_1 = (5 - 3x)/4$$

and

$$y_2 = x + 1.$$

Use the intersect feature of your calculator to find the point of intersection.

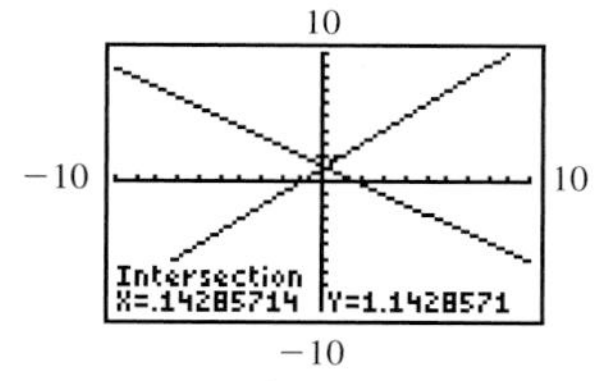

For substitution we must have one of the equations solved for x or y in terms of the other variable. In Example 1 we were given $x = y - 1$. So we replaced x with $y - 1$. In Example 2 we must rewrite one of the equations before substituting. Note how the five steps in the following strategy are used in Example 2.

Strategy for Solving a System by Substitution

1. If necessary, solve one of the equations for one variable in terms of the other. Choose the equation that is easiest to solve for x or y.
2. Substitute into the other equation to eliminate one of the variables.
3. Solve the resulting equation in one variable.
4. Insert the solution found in the last step into one of the original equations and solve for the other variable.
5. Check your solution in both equations.

EXAMPLE 2

Solving a system by substitution

Solve:

$$2x - 3y = 9$$
$$y - 4x = -8$$

‹ Teaching Tip ›

Caution students about getting the signs correct when using the distributive property in the substitution method.

Solution

(1) Solve the second equation for y:

$$y - 4x = -8$$
$$y = 4x - 8$$

(2) Substitute $4x - 8$ for y in the first equation:

$$2x - 3y = 9$$
$$2x - 3(4x - 8) = 9 \quad \text{Replace } y \text{ with } 4x - 8.$$

(3) Solve the equation for x:

$$2x - 12x + 24 = 9 \quad \text{Simplify.}$$
$$-10x + 24 = 9$$
$$-10x = -15$$
$$x = \frac{-15}{-10}$$
$$= \frac{3}{2}$$

(4) Use the value $x = \frac{3}{2}$ in $y = 4x - 8$ to find y:

$$y = 4 \cdot \frac{3}{2} - 8$$
$$= -2$$

(5) Check $x = \frac{3}{2}$ and $y = -2$ in both of the original equations:

$$2\left(\frac{3}{2}\right) - 3(-2) = 9 \quad \text{Correct}$$
$$-2 - 4\left(\frac{3}{2}\right) = -8 \quad \text{Correct}$$

Since both are correct, the solution to the system is $\left(\frac{3}{2}, -2\right)$.

Now do Exercises 15–22

‹2› Dependent and Inconsistent Systems

Examples 3 and 4 illustrate how to solve dependent and inconsistent systems by substitution.

EXAMPLE 3

A system with infinitely many solutions

Solve:

$$2(y - x) = x + y - 1$$
$$y = 3x - 1$$

Solution

Because the second equation is solved for y, we will eliminate the variable y in the substitution. Substitute $y = 3x - 1$ into the first equation:

$$2(3x - 1 - x) = x + (3x - 1) - 1$$
$$2(2x - 1) = 4x - 2$$
$$4x - 2 = 4x - 2$$

Every real number satisfies $4x - 2 = 4x - 2$ because both sides are identical. So every real number can be used for x in the original system as long as we choose $y = 3x - 1$. The system is dependent. The graphs of these two equations are the same line. So the solution to the system is the set of all points on that line, $\{(x, y) \mid y = 3x - 1\}$.

Now do Exercises 23–26

EXAMPLE 4

A system with no solution

Solve by substitution:

$$3x - 6y = 9$$
$$x = 2y + 5$$

Solution

Use $x = 2y + 5$ to replace x in the first equation:

$$3x - 6y = 9$$
$$3(2y + 5) - 6y = 9 \quad \text{Replace } x \text{ by } 2y + 5.$$
$$6y + 15 - 6y = 9 \quad \text{Simplify.}$$
$$15 = 9$$

No values for x and y will make 15 equal to 9. So there is no ordered pair that satisfies both equations. This system is inconsistent. It has no solution. The equations are the equations of parallel lines.

Now do Exercises 27–32

‹ Calculator Close-Up ›

To check Example 4, graph $y_1 = (3x - 9)/6$ and $y_2 = (x - 5)/2$. Since the lines appear to be parallel, there is no solution to the system.

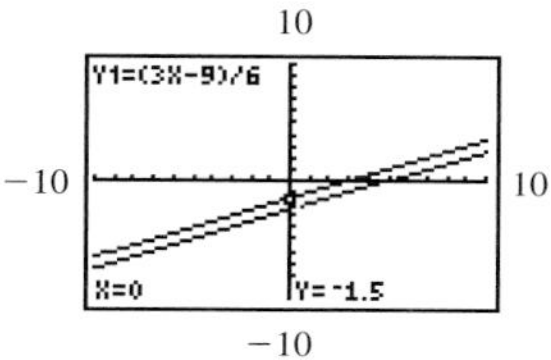

‹ Helpful Hint ›

The purpose of Examples 3 and 4 is to show what happens when substitution is used on dependent and inconsistent systems. If we had first written the equations in slope-intercept form, we would see that the lines in Example 3 are the same, and the lines in Example 4 are parallel.

When solving a system by substitution we can recognize a dependent system or an inconsistent system as follows.

Recognizing Dependent or Inconsistent Systems

Substitution in a dependent system results in an equation that is always true.
Substitution in an inconsistent system results in a false equation.

‹3› Applications

Many of the problems that we solved in previous chapters had two unknown quantities, but we wrote only one equation to solve the problem. For problems with two unknown quantities we can use two variables and a system of equations.

EXAMPLE 5

Two investments

Mrs. Robinson invested a total of \$25,000 in two investments, one paying 6% and the other paying 8%. If her total income from these investments was \$1790, then how much money did she invest in each?

Solution

Let x represent the amount invested at 6%, and let y represent the amount invested at 8%. The following table organizes the given information.

	Interest Rate	Amount Invested	Amount of Interest
First investment	6%	x	$0.06x$
Second investment	8%	y	$0.08y$

Helpful Hint

In Chapter 2, we would have done Example 5 with one variable by letting x represent the amount invested at 6% and $25{,}000 - x$ represent the amount invested at 8%.

Teaching Tip

Note that the decimals could be eliminated by multiplying by 100.

Calculator Close-Up

You can use a calculator to check the answers in Example 5:

```
10500+14500
                 25000
.06*10500+.08*14
500
                  1790
```

Write one equation describing the total of the investments, and the other equation describing the total interest:

$$x + y = 25{,}000 \quad \text{Total investments}$$
$$0.06x + 0.08y = 1790 \quad \text{Total interest}$$

To solve the system, we solve the first equation for y:

$$y = 25{,}000 - x$$

Substitute $25{,}000 - x$ for y in the second equation:

$$\begin{aligned} 0.06x + 0.08(25{,}000 - x) &= 1790 \\ 0.06x + 2000 - 0.08x &= 1790 \\ -0.02x + 2000 &= 1790 \\ -0.02x &= -210 \\ x &= \frac{-210}{-0.02} \\ &= 10{,}500 \end{aligned}$$

Let $x = 10{,}500$ in the equation $y = 25{,}000 - x$ to find y:

$$\begin{aligned} y &= 25{,}000 - 10{,}500 \\ &= 14{,}500 \end{aligned}$$

Check these values for x and y in the original problem. Mrs. Robinson invested \$10,500 at 6% and \$14,500 at 8%.

Now do Exercises 47–58

Warm-Ups

True or false? Explain your answer.

For Exercises 1–7, use the following systems:

a) $y = x - 7$
$2x + 3y = 4$

b) $x + 2y = 1$
$2x - 4y = 0$

1. If we substitute $x - 7$ for y in system (a), we get $2x + 3(x - 7) = 4$. True

2. The x-coordinate of the solution to system (a) is 5. True

3. The solution to system (a) is $(5, -2)$. True

4. The point $\left(\frac{1}{2}, \frac{1}{4}\right)$ satisfies system (b). True

5. It would be difficult to solve system (b) by graphing. True

6. Either x or y could be eliminated by substitution in system (b). True

7. System (b) is a dependent system. False

8. Solving an inconsistent system by substitution will result in a false statement. True

9. Solving a dependent system by substitution results in an equation that is always true. True

10. Any system of two linear equations can be solved by substitution. True

Boost your grade at mathzone.com!
- Practice Problems
- NetTutor
- Self-Tests
- e-Professors
- Videos

Exercises 4.2

‹ Study Tips ›

- Students who have difficulty with a subject often schedule a class that meets one day per week so that they do not have to see it too often. It is better to be in a class that meets more often for shorter time periods.
- Students who explain things to others often learn from it. If you must work on math alone, try explaining things to yourself.

Reading and Writing *After reading this section, write out the answers to these questions. Use complete sentences.*

1. What method is used in this section to solve systems of equations?
   In this section we used the substitution method.
2. What is wrong with the graphing method for solving systems?
   Graphing is not accurate enough.
3. What is a dependent system?
   A dependent system is one that has infinitely many solutions.
4. What is an inconsistent system?
   An inconsistent system is one with no solution.
5. What happens when you try to solve a dependent system by substitution? Using substitution on a dependent system results in an equation that is always true.
6. What happens when you try to solve an inconsistent system by substitution? Using substitution on an inconsistent system results in a false equation.

‹1› Solving a System by Substitution

Solve each system by substitution.

See Examples 1 and 2.

See the Strategy for Solving a System by Substitution box on page 251.

7. $y = x + 2$
$x + y = 8$ $(3, 5)$

8. $y = x - 4$
$x + y = 12$ $(8, 4)$

9. $x = y - 3$
$x + y = 11$ $(4, 7)$

10. $x = y + 1$
$x + y = 7$ $(4, 3)$

11. $y = x + 3$
$2x - 3y = -11$ $(2, 5)$

VIDEO **12.** $y = x - 5$
$x + 2y = 8$ $(6, 1)$

13. $x = 2y - 4$
$2x + y = 7$ $(2, 3)$

14. $x = y - 2$
$-2x + y = -1$ $(3, 5)$

15. $2x + y = 5$
$5x + 2y = 8$ $(-2, 9)$

16. $5y - x = 0$
$6x - y = 29$ $(5, 1)$

17. $x + y = 0$
$3x + 2y = -5$ $(-5, 5)$

18. $x - y = 6$
$3x + 4y = -3$ $(3, -3)$

19. $x + y = 1$
$4x - 8y = -4$ $\left(\frac{1}{3}, \frac{2}{3}\right)$

20. $x - y = 2$
$3x - 6y = 8$ $\left(\frac{4}{3}, -\frac{2}{3}\right)$

21. $2x + 3y = 2$
$4x - 9y = -1$ $\left(\frac{1}{2}, \frac{1}{3}\right)$

22. $x - 2y = 1$
$3x + 10y = -1$ $\left(\frac{1}{2}, -\frac{1}{4}\right)$

‹2› Dependent and Inconsistent Systems

Solve each system by substitution. Indicate whether each system is independent, dependent, or inconsistent. See Examples 1–4.

23. $21x - 35 = 7y$
$3x - y = 5$ $\{(x, y) \mid 3x - y = 5\}$, dependent

24. $2x + y = 3x$
$3x - y = 2y$ $\{(x, y) \mid y = x\}$, dependent

25. $x - 2y = -2$
$x + 2y = 8$ $\left(3, \frac{5}{2}\right)$, independent

26. $y = -3x + 1$
$y = 2x + 4$ $\left(-\frac{3}{5}, \frac{14}{5}\right)$, independent

VIDEO **27.** $x = 4 - 2y$
$4y + 2x = -8$ No solution, inconsistent

28. $y - 3 = 2(x - 1)$
$y = 2x + 3$ No solution, inconsistent

29. $y + 1 = 5(x + 1)$
$y = 5x - 1$ No solution, inconsistent

30. $3x - 2y = 7$
$3x + 2y = 7$ $\left(\frac{7}{3}, 0\right)$, independent

31. $2x + 5y = 5$
$3x - 5y = 6$ $\left(\frac{11}{5}, \frac{3}{25}\right)$, independent

VIDEO **32.** $x + 5y = 4$
$x + 5y = 4y$ $(-1, 1)$, independent

Solve each system by the graphing method shown in Section 4.1 and by substitution.

33. $x + y = 5$
$x - y = 1$ $(3, 2)$

34. $x + y = 6$
$2x - y = 3$ $(3, 3)$

35. $y = x - 2$
$y = 4 - x$ $(3, 1)$

36. $y = 2x - 3$
$y = -x + 3$ $(2, 1)$

37. $y = 3x - 2$
$y - 3x = 1$ No solution

38. $x + y = 5$
$y = 2 - x$ No solution

Determine whether each system is independent, dependent, or inconsistent.

39. $y = -4x + 3$
$y = -4x - 6$
Inconsistent

40. $y = -3x - 6$
$y = 3x - 6$
Independent

41. $y = x$
$x = y$
Dependent

42. $y = x$
$y = x + 5$
Inconsistent

43. $y = x$
$y = -x$
Independent

44. $y = 3x$
$3x - y = 0$
Dependent

45. $x - y = 4$
$x - y = 5$
Inconsistent

46. $y = 1$
$y + 3 = 4$
Dependent

⟨3⟩ Applications

Write a system of two equations in two unknowns for each problem. Solve each system by substitution. See Example 5.

47. ***Rectangular patio.*** The length of a rectangular patio is twice the width. If the perimeter is 84 feet, then what are the length and width? Length 28 ft, width 14 ft

48. ***Rectangular lot.*** The width of a rectangular lot is 50 feet less than the length. If the perimeter is 900 feet, then what are the length and width? Length 250 ft, width 200 ft

49. ***Investing in the future.*** Mrs. Miller invested \$20,000 and received a total of \$1600 in interest. If she invested part of the money at 10% and the remainder at 5%, then how much did she invest at each rate?
\$12,000 at 10%, \$8000 at 5%

VIDEO **50.** ***Stocks and bonds.*** Mr. Walker invested \$30,000 in stocks and bonds and had a total return of \$2880 in one year. If his stock investment returned 10% and his bond investment returned 9%, then how much did he invest in each?
\$18,000 at 10%, \$12,000 at 9%

51. ***Gross receipts.*** Two of the highest grossing movies of all time were *Titanic* and *Star Wars* with total receipts of \$1062 million (www.movieweb.com). If the gross receipts for *Titanic* exceeded the gross receipts for *Star Wars* by \$140 million, then what were the gross receipts for each movie? *Titanic* \$601 million, *Star Wars* \$461 million

VIDEO **52.** ***Tennis court dimensions.*** The singles court in tennis is four yards longer than it is wide. If its perimeter is 44 yards, then what are the length and width?
Length 13 yd, width 9 yd

53. ***Mowing and shoveling.*** When Mr. Wilson came back from his vacation, he paid Frank \$50 for mowing his lawn three times and shoveling his sidewalk two times. During Mr. Wilson's vacation last year, Frank earned \$45 for mowing the lawn two times and shoveling the sidewalk three times. How much does Frank make for mowing the lawn once? How much does Frank make for shoveling the sidewalk once? Lawn \$12, sidewalk \$7

54. ***Burgers and fries.*** Donna ordered four burgers and one order of fries at the Hamburger Palace. However, the waiter put three burgers and two orders of fries in the bag and charged Donna the correct price for three burgers and two orders of fries, \$3.15. When Donna discovered the mistake, she went back to complain. She found out that the price for four burgers and one order of fries is \$3.45 and decided to keep what she had. What is the price of one burger, and what is the price of one order of fries? Burger \$0.75, fries \$0.45

55. ***Racing rules.*** According to NASCAR rules, no more than 52% of a car's total weight can be on any pair of tires. For optimal performance a driver of a 1150-pound car wants to have 50% of its weight on the left rear and left front tires and 48% of its weight on the left rear and right front tires. If the right front weight is determined to be 264 pounds, then what amount of weight should be on the left rear and left front? Are the NASCAR rules satisfied with this weight distribution?
Left rear 288 pounds, left front 287 pounds, no

56. ***Weight distribution.*** A driver of a 1200-pound car wants to have 50% of the car's weight on the left front and left rear tires, 48% on the left rear and right front tires, and 51% on the left rear and right rear tires. How much weight should be on each of these tires?
Left front 306, left rear 294, right front 282, right rear 318 pounds

57. ***Price of hamburger.*** A grocer will supply y pounds of ground beef per day when the retail price is x dollars per pound, where $y = 200x + 60$. Consumer studies show that consumer demand for ground beef is y pounds per day, where $y = -150x + 900$. What is the price at which the supply is equal to the demand, the equilibrium price? See the accompanying figure. \$2.40 per pound

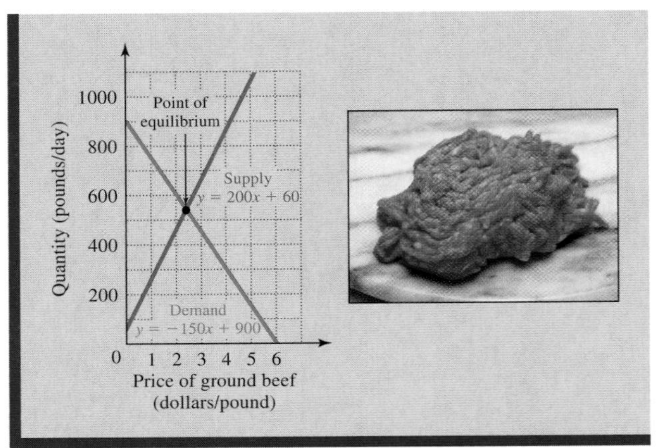

Figure for Exercise 57

58. ***Tweedle Dum and Dee.*** Tweedle Dum said to Tweedle Dee "The sum of my weight and twice yours is 361 pounds." Tweedle Dee said to Tweedle Dum "Contrariwise the sum of my weight and twice yours is 362 pounds." Find the weight of each. Dum 121 lb, Dee 120 lb

Graphing Calculator Exercise

59. ***Life expectancy.*** Since 1950, the life expectancy of a U.S. male born in year x is modeled by the formula

$$y = 0.165x - 256.7,$$

and the life expectancy of a U.S. female born in year x is modeled by

$$y = 0.186x - 290.6$$

(National Center for Health Statistics, www.cdc.gov).

a) Find the life expectancy of a U.S. male born in 1975 and a U.S. female born in 1975.

b) Graph both equations on your graphing calculator for $1950 < x < 2050$.

c) Will U.S. males ever catch up with U.S. females in life expectancy?

d) Assuming that these equations were valid before 1950, solve the system to find the year of birth for which U.S. males and females had the same life expectancy.

a) 69.2 years, 76.8 years

b)

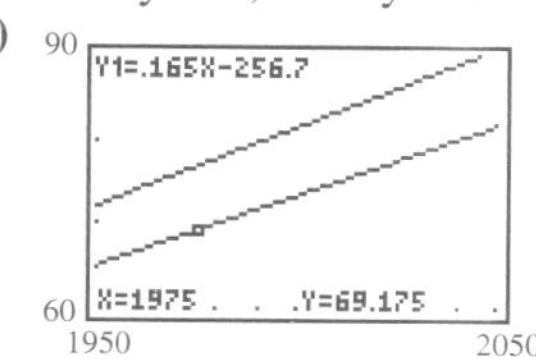

c) No **d)** 1614

Math *at Work* — Audiograms

Mathematics can determine the frequencies that a person can't hear, the volume of the ear canal, and how much hearing a person has lost. Computers do the calculations and audiologists interpret and assess the results.

The results of a hearing test are charted on an audiogram, as shown in the accompanying figure. Frequency is on the horizontal axis and sound level is on the vertical axis. The frequencies tested range from 125 Hz to 8000 Hz. Frequencies around 125 Hz are like the lowest notes on a piano. High frequencies of 8000 Hz are like the highest notes on a piano. The level of the sound ranges from zero decibels to 110 decibels. Normal speech is around 45 dB. The softest sound that a person can hear one-half of the time is considered his or her hearing threshold. These thresholds are measured and marked by an audiologist on the audiogram. Sounds below the marks are sounds that the patient cannot hear. The normal hearing range is 10 dB to 25 dB. Hearing loss is described as mild (26 to 40 dB), moderate (41 to 55 dB), moderately severe (56 to 70 dB), severe (71 to 90 dB), or profound (over 90 dB).

The accompanying audiogram shows a typical plot for conductive and sensorineural hearing loss, which are the two main types. Conductive hearing loss occurs when the outer or middle ear doesn't work properly. Sounds are blocked by fluid or ear wax and do not make it into the inner ear. Conductive hearing loss is usually treatable. Sensorineural hearing loss occurs when the inner ear or hearing nerve becomes damaged from loud noises or aging. From the audiogram, an audiologist can identify which type of hearing loss has occurred.

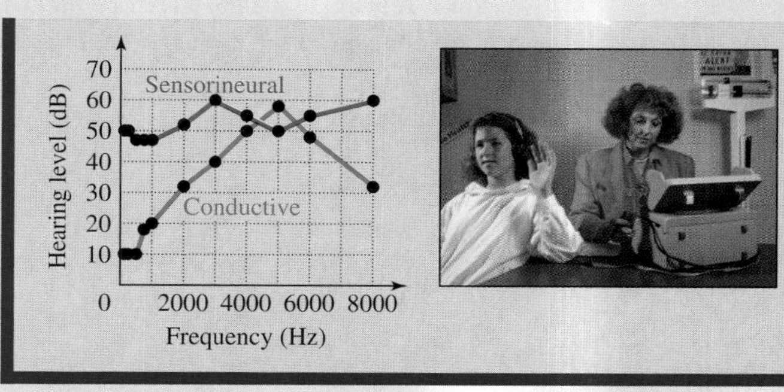

4.3 The Addition Method

In This Section

In Section 4.2, we solved systems of equations by using substitution. We substituted one equation into the other to eliminate a variable. The addition method of this section is another method for eliminating a variable to solve a system of equations.

⟨1⟩ Solving a System by Addition

In the substitution method we most often solve one equation for one variable in terms of the other. When doing this, we may get an expression involving fractions, which must be substituted into the other equation. The addition method avoids fractions and works better than substitution for certain systems. The steps to follow for the addition method are stated in the following strategy.

Strategy for Solving a System by Addition

1. Write both equations in standard form.
2. If a variable will be eliminated by adding, then add the equations.
3. If necessary multiply one or both equations by the appropriate integer to obtain opposite coefficients on one of the variables. Then add the equations.
4. After one variable is eliminated, solve for the remaining variable.
5. Use the value of the remaining variable to find the value of the eliminated variable.
6. Check the solution in the original system.

EXAMPLE 1

Solving a system by addition

Solve:

$$3x - y = 5 \quad \text{(A)}$$
$$2x + y = 10 \quad \text{(B)}$$

Solution

Since the equations are given in standard form, no rewriting is necessary. Since y occurs with opposite signs in the two equations, y will be eliminated if we add the equations.

$$\begin{aligned} \text{(A)} \quad & 3x - y = 5 \\ \text{(B)} \quad & \underline{2x + y = 10} \quad \text{Add.} \\ & 5x \quad = 15 \quad -y + y = 0 \\ & x = 3 \end{aligned}$$

Now use $x = 3$ in either one of the original equations to find y:

$$\begin{aligned} 2x + y &= 10 \\ 2(3) + y &= 10 \quad \text{Let } x = 3. \\ y &= 4 \end{aligned}$$

⟨ Calculator Close-Up ⟩

To check Example 1, graph $y_1 = 3x - 5$ and $y_2 = 10 - 2x$. The lines appear to intersect at (3, 4).

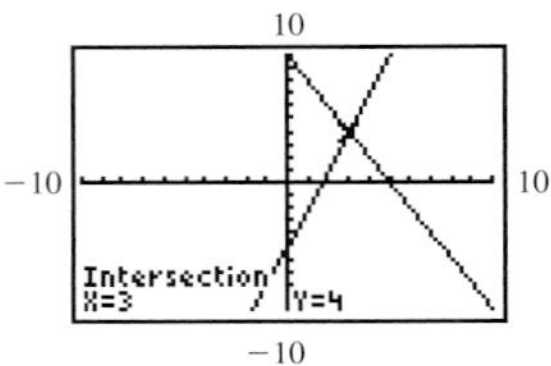

Check (3, 4) in both equations:

$$3(3) - 4 = 5 \quad \text{Correct}$$
$$2(3) + 4 = 10 \quad \text{Correct}$$

The solution to the system is (3, 4).

Now do Exercises 7–12

The addition method is based on the addition property of equality. We are simply adding equal quantities from one equation to each side of the other equation. It is not absolutely necessary to have the equations in standard form. Any form will work as long as the equal signs and the like terms are in line vertically.

In Example 2, adding the given equations will not eliminate a variable. However, we can use the multiplication property of equality to adjust one of the equations so that a variable will be eliminated when the equations are added.

EXAMPLE 2

‹ Teaching Tip ›

Students often multiply on the left side and forget the right side. Encourage them to show the multiplication as done in this example.

Solving a system by addition

Solve:
$$-x + 4y = -14 \quad \text{(A)}$$
$$2x - 3y = 18 \quad \text{(B)}$$

Solution

If we add these equations as they are written, we will not eliminate any variables. However, if we multiply each side of the first equation by 2, then we will be adding $-2x$ and $2x$, and x will be eliminated:

$$
\begin{array}{lrl}
\text{(A) multiplied by 2} & 2(-x + 4y) = 2(-14) & \\
\text{(B)} & 2x - 3y = 18 & \\
\text{(A) multiplied by 2} & -2x + 8y = -28 & \\
\text{(B)} & \underline{2x - 3y = 18} & \text{Add.} \\
 & 5y = -10 & \\
 & y = -2 &
\end{array}
$$

Replace y by -2 in either of the original equations:

$$
\begin{aligned}
-x + 4y &= -14 \\
-x + 4(-2) &= -14 \\
-x - 8 &= -14 \\
-x &= -6 \\
x &= 6
\end{aligned}
$$

Check $x = 6$ and $y = -2$ in the original equations.

$$-6 + 4(-2) = -14 \quad \text{Correct}$$
$$2(6) - 3(-2) = 18 \quad \text{Correct}$$

The solution to the system is $(6, -2)$.

Now do Exercises 13–22

In Example 3 we need to use a multiple of each equation to eliminate a variable by addition.

EXAMPLE 3

Solving a system by addition

Solve: $2x + 3y = 7$ (A)

$3x + 4y = 10$ (B)

Solution

To eliminate x by addition, the coefficients of x in the two equations must be opposites. So we multiply the first equation by -3 and the second by 2:

(A) multiplied by -3 $\quad -3(2x + 3y) = -3(7)$

(B) multiplied by 2 $\quad 2(3x + 4y) = 2(10)$

(A) multiplied by -3 $\quad -6x - 9y = -21$

(B) multiplied by 2 $\quad 6x + 8y = 20$ Add

$$-y = -1$$
$$y = 1$$

Replace y with 1 in one of the original equations:

$$2x + 3y = 7$$
$$2x + 3(1) = 7$$
$$2x + 3 = 7$$
$$2x = 4$$
$$x = 2$$

Check $x = 2$ and $y = 1$ in the original equations.

$$2(2) + 3(1) = 7$$
$$3(2) + 4(1) = 10$$

The solution to the system is (2, 1).

Now do Exercises 23–28

If either equation contains fractions, multiply by the least common denominator to eliminate the fractions. Once the fractions are cleared, it is easier to proceed with the addition method.

EXAMPLE 4

A system involving fractions

Solve: $\frac{1}{2}x - \frac{2}{3}y = 2$

$\frac{1}{4}x + \frac{1}{2}y = 6$

‹ **Teaching Tip** ›

Remind students to show the multiplication on each side as done here.

Solution

Multiply the first equation by 6 and the second by 4 to eliminate the fractions:

$$6\left(\frac{1}{2}x - \frac{2}{3}y\right) = 6 \cdot 2$$
$$4\left(\frac{1}{4}x + \frac{1}{2}y\right) = 4 \cdot 6$$

The result is a system without fractions:

$$3x - 4y = 12$$
$$x + 2y = 24$$

Now multiply $x + 2y = 24$ by 2 to get $2x + 4y = 48$, and then add:

$$\begin{aligned} 3x - 4y &= 12 \\ 2x + 4y &= 48 \\ \hline 5x \qquad &= 60 \\ x &= 12 \end{aligned}$$

Let $x = 12$ in $x + 2y = 24$:

$$\begin{aligned} 12 + 2y &= 24 \\ 2y &= 12 \\ y &= 6 \end{aligned}$$

Check $x = 12$ and $y = 6$ in the original equations. The solution is $(12, 6)$.

Now do Exercises 29–32

‹2› Dependent and Inconsistent Systems

You can recognize dependent and inconsistent systems with the addition method the same way we recognized them when using substitution. If the result of the addition is an equation that is always true, the equations are dependent. If the result is an equation that is false, the equations are inconsistent.

EXAMPLE 5

Dependent and inconsistent systems

Use the addition method to solve each system.

a) $2x - y = 1$
$4x - 2y = 2$

b) $-2x + 3y = 9$
$2x - 3y = 18$

Solution

a) Multiply the first equation by -2, and then add the equations:

$$-2(2x - y) = -2(1)$$
$$4x - 2y = 2$$

$$\begin{aligned} -4x + 2y &= -2 \\ 4x - 2y &= 2 \\ \hline 0 &= 0 \quad \text{True} \end{aligned}$$

Because the equation $0 = 0$ is correct for any value of x, the system is dependent. The graphs of the two equations are the same line and any point on that line satisfies both equations of the system. The solution set is the set of points on the line $2x - y = 1$, which is written in set notation as $\{(x, y) \mid 2x - y = 1\}$.

b) Add the equations:

$$\begin{array}{r} -2x + 3y = 9 \\ 2x - 3y = 18 \\ \hline 0 = 27 \end{array} \quad \text{False}$$

Because $0 = 27$ is a false equation, the system is inconsistent. There is no solution to the system.

Now do Exercises 33–48

‹3› Applications

In Example 6 we solve a problem using a system of equations and the addition method.

EXAMPLE 6

Milk and bread

Lea purchased two gallons of milk and three loaves of bread for \$8.25. Yesterday she purchased five gallons of milk and two loaves of bread for \$13.75. What is the price of a single gallon of milk? What is the price of a single loaf of bread?

‹ Helpful Hint ›

You can see from Example 6 that the standard form $Ax + By = C$ occurs naturally in accounting. This form will occur whenever we have the price each and quantity of two items and we want to express the total cost.

Solution

Let x represent the price of one gallon of milk. Let y represent the price of one loaf of bread. We can write two equations about the milk and bread:

$$2x + 3y = 8.25 \quad \text{Today's purchase}$$
$$5x + 2y = 13.75 \quad \text{Yesterday's purchase}$$

To eliminate x, multiply the first equation by -5 and the second by 2:

$$-5(2x + 3y) = -5(8.25)$$
$$2(5x + 2y) = 2(13.75)$$

$$\begin{array}{r} -10x - 15y = -41.25 \\ 10x + 4y = 27.50 \\ \hline -11y = -13.75 \\ y = 1.25 \end{array} \quad \text{Add.}$$

Replace y by 1.25 in the first equation:

$$2x + 3(1.25) = 8.25$$
$$2x + 3.75 = 8.25$$
$$2x = 4.50$$
$$x = 2.25$$

A gallon of milk costs \$2.25, and a loaf of bread costs \$1.25.

Now do Exercises 57–84

‹ Teaching Tip ›

Note that multiplying by 100 to eliminate all decimals might make this solution look rather complicated.

Warm-Ups ▼

True or false? Explain your answer.

Use the following systems for these exercises:

a) $3x + 2y = 7$
$4x - 5y = -6$

b) $y = -3x + 2$
$2y + 6x - 4 = 0$

c) $y = x - 5$
$x = y + 6$

1. To eliminate x by addition in system (a), we multiply the first equation by 4 and the second equation by 3. False
2. Either variable in system (a) can be eliminated by the addition method. True
3. The ordered pair (1, 2) is a solution to system (a). True
4. The addition method can be used to eliminate a variable in system (b). True
5. Both (0, 2) and (1, −1) satisfy system (b). True
6. The solution to system (c) is $\{(x, y) \mid y = x - 5\}$. False
7. System (c) is independent. False
8. System (b) is inconsistent. False
9. System (a) is dependent. False
10. The graphs of the equations in system (c) are parallel lines. True

Exercises

‹ Study Tips ›

- Keep reviewing. When you are done with your current assignment, go back and work a few problems from the past. You will be amazed at how much your knowledge will improve with a regular review.
- Play offensive math not defensive math. A student who takes an active approach and knows the usual questions and answers is playing offensive math. Don't wait for a question to hit you on the head.

Reading and Writing *After reading this section, write out the answers to these questions. Use complete sentences.*

1. What method is used in this section to solve systems of equations?
   In this section we learned to solve systems by the addition method.
2. What three methods have now been presented for solving a system of linear equations?
   The three methods presented are graphing, substitution, and addition.
3. What do the addition method and the substitution method have in common?
   In addition and substitution we eliminate a variable and solve for the remaining variable.
4. What do we sometimes do before we add the equations?
   It is sometimes necessary to use the multiplication property of equality before adding the equations.
5. How do you decide which variable to eliminate when using the addition method?
   Eliminate the variable that is easiest to eliminate.
6. How do you identify inconsistent and dependent systems when using the addition method?
   In the addition method inconsistent systems result in a false equation and dependent systems result in an equation that is always true.

⟨1⟩ Solving a System by Addition

Solve each system by addition.

See Examples 1–4.

See the Strategy for Solving a System by Addition box on page 258.

7. $x + y = 5$
$x - y = 3$ (4, 1)

8. $-2x + y = 6$
$2x + y = 10$ (1, 8)

9. $2x + y = 5$
$3x - y = 10$ (3, −1)

10. $3x - y = 3$
$4x + y = 11$ (2, 3)

11. $x + 2y = 7$
$-x + 3y = 18$ (−3, 5)

VIDEO **12.** $x + 2y = 7$
$-x + 4y = 5$ (3, 2)

13. $x + 2y = 2$
$-4x + 3y = 25$ (−4, 3)

14. $2x - 3y = -7$
$5x + y = -9$ (−2, 1)

15. $x + 3y = 4$
$2x - y = 22$ (10, −2)

16. $x - y = 0$
$x - 2y = 0$ (0, 0)

17. $y = 4x - 1$
$y = 3x + 7$ (8, 31)

18. $x = 3y + 45$
$x = 2y + 40$ (30, −5)

19. $4x = 3y + 1$
$2x = y - 1$ (−2, −3)

20. $2x = y - 9$
$x = -1 - 3y$ (−4, 1)

21. $2x - 5y = -22$
$-6x + 3y = 18$ (−1, 4)

22. $4x - 3y = 7$
$5x + 6y = -1$ (1, −1)

VIDEO **23.** $2x + 3y = 4$
$-3x + 5y = 13$ (−1, 2)

24. $-5x + 3y = 1$
$2x - 7y = 17$ (−2, −3)

25. $2x - 5y = 11$
$3x - 2y = 11$ (3, −1)

26. $4x - 3y = 17$
$3x - 5y = 21$ (2, −3)

27. $5x + 4y = 13$
$2x + 3y = 8$ (1, 2)

28. $4x + 3y = 8$
$6x + 5y = 14$ (−1, 4)

29. $\frac{1}{2}x + \frac{1}{3}y = 8$
$\frac{1}{3}x - \frac{1}{2}y = 1$ (12, 6)

30. $\frac{1}{5}x + \frac{1}{10}y = 5$
$\frac{1}{2}x - \frac{1}{5}y = 8$ (20, 10)

31. $\frac{2}{3}x + \frac{3}{4}y = 28$
$\frac{1}{2}x - \frac{3}{8}y = 6$ (24, 16)

32. $\frac{2}{5}x - \frac{1}{10}y = 1$
$\frac{3}{10}x + \frac{2}{3}y = 23$ (10, 30)

⟨2⟩ Dependent and Inconsistent Systems

Solve each system by addition or substitution. Indicate whether each system is independent, dependent, or inconsistent. See Examples 1–5.

33. $x + y = 5$
$x + y = 6$ No solution, inconsistent

34. $x + y = 5$
$x + 2y = 6$ (4, 1), independent

VIDEO **35.** $x + y = 5$
$2x + 2y = 10$ $\{(x, y) \mid x + y = 5\}$, dependent

36. $2x + 3y = 4$
$2x - 3y = 4$ (2, 0), independent

37. $2x = y + 3$
$2y = 4x - 6$ $\{(x, y) \mid 2x = y + 3\}$, dependent

38. $y = 2x - 1$
$2x - y + 5 = 0$ No solution, inconsistent

39. $x + 3y = 3$
$5x = 15 - 15y$ $\{(x, y) \mid x + 3y = 3\}$, dependent

40. $y - 3x = 2$
$5y = -15x + 10$ (0, 2), independent

41. $6x - 2y = -2$
$\frac{1}{3}y = x + \frac{4}{3}$ No solution, inconsistent

VIDEO **42.** $x + y = 8$
$\frac{1}{3}x - \frac{1}{2}y = 1$ (6, 2), independent

43. $\frac{1}{2}x - \frac{2}{3}y = -6$
$-\frac{3}{4}x - \frac{1}{2}y = -18$ (12, 18), independent

44. $\frac{1}{2}x - y = 3$
$\frac{1}{5}x + 2y = 6$ (10, 2), independent

45. $0.04x + 0.09y = 7$
$x + y = 100$ (40, 60), independent

46. $0.08x - 0.05y = 0.2$
$2x + y = 140$ (40, 60), independent

47. $0.1x - 0.2y = -0.01$
$0.3x + 0.5y = 0.08$ (0.1, 0.1), independent

48. $0.5y = 0.2x - 0.25$
$0.1y = 0.8x - 1.57$ (2, 0.3), independent

Use a calculator to assist you in finding the exact solution to each system.

49. $2.33x - 4.58y = 16.319$
$4.98x + 3.44y = -2.162$
(1.5, −2.8)

50. $234x - 499y = 1337$
$282x + 312y = 51{,}846$
(123, 55)

Solve each system by graphing (Section 4.1), by substitution (Section 4.2), and by addition.

51. $x + y = 7$
$x - y = 1$ (4, 3)

52. $x + y = 8$
$2x - y = 4$ (4, 4)

53. $y = x - 3$
$y = 5 - x$ (4, 1)

54. $y = 2x - 5$
$y = -x + 4$ (3, 1)

55. $y = 2x - 1$
$y - 2x = 3$ No solution

56. $x + y = 3$
$y = 4 - x$ No solution

⟨3⟩ Applications

Use two variables and a system of equations to solve each problem. See Example 6.

57. ***Cars and trucks.*** An automobile dealer had 250 vehicles on his lot during the month of June. He must pay a monthly inventory tax of \$3 per car and \$4 per truck. If his tax bill for June was \$850, then how many cars and how many trucks did he have on his lot during June? 150 cars, 100 trucks

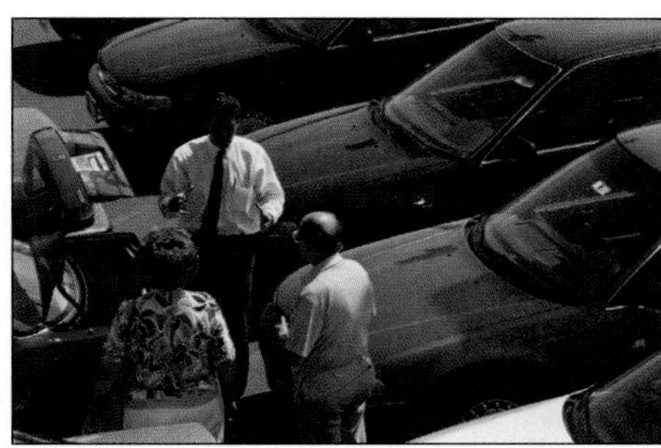

Photo for Exercise 57

58. ***Inventory tax.*** A dealer had 120 vehicles on his lot during June. He must pay a monthly inventory tax of \$6 per car and \$5 per truck. If his tax bill for June was \$640, then how many cars and how many trucks did he have on his lot during June?
40 cars, 80 trucks

59. ***The meter maid.*** Rita opened a parking meter and removed 40 coins consisting of dimes and nickels. If the value of these coins is \$3.20, then how many coins of each type does she have?
24 dimes, 16 nickels

60. ***Paying the penalty.*** Candy paid her library fine with 30 coins consisting of nickels and dimes. If the fine was \$2.40, then how many coins of each type did she use?
12 nickels, 18 dimes

61. ***A great start.*** George paid for his \$4.15 breakfast with 31 coins consisting of dimes and quarters. How many coins of each type did he use?
24 dimes, 7 quarters

62. ***Coin collecting.*** Andrew paid \$2000 for 24 rare coins from a dealer. If all of them were nickels and quarters and the total face value was \$4.40, then how many coins of each type did he buy?
8 nickels, 16 quarters

63. ***Adults and children.*** The Audubon Zoo charges \$5.50 for each adult admission and \$2.75 for each child. The total bill for the 30 people on the Spring Creek Elementary School kindergarten field trip was \$99. How many adults and how many children went on the field trip?
6 adults, 24 children

Photo for Exercise 63

64. ***Concert revenue.*** A total of 1000 tickets were sold for *The Grinch Who Stole Christmas*. Children's tickets were \$6 each and adult tickets were \$10 each. If the total revenue was \$8400, then how many children's tickets and how many adult tickets were sold?
400 children's tickets, 600 adult's tickets

65. ***Coffee and doughnuts.*** Jorge has worked at Dandy Doughnuts so long that he has memorized the amounts for many of the common orders. For example, six doughnuts and five coffees cost \$4.35, while four doughnuts and three coffees cost \$2.75. What are the prices of one cup of coffee and one doughnut?
Coffee \$0.45, doughnut \$0.35

66. ***Time for a change.*** Jimmy has worked at the Donut Shop so long that he has memorized the amounts of the common orders. For example, four doughnuts and two coffees cost \$4.80, while five doughnuts and three coffees cost \$6.45. What are the prices for one doughnut and for one coffee?
Doughnut \$0.75, coffee \$0.90.

67. ***Marketing research.*** American Marketing Corporation found 147 smokers among 660 adults surveyed. If one-fourth of the men and one-fifth of the women were smokers, then how many men and how many women were surveyed?
300 men, 360 women

VIDEO **68.** ***Marketing research.*** The Independent Marketing Research Corporation found 130 smokers among 300 adults surveyed. If one-half of the men and one-third of the women were smokers, then how many men and how many women were in the survey? 180 men, 120 women

69. ***Time and a half.*** In one month, Shelly earned \$1800 for 210 hours of work. If she earns \$8 per hour for regular time and \$12 per hour for overtime, then how many hours of each type did she work?
180 hours regular time, 30 hours overtime

70. ***Good job.*** In one month Hector worked 210 hours and earned \$3276. If he makes \$14 per hour for regular time and \$21 per hour for overtime, then how many hours of each type did he work?
162 hours regular time, 48 hours overtime

71. ***Investing wisely.*** Janet invested a total of \$8000. Part of the money was placed into an account that earned an annual simple interest rate of 7%. The rest of the money was placed into an account that earned an annual simple interest rate of 10%. If the total interest earned in 1 year was \$710, then how much was invested at each rate? \$3000 at 7%, \$5000 at 10%

72. ***Group investing.*** An investment club split a total of \$10,000 into two investments. One of the investments returned 7.5% (simple interest) and the other returned 9% after 1 year. If the total amount of the return for 1 year was \$810, then how much was placed in each investment? \$6000 at 7.5%, \$4000 at 9%

73. ***Stocks and bonds.*** Mr. Taylor invested a total of \$21,000 in stocks and bonds and realized a total return of \$1950 in 1 year. If his stock investment returned 11% and his bond investment returned 7%, then how much did he invest in each? \$12,000 in stocks, \$9000 in bonds

74. ***Mutual funds.*** Belinda split her total investment of \$40,000 between a Dreyfus fund with an annual yield of 15% and a Templeton fund with an annual yield of 12%. If she made \$5460 on these investments in one year, then how much did she invest in each fund? \$22,000 in Dreyfus, \$18,000 in Templeton

75. ***Equal interest.*** John invested a total of \$4800 in two business ventures. One investment returned 15% and the other returned 9% after one year. If the dollar amount of the return for each investment was the same, then how much did he invest in each venture? \$1800 at 15%, \$3000 at 9%

76. ***Earning a tenth.*** Latonya invested \$5000 in a safe investment that she figured would return 8% after 1 year. She plans to invest in a riskier investment that should earn 15% in 1 year. How much should she put in the riskier investment so that her total return is 10% of her total investment? \$2000 at 15%

77. ***Making cloth.*** A manufacturer uses fibers that are 20% synthetic along with fibers that are 40% synthetic to make a fabric. If 800 pounds of 35% synthetic fabric are made from these fibers, then how many pounds of each type of fiber were used in making the fabric? 200 pounds of 20% synthetic, 600 pounds of 40% synthetic

78. ***Mixing acid.*** How many gallons of a 14% acid solution must be mixed with 10 gallons of a 30% acid solution to make a 19% acid solution? 22 gallons of 14% solution

79. ***Mixing fertilizer.*** How many ounces of 10% nitrogen fertilizer must be combined with 22% nitrogen fertilizer to make 120 ounces of an 18% nitrogen fertilizer? 40 ounces of 10%, 80 ounces of 22%

80. ***Chocolate sauce.*** How many ounces of pure Swiss chocolate must be added to 100 ounces of chocolate topping that is 20% Swiss chocolate to get a mixture that is 60% Swiss chocolate? 100 ounces of pure Swiss chocolate

81. ***Mixing metals.*** A metallurgist combined a metal that costs \$4.40 per ounce with a metal that costs \$2.40 per ounce. How many ounces of each were used to make a mixture of 100 ounces costing \$3.68 per ounce? 64 ounces of \$4.40 metal, 36 ounces of \$2.40 metal

82. ***Caramel corn.*** A snack food is made by mixing 190 pounds of caramel corn that costs \$0.60 per pound with nuts that cost \$4.00 per pound. How many pounds of nuts are needed to get a mixture that costs \$0.77 per pound? 10 pounds of nuts

83. ***Middle grade.*** A butcher combined \$4.20 per pound hamburger with \$3.10 per pound hamburger. How many pounds of each were used to get a 100-pound mixture that is worth \$3.76 per pound? 60 pounds of \$4.20 hamburger, 40 pounds of \$3.10 hamburger

84. ***Chocolate mix.*** Find the selling price per pound of a mixture made from 25 pounds of chocolate which costs \$6.60 per pound and 75 pounds of fudge that costs \$4.80 per pound. \$5.25 per pound

Getting More Involved

85. ***Discussion***

Compare and contrast the three methods for solving systems of linear equations in two variables that were presented in this chapter. What are the advantages and disadvantages of each method? How do you choose which method to use?

86. ***Exploration***

Consider the following system:

$$a_1x + b_1y = c_1$$
$$a_2x + b_2y = c_2$$

a) Multiply the first equation by a_2 and the second equation by $-a_1$. Add the resulting equations and solve for y to get a formula for y in terms of the a's, b's, and c's.

$$y = \frac{a_2c_1 - a_1c_2}{a_2b_1 - a_1b_2}$$

b) Multiply the first equation by b_2 and the second by $-b_1$. Add the resulting equations and solve for x to get a formula for x in terms of the a's, b's, and c's.

$$x = \frac{b_2c_1 - b_1c_2}{b_2a_1 - b_1a_2}$$

c) Use the formulas that you found in (a) and (b) to find the solution to the following system:

$$2x + 3y = 7$$
$$5x + 4y = 14$$

(2, 1)

4.4 Graphing Linear Inequalities in Two Variables

In This Section

You studied linear equations and inequalities in one variable in Chapter 2. In this section we extend the ideas of linear equations in two variables to study linear inequalities in two variables.

⟨1⟩ Linear Inequalities

If we replace the equals sign in any linear equation with any one of the inequality symbols $<$, $\le$, $>$, or $\ge$ we have a *linear inequality.* For example, $x + y = 5$ is a linear equation and $x + y < 5$ is a linear inequality.

Linear Inequality in Two Variables

If A, B, and C are real numbers with A and B not both zero, then

$$Ax + By < C$$

is called a **linear inequality in two variables.** In place of $<$, we could have $\le$, $>$, or $\ge$.

The inequalities

$$3x - 4y \le 8, \qquad y > 2x - 3, \qquad \text{and} \qquad x - y + 9 < 0$$

are linear inequalities. Not all of these are in the form of the definition, but they could all be rewritten in that form.

A point (or ordered pair) is a solution to an inequality in two variables if the ordered pair satisfies the inequality.

EXAMPLE 1

Satisfying a linear inequality

Determine whether each point satisfies the inequality $2x - 3y \ge 6$.

a) (4, 1) **b)** (3, 0) **c)** (3, −2)

Solution

a) To determine whether (4, 1) is a solution to the inequality, we replace x by 4 and y by 1 in the inequality $2x - 3y \ge 6$:

$$2(4) - 3(1) \ge 6$$
$$8 - 3 \ge 6$$
$$5 \ge 6 \quad \text{Incorrect}$$

So (4, 1) does not satisfy the inequality $2x - 3y \ge 6$.

b) Replace x by 3 and y by 0:

$$2(3) - 3(0) \ge 6$$
$$6 \ge 6 \quad \text{Correct}$$

So the point (3, 0) satisfies the inequality $2x - 3y \ge 6$.

c) Replace x by 3 and y by -2:

$$2(3) - 3(-2) \geq 6$$
$$6 + 6 \geq 6$$
$$12 \geq 6 \quad \text{Correct}$$

So the point $(3, -2)$ satisfies the inequality $2x - 3y \geq 6$.

Now do Exercises 7–14

⟨2⟩ Graphing a Linear Inequality

The solution set to an equation in one variable such as $x = 3$ is $\{3\}$. This single number divides the number line into two regions as shown in Fig. 4.7. Every number to the right of 3 satisfies $x > 3$, and every number to the left satisfies $x < 3$.

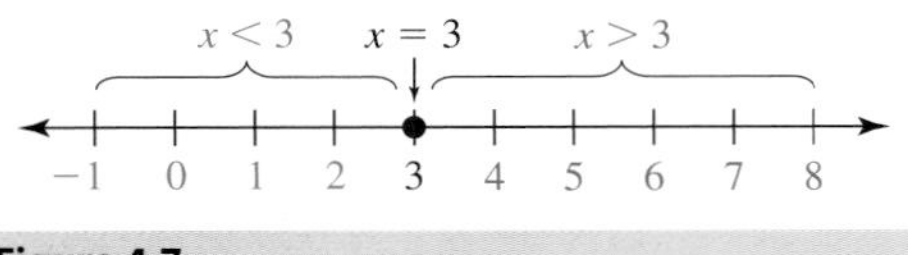

Figure 4.7

A similar situation occurs for linear equations in two variables. For example, the solution set to $y = x + 2$ consists of all ordered pairs on the line shown in Fig. 4.8. This line divides the coordinate plane into two regions. Every ordered pair above the line satisfies $y > x + 2$, and every ordered pair below the line satisfies $y < x + 2$. To see that this statement is correct, check a point such as (3, 5), which is on the line. A point with a larger y-coordinate such as (3, 6) is certainly above the line and satisfies $y > x + 2$. A point with a smaller y-coordinate such as (3, 4) is certainly below the line and satisfies $y < x + 2$.

⟨ Helpful Hint ⟩

Why do we keep drawing graphs? When we solve $2x + 1 = 7$, we don't bother to draw a graph showing 3, because the solution set is so simple. However, the solution set to a linear inequality is an infinite set of ordered pairs. Graphing gives us a way to visualize the solution set.

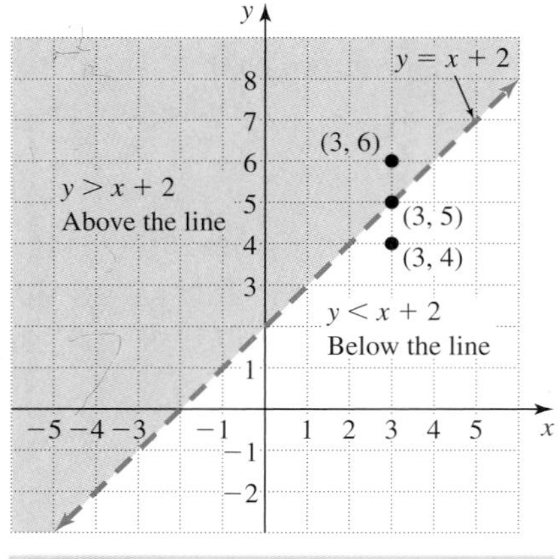

Figure 4.8

So the graph of a linear inequality consists of all ordered pairs that satisfy the inequality and they all lie on one side of the boundary line. If the inequality symbol is $<$ or $>$ the line is not included and it is drawn dashed. If the inequality symbol is $\leq$ or $\geq$ the line is included and it is drawn solid.

‹ **Teaching Tip** ›

The test-point method will work for an inequality in any form. However, it is convenient to know that values of y are larger above the line and smaller below the line.

Strategy for Graphing a Linear Inequality in Two Variables

1. Solve the inequality for y, then graph $y = mx + b$.

$y > mx + b$ is the region above the line.
$y = mx + b$ is the line itself.
$y < mx + b$ is the region below the line.

2. If the inequality involves only x, then graph the vertical line $x = k$.

$x > k$ is the region to the right of the line.
$x = k$ is the line itself.
$x < k$ is the region to the left of the line.

3. If the inequality involves only y, then graph the horizontal line $y = k$.

$y > k$ is the region above the line.
$y = k$ is the line itself.
$y < k$ is the region below the line.

Note that this case is included in part 1, but is restated for clarity.

CAUTION The symbol $>$ corresponds to "above" and the symbol $<$ corresponds to "below" only when the inequality is solved for y. You would certainly *not* shade below the line for $x - y < 0$, because $x - y < 0$ is equivalent to $y > x$. The graph of $y > x$ is the region above $y = x$.

EXAMPLE 2

Graphing a linear inequality

Graph each inequality.

a) $y < \frac{1}{3}x + 1$

b) $y \geq -2x + 3$

c) $2x - 3y < 6$

‹ **Teaching Tip** ›

It is a good idea to review graphing using slope and y-intercept and graphing using both intercepts at this time.

Solution

a) The set of points satisfying this inequality is the region below the line

$$y = \frac{1}{3}x + 1.$$

To show this region, we first graph the boundary line. The slope of the line is $\frac{1}{3}$, and the y-intercept is $(0, 1)$. We draw the line dashed because it is not part of the graph of $y < \frac{1}{3}x + 1$. In Fig. 4.9 on the next page, the graph is the shaded region.

b) Because the inequality symbol is $\geq$, every point on or above the line satisfies this inequality. We use the fact that the slope of this line is -2 and the y-intercept is $(0, 3)$ to draw the graph of the line. To show that the line $y = -2x + 3$ is included in the graph, we make it a solid line and shade the region above. See Fig. 4.10 on the next page.

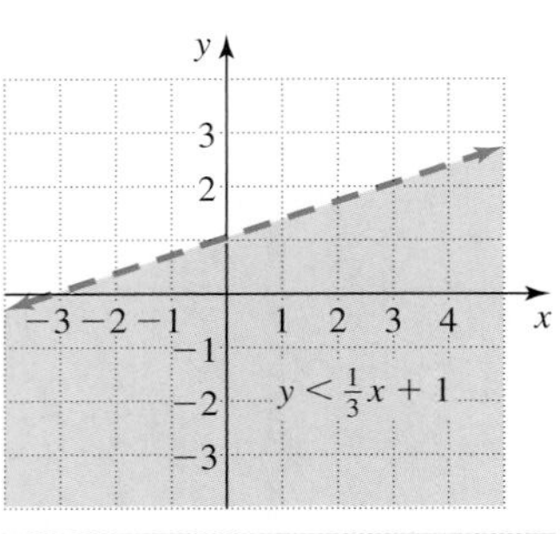

Figure 4.9

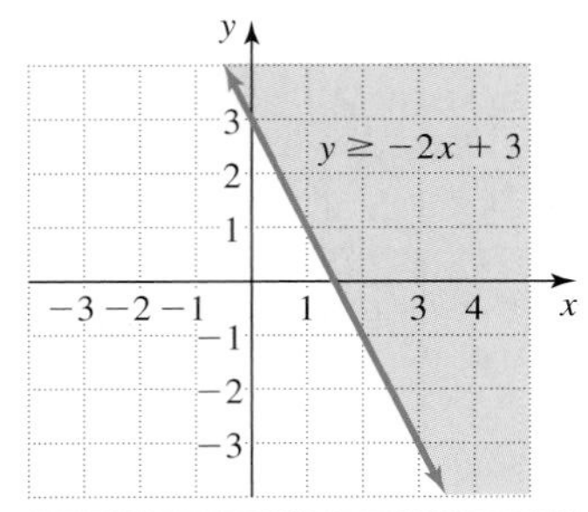

Figure 4.10

c) First solve for y:

$$2x - 3y < 6$$
$$-3y < -2x + 6$$
$$y > \frac{2}{3}x - 2 \quad \text{Divide by } -3 \text{ and reverse the inequality.}$$

To graph this inequality, we first graph the line with slope $\frac{2}{3}$ and y-intercept $(0, -2)$. We use a dashed line for the boundary because it is not included, and we shade the region above the line. Remember, "less than" means below the line and "greater than" means above the line only when the inequality is solved for y. See Fig. 4.11 for the graph.

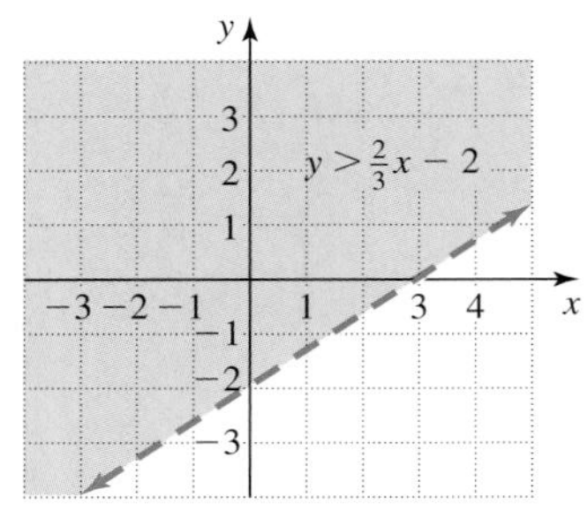

Figure 4.11

Now do Exercises 15–28

EXAMPLE 3

Horizontal and vertical boundary lines

Graph each inequality.

a) $y \leq 4$ **b)** $x > 3$

‹ Teaching Tip ›

Point out that $x > 3$ is an interval of real numbers if the context is inequalities in one variable. The context is important.

Solution

a) The line $y = 4$ is the horizontal line with y-intercept $(0, 4)$. We draw a solid horizontal line and shade below it as in Fig. 4.12.

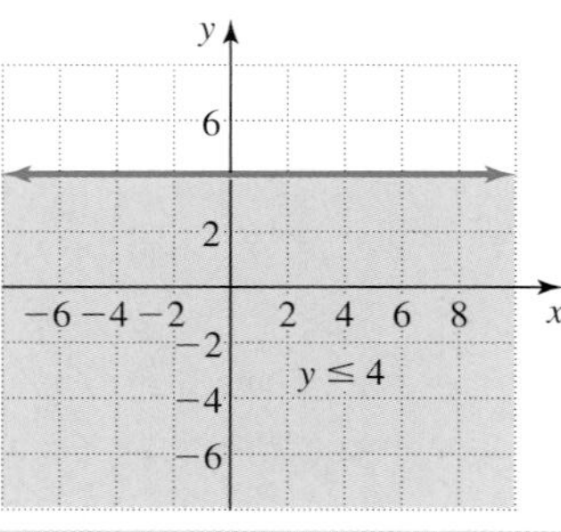

Figure 4.12

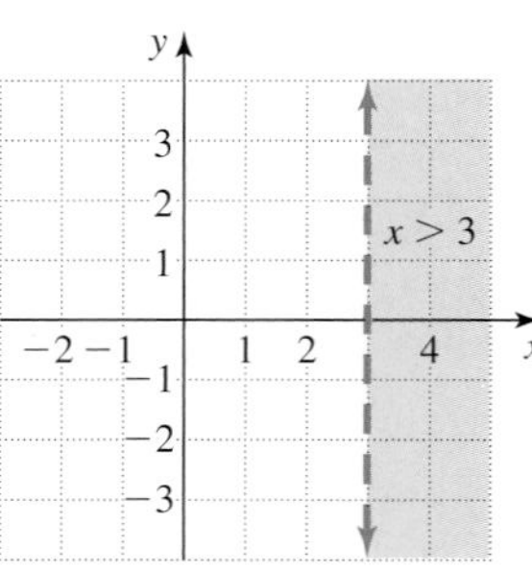

Figure 4.13

b) The line $x = 3$ is a vertical line through $(3, 0)$. Any point to the right of this line has an x-coordinate larger than 3. The graph is shown in Fig. 4.13.

Now do Exercises 29–32

⟨3⟩ The Test-Point Method

The graph of the linear equation $Ax + By = C$ separates the coordinate plane into two regions. All points in one region satisfy $Ax + By > C$ and all points in the other region satisfy $Ax + By < C$. To see which region satisfies which inequality we test a point in one of the regions. With this **test-point method** the form of the inequality does not matter and it does not matter how you graph the line. Here are the steps to follow.

Strategy for the Test-Point Method

To graph a linear inequality follow these steps.

1. Replace the inequality symbol with the equals symbol and graph the resulting boundary line by using any appropriate method. Use a solid line for $\geq$ or $\leq$ and dashed line for $>$ or $<$.
2. Select any point that is not on the line. Pick one with simple coordinates.
3. Check whether the selected point satisfies the inequality.
4. If the inequality is satisfied shade the region containing the test point. If not, shade the other region.

EXAMPLE 4

The test-point method

Graph each inequality.

a) $2x - 3y > 6$ **b)** $x - y \leq 0$

Solution

a) First graph the equation $2x - 3y = 6$ using the x-intercept $(3, 0)$ and the y-intercept $(0, -2)$ as shown in Fig. 4.14. Select a point on one side of the line, say $(0, 1)$ and check to see if it satisfies the inequality. Since $2(0) - 3(1) > 6$ is false, points on the other side of the line must satisfy the inequality. So shade the region on the other side of the line to get the graph of $2x - 3y > 6$, as shown in Fig. 4.15. The boundary line is dashed because the inequality symbol is $>$.

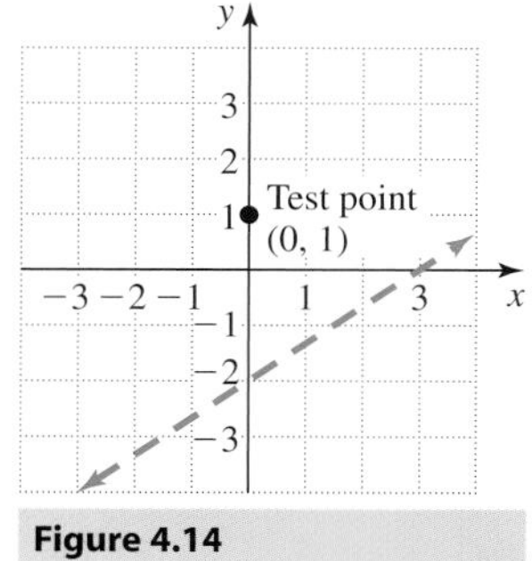

Figure 4.14

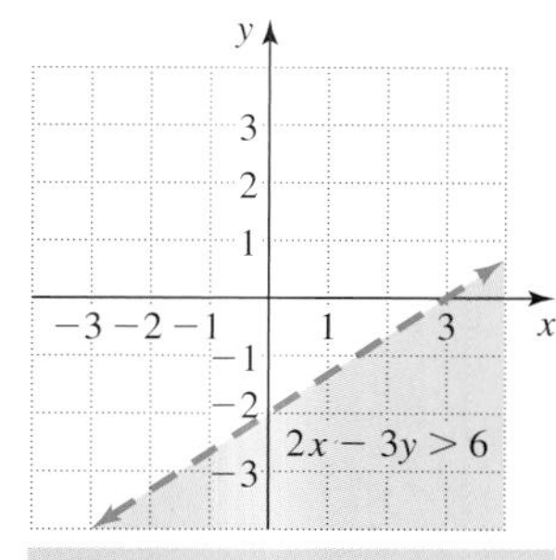

Figure 4.15

b) First graph $x - y = 0$. This line goes through $(1, 1)$, $(2, 2)$, $(3, 3)$, and so on. Select a point not on this line, say, $(1, 3)$, and test it in the inequality. Since $1 - 3 < 0$ is true, shade the region containing $(1, 3)$, as shown in Fig. 4.16. The boundary line is solid because the inequality symbol is $\leq$.

Now do Exercises 39–50

⟨ Helpful Hint ⟩

Some people always like to choose (0, 0) as the test point for lines that do not go through (0, 0). The arithmetic for testing (0, 0) is generally easier than for any other point.

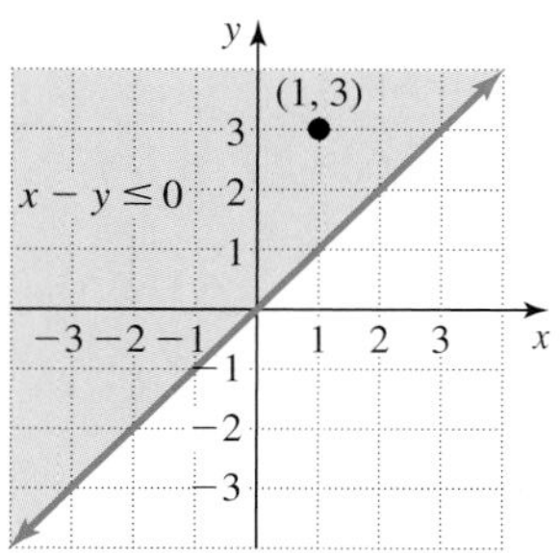

Figure 4.16

The test-point method could be used on inequalities in one variable. For example, to solve $x > 2$ first replace the inequality symbol with equals, to get $x = 2$. The graph of $x = 2$ is a single point at 2 on the number line shown in Fig. 4.17. That point divides the number line into two regions. Every point in one region satisfies $x > 2$, and every point in the other satisfies $x < 2$. Selecting a test point such as 4 and checking that $4 > 2$ is correct, tells us that the region to the right of 2 is the solution set to $x > 2$.

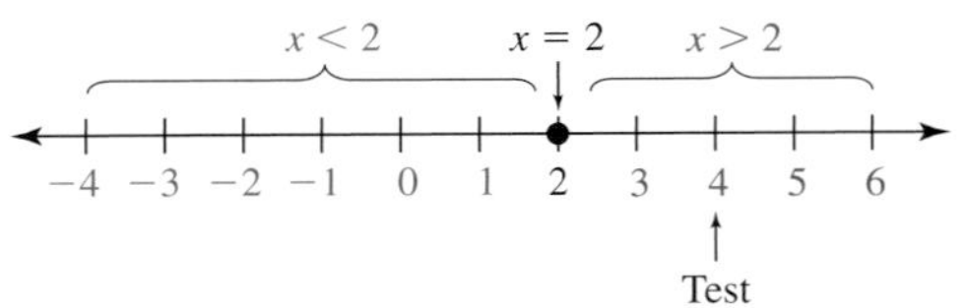

Figure 4.17

‹4› Applications

The values of variables used in applications are often restricted to nonnegative numbers. So solutions to inequalities in these applications are graphed in the first quadrant only.

EXAMPLE 5

Manufacturing tables

The Ozark Furniture Company can obtain at most 8000 board feet of oak lumber for making two types of tables. It takes 50 board feet to make a round table and 80 board feet to make a rectangular table. Write an inequality that limits the possible number of tables of each type that can be made. Draw a graph showing all possibilities for the number of tables that can be made.

‹ Teaching Tip ›

This is a good time to discuss the domain of a variable. In Example 5, the variables are understood to represent nonnegative integers.

Solution

If x is the number of round tables and y is the number of rectangular tables, then x and y satisfy the inequality

$$50x + 80y \le 8000.$$

Now find the intercepts for the line $50x + 80y = 8000$:

$$\begin{aligned} 50 \cdot 0 + 80y &= 8000 \\ 80y &= 8000 \\ y &= 100 \end{aligned} \qquad\qquad \begin{aligned} 50x + 80 \cdot 0 &= 8000 \\ 50x &= 8000 \\ x &= 160 \end{aligned}$$

Draw the line through (0, 100) and (160, 0). Because (0, 0) satisfies the inequality, the number of tables must be below the line. Since the number of tables cannot be negative, the number of tables made must be below the line and in the first quadrant as shown in Fig. 4.18. Assuming that Ozark will not make a fraction of a table, only points in Fig. 4.18 with whole-number coordinates are practical.

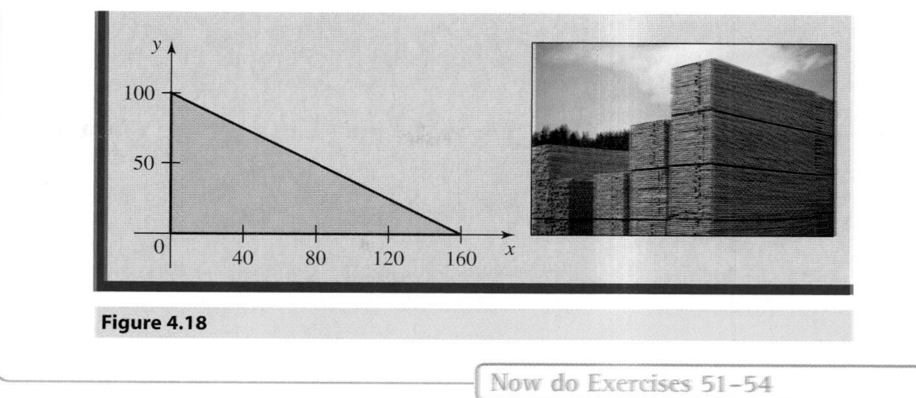

Figure 4.18

Now do Exercises 51–54

Graphical Summary of Equations and Inequalities

The graphs that follow summarize the different types of graphs that can occur for equations and inequalities in two variables. For these graphs m, b, and k are positive. Similar graphs could be made with negative numbers.

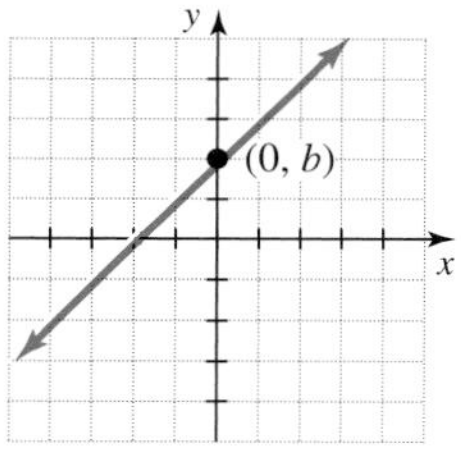

(0, b)

$y = mx + b$ 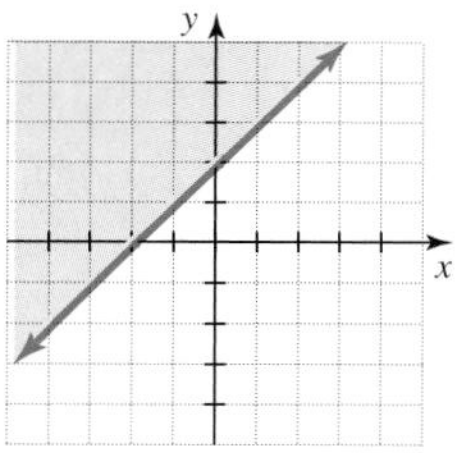 $\quad$ $y \geq mx + b$ 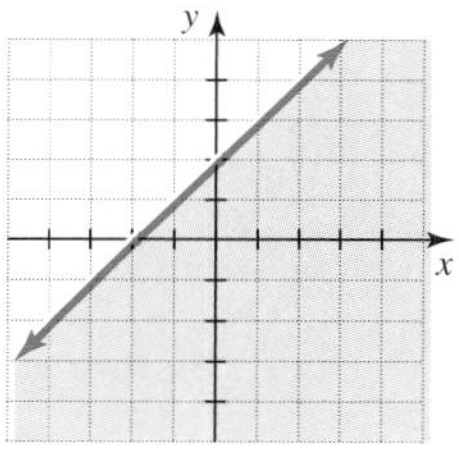 $\quad$ $y \leq mx + b$ 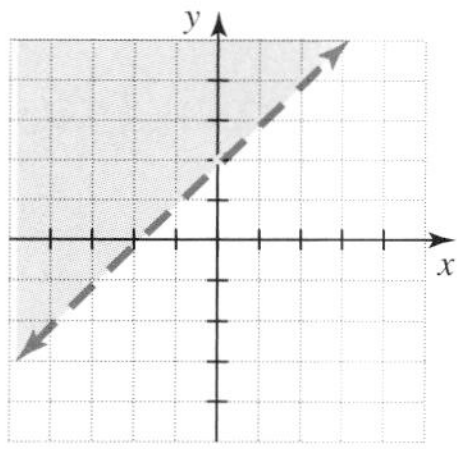 $\quad$ $y > mx + b$ 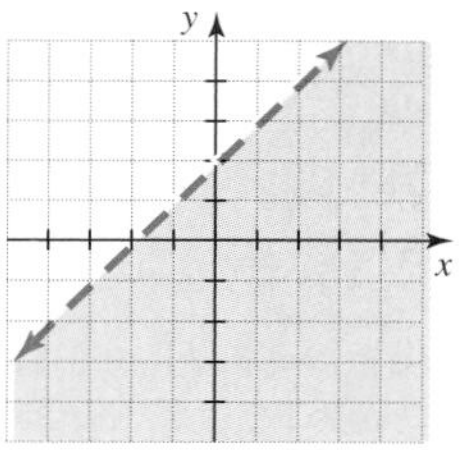 $\quad$ $y < mx + b$

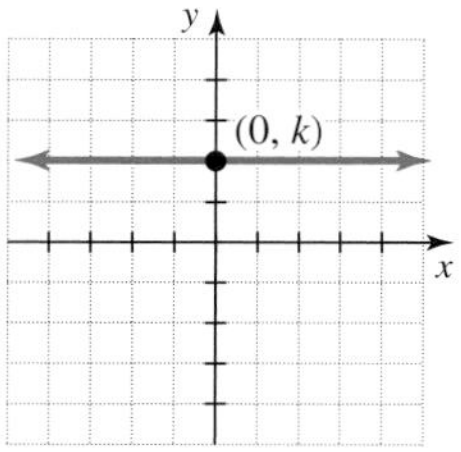

(0, k)

$y = k$ 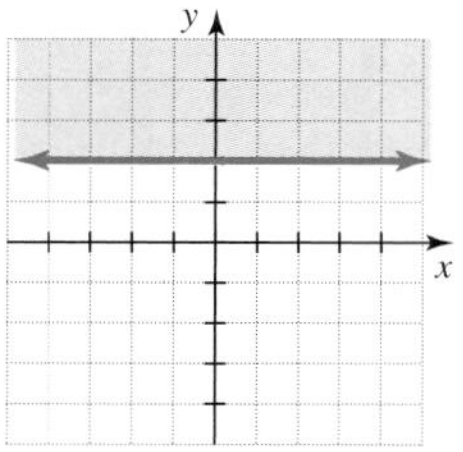 $\quad$ $y \geq k$ 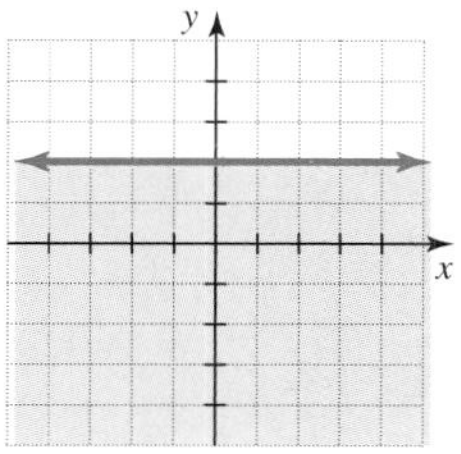 $\quad$ $y \leq k$ 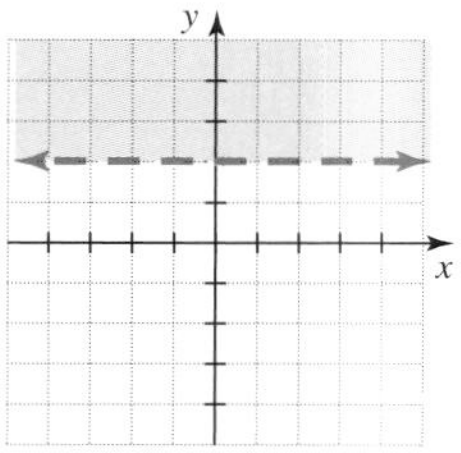 $\quad$ $y > k$ 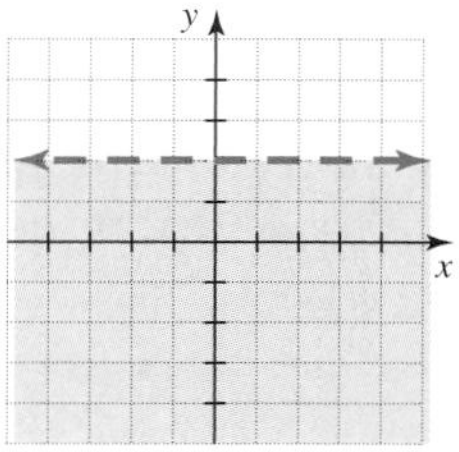 $\quad$ $y < k$

(k, 0)

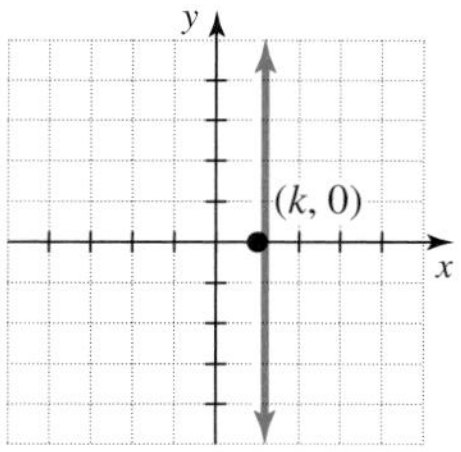

$x = k$ 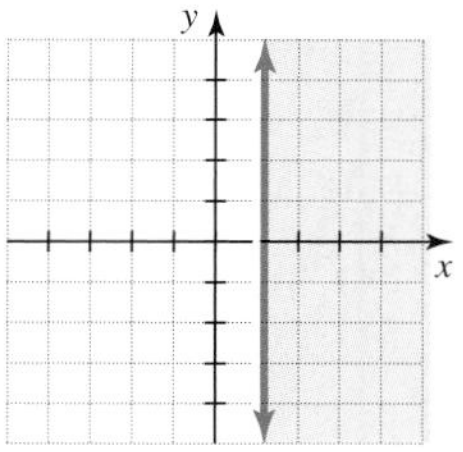 $\quad$ $x \geq k$ 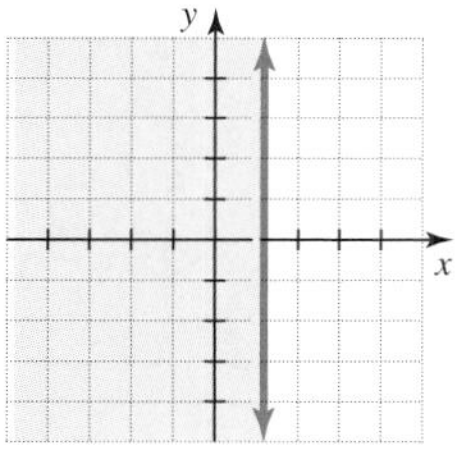 $\quad$ $x \leq k$ 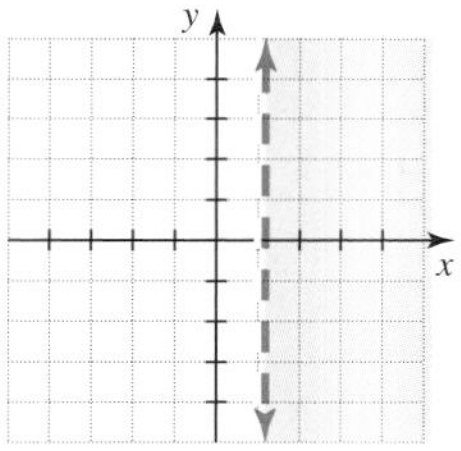 $\quad$ $x > k$ 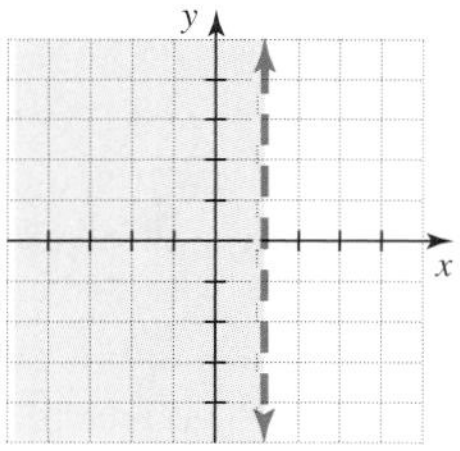 $\quad$ $x < k$

Warm-Ups ▼

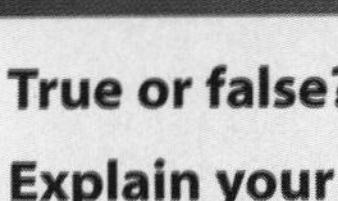

True or false? Explain your answer.

1. The point $(-1, 4)$ satisfies the inequality $y > 3x + 1$. True
2. The point $(2, -3)$ satisfies the inequality $3x - 2y \geq 12$. True
3. The graph of the inequality $y > x + 9$ is the region above the line $y = x + 9$. True
4. The graph of the inequality $x < y + 2$ is the region below the line $x = y + 2$. False
5. The graph of $x = 3$ is a single point on the x-axis. False
6. The graph of $y \leq 5$ is the region below the horizontal line $y = 5$. False
7. The graph of $x < 3$ is the region to the left of the vertical line $x = 3$. True
8. In graphing the inequality $y \geq x$ we use a dashed boundary line. False
9. The point $(0, 0)$ is on the graph of the inequality $y \geq x$. True
10. The point $(0, 0)$ lies above the line $y = 2x + 1$. False

4.4 Exercises

‹ Study Tips ›

- Everyone knows that you must practice to be successful with musical instruments, foreign languages, and sports. Success in algebra also requires regular practice.
- As soon as possible after class find a quiet place to work on your homework. The longer you wait, the harder it is to remember what happened in class.

Reading and Writing *After reading this section, write out the answers to these questions. Use complete sentences.*

1. What is a linear inequality in two variables?
A linear inequality has the same form as a linear equation except that an inequality symbol is used.
2. How can you tell if an ordered pair satisfies a linear inequality in two variables?
An ordered pair satisfies a linear inequality if the inequality is correct when the variables are replaced by the coordinates of the ordered pair.
3. How do you determine whether to draw the boundary line of the graph of a linear inequality dashed or solid?
If the inequality symbol includes equality, then the boundary line is solid; otherwise it is dashed.
4. How do you decide which side of the boundary line to shade?
We shade the side that satisfies the inequality.
5. What is the test-point method?
In the test-point method we test a point to see which side of the boundary line satisfies the inequality.
6. What is the advantage of the test-point method? With the test-point method you can use the inequality in any form.

‹1› Linear Inequalities

Determine which of the points following each inequality satisfy that inequality. See Example 1.

7. $x + y > 0$ $(0, 0), (3, -1), (-5, 4)$ $(3, -1)$
8. $x + y \leq 0$ $(0, 0), (2, -1), (-6, 3)$ $(0, 0), (-6, 3)$
9. $x - y > 5$ $(2, 3), (-3, -9), (8, 3)$ $(-3, -9)$
10. (VIDEO) $2x + y < 3$ $(-2, 6), (0, 3), (3, 0)$ $(-2, 6)$
11. $y \geq -2x + 5$ $(3, 0), (1, 3), (-2, 5)$ $(3, 0), (1, 3)$
12. $y \leq -x + 6$ $(2, 0), (-3, 9), (-4, 12)$ $(2, 0), (-3, 9)$

13. $x > -3y + 4$ (2, 3), (7, −1), (0, 5) (2, 3), (0, 5)

14. $x < -y - 3$ (1, 2), (−3, −4), (0, −3) (−3, −4)

⟨2⟩ Graphing a Linear Inequality

Graph each inequality.

See Examples 2 and 3.

See the Strategy for Graphing a Linear Inequality in Two Variables box on page 269.

15. $y < x + 4$

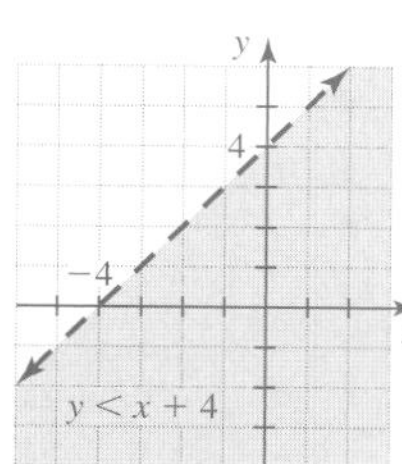

16. $y < 2x + 2$

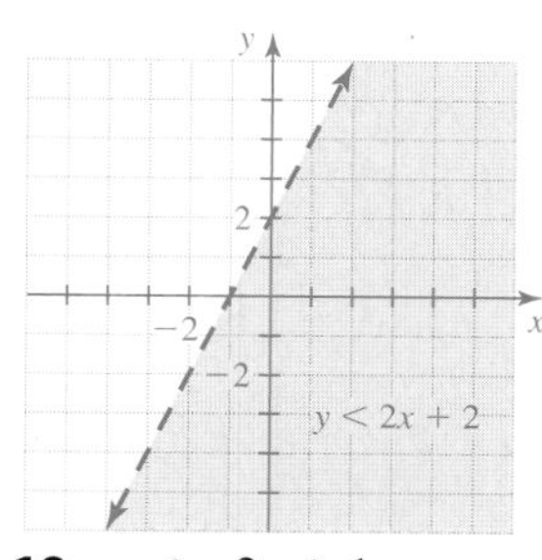

17. $y > -x + 3$

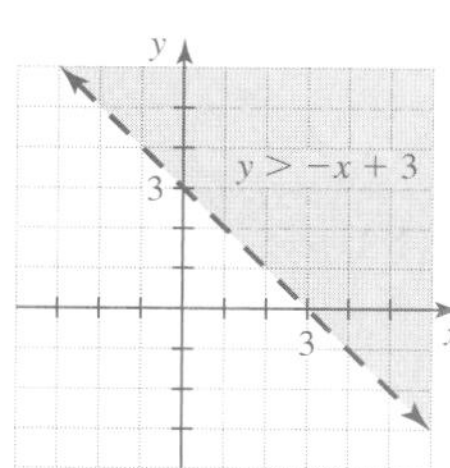

VIDEO **18.** $y < -2x + 1$

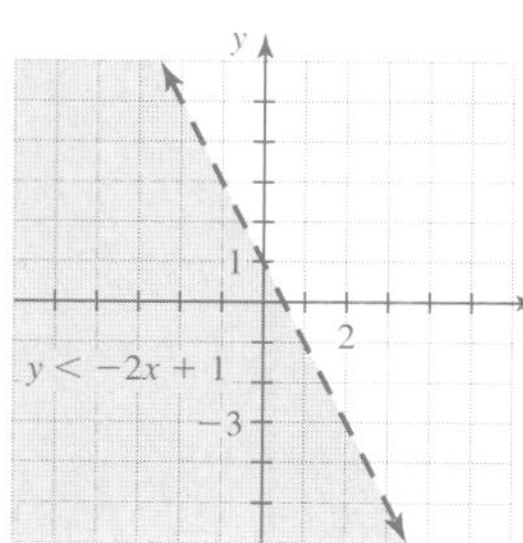

19. $y > \frac{2}{3}x - 3$

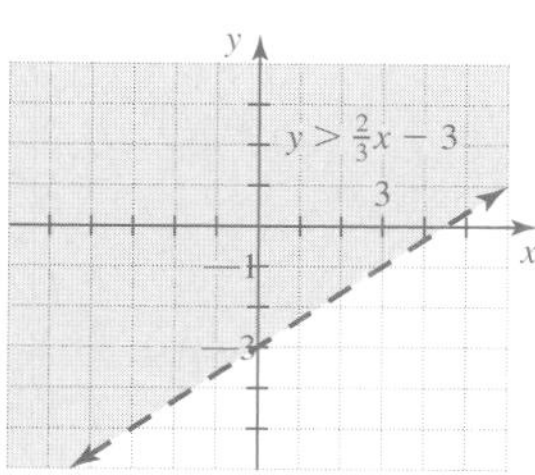

20. $y < \frac{1}{2}x + 1$

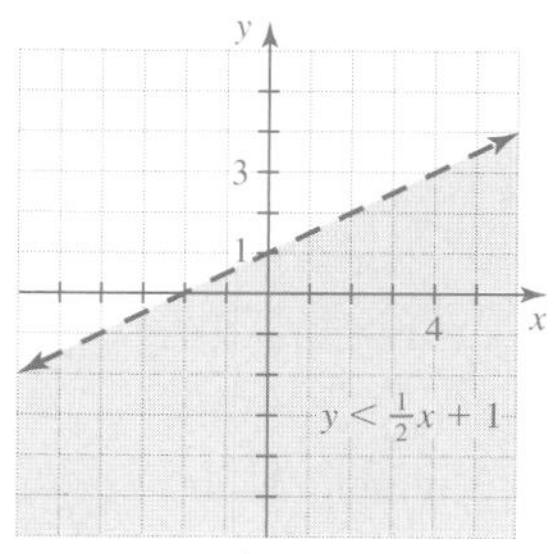

21. $y \leq -\frac{2}{5}x + 2$

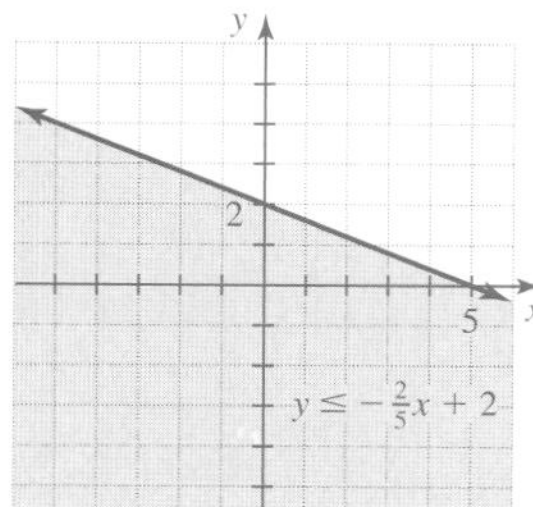

22. $y \geq -\frac{1}{2}x + 3$

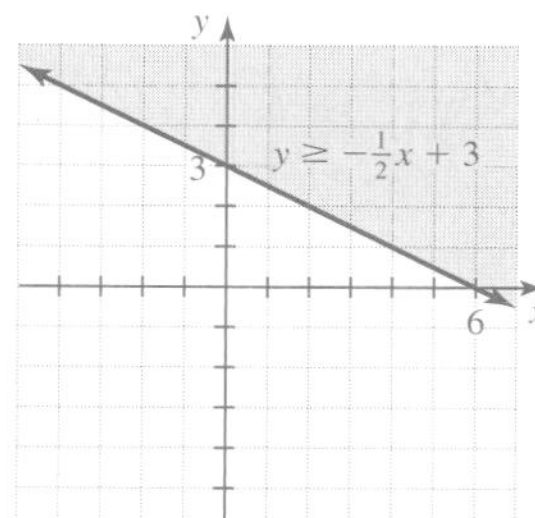

23. $y - x \geq 0$

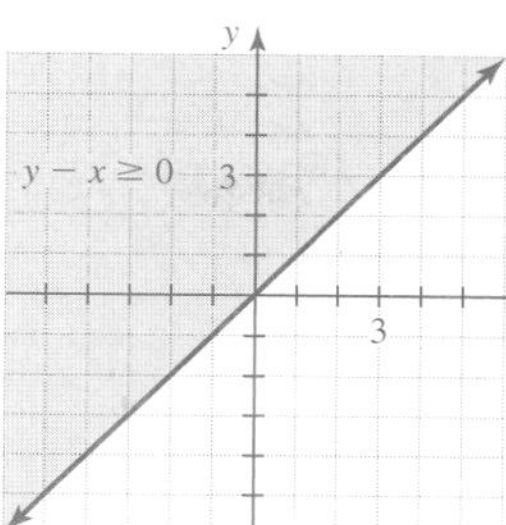

24. $x - 2y \leq 0$

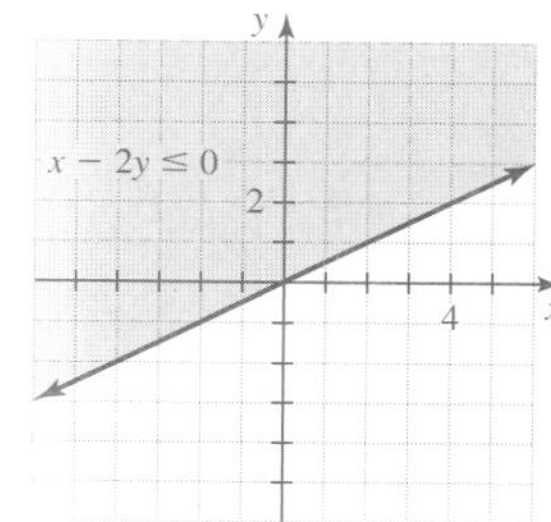

25. $x > y - 5$

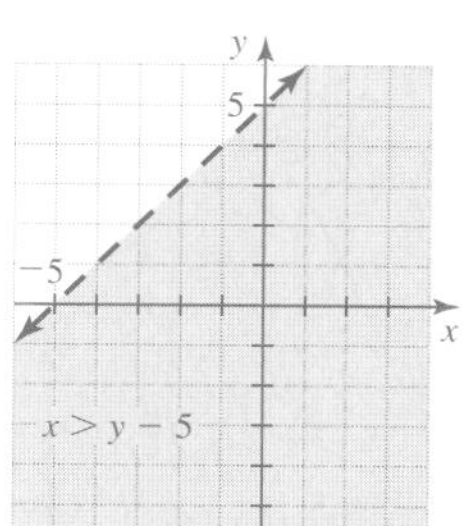

26. $2x < 3y + 6$

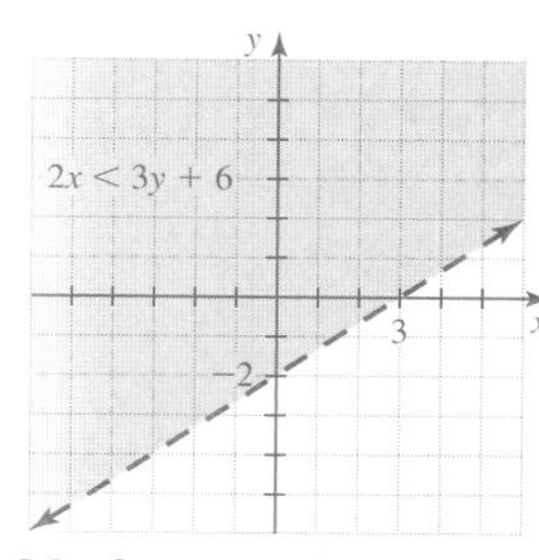

27. $x - 2y + 4 \leq 0$

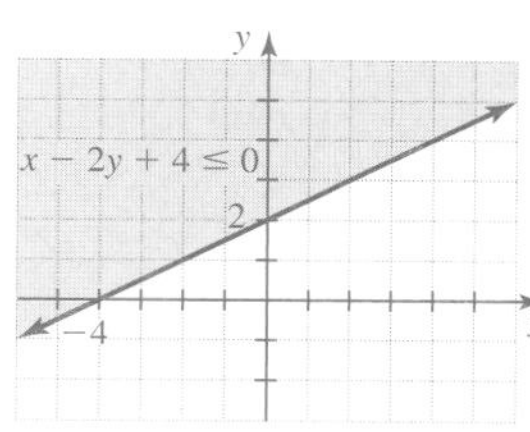

28. $2x - y + 3 \geq 0$

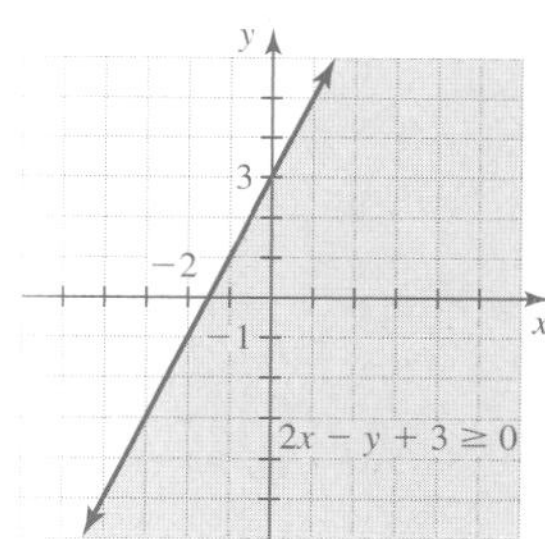

29. $y \geq 2$

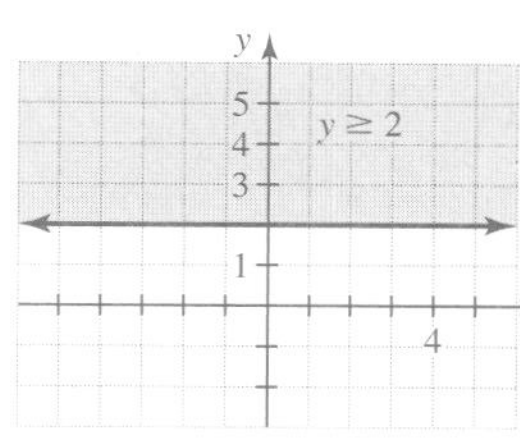

VIDEO **30.** $y < 7$

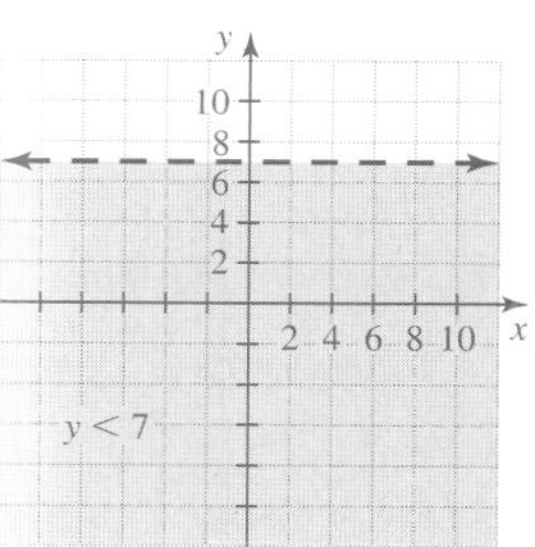

31. $x > 9$

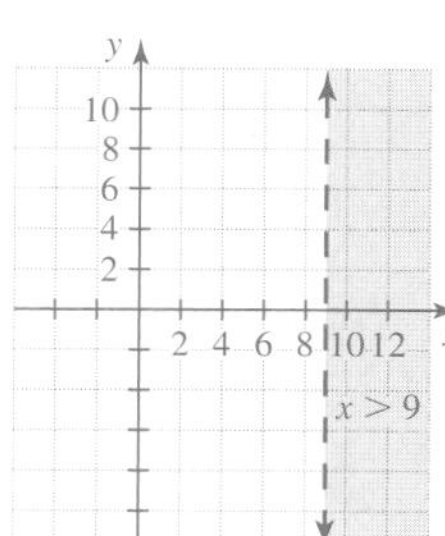

VIDEO **32.** $x \leq 1$

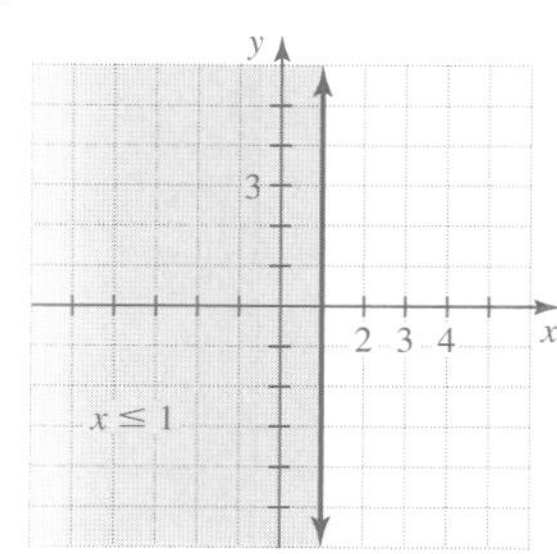

33. $x + y \le 60$

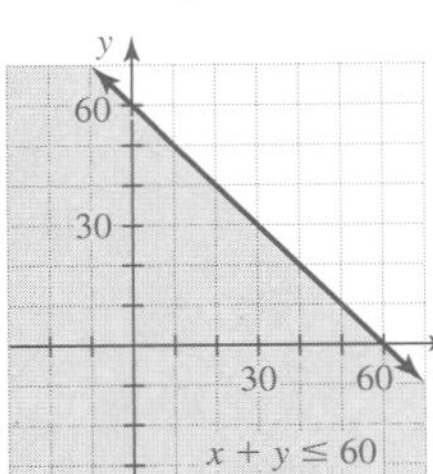

34. $x - y \le 90$

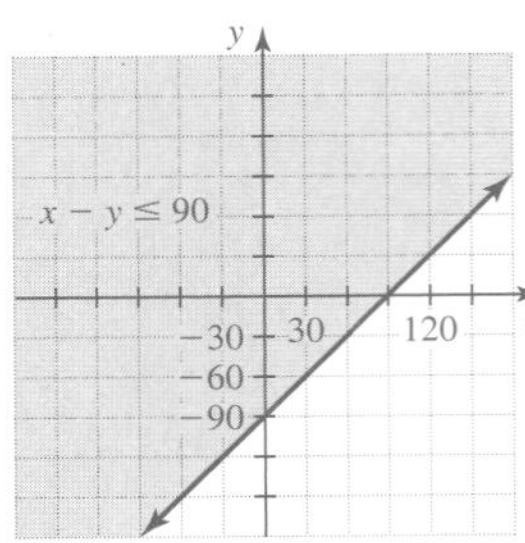

35. $x \le 100y$

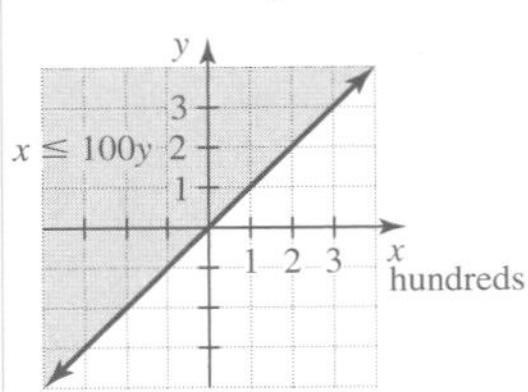

36. $y \ge 600x$

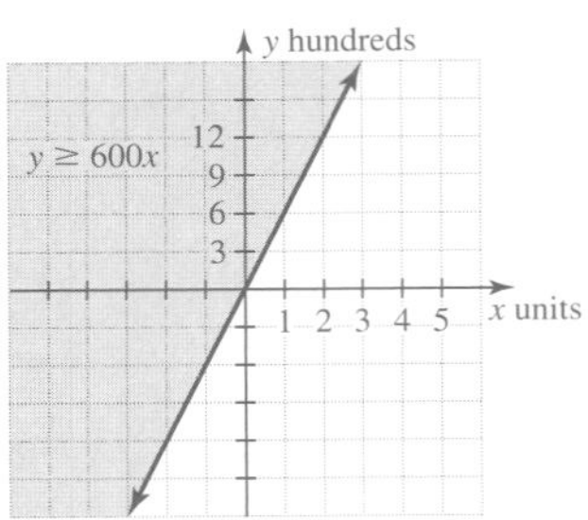

37. $3x - 4y \le 8$

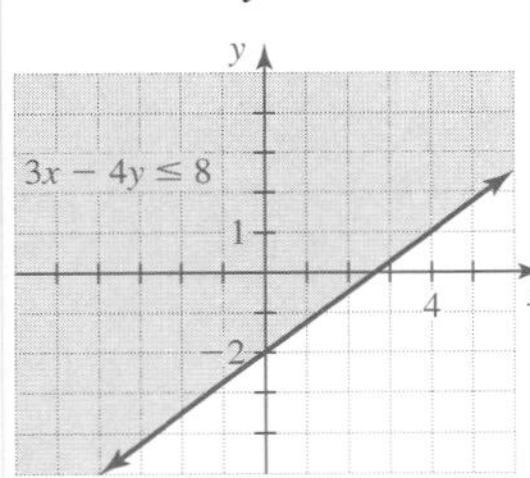

38. $2x + 5y \ge 10$

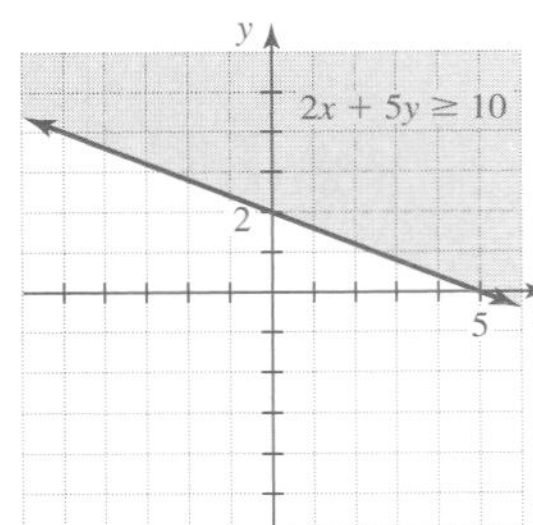

3 The Test-Point Method

Graph each inequality using a test point.

See Example 4.

See the Strategy for the Test-Point Method box on page 271.

39. $2x - 3y < 6$

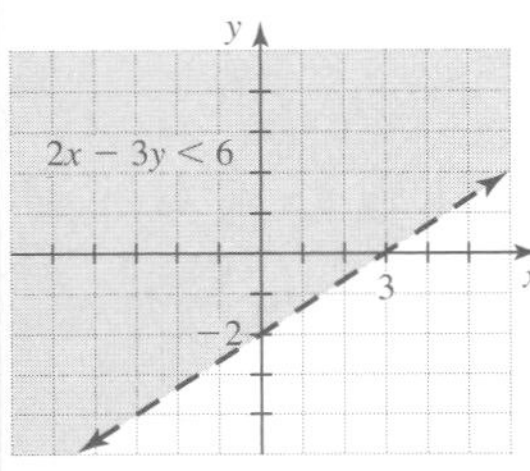

40. $x - 4y > 4$

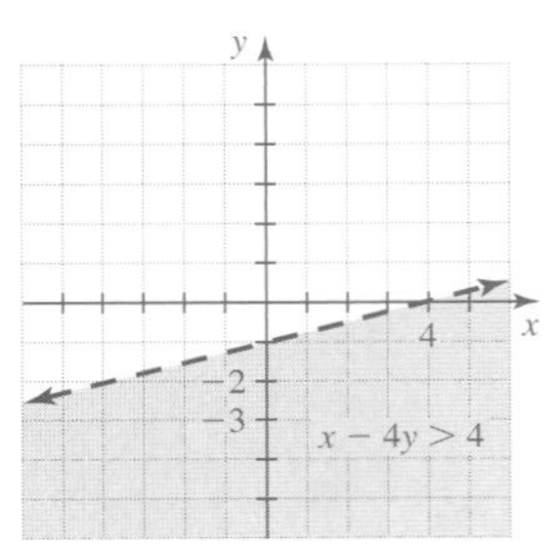

41. $x - 4y \le 8$

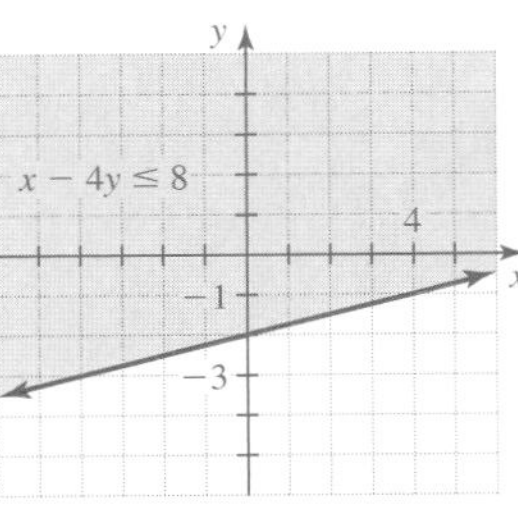

42. $3y - 5x \ge 15$

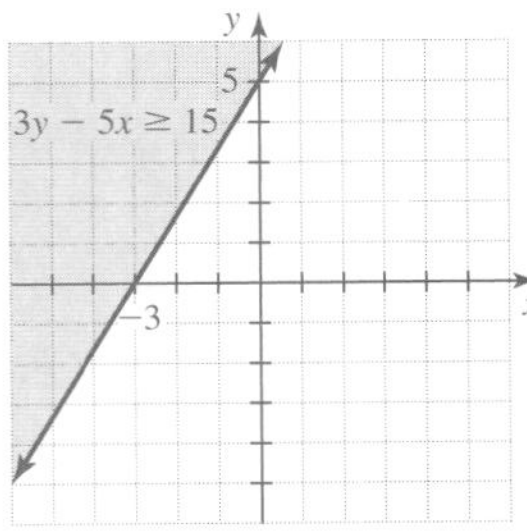

43. $y - \frac{7}{2}x \le 7$

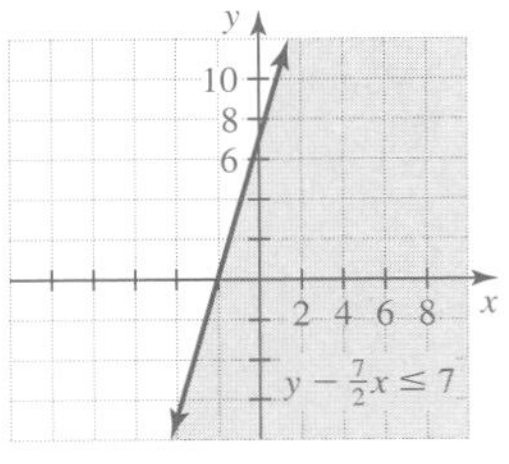

44. $\frac{2}{3}x + 3y \le 12$

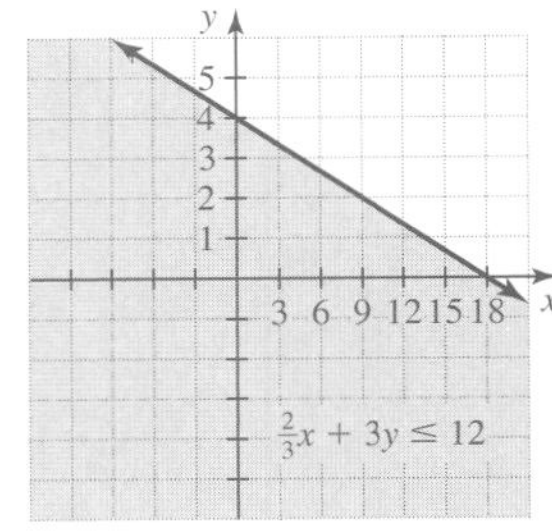

45. $x - y < 5$

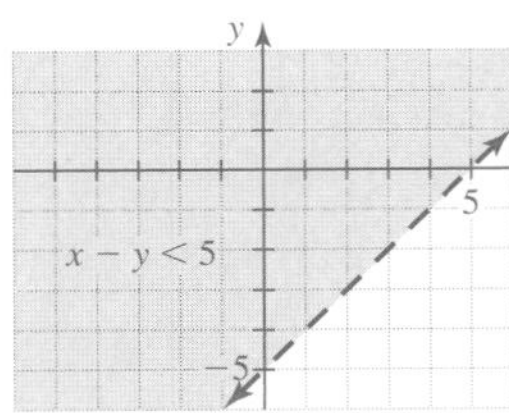

46. $y - x > -3$

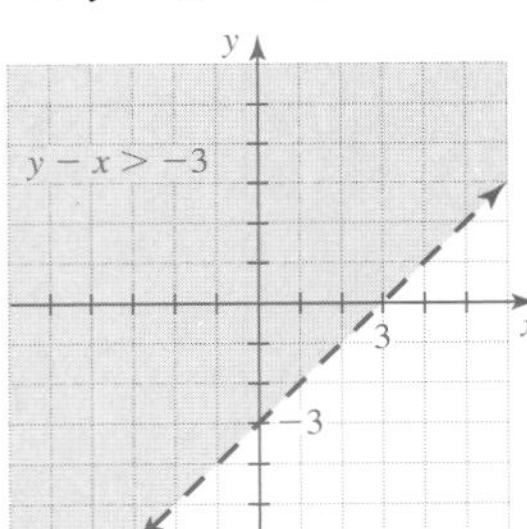

47. $3x - 4y < -12$

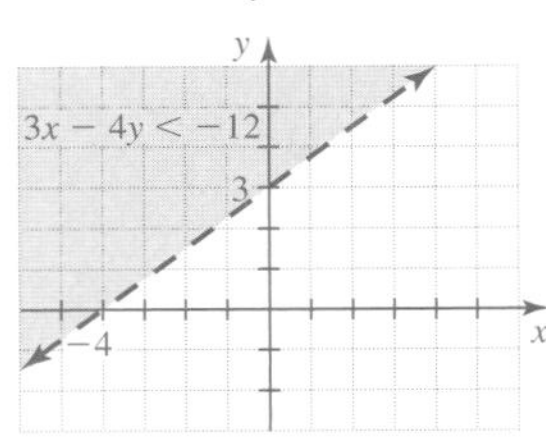

48. $4x + 3y > 24$

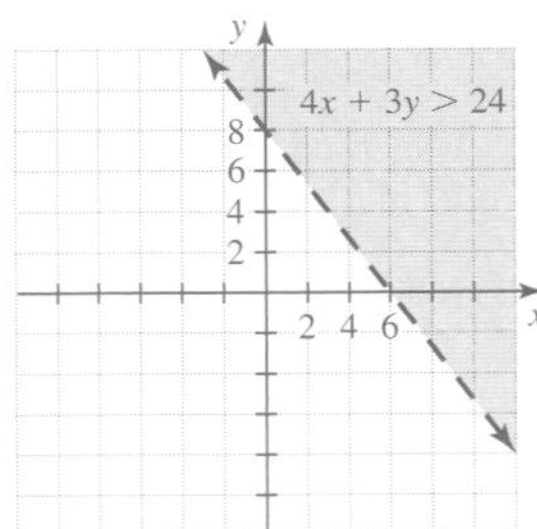

49. $x < 5y - 100$

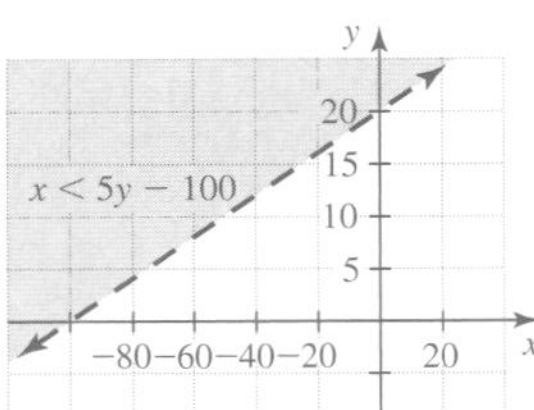

50. $-x > 70 - y$

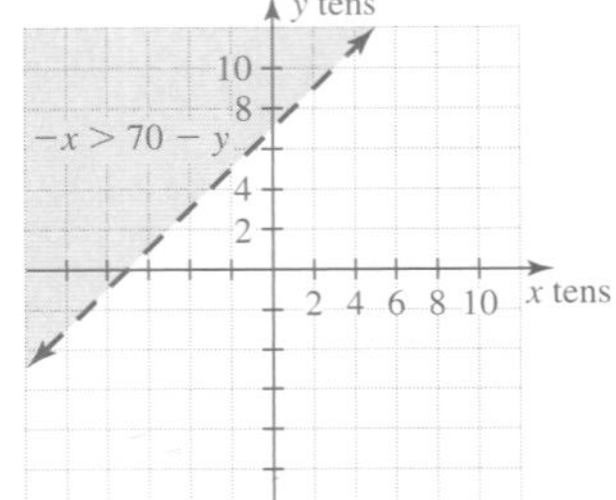

‹4› Applications

Solve each problem. See Example 5.

51. ***Storing the tables.*** Ozark Furniture Company must store its oak tables before shipping. A round table is packaged in a carton with a volume of 25 cubic feet (ft^3), and a rectangular table is packaged in a carton with a volume of 35 ft^3. The warehouse has at most 3850 ft^3 of space available for these tables. Write an inequality that limits the possible number of tables of each type that can be stored, and graph the inequality in the first quadrant. $5x + 7y \le 770$

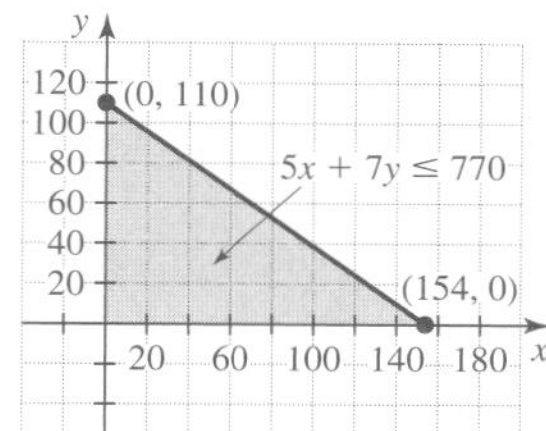

52. ***Maple rockers.*** Ozark Furniture Company can obtain at most 3000 board feet of maple lumber for making its classic and modern maple rocking chairs. A classic maple rocker requires 15 board feet of maple, and a modern rocker requires 12 board feet of maple. Write an inequality that limits the possible number of maple rockers of each type that can be made, and graph the inequality in the first quadrant. $5x + 4y \le 1000$

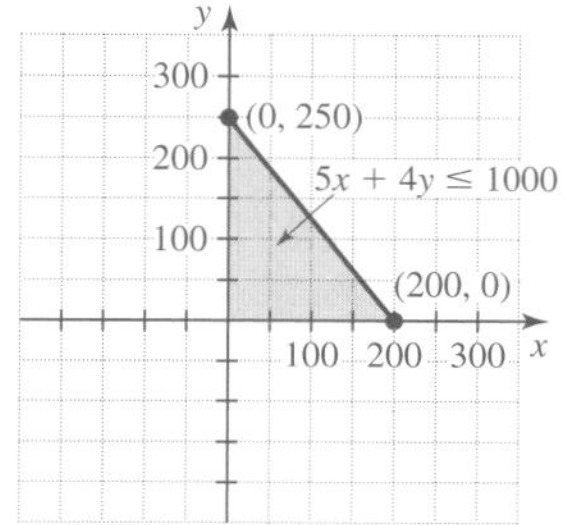

53. ***Pens and notebooks.*** A student has at most \$4 to spend on pens at \$0.25 each and notebooks at \$0.40 each. Write an inequality that limits the possibilities for the number of pens (x) and the number of notebooks (y) that can be purchased. Graph the inequality in the first quadrant. $5x + 8y \le 80$

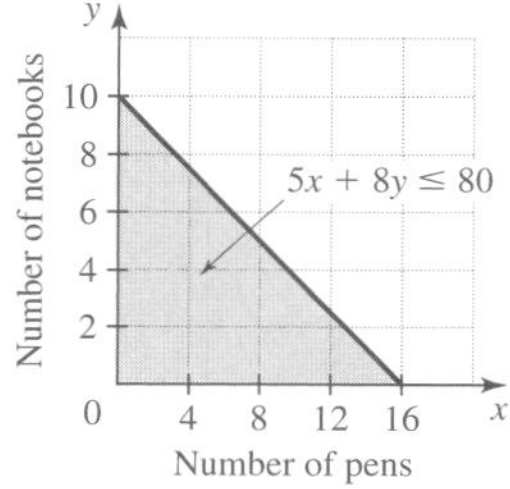

Photo for Exercise 52

54. ***Enzyme concentration.*** A food chemist tests enzymes for their ability to break down pectin in fruit juices (Dennis Callas, *Snapshots of Applications in Mathematics*). Excess pectin makes juice cloudy. In one test, the chemist measures the concentration of the enzyme, c, in milligrams per milliliter and the fraction of light absorbed by the liquid, a. If $a > 0.07c + 0.02$, then the enzyme is working as it should. Graph the inequality in the first quadrant.

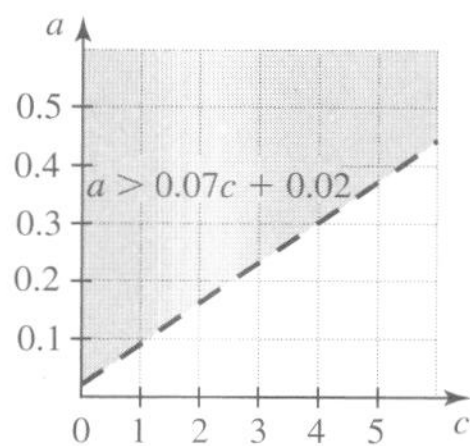

Getting More Involved

55. ***Discussion***

When asked to graph the inequality $x + 2y < 12$, a student found that (0, 5) and (8, 0) both satisfied $x + 2y < 12$. The student then drew a dashed line through these two points and shaded the region below the line. What is wrong with this method? Do all of the points graphed by this student satisfy the inequality?

56. ***Writing***

Compare and contrast the two methods presented in this section for graphing linear inequalities. What are the advantages and disadvantages of each method? How do you choose which method to use?

4.5 Graphing Systems of Linear Inequalities

In Section 4.4, you learned how to solve a linear inequality. In this section, you will solve systems of linear inequalities.

In This Section

⟨1⟩ The Solution to a System of Inequalities

A point is a solution to a system of two equations if it satisfies both equations. Similarly, a point is a solution to a system of two inequalities if it satisfies both inequalities.

EXAMPLE 1 Satisfying a system of inequalities

Determine whether each point is a solution to the system of inequalities:

$$2x + 3y < 6$$
$$y > 2x - 1$$

a) $(-3, 2)$ **b)** $(4, -3)$ **c)** $(5, 1)$

Solution

a) The point $(-3, 2)$ is a solution to the system if it satisfies both inequalities. Let $x = -3$ and $y = 2$ in each inequality:

$$2x + 3y < 6 \qquad y > 2x - 1$$
$$2(-3) + 3(2) < 6 \qquad 2 > 2(-3) - 1$$
$$0 < 6 \quad \text{True} \qquad 2 > -7 \quad \text{True}$$

Because both inequalities are satisfied, the point $(-3, 2)$ is a solution to the system.

b) Let $x = 4$ and $y = -3$ in each inequality:

$$2x + 3y < 6 \qquad y > 2x - 1$$
$$2(4) + 3(-3) < 6 \qquad -3 > 2(4) - 1$$
$$-1 < 6 \quad \text{True} \qquad -3 > 7 \quad \text{False}$$

Because only one inequality is satisfied, the point $(4, -3)$ is not a solution to the system.

c) Let $x = 5$ and $y = 1$ in each inequality:

$$2x + 3y < 6 \qquad y > 2x - 1$$
$$2(5) + 3(1) < 6 \qquad 1 > 2(5) - 1$$
$$13 < 6 \quad \text{False} \qquad 1 > 9 \quad \text{False}$$

Because neither inequality is satisfied, the point $(5, 1)$ is not a solution to the system.

Now do Exercises 7–14

⟨2⟩ Graphing a System of Inequalities

There are infinitely many points that satisfy a typical system of inequalities. The best way to describe the solution to a system of inequalities is with a graph showing all points that satisfy the system. When we graph the points that satisfy a system, we say that we are graphing the system.

EXAMPLE 2

Graphing a system of inequalities

Graph all ordered pairs that satisfy the following system of inequalities:

$$y > x - 2$$
$$y < -2x + 3$$

‹ Teaching Tip ›

Remind students that if no word is used with a pair of equations or inequalities, the word is understood to be "and." We want points for which

$y > x - 2$ and $y < -2x + 3$.

Solution

First graph $y = x - 2$ with slope 1 and y-intercept $(0, -2)$ as a dashed line (because the inequality symbol is $>$). Next graph $y = -2x + 3$ with slope -2 and y-intercept $(0, 3)$ as a dashed line (because the inequality symbol is $<$). The two lines divide the coordinate plane into four regions shown in Fig. 4.19. To determine where the system is satisfied, we test one point in each region. Any four points will do, as long as you choose one in each region. The arbitrary test points chosen here are $(0, -5)$, $(0, 0)$, $(0, 5)$, and $(4, 0)$ as shown in Fig. 4.19. Now check whether each test point satisfies the system, as was done in Example 1. You can keep the checking organized with a table as follows.

Test Points	$y > x - 2$	$y < -2x + 2$	$y > x - 2$ and $y < -2x + 3$
$(0, -5)$	False	True	False
$(0, 0)$	True	True	**True**
$(0, 5)$	True	False	False
$(4, 0)$	False	False	False

The only point that satisfies both inequalities of the system is $(0, 0)$. So every point in the region containing $(0, 0)$ also satisfies both inequalities. The points that satisfy the system are graphed in Fig. 4.20.

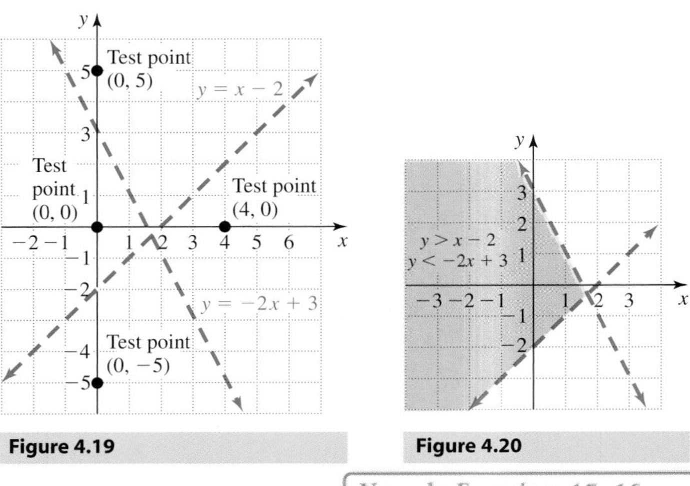

Figure 4.19

Figure 4.20

Now do Exercises 15–16

EXAMPLE 3

Graphing a system of inequalities

Graph all ordered pairs that satisfy the following system of inequalities:

$$y > -3x + 4$$
$$2y - x > 2$$

Solution

First graph the equations $y = -3x + 4$ and $2y - x = 2$ as dashed lines, as shown in Fig. 4.21. Now arbitrarily select one point in each of the four regions determined by the lines, say (0, 0), (0, 2), (0, 6), and (5, 0). Check each point in the system. You can keep all of the checking organized with a table like the following.

Test Points	$y > -3x + 4$	$2y - x > 2$	$y > -3x + 4$ and $2y - x > 2$
(0, 0)	False	False	False
(0, 2)	False	True	False
(0, 6)	True	True	**True**
(5, 0)	True	False	False

Only (0, 6) satisfies both inequalities and satisfies the system. So only the region containing (0, 6) is the solution set and only that region is shaded in Fig. 4.21.

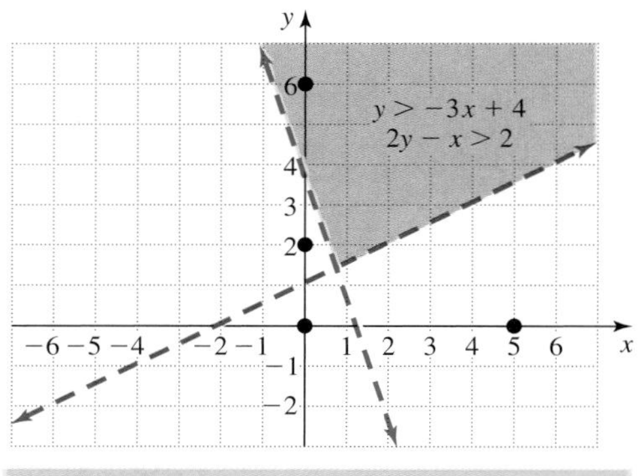

Figure 4.21

Now do Exercises 17–20

To solve a system without using test points, shade the region that satisfies each inequality. The solution set to the system consists of all points that are shaded twice. This method works best when the inequalities are solved for y. In this case, the boundary lines are easy to graph (using slope and y-intercept) and it is easy to decide which side of the boundary line to shade ($y > mx + b$ is above and $y < mx + b$ is below).

EXAMPLE 4

Graphing a system without using test points

Graph the system:

$$y > x$$

$$y < -x + 3$$

Solution

The solution to $y > x$ consists of all points above the line $y = x$ shaded in red in Fig. 4.22(a). The solution to $y < -x + 3$ consists of all points below the line $y = -x + 3$ shaded in blue in Fig. 4.22(a). The points that are shaded twice in Fig. 4.22(a) satisfy the system. They are the points that are above $y = x$ and below $y = -x + 3$. The graph of the system is shown in Fig. 4.22(b).

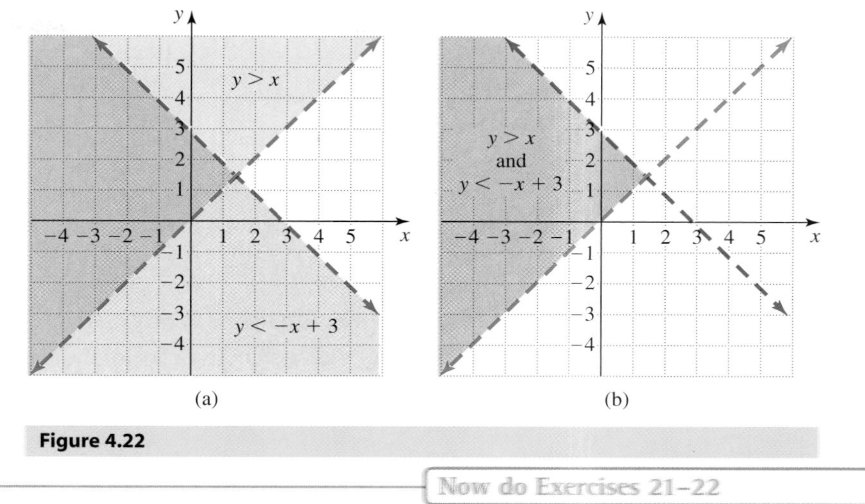

Figure 4.22

Now do Exercises 21–22

CAUTION Figure 4.22(a) is not the answer to Example 4. Figure 4.22(a) is drawn as an aid to getting the graph of the system shown in Fig. 4.22(b).

EXAMPLE 5 Horizontal and vertical boundary lines

Graph the system of inequalities:

$$x > 4$$
$$y < 3$$

Solution

First graph the vertical line $x = 4$ and the horizontal line $y = 3$ as dashed lines, as shown in Fig. 4.23. We could select a point in each region as in the last example, but that is not really necessary here. It is clear that $x > 4$ and $y < 3$ only for a point such as (6, 0). So we shade the region containing (6, 0), as shown in Fig. 4.23. Notice that $x > 4$ is satisfied to the right of the vertical line, and $y < 3$ is satisfied below the horizontal line. Only points that are to the right of $x = 4$ and below $y = 3$ are shaded.

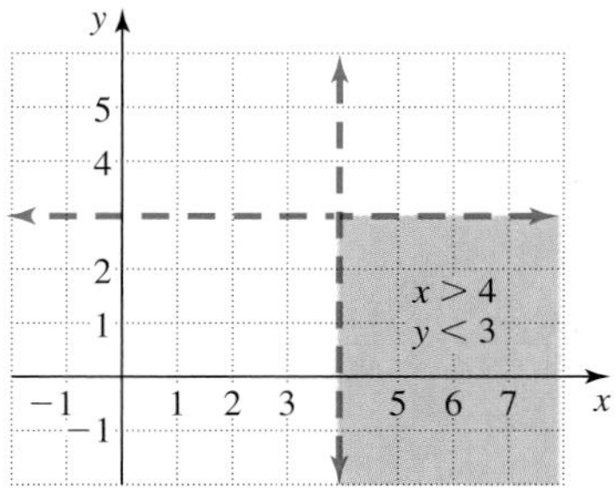

Figure 4.23

Now do Exercises 23–26

EXAMPLE 6 Between parallel lines

Graph the system of inequalities:

$$y < x + 4$$
$$y > x - 1$$

Solution

First graph the lines $y = x + 4$ and $y = x - 1$, as shown in Fig. 4.24 on the next page. Because these lines are parallel, they divide the coordinate plane into only three regions.

Helpful Hint

We could use the notation from Chapter 2 and write the inequalities in Example 6 as the compound inequality

$$x - 1 < y < x + 4.$$

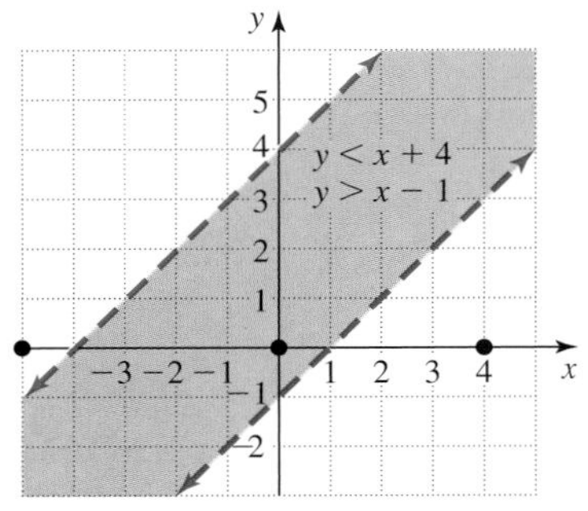

Figure 4.24

Select a point in each region, say, $(-5, 0)$, $(0, 0)$, and $(4, 0)$. Check each point in the system:

Test Points	$y < x + 4$	$y > x - 1$	$y < x + 4$ and $y > x - 1$
$(-5, 0)$	False	True	False
$(0, 0)$	True	True	**True**
$(4, 0)$	True	False	False

Only $(0, 0)$ satisfies both inequalities and satisfies the system. So only the region containing $(0, 0)$ is the solution set to the system and only that region is shaded in Fig. 4.24. Notice that $y < x + 4$ is satisfied below the top line and $y > x - 1$ is satisfied above the bottom line. Only points in between the lines satisfy both inequalities.

Now do Exercises 27–46

⟨3⟩ Systems with No Solution

The solution set to a system of inequalities can be empty even when the solution sets to the individual inequalities are not empty.

EXAMPLE 7 Systems of inequalities with no solution

Solve each system of inequalities.

a) $y > x + 5$
$y < x - 5$

b) $x \geq 2$
$x \leq -3$

c) $y > 5$
$y < 1$

Solution

a) The lines $y = x + 5$ and $y = x - 5$ are parallel lines, as shown in Fig. 4.25. Points that satisfy $y > x + 5$ lie above $y = x + 5$, and points that satisfy $y < x - 5$ lie below $y = x - 5$. Because of the positions of these lines, there are no points that are above $y = x + 5$ and below $y = x - 5$. So the solution set to the system is the empty set $\emptyset$.

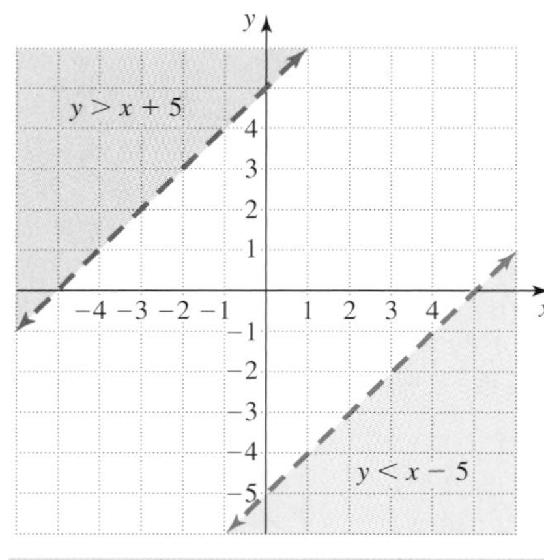

Figure 4.25

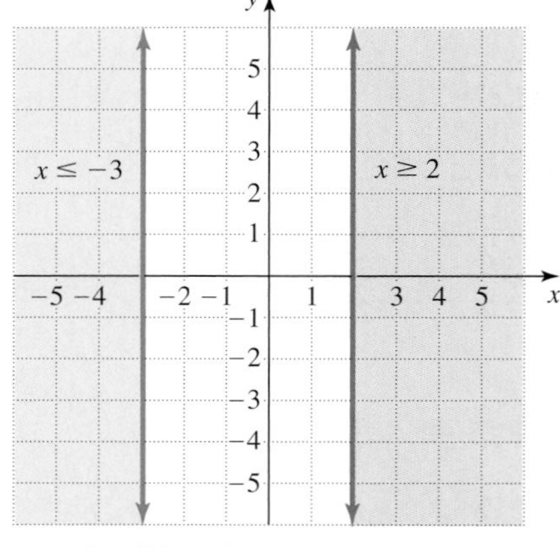

Figure 4.26

b) The lines $x = 2$ and $x = -3$ are vertical parallel lines, as shown in Fig. 4.26. Points that satisfy $x \geq 2$ lie on or to the right of $x = 2$, and points that satisfy $x \leq -3$ lie on or to the left of $x = -3$. Because of the positions of these lines, there are no points that do both. So the solution set is the empty set $\emptyset$.

c) The graph of $y > 5$ is the region above $y = 5$, and the graph of $y < 1$ is the region below $y = 1$. See Fig. 4.27. Since the lines $y = 5$ and $y = 1$ are parallel, there are no points that satisfy both inequalities. The solution set is the empty set $\emptyset$.

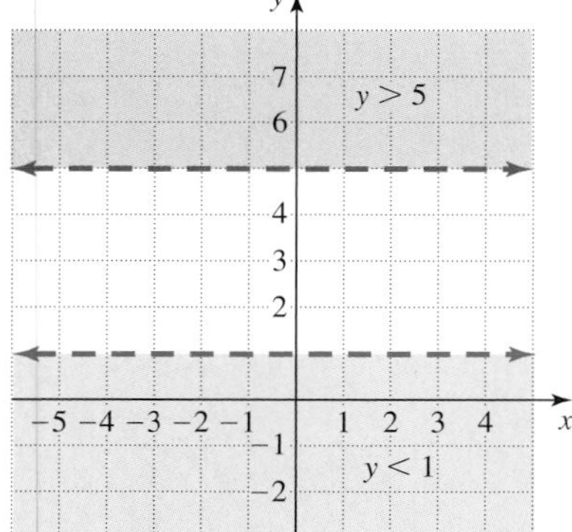

Figure 4.27

Now do Exercises 47–56

⟨4⟩ Applications

EXAMPLE 8

Allocating resources

A small computer shop assembles desktop computers and laptop computers. The cost of material for a desktop is \$300, and the cost for a laptop is \$400. It takes 2 hours to assemble a desktop and 6 hours to assemble a laptop. The shop has at most \$6000 to spend on materials and at most 60 hours of labor available. Write a system of inequalities that limits the number of computers of each type that can be built. Graph the system.

Solution

Let x represent the number of desktop computers and y represent the number of laptop computers. We can write an inequality about the cost of materials and one about the available hours of labor.

$$300x + 400y \le 6000 \quad \text{Total cost of materials} \le \$6000.$$
$$2x + 6y \le 60 \quad \text{Total hours of labor} \le 60.$$

We could also use the inequalities $x \ge 0$ and $y \ge 0$ since negative numbers of computers do not make sense. So the graph is in the first quadrant only. Simplify the inequalities:

$$3x + 4y \le 60 \quad \text{Material inequality}$$
$$x + 3y \le 30 \quad \text{Labor inequality}$$

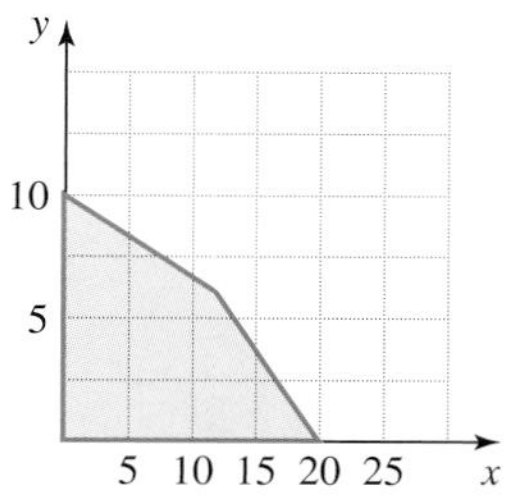

Graph the inequalities as shown in Fig. 4.28. Any point within the shaded region is a possible way for the shop to allocate its resources.

Figure 4.28

Now do Exercises 61–64

Warm-Ups ▼

True or false? Explain your answer.

Use the following systems for Exercises 1–7.

a) $y > -3x + 5$, $y < 2x - 3$ **b)** $y > 2x - 3$, $y < 2x + 3$ **c)** $x + y > 4$, $x - y < 0$

1. The point $(2, -3)$ is a solution to system (a). False
2. The point $(5, 0)$ is a solution to system (a). True
3. The point $(0, 0)$ is a solution to system (b). True
4. The graph of system (b) is the region between two parallel lines. True
5. You can use $(0, 0)$ as a test point for system (c). False
6. The point $(2, 2)$ satisfies system (c). False
7. The point $(4, 5)$ satisfies system (c). True
8. The inequality $x + y > 4$ is equivalent to the inequality $y < -x + 4$. False
9. The graph of $y < 2x + 3$ is the region below the line $y = 2x + 3$. True
10. There is no ordered pair that satisfies $y < 2x - 3$ and $y > 2x + 3$. True

4.5 Exercises

MathZone

Boost your grade at mathzone.com!

- > Practice Problems
- > NetTutor
- > Self-Tests
- > e-Professors
- > Videos

‹ Study Tips ›

- Relax and don't worry about grades. If you are doing everything that you can and should be doing, then there is no reason to worry.
- Be active in class. Don't be embarrassed to ask questions or answer questions. You can often learn more from a wrong answer than a right one.

Reading and Writing *After reading this section, write out the answers to these questions. Use complete sentences.*

1. What is a system of linear inequalities in two variables?
A system of linear inequalities in two variables is a pair of linear inequalities in two variables.

2. How can you tell if an ordered pair satisfies a system of linear inequalities in two variables?
To see if an ordered pair satisfies a system of inequalities, we can check to see if it satisfies both inequalities.

3. How do we usually describe the solution set to a system of inequalities in two variables?
The solution set to a system of inequalities is usually described with a graph.

4. How do you decide whether the boundary lines are solid or dashed?
A boundary line is solid if the inequality symbol includes equality; otherwise it is dashed.

5. How do you use the test-point method for a system of linear inequalities?
To use the test-point method, select a point in each region determined by the graphs of the boundary lines.

6. How do you select test points?
Any point will work as a test point, but it is usually simplest to select points on the axes.

‹1› The Solution to a System of Inequalities

Determine which of the points following each system is a solution to the system. See Example 1.

7. $x > 3$ $(-5, 4), (9, -5), (6, 0)$
$y < -2$ $(9, -5)$

8. $y < -5$ $(-2, 4), (0, -7), (6, -9)$
$x < 1$ $(0, -7)$

9. $x + y > 0$ $(1, 3), (1, -3), (3, 1)$
$x - y < 0$ $(1, 3)$

10. $x + y < 0$ $(2, 4), (2, -4), (-2, 4)$
$x - y > 0$ $(2, -4)$

11. $x - y < 5$ $(4, 3), (8, 2), (-3, 0)$
$2x + y > 3$ $(4, 3)$

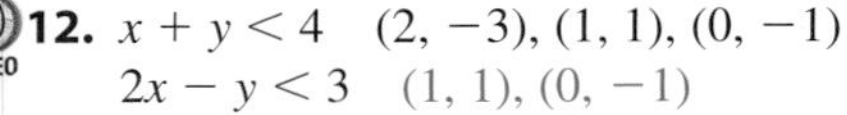

VIDEO **12.** $x + y < 4$ $(2, -3), (1, 1), (0, -1)$
$2x - y < 3$ $(1, 1), (0, -1)$

13. $y > -2x + 1$ $(-3, 2), (-1, 5), (3, 6)$
$y < 3x + 5$ $(3, 6)$

14. $y < -x + 7$ $(-3, 8), (0, 8), (-5, 15)$
$y < -x + 9$ $(-3, 8)$

‹2› Graphing a System of Inequalities

Graph each system of inequalities. See Examples 2–6.

15. $y > -x - 1$
$y > x + 1$

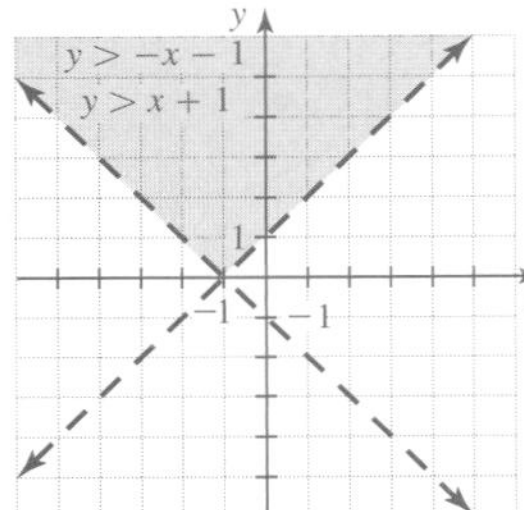

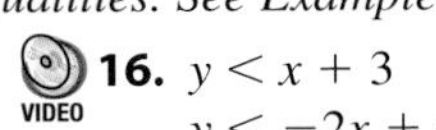

VIDEO **16.** $y < x + 3$
$y < -2x + 4$

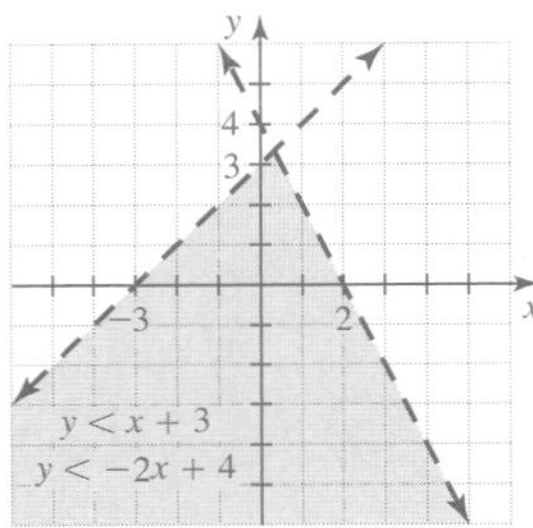

17. $x + y > 5$
$x - y < 3$

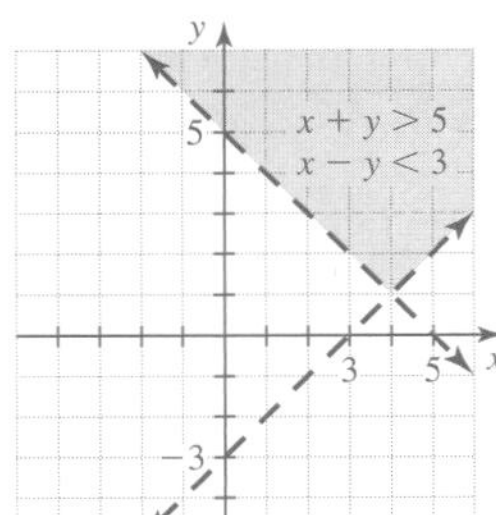

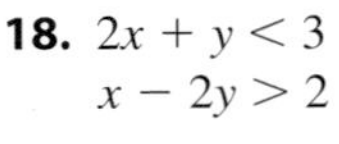

18. $2x + y < 3$
$x - 2y > 2$

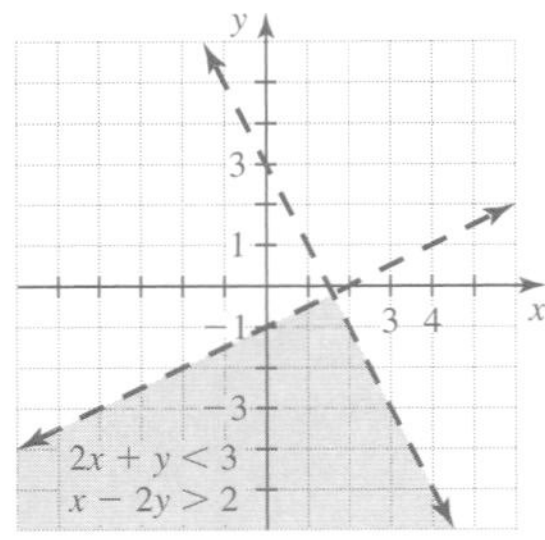

19. $2x - 3y < 6$
$x - y > 3$

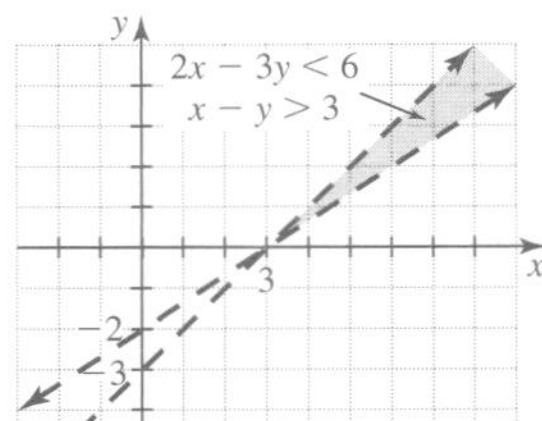

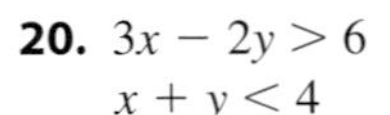

20. $3x - 2y > 6$
$x + y < 4$

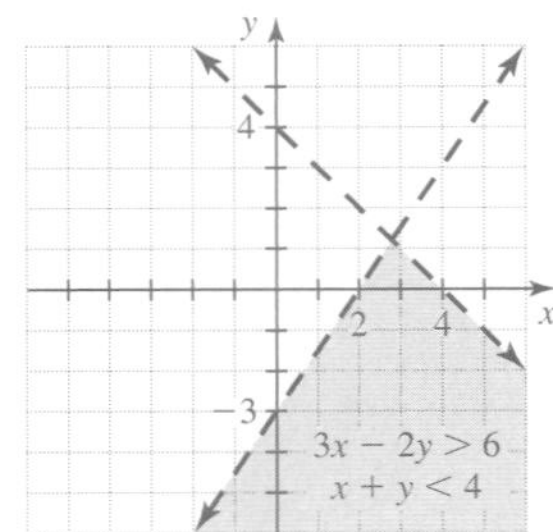

21. $y < 2x - 3$
$y > -x + 2$

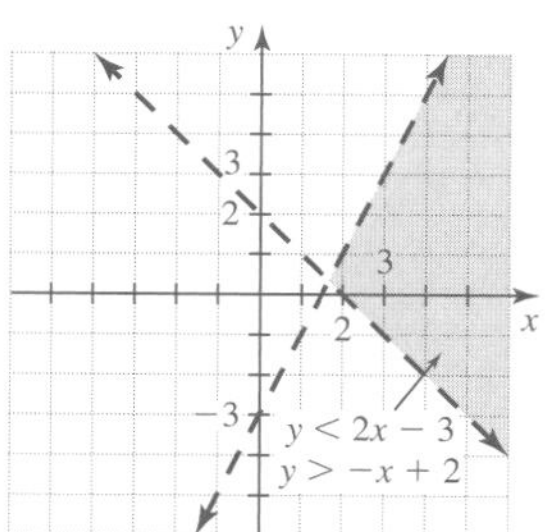

22. $y > 2x - 1$
$y < -x - 4$

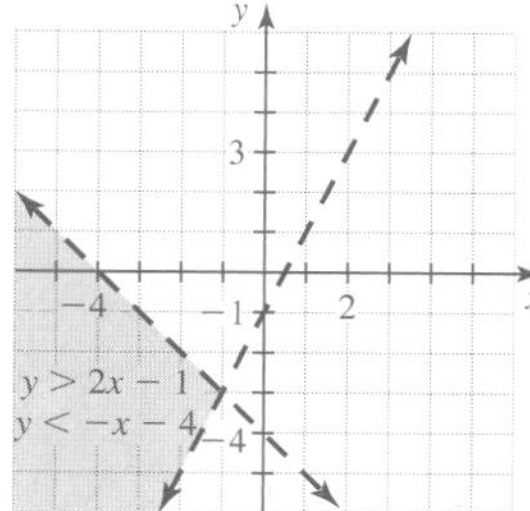

23. $x > 5$
$y > 5$

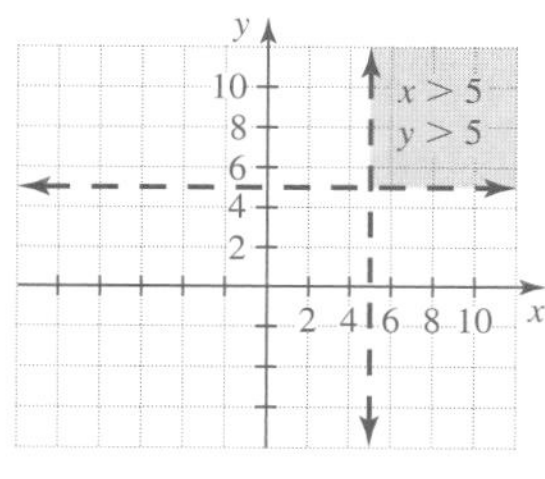

VIDEO **24.** $x < 3$
$y > 2$

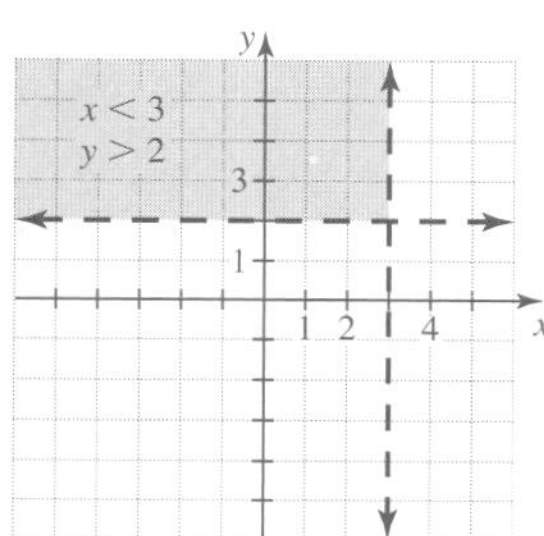

25. $y < -1$
$x > -3$

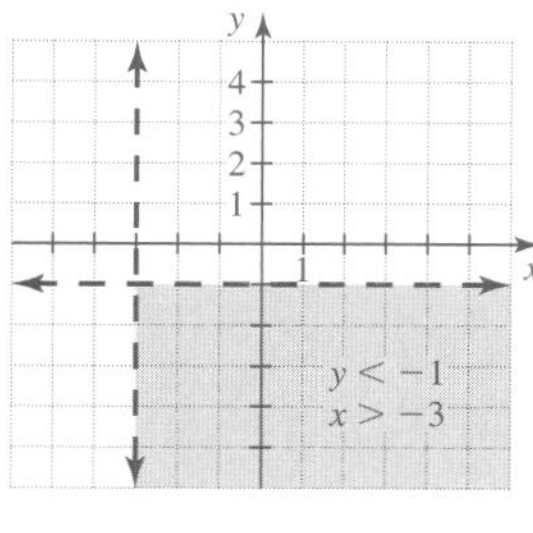

26. $y > -2$
$x < 1$

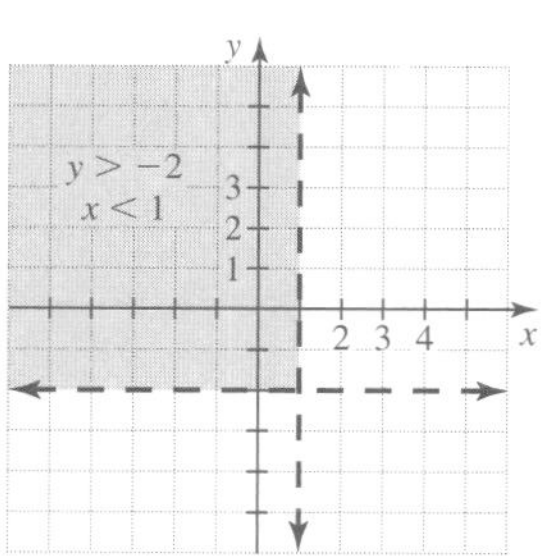

VIDEO **27.** $y > 2x - 4$
$y < 2x + 1$

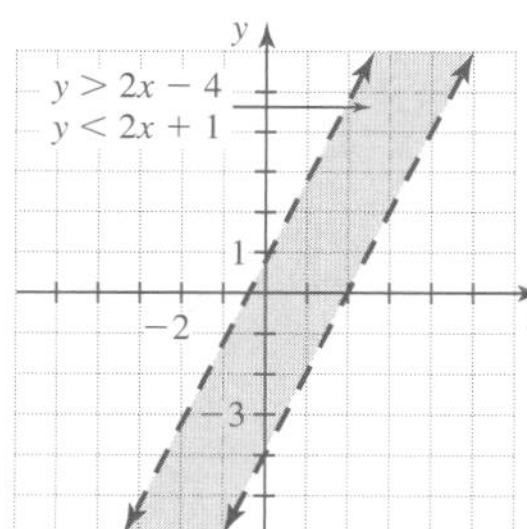

28. $y < -2x + 3$
$y > -2x$

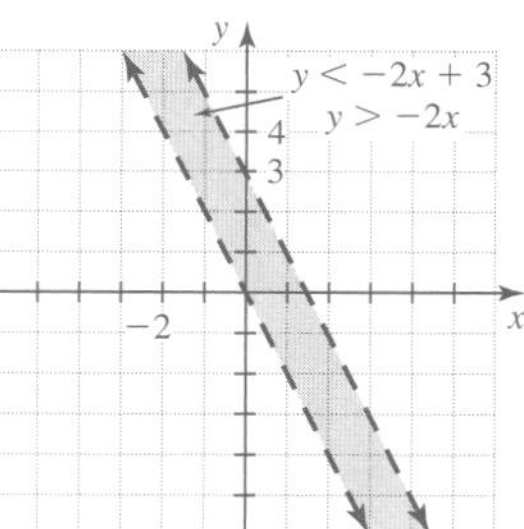

29. $y > x$
$x > 3$

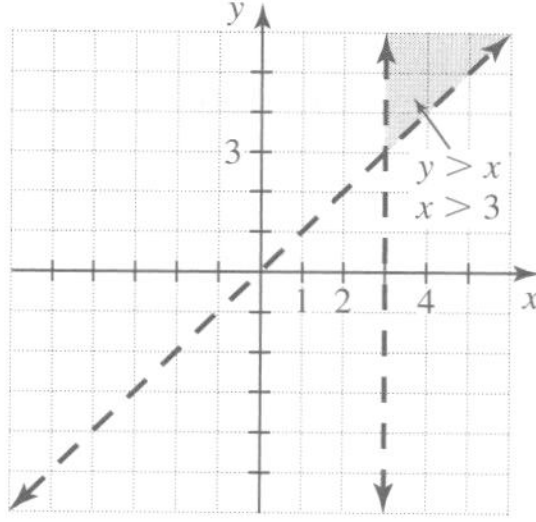

30. $y < x$
$y < 1$

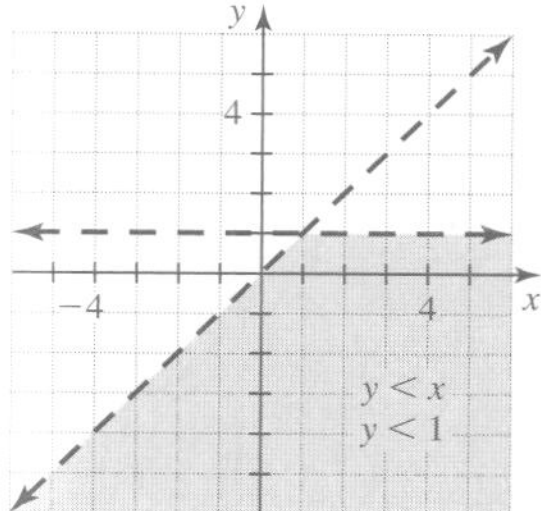

31. $y > -x$
$x < -1$

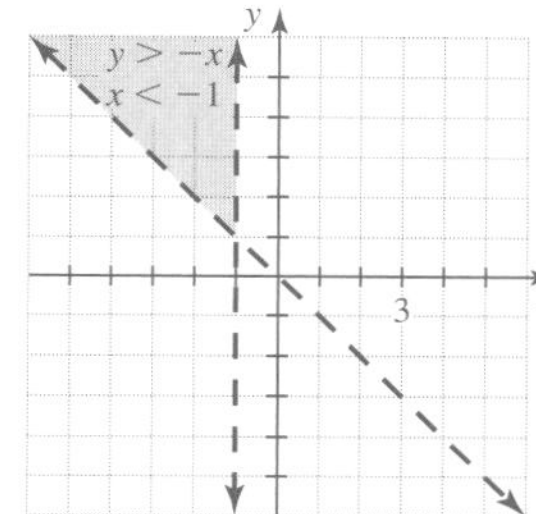

32. $y < -x$
$y > -3$

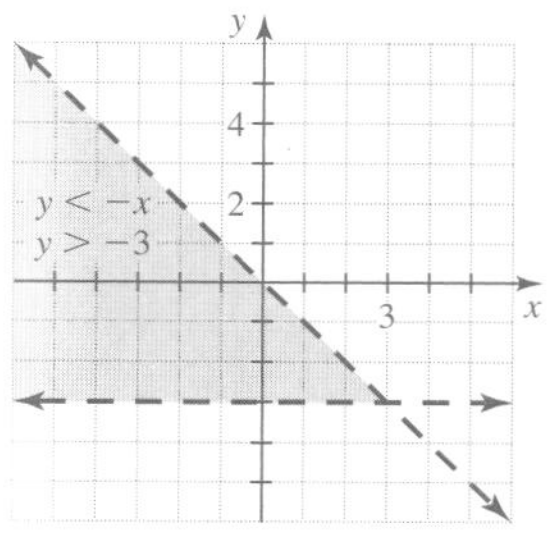

33. $x > 1$
$y - 2x < 3$

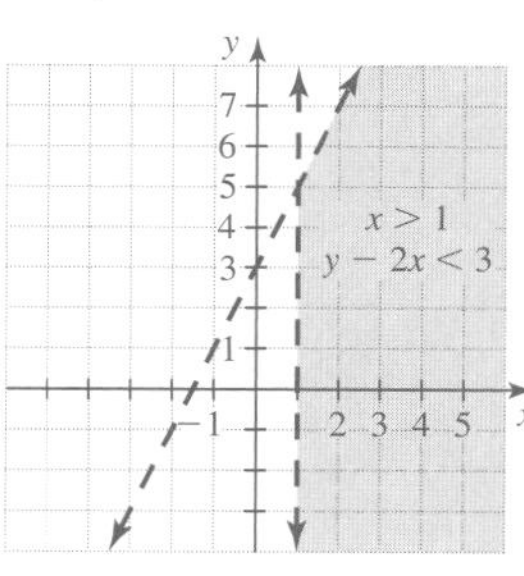

34. $y < 2$
$2x + 3y < 6$

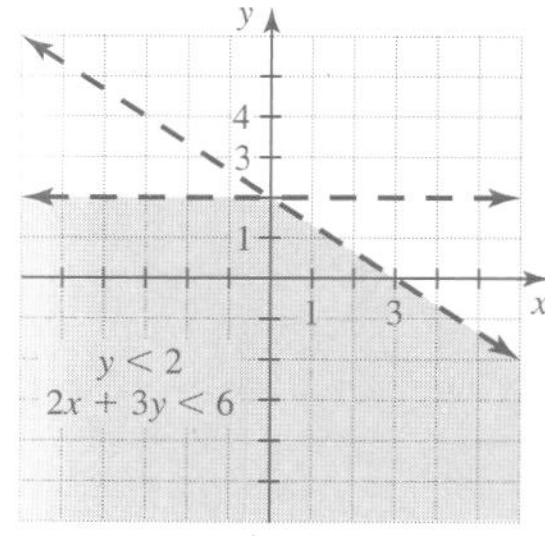

35. $2x - 5y < 5$
$x + 2y > 4$

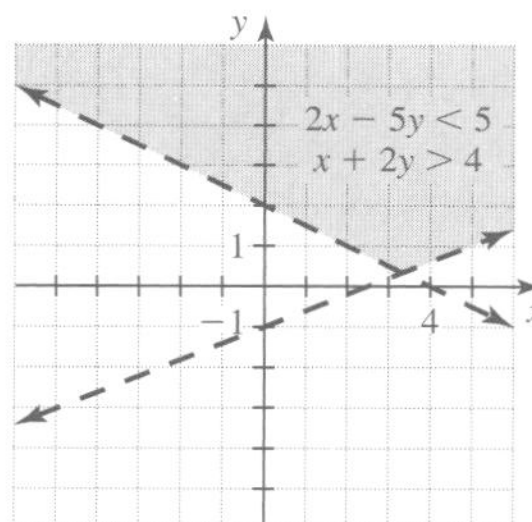

36. $3x + 2y < 2$
$-x - 2y > 4$

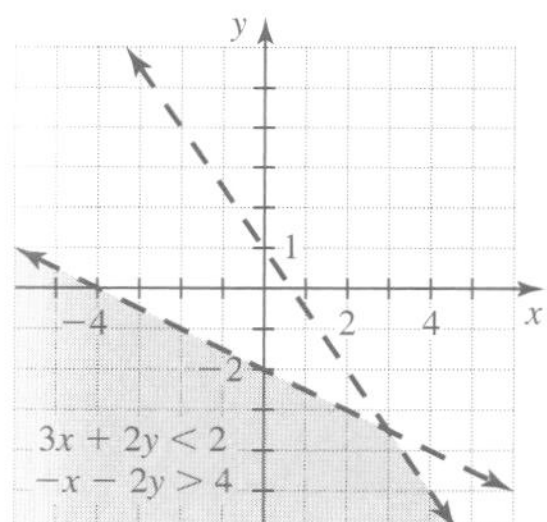

37. $x + y > 3$
$x + y > 1$

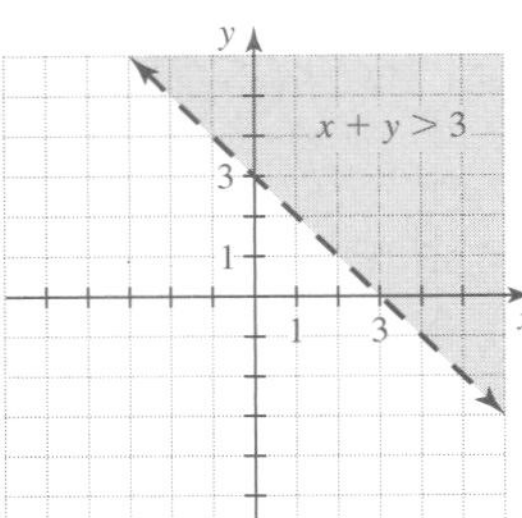

38. $x - y < 5$
$x - y < 3$

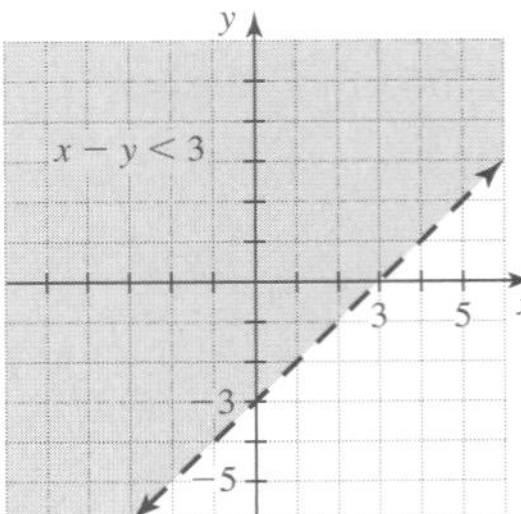

39. $y > 3x + 2$
$y < 3x + 3$

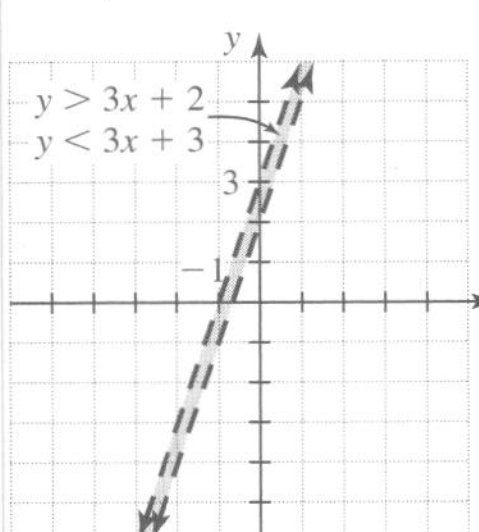

40. $y > x$
$y < -x$

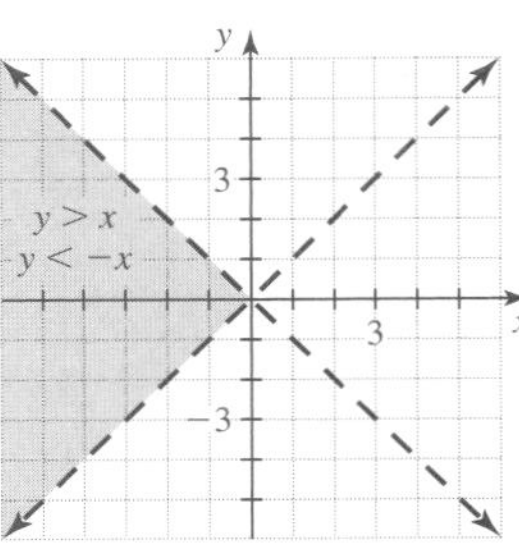

41. $x + y < 5$
$x - y > -1$

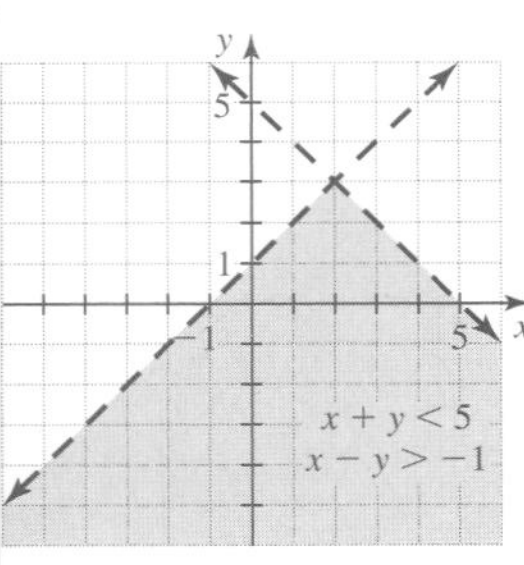

42. $2x - y > 4$
$x - 5y < 5$

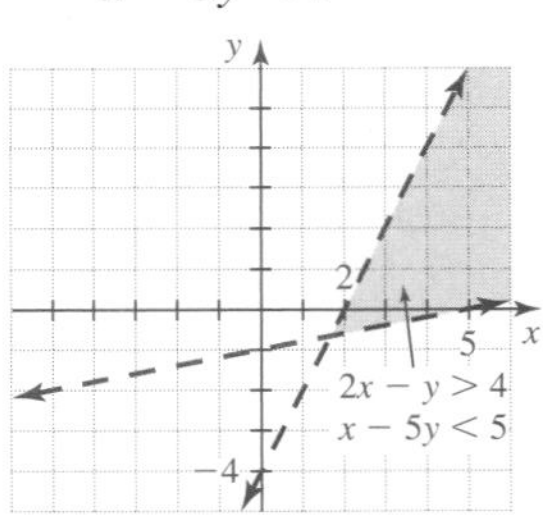

43. $2x - 3y < 6$
$3x + 4y < 12$

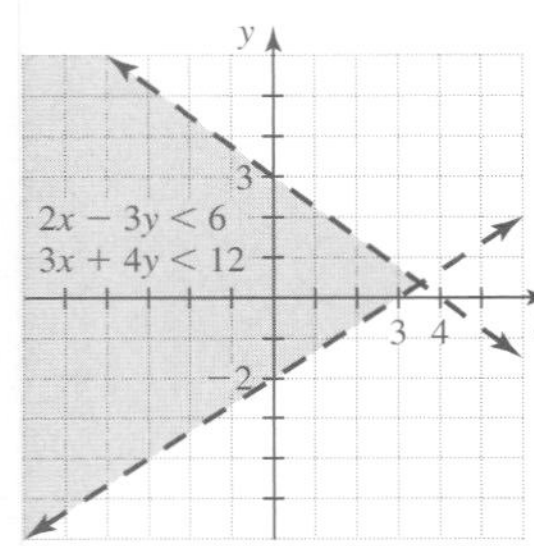

44. $x - 3y > 3$
$x + 2y < 4$

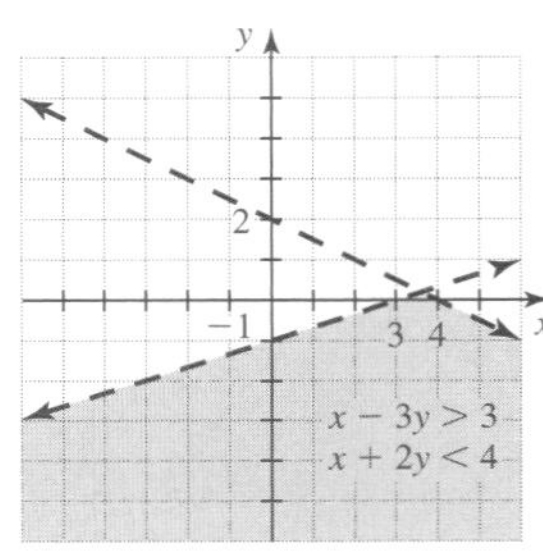

45. $3x - 5y < 15$
$3x + 2y < 12$

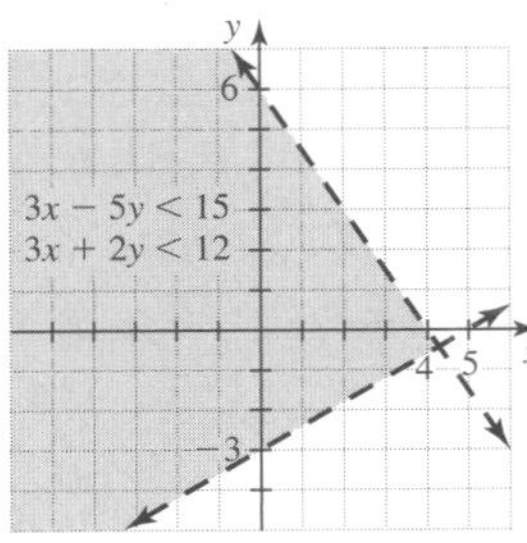

46. $x - 4y < 0$
$x + y > 0$

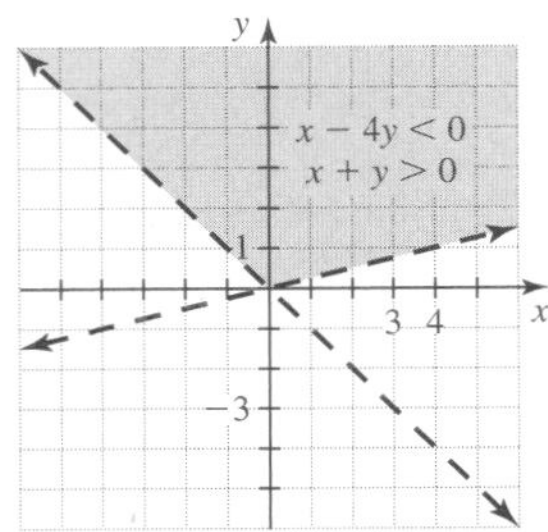

⟨3⟩ Systems with No Solution

Determine whether or not the solution set to each system of inequalities is the empty set. See Example 7.

47. $y > x$
$y < x - 2$ ∅

48. $y < x + 1$
$y > x + 9$ ∅

49. $y < 2x$
$y > 3x$
Not the empty set

50. $y \geq -9x$
$y \leq 9x$
Not the empty set

51. $y \leq 5x - 1$
$y \geq 5x + 2$ ∅

52. $y \geq 3x + 8$
$y \leq 3x - 8$ ∅

53. $y < 2$
$y > 3$
∅

54. $y < 5$
$y > -5$
Not the empty set

55. $x < 4$
$x > -1$
Not the empty set

56. $x < -5$
$x > 5$
∅

Miscellaneous

The graph of each of the following systems is one of the four quadrants in the rectangular coordinate system. Name the quadrant.

57. $y < 0$
$x < 0$
Quadrant III

58. $y < 0$
$x > 0$
Quadrant IV

59. $y > 0$
$x < 0$
Quadrant II

60. $y > 0$
$x > 0$
Quadrant I

⟨4⟩ Applications

Solve each problem. See Example 8.

61. ***Strawberries and blueberries.*** A manager of a produce stand has at most \$60 to spend on strawberries at \$2 per pint and blueberries at \$3 per pint. If x represents the number of pints of strawberries and y represents the number of pints of blueberries, then x and y must satisfy $2x + 3y \leq 60$. Since she cannot purchase a negative number of pints, we also have $x \geq 0$ and $y \geq 0$. Graph this system of three inequalities.

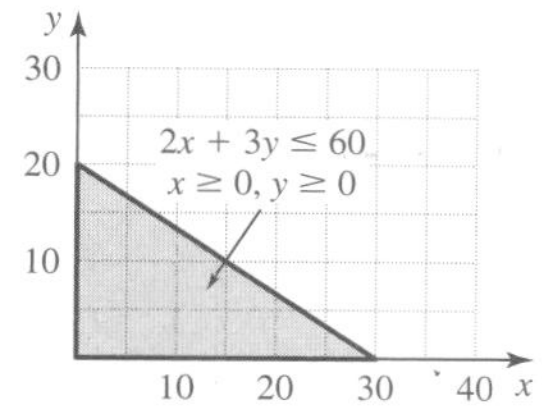

62. ***Target heart rate.*** For beneficial exercise, experts recommend that your target heart rate y should be between 65% and 75% of the maximum heart rate for your age x. That is,

$$y > 0.65(220 - x) \quad \text{and} \quad y < 0.75(220 - x).$$

Graph this system of inequalities for $20 < x < 70$.

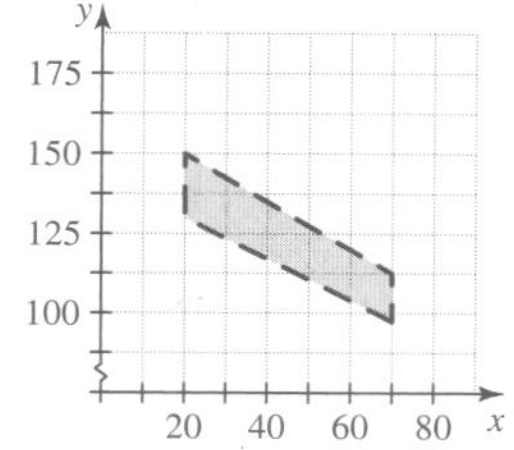

63. ***Making and storing the tables.*** The Ozark Furniture Company can obtain at most 8000 board feet of oak lumber for making round and rectangular tables. The tables must be stored in a warehouse that has at most 3850 ft^3 of space available for the tables. A round table requires 50 board feet of lumber and 25 ft^3 of warehouse space. A rectangular table requires 80 board feet of lumber and 35 ft^3 of warehouse space. Write a system of inequalities that limits the possible number of tables of each type that can be made and stored. Graph the system.

$5x + 8y \leq 800$
$5x + 7y \leq 770$

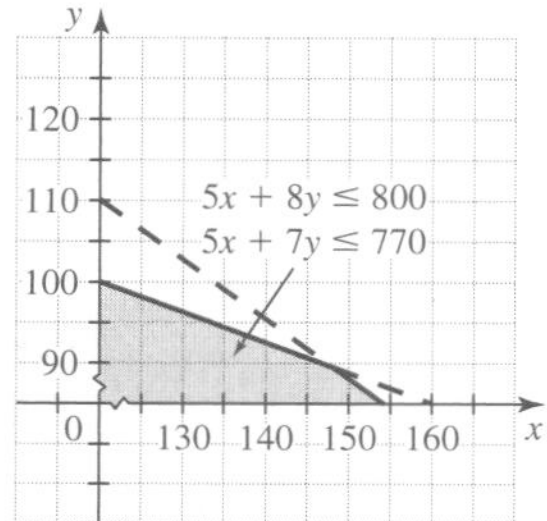

64. ***Allocating resources.*** Wausaukee Enterprises makes yard barns in two sizes. One small barn requires $250 in materials and 20 hours of labor, and one large barn requires $400 in materials and 30 hours of labor. Wausaukee has at most $4000 to spend on materials and at most 300 hours of labor available. Write a system of inequalities that limits the possible number of barns of each type that can be built. Graph the system.

$5x + 8y \leq 80$
$2x + 3y \leq 30$

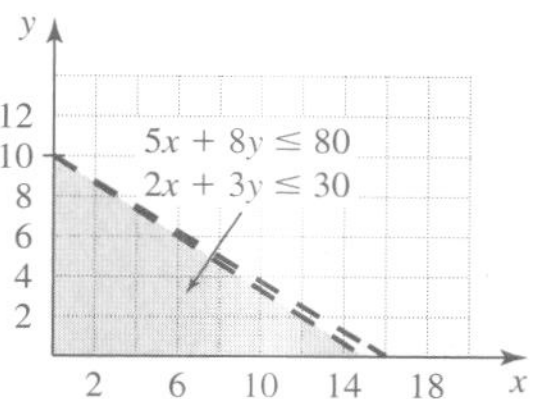

Photo for Exercise 64

Wrap-Up

Summary

Systems of Linear Equations in Two Variables		**Examples**
Graphing method	Sketch each graph and identify the points they have in common.	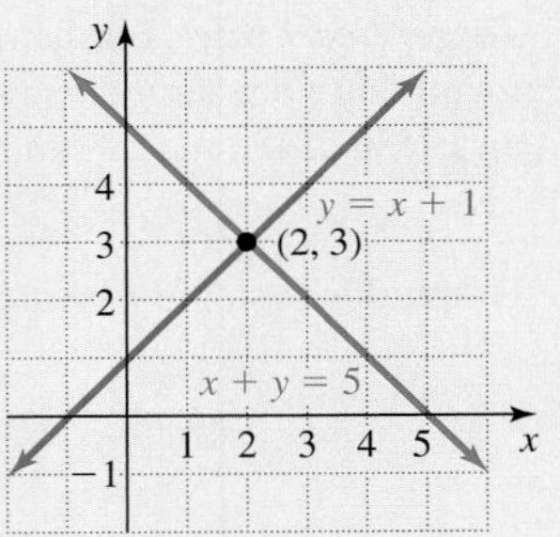
Substitution method	Solve one equation for one variable in terms of the other, then substitute into the other equation.	$y = x - 4$ $x + y = 9$ $x + (x - 4) = 9$
Addition method	Multiply each equation as necessary to eliminate a variable upon addition of the equations.	$5x - 3y = 4$ $x + 3y = 1$ $6x \quad = 5$
Independent	Only one point satisfies both equations. The graphs cross at one point.	$y = x - 4$ $y = 2x + 5$
Dependent	Infinitely many solutions One equation is a multiple of the other. The graphs coincide.	$5x + 3y = 2$ $10x + 6y = 4$
Inconsistent	No solution The graphs are parallel lines.	$y = 5x - 3$ $y = 5x + 1$

Linear Inequalities in Two Variables		**Examples**
Graphing the solution to an inequality in two variables	1. Solve the inequality for y, then graph $y = mx + b$. $y > mx + b$ is the region above the line. $y = mx + b$ is the line itself. $y < mx + b$ is the region below the line. Remember that "less than" means below the line and "greater than" means above the line only when the inequality is solved for y.	 $y > x + 3$ $y = x + 3$ $y < x + 3$

	2. If the inequality involves only x, then graph the vertical line $x = k$. $x > k$ is the region to the right of the line. $x = k$ is the line itself. $x < k$ is the region to the left of the line.	$x > 5$ Region to right of vertical line $x = 5$
Test points	A linear inequality may also be graphed by graphing the equation and then testing a point to determine which region satisfies the inequality.	$x + y > 4$ (0, 6) satisfies the inequality.
Graphing a system of inequalities	Graph the equations and use test points to see which regions satisfy both inequalities.	$x + y > 4$ $x - y < 1$ (0, 6) satisfies the system.

Enriching Your Mathematical Word Power

For each mathematical term, choose the correct meaning.

1. system of equations
a. a systematic method for classifying equations
b. a method for solving an equation
c. two or more equations
d. the properties of equality c

2. independent linear system
a. a system with exactly one solution
b. an equation that is satisfied by every real number
c. equations that are identical
d. a system of lines a

3. inconsistent system
a. a system with no solution
b. a system of inconsistent equations
c. a system that is incorrect
d. a system that we are not sure how to solve a

4. dependent system
a. a system that is independent
b. a system that depends on a variable
c. a system that has no solution
d. a system for which the graphs coincide d

5. substitution method
a. replacing the variables by the correct answer
b. a method of eliminating a variable by substituting one equation into the other
c. the replacement method
d. any method of solving a system b

6. linear inequality in two variables
a. when two lines are not equal
b. line segments that are unequal in length
c. an inequality of the form $Ax + By \geq C$ or with another symbol of inequality
d. an inequality of the form $Ax^2 + By^2 < C^2$ c

7. rational numbers
a. the numbers 1, 2, 3, and so on
b. the integers
c. numbers that make sense
d. numbers of the form a/b where a and b are integers with $b \neq 0$ d

8. irrational numbers
a. the cube roots
b. numbers that cannot be expressed as a ratio of integers
c. numbers that do not make sense
d. the integers b

9. additive identity
a. the number 0
b. the number 1
c. the opposite of a number
d. when two sums are identical a

10. multiplicative identity
a. the number 0
b. the number 1
c. the reciprocal
d. when two products are identical b

Review Exercises

4.1 The Graphing Method

Solve each system by graphing.

1. $y = 2x + 1$
$x + y = 4$ (1, 3)

2. $y = -x + 1$
$y = -x + 3$ No solution

3. $y = 2x + 3$
$y = -2x - 1$ (−1, 1)

4. $x + y = 6$
$x - y = -10$ (−2, 8)

4.2 The Substitution Method

Solve each system by the substitution method.

5. $y = 3x$
$2x + 3y = 22$ (2, 6)

6. $x + y = 3$
$3x - 2y = -11$ (−1, 4)

7. $x = y - 5$
$2x - 3y = -7$ (−8, −3)

8. $2x + y = 5$
$6x - 9 = 3y$ (2, 1)

4.3 The Addition Method

Solve each system by the addition method. Indicate whether each system is independent, dependent, or inconsistent.

9. $x - y = 4$
$2x + y = 5$ (3, −1), independent

10. $x + 2y = -5$
$x - 3y = 10$ (1, −3), independent

11. $2x - 4y = 8$
$x - 2y = 4$ $\{(x, y) \mid x - 2y = 4\}$, dependent

12. $x + 3y = 7$
$2x + 6y = 5$ No solution, inconsistent

13. $y = 3x - 5$
$2y = -x - 3$ (1, −2), independent

14. $3x + 4y = 6$
$4x + 3y = 1$ (−2, 3), independent

15. $2x + 7y = 0$
$7x + 2y = 0$ (0, 0), independent

16. $3x - 5y = 1$
$10y = 6x - 1$ No solution, inconsistent

17. $x - y = 6$
$2x - 12 = 2y$ $\{(x, y) \mid x - y = 6\}$, dependent

18. $y = 4x$
$y = 3x$ (0, 0), independent

19. $y = 4x$
$y = 4x + 3$ No solution, inconsistent

20. $3x - 5y = 21$
$4x + 7y = -13$ (2, −3), independent

4.4 Graphing Linear Inequalities in Two Variables

Graph each inequality.

21. $y > \frac{1}{3}x - 5$

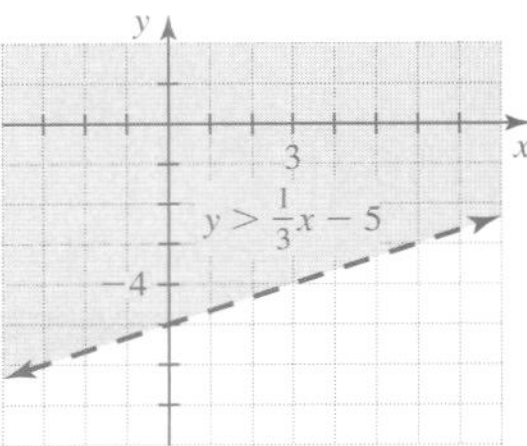

22. $y < \frac{1}{2}x + 2$

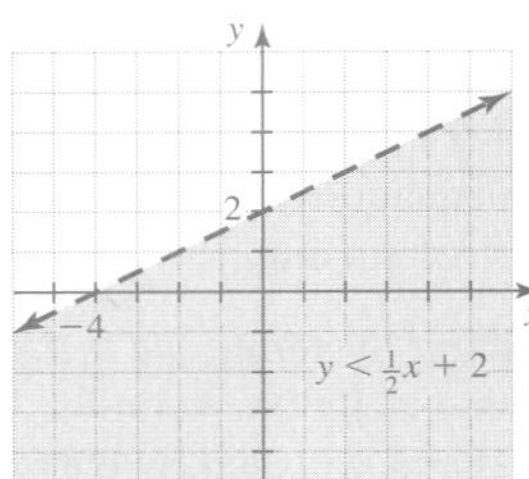

23. $y \le -2x + 7$

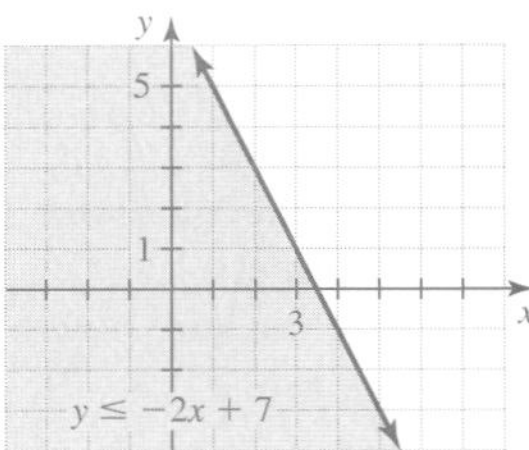

24. $y \ge x - 6$

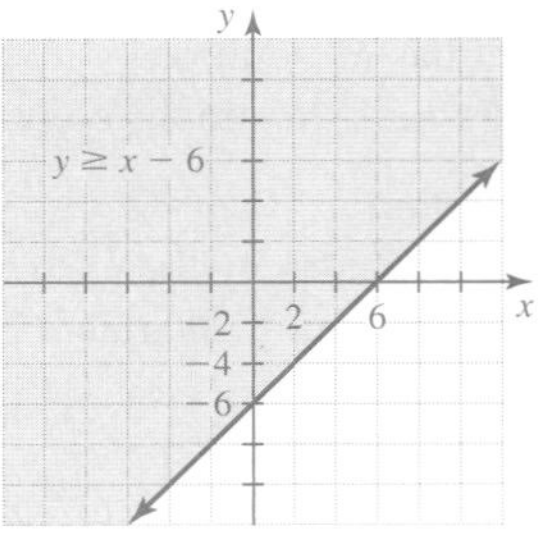

25. $y \le 8$

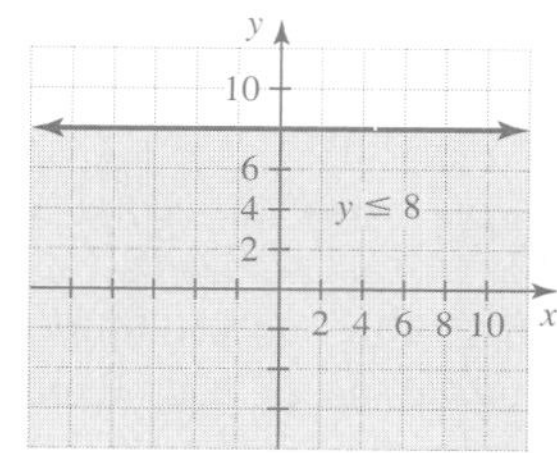

26. $x \ge -6$

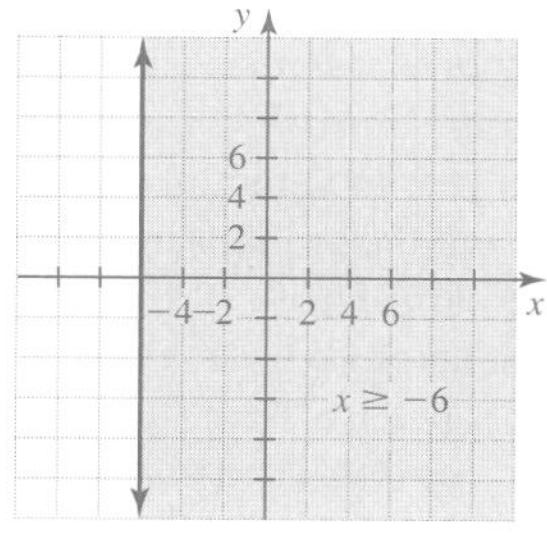

27. $2x + 3y \le -12$

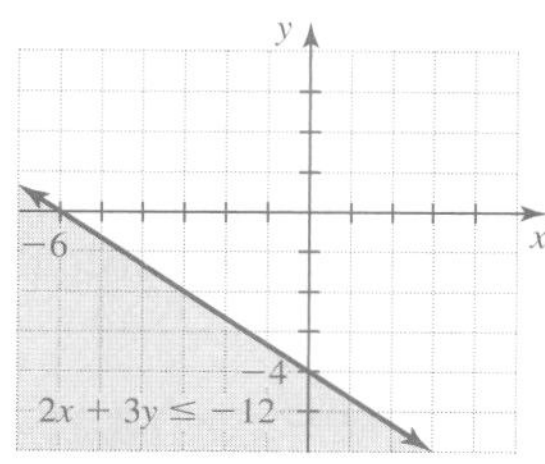

28. $x - 3y < 9$

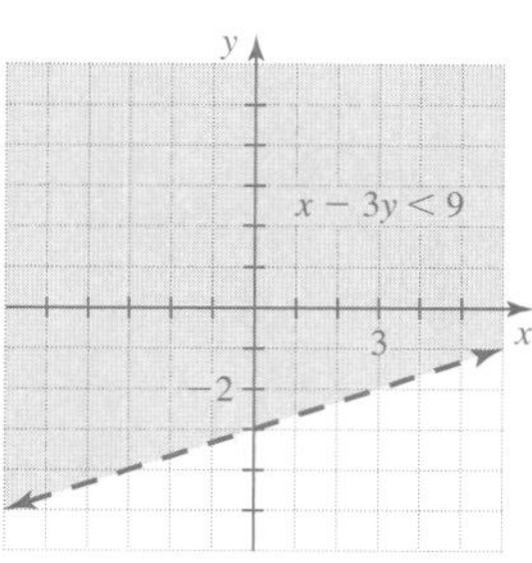

4.5 Graphing Systems of Linear Inequalities

Graph each system of inequalities.

29. $x < 5$
$y < 4$

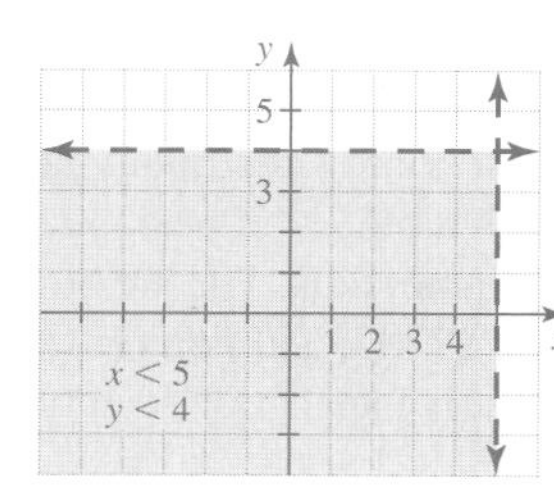

30. $y > -2$
$x < 1$

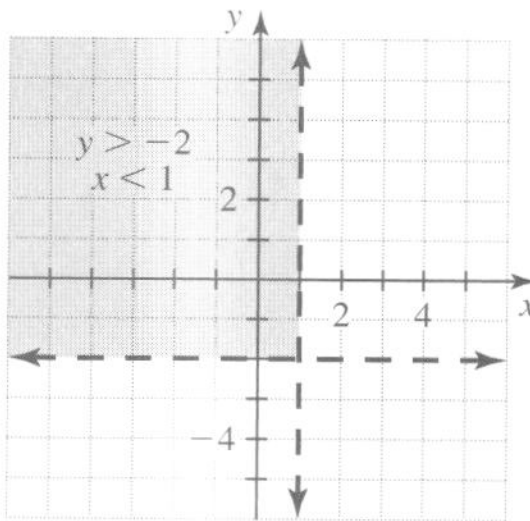

31. $x + y < 2$
$y > 2x - 3$

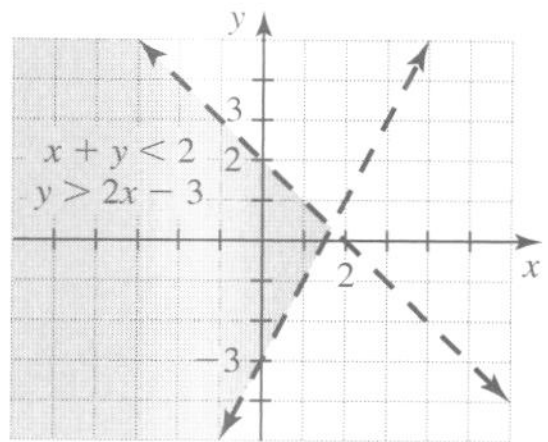

32. $x - y > 4$
$2y > x - 4$

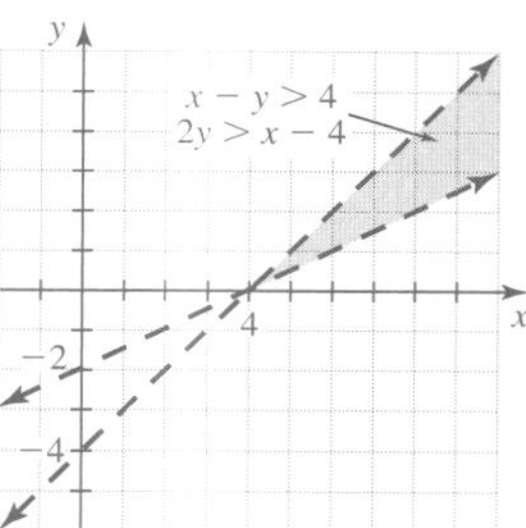

33. $y > 5x - 7$
$y < 5x + 1$

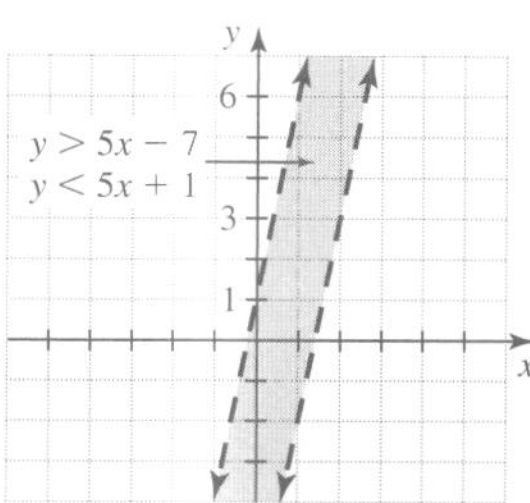

34. $y > x - 6$
$y < x - 5$

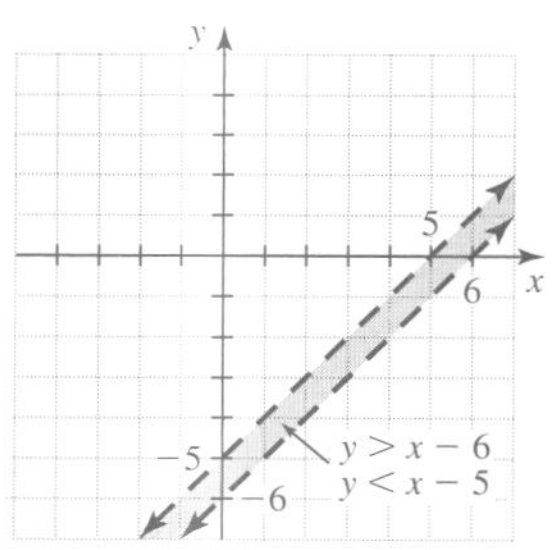

35. $y < 3x + 5$
$y < 3x$

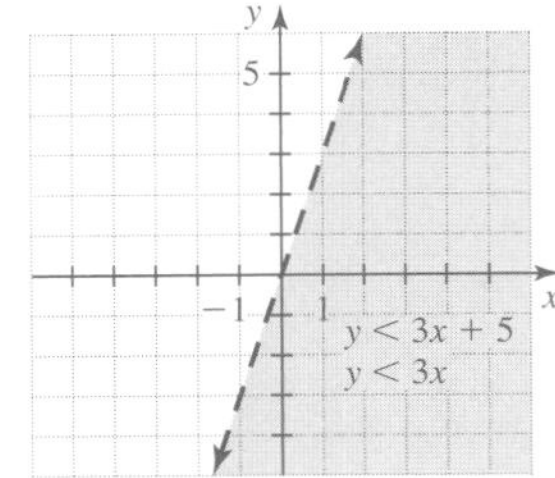

36. $y > -2x$
$y > -3x$

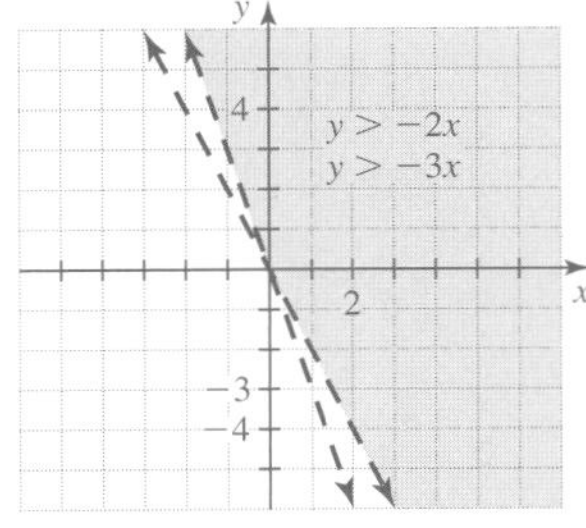

Miscellaneous

Solve each system by the method of your choice.

37. $x - y = 9$
$x + y = 37$ (23, 14)

38. $x + 2y = 20$
$x - 2y = 4$ (12, 4)

39. $y = 3x$
$2x - 6y = 32$ (−2, −6)

40. $y = -2x$
$5x + 3y = 3$ (−3, 6)

41. $y - x = 2$
$4x - 3y = 1$ (7, 9)

42. $x - y = -4$
$3y - 7x = -12$ (6, 10)

43. $2x - 3y = -10$
$3x + 5y = 23$ (1, 4)

44. $3x + 5y = -9$
$4x + 3y = -1$ (2, −3)

Use a system of equations in two variables to solve each problem. Solve the system by the method of your choice.

45. ***Apples and oranges.*** Two apples and three oranges cost \$1.95, and three apples and two oranges cost \$2.05. What are the costs of one apple and one orange?
Apple \$0.45, orange \$0.35

Photo for Exercise 45

46. ***Small or medium.*** Three small drinks and one medium drink cost \$2.30, and two small drinks and four medium drinks cost \$3.70. What is the cost of one small drink? What is the cost of one medium drink?
Small \$0.55, medium \$0.65

47. ***Gambling fever.*** After a long day at the casinos in Biloxi, Louis returned home and told his wife Lois that he had won \$430 in \$5 bills and \$10 bills. On counting them again, he realized that he had mixed up the number of bills of each denomination, and he had really won only \$380. How many bills of each denomination does Louis have?
32 fives, 22 tens

48. ***Diversifying investments.*** Diane invested her \$10,000 bonus in a municipal bond fund and an emerging market fund. In one year the amount invested in the bond fund earned 8%, and the amount invested in the emerging market fund earned 10%. If the total income from these two investments for one year was \$880, then how much did she invest in each fund?
\$6000 at 8%, \$4000 at 10%

49. ***Protein and carbohydrates.*** One serving of green beans contains 1 gram of protein and 4 grams of carbohydrates. One serving of chicken soup contains 3 grams of protein and 9 grams of carbohydrates. The Westdale Diet recommends a lunch of 13 grams of protein and 43 grams of carbohydrates. How many servings of each are necessary to obtain the recommended amounts?
4 servings green beans, 3 servings chicken soup

Photo for Exercise 49

50. ***Advertising revenue.*** A television station aired four 30-second commercials and three 60-second commercials during the first hour of the midnight movie. During the second hour, it aired six 30-second commercials and five 60-second commercials. The advertising revenue for the first hour was \$7700, and that for the second hour was \$12,300. What is the cost of each type of commercial?
30-second \$800, 60-second \$1500

Chapter 4 Test

Solve the system by graphing.

1. $x + y = 2$
$y = 2x + 5$ $(-1, 3)$

Solve each system by substitution.

2. $y = 2x - 3$
$2x + 3y = 7$ $(2, 1)$

3. $x - y = 4$
$3x - 2y = 11$ $(3, -1)$

Solve each system by the addition method.

4. $2x + 5y = 19$
$4x - 3y = -1$ $(2, 3)$

5. $3x - 2y = 10$
$2x + 5y = 13$ $(4, 1)$

Determine whether each system is independent, dependent, or inconsistent.

6. $y = 4x - 9$
$y = 4x + 8$ Inconsistent

7. $3x - 3y = 12$
$y = x - 4$ Dependent

8. $y = 2x$
$y = 5x$ Independent

Graph each inequality.

9. $y > 3x - 5$

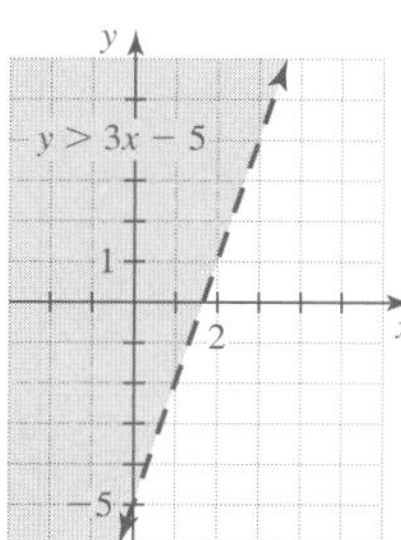

10. $x - y < 3$

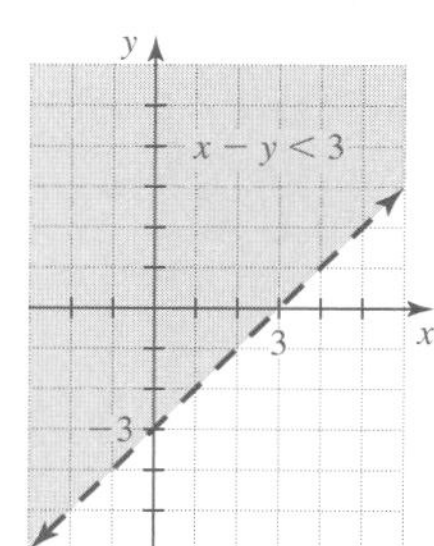

11. $x - 2y \geq 4$

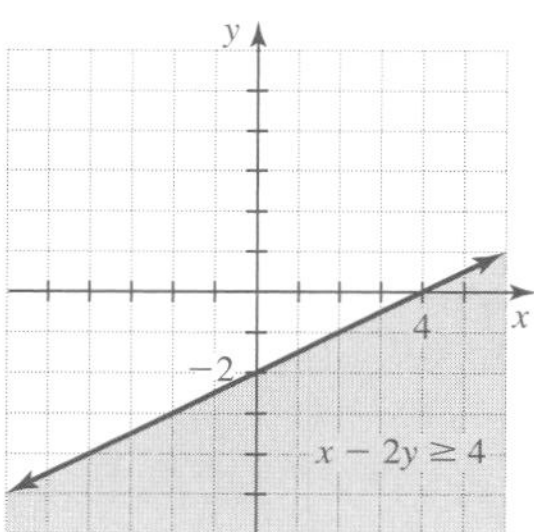

Graph each system of inequalities.

12. $x < 6$
$y > -1$

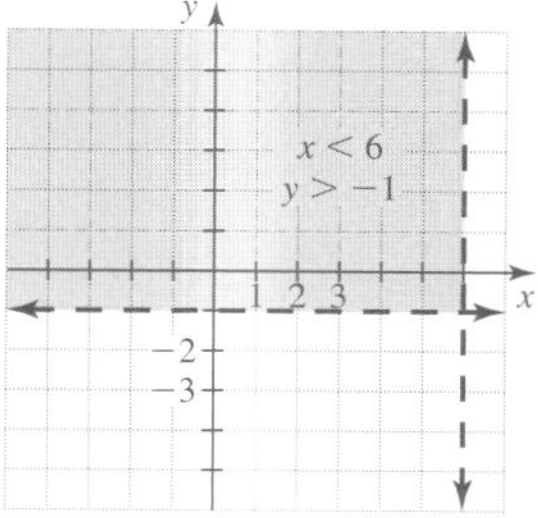

13. $2x + 3y > 6$
$3x - y < 3$

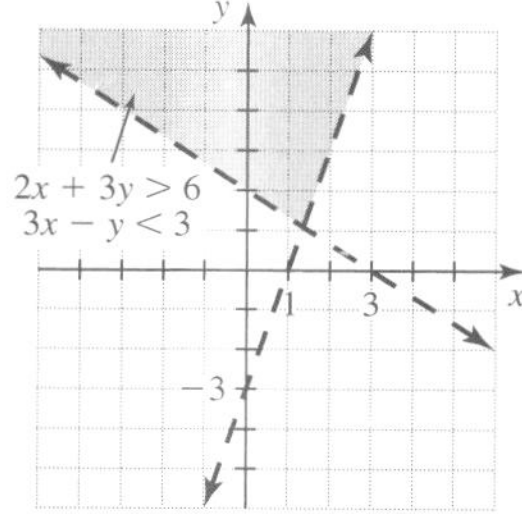

14. $y > 3x - 4$
$3x - y > 3$

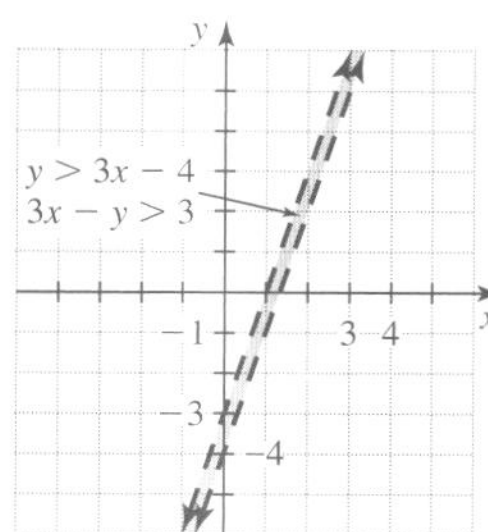

For each problem, write a system of equations in two variables. Use the method of your choice to solve each system.

15. Kathy and Chris studied a total of 54 hours for the CPA exam. If Chris studied only one-half as many hours as Kathy, then how many hours did each of them study?
Kathy 36 hours, Chris 18 hours

16. The Rest-Is-Easy Motel just outside Amarillo rented five singles and three doubles on Monday night for a total of \$188. On Tuesday night it rented three singles and four doubles for a total of \$170. On Wednesday night it rented only one single and one double. How much rent did the motel receive on Wednesday night? \$48

*Making*Connections | A Review of Chapters 1–4

Solve each equation.

1. $2(x - 5) + 3x = 25$ $\{7\}$

2. $3x - 5 = 0$ $\left\{\frac{5}{3}\right\}$

3. $\frac{x}{3} - \frac{2}{5} = \frac{x}{2} - \frac{12}{5}$ $\{12\}$

4. $x - 0.05x = 950$ $\{1000\}$

5. $3(x - 5) - 5x = 5 - 2(x - 4)$ $\varnothing$

6. $7x - 4(5 - x) = 5(2x - 4) + x$ All real numbers

Solve each inequality in one variable. State the solution set using interval notation and sketch the graph on a number line.

7. $3(2 - x) < -6$
$(4, \infty)$

8. $-3 \le 2x - 4 \le 6$
$\left[\frac{1}{2}, 5\right]$

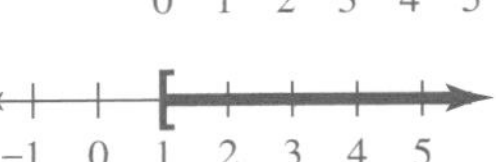

9. $4 \ge 5 - x$
$[1, \infty)$

Sketch the graph of each equation.

10. $y = 3x - 7$

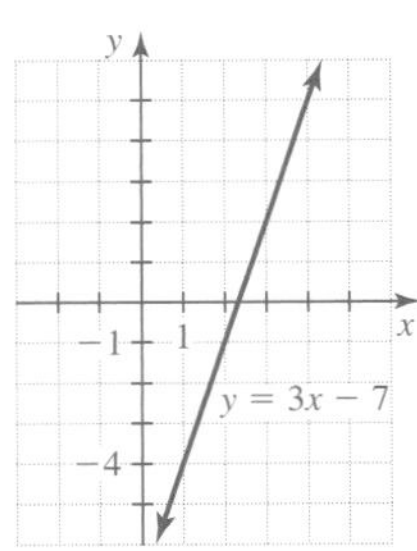

11. $y = 5 - x$

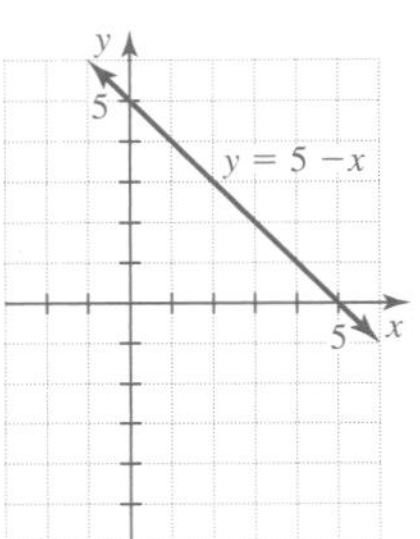

12. $y = x - 1$

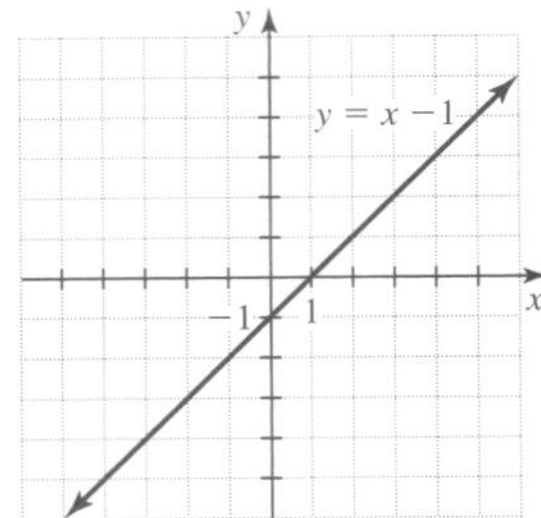

13. $y = x + 1$

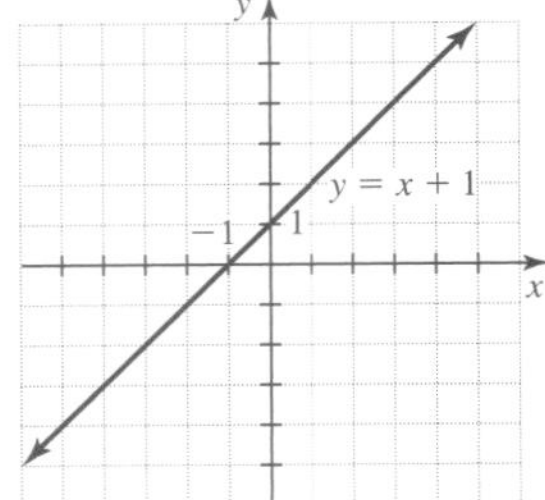

14. $y = -2x + 4$

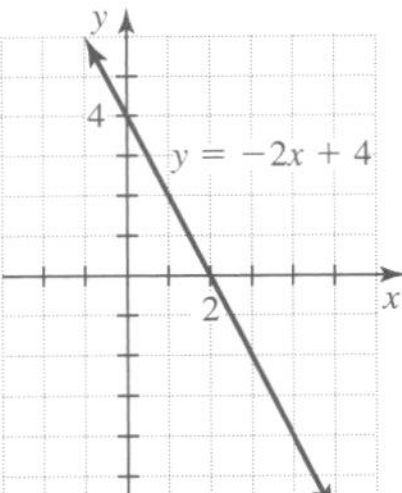

15. $y = -4x - 1$

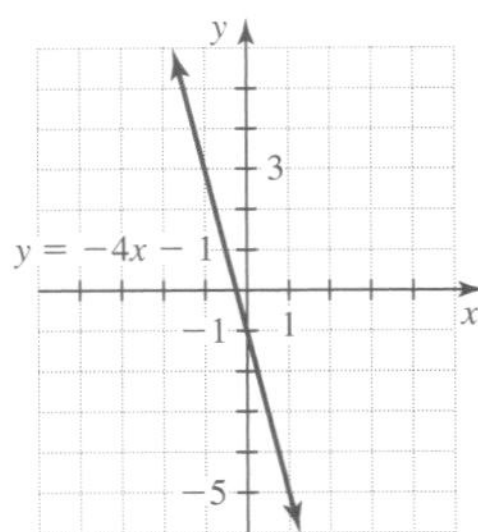

Graph each inequality in two variables.

16. $y \ge 3x - 7$

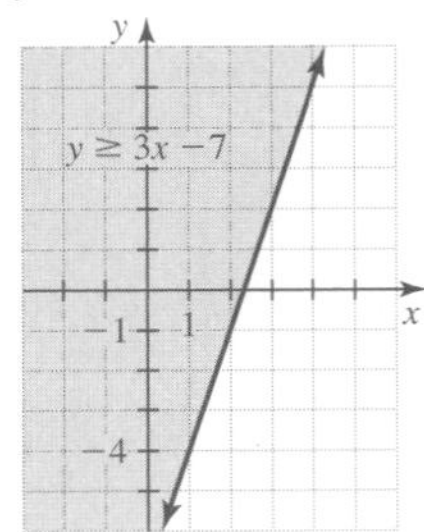

17. $x - 2y < 6$

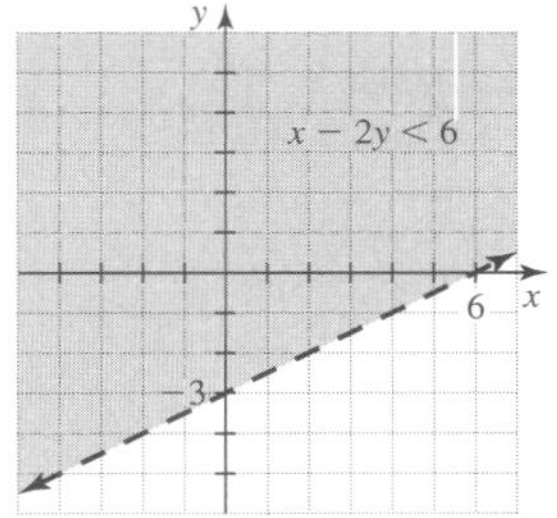

18. $x > 1$

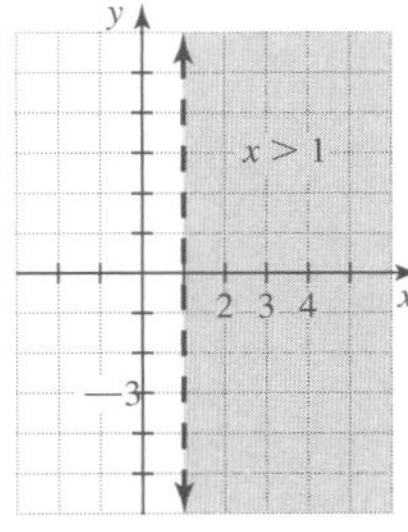

Write the equation of the line going through each pair of points.

19. (0, 36) and (8, 84) $y = 6x + 36$

20. (1, 88) and (12, 11) $y = -7x + 95$

Simplify each expression.

21. $4 - 5x + 6 - 8x$ $-13x + 10$

22. $5x + 3 - 4x + 9$ $x + 12$

23. $(3a - 9) - (a - 9)$ $2a$

24. $(4b - 1) - (5 - b)$ $5b - 6$

25. $5 - 4(c - 3)$ $-4c + 17$

26. $10 - 6(d - 4)$ $-6d + 34$

27. $-2(m - 3) + 5(m - 4)$ $3m - 14$

28. $3(n - 4) - 5(n - 6)$ $-2n + 18$

Evaluate each arithmetic expression.

29. $\dfrac{5 - 9}{3 - 5}$ 2

30. $\dfrac{-2 - 7}{-3 + 6}$ -3

31. $\dfrac{6 - 3 \cdot 12}{5 \cdot 7 - 20}$ -2

32. $\dfrac{-2 - 4 \cdot 10}{-5 \cdot 4 + 6}$ 3

33. $\dfrac{\frac{1}{2} - \frac{1}{2}}{\frac{1}{2} + \frac{1}{2}}$ 0

34. $\dfrac{\frac{1}{2} - \frac{1}{4}}{\frac{1}{8} + \frac{1}{8}}$ 1

35. $\dfrac{6 - 3 \cdot 2^3}{2 \cdot 3^2}$ -1

36. $\dfrac{-2^2 - 4^2}{-5^2 + 5}$ 1

37. $|-2^4 - 3| - |6 - 5|$ 18

38. $|-3^2 - 5| - |-4|$ 10

Solve the problem.

39. ***Decreasing market share.*** The market share for Toys "R" Us went from 25% of the toy market in 1990 to 16% in 2000 as shown in the accompanying graph (*Forbes*, www.forbes.com).

a) Write the market share p in terms of x, where x is the number of years since 1990.

$p = -\dfrac{9}{10}x + 25$

b) Wal-Mart's market share of the toy market went from 10% in 1990 to 19% in 2000. Write Wal-Mart's market share p in terms of x, where x is the number of years since 1990.

$p = \dfrac{9}{10}x + 10$

c) Solve the system of equations that you found in parts (a) and (b) to find the year in which Wal-Mart passed up Toys "R" Us in market share for toys.

$8\frac{1}{3}$ years after 1990 or 1998

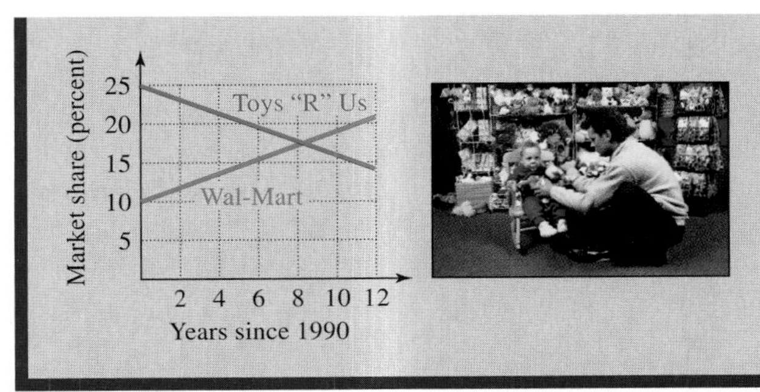

Figure for Exercise 39

Critical **Thinking** | For Individual or Group Work | Chapter 4

These exercises can be solved by a variety of techniques, which may or may not require algebra. So be creative and think critically. Explain all answers. Answers are in the Instructor's Edition of this text.

1. ***Throwing darts.*** A dart board contains a region worth 9 points and a region worth 4 points as shown in the accompanying figure. If you are allowed to throw as many darts as you wish, then what is the largest possible total score that you *cannot* get?

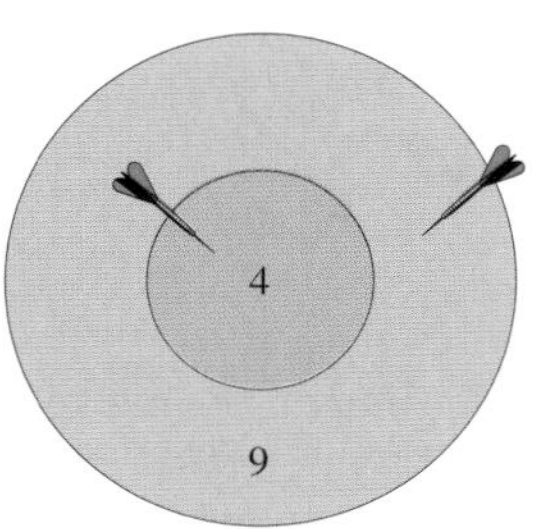

Figure for Exercise 1

2. ***Counting squares.*** A square checkerboard is made up of 36 alternately colored 1 inch by 1 inch squares.

a) What is the total number of squares that are visible on this checkerboard? (*Hint:* Count the 6 by 6 squares, then the 5 by 5 squares, and so on.)

b) How many are visible on a checkerboard that has 64 alternately colored 1 inch by 1 inch squares?

3. ***Four fours.*** Check out these equations:

$$\frac{4+4}{4+4} = 1, \quad \frac{4}{4} + \frac{4}{4} = 2, \quad 4 - 4^{4-4} = 3.$$

a) Using exactly four 4's write arithmetic expressions whose values are 4, 5, 6, and so on. How far can you go?

b) Repeat this exercise using four 5's, three 4's, and three 5's.

4. ***Four coins.*** Place four coins on a table with heads facing downward. On each move you must turn over exactly three coins. Count the number of moves it takes to get all four coins with heads facing upward. What is the minimum number of moves necessary to get all four heads facing upward?

5. ***Snakes and iguanas.*** A woman has a collection of snakes and iguanas. Her young son observed that the reptiles have a total of 50 eyes and 56 feet. How many reptiles of each type does the woman have?

Photo for Exercise 5

6. ***Hungry bugs.*** If it takes a colony of termites one day to devour a block of wood that is 2 inches wide, 2 inches long, and 2 inches high, then how long will it take them to devour a block of wood that is 4 inches wide, 4 inches long, and 4 inches high? Assume that they keep eating at the same rate.

7. ***Ancient history.*** This problem is from the second century. Four numbers have a sum of 9900. The second exceeds the first by one-seventh of the first. The third exceeds the sum of the first two by 300. The fourth exceeds the sum of the first three by 300. Find the four numbers.

8. ***Related digits.*** What is the largest four-digit number such that the second digit is one-fourth of the third digit, the third digit is twice the first digit, and the last digit is the same as the first digit?

1. 23 **2. a)** 91 **b)** 204 **3. a)** $4^{4-4} \cdot 4 = 4$, $4^{4-4} + 4 = 5$, $(4!)/4 + 4 - 4 = 6$ **4.** 4 **5.** 11 snakes and 14 iguanas **6.** 8 days **7.** 1050, 1200, 2550, 5100 **8.** 4284

Chapter 5

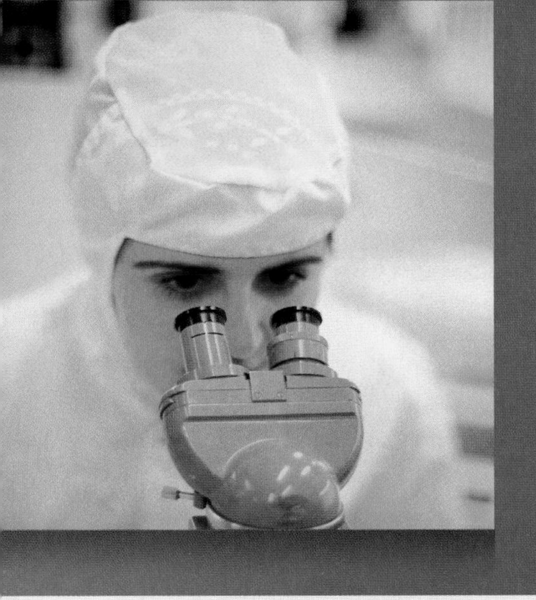

Exponents and Polynomials

The nineteenth-century physician and physicist Jean Louis Marie Poiseuille (1799–1869) is given credit for discovering a formula associated with the circulation of blood through arteries. Poiseuille's law, as it is known, can be used to determine the velocity of blood in an artery at a given distance from the center of the artery. The formula states that the flow of blood in an artery is faster toward the center of the blood vessel and is slower toward the outside. Blood flow can also be affected by a person's blood pressure, the length of the blood vessel, and the viscosity of the blood itself.

In later years, Poiseuille's continued interest in blood circulation led him to experiments to show that blood pressure rises and falls when a person exhales and inhales. In modern medicine, physicians can use Poiseuille's law to determine how much the radius of a blocked blood vessel must be widened to create a healthy flow of blood.

In this chapter, you will study polynomials, the fundamental expressions of algebra. Polynomials are to algebra what integers are to arithmetic. We use polynomials to represent quantities in general, such as perimeter, area, revenue, and the volume of blood flowing through an artery.

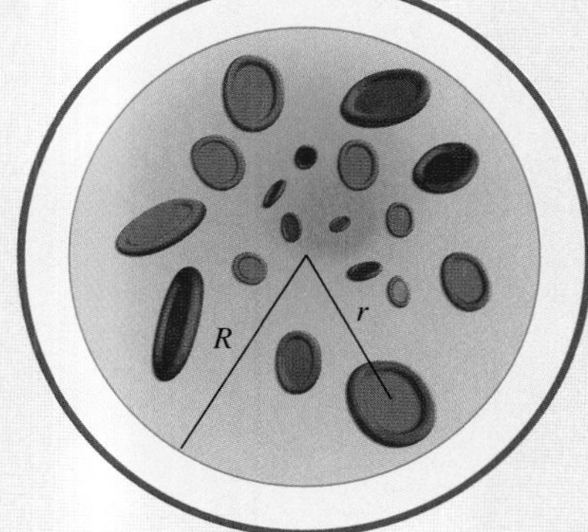

In Exercise 93 of Section 5.6, you will see Poiseuille's law represented by a polynomial.

5.1 The Rules of Exponents

In This Section

We defined exponential expressions with positive integral exponents in Chapter 1. In this section, we will review that definition and then learn the rules for positive integral exponents.

⟨1⟩ The Product Rule for Exponents

Exponents were defined in Chapter 1 as a simple way of expressing repeated multiplication. For example,

$$x^1 = x, \quad y^2 = y \cdot y, \quad 5^3 = 5 \cdot 5 \cdot 5, \quad \text{and} \quad a^4 = a \cdot a \cdot a \cdot a.$$

To find the product of the exponential expressions x^3 and x^5 we could simply count the number of times x appears in the product:

$$x^3 \cdot x^5 = \underbrace{\overbrace{(x \cdot x \cdot x)}^{3\text{ factors}}\overbrace{(x \cdot x \cdot x \cdot x \cdot x)}^{5\text{ factors}}}_{8\text{ factors}} = x^8$$

Instead of counting to find that x occurs 8 times it is easier to add 3 and 5 to get 8. This example illustrates the **product rule for exponents.**

Product Rule for Exponents

If a is any real number, and m and n are positive integers, then

$$a^m \cdot a^n = a^{m+n}.$$

CAUTION By the product rule $2^3 \cdot 2^2 = 2^5$. Note that $2^3 \cdot 2^2 \neq 4^5$ and $2^3 \cdot 2^2 \neq 2^6$. The bases are not multiplied in the product rule and neither are the exponents.

EXAMPLE 1

Using the product rule for exponents

Find the indicated products.

a) $2^3 \cdot 2^2$ **b)** $x^2 \cdot x^4 \cdot x$ **c)** $2y^3 \cdot 4y^8$ **d)** $-4a^2b^3(-3a^5b^9)$

Solution

a) $2^3 \cdot 2^2 = 2^5$ Product rule for exponents
$= 32$ Simplify.

b) $x^2 \cdot x^4 \cdot x = x^2 \cdot x^4 \cdot x^1$ Product rule for exponents
$= x^7$

c) $2y^3 \cdot 4y^8 = (2)(4)y^3y^8$ Product rule for exponents
$= 8y^{11}$

d) $-4a^2b^3(-3a^5b^9) = (-4)(-3)a^2a^5b^3b^9$
$= 12a^7b^{12}$ Product rule for exponents

Now do Exercises 7–18

⟨2⟩ Zero Exponent

A positive integer exponent indicates the number of times that the base is used as a factor. But that idea does not make sense for 0 as an exponent. To see what would make sense for the definition of 0 as an exponent, look at a table of the powers of 2:

2^6	2^5	2^4	2^3	2^2	2^1	2^0
64	32	16	8	4	2	?

⟨ Teaching Tip ⟩

Some expressions like 0^0 look nice, but are left undefined because any definition of them would cause inconsistencies with other rules or definitions.

The value of each expression in the table is one-half of the value of the preceding expression. So it would seem reasonable to define 2^0 to be half of 2 or 1. So the zero power of any nonzero real number is defined to be 1. We do not define the expression 0^0.

Zero Exponent

For any nonzero real number a,

$$a^0 = 1.$$

Note that defining a^0 to be 1 is consistent with the product rule for exponents, because $a^0 \cdot a^n = 1 \cdot a^n = a^n$ and $a^0 \cdot a^n = a^{0+n} = a^n$. So the product rule is now valid for nonnegative integral exponents.

EXAMPLE 2

Using the definition of zero exponent

Simplify each expression. Assume that all variables represent nonzero real numbers.

a) 5^0 **b)** $(3xy)^0$ **c)** $b^0 \cdot b^9$ **d)** $2^0 + 3^0$

Solution

a) $5^0 = 1$ Definition of zero exponent

b) $(3xy)^0 = 1$ Definition of zero exponent

c) If we use the fact that $b^0 = 1$, then $b^0 \cdot b^9 = 1 \cdot b^9 = b^9$. If we use the product rule for exponents, then $b^0 \cdot b^9 = b^{0+9} = b^9$.

d) $2^0 + 3^0 = 1 + 1 = 2$ Definition of zero exponent

Now do Exercises 19–28

⟨3⟩ The Quotient Rule for Exponents

To find the quotient of x^7 and x^3 we can write the quotient as a fraction and divide out or cancel the common factors. Then count the remaining factors:

$$x^7 \div x^3 = \frac{x^7}{x^3} = \frac{\cancel{x} \cdot \cancel{x} \cdot \cancel{x} \cdot x \cdot x \cdot x \cdot x}{\cancel{x} \cdot \cancel{x} \cdot \cancel{x}} = x^4$$

Instead of counting to find that there are four x's left, we can simply subtract 3 from 7 to get 4. This example illustrates the **quotient rule for exponents.**

Quotient Rule for Exponents

If a is a nonzero real number, and m and n are nonnegative integers (with $m \geq n$), then

$$\frac{a^m}{a^n} = a^{m-n}.$$

Note that $\frac{2^3}{2^3} = \frac{8}{8} = 1$, but we also have $\frac{2^3}{2^3} = 2^{3-3} = 2^0 = 1$. So the quotient rule is consistent with the definition of zero exponent. In this section, we will use the quotient rule only when $m \geq n$. The exponent in the numerator must be greater than or equal to the exponent in the denominator. In Section 5.2, we will define negative exponents and see that the quotient rule is valid also when $m < n$.

EXAMPLE 3

Using the quotient rule for exponents

Simplify each expression. Assume that all variables represent nonzero real numbers.

a) $x^7 \div x^4$ **b)** $w^5 \div w^3$ **c)** $\frac{2x^9}{-4x^3}$ **d)** $\frac{6a^{12}b^6}{-3a^9b^6}$

Solution

a) $x^7 \div x^4 = x^{7-4}$ Quotient rule for exponents

$= x^3$ Simplify.

b) $w^5 \div w^3 = w^{5-3}$ Quotient rule for exponents

$= w^2$ Simplify.

c) $\frac{2x^9}{-4x^3} = -\frac{2}{4} \cdot \frac{x^9}{x^3} = -\frac{1}{2} \cdot x^{9-3}$ Quotient rule for exponents

$= -\frac{1}{2} \cdot x^6$ Simplify.

$= -\frac{x^6}{2}$

d) $\frac{6a^{12}b^6}{-3a^9b^6} = \frac{6}{-3} \cdot \frac{a^{12}}{a^9} \cdot \frac{b^6}{b^6}$ Definition of fraction multiplication

$= -2a^{12-9}b^{6-6}$ Quotient rule for exponents

$= -2a^3$ $b^0 = 1$

Now do Exercises 29–40

‹ Helpful Hint ›

Note that these rules of exponents are not absolutely necessary. We could simplify every expression here by using only the definition of exponent. However, these rules make it a lot simpler.

‹4› The Power of a Power Rule

The expression $(a^m)^n$ in which the mth power of a is raised to the nth power is called a **power of a power.** We can simplify a power of a power using the product rule:

$$(x^2)^4 = x^2 \cdot x^2 \cdot x^2 \cdot x^2 = x^8$$

Note that the exponent in the answer is the product of the two original exponents: $4 \cdot 2 = 8$. This example illustrates the **power of a power rule.**

Power of a Power Rule

If a is any real number, and m and n are positive integers, then

$$(a^m)^n = a^{mn}.$$

The power of a power rule is valid also if either of the exponents is zero. In that case, a must not be zero, because 0^0 is undefined.

EXAMPLE 4

Using the power of a power rule

Simplify each expression. Assume that all variables represent nonzero real numbers.

a) $(2^3)^8$ **b)** $(x^2)^5$ **c)** $3x^8(x^3)^6$ **d)** $\frac{-6(b^4)^3}{3b^2}$

Solution

a) $(2^3)^8 = 2^{3\cdot8} = 2^{24}$ Power of a power rule

b) $(x^2)^5 = x^{2\cdot5} = x^{10}$ Power of a power rule

c) $3x^8(x^3)^6 = 3x^8 \cdot x^{18}$ Power of a power rule

$= 3x^{26}$ Product rule for exponents

d) $\frac{-6(b^4)^3}{3b^2} = \frac{-6b^{12}}{3b^2}$ Power of a power rule

$= -2b^{10}$ Quotient rule for exponents

Now do Exercises 41–50

‹ Teaching Tip ›

Remind students that the rules of exponents work so nicely here because these expressions do not involve addition or subtraction.

‹5› The Power of a Product Rule

The expression $(ab)^n$ is a power of the product ab. We can simplify a power of a product using rules that we already know:

$$(5w^2)^3 = \overbrace{5w^2 \cdot 5w^2 \cdot 5w^2}^{\text{3 factors of } 5w^2} = 5^3 \cdot w^6 = 125w^6$$

Note that the exponent is applied to each factor of the product. So we have a new rule, the **power of a product rule,** which makes it easier to simplify this expression.

Power of a Product Rule

If a and b are real numbers, and n is any positive integer, then

$$(ab)^n = a^n \cdot b^n.$$

The power of a power rule is valid also if $n = 0$. In that case, both a and b must be nonzero.

EXAMPLE 5

Using the power of a product rule

Simplify each expression. Assume that all variables represent nonzero real numbers.

a) $(-2x)^3$ **b)** $(-3a^2)^4$ **c)** $(5x^3y^2)^3$

Solution

a) $(-2x)^3 = (-2)^3x^3$ Power of a product rule

$= -8x^3$ Simplify.

b) $(-3a^2)^4 = (-3)^4(a^2)^4$ Power of a product rule
$= 81a^8$ Power of a power rule

c) $(5x^3y^2)^3 = 5^3(x^3)^3(y^2)^3$ Power of a product rule
$= 125x^9y^6$ Power of a power rule

Now do Exercises 51–58

‹6› The Power of a Quotient Rule

The expression $\left(\frac{a}{b}\right)^n$ is a power of the quotient $\frac{a}{b}$. We can simplify a power of a quotient using the definition of exponent and the rule for multiplying fractions:

$$\left(\frac{x}{2}\right)^3 = \frac{x}{2} \cdot \frac{x}{2} \cdot \frac{x}{2} = \frac{x^3}{2^3}$$

Note that the exponent is applied to both the numerator and denominator. So we have a new rule, the **power of a quotient rule,** which makes it easier to simplify this expression.

Power of a Quotient Rule

If a and b are nonzero real numbers, and n is a nonnegative integer, then

$$\left(\frac{a}{b}\right)^n = \frac{a^n}{b^n}.$$

EXAMPLE 6

Using the power of a quotient rule

Simplify each expression. Assume that all variables represent nonzero real numbers.

a) $\left(\frac{y}{4}\right)^3$ **b)** $\left(-\frac{2x^2}{3y}\right)^4$ **c)** $\left(\frac{x^3}{y^5}\right)^4$

Solution

a) $\left(\frac{y}{4}\right)^3 = \frac{y^3}{4^3}$ Power of a quotient rule
$= \frac{y^3}{64}$ Simplify.

b) $\left(-\frac{2x^2}{3y}\right)^4 = \frac{(-2x^2)^4}{(3y)^4}$ Power of a quotient rule
$= \frac{(-2)^4(x^2)^4}{3^4y^4}$ Power of a product rule
$= \frac{16x^8}{81y^4}$ Power of a power rule

c) $\left(\frac{x^3}{y^5}\right)^4 = \frac{(x^3)^4}{(y^5)^4}$ Power of a quotient rule
$= \frac{x^{12}}{y^{20}}$ Power of a power rule

Now do Exercises 59–66

‹ Teaching Tip ›

Emphasize the importance of doing one step at a time, having a reason for each step, and writing neatly.

The five rules that we studied in this section are summarized as follows.

‹ Helpful Hint ›

The exponent rules in this section apply to expressions that involve only multiplication and division. This is not too surprising since exponents, multiplication, and division are closely related.

Rules for Nonnegative Integral Exponents

If a and b are nonzero real numbers, and m and n are nonnegative integers, then

1. $a^m a^n = a^{m+n}$ Product rule for exponents
2. $\dfrac{a^m}{a^n} = a^{m-n}$ Quotient rule for exponents ($m \ge n$)
3. $(a^m)^n = a^{mn}$ Power of a power rule
4. $(ab)^n = a^n b^n$ Power of a product rule
5. $\left(\dfrac{a}{b}\right)^n = \dfrac{a^n}{b^n}$ Power of a quotient rule

‹7› The Amount Formula

The amount of money invested is the **principal,** and the value of the principal after a certain time period is the **amount.** Interest rates are annual percentage rates.

Amount Formula

The amount A of an investment of P dollars with annual interest rate r compounded annually for n years is given by the formula

$$A = P(1 + r)^n.$$

EXAMPLE 7

Using the amount formula

A teacher invested \$10,000 in a bond fund that should have an average annual return of 6% per year for the next 20 years. What will be the amount of the investment in 20 years?

Solution

Use $n = 20$, $P = \$10{,}000$, and $r = 0.06$ in the amount formula:

$$A = P(1 + r)^n$$
$$A = 10{,}000(1 + 0.06)^{20}$$
$$= 10{,}000(1.06)^{20}$$
$$\approx 32{,}071.35$$

So the \$10,000 investment will amount to \$32,071.35 in 20 years.

Now do Exercises 89–94

Warm-Ups ▼

True or false? Explain your answer.

1. $x^3 = x \cdot x \cdot x$ True
2. $3^5 \cdot 3^6 = 3^{11}$ True
3. $2^3 \cdot 3^2 = 6^5$ False
4. $\dfrac{5^{13}}{5^{10}} = 125$ True
5. $(2^3)^2 = 64$ True
6. $(q^3)^5 = q^8$ False
7. $\dfrac{a^{12}}{a^4} = a^3$ False
8. $(2a^3)^4 = 8a^{12}$ False
9. $\dfrac{6w^9}{3w^4} = 2w^5$ True
10. $\left(\dfrac{m^3}{2}\right)^4 = \dfrac{m^{12}}{16}$ True

5.1 Exercises

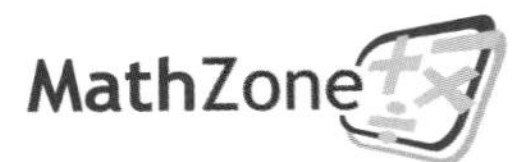

‹ Study Tips ›

- Don't try to get everything done before you start studying. Since the average attention span for a task is only 20 minutes, it is better to study and take breaks from studying to do other duties.
- Your mood for studying should match the mood in which you are tested. Being too relaxed in studying will not match the increased anxiety that you feel during a test.

Reading and Writing *After reading this section, write out the answers to these questions. Use complete sentences.*

1. What is the product rule for exponents?
   The product rule for exponents says that $a^m \cdot a^n = a^{m+n}$.
2. What is the quotient rule for exponents?
   The quotient rule for exponents says that $\frac{a^m}{a^n} = a^{m-n}$.
3. What is the power of a power rule?
   The power of a power rule says that $(a^m)^n = a^{mn}$.
4. What is the power of a product rule?
   The power of a product rule says that $(ab)^n = a^n b^n$.
5. What is the power of a quotient rule?
   The power of a quotient rule says that $\left(\frac{a}{b}\right)^n = \frac{a^n}{b^n}$.
6. What is the definition of zero as an exponent?
   The definition says that $a^0 = 1$ provided $a \neq 0$.

‹1› The Product Rule for Exponents

Find each product. See Example 1.

7. $3x^2 \cdot 9x^3$
   $27x^5$
8. $5x^7 \cdot 3x^5$
   $15x^{12}$
9. $2a^3 \cdot 7a^8$
   $14a^{11}$
10. $3y^{12} \cdot 5y^{15}$
    $15y^{27}$
11. $-6x^2 \cdot 5x^2$
    $-30x^4$
12. $-2x^2 \cdot 8x^5$
    $-16x^7$
13. $(-9x^{10})(-3x^7)$
    $27x^{17}$
14. $(-2x^2)(-8x^9)$
    $16x^{11}$
15. $-6st \cdot 9st$
    $-54s^2t^2$
16. $-12sq \cdot 3s$
    $-36qs^2$
17. $3wt \cdot 8w^7t^6$
    $24t^7w^8$
18. $h^8k^3 \cdot 5h$
    $5h^9k^3$

⟨2⟩ Zero Exponent

Simplify each expression. All variables represent nonzero real numbers. See Example 2.

19. 9^0 1

20. m^0 1

21. $(-2x^3)^0$ 1

22. $(5a^3b)^0$ 1

23. $2 \cdot 5^0 - 5$ -3

24. $-4^0 - 8^0$ -2

25. $(2x - y)^0$ 1

26. $(a^2 + b^2)^0$ 1

27. $x^0 \cdot x^3$ x^3

28. $a^0 \cdot a^2$ a^2

⟨3⟩ The Quotient Rule for Exponents

Find each quotient. All variables represent nonzero real numbers. See Example 3.

29. $m^{18} \div m^6$ m^{12}

30. $a^{12} \div a^3$ a^9

31. $\dfrac{u^6}{u^3}$ u^3

32. $\dfrac{w^{12}}{w^6}$ w^6

33. $b^3 \div b^3$ 1

34. $q^5 \div q^5$ 1

35. $\dfrac{-6a^{10}}{2a^8}$ $-3a^2$

36. $\dfrac{8m^{17}}{-2m^{13}}$ $-4m^4$

37. $\dfrac{8s^2t^{13}}{-2st^5}$ $-4st^8$

38. $\dfrac{-22v^3w^9}{-11v^2w^3}$ $2vw^6$

39. $\dfrac{-6x^8y^4}{-3x^2y^4}$ $2x^6$

40. $\dfrac{-51y^{16}z^3}{17y^9z^3}$ $-3y^7$

⟨4⟩ The Power of a Power Rule

Simplify. All variables represent nonzero real numbers. See Example 4.

41. $(x^2)^3$ x^6

42. $(y^2)^4$ y^8

43. $2x^2 \cdot (x^2)^5$ $2x^{12}$

VIDEO **44.** $(y^2)^6 \cdot 3y^5$ $3y^{17}$

45. $\dfrac{(t^2)^5}{(t^3)^3}$ t

46. $\dfrac{(r^4)^5}{(r^5)^3}$ r^5

47. $\dfrac{(x^3)^4}{(x^6)^2}$ 1

48. $\dfrac{(w^3)^6}{(w^2)^9}$ 1

49. $\dfrac{-3x(x^5)^2}{6x^3(x^2)^4}$ $-\dfrac{1}{2}$

50. $\dfrac{-5y^4(y^5)^2}{15y^7(y^2)^3}$ $-\dfrac{y}{3}$

⟨5⟩ The Power of a Product Rule

Simplify. All variables represent nonzero real numbers. See Example 5.

51. $(xy^2)^3$ x^3y^6

52. $(wy^2)^6$ w^6y^{12}

53. $(-2t^5)^3$ $-8t^{15}$

54. $(-3r^3)^3$ $-27r^9$

55. $(-2x^2y^5)^3$ $-8x^6y^{15}$

VIDEO **56.** $(-3y^2z^3)^3$ $-27y^6z^9$

57. $\dfrac{(a^3b^4c^5)^4}{(a^2b^3c^4)^2}$ $a^8b^{10}c^{12}$

58. $\dfrac{(2a^2b^3)^6}{(4ab^3)^3}$ a^9b^9

⟨6⟩ The Power of a Quotient Rule

Simplify. All variables represent nonzero real numbers. See Example 6.

59. $\left(\dfrac{x}{2}\right)^3$ $\dfrac{x^3}{8}$

60. $\left(\dfrac{y}{3}\right)^4$ $\dfrac{y^4}{81}$

61. $\left(\dfrac{a^4}{4}\right)^3$ $\dfrac{a^{12}}{64}$

62. $\left(\dfrac{w^2}{2}\right)^3$ $\dfrac{w^6}{8}$

63. $\left(\dfrac{-2a^2}{b^3}\right)^4$ $\dfrac{16a^8}{b^{12}}$

VIDEO **64.** $\left(\dfrac{-9r^3}{t^5}\right)^2$ $\dfrac{81r^6}{t^{10}}$

65. $\left(\dfrac{2x^2y^3}{-4y^2}\right)^3$ $-\dfrac{x^6y^3}{8}$

66. $\left(\dfrac{3y^8}{2zy^2}\right)^4$ $\dfrac{81y^{24}}{16z^4}$

Miscellaneous

Simplify. All variables represent nonzero real numbers.

67. $5^2 \cdot 2^3$ 200

68. $10^3 \cdot 3^3$ $27{,}000$

69. $10^2 \cdot 10^4$ $1{,}000{,}000$

70. $2^3 \cdot 2^4$ 128

71. $\left(\dfrac{2^5}{2^3}\right)^3$ 64

72. $\left(\dfrac{3^3}{3}\right)^2$ 81

73. $x^4 \cdot x^3$ x^7

74. $x^5 \cdot x^8$ x^{13}

75. $x^0 \cdot x^5$ x^5

76. $a^9 \cdot a^0$ a^9

77. $a^0 \cdot b^0$ 1

78. $a^0 + b^0$ 2

79. $(a^8)^4$ a^{32}

80. $(b^5)^8$ b^{40}

81. $(a^4b^2)^3$ $a^{12}b^6$

82. $(x^2t^4)^6$ $x^{12}t^{24}$

83. $\dfrac{x^7}{x^4}$ x^3

84. $\dfrac{m^{10}}{m^8}$ m^2

85. $\left(\dfrac{a^3}{b^4}\right)^3$ $\dfrac{a^9}{b^{12}}$

86. $\left(\dfrac{t}{m^2}\right)^4$ $\dfrac{t^4}{m^8}$

87. $(2a^3b)^2(3a^2b^3)^2$ $36a^{10}b^8$

88. $(-2x^2y^3)^4(4xy^3)$ $64x^9y^{15}$

⟨7⟩ The Amount Formula

Solve each problem. See Example 7.

89. ***CD investment.*** Ernesto invested \$25,000 in a CD that paid 5% compounded annually for 6 years. What was the value of his investment at the end of the sixth year? \$33,502.39

90. ***Venture capital.*** Alberto invested \$80,000 in his brother's restaurant. His brother did well and paid him back after 5 years with 10% interest compounded annually. What was the amount that Alberto received? \$128,840.80

91. ***Mutual fund.*** Beryl invested \$40,000 in a mutual fund that had an average annual return of 8%. What was the amount of his investment after 10 years? \$86,357.00

92. ***Savings account.*** Helene put her \$30,000 inheritance into a savings account at her bank and earned 2.2% compounded annually for 10 years. How much did she have after the tenth year? \$37,293.25

93. ***Long-term investing.*** Sheila invested P dollars at annual rate r for 10 years. At the end of 10 years her investment was worth $P(1 + r)^{10}$ dollars. She then reinvested this money for another 5 years at annual rate r. At the end of the second time period her investment was worth $P(1 + r)^{10}(1 + r)^5$ dollars. Which rule of exponents can be used to simplify the expression? Simplify it. Product rule for exponents, $P(1 + r)^{15}$

94. ***CD rollover.*** Ronnie invested P dollars in a 2-year CD with an annual return of r. After the CD rolled over three times, its value was $P((1 + r)^2)^3$ dollars. Which rule of exponents can be used to simplify the expression? Simplify it. Power of a power rule, $P(1 + r)^6$

Getting More Involved

95. ***Writing***

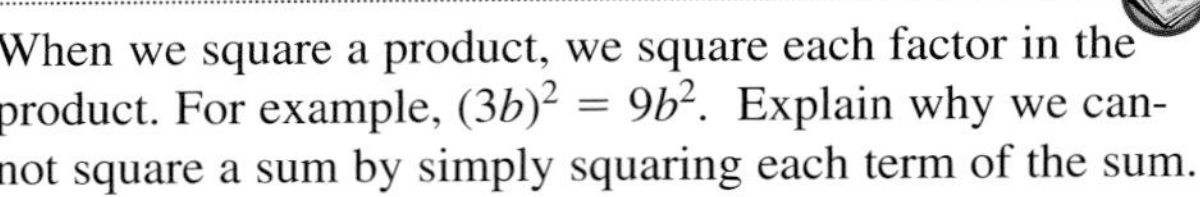

When we square a product, we square each factor in the product. For example, $(3b)^2 = 9b^2$. Explain why we cannot square a sum by simply squaring each term of the sum.

96. ***Writing***

Explain why we defined 2^0 to be 1. Explain why $-2^0 \neq 1$.

5.2 Negative Exponents and Scientific Notation

In This Section

We defined exponential expressions with positive integral exponents in Chapter 1 and learned five rules for exponents in Section 5.1. In this section, we will define negative integral exponents and see how integral exponents are used in scientific notation.

⟨1⟩ Negative Integral Exponents

A positive integral exponent indicates the number of times that the base is used as a factor. For example, $x^2 = x \cdot x$ and $a^3 = a \cdot a \cdot a$. A negative integral exponent indicates the number of times that the reciprocal of the base is used as a factor. So

$$x^{-2} = \frac{1}{x} \cdot \frac{1}{x} \quad \text{and} \quad a^{-3} = \frac{1}{a} \cdot \frac{1}{a} \cdot \frac{1}{a}.$$

Multiplying the fractions yields

$$x^{-2} = \frac{1}{x^2} \quad \text{and} \quad a^{-3} = \frac{1}{a^3}.$$

In general, we have the following definition.

Negative Integral Exponents

If a is a nonzero real number and n is a positive integer, then

$$a^{-n} = \frac{1}{a^n}. \quad \text{(If } n \text{ is positive, } -n \text{ is negative.)}$$

EXAMPLE 1

Simplifying expressions with negative exponents

Simplify.

a) 2^{-5} **b)** $(-2)^{-5}$ **c)** -9^{-2} **d)** $\frac{2^{-3}}{3^{-2}}$

‹ Calculator Close-Up ›

You can evaluate expressions with negative exponents on a calculator as shown here.

```
2^-5▸Frac
                 1/32
(-2)^-5▸Frac
                -1/32
2^-3/3^-2▸Frac
                  9/8
```

Solution

a) $2^{-5} = \frac{1}{2^5} = \frac{1}{32}$

b) $(-2)^{-5} = \frac{1}{(-2)^5}$ Definition of negative exponent

$= \frac{1}{-32} = -\frac{1}{32}$

c) $-9^{-2} = -(9^{-2}) = -\frac{1}{9^2} = -\frac{1}{81}$

d) $\frac{2^{-3}}{3^{-2}} = 2^{-3} \div 3^{-2}$

$= \frac{1}{2^3} \div \frac{1}{3^2}$

$= \frac{1}{8} \div \frac{1}{9} = \frac{1}{8} \cdot \frac{9}{1} = \frac{9}{8}$

Now do Exercises 7–16

CAUTION A negative sign preceding an exponential expression is handled last for any exponents, resulting in a negative value for the expression:

$$-3^{-2} = -\frac{1}{3^2} = -\frac{1}{9}, \quad -3^2 = -9, \quad \text{and} \quad -3^0 = -1.$$

If the base is negative, the value could be positive or negative:

$$(-2)^{-4} = \frac{1}{(-2)^4} = \frac{1}{16} \quad \text{and} \quad (-2)^{-3} = \frac{1}{(-2)^3} = \frac{1}{-8} = -\frac{1}{8}.$$

To evaluate a^{-n}, you can first find the nth power of a and then find the reciprocal. However, the result is the same if you first find the reciprocal of a and then find the nth power of the reciprocal. For example,

$$3^{-2} = \frac{1}{3^2} = \frac{1}{9} \quad \text{or} \quad 3^{-2} = \left(\frac{1}{3}\right)^2 = \frac{1}{3} \cdot \frac{1}{3} = \frac{1}{9}.$$

So the power and the reciprocal can be found in either order. If the exponent is -1, we simply find the reciprocal. For example,

$$5^{-1} = \frac{1}{5}, \quad \left(\frac{1}{4}\right)^{-1} = 4, \quad \text{and} \quad \left(-\frac{3}{5}\right)^{-1} = -\frac{5}{3}.$$

Because $3^{-2} \cdot 3^2 = 1$, the reciprocal of 3^{-2} is 3^2, and we have

$$\frac{1}{3^{-2}} = 3^2.$$

Remember that if a negative sign in a negative exponent is deleted, then you must find a reciprocal. Four situations where this idea occurs are listed in the following box. Don't think of this as four more rules to be memorized. Remember the idea.

‹ Teaching Tip ›

Ask students why we specify that $a \neq 0$. Why do we specify that n is a positive integer? What are the positive integers?

Rules for Negative Exponents

If a is a nonzero real number, and n is a positive integer, then

1. $a^{-1} = \dfrac{1}{a}$

2. $\dfrac{1}{a^{-n}} = a^n$

3. $a^{-n} = \left(\dfrac{1}{a}\right)^n$

4. $\left(\dfrac{a}{b}\right)^{-n} = \left(\dfrac{b}{a}\right)^n$

CAUTION Note that a^{-1} is the multiplicative inverse of a and $-a$ is the additive inverse of a. For example, $2 \cdot 2^{-1} = 2 \cdot \frac{1}{2} = 1$ and $2 + (-2) = 0$.

With our definitions of the integral exponents, we get a nice pattern for the integral powers of 2 as shown in the following table. Whenever the exponent increases by 1, the value of the exponential expression is doubled.

2^{-5}	2^{-4}	2^{-3}	2^{-2}	2^{-1}	2^0	2^1	2^2	2^3	2^4	2^5
$\frac{1}{32}$	$\frac{1}{16}$	$\frac{1}{8}$	$\frac{1}{4}$	$\frac{1}{2}$	1	2	4	8	16	32

EXAMPLE 2

Using the rules for negative exponents

Simplify. Use only positive exponents in the answers.

a) $10^{-1} + 10^{-1}$ **b)** $\dfrac{2y^{-8}}{x^{-3}}$ **c)** 7^{-2} **d)** $\left(\dfrac{3}{4}\right)^{-3}$

Solution

a) $10^{-1} + 10^{-1} = \dfrac{1}{10} + \dfrac{1}{10} = \dfrac{2}{10} = \dfrac{1}{5}$ First rule for negative exponents

b) $\dfrac{2y^{-8}}{x^{-3}} = 2 \cdot y^{-8} \cdot \dfrac{1}{x^{-3}}$ $a \div b = a \cdot \dfrac{1}{b}$

$= 2 \cdot \dfrac{1}{y^8} \cdot x^3$ Second rule for negative exponents

$= \dfrac{2x^3}{y^8}$ Multiply.

Note that a negative exponent in the numerator or denominator can be changed to positive by simply relocating the expression.

c) $7^{-2} = \left(\dfrac{1}{7}\right)^2 = \dfrac{1}{7} \cdot \dfrac{1}{7} = \dfrac{1}{49}$ Third rule for negative exponents

d) We can find the power and the reciprocal in either order:

$$\left(\frac{3}{4}\right)^{-3} = \left(\frac{4}{3}\right)^3 = \frac{4}{3} \cdot \frac{4}{3} \cdot \frac{4}{3} = \frac{64}{27} \qquad \left(\frac{3}{4}\right)^{-3} = \left(\frac{27}{64}\right)^{-1} = \frac{64}{27}$$

Now try Exercises 17–26

CAUTION You cannot change negative exponents to positive so easily if addition or subtraction is present: $\frac{1 + 2^{-3}}{5^{-2}} \neq \frac{1 + 5^2}{2^3}$

⟨2⟩ The Rules for Integral Exponents

To find the product of y^{-2} and y^{-6} we could convert to positive exponents:

$$y^{-2} \cdot y^{-6} = \frac{1}{y^2} \cdot \frac{1}{y^6} = \frac{1}{y^8} = y^{-8}$$

To find the quotient of y^{-2} and y^{-6} we could again convert to positive exponents:

$$\frac{y^{-2}}{y^{-6}} = \frac{\frac{1}{y^2}}{\frac{1}{y^6}} = \frac{1}{y^2} \cdot \frac{y^6}{1} = \frac{y^6}{y^2} = y^{6-2} = y^4$$

However, it is not necessary to convert to positive exponents. The exponent for the product is the sum of the exponents and the exponent for the quotient is the difference: $-2 + (-6) = -8$ and $-2 - (-6) = 4$. These examples illustrate the fact that the product and quotient rules hold for negative exponents as well as positive exponents. In fact, *all five of the rules for exponents from Section 5.1 are valid for any integer exponents!*

The definitions and rules that we studied in this section and the last are summarized as follows. Note the rules apply to any integers as exponents: positive, negative, or zero.

‹ Calculator Close-Up ›

You can use a calculator to demonstrate that the product rule for exponents holds when the exponents are negative numbers.

```
2^-3*2^-5
         .00390625
2^(-3+-5)
         .00390625
```

‹ Helpful Hint ›

The definitions of the different types of exponents are a really clever mathematical invention. The fact that we have rules for performing arithmetic with those exponents makes the notation of exponents even more amazing.

Rules for Integral Exponents

If a and b are nonzero real numbers, and m and n are integers, then

1. $a^{-n} = \frac{1}{a^n}$ Definition of negative exponent
2. $a^{-1} = \frac{1}{a}$, $\frac{1}{a^{-n}} = a^n$, $a^{-n} = \left(\frac{1}{a}\right)^n$, $\left(\frac{a}{b}\right)^{-n} = \left(\frac{b}{a}\right)^n$ Negative exponent rules
3. $a^0 = 1$ Definition of zero exponent
4. $a^m a^n = a^{m+n}$ Product rule for exponents
5. $\frac{a^m}{a^n} = a^{m-n}$ Quotient rule for exponents
6. $(a^m)^n = a^{mn}$ Power of a power rule
7. $(ab)^n = a^n b^n$ Power of a product rule
8. $\left(\frac{a}{b}\right)^n = \frac{a^n}{b^n}$ Power of a quotient rule

In Example 3, we use the product and quotient rules (rules 4 and 5) to simplify some expressions involving positive and negative exponents. Note that we specify that the answers are to be written without negative exponents. We do this to make the answers look simpler and so that there is only one correct answer. It is not wrong to use negative exponents in an answer.

EXAMPLE 3

Using the product and quotient rules with integral exponents

Simplify. Write answers without negative exponents. Assume that the variables represent nonzero real numbers.

a) $b^{-3}b^5$ **b)** $-3x^{-3} \cdot 5x^2$ **c)** $\frac{m^{-6}}{m^{-2}}$ **d)** $\frac{4x^{-6}y^5}{-12x^{-6}y^{-3}}$

Solution

a) $b^{-3}b^5 = b^{-3+5}$ Product rule for exponents

$= b^2$ Simplify.

b) $-3x^{-3} \cdot 5x^2 = -15x^{-3+2}$ Product rule for exponents

$= -15x^{-1}$ Simplify.

$= -15 \cdot \frac{1}{x}$ Definition of negative exponent (to get answer without negative exponents)

$= -\frac{15}{x}$ Simplify.

c) $\frac{m^{-6}}{m^{-2}} = m^{-6-(-2)}$ Quotient rule for exponents

$= m^{-4}$ Simplify.

$= \frac{1}{m^4}$ Definition of negative exponent (to get answer without negative exponents)

d) $\frac{4x^{-6}y^5}{-12x^{-6}y^{-3}} = \frac{x^{-6-(-6)}y^{5-(-3)}}{-3} = \frac{x^0y^8}{-3} = -\frac{y^8}{3}$

Now do Exercises 27–42

In Example 4, we use the power rules (rules 6–8) to simplify some expressions involving positive and negative exponents.

EXAMPLE 4

Using the power rules with integral exponents

Simplify. Write answers without negative exponents. Assume that the variables represent nonzero real numbers.

a) $(a^{-3})^2$ **b)** $(10x^{-3})^{-2}$ **c)** $\left(\frac{4x^{-5}}{y^2}\right)^{-2}$

Solution

a) $(a^{-3})^2 = a^{-3 \cdot 2}$ Power of a power rule

$= a^{-6}$ Simplify.

$= \frac{1}{a^6}$ Definition of negative exponent (to get answer without negative exponents)

b) $(10x^{-3})^{-2} = 10^{-2}(x^{-3})^{-2}$ Power of a product rule

$= \frac{1}{10^2}x^6$ Power of a power rule

$= \frac{x^6}{100}$ Simplify.

‹ Calculator Close-Up ›

You can use a calculator to demonstrate that the power of a power rule for exponents holds when the exponents are negative integers.

```
(3^-2)^-5
                59049
3^(-2*-5)
                59049
```

c) $\left(\frac{4x^{-5}}{y^2}\right)^{-2} = \frac{(4x^{-5})^{-2}}{(y^2)^{-2}}$ Power of a quotient rule

$= \frac{4^{-2}x^{10}}{y^{-4}}$ Power of a product and power of a power rule

$= 4^{-2} \cdot x^{10} \cdot \frac{1}{y^{-4}}$ Because $\frac{a}{b} = a \cdot \frac{1}{b}$

$= \frac{1}{4^2} \cdot x^{10} \cdot y^4$ Definition of negative exponent

$= \frac{x^{10}y^4}{16}$ Simplify.

Now do Exercises 43–58

⟨3⟩ The Present Value Formula

In Section 5.1, we studied the amount formula $A = P(1 + r)^n$. If we are interested in the principal P that must be invested today to grow to a specified amount A in the future, then the principal is called the **present value** of the investment. We can find a formula for present value by solving the amount formula for P:

$A = P(1 + r)^n$ The amount formula

$P = \frac{A}{(1 + r)^n}$ Divide each side by $(1 + r)^n$

$P = A(1 + r)^{-n}$ Definition of negative exponent

Present Value Formula

The present value P that will amount to A dollars after n years with interest compounded annually at annual interest rate r is given by the formula

$$P = A(1 + r)^{-n}.$$

EXAMPLE 5

Using the present value formula

A new parent wants to have $20,000 in his child's college fund when his infant is ready for college in 18 years. How much must he invest now at 8% compounded annually to achieve this goal?

Solution

Use $n = 18$, $A = \$20{,}000$, and $r = 0.08$ in the present value formula:

$$P = A(1 + r)^{-n}$$
$$P = 20{,}000(1 + 0.08)^{-18}$$
$$P = 20{,}000(1.08)^{-18}$$
$$\approx 5004.98$$

An investment today of $5004.98 will amount to $20,000 in 18 years.

Now do Exercises 59–64

⟨4⟩ Scientific Notation

Many of the numbers occurring in science are either very large or very small. The speed of light is 983,571,000 feet per second. One millimeter is equal to 0.000001 kilometer. Numbers larger than 10 or smaller than 1 can be written using positive or negative integral exponents.

Scientific Notation

A number in **scientific notation** is written using the times symbol $\times$ in the form

$$a \times 10^n$$

where $1 \le a < 10$ and n is a positive or negative integer.

⟨ Calculator Close-Up ⟩

On a graphing calculator you can write scientific notation by actually using the power of 10 or press EE to get the letter E, which indicates that the following number is the power of 10.

```
3.27*10^9
           3270000000
3.27E9
           3270000000
```

Note that if the exponent is not too large, scientific notation is converted to standard notation when you press ENTER.

In scientific notation, the speed of light is 9.83571×10^8 feet per second and one millimeter is 1×10^{-6} kilometer. Since a is between 1 and 10, there is always one digit to the left of the decimal point.

Scientific notation is based on multiplication by integral powers of 10. Multiplying a number by a positive power of 10 moves the decimal point to the right:

$$10(5.32) = 53.2$$

$$10^2(5.32) = 100(5.32) = 532$$

$$10^3(5.32) = 1000(5.32) = 5320$$

Multiplying by a negative power of 10 moves the decimal point to the left:

$$10^{-1}(5.32) = \frac{1}{10}(5.32) = 0.532$$

$$10^{-2}(5.32) = \frac{1}{100}(5.32) = 0.0532$$

$$10^{-3}(5.32) = \frac{1}{1000}(5.32) = 0.00532$$

So if n is a positive integer, multiplying by 10^n moves the decimal point n places to the right and multiplying by 10^{-n} moves it n places to the left.

To convert a number in scientific notation to standard notation, we simply multiply by the indicated power of 10, where multiplication is accomplished by moving the decimal point. We can use the following strategy.

Strategy for Converting to Standard Notation

1. Determine the number of places to move the decimal point by examining the exponent on the 10.
2. Move to the right for a positive exponent and to the left for a negative exponent.

EXAMPLE 6

Converting scientific notation to standard notation

Write in standard notation.

a) 7.02×10^6 **b)** 8.13×10^{-5}

Solution

a) Because the exponent is positive, move the decimal point six places to the right:

$$7.02 \times 10^6 = 7020000. = 7{,}020{,}000$$

b) Because the exponent is negative, move the decimal point five places to the left:

$$8.13 \times 10^{-5} = 0.0000813$$

Now do Exercises 65–72

To convert a positive number to scientific notation, we just reverse the strategy for converting from scientific notation.

Strategy for Converting to Scientific Notation

1. Count the number of places (n) that the decimal must be moved so that it will follow the first nonzero digit of the number.
2. If the original number was larger than 10, use 10^n.
3. If the original number was smaller than 1, use 10^{-n}.

Remember that the scientific notation for a number larger than 10 will have a positive power of 10 and the scientific notation for a number between 0 and 1 will have a negative power of 10.

EXAMPLE 7

Converting numbers to scientific notation

Write in scientific notation.

a) 7,346,200 **b)** 0.0000348 **c)** 135×10^{-12}

Solution

a) Because 7,346,200 is larger than 10, the exponent on the 10 will be positive:

$$7{,}346{,}200 = 7.3462 \times 10^6$$

b) Because 0.0000348 is smaller than 1, the exponent on the 10 will be negative:

$$0.0000348 = 3.48 \times 10^{-5}$$

c) There should be only one nonzero digit to the left of the decimal point:

$$135 \times 10^{-12} = 1.35 \times 10^2 \times 10^{-12} \quad \text{Convert 135 to scientific notation.}$$
$$= 1.35 \times 10^{-10} \quad \text{Product rule for exponents}$$

Now do Exercises 73–80

‹ Calculator Close-Up ›

To convert to scientific notation, set the mode to scientific. In scientific mode all results are given in scientific notation.

```
7346200
           7.3462E6
.0000348
             3.48E-5
135E-12
            1.35E-10
```

‹5› Computations with Scientific Notation

An important feature of scientific notation is its use in computations. Numbers in scientific notation are nothing more than exponential expressions, and you have already studied operations with exponential expressions in this section. We use the same rules of exponents on numbers in scientific notation that we use on any other exponential expressions.

EXAMPLE 8

Using the rules of exponents with scientific notation

Perform the indicated computations. Write the answers in scientific notation.

a) $(3 \times 10^6)(2 \times 10^8)$ **b)** $\dfrac{4 \times 10^5}{8 \times 10^{-2}}$ **c)** $(5 \times 10^{-7})^3$

‹ Calculator Close-Up ›

With a calculator's built-in scientific notation, some parentheses can be omitted as shown below. Writing out the powers of 10 can lead to errors.

```
4E5/8E-2
                5E6
4*10^5/8*10^-2
                5E2
```

Try these computations with your calculator.

Solution

a) $(3 \times 10^6)(2 \times 10^8) = 3 \cdot 2 \cdot 10^6 \cdot 10^8 = 6 \times 10^{14}$

b) $\dfrac{4 \times 10^5}{8 \times 10^{-2}} = \dfrac{4}{8} \cdot \dfrac{10^5}{10^{-2}} = \dfrac{1}{2} \cdot 10^{5-(-2)}$ Quotient rule for exponents

$= (0.5)10^7$ $\quad \frac{1}{2} = 0.5$

$= 5 \times 10^{-1} \cdot 10^7$ Write 0.5 in scientific notation.

$= 5 \times 10^6$ Product rule for exponents

c) $(5 \times 10^{-7})^3 = 5^3(10^{-7})^3$ Power of a product rule

$= 125 \cdot 10^{-21}$ Power of a power rule

$= 1.25 \times 10^2 \times 10^{-21}$ $\quad 125 = 1.25 \times 10^2$

$= 1.25 \times 10^{-19}$ Product rule for exponents

Now do Exercises 81–92

EXAMPLE 9

Converting to scientific notation for computations

Perform these computations by first converting each number into scientific notation. Give your answer in scientific notation.

a) (3,000,000)(0.0002) **b)** $(20{,}000{,}000)^3(0.0000003)$

‹ Teaching Tip ›

Many students have trouble converting 24×10^{14} to scientific notation. Be sure they write $2.4 \times 10^1 \times 10^{14}$ and then add exponents.

Solution

a) $(3{,}000{,}000)(0.0002) = 3 \times 10^6 \cdot 2 \times 10^{-4}$ Scientific notation

$= 6 \times 10^2$ Product rule for exponents

b) $(20{,}000{,}000)^3(0.0000003) = (2 \times 10^7)^3(3 \times 10^{-7})$ Scientific notation

$= 8 \times 10^{21} \cdot 3 \times 10^{-7}$ Power of a product rule

$= 24 \times 10^{14}$

$= 2.4 \times 10^1 \times 10^{14}$ $\quad 24 = 2.4 \times 10^1$

$= 2.4 \times 10^{15}$ Product rule for exponents

Now do Exercises 93–100

Warm-Ups ▼

True or false? Explain your answer.

1. $10^{-2} = \dfrac{1}{100}$ True

2. $\left(-\dfrac{1}{5}\right)^{-1} = 5$ False

3. $3^{-2} \cdot 2^{-1} = 6^{-3}$ False

4. $\dfrac{3^{-2}}{3^{-1}} = \dfrac{1}{3}$ True

5. $(2^{-3})^{-2} = 64$ True
6. $-2^{-4} = \frac{1}{16}$ False
7. $23.7 = 2.37 \times 10^{-1}$ False
8. $0.000036 = 3.6 \times 10^{-5}$ True
9. $(3 \times 10^{-9})^2 = 9 \times 10^{-18}$ True
10. $(2 \times 10^{-5})(4 \times 10^4) = 8 \times 10^{-20}$ False

Exercises 5.2

‹ Study Tips ›

- Studying in an environment similar to the one in which you will be tested can increase your chances of recalling information.
- If possible, do some studying in the classroom where you will be taking the test.

Reading and Writing *After reading this section, write out the answers to these questions. Use complete sentences.*

1. What does a negative exponent mean?
A negative exponent means "reciprocal," as in $a^{-n} = \frac{1}{a^n}$.
2. What is the proper order for evaluating the operations indicated by a negative exponent?
The operations can be evaluated in any order.
3. For what exponents is the product rule valid?
The product rule is valid for any integral exponents.
4. How do you convert a number from scientific notation to standard notation?
Convert from scientific notation by multiplying by the appropriate power of 10.
5. How do you convert a number from standard notation to scientific notation?
Convert from standard notation by counting the number of places the decimal point must move so that there is one nonzero digit to the left of the decimal point.
6. Which numbers are not usually written in scientific notation?
Numbers between 1 and 10 are not written in scientific notation.

Variables in all exercises represent nonzero real numbers. Write all answers without negative exponents.

‹1› Negative Integral Exponents

Evaluate each expression. See Example 1.

7. 3^{-1} $\frac{1}{3}$
8. 3^{-3} $\frac{1}{27}$
9. $(-2)^{-4}$ $\frac{1}{16}$ (VIDEO)
10. $(-3)^{-4}$ $\frac{1}{81}$
11. -4^{-2} $-\frac{1}{16}$
12. -2^{-4} $-\frac{1}{16}$
13. -3^{-3} $-\frac{1}{27}$
14. -5^{-3} $-\frac{1}{125}$
15. $\frac{5^{-2}}{10^{-2}}$ 4
16. $\frac{3^{-4}}{6^{-2}}$ $\frac{4}{9}$

Simplify. See Example 2.

17. $6^{-1} + 6^{-1}$ $\frac{1}{3}$
18. $2^{-1} + 4^{-1}$ $\frac{3}{4}$
19. $\frac{10}{5^{-3}}$ 1250
20. $\frac{1}{25 \cdot 10^{-4}}$ 400
21. $\frac{3a^{-3}}{b^{-9}}$ $\frac{3b^9}{a^3}$
22. $\frac{6x^{-5}}{5y^{-1}}$ $\frac{6y}{5x^5}$
23. $\left(\frac{1}{b}\right)^{-7}$ b^7
24. $\left(\frac{1}{y}\right)^{-4}$ y^4
25. $\left(\frac{5}{2}\right)^{-3}$ $\frac{8}{125}$
26. $\left(\frac{4}{3}\right)^{-2}$ $\frac{9}{16}$

‹2› The Rules for Integral Exponents

Simplify. See Example 3.

27. $x^{-1} \cdot x^5$ x^4
28. $y^{-3} \cdot y^5$ y^2
29. $x^3 \cdot x \cdot x^{-7}$ $\frac{1}{x^3}$
30. $y \cdot y^{-8} \cdot y$ $\frac{1}{y^6}$

31. $y^{-3} \cdot y^{-5}$ $\frac{1}{y^8}$

32. $w^{-8} \cdot w^{-3}$ $\frac{1}{w^{11}}$

33. $-2x^2 \cdot 8x^{-6}$ $-\frac{16}{x^4}$

34. $5y^5(-6y^{-7})$ $-\frac{30}{y^2}$

35. $b^3 \div b^9$ $\frac{1}{b^6}$

36. $q^5 \div q^7$ $\frac{1}{q^2}$

37. $\frac{-6a^6}{2a^8}$ $-\frac{3}{a^2}$

38. $\frac{2m^{13}}{-8m^{17}}$ $-\frac{1}{4m^4}$

39. $\frac{u^{-5}}{u^3}$ $\frac{1}{u^8}$

40. $\frac{w^{-4}}{w^6}$ $\frac{1}{w^{10}}$

41. $\frac{8t^{-3}}{-2t^{-5}}$ $-4t^2$

VIDEO **42.** $\frac{-22w^{-4}}{-11w^{-3}}$ $\frac{2}{w}$

Simplify. See Example 4.

43. $(y^{-3})^4$ $\frac{1}{y^{12}}$

44. $(a^5)^{-3}$ $\frac{1}{a^{15}}$

45. $2x^{-3}(x^{-2})^{-5}$ $2x^7$

46. $3x^{16}(x^{-2})^6$ $3x^4$

47. $\frac{(b^3)^{-3}}{(b^{-2})^5}$ b

48. $\frac{(a^{-3})^{-3}}{(a^{-1})^{-4}}$ a^5

49. $(2x)^{-4}$ $\frac{1}{16x^4}$

50. $(3a)^{-3}$ $\frac{1}{27a^3}$

51. $(xy^{-2})^{-3}$ $\frac{y^6}{x^3}$

52. $(a^{-3}b)^4$ $\frac{b^4}{a^{12}}$

53. $\left(\frac{x^{-4}}{9^{-1}}\right)^2$ $\frac{81}{x^8}$

54. $\left(\frac{w^{-3}}{2^{-2}}\right)^3$ $\frac{64}{w^9}$

55. $\left(\frac{-2m^{-3}}{n^{-2}}\right)^4$ $\frac{16n^8}{m^{12}}$

56. $\left(\frac{-3b^{-1}}{a^4}\right)^{-2}$ $\frac{a^8b^2}{9}$

57. $\left(\frac{6ab^{-2}}{3a^2b^{-4}}\right)^3$ $\frac{8b^6}{a^3}$

58. $\left(\frac{2s^{-1}t^3}{6s^2t^{-4}}\right)^{-3}$ $\frac{27s^9}{t^{21}}$

⟨3⟩ The Present Value Formula

Solve each problem. See Example 5.

59. ***Saving for a car.*** How much would Florence have to invest today at 6.2% compounded annually so that she would have \$20,000 to buy a new car in 6 years? \$13,940.65

60. ***Saving for college.*** Mr. Isaacs wants to have \$60,000 in 18 years when little Debby will start college. How much would he have to invest today in high-yield bonds that pay 9% compounded annually to achieve his goal? \$12,719.62

61. ***Saving for retirement.*** Nadine inherited a large sum of money and wants to make sure her son will have a comfortable retirement. How much should she invest today in Treasury Bills paying 4.5% compounded annually so that her son will have \$1,000,000 in 40 years when he retires? \$171,928.70

62. ***Saving for a boat.*** Oscar has an account that is earmarked for a sailboat. He needs \$200,000 for the boat when he retires in 10 years. If he averages 7% annually on this account, how much should he have in the account now so that his goal will be reached with no additional deposits? \$101,669.86

63. ***Present value.*** Find the present value that will amount to \$50,000 in 20 years at 8% compounded annually. \$10,727.41

64. ***Investing in stocks.*** U.S. small company stocks have returned an average of 14.9% annually for the last 50 years (T. Rowe Price, www.troweprice.com). Find the amount invested today in small company stocks that would be worth \$1 million in 50 years, assuming that small company stocks continue to return 14.9% annually for the next 50 years. \$963.83

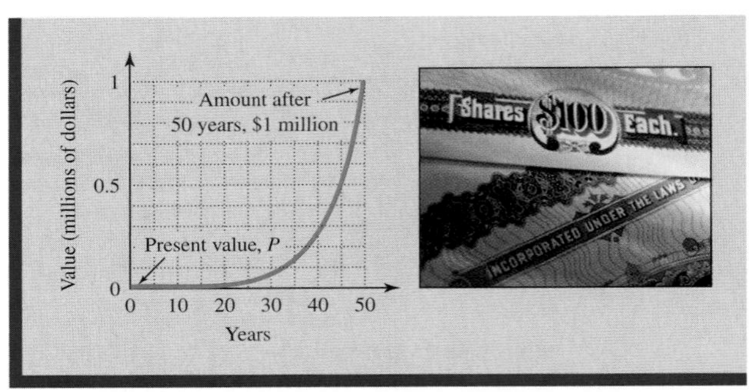

Figure for Exercise 64

⟨4⟩ Scientific Notation

Write each number in standard notation.

See Example 6.

See the Strategy for Converting to Standard Notation box on page 312.

65. 9.86×10^9 9,860,000,000

66. 4.007×10^4 40,070

67. 1.37×10^{-3} 0.00137

68. 9.3×10^{-5} 0.000093

69. 1×10^{-6} 0.000001

70. 3×10^{-1} 0.3

71. 6×10^5 600,000

72. 8×10^6 8,000,000

Write each number in scientific notation.

See Example 7.

See the Strategy for Converting to Scientific Notation box on page 313.

VIDEO **73.** 9000 9×10^3

74. 5,298,000 5.298×10^6

75. 0.00078 7.8×10^{-4}

76. 0.000214 2.14×10^{-4}

77. 0.0000085 8.5×10^{-6}

78. 5,670,000,000 5.67×10^9

79. 525×10^9 5.25×10^{11}

80. 0.0034×10^{-8} 3.4×10^{-11}

⟨5⟩ Computations with Scientific Notation

Perform the computations. Write answers in scientific notation. See Example 8.

81. $(3 \times 10^5)(2 \times 10^{-15})$ 6×10^{-10}

82. $(2 \times 10^{-9})(4 \times 10^{23})$ 8×10^{14}

83. $\dfrac{4 \times 10^{-8}}{2 \times 10^{30}}$ 2×10^{-38}

84. $\dfrac{9 \times 10^{-4}}{3 \times 10^{-6}}$ 3×10^2

85. $\dfrac{3 \times 10^{20}}{6 \times 10^{-8}}$ 5×10^{27}

86. $\dfrac{1 \times 10^{-8}}{4 \times 10^7}$ 2.5×10^{-16}

87. $(3 \times 10^{12})^2$ 9×10^{24}

88. $(2 \times 10^{-5})^3$ 8×10^{-15}

89. $(5 \times 10^4)^3$ 1.25×10^{14}

90. $(5 \times 10^{14})^{-1}$ 2×10^{-15}

91. $(4 \times 10^{32})^{-1}$ 2.5×10^{-33}

92. $(6 \times 10^{11})^2$ 3.6×10^{23}

Perform the following computations by first converting each number into scientific notation. Write answers in scientific notation. See Example 9.

93. (4300)(2,000,000) 8.6×10^9

94. (40,000)(4,000,000,000) 1.6×10^{14}

95. (4,200,000)(0.00005) 2.1×10^2

96. (0.00075)(4,000,000) 3×10^3

97. $(300)^3(0.000001)^5$ 2.7×10^{-23}

98. $(200)^4(0.0005)^3$ 2×10^{-1}

99. $\dfrac{(4000)(90{,}000)}{0.00000012}$ 3×10^{15}

100. $\dfrac{(30{,}000)(80{,}000)}{(0.000006)(0.002)}$ 2×10^{17}

Perform the following computations with the aid of a calculator. Write answers in scientific notation. Round to three decimal places.

101. $(6.3 \times 10^6)(1.45 \times 10^{-4})$ 9.135×10^2

102. $(8.35 \times 10^9)(4.5 \times 10^3)$ 3.758×10^{13}

103. $(5.36 \times 10^{-4}) + (3.55 \times 10^{-5})$ 5.715×10^{-4}

104. $(8.79 \times 10^8) + (6.48 \times 10^9)$ 7.359×10^9

105. $\dfrac{(3.5 \times 10^5)(4.3 \times 10^{-6})}{3.4 \times 10^{-8}}$ 4.426×10^7

106. $\dfrac{(3.5 \times 10^{-8})(4.4 \times 10^{-4})}{2.43 \times 10^{45}}$ 6.337×10^{-57}

107. $(3.56 \times 10^{85})(4.43 \times 10^{96})$ 1.577×10^{182}

108. $(8 \times 10^{99}) + (3 \times 10^{99})$ 1.1×10^{100}

Applications

Solve each problem.

109. ***Distance to the sun.*** The distance from the earth to the sun is 93 million miles. Express this distance in feet. (1 mile = 5280 feet.) 4.910×10^{11} feet

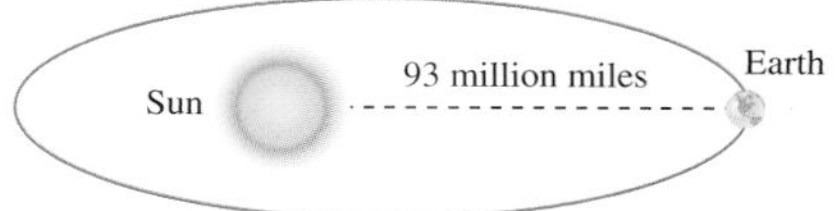

Figure for Exercise 109

110. ***Speed of light.*** The speed of light is 9.83569×10^8 feet per second. How long does it take light to travel from the sun to the earth? See Exercise 109. 8.3 minutes

111. ***Warp drive, Scotty.*** How long does it take a spacecraft traveling at 2×10^{35} miles per hour (warp factor 4) to travel 93 million miles? 4.65×10^{-28} hours

112. ***Area of a dot.*** If the radius of a very small circle is 2.35×10^{-8} centimeters, then what is the circle's area? 1.735×10^{-15} cm^2

113. ***Circumference of a circle.*** If the circumference of a circle is 5.68×10^9 feet, then what is its radius? 9.040×10^8 feet

114. ***Diameter of a circle.*** If the diameter of a circle is 1.3×10^{-12} meters, then what is its radius? 6.5×10^{-13} meters

Getting More Involved

115. ***Exploration***

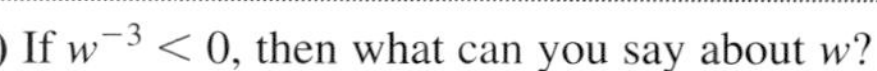

a) If $w^{-3} < 0$, then what can you say about w?

b) If $(-5)^m < 0$, then what can you say about m?

c) What restriction must be placed on w and m so that $w^m < 0$? a) $w < 0$ b) m is odd c) $w < 0$ and m odd

116. ***Discussion***

Which of the following expressions is not equal to -1? Explain your answer.

a) -1^{-1} **b)** -1^{-2} **c)** $(-1^{-1})^{-1}$
d) $(-1)^{-1}$ **e)** $(-1)^{-2}$ e

Math at Work Aerospace Engineering

Aircraft design is a delicate balance between weight and strength. Saving 1 pound of weight could save the plane's operators \$5000 over 20 years. Mathematics is used to calculate the strength of each of a plane's parts and to predict when the material making up a part will fail. If calculations show that one kind of metal isn't strong enough, designers usually have to choose another material or change the design.

As an example, consider an aluminum stringer with a circular cross section. The stringer is used inside the wing of an airplane as shown in the accompanying figure. The aluminum rod has a diameter of 20 mm and will support a load of 5×10^4 Newtons (N). The maximum stress on aluminum is 1×10^8 Pascals (Pa), where 1 Pa = 1 N/m^2. To calculate the stress S on the rod we use S = (load)/(cross sectional area). Note that we must divide the diameter by 2 to get the radius and convert square millimeters to square meters:

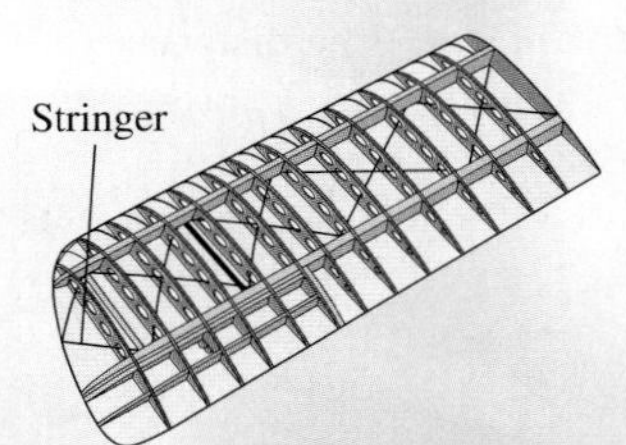

$$S = \frac{L}{\pi r^2} = \frac{5 \times 10^4\text{ N}}{\pi(10\text{ mm})^2} \cdot \left(\frac{1000\text{ mm}}{1\text{ m}}\right)^2 \approx 1.6 \times 10^8\text{ Pa}$$

Since the stress is 1.6×10^8 Pa and the maximum stress on aluminum is 1×10^8 Pa, the aluminum rod is not strong enough. The design must be changed. The diameter of the aluminum rod could be increased or stronger/lighter metal such as titanium could be used.

5.3 Addition and Subtraction of Polynomials

In This Section

- ⟨1⟩ Polynomials
- ⟨2⟩ Evaluating Polynomials
- ⟨3⟩ Addition of Polynomials
- ⟨4⟩ Subtraction of Polynomials
- ⟨5⟩ Applications

We first used polynomials in Chapter 1, but did not identify them as polynomials. Polynomials also occurred in the equations and inequalities of Chapter 2. In this section, we will define polynomials and begin a thorough study of polynomials.

⟨1⟩ Polynomials

In Chapter 1 we defined a **term** as an expression containing a number or the product of a number and one or more variables raised to powers. If the number is 1 or the power is 1 we usually omit it, as in $1x^1 = x$. Some examples of terms are

$$4x^3, \quad -x^2y^3, \quad abc, \quad \text{and} \quad -2.$$

The number preceding the variable in a term is the **coefficient** of the variable or the coefficient of the term. The coefficients of the terms $4x^3$, $-x^2y^3$, and abc are 4, -1, and 1, respectively. The **degree** of a term in one variable is the power of the variable. So the degree of $4x^3$ is 3.

A **polynomial** is a single term or a finite sum of terms in which the powers of the variables are positive integers. If the coefficient of a term is negative we use subtraction, as in $x^4 - 6y^4$ rather than $x^4 + (-6y^4)$. So

$$4x^3 + 3x + 2, \quad a^2 + 2ab + b^2, \quad x^4 - 6y^4, \quad \text{and} \quad x$$

are polynomials. The **degree of a polynomial** in one variable is the highest degree of its terms. Consider the polynomial

$$4x^3 - 15x^2 + x - 2.$$

The degree of $4x^3$ is 3 and the degree of $-15x^2$ is 2. Since $x = x^1$, the degree of x is 1. Since $-2 = -2x^0$, the degree of -2 is 0. So the degree of the polynomial is 3. A single number is called a **constant** and so the zero-degree term is also called the **constant term.** The degree of a polynomial consisting of a single number is 0.

$$4x^3 - 15x^2 + x - 2$$

Third-degree term — Second-degree term — First-degree term — Zero-degree term

In $4x^3 - 15x^2 + x - 2$, the coefficient of x^3 (or the term $4x^3$) is 4. The coefficient of x^2 is -15 and the coefficient of x is 1.

EXAMPLE 1

Identifying coefficients

Determine the coefficients of x^3 and x^2 in each polynomial:

a) $x^3 + 5x^2 - 6$ **b)** $4x^6 - x^3 + x$

Solution

a) Write the polynomial as $1 \cdot x^3 + 5x^2 - 6$ to see that the coefficient of x^3 is 1 and the coefficient of x^2 is 5.

b) The x^2-term is missing in $4x^6 - x^3 + x$. Because $4x^6 - x^3 + x$ can be written as

$$4x^6 - 1 \cdot x^3 + 0 \cdot x^2 + x,$$

the coefficient of x^3 is -1 and the coefficient of x^2 is 0.

Now do Exercises 7–12

For simplicity we generally write polynomials in one variable with the exponents decreasing from left to right and the constant term last. So we write

$$x^3 - 4x^2 + 5x + 1 \qquad \text{rather than} \qquad -4x^2 + 1 + 5x + x^3.$$

When a polynomial is written with decreasing exponents, the coefficient of the first term is called the **leading coefficient.**

Certain polynomials are given special names. A **monomial** is a polynomial that has one term, a **binomial** is a polynomial that has two terms, and a **trinomial** is a polynomial that has three terms. For example, $3x^5$ is a monomial, $2x - 1$ is a binomial, and $4x^6 - 3x + 2$ is a trinomial.

EXAMPLE 2

Types of polynomials

Identify each polynomial as a monomial, binomial, or trinomial and state its degree.

a) $5x^2 - 7x^3 + 2$ **b)** $x^{43} - x^2$ **c)** $5x$ **d)** -12

Solution

a) The polynomial $5x^2 - 7x^3 + 2$ is a third-degree trinomial.

b) The polynomial $x^{43} - x^2$ is a binomial with degree 43.

c) Because $5x = 5x^1$, this polynomial is a monomial with degree 1.

d) The polynomial -12 is a monomial with degree 0.

Now do Exercises 13–24

⟨2⟩ Evaluating Polynomials

A polynomial with a variable in it has no value until the variable is replaced with a number. Example 3 shows how to evaluate a polynomial.

EXAMPLE 3

Evaluating polynomials

a) Find the value of $-3x^4 - x^3 + 20x + 3$ when $x = 1$.

b) Find the value of $-3x^4 - x^3 + 20x + 3$ when $x = -2$.

Solution

a) Replace x by 1 in the polynomial:

$$\begin{aligned} -3x^4 - x^3 + 20x + 3 &= -3(1)^4 - (1)^3 + 20(1) + 3 \\ &= -3 - 1 + 20 + 3 \\ &= 19 \end{aligned}$$

So the value of the polynomial is 19 when $x = 1$.

b) Replace x by -2 in the polynomial:

$$\begin{aligned} -3x^4 - x^3 + 20x + 3 &= -3(-2)^4 - (-2)^3 + 20(-2) + 3 \\ &= -3(16) - (-8) - 40 + 3 \\ &= -48 + 8 - 40 + 3 \\ &= -77 \end{aligned}$$

So the value of the polynomial is -77 when $x = -2$.

Now do Exercises 25–32

A common notation used for evaluating polynomials in mathematics, computer science, and on graphing calculators is **function notation.** In function notation, a polynomial is named with a letter. The variable used in the polynomial is written in parentheses following the letter. For example,

$$P(x) = x^2 - 1$$

is a polynomial expressed in function notation. [Read $P(x)$ as "P of x."] To evaluate this polynomial when $x = 3$, we replace x with 3 in $P(x) = x^2 - 1$:

$$P(3) = 3^2 - 1 = 8$$

So $P(3) = 8$. [Read "P of 3 is 8."] So $P(3) = 8$ is simply a short way of saying that the value of the polynomial $P(x)$ when $x = 3$ is 8. Function notation is very useful when evaluating a polynomial for several values of x. For example, if $P(x) = x^2 - 1$, then $P(0) = -1$, $P(1) = 0$, and $P(2) = 3$. Note that $P(x)$ does *not* mean P times x. (See Section 9.7 for more information on functions.)

‹ Teaching Tip ›

Using function notation for polynomials will get students familiar with the notation before they study functions in detail.

EXAMPLE 4

Evaluating polynomials using function notation

a) If $P(x) = -3x^4 - x^3 + 20x + 3$, find $P(1)$.

b) If $D(a) = a^3 - 5$, find $D(0)$, $D(1)$, and $D(2)$.

Solution

a) To find $P(1)$, replace x by 1 in the formula for $P(x)$:

$$P(x) = -3x^4 - x^3 + 20x + 3$$
$$P(1) = -3(1)^4 - (1)^3 + 20(1) + 3$$
$$= 19$$

So $P(1) = 19$. The value of the polynomial when $x = 1$ is 19.

b) To find $D(0)$, $D(1)$, and $D(2)$ replace a with 0, 1, and 2:

$$D(0) = 0^3 - 5 = -5, \quad D(1) = 1^3 - 5 = -4, \quad D(2) = 2^3 - 5 = 3$$

So $D(0) = -5$, $D(1) = -4$, and $D(2) = 3$.

Now do Exercises 33–38

Calculator Close-Up

To evaluate the polynomial in Example 4(a) with a calculator, first use Y = to define the polynomial.

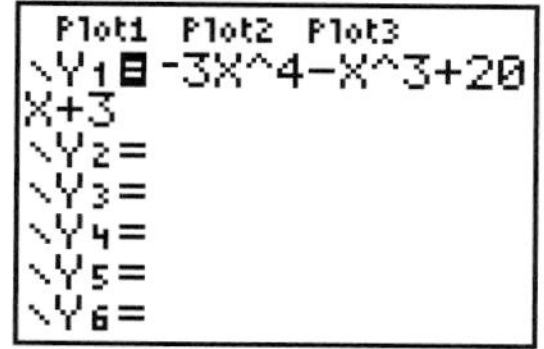

Then find $y_1(1)$.

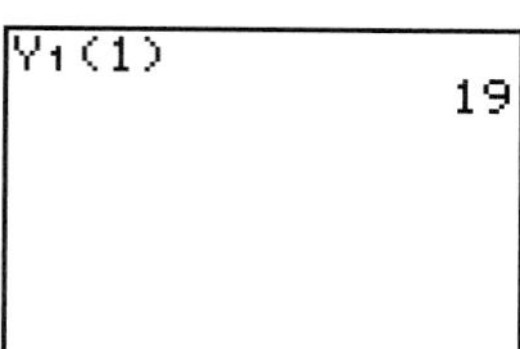

〈3〉 Addition of Polynomials

You learned how to combine like terms in Chapter 1. Also, you combined like terms when solving equations in Chapter 2. Addition of polynomials is done simply by adding the like terms.

Addition of Polynomials

To add two polynomials, add the like terms.

Polynomials can be added horizontally or vertically, as shown in Example 5.

EXAMPLE 5

Adding polynomials

Perform the indicated operation.

a) $(x^2 - 6x + 5) + (-3x^2 + 5x - 9)$

b) $(-5a^3 + 3a - 7) + (4a^2 - 3a + 7)$

Solution

a) The commutative and associative properties enable us to remove the parentheses and rearrange the terms with like terms next to each other:

$$(x^2 - 6x + 5) + (-3x^2 + 5x - 9) = x^2 - 3x^2 - 6x + 5x + 5 - 9$$
$$= -2x^2 - x - 4$$

Note that $x^2 - 3x^2 = (1 - 3)x^2 = -2x^2$ and $-6x + 5x = (-6 + 5)x = -x$ because of the distributive property. It is not necessary to write all of these details. You can simply pick out the like terms from each polynomial and combine them.

b) When adding vertically, we line up the like terms:

$$\begin{array}{rrrr} -5a^3 & & +\ 3a & -\ 7 \\ & 4a^2 & -\ 3a & +\ 7 \\ \hline -5a^3 & +\ 4a^2 & & \end{array} \quad \text{Add.}$$

Now do Exercises 39–52

Helpful Hint

When we perform operations with polynomials and write the results as equations, those equations are identities. For example,

$$(x + 1) + (3x + 5) = 4x + 6$$

is an identity. This equation is satisfied by every real number.

⟨4⟩ Subtraction of Polynomials

To add polynomials we add the like terms and to subtract polynomials we subtract the like terms. However, since $a - b = a + (-b)$, it is usually simplest to change the signs of all terms in the second polynomial and then add.

Subtraction of Polynomials

To subtract two polynomials subtract the like terms, or change the signs of all terms in the second polynomial and then add.

Polynomials can be subtracted horizontally or vertically, as shown in Example 6. Vertical subtraction is used in the long division algorithm in Section 5.7.

EXAMPLE 6

Subtracting polynomials

Perform the indicated operation.

a) $(x^2 - 5x - 3) - (4x^2 + 8x - 9)$ **b)** $(4y^3 - 3y + 2) - (5y^2 - 7y - 6)$

Solution

a)
$$(x^2 - 5x - 3) - (4x^2 + 8x - 9) = x^2 - 5x - 3 - 4x^2 - 8x + 9 \quad \text{Change signs.}$$
$$= x^2 - 4x^2 - 5x - 8x - 3 + 9 \quad \text{Rearrange.}$$
$$= -3x^2 - 13x + 6 \quad \text{Add.}$$

b) To subtract $5y^2 - 7y - 6$ from $4y^3 - 3y + 2$ vertically, we line up the like terms as we do for addition:

$$\begin{array}{r} 4y^3 \qquad\quad - 3y + 2 \\ - \quad (5y^2 - 7y - 6) \\ \hline \end{array}$$

Now change the signs of $5y^2 - 7y - 6$ and add the like terms:

$$\begin{array}{r} 4y^3 \qquad\quad - 3y + 2 \\ -5y^2 + 7y + 6 \\ \hline 4y^3 - 5y^2 + 4y + 8 \end{array}$$

Now do Exercises 53–66

‹ Helpful Hint ›

For subtraction, write the original problem and then rewrite it as addition with the signs changed. Many students have trouble when they write the original problem and then overwrite the signs. Vertical subtraction is essential for performing long division of polynomials in Section 5.7.

CAUTION When adding or subtracting polynomials vertically, be sure to line up the like terms.

In Example 7 we combine addition and subtraction of polynomials.

EXAMPLE 7

Adding and subtracting

Perform the indicated operations:

$$(2x^2 - 3x) + (x^3 + 6) - (x^4 - 6x^2 - 9)$$

Solution

Remove the parentheses and combine the like terms:

$$(2x^2 - 3x) + (x^3 + 6) - (x^4 - 6x^2 - 9) = 2x^2 - 3x + x^3 + 6 - x^4 + 6x^2 + 9$$
$$= -x^4 + x^3 + 8x^2 - 3x + 15$$

Now do Exercises 83–90

‹ Teaching Tip ›

Ask students to identify the values of x for which the equation is true. What is the equation called?

‹5› Applications

Polynomials are often used to represent unknown quantities. In certain situations it is necessary to add or subtract such polynomials.

EXAMPLE 8

Profit from prints

Trey pays \$60 per day for a permit to sell famous art prints in the Student Union Mall. Each print costs him \$4, so the polynomial $C(x) = 4x + 60$ represents his daily cost in dollars for x prints sold. He sells the prints for \$10 each. So the polynomial $R(x) = 10x$ represents his daily revenue for x prints sold. Find a polynomial $P(x)$ that represents his daily profit from selling x prints. Evaluate the profit polynomial for $x = 30$.

‹ Teaching Tip ›

Point out how function notation makes it easy to indicate in symbols that the profit for 30 prints is \$120: $P(30) = 120$.

Solution

Because profit is revenue minus cost, we can subtract the corresponding polynomials to get a polynomial that represents the daily profit:

$$\begin{aligned} P(x) &= R(x) - C(x) \\ &= 10x - (4x + 60) \\ &= 10x - 4x - 60 \\ &= 6x - 60 \end{aligned}$$

So the daily profit polynomial is $P(x) = 6x - 60$. Now evaluate this profit polynomial for $x = 30$:

$$\begin{aligned} P(30) &= 6(30) - 60 \\ &= 120 \end{aligned}$$

So if Trey sells 30 prints, his profit is \$120.

Now do Exercises 91–100

Warm-Ups ▼

True or false? Explain your answer.

1. In the polynomial $2x^2 - 4x + 7$ the coefficient of x is 4. False
2. The degree of the polynomial $x^2 + 5x - 9x^3 + 6$ is 2. False
3. In the polynomial $x^2 - x$ the coefficient of x is -1. True
4. The degree of the polynomial $x^2 - x$ is 2. True
5. A binomial always has a degree of 2. False
6. If $P(x) = 3x - 1$, then $P(5) = 14$. True
7. Every trinomial has degree 2. False
8. $x^2 - 7x^2 = -6x^2$ for any value of x. True
9. $(3x^2 - 8x + 6) + (x^2 + 4x - 9) = 4x^2 - 4x - 3$ for any value of x. True
10. $(x^2 - 4x) - (x^2 - 3x) = -7x$ for any value of x. False

5.3 Exercises

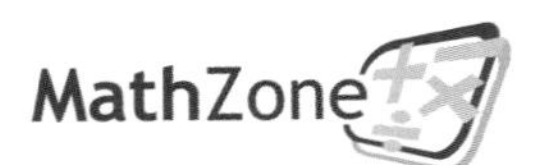

Boost your grade at mathzone.com!
- Practice Problems
- NetTutor
- Self-Tests
- e-Professors
- Videos

‹ Study Tips ›

- Everything we do in solving problems is based on definitions, rules, and theorems. If you just memorize procedures without understanding the principles, you will soon forget the procedures.
- The keys to college success are motivation and time management. Students who tell you that they are making great grades without studying are probably not telling the truth. Success takes lots of effort.

Reading and Writing *After reading this section, write out the answers to these questions. Use complete sentences.*

1. What is a term?
   A term is a single number or the product of a number and one or more variables raised to powers.
2. What is a polynomial?
   A polynomial is a single term or a finite sum of terms.
3. What is the degree of a polynomial?
   The degree of a polynomial in one variable is the highest power of the variable in the polynomial.
4. What is the value of a polynomial?
   The value of a polynomial is the number obtained when the variable is replaced by a number.
5. How do we add polynomials?
   Polynomials are added by adding the like terms.
6. How do we subtract polynomials?
   Polynomials are subtracted by subtracting like terms.

‹1› Polynomials

Determine the coefficients of x^3 and x^2 in each polynomial. See Example 1.

7. $-3x^3 + 7x^2$ $\quad -3, 7$
8. $10x^3 - x^2$ $\quad 10, -1$
9. $x^4 + 6x^2 - 9$ $\quad 0, 6$
10. $x^5 - x^3 + 3$ $\quad -1, 0$
11. $\frac{x^3}{3} + \frac{7x^2}{2} - 4$ $\quad \frac{1}{3}, \frac{7}{2}$
12. $\frac{x^3}{2} - \frac{x^2}{4} + 2x + 1$ $\quad \frac{1}{2}, -\frac{1}{4}$

Identify each polynomial as a monomial, binomial, or trinomial and state its degree. See Example 2.

13. -1 Monomial, 0
14. 5 Monomial, 0
15. m^3 Monomial, 3
16. $3a^8$ Monomial, 8
17. $4x + 7$ Binomial, 1
18. $a + 6$ Binomial, 1
19. $x^{10} - 3x^2 + 2$ Trinomial, 10
20. $y^6 - 6y^3 + 9$ Trinomial, 6
21. $x^6 + 1$ Binomial, 6
22. $b^2 - 4$ Binomial, 2
23. $a^3 - a^2 + 5$ Trinomial, 3
24. $-x^2 + 4x - 9$ Trinomial, 2

‹2› Evaluating Polynomials

Evaluate each polynomial as indicated. See Examples 3 and 4.

25. Evaluate $x^2 + 1$ for $x = 3$. $\quad 10$
26. Evaluate $x^2 - 1$ for $x = -3$. $\quad 8$
27. Evaluate $2x^2 - 3x + 1$ for $x = -1$. $\quad 6$
28. VIDEO Evaluate $3x^2 - x + 2$ for $x = -2$. $\quad 16$
29. Evaluate $\frac{1}{2}x^2 - x + 1$ for $x = \frac{1}{2}$. $\quad \frac{5}{8}$
30. Evaluate $3x^2 + \frac{1}{2}x - 1$ for $x = \frac{1}{3}$. $\quad -\frac{1}{2}$
31. Evaluate $-3x^3 - x^2 + 3x - 4$ for $x = 3$. $\quad -85$
32. Evaluate $-2x^4 - 3x^2 + 5x - 9$ for $x = 2$. $\quad -43$
33. If $P(x) = x^2 - 4$, find $P(3)$. $\quad 5$
34. If $P(x) = x^3 + 1$, find $P(2)$. $\quad 9$
35. If $P(x) = 3x^4 - 2x^3 + 7$, find $P(-2)$. $\quad 71$
36. If $P(x) = -2x^3 + 5x^2 - 12$, find $P(5)$. $\quad -137$
37. If $P(x) = 1.2x^3 - 4.3x - 2.4$, find $P(1.45)$. $\quad -4.97665$
38. If $P(x) = -3.5x^4 - 4.6x^3 + 5.5$, find $P(-2.36)$. $\quad -42.608$

‹3› Addition of Polynomials

Perform the indicated operation. See Example 5.

39. $(x - 3) + (3x - 5)$ $\quad 4x - 8$
40. $(x - 2) + (x + 3)$ $\quad 2x + 1$
41. $(q - 3) + (q + 3)$ $\quad 2q$
42. $(q + 4) + (q + 6)$ $\quad 2q + 10$
43. $(3x + 2) + (x^2 - 4)$ $\quad x^2 + 3x - 2$
44. $(5x^2 - 2) + (-3x^2 - 1)$ $\quad 2x^2 - 3$
45. VIDEO $(4x - 1) + (x^3 + 5x - 6)$ $\quad x^3 + 9x - 7$
46. $(3x - 7) + (x^2 - 4x + 6)$ $\quad x^2 - x - 1$
47. $(a^2 - 3a + 1) + (2a^2 - 4a - 5)$ $\quad 3a^2 - 7a - 4$
48. $(w^2 - 2w + 1) + (2w - 5 + w^2)$ $\quad 2w^2 - 4$
49. $(w^2 - 9w - 3) + (w - 4w^2 + 8)$ $\quad -3w^2 - 8w + 5$
50. $(a^3 - a^2 - 5a) + (6 - a - 3a^2)$ $\quad a^3 - 4a^2 - 6a + 6$
51. $(5.76x^2 - 3.14x - 7.09) + (3.9x^2 + 1.21x + 5.6)$ $\quad 9.66x^2 - 1.93x - 1.49$
52. $(8.5x^2 + 3.27x - 9.33) + (x^2 - 4.39x - 2.32)$ $\quad 9.5x^2 - 1.12x - 11.65$

‹4› Subtraction of Polynomials

Perform the indicated operation. See Example 6.

53. $(x - 2) - (5x - 8)$ $\quad -4x + 6$
54. $(x - 7) - (3x - 1)$ $\quad -2x - 6$
55. $(m - 2) - (m + 3)$ $\quad -5$
56. $(m + 5) - (m + 9)$ $\quad -4$

57. $(2z^2 - 3z) - (3z^2 - 5z)$ $-z^2 + 2z$

58. $(z^2 - 4z) - (5z^2 - 3z)$ $-4z^2 - z$

59. $(w^5 - w^3) - (-w^4 + w^2)$ $w^5 + w^4 - w^3 - w^2$

60. $(w^6 - w^3) - (-w^2 + w)$ $w^6 - w^3 + w^2 - w$

61. $(t^2 - 3t + 4) - (t^2 - 5t - 9)$ $2t + 13$

62. $(t^2 - 6t + 7) - (5t^2 - 3t - 2)$ $-4t^2 - 3t + 9$

63. $(9 - 3y - y^2) - (2 + 5y - y^2)$ $-8y + 7$

VIDEO **64.** $(4 - 5y + y^3) - (2 - 3y + y^2)$ $y^3 - y^2 - 2y + 2$

65. $(3.55x - 879) - (26.4x - 455.8)$ $-22.85x - 423.2$

66. $(345.56x - 347.4) - (56.6x + 433)$ $288.96x - 780.4$

Add or subtract the polynomials as indicated. See Examples 5 and 6.

67. Add:
$$\begin{array}{r} 3a - 4 \\ \underline{a + 6} \\ 4a + 2 \end{array}$$

68. Add:
$$\begin{array}{r} 2w - 8 \\ \underline{w + 3} \\ 3w - 5 \end{array}$$

69. Subtract:
$$\begin{array}{r} 3x + 11 \\ \underline{-(5x + 7)} \\ -2x + 4 \end{array}$$

70. Subtract:
$$\begin{array}{r} 4x + 3 \\ \underline{-(2x + 9)} \\ 2x - 6 \end{array}$$

71. Add:
$$\begin{array}{r} a - b \\ \underline{a + b} \\ 2a \end{array}$$

72. Add:
$$\begin{array}{r} s - 6 \\ \underline{s - 1} \\ 2s - 7 \end{array}$$

73. Subtract:
$$\begin{array}{r} -3m + 1 \\ \underline{-(2m - 6)} \\ -5m + 7 \end{array}$$

74. Subtract:
$$\begin{array}{r} -5n + 2 \\ \underline{-(3n - 4)} \\ -8n + 6 \end{array}$$

Add or subtract as indicated. Arrange the polynomials vertically as in Exercises 67–74. See Examples 5 and 6.

75. Add $2x^2 - x - 3$ and $2x^2 + x + 4$. $4x^2 + 1$

76. Add $-x^2 + 4x - 6$ and $3x^2 - x - 5$. $2x^2 + 3x - 11$

77. Subtract $2a^3 + 4a^2 - 2a$ from $3a^3 - 5a^2 + 7$.
$a^3 - 9a^2 + 2a + 7$

78. Subtract $b^3 - 4b - 2$ from $-2b^3 + 7b^2 - 9$.
$-3b^3 + 7b^2 + 4b - 7$

79. $(x^2 - 3x + 6) - (x^2 - 3)$ $-3x + 9$

80. $(x^4 - 3x^2 + 2) - (3x^4 - 2x)$ $-2x^4 - 3x^2 + 2x + 2$

81. $(y^3 + 4y^2 - 6y - 5) + (y^3 + 3y - 9)$
$2y^3 + 4y^2 - 3y - 14$

82. $(q^2 - 4q + 9) + (-3q^3 - 7q + 5)$
$-3q^3 + q^2 - 11q + 14$

Perform the indicated operations. See Example 7.

83. $(4m - 2) + (2m + 4) - (9m - 1)$ $-3m + 3$

84. $(-5m - 6) + (8m - 3) - (-5m + 3)$ $8m - 12$

85. $(6y - 2) - (8y + 3) - (9y - 2)$ $-11y - 3$

VIDEO **86.** $(-5y - 1) - (8y - 4) - (y + 3)$ $-14y$

87. $(-x^2 - 5x + 4) + (6x^2 - 8x + 9) - (3x^2 - 7x + 1)$
$2x^2 - 6x + 12$

88. $(-8x^2 + 5x - 12) + (-3x^2 - 9x + 18)$
$- (-3x^2 + 9x - 4)$ $-8x^2 - 13x + 10$

89. $(-6z^4 - 3z^3 + 7z^2) - (5z^3 + 3z^2 - 2) + (z^4 - z^2 + 5)$
$-5z^4 - 8z^3 + 3z^2 + 7$

90. $(-v^3 - v^2 - 1) - (v^4 - v^2 - v - 1) + (v^3 - 3v^2 + 6)$
$-v^4 - 3v^2 + v + 6$

⟨5⟩ Applications

Solve each problem. See Example 8.

91. ***Water pumps.*** Walter uses the polynomials $R(x) = 400x$ and $C(x) = 120x + 800$ to estimate his monthly revenue and cost in dollars for producing x water pumps per month.

a) Write a polynomial $P(x)$ for his monthly profit.
$P(x) = 280x - 800$

b) Find the monthly profit for $x = 50$. $13,200

92. ***Manufacturing costs.*** Ace manufacturing has determined that the cost of labor for producing x transmissions is $L(x) = 0.3x^2 + 400x + 550$ dollars, while the cost of materials is $M(x) = 0.1x^2 + 50x + 800$ dollars.

a) Write a polynomial $T(x)$ that represents the total cost of materials and labor for producing x transmissions.

b) Evaluate the total cost polynomial for $x = 500$.

c) Find the cost of labor for 500 transmissions and the cost of materials for 500 transmissions.

a) $T(x) = 0.4x^2 + 450x + 1350$ **b)** $326,350
c) $275,550, $50,800

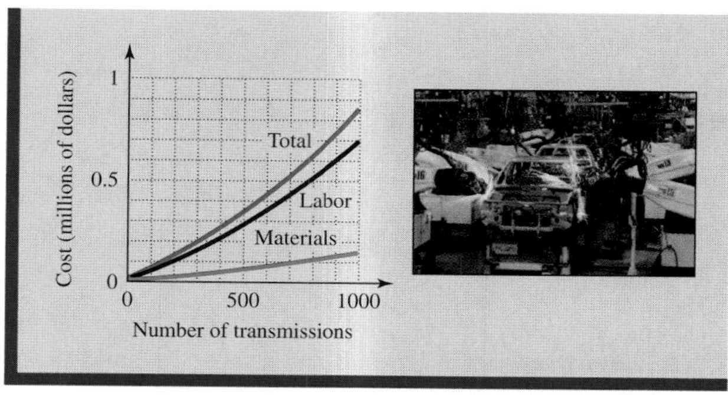

Figure for Exercise 92

93. ***Perimeter of a triangle.*** The shortest side of a triangle is x meters, and the other two sides are $3x - 1$ and $2x + 4$ meters. Write a polynomial $P(x)$ that represents the perimeter and then evaluate the perimeter polynomial if x is 4 meters. $P(x) = 6x + 3$, $P(4) = 27$ meters

94. ***Perimeter of a rectangle.*** The width of a rectangular playground is $2x - 5$ feet, and the length is $3x + 9$ feet. Write a polynomial $P(x)$ that represents the perimeter and then evaluate this perimeter polynomial if x is 4 feet. See the figure on the next page. $P(x) = 10x + 8$, $P(4) = 48$ feet

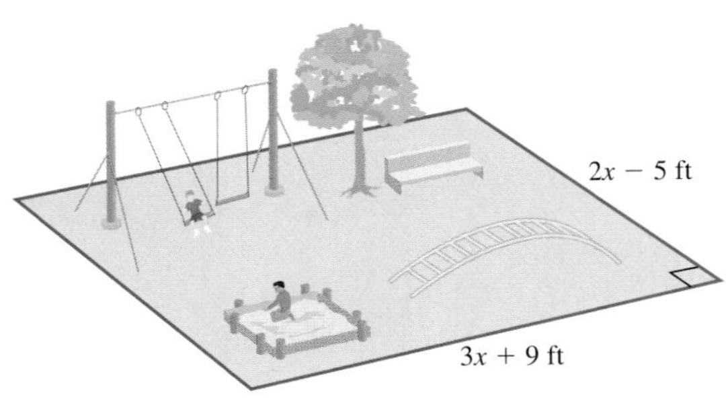

Figure for Exercise 94

95. ***Total distance.*** Hanson drove his rig at x mph for 3 hours, then increased his speed to $x + 15$ mph and drove 2 more hours. Write a polynomial $D(x)$ that represents the total distance that he traveled. Find $D(45)$.
$D(x) = 5x + 30$, 255 miles

96. ***Before and after.*** Jessica traveled $2x + 50$ miles in the morning and $3x - 10$ miles in the afternoon. Write a polynomial $T(x)$ that represents the total distance that she traveled. Find the $T(20)$. $T(x) = 5x + 40$, 140 miles

97. ***Sky divers.*** Bob and Betty simultaneously jump from two airplanes at different altitudes. Bob's altitude t seconds after leaving his plane is $-16t^2 + 6600$ feet. Betty's altitude t seconds after leaving her plane is $-16t^2 + 7400$ feet. Write a polynomial that represents the difference between their altitudes t seconds after leaving the planes. What is the difference between their altitudes 3 seconds after leaving the planes? 800 feet, 800 feet

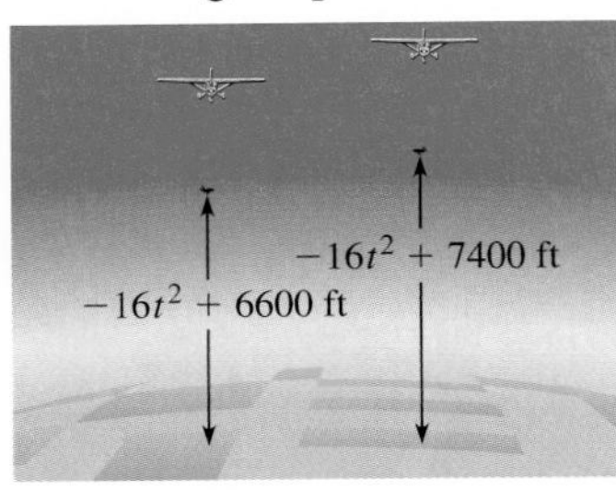

Figure for Exercise 97

98. ***Height difference.*** A red ball and a green ball are simultaneously tossed into the air. The red ball is given an initial velocity of 96 feet per second, and its height t seconds after it is tossed is $-16t^2 + 96t$ feet. The green ball is given an initial velocity of 80 feet per second, and its height t seconds after it is tossed is $-16t^2 + 80t$ feet.

a) Find a polynomial $D(t)$ that represents the difference in the heights of the two balls. $D(t) = 16t$ feet

b) How much higher is the red ball 2 seconds after the balls are tossed? 32 feet

c) In reality, when does the difference in the heights stop increasing? when green ball hits ground

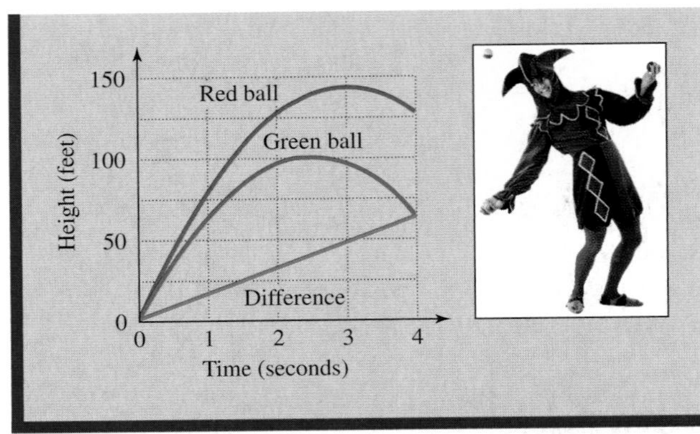

Figure for Exercise 98

99. ***Total interest.*** Donald received $0.08(x + 554)$ dollars interest on one investment and $0.09(x + 335)$ interest on another investment. Write a polynomial $T(x)$ that represents the total interest he received. What is the total interest if $x = 1000$? $T(x) = 0.17x + 74.47$ dollars, \$244.47

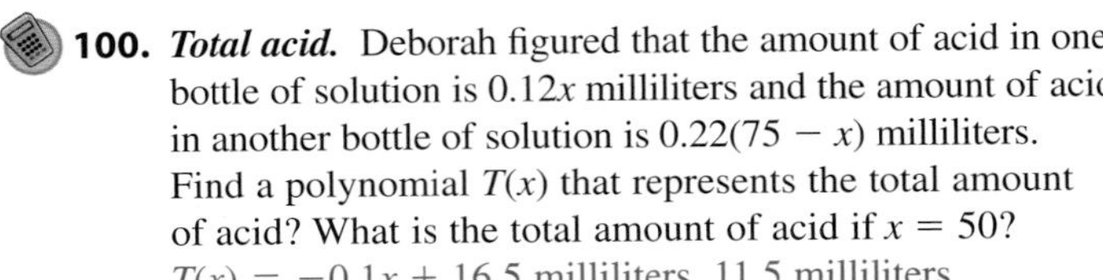

100. ***Total acid.*** Deborah figured that the amount of acid in one bottle of solution is $0.12x$ milliliters and the amount of acid in another bottle of solution is $0.22(75 - x)$ milliliters. Find a polynomial $T(x)$ that represents the total amount of acid? What is the total amount of acid if $x = 50$?
$T(x) = -0.1x + 16.5$ milliliters, 11.5 milliliters

Getting More Involved

101. ***Discussion***

Is the sum of two natural numbers always a natural number? Is the sum of two integers always an integer? Is the sum of two polynomials always a polynomial? Explain. Yes, yes, yes

102. ***Discussion***

Is the difference of two natural numbers always a natural number? Is the difference of two rational numbers always a rational number? Is the difference of two polynomials always a polynomial? Explain. No, yes, yes

103. ***Writing***

Explain why the polynomial $2^4 - 7x^3 + 5x^2 - x$ has degree 3 and not degree 4.
The highest power of x is 3.

104. ***Discussion***

Which of the following polynomials does not have degree 2? Explain.

a) πr^2 b) $\pi^2 - 4$ c) $y^2 - 4$
d) $x^2 - x^4$ e) $a^2 - 3a + 9$ b and d

5.4 Multiplication of Polynomials

In This Section

You learned to multiply some polynomials in Chapter 1. In this section, you will learn how to multiply any two polynomials.

⟨1⟩ Multiplying Monomials

Monomials are the simplest polynomials. We learned to multiply monomials in Section 5.1 using the product rule for exponents.

EXAMPLE 1

Multiplying monomials

Find the indicated products.

a) $2x^3 \cdot 3x^4$ **b)** $(-2ab^2)(-3ab^4)$ **c)** $(3a^2)^3$

Solution

a) $2x^3 \cdot 3x^4 = 6x^7$ Product rule for exponents

b) $(-2ab^2)(-3ab^4) = 6a^2b^6$ Product rule for exponents

c) $(3a^2)^3 = 3^3(a^2)^3$ Power of a product rule

$= 27a^6$ Power of a power rule

Now do Exercises 7–22

CAUTION Be sure to distinguish between adding and multiplying monomials. You can add like terms to get $3x^4 + 2x^4 = 5x^4$, but you cannot combine the terms in $3w^5 + 6w^2$. However, you can multiply any two monomials: $3x^4 \cdot 2x^4 = 6x^8$ and $3w^5 \cdot 6w^2 = 18w^7$. Note that the exponents are added, not multiplied.

⟨2⟩ Multiplying Polynomials

To multiply a monomial and a polynomial, we use the distributive property.

EXAMPLE 2

Multiplying monomials and polynomials

Find each product.

a) $3x^2(x^3 - 4x)$ **b)** $(y^2 - 3y + 4)(-2y)$ **c)** $-a(b - c)$

Solution

a) $3x^2(x^3 - 4x) = 3x^2 \cdot x^3 - 3x^2 \cdot 4x$ Distributive property

$= 3x^5 - 12x^3$

b) $(y^2 - 3y + 4)(-2y) = y^2(-2y) - 3y(-2y) + 4(-2y)$ Distributive property

$= -2y^3 - (-6y^2) + (-8y)$

$= -2y^3 + 6y^2 - 8y$

c) $-a(b - c) = (-a)b - (-a)c$ Distributive property

$= -ab + ac$

$= ac - ab$

Note in part (c) that either of the last two binomials is the correct answer. The last one is just a little simpler to read.

Now do Exercises 23–36

Just as we use the distributive property to find the product of a monomial and a polynomial, we can use it to find the product of any two polynomials.

EXAMPLE 3

Multiplying polynomials

Use the distributive property to find each product.

a) $(x + 2)(x + 5)$ **b)** $(x + 3)(x^2 + 2x - 7)$

Solution

a) First multiply each term of $x + 5$ by $x + 2$:

$(x + 2)(x + 5) = (x + 2)x + (x + 2)5$ Distributive property

$= x^2 + 2x + 5x + 10$ Distributive property

$= x^2 + 7x + 10$ Combine like terms

b) First multiply each term of the trinomial by $x + 3$:

$(x + 3)(x^2 + 2x - 7) = (x + 3)x^2 + (x + 3)2x + (x + 3)(-7)$ Distributive property

$= x^3 + 3x^2 + 2x^2 + 6x - 7x - 21$ Distributive property

$= x^3 + 5x^2 - x - 21$ Combine like terms

Now do Exercises 37–48

Examples 2 and 3 illustrate the following rule.

Multiplication of Polynomials

To multiply polynomials, multiply each term of one polynomial by every term of the other polynomial, then combine like terms.

⟨3⟩ The Additive Inverse of a Polynomial

The additive inverse of a is $-a$, because $a + (-a) = 0$. Since $-1 \cdot a = -a$, multiplying an expression by -1 produces that additive inverse of the expression. To find the additive inverse of $a - b$ multiply by -1:

$$-1(a - b) = -1 \cdot a - (-1)b = -a + b = b - a$$

By the distributive property, every term is multiplied by -1, causing every term to change sign. So the additive inverse (or opposite) of $a - b$ is $-a + b$ or $b - a$. In symbols,

$$-(a - b) = b - a$$

⟨ Teaching Tip ⟩

Knowing that $b - a = -1(a - b)$ will help with rational expressions in Chapter 7.

CAUTION The additive inverse of $a + b$ is $-a - b$ *not* $a - b$.

The additive inverse of any polynomial can be found by multiplying each term by -1 or simply changing the sign of each term, as shown in Example 4.

EXAMPLE 4

Additive inverse of a polynomial

Simplify each expression.

a) $-(x - 2)$
b) $-(9 - y^2)$
c) $-(a + 4)$
d) $-(-x^2 + 6x - 3)$

Solution

a) $-(x - 2) = 2 - x$
b) $-(9 - y^2) = y^2 - 9$
c) $-(a + 4) = -a - 4$
d) $-(-x^2 + 6x - 3) = x^2 - 6x + 3$

Now do Exercises 49–56

⟨4⟩ Applications

EXAMPLE 5

Multiplying polynomials

A parking lot is 20 yards wide and 30 yards long. If the college increases the length and width by the same amount to handle an increasing number of cars, then what polynomial represents the area of the new lot? What is the new area if the increase is 15 yards?

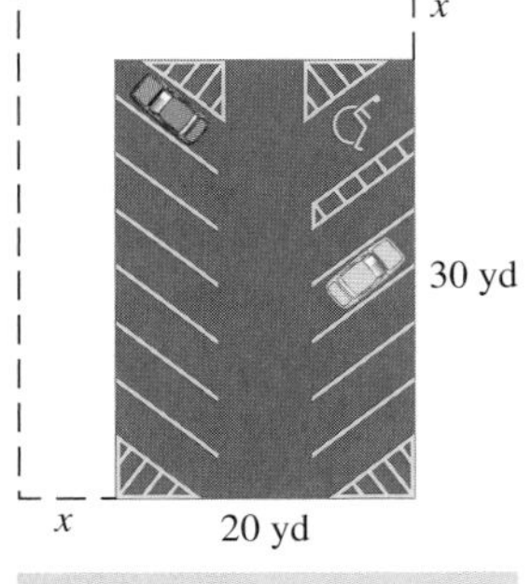

Figure 5.1

Solution

If x is the amount of increase in yards, then the new lot will be $x + 20$ yards wide and $x + 30$ yards long as shown in Fig. 5.1. Multiply the length and width to get the area:

$$\begin{aligned}(x + 20)(x + 30) &= (x + 20)x + (x + 20)30 \\ &= x^2 + 20x + 30x + 600 \\ &= x^2 + 50x + 600\end{aligned}$$

The polynomial $x^2 + 50x + 600$ represents the area of the new lot. If $x = 15$, then

$$x^2 + 50x + 600 = (15)^2 + 50(15) + 600 = 1575.$$

If the increase is 15 yards, then the area of the lot will be 1575 square yards.

Now do Exercises 77–86

Warm-Ups ▼

True or false? Explain your answer.

1. $3x^3 \cdot 5x^4 = 15x^{12}$ for any value of x. False
2. $3x^2 \cdot 2x^7 = 5x^9$ for any value of x. False
3. $(3y^3)^2 = 9y^6$ for any value of y. True
4. $-3x(5x - 7x^2) = -15x^3 + 21x^2$ for any value of x. False
5. $2x(x^2 - 3x + 4) = 2x^3 - 6x^2 + 8x$ for any number x. True
6. $-2(3 - x) = 2x - 6$ for any number x. True

7. $(a + b)(c + d) = ac + ad + bc + bd$ for any values of a, b, c, and d. True
8. $-(x - 7) = 7 - x$ for any value of x. True
9. $83 - 37 = -(37 - 83)$ True
10. The opposite of $x + 3$ is $x - 3$ for any number x. False

5.4 Exercises

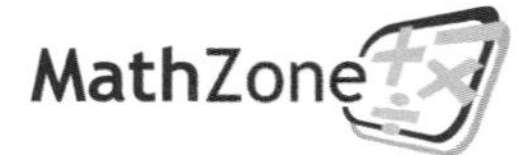

Boost your grade at mathzone.com!
> Practice Problems
> NetTutor
> Self-Tests
> e-Professors
> Videos

‹ Study Tips ›

- Effective time management will allow adequate time for school, work, social life, and free time. However at times you will have to sacrifice to do well.
- Everyone has different attention spans. Start by studying 10 to 15 minutes at a time and then build up to longer periods. Be realistic. When you can no longer concentrate take a break.

Reading and Writing *After reading this section, write out the answers to these questions. Use complete sentences.*

1. What is the product rule for exponents?
   The product rule for exponents says that $a^m \cdot a^n = a^{m+n}$.
2. Why is the sum of two monomials not necessarily a monomial?
   The sum of two monomials can be a binomial if the terms are not like terms.
3. What property of the real numbers is used when multiplying a monomial and a polynomial?
   To multiply a monomial and a polynomial we use the distributive property.
4. What property of the real numbers is used when multiplying two binomials?
   To multiply two binomials we use the distributive property twice.
5. How do we multiply any two polynomials?
   To multiply any two polynomials we multiply each term of the first polynomial by every term of the second polynomial.
6. How do we find the opposite of a polynomial?
   To find the opposite of a polynomial, change the sign of each term in the polynomial.

‹1› Multiplying Monomials

Find each product. See Example 1.

7. $3x^2 \cdot 9x^3$ $27x^5$
8. $5x^7 \cdot 3x^5$ $15x^{12}$
9. (VIDEO) $2a^3 \cdot 7a^8$ $14a^{11}$
10. $3y^{12} \cdot 5y^{15}$ $15y^{27}$
11. $-6x^2 \cdot 5x^2$ $-30x^4$
12. $-2x^2 \cdot 8x^5$ $-16x^7$
13. $(-9x^{10})(-3x^7)$ $27x^{17}$
14. $(-2x^2)(-8x^9)$ $16x^{11}$
15. $-6st \cdot 9st$ $-54s^2t^2$
16. $-12sq \cdot 3s$ $-36qs^2$
17. $3wt \cdot 8w^7t^6$ $24t^7w^8$
18. $h^8k^3 \cdot 5h$ $5h^9k^3$
19. $(5y)^2$ $25y^2$
20. $(6x)^2$ $36x^2$
21. $(2x^3)^2$ $4x^6$
22. $(3y^5)^2$ $9y^{10}$

‹2› Multiplying Polynomials

Find each product. See Example 2.

23. $x(x + y^2)$ $x^2 + xy^2$
24. $x^2(x - y)$ $x^3 - x^2y$
25. $4y^2(y^5 - 2y)$ $4y^7 - 8y^3$
26. (VIDEO) $6t^3(t^5 + 3t^2)$ $6t^8 + 18t^5$
27. $-3y(6y - 4)$ $-18y^2 + 12y$
28. $-9y(y^2 - 1)$ $-9y^3 + 9y$
29. $(y^2 - 5y + 6)(-3y)$ $-3y^3 + 15y^2 - 18y$
30. $(x^3 - 5x^2 - 1)7x^2$ $7x^5 - 35x^4 - 7x^2$
31. $-x(y^2 - x^2)$ $-xy^2 + x^3$
32. $-ab(a^2 - b^2)$ $ab^3 - a^3b$
33. $(3ab^3 - a^2b^2 - 2a^3b)5a^3$ $15a^4b^3 - 5a^5b^2 - 10a^6b$
34. $(3c^2d - d^3 + 1)8cd^2$ $24c^3d^3 - 8cd^5 + 8cd^2$

35. $-\frac{1}{2}t^2v(4t^3v^2 - 6tv - 4v)$ $-2t^5v^3 + 3t^3v^2 + 2t^2v^2$

36. $-\frac{1}{3}m^2n^3(-6mn^2 + 3mn - 12)$ $2m^3n^5 - m^3n^4 + 4m^2n^3$

Use the distributive property to find each product. See Example 3.

37. $(x + 1)(x + 2)$
$x^2 + 3x + 2$

38. $(x + 6)(x + 3)$
$x^2 + 9x + 18$

39. $(x - 3)(x + 5)$
$x^2 + 2x - 15$

40. $(y - 2)(y + 4)$
$y^2 + 2y - 8$

41. $(t - 4)(t - 9)$
$t^2 - 13t + 36$

VIDEO **42.** $(w - 3)(w - 5)$
$w^2 - 8w + 15$

43. $(x + 1)(x^2 + 2x + 2)$
$x^3 + 3x^2 + 4x + 2$

44. $(x - 1)(x^2 + x + 1)$
$x^3 - 1$

45. $(3y + 2)(2y^2 - y + 3)$
$6y^3 + y^2 + 7y + 6$

46. $(4y + 3)(y^2 + 3y + 1)$
$4y^3 + 15y^2 + 13y + 3$

47. $(y^2z - 2y^4)(y^2z + 3z^2 - y^4)$
$2y^8 - 3y^6z - 5y^4z^2 + 3y^2z^3$

48. $(m^3 - 4mn^2)(6m^4n^2 - 3m^6 + m^2n^4)$
$-3m^9 + 18m^7n^2 - 23m^5n^4 - 4m^3n^6$

‹3› The Additive Inverse of a Polynomial

Simplify each expression. See Example 4.

49. $-(3t - u)$ $u - 3t$

50. $-(-4 - u)$ $4 + u$

51. $-(3x + y)$ $-3x - y$

52. $-(x - 5b)$ $5b - x$

53. $-(-3a^2 - a + 6)$ $3a^2 + a - 6$

54. $-(5b^2 - b - 7)$ $-5b^2 + b + 7$

55. $-(3w^2 + w - 6)$ $-3w^2 - w + 6$

56. $-(-4t^2 + t - 6)$ $4t^2 - t + 6$

Miscellaneous

Perform the indicated operation.

57. $-3x(2x - 9)$
$-6x^2 + 27x$

58. $-1(2 - 3x)$
$3x - 2$

59. $2 - 3x(2x - 9)$
$-6x^2 + 27x + 2$

60. $6 - 3(4x - 8)$
$-12x + 30$

61. $(2 - 3x) + (2x - 9)$
$-x - 7$

62. $(2 - 3x) - (2x - 9)$
$-5x + 11$

63. $(6x^6)^2$ $36x^{12}$

VIDEO **64.** $(-3a^3b)^2$ $9a^6b^2$

65. $3ab^3(-2a^2b^7)$
$-6a^3b^{10}$

66. $-4xst \cdot 8xs$
$-32s^2tx^2$

67. $(5x + 6)(5x + 6)$
$25x^2 + 60x + 36$

68. $(5x - 6)(5x - 6)$
$25x^2 - 60x + 36$

69. $(5x - 6)(5x + 6)$
$25x^2 - 36$

70. $(2x - 9)(2x + 9)$
$4x^2 - 81$

71. $2x^2(3x^5 - 4x^2)$
$6x^7 - 8x^4$

72. $4a^3(3ab^3 - 2ab^3)$
$4a^4b^3$

73. $(m - 1)(m^2 + m + 1)$
$m^3 - 1$

74. $(a + b)(a^2 - ab + b^2)$
$a^3 + b^3$

75. $(3x - 2)(x^2 - x - 9)$ $3x^3 - 5x^2 - 25x + 18$

76. $(5 - 6y)(3y^2 - y - 7)$ $-18y^3 + 21y^2 + 37y - 35$

‹4› Applications

Solve each problem. See Example 5.

77. ***Office space.*** The length of a professor's office is x feet and the width is $x + 4$ feet. Write a polynomial $A(x)$ that represents the area of the office. Find $A(10)$.
$A(x) = x^2 + 4x$, 140 square feet

78. ***Swimming space.*** The length of a rectangular swimming pool is $2x - 1$ meters, and the width is $x + 2$ meters. Write a polynomial $A(x)$ that represents the area. Find $A(5)$.
$A(x) = 2x^2 + 3x - 2$, 63 square meters

79. ***Area.*** A roof truss is in the shape of a triangle with height of x feet and a base of $2x + 1$ feet. Write a polynomial $A(x)$ that represents the area of the triangle. Find $A(5)$. See the accompanying figure.

$A(x) = x^2 + \frac{1}{2}x$, $A(5) = 27.5$ square feet

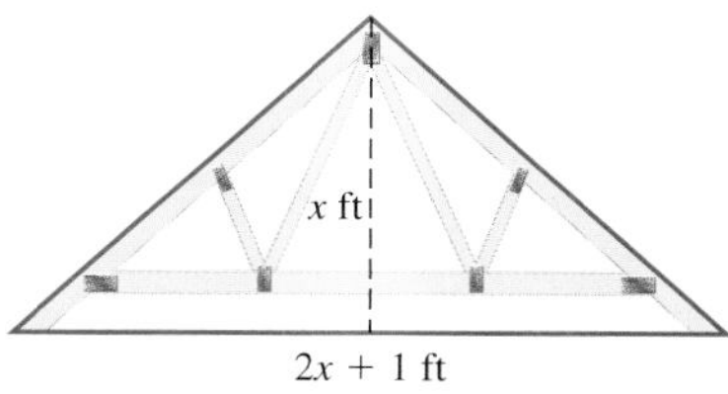

Figure for Exercise 79

80. ***Volume.*** The length, width, and height of a box are x, $2x$, and $3x - 5$ inches, respectively. Write a polynomial $V(x)$ that represents its volume. Find $V(3)$.
$V(x) = 6x^3 - 10x^2$, $V(3) = 72$ cubic inches

3x − 5
2x
x

Figure for Exercise 80

81. ***Number pairs.*** If two numbers differ by 5, then what polynomial represents their product?
$x^2 + 5x$ or $x^2 - 5x$

82. ***Number pairs.*** If two numbers have a sum of 9, then what polynomial represents their product?
$9x - x^2$

83. ***Area of a rectangle.*** The length of a rectangle is $2.3x + 1.2$ meters, and its width is $3.5x + 5.1$ meters. What polynomial represents its area?
$8.05x^2 + 15.93x + 6.12$ square meters

84. ***Patchwork.*** A quilt patch cut in the shape of a triangle has a base of $5x$ inches and a height of $1.732x$ inches. What polynomial represents its area? $4.33x^2$ square inches

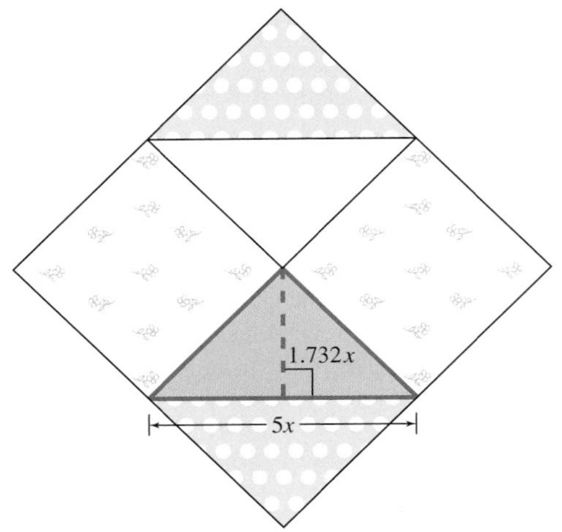

Figure for Exercise 84

85. ***Total revenue.*** At p dollars per ticket, a promoter expects to sell $40{,}000 - 1000p$ tickets to a concert.

a) How many tickets will she sell at \$10 each? 30,000

b) At \$10 per ticket, what is the total revenue? \$300,000

c) Find a polynomial $R(p)$ that represents the total revenue when tickets are p dollars each.
$R(p) = 40{,}000p - 1000p^2$

d) Find $R(20)$, $R(30)$, and $R(35)$.
\$400,000, \$300,000, \$175,000

86. ***Selling shirts.*** If a vendor charges p dollars each for rugby shirts, then he expects to sell $2000 - 100p$ shirts at a tournament.

a) Find a polynomial $R(p)$ that represents the total revenue when the shirts are p dollars each.
$R(p) = 2000p - 100p^2$

b) Find $R(5)$, $R(10)$, and $R(20)$.
\$7500, \$10,000, \$0

c) Use the bar graph to determine the price that will give the maximum total revenue. \$10

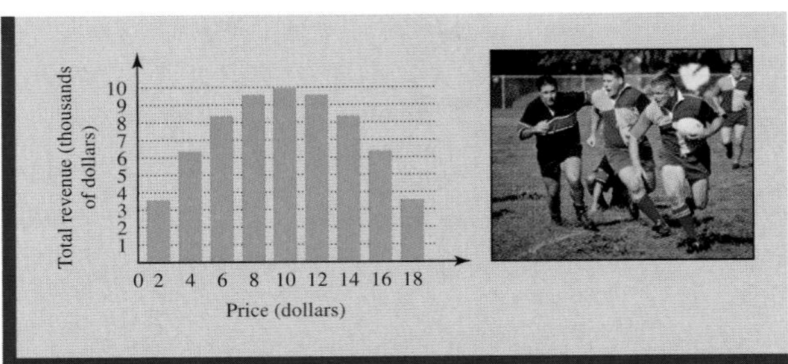

Figure for Exercise 86

Getting More Involved

87. ***Discussion***

Name all properties of the real numbers that are used in finding the following products:

a) $-2ab^3c^2 \cdot 5a^2bc$ **b)** $(x^2 + 3)(x^2 - 8x - 6)$

88. ***Discussion***

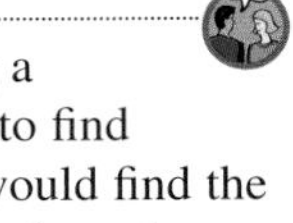

Find the product of 27 and 436 without using a calculator. Then use the distributive property to find the product $(20 + 7)(400 + 30 + 6)$ as you would find the product of a binomial and a trinomial. Explain how the two methods are related.

5.5 Multiplication of Binomials

In This Section

In Section 5.4, you learned to multiply polynomials. In this section, you will learn a rule that makes multiplication of binomials simpler.

⟨1⟩ The FOIL Method

We can use the distributive property to find the product of two binomials. For example,

$$(x + 2)(x + 3) = (x + 2)x + (x + 2)3 \quad \text{Distributive property}$$
$$= x^2 + 2x + 3x + 6 \quad \text{Distributive property}$$
$$= x^2 + 5x + 6 \quad \text{Combine like terms.}$$

There are four terms in $x^2 + 2x + 3x + 6$. The term x^2 is the product of the *first* terms of each binomial, x and x. The term $3x$ is the product of the two *outer* terms, 3 and x.

The term $2x$ is the product of the two *inner* terms, 2 and x. The term 6 is the product of the last terms of each binomial, 2 and 3. We can connect the terms multiplied by lines as follows:

‹ Teaching Tip ›

Have students actually draw lines connecting the first, inner, outer, and last terms of the binomials when they first learn FOIL.

$$(x + 2)(x + 3)$$

F = First terms
O = Outer terms
I = Inner terms
L = Last terms

If you remember the word FOIL, you can get the product of the two binomials much faster than writing out all of the steps above. This method is called the **FOIL method.** The name should make it easier to remember.

EXAMPLE 1

Using the FOIL method

Find each product.

a) $(x + 2)(x - 4)$ **b)** $(2x + 5)(3x - 4)$

c) $(a - b)(2a - b)$ **d)** $(x + 3)(y + 5)$

‹ Helpful Hint ›

You may have to practice FOIL a while to get good at it. However, the better you are at FOIL, the easier you will find factoring in Chapter 6.

Solution

a) $(x + 2)(x - 4) \overset{\text{F}\quad\text{O}\quad\text{I}\quad\text{L}}{= x^2 - 4x + 2x - 8}$

$= x^2 - 2x - 8$ Combine the like terms.

b) $(2x + 5)(3x - 4) = 6x^2 - 8x + 15x - 20$

$= 6x^2 + 7x - 20$ Combine the like terms.

c) $(a - b)(2a - b) = 2a^2 - ab - 2ab + b^2$

$= 2a^2 - 3ab + b^2$

d) $(x + 3)(y + 5) = xy + 5x + 3y + 15$ There are no like terms to combine.

Now do Exercises 5–28

FOIL can be used to multiply any two binomials. The binomials in Example 2 have higher powers than those of Example 1.

EXAMPLE 2

Using the FOIL method

Find each product.

a) $(x^3 - 3)(x^3 + 6)$ **b)** $(2a^2 + 1)(a^2 + 5)$

Solution

a) $(x^3 - 3)(x^3 + 6) = x^6 + 6x^3 - 3x^3 - 18$

$= x^6 + 3x^3 - 18$

b) $(2a^2 + 1)(a^2 + 5) = 2a^4 + 10a^2 + a^2 + 5$

$= 2a^4 + 11a^2 + 5$

Now do Exercises 29–40

⟨2⟩ Multiplying Binomials Quickly

The outer and inner products in the FOIL method are often like terms, and we can combine them without writing them down. Once you become proficient at using FOIL, you can find the product of two binomials without writing anything except the answer.

EXAMPLE 3

Using FOIL to find a product quickly

Find each product. Write down only the answer.

a) $(x + 3)(x + 4)$ **b)** $(2x - 1)(x + 5)$ **c)** $(a - 6)(a + 6)$

Solution

a) $(x + 3)(x + 4) = x^2 + 7x + 12$ Combine like terms: $3x + 4x = 7x$.

b) $(2x - 1)(x + 5) = 2x^2 + 9x - 5$ Combine like terms: $10x - x = 9x$.

c) $(a - 6)(a + 6) = a^2 - 36$ Combine like terms: $6a - 6a = 0$.

Now do Exercises 41–66

EXAMPLE 4

Products of three binomials

Find each product.

a) $(b - 1)(b + 2)(b - 3)$ **b)** $\left(\frac{1}{2}x + 3\right)\left(\frac{1}{2}x - 3\right)(2x + 5)$

Solution

a) Use FOIL to find $(b - 1)(b + 2) = b^2 + b - 2$. Then use the distributive property to multiply $b^2 + b - 2$ and $b - 3$:

$$\begin{aligned}(b - 1)(b + 2)(b - 3) &= (b^2 + b - 2)(b - 3) && \text{FOIL}\\ &= (b^2 + b - 2)b + (b^2 + b - 2)(-3) && \text{Distributive property}\\ &= b^3 + b^2 - 2b - 3b^2 - 3b + 6 && \text{Distributive property}\\ &= b^3 - 2b^2 - 5b + 6 && \text{Combine like terms.}\end{aligned}$$

b)
$$\begin{aligned}\left(\frac{1}{2}x + 3\right)\left(\frac{1}{2}x - 3\right)(2x + 5) &= \left(\frac{1}{4}x^2 - 9\right)(2x + 5) && \text{FOIL}\\ &= \frac{1}{2}x^3 + \frac{5}{4}x^2 - 18x - 45 && \text{FOIL}\end{aligned}$$

Now do Exercises 67–74

⟨3⟩ Applications

EXAMPLE 5

Area of a garden

Sheila has a square garden with sides of length x feet. If she increases the length by 7 feet and decreases the width by 2 feet, then what trinomial represents the area of the new rectangular garden?

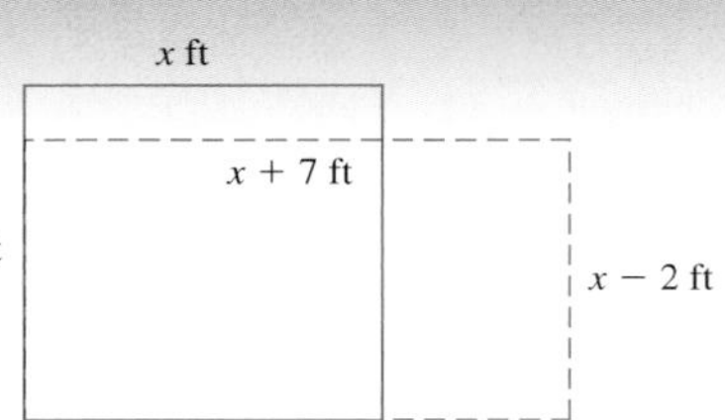

Figure 5.2

Solution

The length of the new garden is $x + 7$ feet and the width is $x - 2$ feet as shown in Fig. 5.2. The area is $(x + 7)(x - 2)$ or $x^2 + 5x - 14$ square feet.

Now do Exercises 97–100

Warm-Ups

True or false? Explain your answer.

1. $(x + 3)(x + 2) = x^2 + 6$ False
2. $(x + 2)(y + 1) = xy + x + 2y + 2$ True
3. $(3a - 5)(2a + 1) = 6a^2 + 3a - 10a - 5$ True
4. $(y + 3)(y - 2) = y^2 + y - 6$ True
5. $(x^2 + 2)(x^2 + 3) = x^4 + 5x^2 + 6$ True
6. $(3a^2 - 2)(3a^2 + 2) = 9a^2 - 4$ False
7. $(t + 3)(t + 5) = t^2 + 8t + 15$ True
8. $(y - 9)(y - 2) = y^2 - 11y - 18$ False
9. $(x + 4)(x - 7) = x^2 + 4x - 28$ False
10. $(a - 8)(a + 8) = a^2 - 64$ True

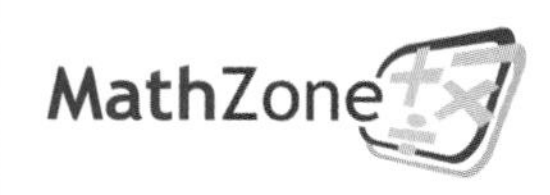

Exercises 5.5

‹ Study Tips ›

- Set short-term goals and reward yourself for accomplishing them. When you have solved 10 problems take a short break and listen to your favorite music.
- Study in a clean, comfortable, well-lit place, but don't get too comfortable. Study at a desk, not in bed.

Reading and Writing *After reading this section, write out the answers to these questions. Use complete sentences.*

1. What property of the real numbers do we usually use to find the product of two binomials?
   We use the distributive property to find the product of two binomials.
2. What does FOIL stand for?
   FOIL stands for first, outer, inner, and last.
3. What is the purpose of FOIL?
   The purpose of FOIL is to provide a faster method for finding the product of two binomials.
4. What is the maximum number of terms that can be obtained when two binomials are multiplied?
   The maximum number of terms obtained in multiplying binomials is four.

‹1› The FOIL Method

Use FOIL to find each product. See Example 1.

5. $(x + 2)(x + 4)$ $x^2 + 6x + 8$
6. $(x + 3)(x + 5)$ $x^2 + 8x + 15$
7. $(a + 1)(a + 4)$ $a^2 + 5a + 4$
8. $(w + 3)(w + 6)$ $w^2 + 9w + 18$
9. $(x + 9)(x + 10)$ $x^2 + 19x + 90$
10. $(x + 5)(x + 7)$ $x^2 + 12x + 35$
11. $(2x + 1)(x + 3)$ $2x^2 + 7x + 3$
12. $(3x + 2)(2x + 1)$ $6x^2 + 7x + 2$
13. $(a - 3)(a + 2)$ $a^2 - a - 6$
14. $(b - 1)(b + 2)$ $b^2 + b - 2$
15. $(2x - 1)(x - 2)$ $2x^2 - 5x + 2$

VIDEO **16.** $(2y - 5)(y - 2)$ $2y^2 - 9y + 10$

17. $(2a - 3)(a + 1)$ $2a^2 - a - 3$

18. $(3x - 5)(x + 4)$ $3x^2 + 7x - 20$

19. $(w - 50)(w - 10)$ $w^2 - 60w + 500$

20. $(w - 30)(w - 20)$ $w^2 - 50w + 600$

21. $(y - a)(y + 5)$ $y^2 + 5y - ay - 5a$

22. $(a + t)(3 - y)$ $3a - ay + 3t - ty$

23. $(5 - w)(w + m)$ $5w + 5m - w^2 - mw$

24. $(a - h)(b + t)$ $ab + at - bh - ht$

VIDEO **25.** $(2m - 3t)(5m + 3t)$ $10m^2 - 9mt - 9t^2$

26. $(2x - 5y)(x + y)$ $2x^2 - 3xy - 5y^2$

27. $(5a + 2b)(9a + 7b)$ $45a^2 + 53ab + 14b^2$

28. $(11x + 3y)(x + 4y)$ $11x^2 + 47xy + 12y^2$

Use FOIL to find each product. See Example 2.

29. $(x^2 - 5)(x^2 + 2)$ $x^4 - 3x^2 - 10$

VIDEO **30.** $(y^2 + 1)(y^2 - 2)$ $y^4 - y^2 - 2$

31. $(h^3 + 5)(h^3 + 5)$ $h^6 + 10h^3 + 25$

32. $(y^6 + 1)(y^6 - 4)$ $y^{12} - 3y^6 - 4$

33. $(3b^3 + 2)(b^3 + 4)$ $3b^6 + 14b^3 + 8$

34. $(5n^4 - 1)(n^4 + 3)$ $5n^8 + 14n^4 - 3$

35. $(y^2 - 3)(y - 2)$ $y^3 - 2y^2 - 3y + 6$

36. $(x - 1)(x^2 - 1)$ $x^3 - x^2 - x + 1$

37. $(3m^3 - n^2)(2m^3 + 3n^2)$ $6m^6 + 7m^3n^2 - 3n^4$

38. $(6y^4 - 2z^2)(6y^4 - 3z^2)$ $36y^8 - 30y^4z^2 + 6z^4$

39. $(3u^2v - 2)(4u^2v + 6)$ $12u^4v^2 + 10u^2v - 12$

40. $(5y^3w^2 + z)(2y^3w^2 + 3z)$ $10y^6w^4 + 17y^3w^2z + 3z^2$

⟨2⟩ Multiplying Binomials Quickly

Find each product. Try to write only the answer. See Example 3.

41. $(w + 2)(w + 1)$ $w^2 + 3w + 2$

42. $(q + 2)(q + 3)$ $q^2 + 5q + 6$

43. $(b + 4)(b + 5)$ $b^2 + 9b + 20$

44. $(y + 8)(y + 4)$ $y^2 + 12y + 32$

45. $(x - 3)(x + 9)$ $x^2 + 6x - 27$

46. $(m + 7)(m - 8)$ $m^2 - m - 56$

47. $(a + 5)(a + 5)$ $a^2 + 10a + 25$

48. $(t - 4)(t - 4)$ $t^2 - 8t + 16$

49. $(2x - 1)(2x - 1)$ $4x^2 - 4x + 1$

VIDEO **50.** $(3y + 4)(3y + 4)$ $9y^2 + 24y + 16$

51. $(z - 10)(z + 10)$ $z^2 - 100$

52. $(3h - 5)(3h + 5)$ $9h^2 - 25$

53. $(a + b)(a + b)$ $a^2 + 2ab + b^2$

54. $(x - y)(x - y)$ $x^2 - 2xy + y^2$

55. $(a - 1)(a - 2)$ $a^2 - 3a + 2$

56. $(b - 8)(b - 1)$ $b^2 - 9b + 8$

57. $(2x - 1)(x + 3)$ $2x^2 + 5x - 3$

58. $(3y + 5)(y - 3)$ $3y^2 - 4y - 15$

59. $(5t - 2)(t - 1)$ $5t^2 - 7t + 2$

60. $(2t - 3)(2t - 1)$ $4t^2 - 8t + 3$

61. $(h - 7)(h - 9)$ $h^2 - 16h + 63$

62. $(h - 7w)(h - 7w)$ $h^2 - 14hw + 49w^2$

63. $(h + 7w)(h + 7w)$ $h^2 + 14hw + 49w^2$

64. $(h - 7q)(h + 7q)$ $h^2 - 49q^2$

65. $(2h^2 - 1)(2h^2 - 1)$ $4h^4 - 4h^2 + 1$

66. $(3h^2 + 1)(3h^2 + 1)$ $9h^4 + 6h^2 + 1$

Find each product. See Example 4.

67. $(a + 1)(a - 2)(a + 5)$ $a^3 + 4a^2 - 7a - 10$

68. $(y - 1)(y + 3)(y - 4)$ $y^3 - 2y^2 - 11y + 12$

69. $(h + 2)(h + 3)(h + 4)$ $h^3 + 9h^2 + 26h + 24$

70. $(m - 1)(m - 3)(m - 5)$ $m^3 - 9m^2 + 23m - 15$

71. $\left(\frac{1}{2}x + 4\right)\left(\frac{1}{2}x - 4\right)(4x - 8)$ $x^3 - 2x^2 - 64x + 128$

72. $\left(\frac{1}{3}w - 3\right)\left(\frac{1}{3}w + 3\right)(w - 6)$ $\frac{1}{9}w^3 - \frac{2}{3}w^2 - 9w + 54$

73. $\left(x + \frac{1}{2}\right)\left(x - \frac{1}{2}\right)(x + 8)$ $x^3 + 8x^2 - \frac{1}{4}x - 2$

74. $\left(x + \frac{1}{3}\right)\left(x - \frac{1}{3}\right)(x + 9)$ $x^3 + 9x^2 - \frac{1}{9}x - 1$

Miscellaneous

Perform the indicated operations.

75. $(x + 10)(x + 5)$ $x^2 + 15x + 50$

76. $(x + 4)(x + 8)$ $x^2 + 12x + 32$

77. $\left(x + \frac{1}{2}\right)\left(x + \frac{1}{2}\right)$ $x^2 + x + \frac{1}{4}$

78. $\left(x + \frac{1}{3}\right)\left(x + \frac{1}{6}\right)$ $x^2 + \frac{1}{2}x + \frac{1}{18}$

79. $\left(4x + \frac{1}{2}\right)\left(2x + \frac{1}{4}\right)$ $8x^2 + 2x + \frac{1}{8}$

80. $\left(3x + \frac{1}{6}\right)\left(6x + \frac{1}{3}\right)$ $18x^2 + 2x + \frac{1}{18}$

81. $\left(2a + \frac{1}{2}\right)\left(4a - \frac{1}{2}\right)$ $8a^2 + a - \frac{1}{4}$

82. $\left(3b + \frac{2}{3}\right)\left(6b - \frac{1}{3}\right)$ $18b^2 + 3b - \frac{2}{9}$

83. $\left(\frac{1}{2}x - \frac{1}{3}\right)\left(\frac{1}{4}x + \frac{1}{2}\right)$ $\frac{1}{8}x^2 + \frac{1}{6}x - \frac{1}{6}$

84. $\left(\frac{2}{3}t - \frac{1}{4}\right)\left(\frac{1}{2}t - \frac{1}{2}\right)$ $\frac{1}{3}t^2 - \frac{11}{24}t + \frac{1}{8}$

85. $a(a + 3)(a + 4)$ $a^3 + 7a^2 + 12a$

86. $w(w + 5)(w + 9)$ $w^3 + 14w^2 + 45w$

87. $x^3(x + 6)(x + 7)$ $x^5 + 13x^4 + 42x^3$

88. $x^2(x^2 + 1)(x^2 + 8)$ $x^6 + 9x^4 + 8x^2$

89. $-2x^4(3x - 1)(2x + 5)$ $-12x^6 - 26x^5 + 10x^4$

90. $4xy^3(2x - y)(3x + y)$ $24x^3y^3 - 4x^2y^4 - 4xy^5$

91. $(x - 1)(x + 1)(x + 3)$ $x^3 + 3x^2 - x - 3$

VIDEO **92.** $(a - 3)(a + 4)(a - 5)$ $a^3 - 4a^2 - 17a + 60$

93. $(3x - 2)(3x + 2)(x + 5)$ $9x^3 + 45x^2 - 4x - 20$

94. $(x - 6)(9x + 4)(9x - 4)$ $81x^3 - 486x^2 - 16x + 96$

95. $(x - 1)(x + 2) - (x + 3)(x - 4)$ $2x + 10$

96. $(k - 4)(k + 9) - (k - 3)(k + 7)$ $k - 15$

‹3› Applications

Solve each problem. See Example 5.

97. ***Area of a rug.*** Find a trinomial $A(x)$ that represents the area of a rectangular rug whose sides are $x + 3$ feet and $2x - 1$ feet. Find $A(4)$.
$A(x) = 2x^2 + 5x - 3$, 49 square feet

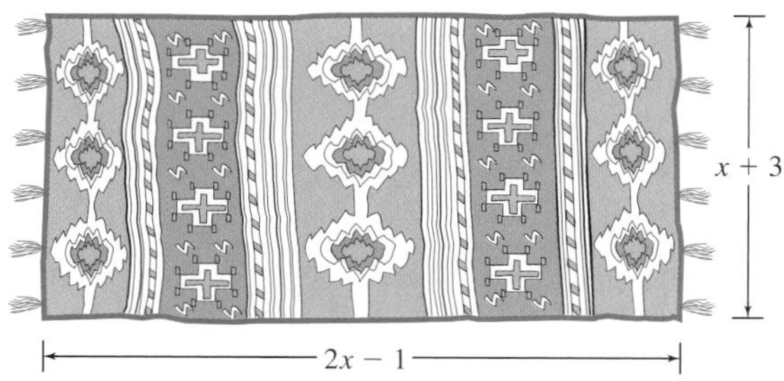

Figure for Exercise 97

98. ***Area of a parallelogram.*** Find a trinomial $A(x)$ that represents the area of a parallelogram whose base is $3x + 2$ meters and whose height is $2x + 3$ meters. Find $A(3)$.
$A(x) = 6x^2 + 13x + 6$, 99 square meters

99. ***Area of a sail.*** A sail is triangular in shape with a base of $2x - 1$ meters and a height of $4x - 4$ meters. Find a polynomial $A(x)$ that represents the area of the sail. Find $A(5)$.
$A(x) = 4x^2 - 6x + 2$, 72 square meters

100. ***Area of a square.*** A square has sides of length $3x + 1$ meters. Find a polynomial $A(x)$ that represents the area of the square. Find $A(1)$.
$A(x) = 9x^2 + 6x + 1$, 16 square meters

Getting More Involved

101. ***Exploration***

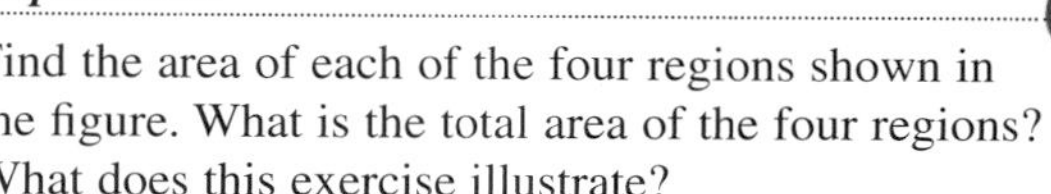

Find the area of each of the four regions shown in the figure. What is the total area of the four regions? What does this exercise illustrate?
12 ft², $3h$ ft², $4h$ ft², h^2 ft²; $h^2 + 7h + 12$ ft²; $(h + 3)(h + 4) = h^2 + 7h + 12$

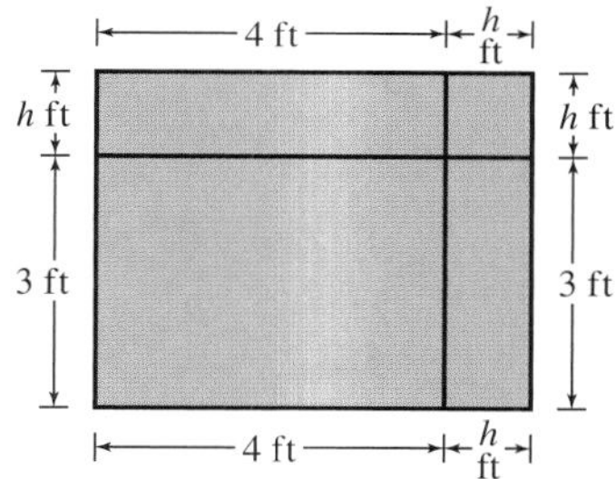

Figure for Exercise 101

102. ***Exploration***

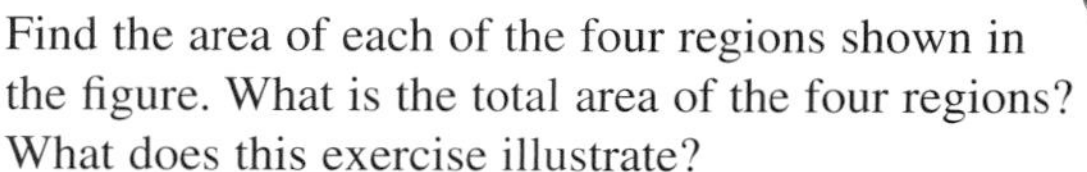

Find the area of each of the four regions shown in the figure. What is the total area of the four regions? What does this exercise illustrate?
a^2, ab, ab, b^2; $a^2 + 2ab + b^2$; $(a + b)(a + b) = a^2 + 2ab + b^2$

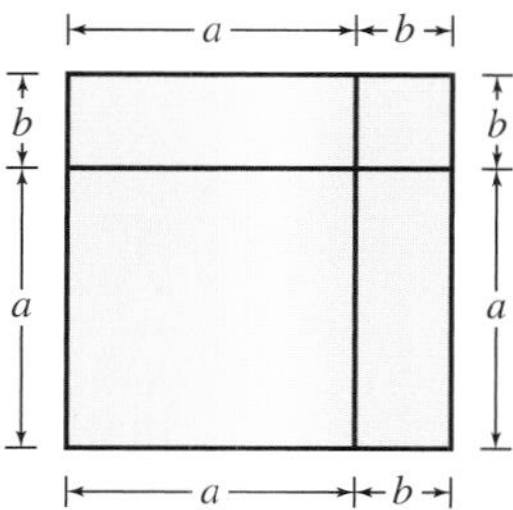

Figure for Exercise 102

5.6 Special Products

In This Section

⟨ Helpful Hint ⟩

To visualize the square of a sum, draw a square with sides of length $a + b$ as shown.

	a	b
a	a^2	ab
b	ab	b^2

The area of the large square is $(a + b)^2$. You get the same area if you add the areas of the four smaller regions: $(a + b)^2 = a^2 + 2(ab) + b^2$.

In Section 5.5, you learned the FOIL method to make multiplying binomials simpler. In this section, you will learn rules for squaring binomials and for finding the product of a sum and a difference. These products are called **special products.**

⟨1⟩ The Square of a Sum or Difference

To compute $(a + b)^2$, the square of a sum, we can write it as $(a + b)(a + b)$ and use FOIL:

$$\begin{aligned}(a + b)^2 &= (a + b)(a + b)\\ &= a^2 + ab + ab + b^2\\ &= a^2 + 2ab + b^2\end{aligned}$$

So to square $a + b$, *we square the first term* (a^2), *add twice the product of the two terms* $(2ab)$, *then add the square of the last term* (b^2). The square of a sum occurs so frequently that it is helpful to learn this new rule to find it. The rule for squaring a sum is given symbolically as follows.

The Square of a Sum

$$(a + b)^2 = a^2 + 2ab + b^2$$

EXAMPLE 1

Using the rule for squaring a sum

Find the square of each sum.

a) $(x + 3)^2$

b) $(2a + 5)^2$

Solution

a) $(x + 3)^2 = x^2 + 2(x)(3) + 3^2 = x^2 + 6x + 9$

(x^2: Square of first; $2(x)(3)$: Twice the product; 3^2: Square of last)

b) $$\begin{aligned}(2a + 5)^2 &= (2a)^2 + 2(2a)(5) + 5^2\\ &= 4a^2 + 20a + 25\end{aligned}$$

Now do Exercises 7–22

CAUTION Don't forget the middle term when squaring a sum. The square of $x + 3$ is $x^2 + 6x + 9$; it is not $x^2 + 9$. The equation $(x + 3)^2 = x^2 + 6x + 9$ is an identity. It is true for every real number x. The equation $(x + 3)^2 = x^2 + 9$ is true only if $x = 0$.

When we use FOIL to find $(a - b)^2$, we see that

$$(a - b)^2 = (a - b)(a - b)$$
$$= a^2 - ab - ab + b^2$$
$$= a^2 - 2ab + b^2.$$

So to square $a - b$, *we square the first term* (a^2), *subtract twice the product of the two terms* $(-2ab)$, *and add the square of the last term* (b^2). The rule for squaring a difference is given symbolically as follows.

The Square of a Difference

$$(a - b)^2 = a^2 - 2ab + b^2$$

EXAMPLE 2

Using the rule for squaring a difference

Find the square of each difference.

a) $(x - 4)^2$ **b)** $(4b - 5y)^2$

Solution

a) $(x - 4)^2 = x^2 - 2(x)(4) + 4^2$
$= x^2 - 8x + 16$

b) $(4b - 5y)^2 = (4b)^2 - 2(4b)(5y) + (5y)^2$
$= 16b^2 - 40by + 25y^2$

Now do Exercises 23–36

‹ Helpful Hint ›

Many students keep using FOIL to find the square of a sum or difference. However, learning the new rules for these special cases will pay off in the future.

‹2› Product of a Sum and a Difference

If we multiply the sum $a + b$ and the difference $a - b$ by using FOIL, we get

$$(a + b)(a - b) = a^2 - ab + ab - b^2$$
$$= a^2 - b^2.$$

The inner and outer products have a sum of 0. So *the product of the sum* $a + b$ *and the difference* $a - b$ *is equal to the difference of two squares* $a^2 - b^2$.

The Product of a Sum and a Difference

$$(a + b)(a - b) = a^2 - b^2$$

EXAMPLE 3

Product of a sum and a difference

Find each product.

a) $(x + 2)(x - 2)$

b) $(b + 7)(b - 7)$

c) $(3x - 5)(3x + 5)$

Solution

a) $(x + 2)(x - 2) = x^2 - 4$

b) $(b + 7)(b - 7) = b^2 - 49$

c) $(3x - 5)(3x + 5) = 9x^2 - 25$

Now do Exercises 37–48

‹ Helpful Hint ›

You can use

$$(a + b)(a - b) = a^2 - b^2$$

to perform mental arithmetic tricks like

$$19 \cdot 21 = (20 - 1)(20 + 1)$$
$$= 400 - 1$$
$$= 399.$$

What is $29 \cdot 31$? $28 \cdot 32$?

⟨3⟩ Higher Powers of Binomials

To find a power of a binomial that is higher than 2, we can use the rule for squaring a binomial along with the method of multiplying binomials using the distributive property. Finding the second or higher power of a binomial is called **expanding the binomial** because the result has more terms than the original.

EXAMPLE 4

Higher powers of a binomial

Expand each binomial.

a) $(x + 4)^3$ **b)** $(y - 2)^4$

Solution

a) $(x + 4)^3 = (x + 4)^2(x + 4)$

$= (x^2 + 8x + 16)(x + 4)$ Square of a sum

$= (x^2 + 8x + 16)x + (x^2 + 8x + 16)4$ Distributive property

$= x^3 + 8x^2 + 16x + 4x^2 + 32x + 64$

$= x^3 + 12x^2 + 48x + 64$

b) $(y - 2)^4 = (y - 2)^2(y - 2)^2$

$= (y^2 - 4y + 4)(y^2 - 4y + 4)$

$= (y^2 - 4y + 4)(y^2) + (y^2 - 4y + 4)(-4y) + (y^2 - 4y + 4)(4)$

$= y^4 - 4y^3 + 4y^2 - 4y^3 + 16y^2 - 16y + 4y^2 - 16y + 16$

$= y^4 - 8y^3 + 24y^2 - 32y + 16$

Now do Exercises 49–56

⟨4⟩ Applications

EXAMPLE 5

Area

a) A square patio has sides of length x feet. If the length and width are increased by 2 feet, then what trinomial represents the area of the larger patio?

b) A pizza parlor makes all of its pizzas one inch smaller in radius than advertised. If x is the advertised radius, then what trinomial represents the actual area?

Solution

a) The area of a square is given by $A = s^2$. Since the larger patio has sides of length $x + 2$ feet its area is $(x + 2)^2$ or $x^2 + 4x + 4$ square feet.

b) The area of a circle is given by $A = \pi r^2$. If the advertised radius is x inches, then the actual radius is $x - 1$ inches. The actual area is $\pi(x - 1)^2$:

$$\pi(x - 1)^2 = \pi(x^2 - 2x + 1) = \pi x^2 - 2\pi x + \pi$$

So the actual area is $\pi x^2 - 2\pi x + \pi$ square inches. Since π is a number, this trinomial is a trinomial in one variable, x.

Now do Exercises 87–98

⟨ Teaching Tip ⟩

A good outside exercise is to ask students to price their favorite pizza in two sizes and determine which is the better value. Does the pizza maker size the pizzas by radius or diameter?

Warm-Ups

True or false? Explain your answer.

1. $(2 + 3)^2 = 2^2 + 3^2$ False
2. $(x + 3)^2 = x^2 + 6x + 9$ for any value of x. True
3. $(3 + 5)^2 = 9 + 30 + 25$ True
4. $(2x + 7)^2 = 4x^2 + 28x + 49$ for any value of x. True
5. $(y + 8)^2 = y^2 + 64$ for any value of y. False
6. The product of a sum and a difference of the same two terms is equal to the difference of two squares. True
7. $(40 - 1)(40 + 1) = 1599$ True
8. $49 \cdot 51 = 2499$ True
9. $(x - 3)^2 = x^2 - 3x + 9$ for any value of x. False
10. The square of a sum is equal to a sum of two squares. False

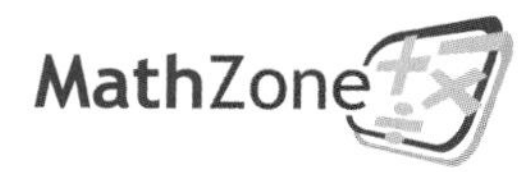

5.6 Exercises

‹ Study Tips ›

- We are all creatures of habit. When you find a place in which you study successfully, stick with it.
- Studying in a quiet place is better than studying in a noisy place. There are very few people who can listen to music or conversation and study effectively.

Reading and Writing *After reading this section, write out the answers to these questions. Use complete sentences.*

1. What are the special products?
   The special products are $(a + b)^2$, $(a - b)^2$, and $(a + b)(a - b)$.
2. What is the rule for squaring a sum?
   $(a + b)^2 = a^2 + 2ab + b^2$
3. Why do we need a new rule to find the square of a sum when we already have FOIL?
   It is faster to do by the new rule than with FOIL.
4. What happens to the inner and outer products in the product of a sum and a difference?
   In $(a + b)(a - b)$ the inner and outer products have a sum of zero.
5. What is the rule for finding the product of a sum and a difference?
   $(a + b)(a - b) = a^2 - b^2$
6. How can you find higher powers of binomials?
   Higher powers of binomials are found by using the distributive property.

‹1› The Square of a Sum or Difference

Square each binomial. See Example 1.

7. $(x + 1)^2$
   $x^2 + 2x + 1$
8. $(y + 2)^2$
   $y^2 + 4y + 4$
9. $(y + 4)^2$
   $y^2 + 8y + 16$
10. $(z + 3)^2$
   $z^2 + 6z + 9$
11. $(m + 6)^2$
   $m^2 + 12m + 36$
12. $(w + 7)^2$
   $w^2 + 14w + 49$
13. $(a + 9)^2$ $a^2 + 18a + 81$
14. $(b + 10)^2$ $b^2 + 20b + 100$
15. $(3x + 8)^2$
   $9x^2 + 48x + 64$

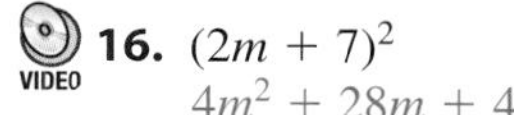

16. $(2m + 7)^2$
   $4m^2 + 28m + 49$

17. $(s + t)^2$ $s^2 + 2st + t^2$

18. $(x + z)^2$ $x^2 + 2xz + z^2$

19. $(2x + y)^2$ $4x^2 + 4xy + y^2$

20. $(3t + v)^2$ $9t^2 + 6tv + v^2$

21. $(2t + 3h)^2$ $4t^2 + 12ht + 9h^2$

22. $(3z + 5k)^2$ $9z^2 + 30kz + 25k^2$

Square each binomial. See Example 2.

23. $(p - 2)^2$ $p^2 - 4p + 4$

24. $(b - 5)^2$ $b^2 - 10b + 25$

25. $(a - 3)^2$ $a^2 - 6a + 9$

26. $(w - 4)^2$ $w^2 - 8w + 16$

27. $(t - 1)^2$ $t^2 - 2t + 1$

VIDEO **28.** $(t - 6)^2$ $t^2 - 12t + 36$

29. $(3t - 2)^2$ $9t^2 - 12t + 4$

30. $(5a - 6)^2$ $25a^2 - 60a + 36$

31. $(s - t)^2$ $s^2 - 2st + t^2$

32. $(r - w)^2$ $r^2 - 2rw + w^2$

33. $(3a - b)^2$ $9a^2 - 6ab + b^2$

34. $(4w - 7)^2$ $16w^2 - 56w + 49$

35. $(3z - 5y)^2$ $9z^2 - 30yz + 25y^2$

36. $(2z - 3w)^2$ $4z^2 - 12wz + 9w^2$

⟨2⟩ Product of a Sum and a Difference

Find each product. See Example 3.

37. $(a - 5)(a + 5)$ $a^2 - 25$

38. $(x - 6)(x + 6)$ $x^2 - 36$

39. $(y - 1)(y + 1)$ $y^2 - 1$

40. $(p + 2)(p - 2)$ $p^2 - 4$

VIDEO **41.** $(3x - 8)(3x + 8)$ $9x^2 - 64$

42. $(6x + 1)(6x - 1)$ $36x^2 - 1$

43. $(r + s)(r - s)$ $r^2 - s^2$

44. $(b - y)(b + y)$ $b^2 - y^2$

45. $(8y - 3a)(8y + 3a)$ $64y^2 - 9a^2$

46. $(4u - 9v)(4u + 9v)$ $16u^2 - 81v^2$

47. $(5x^2 - 2)(5x^2 + 2)$ $25x^4 - 4$

48. $(3y^2 + 1)(3y^2 - 1)$ $9y^4 - 1$

⟨3⟩ Higher Powers of Binomials

Expand each binomial. See Example 4.

49. $(x + 1)^3$ $x^3 + 3x^2 + 3x + 1$

50. $(y - 1)^3$ $y^3 - 3y^2 + 3y - 1$

VIDEO **51.** $(2a - 3)^3$ $8a^3 - 36a^2 + 54a - 27$

52. $(3w - 1)^3$ $27w^3 - 27w^2 + 9w - 1$

53. $(a - 3)^4$ $a^4 - 12a^3 + 54a^2 - 108a + 81$

54. $(2b + 1)^4$ $16b^4 + 32b^3 + 24b^2 + 8b + 1$

55. $(a + b)^4$ $a^4 + 4a^3b + 6a^2b^2 + 4ab^3 + b^4$

56. $(2a - 3b)^4$ $16a^4 - 96a^3b + 216a^2b^2 - 216ab^3 + 81b^4$

Miscellaneous

Find each product.

57. $(a - 20)(a + 20)$ $a^2 - 400$

58. $(1 - x)(1 + x)$ $1 - x^2$

59. $(x + 8)(x + 7)$ $x^2 + 15x + 56$

60. $(x - 9)(x + 5)$ $x^2 - 4x - 45$

61. $(4x - 1)(4x + 1)$ $16x^2 - 1$

62. $(9y - 1)(9y + 1)$ $81y^2 - 1$

63. $(9y - 1)^2$ $81y^2 - 18y + 1$

64. $(4x - 1)^2$ $16x^2 - 8x + 1$

65. $(2t - 5)(3t + 4)$ $6t^2 - 7t - 20$

66. $(2t + 5)(3t - 4)$ $6t^2 + 7t - 20$

67. $(2t - 5)^2$ $4t^2 - 20t + 25$

68. $(2t + 5)^2$ $4t^2 + 20t + 25$

69. $(2t + 5)(2t - 5)$ $4t^2 - 25$

70. $(3t - 4)(3t + 4)$ $9t^2 - 16$

VIDEO **71.** $(x^2 - 1)(x^2 + 1)$ $x^4 - 1$

72. $(y^3 - 1)(y^3 + 1)$ $y^6 - 1$

73. $(2y^3 - 9)^2$ $4y^6 - 36y^3 + 81$

74. $(3z^4 - 8)^2$ $9z^8 - 48z^4 + 64$

75. $(2x^3 + 3y^2)^2$ $4x^6 + 12x^3y^2 + 9y^4$

76. $(4y^5 + 2w^3)^2$ $16y^{10} + 16y^5w^3 + 4w^6$

77. $\left(\frac{1}{2}x + \frac{1}{3}\right)^2$ $\frac{1}{4}x^2 + \frac{1}{3}x + \frac{1}{9}$

78. $\left(\frac{2}{3}y - \frac{1}{2}\right)^2$ $\frac{4}{9}y^2 - \frac{2}{3}y + \frac{1}{4}$

79. $(0.2x - 0.1)^2$ $0.04x^2 - 0.04x + 0.01$

80. $(0.1y + 0.5)^2$ $0.01y^2 + 0.1y + 0.25$

81. $(a + b)^3$ $a^3 + 3a^2b + 3ab^2 + b^3$

82. $(2a - 3b)^3$ $8a^3 - 36a^2b + 54ab^2 - 27b^3$

83. $(1.5x + 3.8)^2$ $2.25x^2 + 11.4x + 14.44$

84. $(3.45a - 2.3)^2$ $11.9025a^2 - 15.87a + 5.29$

85. $(3.5t - 2.5)(3.5t + 2.5)$ $12.25t^2 - 6.25$

86. $(4.5h + 5.7)(4.5h - 5.7)$ $20.25h^2 - 32.49$

⟨4⟩ Applications

Solve each problem. See Example 5.

87. ***Area of a square.*** Find a polynomial $A(x)$ that represents the area of the shaded region in the accompanying figure. $A(x) = x^2 + 6x + 9$

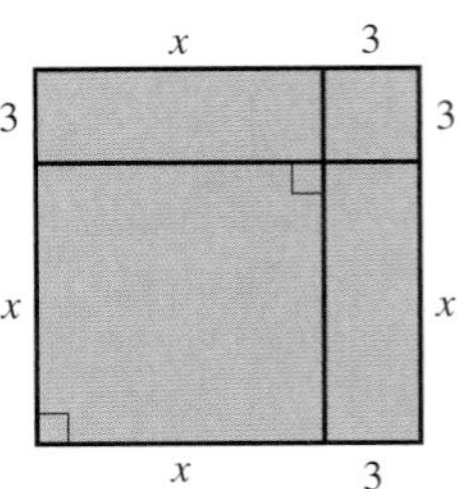

Figure for Exercise 87

88. ***Area of a square.*** Find a polynomial $A(x)$ that represents the area of the shaded region in the accompanying figure. $A(x) = x^2 - 6x + 9$

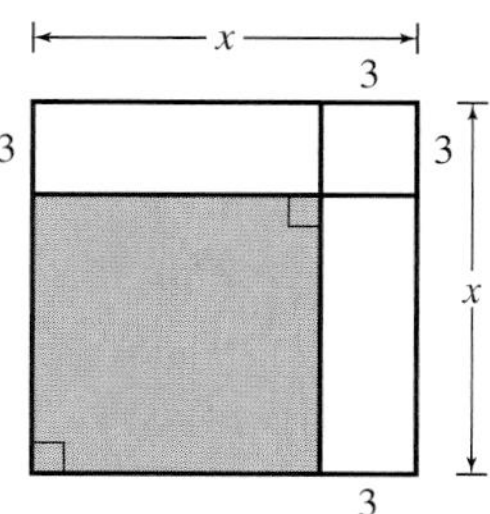

Figure for Exercise 88

89. ***Shrinking garden.*** Rose's garden is a square with sides of length x feet. Next spring she plans to make it rectangular by lengthening one side 5 feet and shortening the other side by 5 feet.

a) Find a polynomial $A(x)$ that represents the new area. $A(x) = x^2 - 25$

b) By how much will the area of the new garden differ from that of the old garden? 25 square feet

90. ***Square lot.*** Sam has a lot that he thought was a square, 200 feet by 200 feet. When he had it surveyed, he discovered that one side was x feet longer than he thought and the other side was x feet shorter than he thought.

a) Find a polynomial $A(x)$ that represents the new area. $A(x) = 40{,}000 - x^2$

b) Find $A(2)$. 39,996 square feet

c) If $x = 2$ feet, then how much less area does he have than he thought he had? 4 square feet

91. ***Area of a circle.*** Find a polynomial $A(b)$ that represents the area of a circle whose radius is $b + 1$. Use 3.14 for π. $A(b) = 3.14b^2 + 6.28b + 3.14$

92. ***Comparing dart boards.*** A small circular dart board has radius t inches and a larger one has radius that is 3 inches larger.

a) Find a polynomial $D(t)$ that represents the difference in area between the two dart boards. Use 3.14 for π. $D(t) = 18.84t + 28.26$

b) Find $D(4)$. 103.62 square inches

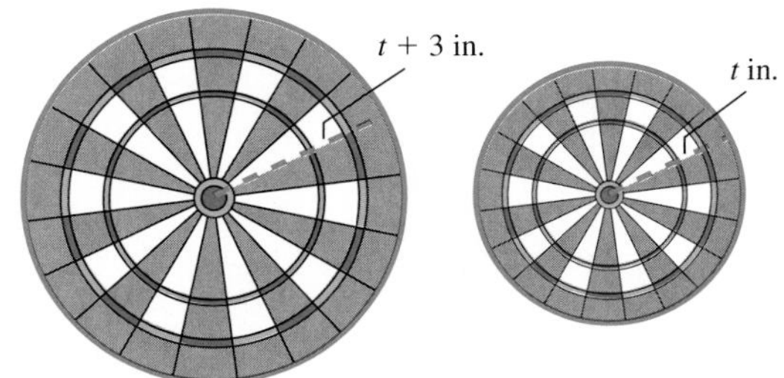

Figure for Exercise 92

93. ***Poiseuille's law.*** According to the nineteenth-century physician Jean Poiseuille, the velocity (in centimeters per second) of blood r centimeters from the center of an artery of radius R centimeters is given by

$$v = k(R - r)(R + r),$$

where k is a constant. Rewrite the formula using a special product rule. $v = k(R^2 - r^2)$

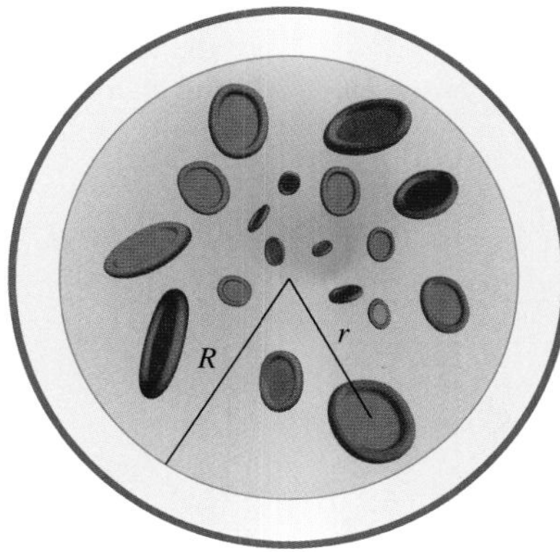

Figure for Exercise 93

94. ***Going in circles.*** A promoter is planning a circular race track with an inside radius of r feet and a width of w feet. The cost in dollars for paving the track is given by the formula

$$C = 1.2\pi[(r + w)^2 - r^2].$$

Use a special product rule to simplify this formula. What is the cost of paving the track if the inside radius is 1000 feet and the width of the track is 40 feet?
$C = 1.2\pi(2rw + w^2)$, \$307,624.75

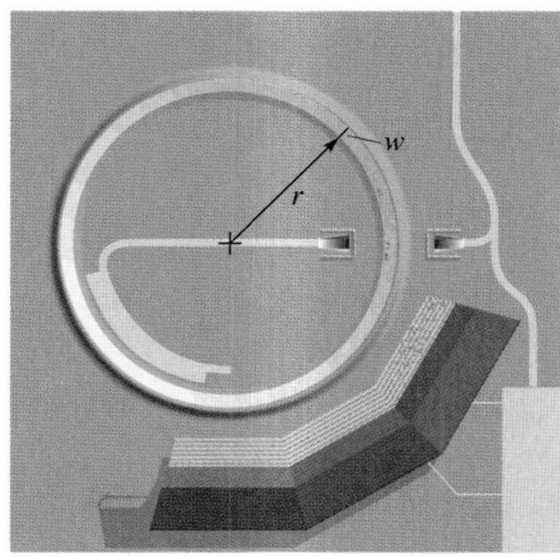

Figure for Exercise 94

95. ***Compounded annually.*** P dollars is invested at annual interest rate r for 2 years. If the interest is compounded annually, then the polynomial $P(1 + r)^2$ represents the value of the investment after 2 years. Rewrite this expression without parentheses. Evaluate the polynomial if $P = \$200$ and $r = 10\%$.
$P + 2Pr + Pr^2$, \$242

96. ***Compounded semiannually.*** P dollars is invested at annual interest rate r for 1 year. If the interest is compounded semiannually, then the polynomial $P\left(1 + \frac{r}{2}\right)^2$ represents the value of the investment after 1 year. Rewrite this expression without parentheses. Evaluate the polynomial if $P = \$200$ and $r = 10\%$. $P + Pr + \frac{Pr^2}{4}$, \$220.50

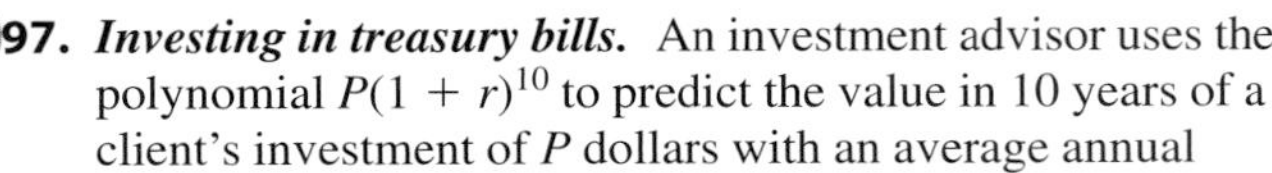

97. ***Investing in treasury bills.*** An investment advisor uses the polynomial $P(1 + r)^{10}$ to predict the value in 10 years of a client's investment of P dollars with an average annual return r. The accompanying graph shows historic average annual returns for the last 20 years for various asset classes (T. Rowe Price, www.troweprice.com). Use the historical average return to predict the value in 10 years of an investment of \$10,000 in U.S. treasury bills. \$20,230.06

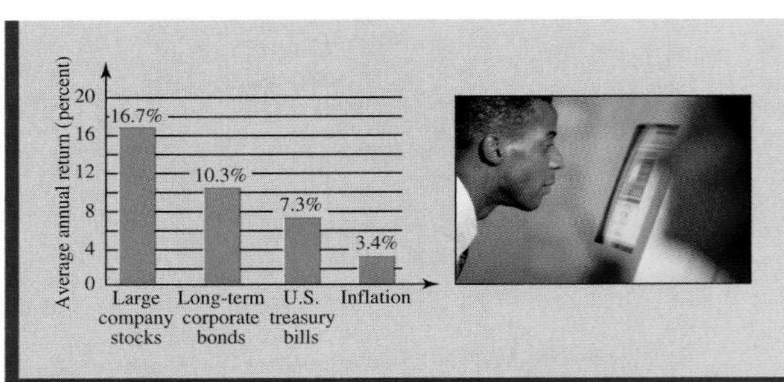

Figure for Exercises 97 and 98

98. ***Comparing investments.*** How much more would the investment in Exercise 97 be worth in 10 years if the client invests in large company stocks rather than U.S. treasury bills? \$26,619.83

Getting More Involved

99. ***Writing***

What is the difference between the equations $(x + 5)^2 = x^2 + 10x + 25$ and $(x + 5)^2 = x^2 + 25$?
The first is an identity and the second is a conditional equation.

100. ***Writing***

Is it possible to square a sum or a difference without using the rules presented in this section? Why should you learn the rules given in this section?
A sum or difference can be squared with the distributive property, FOIL, or the special product rules. It is easier with the special product rules.

5.7 Division of Polynomials

In This Section

You multiplied polynomials in Section 5.4. In this section, you will learn to divide polynomials.

⟨1⟩ Dividing Monomials

We actually divided some monomials in Section 5.1 using the quotient rule for exponents. We use the quotient rule here also. In Section 5.2, we divided expressions with positive and negative exponents. Since monomials and polynomials have nonnegative exponents only, we will not be using negative exponents here.

EXAMPLE 1

Dividing monomials

Find each quotient. All variables represent nonzero real numbers.

a) $(12x^5) \div (3x^2)$ **b)** $\frac{-4x^3}{2x^3}$ **c)** $\frac{-10a^2b^4}{-2a^2b^2}$

Solution

a) $(12x^5) \div (3x^2) = \frac{12x^5}{3x^2} = 4x^{5-2} = 4x^3$

The quotient is $4x^3$. Use the definition of division to check that $4x^3 \cdot 3x^2 = 12x^5$.

b) $\frac{-4x^3}{2x^3} = -2x^{3-3} = -2x^0 = -2 \cdot 1 = -2$

The quotient is -2. Use the definition of division to check that $-2 \cdot 2x^3 = -4x^3$.

c) $\frac{-10a^3b^4}{-2a^2b^2} = 5a^{3-2}b^{4-2} = 5ab^2$

The quotient is $5ab^2$. Check that $5ab^2(-2a^2b^2) = -10a^3b^4$.

Now do Exercises 7–24

If $a \div b = c$, then a is called the **dividend,** b is called the **divisor,** and c is called the **quotient.** We use these terms with division of real numbers or division of polynomials.

⟨2⟩ Dividing a Polynomial by a Monomial

‹ Teaching Tip ›

Emphasize that each term in the numerator is divided by the denominator.

We divided some simple polynomials by monomials in Chapter 1 using the distributive property. Now that we have the rules of exponents, we can use them to divide polynomials of higher degrees by monomials. Because of the distributive property, each term of the polynomial in the numerator is divided by the monomial from the denominator.

EXAMPLE 2

Dividing a polynomial by a monomial

Find the quotient.

a) $(5x - 10) \div 5$ b) $(-8x^6 + 12x^4 - 4x^2) \div (4x^2)$

Solution

a) By the distributive property, each term of $5x - 10$ is divided by 5:

$$\frac{5x - 10}{5} = \frac{5x}{5} - \frac{10}{5} = x - 2$$

The quotient is $x - 2$. Check by multiplying: $5(x - 2) = 5x - 10$.

b) By the distributive property, each term of $-8x^6 + 12x^4 - 4x^2$ is divided by $4x^2$:

$$\frac{-8x^6 + 12x^4 - 4x^2}{4x^2} = \frac{-8x^6}{4x^2} + \frac{12x^4}{4x^2} - \frac{4x^2}{4x^2}$$
$$= -2x^4 + 3x^2 - 1$$

The quotient is $-2x^4 + 3x^2 - 1$. We can check by multiplying.

$$4x^2(-2x^4 + 3x^2 - 1) = -8x^6 + 12x^4 - 4x^2$$

Now do Exercises 25–32

Because division by zero is undefined, we will always assume that the divisor is nonzero in any quotient involving variables. For example, the division in Example 3 is valid only if $4x^2 \neq 0$, or $x \neq 0$.

⟨3⟩ Dividing a Polynomial by a Binomial

Division of whole numbers is often done with a procedure called **long division.** For example, 253 is divided by 7 as follows:

```
               36    ← Quotient
Divisor →   7)253    ← Dividend
              21
               43
               42
                1    ← Remainder
```

Note that the remainder must be smaller than the divisor and

$$\text{dividend} = (\text{quotient})(\text{divisor}) + (\text{remainder}).$$

This fact is used to check. Since $253 = 36 \cdot 7 + 1$ the division was done correctly. Dividing each side of this last equation by "divisor" yields the equation

$$\frac{\text{dividend}}{\text{divisor}} = \text{quotient} + \frac{\text{remainder}}{\text{divisor}}.$$

There are two ways to express the result of dividing 253 by 7. One is to state that the quotient is 36 and the remainder is 1. The other is to write the equation

$$\frac{253}{7} = 36 + \frac{1}{7} = 36\frac{1}{7}.$$

If the division is done in a context where fractions are allowed then $36\frac{1}{7}$ could be called the quotient. For example dividing \$9 among 2 people results in $\$4\frac{1}{2}$ each. However, dividing 9 people into groups of 2 to play tennis results in 4 groups with a remainder of 1 person.

To divide a polynomial by a binomial, we perform the division like long division of whole numbers. For example, to divide $x^2 - 3x - 10$ by $x + 2$, we get the first term of the quotient by dividing the first term of $x + 2$ into the first term of $x^2 - 3x - 10$. So divide x^2 by x to get x, then multiply and subtract as follows:

‹ Teaching Tip ›

Students often have trouble with the subtraction part of the division process.

1 Divide:	x	$x^2 \div x = x$
2 Multiply:	$x + 2\overline{)x^2 - 3x - 10}$	
	$x^2 + 2x$	$x \cdot (x + 2) = x^2 + 2x$
3 Subtract:	$-5x$	$-3x - 2x = -5x$

Now bring down -10 and continue the process. We get the second term of the quotient (below) by dividing the first term of $x + 2$ into the first term of $-5x - 10$. So divide $-5x$ by x to get -5:

1 Divide:	$x - 5$	$-5x \div x = -5$
2 Multiply:	$x + 2\overline{)x^2 - 3x - 10}$	
	$x^2 + 2x \quad \downarrow$	Bring down -10.
	$-5x - 10$	
	$-5x - 10$	$-5(x + 2) = -5x - 10$
3 Subtract:	0	$-10 - (-10) = 0$

So the quotient is $x - 5$, and the remainder is 0.

In Example 3, there is a term missing in the dividend. To account for the missing term we insert a term with a zero coefficient.

EXAMPLE 3

Dividing a polynomial by a binomial

Determine the quotient and remainder when $x^3 - 5x - 1$ is divided by $x - 4$.

Solution

Because the x^2-term in the dividend $x^3 - 5x - 1$ is missing, we write $0 \cdot x^2$ for it:

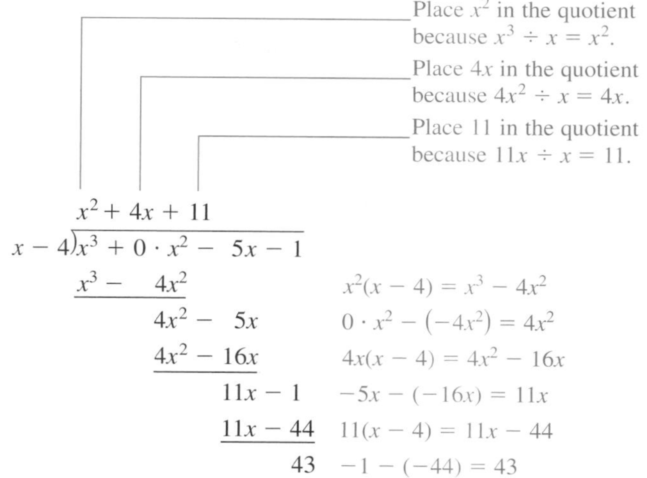

So the quotient is $x^2 + 4x + 11$ and the remainder is 43. To check, multiply the quotient by divisor $x - 4$ and add the remainder to see if you get the dividend $x^3 - 5x - 1$:

$$\begin{aligned}(x - 4)(x^2 + 4x + 11) + 43 &= x(x^2 + 4x + 11) - 4(x^2 + 4x + 11) + 43\\ &= x^3 + 4x^2 + 11x - 4x^2 - 16x - 44 + 43\\ &= x^3 - 5x - 1 \quad \text{The dividend}\end{aligned}$$

Now do Exercises 33–36

In Example 4, the terms of the dividend are not in order of decreasing exponents and there is a missing term.

EXAMPLE 4

Dividing a polynomial by a binomial

Divide $2x^3 - 4 - 7x^2$ by $2x - 3$, and identify the quotient and the remainder.

Solution

Rearrange the dividend as $2x^3 - 7x^2 - 4$. Because the x-term in the dividend is missing, we write $0 \cdot x$ for it:

$$\begin{array}{rll} & x^2 - 2x - 3 & 2x^3 \div (2x) = x^2 \\ 2x - 3 & \overline{)2x^3 - 7x^2 + 0 \cdot x - 4} & \\ & \underline{2x^3 - 3x^2} & x^2(2x - 3) = 2x^3 - 3x^2 \\ & -4x^2 + 0 \cdot x & -7x^2 - (-3x^2) = -4x^2 \\ & \underline{-4x^2 + 6x} & -2x(2x - 3) = -4x^2 + 6x \\ & -6x - 4 & 0 \cdot x - 6x = -6x \\ & \underline{-6x + 9} & -3(2x - 3) = -6x + 9 \\ & -13 & -4 - (9) = -13 \end{array}$$

The quotient is $x^2 - 2x - 3$ and the remainder is -13. To check, multiply the quotient by the divisor $2x - 3$ and add the remainder -13 to see if you get the dividend

‹ Helpful Hint ›

Students usually have the most difficulty with the subtraction part of long division. So pay particular attention to that step and double check your work.

$2x^3 - 7x^2 - 4$:

$$\begin{aligned}(2x - 3)(x^2 - 2x - 3) - 13 &= 2x(x^2 - 2x - 3) - 3(x^2 - 2x - 3) - 13\\ &= 2x^3 - 4x^2 - 6x - 3x^2 + 6x + 9 - 13\\ &= 2x^3 - 7x^2 - 4 \quad \text{The dividend}\end{aligned}$$

Now do Exercises 37–50

CAUTION To avoid errors, always write the terms of the divisor and the dividend in descending order of the exponents and insert a zero for any term that is missing.

EXAMPLE 5

Rewriting algebraic fractions

Express $\frac{-3x}{x-2}$ in the form

$$\text{quotient} + \frac{\text{remainder}}{\text{divisor}}.$$

‹ Teaching Tip ›

Note that the form of the result is specified here so that students don't simply list the quotient and remainder.

Solution

Use long division to get the quotient and remainder:

$$\begin{array}{r} -3 \\ x - 2 \overline{)-3x + 0} \\ \underline{-3x + 6} \\ -6 \end{array}$$

To check, multiply the divisor and quotient and add the remainder to see if you get the dividend $-3x$:

$$-3(x - 2) - 6 = -3x + 6 - 6 = -3x$$

Because the quotient is -3 and the remainder is -6, we can write

$$\frac{-3x}{x-2} = -3 + \frac{-6}{x-2}.$$

Now do Exercises 51–66

CAUTION When dividing polynomials by long division, we do not stop until the remainder is 0 or the degree of the remainder is smaller than the degree of the divisor. For example, we stop dividing in Example 5 because the degree of the remainder -6 is 0 and the degree of the divisor $x - 2$ is 1.

Warm-Ups ▼

True or false? Explain your answer.

1. $y^{10} \div y^2 = y^5$ for any nonzero value of y. False
2. $\frac{7x + 2}{7} = x + 2$ for any value of x. False
3. $\frac{7x^2}{7} = x^2$ for any value of x. True
4. If $3x^2 + 6$ is divided by 3, the quotient is $x^2 + 6$. False

5. If $4y^2 - 6y$ is divided by $2y$, the quotient is $2y - 3$. True
6. The quotient times the remainder plus the dividend equals the divisor. False
7. $(x + 2)(x + 1) + 3 = x^2 + 3x + 5$ for any value of x. True
8. If $x^2 + 3x + 5$ is divided by $x + 2$, then the quotient is $x + 1$. True
9. If $x^2 + 3x + 5$ is divided by $x + 2$, the remainder is 3. True
10. If the remainder is zero, then (divisor)(quotient) = dividend. True

Boost your grade at mathzone.com!
- Practice Problems
- NetTutor
- Self-Tests
- e-Professors
- Videos

Exercises 5.7

‹ Study Tips ›

- Eliminate the obvious distractions when you study. Disconnect the telephone and put away newspapers, magazines, and unfinished projects.
- The sight of a textbook from another class might be a distraction if you have a lot of work to do in that class.

Reading and Writing *After reading this section, write out the answers to these questions. Use complete sentences.*

1. What rule is important for dividing monomials?
   The quotient rule is used for dividing monomials.
2. What is the meaning of a zero exponent?
   The zero power of a nonzero real number is 1.
3. How many terms should you get when dividing a polynomial by a monomial?
   When dividing a polynomial by a monomial, the quotient should have the same number of terms as the polynomial.
4. How should the terms of the polynomials be written when dividing with long division?
   The terms of a polynomial should be written in descending order of the exponents.
5. How do you know when to stop the process in long division of polynomials?
   The long division process stops when the degree of the remainder is less than the degree of the divisor.
6. How do you handle missing terms in the dividend polynomial when doing long division?
   Insert a term with zero coefficient for each missing term when doing long division.

‹1› Dividing Monomials

Find each quotient. Try to write only the answer. See Example 1.

7. $\frac{x^8}{x^2}$ x^6
8. $\frac{y^9}{y^3}$ y^6
9. $\frac{w^{12}}{w^3}$ w^9
10. $\frac{m^{20}}{m^{10}}$ m^{10}
11. $\frac{a^{14}}{a^5}$ a^9
12. $\frac{b^{19}}{b^{12}}$ b^7
13. $\frac{6a^{12}}{2a^7}$ $3a^5$
14. $\frac{30b^6}{3b^2}$ $10b^4$
15. $a^9 \div a^3$ a^6
16. $b^{12} \div b^4$ b^8
17. $-12x^9 \div (3x^5)$ $-4x^4$
18. $-6y^{10} \div (-3y^5)$ $2y^5$
19. $-6y^2 \div (6y)$ $-y$
20. $-3a^2b \div (3ab)$ $-a$
21. (VIDEO) $\frac{-6x^3y^2}{2x^2y^2}$ $-3x$
22. $\frac{-4h^2k^4}{-2hk^3}$ $2hk$
23. $\frac{-9x^5y^2}{3x^2y^2}$ $-3x^3$
24. $\frac{-12z^{10}y^2}{-2z^4y^2}$ $6z^6$

⟨2⟩ Dividing a Polynomial by a Monomial

Find the quotients. See Example 2.

25. $\dfrac{3x - 6}{3}$ $x - 2$

26. $\dfrac{5y - 10}{-5}$ $-y + 2$

27. $\dfrac{x^5 + 3x^4 - x^3}{x^2}$ $x^3 + 3x^2 - x$

28. $\dfrac{6y^6 - 9y^4 + 12y^2}{3y^2}$ $2y^4 - 3y^2 + 4$

VIDEO

29. $\dfrac{-8x^2y^2 + 4x^2y - 2xy^2}{-2xy}$ $4xy - 2x + y$

30. $\dfrac{-9ab^2 - 6a^3b^3}{-3ab^2}$ $3 + 2a^2b$

31. $(x^2y^3 - 3x^3y^2) \div (x^2y)$ $y^2 - 3xy$

32. $(4h^5k - 6h^2k^2) \div (-2h^2k)$ $-2h^3 + 3k$

⟨3⟩ Dividing a Polynomial by a Binomial

Complete each division and identify the quotient and remainder. See Example 3.

33. $\begin{array}{r} 2 \\ x - 1\overline{)2x - 3} \\ \underline{2x - 2} \end{array}$

$2, -1$

34. $\begin{array}{r} -3 \\ x + 2\overline{)-3x + 4} \\ \underline{-3x - 6} \end{array}$

VIDEO

$-3, 10$

35. $\begin{array}{r} x \\ x - 3\overline{)x^2 + 2x + 1} \\ \underline{x^2 - 3x} \end{array}$

$x + 5, 16$

36. $\begin{array}{r} x \\ x + 4\overline{)x^2 - 3x + 2} \\ \underline{x^2 + 4x} \end{array}$

$x - 7, 30$

Find the quotient and remainder for each division. Check by using the fact that dividend = (quotient)(divisor) + remainder. See Example 4.

37. $(x^2 + 5x + 13) \div (x + 3)$ $x + 2, 7$

38. $(x^2 + 3x + 6) \div (x + 3)$ $x, 6$

39. $(2x) \div (x + 5)$ $2, -10$

40. $(5x) \div (x - 1)$ $5, 5$

41. $(a^3 + 4a - 3) \div (a - 2)$ $a^2 + 2a + 8, 13$

42. $(w^3 + 2w^2 - 3) \div (w - 2)$ $w^2 + 4w + 8, 13$

VIDEO

43. $(x^2 - 3x) \div (x + 1)$ $x - 4, 4$

44. $(3x^2) \div (x + 1)$ $3x - 3, 3$

45. $(h^3 - 27) \div (h - 3)$ $h^2 + 3h + 9, 0$

46. $(w^3 + 1) \div (w + 1)$ $w^2 - w + 1, 0$

47. $(6x^2 - 13x + 7) \div (3x - 2)$ $2x - 3, 1$

48. $(4b^2 + 25b - 3) \div (4b + 1)$ $b + 6, -9$

49. $(x^3 - x^2 + x - 2) \div (x - 1)$ $x^2 + 1, -1$

50. $(a^3 - 3a^2 + 4a - 4) \div (a - 2)$ $a^2 - a + 2, 0$

Write each expression in the form

$$\textit{quotient} + \frac{\textit{remainder}}{\textit{divisor}}.$$

See Example 5.

51. $\dfrac{3x}{x - 5}$ $3 + \dfrac{15}{x - 5}$

52. $\dfrac{2x}{x - 1}$ $2 + \dfrac{2}{x - 1}$

53. $\dfrac{-x}{x + 3}$ $-1 + \dfrac{3}{x + 3}$

54. $\dfrac{-3x}{x + 1}$ $-3 + \dfrac{3}{x + 1}$

55. $\dfrac{x - 1}{x}$ $1 - \dfrac{1}{x}$

56. $\dfrac{a - 5}{a}$ $1 - \dfrac{5}{a}$

57. $\dfrac{3x + 1}{x}$ $3 + \dfrac{1}{x}$

58. $\dfrac{2y + 1}{y}$ $2 + \dfrac{1}{y}$

59. $\dfrac{x^2}{x + 1}$ $x - 1 + \dfrac{1}{x + 1}$

60. $\dfrac{x^2}{x - 1}$ $x + 1 + \dfrac{1}{x - 1}$

61. $\dfrac{x^2 + 4}{x + 2}$ $x - 2 + \dfrac{8}{x + 2}$

62. $\dfrac{x^2 + 1}{x - 1}$ $x + 1 + \dfrac{2}{x - 1}$

63. $\dfrac{x^3}{x - 2}$ $x^2 + 2x + 4 + \dfrac{8}{x - 2}$

64. $\dfrac{x^3 - 1}{x + 1}$ $x^2 - x + 1 + \dfrac{-2}{x + 1}$

65. $\dfrac{x^3 + 3}{x}$ $x^2 + \dfrac{3}{x}$

66. $\dfrac{2x^2 + 4}{2x}$ $x + \dfrac{2}{x}$

Miscellaneous

Find each quotient.

67. $-6a^3b \div (2a^2b)$ $-3a$

68. $-14x^7 \div (-7x^2)$ $2x^5$

69. $-8w^9t^7 \div (-2w^4t^3)$ $4w^5t^4$

70. $-9y^7z^{11} \div (3y^3z^4)$ $-3y^4z^7$

71. $(3a - 12) \div (-3)$ $-a + 4$

72. $(-6z + 3z^2) \div (-3z)$ $2 - z$

73. $(3x^2 - 9x) \div (3x)$ $x - 3$

74. $(5x^3 + 15x^2 - 25x) \div (5x)$ $x^2 + 3x - 5$

75. $(12x^4 - 4x^3 + 6x^2) \div (-2x^2)$ $-6x^2 + 2x - 3$

76. $(-9x^3 + 3x^2 - 15x) \div (-3x)$ $3x^2 - x + 5$

77. $(t^2 - 5t - 36) \div (t - 9)$ $t + 4$

78. $(b^2 + 2b - 35) \div (b - 5)$ $b + 7$

VIDEO

79. $(6w^2 - 7w - 5) \div (3w - 5)$ $2w + 1$

80. $(4z^2 + 23z - 6) \div (4z - 1)$ $z + 6$

81. $(8x^3 + 27) \div (2x + 3)$ $4x^2 - 6x + 9$

82. $(8y^3 - 1) \div (2y - 1)$ $4y^2 + 2y + 1$

83. $(t^3 - 3t^2 + 5t - 6) \div (t - 2)$ $t^2 - t + 3$

84. $(2u^3 - 13u^2 - 8u + 7) \div (u - 7)$ $2u^2 + u - 1$

85. $(-6v^2 - 4 + 9v + v^3) \div (v - 4)$ $v^2 - 2v + 1$

86. $(14y + 8y^2 + y^3 + 12) \div (6 + y)$ $y^2 + 2y + 2$

Solve each problem.

87. ***Area of a rectangle.*** The area of a rectangular billboard is $x^2 + x - 30$ square meters. If the length is $x + 6$ meters, find a binomial that represents the width. $x - 5$ meters

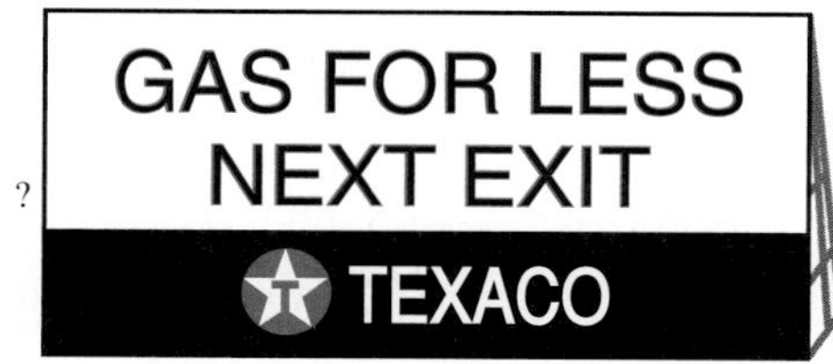

Figure for Exercise 87

88. ***Perimeter of a rectangle.*** The perimeter of a rectangular backyard is $6x + 6$ yards. If the width is x yards, find a binomial that represents the length. $2x + 3$ yards

Figure for Exercise 88

Getting More Involved

89. ***Exploration***

Divide $x^3 - 1$ by $x - 1$, $x^4 - 1$ by $x - 1$, and $x^5 - 1$ by $x - 1$. What is the quotient when $x^9 - 1$ is divided by $x - 1$?
$x^8 + x^7 + x^6 + x^5 + x^4 + x^3 + x^2 + x + 1$

90. ***Exploration***

Divide $a^3 - b^3$ by $a - b$ and $a^4 - b^4$ by $a - b$. What is the quotient when $a^8 - b^8$ is divided by $a - b$?
$a^7 + a^6b + a^5b^2 + a^4b^3 + a^3b^4 + a^2b^5 + ab^6 + b^7$

91. ***Discussion***

Are the expressions $\frac{10x}{5x}$, $10x \div 5x$, and $(10x) \div (5x)$ equivalent? Before you answer, review the order of operations in Section 1.5 and evaluate each expression for $x = 3$.
$10x \div 5x$ is not equivalent to the other two.

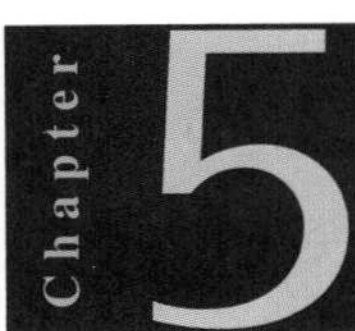

Wrap-Up

Summary

The Rules of Exponents		**Examples**
The following rules hold for any integers m and n, and nonzero real numbers a and b.		
Zero exponent	$a^0 = 1$	$(-3)^0 = 1, \quad -3^0 = -1$
Product rule for exponents	$a^m \cdot a^n = a^{m+n}$	$a^2 \cdot a^3 = a^5, \quad b^{-5} \cdot b^3 = b^{-2}$
Quotient rule for exponents	$\dfrac{a^m}{a^n} = a^{m-n}$	$x^8 \div x^2 = x^6, \quad \dfrac{y^{-3}}{y^{-7}} = y^4$
Power of a power rule	$(a^m)^n = a^{mn}$	$(2^2)^3 = 2^6, \quad (w^{-3})^{-4} = w^{12}$
Power of a product rule	$(ab)^n = a^n b^n$	$(2t)^3 = 8t^3, \quad (3t^{-2})^4 = 81t^{-8}$
Power of a quotient rule	$\left(\dfrac{a}{b}\right)^n = \dfrac{a^n}{b^n}$	$\left(\dfrac{x}{3}\right)^3 = \dfrac{x^3}{27}, \quad \left(\dfrac{a^{-3}}{b^{-4}}\right)^{-2} = \dfrac{a^6}{b^8}$

Negative Exponents		**Examples**
Negative integral exponents	If n is a positive integer and a is a nonzero real number, then $a^{-n} = \dfrac{1}{a^n}$.	$3^{-2} = \dfrac{1}{3^2}, \quad x^{-5} = \dfrac{1}{x^5}$
Rules for negative exponents	If a is a nonzero real number and n is a positive integer, then $a^{-1} = \dfrac{1}{a}, \dfrac{1}{a^{-n}} = a^n, a^{-n} = \left(\dfrac{1}{a}\right)^n,$ and $\left(\dfrac{a}{b}\right)^{-n} = \left(\dfrac{b}{a}\right)^n$.	$5^{-1} = \dfrac{1}{5}, \quad \dfrac{1}{x^{-3}} = x^3$ $2^{-3} = \left(\dfrac{1}{2}\right)^3$ $\left(\dfrac{2}{3}\right)^{-3} = \left(\dfrac{3}{2}\right)^3$

Scientific Notation

		Examples
Converting from scientific notation	1. Find the number of places to move the decimal point by examining the exponent on the 10. 2. Move to the right for a positive exponent and to the left for a negative exponent.	$5.6 \times 10^3 = 5600$ $9 \times 10^{-4} = 0.0009$
Converting into scientific notation (positive numbers)	1. Count the number of places (n) that the decimal point must be moved so that it will follow the first nonzero digit of the number. 2. If the original number was larger than 10, use 10^n. 3. If the original number was smaller than 1, use 10^{-n}.	$304.6 = 3.046 \times 10^2$ $0.0035 = 3.5 \times 10^{-3}$

Polynomials

		Examples
Term	A number or the product of a number and one or more variables raised to powers	$5x^3, -4x, 7$
Polynomial	A single term or a finite sum of terms	$2x^5 - 9x^2 + 11$
Degree of a polynomial	The highest degree of any of the terms	Degree of $2x - 9$ is 1. Degree of $5x^3 - x^2$ is 3.
Naming a polynomial	A polynomial can be named with a letter such as P or $P(x)$ (function notation).	$P = x^2 - 1$ $P(x) = x^2 - 1$
Evaluating a polynomial	The value of a polynomial is the real number that is obtained when the variable (x) is replaced with a real number.	If $x = 3$ then $P = 8$, or $P(3) = 8$.

Adding, Subtracting, and Multiplying Polynomials

		Examples
Add or subtract polynomials	Add or subtract the like terms.	$(x + 1) + (x - 4) = 2x - 3$ $(x^2 - 3x) - (4x^2 - x)$ $= -3x^2 - 2x$
Multiply monomials	Use the product rule for exponents.	$-2x^5 \cdot 6x^8 = -12x^{13}$
Multiply polynomials	Multiply each term of one polynomial by every term of the other polynomial, then combine like terms.	$(x - 1)(x^2 + 2x + 5)$ $= x(x^2 + 2x + 5) - 1(x^2 + 2x + 5)$ $= x^3 + 2x^2 + 5x - x^2 - 2x - 5$ $= x^3 + x^2 + 3x - 5$

Binomials		**Examples**
FOIL	A method for multiplying two binomials quickly	$(x - 2)(x + 3) = x^2 + x - 6$
Square of a sum	$(a + b)^2 = a^2 + 2ab + b^2$	$(x + 3)^2 = x^2 + 6x + 9$
Square of a difference	$(a - b)^2 = a^2 - 2ab + b^2$	$(m - 5)^2 = m^2 - 10m + 25$
Product of a sum and a difference	$(a - b)(a + b) = a^2 - b^2$	$(x + 2)(x - 2) = x^2 - 4$

Dividing Polynomials		**Examples**
Dividing monomials	Use the quotient rule for exponents	$8x^5 \div (2x^2) = 4x^3$
Divide a polynomial by a monomial	Divide each term of the polynomial by the monomial.	$\dfrac{3x^5 + 9x}{3x} = x^4 + 3$
Divide a polynomial by a binomial	If the divisor is a binomial, use long division. (quotient)(divisor) + (remainder) = dividend	$x - 7 \leftarrow$ Quotient Divisor $\rightarrow x + 2\overline{)x^2 - 5x - 4} \leftarrow$ Dividend $\underline{x^2 + 2x}$ $-7x - 4$ $\underline{-7x - 14}$ $10 \leftarrow$ Remainder

Enriching Your Mathematical Word Power

For each mathematical term, choose the correct meaning.

1. integral exponent
a. an exponent that is an integer
b. a positive exponent
c. a rational exponent
d. a fractional exponent a

2. scientific notation
a. the notation of rational exponents
b. the notation of algebra
c. a notation for expressing large or small numbers with powers of 10
d. radical notation c

3. term
a. an expression containing a number or the product of a number and one or more variables
b. the amount of time spent in this course
c. a word that describes a number
d. a variable a

4. polynomial
a. four or more terms
b. many numbers
c. a sum of four or more numbers
d. a single term or a finite sum of terms d

5. degree of a polynomial
a. the number of terms in a polynomial
b. the highest degree of any of the terms of a polynomial
c. the value of a polynomial when $x = 0$
d. the largest coefficient of any of the terms of a polynomial b

6. leading coefficient
a. the first coefficient
b. the largest coefficient
c. the coefficient of the first term when a polynomial is written with decreasing exponents
d. the most important coefficient c

7. monomial
a. a single polynomial
b. one number
c. an equation that has only one solution
d. a polynomial that has one term d

8. FOIL
a. a method for adding polynomials
b. first, outer, inner, last
c. an equation with no solution
d. a polynomial with five terms b

9. dividend
a. a in a/b
b. b in a/b
c. the result of a/b
d. what a bank pays on deposits a

10. divisor
a. a in a/b
b. b in a/b
c. the result of a/b
d. two visors b

11. quotient
a. a in a/b
b. b in a/b
c. a/b
d. the divisor plus the remainder c

12. binomial
a. a polynomial with two terms
b. any two numbers
c. the two coordinates in an ordered pair
d. an equation with two variables a

Review Exercises

5.1 The Rules of Exponents

Simplify each expression. Assume all variables represent nonzero real numbers.

1. $-5^0 + 3^0$ 0
2. $-4^0 - 3^0$ -2
3. $-3a^3 \cdot 2a^4$ $-6a^7$
4. $2y^{10}(-3y^{20})$ $-6y^{30}$
5. $\dfrac{-10b^5c^9}{2b^5c^3}$ $-5c^6$
6. $\dfrac{-30k^3y^9}{15k^3y^2}$ $-2y^7$
7. $(b^5)^6$ b^{30}
8. $(y^5)^8$ y^{40}
9. $(-2x^3y^2)^3$ $-8x^9y^6$
10. $(-3a^4b^6)^4$ $81a^{16}b^{24}$
11. $\left(\dfrac{2a}{b^2}\right)^3$ $\dfrac{8a^3}{b^6}$
12. $\left(\dfrac{3y^2}{2}\right)^3$ $\dfrac{27y^6}{8}$
13. $\left(\dfrac{-6x^2y^5}{-3z^6}\right)^3$ $\dfrac{8x^6y^{15}}{z^{18}}$
14. $\left(\dfrac{-3a^4b^8}{6a^3b^{12}}\right)^4$ $\dfrac{a^4}{16b^{16}}$

5.2 Negative Exponents and Scientific Notation

Simplify each expression. Assume all variables represent nonzero real numbers. Use only positive exponents in answers.

15. 2^{-3} $\dfrac{1}{8}$
16. -2^{-4} $-\dfrac{1}{16}$
17. $\left(\dfrac{1}{7}\right)^{-1}$ 7
18. $\left(\dfrac{1}{2}\right)^{-2}$ 4
19. $x^5 \cdot x^{-8}$ $\dfrac{1}{x^3}$
20. $a^{-3}a^{-9}$ $\dfrac{1}{a^{12}}$
21. $\dfrac{a^{-8}}{a^{-12}}$ a^4
22. $\dfrac{a^{10}}{a^{-4}}$ a^{14}
23. $(x^{-3})^4$ $\dfrac{1}{x^{12}}$
24. $(x^5)^{-10}$ $\dfrac{1}{x^{50}}$
25. $(2x^{-3})^{-3}$ $\dfrac{x^9}{8}$
26. $(3y^{-5})^2$ $\dfrac{9}{y^{10}}$
27. $\left(\dfrac{a}{3b^{-3}}\right)^{-2}$ $\dfrac{9}{a^2b^6}$
28. $\left(\dfrac{a^{-2}}{5b}\right)^{-3}$ $125a^6b^3$

Write each number in standard notation.

29. 8.36×10^6 8,360,000
30. 3.4×10^7 34,000,000
31. 5.7×10^{-4} 0.00057
32. 4×10^{-3} 0.004

Write each number in scientific notation.

33. 8,070,000 8.07×10^6
34. 90,000 9×10^4
35. 0.000709 7.09×10^{-4}
36. 0.0000005 5×10^{-7}

Perform each computation without a calculator. Write the answer in scientific notation.

37. $(5(2 \times 10^4))^3$ 1×10^{15}
38. $(6(2 \times 10^{-3}))^2$ 1.44×10^{-4}
39. $\dfrac{(2 \times 10^{-9})(3 \times 10^7)}{5(6 \times 10^{-4})}$ 2×10^1
40. $\dfrac{(3 \times 10^{12})(5 \times 10^4)}{30 \times 10^{-9}}$ 5×10^{24}
41. $\dfrac{(4{,}000{,}000{,}000)(0.0000006)}{(0.000012)(2{,}000{,}000)}$ 1×10^2
42. $\dfrac{(1200)(0.00002)}{0.0000004}$ 6×10^4

5.3 Addition and Subtraction of Polynomials

Perform the indicated operations.

43. $(2w - 6) + (3w + 4)$ $5w - 2$
44. $(1 - 3y) + (4y - 6)$ $y - 5$
45. $(x^2 - 2x - 5) - (x^2 + 4x - 9)$ $-6x + 4$
46. $(3 - 5x - x^2) - (x^2 - 7x + 8)$ $-2x^2 + 2x - 5$
47. $(5 - 3w + w^2) + (w^2 - 4w - 9)$ $2w^2 - 7w - 4$
48. $(-2t^2 + 3t - 4) + (t^2 - 7t + 2)$ $-t^2 - 4t - 2$
49. $(4 - 3m - m^2) - (m^2 - 6m + 5)$ $-2m^2 + 3m - 1$
50. $(n^3 - n^2 + 9) - (n^4 - n^3 + 5)$ $-n^4 + 2n^3 - n^2 + 4$

Find the following values.

51. Find the value of the polynomial $x^3 - 9x$ if $x = 3$. 0

52. Find the value of the polynomial $x^2 - 7x + 1$ if $x = 4$. -11

53. Suppose that $P(x) = x^3 - x^2 + x - 1$. Find $P(2)$. 5

54. Suppose that $Q(x) = x^2 - 6x - 8$. Find $Q(-3)$. 19

5.4 Multiplication of Polynomials

Perform the indicated operations.

55. $5x^2 \cdot (-10x^9)$ $-50x^{11}$ **56.** $3h^3t^2 \cdot 2h^2t^5$ $6h^5t^7$

57. $(-11a^7)^2$ $121a^{14}$ **58.** $(12b^3)^2$ $144b^6$

59. $x - 5(x - 3)$ $-4x + 15$

60. $x - 4(x - 9)$ $-3x + 36$

61. $5x + 3(x^2 - 5x + 4)$ $3x^2 - 10x + 12$

62. $5 + 4x^2(x - 5)$ $4x^3 - 20x^2 + 5$

63. $3m^2(5m^3 - m + 2)$ $15m^5 - 3m^3 + 6m^2$

64. $-4a^4(a^2 + 2a + 4)$ $-4a^6 - 8a^5 - 16a^4$

65. $(x - 5)(x^2 - 2x + 10)$ $x^3 - 7x^2 + 20x - 50$

66. $(x + 2)(x^2 - 2x + 4)$ $x^3 + 8$

67. $(x^2 - 2x + 4)(3x - 2)$ $3x^3 - 8x^2 + 16x - 8$

68. $(5x + 3)(x^2 - 5x + 4)$ $5x^3 - 22x^2 + 5x + 12$

5.5 Multiplication of Binomials

Perform the indicated operations.

69. $(q - 6)(q + 8)$ $q^2 + 2q - 48$

70. $(w + 5)(w + 12)$ $w^2 + 17w + 60$

71. $(2t - 3)(t - 9)$ $2t^2 - 21t + 27$

72. $(5r + 1)(5r + 2)$ $25r^2 + 15r + 2$

73. $(4y - 3)(5y + 2)$ $20y^2 - 7y - 6$

74. $(11y + 1)(y + 2)$ $11y^2 + 23y + 2$

75. $(3x^2 + 5)(2x^2 + 1)$ $6x^4 + 13x^2 + 5$

76. $(x^3 - 7)(2x^3 + 7)$ $2x^6 - 7x^3 - 49$

5.6 Special Products

Perform the indicated operations. Try to write only the answers.

77. $(z - 7)(z + 7)$ $z^2 - 49$

78. $(a - 4)(a + 4)$ $a^2 - 16$

79. $(y + 7)^2$ $y^2 + 14y + 49$

80. $(a + 5)^2$ $a^2 + 10a + 25$

81. $(w - 3)^2$ $w^2 - 6w + 9$

82. $(a - 6)^2$ $a^2 - 12a + 36$

83. $(x^2 - 3)(x^2 + 3)$ $x^4 - 9$

84. $(2b^2 - 1)(2b^2 + 1)$ $4b^4 - 1$

85. $(3a + 1)^2$ $9a^2 + 6a + 1$

86. $(1 - 3c)^2$ $1 - 6c + 9c^2$

87. $(4 - y)^2$ $16 - 8y + y^2$

88. $(9 - t)^2$ $81 - 18t + t^2$

5.7 Division of Polynomials

Find each quotient.

89. $-10x^5 \div (2x^3)$ $-5x^2$

90. $-6x^4y^2 \div (-2x^2y^2)$ $3x^2$

91. $\dfrac{6a^5b^9c^6}{-3a^3b^7c^6}$ $-2a^2b^2$ **92.** $\dfrac{-9h^7t^9r^2}{3h^5t^6r^2}$ $-3h^2t^3$

93. $\dfrac{3x - 9}{-3}$ $-x + 3$ **94.** $\dfrac{7 - y}{-1}$ $y - 7$

95. $\dfrac{9x^3 - 6x^2 + 3x}{-3x}$ $-3x^2 + 2x - 1$

96. $\dfrac{-8x^3y^5 + 4x^2y^4 - 2xy^3}{2xy^2}$ $-4x^2y^3 + 2xy^2 - y$

97. $(a - 1) \div (1 - a)$ -1

98. $(t - 3) \div (3 - t)$ -1

99. $(m^4 - 16) \div (m - 2)$ $m^3 + 2m^2 + 4m + 8$

100. $(x^4 - 1) \div (x - 1)$ $x^3 + x^2 + x + 1$

Find the quotient and remainder.

101. $(3m^3 - 9m^2 + 18m) \div (3m)$ $m^2 - 3m + 6,\ 0$

102. $(8x^3 - 4x^2 - 18x) \div (2x)$ $4x^2 - 2x - 9,\ 0$

103. $(b^2 - 3b + 5) \div (b + 2)$ $b - 5,\ 15$

104. $(r^2 - 5r + 9) \div (r - 3)$ $r - 2,\ 3$

105. $(4x^2 - 9) \div (2x + 1)$ $2x - 1,\ -8$

106. $(9y^3 + 2y) \div (3y + 2)$ $3y^2 - 2y + 2,\ -4$

107. $(x^3 + x^2 - 11x + 10) \div (x - 1)$ $x^2 + 2x - 9,\ 1$

108. $(y^3 - 9y^2 + 3y - 6) \div (y + 1)$ $y^2 - 10y + 13,\ -19$

Write each expression in the form

$$\text{quotient} + \frac{\text{remainder}}{\text{divisor}}.$$

109. $\dfrac{2x}{x - 3}$ $2 + \dfrac{6}{x - 3}$

110. $\dfrac{3x}{x - 4}$ $3 + \dfrac{12}{x - 4}$

111. $\dfrac{2x}{1 - x}$ $-2 + \dfrac{2}{1 - x}$

112. $\dfrac{3x}{5 - x}$ $-3 + \dfrac{15}{5 - x}$

113. $\dfrac{x^2 - 3}{x + 1}$ $x - 1 + \dfrac{-2}{x + 1}$

114. $\dfrac{x^2 + 3x + 1}{x - 3}$ $x + 6 + \dfrac{19}{x - 3}$

115. $\frac{x^2}{x+1}$ $x - 1 + \frac{1}{x+1}$

116. $\frac{-2x^2}{x-3}$ $-2x - 6 + \frac{-18}{x-3}$

Miscellaneous

Perform the indicated operations.

117. $(x + 3)(x + 7)$ $x^2 + 10x + 21$

118. $(k + 5)(k + 4)$ $k^2 + 9k + 20$

119. $(t - 3y)(t - 4y)$ $t^2 - 7ty + 12y^2$

120. $(t + 7z)(t + 6z)$ $t^2 + 13tz + 42z^2$

121. $(2x^3)^0 + (2y)^0$ 2 **122.** $(4y^2 - 9)^0$ 1

123. $(-3ht^6)^3$ $-27h^3t^{18}$

124. $(-9y^3c^4)^2$ $81y^6c^8$

125. $(2w + 3)(w - 6)$ $2w^2 - 9w - 18$

126. $(3x + 5)(2x - 6)$ $6x^2 - 8x - 30$

127. $(3u - 5v)(3u + 5v)$ $9u^2 - 25v^2$

128. $(9x^2 - 2)(9x^2 + 2)$ $81x^4 - 4$

129. $(3h + 5)^2$ $9h^2 + 30h + 25$

130. $(4v - 3)^2$ $16v^2 - 24v + 9$

131. $(x + 3)^3$ $x^3 + 9x^2 + 27x + 27$

132. $(k - 10)^3$ $k^3 - 30k^2 + 300k - 1000$

133. $(-7s^2t)(-2s^3t^5)$ $14s^5t^6$

134. $-5w^3r^2 \cdot 2w^4r^8$ $-10w^7r^{10}$

135. $\left(\frac{k^4m^2}{2k^2m^2}\right)^4$ $\frac{k^8}{16}$ **136.** $\left(\frac{-6h^3y^5}{2h^7y^2}\right)^4$ $\frac{81y^{12}}{h^{16}}$

137. $(5x^2 - 8x - 8) - (4x^2 + x - 3)$ $x^2 - 9x - 5$

138. $(4x^2 - 6x - 8) - (9x^2 - 5x + 7)$ $-5x^2 - x - 15$

139. $(2x^2 - 2x - 3) + (3x^2 + x - 9)$ $5x^2 - x - 12$

140. $(x^2 - 3x - 1) + (x^2 - 2x + 1)$ $2x^2 - 5x$

141. $(x + 4)(x^2 - 5x + 1)$ $x^3 - x^2 - 19x + 4$

142. $(2x^2 - 7x + 4)(x + 3)$ $2x^3 - x^2 - 17x + 12$

143. $(x^2 + 4x - 12) \div (x - 2)$ $x + 6$

144. $(a^2 - 3a - 10) \div (a - 5)$ $a + 2$

Applications

Solve each problem.

145. ***Roundball court.*** The length of a basketball court is 44 feet more than its width w. Find polynomials $P(w)$ and $A(w)$ that represent its perimeter and area. Find $P(50)$ and $A(50)$. $P(w) = 4w + 88, A(w) = w^2 + 44w$, $P(50) = 288$ ft, $A(50) = 4700$ ft^2

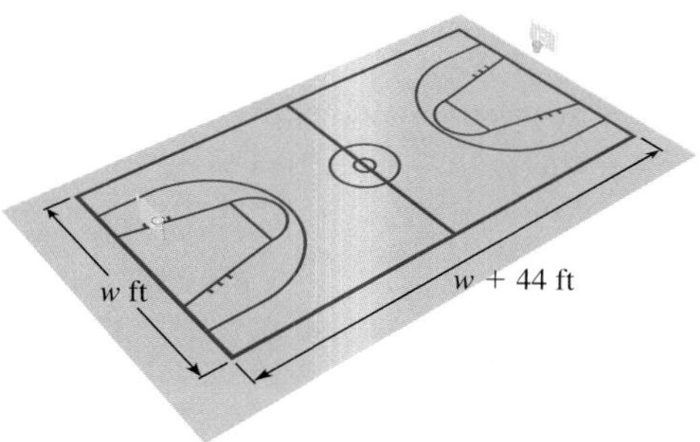

Figure for Exercise 145

146. ***Badminton court.*** The width of a badminton court is 24 feet less than its length x. Find polynomials $P(x)$ and $A(x)$ that represent its perimeter and area. Find $P(44)$ and $A(44)$. $P(x) = 4x - 48, A(x) = x^2 - 24x$, $P(44) = 128$ ft, $A(44) = 880$ ft^2

147. ***Smoke alert.*** A retailer of smoke alarms knows that at a price of p dollars each, she can sell $600 - 15p$ smoke alarms per week. Find a polynomial $R(p)$ that represents the weekly revenue for the smoke alarms. Find the revenue for a week in which the price is \$12 per smoke alarm. Use the bar graph to find the price per smoke alarm that gives the maximum weekly revenue. $R(p) = -15p^2 + 600p$, \$5040, \$20

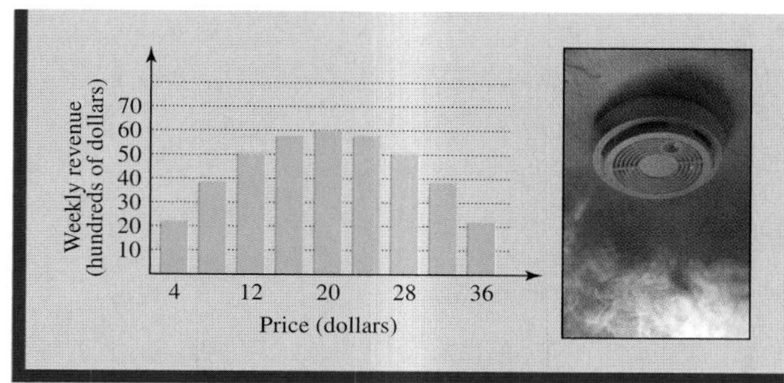

Figure for Exercise 147

148. ***Boom box sales.*** A retailer of boom boxes knows that at a price of q dollars each, he can sell $900 - 3q$ boom boxes per month. Find a polynomial $R(q)$ that represents the monthly revenue for the boom boxes. How many boom boxes will he sell if the price is \$300 each? $R(q) = -3q^2 + 900q$, 0

149. ***CD savings.*** Valerie invested \$12,000 in a CD that paid 6% compounded annually for 8 years. What was the value of her investment at the end of the eighth year? \$19,126.18

150. ***Risky business.*** Tony invested \$45,000 in Kirk's new business. If Kirk does well he will pay Tony back in 5 years with interest at 5% compounded annually. If the business succeeds, then how much will Tony receive in 5 years? \$57,432.67

151. ***Saving for a house.*** Newlyweds Michael and Leslie want to have \$30,000 for a down payment on a house in 4 years. If they can earn 9% interest compounded annually, then how much would they have to have now to reach this goal? \$21,252.76

152. ***Opening a business.*** Sandy wants to start a florist shop in 6 years and figures that she will need \$20,000 to do it. If she can earn 7% interest compounded annually, then how much does she need now to reach this goal? \$13,326.84

Chapter 5 Test

Use the rules of exponents to simplify each expression. Write answers without negative exponents.

1. $-5x^3 \cdot 7x^5$ $-35x^8$

2. $3x^3y \cdot (2xy^4)^2$ $12x^5y^9$

3. $-4a^6b^5 \div (2a^5b)$ $-2ab^4$

4. $3x^{-2} \cdot 5x^7$ $15x^5$

5. $\left(\frac{-2a}{b^2}\right)^5$ $\frac{-32a^5}{b^{10}}$

6. $\frac{-6a^7b^6c^2}{-2a^3b^8c^2}$ $\frac{3a^4}{b^2}$

7. $\frac{6t^{-7}}{2t^9}$ $\frac{3}{t^{16}}$

8. $\frac{w^{-6}}{w^{-4}}$ $\frac{1}{w^2}$

9. $(-3s^{-3}t^2)^{-2}$ $\frac{s^6}{9t^4}$

10. $(-2x^{-6}y)^3$ $\frac{-8y^3}{x^{18}}$

Convert to scientific notation.

11. 5,433,000 5.433×10^6

12. 0.0000065 6.5×10^{-6}

Perform each computation by converting to scientific notation. Give answers in scientific notation.

13. (80,000)(0.000006) 4.8×10^{-1}

14. $(0.0000003)^4$ 8.1×10^{-27}

Perform the indicated operations.

15. $(7x^3 - x^2 - 6) + (5x^2 + 2x - 5)$ $7x^3 + 4x^2 + 2x - 11$

16. $(x^2 - 3x - 5) - (2x^2 + 6x - 7)$ $-x^2 - 9x + 2$

17. $\frac{6y^3 - 9y^2}{-3y}$ $-2y^2 + 3y$

18. $(x - 2) \div (2 - x)$ -1

19. $(x^3 - 2x^2 - 4x + 3) \div (x - 3)$ $x^2 + x - 1$

20. $3x^2(5x^3 - 7x^2 + 4x - 1)$ $15x^5 - 21x^4 + 12x^3 - 3x^2$

Find the products.

21. $(x + 5)(x - 2)$ $x^2 + 3x - 10$

22. $(3a - 7)(2a + 5)$ $6a^2 + a - 35$

23. $(a - 7)^2$ $a^2 - 14a + 49$

24. $(4x + 3y)^2$ $16x^2 + 24xy + 9y^2$

25. $(b - 3)(b + 3)$ $b^2 - 9$

26. $(3t^2 - 7)(3t^2 + 7)$ $9t^4 - 49$

27. $(4x^2 - 3)(x^2 + 2)$ $4x^4 + 5x^2 - 6$

28. $(x - 2)(x + 3)(x - 4)$ $x^3 - 3x^2 - 10x + 24$

Write each expression in the form

$$quotient + \frac{remainder}{divisor}.$$

29. $\frac{2x}{x - 3}$ $2 + \frac{6}{x - 3}$

30. $\frac{x^2 - 3x + 5}{x + 2}$ $x - 5 + \frac{15}{x + 2}$

Solve each problem.

31. Find the value of the polynomial $x^3 - 5x + 1$ when $x = 3$. 13

32. Suppose that $P(x) = x^2 - 5x + 2$. Find $P(0)$ and $P(3)$. 2, -4

33. Find the quotient and remainder when $x^2 - 5x + 9$ is divided by $x - 3$. $x - 2$, 3

34. Subtract $3x^2 - 4x - 9$ from $x^2 - 3x + 6$. $-2x^2 + x + 15$

35. The width of a pool table is x feet, and the length is 4 feet longer than the width. Find polynomials $A(x)$ and $P(x)$ that represent the area and perimeter of the pool table. Find $A(4)$ and $P(4)$.
$A(x) = x^2 + 4x$, $P(x) = 4x + 8$, $A(4) = 32$ ft², $P(4) = 24$ ft

36. If a manufacturer charges q dollars each for footballs, then he can sell $3000 - 150q$ footballs per week. Find a polynomial $R(q)$ that represents the revenue for one week. Find the weekly revenue if the price is \$8 for each football.
$R(q) = -150q^2 + 3000q$, \$14,400

37. Gordon got a \$15,000 bonus and has decided to invest it in the stock market until he retires in 35 years. If he averages 9% return on the investment compounded annually, then how much will he have in 35 years? \$306,209.52

Making Connections | A Review of Chapters 1–5

Evaluate each arithmetic expression.

1. $-16 \div (-2)$ 8

2. $-16 \div \left(-\frac{1}{2}\right)$ 32

3. $(-5)^2 - 3(-5) + 1$ 41

4. $-5^2 - 4(-5) + 3$ -2

5. $2^{15} \div 2^{10}$ 32

6. $2^6 - 2^5$ 32

7. $-3^2 \cdot 4^2$ -144

8. $(-3 \cdot 4)^2$ 144

9. $\left(\frac{1}{2}\right)^3 + \frac{1}{2}$ $\frac{5}{8}$

10. $\left(\frac{2}{3}\right)^2 - \frac{1}{3}$ $\frac{1}{9}$

11. $(5 + 3)^2$ 64

12. $5^2 + 3^2$ 34

13. $3^{-1} + 2^{-1}$ $\frac{5}{6}$

14. $2^{-2} - 3^{-2}$ $\frac{5}{36}$

15. $(30 - 1)(30 + 1)$ 899

16. $(30 - 1) \div (1 - 30)$ -1

Perform the indicated operations.

17. $(x + 3)(x + 5)$
$x^2 + 8x + 15$

18. $x + 3(x + 5)$
$4x + 15$

19. $-5t^3v \cdot 3t^2v^6$
$-15t^5v^7$

20. $(-10t^3v^2) \div (-2t^2v)$
$5tv$

21. $(x^2 + 8x + 15) + (x + 5)$ $x^2 + 9x + 20$

22. $(x^2 + 8x + 15) - (x + 5)$ $x^2 + 7x + 10$

23. $(x^2 + 8x + 15) \div (x + 5)$ $x + 3$

24. $(x^2 + 8x + 15)(x + 5)$ $x^3 + 13x^2 + 55x + 75$

25. $(-6y^3 + 8y^2) \div (-2y^2)$ $3y - 4$

26. $(18y^4 - 12y^3 + 3y^2) \div (3y^2)$ $6y^2 - 4y + 1$

Solve each equation.

27. $2x + 1 = 0$ $\left\{-\frac{1}{2}\right\}$

28. $x - 7 = 0$ $\{7\}$

29. $\frac{3}{4}x - 3 = \frac{1}{2}$ $\left\{\frac{14}{3}\right\}$

30. $\frac{x}{2} - \frac{3}{4} = \frac{1}{8}$ $\left\{\frac{7}{4}\right\}$

31. $2(x - 3) = 3(x - 2)$ $\{0\}$

32. $2(3x - 3) = 3(2x - 2)$ All real numbers

Solve.

33. Find the x-intercept for the line $y = 2x + 1$. $\left(-\frac{1}{2}, 0\right)$

34. Find the y-intercept for the line $y = x - 7$. $(0, -7)$

35. Find the slope of the line $y = 2x + 1$. 2

36. Find the slope of the line that goes through (0, 0) and $\left(\frac{1}{2}, \frac{1}{3}\right)$. $\frac{2}{3}$

37. If $y = \frac{3}{4}x - 3$ and y is $\frac{1}{2}$, then what is x? $\frac{14}{3}$

38. Find y if $y = \frac{x}{2} - \frac{3}{4}$ and x is $\frac{1}{2}$. $-\frac{1}{2}$

Solve the problem.

39. ***Average cost.*** Pineapple Recording plans to spend \$100,000 to record a new CD by the Woozies and \$2.25 per CD to manufacture the disks. The polynomial $2.25n + 100{,}000$ represents the total cost in dollars for recording and manufacturing n disks. Find an expression that represents the average cost per disk by dividing the total cost by n. Find the average cost per disk for $n = 1000$, 100,000, and 1,000,000. What happens to the large initial investment of \$100,000 if the company sells one million CDs?

$\frac{2.25n + 100{,}000}{n}$; \$102.25, \$3.25, \$2.35; It averages out to 10 cents per disk.

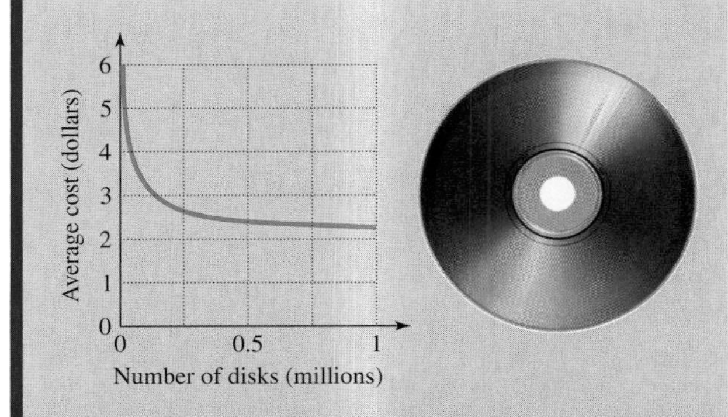

Figure for Exercise 39

Critical Thinking | For Individual or Group Work | Chapter 5

These exercises can be solved by a variety of techniques, which may or may not require algebra. So be creative and think critically. Explain all answers. Answers are in the Instructor's Edition of this text.

1. ***Counting cubes.*** What is the total number of cubes that are in each of the following diagrams?

a) 

b) 

c) 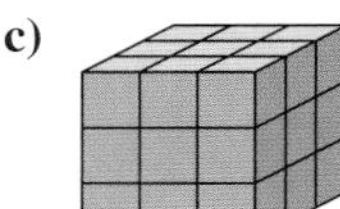

d) 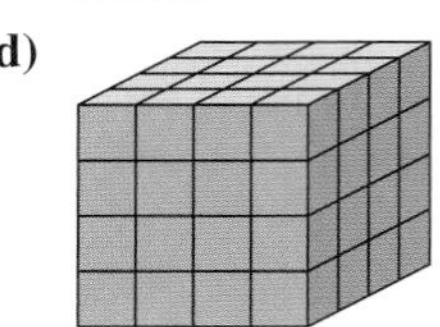

2. ***More cubes.*** Imagine a large cube that is made up of 125 small cubes like those in the previous exercise. What is the total number of cubes that could be found in this arrangement?

3. ***Timely coincidence.*** Starting at 8 A.M. determine the number of times in the next 24 hours for which the hour and minute hands on a clock coincide.

Photo for Exercise 3

4. ***Chess board.*** There are 64 squares on a square chess board. How many squares are neither diagonal squares nor edge squares?

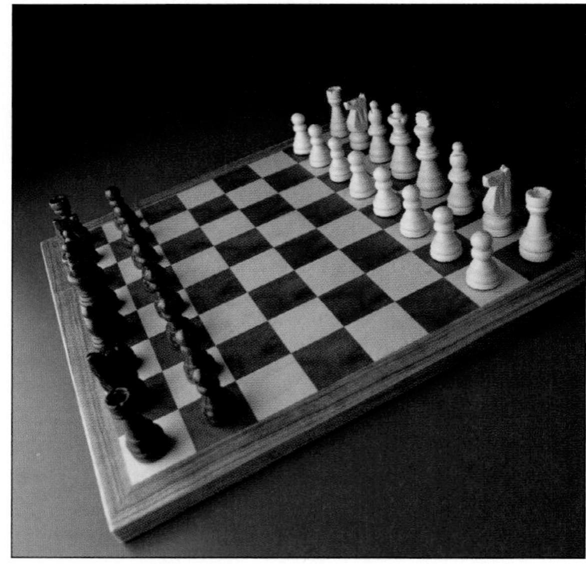

Photo for Exercise 4

5. ***Last digit.*** Find the last digit in 3^{9999}.

6. ***Reconciling remainders.*** Find a positive integer smaller than 500 that has a remainder of 3 when divided by 5, a remainder of 6 when divided by 9, and a remainder of 8 when divided by 11.

7. ***Exact sum.*** Find this sum exactly:

$$\frac{1}{2} + \frac{1}{2^2} + \frac{1}{2^3} + \frac{1}{2^4} + \cdots + \frac{1}{2^{19}}$$

8. ***Ten-digit number.*** Find a 10-digit number whose first digit is the number of 1's in the 10-digit number, whose second digit is the number of 2's in the 10-digit number, whose third digit is the number of 3's in the 10-digit number, and so on. The ninth digit must be the number of nines in the 10-digit number and the tenth digit must be the number of zeros in the 10-digit number.

1. a) 1 **b)** 9 **c)** 36 **d)** 100 **2.** 225 **3.** 22 **4.** 24 **5.** 7 **6.** 393 **7.** $\frac{524{,}287}{524{,}288}$ **8.** 2,100,010,006.

Chapter

6

Factoring

The sport of skydiving was born in the 1930s soon after the military began using parachutes as a means of deploying troops. Today, skydiving is a popular sport around the world.

With as little as 8 hours of ground instruction, first-time jumpers can be ready to make a solo jump. Without the assistance of oxygen, skydivers can jump from as high as 14,000 feet and reach speeds of more than 100 miles per hour as they fall toward the earth. Jumpers usually open their parachutes between 2000 and 3000 feet and then gradually glide down to their landing area. If the jump and the parachute are handled correctly, the landing can be as gentle as jumping off two steps.

Making a jump and floating to earth are only part of the sport of skydiving. For example, in an activity called "relative work skydiving," a team of as many as 920 free-falling skydivers join together to make geometrically-shaped formations. In a related exercise called "canopy relative work," the team members form geometric patterns after their parachutes or canopies have opened. This kind of skydiving takes skill and practice, and teams are not always successful in their attempts.

The amount of time a skydiver has for a free fall depends on the height of the jump and how much the skydiver uses the air to slow the fall.

In Exercises 89 and 90 of Section 6.6 we find the amount of time that it takes a skydiver to fall from a given height.

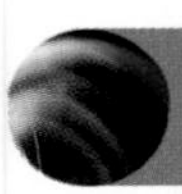

6.1 Factoring Out Common Factors

In This Section

In Chapter 5, you learned how to multiply a monomial and a polynomial. In this section, you will learn how to reverse that multiplication by finding the greatest common factor for the terms of a polynomial and then factoring the polynomial.

⟨1⟩ Prime Factorization of Integers

To **factor** an expression means to write the expression as a product. For example, if we start with 12 and write $12 = 4 \cdot 3$, we have factored 12. Both 4 and 3 are **factors** or **divisors** of 12. There are other factorizations of 12:

$$12 = 2 \cdot 6 \qquad 12 = 1 \cdot 12 \qquad 12 = 2 \cdot 2 \cdot 3 = 2^2 \cdot 3$$

The one that is most useful to us is $12 = 2^2 \cdot 3$, because it expresses 12 as a product of *prime numbers.*

⟨ Teaching Tip ⟩

The fundamental theorem of arithmetic says that the prime factorization is unique. If 1 were allowed to be prime, that would be false. For example, $6 = 2 \cdot 3$ and $6 = 1 \cdot 2 \cdot 3$.

Prime Number

A positive integer larger than 1 that has no positive integral factors other than itself and 1 is called a **prime number.**

The numbers 2, 3, 5, 7, 11, 13, 17, 19, and 23 are the first nine prime numbers. A positive integer larger than 1 that is not a prime is a **composite number.** The numbers 4, 6, 8, 9, 10, and 12 are the first six composite numbers. Every composite number is a product of prime numbers. The **prime factorization** for 12 is $2^2 \cdot 3$.

EXAMPLE 1

Prime factorization

Find the prime factorization for 36.

Solution

We start by writing 36 as a product of two integers:

$36 = 2 \cdot 18$	Write 36 as $2 \cdot 18$.
$= 2 \cdot 2 \cdot 9$	Replace 18 by $2 \cdot 9$.
$= 2 \cdot 2 \cdot 3 \cdot 3$	Replace 9 by $3 \cdot 3$.
$= 2^2 \cdot 3^2$	Use exponential notation.

The prime factorization for 36 is $2^2 \cdot 3^2$.

Now do Exercises 7–12

⟨ Helpful Hint ⟩

The prime factorization of 36 can be found also with a *factoring tree:*

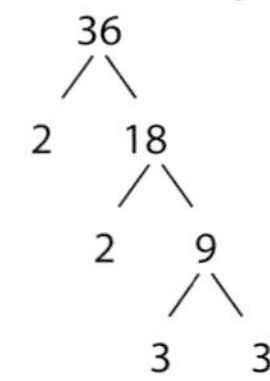

So $36 = 2 \cdot 2 \cdot 3 \cdot 3$.

For larger integers, it is better to use the method shown in Example 2 and to recall some divisibility rules. Even numbers are divisible by 2. If the sum of the digits of a number is divisible by 3, then the number is divisible by 3. Numbers that end in 0 or 5 are divisible by 5. Two-digit numbers with repeated digits (11, 22, 33, . . .) are divisible by 11.

EXAMPLE 2

Factoring a large number

Find the prime factorization for 420.

Solution

Start by dividing 420 by the smallest prime number that will divide into it evenly (without remainder). The smallest prime divisor of 420 is 2.

$$2\overline{)420}\quad 210$$

Now find the smallest prime that will divide evenly into the quotient, 210. The smallest prime divisor of 210 is 2. Continue this procedure, as follows, until the quotient is a prime number:

$$\begin{array}{rl} 2\overline{)420} & \\ 2\overline{)210} & 420 \div 2 = 210 \\ 3\overline{)105} & 210 \div 2 = 105 \\ 5\overline{)35} & 105 \div 3 = 35 \\ 7 & \end{array}$$

The product of all of the prime numbers in this procedure is 420:

$$420 = 2 \cdot 2 \cdot 3 \cdot 5 \cdot 7$$

So the prime factorization of 420 is $2^2 \cdot 3 \cdot 5 \cdot 7$. Note that it is not necessary to divide by the smallest prime divisor at each step. We get the same factorization if we divide by any prime divisor.

Now do Exercises 13–18

‹ Helpful Hint ›

The fact that every composite number has a unique prime factorization is known as the fundamental theorem of arithmetic.

‹2› Greatest Common Factor

The largest integer that is a factor of two or more integers is called the **greatest common factor (GCF)** of the integers. For example, 1, 2, 3, and 6 are common factors of 18 and 24. Because 6 is the largest, 6 is the GCF of 18 and 24. We can use prime factorizations to find the GCF. For example, to find the GCF of 8 and 12, we first factor 8 and 12:

$$8 = 2 \cdot 2 \cdot 2 = 2^3 \qquad 12 = 2 \cdot 2 \cdot 3 = 2^2 \cdot 3$$

We see that the factor 2 appears twice in both 8 and 12. So 2^2, or 4, is the GCF of 8 and 12. Notice that 2 is a factor in both 2^3 and $2^2 \cdot 3$ and that 2^2 is the smallest power of 2 in these factorizations. In general, we can use the following strategy to find the GCF.

Strategy for Finding the GCF for Positive Integers

1. Find the prime factorization for each integer.
2. The GCF is the product of the common prime factors using the smallest exponent that appears on each of them.

If two integers have no common prime factors, then their greatest common factor is 1, because 1 is a factor of every integer. For example, 6 and 35 have no common prime factors because $6 = 2 \cdot 3$ and $35 = 5 \cdot 7$. However, because $6 = 1 \cdot 6$ and $35 = 1 \cdot 35$, the GCF for 6 and 35 is 1.

EXAMPLE 3

Greatest common factor

Find the GCF for each group of numbers.

a) 150, 225 **b)** 216, 360, 504 **c)** 55, 168

‹ Teaching Tip ›

Students often find the GCF for small numbers without factoring. With larger numbers factoring is essential.

Solution

a) First find the prime factorization for each number:

$$\begin{array}{r} 2\underline{)150} \\ 3\underline{)75} \\ 5\underline{)25} \\ 5 \end{array} \qquad \begin{array}{r} 3\underline{)225} \\ 3\underline{)75} \\ 5\underline{)25} \\ 5 \end{array}$$

$$150 = 2 \cdot 3 \cdot 5^2 \qquad 225 = 3^2 \cdot 5^2$$

Because 2 is not a factor of 225, it is not a common factor of 150 and 225. Only 3 and 5 appear in both factorizations. Looking at both $2 \cdot 3 \cdot 5^2$ and $3^2 \cdot 5^2$, we see that the smallest power of 5 is 2 and the smallest power of 3 is 1. So the GCF for 150 and 225 is $3 \cdot 5^2$, or 75.

b) First find the prime factorization for each number:

$$216 = 2^3 \cdot 3^3 \qquad 360 = 2^3 \cdot 3^2 \cdot 5 \qquad 504 = 2^3 \cdot 3^2 \cdot 7$$

The only common prime factors are 2 and 3. The smallest power of 2 in the factorizations is 3, and the smallest power of 3 is 2. So the GCF is $2^3 \cdot 3^2$, or 72.

c) First find the prime factorization for each number:

$$55 = 5 \cdot 11 \qquad 168 = 2^3 \cdot 3 \cdot 7$$

Because there are no common factors other than 1, the GCF is 1.

Now do Exercises 19–28

‹3› Greatest Common Factor for Monomials

To find the GCF for a group of monomials, we use the same procedure as that used for integers.

Strategy for Finding the GCF for Monomials

1. Find the GCF for the coefficients of the monomials.
2. Form the product of the GCF for the coefficients and each variable that is common to all of the monomials, where the exponent on each variable is the smallest power of that variable in any of the monomials.

EXAMPLE 4

Greatest common factor for monomials

Find the greatest common factor for each group of monomials.

a) $15x^2, 9x^3$ **b)** $12x^2y^2, 30x^2yz, 42x^3y$

Solution

a) Since $15 = 3 \cdot 5$ and $9 = 3^2$, the GCF for 15 and 9 is 3. Since the smallest power of x in $15x^2$ and $9x^3$ is 2, the GCF is $3x^2$. If we write these monomials as

$$15x^2 = 5 \cdot 3 \cdot x \cdot x \quad \text{and} \quad 9x^3 = 3 \cdot 3 \cdot x \cdot x \cdot x,$$

we can see that $3x^2$ is the GCF.

b) Since $12 = 2^2 \cdot 3$, $30 = 2 \cdot 3 \cdot 5$, and $42 = 2 \cdot 3 \cdot 7$, the GCF for 12, 30, and 42 is $2 \cdot 3$ or 6. For the common variables x and y, 2 is the smallest power of x and 1 is the smallest power of y. So the GCF for the three monomials is $6x^2y$. Note that z is not in the GCF because it is not in all three monomials.

Now do Exercises 29–40

⟨4⟩ Factoring Out the Greatest Common Factor

In Chapter 5, we used the distributive property to multiply monomials and polynomials. For example,

$$6(5x - 3) = 30x - 18.$$

If we start with $30x - 18$ and write

$$30x - 18 = 6(5x - 3),$$

we have factored $30x - 18$. Because multiplication is the last operation to be performed in $6(5x - 3)$, the expression $6(5x - 3)$ is a product. Because 6 is the GCF for 30 and 18, we have **factored out** the GCF.

EXAMPLE 5

Factoring out the greatest common factor

Factor the following polynomials by factoring out the GCF.

a) $25a^2 + 40a$ **b)** $6x^4 - 12x^3 + 3x^2$ **c)** $x^2y^5 + x^6y^3$

Solution

a) The GCF for the coefficients 25 and 40 is 5. Because the smallest power of the common factor a is 1, we can factor $5a$ out of each term:

$$\begin{aligned} 25a^2 + 40a &= 5a \cdot 5a + 5a \cdot 8 \\ &= 5a(5a + 8) \end{aligned}$$

b) The GCF for 6, 12, and 3 is 3. We can factor x^2 out of each term, since the smallest power of x in the three terms is 2. So factor $3x^2$ out of each term as follows:

$$\begin{aligned} 6x^4 - 12x^3 + 3x^2 &= 3x^2 \cdot 2x^2 - 3x^2 \cdot 4x + 3x^2 \cdot 1 \\ &= 3x^2(2x^2 - 4x + 1) \end{aligned}$$

Check by multiplying: $3x^2(2x^2 - 4x + 1) = 6x^4 - 12x^3 + 3x^2$.

c) The GCF for the numerical coefficients is 1. Both x and y are common to each term. Using the lowest powers of x and y, we get

$$x^2y^5 + x^6y^3 = x^2y^3 \cdot y^2 + x^2y^3 \cdot x^4$$
$$= x^2y^3(y^2 + x^4).$$

Check by multiplying.

Now do Exercises 41–68

Because of the commutative property of multiplication, the common factor can be placed on either side of the other factor. So in Example 5, the answers could be written as $(5a + 8)5a$, $(2x^2 - 4x + 1)3x^2$, and $(y^2 + x^4)x^2y^3$.

‹ Teaching Tip ›

Emphasize the 1 here. Students often write $ab + b = a(b)$.

CAUTION If the GCF is one of the terms of the polynomial, then you must remember to leave a 1 in place of that term when the GCF is factored out. For example,

$$ab + b = a \cdot b + 1 \cdot b = b(a + 1).$$

You should always check your answer by multiplying the factors.

In Example 6, the greatest common factor is a binomial. This type of factoring will be used in factoring trinomials by grouping in Section 6.2.

EXAMPLE 6

A binomial factor

Factor out the greatest common factor.

a) $(a + b)w + (a + b)6$

b) $x(x + 2) + 3(x + 2)$

c) $y(y - 3) - (y - 3)$

‹ Teaching Tip ›

Remind students that the commutative property enables us to place the GCF on the left or right when it is factored out.

Solution

a) The greatest common factor is $a + b$:

$$(a + b)w + (a + b)6 = (a + b)(w + 6)$$

b) The greatest common factor is $x + 2$:

$$x(x + 2) + 3(x + 2) = (x + 3)(x + 2)$$

c) The greatest common factor is $y - 3$:

$$y(y - 3) - (y - 3) = y(y - 3) - 1(y - 3)$$
$$= (y - 1)(y - 3)$$

Now do Exercises 69–76

‹ Teaching Tip ›

Ask students why we say opposite of the GCF rather than negative GCF.

‹5› Factoring Out the Opposite of the GCF

The greatest common factor for $-4x + 2xy$ is $2x$. Note that you can factor out the GCF $(2x)$ or the opposite of the GCF $(-2x)$:

$$-4x + 2xy = 2x(-2 + y) \qquad -4x + 2xy = -2x(2 - y)$$

It is useful to know both of these factorizations. Factoring out the opposite of the GCF will be used in factoring by grouping in Section 6.2 and in factoring trinomials with negative leading coefficients in Section 6.4. Remember to check all factoring by multiplying the factors to see if you get the original polynomial.

EXAMPLE 7

Factoring out the opposite of the GCF

Factor each polynomial twice. First factor out the greatest common factor, and then factor out the opposite of the GCF.

a) $3x - 3y$ **b)** $a - b$

c) $-x^3 + 2x^2 - 8x$

Solution

a) $3x - 3y = 3(x - y)$ Factor out 3.

$= -3(-x + y)$ Factor out -3.

Note that the signs of the terms in parentheses change when -3 is factored out. Check the answers by multiplying.

b) $a - b = 1(a - b)$ Factor out 1, the GCF of a and b.

$= -1(-a + b)$ Factor out -1, the opposite of the GCF.

We can also write $a - b = -1(b - a)$.

c) $-x^3 + 2x^2 - 8x = x(-x^2 + 2x - 8)$ Factor out x.

$= -x(x^2 - 2x + 8)$ Factor out $-x$.

Now do Exercises 77–92

CAUTION Be sure to change the sign of each term in parentheses when you factor out the opposite of the greatest common factor.

Warm-Ups

True or false? Explain your answer.

1. There are only nine prime numbers. False
2. The prime factorization of 32 is $2^3 \cdot 3$. False
3. The integer 51 is a prime number. False
4. The GCF for the integers 12 and 16 is 4. True
5. The GCF for the integers 10 and 21 is 1. True
6. The GCF for the polynomial $x^5y^3 - x^4y^7$ is x^4y^3. True
7. For the polynomial $2x^2y - 6xy^2$ we can factor out either $2xy$ or $-2xy$. True
8. The greatest common factor for the polynomial $8a^3b - 12a^2b$ is $4ab$. False
9. $x - 7 = 7 - x$ for any real number x. False
10. $-3x^2 + 6x = -3x(x - 2)$ for any real number x. True

6.1 Exercises

‹ Study Tips ›

- To get the big picture, survey the chapter that you are studying. Read the headings to get the general idea of the chapter content.
- Read the chapter summary several times while you are working in a chapter to see what's important in the chapter.

Reading and Writing *After reading this section, write out the answers to these questions. Use complete sentences.*

1. What does it mean to factor an expression?
   To factor means to write as a product.
2. What is a prime number? A prime number is an integer greater than 1 that has no factors besides itself and 1.
3. How do you find the prime factorization for a number?
   You can find the prime factorization by dividing by prime factors until the result is prime.
4. What is the greatest common factor for two numbers?
   The GCF for two numbers is the largest number that is a factor of both.
5. What is the greatest common factor for two monomials?
   The GCF for two monomials consists of the GCF of their coefficients and every variable that they have in common raised to the lowest power that appears on the variable.
6. How can you check if you have factored an expression correctly?
   You can check all factoring by multiplying the factors.

‹1› Prime Factorization of Integers

Find the prime factorization of each integer. See Examples 1 and 2.

7. 18 $2 \cdot 3^2$
8. 20 $2^2 \cdot 5$
9. 52 $2^2 \cdot 13$
10. 76 $2^2 \cdot 19$
11. 98 $2 \cdot 7^2$
12. 100 $2^2 \cdot 5^2$
13. 216 $2^3 \cdot 3^3$
14. 248 $2^3 \cdot 31$
15. 460 $2^2 \cdot 5 \cdot 23$
16. 345 $3 \cdot 5 \cdot 23$
17. 924 $2^2 \cdot 3 \cdot 7 \cdot 11$
18. 585 $3^2 \cdot 5 \cdot 13$

‹2› Greatest Common Factor

Find the greatest common factor for each group of integers. See Example 3.

See the Strategy for Finding the GCF for Positive Integers box on page 363.

19. 8, 20 4
20. 18, 42 6
21. 36, 60 12
22. 42, 70 14
23. 40, 48, 88 8
24. 15, 35, 45 5
25. 76, 84, 100 4
26. 66, 72, 120 6
27. 39, 68, 77 1
28. 81, 200, 539 1

‹3› Greatest Common Factor for Monomials

Find the greatest common factor for each group of monomials. See Example 4.

See the Strategy for Finding the GCF for Monomials box on page 364.

29. $6x, 8x^3$ $2x$
30. $12x^2, 4x^3$ $4x^2$
31. $12x^3, 4x^2, 6x$ $2x$
32. $3y^5, 9y^4, 15y^3$ $3y^3$
33. $3x^2y, 2xy^2$ xy
34. $7a^2x^3, 5a^3x$ a^2x
35. $24a^2bc, 60ab^2$ $12ab$
36. $30x^2yz^3, 75x^3yz^6$ $15x^2yz^3$
37. $12u^3v^2, 25s^2t^4$ 1
38. $45m^2n^5, 56a^4b^8$ 1
39. $18a^3b, 30a^2b^2, 54ab^3$ $6ab$
40. $16x^2z, 40xz^2, 72z^3$ $8z$

‹4› Factoring Out the Greatest Common Factor

Complete the factoring of each monomial.

41. $27x = 9(3x)$
42. $51y = 3y(17)$
43. $24t^2 = 8t(3t)$
44. $18u^2 = 3u(6u)$ VIDEO
45. $36y^5 = 4y^2(9y^3)$
46. $42z^4 = 3z^2(14z^2)$
47. $u^4v^3 = uv(u^3v^2)$
48. $x^5y^3 = x^2y(x^3y^2)$
49. $-14m^4n^3 = 2m^4(-7n^3)$
50. $-8y^3z^4 = 4z^3(-2y^3z)$
51. $-33x^4y^3z^2 = -3x^3yz(11xy^2z)$
52. $-96a^3b^4c^5 = -12ab^3c^3(8a^2bc^2)$

Factor out the GCF in each expression. See Example 5.

53. $2w + 4t$ $2(w + 2t)$
54. $6y + 3$ $3(2y + 1)$
55. $12x - 18y$ $6(2x - 3y)$
56. $24a - 36b$ $12(2a - 3b)$
57. $x^3 - 6x$ $x(x^2 - 6)$
58. $10y^4 - 30y^2$ $10y^2(y^2 - 3)$ VIDEO
59. $5ax + 5ay$ $5a(x + y)$
60. $6wz + 15wa$ $3w(2z + 5a)$
61. $h^5 + h^3$ $h^3(h^2 + 1)$
62. $y^6 + y^5$ $y^5(y + 1)$ VIDEO
63. $-2k^7m^4 + 4k^3m^6$ $2k^3m^4(-k^4 + 2m^2)$
64. $-6h^5t^2 + 3h^3t^6$ $3h^3t^2(-2h^2 + t^4)$
65. $2x^3 - 6x^2 + 8x$ $2x(x^2 - 3x + 4)$
66. $6x^3 + 18x^2 + 24x$ $6x(x^2 + 3x + 4)$
67. $12x^4t + 30x^3t - 24x^2t^2$ $6x^2t(2x^2 + 5x - 4t)$
68. $15x^2y^2 - 9xy^2 + 6x^2y$ $3xy(5xy - 3y + 2x)$

Factor out the GCF in each expression. See Example 6.

69. $(x - 3)a + (x - 3)b$ $(x - 3)(a + b)$

70. $(y + 4)3 + (y + 4)z$ $(y + 4)(3 + z)$

71. $x(x - 1) - 5(x - 1)$ $(x - 5)(x - 1)$

VIDEO **72.** $a(a + 1) - 3(a + 1)$ $(a - 3)(a + 1)$

73. $m(m + 9) + (m + 9)$ $(m + 1)(m + 9)$

74. $(x - 2)x - (x - 2)$ $(x - 2)(x - 1)$

75. $a(y + 1)^2 + b(y + 1)^2$ $(a + b)(y + 1)^2$

76. $w(w + 2)^2 + 8(w + 2)^2$ $(w + 8)(w + 2)^2$

⟨5⟩ Factoring Out the Opposite of the GCF

First factor out the GCF, and then factor out the opposite of the GCF. See Example 7.

77. $8x - 8y$ $8(x - y), -8(-x + y)$

78. $2a - 6b$ $2(a - 3b), -2(-a + 3b)$

79. $-4x + 8x^2$ $4x(-1 + 2x), -4x(1 - 2x)$

80. $-5x^2 + 10x$ $5x(-x + 2), -5x(x - 2)$

81. $x - 5$ $1(x - 5), -1(-x + 5)$

82. $a - 6$ $1(a - 6), -1(-a + 6)$

83. $4 - 7a$ $1(4 - 7a), -1(-4 + 7a)$

84. $7 - 5b$ $1(7 - 5b), -1(-7 + 5b)$

85. $-24a^3 + 16a^2$ $8a^2(-3a + 2), -8a^2(3a - 2)$

86. $-30b^4 + 75b^3$ $15b^3(-2b + 5), -15b^3(2b - 5)$

87. $-12x^2 - 18x$ $6x(-2x - 3), -6x(2x + 3)$

88. $-20b^2 - 8b$ $4b(-5b - 2), -4b(5b + 2)$

89. $-2x^3 - 6x^2 + 14x$ $2x(-x^2 - 3x + 7), -2x(x^2 + 3x - 7)$

VIDEO **90.** $-8x^4 + 6x^3 - 2x^2$
$2x^2(-4x^2 + 3x - 1), -2x^2(4x^2 - 3x + 1)$

91. $4a^3b - 6a^2b^2 - 4ab^3$
$2ab(2a^2 - 3ab - 2b^2), -2ab(-2a^2 + 3ab + 2b^2)$

92. $12u^5v^6 + 18u^2v^3 - 15u^4v^5$
$3u^2v^3(4u^3v^3 + 6 - 5u^2v^2), -3u^2v^3(-4u^3v^3 - 6 + 5u^2v^2)$

Applications

Solve each problem by factoring.

93. ***Uniform motion.*** Helen traveled a distance of $20x + 40$ miles at 20 miles per hour on the Yellowhead Highway. Find a binomial that represents the time that she traveled. $x + 2$ hours

94. ***Area of a painting.*** A rectangular painting with a width of x centimeters has an area of $x^2 + 50x$ square centimeters. Find a binomial that represents the length. See the accompanying figure. $x + 50$ cm

Figure for Exercise 94

95. ***Tomato soup.*** The amount of metal S (in square inches) that it takes to make a can for tomato soup depends on the radius r and height h:

$$S = 2\pi r^2 + 2\pi rh$$

a) Rewrite this formula by factoring out the greatest common factor on the right-hand side. $S = 2\pi r(r + h)$

b) Let $h = 5$ in. and write a formula that expresses S in terms of r. $S = 2\pi r^2 + 10\pi r$

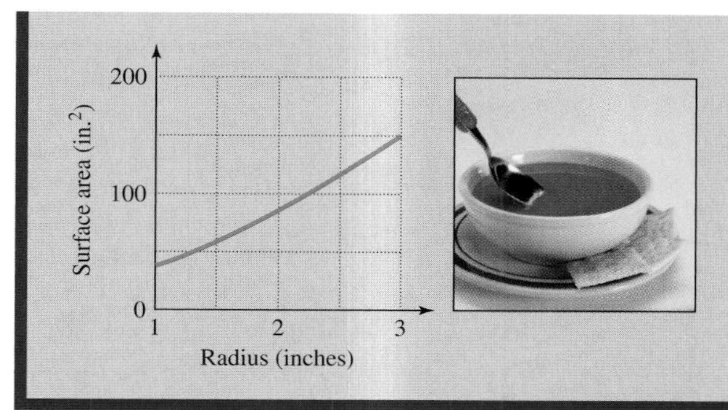

Figure for Exercise 95

c) The accompanying graph shows S for r between 1 in. and 3 in. (with $h = 5$ in.). Which of these r-values gives the maximum surface area? 3 in.

96. ***Amount of an investment.*** The amount of an investment of P dollars for t years at simple interest rate r is given by $A = P + Prt$.

a) Rewrite this formula by factoring out the greatest common factor on the right-hand side.
$A = P(1 + rt)$

b) Find A if \$8300 is invested for 3 years at a simple interest rate of 15%. \$12,035

Getting More Involved

97. ***Discussion***

Is the greatest common factor of $-6x^2 + 3x$ positive or negative? Explain.
The GCF is an algebraic expression.

98. ***Writing***

Explain in your own words why you use the smallest power of each common prime factor when finding the GCF of two or more integers.

Math *at Work* Kayak Design

Kayaks have been built by the Aleut and Inuit peoples for the past 4000 years. Today's builders have access to materials and techniques unavailable to the original kayak builders. Modern kayakers incorporate hydrodynamics and materials technology to create designs that are efficient and stable. Builders measure how well their designs work by calculating indicators such as prismatic coefficient, block coefficient, and the midship area coefficient, to name a few.

Even the fitting of a kayak to the paddler is done scientifically. For example, the formula

$$PL = 2 \cdot BL + BS\left(0.38 \cdot EE + 1.2\sqrt{\left(\frac{BW}{2} - \frac{SW}{2}\right)^2 + (SL)^2}\right)$$

can be used to calculate the appropriate paddle length. *BL* is the length of the paddle's blade. *BS* is a boating style factor, which is 1.2 for touring, 1.0 for river running, and 0.95 for play boating. *EE* is the elbow to elbow distance with the paddler's arms straight out to the sides. *BW* is the boat width and *SW* is the shoulder width. *SL* is the spine length, which is the distance measured in a sitting position from the chair seat to the top of the paddler's shoulder. All lengths are in centimeters.

The degree of control a kayaker exerts over the kayak depends largely on the body contact with it. A kayaker wears the kayak. So the choice of a kayak should hinge first on the right body fit and comfort and second on the skill level or intended paddling style. So designing, building, and even fitting a kayak is a blend of art and science.

6.2 Special Products and Grouping

In This Section

In Section 5.6, you learned how to find the special products: the square of a sum, the square of a difference, and the product of a sum and a difference. In this section you will learn how to reverse those operations.

⟨1⟩ Factoring a Difference of Two Squares

In Section 5.6, you learned that the product of a sum and a difference is a difference of two squares:

$$(a + b)(a - b) = a^2 - ab + ab - b^2 = a^2 - b^2$$

So a difference of two squares can be factored as a product of a sum and a difference, using the following rule.

Factoring a Difference of Two Squares

For any real numbers a and b,

$$a^2 - b^2 = (a + b)(a - b).$$

Note that the square of an integer is a perfect square. For example, 64 is a perfect square because $64 = 8^2$. The square of a monomial in which the coefficient is an integer is also called a **perfect square** or simply a **square.** For example, $9m^2$ is a perfect square because $9m^2 = (3m)^2$.

EXAMPLE 1

Factoring a difference of two squares

Factor each polynomial.

a) $y^2 - 81$ **b)** $9m^2 - 16$ **c)** $4x^2 - 9y^2$

Solution

a) Because $81 = 9^2$, the binomial $y^2 - 81$ is a difference of two squares:

$$y^2 - 81 = y^2 - 9^2 \quad \text{Rewrite as a difference of two squares.}$$
$$= (y + 9)(y - 9) \quad \text{Factor.}$$

Check by multiplying.

b) Because $9m^2 = (3m)^2$ and $16 = 4^2$, the binomial $9m^2 - 16$ is a difference of two squares:

$$9m^2 - 16 = (3m)^2 - 4^2 \quad \text{Rewrite as a difference of two squares.}$$
$$= (3m + 4)(3m - 4) \quad \text{Factor.}$$

Check by multiplying.

c) Because $4x^2 = (2x)^2$ and $9y^2 = (3y)^2$, the binomial $4x^2 - 9y^2$ is a difference of two squares:

$$4x^2 - 9y^2 = (2x + 3y)(2x - 3y)$$

Now do Exercises 7–20

CAUTION Don't confuse a difference of two squares $a^2 - b^2$ with a sum of two squares $a^2 + b^2$. The sum $a^2 + b^2$ is not one of the special products and it can't be factored.

⟨2⟩ Factoring a Perfect Square Trinomial

In Section 5.6 you learned how to square a binomial using the rule

$$(a + b)^2 = a^2 + 2ab + b^2.$$

You can reverse this rule to factor a trinomial such as $x^2 + 6x + 9$. Notice that

$$x^2 + 6x + 9 = \underset{\underset{a^2}{\uparrow}}{x^2} + \underbrace{2 \cdot x \cdot 3}_{2ab} + \underset{\underset{b^2}{\uparrow}}{3^2}.$$

So if $a = x$ and $b = 3$, then $x^2 + 6x + 9$ fits the form $a^2 + 2ab + b^2$, and

$$x^2 + 6x + 9 = (x + 3)^2.$$

A trinomial that is of the form $a^2 + 2ab + b^2$ or $a^2 - 2ab + b^2$ is called a **perfect square trinomial.** A perfect square trinomial is the square of a binomial. Perfect square trinomials will be used in solving quadratic equations by completing the square in Chapter 9. Perfect square trinomials can be identified using the following strategy.

Strategy for Identifying a Perfect Square Trinomial

A trinomial is a perfect square trinomial if

1. the first and last terms are of the form a^2 and b^2 (perfect squares).
2. the middle term is $2ab$ or $-2ab$.

EXAMPLE 2

Identifying the special products

Determine whether each binomial is a difference of two squares and whether each trinomial is a perfect square trinomial.

a) $x^2 - 14x + 49$
b) $4x^2 - 81$
c) $4a^2 + 24a + 25$
d) $9y^2 - 24y - 16$

Solution

a) The first term is x^2, and the last term is 7^2. The middle term, $-14x$, is $-2 \cdot x \cdot 7$. So this trinomial is a perfect square trinomial.

b) Both terms of $4x^2 - 81$ are perfect squares, $(2x)^2$ and 9^2. So $4x^2 - 81$ is a difference of two squares.

c) The first term of $4a^2 + 24a + 25$ is $(2a)^2$ and the last term is 5^2. However, $2 \cdot 2a \cdot 5$ is $20a$. Because the middle term is $24a$, this trinomial is not a perfect square trinomial.

d) The first and last terms in a perfect square trinomial are both positive. Because the last term in $9y^2 - 24y - 16$ is negative, the trinomial is not a perfect square trinomial.

Now do Exercises 21–32

Note that the middle term in a perfect square trinomial may have a positive or a negative coefficient, while the first and last terms must be positive. Any perfect square trinomial can be factored as the square of a binomial by using the following rule.

Factoring Perfect Square Trinomials

For any real numbers a and b,

$$a^2 + 2ab + b^2 = (a + b)^2$$
$$a^2 - 2ab + b^2 = (a - b)^2.$$

EXAMPLE 3

Factoring perfect square trinomials

Factor.

a) $x^2 - 4x + 4$ **b)** $a^2 + 16a + 64$ **c)** $4x^2 - 12x + 9$

Solution

a) The first term is x^2, and the last term is 2^2. Because the middle term is $-2 \cdot 2 \cdot x$, or $-4x$, this polynomial is a perfect square trinomial:

$$x^2 - 4x + 4 = (x - 2)^2$$

Check by expanding $(x - 2)^2$.

b) $a^2 + 16a + 64 = (a + 8)^2$

Check by expanding $(a + 8)^2$.

c) The first term is $(2x)^2$, and the last term is 3^2. Because $-2 \cdot 2x \cdot 3 = -12x$, the polynomial is a perfect square trinomial. So

$$4x^2 - 12x + 9 = (2x - 3)^2.$$

Check by expanding $(2x - 3)^2$.

Now do Exercises 33–50

⟨3⟩ Factoring Completely

To factor a polynomial means to write it as a product of simpler polynomials. A polynomial that can't be factored using integers is called a **prime** or **irreducible polynomial.** The polynomials $3x$, $w + 1$, and $4m - 5$ are prime polynomials. Note that $4m - 5 = 4\left(m - \frac{5}{4}\right)$, but $4m - 5$ is a prime polynomial because it can't be factored using integers only.

A polynomial is **factored completely** when it is written as a product of prime polynomials. So $(y - 8)(y + 1)$ is a complete factorization. When factoring polynomials we usually do not factor integers that occur as common factors. So $6x(x - 7)$ is considered to be factored completely even though 6 could be factored.

Some polynomials have a factor common to all terms. To factor such polynomials completely, it is simpler to factor out the greatest common factor (GCF) and then factor the remaining polynomial. Example 4 illustrates factoring completely.

EXAMPLE 4

Factoring completely

Factor each polynomial completely.

a) $2x^3 - 50x$ **b)** $8x^2y - 32xy + 32y$

Solution

a) The greatest common factor of $2x^3$ and $50x$ is $2x$:

$$\begin{aligned} 2x^3 - 50x &= 2x(x^2 - 25) && \text{Check this step by multiplying.} \\ &= 2x(x + 5)(x - 5) && \text{Difference of two squares} \end{aligned}$$

b)
$$\begin{aligned} 8x^2y - 32xy + 32y &= 8y(x^2 - 4x + 4) && \text{Check this step by multiplying.} \\ &= 8y(x - 2)^2 && \text{Perfect square trinomial} \end{aligned}$$

Now do Exercises 51–70

Remember that factoring reverses multiplication and *every step of factoring can be checked by multiplication.*

⟨4⟩ Factoring by Grouping

The product of two binomials may be a polynomial with four terms. For example,

$$(x + a)(x + 3) = (x + a)x + (x + a)3$$
$$= x^2 + ax + 3x + 3a.$$

We can factor a polynomial of this type by simply reversing the steps we used to find the product. To reverse these steps, we factor out common factors from the first two terms and from the last two terms. This procedure is called **factoring by grouping.**

EXAMPLE 5

Factoring by grouping

Use grouping to factor each polynomial completely.

a) $xy + 2y + 3x + 6$ **b)** $2x^3 - 3x^2 - 2x + 3$ **c)** $ax + 3y - 3x - ay$

Solution

a) Notice that the first two terms have a common factor of y and the last two terms have a common factor of 3:

$$xy + 2y + 3x + 6 = (xy + 2y) + (3x + 6) \quad \text{Use the associative property to group the terms.}$$
$$= y(x + 2) + 3(x + 2) \quad \text{Factor out the common factors in each group.}$$
$$= (y + 3)(x + 2) \quad \text{Factor out } x + 2.$$

b) We can factor x^2 out of the first two terms and 1 out of the last two terms:

$$2x^3 - 3x^2 - 2x + 3 = (2x^3 - 3x^2) + (-2x + 3) \quad \text{Group the terms.}$$
$$= x^2(2x - 3) + 1(-2x + 3)$$

However, we cannot proceed any further because $2x - 3$ and $-2x + 3$ are not the same. To get $2x - 3$ as a common factor, we must factor out -1 from the last two terms:

$$2x^3 - 3x^2 - 2x + 3 = x^2(2x - 3) - 1(2x - 3) \quad \text{Factor out the common factors.}$$
$$= (x^2 - 1)(2x - 3) \quad \text{Factor out } 2x - 3.$$
$$= (x - 1)(x + 1)(2x - 3) \quad \text{Difference of two squares}$$

c) In $ax + 3y - 3x - ay$ there are no common factors in the first two or the last two terms. However, if we use the commutative property to rewrite the polynomial as $ax - 3x - ay + 3y$, then we can factor by grouping:

$$ax + 3y - 3x - ay = ax - 3x - ay + 3y \quad \text{Rearrange the terms.}$$
$$= x(a - 3) - y(a - 3) \quad \text{Factor out } x \text{ and } -y.$$
$$= (x - y)(a - 3) \quad \text{Factor out } a - 3.$$

Now do Exercises 71–86

⟨ Teaching Tip ⟩

Some students always put the common factor on the left. So they might write $(x + 2)(y + 3)$, which of course is also correct.

Warm-Ups 

True or false? Explain your answer.

1. The polynomial $x^2 + 16$ is a difference of two squares. False
2. The polynomial $x^2 - 8x + 16$ is a perfect square trinomial. True
3. The polynomial $9x^2 + 21x + 49$ is a perfect square trinomial. False
4. $4x^2 + 4 = (2x + 2)^2$ for any real number x. False
5. A difference of two squares is equal to a product of a sum and a difference. True
6. The polynomial $16y + 1$ is a prime polynomial. True
7. The polynomial $x^2 + 9$ can be factored as $(x + 3)(x + 3)$. False
8. The polynomial $4x^2 - 4$ is factored completely as $4(x^2 - 1)$. False
9. $y^2 - 2y + 1 = (y - 1)^2$ for any real number y. True
10. $2x^2 - 18 = 2(x - 3)(x + 3)$ for any real number x. True

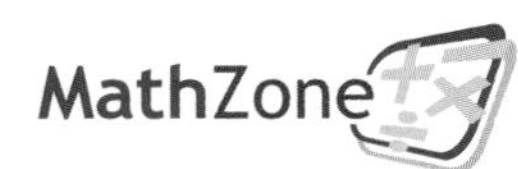

Exercises 6.2

‹ Study Tips ›

- As you study a chapter, make a list of topics and questions that you would put on the test, if you were to write it.
- Write about what you read in the text. Sum things up in your own words.

Reading and Writing *After reading this section, write out the answers to these questions. Use complete sentences.*

1. What is a perfect square? A perfect square is the square of an integer or an algebraic expression.
2. How do we factor a difference of two squares? $a^2 - b^2 = (a + b)(a - b)$
3. How can you recognize if a trinomial is a perfect square? A perfect square trinomial is of the form $a^2 + 2ab + b^2$ or $a^2 - 2ab + b^2$.
4. What is a prime polynomial? A prime polynomial is a polynomial that cannot be factored.
5. When is a polynomial factored completely? A polynomial is factored completely when it is a product of prime polynomials.
6. What should you always look for first when attempting to factor a polynomial completely? Always factor out the GCF first.

‹1› Factoring a Difference of Two Squares

Factor each polynomial. See Example 1.

7. $a^2 - 4$ $(a - 2)(a + 2)$
8. $h^2 - 9$ $(h - 3)(h + 3)$
9. $x^2 - 49$ $(x - 7)(x + 7)$
10. $y^2 - 36$ $(y - 6)(y + 6)$ (VIDEO)
11. $a^2 - 121$ $(a + 11)(a - 11)$
12. $w^2 - 81$ $(w + 9)(w - 9)$
13. $y^2 - 9x^2$ $(y + 3x)(y - 3x)$
14. $16x^2 - y^2$ $(4x - y)(4x + y)$
15. $25a^2 - 49b^2$ $(5a + 7b)(5a - 7b)$
16. $9a^2 - 64b^2$ $(3a - 8b)(3a + 8b)$
17. $121m^2 - 1$ $(11m + 1)(11m - 1)$
18. $144n^2 - 1$ $(12n - 1)(12n + 1)$

19. $9w^2 - 25c^2$ $(3w - 5c)(3w + 5c)$

20. $144w^2 - 121a^2$ $(12w - 11a)(12w + 11a)$

⟨2⟩ Factoring a Perfect Square Trinomial

Determine whether each polynomial is a difference of two squares, a perfect square trinomial, or neither of these.

See Example 2.

See the Strategy for Identifying Perfect Square Trinomials box on page 372.

21. $x^2 - 20x + 100$ Perfect square trinomial

22. $x^2 - 10x - 25$ Neither

23. $y^2 - 40$ Neither

24. $a^2 - 49$ Difference of two squares

25. $4y^2 + 12y + 9$ Perfect square trinomial

26. $9a^2 - 30a - 25$ Neither

27. $x^2 - 8x + 64$ Neither

28. $x^2 + 4x + 4$ Perfect square trinomial

29. $9y^2 - 25c^2$ Difference of two squares

30. $9x^2 + 4$ Neither

31. $9a^2 + 6ab + b^2$ Perfect square trinomial

32. $4x^2 - 4xy + y^2$ Perfect square trinomial

Factor each perfect square trinomial. See Example 3.

33. $x^2 + 2x + 1$ $(x + 1)^2$

34. $y^2 + 4y + 4$ $(y + 2)^2$

35. $a^2 + 6a + 9$ $(a + 3)^2$

36. $w^2 + 10w + 25$ $(w + 5)^2$

37. $x^2 + 12x + 36$ $(x + 6)^2$

38. $y^2 + 14y + 49$ $(y + 7)^2$

39. $a^2 - 4a + 4$ $(a - 2)^2$

40. $b^2 - 6b + 9$ $(b - 3)^2$

41. $4w^2 + 4w + 1$ $(2w + 1)^2$

VIDEO **42.** $9m^2 + 6m + 1$ $(3m + 1)^2$

43. $16x^2 - 8x + 1$ $(4x - 1)^2$

44. $25y^2 - 10y + 1$ $(5y - 1)^2$

45. $4t^2 + 20t + 25$ $(2t + 5)^2$

46. $9y^2 - 12y + 4$ $(3y - 2)^2$

47. $9w^2 + 42w + 49$ $(3w + 7)^2$

48. $144x^2 + 24x + 1$ $(12x + 1)^2$

49. $n^2 + 2nt + t^2$ $(n + t)^2$

50. $x^2 - 2xy + y^2$ $(x - y)^2$

⟨3⟩ Factoring Completely

Factor each polynomial completely. See Example 4.

51. $5x^2 - 125$ $5(x - 5)(x + 5)$

52. $3y^2 - 27$ $3(y - 3)(y + 3)$

53. $-2x^2 + 18$ $-2(x - 3)(x + 3)$

54. $-5y^2 + 20$ $-5(y - 2)(y + 2)$

55. $a^3 - ab^2$ $a(a - b)(a + b)$

VIDEO **56.** $x^2y - y$ $y(x - 1)(x + 1)$

57. $3x^2 + 6x + 3$ $3(x + 1)^2$

58. $12a^2 + 36a + 27$ $3(2a + 3)^2$

59. $-5y^2 + 50y - 125$ $-5(y - 5)^2$

60. $-2a^2 - 16a - 32$ $-2(a + 4)^2$

61. $x^3 - 2x^2y + xy^2$ $x(x - y)^2$

62. $x^3y + 2x^2y^2 + xy^3$ $xy(x + y)^2$

63. $-3x^2 + 3y^2$ $-3(x - y)(x + y)$

64. $-8a^2 + 8b^2$ $-8(a - b)(a + b)$

VIDEO **65.** $2ax^2 - 98a$ $2a(x - 7)(x + 7)$

66. $32x^2y - 2y^3$ $2y(4x - y)(4x + y)$

67. $3ab^2 - 18ab + 27a$ $3a(b - 3)^2$

68. $-2a^2b + 8ab - 8b$ $-2b(a - 2)^2$

69. $-4m^3 + 24m^2n - 36mn^2$ $-4m(m - 3n)^2$

70. $10a^3 - 20a^2b + 10ab^2$ $10a(a - b)^2$

⟨4⟩ Factoring by Grouping

Use grouping to factor each polynomial completely. See Example 5.

71. $bx + by + cx + cy$ $(b + c)(x + y)$

72. $3x + 3z + ax + az$ $(3 + a)(x + z)$

73. $x^3 + x^2 - 4x - 4$ $(x - 2)(x + 2)(x + 1)$

74. $x^3 + x^2 - x - 1$ $(x - 1)(x + 1)^2$

75. $3a - 3b - xa + xb$ $(3 - x)(a - b)$

76. $ax - bx - 4a + 4b$ $(x - 4)(a - b)$

77. $a^3 + 3a^2 + a + 3$ $(a^2 + 1)(a + 3)$

78. $y^3 - 5y^2 + 8y - 40$ $(y^2 + 8)(y - 5)$

VIDEO **79.** $xa + ay + 3y + 3x$ $(a + 3)(x + y)$

80. $x^3 + ax + 3a + 3x^2$ $(x + 3)(x^2 + a)$

81. $abc - 3 + c - 3ab$ $(c - 3)(ab + 1)$

82. $xa + tb + ba + tx$ $(a + t)(x + b)$

83. $x^2a - b + bx^2 - a$ $(a + b)(x - 1)(x + 1)$

84. $a^2m - b^2n + a^2n - b^2m$ $(m + n)(a - b)(a + b)$

85. $y^2 + y + by + b$ $(y + b)(y + 1)$

86. $ac + mc + aw^2 + mw^2$ $(c + w^2)(a + m)$

Miscellaneous

Factor each polynomial completely.

87. $6a^3y + 24a^2y^2 + 24ay^3$ $6ay(a + 2y)^2$

88. $8b^5c - 8b^4c^2 + 2b^3c^3$ $2b^3c(2b - c)^2$

89. $24a^3y - 6ay^3$ $6ay(2a - y)(2a + y)$

90. $27b^3c - 12bc^3$ $3bc(3b - 2c)(3b + 2c)$

91. $2a^3y^2 - 6a^2y$ $2a^2y(ay - 3)$

92. $9x^3y - 18x^2y^2$ $9x^2y(x - 2y)$

93. $ab + 2bw - 4aw - 8w^2$ $(b - 4w)(a + 2w)$

94. $3am - 6n - an + 18m$ $(3m - n)(a + 6)$

95. $(a - b) - b(a - b)$ $(a - b)(1 - b)$

96. $(a + b)w - (a + b)$ $(a + b)(w - 1)$

97. $(4x^2 - 1)2x - (4x^2 - 1)$ $(2x - 1)^2(2x + 1)$

98. $(a^2 - 9)a + 3(a^2 - 9)$ $(a + 3)^2(a - 3)$

Applications

Use factoring to solve each problem.

99. ***Skydiving.*** The height in feet above the earth for skydiver t seconds after jumping from an airplane at 6400 ft is approximated by the formula $h(t) = -16t^2 + 6400$, provided $t < 5$.

a) Rewrite the formula with the right-hand side factored completely. $h(t) = -16(t - 20)(t + 20)$

b) Use the result of part (a) to find $h(2)$. 6336 feet

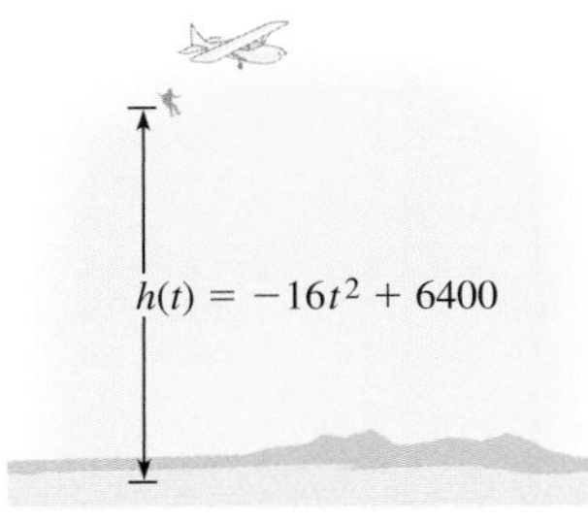

Figure for Exercise 99

100. ***Demand for pools.*** Tropical Pools sells an aboveground model for p dollars each. The monthly revenue for this model is given by the formula

$$R(p) = -0.08p^2 + 300p.$$

Revenue is the product of the price p and the demand (quantity sold).

a) Factor out the price on the right-hand side of the formula. $R(p) = p(-0.08p + 300)$

b) Write a formula $D(p)$ for the monthly demand. $D(p) = -0.08p + 300$

c) Find $D(3000)$. 60 pools

d) Use the accompanying graph to estimate the price at which the revenue is maximized. Approximately how many pools will be sold monthly at this price? \$2000, 140 pools

e) What is the approximate maximum revenue? \$280,000

f) Use the accompanying graph to estimate the price at which the revenue is zero. \$0 or \$3800

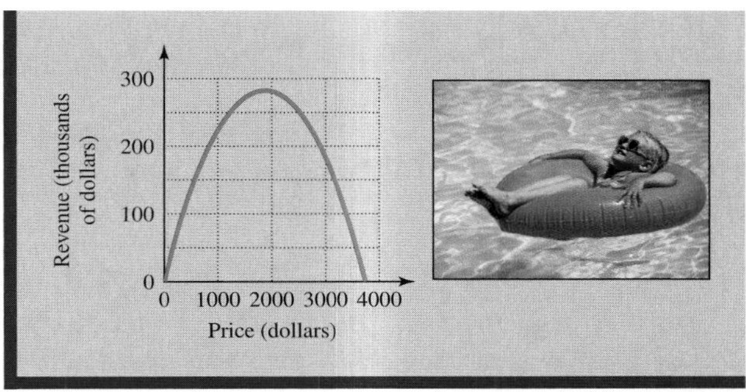

Figure for Exercise 100

101. ***Volume of a tank.*** The volume in cubic inches for a fish tank with a square base and height x is given by the formula

$$V(x) = x^3 - 6x^2 + 9x.$$

a) Rewrite the formula with the right-hand side factored completely. $V(x) = x(x - 3)^2$

b) Find an expression for the length of a side of the square base. $x - 3$ inches

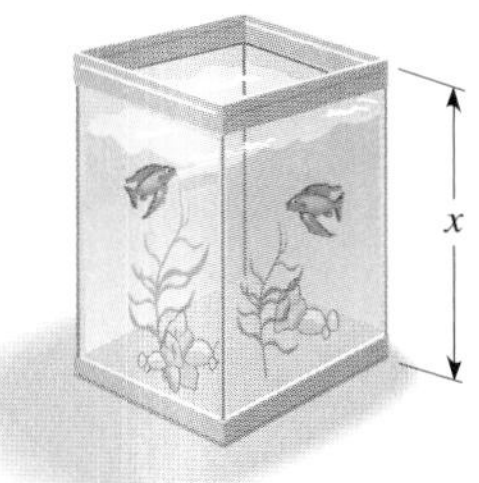

Figure for Exercise 101

Getting More Involved

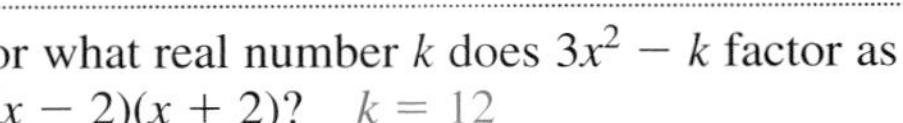

102. ***Discussion***

For what real number k does $3x^2 - k$ factor as $3(x - 2)(x + 2)$? $k = 12$

103. ***Writing***

Explain in your own words how to factor a four-term polynomial by grouping.

104. ***Writing***

Explain how you know that $x^2 + 1$ is a prime polynomial.

6.3 Factoring the Trinomial $ax^2 + bx + c$ with $a = 1$

In This Section

In this section, we will factor the type of trinomials that result from multiplying two different binomials. We will do this only for trinomials in which the coefficient of x^2, the leading coefficient, is 1. Factoring trinomials with leading coefficient not equal to 1 will be done in Section 6.4.

⟨1⟩ Factoring $ax^2 + bx + c$ with $a = 1$

To find the product of the binomials $x + m$ and $x + n$, where x is the variable and m and n are constants, we use the distributive property as follows:

$$\begin{aligned}(x + m)(x + n) &= (x + m)x + (x + m)n && \text{Distributive property}\\ &= x^2 + mx + nx + mn && \text{Distributive property}\\ &= x^2 + (m + n)x + mn && \text{Combine like terms.}\end{aligned}$$

Notice that in the trinomial the coefficient of x is the sum $m + n$ and the constant term is the product mn. This observation is the key to factoring the trinomial $ax^2 + bx + c$ with $a = 1$. We first find two numbers that have a product of c (the constant term) and a sum of b (the coefficient of x). Then we simply reverse the steps in the process, as shown in Example 1.

EXAMPLE 1 Factoring a trinomial

Factor.

a) $x^2 + 5x + 6$ b) $x^2 + 8x + 12$ c) $a^2 - 9a + 20$

Solution

a) We first find two integers with a product of 6 and a sum of 5. If the product is positive and the sum is positive, then both integers must be positive. So the only possibilities for a product of 6 are 1 and 6 or 2 and 3. Only 2 and 3 have a sum of 5. So we replace $5x$ with $2x + 3x$, then factor by grouping:

$$\begin{aligned}x^2 + 5x + 6 &= x^2 + 2x + 3x + 6 && \text{Replace } 5x \text{ by } 2x + 3x.\\ &= (x^2 + 2x) + (3x + 6) && \text{Group terms together.}\\ &= x(x + 2) + 3(x + 2) && \text{Factor out common factors.}\\ &= (x + 2)(x + 3) && \text{Factor out } x + 2.\end{aligned}$$

⟨ Teaching Tip ⟩

Note that in Example 1 the common factor is factored out sometimes to the left and sometimes to the right to show that it can be done either way.

b) To factor $x^2 + 8x + 12$, we first find two integers that have a product of 12 and a sum of 8. If the product is positive and the sum is positive, then both integers must be positive. So for a product of 12 we have $1 \cdot 12$, $2 \cdot 6$, or $3 \cdot 4$. Only 2 and 6 have a sum of 8. So replace $8x$ with $2x + 6x$, then factor by grouping:

$$\begin{aligned}x^2 + 8x + 12 &= x^2 + 2x + 6x + 12\\ &= (x + 2)x + (x + 2)6 && \text{Factor out the common factors.}\\ &= (x + 2)(x + 6) && \text{Factor out } x + 2.\end{aligned}$$

Check by using FOIL: $(x + 2)(x + 6) = x^2 + 8x + 12$.

c) To factor $a^2 - 9a + 20$, we first find two integers that have a product of 20 and a sum of -9. Since the product is positive and the sum is negative, both numbers must be negative. So for a product of 20 we have $(-1)(-20)$, $(-2)(-10)$, or $(-4)(-5)$. Only -4 and -5 have a sum of -9. So replace $-9a$ with $-4a - 5a$ and factor by grouping.

$$a^2 - 9a + 20 = a^2 - 4a - 5a + 20 \quad \text{Replace } -9a \text{ by } -4a - 5a.$$
$$= a(a - 4) - 5(a - 4) \quad \text{Factor by grouping.}$$
$$= (a - 5)(a - 4) \quad \text{Factor out } a - 4.$$

Now do Exercises 7–20

We usually do not write out all of the steps shown in Example 1. We saw prior to Example 1 that

$$x^2 + (m + n)x + mn = (x + m)(x + n).$$

So once you know m and n, you can simply write the factors, as shown in Example 2.

EXAMPLE 2

Factoring trinomials

Factor.

a) $x^2 + 5x + 4$

b) $y^2 + 6y - 16$

c) $w^2 - 5w - 24$

Solution

a) To factor $x^2 + 5x + 4$ we need two integers with a product of 4 and a sum of 5. The only possibilities for a product of 4 are

$$(1)(4), (-1)(-4), (2)(2), \quad \text{and} \quad (-2)(-2).$$

Only 1 and 4 have a sum of 5. So

$$x^2 + 5x + 4 = (x + 1)(x + 4).$$

Check by using FOIL on $(x + 1)(x + 4)$ to get $x^2 + 5x + 4$.

b) To factor $y^2 + 6y - 16$ we need two integers with a product of -16 and a sum of 6. The only possibilities for a product of -16 are

$$(-1)(16), (1)(-16), (-2)(8), (2)(-8), \quad \text{and} \quad (-4)(4).$$

Only -2 and 8 have a sum of 6. So

$$y^2 + 6y - 16 = (y + 8)(y - 2).$$

Check by using FOIL on $(y + 8)(y - 2)$ to get $y^2 + 6y - 16$.

c) To factor $w^2 - 5w - 24$ we need two integers with a product of -24 and a sum of -5. The only possibilities for a product of -24 are

$(-1)(24)$, $(1)(-24)$, $(-2)(12)$, $(2)(-12)$, $(-3)(8)$, $(3)(-8)$, $(-4)(6)$, and $(4)(-6)$.

Only -8 and 3 have a sum of -5. So

$$w^2 - 5w - 24 = (w - 8)(w + 3).$$

Check by using FOIL on $(w - 8)(w + 3)$ to get $w^2 - 5w - 24$.

Now do Exercises 21–28

Polynomials are easiest to factor when they are in the form $ax^2 + bx + c$. So if a polynomial can be rewritten into that form, rewrite it before attempting to factor it. In Example 3, we factor polynomials that need to be rewritten.

EXAMPLE 3

Factoring trinomials

Factor.

a) $2x - 8 + x^2$

b) $-36 + t^2 - 9t$

Solution

a) Before factoring, write the trinomial as $x^2 + 2x - 8$. Now, to get a product of -8 and a sum of 2, use -2 and 4:

$$\begin{aligned} 2x - 8 + x^2 &= x^2 + 2x - 8 && \text{Write in } ax^2 + bx + c \text{ form.} \\ &= (x + 4)(x - 2) && \text{Factor and check by multiplying.} \end{aligned}$$

b) Before factoring, write the trinomial as $t^2 - 9t - 36$. Now, to get a product of -36 and a sum of -9, use -12 and 3:

$$\begin{aligned} -36 + t^2 - 9t &= t^2 - 9t - 36 && \text{Write in } ax^2 + bx + c \text{ form.} \\ &= (t - 12)(t + 3) && \text{Factor and check by multiplying.} \end{aligned}$$

Now do Exercises 29–30

To factor $x^2 + bx + c$, we search through all pairs of integers that have a product of c until we find a pair that has a sum of b. If there is no such pair of integers, then the polynomial cannot be factored and it is a prime polynomial. Before you can conclude that a polynomial is prime, be sure that you have tried *all* possibilities.

EXAMPLE 4

Prime polynomials

Factor.

a) $x^2 + 7x - 6$

b) $x^2 + 9$

Solution

a) Because the last term is -6, we want a positive integer and a negative integer that have a product of -6 and a sum of 7. Check all possible pairs of integers:

Product	**Sum**
$-6 = (-1)(6)$	$-1 + 6 = 5$
$-6 = (1)(-6)$	$1 + (-6) = -5$
$-6 = (2)(-3)$	$2 + (-3) = -1$
$-6 = (-2)(3)$	$-2 + 3 = 1$

None of these possible factors of -6 have a sum of 7, so we can be certain that $x^2 + 7x - 6$ cannot be factored. It is a prime polynomial.

b) Because the x-term is missing in $x^2 + 9$, its coefficient is 0. That is, $x^2 + 9 = x^2 + 0x + 9$. So we seek two positive integers or two negative integers that have a product of 9 and a sum of 0. Check all possibilities:

Product	**Sum**
$9 = (1)(9)$	$1 + 9 = 10$
$9 = (-1)(-9)$	$-1 + (-9) = -10$
$9 = (3)(3)$	$3 + 3 = 6$
$9 = (-3)(-3)$	$-3 + (-3) = -6$

None of these pairs of integers have a sum of 0, so we can conclude that $x^2 + 9$ is a prime polynomial. Note that $x^2 + 9$ does not factor as $(x + 3)^2$ because $(x + 3)^2$ has a middle term: $(x + 3)^2 = x^2 + 6x + 9$.

Now do Exercises 31–58

‹ Helpful Hint ›

Don't confuse $a^2 + b^2$ with the difference of two squares $a^2 - b^2$ which is not a prime polynomial:

$$a^2 - b^2 = (a + b)(a - b)$$

The prime polynomial $x^2 + 9$ in Example 4(b) is a sum of two squares. It can be shown that any sum of two squares (in which there are no common factors) is a prime polynomial.

‹ Teaching Tip ›

Note that a sum of two squares of the type $(a^3)^2 + (b^3)^2$ is not prime because it is also a sum of two cubes, $(a^2)^3 + (b^2)^3$.

Sum of Two Squares

If a sum of two squares, $a^2 + b^2$, has no common factor other than 1, then it is a prime polynomial.

‹2› Factoring with Two Variables

In Example 5, we factor polynomials that have two variables using the same technique that we used for one variable.

EXAMPLE 5 **Polynomials with two variables**

Factor.

a) $x^2 + 2xy - 8y^2$

b) $a^2 - 7ab + 10b^2$

Solution

a) To factor $x^2 + 2xy - 8y^2$ we need two integers with a product of -8 and a sum of 2. The only possibilities for a product of -8 are

$$(-1)(8),\ (1)(-8),\ (-2)(4),\ \text{and}\ (2)(-4).$$

Only -2 and 4 have a sum of 2. Since $(-2y)(4y) = -8y^2$, we have

$$x^2 + 2xy - 8y^2 = (x - 2y)(x + 4y).$$

Check by using FOIL on $(x - 2y)(x + 4y)$ to get $x^2 + 2xy - 8y^2$.

b) To factor $a^2 - 7ab + 10b^2$ we need two integers with a product of 10 and a sum of -7. The only possibilities for a product of 10 are

$$(-1)(-10),\ (1)(10),\ (-2)(-5),\ \text{and}\ (2)(5).$$

Only -2 and -5 have a sum of -7. Since $(-2b)(-5b) = 10b^2$, we have

$$a^2 - 7ab + 10b^2 = (a - 5b)(a - 2b).$$

Check by using FOIL on $(a - 2b)(a - 5b)$ to get $a^2 - 7ab + 10b^2$.

Now do Exercises 59–66

‹3› Factoring Completely

In Section 6.2 you learned that binomials such as $3x - 5$ (with no common factor) are prime polynomials. In Example 4 of this section we saw a trinomial that is a prime polynomial. There are infinitely many prime trinomials. When factoring a polynomial completely, we could have a factor that is a prime trinomial.

EXAMPLE 6

Factoring completely

Factor each polynomial completely.

a) $x^3 - 6x^2 - 16x$

b) $4x^3 + 4x^2 + 4x$

Solution

a) $x^3 - 6x^2 - 16x = x(x^2 - 6x - 16)$ Factor out the GCF.

$= x(x - 8)(x + 2)$ Factor $x^2 - 6x - 16$.

b) First factor out $4x$, the greatest common factor:

$$4x^3 + 4x^2 + 4x = 4x(x^2 + x + 1)$$

To factor $x^2 + x + 1$, we would need two integers with a product of 1 and a sum of 1. Because there are no such integers, $x^2 + x + 1$ is prime, and the factorization is complete.

Now do Exercises 67–108

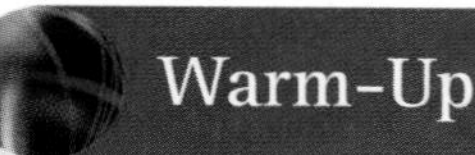

Warm-Ups ▼

True or false? Explain your answer.

1. $x^2 - 6x + 9 = (x - 3)^2$ True
2. $x^2 + 6x + 9 = (x + 3)^2$ True
3. $x^2 + 10x + 9 = (x - 9)(x - 1)$ False
4. $x^2 - 8x - 9 = (x - 8)(x - 9)$ False
5. $x^2 + 8x - 9 = (x + 9)(x - 1)$ True
6. $x^2 + 8x + 9 = (x + 3)^2$ False
7. $x^2 - 10xy + 9y^2 = (x - y)(x - 9y)$ True
8. $x^2 + x + 1 = (x + 1)(x + 1)$ False
9. $x^2 + xy + 20y^2 = (x + 5y)(x - 4y)$ False
10. $x^2 + 1 = (x + 1)(x + 1)$ False

Exercises 6.3

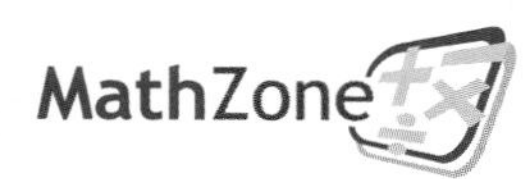

Boost your grade at mathzone.com!
- Practice Problems
- NetTutor
- Self-Tests
- e-Professors
- Videos

‹ Study Tips ›

- Put important facts on note cards. Work on memorizing the note cards when you have a few spare minutes.
- Post some note cards on your refrigerator door. Make this course a part of your life.

Reading and Writing *After reading this section, write out the answers to these questions. Use complete sentences.*

1. What types of polynomials did we factor in this section?
   We factored $ax^2 + bx + c$ with $a = 1$.
2. How can you check if you have factored a trinomial correctly?
   You can check all factoring by multiplying the factors.
3. How can you determine if $x^2 + bx + c$ is prime?
   If there are no two integers that have a product of c and a sum of b, then $x^2 + bx + c$ is prime.
4. How do you factor a sum of two squares?
   A sum of two squares with no common factor is prime.
5. When is a polynomial factored completely?
   A polynomial is factored completely when all of the factors are prime polynomials.
6. What should you always look for first when attempting to factor a polynomial completely?
   Always look for the GCF first.

‹1› Factoring $ax^2 + bx + c$ with $a = 1$

Factor each trinomial. Write out all of the steps as shown in Example 1.

7. $x^2 + 4x + 3$
   $(x + 3)(x + 1)$
8. $y^2 + 6y + 5$
   $(y + 5)(y + 1)$
9. $x^2 + 9x + 18$
   $(x + 3)(x + 6)$
10. $w^2 + 6w + 8$
    $(w + 2)(w + 4)$
11. $a^2 + 7a + 10$
    $(a + 2)(a + 5)$
12. $b^2 + 7b + 12$
    $(b + 3)(b + 4)$
13. $a^2 - 7a + 12$
    $(a - 3)(a - 4)$
14. $m^2 - 9m + 14$
    $(m - 2)(m - 7)$

15. $b^2 - 5b - 6$ $(b - 6)(b + 1)$

16. $a^2 + 5a - 6$ $(a + 6)(a - 1)$

17. $x^2 + 3x - 10$ $(x - 2)(x + 5)$

18. $x^2 - x - 12$ $(x + 3)(x - 4)$

19. $x^2 + 5x - 24$ $(x + 8)(x - 3)$

20. $a^2 - 5a - 50$ $(a + 5)(a - 10)$

Factor each polynomial. If the polynomial is prime, say so. See Examples 2–4.

21. $y^2 + 7y + 10$ $(y + 2)(y + 5)$

22. $x^2 + 8x + 15$ $(x + 3)(x + 5)$

23. $a^2 - 6a + 8$ $(a - 2)(a - 4)$

24. $b^2 - 8b + 15$ $(b - 3)(b - 5)$

VIDEO **25.** $m^2 - 10m + 16$ $(m - 8)(m - 2)$

26. $m^2 - 17m + 16$ $(m - 16)(m - 1)$

27. $w^2 + 9w - 10$ $(w + 10)(w - 1)$

28. $m^2 + 6m - 16$ $(m + 8)(m - 2)$

29. $w^2 - 8 - 2w$ $(w - 4)(w + 2)$

30. $-16 + m^2 - 6m$ $(m - 8)(m + 2)$

31. $a^2 - 2a - 12$ Prime

VIDEO **32.** $x^2 + 3x + 3$ Prime

33. $15m - 16 + m^2$ $(m + 16)(m - 1)$

34. $3y + y^2 - 10$ $(y + 5)(y - 2)$

35. $a^2 - 4a + 12$ Prime

36. $y^2 - 6y - 8$ Prime

37. $z^2 - 25$ $(z - 5)(z + 5)$

38. $p^2 - 1$ $(p - 1)(p + 1)$

39. $h^2 + 49$ Prime

40. $q^2 + 4$ Prime

41. $m^2 + 12m + 20$ $(m + 2)(m + 10)$

42. $m^2 + 21m + 20$ $(m + 1)(m + 20)$

43. $t^2 - 3t + 10$ Prime

44. $x^2 - 5x - 3$ Prime

VIDEO **45.** $m^2 - 18 - 17m$ $(m - 18)(m + 1)$

46. $h^2 - 36 + 5h$ $(h + 9)(h - 4)$

47. $m^2 - 23m + 24$ Prime

48. $m^2 + 23m + 24$ Prime

49. $5t - 24 + t^2$ $(t + 8)(t - 3)$

50. $t^2 - 24 - 10t$ $(t - 12)(t + 2)$

51. $t^2 - 2t - 24$ $(t - 6)(t + 4)$

52. $t^2 + 14t + 24$ $(t + 12)(t + 2)$

53. $t^2 - 10t - 200$ $(t - 20)(t + 10)$

54. $t^2 + 30t + 200$ $(t + 20)(t + 10)$

55. $x^2 - 5x - 150$ $(x - 15)(x + 10)$

56. $x^2 - 25x + 150$ $(x - 15)(x - 10)$

57. $13y + 30 + y^2$ $(y + 3)(y + 10)$

58. $18z + 45 + z^2$ $(z + 3)(z + 15)$

⟨2⟩ Factoring with Two Variables

Factor each polynomial. See Example 5.

59. $x^2 + 5ax + 6a^2$ $(x + 3a)(x + 2a)$

60. $a^2 + 7ab + 10b^2$ $(a + 2b)(a + 5b)$

61. $x^2 - 4xy - 12y^2$ $(x - 6y)(x + 2y)$

62. $y^2 + yt - 12t^2$ $(y + 4t)(y - 3t)$

63. $x^2 - 13xy + 12y^2$ $(x - 12y)(x - y)$

64. $h^2 - 9hs + 9s^2$ Prime

65. $x^2 + 4xz - 33z^2$ Prime

66. $x^2 - 5xs - 24s^2$ $(x - 8s)(x + 3s)$

⟨3⟩ Factoring Completely

Factor each polynomial completely. Use the methods discussed in Sections 6.1 through 6.3. If the polynomial is prime say so. See Example 6.

67. $5x^3 + 5x$ $5x(x^2 + 1)$

68. $b^3 + 49b$ $b(b^2 + 49)$

69. $w^2 - 8w$ $w(w - 8)$

70. $x^4 - x^3$ $x^3(x - 1)$

71. $2w^2 - 162$ $2(w - 9)(w + 9)$

72. $6w^4 - 54w^2$ $6w^2(w - 3)(w + 3)$

73. $-2b^2 - 98$ $-2(b^2 + 49)$

74. $-a^3 - 100a$ $-a(a^2 + 100)$

75. $x^3 - 2x^2 - 9x + 18$ $(x + 3)(x - 3)(x - 2)$

76. $x^3 + 7x^2 - x - 7$ $(x + 7)(x + 1)(x - 1)$

77. $4r^2 + 9$ Prime

78. $t^2 + 4z^2$ Prime

79. $x^2w^2 + 9x^2$ $x^2(w^2 + 9)$

80. $a^4b + a^2b^3$ $a^2b(a^2 + b^2)$

81. $w^2 - 18w + 81$ $(w - 9)^2$

82. $w^2 + 30w + 81$ $(w + 3)(w + 27)$

83. $6w^2 - 12w - 18$ $6(w - 3)(w + 1)$

84. $9w - w^3$ $w(3 - w)(3 + w)$

85. $3y^2 + 75$ $3(y^2 + 25)$

86. $5x^2 + 500$ $5(x^2 + 100)$

87. $ax + ay + cx + cy$ $(a + c)(x + y)$

88. $y^3 + y^2 - 4y - 4$ $(y - 2)(y + 2)(y + 1)$

89. $-2x^2 - 10x - 12$ $-2(x + 2)(x + 3)$

90. $-a^3 - 2a^2 - a$ $-a(a + 1)^2$

91. $32x^2 - 2x^4$ $2x^2(4 - x)(4 + x)$

92. $20w^2 + 100w + 40$ $20(w^2 + 5w + 2)$

93. $3w^2 + 27w + 54$ $3(w + 3)(w + 6)$

94. $w^3 - 3w^2 - 18w$ $w(w - 6)(w + 3)$

95. $18w^2 + w^3 + 36w$ $w(w^2 + 18w + 36)$

96. $18a^2 + 3a^3 + 36a$ $3a(a^2 + 6a + 12)$

97. $9y^2 + 1 + 6y$ $(3y + 1)^2$

98. $2a^2 + 1 + 3a$ $(2a + 1)(a + 1)$

99. $8vw^2 + 32vw + 32v$ $8v(w + 2)^2$

VIDEO 100. $3h^2t + 6ht + 3t$ $3t(h + 1)^2$

101. $6x^3y + 30x^2y^2 + 36xy^3$ $6xy(x + 3y)(x + 2y)$

102. $3x^3y^2 - 3x^2y^2 + 3xy^2$ $3xy^2(x^2 - x + 1)$

103. $5 + 8w + 3w^2$ $(3w + 5)(w + 1)$

104. $-3 + 2y + 21y^2$ $(3y - 1)(7y + 3)$

105. $-3y^3 + 6y^2 - 3y$ $-3y(y - 1)^2$

106. $-4w^3 - 16w^2 + 20w$ $-4w(w - 1)(w + 5)$

107. $a^3 + ab + 3b + 3a^2$ $(a + 3)(a^2 + b)$

108. $ac + xc + aw^2 + xw^2$ $(a + x)(c + w^2)$

Applications

Use factoring to solve each problem.

109. ***Area of a deck.*** The area in square feet for a rectangular deck is given by $A(x) = x^2 + 6x + 8$.

a) Find $A(6)$. 80 square feet

b) If the width of the deck is $x + 2$ feet, then what is the length? $x + 4$ feet

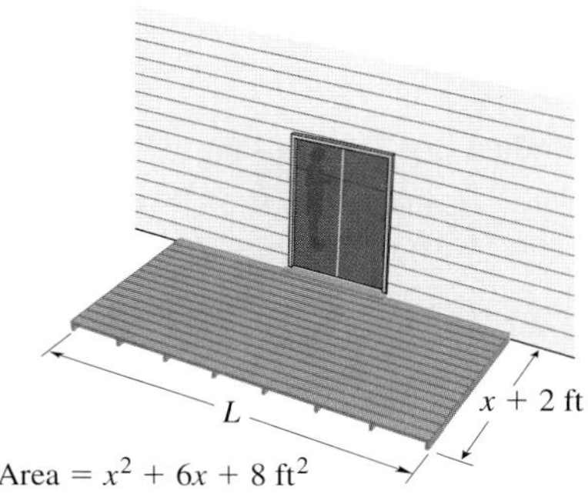

Figure for Exercise 109

110. ***Area of a sail.*** The area in square meters for a triangular sail is given by $A(x) = x^2 + 5x + 6$.

a) Find $A(5)$. 56 square meters

b) If the height of the sail is $x + 3$ meters, then what is the length of the base of the sail? $2x + 4$ meters

x + 3 m
Base
Area = $x^2 + 5x + 6$ m^2

Figure for Exercise 110

111. ***Volume of a cube.*** Hector designed a cubic box with volume x^3 cubic feet. After increasing the dimensions of the bottom, the box has a volume of $x^3 + 8x^2 + 15x$ cubic feet. If each of the dimensions of the bottom was increased by a whole number of feet, then how much was each increase?
3 feet and 5 feet

112. ***Volume of a container.*** A cubic shipping container had a volume of a^3 cubic meters. The height was decreased by a whole number of meters and the width was increased by a whole number of meters so that the volume of the container is now $a^3 + 2a^2 - 3a$ cubic meters. By how many meters were the height and width changed?
Height 1 meter smaller, width 3 meters larger

Getting More Involved

113. ***Discussion***

Which of the following products is not equivalent to the others? Explain your answer.

a) $(2x - 4)(x + 3)$ b) $(x - 2)(2x + 6)$
c) $2(x - 2)(x + 3)$ d) $(2x - 4)(2x + 6)$ d

114. ***Discussion***

When asked to factor completely a certain polynomial, four students gave the following answers. Only one student gave the correct answer. Which one must it be? Explain your answer.

a) $3(x^2 - 2x - 15)$ b) $(3x - 5)(5x - 15)$
c) $3(x - 5)(x - 3)$ d) $(3x - 15)(x - 3)$ c

6.4 Factoring the Trinomial $ax^2 + bx + c$ with $a \neq 1$

In This Section

In Section 6.3, we used grouping to factor trinomials with a leading coefficient of 1. In this section we will also use grouping to factor trinomials with a leading coefficient that is not equal to 1.

⟨1⟩ The *ac* Method

The first step in factoring $ax^2 + bx + c$ with $a = 1$ is to find two numbers with a product of c and a sum of b. If $a \neq 1$, then the first step is to find two numbers with a product of ac and a sum of b. This method is called the ***ac* method.** The strategy for factoring by the ac method follows. Note that this strategy works whether or not the leading coefficient is 1.

Strategy for Factoring $ax^2 + bx + c$ by the *ac* Method

To factor the trinomial $ax^2 + bx + c$:

1. Find two numbers that have a product equal to ac and a sum equal to b.
2. Replace bx by two terms using the two new numbers as coefficients.
3. Factor the resulting four-term polynomial by grouping.

EXAMPLE 1

The *ac* method

Factor each trinomial.

a) $2x^2 + 7x + 6$

b) $2x^2 + x - 6$

c) $10x^2 + 13x - 3$

Solution

a) In $2x^2 + 7x + 6$ we have $a = 2$, $b = 7$, and $c = 6$. So

$$ac = 2 \cdot 6 = 12.$$

Now we need two integers with a product of 12 and a sum of 7. The pairs of integers with a product of 12 are 1 and 12, 2 and 6, and 3 and 4. Only 3 and 4 have a sum of 7. Replace $7x$ by $3x + 4x$ and factor by grouping:

$$\begin{aligned} 2x^2 + 7x + 6 &= 2x^2 + 3x + 4x + 6 && \text{Replace } 7x \text{ by } 3x + 4x. \\ &= (2x + 3)x + (2x + 3)2 && \text{Factor out the common factors.} \\ &= (2x + 3)(x + 2) && \text{Factor out } 2x + 3. \end{aligned}$$

Check by FOIL.

b) In $2x^2 + x - 6$ we have $a = 2$, $b = 1$, and $c = -6$. So

$$ac = 2(-6) = -12.$$

Now we need two integers with a product of -12 and a sum of 1. We can list the possible pairs of integers with a product of -12 as follows:

1 and -12	2 and -6	3 and -4
-1 and 12	-2 and 6	-3 and 4

Only -3 and 4 have a sum of 1. Replace x by $-3x + 4x$ and factor by grouping:

$$\begin{aligned} 2x^2 + x - 6 &= 2x^2 - 3x + 4x - 6 && \text{Replace } x \text{ by } -3x + 4x. \\ &= (2x - 3)x + (2x - 3)2 && \text{Factor out the common factors.} \\ &= (2x - 3)(x + 2) && \text{Factor out } 2x - 3. \end{aligned}$$

Check by FOIL.

c) Because $ac = 10(-3) = -30$, we need two integers with a product of -30 and a sum of 13. The product is negative, so the integers must have opposite signs. We can list all pairs of factors of -30 as follows:

1 and -30	2 and -15	3 and -10	5 and -6
-1 and 30	-2 and 15	-3 and 10	-5 and 6

The only pair that has a sum of 13 is -2 and 15:

$$\begin{aligned} 10x^2 + 13x - 3 &= 10x^2 - 2x + 15x - 3 && \text{Replace } 13x \text{ by } -2x + 15x. \\ &= (5x - 1)2x + (5x - 1)3 && \text{Factor out the common factors.} \\ &= (5x - 1)(2x + 3) && \text{Factor out } 5x - 1. \end{aligned}$$

Check by FOIL.

Now do Exercises 5–42

‹ Teaching Tip ›

Many students like the *ac* method because it is systematic. However, when factoring appears in a later course, students generally remember only trial and error.

EXAMPLE 2

Factoring a trinomial in two variables by the *ac* method

Factor $8x^2 - 14xy + 3y^2$

Solution

Since $a = 8$, $b = -14$, and $c = 3$, we have $ac = 24$. Two numbers with a product of 24 and a sum of -14 must both be negative. The possible pairs with a product of 24 follow:

-1 and -24	-3 and -8
-2 and -12	-4 and -6

Only -2 and -12 have a sum of -14. Replace $-14xy$ by $-2xy - 12xy$ and factor by grouping:

$$\begin{aligned} 8x^2 - 14xy + 3y^2 &= 8x^2 - 2xy - 12xy + 3y^2 \\ &= (4x - y)2x + (4x - y)(-3y) \\ &= (4x - y)(2x - 3y) \end{aligned}$$

Check by FOIL.

Now do Exercises 43–48

‹2› Trial and Error

After you have gained some experience at factoring by the *ac* method, you can often find the factors without going through the steps of grouping. For example, consider the polynomial

$$3x^2 + 7x - 6.$$

‹ Helpful Hint ›

The *ac* method is more systematic than trial and error. However, trial and error can be faster and easier, especially if your first or second trial is correct.

The factors of $3x^2$ can only be $3x$ and x. The factors of 6 could be 2 and 3 or 1 and 6. We can list all of the possibilities that give the correct first and last terms, without regard to the signs:

$$(3x \quad 3)(x \quad 2) \qquad (3x \quad 2)(x \quad 3) \qquad (3x \quad 6)(x \quad 1) \qquad (3x \quad 1)(x \quad 6)$$

Because the factors of -6 have unlike signs, one binomial factor is a sum and the other binomial is a difference. Now we try some products to see if we get a middle term of $7x$:

$$(3x + 3)(x - 2) = 3x^2 - 3x - 6 \quad \text{Incorrect}$$
$$(3x - 3)(x + 2) = 3x^2 + 3x - 6 \quad \text{Incorrect}$$

Actually, there is no need to try $(3x \quad 3)(x \quad 2)$ or $(3x \quad 6)(x \quad 1)$ because each contains a binomial with a common factor. A common factor in the binomial causes a common factor in the product. But $3x^2 + 7x - 6$ has no common factor. So the factors must come from either $(3x \quad 2)(x \quad 3)$ or $(3x \quad 1)(x \quad 6)$. So we try again:

$$(3x + 2)(x - 3) = 3x^2 - 7x - 6 \quad \text{Incorrect}$$
$$(3x - 2)(x + 3) = 3x^2 + 7x - 6 \quad \text{Correct}$$

Even though there may be many possibilities in some factoring problems, it is often possible to find the correct factors without writing down every possibility. We can use a bit of guesswork in factoring trinomials. *Try* whichever possibility you think might work. *Check* it by multiplying. If it is not right, then *try again.* That is why this method is called **trial and error.**

EXAMPLE 3

Trial and error

Factor each trinomial using trial and error.

a) $2x^2 + 5x - 3$

b) $3x^2 - 11x + 6$

Solution

a) Because $2x^2$ factors only as $2x \cdot x$ and 3 factors only as $1 \cdot 3$, there are only two possible ways to get the correct first and last terms, without regard to the signs:

$$(2x \quad 1)(x \quad 3) \qquad \text{and} \qquad (2x \quad 3)(x \quad 1)$$

Because the last term of the trinomial is negative, one of the missing signs must be $+$, and the other must be $-$. The trinomial is factored correctly as

$$2x^2 + 5x - 3 = (2x - 1)(x + 3).$$

Check by using FOIL.

b) There are four possible ways to factor $3x^2 - 11x + 6$:

$$(3x \quad 1)(x \quad 6) \qquad (3x \quad 2)(x \quad 3)$$
$$(3x \quad 6)(x \quad 1) \qquad (3x \quad 3)(x \quad 2)$$

Because the last term in $3x^2 - 11x + 6$ is positive and the middle term is negative, both signs in the factors must be negative. Because $3x^2 - 11x + 6$ has no common factor, we can rule out $(3x \quad 6)(x \quad 1)$ and $(3x \quad 3)(x \quad 2)$. So the only possibilities left are $(3x - 1)(x - 6)$ and $(3x - 2)(x - 3)$. The trinomial is factored correctly as

$$3x^2 - 11x + 6 = (3x - 2)(x - 3).$$

Check by using FOIL.

Now do Exercises 49–68

Factoring by trial and error is not just guessing. In fact, if the trinomial has a positive leading coefficient, we can determine in advance whether its factors are sums or differences.

Using Signs in Trial and Error

1. If the signs of the terms of a trinomial are + + + then both factors are sums: $x^2 + 5x + 6 = (x + 2)(x + 3)$.
2. If the signs are + − + then both factors are differences: $x^2 - 5x + 6 = (x - 2)(x - 3)$.
3. If the signs are + + − or + − − then one factor is a sum and the other is a difference: $x^2 + x - 6 = (x + 3)(x - 2)$ and $x^2 - x - 6 = (x - 3)(x + 2)$.

In Example 4 we factor a trinomial that has two variables.

EXAMPLE 4

Factoring a trinomial with two variables by trial and error

Factor $6x^2 - 7xy + 2y^2$.

Solution

We list the possible ways to factor the trinomial:

$$(3x \quad 2y)(2x \quad y) \qquad (3x \quad y)(2x \quad 2y) \qquad (6x \quad 2y)(x \quad y) \qquad (6x \quad y)(x \quad 2y)$$

Note that there is a common factor 2 in $(2x \quad 2y)$ and in $(6x \quad 2y)$. Since there is no common factor of 2 in the original trinomial, the second and third possibilities will not work. Because the last term of the trinomial is positive and the middle term is negative, both factors must contain subtraction symbols. Only the first possibility will give a middle term of $-7xy$ when subtraction symbols are used in both factors. So

$$6x^2 - 7xy + 2y^2 = (3x - 2y)(2x - y).$$

Now do Exercises 69–72

⟨3⟩ Factoring Completely

You can use the latest factoring technique along with the techniques that you learned earlier to factor polynomials completely. Remember always to first factor out the greatest common factor (if it is not 1).

EXAMPLE 5

Factoring completely

Factor each polynomial completely.

a) $4x^3 + 14x^2 + 6x$

b) $12x^2y + 6xy + 6y$

Solution

a) $4x^3 + 14x^2 + 6x = 2x(2x^2 + 7x + 3)$ Factor out the GCF, $2x$.

$= 2x(2x + 1)(x + 3)$ Factor $2x^2 + 7x + 3$.

Check by multiplying.

b) $12x^2y + 6xy + 6y = 6y(2x^2 + x + 1)$ Factor out the GCF, $6y$.

To factor $2x^2 + x + 1$ by the ac method, we need two numbers with a product of 2 and a sum of 1. Because there are no such numbers, $2x^2 + x + 1$ is prime and the factorization is complete.

Now do Exercises 79–88

Our first step in factoring is to factor out the greatest common factor (if it is not 1). If the first term of a polynomial has a negative coefficient, then it is better to factor out the opposite of the GCF so that the resulting polynomial will have a positive leading coefficient.

EXAMPLE 6

Factoring out the opposite of the GCF

Factor each polynomial completely.

a) $-18x^3 + 51x^2 - 15x$

b) $-3a^2 + 2a + 21$

‹ Teaching Tip ›

If the leading coefficient is negative, both ac and trial and error will work, but students find it easier to have a positive leading coefficient.

Solution

a) The GCF is $3x$. Because the first term has a negative coefficient, we factor out $-3x$:

$-18x^3 + 51x^2 - 15x = -3x(6x^2 - 17x + 5)$ Factor out $-3x$.

$= -3x(3x - 1)(2x - 5)$ Factor $6x^2 - 17x + 5$.

b) The GCF for $-3a^2 + 2a + 21$ is 1. Because the first term has a negative coefficient, factor out -1:

$-3a^2 + 2a + 21 = -1(3a^2 - 2a - 21)$ Factor out -1.

$= -1(3a + 7)(a - 3)$ Factor $3a^2 - 2a - 21$.

Now do Exercises 89–104

Warm-Ups ▼

True or false? Explain your answer.

1. $2x^2 + 3x + 1 = (2x + 1)(x + 1)$ True
2. $2x^2 + 5x + 3 = (2x + 1)(x + 3)$ False
3. $3x^2 + 10x + 3 = (3x + 1)(x + 3)$ True
4. $15x^2 + 31x + 14 = (3x + 7)(5x + 2)$ False
5. $2x^2 - 7x - 9 = (2x - 9)(x + 1)$ True
6. $2x^2 + 3x - 9 = (2x + 3)(x - 3)$ False
7. $2x^2 - 16x - 9 = (2x - 9)(2x + 1)$ False
8. $8x^2 - 22x - 5 = (4x - 1)(2x + 5)$ False
9. $9x^2 + x - 1 = (5x - 1)(4x + 1)$ False
10. $12x^2 - 13x + 3 = (3x - 1)(4x - 3)$ True

Exercises

‹ Study Tips ›

- Pay particular attention to the examples that your instructor works in class or presents to you online.
- The examples and homework assignments should give you a good idea of what your instructor expects from you.

Reading and Writing *After reading this section, write out the answers to these questions. Use complete sentences.*

1. What types of polynomials did we factor in this section? We factored $ax^2 + bx + c$ with $a \neq 1$.
2. What is the ac method of factoring? In the ac method we find two integers whose product is equal to ac and whose sum is b, and then we use factoring by grouping.
3. How can you determine if $ax^2 + bx + c$ is prime? If there are no two integers whose product is ac and whose sum is b, then $ax^2 + bx + c$ is prime.
4. What is the trial-and-error method of factoring? In trial and error, we make an educated guess at the factors and then check by FOIL.

‹1› The *ac* Method

Find the following. See Example 1.

5. Two integers that have a product of 12 and a sum of 7
 3 and 4
6. Two integers that have a product of 20 and a sum of 12
 2 and 10
7. Two integers that have a product of 30 and a sum of -17
 -2 and -15
8. Two integers that have a product of 36 and a sum of -20
 -2 and -18
9. Two integers that have a product of -12 and a sum of -4
 -6 and 2
10. Two integers that have a product of -8 and a sum of 7
 8 and -1

Each of the following trinomials is in the form $ax^2 + bx + c$. For each trinomial, find two integers that have a product of ac and a sum of b. Do not factor the trinomials. See Example 1.

11. $6x^2 + 7x + 2$
 3 and 4
12. $5x^2 + 17x + 6$
 2 and 15
13. $6y^2 - 11y + 3$
 -2 and -9
14. $6z^2 - 19z + 10$
 -4 and -15

15. $12w^2 + w - 1$
-3 and 4

16. $15t^2 - 17t - 4$
-20 and 3

Factor each trinomial using the ac method.
See Example 1.
See the Strategy for Factoring $ax^2 + bx + c$ by the ac Method box on page 386.

17. $2x^2 + 3x + 1$
$(2x + 1)(x + 1)$

18. $2x^2 + 11x + 5$
$(2x + 1)(x + 5)$

19. $2x^2 + 9x + 4$
$(2x + 1)(x + 4)$

20. $2h^2 + 7h + 3$
$(2h + 1)(h + 3)$

21. $3t^2 + 7t + 2$
$(3t + 1)(t + 2)$

22. $3t^2 + 8t + 5$
$(3t + 5)(t + 1)$

23. $2x^2 + 5x - 3$
$(2x - 1)(x + 3)$

24. $3x^2 - x - 2$
$(3x + 2)(x - 1)$

25. $6x^2 + 7x - 3$
$(3x - 1)(2x + 3)$

26. $21x^2 + 2x - 3$
$(3x - 1)(7x + 3)$

27. $3x^2 - 5x + 4$ Prime

28. $6x^2 - 5x + 3$ Prime

29. $2x^2 - 7x + 6$
$(2x - 3)(x - 2)$

30. $3a^2 - 14a + 15$
$(3a - 5)(a - 3)$

31. $5b^2 - 13b + 6$
$(5b - 3)(b - 2)$

32. $7y^2 + 16y - 15$
$(7y - 5)(y + 3)$

33. $4y^2 - 11y - 3$
$(4y + 1)(y - 3)$

34. $35x^2 - 2x - 1$
$(7x + 1)(5x - 1)$

35. $3x^2 + 2x + 1$
Prime

36. $6x^2 - 4x - 5$
Prime

37. $8x^2 - 2x - 1$
$(4x + 1)(2x - 1)$

38. $8x^2 - 10x - 3$
$(4x + 1)(2x - 3)$

39. $9t^2 - 9t + 2$
$(3t - 1)(3t - 2)$

40. $9t^2 + 5t - 4$
$(9t - 4)(t + 1)$

41. $15x^2 + 13x + 2$
$(5x + 1)(3x + 2)$

42. $15x^2 - 7x - 2$
$(5x + 1)(3x - 2)$

Use the ac method to factor each trinomial. See Example 2.

43. $4a^2 + 16ab + 15b^2$
$(2a + 3b)(2a + 5b)$

44. $10x^2 + 17xy + 3y^2$
$(5x + y)(2x + 3y)$

45. $6m^2 - 7mn - 5n^2$
$(3m - 5n)(2m + n)$

46. $3a^2 + 2ab - 21b^2$
$(3a - 7b)(a + 3b)$

47. $3x^2 - 8xy + 5y^2$
$(x - y)(3x - 5y)$

48. $3m^2 - 13mn + 12n^2$
$(m - 3n)(3m - 4n)$

⟨2⟩ Trial and Error

Factor each trinomial using trial and error. See Examples 3 and 4.

49. $5a^2 + 6a + 1$
$(5a + 1)(a + 1)$

50. $7b^2 + 8b + 1$
$(7b + 1)(b + 1)$

51. $6x^2 + 5x + 1$
$(2x + 1)(3x + 1)$

52. $15y^2 + 8y + 1$
$(3y + 1)(5y + 1)$

53. $5a^2 + 11a + 2$
$(5a + 1)(a + 2)$

54. $3y^2 + 10y + 7$
$(3y + 7)(y + 1)$

55. $4w^2 + 8w + 3$
$(2w + 3)(2w + 1)$

56. $6z^2 + 13z + 5$
$(2z + 1)(3z + 5)$

57. $15x^2 - x - 2$
$(5x - 2)(3x + 1)$

58. $15x^2 + 13x - 2$
$(15x - 2)(x + 1)$

59. $8x^2 - 6x + 1$
$(4x - 1)(2x - 1)$

60. $8x^2 - 22x + 5$
$(4x - 1)(2x - 5)$

61. $15x^2 - 31x + 2$
$(15x - 1)(x - 2)$

62. $15x^2 + 31x + 2$
$(15x + 1)(x + 2)$

63. $4x^2 - 4x + 3$
Prime

64. $4x^2 + 12x - 5$
Prime

65. $2x^2 + 18x - 90$
$2(x^2 + 9x - 45)$

66. $3x^2 + 11x + 10$
$(x + 2)(3x + 5)$

67. $3x^2 + x - 10$
$(3x - 5)(x + 2)$

68. $3x^2 - 17x + 10$
$(3x - 2)(x - 5)$

69. $10x^2 - 3xy - y^2$
$(5x + y)(2x - y)$

70. $8x^2 - 2xy - y^2$
$(4x + y)(2x - y)$

71. $42a^2 - 13ab + b^2$
$(6a - b)(7a - b)$

72. $10a^2 - 27ab + 5b^2$
$(5a - b)(2a - 5b)$

Complete the factoring.

73. $3x^2 + 7x + 2 = (x + 2)(\ 3x + 1)$

74. $2x^2 - x - 15 = (x - 3)(\ 2x + 5)$

75. $5x^2 + 11x + 2 = (5x + 1)(\ x + 2)$

76. $4x^2 - 19x - 5 = (4x + 1)(\ x - 5)$

77. $6a^2 - 17a + 5 = (3a - 1)(\ 2a - 5)$

78. $4b^2 - 16b + 15 = (2b - 5)(\ 2b - 3)$

⟨3⟩ Factoring Completely

Factor each polynomial completely. See Examples 5 and 6.

79. $81w^3 - w$
$w(9w - 1)(9w + 1)$

80. $81w^3 - w^2$
$w^2(81w - 1)$

81. $4w^2 + 2w - 30$
$2(2w - 5)(w + 3)$

82. $2x^2 - 28x + 98$
$2(x - 7)^2$

83. $27 + 12x^2 + 36x$
$3(2x + 3)^2$

84. $24y + 12y^2 + 12$
$12(y + 1)^2$

85. $6w^2 - 11w - 35$
$(3w + 5)(2w - 7)$

86. $8y^2 - 14y - 15$
$(2y - 5)(4y + 3)$

87. $3x^2z - 3zx - 18z$
$3z(x - 3)(x + 2)$

88. $a^2b + 2ab - 15b$
$b(a + 5)(a - 3)$

89. $9x^3 - 21x^2 + 18x$
$3x(3x^2 - 7x + 6)$

90. $-8x^3 + 4x^2 - 2x$
$-2x(4x^2 - 2x + 1)$

91. $a^2 + 2ab - 15b^2$
$(a + 5b)(a - 3b)$

92. $a^2b^2 - 2a^2b - 15a^2$
$a^2(b - 5)(b + 3)$

93. $2x^2y^2 + xy^2 + 3y^2$
$y^2(2x^2 + x + 3)$

94. $18x^2 - 6x + 6$
$6(3x^2 - x + 1)$

95. $-6t^3 - t^2 + 2t$
$-t(3t + 2)(2t - 1)$

96. $-36t^2 - 6t + 12$
$-6(3t + 2)(2t - 1)$

97. $12t^4 - 2t^3 - 4t^2$
$2t^2(3t - 2)(2t + 1)$

98. $12t^3 + 14t^2 + 4t$
$2t(3t + 2)(2t + 1)$

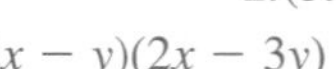

99. $4x^2y - 8xy^2 + 3y^3$ $y(2x - y)(2x - 3y)$

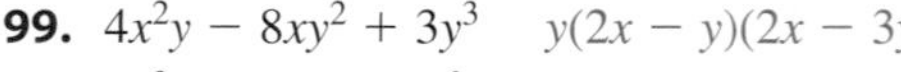

100. $9x^2 + 24xy - 9y^2$ $3(3x - y)(x + 3y)$

101. $-4w^2 + 7w - 3$ $-1(w - 1)(4w - 3)$

102. $-30w^2 + w + 1$ $-1(5w - 1)(6w + 1)$

103. $-12a^3 + 22a^2b - 6ab^2$ $\quad -2a(2a - 3b)(3a - b)$

104. $-36a^2b + 21ab^2 - 3b^3$ $\quad -3b(3a - b)(4a - b)$

Applications

Solve each problem.

105. ***Height of a ball.*** If a ball is thrown straight upward at 40 feet per second from a rooftop 24 feet above the ground, then its height in feet above the ground t seconds after it is thrown is given by

$$h(t) = -16t^2 + 40t + 24.$$

a) Find $h(0)$, $h(1)$, $h(2)$, and $h(3)$. 24, 48, 40, 0 feet

b) Rewrite the formula with the polynomial factored completely. $h(t) = -8(2t + 1)(t - 3)$

c) Find $h(3)$ using the result of part (b). 0 feet

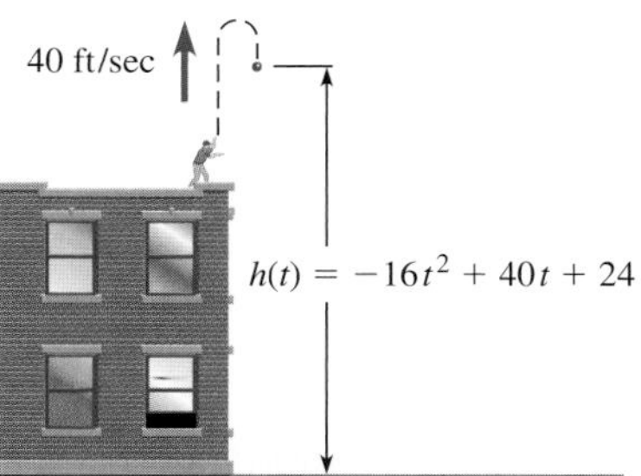

Figure for Exercise 105

106. ***Worker efficiency.*** In a study of worker efficiency at Wong Laboratories it was found that the number of components assembled per hour by the average worker t hours after starting work could be modeled by the formula

$$N(t) = -3t^3 + 23t^2 + 8t.$$

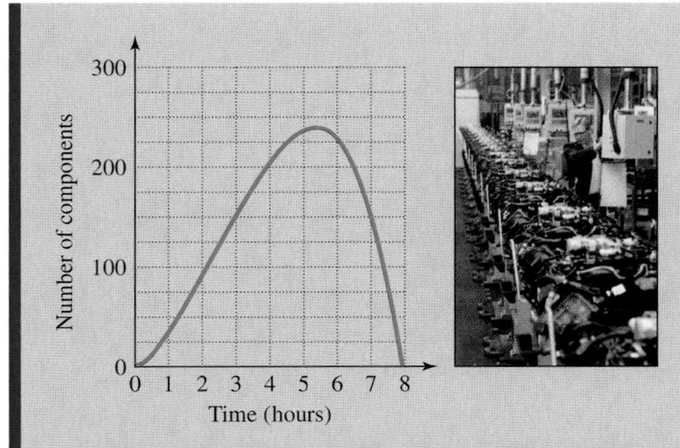

Figure for Exercise 106

a) Rewrite the formula by factoring the right-hand side completely. $N(t) = -t(3t + 1)(t - 8)$

b) Use the factored version of the formula to find $N(3)$. 150 components

c) Use the accompanying graph to estimate the time at which the workers are most efficient. 5 hr

d) Use the accompanying graph to estimate the maximum number of components assembled per hour during an 8-hour shift. 250 components

Getting More Involved

107. ***Exploration***

Find all positive and negative integers b for which each polynomial can be factored.

a) $x^2 + bx + 3$ $\quad \pm 4$ **b)** $3x^2 + bx + 5$ $\quad \pm 8, \pm 16$

c) $2x^2 + bx - 15$ $\quad \pm 1, \pm 7, \pm 13, \pm 29$

108. ***Exploration***

Find two integers c (positive or negative) for which each polynomial can be factored. Many answers are possible.

a) $x^2 + x + c$ $\quad -2, -6$

b) $x^2 - 2x + c$ $\quad 1, -8$

c) $2x^2 - 3x + c$ $\quad 1, -9$

109. ***Cooperative learning***

Working in groups, cut two large squares, three rectangles, and one small square out of paper that are exactly the same size as shown in the accompanying figure. Then try to place the six figures next to one another so that they form a large rectangle. Do not overlap the pieces or leave any gaps. Explain how factoring $2x^2 + 3x + 1$ can help you solve this puzzle.

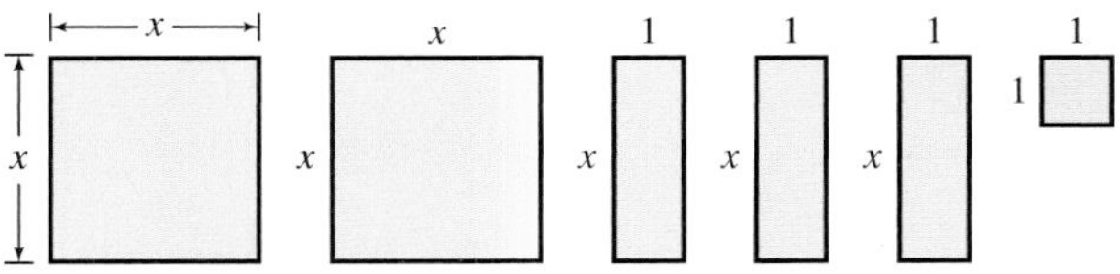

Figure for Exercise 109

110. ***Cooperative learning***

Working in groups, cut four squares and eight rectangles out of paper as in the previous exercise to illustrate the trinomial $4x^2 + 7x + 3$. Select one group to demonstrate how to arrange the 12 pieces to form a large rectangle. Have another group explain how factoring the trinomial can help you solve this puzzle.

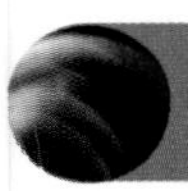

6.5 The Factoring Strategy

In This Section

In Sections 6.1 to 6.4, we established the general idea of factoring and some special cases. In this section we will see how division relates to factoring and see two more special cases. We will then summarize all of the factoring that we have done with a factoring strategy.

⟨1⟩ Using Division in Factoring

To find the prime factorization for a large integer such as 1001, you could divide possible factors (prime numbers) into 1001 until you find one that leaves no remainder. If you are told that 13 is a factor (or make a lucky guess), then you could divide 1001 by 13 to get the quotient 77. With this information you can factor 1001:

$$1001 = 77 \cdot 13$$

Now you can factor 77 to get the prime factorization of 1001:

$$1001 = 7 \cdot 11 \cdot 13$$

We can use this same idea with polynomials that are of higher degree than the ones we have been factoring. If we can guess a factor or if we are given a factor, we can use division to find the other factor and then proceed to factor the polynomial completely. Of course, it is harder to guess a factor of a polynomial than it is to guess a factor of an integer. In Example 1 we will factor a third-degree polynomial completely, given one factor.

EXAMPLE 1

Using division in factoring

Factor the polynomial $x^3 + 2x^2 - 5x - 6$ completely, given that the binomial $x + 1$ is a factor of the polynomial.

Solution

Divide the polynomial by the binomial:

$$\begin{array}{r l}
 & x^2 + x - 6 \\
x + 1 \overline{)} & x^3 + 2x^2 - 5x - 6 \\
 & \underline{x^3 + x^2} \\
 & x^2 - 5x \\
 & \underline{x^2 + x} \\
 & -6x - 6 \quad -5x - x = -6x \\
 & \underline{-6x - 6} \\
 & 0 \quad -6 - (-6) = 0
\end{array}$$

Because the remainder is 0, the dividend is the divisor times the quotient:

$$x^3 + 2x^2 - 5x - 6 = (x + 1)(x^2 + x - 6)$$

Now we factor the remaining trinomial to get the complete factorization:

$$x^3 + 2x^2 - 5x - 6 = (x + 1)(x + 3)(x - 2)$$

Now do Exercises 7–18

‹ Teaching Tip ›

It is a good exercise to have the students actually perform these two divisions and discover the rules for themselves.

‹2› Factoring a Difference or Sum of Two Cubes

We can use division to discover that $a - b$ is a factor of $a^3 - b^3$ (a difference of two cubes) and $a + b$ is a factor of $a^3 + b^3$ (a sum of two cubes):

$$\begin{array}{r} a^2 + ab + b^2 \\ a - b\overline{)a^3 + 0a^2b + 0ab^2 - b^3} \\ \underline{a^3 - a^2b} \qquad\qquad\qquad \\ a^2b + 0ab^2 \qquad \\ \underline{a^2b - ab^2} \qquad \\ ab^2 - b^3 \\ \underline{ab^2 - b^3} \\ 0 \end{array} \qquad \begin{array}{r} a^2 - ab + b^2 \\ a + b\overline{)a^3 + 0a^2b + 0ab^2 + b^3} \\ \underline{a^3 + a^2b} \qquad\qquad\qquad \\ -a^2b + 0ab^2 \qquad \\ \underline{-a^2b - ab^2} \qquad \\ ab^2 + b^3 \\ \underline{ab^2 + b^3} \\ 0 \end{array}$$

So $a - b$ is a factor of $a^3 - b^3$, and $a + b$ is a factor of $a^3 + b^3$. These results give us two more factoring rules.

Factoring a Difference or Sum of Two Cubes

$$a^3 - b^3 = (a - b)(a^2 + ab + b^2)$$
$$a^3 + b^3 = (a + b)(a^2 - ab + b^2)$$

Note that $a^2 + ab + b^2$ and $a^2 - ab + b^2$ are prime. Do not confuse them with $a^2 + 2ab + b^2$ and $a^2 - 2ab + b^2$, which are not prime because

$$a^2 + 2ab + b^2 = (a + b)^2 \qquad \text{and} \qquad a^2 - 2ab + b^2 = (a - b)^2.$$

These similarities can help you remember the rules for factoring $a^3 - b^3$ and $a^3 + b^3$. Note also how $a^3 - b^3$ compares with $a^2 - b^2$:

$$a^2 - b^2 = (a - b)(a + b)$$
$$a^3 - b^3 = (a - b)(a^2 + ab + b^2)$$

EXAMPLE 2

Factoring a difference or sum of two cubes

Factor each polynomial.

a) $w^3 - 8$ **b)** $x^3 + 1$ **c)** $8y^3 - 27$

Solution

a) Because $8 = 2^3$, $w^3 - 8$ is a difference of two cubes. To factor $w^3 - 8$, let $a = w$ and $b = 2$ in the formula $a^3 - b^3 = (a - b)(a^2 + ab + b^2)$:

$$w^3 - 8 = (w - 2)(w^2 + 2w + 4)$$

b) Because $1 = 1^3$, the binomial $x^3 + 1$ is a sum of two cubes. Let $a = x$ and $b = 1$ in the formula $a^3 + b^3 = (a + b)(a^2 - ab + b^2)$:

$$x^3 + 1 = (x + 1)(x^2 - x + 1)$$

c) $8y^3 - 27 = (2y)^3 - 3^3$ This is a difference of two cubes.
$= (2y - 3)(4y^2 + 6y + 9)$ Let $a = 2y$ and $b = 3$ in the formula.

Now do Exercises 19–34

‹ Teaching Tip ›

This is a good opportunity to discuss the differences between $(a + b)^3$, $a^3 + b^3$, and $(ab)^3$.

In Example 2, we used the first three perfect cubes, 1, 8, and 27. You should verify that 1, 8, 27, 64, 125, 216, 343, 512, 729, and 1000 are the first 10 perfect cubes.

CAUTION The polynomial $(a - b)^3$ is not equivalent to $a^3 - b^3$ because if $a = 2$ and $b = 1$, then

$$(a - b)^3 = (2 - 1)^3 = 1^3 = 1$$

and

$$a^3 - b^3 = 2^3 - 1^3 = 8 - 1 = 7.$$

Likewise, $(a + b)^3$ is not equivalent to $a^3 + b^3$.

‹3› Factoring a Difference of Two Fourth Powers

A difference of two fourth powers of the form $a^4 - b^4$ is also a difference of two squares, $(a^2)^2 - (b^2)^2$. It can be factored by the rule for factoring a difference of two squares:

$$\begin{aligned} a^4 - b^4 &= (a^2)^2 - (b^2)^2 && \text{Write as a difference of two squares.} \\ &= (a^2 - b^2)(a^2 + b^2) && \text{Difference of two squares} \\ &= (a - b)(a + b)(a^2 + b^2) && \text{Factor completely.} \end{aligned}$$

Note that the sum of two squares $a^2 + b^2$ is prime and cannot be factored.

EXAMPLE 3

Factoring a difference of two fourth powers

Factor each polynomial completely.

a) $x^4 - 16$ **b)** $81m^4 - n^4$

Solution

a) $$\begin{aligned} x^4 - 16 &= (x^2)^2 - 4^2 && \text{Write as a difference of two squares.} \\ &= (x^2 - 4)(x^2 + 4) && \text{Difference of two squares} \\ &= (x - 2)(x + 2)(x^2 + 4) && \text{Factor completely.} \end{aligned}$$

b) $$\begin{aligned} 81m^4 - n^4 &= (9m^2)^2 - (n^2)^2 && \text{Write as a difference of two squares.} \\ &= (9m^2 - n^2)(9m^2 + n^2) && \text{Factor.} \\ &= (3m - n)(3m + n)(9m^2 + n^2) && \text{Factor completely.} \end{aligned}$$

Now do Exercises 35–42

CAUTION A difference of two squares or cubes can be factored and a sum of two cubes can be factored. But the sums of two squares $x^2 + 4$ and $9m^2 + n^2$ in Example 3 are prime.

‹4› The Factoring Strategy

The following is a summary of the ideas that we use to factor a polynomial completely.

Strategy for Factoring Polynomials Completely

1. If there are any common factors, factor them out first.
2. When factoring a binomial, check to see whether it is a difference of two squares, a difference of two cubes, or a sum of two cubes. *A sum of two squares does not factor.*
3. When factoring a trinomial, check to see whether it is a perfect square trinomial.
4. When factoring a trinomial that is not a perfect square, use the *ac* method or the trial-and-error method.
5. If the polynomial has four terms, try factoring by grouping.
6. Check to see whether any of the factors can be factored again.

We will use the factoring strategy in Example 4.

EXAMPLE 4

Factoring polynomials

Factor each polynomial completely.

a) $2a^2b - 24ab + 72b$ **b)** $3x^3 + 6x^2 - 75x - 150$

c) $-3x^4 - 15x^3 + 72x^2$ **d)** $60y^3 - 85y^2 - 25y$

Solution

a)
$$\begin{aligned} 2a^2b - 24ab + 72b &= 2b(a^2 - 12a + 36) && \text{First factor out the GCF, } 2b. \\ &= 2b(a - 6)^2 && \text{Factor the perfect square trinomial.} \end{aligned}$$

b)
$$\begin{aligned} 3x^3 + 6x^2 - 75x - 150 &= 3[x^3 + 2x^2 - 25x - 50] && \text{Factor out the GCF, 3.} \\ &= 3[x^2(x + 2) - 25(x + 2)] && \text{Factor out common factors.} \\ &= 3(x^2 - 25)(x + 2) && \text{Factor by grouping.} \\ &= 3(x + 5)(x - 5)(x + 2) && \text{Factor the difference of two squares.} \end{aligned}$$

c) Factor out $-3x^2$ to get $-3x^4 - 15x^3 + 72x^2 = -3x^2(x^2 + 5x - 24)$. To factor the trinomial, find two numbers with a product of -24 and a sum of 5. For a product of 24 we have $1 \cdot 24$, $2 \cdot 12$, $3 \cdot 8$, and $4 \cdot 6$. To get a sum of 5 and a product of -24 choose 8 and -3:

$$\begin{aligned} -3x^4 - 15x^3 + 72x^2 &= -3x^2(x^2 + 5x - 24) \\ &= -3x^2(x - 3)(x + 8) \end{aligned}$$

d) Factor out $5y$ to get $60y^3 - 85y^2 - 25y = 5y(12y^2 - 17y - 5)$. By the *ac* method we need two numbers that have a product of -60 (ac) and a sum of -17. The numbers are -20 and 3. Now factor by grouping:

$$\begin{aligned} 60y^3 - 85y^2 - 25y &= 5y(12y^2 - 17y - 5) && \text{Factor out } 5y. \\ &= 5y(12y^2 - 20y + 3y - 5) && -17y = -20y + 3y \\ &= 5y[4y(3y - 5) + 1(3y - 5)] && \text{Factor by grouping.} \\ &= 5y(3y - 5)(4y + 1) && \text{Factor out } 3y - 5. \end{aligned}$$

Now do Exercises 43–110

Warm-Ups

True or false? Explain your answer.

1. $x^2 - 4 = (x - 2)^2$ for any real number x. False
2. The trinomial $4x^2 + 6x + 9$ is a perfect square trinomial. False
3. The polynomial $4y^2 + 25$ is a prime polynomial. True
4. $3y + ay + 3x + ax = (x + y)(3 + a)$ for any values of the variables. True
5. The polynomial $3x^2 + 51$ cannot be factored. False
6. If the GCF is not 1, then you should factor it out first. True
7. $x^2 + 9 = (x + 3)^2$ for any real number x. False
8. The polynomial $x^2 - 3x - 5$ is a prime polynomial. True
9. The polynomial $y^2 - 5y - my + 5m$ can be factored by grouping. True
10. The polynomial $x^2 + ax - 3x + 3a$ can be factored by grouping. False

6.5 Exercises

Study Tips

- If you have a choice, sit at the front of the class. It is easier to stay alert when you are at the front.
- If you miss what is going on in class, you miss what your instructor feels is important and most likely to appear on tests and quizzes.

Reading and Writing *After reading this section, write out the answers to these questions. Use complete sentences.*

1. What is the relationship between division and factoring? If there is no remainder, then the dividend factors as the divisor times the quotient.
2. How do we know that $a - b$ is a factor of $a^3 - b^3$? If you divide $a^3 - b^3$ by $a - b$ there will be no remainder.
3. How do we know that $a + b$ is a factor of $a^3 + b^3$? If you divide $a^3 + b^3$ by $a + b$ there will be no remainder.
4. How do you recognize if a polynomial is a sum of two cubes? A sum of two cubes is of the form $a^3 + b^3$.
5. How do you factor a sum of two cubes? $a^3 + b^3 = (a + b)(a^2 - ab + b^2)$
6. How do you factor a difference of two cubes? $a^3 - b^3 = (a - b)(a^2 + ab + b^2)$

‹1› Using Division in Factoring

Factor each polynomial completely, given that the binomial following it is a factor of the polynomial. See Example 1.

7. $x^3 + 6x^2 + 11x + 6,\ x + 1$ $(x + 1)(x + 2)(x + 3)$
8. $x^3 + 9x^2 + 26x + 24,\ x + 2$ $(x + 2)(x + 3)(x + 4)$
9. $x^3 + 3x^2 - 10x - 24,\ x + 4$ $(x + 4)(x - 3)(x + 2)$
10. $x^3 - 7x + 6,\ x - 1$ $(x - 1)(x + 3)(x - 2)$
11. $x^3 + 4x^2 + x - 6,\ x - 1$ $(x - 1)(x + 3)(x + 2)$
12. $x^3 - 5x^2 - 2x + 24,\ x + 2$ $(x + 2)(x - 3)(x - 4)$
13. $x^3 - 8,\ x - 2$ $(x - 2)(x^2 + 2x + 4)$
14. VIDEO $x^3 + 27,\ x + 3$ $(x + 3)(x^2 - 3x + 9)$
15. $x^3 + 4x^2 - 3x + 10,\ x + 5$ $(x + 5)(x^2 - x + 2)$
16. $2x^3 - 5x^2 - x - 6,\ x - 3$ $(x - 3)(2x^2 + x + 2)$

17. $x^3 + 2x^2 + 2x + 1, x + 1$ $(x + 1)(x^2 + x + 1)$

18. $x^3 + 2x^2 - 5x - 6, x + 3$ $(x + 3)(x - 2)(x + 1)$

⟨2⟩ Factoring a Difference or Sum of Two Cubes

Factor each difference or sum of cubes. See Example 2.

19. $m^3 - 1$ $(m - 1)(m^2 + m + 1)$

20. $z^3 - 27$ $(z - 3)(z^2 + 3z + 9)$

21. $x^3 + 8$ $(x + 2)(x^2 - 2x + 4)$

22. $y^3 + 27$ $(y + 3)(y^2 - 3y + 9)$

VIDEO **23.** $a^3 + 125$ $(a + 5)(a^2 - 5a + 25)$

24. $b^3 - 216$ $(b - 6)(b^2 + 6b + 36)$

25. $c^3 - 343$ $(c - 7)(c^2 + 7c + 49)$

26. $d^3 + 1000$ $(d + 10)(d^2 - 10d + 100)$

27. $8w^3 + 1$ $(2w + 1)(4w^2 - 2w + 1)$

28. $125m^3 + 1$ $(5m + 1)(25m^2 - 5m + 1)$

29. $8t^3 - 27$ $(2t - 3)(4t^2 + 6t + 9)$

VIDEO **30.** $125n^3 - 8$ $(5n - 2)(25n^2 + 10n + 4)$

31. $x^3 - y^3$ $(x - y)(x^2 + xy + y^2)$

32. $m^3 + n^3$ $(m + n)(m^2 - mn + n^2)$

33. $8t^3 + y^3$ $(2t + y)(4t^2 - 2ty + y^2)$

34. $u^3 - 125v^3$ $(u - 5v)(u^2 + 5uv + 25v^2)$

⟨3⟩ Factoring a Difference of Two Fourth Powers

Factor each polynomial completely. See Example 3.

35. $x^4 - y^4$ $(x - y)(x + y)(x^2 + y^2)$

36. $m^4 - n^4$ $(m - n)(m + n)(m^2 + n^2)$

37. $x^4 - 1$ $(x - 1)(x + 1)(x^2 + 1)$

38. $a^4 - 81$ $(a - 3)(a + 3)(a^2 + 9)$

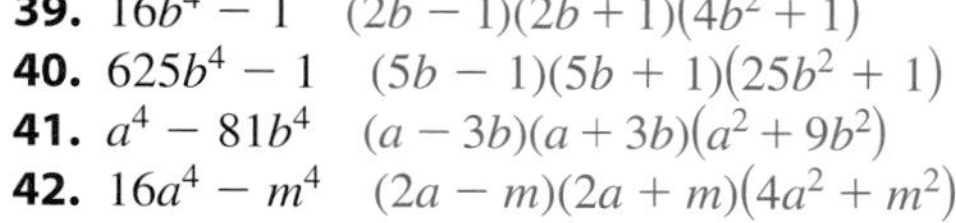

VIDEO **39.** $16b^4 - 1$ $(2b - 1)(2b + 1)(4b^2 + 1)$

40. $625b^4 - 1$ $(5b - 1)(5b + 1)(25b^2 + 1)$

41. $a^4 - 81b^4$ $(a - 3b)(a + 3b)(a^2 + 9b^2)$

42. $16a^4 - m^4$ $(2a - m)(2a + m)(4a^2 + m^2)$

⟨4⟩ The Factoring Strategy

Factor each polynomial completely. If a polynomial is prime, say so.

See Example 4.

See the Strategy for Factoring Polynomials Completely box on page 397.

43. $2x^2 - 18$ $2(x - 3)(x + 3)$

44. $3x^3 - 12x$ $3x(x - 2)(x + 2)$

45. $a^2 + 4$ Prime

46. $x^2 + y^2$ Prime

47. $4x^2 + 8x - 60$ $4(x + 5)(x - 3)$

48. $3x^2 + 18x + 27$ $3(x + 3)^2$

49. $x^3 + 4x^2 + 4x$ $x(x + 2)^2$

50. $a^3 - 5a^2 + 6a$ $a(a - 2)(a - 3)$

51. $5max^2 + 20ma$ $5am(x^2 + 4)$

52. $3bmw^2 - 12bm$ $3bm(w - 2)(w + 2)$

53. $2x^2 - 3x - 1$ Prime

54. $3x^2 - 8x - 5$ Prime

55. $9x^2 + 6x + 1$ $(3x + 1)^2$

56. $9x^2 + 6x + 3$ $3(3x^2 + 2x + 1)$

57. $9m^2 + 1$ Prime

58. $4b^2 + 25$ Prime

59. $w^4 - z^4$ $(w - z)(w + z)(w^2 + z^2)$

60. $y^4 - 1$ $(y - 1)(y + 1)(y^2 + 1)$

61. $6x^2y + xy - 2y$ $y(3x + 2)(2x - 1)$

62. $5x^2y^2 - xy^2 - 6y^2$ $y^2(5x - 6)(x + 1)$

63. $y^2 + 10y - 25$ Prime

64. $x^2 - 20x + 25$ Prime

65. $48a^2 - 24a + 3$ $3(4a - 1)^2$

66. $8b^2 + 24b + 18$ $2(2b + 3)^2$

67. $16m^2 - 4m - 2$ $2(4m + 1)(2m - 1)$

68. $32a^2 + 4a - 6$ $2(2a + 1)(8a - 3)$

69. $s^4 - 16t^4$ $(s - 2t)(s + 2t)(s^2 + 4t^2)$

70. $81 - q^4$ $(3 - q)(3 + q)(9 + q^2)$

71. $9a^2 + 24a + 16$ $(3a + 4)^2$

72. $3x^2 - 18x - 48$ $3(x - 8)(x + 2)$

VIDEO **73.** $24x^2 - 26x + 6$ $2(3x - 1)(4x - 3)$

74. $4x^2 - 6x - 12$ $2(2x^2 - 3x - 6)$

75. $3m^2 + 27$ $3(m^2 + 9)$

76. $5a^2 + 20b^2$ $5(a^2 + 4b^2)$

77. $3a^2 - 27a$ $3a(a - 9)$

78. $a^2 - 25a$ $a(a - 25)$

79. $8 - 2x^2$ $2(2 - x)(2 + x)$

80. $x^3 + 6x^2 + 9x$ $x(x + 3)^2$

81. $w^2 + 4t^2$ Prime

82. $9x^2 + 4y^2$ Prime

83. $6x^3 - 5x^2 + 12x$ $x(6x^2 - 5x + 12)$

84. $x^3 + 2x^2 - x - 2$ $(x - 1)(x + 1)(x + 2)$

85. $a^3b - 4ab$ $ab(a - 2)(a + 2)$

86. $2m^2 - 1800$ $2(m - 30)(m + 30)$

87. $x^3 + 2x^2 - 4x - 8$ $(x - 2)(x + 2)^2$

88. $-2x^3 - 50x$ $-2x(x^2 + 25)$

89. $-7m^3n - 28mn^3$ $-7mn(m^2 + 4n^2)$

90. $x^3 - x^2 - x + 1$ $(x + 1)(x - 1)^2$

91. $2x^3 + 16$ $2(x + 2)(x^2 - 2x + 4)$

VIDEO **92.** $m^2a + 2ma^2 + a^3$ $a(m + a)^2$

93. $2w^4 - 16w$ $2w(w - 2)(w^2 + 2w + 4)$

94. $m^4n + mn^4$ $mn(m + n)(m^2 - mn + n^2)$

95. $3a^2w - 18aw + 27w$ $3w(a - 3)^2$

96. $8a^3 + 4a$ $4a(2a^2 + 1)$

97. $5x^2 - 500$ $5(x - 10)(x + 10)$

98. $25x^2 - 16y^2$ $(5x - 4y)(5x + 4y)$

99. $2m + 2n - wm - wn$ $(2 - w)(m + n)$

100. $aw - 5b - bw + 5a$ $(w + 5)(a - b)$

101. $3x^4 + 3x$ $3x(x + 1)(x^2 - x + 1)$

102. $3a^5 - 81a^2$ $3a^2(a - 3)(a^2 + 3a + 9)$

103. $4w^2 + 4w - 4$ $4(w^2 + w - 1)$

104. $4w^2 + 8w - 5$ $(2w + 5)(2w - 1)$

105. $a^4 + 7a^3 - 30a^2$ $a^2(a + 10)(a - 3)$

106. $2y^5 + 3y^4 - 20y^3$ $y^3(2y - 5)(y + 4)$

107. $4aw^3 - 12aw^2 + 9aw$ $aw(2w - 3)^2$

108. $9bn^3 + 15bn^2 - 14bn$ $bn(3n - 2)(3n + 7)$
109. $t^2 + 6t + 9$ $(t + 3)^2$
110. $t^3 + 12t^2 + 36t$ $t(t + 6)^2$

Applications

Solve each problem.

111. ***Increasing cube.*** Each of the three sides of a cube with sides of x centimeters is increased by a whole number of centimeters. The new volume in cubic centimeters is given by

$$V(x) = x^3 + 10x^2 + 31x + 30.$$

a) Find $V(3)$. 240 cubic centimeters
b) If the new height is $x + 2$ centimeters, then what are the new length and width? Length $x + 5$ cm, width $x + 3$ cm
c) Find the volume when $x = 3$ by multiplying the length, width, and height. 240 cubic centimeters

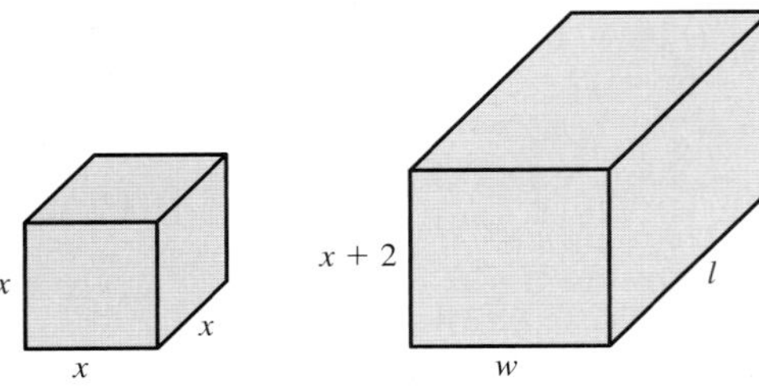

Figure for Exercise 111

112. ***Decreasing cube.*** Each of the three dimensions of a cube with sides of length s centimeters is decreased by a whole number of centimeters. The new volume in cubic centimeters is given by

$$V(s) = s^3 - 13s^2 + 54s - 72.$$

a) Find $V(10)$. 168 cubic centimeters
b) If the new width is $s - 6$ centimeters, then what are the new length and height?
Length $s - 3$ cm, height $s - 4$ cm
c) Find the volume when $s = 10$ by multiplying the length, width, and height.
168 cubic centimeters

Getting More Involved

113. ***Discussion***

Are there any values for a and b for which $(a + b)^3 = a^3 + b^3$? Find a pair of values for a and b for which $(a + b)^3 \neq a^3 + b^3$. Is $(a + b)^3$ equivalent to $a^3 + b^3$? Explain your answers.
$(-1 + 1)^3 = (-1)^3 + 1^3$, $(1 + 2)^3 \neq 1^3 + 2^3$

114. ***Writing***

Explain why $a^2 + ab + b^2$ and $a^2 - ab + b^2$ are prime polynomials.

Extra Factoring Exercises

Factor each polynomial completely.

115. $3w^2 + 30w + 75$ $3(w + 5)^2$
116. $4z^2 + 16z + 16$ $4(z + 2)^2$
117. $81 - b^2$ $(9 + b)(9 - b)$
118. $9 - 4p^2$ $(3 + 2p)(3 - 2p)$
119. $w^2 - 8w$ $w(w - 8)$
120. $6z^2 + 12z$ $6z(z + 2)$
121. $3x^2 + 6x - 105$ $3(x - 5)(x + 7)$
122. $6m^2 - 36m - 96$ $6(m + 2)(m - 8)$
123. $ax - 5a + 4x - 20$ $(x - 5)(a + 4)$
124. $w^2 + 3w - 3c - cw$ $(w + 3)(w - c)$
125. $12x^2 - 7x - 12$ $(3x - 4)(4x + 3)$
126. $8x^2 - 6x - 27$ $(4x - 9)(2x + 3)$
127. $-9x^2 - 15x + 6$ $-3(3x - 1)(x + 2)$
128. $-8x^2 - 4x + 40$ $-4(x - 2)(2x + 5)$
129. $w^3 - 27$ $(w - 3)(w^2 + 3w + 9)$
130. $y^3 + 1$ $(y + 1)(y^2 - y + 1)$
131. $y^3 + y^2 + y + 1$ $(y + 1)(y^2 + 1)$
132. $a^3 + 2a^2 + 4a + 8$ $(a + 2)(a^2 + 4)$
133. $m^4 - 81$ $(m + 3)(m - 3)(m^2 + 9)$
134. $t^4 - 256$ $(t + 4)(t - 4)(t^2 + 16)$
135. $a^2 - 2ab - 8b^2$ $(a + 2b)(a - 4b)$
136. $x^2 - xy - 12y^2$ $(x + 3y)(x - 4y)$
137. $m^3y + 6m^2y^2 + 9my^3$ $my(m + 3y)^2$
138. $w^4a - 10w^3a^2 + 25w^2a^3$ $w^2a(w - 5a)^2$
139. $x^4 + 2x^3 + 4x^2$ $x^2(x^2 + 2x + 4)$
140. $y^5 - 6y^4 - 9y^3$ $y^3(y^2 - 6y - 9)$
141. $y^7 - y^3$ $y^3(y + 1)(y - 1)(y^2 + 1)$
142. $a^6 - 16a^2$ $a^2(a + 2)(a - 2)(a^2 + 4)$
143. $x^2 - 18x + 72$ $(x - 6)(x - 12)$
144. $m^2 - 17m + 72$ $(m - 8)(m - 9)$
145. $-6a^3 + 5a^2 + 4a$ $-a(2a + 1)(3a - 4)$
146. $-12x^2 + 15x + 18$ $-3(4x + 3)(x - 2)$
147. $x^4 - 8x$ $x(x - 2)(x^2 + 2x + 4)$
148. $a^4 + ab^3$ $a(a + b)(a^2 - ab + b^2)$
149. $16t^2 - 24tx + 9x^2$ $(4t - 3x)^2$
150. $9y^2 + 30yz + 25z^2$ $(3y + 5z)^2$

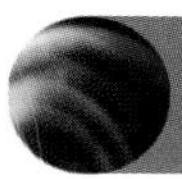

6.6 Solving Quadratic Equations by Factoring

In This Section

The techniques of factoring can be used to solve equations involving polynomials. These equations cannot be solved by the other methods that you have learned. After you learn to solve equations by factoring, you will use this technique to solve some new types of problems.

⟨1⟩ The Zero Factor Property

In this chapter you learned to factor polynomials such as $x^2 + x - 6$. The equation $x^2 + x - 6 = 0$ is called a *quadratic equation.*

Quadratic Equation

If a, b, and c are real numbers with $a \neq 0$, then

$$ax^2 + bx + c = 0$$

is called a **quadratic equation.**

A quadratic equation always has a second-degree term because it is specified in the definition that a is not zero. The main idea used to solve quadratic equations, the **zero factor property,** is simply a fact about multiplication by zero.

The Zero Factor Property

The equation $a \cdot b = 0$ is equivalent to

$$a = 0 \quad \text{or} \quad b = 0.$$

We will use the zero factor property most often to solve quadratic equations that have two factors, as shown in Example 1. However, this property holds for more than two factors as well. If a product of any number of factors is zero, then at least one of the factors is zero.

The following strategy gives the steps to follow when solving a quadratic equation by factoring. Of course, this method applies only to quadratic equations in which the quadratic polynomial can be factored. Methods that can be used for solving all quadratic equations are presented in Chapter 9.

Strategy for Solving an Equation by Factoring

1. Rewrite the equation with 0 on one side.
2. Factor the other side completely.
3. Use the zero factor property to get simple linear equations.
4. Solve the linear equations.
5. Check the answer in the original equation.
6. State the solution(s) to the original equation.

EXAMPLE 1

Using the zero factor property

Solve $x^2 + x - 6 = 0$.

Solution

First factor the polynomial on the left-hand side:

$$x^2 + x - 6 = 0$$

$$(x + 3)(x - 2) = 0 \quad \text{Factor the left-hand side.}$$

$$x + 3 = 0 \quad \text{or} \quad x - 2 = 0 \quad \text{Zero factor property}$$

$$x = -3 \quad \text{or} \quad x = 2 \quad \text{Solve each equation.}$$

We now check that -3 and 2 satisfy the original equation.

For $x = -3$:

$$x^2 + x - 6 = (-3)^2 + (-3) - 6 = 9 - 3 - 6 = 0$$

For $x = 2$:

$$x^2 + x - 6 = (2)^2 + (2) - 6 = 4 + 2 - 6 = 0$$

The solutions to $x^2 + x - 6 = 0$ are -3 and 2. Checking -3 and 2 in the factored form of the equation $(x + 3)(x - 2) = 0$ will help you understand the zero factor property:

$$(-3 + 3)(-3 - 2) = (0)(-5) = 0$$

$$(2 + 3)(2 - 2) = (5)(0) = 0$$

For each solution to the equation, one of the factors is zero and the other is not zero. All it takes to get a product of zero is one of the factors being zero.

Now do Exercises 7–18

‹ Helpful Hint ›

Some students grow up believing that the only way to solve an equation is to "do the same thing to each side." Then along come quadratic equations and the zero factor property. For a quadratic equation, we write an equivalent compound equation that is not obtained by "doing the same thing to each side."

A sentence such as $x = -3$ or $x = 2$, which is made up of two or more equations connected with the word "or," is called a **compound equation.** In Example 2, we again solve a quadratic equation by using the zero factor property to write a compound equation.

EXAMPLE 2

Using the zero factor property

Solve the equation $3x^2 = -3x$.

Solution

First rewrite the equation with 0 on the right-hand side:

$$3x^2 = -3x$$

$$3x^2 + 3x = 0 \quad \text{Add } 3x \text{ to each side.}$$

$$3x(x + 1) = 0 \quad \text{Factor the left-hand side.}$$

$$3x = 0 \quad \text{or} \quad x + 1 = 0 \quad \text{Zero factor property}$$

$$x = 0 \quad \text{or} \quad x = -1 \quad \text{Solve each equation.}$$

Check 0 and -1 in the original equation $3x^2 = -3x$.

For $x = 0$:

$$3(0)^2 = -3(0)$$

$$0 = 0$$

For $x = -1$:

$$3(-1)^2 = -3(-1)$$

$$3 = 3$$

There are two solutions to the original equation, 0 and -1.

Now do Exercises 19–26

‹ Teaching Tip ›

Another good example to work at this point is to solve $x^2 = x$.

CAUTION If in Example 2 you divide each side of $3x^2 = -3x$ by $3x$, you would get $x = -1$ but not the solution $x = 0$. For this reason we usually do not divide each side of an equation by a variable.

EXAMPLE 3

Using the zero factor property

Solve $(2x + 1)(x - 1) = 14$.

Solution

To write the equation with 0 on the right-hand side, multiply the binomials on the left and then subtract 14 from each side:

$$
\begin{aligned}
(2x + 1)(x - 1) &= 14 && \text{Original equation} \\
2x^2 - x - 1 &= 14 && \text{Multiply the binomials.} \\
2x^2 - x - 15 &= 0 && \text{Subtract 14 from each side.} \\
(2x + 5)(x - 3) &= 0 && \text{Factor.} \\
2x + 5 = 0 \quad \text{or} \quad x - 3 &= 0 && \text{Zero factor property} \\
2x = -5 \quad \text{or} \quad x &= 3 \\
x = -\frac{5}{2} \quad \text{or} \quad x &= 3
\end{aligned}
$$

Check $-\frac{5}{2}$ and 3 in the original equation:

$$
\begin{aligned}
\left(2 \cdot -\frac{5}{2} + 1\right)\left(-\frac{5}{2} - 1\right) &= (-5 + 1)\left(-\frac{5}{2} - \frac{2}{2}\right) \\
&= (-4)\left(-\frac{7}{2}\right) \\
&= 14 \\
(2 \cdot 3 + 1)(3 - 1) &= (7)(2) \\
&= 14
\end{aligned}
$$

So the solutions are $-\frac{5}{2}$ and 3.

Now do Exercises 27–32

‹ Teaching Tip ›

Show students how to make up a problem like this example: If $x = 5$, then $(5 - 2)(5 + 7) = 36$. So one of the solutions to $(x - 2)(x + 7) = 36$ is 5. Now solve it to find both solutions.

CAUTION In Example 3, we started with a product equal to 14. Because $1 \cdot 14 = 14$, $2 \cdot 7 = 14$, $\frac{1}{2} \cdot 28 = 14$, $\frac{1}{3} \cdot 42 = 14$, and so on, we cannot make any conclusion about the factors that have a product of 14. If the product of two factors is zero, then we can conclude that one or the other factor is zero.

If a perfect square trinomial occurs in a quadratic equation with 0 on one side, then there are two identical factors of the trinomial. In this case it is not necessary to set both factors equal to zero. The solution can be found from one factor.

EXAMPLE 4

An equation with a repeated factor

Solve $5x^2 - 30x + 45 = 0$.

Solution

Notice that the trinomial on the left-hand side has a common factor:

$$
\begin{aligned}
5x^2 - 30x + 45 &= 0 \\
5(x^2 - 6x + 9) &= 0 \quad \text{Factor out the GCF.} \\
5(x - 3)^2 &= 0 \quad \text{Factor the perfect square trinomial.} \\
(x - 3)^2 &= 0 \quad \text{Divide each side by 5.} \\
x - 3 &= 0 \quad \text{Zero factor property} \\
x &= 3
\end{aligned}
$$

Even though $x - 3$ occurs twice as a factor, it is not necessary to write $x - 3 = 0$ or $x - 3 = 0$. If $x = 3$ in $5x^2 - 30x + 45 = 0$, we get

$$5 \cdot 3^2 - 30 \cdot 3 + 45 = 0,$$

which is correct. So the only solution to the equation is 3.

Now do Exercises 33–36

‹ Teaching Tip ›

There are two trouble spots here, the constant factor and the repeated factor. You might need to work another example: $-12x^2 - 36x - 27 = 0$.

CAUTION Do not include 5 in the solution set to Example 4. Dividing by 5 eliminates it. Instead of dividing by 5 we could have applied the zero factor property to $5(x - 3)^2 = 0$. Since 5 is not 0, we must have $(x - 3)^2 = 0$ or $x - 3 = 0$.

If the left-hand side of the equation has more than two factors, we can write an equivalent equation by setting each factor equal to zero.

EXAMPLE 5

An equation with three solutions

Solve $2x^3 - x^2 - 8x + 4 = 0$.

Solution

We can factor the four-term polynomial by grouping:

$$
\begin{aligned}
2x^3 - x^2 - 8x + 4 &= 0 \\
x^2(2x - 1) - 4(2x - 1) &= 0 \quad \text{Factor out the common factors.} \\
(x^2 - 4)(2x - 1) &= 0 \quad \text{Factor out } 2x - 1. \\
(x - 2)(x + 2)(2x - 1) &= 0 \quad \text{Difference of two squares}
\end{aligned}
$$

$$x - 2 = 0 \quad \text{or} \quad x + 2 = 0 \quad \text{or} \quad 2x - 1 = 0 \quad \text{Zero factor property}$$

$$x = 2 \quad \text{or} \quad x = -2 \quad \text{or} \quad x = \frac{1}{2} \quad \text{Solve each equation.}$$

To check let $x = -2, \frac{1}{2}$, and 2 in $2x^3 - x^2 - 8x + 4 = 0$:

$$
\begin{aligned}
2(-2)^3 - (-2)^2 - 8(-2) + 4 &= 0 \\
2\left(\frac{1}{2}\right)^3 - \left(\frac{1}{2}\right)^2 - 8\left(\frac{1}{2}\right) + 4 &= 0 \\
2(2)^3 - 2^2 - 8(2) + 4 &= 0
\end{aligned}
$$

Since all of these equations are correct, the solutions are $-2, \frac{1}{2}$, and 2.

Now do Exercises 37–44

‹ Helpful Hint ›

Compare the number of solutions in Examples 1 through 5 to the degree of the polynomial. The number of real solutions to any polynomial equation is less than or equal to the degree of the polynomial. This fact is known as the fundamental theorem of algebra.

⟨2⟩ Fractions and Decimals

If the coefficients in an equation are not integers, we might be able to convert them into integers. Fractions can be eliminated by multiplying each side of the equation by the least common denominator (LCD). To eliminate decimals multiply each side by the smallest power of 10 that will eliminate all of the decimals.

EXAMPLE 6

Converting to Integers

Solve.

a) $\frac{1}{12}x^2 + \frac{1}{6}x - 2 = 0$

b) $0.02x^2 - 0.19x = 0.1$

Solution

a) The LCD for 6 and 12 is 12. So multiply each side of the equation by 12:

$$\frac{1}{12}x^2 + \frac{1}{6}x - 2 = 0 \quad \text{Original equation}$$

$$12\left(\frac{1}{12}x^2 + \frac{1}{6}x - 2\right) = 12(0) \quad \text{Multiply each side by 12.}$$

$$x^2 + 2x - 24 = 0 \quad \text{Simplify.}$$

$$(x + 6)(x - 4) = 0 \quad \text{Factor.}$$

$$x + 6 = 0 \quad \text{or} \quad x - 4 = 0 \quad \text{Zero factor property}$$

$$x = -6 \quad \text{or} \quad x = 4$$

Check:

$$\frac{1}{12}(-6)^2 + \frac{1}{6}(-6) - 2 = 3 - 1 - 2 = 0$$

$$\frac{1}{12}(4)^2 + \frac{1}{6}(4) - 2 = \frac{4}{3} + \frac{2}{3} - 2 = 0$$

The solutions are -6 and 4.

b) Multiply each side by 100 to eliminate the decimals:

$$0.02x^2 - 0.19x = 0.1 \quad \text{Original equation}$$

$$100(0.02x^2 - 0.19x) = 100(0.1) \quad \text{Multiply each side by 100.}$$

$$2x^2 - 19x = 10 \quad \text{Simplify.}$$

$$2x^2 - 19x - 10 = 0 \quad \text{Get 0 on one side.}$$

$$(2x + 1)(x - 10) = 0 \quad \text{Factor.}$$

$$2x + 1 = 0 \quad \text{or} \quad x - 10 = 0 \quad \text{Zero factor property}$$

$$x = -\frac{1}{2} \quad \text{or} \quad x = 10$$

The solutions are $-\frac{1}{2}$ and 10. You might want to use a calculator to check.

Now do Exercises 45–52

CAUTION You can multiply each side of the equation in Example 6(a) by 12 to clear the fractions and get an equivalent equation, but multiplying the polynomial $\frac{1}{12}x^2 + \frac{1}{6}x - 2$ by 12 to clear the fractions is not allowed. It would result in an expression that is not equivalent to the original.

Note that all of the equations in this section can be solved by factoring. However, we can have equations involving prime polynomials. Such equations cannot be solved by factoring but can be solved by the methods in Chapter 9.

⟨3⟩ Applications

There are many problems that can be solved by equations like those we have just discussed.

EXAMPLE 7

Area of a garden

Merida's garden has a rectangular shape with a length that is 1 foot longer than twice the width. If the area of the garden is 55 square feet, then what are the dimensions of the garden?

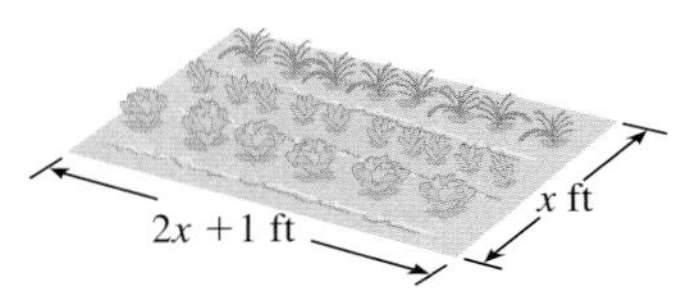

Figure 6.1

Solution

If x represents the width of the garden, then $2x + 1$ represents the length. See Fig. 6.1. Because the area of a rectangle is the length times the width, we can write the equation

$$x(2x + 1) = 55.$$

We must have zero on the right-hand side of the equation to use the zero factor property. So we rewrite the equation and then factor:

$$2x^2 + x - 55 = 0$$

$$(2x + 11)(x - 5) = 0 \quad \text{Factor.}$$

$$2x + 11 = 0 \quad \text{or} \quad x - 5 = 0 \quad \text{Zero factor property}$$

$$x = -\frac{11}{2} \quad \text{or} \quad x = 5$$

The width is certainly not $-\frac{11}{2}$. So we use $x = 5$ to get the length:

$$2x + 1 = 2(5) + 1 = 11$$

We check by multiplying 11 feet and 5 feet to get the area of 55 square feet. So the width is 5 ft, and the length is 11 ft.

Now do Exercises 71–72

⟨ Helpful Hint ⟩

To prove the Pythagorean theorem, draw two squares with sides of length $a + b$, and partition them as shown.

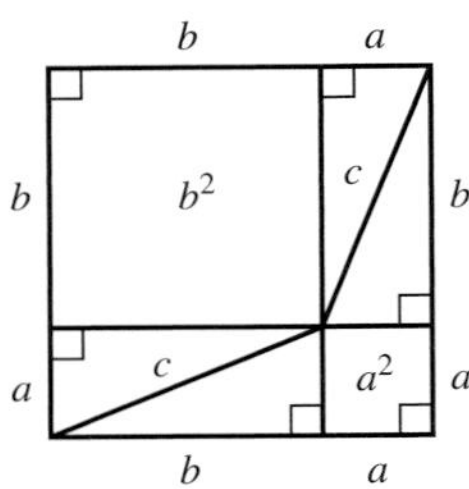

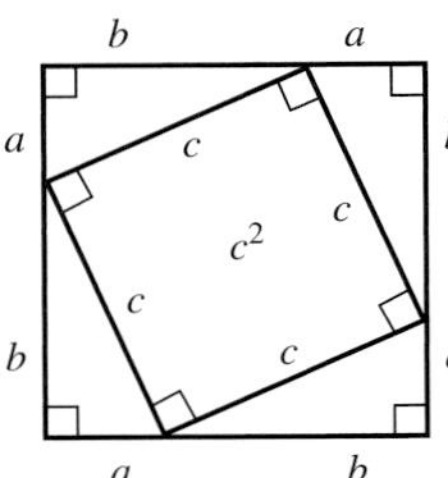

Erasing the four identical triangles from each picture will subtract the same amount of area from each original square. Since we started with equal areas, we will have equal areas after erasing the triangles:

$$a^2 + b^2 = c^2$$

The next application involves a theorem from geometry called the **Pythagorean theorem.** This theorem says that in any right triangle the sum of the squares of the lengths of the legs is equal to the square of the length of the hypotenuse.

The Pythagorean Theorem

The triangle shown in Fig. 6.2 is a right triangle if and only if

$$a^2 + b^2 = c^2.$$

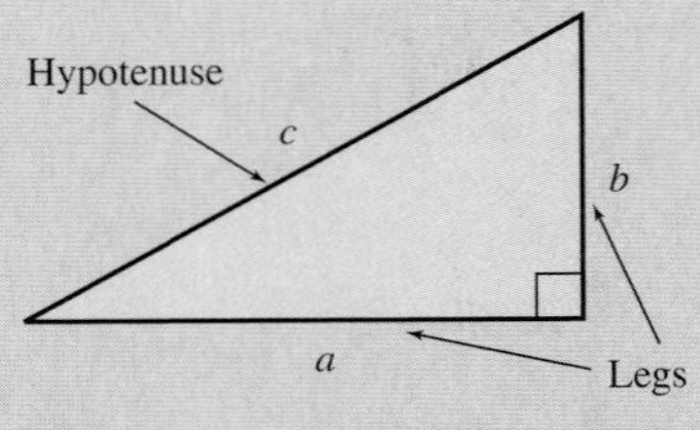

Figure 6.2

EXAMPLE 8

Using the Pythagorean theorem

The length of a rectangle is 1 meter longer than the width, and the diagonal measures 5 meters. What are the length and width?

Solution

If x represents the width of the rectangle, then $x + 1$ represents the length. Because the two sides are the legs of a right triangle, we can use the Pythagorean theorem to get a relationship between the length, width, and diagonal. See Fig. 6.3.

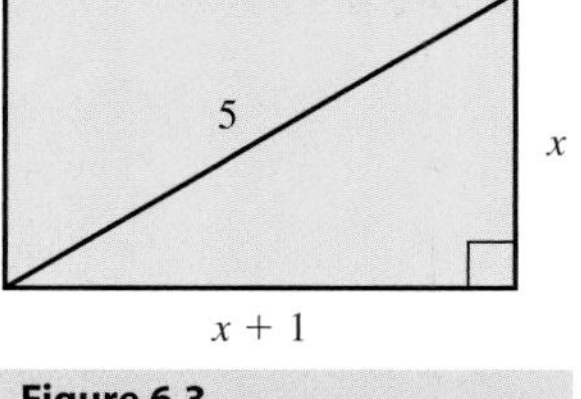

Figure 6.3

$$x^2 + (x + 1)^2 = 5^2 \quad \text{Pythagorean theorem}$$
$$x^2 + x^2 + 2x + 1 = 25 \quad \text{Simplify.}$$
$$2x^2 + 2x - 24 = 0$$
$$x^2 + x - 12 = 0 \quad \text{Divide each side by 2.}$$
$$(x - 3)(x + 4) = 0$$
$$x - 3 = 0 \quad \text{or} \quad x + 4 = 0 \quad \text{Zero factor property}$$
$$x = 3 \quad \text{or} \quad x = -4 \quad \text{The length cannot be negative.}$$
$$x + 1 = 4$$

To check this answer, we compute $3^2 + 4^2 = 5^2$, or $9 + 16 = 25$. So the rectangle is 3 meters by 4 meters.

Now do Exercises 73–74

CAUTION The hypotenuse is the longest side of a right triangle. So if the lengths of the sides of a right triangle are 5 meters, 12 meters, and 13 meters, then the length of the hypotenuse is 13 meters, and $5^2 + 12^2 = 13^2$.

Warm-Ups ▼

True or false? Explain your answer.

1. The equation $x(x + 2) = 3$ is equivalent to $x = 3$ or $x + 2 = 3$. False
2. Equations solved by factoring always have two different solutions. False
3. The equation $a \cdot d = 0$ is equivalent to $a = 0$ or $d = 0$. True
4. If x is the width in feet of a rectangular room and the length is 5 feet longer than the width, then the area is $x^2 + 5x$ square feet. True
5. Both 1 and -4 are solutions to the equation $(x - 1)(x + 4) = 0$. True
6. If a, b, and c are the sides of any triangle, then $a^2 + b^2 = c^2$. False
7. If the perimeter of a rectangular room is 50 feet, then the sum of the length and width is 25 feet. True
8. Equations solved by factoring may have more than two solutions. True
9. Both 0 and 2 are solutions to the equation $x(x - 2) = 0$. True
10. The solutions to $3(x - 2)(x + 5) = 0$ are 3, 2, and -5. False

6.6 Exercises

MathZone

Boost your grade at mathzone.com!
- Practice Problems
- NetTutor
- Self-Tests
- e-Professors
- Videos

‹ Study Tips ›

- Avoid cramming. When you have limited time to study for a test, start with class notes and homework assignments. Work one or two problems of each type.
- Don't get discouraged if you cannot work the hardest problems. Instructors often ask some relatively easy questions to see if you understand the basics.

Reading and Writing *After reading this section, write out the answers to these questions. Use complete sentences.*

1. What is a quadratic equation? A quadratic equation has the form $ax^2 + bx + c = 0$ with $a \neq 0$.
2. What is a compound equation? A compound equation is two equations connected with the word "or."
3. What is the zero factor property? The zero factor property says that if $ab = 0$ then $a = 0$ or $b = 0$.
4. What method is used to solve quadratic equations in this section? Quadratic equations are solved by factoring in this section.
5. Why don't we usually divide each side of an equation by a variable? Dividing each side by a variable is not usually done because the variable might have a value of zero.
6. What is the Pythagorean theorem? A triangle is a right triangle if and only if the sum of the squares of the legs is equal to the square of the hypotenuse.

‹1› The Zero Factor Property

Solve by factoring.

See Example 1.

See the Strategy for Solving an Equation by Factoring box on page 401.

7. $(x + 5)(x + 4) = 0$ $-4, -5$
8. $(a + 6)(a + 5) = 0$ $-6, -5$
9. $(2x + 5)(3x - 4) = 0$ $-\frac{5}{2}, \frac{4}{3}$
10. $(3k - 8)(4k + 3) = 0$ $\frac{8}{3}, -\frac{3}{4}$
11. $x^2 + 3x + 2 = 0$ $-2, -1$
12. $x^2 + 7x + 12 = 0$ $-4, -3$
13. $w^2 - 9w + 14 = 0$ $2, 7$
14. VIDEO $t^2 + 6t - 27 = 0$ $-9, 3$
15. $y^2 - 2y - 24 = 0$ $-4, 6$
16. $q^2 + 3q - 18 = 0$ $-6, 3$
17. $2m^2 + m - 1 = 0$ $-1, \frac{1}{2}$
18. $2h^2 - h - 3 = 0$ $-1, \frac{3}{2}$

Solve each equation. See Examples 2 and 3.

19. $x^2 = x$ $0, 1$
20. $w^2 = 2w$ $0, 2$
21. $m^2 = -7m$ $0, -7$
22. $h^2 = -5h$ $0, -5$
23. $a^2 + a = 20$ $-5, 4$
24. $p^2 + p = 42$ $-7, 6$
25. $2x^2 + 5x = 3$ $\frac{1}{2}, -3$
26. $3x^2 - 10x = -7$ $1, \frac{7}{3}$
27. $(x + 2)(x + 6) = 12$ $0, -8$
28. VIDEO $(x + 2)(x - 6) = 20$ $-4, 8$
29. $(a + 3)(2a - 1) = 15$ $-\frac{9}{2}, 2$
30. $(b - 3)(3b + 4) = 10$ $\frac{11}{3}, -2$
31. $2(4 - 5h) = 3h^2$ $\frac{2}{3}, -4$
32. $2w(4w + 1) = 1$ $-\frac{1}{2}, \frac{1}{4}$

Solve each equation. See Examples 4 and 5.

33. $2x^2 + 50 = 20x$ 5
34. $3x^2 + 48 = 24x$ 4
35. $4m^2 - 12m + 9 = 0$ $\frac{3}{2}$
36. $25y^2 + 20y + 4 = 0$ $-\frac{2}{5}$
37. VIDEO $x^3 - 9x = 0$ $0, -3, 3$
38. $25x - x^3 = 0$ $-5, 0, 5$
39. $w^3 + 4w^2 - 4w = 16$ $-4, -2, 2$
40. $a^3 + 2a^2 - a = 2$ $-2, -1, 1$
41. $n^3 - 3n^2 + 3 = n$ $-1, 1, 3$
42. $w^3 + w^2 - 25w = 25$ $-5, -1, 5$
43. $6y^3 - y^2 - 2y = 0$ $-\frac{1}{2}, 0, \frac{2}{3}$
44. $12m^3 - 13m^2 + 3m = 0$ $0, \frac{1}{3}, \frac{3}{4}$

⟨2⟩ Fractions and Decimals

Solve each equation. See Example 6.

45. $\frac{1}{6}x^2 - \frac{5}{6}x - 1 = 0$ $-1, 6$

46. $\frac{1}{10}x^2 + \frac{3}{10}x - 1 = 0$ $-5, 2$

47. $\frac{1}{9}x^2 + \frac{2}{3}x - 3 = 0$ $-9, 3$

48. $\frac{1}{10}x^2 - \frac{3}{2}x + 5 = 0$ $5, 10$

49. $0.01x^2 + 0.08x = 0.2$ $-10, 2$

50. $0.01x^2 - 0.07x = -0.1$ $2, 5$

51. $0.3x^2 + 0.7x - 2 = 0$ $-4, \frac{5}{3}$

52. $0.1x^2 + 0.7x + 1 = 0$ $-2, -5$

Miscellaneous

Solve each equation.

53. $x^2 - 16 = 0$ $-4, 4$

54. $x^2 - 36 = 0$ $-6, 6$

55. $4x^2 = 9$ $-\frac{3}{2}, \frac{3}{2}$

56. $25x^2 = 1$ $-\frac{1}{5}, \frac{1}{5}$

57. $a^3 = a$ $0, -1, 1$

58. $x^3 = 4x$ $-2, 0, 2$

59. $3x^2 + 15x + 18 = 0$ $-3, -2$

60. $-2x^2 - 2x + 24 = 0$ $-4, 3$

61. $z^2 + \frac{11}{2}z = -6$ $-\frac{3}{2}, -4$

62. $m^2 + \frac{8}{3}m = 1$ $-3, \frac{1}{3}$

63. $(t - 3)(t + 5) = 9$ $-6, 4$

64. $3x(2x + 1) = 18$ $-2, \frac{3}{2}$

65. $(x - 2)^2 + x^2 = 10$ $-1, 3$

66. $(x - 3)^2 + (x + 2)^2 = 17$ $-1, 2$

67. $\frac{1}{16}x^2 + \frac{1}{8}x = \frac{1}{2}$ $-4, 2$

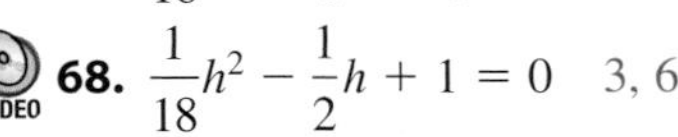

68. $\frac{1}{18}h^2 - \frac{1}{2}h + 1 = 0$ $3, 6$

69. $a^3 + 3a^2 - 25a = 75$ $-5, -3, 5$

70. $m^4 + m^3 = 100m^2 + 100m$ $-10, -1, 0, 10$

⟨3⟩ Applications

Solve each problem. See Examples 7 and 8.

71. ***Dimensions of a rectangle.*** The perimeter of a rectangle is 34 feet, and the diagonal is 13 feet long. What are the length and width of the rectangle?   Length 12 ft, width 5 ft

72. ***Address book.*** The perimeter of the cover of an address book is 14 inches, and the diagonal measures 5 inches. What are the length and width of the cover?   Width 3 in., length 4 in.

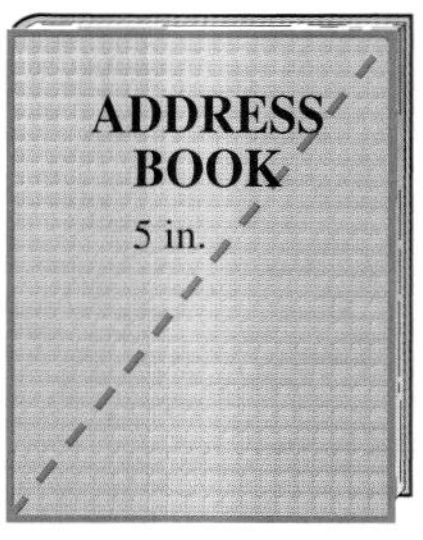

Figure for Exercise 72

73. ***Violla's bathroom.*** The length of Violla's bathroom is 2 feet longer than twice the width. If the diagonal measures 13 feet, then what are the length and width?   Width 5 ft, length 12 ft

74. ***Rectangular stage.*** One side of a rectangular stage is 2 meters longer than the other. If the diagonal is 10 meters, then what are the lengths of the sides?   6 m and 8 m

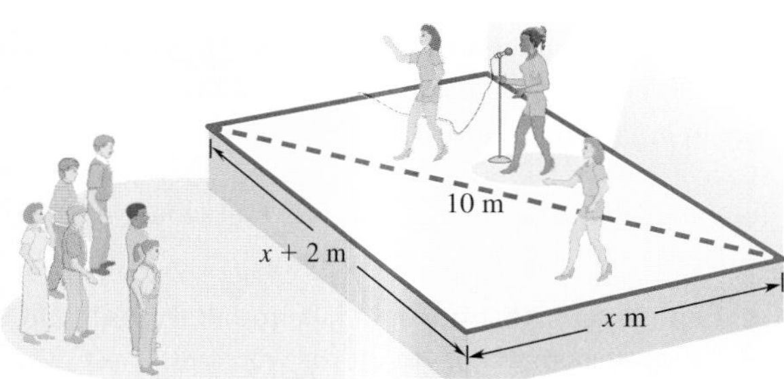

Figure for Exercise 74

75. ***Consecutive integers.*** The sum of the squares of two consecutive integers is 13. Find the integers.
2 and 3, or -3 and -2

76. ***Consecutive integers.*** The sum of the squares of two consecutive even integers is 52. Find the integers.
-6 and -4, or 4 and 6

77. ***Two numbers.*** The sum of two numbers is 11, and their product is 30. Find the numbers.   5 and 6

78. ***Missing ages.*** Molly's age is twice Anita's. If the sum of the squares of their ages is 80, then what are their ages?
Anita 4, Molly 8

79. ***Three even integers.*** The sum of the squares of three consecutive even integers is 116. Find the integers.
$-8, -6, -4$, or 4, 6, 8

80. ***Two odd integers.*** The product of two consecutive odd integers is 63. Find the integers. -9 and -7, or 7 and 9

81. ***Consecutive integers.*** The product of two consecutive integers is 5 more than their sum. Find the integers.
-2 and -1, or 3 and 4

82. ***Consecutive even integers.*** If the product of two consecutive even integers is 34 larger than their sum, then what are the integers? -6 and -4, or 6 and 8

83. ***Two integers.*** Two integers differ by 5. If the sum of their squares is 53, then what are the integers? -7 and -2, or 2 and 7

84. ***Two negative integers.*** Two negative integers have a sum of -10. If the sum of their squares is 68, then what are the integers? -8 and -2

85. ***Area of a rectangle.*** The area of a rectangle is 72 square feet. If the length is 6 feet longer than the width, then what are the length and the width? Length 12 feet, width 6 feet

86. ***Area of a triangle.*** The base of a triangle is 4 inches longer than the height. If its area is 70 square inches, then what are the base and the height? Base 14 inches, height 10 inches

87. ***Legs of a right triangle.*** The hypotenuse of a right triangle is 15 meters. If one leg is 3 meters longer than the other, then what are the lengths of the legs? 9 meters and 12 meters

88. ***Legs of a right triangle.*** If the longer leg of a right triangle is 1 cm longer than the shorter leg and the hypotenuse is 5 cm, then what are the lengths of the legs? 3 cm and 4 cm

89. ***Skydiving.*** If there were no air resistance, then the height (in feet) above the earth for a skydiver t seconds after jumping from an airplane at 10,000 feet would be given by

$$h(t) = -16t^2 + 10{,}000.$$

a) Find the time that it would take to fall to earth with no air resistance; that is, find t for which $h(t) = 0$. A skydiver actually gets about twice as much free fall time due to air resistance. 25 sec

b) Use the accompanying graph to determine whether the skydiver (with no air resistance) falls farther in the first 5 seconds or the last 5 seconds of the fall. last 5 sec

c) Is the skydiver's velocity increasing or decreasing as she falls? increasing

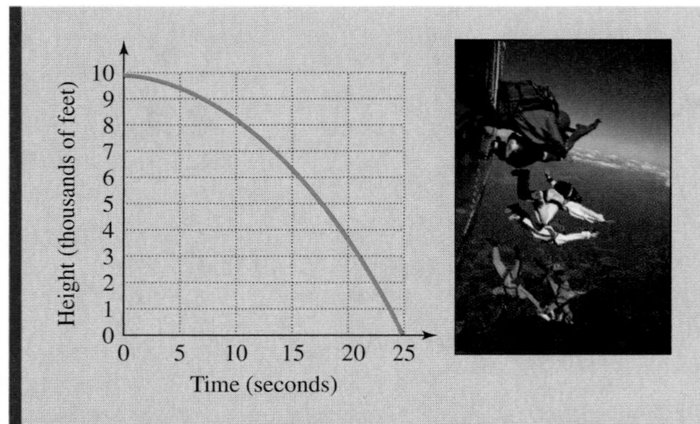

Figure for Exercise 89

90. ***Skydiving.*** If a skydiver jumps from an airplane at a height of 8256 feet, then for the first five seconds, her height above the earth is approximated by the formula $h(t) = -16t^2 + 8256$. How many seconds does it take her to reach 8000 feet? 4 sec

91. ***Throwing a sandbag.*** A balloonist throws a sandbag downward at 24 feet per second from an altitude of 720 feet. Its height (in feet) above the ground after t seconds is given by $S(t) = -16t^2 - 24t + 720$.

a) Find $S(1)$. 680 feet

b) What is the height of the sandbag 2 seconds after it is thrown? 608 feet

c) How long does it take for the sandbag to reach the ground? [On the ground, $S(t) = 0$.] 6 sec

92. ***Throwing a wrench.*** An angry construction worker throws his wrench downward from a height of 128 feet with an initial velocity of 32 feet per second. The height of the wrench above the ground after t seconds is given by $S(t) = -16t^2 - 32t + 128$.

a) What is the height of the wrench after 1 second? 80 feet

b) How long does it take for the wrench to reach the ground? 2 sec

93. ***Glass prism.*** One end of a glass prism is in the shape of a triangle with a height that is 1 inch longer than twice the base. If the area of the triangle is 39 square inches, then how long are the base and height? Base 6 in., height 13 in.

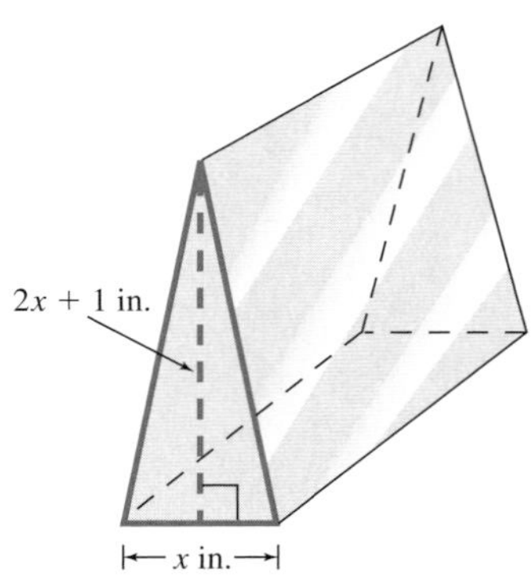

Figure for Exercise 93

94. ***Areas of two circles.*** The radius of a circle is 1 meter longer than the radius of another circle. If their areas differ by 5π square meters, then what is the radius of each? 2 m and 3 m

95. ***Changing area.*** Last year Otto's garden was square. This year he plans to make it smaller by shortening one side 5 feet and the other 8 feet. If the area of the smaller garden will be 180 square feet, then what was the size of Otto's garden last year? 20 ft by 20 ft

96. ***Dimensions of a box.*** Rosita's Christmas present from Carlos is in a box that has a width that is 3 inches shorter than the height. The length of the base is 5 inches longer than the height. If the area of the base is 84 square inches, then what is the height of the package? 9 in.

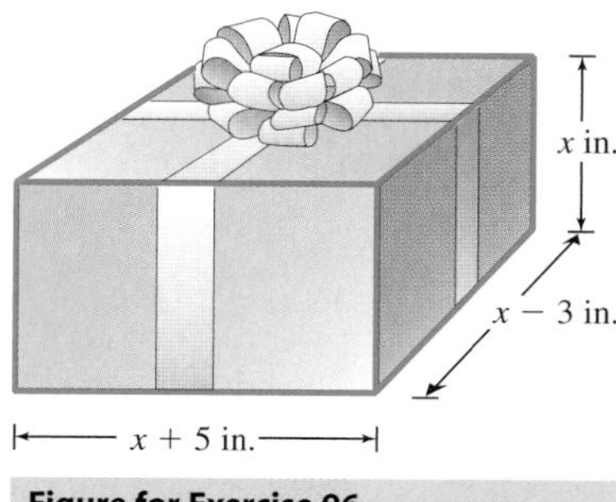

Figure for Exercise 96

97. ***Flying a kite.*** Imelda and Gordon have designed a new kite. While Imelda is flying the kite, Gordon is standing directly below it. The kite is designed so that its altitude is always 20 feet larger than the distance between Imelda and Gordon. What is the altitude of the kite when it is 100 feet from Imelda? 80 ft

98. ***Avoiding a collision.*** A car is traveling on a road that is perpendicular to a railroad track. When the car is 30 meters from the crossing, the car's new collision detector warns the driver that there is a train 50 meters from the car and heading toward the same crossing. How far is the train from the crossing? 40 m

99. ***Carpeting two rooms.*** Virginia is buying carpet for two square rooms. One room is 3 yards wider than the other. If she needs 45 square yards of carpet, then what are the dimensions of each room?
3 yd by 3 yd, 6 yd by 6 yd

100. ***Winter wheat.*** While finding the amount of seed needed to plant his three square wheat fields, Hank observed that the side of one field was 1 kilometer longer than the side of the smallest field and that the side of the largest field was 3 kilometers longer than the side of the smallest field. If the total area of the three fields is 38 square kilometers, then what is the area of each field?
4 km^2, 9 km^2, 25 km^2

101. ***Sailing to Miami.*** At point A the captain of a ship determined that the distance to Miami was 13 miles. If she sailed north to point B and then west to Miami, the distance would be 17 miles. If the distance from point A to point B is greater than the distance from point B to Miami, then how far is it from point A to point B?
12 mi

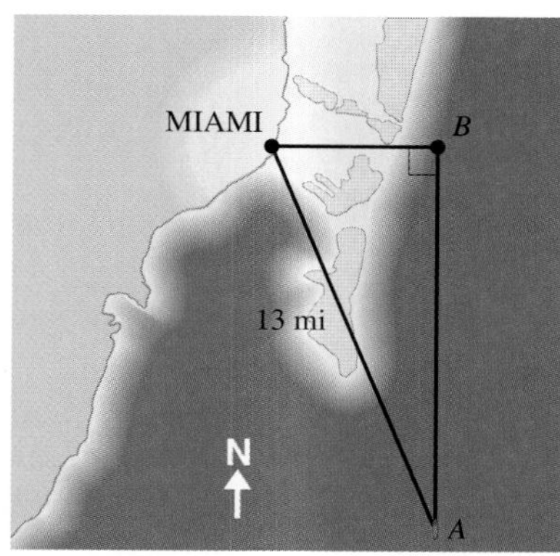

Figure for Exercise 101

102. ***Buried treasure.*** Ahmed has half of a treasure map, which indicates that the treasure is buried in the desert $2x + 6$ paces from Castle Rock. Vanessa has the other half of the map. Her half indicates that to find the treasure, one must get to Castle Rock, walk x paces to the north, and then walk $2x + 4$ paces to the east. If they share their information, then they can find x and save a lot of digging. What is x?
10 paces

103. ***Emerging markets.*** Catarina's investment of \$16,000 in an emerging market fund grew to \$25,000 in two years. Find the average annual rate of return by solving the equation $16{,}000(1 + r)^2 = 25{,}000$.
25%

104. ***Venture capital.*** Henry invested \$12,000 in a new restaurant. When the restaurant was sold two years later, he received \$27,000. Find his average annual return by solving the equation $12{,}000(1 + r)^2 = 27{,}000$. 50%

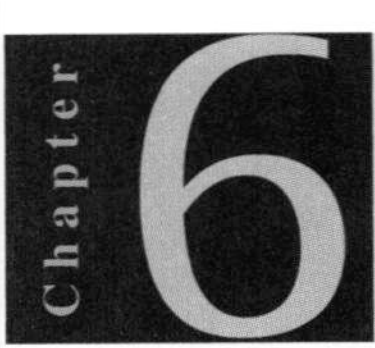

Wrap-Up

Summary

Factoring		**Examples**
Prime number	A positive integer larger than 1 that has no integral factors other than 1 and itself	2, 3, 5, 7, 11
Prime polynomial	A polynomial that cannot be factored is prime.	$x^2 + 3$ and $x^2 - x + 5$ are prime.
Strategy for finding the GCF for monomials	1. Find the GCF for the coefficients of the monomials. 2. Form the product of the GCF of the coefficients and each variable that is common to all of the monomials, where the exponent on each variable equals the smallest power of that variable in any of the monomials.	$12x^3yz$, $8x^2y^3$ GCF $= 4x^2y$
Factoring out the GCF	Use the distributive property to factor out the GCF from all terms of a polynomial.	$2x^3 - 4x = 2x(x^2 - 2)$

Special Cases		**Examples**
Difference of two squares	$a^2 - b^2 = (a + b)(a - b)$	$m^2 - 9 = (m - 3)(m + 3)$
Perfect square trinomial	$a^2 + 2ab + b^2 = (a + b)^2$ $a^2 - 2ab + b^2 = (a - b)^2$	$x^2 + 6x + 9 = (x + 3)^2$ $4h^2 - 12h + 9 = (2h - 3)^2$
Difference or sum of two cubes	$a^3 - b^3 = (a - b)(a^2 + ab + b^2)$ $a^3 + b^3 = (a + b)(a^2 - ab + b^2)$	$t^3 - 8 = (t - 2)(t^2 + 2t + 4)$ $p^3 + 1 = (p + 1)(p^2 - p + 1)$

Factoring Polynomials		**Examples**
Factoring by grouping	Factor out common factors from groups of terms.	$6x + 6w + ax + aw$ $= 6(x + w) + a(x + w)$ $= (6 + a)(x + w)$
Strategy for factoring $ax^2 + bx + c$ by the *ac* method	1. Find two numbers that have a product equal to *ac* and a sum equal to *b*. 2. Replace *bx* by two terms using the two new numbers as coefficients. 3. Factor the resulting four-term polynomial by grouping.	$6x^2 + 17x + 12$ $= 6x^2 + 9x + 8x + 12$ $= (2x + 3)3x + (2x + 3)4$ $= (2x + 3)(3x + 4)$
Factoring by trial and error	Try possible factors of the trinomial and check by using FOIL. If incorrect, try again.	$2x^2 + 5x - 12 = (2x - 3)(x + 4)$

Strategy for factoring polynomials completely	1. First factor out the greatest common factor.	$x^4 - 4x^2 = x^2(x^2 - 4)$
	2. When factoring a binomial, check to see whether it is a difference of two squares, a difference of two cubes, or a sum of two cubes. The sum of two squares (with no common factor) is prime.	$x^2 - 4 = (x + 2)(x - 2)$ $x^3 - 8 = (x - 2)(x^2 + 2x + 4)$ $x^3 + 8 = (x + 2)(x^2 - 2x + 4)$ $x^2 + 4$ is prime.
	3. When factoring a trinomial, check to see whether it is a perfect square trinomial.	$x^2 + 6x + 9 = (x + 3)^2$ $x^2 - 6x + 9 = (x - 3)^2$
	4. When factoring a trinomial that is not a perfect square, use the *ac* method or trial and error.	$x^2 + 7x + 12 = (x + 3)(x + 4)$
	5. If the polynomial has four terms, try factoring by grouping.	$x^2 + bx + 2x + 2b = x(x + b) + 2(x + b)$ $= (x + 2)(x + b)$
	6. Check to see whether any factors can be factored again.	$x^4 - 4x^2 = x^2(x^2 - 4)$ $= x^2(x + 2)(x - 2)$

Solving Equations		**Examples**
Zero factor property	The equation $a \cdot b = 0$ is equivalent to $a = 0$ or $b = 0$.	$x(x - 1) = 0$ $x = 0$ or $x - 1 = 0$
Strategy for solving an equation by factoring	1. Rewrite the equation with 0 on the right-hand side. 2. Factor the left-hand side completely. 3. Set each factor equal to zero to get linear equations. 4. Solve the linear equations. 5. Check the answers in the original equation. 6. State the solution(s) to the original equation.	$x^2 + 3x = 18$ $x^2 + 3x - 18 = 0$ $(x + 6)(x - 3) = 0$ $x + 6 = 0$ or $x - 3 = 0$ $x = -6$ or $x = 3$

Enriching Your Mathematical Word Power

For each mathematical term, choose the correct meaning.

1. factor
a. to write an expression as a product
b. to multiply
c. what two numbers have in common
d. to FOIL a

2. prime number
a. a polynomial that cannot be factored
b. a number with no divisors
c. an integer between 1 and 10
d. an integer larger than 1 that has no integral factors other than itself and 1 d

3. greatest common factor
a. the least common multiple
b. the least common denominator
c. the largest integer that is a factor of two or more integers
d. the largest number in a product c

4. prime polynomial
a. a polynomial that has no factors
b. a product of prime numbers
c. a first-degree polynomial
d. a monomial a

5. factor completely
a. to factor by grouping
b. to factor out a prime number
c. to write as a product of primes
d. to factor by trial and error c

6. sum of two cubes
a. $(a + b)^3$
b. $a^3 + b^3$
c. $a^3 - b^3$
d. a^3b^3 b

7. quadratic equation
a. $ax + b = 0$ where $a \neq 0$
b. $ax + b = cx + d$
c. $ax^2 + bx + c = 0$ where $a \neq 0$
d. any equation with four terms c

8. zero factor property
a. If $ab = 0$ then $a = 0$ or $b = 0$
b. $a \cdot 0 = 0$ for any a
c. $a = a + 0$ for any real number a
d. $a + (-a) = 0$ for any real number a a

9. Pythagorean theorem
a. $a^2 + b^2 = (a + b)^2$
b. a triangle is a right triangle if and only if it has one right angle
c. the legs of a right triangle meet at a 90° angle
d. a theorem that gives a relationship between the two legs and the hypotenuse of a right triangle d

10. difference of two squares
a. $a^3 - b^3$
b. $2a - 2b$
c. $a^2 - b^2$
d. $(a - b)^2$ c

Review Exercises

6.1 Factoring Out Common Factors

Find the prime factorization for each integer.

1. 144 $2^4 \cdot 3^2$
2. 121 11^2
3. 58 $2 \cdot 29$
4. 76 $2^2 \cdot 19$
5. 150 $2 \cdot 3 \cdot 5^2$
6. 200 $2^3 \cdot 5^2$

Find the greatest common factor for each group.

7. 36, 90 18
8. 30, 42, 78 6
9. $8x$, $12x^2$ $4x$
10. $6a^2b$, $9ab^2$, $15a^2b^2$ $3ab$

Complete the factorization of each binomial.

11. $3x + 6 = 3(x + 2)$
12. $7x^2 + x = x(7x + 1)$
13. $2a - 20 = -2(-a + 10)$
14. $a^2 - a = -a(-a + 1)$

Factor each polynomial by factoring out the GCF.

15. $2a - a^2$ $a(2 - a)$
16. $9 - 3b$ $3(3 - b)$
17. $6x^2y^2 - 9x^5y$
$3x^2y(2y - 3x^3)$
18. $a^3b^5 + a^3b^2$
$a^3b^2(b^3 + 1)$
19. $3x^2y - 12xy - 9y^2$
$3y(x^2 - 4x - 3y)$
20. $2a^2 - 4ab^2 - ab$
$a(2a - 4b^2 - b)$

6.2 Special Products and Grouping

Factor each polynomial completely.

21. $y^2 - 400$
$(y - 20)(y + 20)$
22. $4m^2 - 9$
$(2m - 3)(2m + 3)$
23. $w^2 - 8w + 16$
$(w - 4)^2$
24. $t^2 + 20t + 100$
$(t + 10)^2$
25. $4y^2 + 20y + 25$
$(2y + 5)^2$
26. $2a^2 - 4a - 2$
$2(a^2 - 2a - 1)$
27. $r^2 - 4r + 4$
$(r - 2)^2$
28. $3m^2 - 75$
$3(m - 5)(m + 5)$
29. $8t^3 - 24t^2 + 18t$
$2t(2t - 3)^2$
30. $t^2 - 9w^2$
$(t - 3w)(t + 3w)$
31. $x^2 + 12xy + 36y^2$
$(x + 6y)^2$
32. $9y^2 - 12xy + 4x^2$
$(3y - 2x)^2$
33. $x^2 + 5x - xy - 5y$
$(x - y)(x + 5)$
34. $x^2 + xy + ax + ay$
$(x + a)(x + y)$

6.3 Factoring the Trinomial $ax^2 + bx + c$ with $a = 1$

Factor each polynomial.

35. $b^2 + 5b - 24$
$(b + 8)(b - 3)$
36. $a^2 - 2a - 35$
$(a - 7)(a + 5)$
37. $r^2 - 4r - 60$
$(r - 10)(r + 6)$
38. $x^2 + 13x + 40$
$(x + 8)(x + 5)$
39. $y^2 - 6y - 55$
$(y - 11)(y + 5)$
40. $a^2 + 6a - 40$
$(a + 10)(a - 4)$
41. $u^2 + 26u + 120$
$(u + 20)(u + 6)$
42. $v^2 - 22v - 75$
$(v - 25)(v + 3)$

Factor completely.

43. $3t^3 + 12t^2$
$3t^2(t + 4)$
44. $-4m^4 - 36m^2$
$-4m^2(m^2 + 9)$
45. $5w^3 + 25w^2 + 25w$
$5w(w^2 + 5w + 5)$
46. $-3t^3 + 3t^2 - 6t$
$-3t(t^2 - t + 2)$
47. $2a^3b + 3a^2b^2 + ab^3$
$ab(2a + b)(a + b)$
48. $6x^2y^2 - xy^3 - y^4$
$y^2(2x - y)(3x + y)$
49. $9x^3 - xy^2$
$x(3x - y)(3x + y)$
50. $h^4 - 100h^2$
$h^2(h - 10)(h + 10)$

6.4 Factoring the Trinomial $ax^2 + bx + c$ with $a \neq 1$

Factor each polynomial completely.

51. $14t^2 + t - 3$
$(7t - 3)(2t + 1)$
52. $15x^2 - 22x - 5$
$(5x + 1)(3x - 5)$
53. $6x^2 - 19x - 7$
$(3x + 1)(2x - 7)$
54. $2x^2 - x - 10$
$(x + 2)(2x - 5)$
55. $6p^2 + 5p - 4$
$(3p + 4)(2p - 1)$
56. $3p^2 + 2p - 5$
$(p - 1)(3p + 5)$
57. $-30p^3 + 8p^2 + 8p$
$-2p(5p + 2)(3p - 2)$
58. $-6q^2 - 40q - 50$
$-2(3q + 5)(q + 5)$
59. $6x^2 - 29xy - 5y^2$
$(6x + y)(x - 5y)$
60. $10a^2 + ab - 2b^2$
$(5a - 2b)(2a + b)$
61. $32x^2 + 16xy + 2y^2$
$2(4x + y)^2$
62. $8a^2 + 40ab + 50b^2$
$2(2a + 5b)^2$

6.5 The Factoring Strategy

Factor completely.

63. $5x^3 + 40x$ $5x(x^2 + 8)$
64. $w^2 + 6w + 9$ $(w + 3)^2$

65. $9x^2 + 3x - 2$
$(3x - 1)(3x + 2)$

66. $ax^3 + ax$
$ax(x^2 + 1)$

67. $n^2 + 64$
Prime

68. $4t^2 + h^2$
Prime

69. $x^3 + 2x^2 - x - 2$
$(x + 2)(x - 1)(x + 1)$

70. $16x^2 - 2x - 3$
$(8x + 3)(2x - 1)$

71. $x^2y - 16xy^2$
$xy(x - 16y)$

72. $-3x^2 + 27$
$-3(x - 3)(x + 3)$

73. $w^2 + 4w + 5$
Prime

74. $2n^2 + 3n - 1$
Prime

75. $a^2 + 2a + 1$
$(a + 1)^2$

76. $-2w^2 - 12w - 18$
$-2(w + 3)^2$

77. $x^3 - x^2 + x - 1$
$(x^2 + 1)(x - 1)$

78. $9x^2y^2 - 9y^2$
$9y^2(x - 1)(x + 1)$

79. $a^2 + ab + 2a + 2b$
$(a + 2)(a + b)$

80. $4m^2 + 20m + 25$
$(2m + 5)^2$

81. $-2x^2 + 16x - 24$
$-2(x - 6)(x - 2)$

82. $6x^2 + 21x - 45$
$3(2x - 3)(x + 5)$

83. $m^3 - 1000$
$(m - 10)(m^2 + 10m + 100)$

84. $8p^3 + 1$
$(2p + 1)(4p^2 - 2p + 1)$

85. $p^4 - q^4$
$(p - q)(p + q)(p^2 + q^2)$

86. $z^4 - 81$
$(z - 3)(z + 3)(z^2 + 9)$

Factor each polynomial completely, given that the binomial following it is a factor of the polynomial.

87. $x^3 + x + 10,\ x + 2$
$(x + 2)(x^2 - 2x + 5)$

88. $x^3 - 5x - 12,\ x - 3$
$(x - 3)(x^2 + 3x + 4)$

89. $x^3 + 6x^2 - 7x - 60,\ x + 4$
$(x + 4)(x + 5)(x - 3)$

90. $x^3 - 4x^2 - 3x - 10,\ x - 5$
$(x - 5)(x^2 + x + 2)$

6.6 Solving Quadratic Equations by Factoring

Solve each equation.

91. $x^3 = 5x^2$
0, 5

92. $2m^2 + 10m = -12$
$-3, -2$

93. $(a - 2)(a - 3) = 6$
0, 5

94. $(w - 2)(w + 3) = 50$
$-8, 7$

95. $2m^2 - 9m - 5 = 0$
$-\frac{1}{2}, 5$

96. $12x^2 + 5x - 3 = 0$
$-\frac{3}{4}, \frac{1}{3}$

97. $m^3 + 4m^2 - 9m = 36$
$-4, -3, 3$

98. $w^3 + 5w^2 - w = 5$
$-5, -1, 1$

99. $(x + 3)^2 + x^2 = 5$
$-2, -1$

100. $(h - 2)^2 + (h + 1)^2 = 9$
$-1, 2$

101. $p^2 + \frac{1}{4}p - \frac{1}{8} = 0$
$-\frac{1}{2}, \frac{1}{4}$

102. $t^2 + 1 = \frac{13}{6}t$
$\frac{2}{3}, \frac{3}{2}$

103. $0.1x^2 + 0.01 = 0.07x$
$\frac{1}{5}, \frac{1}{2}$

104. $0.2y^2 + 0.03y = 0.02$
$-\frac{2}{5}, \frac{1}{4}$

Applications

Solve each problem.

105. ***Positive numbers.*** Two positive numbers differ by 6, and their squares differ by 96. Find the numbers. 5, 11

106. ***Consecutive integers.*** Find three consecutive integers such that the sum of their squares is 77.
$-6, -5, -4$ or 4, 5, 6

107. ***Dimensions of a notebook.*** The perimeter of a notebook is 28 inches, and the diagonal measures 10 inches. What are the length and width of the notebook?
6 in. by 8 in.

108. ***Two numbers.*** The sum of two numbers is 8.5, and their product is 18. Find the numbers.
4 and 4.5

109. ***Poiseuille's law.*** According to the nineteenth-century physician Poiseuille, the velocity (in centimeters per second) of blood r centimeters from the center of an artery of radius R centimeters is given by $v = kR^2 - kr^2$, where k is a constant. Rewrite the formula by factoring the right-hand side completely.
$v = k(R - r)(R + r)$

110. ***Racquetball.*** The volume of rubber (in cubic centimeters) in a hollow rubber ball used in racquetball is given by

$$V = \frac{4}{3}\pi R^3 - \frac{4}{3}\pi r^3,$$

where the inside radius is r centimeters and the outside radius is R centimeters.

a) Rewrite the formula by factoring the right-hand side completely.
$V = \frac{4}{3}\pi(R - r)(R^2 + Rr + r^2)$

b) The accompanying graph shows the relationship between r and V when $R = 3$. Use the graph to estimate the value of r for which $V = 100$ cm^3.
1.5 cm

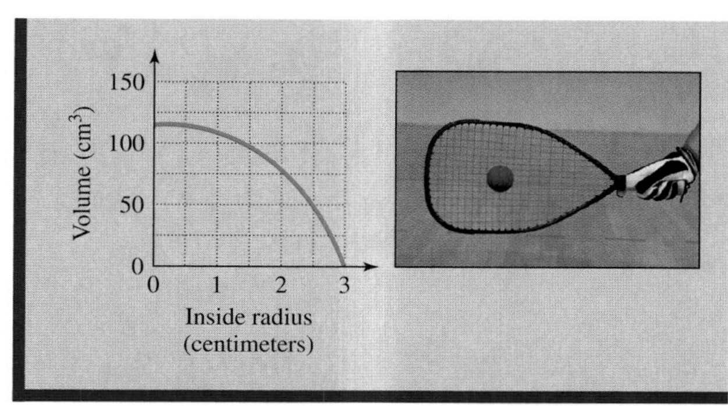

Figure for Exercise 110

111. ***Leaning ladder.*** A 10-foot ladder is placed against a building so that the distance from the bottom of the ladder to the building is 2 feet less than the

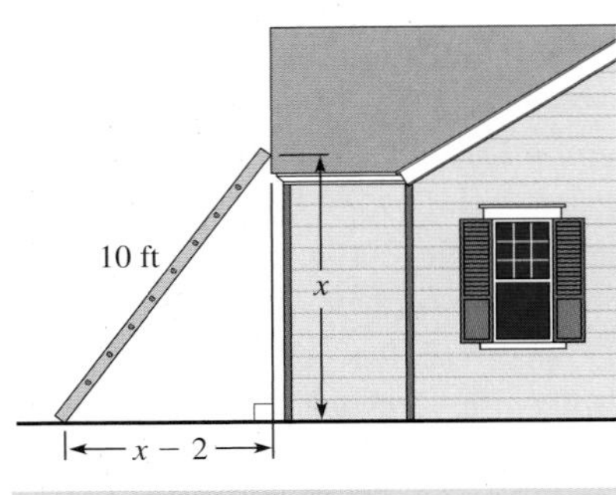

Figure for Exercise 111

distance from the top of the ladder to the ground. What is the distance from the bottom of the ladder to the building? 6 ft

112. ***Towering antenna.*** A guy wire of length 50 feet is attached to the ground and to the top of an antenna. The height of the antenna is 10 feet larger than the distance from the base of the antenna to the point where the guy wire is attached to the ground. What is the height of the antenna? 40 ft

Chapter 6 Test

Give the prime factorization for each integer.

1. 66 $2 \cdot 3 \cdot 11$

2. 336 $2^4 \cdot 3 \cdot 7$

Find the greatest common factor (GCF) for each group.

3. 48, 80 16

4. 42, 66, 78 6

5. $6y^2, 15y^3$ $3y^2$

6. $12a^2b, 18ab^2, 24a^3b^3$ $6ab$

Factor each polynomial completely.

7. $5x^2 - 10x$
$5x(x - 2)$

8. $6x^2y^2 + 12xy^2 + 12y^2$
$6y^2(x^2 + 2x + 2)$

9. $3a^3b - 3ab^3$
$3ab(a - b)(a + b)$

10. $a^2 + 2a - 24$
$(a + 6)(a - 4)$

11. $4b^2 - 28b + 49$
$(2b - 7)^2$

12. $3m^3 + 27m$
$3m(m^2 + 9)$

13. $ax - ay + bx - by$
$(a + b)(x - y)$

14. $ax - 2a - 5x + 10$
$(a - 5)(x - 2)$

15. $6b^2 - 7b - 5$
$(3b - 5)(2b + 1)$

16. $m^2 + 4mn + 4n^2$
$(m + 2n)^2$

17. $2a^2 - 13a + 15$
$(2a - 3)(a - 5)$

18. $z^3 + 9z^2 + 18z$
$z(z + 3)(z + 6)$

19. $x^3 + 125$
$(x + 5)(x^2 - 5x + 25)$

20. $a^4 - ab^3$
$a(a - b)(a^2 + ab + b^2)$

Factor the polynomial completely, given that $x - 1$ is a factor.

21. $x^3 - 6x^2 + 11x - 6$ $(x - 1)(x - 2)(x - 3)$

Solve each equation.

22. $x^2 + 6x + 9 = 0$
-3

23. $2x^2 + 5x - 12 = 0$
$\frac{3}{2}, -4$

24. $3x^3 = 12x$
$0, -2, 2$

25. $(2x - 1)(3x + 5) = 5$
$-2, \frac{5}{6}$

26. $\frac{1}{8}x^2 - \frac{3}{4}x + 1 = 0$
$2, 4$

27. $0.3x^2 - 1.7x + 1 = 0$
$\frac{2}{3}, 5$

Write a complete solution to each problem.

28. If the length of a rectangle is 3 feet longer than the width and the diagonal is 15 feet, then what are the length and width?
Length 12 ft, width 9 ft

29. The sum of two numbers is 4, and their product is −32. Find the numbers.
−4 and 8

30. A ball is dropped from a height of 64 feet. Its height above the earth in feet is given by $h(t) = -16t^2 + 64$, where t is the number of seconds after it is dropped.

a) Find $h(1)$. 48 feet

b) How long does it take the ball to fall to the earth?
2 seconds

*Making*Connections | A Review of Chapters 1–6

Simplify each expression.

1. $\frac{91 - 17}{17 - 91}$ -1

2. $\frac{4 - 18}{-6 - 1}$ 2

3. $5 - 2(7 - 3)$ -3

4. $3^2 - 4(6)(-2)$ 57

5. $2^5 - 2^4$ 16

6. $0.07(37) + 0.07(63)$ 7

Perform the indicated operations.

7. $x \cdot 2x$ $2x^2$

8. $x + 2x$ $3x$

9. $\frac{6 + 2x}{2}$ $3 + x$

10. $\frac{6 \cdot 2x}{2}$ $6x$

11. $2 \cdot 3y \cdot 4z$ $24yz$

12. $2(3y + 4z)$ $6y + 8z$

13. $2 - (3 - 4z)$ $4z - 1$

14. $-(x - 3) - 2(5 - x)$ $x - 7$

Simplify each expression. Write answers without negative exponents. All variables represent nonzero real numbers.

15. $t^8 \div t^2$ t^6

16. $t^8 \cdot t^2$ t^{10}

17. $t^2 \div t^8$ $\frac{1}{t^6}$

18. $(t^8)^2$ t^{16}

19. $\frac{8t^8}{2t^2}$ $4t^6$

20. $\frac{3y^{-5}}{9y^2}$ $\frac{1}{3y^7}$

21. $\frac{6x^{-6}}{15x^{-8}}$ $\frac{2x^2}{5}$

22. $\frac{(4w^{-3})^2}{24w^{-6}}$ $\frac{2}{3}$

23. $(-2x^{-3}y^2)^3$ $-\frac{8y^6}{x^9}$

24. $\left(\frac{x^{-2}}{3y^3}\right)^{-2}$ $9x^4y^6$

25. $-3^2 + \left(\frac{1}{2}\right)^{-2}$ -5

26. $-4^0 + \left(-\frac{1}{3}\right)^{-3}$ -28

Solve each inequality. State the solution set in interval notation and sketch its graph.

27. $2x - 5 > 3x + 4$ $(-\infty, -9)$

−13 −12 −11 −10 −9 −8 −7

28. $4 - 5x \le -11$ $[3, \infty)$

1 2 3 4 5 6 7

29. $-\frac{2}{3}x + 3 < -5$ $(12, \infty)$

10 11 12 13 14 15 16

30. $0.05(x - 120) - 24 < 0$ $(-\infty, 600)$

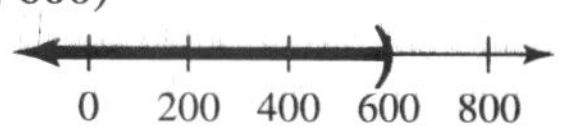

Find the solution set to each equation.

31. $2x - 3 = 0$ $\left\{\frac{3}{2}\right\}$

32. $2x + 1 = 0$ $\left\{-\frac{1}{2}\right\}$

33. $(x - 3)(x + 5) = 0$ $\{3, -5\}$

34. $(2x - 3)(2x + 1) = 0$ $\left\{\frac{3}{2}, -\frac{1}{2}\right\}$

35. $3x(x - 3) = 0$ $\{0, 3\}$

36. $x^2 = x$ $\{0, 1\}$

37. $3x - 3x = 0$ R

38. $3x - 3x = 1$ No solution or $\varnothing$

39. $0.01x - x + 14.9 = 0.5x$ $\{10\}$

40. $0.05x + 0.04(x - 40) = 2$ $\{40\}$

41. $2x^2 = 18$ $\{-3, 3\}$

42. $2x^2 + 7x - 15 = 0$ $\left\{-5, \frac{3}{2}\right\}$

Solve the problem.

43. ***Another ace.*** Professional tennis players can serve a tennis ball at speeds over 120 mph into a rectangular region that has a perimeter of 69 feet and an area of 283.5 square feet. Find the length and width of the service region.
Length 21 ft, width 13.5 ft

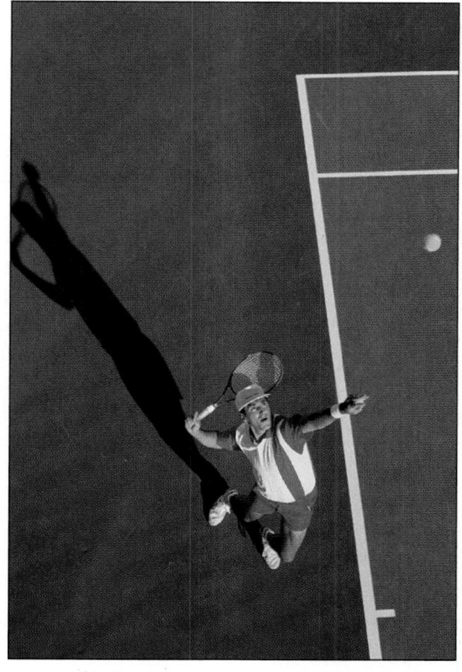

Photo for Exercise 43

Critical **Thinking** | For Individual or Group Work | Chapter 6

These exercises can be solved by a variety of techniques, which may or may not require algebra. So be creative and think critically. Explain all answers. Answers are in the Instructor's Edition of this text.

1. ***Equilateral triangles.*** Consider the sequence of three equilateral triangles shown in the accompanying figure.

a) How many equilateral triangles are there in (a) of the accompanying figure?

b) How many equilateral triangles congruent to the one in (a) can be found in (b) of the accompanying figure? How many are found in (c)?

c) Suppose the sequence of equilateral triangles shown in (a), (b), and (c) is continued. How many equilateral triangles [congruent to the one in (a)] could be found in the *n*th such figure?

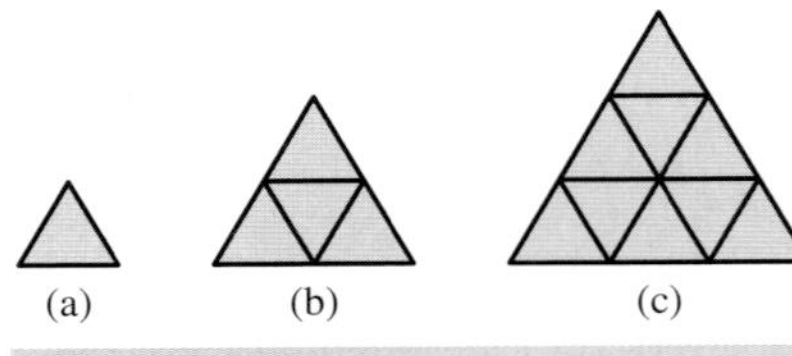

Figure for Exercise 1

2. ***The amazing Amber.*** Amber has been amazing her friends with a math trick. Amber has a friend select a three-digit number and reverse the digits. The friend then finds the difference of the two numbers and reads the first two digits of the difference (from left to right). Amber can always tell the last digit of the difference. Explain how Amber does this.

3. ***Missing proceeds.*** Ruth and Betty sell apples at a farmers market. Ruth's apples sell at 2 for \$1 while Betty's slightly smaller apples sell at 3 for \$1. When Betty leaves to pick up her kids they each have 30 apples and Ruth takes charge of both businesses. To simplify things, Ruth puts all 60 of the apples together and sells them at 5 for \$2. When Betty returns, all of the apples have been sold, but they begin arguing over how to divide up the proceeds. What is the problem? Explain what went wrong.

4. ***Eyes and feet.*** A rancher has some sheep and ostriches. His young daughter observed that the animals have a total of 60 eyes and 86 feet. How many animals of each type does the rancher have?

Photo for Exercise 4

5. ***Evaluation nightmare.*** Evaluate:

$$\frac{9{,}876{,}543{,}210}{9{,}876{,}543{,}211^2 - 9{,}876{,}543{,}210 \cdot 9{,}876{,}543{,}212}$$

6. ***Perfect squares.*** Find a positive integer such that the integer increased by 1 is a perfect square and one-half of the integer increased by 1 is a perfect square. Also find the next two larger positive integers that have this same property.

7. ***Multiplying primes.*** Find the units digit of the product of the first 500 prime numbers.

8. ***Ones and zeros.*** Find the sum of all seven-digit numbers that can be written using only ones or zeros.

1. a) 1 **b)** 4, 9 **c)** n^2 **2.** The difference is a multiple of 99 and the last digit is the difference between the first two. **3.** If they had sold separately they would have \$15 and \$10, but together have only \$24. The average price of an apple before combining is $\left(50 + 33\frac{1}{3}\right)/2$, or $41\frac{2}{3}$ cents, but Ruth sold them for an average of 40 cents each. **4.** 17 ostriches, 13 sheep **5.** 9,876,543,210 **6.** 48, 1680, 57,120 **7.** 0 **8.** 67,555,552

Chapter 7

Rational Expressions

Advanced technical developments have made sports equipment faster, lighter, and more responsive to the human body. Behind the more flexible skis, lighter bats, and comfortable athletic shoes lies the science of biomechanics, which is the study of human movement and the factors that influence it.

Designing and testing an athletic shoe go hand in hand. While a shoe is being designed, it is tested in a multitude of ways, including long-term wear, rear foot stability, and strength of materials. Testing basketball shoes usually includes an evaluation of the force applied to the ground by the foot during running, jumping, and landing. Many biomechanics laboratories have a special platform that can measure the force exerted when a player cuts from side to side, as well as the force against the bottom of the shoe. Force exerted in landing from a lay-up shot can be as high as 14 times the weight of the body. Side-to-side force is usually about 1 to 2 body weights in a cutting movement.

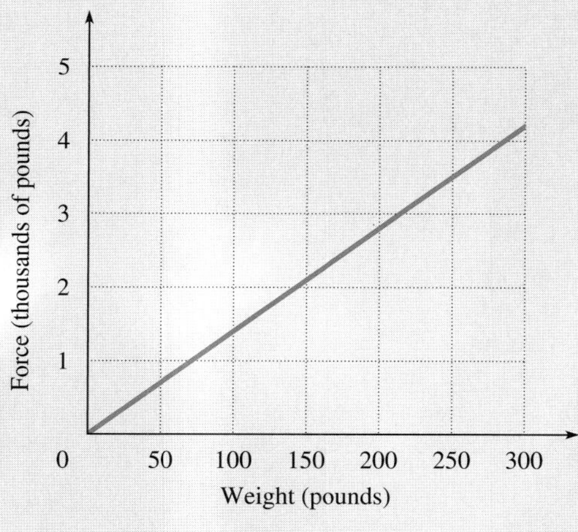

In Exercises 59 and 60 of Section 7.7 you will see how designers of athletic shoes use proportions to find the amount of force on the foot and soles of shoes for activities such as running and jumping.

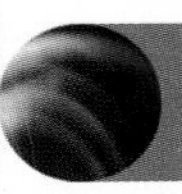

7.1 Reducing Rational Expressions

In This Section

Rational expressions in algebra are similar to the rational numbers in arithmetic. In this section, you will learn the basic ideas of rational expressions.

⟨1⟩ Rational Expressions

A rational number is the ratio of two integers with the denominator not equal to 0. For example,

$$\frac{3}{4}, \quad \frac{-9}{-6}, \quad \frac{-7}{1}, \quad \text{and} \quad \frac{0}{2}$$

are rational numbers. Of course, we usually write the last three of these rational numbers in their simpler forms $\frac{3}{2}$, -7, and 0. A **rational expression** is the ratio of two polynomials with the denominator not equal to 0. Because an integer is a monomial, a rational number is also a rational expression. As with rational numbers, if the denominator is 1, it can be omitted. Some examples of rational expressions are

$$\frac{x^2 - 1}{x + 8}, \quad \frac{3a^2 + 5a - 3}{a - 9}, \quad \frac{3}{7}, \quad \text{and} \quad 9x.$$

A rational expression involving a variable has no value unless we assign a value to the variable. Once the variable is given a value, we can evaluate the expression. We can discuss the value of a rational expression using the notation that we used for evaluating polynomials in Chapter 5.

EXAMPLE 1 Evaluating a rational expression

a) Find the value of $\frac{4x - 1}{x + 2}$ for $x = -3$.

b) If $R(x) = \frac{3x + 2}{2x - 1}$, find $R(4)$.

Solution

a) To find the value of $\frac{4x - 1}{x + 2}$ for $x = -3$, replace x by -3 in the rational expression:

$$\frac{4(-3) - 1}{-3 + 2} = \frac{-13}{-1} = 13$$

So the value of the rational expression is 13. The Calculator Close-Up shows how to evaluate the expression with a graphing calculator using a variable. With a scientific or graphing calculator you could also evaluate the expression by entering $(4(-3) - 1)/(-3 + 2)$. Be sure to enclose the numerator and denominator in parentheses.

b) $R(4)$ is the value of the rational expression when $x = 4$. To find $R(4)$, replace x by 4 in $R(x) = \frac{3x + 2}{2x - 1}$:

$$R(4) = \frac{3(4) + 2}{2(4) - 1}$$

$$R(4) = \frac{14}{7} = 2$$

So the value of the rational expression is 2 when $x = 4$, or $R(4) = 2$ (read "R of 4 is 2").

Now do Exercises 7–12

⟨ Calculator Close-Up ⟩

To evaluate the rational expression in Example 1(a) with a calculator, first use Y= to define the rational expression. Be sure to enclose both numerator and denominator in parentheses.

```
Plot1 Plot2 Plot3
\Y1=(4X-1)/(X+2)
\Y2=
\Y3=
\Y4=
\Y5=
\Y6=
```

Then find $y_1(-3)$.

```
Y1(-3)
                 13
```

An expression such as $\frac{5}{0}$ is an **undefined** expression because the definition of rational numbers does not allow zero in the denominator. When a variable occurs in a denominator, any real number can be used for the variable *except* numbers that make the expression undefined.

EXAMPLE 2

Ruling out values for *x*

Which numbers cannot be used in place of x in each rational expression?

a) $\dfrac{x^2 - 1}{x + 8}$ **b)** $\dfrac{x + 2}{2x + 1}$ **c)** $\dfrac{x + 5}{x^2 - 4}$

‹ Teaching Tip ›

It is more difficult for students to state which numbers can be used for x, rather than which numbers cannot be used for x.

Solution

a) The denominator is 0 if $x + 8 = 0$, or $x = -8$. So -8 cannot be used in place of x. (All real numbers except -8 can be used in place of x.)

b) The denominator is zero if $2x + 1 = 0$, or $x = -\frac{1}{2}$. So we cannot use $-\frac{1}{2}$ in place of x. (All real numbers except $-\frac{1}{2}$ can be used in place of x.)

c) The denominator is zero if $x^2 - 4 = 0$. Solve this equation:

$$x^2 - 4 = 0$$

$$(x - 2)(x + 2) = 0 \quad \text{Factor.}$$

$$x - 2 = 0 \quad \text{or} \quad x + 2 = 0 \quad \text{Zero factor property}$$

$$x = 2 \quad \text{or} \quad x = -2$$

So 2 and -2 cannot be used in place of x. (All real numbers except 2 and -2 can be used in place of x.)

Now do Exercises 13–20

In Example 2 we determined the real numbers that could not be used in place of the variable in a rational expression. The **domain** of any algebraic expression in one variable is the set of all real numbers that *can* be used in place of the variable. For rational expressions, the domain must exclude any real numbers that cause the denominator to be zero.

EXAMPLE 3

Domain

Find the domain of each expression.

a) $\dfrac{x^2 - 9}{x + 3}$ **b)** $\dfrac{x}{x^2 - x - 6}$ **c)** $\dfrac{x - 5}{4}$

Solution

a) The denominator is 0 if $x + 3 = 0$, or $x = -3$. So -3 can't be used for x. The domain is the set of all real numbers except -3, which is written in set notation as $\{x \mid x \neq -3\}$.

b) The denominator is 0 if $x^2 - x - 6 = 0$:

$$x^2 - x - 6 = 0$$

$$(x - 3)(x + 2) = 0$$

$$x - 3 = 0 \quad \text{or} \quad x + 2 = 0$$

$$x = 3 \quad \text{or} \quad x = -2$$

So -2 and 3 can't be used in place of x. The domain is the set of all real numbers except -2 and 3, which is written as $\{x \mid x \neq -2 \text{ and } x \neq 3\}$.

c) Since the denominator is 4, the denominator can't be 0 no matter what number is used for x. The domain is the set of all real numbers, R.

Now do Exercises 21–28

When dealing with rational expressions in this book, we will generally assume that the variables represent numbers for which the denominator is not zero.

⟨2⟩ Reducing to Lowest Terms

Rational expressions are a generalization of rational numbers. The operations that we perform on rational numbers can be performed on rational expressions in exactly the same manner.

Each rational number can be written in infinitely many equivalent forms. For example,

$$\frac{3}{5} = \frac{6}{10} = \frac{9}{15} = \frac{12}{20} = \frac{15}{25} = \cdots.$$

Each equivalent form of $\frac{3}{5}$ is obtained from $\frac{3}{5}$ by multiplying both numerator and denominator by the same nonzero number. This is equivalent to multiplying the fraction by 1, which does not change its value. For example,

$$\frac{3}{5} = \frac{3}{5} \cdot 1 = \frac{3}{5} \cdot \frac{2}{2} = \frac{6}{10} \quad \text{and} \quad \frac{3}{5} = \frac{3 \cdot 3}{5 \cdot 3} = \frac{9}{15}.$$

⟨ Helpful Hint ⟩

How would you fill in the blank in $\frac{3}{5} = \frac{\ }{10}$? Most students learn to divide 5 into 10 to get 2, then multiply 3 by 2 to get 6. In algebra, it is better to multiply the numerator and denominator of $\frac{3}{5}$ by 2, as shown here.

If we start with $\frac{6}{10}$ and convert it into $\frac{3}{5}$, we say that we are **reducing $\frac{6}{10}$ to lowest terms.** We reduce by dividing the numerator and denominator by the common factor 2:

$$\frac{6}{10} = \frac{\cancel{2} \cdot 3}{\cancel{2} \cdot 5} = \frac{3}{5}$$

A rational number is expressed in lowest terms when the numerator and the denominator have no common factors other than 1.

CAUTION We can reduce fractions only by dividing the numerator and the denominator by a common factor. Although it is true that

$$\frac{6}{10} = \frac{2 + 4}{2 + 8},$$

we cannot eliminate the 2's, because they are not factors. Removing them from the sums in the numerator and denominator would not result in $\frac{3}{5}$.

Reducing Fractions

If $a \neq 0$ and $c \neq 0$, then

$$\frac{ab}{ac} = \frac{b}{c}.$$

To reduce rational expressions to lowest terms, we use exactly the same procedure as with fractions:

Reducing Rational Expressions

1. Factor the numerator and denominator completely.
2. Divide the numerator and denominator by the greatest common factor.

Dividing the numerator and denominator by the GCF is often referred to as **dividing out** or **canceling** the GCF.

EXAMPLE 4

Reducing

Reduce to lowest terms.

a) $\frac{30}{42}$ **b)** $\frac{x^2 - 9}{6x + 18}$ **c)** $\frac{3x^2 + 9x + 6}{2x^2 - 8}$

Solution

a) $\frac{30}{42} = \frac{\not{2} \cdot \not{3} \cdot 5}{\not{2} \cdot \not{3} \cdot 7}$ Factor.

$= \frac{5}{7}$ Divide out the GCF: $2 \cdot 3$ or 6.

b) Since $\frac{9}{18} = \frac{9 \cdot 1}{9 \cdot 2} = \frac{1}{2}$, it is tempting to apply that fact here. However, 9 is not a common factor of the numerator and denominator of $\frac{x^2 - 9}{6x + 18}$, as it is in $\frac{9}{18}$. You must factor the numerator and denominator completely before reducing.

$$\frac{x^2 - 9}{6x + 18} = \frac{(x - 3)\cancel{(x + 3)}}{6\cancel{(x + 3)}} \quad \text{Factor.}$$

$$= \frac{x - 3}{6} \quad \text{Divide out the GCF: } x + 3.$$

This reduction is valid for all real numbers except -3, because that is the domain of the original expression. If $x = -3$, then $x + 3 = 0$ and we would be dividing out 0 from the numerator and denominator, which is prohibited in the rule for reducing fractions.

c) $\frac{3x^2 + 9x + 6}{2x^2 - 8} = \frac{3\cancel{(x + 2)}(x + 1)}{2\cancel{(x + 2)}(x - 2)}$ Factor completely.

$= \frac{3x + 3}{2(x - 2)}$ Divide out the GCF: $x + 2$.

This reduction is valid for all real numbers except -2 and 2, because that is the domain of the original expression.

Now do Exercises 29–52

CAUTION In reducing, you can divide out or cancel common factors only. You cannot cancel x from $\frac{x + 3}{x + 2}$, because it is not a factor of either $x + 3$ or $x + 2$. But x is a common factor in $\frac{3x}{2x}$, and $\frac{3x}{2x} = \frac{3}{2}$.

Note that there are four ways to write the answer to Example 3(c) depending on whether the numerator and denominator are factored. Since

$$\frac{3x + 3}{2(x - 2)} = \frac{3(x + 1)}{2(x - 2)} = \frac{3(x + 1)}{2x - 4} = \frac{3x + 3}{2x - 4},$$

any of these four rational expressions is correct. We usually give such answers with the denominator factored and the numerator not factored. With the denominator factored you can easily spot the values for x that will cause an undefined expression.

‹3› Reducing with the Quotient Rule for Exponents

To reduce rational expressions involving exponential expressions, we use the quotient rule for exponents from Chapter 5. We restate it here for reference.

Quotient Rule for Exponents

If $a \neq 0$, and m and n are any integers, then

$$\frac{a^m}{a^n} = a^{m-n}.$$

EXAMPLE 5

Using the quotient rule in reducing

Reduce to lowest terms.

a) $\dfrac{3a^{15}}{6a^7}$ b) $\dfrac{6x^4y^2}{4xy^5}$

‹ Teaching Tip ›

We did problems like this in Chapter 5 when we introduced the quotient rule. We repeat them here because they are also problems in reducing rational expressions.

Solution

a) $\dfrac{3a^{15}}{6a^7} = \dfrac{\cancel{3}a^{15}}{\cancel{3} \cdot 2a^7}$ Factor.

$= \dfrac{a^{15-7}}{2}$ Quotient rule for exponents

$= \dfrac{a^8}{2}$

b) $\dfrac{6x^4y^2}{4xy^5} = \dfrac{\cancel{2} \cdot 3x^4y^2}{\cancel{2} \cdot 2xy^5}$ Factor.

$= \dfrac{3x^{4-1}y^{2-5}}{2}$ Quotient rule for exponents

$= \dfrac{3x^3y^{-3}}{2} = \dfrac{3x^3}{2y^3}$

Now do Exercises 53–64

The essential part of reducing is getting a complete factorization for the numerator and denominator. To get a complete factorization, you must use the techniques for factoring from Chapter 6. If there are large integers in the numerator and denominator, you can use the technique shown in Section 6.1 to get a prime factorization of each integer.

EXAMPLE 6

Reducing expressions involving large integers

Reduce $\frac{420}{616}$ to lowest terms.

Solution

Use the method of Section 6.1 to get a prime factorization of 420 and 616:

$$\begin{array}{r} 2\overline{)420} \\ 2\overline{)210} \\ 3\overline{)105} \\ 5\overline{)35} \\ 7 \end{array} \qquad \begin{array}{r} 2\overline{)616} \\ 2\overline{)308} \\ 2\overline{)154} \\ 7\overline{)77} \\ 11 \end{array}$$

The complete factorization for 420 is $2^2 \cdot 3 \cdot 5 \cdot 7$, and the complete factorization for 616 is $2^3 \cdot 7 \cdot 11$. To reduce the fraction, we divide out the common factors:

$$\frac{420}{616} = \frac{2^2 \cdot 3 \cdot 5 \cdot 7}{2^3 \cdot 7 \cdot 11} = \frac{3 \cdot 5}{2 \cdot 11} = \frac{15}{22}$$

Now do Exercises 65–72

⟨4⟩ Dividing $a - b$ by $b - a$

In Section 5.4 you learned that $a - b = -(b - a) = -1(b - a)$. So if $a - b$ is divided by $b - a$, the quotient is -1:

$$\frac{a - b}{b - a} = \frac{-1(b - a)}{b - a} = -1$$

We will use this fact in Example 7.

EXAMPLE 7 Expressions with $a - b$ and $b - a$

Reduce to lowest terms.

a) $\dfrac{5x - 5y}{4y - 4x}$ **b)** $\dfrac{m^2 - n^2}{n - m}$

Solution

a) Factor out 5 from the numerator and 4 from the denominator and use $\frac{x - y}{y - x} = -1$:

$$\frac{5x - 5y}{4y - 4x} = \frac{5(x - y)}{4(y - x)} = \frac{5}{4}(-1) = -\frac{5}{4}$$

Another way is to factor out -5 from the numerator and 4 from the denominator and then use $\frac{y - x}{y - x} = 1$:

$$\frac{5x - 5y}{4y - 4x} = \frac{-5(y - x)}{4(y - x)} = \frac{-5}{4}(1) = -\frac{5}{4}$$

b) $\dfrac{m^2 - n^2}{n - m} = \dfrac{\overset{-1}{\cancel{(m - n)}}(m + n)}{\cancel{n - m}}$ Factor.

$= -1(m + n)$ $\quad \frac{m - n}{n - m} = -1$

$= -m - n$

Now do Exercises 73–80

CAUTION We can reduce $\frac{a - b}{b - a}$ to -1, but we cannot reduce $\frac{a - b}{a + b}$. There is no factor that is common to the numerator and denominator of $\frac{a - b}{a + b}$ or $\frac{a + b}{a - b}$.

⟨5⟩ Factoring Out the Opposite of a Common Factor

If we can factor out a common factor, we can also factor out the opposite of that common factor. For example, from $-3x - 6y$ we can factor out the common factor 3 or the common factor -3:

$$-3x - 6y = 3(-x - 2y) \quad \text{or} \quad -3x - 6y = -3(x + 2y)$$

To reduce an expression, it is sometimes necessary to factor out the opposite of a common factor.

EXAMPLE 8

Factoring out the opposite of a common factor

Reduce $\frac{-3w - 3w^2}{w^2 - 1}$ to lowest terms.

Solution

We can factor $3w$ or $-3w$ from the numerator. If we factor out $-3w$, we get a common factor in the numerator and denominator:

$$\frac{-3w - 3w^2}{w^2 - 1} = \frac{-3w(1 + w)}{(w - 1)(w + 1)} \quad \text{Factor.}$$

$$= \frac{-3w}{w - 1} \quad \text{Since } 1 + w = w + 1 \text{, we divide out } w + 1.$$

$$= \frac{3w}{1 - w} \quad \text{Multiply numerator and denominator by } -1.$$

The last step is not absolutely necessary, but we usually perform it to express the answer with one less negative sign.

Now do Exercises 81–90

The main points to remember for reducing rational expressions are summarized in the following reducing strategy.

Strategy for Reducing Rational Expressions

1. Factor the numerator and denominator completely. Factor out a common factor with a negative sign if necessary.
2. Divide out all common factors. Use the quotient rule if the common factors are powers.

‹6› Writing Rational Expressions

Rational expressions occur in applications involving rates. For uniform motion, rate is distance divided by time, $R = \frac{D}{T}$. For example, if you drive 500 miles in 10 hours, your rate is $\frac{500}{10}$ or 50 mph. If you drive 500 miles in x hours, your rate is $\frac{500}{x}$ mph. In work problems, rate is work divided by time, $R = \frac{W}{T}$. For example, if you lay 400 tiles in 4 hours, your rate is $\frac{400}{4}$ or 100 tiles/hour. If you lay 400 tiles in x hours, your rate is $\frac{400}{x}$ tiles/hour.

EXAMPLE 9

Writing rational expressions

Answer each question with a rational expression.

a) If a trucker drives 500 miles in $x + 1$ hours, then what is his average speed?

b) If a wholesaler buys 100 pounds of shrimp for x dollars, then what is the price per pound?

c) If a painter completes an entire house in $2x$ hours, then at what rate is she painting?

Solution

a) Because $R = \frac{D}{T}$, he is averaging $\frac{500}{x + 1}$ mph.

b) At x dollars for 100 pounds, the wholesaler is paying $\frac{x}{100}$ dollars per pound or $\frac{x}{100}$ dollars/pound.

c) By completing 1 house in $2x$ hours, her rate is $\frac{1}{2x}$ house/hour.

Now do Exercises 113–118

‹ Teaching Tip ›

These are good exercises to get students ready for word problems involving rational expressions.

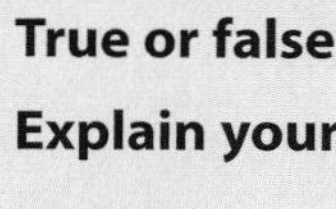

Warm-Ups

True or false? Explain your answer.

1. A complete factorization of 3003 is $2 \cdot 3 \cdot 7 \cdot 11 \cdot 13$. False
2. A complete factorization of 120 is $2^3 \cdot 3 \cdot 5$. True
3. Any number can be used in place of x in the expression $\frac{x-2}{5}$. True
4. We cannot replace x by -1 or 3 in the expression $\frac{x+1}{x-3}$. False
5. The rational expression $\frac{x+2}{2}$ reduces to x. False
6. $\frac{2x}{2} = x$ for any real number x. True
7. $\frac{x^{13}}{x^{20}} = \frac{1}{x^7}$ for any nonzero value of x. True
8. $\frac{a^2+b^2}{a+b}$ reduced to lowest terms is $a + b$. False
9. If $a \neq b$, then $\frac{a-b}{b-a} = 1$. False
10. The expression $\frac{-3x-6}{x+2}$ reduces to -3. True

7.1 Exercises

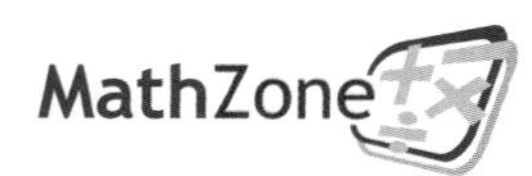

Boost your grade at mathzone.com!
- Practice Problems
- NetTutor
- Self-Tests
- e-Professors
- Videos

‹ Study Tips ›

- If you must miss class, let your instructor know. Be sure to get notes from a reliable classmate.
- Take good notes in class for yourself and your classmates. You never know when a classmate will ask to see your notes.

Reading and Writing *After reading this section, write out the answers to these questions. Use complete sentences.*

1. What is a rational number?
A rational number is a ratio of two integers with the denominator not 0.
2. What is a rational expression?
A rational expression is a ratio of two polynomials with the denominator not 0.
3. How do you reduce a rational number to lowest terms?
A rational number is reduced to lowest terms by dividing the numerator and denominator by the GCF.
4. How do you reduce a rational expression to lowest terms?
A rational expression is reduced to lowest terms by dividing the numerator and denominator by the GCF.
5. How is the quotient rule used in reducing rational expressions?
The quotient rule is used in reducing ratios of monomials.
6. What is the relationship between $a - b$ and $b - a$?
The expressions $a - b$ and $b - a$ are opposites.

‹1› Rational Expressions

Evaluate each rational expression. See Example 1.

7. Evaluate $\frac{3x-3}{x+5}$ for $x = -2$. -3
8. Evaluate $\frac{3x+1}{4x-4}$ for $x = 5$. 1
9. If $R(x) = \frac{2x+9}{x}$, find $R(3)$. 5
10. (VIDEO) If $R(x) = \frac{-20x-2}{x-8}$, find $R(-1)$. -2
11. If $R(x) = \frac{x-5}{x+3}$, find $R(2)$, $R(-4)$, $R(-3.02)$, and $R(-2.96)$. Note how a small difference in x (-3.02 to -2.96) can make a big difference in $R(x)$.
$-0.6, 9, 401, -199$

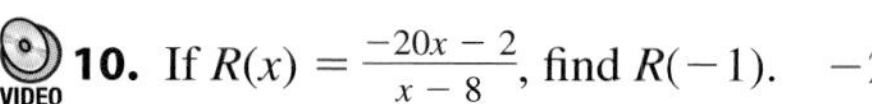

12. If $R(x) = \frac{x^2-2x-3}{x-2}$, find $R(3)$, $R(5)$, $R(2.05)$, and $R(1.999)$. 0, 4, -57.95, 3001.999

Which numbers cannot be used in place of the variable in each rational expression? See Example 2.

13. $\frac{x}{x+1}$ -1

14. $\frac{3x}{x-7}$ 7

15. $\frac{7a}{3a-5}$ $\frac{5}{3}$

16. $\frac{84}{3-2a}$ $\frac{3}{2}$

VIDEO **17.** $\frac{2x+3}{x^2-16}$ $4, -4$

18. $\frac{2y+1}{y^2-y-6}$ $-2, 3$

19. $\frac{p-1}{2}$ Any number can be used.

20. $\frac{m+31}{5}$ Any number can be used.

Find the domain of each rational expression. See Example 3.

21. $\frac{x^2+x}{x-2}$ All real numbers except 2

22. $\frac{x+4}{x-5}$ All real numbers except 5

23. $\frac{x}{x^2+5x+6}$ All real numbers except -3 and -2

24. $\frac{x^2+2}{x^2-x-12}$ All real numbers except -3 and 4

25. $\frac{x^2-4}{2}$ R

26. $\frac{x^2-3x}{9}$ R

27. $\frac{x-5}{x}$ All real numbers except 0

28. $\frac{x^2-3}{x+9}$ All real numbers except -9

⟨2⟩ Reducing to Lowest Terms

Reduce each rational expression to lowest terms. Assume that the variables represent only numbers for which the denominators are nonzero. See Example 4.

29. $\frac{6}{27}$ $\frac{2}{9}$

30. $\frac{14}{21}$ $\frac{2}{3}$

31. $\frac{42}{90}$ $\frac{7}{15}$

32. $\frac{42}{54}$ $\frac{7}{9}$

33. $\frac{36a}{90}$ $\frac{2a}{5}$

34. $\frac{56y}{40}$ $\frac{7y}{5}$

35. $\frac{78}{30w}$ $\frac{13}{5w}$

36. $\frac{68}{44y}$ $\frac{17}{11y}$

37. $\frac{6x+2}{6}$ $\frac{3x+1}{3}$

38. $\frac{2w+2}{2w}$ $\frac{w+1}{w}$

39. $\frac{2x+4y}{6y+3x}$ $\frac{2}{3}$

40. $\frac{5x-10a}{10x-20a}$ $\frac{1}{2}$

41. $\frac{3b-9}{6b-15}$ $\frac{b-3}{2b-5}$

42. $\frac{3m+9w}{3m-6w}$ $\frac{m+3w}{m-2w}$

43. $\frac{w^2-49}{w+7}$ $w-7$

44. $\frac{a^2-b^2}{a-b}$ $a+b$

45. $\frac{a^2-1}{a^2+2a+1}$ $\frac{a-1}{a+1}$

VIDEO **46.** $\frac{x^2-y^2}{x^2+2xy+y^2}$ $\frac{x-y}{x+y}$

47. $\frac{2x^2+4x+2}{4x^2-4}$ $\frac{x+1}{2(x-1)}$

48. $\frac{2x^2+10x+12}{3x^2-27}$ $\frac{2x+4}{3(x-3)}$

49. $\frac{3x^2+18x+27}{21x+63}$ $\frac{x+3}{7}$

50. $\frac{x^3-3x^2-4x}{x^2-4x}$ $x+1$

51. $\frac{2a^3+16}{4a+8}$ $\frac{a^2-2a+4}{2}$

52. $\frac{w^3-27}{w^2-3w}$ $\frac{w^2+3w+9}{w}$

⟨3⟩ Reducing with the Quotient Rule for Exponents

Reduce each expression to lowest terms. Assume that all variables represent nonzero real numbers and use only positive exponents in your answers. See Example 5.

53. $\frac{x^{10}}{x^7}$ x^3

54. $\frac{y^8}{y^5}$ y^3

55. $\frac{z^3}{z^8}$ $\frac{1}{z^5}$

56. $\frac{w^9}{w^{12}}$ $\frac{1}{w^3}$

57. $\frac{4x^7}{-2x^5}$ $-2x^2$

58. $\frac{-6y^3}{3y^9}$ $\frac{-2}{y^6}$

59. $\frac{-12m^9n^{18}}{8m^6n^{16}}$ $\frac{-3m^3n^2}{2}$

60. $\frac{-9u^9v^{19}}{6u^9v^{14}}$ $\frac{-3v^5}{2}$

61. $\frac{6b^{10}c^4}{-8b^{10}c^7}$ $\frac{-3}{4c^3}$

62. $\frac{9x^{20}y}{-6x^{25}y^3}$ $\frac{-3}{2x^5y^2}$

VIDEO **63.** $\frac{30a^3bc}{18a^7b^{17}}$ $\frac{5c}{3a^4b^{16}}$

64. $\frac{15m^{10}n^3}{24m^{12}np}$ $\frac{5n^2}{8m^2p}$

Reduce each expression to lowest terms. Assume that all variables represent nonzero real numbers and use only positive exponents in your answers. See Example 6.

65. $\frac{210}{264}$ $\frac{35}{44}$

66. $\frac{616}{660}$ $\frac{14}{15}$

67. $\frac{231}{168}$ $\frac{11}{8}$

68. $\frac{936}{624}$ $\frac{3}{2}$

69. $\frac{630x^5}{300x^9}$ $\frac{21}{10x^4}$

70. $\frac{96y^2}{108y^5}$ $\frac{8}{9y^3}$

71. $\frac{924a^{23}}{448a^{19}}$ $\frac{33a^4}{16}$

72. $\frac{270b^{75}}{165b^{12}}$ $\frac{18b^{63}}{11}$

⟨4⟩ Dividing *a* − *b* by *b* − *a*

Reduce each expression to lowest terms. See Example 7.

73. $\dfrac{3a - 2b}{2b - 3a}$ -1

74. $\dfrac{5m - 6n}{6n - 5m}$ -1

75. $\dfrac{h^2 - t^2}{t - h}$ $-h - t$

76. $\dfrac{r^2 - s^2}{s - r}$ $-r - s$

77. $\dfrac{2g - 6h}{9h^2 - g^2}$ $\dfrac{-2}{3h + g}$

78. $\dfrac{5a - 10b}{4b^2 - a^2}$ $\dfrac{-5}{2b + a}$

79. $\dfrac{x^2 - x - 6}{9 - x^2}$ $\dfrac{-x - 2}{x + 3}$

80. $\dfrac{1 - a^2}{a^2 + a - 2}$ $-\dfrac{a + 1}{a + 2}$

⟨5⟩ Factoring Out the Opposite of a Common Factor

Reduce each expression to lowest terms. See Example 8.

81. $\dfrac{-x - 6}{x + 6}$ -1

82. $\dfrac{-5x - 20}{3x + 12}$ $-\dfrac{5}{3}$

83. $\dfrac{-2y - 6y^2}{3 + 9y}$ $\dfrac{-2y}{3}$

84. $\dfrac{y^2 - 16}{-8 - 2y}$ $\dfrac{4 - y}{2}$

85. $\dfrac{-3x - 6}{3x - 6}$ $\dfrac{x + 2}{2 - x}$

86. $\dfrac{8 - 4x}{-8x - 16}$ $\dfrac{x - 2}{2(x + 2)}$

87. $\dfrac{-12a - 6}{2a^2 + 7a + 3}$ $\dfrac{-6}{a + 3}$

88. $\dfrac{-2b^2 - 6b - 4}{b^2 - 1}$ $\dfrac{-2b - 4}{b - 1}$

89. $\dfrac{a^3 - b^3}{2b^2 - 2ab}$ $\dfrac{-a^2 - ab - b^2}{2b}$

90. $\dfrac{x^3 - 1}{x - x^2}$ $\dfrac{-x^2 - x - 1}{x}$

Reduce each expression to lowest terms.

See the Strategy for Reducing Rational Expressions box on page 426.

91. $\dfrac{2x^{12}}{4x^8}$ $\dfrac{x^4}{2}$

92. $\dfrac{4x^2}{2x^9}$ $\dfrac{2}{x^7}$

93. $\dfrac{2x + 4}{4x}$ $\dfrac{x + 2}{2x}$

94. $\dfrac{2x + 4x^2}{4x}$ $\dfrac{1 + 2x}{2}$

95. $\dfrac{a - 4}{4 - a}$ -1

96. $\dfrac{2b - 4}{2b + 4}$ $\dfrac{b - 2}{b + 2}$

97. $\dfrac{2c - 4}{4 - c^2}$ $\dfrac{-2}{c + 2}$

98. $\dfrac{-2t - 4}{4 - t^2}$ $\dfrac{2}{t - 2}$

99. $\dfrac{x^2 + 4x + 4}{x^2 - 4}$ $\dfrac{x + 2}{x - 2}$

100. $\dfrac{3x - 6}{x^2 - 4x + 4}$ $\dfrac{3}{x - 2}$

101. $\dfrac{-2x - 4}{x^2 + 5x + 6}$ $\dfrac{-2}{x + 3}$

102. $\dfrac{-2x - 8}{x^2 + 2x - 8}$ $\dfrac{-2}{x - 2}$

103. $\dfrac{2q^8 + q^7}{2q^6 + q^5}$ q^2

104. $\dfrac{8s^{12}}{12s^6 - 16s^5}$ $\dfrac{2s^7}{3s - 4}$

105. $\dfrac{u^2 - 6u - 16}{u^2 - 16u + 64}$ $\dfrac{u + 2}{u - 8}$

106. $\dfrac{v^2 + 3v - 18}{v^2 + 12v + 36}$ $\dfrac{v - 3}{v + 6}$

107. $\dfrac{a^3 - 8}{2a - 4}$ $\dfrac{a^2 + 2a + 4}{2}$

108. $\dfrac{4w^2 - 12w + 36}{2w^3 + 54}$ $\dfrac{2}{w + 3}$

109. $\dfrac{y^3 - 2y^2 - 4y + 8}{y^2 - 4y + 4}$ $y + 2$

110. $\dfrac{mx + 3x + my + 3y}{m^2 - 3m - 18}$ $\dfrac{x + y}{m - 6}$

111. $\dfrac{2x + 2w - ax - aw}{x^3 - xw^2}$ $\dfrac{2 - a}{x(x - w)}$

112. $\dfrac{x^2 + ax - 4x - 4a}{x^2 - 16}$ $\dfrac{x + a}{x + 4}$

⟨6⟩ Writing Rational Expressions

Answer each question with a rational expression. Be sure to include the units. See Example 9.

113. If Sergio drove 300 miles at $x + 10$ miles per hour, then how many hours did he drive?
$\dfrac{300}{x + 10}$ hr

114. If Carrie walked 40 miles in x hours, then how fast did she walk?
$\dfrac{40}{x}$ mph

115. If $x + 4$ pounds of peaches cost \$4.50, then what is the cost per pound?
$\dfrac{4.50}{x + 4}$ dollars/lb

116. If nine pounds of pears cost x dollars, then what is the price per pound?
$\dfrac{x}{9}$ dollars/lb

117. If Ayesha can clean the entire swimming pool in x hours, then how much of the pool does she clean per hour?
$\dfrac{1}{x}$ pool/hr

118. If Ramon can mow the entire lawn in $x - 3$ hours, then how much of the lawn does he mow per hour?
$\dfrac{1}{x - 3}$ lawn/hr

Applications

Solve each problem.

119. ***Annual reports.*** The Crest Meat Company found that the cost per report for printing x annual reports at Peppy Printing is given by the formula

$$C(x) = \frac{150 + 0.60x}{x},$$

where $C(x)$ is in dollars.

a) Use the accompanying graph to estimate the cost per report for printing 1000 reports.

b) Use the formula to find $C(1000)$, $C(5000)$, and $C(10{,}000)$.

c) What happens to the cost per report as the number of reports gets very large?

a) \$0.75 b) \$0.75, \$0.63, \$0.615

c) Approaches \$0.60

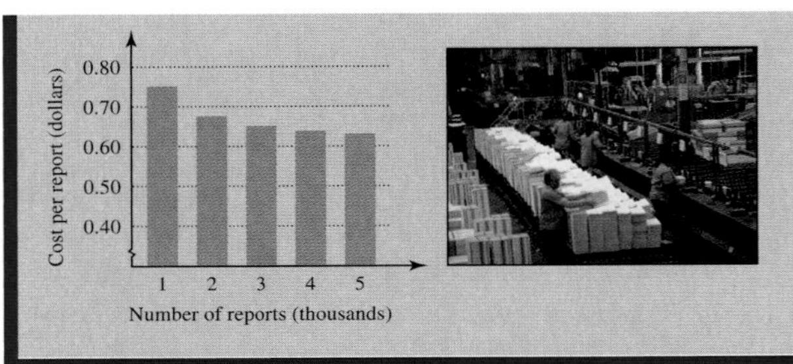

Figure for Exercise 119

120. ***Toxic pollutants.*** The annual cost in dollars for removing $p\%$ of the toxic chemicals from a town's water supply is given by the formula

$$C(p) = \frac{500{,}000}{100 - p}.$$

a) Use the accompanying graph to estimate the cost for removing 90% and 95% of the toxic chemicals.

b) Use the formula to find $C(99.5)$ and $C(99.9)$.

c) What happens to the cost as the percentage of pollutants removed approaches 100%?

a) \$50,000, \$100,000

b) \$1,000,000, \$5,000,000

c) Gets larger and larger without bound

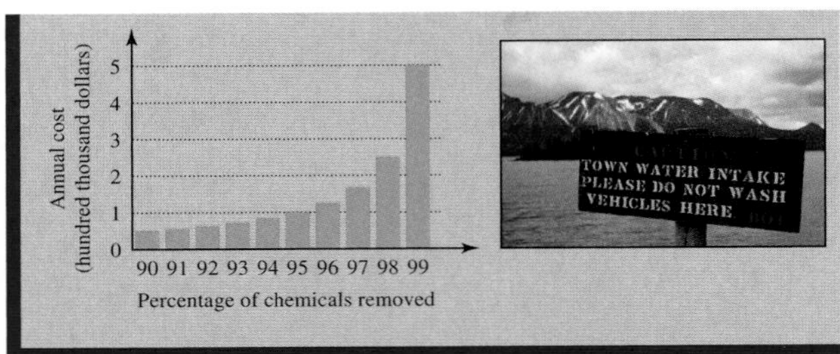

Figure for Exercise 120

7.2 Multiplication and Division

In This Section

- ⟨1⟩ Multiplication of Rational Numbers
- ⟨2⟩ Multiplication of Rational Expressions
- ⟨3⟩ Division of Rational Numbers
- ⟨4⟩ Division of Rational Expressions
- ⟨5⟩ Applications

In Section 7.1, you learned to reduce rational expressions in the same way that we reduce rational numbers. In this section, we will multiply and divide rational expressions using the same procedures that we use for rational numbers.

⟨1⟩ Multiplication of Rational Numbers

Two rational numbers are multiplied by multiplying their numerators and multiplying their denominators.

Multiplication of Rational Numbers

If $b \neq 0$ and $d \neq 0$, then

$$\frac{a}{b} \cdot \frac{c}{d} = \frac{ac}{bd}.$$

EXAMPLE 1

Multiplying rational numbers

Find the product $\frac{6}{7} \cdot \frac{14}{15}$.

Solution

The product is found by multiplying the numerators and multiplying the denominators:

$$\frac{6}{7} \cdot \frac{14}{15} = \frac{84}{105}$$

$$= \frac{21 \cdot 4}{21 \cdot 5} \quad \text{Factor the numerator and denominator.}$$

$$= \frac{4}{5} \quad \text{Divide out the GCF 21.}$$

The reducing that we did after multiplying is easier to do before multiplying. First factor all terms, reduce, and then multiply:

$$\frac{6}{7} \cdot \frac{14}{15} = \frac{2 \cdot \cancel{3}}{\cancel{7}} \cdot \frac{2 \cdot \cancel{7}}{\cancel{3} \cdot 5}$$

$$= \frac{4}{5}$$

Now do Exercises 5–12

‹ **Helpful Hint** ›

Did you know that the line separating the numerator and denominator in a fraction is called the *vinculum?*

‹2› Multiplication of Rational Expressions

Rational expressions are multiplied just like rational numbers: factor, reduce, and then multiply. A rational number cannot have zero in its denominator and neither can a rational expression. Since a rational expression can have variables in its denominator, the results obtained in Examples 2 and 3 are valid only for values of the variable(s) that would not cause a denominator to be 0.

EXAMPLE 2

Multiplying rational expressions

Find the indicated products.

a) $\frac{9x}{5y} \cdot \frac{10y}{3xy}$

b) $\frac{-8xy^4}{3z^3} \cdot \frac{15z}{2x^5y^3}$

Solution

a) $$\frac{9x}{5y} \cdot \frac{10y}{3xy} = \frac{3 \cdot \cancel{3}\cancel{x}}{\cancel{5}\cancel{y}} \cdot \frac{2 \cdot \cancel{5}\cancel{y}}{\cancel{3}\cancel{x}y} \quad \text{Factor.}$$

$$= \frac{6}{y}$$

b) $$\frac{-8xy^4}{3z^3} \cdot \frac{15z}{2x^5y^3} = \frac{-2 \cdot 2 \cdot \cancel{2}xy^4}{\cancel{3}z^3} \cdot \frac{\cancel{3} \cdot 5z}{\cancel{2}x^5y^3} \quad \text{Factor.}$$

$$= \frac{-20xy^4z}{z^3x^5y^3} \quad \text{Reduce.}$$

$$= \frac{-20y}{z^2x^4} \quad \text{Quotient rule}$$

Now do Exercises 13–22

‹ **Teaching Tip** ›

Since students find multiplication and division easier than addition and subtraction, we study them first.

EXAMPLE 3

Multiplying rational expressions

Find the indicated products.

a) $\dfrac{2x-2y}{4} \cdot \dfrac{2x}{x^2-y^2}$ **b)** $\dfrac{x^2+7x+12}{2x+6} \cdot \dfrac{x}{x^2-16}$ **c)** $\dfrac{a+b}{6a} \cdot \dfrac{8a^2}{a^2+2ab+b^2}$

Solution

a) $\dfrac{2x-2y}{4} \cdot \dfrac{2x}{x^2-y^2} = \dfrac{\cancel{2}\cancel{(x-y)}}{\cancel{2} \cdot 2} \cdot \dfrac{\cancel{2} \cdot x}{\cancel{(x-y)}(x+y)}$ Factor.

$= \dfrac{x}{x+y}$ Reduce.

b) $\dfrac{x^2+7x+12}{2x+6} \cdot \dfrac{x}{x^2-16} = \dfrac{\cancel{(x+3)}\cancel{(x+4)}}{2\cancel{(x+3)}} \cdot \dfrac{x}{(x-4)\cancel{(x+4)}}$ Factor.

$= \dfrac{x}{2(x-4)}$ Reduce.

c) $\dfrac{a+b}{6a} \cdot \dfrac{8a^2}{a^2+2ab+b^2} = \dfrac{a+b}{2 \cdot 3a} \cdot \dfrac{2 \cdot 4a^2}{(a+b)^2}$ Factor.

$= \dfrac{4a}{3(a+b)}$ Reduce.

Now do Exercises 23–30

‹3› Division of Rational Numbers

By the definition of division, a quotient is found by multiplying the dividend by the reciprocal of the divisor. If the divisor is a rational number $\frac{c}{d}$, its reciprocal is simply $\frac{d}{c}$.

Division of Rational Numbers

If $b \neq 0$, $c \neq 0$, and $d \neq 0$, then

$$\frac{a}{b} \div \frac{c}{d} = \frac{a}{b} \cdot \frac{d}{c}.$$

EXAMPLE 4

Dividing rational numbers

Find each quotient.

a) $5 \div \dfrac{1}{2}$ **b)** $\dfrac{6}{7} \div \dfrac{3}{14}$

Solution

a) $5 \div \dfrac{1}{2} = 5 \cdot 2 = 10$

b) $\dfrac{6}{7} \div \dfrac{3}{14} = \dfrac{6}{7} \cdot \dfrac{14}{3} = \dfrac{2 \cdot \cancel{3}}{\cancel{7}} \cdot \dfrac{2 \cdot \cancel{7}}{\cancel{3}} = 4$

Now do Exercises 31–38

‹4› Division of Rational Expressions

We divide rational expressions in the same way we divide rational numbers: Invert the divisor and multiply.

EXAMPLE 5

Dividing rational expressions

Find each quotient.

a) $\dfrac{5}{3x} \div \dfrac{5}{6x}$ **b)** $\dfrac{x^7}{2} \div (2x^2)$ **c)** $\dfrac{4 - x^2}{x^2 + x} \div \dfrac{x - 2}{x^2 - 1}$

Solution

a) $\dfrac{5}{3x} \div \dfrac{5}{6x} = \dfrac{5}{3x} \cdot \dfrac{6x}{5}$ Invert the divisor and multiply.

$= \dfrac{\cancel{5}}{\cancel{3x}} \cdot \dfrac{2 \cdot \cancel{3x}}{\cancel{5}}$ Factor.

$= 2$ Divide out the common factors.

b) $\dfrac{x^7}{2} \div (2x^2) = \dfrac{x^7}{2} \cdot \dfrac{1}{2x^2}$ Invert and multiply.

$= \dfrac{x^5}{4}$ Quotient rule

c) $\dfrac{4 - x^2}{x^2 + x} \div \dfrac{x - 2}{x^2 - 1} = \dfrac{4 - x^2}{x^2 + x} \cdot \dfrac{x^2 - 1}{x - 2}$ Invert and multiply.

$= \dfrac{\overset{-1}{\cancel{(2 - x)}}(2 + x)}{x\cancel{(x + 1)}} \cdot \dfrac{\cancel{(x + 1)}(x - 1)}{\cancel{x - 2}}$ Factor.

$= \dfrac{-1(2 + x)(x - 1)}{x}$ $\dfrac{2 - x}{x - 2} = -1$

$= \dfrac{-1(x^2 + x - 2)}{x}$ Simplify.

$= \dfrac{-x^2 - x + 2}{x}$

Now do Exercises 39–52

‹ Helpful Hint ›

A doctor told a nurse to give a patient half of the usual 500-mg dose of a drug. The nurse stated in court, "dividing in half means dividing by 1/2, which means multiply by 2." The nurse was in court because the patient got 1000 mg instead of 250 mg and died (true story). Dividing a quantity in half and dividing by one-half are not the same.

We sometimes write division of rational expressions using the fraction bar. For example, we can write

$$\frac{a + b}{3} \div \frac{1}{6} \quad \text{as} \quad \frac{\frac{a + b}{3}}{\frac{1}{6}}.$$

No matter how division is expressed, we invert the divisor and multiply.

EXAMPLE 6

Division expressed with a fraction bar

Find each quotient.

a) $\dfrac{\frac{a + b}{3}}{\frac{1}{6}}$ **b)** $\dfrac{\frac{x^2 - 1}{2}}{\frac{x - 1}{3}}$ **c)** $\dfrac{\frac{a^2 + 5}{3}}{2}$

‹ Teaching Tip ›

Another example that is good to work here is

$$\frac{\frac{2x+6}{5}}{2} = \frac{x+3}{5}.$$

‹ Helpful Hint ›

In Section 7.5 you will see another technique for finding the quotients in Example 6.

Solution

a) $\dfrac{\frac{a+b}{3}}{\frac{1}{6}} = \dfrac{a+b}{3} \div \dfrac{1}{6}$ Rewrite as division.

$= \dfrac{a+b}{3} \cdot \dfrac{6}{1}$ Invert and multiply.

$= \dfrac{a+b}{\cancel{3}} \cdot \dfrac{2 \cdot \cancel{3}}{1}$ Factor.

$= (a+b)2$ Reduce.

$= 2a + 2b$

b) $\dfrac{\frac{x^2-1}{2}}{\frac{x-1}{3}} = \dfrac{x^2-1}{2} \div \dfrac{x-1}{3}$ Rewrite as division.

$= \dfrac{x^2-1}{2} \cdot \dfrac{3}{x-1}$ Invert and multiply.

$= \dfrac{\cancel{(x-1)}(x+1)}{2} \cdot \dfrac{3}{\cancel{x-1}}$ Factor.

$= \dfrac{3x+3}{2}$ Reduce.

c) $\dfrac{\frac{a^2+5}{3}}{2} = \dfrac{a^2+5}{3} \div 2$ Rewrite as division.

$= \dfrac{a^2+5}{3} \cdot \dfrac{1}{2} = \dfrac{a^2+5}{6}$

Now do Exercises 53–60

‹5› Applications

We saw in Section 7.1 that rational expressions can be used to represent rates. Note that there are several ways to write rates. For example, miles per hour is written mph, mi/hr, or $\frac{\text{mi}}{\text{hr}}$. The last way is best when doing operations with rates because it helps us reconcile our answers. Notice how hours "cancels" when we multiply miles per hour and hours in Example 7, giving an answer in miles, as it should be.

EXAMPLE 7

Using rational expressions with uniform motion

Shasta drove 200 miles on I-10 in x hours before lunch.

a) Write a rational expression for her average speed before lunch.
b) She drives for 3 hours after lunch at the same average speed. Write a rational expression for her distance after lunch.

Solution

a) Because $R = \frac{D}{T}$, her rate before lunch is $\frac{200 \text{ miles}}{x \text{ hours}}$ or $\frac{200}{x}$ mph.

‹ Teaching Tip ›

These exercises are designed to get students ready for word problems. Note the cancellation of units here.

b) Because $D = R \cdot T$, her distance after lunch is the product of $\frac{200}{x}$ mph (her rate) and 3 hours (her time):

$$D = \frac{200 \text{ mi}}{x \text{ hr}} \cdot 3 \text{ hr} = \frac{600}{x} \text{ mi}$$

Now do Exercises 81–82

The amount of work completed is the product of rate and time, $W = R \cdot T$. So if a machine washes cars at the rate of 12 per hour and it works for 3 hours, the amount of work completed is 36 cars washed. Note that the rate is given by $R = \frac{W}{T}$.

EXAMPLE 8

Using rational expressions with work

It takes x minutes to fill a bathtub.

a) Write a rational expression for the rate at which the tub is filling.
b) Write a rational expression for the portion of the tub that is filled in 10 minutes.

Solution

a) The work completed in this situation is 1 tub being filled. Because $R = \frac{W}{T}$, the rate at which the tub is filling is $\frac{1 \text{ tub}}{x \text{ min}}$ or $\frac{1}{x}$ tub/min.

b) Because $W = R \cdot T$, the work completed in 10 minutes or the portion of the tub that is filled in 10 minutes is the product of $\frac{1}{x}$ tub/min (the rate) and 10 minutes (the time):

$$W = \frac{1 \text{ tub}}{x \text{ min}} \cdot 10 \text{ min} = \frac{10}{x} \text{ tub}$$

Now do Exercises 83–84

Warm-Ups ▼

True or false? Explain your answer.

1. $\frac{2}{3} \cdot \frac{5}{3} = \frac{10}{9}$. True
2. The product of $\frac{x-7}{3}$ and $\frac{6}{7-x}$ is -2. True
3. Dividing by 2 is equivalent to multiplying by $\frac{1}{2}$. True
4. $3 \div x = \frac{1}{3} \cdot x$ for any nonzero number x. False
5. Factoring polynomials is essential in multiplying rational expressions. True
6. One-half of one-fourth is one-sixth. False
7. One-half divided by three is three-halves. False
8. The quotient of $(839 - 487)$ and $(487 - 839)$ is -1. True
9. $\frac{a}{3} \div 3 = \frac{a}{9}$ for any value of a. True
10. $\frac{a}{b} \cdot \frac{b}{a} = 1$ for any nonzero values of a and b. True

7.2 Exercises

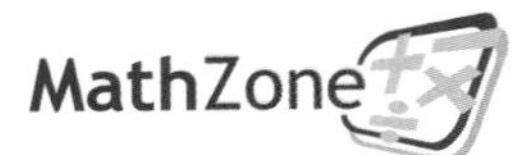

Boost your grade at mathzone.com!
- Practice Problems
- NetTutor
- Self-Tests
- e-Professors
- Videos

‹ Study Tips ›

- Personal issues can have a tremendous effect on your progress in any course. If you need help, get it.
- Most schools have counseling centers that can help you to overcome personal issues that are affecting your studies.

Reading and Writing *After reading this section, write out the answers to these questions. Use complete sentences.*

1. How do you multiply rational numbers?
   Rational numbers are multiplied by multiplying their numerators and their denominators.
2. How do you multiply rational expressions?
   Rational expressions are multiplied by multiplying their numerators and their denominators.
3. What can be done to simplify the process of multiplying rational numbers or rational expressions?
   Reducing can be done before multiplying rational numbers or expressions.
4. How do you divide rational numbers or rational expressions?
   To divide rational expressions, invert the divisor and multiply.

‹1› Multiplication of Rational Numbers

Perform the indicated operation. See Example 1.

5. $\frac{2}{3} \cdot \frac{5}{6}$ $\quad \frac{5}{9}$

6. $\frac{3}{4} \cdot \frac{2}{5}$ $\quad \frac{3}{10}$

7. $\frac{8}{15} \cdot \frac{35}{24}$ $\quad \frac{7}{9}$

8. $\frac{3}{4} \cdot \frac{8}{21}$ $\quad \frac{2}{7}$

9. $\frac{12}{17} \cdot \frac{51}{10}$ $\quad \frac{18}{5}$

10. $\frac{25}{48} \cdot \frac{56}{35}$ $\quad \frac{5}{6}$

11. $24 \cdot \frac{7}{20}$ $\quad \frac{42}{5}$

12. $\frac{3}{10} \cdot 35$ $\quad \frac{21}{2}$

‹2› Multiplication of Rational Expressions

Perform the indicated operation. See Example 2.

13. $\frac{2x}{3} \cdot \frac{5}{4x}$ $\quad \frac{5}{6}$

14. $\frac{3y}{7} \cdot \frac{21}{2y}$ $\quad \frac{9}{2}$

15. $\frac{5x^2}{6} \cdot \frac{3}{x}$ $\quad \frac{5x}{2}$

16. $\frac{9x}{10} \cdot \frac{5}{x^2}$ $\quad \frac{9}{2x}$

17. $\frac{5a}{12b} \cdot \frac{3ab}{55a}$ $\quad \frac{a}{44}$

18. $\frac{3m}{7p} \cdot \frac{35p}{6mp}$ $\quad \frac{5}{2p}$

19. $\frac{-2x^6}{7a^5} \cdot \frac{21a^2}{6x}$ $\quad \frac{-x^5}{a^3}$

20. $\frac{5z^3w}{-9y^3} \cdot \frac{-6y^5}{20z^9}$ $\quad \frac{wy^2}{6z^6}$

21. $\frac{15t^3y^5}{20w^7} \cdot 24t^5w^3y^2$ $\quad \frac{18t^8y^7}{w^4}$

22. $22x^2y^3z \cdot \frac{6x^5}{33y^3z^4}$ $\quad \frac{4x^7}{z^3}$

Perform the indicated operation. See Example 3.

23. $\frac{2x + 2y}{7} \cdot \frac{15}{6x + 6y}$ $\quad \frac{5}{7}$

24. $\frac{3}{a^2 + a} \cdot \frac{2a + 2}{6}$ $\quad \frac{1}{a}$

25. $\frac{3a + 3b}{15} \cdot \frac{10a}{a^2 - b^2}$ $\quad \frac{2a}{a - b}$

26. $\frac{b^3 + b}{5} \cdot \frac{10}{b^2 + b}$ $\quad \frac{2b^2 + 2}{b + 1}$

27. $(x^2 - 6x + 9) \cdot \frac{3}{x - 3}$ $\quad 3x - 9$

28. $\frac{12}{4x + 10} \cdot (4x^2 + 20x + 25)$ $\quad 12x + 30$

29. $\frac{16a + 8}{5a^2 + 5} \cdot \frac{2a^2 + a - 1}{4a^2 - 1}$ $\quad \frac{8a + 8}{5(a^2 + 1)}$

VIDEO **30.** $\frac{6x - 18}{2x^2 - 5x - 3} \cdot \frac{4x^2 + 4x + 1}{6x + 3}$ $\quad 2$

‹3› Division of Rational Numbers

Perform the indicated operation. See Example 4.

31. $\frac{1}{4} \div \frac{1}{2}$ $\quad \frac{1}{2}$

32. $\frac{1}{6} \div \frac{1}{2}$ $\quad \frac{1}{3}$

33. $12 \div \frac{2}{5}$ $\quad 30$

34. $32 \div \frac{1}{4}$ $\quad 128$

35. $\frac{5}{7} \div \frac{15}{14}$ $\quad \frac{2}{3}$

36. $\frac{3}{4} \div \frac{15}{2}$ $\quad \frac{1}{10}$

37. $\frac{40}{3} \div 12$ $\quad \frac{10}{9}$

38. $\frac{22}{9} \div 9$ $\quad \frac{22}{81}$

‹4› Division of Rational Expressions

Perform the indicated operation. See Example 5.

39. $\frac{x^2}{4} \div \frac{x}{2}$ $\quad \frac{x}{2}$

40. $\frac{3}{2a^2} \div \frac{6}{2a}$ $\quad \frac{1}{2a}$

41. $\frac{5x^2}{3} \div \frac{10x}{21}$ $\quad \frac{7x}{2}$

42. $\frac{4u^2}{3v} \div \frac{14u}{15v^6}$ $\quad \frac{10uv^5}{7}$

43. $\frac{8m^3}{n^4} \div (12mn^2)$ $\quad \frac{2m^2}{3n^6}$

44. $\frac{2p^4}{3q^3} \div (4pq^5)$ $\quad \frac{p^3}{6q^8}$

45. $\frac{y - 6}{2} \div \frac{6 - y}{6}$ $\quad -3$

VIDEO **46.** $\frac{4 - a}{5} \div \frac{a^2 - 16}{3}$ $\quad \frac{-3}{5(a + 4)}$

47. $\frac{x^2 + 4x + 4}{8} \div \frac{(x + 2)^3}{16}$ $\frac{2}{x + 2}$

48. $\frac{a^2 + 2a + 1}{3} \div \frac{a^2 - 1}{a}$ $\frac{a^2 + a}{3(a - 1)}$

49. $\frac{t^2 + 3t - 10}{t^2 - 25} \div (4t - 8)$ $\frac{1}{4(t - 5)}$

50. $\frac{w^2 - 7w + 12}{w^2 - 4w} \div (w^2 - 9)$ $\frac{1}{w(w + 3)}$

51. $(2x^2 - 3x - 5) \div \frac{2x - 5}{x - 1}$ $x^2 - 1$

52. $(6y^2 - y - 2) \div \frac{2y + 1}{3y - 2}$ $9y^2 - 12y + 4$

Perform the indicated operation. See Example 6.

53. $\frac{\frac{x - 2y}{5}}{\frac{1}{10}}$ $2x - 4y$

54. $\frac{\frac{3m + 6n}{8}}{\frac{3}{4}}$ $\frac{m + 2n}{2}$

VIDEO **55.** $\frac{\frac{x^2 - 4}{12}}{\frac{x - 2}{6}}$ $\frac{x + 2}{2}$

56. $\frac{\frac{6a^2 + 6}{5}}{\frac{6a + 6}{5}}$ $\frac{a^2 + 1}{a + 1}$

57. $\frac{\frac{x^2 + 9}{3}}{5}$ $\frac{x^2 + 9}{15}$

58. $\frac{\frac{1}{a - 3}}{4}$ $\frac{1}{4(a - 3)}$

59. $\frac{\frac{x^2 - y^2}{x - y}}{9}$ $9x + 9y$

60. $\frac{\frac{x^2 + 6x + 8}{x + 2}}{x + 1}$ $x^2 + 5x + 4$

Miscellaneous

Perform the indicated operation.

61. $\frac{x - 1}{3} \cdot \frac{9}{1 - x}$ -3

62. $\frac{2x - 2y}{3} \cdot \frac{1}{y - x}$ $-\frac{2}{3}$

63. $\frac{3a + 3b}{a} \cdot \frac{1}{3}$ $\frac{a + b}{a}$

64. $\frac{a - b}{2b - 2a} \cdot \frac{2}{5}$ $-\frac{1}{5}$

65. $\frac{\frac{b}{a}}{\frac{1}{2}}$ $\frac{2b}{a}$

66. $\frac{\frac{2g}{3h}}{\frac{1}{h}}$ $\frac{2g}{3}$

67. $\frac{6y}{3} \div (2x)$ $\frac{y}{x}$

68. $\frac{8x}{9} \div (18x)$ $\frac{4}{81}$

69. $\frac{a^3b^4}{-2ab^2} \cdot \frac{a^5b^7}{ab}$ $\frac{-a^6b^8}{2}$

VIDEO **70.** $\frac{-2a^2}{3a^2} \cdot \frac{20a}{15a^3}$ $\frac{-8}{9a^2}$

71. $\frac{2mn^4}{6mn^2} \div \frac{3m^5n^7}{m^2n^4}$ $\frac{1}{9m^3n}$

72. $\frac{rt^2}{rt^2} \div \frac{rt^2}{r^3t^2}$ r^2

73. $\frac{3x^2 + 16x + 5}{x} \cdot \frac{x^2}{9x^2 - 1}$ $\frac{x^2 + 5x}{3x - 1}$

74. $\frac{x^2 + 6x + 5}{x} \cdot \frac{x^4}{3x + 3}$ $\frac{x^4 + 5x^3}{3}$

75. $\frac{a^2 - 2a + 4}{a^2 - 4} \cdot \frac{(a + 2)^3}{2a + 4}$ $\frac{a^3 + 8}{2(a - 2)}$

76. $\frac{w^2 - 1}{(w - 1)^2} \cdot \frac{w - 1}{w^2 + 2w + 1}$ $\frac{1}{w + 1}$

77. $\frac{2x^2 + 19x - 10}{x^2 - 100} \div \frac{4x^2 - 1}{2x^2 - 19x - 10}$ 1

VIDEO **78.** $\frac{x^3 - 1}{x^2 + 1} \div \frac{9x^2 + 9x + 9}{x^2 - x}$ $\frac{x^3 - 2x^2 + x}{9(x^2 + 1)}$

79. $\frac{9 + 6m + m^2}{9 - 6m + m^2} \cdot \frac{m^2 - 9}{m^2 + mk + 3m + 3k}$ $\frac{m^2 + 6m + 9}{(m - 3)(m + k)}$

80. $\frac{3x + 3w + bx + bw}{x^2 - w^2} \cdot \frac{6 - 2b}{9 - b^2}$ $\frac{2}{x - w}$

⟨5⟩ Applications

Solve each problem. Answers could be rational expressions. Be sure to give your answers with appropriate units. See Examples 7 and 8.

81. ***Marathon run.*** Florence ran 26.2 miles in x hours in the Boston Marathon.

a) Write a rational expression for her average speed. $\frac{26.2}{x}$ mph

b) She runs at the same average speed for $\frac{1}{2}$ hour in the Cripple Creek Fun Run. Write a rational expression for her distance at Cripple Creek. $\frac{13.1}{x}$ miles

82. ***Driving marathon.*** Felix drove 800 miles in x hours on Monday.

a) Write a rational expression for his average speed. $\frac{800}{x}$ mph

b) On Tuesday he drove for 6 hours at the same average speed. Write a rational expression for his distance on Tuesday. $\frac{4800}{x}$ miles

83. ***Filling the tank.*** Chantal filled her empty gas tank in x minutes.

a) Write a rational expression for the rate at which she filled her tank.

$\frac{1}{x}$ tank/min

b) Write a rational expression for the portion of the tank that is filled in 2 minutes.

$\frac{2}{x}$ tank

84. ***Magazine sales.*** Henry sold 120 magazine subscriptions in x days.

a) Write a rational expression for the rate at which he sold the subscriptions.

$\frac{120}{x}$ magazines/day

b) Suppose that he continues to sell at the same rate for 5 more days. Write a rational expression for the number of magazines sold in those 5 days.

$\frac{600}{x}$ magazines

85. ***Area of a rectangle.*** If the length of a rectangular flag is x meters and its width is $\frac{5}{x}$ meters, then what is the area of the rectangle? 5 square meters

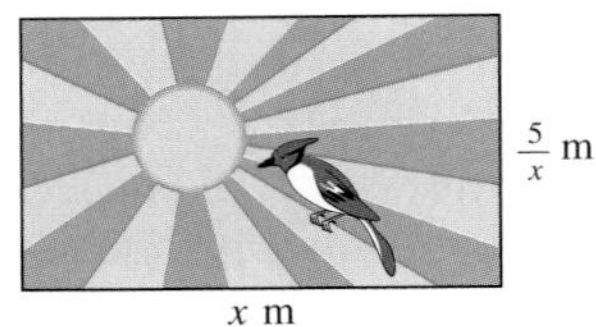

Figure for Exercise 85

86. ***Area of a triangle.*** If the base of a triangle is $8x + 16$ yards and its height is $\frac{1}{x+2}$ yards, then what is the area of the triangle? 4 yd^2

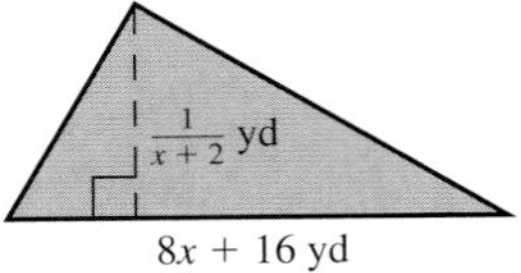

Figure for Exercise 86

Getting More Involved

87. ***Discussion***

Evaluate each expression.

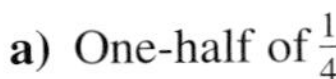

a) One-half of $\frac{1}{4}$ **b)** One-third of 4

c) One-half of $\frac{4x}{3}$ **d)** One-half of $\frac{3x}{2}$

a) $\frac{1}{8}$ b) $\frac{4}{3}$ c) $\frac{2x}{3}$ d) $\frac{3x}{4}$

88. ***Exploration***

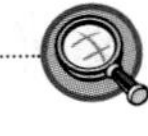

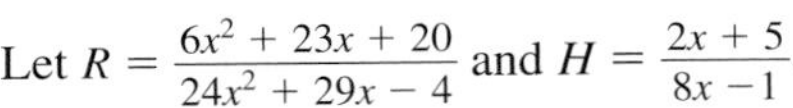

Let $R = \frac{6x^2 + 23x + 20}{24x^2 + 29x - 4}$ and $H = \frac{2x + 5}{8x - 1}$.

a) Find R when $x = 2$ and $x = 3$. Find H when $x = 2$ and $x = 3$.

b) How are these values of R and H related and why?

a) $R = \frac{3}{5}$, $R = \frac{11}{23}$, $H = \frac{3}{5}$, $H = \frac{11}{23}$

b) The values of R and H are the same since R reduces to H.

7.3 Finding the Least Common Denominator

In This Section

⟨1⟩ Building Up the Denominator
⟨2⟩ Finding the Least Common Denominator
⟨3⟩ Converting to the LCD

Every rational expression can be written in infinitely many equivalent forms. Because we can add or subtract only fractions with identical denominators, we must be able to change the denominator of a fraction. You have already learned how to change the denominator of a fraction by reducing. In this section, you will learn the opposite of reducing, which is called **building up the denominator.**

⟨1⟩ Building Up the Denominator

To convert the fraction $\frac{2}{3}$ into an equivalent fraction with a denominator of 21, we factor 21 as $21 = 3 \cdot 7$. Because $\frac{2}{3}$ already has a 3 in the denominator, multiply the numerator and denominator of $\frac{2}{3}$ by the missing factor 7 to get a denominator of 21:

$$\frac{2}{3} = \frac{2}{3} \cdot \frac{7}{7} = \frac{14}{21}$$

For rational expressions the process is the same. To convert the rational expression

$$\frac{5}{x + 3}$$

into an equivalent rational expression with a denominator of $x^2 - x - 12$, first factor $x^2 - x - 12$:

$$x^2 - x - 12 = (x + 3)(x - 4)$$

From the factorization we can see that the denominator $x + 3$ needs only a factor of $x - 4$ to have the required denominator. So multiply the numerator and denominator by the missing factor $x - 4$:

$$\frac{5}{x + 3} = \frac{5(x - 4)}{(x + 3)(x - 4)} = \frac{5x - 20}{x^2 - x - 12}$$

EXAMPLE 1

Building up the denominator

Build each rational expression into an equivalent rational expression with the indicated denominator.

a) $3 = \frac{?}{12}$ **b)** $\frac{3}{w} = \frac{?}{wx}$ **c)** $\frac{2}{3y^3} = \frac{?}{12y^8}$

Solution

a) Because $3 = \frac{3}{1}$, we get a denominator of 12 by multiplying the numerator and denominator by 12:

$$3 = \frac{3}{1} = \frac{3 \cdot 12}{1 \cdot 12} = \frac{36}{12}$$

b) Multiply the numerator and denominator by x:

$$\frac{3}{w} = \frac{3 \cdot x}{w \cdot x} = \frac{3x}{wx}$$

c) Note that $12y^8 = 3y^3 \cdot 4y^5$. So to build $3y^3$ up to $12y^8$ multiply by $4y^5$:

$$\frac{2}{3y^3} = \frac{2 \cdot 4y^5}{3y^3 \cdot 4y^5} = \frac{8y^5}{12y^8}$$

Now do Exercises 5–24

In Example 2 we must factor the original denominator before building up the denominator.

EXAMPLE 2

Building up the denominator

Build each rational expression into an equivalent rational expression with the indicated denominator.

a) $\frac{7}{3x - 3y} = \frac{?}{6y - 6x}$ **b)** $\frac{x - 2}{x + 2} = \frac{?}{x^2 + 8x + 12}$

Helpful Hint

Notice that reducing and building up are exactly the opposite of each other. In reducing you remove a factor that is common to the numerator and denominator, and in building up you put a common factor into the numerator and denominator.

Solution

a) Because $3x - 3y = 3(x - y)$, we factor -6 out of $6y - 6x$. This will give a factor of $x - y$ in each denominator:

$$3x - 3y = 3(x - y)$$
$$6y - 6x = -6(x - y) = -2 \cdot 3(x - y)$$

To get the required denominator, we multiply the numerator and denominator by -2 only:

$$\frac{7}{3x - 3y} = \frac{7(-2)}{(3x - 3y)(-2)}$$
$$= \frac{-14}{6y - 6x}$$

b) Because $x^2 + 8x + 12 = (x + 2)(x + 6)$, we multiply the numerator and denominator by $x + 6$, the missing factor:

$$\frac{x - 2}{x + 2} = \frac{(x - 2)(x + 6)}{(x + 2)(x + 6)}$$
$$= \frac{x^2 + 4x - 12}{x^2 + 8x + 12}$$

Now do Exercises 25–36

CAUTION When building up a denominator, *both* the numerator and the denominator must be multiplied by the appropriate expression.

⟨2⟩ Finding the Least Common Denominator

We can use the idea of building up the denominator to convert two fractions with different denominators into fractions with identical denominators. For example,

$$\frac{5}{6} \quad \text{and} \quad \frac{1}{4}$$

can both be converted into fractions with a denominator of 12, since $12 = 2 \cdot 6$ and $12 = 3 \cdot 4$:

$$\frac{5}{6} = \frac{5 \cdot 2}{6 \cdot 2} = \frac{10}{12} \qquad \frac{1}{4} = \frac{1 \cdot 3}{4 \cdot 3} = \frac{3}{12}$$

The smallest number that is a multiple of all of the denominators is called the **least common denominator (LCD).** The LCD for the denominators 6 and 4 is 12.

To find the LCD in a systematic way, we look at a complete factorization of each denominator. Consider the denominators 24 and 30:

$$24 = 2 \cdot 2 \cdot 2 \cdot 3 = 2^3 \cdot 3$$
$$30 = 2 \cdot 3 \cdot 5$$

Any multiple of 24 must have three 2's in its factorization, and any multiple of 30 must have one 2 as a factor. So a number with three 2's in its factorization will have enough to be a multiple of both 24 and 30. The LCD must also have one 3 and one 5 in its factorization. *We use each factor the maximum number of times it appears in either factorization.* So the LCD is $2^3 \cdot 3 \cdot 5$:

$$2^3 \cdot 3 \cdot 5 = \overbrace{2 \cdot 2 \cdot 2 \cdot 3}^{24} \cdot 5 = 120, \quad \text{where } \underbrace{2 \cdot 3 \cdot 5}_{30}$$

If we omitted any one of the factors in $2 \cdot 2 \cdot 2 \cdot 3 \cdot 5$, we would not have a multiple of both 24 and 30. That is what makes 120 the *least* common denominator. To find the LCD for two polynomials, we use the same strategy.

Strategy for Finding the LCD for Polynomials

1. Factor each denominator completely. Use exponent notation for repeated factors.
2. Write the product of all of the different factors that appear in the denominators.
3. On each factor, use the highest power that appears on that factor in any of the denominators.

EXAMPLE 3

Finding the LCD

If the given expressions were used as denominators of rational expressions, then what would be the LCD for each group of denominators?

a) 20, 50 **b)** x^3yz^2, x^5y^2z, xyz^5 **c)** $a^2 + 5a + 6, a^2 + 4a + 4$

Solution

a) First factor each number completely:

$$20 = 2^2 \cdot 5 \qquad 50 = 2 \cdot 5^2$$

The highest power of 2 is 2, and the highest power of 5 is 2. So the LCD of 20 and 50 is $2^2 \cdot 5^2$, or 100.

b) The expressions x^3yz^2, x^5y^2z, and xyz^5 are already factored. For the LCD, use the highest power of each variable. So the LCD is $x^5y^2z^5$.

c) First factor each polynomial.

$$a^2 + 5a + 6 = (a + 2)(a + 3) \qquad a^2 + 4a + 4 = (a + 2)^2$$

The highest power of $(a + 3)$ is 1, and the highest power of $(a + 2)$ is 2. So the LCD is $(a + 3)(a + 2)^2$.

Now do Exercises 37–50

‹3› Converting to the LCD

When adding or subtracting rational expressions, we must convert the expressions into expressions with identical denominators. To keep the computations as simple as possible, we use the least common denominator.

EXAMPLE 4

Converting to the LCD

Find the LCD for the rational expressions, and convert each expression into an equivalent rational expression with the LCD as the denominator.

a) $\dfrac{4}{9xy}, \dfrac{2}{15xz}$ **b)** $\dfrac{5}{6x^2}, \dfrac{1}{8x^3y}, \dfrac{3}{4y^2}$

Solution

a) Factor each denominator completely:

$$9xy = 3^2xy \qquad 15xz = 3 \cdot 5xz$$

Helpful Hint

What is the difference between LCD, GCF, CBS, and NBC? The LCD for the denominators 4 and 6 is 12. The *least* common denominator is *greater than* or equal to both numbers. The GCF for 4 and 6 is 2. The *greatest* common factor is *less than* or equal to both numbers. CBS and NBC are TV networks.

The LCD is $3^2 \cdot 5xyz$. Now convert each expression into an expression with this denominator. We must multiply the numerator and denominator of the first rational expression by $5z$ and the second by $3y$:

$$\frac{4}{9xy} = \frac{4 \cdot 5z}{9xy \cdot 5z} = \frac{20z}{45xyz}$$

$$\frac{2}{15xz} = \frac{2 \cdot 3y}{15xz \cdot 3y} = \frac{6y}{45xyz}$$

Same denominator

b) Factor each denominator completely:

$$6x^2 = 2 \cdot 3x^2 \qquad 8x^3y = 2^3x^3y \qquad 4y^2 = 2^2y^2$$

The LCD is $2^3 \cdot 3 \cdot x^3y^2$ or $24x^3y^2$. Now convert each expression into an expression with this denominator:

$$\frac{5}{6x^2} = \frac{5 \cdot 4xy^2}{6x^2 \cdot 4xy^2} = \frac{20xy^2}{24x^3y^2}$$

$$\frac{1}{8x^3y} = \frac{1 \cdot 3y}{8x^3y \cdot 3y} = \frac{3y}{24x^3y^2}$$

$$\frac{3}{4y^2} = \frac{3 \cdot 6x^3}{4y^2 \cdot 6x^3} = \frac{18x^3}{24x^3y^2}$$

Now do Exercises 51–62

EXAMPLE 5

Converting to the LCD

Find the LCD for the rational expressions

$$\frac{5x}{x^2 - 4} \quad \text{and} \quad \frac{3}{x^2 + x - 6}$$

and convert each into an equivalent rational expression with that denominator.

Solution

First factor the denominators:

$$x^2 - 4 = (x - 2)(x + 2)$$

$$x^2 + x - 6 = (x - 2)(x + 3)$$

The LCD is $(x - 2)(x + 2)(x + 3)$. Now we multiply the numerator and denominator of the first rational expression by $(x + 3)$ and those of the second rational expression by $(x + 2)$. Because each denominator already has one factor of $(x - 2)$, there is no reason to multiply by $(x - 2)$. We multiply each denominator by the factors in the LCD that are missing from that denominator:

$$\frac{5x}{x^2 - 4} = \frac{5x(x + 3)}{(x - 2)(x + 2)(x + 3)} = \frac{5x^2 + 15x}{(x - 2)(x + 2)(x + 3)}$$

$$\frac{3}{x^2 + x - 6} = \frac{3(x + 2)}{(x - 2)(x + 3)(x + 2)} = \frac{3x + 6}{(x - 2)(x + 2)(x + 3)}$$

Same denominator

Teaching Tip

Point out that the LCD is what you get when you make the denominators the same with the least amount of multiplying.

Now do Exercises 63–74

Warm-Ups

True or false? Explain your answer.

1. To convert $\frac{2}{3}$ into an equivalent fraction with a denominator of 18, we would multiply only the denominator of $\frac{2}{3}$ by 6. False
2. Factoring has nothing to do with finding the least common denominator. False
3. $\frac{3}{2ab^2} = \frac{15a^2b^2}{10a^3b^4}$ for any nonzero values of a and b. True
4. The LCD for the denominators $2^5 \cdot 3$ and $2^4 \cdot 3^2$ is $2^5 \cdot 3^2$. True
5. The LCD for the fractions $\frac{1}{6}$ and $\frac{1}{10}$ is 60. False
6. The LCD for the denominators $6a^2b$ and $4ab^3$ is $2ab$. False
7. The LCD for the denominators $a^2 + 1$ and $a + 1$ is $a^2 + 1$. False
8. $\frac{x}{2} = \frac{x+7}{2+7}$ for any real number x. False
9. The LCD for the rational expressions $\frac{1}{x-2}$ and $\frac{3}{x+2}$ is $x^2 - 4$. True
10. $x = \frac{3x}{3}$ for any real number x. True

7.3 Exercises

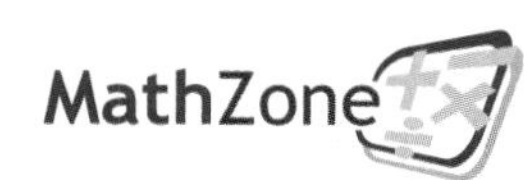

‹ Study Tips ›

- Try changing subjects or tasks every hour when you study. The brain does not easily assimilate the same material hour after hour.
- You will learn more from working on a subject one hour per day than seven hours on Saturday.

Reading and Writing *After reading this section, write out the answers to these questions. Use complete sentences.*

1. What is building up the denominator? We can build up a denominator by multiplying the numerator and denominator of a fraction by the same nonzero number.
2. How do we build up the denominator of a rational expression? To build up the denominator of a rational expression, we can multiply the numerator and denominator by the same polynomial.
3. What is the least common denominator for fractions? For fractions, the LCD is the smallest number that is a multiple of all of the denominators.
4. How do you find the LCD for two polynomial denominators? For polynomial denominators, the LCD consists of every factor that appears, raised to the highest power that appears on the factor.

‹1› Building Up the Denominator

Build each rational expression into an equivalent rational expression with the indicated denominator. See Example 1.

5. $\frac{1}{3} = \frac{?}{27}$ $\frac{9}{27}$
6. $\frac{2}{5} = \frac{?}{35}$ $\frac{14}{35}$
7. $\frac{3}{4} = \frac{?}{16}$ $\frac{12}{16}$
8. $\frac{3}{7} = \frac{?}{28}$ $\frac{12}{28}$
9. $1 = \frac{?}{7}$ $\frac{7}{7}$
10. $1 = \frac{?}{3x}$ $\frac{3x}{3x}$
11. $2 = \frac{?}{6}$ $\frac{12}{6}$
12. $5 = \frac{?}{12}$ $\frac{60}{12}$
13. $\frac{5}{x} = \frac{?}{ax}$ $\frac{5a}{ax}$
14. $\frac{x}{3} = \frac{?}{3x}$ $\frac{x^2}{3x}$

15. $7 = \frac{?}{2x}$ $\frac{14x}{2x}$

16. $6 = \frac{?}{4y}$ $\frac{24y}{4y}$

17. $\frac{5}{b} = \frac{?}{3bt}$ $\frac{15t}{3bt}$

18. $\frac{7}{2ay} = \frac{?}{2ayz}$ $\frac{7z}{2ayz}$

19. $\frac{-9z}{2aw} = \frac{?}{8awz}$ $\frac{-36z^2}{8awz}$

20. $\frac{-7yt}{3x} = \frac{?}{18xyt}$ $\frac{-42y^2t^2}{18xyt}$

21. $\frac{2}{3a} = \frac{?}{15a^3}$ $\frac{10a^2}{15a^3}$

22. $\frac{7b}{12c^5} = \frac{?}{36c^8}$ $\frac{21bc^3}{36c^8}$

23. $\frac{4}{5xy^2} = \frac{?}{10x^2y^5}$ $\frac{8xy^3}{10x^2y^5}$

24. $\frac{5y^2}{8x^3z} = \frac{?}{24x^5z^3}$ $\frac{15x^2y^2z^2}{24x^5z^3}$

Build each rational expression into an equivalent rational expression with the indicated denominator. See Example 2.

25. $\frac{5}{x+3} = \frac{?}{2x+6}$ $\frac{10}{2x+6}$

26. $\frac{4}{a-5} = \frac{?}{3a-15}$ $\frac{12}{3a-15}$

27. $\frac{5}{2x+2} = \frac{?}{-8x-8}$ $\frac{-20}{-8x-8}$

28. $\frac{3}{m-n} = \frac{?}{2n-2m}$ $\frac{-6}{2n-2m}$

VIDEO **29.** $\frac{8a}{5b^2-5b} = \frac{?}{20b^2-20b^3}$ $\frac{-32ab}{20b^2-20b^3}$

30. $\frac{5x}{-6x-9} = \frac{?}{18x^2+27x}$ $\frac{-15x^2}{18x^2+27x}$

31. $\frac{3}{x+2} = \frac{?}{x^2-4}$ $\frac{3x-6}{x^2-4}$

32. $\frac{a}{a+3} = \frac{?}{a^2-9}$ $\frac{a^2-3a}{a^2-9}$

33. $\frac{3x}{x+1} = \frac{?}{x^2+2x+1}$ $\frac{3x^2+3x}{x^2+2x+1}$

34. $\frac{-7x}{2x-3} = \frac{?}{4x^2-12x+9}$ $\frac{-14x^2+21x}{4x^2-12x+9}$

35. $\frac{y-6}{y-4} = \frac{?}{y^2+y-20}$ $\frac{y^2-y-30}{y^2+y-20}$

36. $\frac{z-6}{z+3} = \frac{?}{z^2-2z-15}$ $\frac{z^2-11z+30}{z^2-2z-15}$

⟨2⟩ Finding the Least Common Denominator

If the given expressions were used as denominators of rational expressions, then what would be the LCD for each group of denominators?

See Example 3.

See the Strategy for Finding the LCD for Polynomials box on page 441.

37. 12, 16 48

38. 28, 42 84

39. 12, 18, 20 180

40. 24, 40, 48 240

41. $6a^2$, $15a$ $30a^2$

42. $18x^2$, $20xy$ $180x^2y$

43. $2a^4b$, $3ab^6$, $4a^3b^2$ $12a^4b^6$

44. $4m^3nw$, $6mn^5w^8$, $9m^6nw$ $36m^6n^5w^8$

45. x^2-16, $x^2+8x+16$ $(x-4)(x+4)^2$

VIDEO **46.** x^2-9, x^2+6x+9 $(x-3)(x+3)^2$

47. x, $x+2$, $x-2$ $x(x+2)(x-2)$

48. y, $y-5$, $y+2$ $y(y-5)(y+2)$

49. x^2-4x, x^2-16, $2x$ $2x(x-4)(x+4)$

50. y, y^2-3y, $3y$ $3y(y-3)$

⟨3⟩ Converting to the LCD

Find the LCD for the given rational expressions, and convert each rational expression into an equivalent rational expression with the LCD as the denominator. See Example 4.

51. $\frac{1}{6}, \frac{3}{8}$ $\frac{4}{24}, \frac{9}{24}$

52. $\frac{5}{12}, \frac{3}{20}$ $\frac{25}{60}, \frac{9}{60}$

53. $\frac{1}{2x}, \frac{5}{6x}$ $\frac{3}{6x}, \frac{5}{6x}$

54. $\frac{3}{5x}, \frac{1}{10x}$ $\frac{6}{10x}, \frac{1}{10x}$

55. $\frac{2}{3a}, \frac{1}{2b}$ $\frac{4b}{6ab}, \frac{3a}{6ab}$

56. $\frac{y}{4x}, \frac{x}{6y}$ $\frac{3y^2}{12xy}, \frac{2x^2}{12xy}$

57. $\frac{3}{84a}, \frac{5}{63b}$ $\frac{9b}{252ab}, \frac{20a}{252ab}$

58. $\frac{4b}{75a}, \frac{6}{105ab}$ $\frac{28b^2}{525ab}, \frac{30}{525ab}$

59. $\frac{1}{3x^2}, \frac{3}{2x^5}$ $\frac{2x^3}{6x^5}, \frac{9}{6x^5}$

VIDEO **60.** $\frac{3}{8a^3b^9}, \frac{5}{6a^2c}$ $\frac{9c}{24a^3b^9c}, \frac{20ab^9}{24a^3b^9c}$

61. $\frac{x}{9y^5z}, \frac{y}{12x^3}, \frac{1}{6x^2y}$ $\frac{4x^4}{36x^3y^5z}, \frac{3y^6z}{36x^3y^5z}, \frac{6xy^4z}{36x^3y^5z}$

62. $\frac{5}{12a^6b}, \frac{3b}{14a^3}, \frac{1}{2ab^3}$ $\frac{35b^2}{84a^6b^3}, \frac{18a^3b^4}{84a^6b^3}, \frac{42a^5}{84a^6b^3}$

Find the LCD for the given rational expressions, and convert each rational expression into an equivalent rational expression with the LCD as the denominator. See Example 5.

63. $\frac{2x}{x-3}, \frac{5x}{x+2}$ $\frac{2x^2+4x}{(x-3)(x+2)}, \frac{5x^2-15x}{(x-3)(x+2)}$

64. $\dfrac{2a}{a-5}, \dfrac{3a}{a+2}$ $\quad \dfrac{2a^2+4a}{(a-5)(a+2)}, \dfrac{3a^2-15a}{(a-5)(a+2)}$

65. $\dfrac{4}{a-6}, \dfrac{5}{6-a}$ $\quad \dfrac{4}{a-6}, \dfrac{-5}{a-6}$

66. $\dfrac{4}{x-y}, \dfrac{5x}{2y-2x}$ $\quad \dfrac{8}{2(x-y)}, \dfrac{-5x}{2(x-y)}$

67. $\dfrac{x}{x^2-9}, \dfrac{5x}{x^2-6x+9}$ $\quad \dfrac{x^2-3x}{(x-3)^2(x+3)}, \dfrac{5x^2+15x}{(x-3)^2(x+3)}$

68. $\dfrac{5x}{x^2-1}, \dfrac{-4}{x^2-2x+1}$ $\quad \dfrac{5x^2-5x}{(x+1)(x-1)^2}, \dfrac{-4x-4}{(x+1)(x-1)^2}$

69. $\dfrac{w+2}{w^2-2w-15}, \dfrac{-2w}{w^2-4w-5}$

$\dfrac{w^2+3w+2}{(w-5)(w+3)(w+1)}, \dfrac{-2w^2-6w}{(w-5)(w+3)(w+1)}$

70. $\dfrac{z-1}{z^2+6z+8}, \dfrac{z+1}{z^2+5z+6}$

$\dfrac{z^2+2z-3}{(z+2)(z+4)(z+3)}, \dfrac{z^2+5z+4}{(z+2)(z+4)(z+3)}$

71. $\dfrac{-5}{6x-12}, \dfrac{x}{x^2-4}, \dfrac{3}{2x+4}$

$\dfrac{-5x-10}{6(x-2)(x+2)}, \dfrac{6x}{6(x-2)(x+2)}, \dfrac{9x-18}{6(x-2)(x+2)}$

72. $\dfrac{3}{4b^2-9}, \dfrac{2b}{2b+3}, \dfrac{-5}{2b^2-3b}$

$\dfrac{3b}{b(2b-3)(2b+3)}, \dfrac{4b^3-6b^2}{b(2b-3)(2b+3)},$

$\dfrac{-10b-15}{b(2b-3)(2b+3)}$

73. $\dfrac{2}{2q^2-5q-3}, \dfrac{3}{2q^2+9q+4}, \dfrac{4}{q^2+q-12}$

$\dfrac{2q+8}{(2q+1)(q-3)(q+4)}, \dfrac{3q-9}{(2q+1)(q-3)(q+4)},$

$\dfrac{8q+4}{(2q+1)(q-3)(q+4)}$

74. $\dfrac{-3}{2p^2+7p-15}, \dfrac{p}{2p^2-11p+12}, \dfrac{2}{p^2+p-20}$

$\dfrac{-3p+12}{(2p-3)(p+5)(p-4)}, \dfrac{p^2+5p}{(2p-3)(p+5)(p-4)},$

$\dfrac{4p-6}{(2p-3)(p+5)(p-4)}$

Getting More Involved

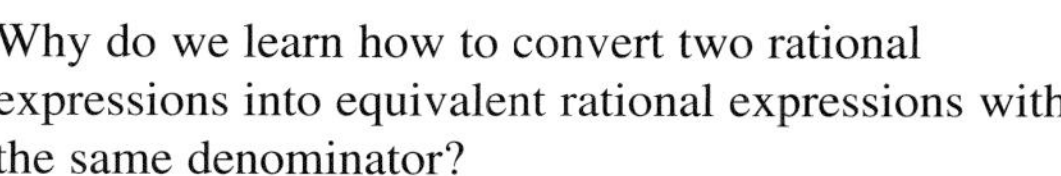

75. ***Discussion***

Why do we learn how to convert two rational expressions into equivalent rational expressions with the same denominator?

Identical denominators are needed for addition and subtraction.

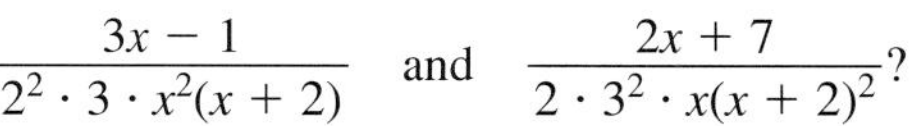

76. ***Discussion***

Which expression is the LCD for

$$\frac{3x-1}{2^2 \cdot 3 \cdot x^2(x+2)} \quad \text{and} \quad \frac{2x+7}{2 \cdot 3^2 \cdot x(x+2)^2}?$$

a) $2 \cdot 3 \cdot x(x+2)$ **b)** $36x(x+2)$

c) $36x^2(x+2)^2$ **d)** $2^3 \cdot 3^3x^3(x+2)^2$ c

7.4 Addition and Subtraction

In This Section

- ⟨1⟩ Addition and Subtraction of Rational Numbers
- ⟨2⟩ Addition and Subtraction of Rational Expressions
- ⟨3⟩ Applications

In Section 7.3, you learned how to find the LCD and build up the denominators of rational expressions. In this section, we will use that knowledge to add and subtract rational expressions with different denominators.

⟨1⟩ Addition and Subtraction of Rational Numbers

We can add or subtract rational numbers (or fractions) only with identical denominators according to the following definition.

Addition and Subtraction of Rational Numbers

If $b \neq 0$, then

$$\frac{a}{b} + \frac{c}{b} = \frac{a+c}{b} \quad \text{and} \quad \frac{a}{b} - \frac{c}{b} = \frac{a-c}{b}.$$

EXAMPLE 1

Adding or subtracting fractions with the same denominator

Perform the indicated operations. Reduce answers to lowest terms.

a) $\frac{1}{12} + \frac{7}{12}$

b) $\frac{1}{4} - \frac{3}{4}$

Solution

a) $\frac{1}{12} + \frac{7}{12} = \frac{8}{12} = \frac{\cancel{4} \cdot 2}{\cancel{4} \cdot 3} = \frac{2}{3}$

b) $\frac{1}{4} - \frac{3}{4} = \frac{-2}{4} = -\frac{1}{2}$

Now do Exercises 5–12

If the rational numbers have different denominators, we must convert them to equivalent rational numbers that have identical denominators and then add or subtract. Of course, it is most efficient to use the least common denominator (LCD), as in Example 2.

EXAMPLE 2

Adding or subtracting fractions with different denominators

Find each sum or difference.

a) $\frac{3}{20} + \frac{7}{12}$

b) $\frac{1}{6} - \frac{4}{15}$

Helpful Hint

Note how all of the operations with rational expressions are performed according to the rules for fractions. So keep thinking of how you perform operations with fractions, and you will improve your skills with fractions and with rational expressions.

Solution

a) Because $20 = 2^2 \cdot 5$ and $12 = 2^2 \cdot 3$, the LCD is $2^2 \cdot 3 \cdot 5$, or 60. Convert each fraction to an equivalent fraction with a denominator of 60:

$$\frac{3}{20} + \frac{7}{12} = \frac{3 \cdot 3}{20 \cdot 3} + \frac{7 \cdot 5}{12 \cdot 5} \quad \text{Build up the denominators.}$$

$$= \frac{9}{60} + \frac{35}{60} \quad \text{Simplify numerators and denominators.}$$

$$= \frac{44}{60} \quad \text{Add the fractions.}$$

$$= \frac{4 \cdot 11}{4 \cdot 15} \quad \text{Factor.}$$

$$= \frac{11}{15} \quad \text{Reduce.}$$

b) Because $6 = 2 \cdot 3$ and $15 = 3 \cdot 5$, the LCD is $2 \cdot 3 \cdot 5$ or 30:

$$\frac{1}{6} - \frac{4}{15} = \frac{1}{2 \cdot 3} - \frac{4}{3 \cdot 5} \quad \text{Factor the denominators.}$$

$$= \frac{1 \cdot 5}{2 \cdot 3 \cdot 5} - \frac{4 \cdot 2}{3 \cdot 5 \cdot 2} \quad \text{Build up the denominators.}$$

$$= \frac{5}{30} - \frac{8}{30}$$ Simplify the numerators and denominators.

$$= \frac{-3}{30}$$ Subtract.

$$= \frac{-1 \cdot 3}{10 \cdot 3}$$ Factor.

$$= -\frac{1}{10}$$ Reduce.

Now do Exercises 13–22

⟨2⟩ Addition and Subtraction of Rational Expressions

Rational expressions are added or subtracted just like rational numbers. We can add or subtract only when we have identical denominators. All answers should be reduced to lowest terms. Remember to factor first when reducing, then divide out any common factors.

EXAMPLE 3

Rational expressions with the same denominator

Perform the indicated operations and reduce answers to lowest terms.

a) $\frac{2}{3y} + \frac{4}{3y}$ **b)** $\frac{2x}{x + 2} + \frac{4}{x + 2}$ **c)** $\frac{x^2 + 2x}{(x - 1)(x + 3)} - \frac{2x + 1}{(x - 1)(x + 3)}$

Solution

a) $$\frac{2}{3y} + \frac{4}{3y} = \frac{6}{3y}$$ Add the fractions.

$$= \frac{2}{y}$$ Reduce.

b) $$\frac{2x}{x + 2} + \frac{4}{x + 2} = \frac{2x + 4}{x + 2}$$ Add the fractions.

$$= \frac{2(x + 2)}{x + 2}$$ Factor the numerator.

$$= 2$$ Reduce.

c) $$\frac{x^2 + 2x}{(x - 1)(x + 3)} - \frac{2x + 1}{(x - 1)(x + 3)} = \frac{x^2 + 2x - (2x + 1)}{(x - 1)(x + 3)}$$ Subtract the fractions.

$$= \frac{x^2 + 2x - 2x - 1}{(x - 1)(x + 3)}$$ Remove parentheses.

$$= \frac{x^2 - 1}{(x - 1)(x + 3)}$$ Combine like terms.

$$= \frac{(x - 1)(x + 1)}{(x - 1)(x + 3)}$$ Factor.

$$= \frac{x + 1}{x + 3}$$ Reduce.

Now do Exercises 23–34

CAUTION When subtracting a numerator containing more than one term, be sure to enclose it in parentheses, as in Example 3(c). Because that numerator is a binomial, the sign of each of its terms must be changed for the subtraction.

In Example 4, the rational expressions have different denominators.

EXAMPLE 4

Rational expressions with different denominators

Perform the indicated operations.

a) $\dfrac{5}{2x} + \dfrac{2}{3}$ **b)** $\dfrac{4}{x^3y} + \dfrac{2}{xy^3}$

c) $\dfrac{a+1}{6} - \dfrac{a-2}{8}$

‹ Helpful Hint ›

You can remind yourself of the difference between addition and multiplication of fractions with a simple example: If you and your spouse each own 1/7 of Microsoft, then together you own 2/7 of Microsoft. If you own 1/7 of Microsoft, and give 1/7 of your stock to your child, then your child owns 1/49 of Microsoft.

Solution

a) The LCD for $2x$ and 3 is $6x$:

$$\frac{5}{2x} + \frac{2}{3} = \frac{5 \cdot 3}{2x \cdot 3} + \frac{2 \cdot 2x}{3 \cdot 2x} \quad \text{Build up both denominators to } 6x.$$

$$= \frac{15}{6x} + \frac{4x}{6x} \quad \text{Simplify numerators and denominators.}$$

$$= \frac{15 + 4x}{6x} \quad \text{Add the rational expressions.}$$

b) The LCD is x^3y^3.

$$\frac{4}{x^3y} + \frac{2}{xy^3} = \frac{4 \cdot y^2}{x^3y \cdot y^2} + \frac{2 \cdot x^2}{xy^3 \cdot x^2} \quad \text{Build up both denominators to the LCD.}$$

$$= \frac{4y^2}{x^3y^3} + \frac{2x^2}{x^3y^3} \quad \text{Simplify numerators and denominators.}$$

$$= \frac{4y^2 + 2x^2}{x^3y^3} \quad \text{Add the rational expressions.}$$

c) Because $6 = 2 \cdot 3$ and $8 = 2^3$, the LCD is $2^3 \cdot 3$, or 24:

$$\frac{a+1}{6} - \frac{a-2}{8} = \frac{(a+1)4}{6 \cdot 4} - \frac{(a-2)3}{8 \cdot 3} \quad \text{Build up both denominators to the LCD 24.}$$

$$= \frac{4a+4}{24} - \frac{3a-6}{24} \quad \text{Simplify numerators and denominators.}$$

$$= \frac{4a + 4 - (3a - 6)}{24} \quad \text{Subtract the rational expressions.}$$

$$= \frac{4a + 4 - 3a + 6}{24} \quad \text{Remove the parentheses.}$$

$$= \frac{a + 10}{24} \quad \text{Combine like terms.}$$

Now do Exercises 35–50

EXAMPLE 5

Rational expressions with different denominators

Perform the indicated operations:

a) $\frac{1}{x^2 - 9} + \frac{2}{x^2 + 3x}$ **b)** $\frac{4}{5 - a} - \frac{2}{a - 5}$

‹ Helpful Hint ›

Once the denominators are factored as in Example 5(a), you can simply look at each denominator and ask, "What factor does the other denominator(s) have that is missing from this one?" Then use the missing factor to build up the denominator. Repeat until all denominators are identical and you will have the LCD.

Solution

a) $\frac{1}{x^2 - 9} + \frac{2}{x^2 + 3x} = \underbrace{\frac{1}{(x - 3)(x + 3)}}_{\text{Needs } x} + \underbrace{\frac{2}{x(x + 3)}}_{\text{Needs } x - 3}$ The LCD is $x(x - 3)(x + 3)$.

$$= \frac{1 \cdot x}{(x - 3)(x + 3)x} + \frac{2(x - 3)}{x(x + 3)(x - 3)}$$

$$= \frac{x}{x(x - 3)(x + 3)} + \frac{2x - 6}{x(x - 3)(x + 3)}$$

$$= \frac{3x - 6}{x(x - 3)(x + 3)}$$ We usually leave the denominator in factored form.

b) Because $-1(5 - a) = a - 5$, we can get identical denominators by multiplying only the first expression by -1 in the numerator and denominator:

$$\frac{4}{5 - a} - \frac{2}{a - 5} = \frac{4(-1)}{(5 - a)(-1)} - \frac{2}{a - 5}$$

$$= \frac{-4}{a - 5} - \frac{2}{a - 5}$$

$$= \frac{-6}{a - 5}$$ $-4 - 2 = -6$

$$= -\frac{6}{a - 5}$$

Now do Exercises 51–68

In Example 6, we combine three rational expressions by addition and subtraction.

EXAMPLE 6

Rational expressions with different denominators

Perform the indicated operations.

$$\frac{x + 1}{x^2 + 2x} + \frac{2x + 1}{6x + 12} - \frac{1}{6}$$

Solution

The LCD for $x(x + 2)$, $6(x + 2)$, and 6 is $6x(x + 2)$.

$$\frac{x + 1}{x^2 + 2x} + \frac{2x + 1}{6x + 12} - \frac{1}{6} = \frac{x + 1}{x(x + 2)} + \frac{2x + 1}{6(x + 2)} - \frac{1}{6}$$ Factor denominators.

$$= \frac{6(x + 1)}{6x(x + 2)} + \frac{x(2x + 1)}{6x(x + 2)} - \frac{1x(x + 2)}{6x(x + 2)}$$ Build up to the LCD.

$$= \frac{6x + 6}{6x(x + 2)} + \frac{2x^2 + x}{6x(x + 2)} - \frac{x^2 + 2x}{6x(x + 2)}$$ Simplify numerators.

$$= \frac{6x + 6 + 2x^2 + x - x^2 - 2x}{6x(x + 2)}$$ Combine the numerators.

$$= \frac{x^2 + 5x + 6}{6x(x + 2)}$$ Combine like terms.

$$= \frac{(x + 3)(x + 2)}{6x(x + 2)}$$ Factor.

$$= \frac{x + 3}{6x}$$ Reduce.

Now do Exercises 69–74

‹3› Applications

We have seen how rational expressions can occur in problems involving rates. In Example 7, we see an applied situation in which we add rational expressions.

EXAMPLE 7

Adding work

Harry takes twice as long as Lucy to proofread a manuscript. Write a rational expression for the amount of work they do in 3 hours working together on a manuscript.

Solution

Let $x =$ the number of hours it would take Lucy to complete the manuscript alone and $2x =$ the number of hours it would take Harry to complete the manuscript alone. Make a table showing rate, time, and work completed:

	Rate	Time	Work
Lucy	$\frac{1}{x}\frac{\text{msp}}{\text{hr}}$	3 hr	$\frac{3}{x}$ msp
Harry	$\frac{1}{2x}\frac{\text{msp}}{\text{hr}}$	3 hr	$\frac{3}{2x}$ msp

Now find the sum of each person's work.

$$\frac{3}{x} + \frac{3}{2x} = \frac{2 \cdot 3}{2 \cdot x} + \frac{3}{2x}$$

$$= \frac{6}{2x} + \frac{3}{2x}$$

$$= \frac{9}{2x}$$

So in 3 hours working together they will complete $\frac{9}{2x}$ of the manuscript.

Now do Exercises 85–90

‹ Teaching Tip ›

Emphasize the importance of tables for keeping all of the information organized. Note that in work problems the product of rate and time is work. In motion problems $RT = D$.

Warm-Ups ▼

True or false? Explain your answer.

1. $\frac{1}{2} + \frac{1}{3} = \frac{2}{5}$ False

2. $\frac{7}{12} - \frac{1}{12} = \frac{1}{2}$ True

3. $\frac{3}{5} + \frac{4}{3} = \frac{29}{15}$ True

4. $\frac{4}{5} - \frac{5}{7} = \frac{3}{35}$ True

5. $\frac{5}{20} + \frac{3}{4} = 1$ True

6. $\frac{2}{x} + 1 = \frac{3}{x}$ for any nonzero value of x. False

7. $1 + \frac{1}{a} = \frac{a+1}{a}$ for any nonzero value of a. True

8. $a - \frac{1}{4} = \frac{3}{4}a$ for any value of a. False

9. $\frac{a}{2} + \frac{b}{3} = \frac{3a + 2b}{6}$ for any values of a and b. True

10. The LCD for the rational expressions $\frac{1}{x}$ and $\frac{3x}{x-1}$ is $x^2 - 1$. False

Exercises 7.4

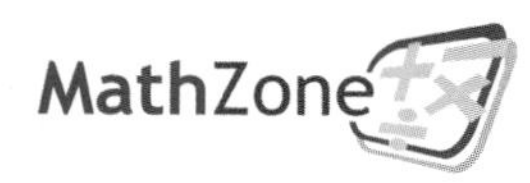

Boost your grade at mathzone.com!
- Practice Problems
- NetTutor
- Self-Tests
- e-Professors
- Videos

‹ Study Tips ›

- When studying for a midterm or final, review the material in the order it was originally presented. This strategy will help you to see connections between the ideas.
- Studying the oldest material first will give top priority to material that you might have forgotten.

Reading and Writing *After reading this section, write out the answers to these questions. Use complete sentences.*

1. How do you add or subtract rational numbers?
   We can add rational numbers with identical denominators as follows: $\frac{a}{c} + \frac{b}{c} = \frac{a+b}{c}$.
2. How do you add or subtract rational expressions?
   Rational expressions with identical denominators are added in the same manner as rational numbers.
3. What is the least common denominator?
   The LCD is the smallest number that is a multiple of all denominators.
4. Why do we use the *least* common denominator when adding rational expressions?
   We use the least common denominator to keep the addition process as simple as possible.

‹1› Addition and Subtraction of Rational Numbers

Perform the indicated operation. Reduce each answer to lowest terms. See Example 1.

5. $\frac{1}{10} + \frac{1}{10}$ $\frac{1}{5}$

6. $\frac{1}{8} + \frac{3}{8}$ $\frac{1}{2}$

7. $\frac{7}{8} - \frac{1}{8}$ $\frac{3}{4}$

8. $\frac{4}{9} - \frac{1}{9}$ $\frac{1}{3}$

9. $\frac{1}{6} - \frac{5}{6}$ $-\frac{2}{3}$

10. $-\frac{3}{8} - \frac{7}{8}$ $-\frac{5}{4}$

11. $-\frac{7}{8} + \frac{1}{8}$ $-\frac{3}{4}$

12. $-\frac{9}{20} + \left(-\frac{3}{20}\right)$ $-\frac{3}{5}$

Perform the indicated operation. Reduce each answer to lowest terms. See Example 2.

13. $\frac{1}{3} + \frac{2}{9}$ $\frac{5}{9}$

14. $\frac{1}{4} + \frac{5}{6}$ $\frac{13}{12}$

15. $\frac{7}{10} + \frac{5}{6}$ $\frac{23}{15}$

16. $\frac{5}{6} + \frac{3}{10}$ $\frac{17}{15}$

17. $\frac{7}{16} + \frac{5}{18}$ $\frac{103}{144}$

18. $\frac{7}{6} + \frac{4}{15}$ $\frac{43}{30}$

19. $\frac{1}{8} - \frac{9}{10}$ $-\frac{31}{40}$

20. $\frac{2}{15} - \frac{5}{12}$ $-\frac{17}{60}$

21. $-\frac{1}{6} - \left(-\frac{3}{8}\right)$ $\frac{5}{24}$

22. $-\frac{1}{5} - \left(-\frac{1}{7}\right)$ $-\frac{2}{35}$

⟨2⟩ Addition and Subtraction of Rational Expressions

Perform the indicated operation. Reduce each answer to lowest terms. See Example 3.

23. $\frac{1}{2x}+\frac{1}{2x}$ $\frac{1}{x}$

24. $\frac{1}{3y}+\frac{2}{3y}$ $\frac{1}{y}$

25. $\frac{3}{2w}+\frac{7}{2w}$ $\frac{5}{w}$

26. $\frac{5x}{3y}+\frac{7x}{3y}$ $\frac{4x}{y}$

27. $\frac{3a}{a+5}+\frac{15}{a+5}$ 3

VIDEO **28.** $\frac{a+7}{a-4}+\frac{9-5a}{a-4}$ -4

29. $\frac{q-1}{q-4}-\frac{3q-9}{q-4}$ -2

30. $\frac{3-a}{3}-\frac{a-5}{3}$ $\frac{8-2a}{3}$

31. $\frac{4h-3}{h(h+1)}-\frac{h-6}{h(h+1)}$ $\frac{3}{h}$

32. $\frac{2t-9}{t(t-3)}-\frac{t-9}{t(t-3)}$ $\frac{1}{t-3}$

VIDEO **33.** $\frac{x^2-x-5}{(x+1)(x+2)}+\frac{1-2x}{(x+1)(x+2)}$ $\frac{x-4}{x+2}$

34. $\frac{2x-5}{(x-2)(x+6)}+\frac{x^2-2x+1}{(x-2)(x+6)}$ $\frac{x+2}{x+6}$

Perform the indicated operation. Reduce each answer to lowest terms. See Example 4.

35. $\frac{1}{a}+\frac{1}{2a}$ $\frac{3}{2a}$

36. $\frac{1}{3w}+\frac{2}{w}$ $\frac{7}{3w}$

37. $\frac{x}{3}+\frac{x}{2}$ $\frac{5x}{6}$

38. $\frac{y}{4}+\frac{y}{2}$ $\frac{3y}{4}$

39. $\frac{m}{5}+m$ $\frac{6m}{5}$

40. $\frac{y}{4}+2y$ $\frac{9y}{4}$

41. $\frac{1}{x}+\frac{2}{y}$ $\frac{2x+y}{xy}$

42. $\frac{2}{a}+\frac{3}{b}$ $\frac{3a+2b}{ab}$

43. $\frac{3}{2a}+\frac{1}{5a}$ $\frac{17}{10a}$

44. $\frac{5}{6y}-\frac{3}{8y}$ $\frac{11}{24y}$

45. $\frac{w-3}{9}-\frac{w-4}{12}$ $\frac{w}{36}$

46. $\frac{y+4}{10}-\frac{y-2}{14}$ $\frac{y+19}{35}$

47. $\frac{b^2}{4a}-c$ $\frac{b^2-4ac}{4a}$

48. $y+\frac{3}{7b}$ $\frac{7by+3}{7b}$

49. $\frac{2}{wz^2}+\frac{3}{w^2z}$ $\frac{2w+3z}{w^2z^2}$

50. $\frac{1}{a^5b}-\frac{5}{ab^3}$ $\frac{b^2-5a^4}{a^5b^3}$

Perform the indicated operation. Reduce each answer to lowest terms. See Examples 5 and 6.

51. $\frac{1}{x}+\frac{1}{x+2}$ $\frac{2x+2}{x(x+2)}$

52. $\frac{1}{y}+\frac{2}{y+1}$ $\frac{3y+1}{y(y+1)}$

53. $\frac{2}{x+1}-\frac{3}{x}$ $\frac{-x-3}{x(x+1)}$

54. $\frac{1}{a-1}-\frac{2}{a}$ $\frac{2-a}{a(a-1)}$

55. $\frac{2}{a-b}+\frac{1}{a+b}$ $\frac{3a+b}{(a-b)(a+b)}$

56. $\frac{3}{x+1}+\frac{2}{x-1}$ $\frac{5x-1}{(x+1)(x-1)}$

VIDEO **57.** $\frac{3}{x^2+x}-\frac{4}{5x+5}$ $\frac{15-4x}{5x(x+1)}$

58. $\frac{3}{a^2+3a}-\frac{2}{5a+15}$ $\frac{15-2a}{5a(a+3)}$

59. $\frac{2a}{a^2-9}+\frac{a}{a-3}$ $\frac{a^2+5a}{(a-3)(a+3)}$

60. $\frac{x}{x^2-1}+\frac{3}{x-1}$ $\frac{4x+3}{(x-1)(x+1)}$

61. $\frac{4}{a-b}+\frac{4}{b-a}$ 0

VIDEO **62.** $\frac{2}{x-3}+\frac{3}{3-x}$ $\frac{1}{3-x}$

63. $\frac{3}{2a-2}-\frac{2}{1-a}$ $\frac{7}{2(a-1)}$

64. $\frac{5}{2x-4}-\frac{3}{2-x}$ $\frac{11}{2(x-2)}$

65. $\frac{1}{x^2-4}-\frac{3}{x^2-3x-10}$ $\frac{-2x+1}{(x-5)(x+2)(x-2)}$

66. $\frac{2x}{x^2-9}+\frac{3x}{x^2+4x+3}$ $\frac{5x^2-7x}{(x-3)(x+3)(x+1)}$

67. $\frac{3}{x^2+x-2}+\frac{4}{x^2+2x-3}$ $\frac{7x+17}{(x+2)(x-1)(x+3)}$

VIDEO **68.** $\frac{x-1}{x^2-x-12}+\frac{x+4}{x^2+5x+6}$ $\frac{2x^2+x-18}{(x+2)(x+3)(x-4)}$

69. $\frac{1}{a}+\frac{1}{b}+\frac{1}{c}$ $\frac{bc+ac+ab}{abc}$

70. $\frac{1}{x}+\frac{1}{x^2}+\frac{1}{x^3}$ $\frac{x^2+x+1}{x^3}$

71. $\frac{2}{x} - \frac{1}{x - 1} + \frac{1}{x + 2}$ $\frac{2x^2 - x - 4}{x(x - 1)(x + 2)}$

72. $\frac{1}{a} - \frac{2}{a + 1} + \frac{3}{a - 1}$ $\frac{2a^2 + 5a - 1}{a(a - 1)(a + 1)}$

73. $\frac{5}{3a - 9} - \frac{3}{2a} + \frac{4}{a^2 - 3a}$ $\frac{a + 51}{6a(a - 3)}$

74. $\frac{3}{4c + 2} - \frac{c - 4}{2c^2 + c} - \frac{5}{6c}$ $\frac{-7c + 19}{6c(2c + 1)}$

Match each expression in (a)–(f) with the equivalent expression in (A)–(F).

75. **a)** $\frac{1}{y} + 2$ F **b)** $\frac{1}{y} + \frac{2}{y}$ A **c)** $\frac{1}{y} + \frac{1}{2}$ E

d) $\frac{1}{y} + \frac{1}{2y}$ B **e)** $\frac{2}{y} + 1$ D **f)** $\frac{y}{2} + 1$ C

A) $\frac{3}{y}$ **B)** $\frac{3}{2y}$ **C)** $\frac{y + 2}{2}$

D) $\frac{y + 2}{y}$ **E)** $\frac{y + 2}{2y}$ **F)** $\frac{2y + 1}{y}$

76. **a)** $\frac{1}{x} - x$ C **b)** $\frac{1}{x} - \frac{1}{x^2}$ F **c)** $\frac{1}{x} - 1$ B

d) $\frac{1}{x^2} - x$ A **e)** $x - \frac{1}{x}$ E **f)** $\frac{1}{x^2} - \frac{1}{x}$ D

A) $\frac{1 - x^3}{x^2}$ **B)** $\frac{1 - x}{x}$ **C)** $\frac{1 - x^2}{x}$

D) $\frac{1 - x}{x^2}$ **E)** $\frac{x^2 - 1}{x}$ **F)** $\frac{x - 1}{x^2}$

Perform the indicated operation. Reduce each answer to lowest terms.

77. $\frac{3}{2p} - \frac{1}{2p + 8}$ $\frac{p + 6}{p(p + 4)}$

78. $\frac{3}{2y} - \frac{3}{2y + 4}$ $\frac{3}{y(y + 2)}$

79. $\frac{3}{a^2 + 3a + 2} + \frac{3}{a^2 + 5a + 6}$ $\frac{6}{(a + 1)(a + 3)}$

80. $\frac{4}{w^2 + w} + \frac{12}{w^2 - 3w}$ $\frac{16}{(w + 1)(w - 3)}$

81. $\frac{2}{b^2 + 4b + 3} - \frac{1}{b^2 + 5b + 6}$ $\frac{1}{(b + 1)(b + 2)}$

82. $\frac{9}{m^2 - m - 2} - \frac{6}{m^2 - 1}$ $\frac{3}{(m - 1)(m - 2)}$

83. $\frac{3}{2t} - \frac{2}{t + 2} - \frac{3}{t^2 + 2t}$ $\frac{-1}{2(t + 2)}$

84. $\frac{4}{3n} + \frac{2}{n + 1} + \frac{2}{n^2 + n}$ $\frac{10}{3n}$

⟨3⟩ Applications

Solve each problem. See Example 7.

85. ***Perimeter of a rectangle.*** Suppose that the length of a rectangle is $\frac{3}{x}$ feet and its width is $\frac{5}{2x}$ feet. Find a rational expression for the perimeter of the rectangle.

$\frac{11}{x}$ feet

86. ***Perimeter of a triangle.*** The lengths of the sides of a triangle are $\frac{1}{x}$, $\frac{1}{2x}$, and $\frac{2}{3x}$ meters. Find a rational expression for the perimeter of the triangle.

$\frac{13}{6x}$ meters

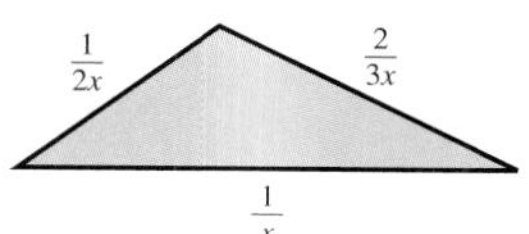

Figure for Exercise 86

87. ***Traveling time.*** Janet drove 120 miles at x mph before 6:00 A.M. After 6:00 A.M., she increased her speed by 5 mph and drove 195 additional miles. Use the fact that $T = \frac{D}{R}$ to complete the following table.

	Rate	Time	Distance
Before	$x \frac{\text{mi}}{\text{hr}}$	$\frac{120}{x}$ hr	120 mi
After	$x + 5 \frac{\text{mi}}{\text{hr}}$	$\frac{195}{x + 5}$ hr	195 mi

Write a rational expression for her total traveling time. Evaluate the expression for $x = 60$.

$\frac{315x + 600}{x(x + 5)}$ hours, 5 hours

88. ***Traveling time.*** After leaving Moose Jaw, Hanson drove 200 kilometers at x km/hr and then decreased his speed by 20 km/hr and drove 240 additional kilometers. Make a table like the one in Exercise 87. Write a rational expression for his total traveling time. Evaluate the expression for $x = 100$.

$\frac{440x - 4000}{x(x - 20)}$ hours, 5 hours

89. ***House painting.*** Kent can paint a certain house by himself in x days. His helper Keith can paint the same house by himself in $x + 3$ days. Suppose that they work together on the job for 2 days. To complete the table on the next page, use the fact that the work completed is the product of the rate and the time.

	Rate	Time	Work
Kent	$\frac{1}{x}\frac{\text{job}}{\text{day}}$	2 days	$\frac{2}{x}$ job
Keith	$\frac{1}{x+3}\frac{\text{job}}{\text{day}}$	2 days	$\frac{2}{x+3}$ job

Write a rational expression for the fraction of the house that they complete by working together for 2 days. Evaluate the expression for $x = 6$.

$\frac{4x+6}{x(x+3)}$ job, $\frac{5}{9}$ job

90. ***Barn painting.*** Melanie can paint a certain barn by herself in x days. Her helper Melissa can paint the same barn by herself in $2x$ days. Write a rational expression for the fraction of the barn that they complete in one day by working together. Evaluate the expression for $x = 5$.

$\frac{3}{2x}$ barn, $\frac{3}{10}$ barn

Photo for Exercise 90

Getting More Involved

91. ***Writing***

Write a step-by-step procedure for adding rational expressions.

92. ***Writing***

Explain why fractions must have the same denominator to be added. Use real-life examples.

Math *at Work* Gravity on the Moon

Hundreds of years before humans even considered traveling beyond the earth, Isaac Newton established the laws of gravity. So when Neil Armstrong made the first human step onto the moon in 1969 he knew what amount of gravitational force to expect. Let's see how he knew.

Newton's equation for the force of gravity between two objects is $F = G\frac{m_1m_2}{d^2}$, where m_1 and m_2 are the masses of the objects (in kilograms), d is the distance (in meters) between the centers of the two objects, and G is the gravitational constant 6.67×10^{-11}. To find the force of gravity for Armstrong on earth, use 5.98×10^{24} kg for the mass of the earth, 6.378×10^6 m for the radius of the earth, and 80 kg for Armstrong's mass. We get

$$F = 6.67 \times 10^{-11} \cdot \frac{5.98 \times 10^{24}\text{ kg} \cdot 80\text{ kg}}{(6.378 \times 10^6\text{ m})^2} \approx 784\text{ Newtons.}$$

To find the force of gravity for Armstrong on the moon, use 7.34×10^{22} kg for the mass of the moon and 1.737×10^6 m for the radius of the moon. We get

$$F = 6.67 \times 10^{-11} \cdot \frac{7.34 \times 10^{22}\text{ kg} \cdot 80\text{ kg}}{(1.737 \times 10^6\text{ m})^2} \approx 130\text{ Newtons.}$$

So the force of gravity for Armstrong on the moon was about one-sixth of the force of gravity for Armstrong on earth. Fortunately, the moon is smaller than the earth. Walking on a planet much larger than the earth would present a real problem in terms of gravitational force.

7.5 Complex Fractions

In This Section

In this section, we will use the idea of least common denominator to simplify complex fractions. Also we will see how complex fractions can arise in applications.

⟨1⟩ Complex Fractions

A **complex fraction** is a fraction having rational expressions in the numerator, denominator, or both. Consider the following complex fraction:

$$\frac{\frac{1}{2}+\frac{2}{3}}{\frac{1}{4}-\frac{5}{8}} \quad \begin{array}{l} \leftarrow \text{Numerator of complex fraction} \\ \\ \leftarrow \text{Denominator of complex fraction} \end{array}$$

Since the fraction bar is a grouping symbol, we can compute the value of the numerator, the value of the denominator, and then divide them, as shown in Example 1.

EXAMPLE 1

Simplifying complex fractions

Simplify.

a) $\dfrac{\frac{1}{2}+\frac{2}{3}}{\frac{1}{4}-\frac{5}{8}}$ **b)** $\dfrac{4-\frac{2}{5}}{\frac{1}{10}+3}$

Solution

a) Combine the fractions in the numerator:

$$\frac{1}{2}+\frac{2}{3}=\frac{1\cdot 3}{2\cdot 3}+\frac{2\cdot 2}{3\cdot 2}=\frac{3}{6}+\frac{4}{6}=\frac{7}{6}$$

Combine the fractions in the denominator as follows:

$$\frac{1}{4}-\frac{5}{8}=\frac{1\cdot 2}{4\cdot 2}-\frac{5}{8}=\frac{2}{8}-\frac{5}{8}=-\frac{3}{8}$$

Now divide the numerator by the denominator:

$$\frac{\frac{1}{2}+\frac{2}{3}}{\frac{1}{4}-\frac{5}{8}}=\frac{\frac{7}{6}}{-\frac{3}{8}}=\frac{7}{6}\div\left(-\frac{3}{8}\right)=\frac{7}{6}\cdot\left(-\frac{8}{3}\right)=-\frac{56}{18}=-\frac{28}{9}$$

b) $$\frac{4-\frac{2}{5}}{\frac{1}{10}+3}=\frac{\frac{20}{5}-\frac{2}{5}}{\frac{1}{10}+\frac{30}{10}}=\frac{\frac{18}{5}}{\frac{31}{10}}=\frac{18}{5}\div\frac{31}{10}=\frac{18}{5}\cdot\frac{10}{31}=\frac{36}{31}$$

Now do Exercises 3–14

‹ Teaching Tip ›

It is good to know both methods for simplifying complex fractions, but in most cases multiplying by the LCD is simpler and it shows another use of the LCD.

‹2› Using the LCD to Simplify Complex Fractions

A complex fraction can be simplified by performing the operations in the numerator and denominator, and then dividing the results, as shown in Example 1. However, there is a better method. All of the fractions in the complex fraction can be eliminated in one step by multiplying by the LCD of all of the single fractions. The strategy for this method is detailed in the following box and illustrated in Example 2.

Strategy for Simplifying a Complex Fraction

1. Find the LCD for all the denominators in the complex fraction.
2. Multiply both the numerator and the denominator of the complex fraction by the LCD. Use the distributive property if necessary.
3. Combine like terms if possible.
4. Reduce to lowest terms when possible.

EXAMPLE 2

Using the LCD to simplify a complex fraction

Use the LCD to simplify

$$\frac{\frac{1}{2}+\frac{2}{3}}{\frac{1}{4}-\frac{5}{8}}.$$

‹ Calculator Close-Up ›

You can check Example 2 with a calculator as shown here.

```
(1/2+2/3)/(1/4-5
/8)▸Frac
              -28/9
```

Solution

The LCD of 2, 3, 4, and 8 is 24. Now multiply the numerator and denominator of the complex fraction by the LCD:

$$\frac{\frac{1}{2}+\frac{2}{3}}{\frac{1}{4}-\frac{5}{8}} = \frac{\left(\frac{1}{2}+\frac{2}{3}\right)24}{\left(\frac{1}{4}-\frac{5}{8}\right)24}$$ Multiply the numerator and denominator by the LCD.

$$= \frac{\frac{1}{2}\cdot 24+\frac{2}{3}\cdot 24}{\frac{1}{4}\cdot 24-\frac{5}{8}\cdot 24}$$ Distributive property

$$= \frac{12+16}{6-15}$$ Simplify.

$$= \frac{28}{-9}$$

$$= -\frac{28}{9}$$

Now do Exercises 15–22

CAUTION We simplify a complex fraction by multiplying the numerator and denominator of the *complex fraction* by the LCD. Do not multiply the numerator and denominator of each fraction in the complex fraction by the LCD.

In Example 3 we simplify a complex fraction involving variables.

EXAMPLE 3

A complex fraction with variables

Simplify

$$\frac{2 - \frac{1}{x}}{\frac{1}{x^2} - \frac{1}{2}}.$$

Helpful Hint

When students see addition or subtraction in a complex fraction, they often convert all fractions to the same denominator. This is not wrong, but it is not necessary. Simply multiplying every fraction by the LCD eliminates the denominators of the original fractions.

Solution

The LCD of the denominators x, x^2, and 2 is $2x^2$:

$$\frac{2 - \frac{1}{x}}{\frac{1}{x^2} - \frac{1}{2}} = \frac{\left(2 - \frac{1}{x}\right)(2x^2)}{\left(\frac{1}{x^2} - \frac{1}{2}\right)(2x^2)} \quad \text{Multiply the numerator and denominator by } 2x^2.$$

$$= \frac{2 \cdot 2x^2 - \frac{1}{x} \cdot 2x^2}{\frac{1}{x^2} \cdot 2x^2 - \frac{1}{2} \cdot 2x^2} \quad \text{Distributive property}$$

$$= \frac{4x^2 - 2x}{2 - x^2} \quad \text{Simplify.}$$

The numerator of this answer can be factored, but the rational expression cannot be reduced.

Now do Exercises 23–32

EXAMPLE 4

Simplifying a complex fraction

Simplify

$$\frac{\frac{1}{x - 2} - \frac{2}{x + 2}}{\frac{3}{2 - x} + \frac{4}{x + 2}}.$$

‹ Teaching Tip ›

If desired you can rewrite $\frac{3}{2-x}$ as $\frac{-3}{x-2}$.

Solution

Because $x - 2$ and $2 - x$ are opposites, we can use $(x - 2)(x + 2)$ as the LCD. Multiply the numerator and denominator by $(x - 2)(x + 2)$:

$$\frac{\frac{1}{x-2} - \frac{2}{x+2}}{\frac{3}{2-x} + \frac{4}{x+2}} = \frac{\frac{1}{x-2}(x-2)(x+2) - \frac{2}{x+2}(x-2)(x+2)}{\frac{3}{2-x}(x-2)(x+2) + \frac{4}{x+2}(x-2)(x+2)}$$

$$= \frac{x + 2 - 2(x-2)}{3(-1)(x+2) + 4(x-2)} \qquad \frac{x-2}{2-x} = -1$$

$$= \frac{x + 2 - 2x + 4}{-3x - 6 + 4x - 8} \qquad \text{Distributive property}$$

$$= \frac{-x + 6}{x - 14} \qquad \text{Combine like terms.}$$

Now do Exercises 33–48

‹3› Applications

As their name suggests, complex fractions arise in some fairly complex situations.

EXAMPLE 5

Fast-food workers

A survey of college students found that $\frac{1}{2}$ of the female students had jobs and $\frac{2}{3}$ of the male students had jobs. It was also found that $\frac{1}{4}$ of the female students worked in fast-food restaurants and $\frac{1}{6}$ of the male students worked in fast-food restaurants. If equal numbers of male and female students were surveyed, then what fraction of the working students worked in fast-food restaurants?

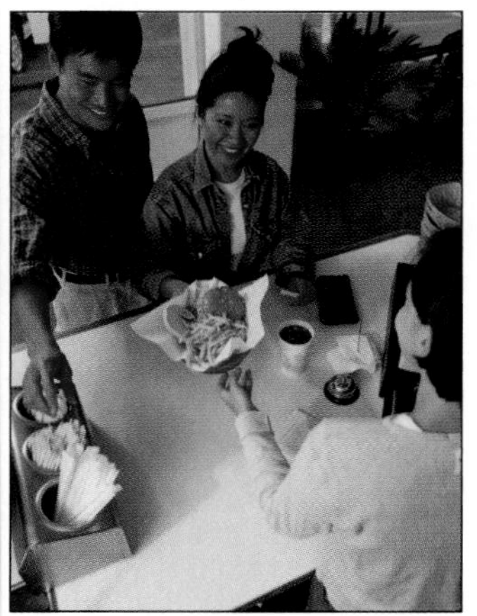

Solution

Let x represent the number of males surveyed. The number of females surveyed is also x. The total number of students working in fast-food restaurants is

$$\frac{1}{4}x + \frac{1}{6}x.$$

The total number of working students in the survey is

$$\frac{1}{2}x + \frac{2}{3}x.$$

So the fraction of working students who work in fast-food restaurants is

$$\frac{\frac{1}{4}x + \frac{1}{6}x}{\frac{1}{2}x + \frac{2}{3}x}.$$

The LCD of the denominators 2, 3, 4, and 6 is 12. Multiply the numerator and denominator by 12 to eliminate the fractions as follows:

$$\frac{\frac{1}{4}x + \frac{1}{6}x}{\frac{1}{2}x + \frac{2}{3}x} = \frac{\left(\frac{1}{4}x + \frac{1}{6}x\right)12}{\left(\frac{1}{2}x + \frac{2}{3}x\right)12} \quad \text{Multiply numerator and denominator by 12.}$$

$$= \frac{3x + 2x}{6x + 8x} \quad \text{Distributive property}$$

$$= \frac{5x}{14x} \quad \text{Combine like terms.}$$

$$= \frac{5}{14} \quad \text{Reduce.}$$

So $\frac{5}{14}$ (or about 36%) of the working students work in fast-food restaurants.

Now do Exercises 63–64

Warm-Ups

True or false? Explain your answer.

1. The LCD for the denominators 4, x, 6, and x^2 is $12x^3$. False
2. The LCD for the denominators $a - b$, $2b - 2a$, and 6 is $6a - 6b$. True
3. The fraction $\frac{4117}{7983}$ is a complex fraction. False
4. The LCD for the denominators $a - 3$ and $3 - a$ is $a^2 - 9$. False
5. The largest common denominator for the fractions $\frac{1}{2}$, $\frac{1}{3}$, and $\frac{1}{4}$ is 24. False

Questions 6–10 refer to the following complex fractions:

a) $\dfrac{\frac{1}{2} + \frac{x}{3}}{\frac{1}{4} + \frac{1}{5}}$ b) $\dfrac{1 + \frac{2}{b}}{\frac{2}{a} + 5}$ c) $\dfrac{x - \frac{1}{2}}{x + \frac{3}{2}}$ d) $\dfrac{\frac{1}{2} + \frac{1}{3}}{1 + \frac{1}{2}}$

6. To simplify (a), we multiply the numerator and denominator by $60x$. False
7. To simplify (b), we multiply the numerator and denominator by $\frac{ab}{ab}$. False
8. The complex fraction (c) is equivalent to $\frac{2x - 1}{2x + 3}$. True
9. If $x \neq -\frac{3}{2}$, then (c) represents a real number. True
10. The complex fraction (d) can be written as $\frac{5}{6} \div \frac{3}{2}$. True

7.5 Exercises

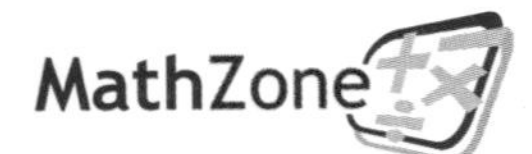

‹ Study Tips ›

- Stay calm and confident. Take breaks when you study. Get 6 to 8 hours of sleep every night.
- Keep reminding yourself that working hard throughout the semester will really pay off in the end.

Reading and Writing *After reading this section, write out the answers to these questions. Use complete sentences.*

1. What is a complex fraction? A complex fraction is a fraction that has fractions in its numerator, denominator, or both.
2. What are the two ways to simplify a complex fraction? You can multiply the numerator and denominator by the LCD or you can simplify the numerator and denominator, and then divide.

‹1› Complex Fractions

Simplify each complex fraction. See Example 1.

3. $\dfrac{\frac{1}{2}+\frac{1}{4}}{\frac{1}{2}+\frac{3}{4}}$ $\frac{3}{5}$

4. $\dfrac{\frac{1}{3}+\frac{5}{6}}{\frac{2}{3}+\frac{1}{6}}$ $\frac{7}{5}$

5. $\dfrac{\frac{1}{2}+\frac{1}{3}}{\frac{1}{4}-\frac{1}{2}}$ $-\frac{10}{3}$

6. $\dfrac{\frac{1}{3}-\frac{1}{4}}{\frac{1}{3}+\frac{1}{6}}$ $\frac{1}{6}$

7. $\dfrac{\frac{2}{5}+\frac{5}{6}-\frac{1}{2}}{\frac{1}{2}-\frac{1}{3}+\frac{1}{15}}$ $\frac{22}{7}$

8. $\dfrac{\frac{2}{5}-\frac{2}{9}-\frac{1}{3}}{\frac{1}{3}+\frac{1}{5}+\frac{2}{15}}$ $-\frac{7}{30}$

9. $\dfrac{1+\frac{1}{2}}{2+\frac{1}{4}}$ $\frac{2}{3}$

10. $\dfrac{\frac{1}{3}+1}{\frac{1}{6}+2}$ $\frac{8}{13}$

11. $\dfrac{3+\frac{1}{2}}{5-\frac{3}{4}}$ $\frac{14}{17}$

12. $\dfrac{1+\frac{1}{12}}{1-\frac{1}{12}}$ $\frac{13}{11}$

13. $\dfrac{1-\frac{1}{6}+\frac{2}{3}}{1+\frac{1}{15}-\frac{3}{10}}$ $\frac{45}{23}$

14. $\dfrac{3-\frac{2}{9}-\frac{1}{6}}{\frac{5}{18}-\frac{1}{3}-2}$ $-\frac{47}{37}$

‹2› Using the LCD to Simplify Complex Fractions

Simplify each complex fraction.

See Examples 2 and 3.

See the Strategy for Simplifying a Complex Fraction box on page 456.

15. $\dfrac{\frac{1}{2}+\frac{1}{3}}{\frac{1}{2}-\frac{1}{4}}$ $\frac{10}{3}$

16. $\dfrac{\frac{1}{4}-\frac{1}{3}}{\frac{1}{4}+\frac{1}{6}}$ $-\frac{1}{5}$

17. $\dfrac{\frac{2}{5}+\frac{1}{10}}{\frac{1}{5}+\frac{1}{4}}$ $\frac{10}{9}$

18. $\dfrac{\frac{3}{10}+\frac{4}{5}}{\frac{1}{2}+\frac{3}{4}}$ $\frac{22}{25}$

19. $\dfrac{1+\frac{2}{3}+\frac{1}{2}}{2-\frac{1}{3}-\frac{3}{2}}$ 13

20. $\dfrac{3-\frac{3}{5}+\frac{1}{10}}{2+\frac{6}{5}-\frac{3}{10}}$ $\frac{25}{29}$

21. $\dfrac{\frac{2}{3}+\frac{5}{6}+\frac{1}{2}}{\frac{1}{6}-\frac{1}{3}-\frac{1}{2}}$ -3

22. $\dfrac{\frac{2}{5}-\frac{3}{2}+\frac{7}{10}}{\frac{1}{5}+\frac{1}{2}-\frac{1}{10}}$ $-\frac{2}{3}$

23. $\dfrac{\frac{1}{a}+\frac{1}{b}}{\frac{2}{a}+\frac{2}{b}}$ $\frac{1}{2}$

24. $\dfrac{\frac{1}{x}+\frac{1}{y}}{\frac{3}{x}+\frac{3}{y}}$ $\frac{1}{3}$

25. $\dfrac{\frac{1}{a}+\frac{3}{b}}{\frac{1}{b}-\frac{3}{a}}$ $\frac{3a+b}{a-3b}$

26. (VIDEO) $\dfrac{\frac{1}{x}-\frac{3}{2}}{\frac{3}{4}+\frac{1}{x}}$ $\frac{4-6x}{3x+4}$

27. $\dfrac{5-\frac{3}{a}}{3+\frac{1}{a}}$ $\frac{5a-3}{3a+1}$

28. $\dfrac{4+\frac{3}{y}}{1-\frac{2}{y}}$ $\frac{4y+3}{y-2}$

29. $\dfrac{\frac{1}{2}-\frac{2}{x}}{3-\frac{1}{x^2}}$ $\frac{x^2-4x}{2(3x^2-1)}$

30. $\dfrac{\frac{2}{a}+\frac{5}{3}}{\frac{3}{a}-\frac{3}{a^2}}$ $\frac{6a+5a^2}{9(a-1)}$

31. $\dfrac{\frac{3}{2b}+\frac{1}{b}}{\frac{3}{4}-\frac{1}{b^2}}$ $\frac{10b}{3b^2-4}$

32. $\dfrac{\frac{3}{2w}+\frac{4}{3w}}{\frac{1}{4w}-\frac{5}{9w}}$ $-\frac{102}{11}$

Simplify each complex fraction. See Example 4.

33. $\dfrac{\frac{1}{x+1}+1}{\frac{3}{x+1}+3}$ $\frac{1}{3}$

34. $\dfrac{\frac{2}{x+3}+1}{\frac{4}{x+3}+2}$ $\frac{1}{2}$

35. $\dfrac{1-\frac{3}{y+1}}{3+\frac{1}{y+1}}$ $\frac{y-2}{3y+4}$

36. $\dfrac{2-\frac{1}{a-3}}{3-\frac{1}{a-3}}$ $\frac{2a-7}{3a-10}$

37. $\dfrac{x + \dfrac{4}{x-2}}{x - \dfrac{x+1}{x-2}}$ $\dfrac{x^2 - 2x + 4}{x^2 - 3x - 1}$

VIDEO **38.** $\dfrac{x - \dfrac{x-6}{x-1}}{x - \dfrac{x+15}{x-1}}$ $\dfrac{x^2 - 2x + 6}{(x-5)(x+3)}$

39. $\dfrac{\dfrac{1}{3-x} - 5}{\dfrac{1}{x-3} - 2}$ $\dfrac{5x - 14}{2x - 7}$

40. $\dfrac{\dfrac{2}{x-5} - x}{\dfrac{3x}{5-x} - 1}$ $\dfrac{x^2 - 5x - 2}{4x - 5}$

VIDEO **41.** $\dfrac{1 - \dfrac{5}{a-1}}{3 - \dfrac{2}{1-a}}$ $\dfrac{a-6}{3a-1}$

42. $\dfrac{\dfrac{1}{3} - \dfrac{2}{9-x}}{\dfrac{1}{6} - \dfrac{1}{x-9}}$ $\dfrac{2x-6}{x-15}$

43. $\dfrac{\dfrac{1}{m-3} - \dfrac{4}{m}}{\dfrac{3}{m-3} + \dfrac{1}{m}}$ $\dfrac{-3m+12}{4m-3}$

44. $\dfrac{\dfrac{1}{y+3} - \dfrac{4}{y}}{\dfrac{1}{y} - \dfrac{2}{y+3}}$ $\dfrac{3y+12}{y-3}$

45. $\dfrac{\dfrac{2}{w-1} - \dfrac{3}{w+1}}{\dfrac{4}{w+1} + \dfrac{5}{w-1}}$ $\dfrac{-w+5}{9w+1}$

46. $\dfrac{\dfrac{1}{x+2} - \dfrac{3}{x+3}}{\dfrac{2}{x+3} + \dfrac{3}{x+2}}$ $\dfrac{-2x-3}{5x+13}$

47. $\dfrac{\dfrac{1}{a-b} - \dfrac{1}{a+b}}{\dfrac{1}{b-a} + \dfrac{1}{b+a}}$ -1

48. $\dfrac{\dfrac{1}{2+x} - \dfrac{1}{2-x}}{\dfrac{1}{x+2} - \dfrac{1}{x-2}}$ $-\dfrac{x}{2}$

Simplify each complex fraction. Reduce each answer to lowest terms.

49. $\dfrac{1 - \dfrac{4}{a^2}}{1 + \dfrac{2}{a} - \dfrac{8}{a^2}}$ $\dfrac{a+2}{a+4}$

50. $\dfrac{\dfrac{1}{3} + \dfrac{1}{y}}{\dfrac{y}{3} - \dfrac{3}{y}}$ $\dfrac{1}{y-3}$

51. $\dfrac{\dfrac{1}{2} + \dfrac{1}{4x}}{\dfrac{x}{3} - \dfrac{1}{12x}}$ $\dfrac{3}{2x-1}$

52. $\dfrac{\dfrac{1}{9} + \dfrac{1}{3x}}{\dfrac{x}{9} - \dfrac{1}{x}}$ $\dfrac{1}{x-3}$

53. $\dfrac{\dfrac{1}{3} - \dfrac{5}{3x} + \dfrac{2}{x^2}}{\dfrac{1}{3} - \dfrac{3}{x^2}}$ $\dfrac{x-2}{x+3}$

54. $\dfrac{\dfrac{1}{2} - \dfrac{3}{2x} + \dfrac{1}{x^2}}{\dfrac{1}{2} - \dfrac{1}{2x^2}}$ $\dfrac{x-2}{x+1}$

55. $\dfrac{\dfrac{2x-9}{6}}{\dfrac{2x-3}{9}}$ $\dfrac{6x-27}{2(2x-3)}$

56. $\dfrac{\dfrac{a-5}{12}}{\dfrac{a+2}{15}}$ $\dfrac{5a-25}{4(a+2)}$

57. $\dfrac{\dfrac{2x-4y}{xy^2}}{\dfrac{3x-6y}{x^3y}}$ $\dfrac{2x^2}{3y}$

VIDEO **58.** $\dfrac{\dfrac{ab+b^2}{4ab^5}}{\dfrac{a+b}{6a^2b^4}}$ $\dfrac{3a}{2}$

59. $\dfrac{\dfrac{a^2+2a-24}{a+1}}{\dfrac{a^2-a-12}{(a+1)^2}}$ $\dfrac{a^2+7a+6}{a+3}$

60. $\dfrac{\dfrac{y^2-3y-18}{y^2-4}}{\dfrac{y^2+5y+6}{y-2}}$ $\dfrac{y-6}{(y+2)^2}$

61. $\dfrac{\dfrac{x}{x+1}}{\dfrac{1}{x^2-1} - \dfrac{1}{x-1}}$ $1-x$

62. $\dfrac{\dfrac{a}{a^2-b^2}}{\dfrac{1}{a+b} + \dfrac{1}{a-b}}$ $\dfrac{1}{2}$

⟨3⟩ Applications

Solve each problem. See Example 5.

63. ***Sophomore math.*** A survey of college sophomores showed that $\frac{5}{6}$ of the males were taking a mathematics class and $\frac{3}{4}$ of the females were taking a mathematics class. One-third of the males were enrolled in calculus, and $\frac{1}{5}$ of the females were enrolled in calculus. If just as many males as females were surveyed, then what fraction of the surveyed students taking mathematics were enrolled in calculus? Rework this problem assuming that the number of females in the survey was twice the number of males. $\frac{32}{95}$, $\frac{11}{35}$

64. ***Commuting students.*** At a well-known university, $\frac{1}{4}$ of the undergraduate students commute, and $\frac{1}{3}$ of the graduate students commute. One-tenth of the undergraduate students drive more than 40 miles daily, and $\frac{1}{6}$ of the graduate students drive more than 40 miles daily. If there are twice as many undergraduate students as there are graduate students, then what fraction of the commuters drive more than 40 miles daily? $\frac{11}{25}$

Photo for Exercise 64

Getting More Involved

65. ***Exploration***

Simplify

$$\frac{1}{1+\frac{1}{2}},\quad \frac{1}{1+\frac{1}{1+\frac{1}{2}}},\quad \text{and}\quad \frac{1}{1+\frac{1}{1+\frac{1}{1+\frac{1}{2}}}}.$$

a) Are these fractions getting larger or smaller as the fractions become more complex? Neither

b) Continuing the pattern, find the next two complex fractions and simplify them. $\frac{8}{13}, \frac{13}{21}$

c) Now what can you say about the values of all five complex fractions? Converging to 0.61803

66. ***Discussion***

A complex fraction can be simplified by writing the numerator and denominator as single fractions and then dividing them or by multiplying the numerator and denominator by the LCD. Simplify the complex fraction

$$\frac{\frac{4}{xy^2} - \frac{6}{xy}}{\frac{2}{x^2} + \frac{4}{x^2y}}$$

by using each of these methods. Compare the number of steps used in each method, and determine which method requires fewer steps.

7.6 Solving Equations with Rational Expressions

In This Section

‹1› Equations with Rational Expressions

‹2› Extraneous Solutions

Many problems in algebra can be solved by using equations involving rational expressions. In this section you will learn how to solve equations that involve rational expressions, and in Sections 7.7 and 7.8 you will solve problems using these equations.

‹1› Equations with Rational Expressions

We solved some equations involving fractions in Section 2.3. In that section, the equations had only integers in the denominators. Our first step in solving those equations was to multiply by the LCD to eliminate all of the denominators.

EXAMPLE 1

Integers in the denominators

Solve $\frac{1}{2} - \frac{x-2}{3} = \frac{1}{6}$.

Solution

The LCD for 2, 3, and 6 is 6. Multiply each side of the equation by 6:

$$\frac{1}{2} - \frac{x-2}{3} = \frac{1}{6} \qquad \text{Original equation}$$

$$6\left(\frac{1}{2} - \frac{x-2}{3}\right) = 6 \cdot \frac{1}{6} \qquad \text{Multiply each side by 6.}$$

$$6 \cdot \frac{1}{2} - \overset{2}{\cancel{6}} \cdot \frac{x-2}{\cancel{3}} = \cancel{6} \cdot \frac{1}{\cancel{6}} \qquad \text{Distributive property}$$

$$3 - 2(x - 2) = 1 \qquad \text{Simplify.}$$

$$3 - 2x + 4 = 1 \qquad \text{Distributive property}$$

$$-2x = -6 \qquad \text{Subtract 7 from each side.}$$

$$x = 3 \qquad \text{Divide each side by } -2.$$

‹ Helpful Hint ›

Note that it is not necessary to convert each fraction into an equivalent fraction with a common denominator here. Since we can multiply both sides of an equation by any expression we choose, we choose to multiply by the LCD. This tactic eliminates the fractions in one step.

‹ Helpful Hint ›

Always check your solution in the original equation by calculating the value of the left-hand side and the value of the right-hand side. If they are the same, your solution is correct.

Check $x = 3$ in the original equation:

$$\frac{1}{2} - \frac{3-2}{3} = \frac{1}{2} - \frac{1}{3} = \frac{3}{6} - \frac{2}{6} = \frac{1}{6}$$

Since the right-hand side of the equation is $\frac{1}{6}$, you can be sure that the solution to the equation is 3.

Now do Exercises 5–16

CAUTION When a numerator contains a binomial, as in Example 1, the numerator must be enclosed in parentheses when the denominator is eliminated.

To solve an equation involving rational expressions, we usually multiply each side of the equation by the LCD for all the denominators involved, just as we do for an equation with fractions.

EXAMPLE 2

Variables in the denominators

Solve $\frac{1}{x} + \frac{1}{6} = \frac{1}{4}$.

‹ Teaching Tip ›

Students often confuse solving equations containing rational expressions with adding or subtracting rational expressions. To solve this problem be sure to assign Exercises 103–122 in the Review Exercises.

Solution

We multiply each side of the equation by $12x$, the LCD for 4, 6, and x:

$$\frac{1}{x} + \frac{1}{6} = \frac{1}{4} \qquad \text{Original equation}$$

$$12x\left(\frac{1}{x} + \frac{1}{6}\right) = 12x\left(\frac{1}{4}\right) \qquad \text{Multiply each side by } 12x.$$

$$12\cancel{x} \cdot \frac{1}{\cancel{x}} + \overset{2}{\cancel{12}}x \cdot \frac{1}{\cancel{6}} = \overset{3}{\cancel{12}}x \cdot \frac{1}{\cancel{4}} \qquad \text{Distributive property}$$

$$12 + 2x = 3x \qquad \text{Simplify.}$$

$$12 = x \qquad \text{Subtract } 2x \text{ from each side.}$$

Check that 12 satisfies the original equation:

$$\frac{1}{12} + \frac{1}{6} = \frac{1}{12} + \frac{2}{12} = \frac{3}{12} = \frac{1}{4}$$

The solution to the equation is 12.

Now do Exercises 17–28

EXAMPLE 3

An equation with two solutions

Solve the equation $\frac{100}{x} + \frac{100}{x+5} = 9$.

Solution

The LCD for the denominators x and $x + 5$ is $x(x + 5)$:

$$\frac{100}{x} + \frac{100}{x+5} = 9 \qquad \text{Original equation}$$

$$x(x+5)\frac{100}{x} + x(x+5)\frac{100}{x+5} = x(x+5)9 \qquad \text{Multiply each side by } x(x+5).$$

$$(x+5)100 + x(100) = (x^2+5x)9 \qquad \text{All denominators are eliminated.}$$

$$100x + 500 + 100x = 9x^2 + 45x \qquad \text{Simplify.}$$

$$500 + 200x = 9x^2 + 45x$$

$$0 = 9x^2 - 155x - 500 \qquad \text{Get 0 on one side.}$$

$$0 = (9x+25)(x-20) \qquad \text{Factor.}$$

$$9x + 25 = 0 \quad \text{or} \quad x - 20 = 0 \qquad \text{Zero factor property}$$

$$x = -\frac{25}{9} \quad \text{or} \quad x = 20$$

A check will show that both $-\frac{25}{9}$ and 20 satisfy the original equation.

Now do Exercises 29–36

⟨2⟩ Extraneous Solutions

In a rational expression, we can replace the variable only by real numbers that do not cause the denominator to be 0. When solving equations involving rational expressions, we must check every solution to see whether it causes 0 to appear in a denominator. If a number causes the denominator to be 0, then it cannot be a solution to the equation. A number that appears to be a solution but causes 0 in a denominator is called an **extraneous solution.** Since a solution to an equation is sometimes called a **root** to the equation, an extraneous solution is also called an **extraneous root.**

EXAMPLE 4

An equation with an extraneous solution

Solve the equation $\frac{1}{x-2} = \frac{x}{2x-4} + 1$.

Solution

Because the denominator $2x - 4$ factors as $2(x - 2)$, the LCD is $2(x - 2)$.

$$2(x-2)\frac{1}{x-2} = 2(x-2)\frac{x}{2(x-2)} + 2(x-2) \cdot 1 \qquad \text{Multiply each side of the original equation by } 2(x-2).$$

$$2 = x + 2x - 4 \qquad \text{Simplify.}$$

$$2 = 3x - 4$$

$$6 = 3x$$

$$2 = x$$

Check 2 in the original equation:

$$\frac{1}{2-2} = \frac{2}{2 \cdot 2 - 4} + 1$$

The denominator $2 - 2$ is 0. So 2 does not satisfy the equation, and it is an extraneous solution. The equation has no solutions.

Now do Exercises 37–40

If the denominators of the rational expressions in an equation are not too complicated, you can tell at a glance which numbers cannot be solutions. For example, the equation $\frac{2}{x} + \frac{3}{x-1} = \frac{x-2}{x+5}$ could not have 0, 1, or -5 as a solution. Any solution to this equation must be in the domain of all three of the rational expressions in the equation.

EXAMPLE 5

Another extraneous solution

Solve the equation $\frac{1}{x} + \frac{1}{x-3} = \frac{x-2}{x-3}$.

Solution

The LCD for the denominators x and $x - 3$ is $x(x - 3)$:

$$\frac{1}{x} + \frac{1}{x-3} = \frac{x-2}{x-3} \quad \text{Original equation}$$

$$x(x-3) \cdot \frac{1}{x} + x(x-3) \cdot \frac{1}{x-3} = x(x-3) \cdot \frac{x-2}{x-3} \quad \text{Multiply each side by } x(x-3).$$

$$x - 3 + x = x(x - 2)$$

$$2x - 3 = x^2 - 2x$$

$$0 = x^2 - 4x + 3$$

$$0 = (x - 3)(x - 1)$$

$$x - 3 = 0 \quad \text{or} \quad x - 1 = 0$$

$$x = 3 \quad \text{or} \quad x = 1$$

If $x = 3$, then the denominator $x - 3$ has a value of 0. If $x = 1$, the original equation is satisfied. The only solution to the equation is 1.

Now do Exercises 41–44

CAUTION Always be sure to check your answers in the original equation to determine whether they are extraneous solutions.

Warm-Ups ▼

True or false? Explain your answers.

1. The LCD is not used in solving equations with rational expressions. False
2. To solve the equation $x^2 = 8x$, we divide each side by x. False
3. An extraneous solution is an irrational number. False

Use the following equations for Questions 4–10.

a) $\frac{3}{x} + \frac{5}{x-2} = \frac{2}{3}$ **b)** $\frac{1}{x} + \frac{1}{2} = \frac{3}{4}$ **c)** $\frac{1}{x-1} + 2 = \frac{1}{x+1}$

4. To solve Eq. (a), we must add the expressions on the left-hand side. False
5. Both 0 and 2 satisfy Eq. (a). False
6. To solve Eq. (a), we multiply each side by $3x^2 - 6x$. True
7. The only solution to Eq. (b) is 4. True
8. Equation (b) is equivalent to $4 + 2x = 3x$. True
9. To solve Eq. (c), we multiply each side by $x^2 - 1$. True
10. The numbers 1 and -1 do not satisfy Eq. (c). True

7.6 Exercises

Boost your grade at mathzone.com!
- Practice Problems
- NetTutor
- Self-Tests
- e-Professors
- Videos

‹ Study Tips ›

- The last couple of weeks of the semester is not the time to slack off. This is the time to double your efforts.
- Make a schedule and plan every hour of your time.

Reading and Writing *After reading this section, write out the answers to these questions. Use complete sentences.*

1. What is the typical first step for solving an equation involving rational expressions?
The first step is usually to multiply each side by the LCD.

2. What is the difference in procedure for solving an equation involving rational expressions and adding rational expressions?
In adding rational expressions we build up each expression to get the LCD as the common denominator.

3. What is an extraneous solution?
An extraneous solution is a number that appears to be a solution when we solve an equation, but it does not check in the original equation.

4. Why is checking essential in solving equations with rational expressions?
We must check because extraneous solutions can occur.

‹1› Equations with Rational Expressions

Solve each equation. See Example 1.

5. $\frac{x}{2} + 1 = \frac{x}{4}$ -4

6. $\frac{x}{3} + 2 = \frac{x}{6}$ -12

7. $\frac{x}{3} - 5 = \frac{x}{2} - 7$ 12

8. $\frac{x}{3} - \frac{x}{2} = \frac{x}{5} - 11$ 30

9. $\frac{y}{5} - \frac{2}{3} = \frac{y}{6} + \frac{1}{3}$ 30

10. $\frac{z}{6} + \frac{5}{4} = \frac{z}{2} - \frac{3}{4}$ 6

11. $\frac{3}{4} - \frac{t-4}{3} = \frac{t}{12}$ 5

12. $\frac{4}{5} - \frac{v-1}{10} = \frac{v-5}{30}$ 8

13. $\frac{x}{3} + \frac{x+1}{4} = \frac{x+15}{12}$ 2

14. $\frac{x}{8} + \frac{x+4}{12} = \frac{6x+5}{24}$ 3

15. $\frac{1}{5} - \frac{w+10}{15} = \frac{1}{10} - \frac{w+1}{6}$ 4

VIDEO **16.** $\frac{q}{5} - \frac{q-1}{2} = \frac{13}{20} - \frac{q+1}{4}$ 2

Solve each equation. See Example 2.

17. $\frac{1}{x} + \frac{1}{2} = 3$ $\frac{2}{5}$

18. $\frac{2}{x} + \frac{3}{4} = 5$ $\frac{8}{17}$

19. $\frac{1}{x} + \frac{2}{x} = 7$ $\frac{3}{7}$

20. $\frac{5}{x} + \frac{6}{x} = 12$ $\frac{11}{12}$

21. $\frac{1}{x} + \frac{1}{2} = \frac{3}{4}$ 4

22. $\frac{3}{x} + \frac{1}{4} = \frac{5}{8}$ 8

23. $\frac{2}{3x} + \frac{1}{2x} = \frac{7}{24}$ 4

24. $\frac{1}{6x} - \frac{1}{8x} = \frac{1}{72}$ 3

25. $\frac{1}{2} + \frac{a-2}{a} = \frac{a+2}{2a}$ 3

26. $\frac{1}{b} + \frac{1}{5} = \frac{b-1}{5b} + \frac{3}{10}$ 4

27. $\frac{1}{3} - \frac{k+3}{6k} = \frac{1}{3k} - \frac{k-1}{2k}$ 2

28. $\frac{3}{p} - \frac{p+3}{3p} = \frac{2p-1}{2p} - \frac{5}{6}$ 5

Solve each equation. See Example 3.

29. $\frac{x}{2} = \frac{5}{x+3}$ $-5, 2$

30. $\frac{x}{3} = \frac{4}{x+1}$ $-4, 3$

VIDEO **31.** $\frac{x}{x+1} = \frac{6}{x+7}$ $-3, 2$

32. $\frac{x}{x+3} = \frac{2}{x-3}$ $-1, 6$

33. $\frac{2}{x+1} = \frac{1}{x} + \frac{1}{6}$ 2, 3

34. $\frac{1}{w+1} - \frac{1}{2w} = \frac{3}{40}$ $\frac{5}{3}, 4$

35. $\frac{a-1}{a^2-4} + \frac{1}{a-2} = \frac{a+4}{a+2}$ $-3, 3$

36. $\frac{b+17}{b^2-1} - \frac{1}{b+1} = \frac{b-2}{b-1}$ $-4, 5$

‹2› Extraneous Solutions

Solve each equation. Watch for extraneous solutions. See Examples 4 and 5.

37. $\frac{1}{x-1} + \frac{2}{x} = \frac{x}{x-1}$ 2

38. $\frac{4}{x} + \frac{3}{x-3} = \frac{x}{x-3} - \frac{1}{3}$ 6

39. $\frac{5}{x+2} + \frac{2}{x-3} = \frac{x-1}{x-3}$ No solution

40. $\frac{6}{y-2} + \frac{7}{y-8} = \frac{y-1}{y-8}$ No solution

41. $1 + \frac{3y}{y-2} = \frac{6}{y-2}$ No solution

VIDEO **42.** $\frac{5}{y-3} = \frac{y+7}{2y-6} + 1$ No solution

43. $\frac{z}{z+1} - \frac{1}{z+2} = \frac{2z+5}{z^2+3z+2}$ 3

44. $\frac{z}{z-2} - \frac{1}{z+5} = \frac{7}{z^2+3z-10}$ 1

Miscellaneous

Solve each equation.

45. $\frac{a}{4} = \frac{5}{2}$ 10

46. $\frac{y}{3} = \frac{6}{5}$ $\frac{18}{5}$

47. $\frac{w}{6} = \frac{3w}{11}$ 0

48. $\frac{2m}{3} = \frac{3m}{2}$ 0

49. $\frac{5}{x} = \frac{x}{5}$ $-5, 5$

50. $\frac{-3}{x} = \frac{x}{-3}$ $-3, 3$

51. $\frac{x-3}{5} = \frac{x-3}{x}$ 3, 5

52. $\frac{a+4}{2} = \frac{a+4}{a}$ $-4, 2$

53. $\frac{1}{x+2} = \frac{x}{x+2}$ 1

54. $\frac{-3}{w+2} = \frac{w}{w+2}$ -3

55. $\frac{1}{2x-4} + \frac{1}{x-2} = \frac{3}{2}$ 3

56. $\frac{7}{3x-9} - \frac{1}{x-3} = \frac{4}{3}$ 4

57. $\frac{3}{a^2-a-6} = \frac{2}{a^2-4}$ 0

58. $\frac{8}{a^2+a-6} = \frac{6}{a^2-9}$ 6

59. $\frac{4}{c-2} - \frac{1}{2-c} = \frac{25}{c+6}$ 4

60. $\frac{3}{x+1} - \frac{1}{1-x} = \frac{10}{x^2-1}$ 3

61. $\frac{1}{x^2-9} + \frac{3}{x+3} = \frac{4}{x-3}$ -20

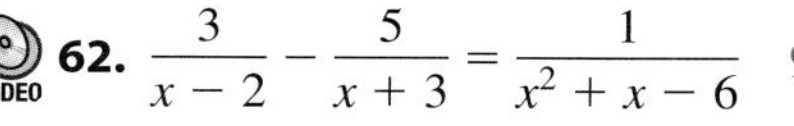

62. $\frac{3}{x-2} - \frac{5}{x+3} = \frac{1}{x^2+x-6}$ 9

63. $\frac{3}{2x+4} - \frac{1}{x+2} = \frac{1}{3x+1}$ 3

64. $\frac{5}{2m+6} - \frac{1}{m+1} = \frac{1}{m+3}$ 3

65. $\frac{2t-1}{3t+3} + \frac{3t-1}{6t+6} = \frac{t}{t+1}$ 3

66. $\frac{4w-1}{3w+6} - \frac{w-1}{3} = \frac{w-1}{w+2}$ 2

Applications

Solve each problem.

67. ***Lens equation.*** The focal length f for a camera lens is related to the object distance o and the image distance i by the formula

$$\frac{1}{f} = \frac{1}{o} + \frac{1}{i}.$$

See the accompanying figure. The image is in focus at distance i from the lens. For an object that is 600 mm from a 50-mm lens, use $f = 50$ mm and $o = 600$ mm to find i.

$54\frac{6}{11}$ mm

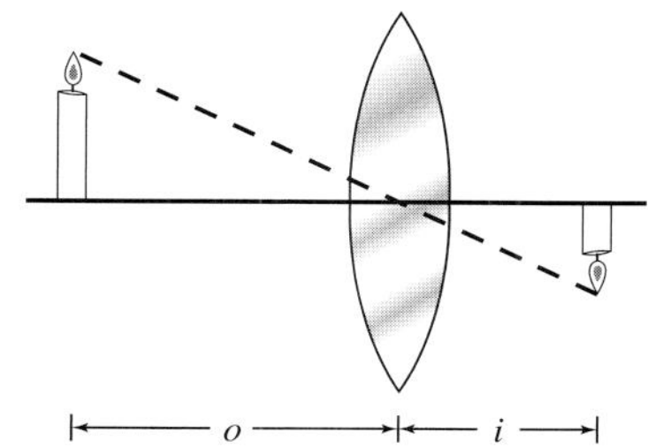

Figure for Exercise 67

68. ***Telephoto lens.*** Use the formula from Exercise 67 to find the image distance i for an object that is 2,000,000 mm from a 250-mm telephoto lens. 250.03 mm

Photo for Exercise 68

7.7 Applications of Ratios and Proportions

In This Section

⟨1⟩ Ratios

⟨2⟩ Proportions

In this section, we will use the ideas of rational expressions in ratio and proportion problems. We will solve proportions in the same way we solved equations in Section 7.6.

⟨1⟩ Ratios

In Chapter 1 we defined a rational number as the *ratio of two integers*. We will now give a more general definition of ratio. If a and b are any real numbers (not just integers), with $b \neq 0$, then the expression $\frac{a}{b}$ is called the **ratio of a and b** or the **ratio of a to b**.

The ratio of a to b is also written as $a:b$. A ratio is a comparison of two numbers. Some examples of ratios are

$$\frac{3}{4}, \quad \frac{4.2}{2.1}, \quad \frac{\frac{1}{4}}{\frac{1}{2}}, \quad \frac{3.6}{5}, \quad \text{and} \quad \frac{100}{1}.$$

Ratios are treated just like fractions. We can reduce ratios, and we can build them up. We generally express ratios as ratios of integers. When possible, we will convert a ratio into an equivalent ratio of integers in lowest terms.

EXAMPLE 1

Finding equivalent ratios

Find an equivalent ratio of integers in lowest terms for each ratio.

a) $\frac{4.2}{2.1}$ **b)** $\frac{\frac{1}{4}}{\frac{1}{2}}$ **c)** $\frac{3.6}{5}$

Solution

a) Because both the numerator and the denominator have one decimal place, we will multiply the numerator and denominator by 10 to eliminate the decimals:

$$\frac{4.2}{2.1} = \frac{4.2(10)}{2.1(10)} = \frac{42}{21} = \frac{21 \cdot 2}{21 \cdot 1} = \frac{2}{1} \quad \text{Do not omit the 1 in a ratio.}$$

So the ratio of 4.2 to 2.1 is equivalent to the ratio 2 to 1.

b) This ratio is a complex fraction. We can simplify this expression using the LCD method as shown in Section 7.5. Multiply the numerator and denominator of this ratio by 4:

$$\frac{\frac{1}{4}}{\frac{1}{2}} = \frac{\frac{1}{4} \cdot 4}{\frac{1}{2} \cdot 4} = \frac{1}{2}$$

c) We can get a ratio of integers if we multiply the numerator and denominator by 10.

$$\frac{3.6}{5} = \frac{3.6(10)}{5(10)} = \frac{36}{50}$$

$$= \frac{18}{25} \quad \text{Reduce to lowest terms.}$$

Now do Exercises 7–22

In Example 2, a ratio is used to compare quantities.

EXAMPLE 2

Nitrogen to potash

In a 50-pound bag of lawn fertilizer there are 8 pounds of nitrogen and 12 pounds of potash. What is the ratio of nitrogen to potash?

Solution

The nitrogen and potash occur in this fertilizer in the ratio of 8 pounds to 12 pounds:

$$\frac{8}{12} = \frac{2 \cdot \not{4}}{3 \cdot \not{4}} = \frac{2}{3}$$

So the ratio of nitrogen to potash is 2 to 3.

Now do Exercises 23–24

EXAMPLE 3

Males to females

In a class of 50 students, there were exactly 20 male students. What was the ratio of males to females in this class?

Solution

Because there were 20 males in the class of 50, there were 30 females. The ratio of males to females was 20 to 30, or 2 to 3.

Now do Exercises 25–26

‹ **Teaching Tip** ›

You can write a ratio of males to females because they are both people. You should not write a ratio of inches to feet, because they are not the same unit.

Ratios give us a means of comparing the size of two quantities. For this reason *the numbers compared in a ratio should be expressed in the same units.* For example, if one dog is 24 inches high and another is 1 foot high, then the ratio of their heights is 2 to 1, not 24 to 1.

EXAMPLE 4

Quantities with different units

What is the ratio of length to width for a poster with a length of 30 inches and a width of 2 feet?

Solution

Because the width is 2 feet, or 24 inches, the ratio of length to width is 30 to 24. Reduce as follows:

$$\frac{30}{24} = \frac{5 \cdot 6}{4 \cdot 6} = \frac{5}{4}$$

So the ratio of length to width is 5 to 4.

Now do Exercises 27–30

‹2› Proportions

A **proportion** is any statement expressing the equality of two ratios. The statement

$$\frac{a}{b} = \frac{c}{d} \qquad \text{or} \qquad a:b = c:d$$

is a proportion. In any proportion the numbers in the positions of a and d shown here are called the **extremes.** The numbers in the positions of b and c as shown are called the **means.** In the proportion

$$\frac{30}{24} = \frac{5}{4},$$

the means are 24 and 5, and the extremes are 30 and 4.

If we multiply each side of the proportion

$$\frac{a}{b} = \frac{c}{d}$$

by the LCD, bd, we get

$$\frac{a}{b} \cdot bd = \frac{c}{d} \cdot bd$$

or

$$a \cdot d = b \cdot c.$$

‹ Helpful Hint ›

The extremes-means property or cross-multiplying is nothing new. You can accomplish the same thing by multiplying each side of the equation by the LCD.

We can express this result by saying *that the product of the extremes is equal to the product of the means*. We call this fact the **extremes-means property** or **cross-multiplying.**

Extremes-Means Property (Cross-Multiplying)

Suppose a, b, c, and d are real numbers with $b \neq 0$ and $d \neq 0$. If

$$\frac{a}{b} = \frac{c}{d}, \quad \text{then} \quad ad = bc.$$

We use the extremes-means property to solve proportions.

EXAMPLE 5

Using the extremes-means property

Solve the proportion $\frac{3}{x} = \frac{5}{x + 5}$ for x.

‹ Teaching Tip ›

Remind students that the extremes-means property works on proportions and not on an equation like $\frac{3}{x} = \frac{8}{x + 1} - 1.$

Solution

Instead of multiplying each side by the LCD, we use the extremes-means property:

$$\frac{3}{x} = \frac{5}{x + 5} \quad \text{Original proportion}$$

$$3(x + 5) = 5x \quad \text{Extremes-means property}$$

$$3x + 15 = 5x \quad \text{Distributive property}$$

$$15 = 2x$$

$$\frac{15}{2} = x$$

Check:

$$\frac{3}{\frac{15}{2}} = 3 \cdot \frac{2}{15} = \frac{2}{5}$$

$$\frac{5}{\frac{15}{2} + 5} = \frac{5}{\frac{25}{2}} = 5 \cdot \frac{2}{25} = \frac{2}{5}$$

So $\frac{15}{2}$ is the solution to the equation or the solution to the proportion.

Now do Exercises 31–44

EXAMPLE 6

Solving a proportion

The ratio of men to women at Brighton City College is 2 to 3. If there are 894 men, then how many women are there?

Solution

Because the ratio of men to women is 2 to 3, we have

$$\frac{\text{Number of men}}{\text{Number of women}} = \frac{2}{3}.$$

If x represents the number of women, then we have the following proportion:

$$\frac{894}{x} = \frac{2}{3}$$

$$2x = 2682 \quad \text{Extremes-means property}$$

$$x = 1341$$

The number of women is 1341.

Now do Exercises 45–48

Note that any proportion can be solved by multiplying each side by the LCD as we did when we solved other equations involving rational expressions. The extremes-means property gives us a shortcut for solving proportions.

EXAMPLE 7

Solving a proportion

In a conservative portfolio the ratio of the amount invested in bonds to the amount invested in stocks should be 3 to 1. A conservative investor invested $2850 more in bonds than she did in stocks. How much did she invest in each category?

Solution

Because the ratio of the amount invested in bonds to the amount invested in stocks is 3 to 1, we have

$$\frac{\text{Amount invested in bonds}}{\text{Amount invested in stocks}} = \frac{3}{1}.$$

If x represents the amount invested in stocks and $x + 2850$ represents the amount invested in bonds, then we can write and solve the following proportion:

$$\frac{x + 2850}{x} = \frac{3}{1}$$

$$3x = x + 2850 \quad \text{Extremes-means property}$$

$$2x = 2850$$

$$x = 1425$$

$$x + 2850 = 4275$$

So she invested $4275 in bonds and $1425 in stocks. As a check, note that these amounts are in the ratio of 3 to 1.

Now do Exercises 49–52

Example 8 shows how conversions from one unit of measurement to another can be done by using proportions.

EXAMPLE 8

Converting measurements

There are 3 feet in 1 yard. How many feet are there in 12 yards?

Solution

Let x represent the number of feet in 12 yards. There are two proportions that we can write to solve the problem:

$$\frac{3 \text{ feet}}{x \text{ feet}} = \frac{1 \text{ yard}}{12 \text{ yards}} \qquad \frac{3 \text{ feet}}{1 \text{ yard}} = \frac{x \text{ feet}}{12 \text{ yards}}$$

The ratios in the second proportion violate the rule of comparing only measurements that are expressed in the same units. Note that each side of the second proportion is actually the ratio 1 to 1, since 3 feet = 1 yard and x feet = 12 yards. For doing conversions we can use ratios like this to compare measurements in different units. Applying the extremes-means property to either proportion gives

$$3 \cdot 12 = x \cdot 1,$$

or

$$x = 36.$$

So there are 36 feet in 12 yards.

Now do Exercises 53–56

‹ Teaching Tip ›

Note that in doing conversions the units can be mixed in a proportion. Note that the ratio of 3 feet to 1 yard is 1.

Warm-Ups ▼

True or false? Explain your answer.

1. The ratio of 40 men to 30 women can be expressed as the ratio 4 to 3. True
2. The ratio of 3 feet to 2 yards can be expressed as the ratio 3 to 2. False
3. If the ratio of men to women in the Chamber of Commerce is 3 to 2 and there are 20 men, then there must be 30 women. False
4. The ratio of 1.5 to 2 is equivalent to the ratio of 3 to 4. True
5. A statement that two ratios are equal is called a proportion. True
6. The product of the extremes is equal to the product of the means. True
7. If $\frac{2}{x} = \frac{3}{5}$, then $5x = 6$. False
8. The ratio of the height of a 12-inch cactus to the height of a 3-foot cactus is 4 to 1. False
9. If 30 out of 100 lawyers preferred aspirin and the rest did not, then the ratio of lawyers that preferred aspirin to those who did not is 30 to 100. False
10. If $\frac{x+5}{x} = \frac{2}{3}$, then $3x + 15 = 2x$. True

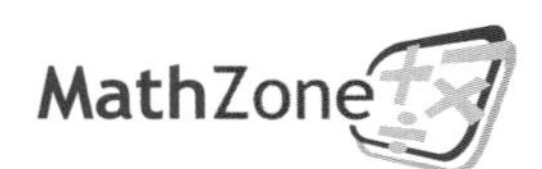

‹ Study Tips ›

- Get an early start studying for your final exams.
- If you have several final exams, it can be difficult to find the time to prepare for all of them in the last couple of days.

Reading and Writing *After reading this section, write out the answers to these questions. Use complete sentences.*

1. What is a ratio?
A ratio is a comparison of two numbers.

2. What are the different ways of expressing a ratio?
The ratio of a to b is also written as $\frac{a}{b}$ or $a : b$.

3. What are equivalent ratios?
Equivalent ratios are ratios that are equivalent as fractions.

4. What is a proportion?
A proportion is an equation that expresses equality of two ratios.

5. What are the means and what are the extremes?
In the proportion $\frac{a}{b} = \frac{c}{d}$ the means are b and c and the extremes are a and d.

6. What is the extremes-means property?
The extremes-means property says that if $\frac{a}{b} = \frac{c}{d}$ then $ad = bc$.

‹1› Ratios

For each ratio, find an equivalent ratio of integers in lowest terms. See Example 1.

7. $\frac{4}{6}$ $\frac{2}{3}$

8. $\frac{10}{20}$ $\frac{1}{2}$

9. $\frac{200}{150}$ $\frac{4}{3}$

10. $\frac{1000}{200}$ $\frac{5}{1}$

11. $\frac{2.5}{3.5}$ $\frac{5}{7}$

12. $\frac{4.8}{1.2}$ $\frac{4}{1}$

13. $\frac{0.32}{0.6}$ $\frac{8}{15}$

14. $\frac{0.05}{0.8}$ $\frac{1}{16}$

15. $\frac{35}{10}$ $\frac{7}{2}$

16. $\frac{88}{33}$ $\frac{8}{3}$

17. $\frac{4.5}{7}$ $\frac{9}{14}$

18. $\frac{3}{2.5}$ $\frac{6}{5}$

19. $\frac{\frac{1}{2}}{\frac{1}{5}}$ $\frac{5}{2}$

20. $\frac{\frac{2}{3}}{\frac{3}{4}}$ $\frac{8}{9}$

21. $\frac{5}{\frac{1}{3}}$ $\frac{15}{1}$

22. $\frac{4}{\frac{1}{4}}$ $\frac{16}{1}$

Find a ratio for each of the following, and write it as a ratio of integers in lowest terms. See Examples 2–4.

23. ***Men and women.*** Find the ratio of men to women in a bowling league containing 12 men and 8 women. 3 to 2

24. ***Coffee drinkers.*** Among 100 coffee drinkers, 36 said that they preferred their coffee black and the rest did not prefer their coffee black. Find the ratio of those who prefer black coffee to those who prefer nonblack coffee. 9 to 16

Photo for Exercise 24

VIDEO **25.** ***Smokers.*** A life insurance company found that among its last 200 claims, there were six dozen smokers. What is the ratio of smokers to nonsmokers in this group of claimants? 9 to 16

26. ***Hits and misses.*** A woman threw 60 darts and hit the target a dozen times. What is her ratio of hits to misses? 1 to 4

27. ***Violence and kindness.*** While watching television for one week, a consumer group counted 1240 acts of violence and 40 acts of kindness. What is the violence to kindness ratio for television, according to this group? 31 to 1

28. ***Length to width.*** What is the ratio of length to width for the rectangle shown? 8 to 5

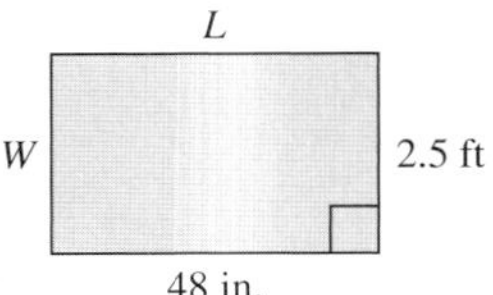

Figure for Exercise 28

29. ***Rise to run.*** What is the ratio of rise to run for the stairway shown in the figure on the next page? 2 to 3

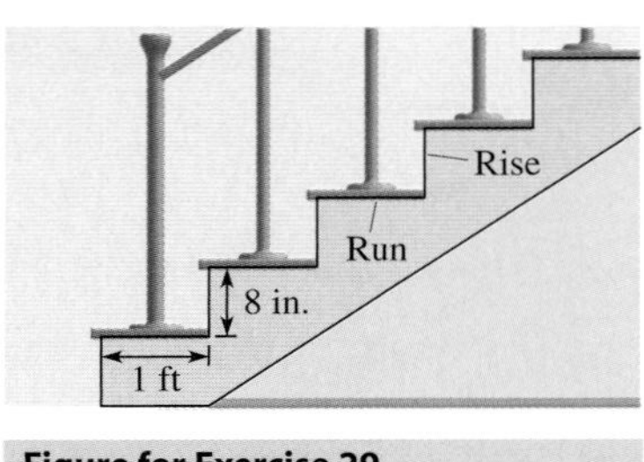

Figure for Exercise 29

30. ***Rise and run.*** If the rise is $\frac{3}{2}$ and the run is 5, then what is the ratio of the rise to the run? 3 to 10

⟨2⟩ Proportions

Solve each proportion. See Example 5.

31. $\frac{4}{x} = \frac{2}{3}$ 6

32. $\frac{9}{x} = \frac{3}{2}$ 6

33. $\frac{a}{2} = \frac{-1}{5}$ $-\frac{2}{5}$

34. $\frac{b}{3} = \frac{-3}{4}$ $-\frac{9}{4}$

35. $-\frac{5}{9} = \frac{3}{x}$ $-\frac{27}{5}$

36. $-\frac{3}{4} = \frac{5}{x}$ $-\frac{20}{3}$

37. $\frac{x-2}{5} = \frac{x}{7}$ 7

38. $\frac{4}{x+1} = \frac{2}{x}$ 1

39. $\frac{10}{x} = \frac{34}{x+12}$ 5

 **40.** $\frac{x}{3} = \frac{x+1}{2}$ -3

41. $\frac{a}{a+1} = \frac{a+3}{a}$ $-\frac{3}{4}$

42. $\frac{c+3}{c-1} = \frac{c+2}{c-3}$ -7

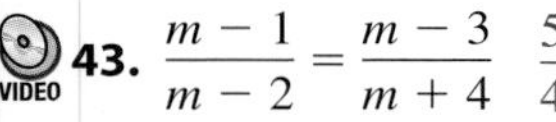 **43.** $\frac{m-1}{m-2} = \frac{m-3}{m+4}$ $\frac{5}{4}$

44. $\frac{h}{h-3} = \frac{h}{h-9}$ 0

Use a proportion to solve each problem. See Examples 6–8.

45. ***New shows and reruns.*** The ratio of new shows to reruns on cable TV is 2 to 27. If Frank counted only eight new shows one evening, then how many reruns were there? 108

46. ***Fast food.*** If four out of five doctors prefer fast food, then at a convention of 445 doctors, how many prefer fast food? 356

47. ***Voting.*** If 220 out of 500 voters surveyed said that they would vote for the incumbent, then how many votes could the incumbent expect out of the 400,000 voters in the state? 176,000

Photo for Exercise 47

 **48.** ***New product.*** A taste test with 200 randomly selected people found that only three of them said that they would buy a box of new Sweet Wheats cereal. How many boxes could the manufacturer expect to sell in a country of 280 million people? 4.2 million

49. ***Basketball blowout.*** As the final buzzer signaled the end of the basketball game, the Lions were 34 points ahead of the Tigers. If the Lions scored 5 points for every 3 scored by the Tigers, then what was the final score? Lions 85, Tigers 51

50. ***The golden ratio.*** The ancient Greeks thought that the most pleasing shape for a rectangle was one for which the ratio of the length to the width was approximately 8 to 5, the golden ratio. If the length of a rectangular painting is 2 ft longer than its width, then for what dimensions would the length and width have the golden ratio?
Length $\frac{16}{3}$ ft, width $\frac{10}{3}$ ft

51. ***Automobile sales.*** The ratio of sports cars to luxury cars sold in Wentworth one month was 3 to 2. If 20 more sports cars were sold than luxury cars, then how many of each were sold that month? 40 luxury cars, 60 sports cars

52. ***Foxes and rabbits.*** The ratio of foxes to rabbits in the Deerfield Forest Preserve is 2 to 9. If there are 35 fewer foxes than rabbits, then how many of each are there?
45 rabbits, 10 foxes

VIDEO **53.** ***Inches and feet.*** If there are 12 inches in 1 foot, then how many inches are there in 7 feet? 84 in.

54. ***Feet and yards.*** If there are 3 feet in 1 yard, then how many yards are there in 28 feet? $\frac{28}{3}$ yd

55. ***Minutes and hours.*** If there are 60 minutes in 1 hour, then how many minutes are there in 0.25 hour? 15 min

56. ***Meters and kilometers.*** If there are 1000 meters in 1 kilometer, then how many meters are there in 2.33 kilometers? 2330 m

57. ***Miles and hours.*** If Alonzo travels 230 miles in 3 hours, then how many miles does he travel in 7 hours?
$\frac{1610}{3}$ or 536.7 mi

58. ***Hiking time.*** If Evangelica can hike 19 miles in 2 days on the Appalachian Trail, then how many days will it take her to hike 63 miles?
$\frac{126}{19}$ days

59. ***Force on basketball shoes.*** The force exerted on shoe soles in a jump shot is proportional to the weight of the person jumping. If a 70-pound boy exerts a force of 980 pounds on his shoe soles when he returns to the court after a jump, then what force does a 6 ft 8 in. professional ball player weighing 280 pounds exert on the soles of his shoes when he returns to the court after a jump? Use the accompanying graph to estimate the force for a 150-pound player. 3920 lb, 2000 lb

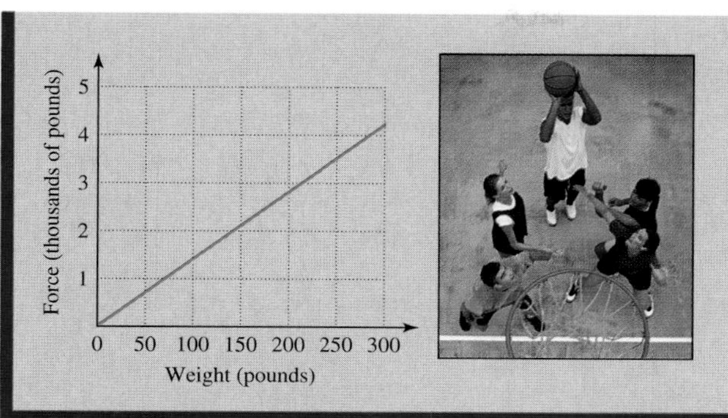

Figure for Exercise 59

60. ***Force on running shoes.*** The ratio of the force on the shoe soles to the weight of a runner is 3 to 1. What force does a 130-pound jogger exert on the soles of her shoes? 390 lb

61. ***Capture-recapture.*** To estimate the number of trout in Trout Lake, rangers used the capture-recapture method. They caught, tagged, and released 200 trout. One week later, they caught a sample of 150 trout and found that 5 of them were tagged. Assuming that the ratio of tagged trout to the total number of trout in the lake is the same as the ratio of tagged trout in the sample to the number of trout in the sample, find the number of trout in the lake. 6000

62. ***Bear population.*** To estimate the size of the bear population on the Keweenaw Peninsula, conservationists captured, tagged, and released 50 bears. One year later, a random sample of 100 bears included only 2 tagged bears. What is the conservationist's estimate of the size of the bear population? 2500

63. ***Fast-food waste.*** The accompanying figure shows the typical distribution of waste at a fast-food restaurant (U.S. Environmental Protection Agency, www.epa.gov).

a) What is the ratio of customer waste to food waste? 3 to 17

b) If a typical McDonald's generates 67 more pounds of food waste than customer waste per day, then how many pounds of customer waste does it generate? $\frac{201}{14}$ or 14.4 lb

64. ***Corrugated waste.*** Use the accompanying figure to find the ratio of waste from corrugated shipping boxes to waste not from corrugated shipping boxes. If a typical McDonald's generates 81 pounds of waste per day from corrugated shipping boxes, then how many pounds of waste per day does it generate that is not from corrugated shipping boxes? 17 to 33, $\frac{2673}{17}$ or 157.2 lb

WASTE GENERATION AT A FAST-FOOD RESTAURANT

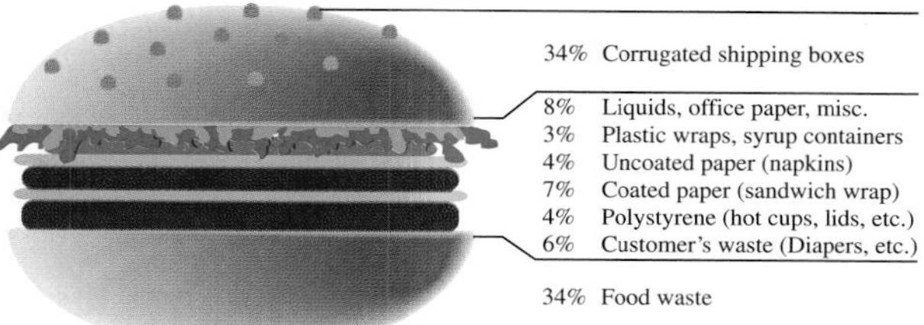

Figure for Exercises 63 and 64

65. ***Mascara needs.*** In determining warehouse needs for a particular mascara for a chain of 2000 stores, Mike Pittman first determines a need B based on sales figures for the past 52 weeks. He then determines the actual need A from the equation $\frac{A}{B} = k$, where

$$k = 1 + V + C + X - D.$$

He uses $V = 0.22$ if there is a national TV ad and $V = 0$ if not, $C = 0.26$ if there is a national coupon and $C = 0$ if not, $X = 0.36$ if there is a chain-specific ad and $X = 0$ if not, and $D = 0.29$ if there is a special display in the chain and $D = 0$ if not. (D is subtracted because less product is needed in the warehouse when more is on display in the store.) If $B = 4200$ units and there is a special display and a national coupon but no national TV ad and no chain-specific ad, then what is the value of A? 4074

Getting More Involved

66. ***Discussion***

Which of the following equations is not a proportion? Explain.

a) $\frac{1}{2} = \frac{1}{2}$ **b)** $\frac{x}{x+2} = \frac{4}{5}$

c) $\frac{x}{4} = \frac{9}{x}$ **d)** $\frac{8}{x+2} - 1 = \frac{5}{x+2}$ d

67. ***Discussion***

Find all of the errors in the following solution to an equation.

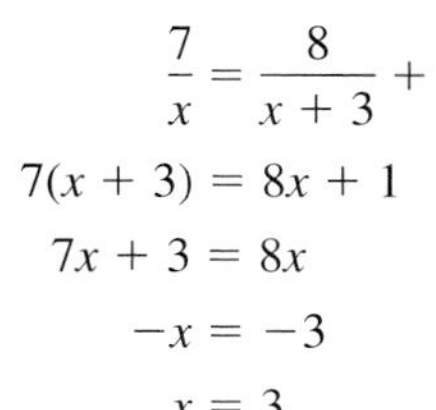

$$\frac{7}{x} = \frac{8}{x+3} + 1$$
$$7(x + 3) = 8x + 1$$
$$7x + 3 = 8x$$
$$-x = -3$$
$$x = 3$$

7.8 Applications of Rational Expressions

In This Section

In this section, we will study additional applications of rational expressions.

⟨1⟩ Formulas

Many formulas involve rational expressions. When solving a formula of this type for a certain variable, we usually multiply each side by the LCD to eliminate the denominators.

EXAMPLE 1

An equation of a line

The equation for the line through $(-2, 4)$ with slope $\frac{3}{2}$ can be written as

$$\frac{y - 4}{x + 2} = \frac{3}{2}.$$

We studied equations of this type in Chapter 3. Solve this equation for y.

Solution

To isolate y on the left-hand side of the equation, we multiply each side by $x + 2$:

$$\frac{y - 4}{x + 2} = \frac{3}{2} \quad \text{Original equation}$$

$$(x + 2) \cdot \frac{y - 4}{x + 2} = (x + 2) \cdot \frac{3}{2} \quad \text{Multiply by } x + 2.$$

$$y - 4 = \frac{3}{2}x + 3 \quad \text{Simplify.}$$

$$y = \frac{3}{2}x + 7 \quad \text{Add 4 to each side.}$$

Because the original equation is a proportion, we could have used the extremes-means property to solve it for y.

Now do Exercises 1–10

⟨ Teaching Tip ⟩

Note that the left side of this equation is the slope of the line through (x, y) and $(-2, 4)$.

EXAMPLE 2

Distance, rate, and time

Solve the formula $\frac{D}{T} = R$ for T.

Solution

Because the only denominator is T, we multiply each side by T:

$$\frac{D}{T} = R \quad \text{Original formula}$$

$$T \cdot \frac{D}{T} = T \cdot R \quad \text{Multiply each side by } T.$$

$$D = TR$$

$$\frac{D}{R} = \frac{TR}{R} \quad \text{Divide each side by } R.$$

$$\frac{D}{R} = T \quad \text{Simplify.}$$

The formula solved for T is $T = \frac{D}{R}$.

Now do Exercises 11–16

In Example 3, different subscripts are used on a variable to indicate that they are different variables. Think of R_1 as the first resistance, R_2 as the second resistance, and R as a combined resistance.

EXAMPLE 3

Total resistance

The formula

$$\frac{1}{R} = \frac{1}{R_1} + \frac{1}{R_2}$$

(from physics) expresses the relationship between different amounts of resistance in a parallel circuit. Solve it for R_2.

Solution

The LCD for R, R_1, and R_2 is RR_1R_2:

$$\frac{1}{R} = \frac{1}{R_1} + \frac{1}{R_2} \quad \text{Original formula}$$

$$RR_1R_2 \cdot \frac{1}{R} = RR_1R_2 \cdot \frac{1}{R_1} + RR_1R_2 \cdot \frac{1}{R_2} \quad \text{Multiply each side by the LCD, } RR_1R_2.$$

$$R_1R_2 = RR_2 + RR_1 \quad \text{All denominators are eliminated.}$$

$$R_1R_2 - RR_2 = RR_1 \quad \text{Get all terms involving } R_2 \text{ onto the left side.}$$

$$R_2(R_1 - R) = RR_1 \quad \text{Factor out } R_2.$$

$$R_2 = \frac{RR_1}{R_1 - R} \quad \text{Divide each side by } R_1 - R.$$

Now do Exercises 17–24

EXAMPLE 4

Finding the value of a variable

In the formula of Example 1, find x if $y = -3$.

Solution

Substitute $y = -3$ into the formula, then solve for x:

$$\frac{y - 4}{x + 2} = \frac{3}{2} \quad \text{Original formula}$$

$$\frac{-3 - 4}{x + 2} = \frac{3}{2} \quad \text{Replace } y \text{ by } -3.$$

$$\frac{-7}{x + 2} = \frac{3}{2} \quad \text{Simplify.}$$

$$3x + 6 = -14 \quad \text{Extremes-means property}$$

$$3x = -20$$

$$x = -\frac{20}{3}$$

Now do Exercises 25–34

⟨2⟩ Uniform Motion Problems

In uniform motion problems we use the formula $D = RT$. In some problems in which the time is unknown, we can use the formula $T = \frac{D}{R}$ to get an equation involving rational expressions.

EXAMPLE 5

Driving to Florida

Susan drove 1500 miles to Daytona Beach for spring break. On the way back she averaged 10 miles per hour less, and the drive back took her 5 hours longer. Find Susan's average speed on the way to Daytona Beach.

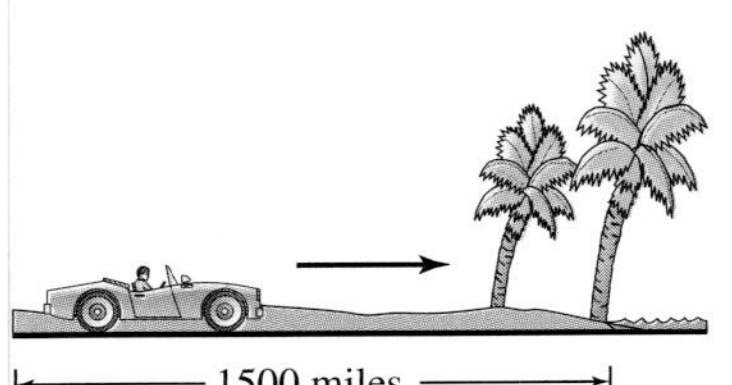

Figure 7.1

Solution

If x represents her average speed going there, then $x - 10$ is her average speed for the return trip. See Fig. 7.1. We use the formula $T = \frac{D}{R}$ to make the following table.

	D	R	T	
Going	1500	x	$\frac{1500}{x}$	← Shorter time
Returning	1500	$x - 10$	$\frac{1500}{x - 10}$	← Longer time

Because the difference between the two times is 5 hours, we have

longer time − shorter time = 5.

Using the time expressions from the table, we get the following equation:

$$\frac{1500}{x - 10} - \frac{1500}{x} = 5$$

$$x(x - 10)\frac{1500}{x - 10} - x(x - 10)\frac{1500}{x} = x(x - 10)5 \quad \text{Multiply by } x(x - 10).$$

$$1500x - 1500(x - 10) = 5x^2 - 50x$$

$$15{,}000 = 5x^2 - 50x \quad \text{Simplify.}$$

$$3000 = x^2 - 10x \quad \text{Divide each side by 5.}$$

$$0 = x^2 - 10x - 3000$$

$$(x + 50)(x - 60) = 0 \quad \text{Factor.}$$

$$x + 50 = 0 \quad \text{or} \quad x - 60 = 0$$

$$x = -50 \quad \text{or} \quad x = 60$$

The answer $x = -50$ is a solution to the equation, but it cannot indicate the average speed of the car. Her average speed going to Daytona Beach was 60 mph.

Now do Exercises 35–40

‹3› Work Problems

If you can complete a job in 3 hours, then you are working at the rate of $\frac{1}{3}$ of the job per hour. If you work for 2 hours at the rate of $\frac{1}{3}$ of the job per hour, then you will complete $\frac{2}{3}$ of the job. The product of the rate and time is the amount of work completed. For problems involving work, we will always assume that the work is done at a constant rate. So if a job takes x hours to complete, then the rate is $\frac{1}{x}$ of the job per hour.

‹ Helpful Hint ›

Notice that a work rate is the same as a slope from Chapter 3. The only difference is that the work rates here can contain a variable.

EXAMPLE 6

Shoveling snow

After a heavy snowfall, Brian can shovel all of the driveway in 30 minutes. If his younger brother Allen helps, the job takes only 20 minutes. How long would it take Allen to do the job by himself?

‹ Helpful Hint ›

The secret to work problems is remembering that the individual rates or the amounts of work can be added when people work together. If your painting rate is 1/10 of the house per day and your helper's rate is 1/5 of the house per day, then your rate together will be 3/10 of the house per day. In 2 days you will paint 2/10 of the house and your helper will paint 2/5 of the house for a total of 3/5 of the house completed.

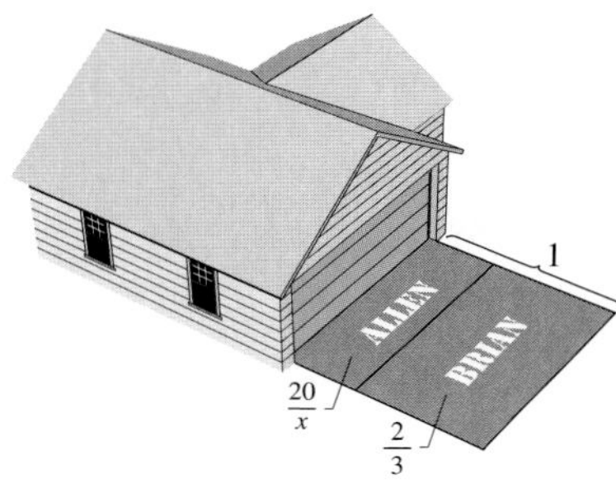

Figure 7.2

Solution

Let x represent the number of minutes it would take Allen to do the job by himself. Brian's rate for shoveling is $\frac{1}{30}$ of the driveway per minute, and Allen's rate for shoveling is $\frac{1}{x}$ of the driveway per minute. We organize all of the information in a table like the table in Example 5.

	Rate	Time	Work
Brian	$\frac{1 \text{ job}}{30 \text{ min}}$	20 min	$\frac{2}{3}$ job
Allen	$\frac{1 \text{ job}}{x \text{ min}}$	20 min	$\frac{20}{x}$ job

If Brian works for 20 min at the rate $\frac{1}{30}$ of the job per minute, then he does $\frac{20}{30}$ or $\frac{2}{3}$ of the job, as shown in Fig. 7.2. The amount of work that each boy does is a fraction of the whole job. So the expressions for work in the last column of the table have a sum of 1:

$$\frac{2}{3} + \frac{20}{x} = 1$$

$$3x \cdot \frac{2}{3} + 3x \cdot \frac{20}{x} = 3x \cdot 1 \quad \text{Multiply each side by } 3x.$$

$$2x + 60 = 3x$$

$$60 = x$$

If it takes Allen 60 min to do the job by himself, then he works at the rate of $\frac{1}{60}$ of the job per minute. In 20 minutes he does $\frac{1}{3}$ of the job while Brian does $\frac{2}{3}$. So it would take Allen 60 minutes to shovel the driveway by himself.

Now do Exercises 41–46

Notice the similarities between the uniform motion problem in Example 5 and the work problem in Example 6. In both cases, it is beneficial to make a table. We use $D = R \cdot T$ in uniform motion problems and $W = R \cdot T$ in work problems. The main points to remember when solving work problems are summarized in the following strategy.

‹ Teaching Tip ›

Note how the tables in Examples 5–8 tie them together. Making tables will help students solve these problems.

Strategy for Solving Work Problems

1. If a job is completed in x hours, then the rate is $\frac{1}{x}$ job/hr.
2. Make a table showing rate, time, and work completed ($W = R \cdot T$) for each person or machine.
3. The total work completed is the sum of the individual amounts of work completed.
4. If the job is completed, then the total work done is 1 job.

⟨4⟩ More Rate Problems

Rates are used in uniform motion and work problems. But rates also occur in other problems. If you make \$400 for x hours of work, then your pay rate is $\frac{400}{x}$ dollars per hour. If you get \$50 for selling x pounds of apples, then you are making money at the rate of $\frac{50}{x}$ dollars per pound.

EXAMPLE 7

Hourly rates

Dr. Watts paid \$80 to her gardener and \$80 to the gardener's helper for a total of 12 hours labor. If the gardener makes \$10 more per hour than the helper, then how many hours did each of them work?

Solution

Let x be the number of hours for the gardener and $12 - x$ be the number of hours for the helper. Make a table as follows.

	Time	Pay	Hourly Rate
Gardener	x hours	80 dollars	$\frac{80}{x}$ dollars/hour
Helper	$12 - x$ hours	80 dollars	$\frac{80}{12 - x}$ dollars/hour

Since the gardener makes \$10 more per hour, we can write the following equation.

$$\frac{80}{12 - x} + 10 = \frac{80}{x}$$

To solve the equation multiply each side by the LCD $x(12 - x)$.

$$x(12 - x)\left(\frac{80}{12 - x} + 10\right) = x(12 - x)\frac{80}{x} \quad \text{Muliply by the LCD.}$$

$$80x + 10x(12 - x) = (12 - x)80 \quad \text{Distributive property}$$

$$80x + 120x - 10x^2 = 960 - 80x \quad \text{Distributive property}$$

$$-10x^2 + 280x - 960 = 0 \quad \text{Get 0 on the right.}$$

$$x^2 - 28x + 96 = 0 \quad \text{Divide each side by } -10.$$

$$(x - 4)(x - 24) = 0 \quad \text{Factor.}$$

$$x - 4 = 0 \quad \text{or} \quad x - 24 = 0$$

$$x = 4 \quad \text{or} \quad x = 24$$

$$12 - x = 8 \qquad 12 - x = -12$$

Since $x = 24$ hours and $12 - x = -12$ hours does not make sense, we must have 4 hours for the gardener and 8 hours for the helper. Check: The gardener worked 4 hours at \$20 per hour and the helper worked 8 hours at \$10 per hour. The gardener made \$10 more per hour than the helper. Note that the problem could be solved also by starting with x as the hourly pay for the gardener and $x - 10$ as the hourly pay for the helper. Try it.

Now do Exercises 47–48

EXAMPLE 8

Oranges and grapefruit

Tamara bought 50 pounds of fruit consisting of Florida oranges and Texas grapefruit. She paid twice as much per pound for the grapefruit as she did for the oranges. If Tamara bought \$12 worth of oranges and \$16 worth of grapefruit, then how many pounds of each did she buy?

x lb

Oranges

$50 - x$ lb

Grapefruit

Figure 7.3

Solution

Let x represent the number of pounds of oranges and $50 - x$ represent the number of pounds of grapefruit. See Fig. 7.3. Make a table.

	Rate	Quantity	Total Cost
Oranges	$\frac{12}{x}$ dollars/pound	x pounds	12 dollars
Grapefruit	$\frac{16}{50 - x}$ dollars/pound	$50 - x$ pounds	16 dollars

Since the price per pound for the grapefruit is twice that for the oranges, we have:

$$2(\text{price per pound for oranges}) = \text{price per pound for grapefruit}$$

$$2\left(\frac{12}{x}\right) = \frac{16}{50 - x}$$

$$\frac{24}{x} = \frac{16}{50 - x}$$

$$16x = 1200 - 24x \quad \text{Extremes-means property}$$

$$40x = 1200$$

$$x = 30$$

$$50 - x = 20$$

If Tamara purchased 20 pounds of grapefruit for \$16, then she paid \$0.80 per pound. If she purchased 30 pounds of oranges for \$12, then she paid \$0.40 per pound. Because \$0.80 is twice \$0.40, we can be sure that she purchased 20 pounds of grapefruit and 30 pounds of oranges.

Now do Exercises 49–50

Warm-Ups ▼

True or false? Explain your answer.

1. The formula $t = \frac{1 - t}{m}$, solved for m, is $m = \frac{1 - t}{t}$. True
2. To solve $\frac{1}{m} + \frac{1}{n} = \frac{1}{2}$ for m, we multiply each side by $2mn$. True
3. If Fiona drives 300 miles in x hours, then her average speed is $\frac{x}{300}$ mph. False
4. If Miguel drives 20 hard bargains in x hours, then he is driving $\frac{20}{x}$ hard bargains per hour. True
5. If Fred can paint a house in y days, then he paints $\frac{1}{y}$ of the house per day. True
6. If $\frac{1}{x}$ is 1 less than $\frac{2}{x + 3}$, then $\frac{1}{x} - 1 = \frac{2}{x + 3}$. False
7. If a and b are nonzero and $a = \frac{m}{b}$, then $b = am$. False
8. If $D = RT$, then $T = \frac{D}{R}$. True
9. Solving $P + Prt = I$ for P gives $P = I - Prt$. False
10. To solve $3R + yR = m$ for R, we must first factor the left-hand side. True

7.8 Exercises

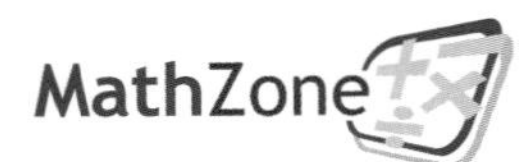

‹ **Study Tips** ›

- Establish a regular routine of eating, sleeping, and exercise.
- The ability to concentrate depends on adequate sleep, decent nutrition, and the physical well-being that comes with exercise.

‹1› Formulas

Solve each equation for y. See Example 1.

1. $\dfrac{y+2}{x+1} = 3$
$y = 3x + 1$

2. $\dfrac{y+5}{x+2} = 6$
$y = 6x + 7$

3. $\dfrac{y-1}{x-3} = 2$
$y = 2x - 5$

4. $\dfrac{y-2}{x-4} = -2$
$y = -2x + 10$

5. $\dfrac{y-1}{x+6} = -\dfrac{1}{2}$
$y = -\dfrac{1}{2}x - 2$

6. $\dfrac{y+5}{x-2} = -\dfrac{1}{2}$
$y = -\dfrac{1}{2}x - 4$

7. $\dfrac{y+a}{x-b} = m$
$y = mx - mb - a$

8. $\dfrac{y-h}{x+k} = a$
$y = ax + ak + h$

VIDEO **9.** $\dfrac{y-1}{x+4} = -\dfrac{1}{3}$
$y = -\dfrac{1}{3}x - \dfrac{1}{3}$

10. $\dfrac{y-1}{x+3} = -\dfrac{3}{4}$
$y = -\dfrac{3}{4}x - \dfrac{5}{4}$

Solve each formula for the indicated variable. See Examples 2 and 3.

11. $A = \dfrac{B}{C}$ for C
$C = \dfrac{B}{A}$

12. $P = \dfrac{A}{C+D}$ for A
$A = PC + PD$

13. $\dfrac{1}{a} + m = \dfrac{1}{p}$ for p
$p = \dfrac{a}{1 + am}$

14. $\dfrac{2}{f} + t = \dfrac{3}{m}$ for m
$m = \dfrac{3f}{2 + ft}$

15. $F = k\dfrac{m_1 m_2}{r^2}$ for m_1
$m_1 = \dfrac{r^2 F}{k m_2}$

VIDEO **16.** $F = \dfrac{mv^2}{r}$ for r
$r = \dfrac{mv^2}{F}$

17. $\dfrac{1}{a} + \dfrac{1}{b} = \dfrac{1}{f}$ for a
$a = \dfrac{bf}{b - f}$

18. $\dfrac{1}{R} = \dfrac{1}{R_1} + \dfrac{1}{R_2}$ for R
$R = \dfrac{R_1 R_2}{R_1 + R_2}$

19. $S = \dfrac{a}{1-r}$ for r
$r = \dfrac{S - a}{S}$

20. $I = \dfrac{E}{R+r}$ for R
$R = \dfrac{E - Ir}{I}$

21. $\dfrac{P_1V_1}{T_1} = \dfrac{P_2V_2}{T_2}$ for P_2
$P_2 = \dfrac{P_1V_1T_2}{T_1V_2}$

22. $\dfrac{P_1V_1}{T_1} = \dfrac{P_2V_2}{T_2}$ for T_1
$T_1 = \dfrac{P_1V_1T_2}{P_2V_2}$

23. $V = \dfrac{4}{3}\pi r^2 h$ for h
$h = \dfrac{3V}{4\pi r^2}$

24. $h = \dfrac{S - 2\pi r^2}{2\pi r}$ for S
$S = 2\pi rh + 2\pi r^2$

Find the value of the indicated variable. See Example 4.

25. In the formula of Exercise 11, if $A = 12$ and $B = 5$, find C. $\dfrac{5}{12}$

26. In the formula of Exercise 12, if $A = 500$, $P = 100$, and $C = 2$, find D. 3

27. In the formula of Exercise 13, if $p = 6$ and $m = 4$, find a. $-\dfrac{6}{23}$

VIDEO **28.** In the formula of Exercise 14, if $m = 4$ and $t = 3$, find f. $-\dfrac{8}{9}$

29. In the formula of Exercise 15, if $F = 32$, $r = 4$, $m_1 = 2$, and $m_2 = 6$, find k. $\dfrac{128}{3}$

30. In the formula of Exercise 16, if $F = 10$, $v = 8$, and $r = 6$, find m. $\dfrac{15}{16}$

31. In the formula of Exercise 17, if $f = 3$ and $a = 2$, find b. -6

32. In the formula of Exercise 18, if $R = 3$ and $R_1 = 5$, find R_2. $\dfrac{15}{2}$

33. In the formula of Exercise 19, if $S = \dfrac{3}{2}$ and $r = \dfrac{1}{5}$, find a. $\dfrac{6}{5}$

34. In the formula of Exercise 20, if $I = 15$, $E = 3$, and $R = 2$, find r. $-\dfrac{9}{5}$

⟨2⟩ Uniform Motion Problems

Show a complete solution to each problem. See Example 5.

VIDEO **35.** ***Fast walking.*** Marcie can walk 8 miles in the same time as Frank walks 6 miles. If Marcie walks 1 mile per hour faster than Frank, then how fast does each person walk? Marcie 4 mph, Frank 3 mph

36. ***Upstream, downstream.*** Junior's boat will go 15 miles per hour in still water. If he can go 12 miles downstream in the same amount of time as it takes to go 9 miles upstream, then what is the speed of the current? $\frac{15}{7}$ mph

37. ***Delivery routes.*** Pat travels 70 miles on her milk route, and Bob travels 75 miles on his route. Pat travels 5 miles per hour slower than Bob, and her route takes her one-half hour longer than Bob's. How fast is each one traveling? Bob 25 mph, Pat 20 mph

38. ***Ride the peaks.*** Smith bicycled 45 miles going east from Durango, and Jones bicycled 70 miles. Jones averaged 5 miles per hour more than Smith, and his trip took one-half hour longer than Smith's. How fast was each one traveling? Smith 15 mph and Jones 20 mph, or Smith 30 mph and Jones 35 mph

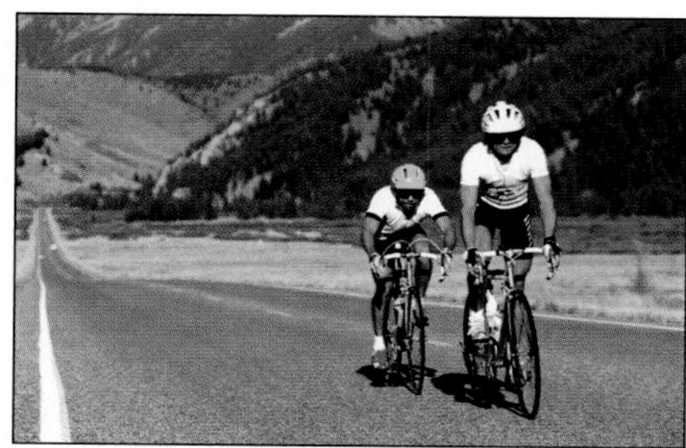

Photo for Exercise 38

39. ***Walking and running.*** Raffaele ran 8 miles and then walked 6 miles. If he ran 5 miles per hour faster than he walked and the total time was 2 hours, then how fast did he walk? 5 mph

40. ***Triathlon.*** Luisa participated in a triathlon in which she swam 3 miles, ran 5 miles, and then bicycled 10 miles. Luisa ran twice as fast as she swam, and she cycled three times as fast as she swam. If her total time for the triathlon was 1 hour and 46 minutes, then how fast did she swim? 5 mph

⟨3⟩ Work Problems

Show a complete solution to each problem.

See Example 6.

See the Strategy for Solving Work Problems on page 479.

41. ***Fence painting.*** Kiyoshi can paint a certain fence in 3 hours by himself. If Red helps, the job takes only 2 hours. How long would it take Red to paint the fence by himself? 6 hours

42. ***Envelope stuffing.*** Every week, Linda must stuff 1000 envelopes. She can do the job by herself in 6 hours. If Laura helps, they get the job done in $5\frac{1}{2}$ hours. How long would it take Laura to do the job by herself? 66 hours

43. ***Garden destroying.*** Mr. McGregor has discovered that a large dog can destroy his entire garden in 2 hours and that a small boy can do the same job in 1 hour. How long would it take the large dog and the small boy working together to destroy Mr. McGregor's garden? 40 minutes

44. ***Draining the vat.*** With only the small valve open, all of the liquid can be drained from a large vat in 4 hours. With only the large valve open, all of the liquid can be drained from the same vat in 2 hours. How long would it take to drain the vat with both valves open? 1 hour 20 minutes

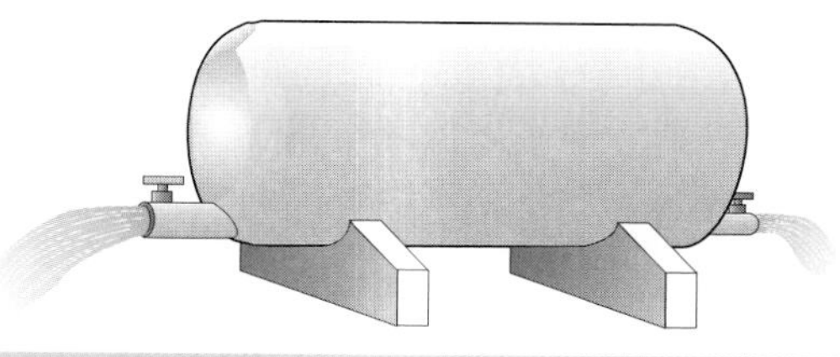

Figure for Exercise 44

45. ***Cleaning sidewalks.*** Edgar can blow the leaves off the sidewalks around the capitol building in 2 hours using a gasoline-powered blower. Ellen can do the same job in 8 hours using a broom. How long would it take them working together? 1 hour 36 minutes

46. ***Computer time.*** It takes a computer 8 days to print all of the personalized letters for a national sweepstakes. A new computer is purchased that can do the same job in 5 days. How long would it take to do the job with both computers working on it? $\frac{40}{13}$ days

⟨4⟩ More Rate Problems

Show a complete solution to each problem. See Examples 7 and 8.

47. ***Repair work.*** Sally received a bill for a total of 8 hours labor on the repair of her bulldozer. She paid \$50 to the master mechanic and \$90 to his apprentice. If the master mechanic gets \$10 more per hour than his apprentice, then how many hours did each work on the bulldozer? Master 2 hours, apprentice 6 hours

48. ***Running backs.*** In the playoff game the ball was carried by either Anderson or Brown on 21 plays. Anderson gained 36 yards, and Brown gained 54 yards. If Brown averaged twice as many yards per carry as Anderson, then on how many plays did Anderson carry the ball? 12

Photo for Exercise 48

49. ***Apples and bananas.*** Bertha bought 18 pounds of fruit consisting of apples and bananas. She paid $9 for the apples and $2.40 for the bananas. If the price per pound of the apples was 3 times that of the bananas, then how many pounds of each type of fruit did she buy?
Bananas 8 pounds, apples 10 pounds

50. ***Fuel efficiency.*** Last week, Joe's Electric Service used 110 gallons of gasoline in its two trucks. The large truck was driven 800 miles, and the small truck was driven 600 miles. If the small truck gets twice as many miles per gallon as the large truck, then how many gallons of gasoline did the large truck use? 80 gallons

Miscellaneous

Show a complete solution to each problem.

51. ***Small plane.*** It took a small plane 1 hour longer to fly 480 miles against the wind than it took the plane to fly the same distance with the wind. If the wind speed was 20 mph, then what is the speed of the plane in calm air?
140 mph

52. ***Fast boat.*** A motorboat at full throttle takes two hours longer to travel 75 miles against the current than it takes to travel the same distance with the current. If the rate of the current is 5 mph, then what is the speed of the boat at full throttle in still water? 20 mph

53. ***Light plane.*** At full throttle a light plane flies 275 miles against the wind in the same time as it flies 325 miles with the wind. If the plane flies at 120 mph at full throttle in still air, then what is the wind speed? 10 mph

54. ***Big plane.*** A six-passenger plane cruises at 180 mph in calm air. If the plane flies 7 miles with the wind in the same amount of time as it flies 5 miles against the wind, then what is the wind speed? 30 mph

55. ***Two cyclists.*** Ben and Jerry start from the same point and ride their bicycles in opposite directions. If Ben rides twice as fast as Jerry and they are 90 miles apart after four hours, then what is the speed of each rider?
Ben 15 mph, Jerry 7.5 mph

56. ***Catching up.*** A sailboat leaves port and travels due south at an average speed of 9 mph. Four hours later a motorboat leaves the same port and travels due south at an average speed of 21 mph. How long will it take the motorboat to catch the sailboat? 3 hours

57. ***Road trip.*** The Griswalds averaged 45 mph on their way to Las Vegas and 60 mph on the way back home using the same route. Find the distance from their home to Las Vegas if the total driving time was 70 hours. 1800 miles

58. ***Meeting cyclists.*** Tanya and Lebron start at the same time from opposite ends of a bicycle trail that is 81 miles long. Tanya averages 12 mph and Lebron averages 15 mph. How long does it take for them to meet? 3 hours

59. ***Filling a fountain.*** Pete's fountain can be filled using a pipe or a hose. The fountain can be filled using the pipe in 6 hours or the hose in 12 hours. How long will it take to fill the fountain using both the pipe and the hose? 4 hours

60. ***Mowing a lawn.*** Albert can mow a lawn in 40 minutes, while his cousin Vinnie can mow the same lawn in one hour. How long would it take to mow the lawn if Albert and Vinnie work together? 24 minutes

61. ***Printing a report.*** Debra plans to use two computers to print all of the copies of the annual report that are needed for the year-end meeting. The new computer can do the whole job in 2 hours while the old computer can do the whole job in 3 hours. How long will it take to get the job done using both computers simultaneously?
1.2 hours or 1 hour 12 minutes

62. ***Installing a dishwasher.*** A plumber can install a dishwasher in 50 min. If the plumber brings his apprentice to help, the job takes 40 minutes. How long would it take the apprentice working alone to install the dishwasher?
200 minutes

63. ***Filling a tub.*** Using the hot and cold water faucets together, a bathtub fills in 8 minutes. Using the hot water faucet alone, the tub fills in 12 minutes. How long does it take to fill the tub using only the cold water faucet? 24 minutes

64. ***Filling a tank.*** A water tank has an inlet pipe and a drain pipe. A full tank can be emptied in 30 minutes if the drain is opened and an empty tank can be filled in 45 minutes with the inlet pipe opened. If both pipes are accidentally opened when the tank is full, then how long will it take to empty the tank? 90 minutes

Wrap-Up

Summary

Rational Expressions		Examples
Rational expression	The ratio of two polynomials with the denominator not equal to 0	$\frac{x-1}{x-3}$ $(x \neq 3)$
Rule for reducing rational expressions	If $a \neq 0$ and $c \neq 0$, then $\frac{ab}{ac} = \frac{b}{c}$. (Divide out the common factors.)	$\frac{8x+2}{4x} = \frac{2(4x+1)}{2(2x)} = \frac{4x+1}{2x}$ $\frac{x^7}{x^5} = x^2$ $\frac{x^2}{x^5} = \frac{1}{x^3}$

Multiplication and Division of Rational Expressions		Examples
Multiplication	If $b \neq 0$ and $d \neq 0$, then $\frac{a}{b} \cdot \frac{c}{d} = \frac{ac}{bd}$.	$\frac{3}{x^3} \cdot \frac{6}{x^5} = \frac{18}{x^8}$
Division	If $b \neq 0$, $c \neq 0$, and $d \neq 0$, then $\frac{a}{b} \div \frac{c}{d} = \frac{a}{b} \cdot \frac{d}{c}$. (Invert the divisor and multiply.)	$\frac{a}{x^3} \div \frac{5}{x^9} = \frac{a}{x^3} \cdot \frac{x^9}{5} = \frac{ax^6}{5}$

Addition and Subtraction of Rational Expressions		Examples
Least common denominator	The LCD of a group of denominators is the smallest number that is a multiple of all of them.	8, 12 LCD = 24
Finding the least common denominator	1. Factor each denominator completely. Use exponent notation for repeated factors. 2. Write the product of all of the different factors that appear in the denominators. 3. On each factor, use the highest power that appears on that factor in any of the denominators.	$4ab^3$, $6a^2b$ $4ab^3 = 2^2ab^3$ $6a^2b = 2 \cdot 3a^2b$ $\text{LCD} = 2^2 \cdot 3a^2b^3 = 12a^2b^3$
Addition and subtraction of rational expressions	If $b \neq 0$, then $\frac{a}{b} + \frac{c}{b} = \frac{a+c}{b}$ and $\frac{a}{b} - \frac{c}{b} = \frac{a-c}{b}$. If the denominators are not identical, change each fraction to an equivalent fraction so that all denominators are identical.	$\frac{2x}{x-3} + \frac{7x}{x-3} = \frac{9x}{x-3}$ $\frac{2}{x} + \frac{1}{3x} = \frac{6}{3x} + \frac{1}{3x} = \frac{7}{3x}$

Complex fraction	A rational expression that has fractions in the numerator and/or the denominator	$\dfrac{\frac{1}{2}+\frac{1}{3}}{\frac{1}{3}-\frac{3}{4}}$
Simplifying complex fractions	Multiply the numerator and denominator by the LCD.	$\dfrac{\left(\frac{1}{2}+\frac{1}{3}\right)12}{\left(\frac{1}{3}-\frac{3}{4}\right)12} = \dfrac{6+4}{4-9} = -2$

Equations with Rational Expressions — **Examples**

Solving equations	Multiply each side by the LCD.	$\frac{1}{x}-\frac{1}{3}=\frac{1}{2x}-\frac{1}{6}$ $6x\left(\frac{1}{x}-\frac{1}{3}\right)=6x\left(\frac{1}{2x}-\frac{1}{6}\right)$ $6-2x=3-x$
Proportion	An equation expressing the equality of two ratios	$\frac{a}{b}=\frac{c}{d}$
Extremes-means property (Cross-multiplying)	If $b \neq 0$ and $d \neq 0$, then $\frac{a}{b}=\frac{c}{d}$ is equivalent to $ad = bc$. Cross-multiplying is a quick way to eliminate the fractions in a proportion.	$\frac{2}{x-3}=\frac{5}{6}$ $2\cdot 6=(x-3)5$ $12=5x-15$

Enriching Your Mathematical Word Power

For each mathematical term, choose the correct meaning.

1. rational expression
   a. a fraction
   b. a ratio of two polynomials with denominator not equal to 0
   c. an expression involving fractions
   d. a fraction in which the numerator and denominator contain fractions b

2. complex fraction
   a. a fraction having rational expressions in the numerator, denominator, or both
   b. a fraction with a large denominator
   c. the sum of two fractions
   d. a fraction with a variable in the denominator a

3. building up the denominator
   a. the opposite of reducing a fraction
   b. finding the least common denominator
   c. adding the same number to the numerator and denominator
   d. writing a fraction larger a

4. least common denominator
   a. the largest number that is a multiple of all denominators
   b. the sum of the denominators
   c. the product of the denominators
   d. the smallest number that is a multiple of all denominators d

5. extraneous solution
   a. a number that appears to be a solution to an equation but does not satisfy the equation
   b. an extra solution to an equation
   c. the second solution
   d. a nonreal solution a

6. ratio of *a* to *b*
   a. b/a b. a/b c. $a/(a+b)$ d. ab b

7. proportion
   a. a ratio
   b. two ratios
   c. the product of the means equals the product of the extremes
   d. a statement expressing the equality of two ratios d

8. extremes
a. a and d in $a/b = c/d$
b. b and c in $a/b = c/d$
c. the extremes-means property
d. if $a/b = c/d$ then $ad = bc$ a

9. means
a. the average of a, b, c, and d
b. a and d in $a/b = c/d$
c. b and c in $a/b = c/d$
d. if $a/b = c/d$, then $(a + b)/2 = (c + d)/2$ c

10. cross-multiplying
a. $ab = ba$ for any real numbers a and b
b. $(a - b)^2 = (b - a)^2$ for any real numbers a and b
c. if $a/b = c/d$, then $ab = cd$
d. if $a/b = c/d$, then $ad = bc$ d

Review Exercises

7.1 Reducing Rational Expressions

Find the domain of each rational expression.

1. $\dfrac{x^2}{4 - x}$ All real numbers except 4

2. $\dfrac{x - 9}{2x + 6}$ All real numbers except -3

3. $\dfrac{x - 5}{x^2 - 4x - 5}$ All real numbers except -1 and 5

4. $\dfrac{x + 2}{x^2 + 6x + 8}$ All real numbers except -4 and -2

Reduce each rational expression to lowest terms.

5. $\dfrac{24}{28}$ $\dfrac{6}{7}$

6. $\dfrac{42}{18}$ $\dfrac{7}{3}$

7. $\dfrac{2a^3c^3}{8a^5c}$ $\dfrac{c^2}{4a^2}$

8. $\dfrac{39x^6}{15x}$ $\dfrac{13x^5}{5}$

9. $\dfrac{6w - 9}{9w - 12}$ $\dfrac{2w - 3}{3w - 4}$

10. $\dfrac{3t - 6}{8 - 4t}$ $-\dfrac{3}{4}$

11. $\dfrac{x^2 - 1}{3 - 3x}$ $-\dfrac{x + 1}{3}$

12. $\dfrac{3x^2 - 9x + 6}{10 - 5x}$ $\dfrac{3 - 3x}{5}$

7.2 Multiplication and Division

Perform the indicated operation.

13. $\dfrac{1}{6k} \cdot 3k^2$ $\dfrac{1}{2}k$

14. $\dfrac{1}{15abc} \cdot 5a^3b^5c^2$ $\dfrac{1}{3}a^2b^4c$

15. $\dfrac{2xy}{3} \div y^2$ $\dfrac{2x}{3y}$

16. $4ab \div \dfrac{1}{2a^4}$ $8a^5b$

17. $\dfrac{a^2 - 9}{a - 2} \cdot \dfrac{a^2 - 4}{a + 3}$ $a^2 - a - 6$

18. $\dfrac{x^2 - 1}{3x} \cdot \dfrac{6x}{2x - 2}$ $x + 1$

19. $\dfrac{w - 2}{3w} \div \dfrac{4w - 8}{6w}$ $\dfrac{1}{2}$

20. $\dfrac{2y + 2x}{x - xy} \div \dfrac{x^2 + 2xy + y^2}{y^2 - y}$ $\dfrac{-2y}{x(x + y)}$

7.3 Finding the Least Common Denominator

Find the least common denominator for each group of denominators.

21. 36, 54 108

22. 10, 15, 35 210

23. $6ab^3$, $8a^7b^2$ $24a^7b^3$

24. $20u^4v$, $18uv^5$, $12u^2v^3$ $180u^4v^5$

25. $4x$, $6x - 6$ $12x(x - 1)$

26. $8a$, $6a$, $2a^2 + 2a$ $24a(a + 1)$

27. $x^2 - 4$, $x^2 - x - 2$ $(x + 1)(x - 2)(x + 2)$

28. $x^2 - 9$, $x^2 + 6x + 9$ $(x - 3)(x + 3)^2$

Convert each rational expression into an equivalent rational expression with the indicated denominator.

29. $\dfrac{5}{12} = \dfrac{?}{36}$ $\dfrac{15}{36}$

30. $\dfrac{2a}{15} = \dfrac{?}{45}$ $\dfrac{6a}{45}$

31. $\dfrac{2}{3xy} = \dfrac{?}{15x^2y}$ $\dfrac{10x}{15x^2y}$

32. $\dfrac{3z}{7x^2y} = \dfrac{?}{42x^3y^8}$ $\dfrac{18xy^7z}{42x^3y^8}$

33. $\dfrac{5}{y - 6} = \dfrac{?}{12 - 2y}$ $\dfrac{-10}{12 - 2y}$

34. $\dfrac{-3}{2 - t} = \dfrac{?}{2t - 4}$ $\dfrac{6}{2t - 4}$

35. $\dfrac{x}{x - 1} = \dfrac{?}{x^2 - 1}$ $\dfrac{x^2 + x}{x^2 - 1}$

36. $\dfrac{t}{t - 3} = \dfrac{?}{t^2 + 2t - 15}$ $\dfrac{t^2 + 5t}{t^2 + 2t - 15}$

7.4 Addition and Subtraction

Perform the indicated operation.

37. $\dfrac{5}{36} + \dfrac{9}{28}$ $\dfrac{29}{63}$

38. $\dfrac{7}{30} - \dfrac{11}{42}$ $-\dfrac{1}{35}$

39. $3 - \dfrac{4}{x}$ $\dfrac{3x - 4}{x}$

40. $1 + \dfrac{3a}{2b}$ $\dfrac{2b + 3a}{2b}$

41. $\dfrac{2}{ab^2} - \dfrac{1}{a^2b}$ $\dfrac{2a - b}{a^2b^2}$

42. $\dfrac{3}{4x^3} + \dfrac{5}{6x^2}$ $\dfrac{10x + 9}{12x^3}$

43. $\dfrac{9a}{2a - 3} + \dfrac{5}{3a - 2}$ $\dfrac{27a^2 - 8a - 15}{(2a - 3)(3a - 2)}$

44. $\dfrac{3}{x - 2} - \dfrac{5}{x + 3}$ $\dfrac{-2x + 19}{(x - 2)(x + 3)}$

45. $\dfrac{1}{a - 8} - \dfrac{2}{8 - a}$ $\dfrac{3}{a - 8}$

46. $\dfrac{5}{x - 14} + \dfrac{4}{14 - x}$ $\dfrac{1}{x - 14}$

47. $\dfrac{3}{2x - 4} + \dfrac{1}{x^2 - 4}$ $\dfrac{3x + 8}{2(x + 2)(x - 2)}$

48. $\dfrac{x}{x^2 - 2x - 3} - \dfrac{3x}{x^2 - 9}$ $\dfrac{-2x^2}{(x - 3)(x + 3)(x + 1)}$

7.5 Complex Fractions

Simplify each complex fraction.

49. $\dfrac{\frac{1}{2}-\frac{3}{4}}{\frac{2}{3}+\frac{1}{2}}$ $-\dfrac{3}{14}$

50. $\dfrac{\frac{2}{3}+\frac{5}{8}}{\frac{1}{2}-\frac{3}{8}}$ $\dfrac{31}{3}$

51. $\dfrac{\frac{1}{a}+\frac{2}{3b}}{\frac{1}{2b}-\frac{3}{a}}$ $\dfrac{6b+4a}{3(a-6b)}$

52. $\dfrac{\frac{3}{xy}-\frac{1}{3y}}{\frac{1}{6x}-\frac{3}{5y}}$ $\dfrac{90-10x}{5y-18x}$

53. $\dfrac{\frac{1}{x-2}-\frac{3}{x+3}}{\frac{2}{x+3}+\frac{1}{x-2}}$ $\dfrac{-2x+9}{3x-1}$

54. $\dfrac{\frac{4}{a+1}+\frac{5}{a^2-1}}{\frac{1}{a^2-1}-\frac{3}{a-1}}$ $\dfrac{4a+1}{-3a-2}$

55. $\dfrac{\frac{x-1}{x-3}}{\frac{1}{x^2-x-6}-\frac{4}{x+2}}$ $\dfrac{x^2+x-2}{-4x+13}$

56. $\dfrac{\frac{6}{a^2+5a+6}-\frac{8}{a+2}}{\frac{2}{a+3}-\frac{4}{a+2}}$ $\dfrac{4a+9}{a+4}$

7.6 Solving Equations with Rational Expressions

Solve each equation.

57. $\dfrac{-2}{5}=\dfrac{3}{x}$ $-\dfrac{15}{2}$

58. $\dfrac{3}{x}+\dfrac{5}{3x}=1$ $\dfrac{14}{3}$

59. $\dfrac{14}{a^2-1}+\dfrac{1}{a-1}=\dfrac{3}{a+1}$ 9

60. $2+\dfrac{3}{y-5}=\dfrac{2y}{y-5}$ No solution

61. $z-\dfrac{3z}{2-z}=\dfrac{6}{z-2}$ -3

62. $\dfrac{1}{x}+\dfrac{1}{3}=\dfrac{1}{2}$ 6

7.7 Applications of Ratios and Proportions

Solve each proportion.

63. $\dfrac{3}{x}=\dfrac{2}{7}$ $\dfrac{21}{2}$

64. $\dfrac{4}{x}=\dfrac{x}{4}$ $-4, 4$

65. $\dfrac{2}{w-3}=\dfrac{5}{w}$ 5

66. $\dfrac{3}{t-3}=\dfrac{5}{t+4}$ $\dfrac{27}{2}$

Solve each problem by using a proportion.

67. ***Taxis in Times Square.*** The ratio of taxis to private automobiles in Times Square at 6:00 P.M. on New Year's Eve was estimated to be 15 to 2. If there were 60 taxis, then how many private automobiles were there? 8

68. ***Student-teacher ratio.*** The student-teacher ratio for Washington High was reported to be 27.5 to 1. If there are 42 teachers, then how many students are there? 1155

Photo for Exercise 67

69. ***Water and rice.*** At Wong's Chinese Restaurant the secret recipe for white rice calls for a 2 to 1 ratio of water to rice. In one batch the chef used 28 more cups of water than rice. How many cups of each did he use?
56 cups water, 28 cups rice

Photo for Exercise 69

70. ***Oil and gas.*** An outboard motor calls for a fuel mixture that has a gasoline-to-oil ratio of 50 to 1. How many pints of oil should be added to 6 gallons of gasoline?
$\dfrac{24}{25}$ pint

7.8 Applications of Rational Expressions

Solve each formula for the indicated variable.

71. $\dfrac{y-b}{m}=x$ for y $y=mx+b$

72. $\dfrac{A}{h}=\dfrac{a+b}{2}$ for a $a=\dfrac{2A-hb}{h}$

73. $F=\dfrac{mv+1}{m}$ for m $m=\dfrac{1}{F-v}$

74. $m=\dfrac{r}{1+rt}$ for r $r=\dfrac{m}{1-mt}$

75. $\dfrac{y+1}{x-3}=4$ for y $y=4x-13$

76. $\dfrac{y-3}{x+2}=\dfrac{-1}{3}$ for y $y=-\dfrac{1}{3}x+\dfrac{7}{3}$

Solve each problem.

77. ***Making a puzzle.*** Tracy, Stacy, and Fred assembled a very large puzzle together in 40 hours. If Stacy worked twice as fast as Fred and Tracy worked just as fast as Stacy, then how long would it have taken Fred to assemble the puzzle alone? 200 hours

78. ***Going skiing.*** Leon drove 270 miles to the lodge in the same time as Pat drove 330 miles to the lodge. If Pat drove 10 miles per hour faster than Leon, then how fast did each of them drive? Leon 45 mph, Pat 55 mph

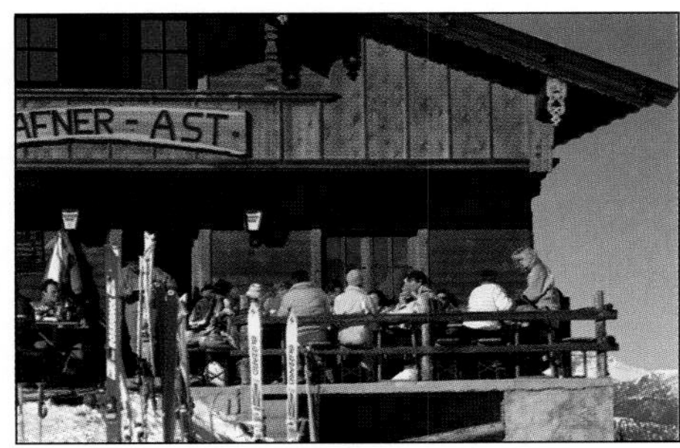

Photo for Exercise 78

79. ***Merging automobiles.*** When Bert and Ernie merged their automobile dealerships, Bert had 10 more cars than Ernie. While 36% of Ernie's stock consisted of new cars, only 25% of Bert's stock consisted of new cars. If they had 33 new cars on the lot after the merger, then how many cars did each one have before the merger? Bert 60 cars, Ernie 50 cars

80. ***Magazine sales.*** A company specializing in magazine sales over the telephone found that in 2500 phone calls, 360 resulted in sales and were made by male callers, and 480 resulted in sales and were made by female callers. If the company gets twice as many sales per call with a woman's voice than with a man's voice, then how many of the 2500 calls were made by females? 1000

2000 Total Waste Generation (before recycling)

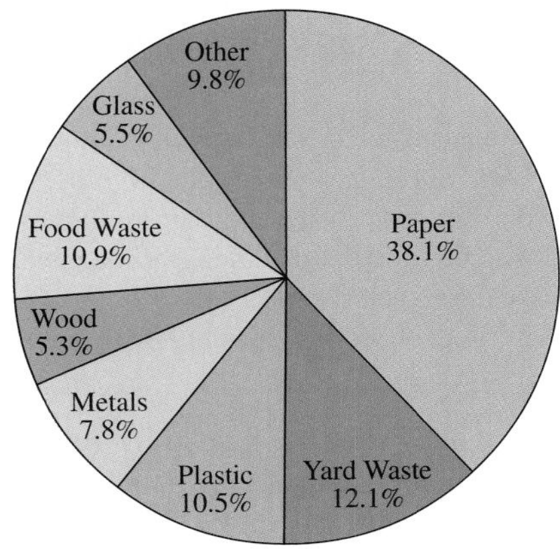

Figure for Exercises 81 and 82

81. ***Distribution of waste.*** The accompanying figure shows the distribution of the total municipal solid waste into various categories in 2000 (U.S. Environmental Protection Agency, www.epa.gov). If the paper waste was 59.8 million tons greater than the yard waste, then what was the amount of yard waste generated? 27.83 million tons

82. ***Total waste.*** Use the information given in Exercise 81 to find the total waste generated in 2000 and the amount of food waste. 230 million tons, 25.07 million tons

Miscellaneous

In place of each question mark, put an expression that makes each equation an identity.

83. $\frac{5}{x} = \frac{?}{2x}$ 10

84. $\frac{?}{a} = \frac{6}{3a}$ 2

85. $\frac{2}{a-5} = \frac{?}{5-a}$ -2

86. $\frac{-1}{a-7} = \frac{1}{?}$ $7-a$

87. $3 = \frac{?}{x}$ $3x$

88. $2a = \frac{?}{b}$ $2ab$

89. $m \div \frac{1}{2} = ?$ $2m$

90. $5x \div \frac{1}{x} = ?$ $5x^2$

91. $2a \div ? = 12a$ $\frac{1}{6}$

92. $10x \div ? = 20x^2$ $\frac{1}{2x}$

93. $\frac{a-1}{a^2-1} = \frac{1}{?}$ $a+1$

94. $\frac{?}{x^2-9} = \frac{1}{x-3}$ $x+3$

95. $\frac{1}{a} - \frac{1}{5} = ?$ $\frac{5-a}{5a}$

96. $\frac{3}{7} - \frac{2}{b} = ?$ $\frac{3b-14}{7b}$

97. $\frac{a}{2} - 1 = \frac{?}{2}$ $a-2$

98. $\frac{1}{a} - 1 = \frac{?}{a}$ $1-a$

99. $(a-b) \div (-1) = ?$ $b-a$

100. $(a-7) \div (7-a) = ?$ -1

101. $\frac{\frac{1}{5a}}{2} = ?$ $\frac{1}{10a}$

102. $\frac{3a}{\frac{1}{2}} = ?$ $6a$

For each expression in Exercises 103–122, either perform the indicated operation or solve the equation, whichever is appropriate.

103. $\frac{1}{x} + \frac{1}{2x}$ $\frac{3}{2x}$

104. $\frac{1}{y} + \frac{1}{3y} = 2$ $\frac{2}{3}$

105. $\frac{2}{3xy} + \frac{1}{6x}$ $\frac{4+y}{6xy}$

106. $\frac{3}{x-1} - \frac{3}{x}$ $\frac{3}{x(x-1)}$

107. $\frac{5}{a-5} - \frac{3}{5-a}$ $\frac{8}{a-5}$

108. $\frac{2}{x-2} - \frac{3}{x} = \frac{-1}{x}$ No solution

109. $\dfrac{2}{x-1} - \dfrac{2}{x} = 1$ $-1, 2$

110. $\dfrac{2}{x-2} \cdot \dfrac{6x-12}{14}$ $\dfrac{6}{7}$

111. $\dfrac{-3}{x+2} \cdot \dfrac{5x+10}{9}$ $-\dfrac{5}{3}$

112. $\dfrac{3}{10} = \dfrac{5}{x}$ $\dfrac{50}{3}$

113. $\dfrac{1}{-3} = \dfrac{-2}{x}$ 6

114. $\dfrac{x^2-4}{x} \div \dfrac{4x-8}{x}$ $\dfrac{x+2}{4}$

115. $\dfrac{ax+am+3x+3m}{a^2-9} \div \dfrac{2x+2m}{a-3}$ $\dfrac{1}{2}$

116. $\dfrac{-2}{x} = \dfrac{3}{x+2}$ $-\dfrac{4}{5}$

117. $\dfrac{2}{x^2-25} + \dfrac{1}{x^2-4x-5}$ $\dfrac{3x+7}{(x-5)(x+5)(x+1)}$

118. $\dfrac{4}{a^2-1} + \dfrac{1}{2a+2}$ $\dfrac{a+7}{2(a+1)(a-1)}$

119. $\dfrac{-3}{a^2-9} - \dfrac{2}{a^2+5a+6}$ $\dfrac{-5a}{(a-3)(a+3)(a+2)}$

120. $\dfrac{-5}{a^2-4} - \dfrac{2}{a^2-3a+2}$ $\dfrac{-7a+1}{(a+2)(a-2)(a-1)}$

121. $\dfrac{1}{a^2-1} + \dfrac{2}{1-a} = \dfrac{3}{a+1}$ $\dfrac{2}{5}$

122. $3 + \dfrac{1}{x-2} = \dfrac{2x-3}{x-2}$ No solution

Chapter 7 Test

What numbers cannot be used for x in each rational expression?

1. $\dfrac{2x-1}{x^2-1}$ $-1, 1$

2. $\dfrac{5}{2-3x}$ $\dfrac{2}{3}$

3. $\dfrac{1}{x}$ 0

Perform the indicated operation. Write each answer in lowest terms.

4. $\dfrac{2}{15} - \dfrac{4}{9}$ $-\dfrac{14}{45}$

5. $\dfrac{1}{y} + 3$ $\dfrac{1+3y}{y}$

6. $\dfrac{3}{a-2} - \dfrac{1}{2-a}$ $\dfrac{4}{a-2}$

7. $\dfrac{2}{x^2-4} - \dfrac{3}{x^2+x-2}$ $\dfrac{-x+4}{(x+2)(x-2)(x-1)}$

8. $\dfrac{m^2-1}{(m-1)^2} \cdot \dfrac{2m-2}{3m+3}$ $\dfrac{2}{3}$

9. $\dfrac{a-b}{3} \div \dfrac{b^2-a^2}{6}$ $\dfrac{-2}{a+b}$

10. $\dfrac{5a^2b}{12a} \cdot \dfrac{2a^3b}{15ab^6}$ $\dfrac{a^3}{18b^4}$

Simplify each complex fraction.

11. $\dfrac{\dfrac{2}{3} + \dfrac{4}{5}}{\dfrac{2}{5} - \dfrac{3}{2}}$ $-\dfrac{4}{3}$

12. $\dfrac{\dfrac{2}{x} + \dfrac{1}{x-2}}{\dfrac{1}{x-2} - \dfrac{3}{x}}$ $\dfrac{-3x+4}{2(x-3)}$

Solve each equation.

13. $\dfrac{3}{x} = \dfrac{7}{5}$ $\dfrac{15}{7}$

14. $\dfrac{x}{x-1} - \dfrac{3}{x} = \dfrac{1}{2}$ $2, 3$

15. $\dfrac{1}{x} + \dfrac{1}{6} = \dfrac{1}{4}$ 12

Solve each formula for the indicated variable.

16. $\dfrac{y-3}{x+2} = \dfrac{-1}{5}$ for y $y = -\dfrac{1}{5}x + \dfrac{13}{5}$

17. $M = \dfrac{1}{3}b(c+d)$ for c $c = \dfrac{3M-bd}{b}$

Solve each problem.

18. If $R(x) = \dfrac{x+2}{1-x}$, then what is $R(0.9)$? 29

19. When all of the grocery carts escape from the supermarket, it takes Reginald 12 minutes to round them up and bring them back. Because Norman doesn't make as much per hour as Reginald, it takes Norman 18 minutes to do the same job. How long would it take them working together to complete the roundup? 7.2 minutes

20. Brenda and her husband Randy bicycled cross-country together. One morning, Brenda rode 30 miles. By traveling only 5 miles per hour faster and putting in one more hour, Randy covered twice the distance Brenda covered. What was the speed of each cyclist?
Brenda 15 mph and Randy 20 mph, or Brenda 10 mph and Randy 15 mph

21. For a certain time period the ratio of the dollar value of exports to the dollar value of imports for the United States was 2 to 3. If the value of exports during that time period was 48 billion dollars, then what was the value of imports? $72 billion

Making Connections | A Review of Chapters 1–7

Solve each equation.

1. $3x - 2 = 5$ $\quad \frac{7}{3}$

2. $\frac{3}{5}x = -2$ $\quad -\frac{10}{3}$

3. $2(x - 2) = 4x$ $\quad -2$

4. $2(x - 2) = 2x$ $\quad$ No solution

5. $2(x + 3) = 6x + 6$ $\quad 0$

6. $2(3x + 4) + x^2 = 0$ $\quad -4, -2$

7. $4x - 4x^3 = 0$ $\quad -1, 0, 1$

8. $\frac{3}{x} = \frac{-2}{5}$ $\quad -\frac{15}{2}$

9. $\frac{3}{x} = \frac{x}{12}$ $\quad -6, 6$

10. $\frac{x}{2} = \frac{4}{x - 2}$ $\quad -2, 4$

11. $\frac{w}{18} - \frac{w - 1}{9} = \frac{4 - w}{6}$ $\quad 5$

12. $\frac{x}{x + 1} + \frac{1}{2x + 2} = \frac{7}{8}$ $\quad 3$

Solve each equation for y.

13. $2x + 3y = c$ $\quad y = \frac{c - 2x}{3}$

14. $\frac{y - 3}{x - 5} = \frac{1}{2}$ $\quad y = \frac{1}{2}x + \frac{1}{2}$

15. $2y = ay + c$ $\quad y = \frac{c}{2 - a}$

16. $\frac{A}{y} = \frac{C}{B}$ $\quad y = \frac{AB}{C}$

17. $\frac{A}{y} + \frac{1}{3} = \frac{B}{y}$ $\quad y = 3B - 3A$

18. $\frac{A}{y} - \frac{1}{2} = \frac{1}{3}$ $\quad y = \frac{6A}{5}$

19. $3y - 5ay = 8$ $\quad y = \frac{8}{3 - 5a}$

20. $y^2 - By = 0$ $\quad y = 0$ or $y = B$

21. $A = \frac{1}{2}h(b + y)$ $\quad y = \frac{2A - hb}{h}$

22. $2(b + y) = b$ $\quad y = -\frac{b}{2}$

Calculate the value of $b^2 - 4ac$ for each choice of a, b, and c.

23. $a = 1, b = 2, c = -15$ $\quad 64$

24. $a = 1, b = 8, c = 12$ $\quad 16$

25. $a = 2, b = 5, c = -3$ $\quad 49$

26. $a = 6, b = 7, c = -3$ $\quad 121$

Perform each indicated operation.

27. $(3x - 5) - (5x - 3)$ $\quad -2x - 2$

28. $(2a - 5)(a - 3)$ $\quad 2a^2 - 11a + 15$

29. $x^7 \div x^3$ $\quad x^4$

30. $\frac{x - 3}{5} + \frac{x + 4}{5}$ $\quad \frac{2x + 1}{5}$

31. $\frac{1}{2} \cdot \frac{1}{x}$ $\quad \frac{1}{2x}$

32. $\frac{1}{2} + \frac{1}{x}$ $\quad \frac{x + 2}{2x}$

33. $\frac{1}{2} \div \frac{1}{x}$ $\quad \frac{x}{2}$

34. $\frac{1}{2} - \frac{1}{x}$ $\quad \frac{x - 2}{2x}$

35. $\frac{x - 3}{5} - \frac{x + 4}{5}$ $\quad -\frac{7}{5}$

36. $\frac{3a}{2} \div 2$ $\quad \frac{3a}{4}$

37. $(x - 8)(x + 8)$ $\quad x^2 - 64$

38. $3x(x^2 - 7)$ $\quad 3x^3 - 21x$

39. $2a^5 \cdot 5a^9$ $\quad 10a^{14}$

40. $x^2 \cdot x^8$ $\quad x^{10}$

41. $(k - 6)^2$ $\quad k^2 - 12k + 36$

42. $(j + 5)^2$ $\quad j^2 + 10j + 25$

43. $(g - 3) \div (3 - g)$ $\quad -1$

44. $(6x^3 - 8x^2) \div (2x)$ $\quad 3x^2 - 4x$

Solve.

45. ***Present value.*** An investor is interested in the amount or present value that she would have to invest today to receive periodic payments in the future. The present value of \$1 in one year and \$1 in 2 years with interest rate r compounded annually is given by the formula

$$P = \frac{1}{1 + r} + \frac{1}{(1 + r)^2}.$$

a) Rewrite the formula so that the right-hand side is a single rational expression.

b) Find P if $r = 7\%$.

c) The present value of \$1 per year for the next 10 years is given by the formula

$$P = \frac{1}{1 + r} + \frac{1}{(1 + r)^2} + \frac{1}{(1 + r)^3} + \cdots + \frac{1}{(1 + r)^{10}}.$$

Use this formula to find P if $r = 5\%$.

a) $P = \frac{r + 2}{(1 + r)^2}$ **b)** \$1.81 **c)** \$7.72

Critical **Thinking** | For Individual or Group Work | Chapter 7

These exercises can be solved by a variety of techniques, which may or may not require algebra. So be creative and think critically. Explain all answers. Answers are in the Instructor's Edition of this text.

1. ***Counting paths.*** How many different paths are there from point A to point B in the accompanying figure? You can only move in a downward direction along the line segments.

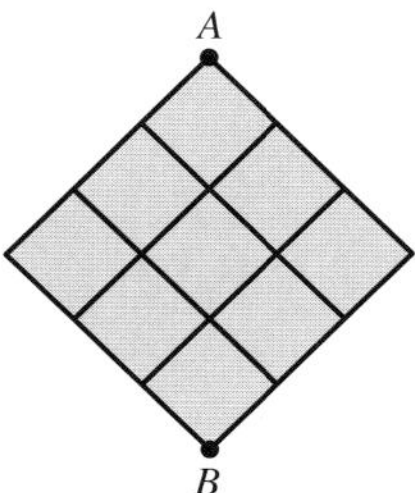

Figure for Exercise 1

2. ***Canadian prime.*** On November 14, 2001, Michael Cameron, a 20-year-old Canadian, discovered the largest known prime number to date,

$$2^{13,466,917} - 1.$$

This number contains 4,053,946 digits. What is the ones digit? What is the tens digit?

3. ***Good excuse.*** A driver was stopped for doing 70 mph in a 60 mph zone. The driver explained to the officer that her speedometer read 60 mph. However, she recently replaced her stock 24-inch-diameter tires with 25-inch-diameter tires, which caused her to do 10 mph over the speed limit. If her speedometer reads 60 mph, then what is her actual speed with the new tires?

4. ***Palindromic dates.*** October 2, 2001, can be written in *abbreviated* form as 10-2-01, or in *complete* form as 10-02-2001, both of which are palindromic dates (they read the same forward or backward). What was the last palindromic date in abbreviated form prior to 10-1-01? What was the last palindromic date in complete form prior to 10-1-01?

5. ***Integral solutions.*** Find all integral solutions to

$$x^2y - y^3 = 105.$$

6. ***Jogging observation.*** While jogging on a circular track, Heather observes that one-fifth of the joggers in front of her plus five-sixths of the joggers behind her is equal to the total number of joggers. How many joggers are on the track?

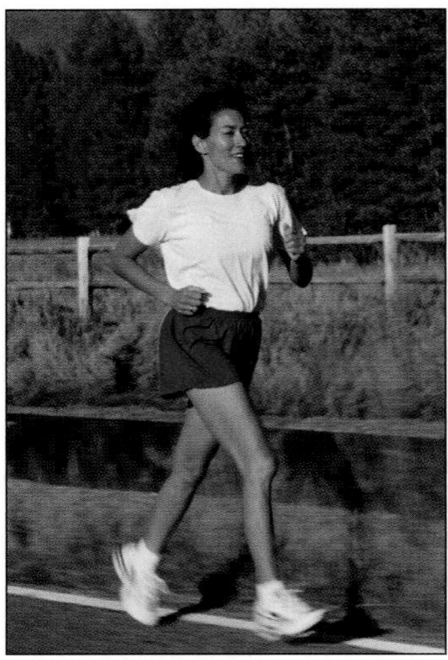

Photo for Exercise 6

7. ***Volume of a box.*** The area of the top of a box is 30 in.^{2} and the area of the front is 12 in.^{2} If the surface area of the box is 164 in.^{2}, then what is the volume of the box?

8. ***Making triangles.*** Brenda has a 12-in. loop necklace that she plays with on her desk by forming triangles with it.

a) Find all possible triangles with integer sides that she can form with her necklace and classify each as a right, obtuse, scalene, equilateral, or isosceles triangle.

b) Which triangle has the largest area?

1. 20 **2.** Ones digit is 1; tens digit is 7. **3.** 62.5 mph **4.** 9-9-99, 12-31-1321 **5.** $(\pm 8, 7)$, $(\pm 2, -5)$ **6.** 31 **7.** 120 in.^{3}
8. a) 3-4-5 right triangle, 4-4-4 acute and equilateral, 2-5-5 scalene and isosceles **b)** The 4-4-4 triangle has the largest area.

Chapter 8

Powers and Roots

Sailing—the very word conjures up images of warm summer breezes, sparkling blue water, and white billowing sails. But to boat builders, sailing is a serious business. Yacht designers know that the ocean is a dangerous and unforgiving place. It is their job to build boats that are not only fast, comfortable, and fun, but capable of withstanding the punishment inflicted by the wind and waves.

Designing sailboats is a technical balancing act. A good boat has just the right combination of length, width (or beam), sail area, and displacement. A boat can always be made faster by increasing the sail area, but too much sail area increases the chance of capsize. Making the boat wider decreases the chance of capsize, but causes more resistance from the water and slows down the boat.

There are four ratios commonly used to measure performance and safety for a yacht: ballast-displacement ratio, displacement-length ratio, sail area-displacement ratio, and capsize screening value. The formulas for these ratios involve powers and roots, which is the subject of this chapter.

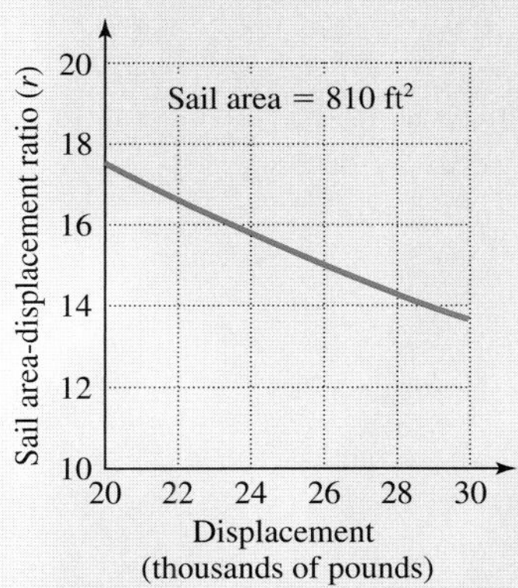

In Exercise 91 of Section 8.5 you will find the sail area-displacement ratio for a sailboat.

8.1 Roots, Radicals, and Rules

In This Section

In Section 5.1, you learned the basic facts about powers. In this section, you will study roots and see how powers and roots are related.

⟨1⟩ Roots

Roots are defined in terms of powers as follows.

nth Roots

If $a = b^n$ for a positive integer n, then b is an ***n*th root of *a*.** If $a = b^2$, then b is a **square root** of a. If $a = b^3$, then b is a **cube root** of a.

EXAMPLE 1

Finding roots

Find the indicated roots:

a) The square roots of 9 **b)** The fourth roots of 16

c) The cube root of 8 **d)** The cube root of -8

Solution

a) Because $3^2 = 9$ and $(-3)^2 = 9$, both 3 and -3 are square roots of 9.

b) Because $2^4 = 16$, and $(-2)^4 = 16$, both 2 and -2 are fourth roots of 16.

c) Because $2^3 = 8$, the cube root of 8 is 2.

d) Because $(-2)^3 = -8$, the cube root of -8 is -2.

Now do Exercises 7–14

⟨ Teaching Tip ⟩

Mention that in the complex number system, discussed in Section 9.5, every real number has n distinct nth roots.

Roots are classified as even or odd according to the following definition.

⟨ Teaching Tip ⟩

Have students list the powers of 2, powers of 3, and so on, where the results are less than 100. This will help them with roots.

Even Roots, Principal Roots, and Odd Roots

If n is a positive *even* integer and a is positive, then there are two real nth roots of a. We call these roots **even roots.**

The positive even root of a positive number is called the **principal root.**

If n is a positive *odd* integer and a is any real number, then there is only one real nth root of a. We call that root an **odd root.**

So the principal square root of 9 is 3 and the principal fourth root of 16 is 2 and these roots are even roots. Because $2^5 = 32$, the fifth root of 32 is 2 and 2 is an odd root.

We use the **radical symbol** $\sqrt{\ }$ to signify roots.

$\sqrt[n]{a}$

If n is a positive *even* integer and a is positive, then $\sqrt[n]{a}$ denotes the principal nth root of a.

If n is a positive *odd* integer, then $\sqrt[n]{a}$ denotes the nth root of a.

If n is any positive integer, then $\sqrt[n]{0} = 0$.

We read $\sqrt[n]{a}$ as "the nth root of a." In the notation $\sqrt[n]{a}$, n is the **index of the radical** and a is the **radicand.** For square roots the index is omitted, and we simply write $\sqrt{a}$.

EXAMPLE 2

Using radical symbols

Translate each verbal expression into an algebraic expression using a radical symbol.

a) The principal square root of 5

b) The cube root of -2

c) The principal fourth root of 10

Solution

a) The principal square root of 5 is written symbolically as $\sqrt{5}$.

b) The cube root of -2 is written symbolically as $\sqrt[3]{-2}$.

c) The principal fourth root of 10 is written symbolically as $\sqrt[4]{10}$.

Now do Exercises 15-22

EXAMPLE 3

Evaluating radical expressions

Find the following roots:

a) $\sqrt{25}$ **b)** $\sqrt[3]{-27}$ **c)** $\sqrt[6]{64}$ **d)** $-\sqrt{4}$

Solution

a) Because $5^2 = 25$, $\sqrt{25} = 5$.

b) Because $(-3)^3 = -27$, $\sqrt[3]{-27} = -3$.

c) Because $2^6 = 64$, $\sqrt[6]{64} = 2$.

d) Because $\sqrt{4} = 2$, $-\sqrt{4} = -(\sqrt{4}) = -2$.

Now do Exercises 23-56

‹ Calculator Close-Up ›

We can use the radical symbol to find a square root on a graphing calculator, but for other roots we use the xth root symbol as shown. The xth root symbol is in the MATH menu.

```
√(25)
                5
3 ×√ -27
               -3
6 ×√64
                2
```

CAUTION In radical notation, $\sqrt{4}$ represents the *principal square root of* 4, so $\sqrt{4} = 2$. Note that -2 is also a square root of 4, but $\sqrt{4} \neq -2$.

Note that even roots of negative numbers are omitted from the definition of nth roots because even powers of real numbers are never negative. So no real number can be an even root of a negative number. Expressions such as

$$\sqrt{-9}, \quad \sqrt[4]{-81}, \quad \text{and} \quad \sqrt[6]{-64}$$

are not real numbers. Square roots of negative numbers will be discussed in Section 9.5 when we discuss the imaginary numbers.

‹2› Roots and Variables

Consider the result of squaring a power of x:

$$(x^1)^2 = x^2, \quad (x^2)^2 = x^4, \quad (x^3)^2 = x^6, \quad \text{and} \quad (x^4)^2 = x^8.$$

When a power of x is squared, the exponent is multiplied by 2. So any even power of x is a perfect square.

Calculator Close-Up

A calculator can provide numerical support for this discussion of roots. Note that $\sqrt{(-3)^2} = 3$, not -3, because $\sqrt{x^2} \neq x$ when x is negative. Note also that the calculator will not evaluate $\sqrt{-3^2}$ because $\sqrt{-3^2} = \sqrt{-9}$.

```
√((-3)²)
                3
√(-3²)
```

Perfect Squares

The following expressions are perfect squares:

$$x^2,\quad x^4,\quad x^6,\quad x^8,\quad x^{10},\quad x^{12},\quad \ldots$$

Since taking a square root reverses the operation of squaring, the square root of an even power of x is found by dividing the exponent by 2. Provided x is nonnegative (see the next Caution), we have

$$\sqrt{x^2} = x^1 = x,\quad \sqrt{x^4} = x^2,\quad \sqrt{x^6} = x^3,\quad \text{and}\quad \sqrt{x^8} = x^4.$$

CAUTION For $x < 0$, $\sqrt{x^2} = x$ and $\sqrt{x^6} = x^3$ are not correct, because x and x^3 are negative. For even roots, the radical symbol means principal square root, which is always positive. For example, $\sqrt{(-2)^2} = \sqrt{4} = 2$, not -2. We can use absolute value and write $\sqrt{x^2} = |x|$ and $\sqrt{x^6} = |x^3|$ or we can assume that x is nonnegative.

If a power of x is cubed, the exponent is multiplied by 3:

$$(x^1)^3 = x^3,\quad (x^2)^3 = x^6,\quad (x^3)^3 = x^9,\quad \text{and}\quad (x^4)^3 = x^{12}$$

So if the exponent is a multiple of 3, we have a perfect cube.

Perfect Cubes

The following expressions are perfect cubes:

$$x^3,\quad x^6,\quad x^9,\quad x^{12},\quad x^{15},\quad \ldots$$

Since the cube root reverses the operation of cubing, the cube root of any of these perfect cubes is found by dividing the exponent by 3:

$$\sqrt[3]{x^3} = x^1 = x,\quad \sqrt[3]{x^6} = x^2,\quad \sqrt[3]{x^9} = x^3,\quad \text{and}\quad \sqrt[3]{x^{12}} = x^4$$

If the exponent is divisible by 4, we have a perfect fourth power, and so on.

EXAMPLE 4

Roots of exponential expressions

Find each root. Assume that all variables represent nonnegative real numbers.

a) $\sqrt{x^{22}}$ **b)** $\sqrt[3]{t^{18}}$ **c)** $\sqrt[5]{s^{30}}$

Solution

a) $\sqrt{x^{22}} = x^{11}$ because $(x^{11})^2 = x^{22}$.

b) $\sqrt[3]{t^{18}} = t^6$ because $(t^6)^3 = t^{18}$.

c) $\sqrt[5]{s^{30}} = s^6$ because one-fifth of 30 is 6.

Now do Exercises 57–72

⟨3⟩ Product Rule for Radicals

Consider the expression $\sqrt{2} \cdot \sqrt{3}$. If we square this product, we get

$$\begin{aligned}(\sqrt{2} \cdot \sqrt{3})^2 &= (\sqrt{2})^2(\sqrt{3})^2 && \text{Power of a product rule} \\ &= 2 \cdot 3 && (\sqrt{2})^2 = 2 \text{ and } (\sqrt{3})^2 = 3 \\ &= 6.\end{aligned}$$

The number $\sqrt{6}$ is the unique positive number whose square is 6. Because we squared $\sqrt{2} \cdot \sqrt{3}$ and obtained 6, we must have $\sqrt{6} = \sqrt{2} \cdot \sqrt{3}$. This example illustrates the product rule for radicals.

⟨ Teaching Tip ⟩

To find $\sqrt{17} \cdot \sqrt{17}$ students often use the product rule to get $\sqrt{289}$ and then get out a calculator. Keep reminding them that $\sqrt{a} \cdot \sqrt{a} = a$ for $a \geq 0$.

Product Rule for Radicals

The *n*th root of a product is equal to the product of the *n*th roots. In symbols,

$$\sqrt[n]{ab} = \sqrt[n]{a} \cdot \sqrt[n]{b},$$

provided all of these roots are real numbers.

EXAMPLE 5

Using the product rule for radicals

Simplify each radical. Assume that all variables represent positive real numbers.

a) $\sqrt{4y}$ **b)** $\sqrt{3y^8}$

Solution

a) $\begin{aligned}\sqrt{4y} &= \sqrt{4} \cdot \sqrt{y} && \text{Product rule for radicals} \\ &= 2\sqrt{y} && \text{Simplify.}\end{aligned}$

b) $\begin{aligned}\sqrt{3y^8} &= \sqrt{3} \cdot \sqrt{y^8} && \text{Product rule for radicals} \\ &= \sqrt{3} \cdot y^4 && \sqrt{y^8} = y^4 \\ &= y^4\sqrt{3} && \text{A radical is usually written last in a product.}\end{aligned}$

Now do Exercises 73–88

⟨4⟩ Quotient Rule for Radicals

Because $\sqrt{2} \cdot \sqrt{3} = \sqrt{6}$, we have $\sqrt{6} \div \sqrt{3} = \sqrt{2}$, or

$$\sqrt{2} = \sqrt{\frac{6}{3}} = \frac{\sqrt{6}}{\sqrt{3}}.$$

This example illustrates the quotient rule for radicals.

Quotient Rule for Radicals

The *n*th root of a quotient is equal to the quotient of the *n*th roots. In symbols,

$$\sqrt[n]{\frac{a}{b}} = \frac{\sqrt[n]{a}}{\sqrt[n]{b}}$$

provided that all of these roots are real numbers and $b \neq 0$.

In Example 6 we use the quotient rule to simplify radical expressions.

EXAMPLE 6

Using the quotient rule for radicals

Simplify each radical. Assume that all variables represent positive real numbers.

a) $\sqrt{\dfrac{t}{9}}$

b) $\sqrt[3]{\dfrac{x^{21}}{y^6}}$

‹ Calculator Close-Up ›

You can illustrate the product and quotient rules for radicals with a calculator.

```
√(2)*√(3)
         2.449489743
√(6)
         2.449489743
```

```
√(6)/√(3)
         1.414213562
√(6/3)
         1.414213562
```

Solution

a) $\sqrt{\dfrac{t}{9}} = \dfrac{\sqrt{t}}{\sqrt{9}}$ Quotient rule for radicals

$= \dfrac{\sqrt{t}}{3}$

b) $\sqrt[3]{\dfrac{x^{21}}{y^6}} = \dfrac{\sqrt[3]{x^{21}}}{\sqrt[3]{y^6}}$ Quotient rule for radicals

$= \dfrac{x^7}{y^2}$

Now do Exercises 89–100

Warm-Ups ▼

True or false? Explain your answer.

1. $\sqrt{2} \cdot \sqrt{2} = 2$ True
2. $\sqrt[3]{2} \cdot \sqrt[3]{2} = 2$ False
3. $\sqrt[3]{-27} = -3$ True
4. $\sqrt{-25} = -5$ False
5. $\sqrt[4]{16} = 2$ True
6. $\sqrt{9} = 3$ True
7. $\sqrt{2^9} = 2^3$ False
8. $\sqrt{17} \cdot \sqrt{17} = 289$ False
9. If $w \geq 0$, then $\sqrt{w^2} = w$. True
10. If $t \geq 0$, then $\sqrt[4]{t^{12}} = t^3$. True

Boost your grade at mathzone.com!
> Practice Problems
> NetTutor
> Self-Tests
> e-Professors
> Videos

Exercises

‹ Study Tips ›

- Keep track of your time for one entire week. Account for every half hour.
- You should be sleeping 50 to 60 hours per week and studying 1 to 2 hours for every credit hour you are taking. For a three-credit hour class you should be studying 3 to 6 hours per week.

Reading and Writing *After reading this section, write out the answers to these questions. Use complete sentences.*

1. How do you know if b is an nth root of a?
If $b^n = a$, then b is an nth root of a.

2. What is a principal root?
The principal root is the positive even root of a positive number.

3. What is the difference between an even root and an odd root?
If $b^n = a$, then b is an even root provided n is even or an odd root provided n is odd.

4. What symbol is used to indicate an nth root?
The nth root of a is written as $\sqrt[n]{a}$.

5. What is the product rule for radicals?
The product rule for radicals says that $\sqrt[n]{a} \cdot \sqrt[n]{b} = \sqrt[n]{ab}$ provided all of these roots are real.

6. What is the quotient rule for radicals?
The quotient rule for radicals says that $\sqrt[n]{a}/\sqrt[n]{b} = \sqrt[n]{a/b}$ provided all of these roots are real.

For all of the exercises in this section, assume that all variables represent positive real numbers.

‹1› Roots

Find the indicated roots. See Example 1.

7. The square roots of 25 -5 and 5
8. The square roots of 36 -6 and 6
9. The cube root of 27 3
10. The cube root of -27 -3
11. The fourth roots of 81 -3 and 3
12. The fourth roots of 256 -4 and 4
13. The fifth root of -32 -2
14. The fifth root of 32 2

Translate each verbal expression into an algebraic expression using a radical symbol. See Example 2.

15. The principal square root of 8 $\sqrt{8}$
16. The principal square root of 13 $\sqrt{13}$
17. The cube root of -7 $\sqrt[3]{-7}$
18. The cube root of 14 $\sqrt[3]{14}$
19. The principal fourth root of 5 $\sqrt[4]{5}$
20. The fifth root of 18 $\sqrt[5]{18}$
21. The principal sixth root of 3 $\sqrt[6]{3}$
22. The principal fourth root of 4 $\sqrt[4]{4}$

Find each root. See Example 3.

23. $\sqrt{36}$ 6
24. $\sqrt{49}$ 7
25. $\sqrt[5]{32}$ 2
26. $\sqrt[4]{81}$ 3
27. $\sqrt[3]{1000}$ 10
VIDEO **28.** $\sqrt[4]{16}$ 2
29. $\sqrt[4]{-16}$ Not a real number
30. $\sqrt{-1}$ Not a real number
31. $\sqrt{0}$ 0
32. $\sqrt{1}$ 1
33. $\sqrt[3]{-1}$ -1
34. $\sqrt[3]{0}$ 0
35. $\sqrt[3]{1}$ 1
36. $\sqrt[4]{1}$ 1
VIDEO **37.** $\sqrt[4]{-81}$ Not a real number
38. $\sqrt[6]{-64}$ Not a real number
39. $\sqrt[6]{64}$ 2
40. $\sqrt[7]{128}$ 2
41. $\sqrt[5]{-32}$ -2
42. $\sqrt[3]{-125}$ -5
43. $-\sqrt{100}$ -10
44. $-\sqrt{36}$ -6
45. $\sqrt[4]{-50}$ Not a real number
46. $-\sqrt{-144}$ Not a real number

Simplify each expression.

47. $\sqrt{9 + 16}$ 5
48. $\sqrt{9} + \sqrt{16}$ 7
49. $\sqrt{9} \cdot \sqrt{4}$ 6
50. $\sqrt{9 \cdot 4}$ 6
51. $\dfrac{\sqrt{36}}{\sqrt{4}}$ 3
52. $\sqrt{\dfrac{36}{4}}$ 3
53. $\sqrt{64 + 36}$ 10
54. $\sqrt{64} + \sqrt{36}$ 14
55. $\sqrt{25 - 16}$ 3
56. $\sqrt{25} - \sqrt{16}$ 1

‹2› Roots and Variables

Find each root. See Example 4.

57. $\sqrt{m^2}$ m
58. $\sqrt{m^6}$ m^3
59. $\sqrt[5]{y^{15}}$ y^3
VIDEO **60.** $\sqrt[4]{m^8}$ m^2

61. $\sqrt[3]{y^{15}}$ y^5
62. $\sqrt{m^8}$ m^4
63. $\sqrt[3]{m^3}$ m
64. $\sqrt[4]{x^4}$ x
65. $\sqrt{3^6}$ 27
66. $\sqrt{4^2}$ 4
67. $\sqrt{2^{10}}$ 32
68. $\sqrt[3]{2^{99}}$ 2^{33}
69. $\sqrt[3]{5^9}$ 125
70. $\sqrt[3]{10^{18}}$ 1,000,000
71. $\sqrt{10^{20}}$ 10^{10}
72. $\sqrt{10^{18}}$ 10^9

‹3› Product Rule for Radicals

Use the product rule for radicals to simplify each expression. See Example 5.

73. $\sqrt{9y}$ $3\sqrt{y}$
74. $\sqrt{16n}$ $4\sqrt{n}$
75. $\sqrt{4a^2}$ $2a$
76. $\sqrt{36n^2}$ $6n$
77. $\sqrt{x^4y^2}$ x^2y
78. $\sqrt{w^6t^2}$ w^3t
VIDEO 79. $\sqrt{5m^{12}}$ $m^6\sqrt{5}$
80. $\sqrt{7z^{16}}$ $z^8\sqrt{7}$
81. $\sqrt[3]{8y}$ $2\sqrt[3]{y}$
82. $\sqrt[3]{27z^2}$ $3\sqrt[3]{z^2}$
83. $\sqrt[3]{-27w^3}$ $-3w$
84. $\sqrt[3]{-125m^6}$ $-5m^2$
85. $\sqrt[4]{16s}$ $2\sqrt[4]{s}$
86. $\sqrt[4]{81w}$ $3\sqrt[4]{w}$
87. $\sqrt[3]{-125a^9y^6}$ $-5a^3y^2$
88. $\sqrt[3]{-27z^3w^{15}}$ $-3zw^5$

‹4› Quotient Rule for Radicals

Simplify each radical. See Example 6.

89. $\sqrt{\dfrac{t}{4}}$ $\dfrac{\sqrt{t}}{2}$
90. $\sqrt{\dfrac{w}{36}}$ $\dfrac{\sqrt{w}}{6}$
91. $\sqrt{\dfrac{625}{16}}$ $\dfrac{25}{4}$
92. $\sqrt{\dfrac{9}{144}}$ $\dfrac{1}{4}$
93. $\sqrt[3]{\dfrac{t}{8}}$ $\dfrac{\sqrt[3]{t}}{2}$
VIDEO 94. $\sqrt[3]{\dfrac{a}{27}}$ $\dfrac{\sqrt[3]{a}}{3}$
95. $\sqrt[3]{\dfrac{-8x^6}{y^3}}$ $\dfrac{-2x^2}{y}$
96. $\sqrt[3]{\dfrac{-27y^{36}}{1000}}$ $\dfrac{-3y^{12}}{10}$
97. $\sqrt{\dfrac{4a^6}{9}}$ $\dfrac{2a^3}{3}$
98. $\sqrt{\dfrac{9a^2}{49b^4}}$ $\dfrac{3a}{7b^2}$
99. $\sqrt[4]{\dfrac{y}{16}}$ $\dfrac{\sqrt[4]{y}}{2}$
100. $\sqrt[4]{\dfrac{5w}{81}}$ $\dfrac{\sqrt[4]{5w}}{3}$

Miscellaneous

Use a calculator to find the approximate value of each expression to three decimal places.

101. $\sqrt{3} + \sqrt{5}$ 3.968
102. $\sqrt{7} - \sqrt{3}$ 0.914
103. $\dfrac{\sqrt{5} + \sqrt{2}}{\sqrt{3} - 4}$ -1.610
104. $\dfrac{\sqrt{2} - \sqrt{3}}{1 - \sqrt{5}}$ 0.257
105. $\sqrt{7.1^2 - 4(1.2)(3)}$ 6.001
106. $\sqrt{3^2 - 4(-2)(0.2)}$ 3.256
107. $\dfrac{-3 + \sqrt{3^2 - 4(1)(-2.9)}}{2}$ 0.769
108. $\dfrac{8 + \sqrt{(-8)^2 - 4(1.3)(-6.2)}}{2(1.3)}$ 6.850

Applications

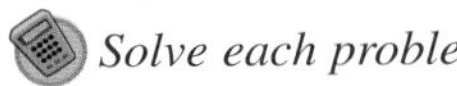

Solve each problem.

109. ***Diagonal of a square.*** The length of the diagonal of a square with sides of length s is given by

$$D(s) = s\sqrt{2}.$$

a) Find $D(3)$ and $D(\sqrt{2})$.
$3\sqrt{2}$, 2

b) Find the length of the diagonal to the nearest tenth of an inch for a square in which each side measures 5 inches.
7.1 inches

110. ***Radius of a circle.*** The radius of a circle with area A is given by

$$r(A) = \sqrt{\frac{A}{\pi}}.$$

a) Find $r(100)$ to the nearest tenth. Use your calculator's value for π. 5.6

b) Find the radius to the nearest hundredth of an inch for a circle whose area is 346 square inches. Use your calculator's value for π.
10.49 inches

111. ***Economic order quantity.*** When a part is needed for a space shuttle external fuel tank, Joseph Bursavich at Martin Marietta determines the most economic order quantity E by using the formula $E = \sqrt{\frac{2AS}{I}}$, where A is the quantity that the plant will use in one year, S is the cost of setup for making the part, and I is the cost of holding one unit in stock for one year.

Find the most economic order quantity if $S = \$5290$, $A = 20$, and $I = \$100$. 46

112. ***Diagonal of a box.*** The length of the diagonal D of the box shown in the figure can be found from the formula

$$D = \sqrt{L^2 + W^2 + H^2},$$

where L, W, and H represent the length, width, and height of the box, respectively. If the box has length 6 inches, width 4 inches, and height 3 inches, then what is the length of the diagonal to the nearest tenth of an inch? 7.8 in.

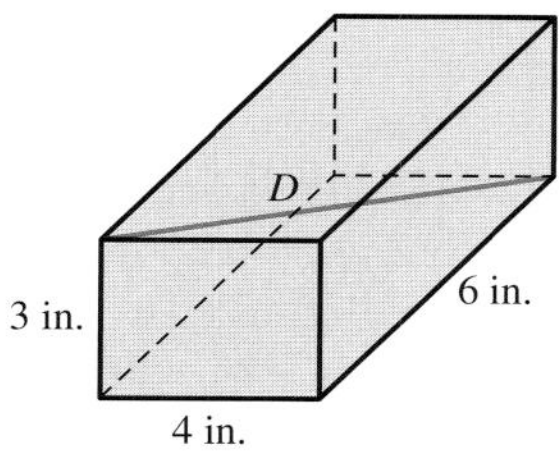

Figure for Exercise 112

113. ***Buena vista.*** The formula $V = 1.22\sqrt{A}$ gives the view in miles from horizon to horizon at an altitude of A feet (Delta Airlines brochure).

a) Use the formula to find the view to the nearest mile from an altitude of 35,000 feet.

b) Use the accompanying graph to estimate the altitude of an airplane from which the view is 100 miles.

a) 228 mi **b)** 7000 ft

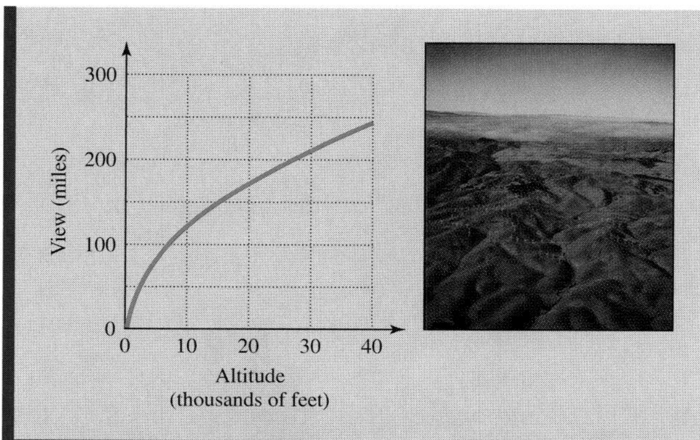

Figure for Exercise 113

114. ***Sailing speed.*** To find the maximum speed in knots (nautical miles per hour) for a sailboat, sailors use the formula $M = 1.3\sqrt{w}$, where w is the length of the waterline in feet.

a) If the length of the waterline for the sloop *John B.* is 38 feet, then what is the maximum speed to the nearest tenth of a knot for the *John B.?*

b) Use the accompanying graph to estimate the length of the waterline for a boat for which the maximum speed is 6 knots.

a) 8.0 knots **b)** 20 ft

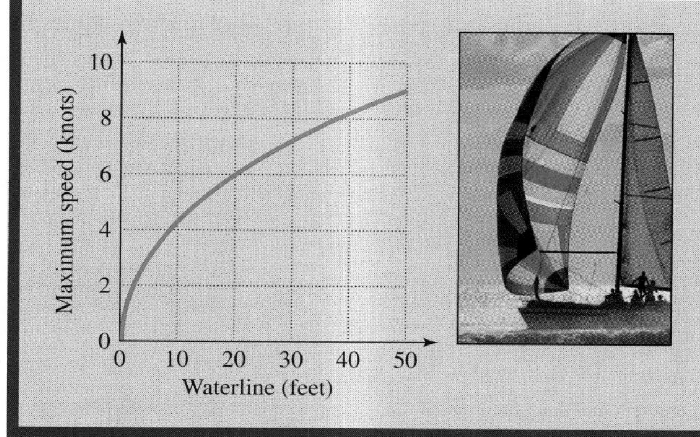

Figure for Exercise 114

Getting More Involved

115. ***Discussion***

Determine whether each equation is correct.

a) $\sqrt{(-5)^2} = -5$

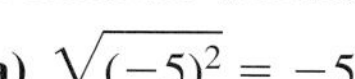

b) $\sqrt[3]{(-2)^3} = -2$

c) $\sqrt[4]{(-3)^4} = -3$

d) $\sqrt[5]{(-7)^5} = -7$

a) No **b)** Yes **c)** No **d)** Yes

116. ***Writing***

If x is a negative number and $\sqrt[n]{x^n} = x$, then what can you say about n? Explain your answer.

n is odd

Math *at Work* Just Average

In common usage the word "average" can mean many things. Average might mean "most common." (The average person works for a living.) Average can also mean "middle." When you average four test scores, you add them and divide by 4. In statistics, this average is actually called the *mean*. The mean is a single number that is used to measure or describe the entire set of test scores. It is an estimate of the "middle" of the scores. There are several other precisely-defined terms in statistics that also are measures of the middle of a set of scores.

The second most popular measure of the center (after the mean) is the *median*. The median is a number that separates the data into two equal parts. Half of the scores are above the median and half below. The median price of a new house in 2006 was \$195,200, whereas the mean was \$242,500. So half of the new houses sold for less than \$195,200 and half sold for more. The mean of \$242,500 is higher than the median due to some very expensive houses.

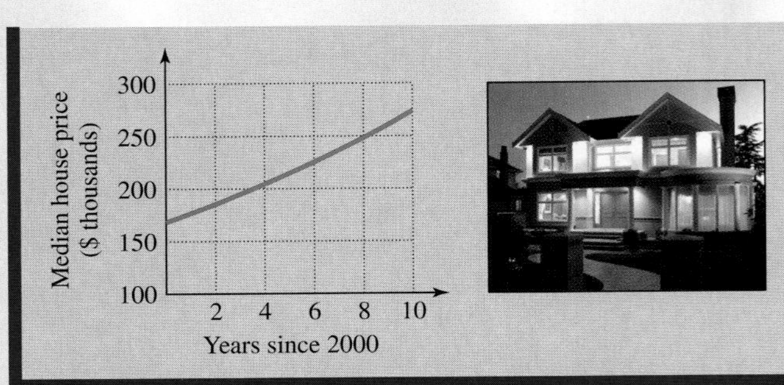

Less popular measures of the middle are the *geometric mean*, the *harmonic mean*, and the *quadratic mean*. The geometric mean is the nth root of the product of the n scores. The harmonic mean is n divided by the sum of the reciprocals of the n scores. For the quadratic mean, we find the sum of the squares of the scores, divide by n, and then take the square root. The test scores 45, 64, 78, and 99 have a mean of 71.5, a geometric mean of 68.7, a harmonic mean of 65.8, and a quadratic mean of 74.2.

So what does average really mean?

8.2 Simplifying Square Roots

In This Section

⟨1⟩ Using the Product Rule for Radicals
⟨2⟩ Rationalizing the Denominator
⟨3⟩ Simplified Form of a Square Root

In Section 8.1, you learned to simplify some radical expressions using the product rule. In this section, you will learn three basic rules to follow for writing expressions involving square roots in simplest form. These rules can be extended to radicals with index greater than 2, but we will not do that in this text.

⟨1⟩ Using the Product Rule for Radicals

We can use the product rule to simplify square roots of certain numbers. For example,

$$\begin{aligned} \sqrt{45} &= \sqrt{9 \cdot 5} && \text{Factor 45 as } 9 \cdot 5. \\ &= \sqrt{9} \cdot \sqrt{5} && \text{Product rule for radicals} \\ &= 3\sqrt{5} && \sqrt{9} = 3 \end{aligned}$$

Because 45 is not a perfect square, we cannot write $\sqrt{45}$ without the radical symbol. However, $3\sqrt{5}$ is considered a simpler expression that represents the exact value of $\sqrt{45}$. When simplifying square roots, we can factor the perfect squares out of the radical and replace them with their square roots. Look for the factors

$$4, \quad 9, \quad 16, \quad 25, \quad 36, \quad 49, \quad \text{and so on.}$$

⟨ Teaching Tip ⟩

Have students start this section with making their own list of perfect squares.

EXAMPLE 1

Simplifying radicals using the product rule for radicals

Simplify.

a) $\sqrt{12}$ **b)** $\sqrt{50}$ **c)** $\sqrt{72}$

‹ **Calculator Close-Up** ›

You can use a calculator to see that $\sqrt{12}$ and $2\sqrt{3}$ agree for the first 10 digits (out of infinitely many). Having the same first 10 digits does not make $\sqrt{12} = 2\sqrt{3}$. The product rule for radicals guarantees that they are equal.

```
√(12)
        3.464101615
2√(3)
        3.464101615
```

Solution

a) Because $12 = 4 \cdot 3$, we can use the product rule to write

$$\sqrt{12} = \sqrt{4} \cdot \sqrt{3} = 2\sqrt{3}.$$

b) $\sqrt{50} = \sqrt{25} \cdot \sqrt{2} = 5\sqrt{2}$

c) Note that 4, 9, and 36 are perfect squares and are factors of 72. In factoring out a perfect square, it is most efficient to use the largest perfect square:

$$\sqrt{72} = \sqrt{36} \cdot \sqrt{2} = 6\sqrt{2}$$

If we had factored out 9, we could still get the correct answer as follows:

$$\sqrt{72} = \sqrt{9} \cdot \sqrt{8} = 3 \cdot \sqrt{8} = 3 \cdot \sqrt{4} \cdot \sqrt{2} = 3 \cdot 2\sqrt{2} = 6\sqrt{2}$$

Now do Exercises 7–18

‹2› Rationalizing the Denominator

Radicals such as $\sqrt{2}$, $\sqrt{3}$, and $\sqrt{5}$ are irrational numbers. So a fraction such as $\frac{3}{\sqrt{5}}$ has an irrational denominator. Because fractions with rational denominators are considered simpler than fractions with irrational denominators, we usually convert fractions with irrational denominators to equivalent ones with rational denominators. That is, we **rationalize the denominator.**

EXAMPLE 2

Rationalizing denominators

Simplify each expression by rationalizing its denominator.

a) $\dfrac{3}{\sqrt{5}}$ **b)** $\dfrac{\sqrt{3}}{\sqrt{7}}$

‹ **Teaching Tip** ›

Students often realize for the first time that $\sqrt{5} \cdot \sqrt{5} = 5$ (skipping $\sqrt{25}$) when they rationalize denominators.

Solution

a) Because $\sqrt{5} \cdot \sqrt{5} = 5$, we multiply numerator and denominator by $\sqrt{5}$:

$$\frac{3}{\sqrt{5}} = \frac{3 \cdot \sqrt{5}}{\sqrt{5} \cdot \sqrt{5}} \quad \text{Multiply numerator and denominator by } \sqrt{5}.$$

$$= \frac{3\sqrt{5}}{5} \quad \sqrt{5} \cdot \sqrt{5} = 5$$

b) Because $\sqrt{7} \cdot \sqrt{7} = 7$, multiply the numerator and denominator by $\sqrt{7}$:

$$\frac{\sqrt{3}}{\sqrt{7}} = \frac{\sqrt{3} \cdot \sqrt{7}}{\sqrt{7} \cdot \sqrt{7}} \quad \text{Multiply numerator and denominator by } \sqrt{7}.$$

$$= \frac{\sqrt{21}}{7} \quad \text{Product rule for radicals}$$

Now do Exercises 19–30

⟨3⟩ Simplified Form of a Square Root

When we simplify any expression, we try to write a "simpler" expression that is equivalent to the original. However, one person's idea of simpler is sometimes different from another person's. For a square root the expression must satisfy three conditions to be in simplified form. These three conditions provide specific rules to follow for simplifying square roots.

Simplified Form for Square Roots

An expression involving a square root is in **simplified form** if it has

1. *no* perfect-square factors inside the radical,
2. *no* fractions inside the radical, and
3. *no* radicals in the denominator.

Because a decimal is a form of a fraction, a simplified square root should not contain any decimal numbers. Also, a simplified expression should use the fewest number of radicals possible. So we write $\sqrt{6}$ rather than $\sqrt{2} \cdot \sqrt{3}$ even though both $\sqrt{2}$ and $\sqrt{3}$ are both in simplified form.

EXAMPLE 3

Simplified form for square roots

Write each radical expression in simplified form.

a) $\sqrt{300}$ **b)** $\sqrt{\frac{2}{5}}$ **c)** $\frac{\sqrt{10}}{\sqrt{6}}$

Solution

a) We must remove the perfect square factor of 100 from inside the radical:

$$\sqrt{300} = \sqrt{100 \cdot 3} = \sqrt{100} \cdot \sqrt{3} = 10\sqrt{3}$$

b) We first use the quotient rule to remove the fraction $\frac{2}{5}$ from inside the radical:

$$\sqrt{\frac{2}{5}} = \frac{\sqrt{2}}{\sqrt{5}} \quad \text{Quotient rule for radicals}$$

$$= \frac{\sqrt{2} \cdot \sqrt{5}}{\sqrt{5} \cdot \sqrt{5}} \quad \text{Rationalize the denominator.}$$

$$= \frac{\sqrt{10}}{5} \quad \text{Product rule for radicals}$$

c) The numerator and denominator have a common factor of $\sqrt{2}$:

$$\frac{\sqrt{10}}{\sqrt{6}} = \frac{\sqrt{2} \cdot \sqrt{5}}{\sqrt{2} \cdot \sqrt{3}} \quad \text{Product rule for radicals}$$

$$= \frac{\sqrt{5}}{\sqrt{3}} \quad \text{Reduce.}$$

$$= \frac{\sqrt{5} \cdot \sqrt{3}}{\sqrt{3} \cdot \sqrt{3}} \quad \text{Rationalize the denominator.}$$

$$= \frac{\sqrt{15}}{3} \quad \text{Product rule for radicals}$$

⟨ Calculator Close-Up ⟩

Using a calculator to check simplification problems will help you to understand the concepts.

```
√(10)/√(6)
        1.290994449
√(15)/3
        1.290994449
```

Note that we could have simplified $\frac{\sqrt{10}}{\sqrt{6}}$ by first using the quotient rule to get $\frac{\sqrt{10}}{\sqrt{6}} = \sqrt{\frac{10}{6}}$ and then reducing $\frac{10}{6}$. Another way to simplify $\frac{\sqrt{10}}{\sqrt{6}}$ is to first multiply the numerator and denominator by $\sqrt{6}$. You should try these alternatives. Of course, the simplified form is $\frac{\sqrt{15}}{3}$ by any method.

Now do Exercises 31–44

In Example 4, we simplify some expressions involving variables. Remember that *any exponential expression with an even exponent is a perfect square.*

EXAMPLE 4

Radicals containing variables

Simplify each expression. All variables represent nonnegative real numbers.

a) $\sqrt{x^3}$ **b)** $\sqrt{8a^9}$ **c)** $\sqrt{18a^4b^7}$

‹ Teaching Tip ›

Have students make their own list of powers of x that are perfect squares ($x^2, x^4, x^6, \ldots$).

Solution

a) $\sqrt{x^3} = \sqrt{x^2 \cdot x}$ The largest perfect square factor of x^3 is x^2.

$= \sqrt{x^2} \cdot \sqrt{x}$ Product rule for radicals

$= x\sqrt{x}$ For any nonnegative x, $\sqrt{x^2} = x$.

b) $\sqrt{8a^9} = \sqrt{4a^8} \cdot \sqrt{2a}$ The largest perfect square factor of $8a^9$ is $4a^8$.

$= 2a^4\sqrt{2a}$ $\sqrt{4a^8} = 2a^4$

c) $\sqrt{18a^4b^7} = \sqrt{9a^4b^6} \cdot \sqrt{2b}$ Factor out the perfect squares.

$= 3a^2b^3\sqrt{2b}$ $\sqrt{9a^4b^6} = 3a^2b^3$

Now do Exercises 45–56

If square roots of variables appear in the denominator, then we rationalize the denominator.

EXAMPLE 5

Radicals containing variables

Simplify each expression. All variables represent positive real numbers.

a) $\frac{5}{\sqrt{a}}$ **b)** $\sqrt{\frac{a}{b}}$ **c)** $\frac{\sqrt{2}}{\sqrt{6a}}$

‹ Helpful Hint ›

If you are going to compute the value of a radical expression with a calculator, it doesn't matter if the denominator is rational. However, rationalizing the denominator provides another opportunity to practice building up the denominator of a fraction and multiplying radicals.

Solution

a) $\frac{5}{\sqrt{a}} = \frac{5 \cdot \sqrt{a}}{\sqrt{a} \cdot \sqrt{a}}$ Multiply numerator and denominator by $\sqrt{a}$.

$= \frac{5\sqrt{a}}{a}$ $\sqrt{a} \cdot \sqrt{a} = a$

b) $\sqrt{\frac{a}{b}} = \frac{\sqrt{a}}{\sqrt{b}}$ Quotient rule for radicals

$= \frac{\sqrt{a} \cdot \sqrt{b}}{\sqrt{b} \cdot \sqrt{b}}$ Rationalize the denominator.

$= \frac{\sqrt{ab}}{b}$ Product rule for radicals

c) $\frac{\sqrt{2}}{\sqrt{6a}} = \frac{\sqrt{2} \cdot \sqrt{6a}}{\sqrt{6a} \cdot \sqrt{6a}}$ Rationalize the denominator.

$= \frac{\sqrt{12a}}{6a}$ Product rule for radicals

$= \frac{\sqrt{4} \cdot \sqrt{3a}}{6a}$ Factor out the perfect square.

$= \frac{2\sqrt{3a}}{6a}$ $\sqrt{4} = 2$

$= \frac{2\sqrt{3a}}{2 \cdot 3a}$ Factor the denominator.

$= \frac{\sqrt{3a}}{3a}$ Divide out the common factor 2.

Now do Exercises 57–68

CAUTION Do not attempt to reduce an expression like the one in Example 5(c):

$$\frac{\sqrt{3a}}{3a}$$

You cannot divide out common factors when one is inside a radical.

Warm-Ups ▼

True or false? Explain your answer.

1. $\sqrt{20} = 2\sqrt{5}$ True

2. $\sqrt{18} = 9\sqrt{2}$ False

3. $\frac{1}{\sqrt{3}} = \frac{\sqrt{3}}{3}$ True

4. $\frac{9}{4} = \frac{3}{2}$ False

5. $\sqrt{a^3} = a\sqrt{a}$ for any positive value of a. True

6. $\sqrt{a^9} = a^3$ for any positive value of a. False

7. $\sqrt{y^{17}} = y^8\sqrt{y}$ for any positive value of y. True

8. $\frac{\sqrt{6}}{2} = \sqrt{3}$ False

9. $\sqrt{4} = \sqrt{2}$ False

10. $\sqrt{283} = 17$ False

Exercises 8.2

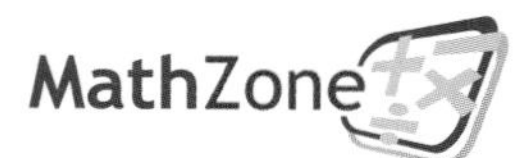

Boost your grade at mathzone.com!
- > Practice Problems
- > NetTutor
- > Self-Tests
- > e-Professors
- > Videos

‹ Study Tips ›

- Success in school depends on effective time management, which is all about goals.
- Write down your long-term, short-term, and daily goals. Assess them, develop methods for meeting them, and reward yourself when you do.

Reading and Writing *After reading this section, write out the answers to these questions. Use complete sentences.*

1. How do we simplify a square root with the product rule? We use the product rule to factor out a perfect square from inside a square root.
2. Which integers are perfect squares? The perfect squares are 1, 4, 9, 16, 25, and so on.
3. What does it mean to rationalize a denominator? To rationalize a denominator means to rewrite the expression so that the denominator is a rational number.
4. What is simplified form for a square root? A square root in simplified form has no perfect squares or fractions inside the radical and no radicals in the denominator.
5. How do you simplify a square root that contains a variable? To simplify square roots containing variables use the same techniques as we use on square roots of numbers.
6. How can you tell if an exponential expression is a perfect square? Any even power of a variable is a perfect square.

Assume that all variables in the exercises represent positive real numbers.

‹1› Using the Product Rule for Radicals

Simplify each radical. See Example 1.

7. $\sqrt{8}$ $2\sqrt{2}$ **8.** $\sqrt{20}$ $2\sqrt{5}$ **9.** $\sqrt{24}$ $2\sqrt{6}$

10. $\sqrt{75}$ $5\sqrt{3}$ **11.** $\sqrt{28}$ $2\sqrt{7}$ **12.** $\sqrt{40}$ $2\sqrt{10}$

13. $\sqrt{90}$ $3\sqrt{10}$ **14.** $\sqrt{200}$ $10\sqrt{2}$ **15.** $\sqrt{500}$ $10\sqrt{5}$

VIDEO **16.** $\sqrt{98}$ $7\sqrt{2}$ **17.** $\sqrt{150}$ $5\sqrt{6}$ **18.** $\sqrt{120}$ $2\sqrt{30}$

‹2› Rationalizing the Denominator

Simplify each expression by rationalizing the denominator. See Example 2.

19. $\dfrac{1}{\sqrt{5}}$ $\dfrac{\sqrt{5}}{5}$ **20.** $\dfrac{1}{\sqrt{6}}$ $\dfrac{\sqrt{6}}{6}$ **21.** $\dfrac{3}{\sqrt{2}}$ $\dfrac{3\sqrt{2}}{2}$

22. $\dfrac{4}{\sqrt{3}}$ $\dfrac{4\sqrt{3}}{3}$ VIDEO **23.** $\dfrac{\sqrt{3}}{\sqrt{2}}$ $\dfrac{\sqrt{6}}{2}$ **24.** $\dfrac{\sqrt{7}}{\sqrt{6}}$ $\dfrac{\sqrt{42}}{6}$

25. $\dfrac{-3}{\sqrt{10}}$ $\dfrac{-3\sqrt{10}}{10}$ **26.** $\dfrac{-4}{\sqrt{5}}$ $-\dfrac{4\sqrt{5}}{5}$ **27.** $\dfrac{-10}{\sqrt{17}}$ $\dfrac{-10\sqrt{17}}{17}$

28. $\dfrac{-3}{\sqrt{19}}$ $-\dfrac{3\sqrt{19}}{19}$ **29.** $\dfrac{\sqrt{11}}{\sqrt{7}}$ $\dfrac{\sqrt{77}}{7}$ **30.** $\dfrac{\sqrt{10}}{\sqrt{3}}$ $\dfrac{\sqrt{30}}{3}$

‹3› Simplified Form of a Square Root

Write each radical expression in simplified form. See Example 3.

31. $\sqrt{63}$ $3\sqrt{7}$ **32.** $\sqrt{48}$ $4\sqrt{3}$ **33.** $\dfrac{3}{\sqrt{2}}$ $\dfrac{3\sqrt{2}}{2}$

34. $\dfrac{2}{\sqrt{5}}$ $\dfrac{2\sqrt{5}}{5}$ **35.** $\sqrt{\dfrac{3}{2}}$ $\dfrac{\sqrt{6}}{2}$ **36.** $\sqrt{\dfrac{3}{5}}$ $\dfrac{\sqrt{15}}{5}$

37. $\sqrt{\dfrac{5}{8}}$ $\dfrac{\sqrt{10}}{4}$ **38.** $\sqrt{\dfrac{5}{18}}$ $\dfrac{\sqrt{10}}{6}$ **39.** $\dfrac{\sqrt{6}}{\sqrt{10}}$ $\dfrac{\sqrt{15}}{5}$

40. $\dfrac{\sqrt{12}}{\sqrt{20}}$ $\dfrac{\sqrt{15}}{5}$ **41.** $\dfrac{\sqrt{75}}{\sqrt{3}}$ 5 **42.** $\dfrac{\sqrt{45}}{\sqrt{5}}$ 3

43. $\dfrac{\sqrt{15}}{\sqrt{10}}$ $\dfrac{\sqrt{6}}{2}$ **44.** $\dfrac{\sqrt{30}}{\sqrt{21}}$ $\dfrac{\sqrt{70}}{7}$

Simplify each expression. See Example 4.

45. $\sqrt{a^8}$ a^4 **46.** $\sqrt{y^{10}}$ y^5 **47.** $\sqrt{a^9}$ $a^4\sqrt{a}$

48. $\sqrt{t^{11}}$ $t^5\sqrt{t}$ **49.** $\sqrt{8a^6}$ $2a^3\sqrt{2}$ **50.** $\sqrt{18w^9}$ $3w^4\sqrt{2w}$

51. $\sqrt{20a^4b^9}$ $2a^2b^4\sqrt{5b}$ VIDEO **52.** $\sqrt{12x^2y^3}$ $2xy\sqrt{3y}$ **53.** $\sqrt{27x^3y^3}$ $3xy\sqrt{3xy}$

54. $\sqrt{45x^5y^3}$ $3x^2y\sqrt{5xy}$ **55.** $\sqrt{27a^3b^8c^2}$ $3ab^4c\sqrt{3a}$ **56.** $\sqrt{125x^3y^9z^4}$ $5xy^4z^2\sqrt{5xy}$

Simplify each expression. See Example 5.

57. $\dfrac{1}{\sqrt{x}}$ $\dfrac{\sqrt{x}}{x}$ **58.** $\dfrac{1}{\sqrt{2x}}$ $\dfrac{\sqrt{2x}}{2x}$ **59.** $\dfrac{\sqrt{2}}{\sqrt{3a}}$ $\dfrac{\sqrt{6a}}{3a}$

60. $\dfrac{\sqrt{5}}{\sqrt{2b}}$ $\dfrac{\sqrt{10b}}{2b}$ **61.** $\dfrac{\sqrt{3}}{\sqrt{15y}}$ $\dfrac{\sqrt{5y}}{5y}$ **62.** $\dfrac{\sqrt{5}}{\sqrt{10x}}$ $\dfrac{\sqrt{2x}}{2x}$

63. $\sqrt{\dfrac{3x}{2y}}$ $\dfrac{\sqrt{6xy}}{2y}$ VIDEO **64.** $\sqrt{\dfrac{6}{5w}}$ $\dfrac{\sqrt{30w}}{5w}$ **65.** $\sqrt{\dfrac{10y}{15x}}$ $\dfrac{\sqrt{6xy}}{3x}$

66. $\sqrt{\dfrac{6x}{4y}}$ $\dfrac{\sqrt{6xy}}{2y}$

67. $\sqrt{\dfrac{8x^3}{y}}$ $\dfrac{2x\sqrt{2xy}}{y}$

68. $\sqrt{\dfrac{8s^5}{t}}$ $\dfrac{2s^2\sqrt{2st}}{t}$

Miscellaneous

Simplify each expression.

69. $\sqrt{8a}$ $2\sqrt{2a}$

70. $\sqrt{12b}$ $2\sqrt{3b}$

71. $\sqrt{w^4}$ w^2

72. $\sqrt{m^6}$ m^3

73. $\sqrt{z^5}$ $z^2\sqrt{z}$

74. $\sqrt{p^9}$ $p^4\sqrt{p}$

75. $\sqrt{\dfrac{p}{3}}$ $\dfrac{\sqrt{3p}}{3}$

76. $\sqrt{\dfrac{a}{7}}$ $\dfrac{\sqrt{7a}}{7}$

77. $\sqrt{\dfrac{b}{a}}$ $\dfrac{\sqrt{ab}}{a}$

78. $\sqrt{\dfrac{w}{2z}}$ $\dfrac{\sqrt{2zw}}{2z}$

79. $\dfrac{ab}{\sqrt{a}}$ $b\sqrt{a}$

80. $\dfrac{wx^2}{\sqrt{wx}}$ $x\sqrt{wx}$

81. $\sqrt{80x^3}$ $4x\sqrt{5x}$

82. $\sqrt{90y^{80}}$ $3y^{40}\sqrt{10}$

83. $\sqrt{9y^9x^{15}}$ $3y^4x^7\sqrt{yx}$

84. $\sqrt{48x^2y^7}$ $4xy^3\sqrt{3y}$

85. $\dfrac{20x^6}{\sqrt{5x^5}}$ $4x^3\sqrt{5x}$

86. $\dfrac{7x^7y}{\sqrt{7x^9}}$ $x^2y\sqrt{7x}$

87. $\dfrac{-22p^2}{p\sqrt{6pq}}$ $\dfrac{-11\sqrt{6pq}}{3q}$

VIDEO **88.** $\dfrac{-30t^5}{t^2\sqrt{3t}}$ $-10t^2\sqrt{3t}$

89. $\dfrac{a^3b^7\sqrt{a^2b^3c^4}}{\sqrt{abc}}$ $a^3b^8c\sqrt{ac}$

90. $\dfrac{3n^4b^5\sqrt{n^2b^2c^7}}{\sqrt{nbc}}$ $3n^4b^5c^3\sqrt{nb}$

91. $\dfrac{\sqrt{4xy^2}}{x^9y^3\sqrt{6xy^3}}$ $\dfrac{\sqrt{6y}}{3x^9y^4}$

92. $\dfrac{\sqrt{8m^3n^2}}{m^3n^2\sqrt{6mn^3}}$ $\dfrac{2\sqrt{3n}}{3m^2n^3}$

Use a calculator to evaluate each expression.

93. $\dfrac{1}{\sqrt{2}} - \dfrac{\sqrt{2}}{2}$ 0

94. $\dfrac{\sqrt{2}}{\sqrt{3}} - \dfrac{\sqrt{6}}{3}$ 0

95. $\dfrac{\sqrt{6}}{\sqrt{2}} - \sqrt{3}$ 0

96. $2 - \dfrac{\sqrt{20}}{\sqrt{5}}$ 0

Applications

Solve each problem.

97. ***Economic order quantity.*** The formula for economic order quantity

$$E = \sqrt{\frac{2AS}{I}}$$

was used in Exercise 111 of Section 8.1.

a) Express the right-hand side in simplified form. $E = \dfrac{\sqrt{2AIS}}{I}$

b) Find E to the nearest tenth when $A = 23$, $S = \$4566$, and $I = \$80$. 51.2

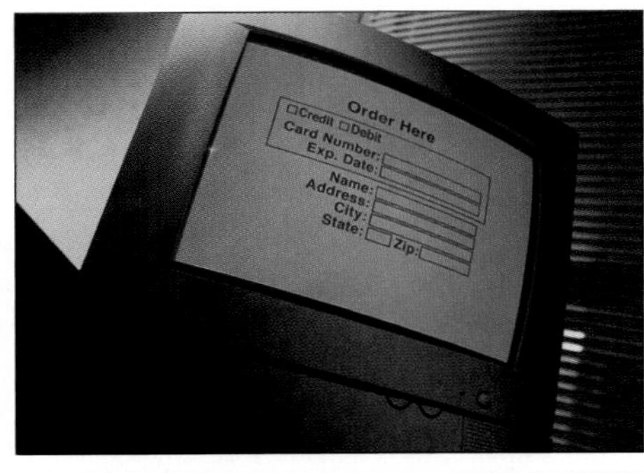

Photo for Exercise 97

98. ***Landing speed.*** Aircraft design engineers determine the proper landing speed V (in ft/sec) by using the formula

$$V = \sqrt{\frac{841L}{CS}},$$

where L is the gross weight of the aircraft in pounds, C is the coefficient of lift, and S is the wing surface area in square feet.

a) Express the right-hand side in simplified form. $V = \dfrac{29\sqrt{LCS}}{CS}$

b) Find V to the nearest tenth when $L = 8600$ pounds, $C = 2.81$, and $S = 200$ square feet. 113.4 ft/sec

Photo for Exercise 98

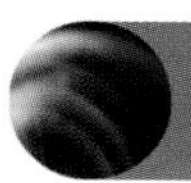

8.3 Operations with Radicals

In This Section

In this section, you will learn how to perform the basic operations of arithmetic with radical expressions.

⟨1⟩ Adding and Subtracting Radicals

Like radicals are radical expressions that have the same index and the same radicand. For example, $2\sqrt{3}$ and $5\sqrt{3}$ are like radicals. They are both square roots and both have the same radicand, 3. When you studied like terms, you learned that

$$2x + 5x = 7x$$

is true for any value of x. If $x = \sqrt{3}$, then

$$2\sqrt{3} + 5\sqrt{3} = 7\sqrt{3}.$$

So like radicals can be combined just as we combine like terms. We can add or subtract them as long as they have the *same index and the same radicand.*

EXAMPLE 1

Combining like radicals

Simplify the following expressions by combining like radicals. Assume that the variables represent nonnegative numbers.

a) $2\sqrt{5} + 7\sqrt{5}$

b) $3\sqrt[3]{2} - 9\sqrt[3]{2}$

c) $\sqrt{2} - 5\sqrt{a} + 4\sqrt{2} - 3\sqrt{a}$

Solution

a) $2\sqrt{5} + 7\sqrt{5} = 9\sqrt{5}$

b) $3\sqrt[3]{2} - 9\sqrt[3]{2} = -6\sqrt[3]{2}$

c) $\sqrt{2} - 5\sqrt{a} + 4\sqrt{2} - 3\sqrt{a} = \sqrt{2} + 4\sqrt{2} - 5\sqrt{a} - 3\sqrt{a}$

$= 5\sqrt{2} - 8\sqrt{a}$ Combine like radicals only.

Now do Exercises 7–18

⟨ Calculator Close-Up ⟩

A calculator can show you when a rule is applied incorrectly. For example, we cannot say that $\sqrt{2} + \sqrt{5}$ is equal to $\sqrt{7}$.

```
√(2)+√(5)
        3.65028154
√(7)
       2.645751311
```

CAUTION We cannot combine the terms in the expressions

$$\sqrt{2} + \sqrt{5}, \quad \sqrt[3]{x} - \sqrt{x}, \quad \text{or} \quad 3\sqrt{2} + \sqrt[4]{6}$$

because the radicands are unequal in the first expression, the indices are unequal in the second, and both the radicands and the indices are unequal in the third.

In Example 2, we simplify the radicals before adding or subtracting.

EXAMPLE 2

Simplifying radicals before combining

Simplify. Assume that all variables represent nonnegative real numbers.

a) $\sqrt{12} + \sqrt{75}$ **b)** $\sqrt{8x^3} + x\sqrt{18x}$ **c)** $\dfrac{4}{\sqrt{2}} - \dfrac{\sqrt{3}}{\sqrt{6}}$

‹ Teaching Tip ›

Part (c) can be difficult for students because it combines radicals and subtraction of fractions with different denominators. You might need to work more examples of this.

Solution

a)
$$\sqrt{12} + \sqrt{75} = \sqrt{4} \cdot \sqrt{3} + \sqrt{25} \cdot \sqrt{3} \quad \text{Product rule for radicals}$$
$$= 2\sqrt{3} + 5\sqrt{3} \quad \text{Simplify.}$$
$$= 7\sqrt{3} \quad \text{Combine like radicals.}$$

b)
$$\sqrt{8x^3} + x\sqrt{18x} = \sqrt{4x^2} \cdot \sqrt{2x} + x\sqrt{9} \cdot \sqrt{2x} \quad \text{Product rule for radicals}$$
$$= 2x\sqrt{2x} + 3x\sqrt{2x} \quad \text{Simplify.}$$
$$= 5x\sqrt{2x} \quad \text{Combine like radicals.}$$

c)
$$\frac{4}{\sqrt{2}} - \frac{\sqrt{3}}{\sqrt{6}} = \frac{4 \cdot \sqrt{2}}{\sqrt{2} \cdot \sqrt{2}} - \frac{\sqrt{3} \cdot \sqrt{6}}{\sqrt{6} \cdot \sqrt{6}} \quad \text{Rationalize the denominators.}$$
$$= \frac{4\sqrt{2}}{2} - \frac{\sqrt{18}}{6} \quad \text{Simplify.}$$
$$= \frac{4\sqrt{2}}{2} - \frac{3\sqrt{2}}{6} \quad \sqrt{18} = \sqrt{9} \cdot \sqrt{2} = 3\sqrt{2}$$
$$= \frac{4\sqrt{2}}{2} - \frac{\sqrt{2}}{2} \quad \text{Reduce } \frac{3\sqrt{2}}{6} \text{ to } \frac{\sqrt{2}}{2}.$$
$$= \frac{3\sqrt{2}}{2} \quad 4\sqrt{2} - \sqrt{2} = 3\sqrt{2}$$

Now do Exercises 19–32

‹2› Multiplying Radicals

We have been using the product rule for radicals

$$\sqrt[n]{ab} = \sqrt[n]{a} \cdot \sqrt[n]{b}$$

to express a root of a product as a product of the roots of the factors. When we rationalized denominators in Section 8.2, we used the product rule to multiply radicals. We will now study multiplication of radicals in more detail.

EXAMPLE 3

Multiplying radical expressions

Multiply and simplify. Assume that variables represent positive numbers.

a) $\sqrt{2} \cdot \sqrt{5}$

b) $2\sqrt{5} \cdot 3\sqrt{6}$

c) $\sqrt{2a^2} \cdot \sqrt{6a}$

d) $\sqrt[3]{4} \cdot \sqrt[3]{2}$

‹ Helpful Hint ›

Students often write

$$\sqrt{15} \cdot \sqrt{15} = \sqrt{225} = 15.$$

Although this is correct, you should get used to the idea that

$$\sqrt{15} \cdot \sqrt{15} = 15.$$

Because of the definition of square root, $\sqrt{a} \cdot \sqrt{a} = a$ for any positive number a.

Solution

a) $\sqrt{2} \cdot \sqrt{5} = \sqrt{2 \cdot 5}$ Product rule for radicals

$= \sqrt{10}$

b) $2\sqrt{5} \cdot 3\sqrt{6} = 2 \cdot 3 \cdot \sqrt{5} \cdot \sqrt{6}$

$= 6\sqrt{30}$ Product rule for radicals

c) $\sqrt{2a^2} \cdot \sqrt{6a} = \sqrt{12a^3}$ Product rule for radicals

$= \sqrt{4a^2} \cdot \sqrt{3a}$ Factor out the perfect square.

$= 2a\sqrt{3a}$ Simplify.

d) $\sqrt[3]{4} \cdot \sqrt[3]{2} = \sqrt[3]{8}$ Product rule for radicals

$= 2$

Now do Exercises 33–44

In Example 4, we use the distributive property to multiply a radical and a sum of two radicals.

EXAMPLE 4

Using the distributive property with radicals

Find the product: $3\sqrt{3}(\sqrt{6} + \sqrt{2})$

Solution

$3\sqrt{3}(\sqrt{6} + \sqrt{2}) = 3\sqrt{3} \cdot \sqrt{6} + 3\sqrt{3} \cdot \sqrt{2}$ Distributive property

$= 3\sqrt{18} + 3\sqrt{6}$ Product rule for radicals

$= 3 \cdot 3\sqrt{2} + 3\sqrt{6}$ $\sqrt{18} = \sqrt{9} \cdot \sqrt{2} = 3\sqrt{2}$

$= 9\sqrt{2} + 3\sqrt{6}$

Now do Exercises 45–50

In Example 5, we use the FOIL method to find products of expressions involving radicals.

EXAMPLE 5

Using FOIL to multiply radicals

Multiply and simplify.

a) $(\sqrt{3} + 5)(\sqrt{3} - 2)$ **b)** $(\sqrt{5} - 2)(\sqrt{5} + 2)$

c) $(2\sqrt{3} + \sqrt{5})(\sqrt{3} - \sqrt{5})$

Solution

a) $(\sqrt{3} + 5)(\sqrt{3} - 2) = \overset{\text{F}}{3} - \overset{\text{O}}{2\sqrt{3}} + \overset{\text{I}}{5\sqrt{3}} - \overset{\text{L}}{10}$

$= 3\sqrt{3} - 7$ Add the like terms.

b) The product $(\sqrt{5} - 2)(\sqrt{5} + 2)$ is the product of a sum and a difference. Recall that $(a - b)(a + b) = a^2 - b^2$.

$$\begin{aligned}(\sqrt{5} - 2)(\sqrt{5} + 2) &= (\sqrt{5})^2 - 2^2 \\ &= 5 - 4 \\ &= 1\end{aligned}$$

c)
$$\begin{aligned}(2\sqrt{3} + \sqrt{5})(\sqrt{3} - \sqrt{5}) &= \overset{\text{F}}{2\sqrt{3}\sqrt{3}} - \overset{\text{O}}{2\sqrt{3}\sqrt{5}} + \overset{\text{I}}{\sqrt{5}\sqrt{3}} - \overset{\text{L}}{\sqrt{5}\sqrt{5}} \\ &= 6 - 2\sqrt{15} + \sqrt{15} - 5 \\ &= 1 - \sqrt{15}\end{aligned}$$

Now do Exercises 51–62

⟨3⟩ Dividing Radicals

In Section 8.1 we used the quotient rule for radicals to write a square root of a quotient as a quotient of square roots. We can also use the quotient rule for radicals to divide radicals of the same index. For example,

$$\frac{\sqrt{10}}{\sqrt{2}} = \sqrt{\frac{10}{2}} = \sqrt{5}.$$

Division of radicals is simplest when the quotient of the radicands is a whole number, as it was in the example $\sqrt{10} \div \sqrt{2} = \sqrt{5}$. If the quotient of the radicands is not a whole number, then we divide by rationalizing the denominator, as shown in Example 6.

EXAMPLE 6

Dividing radicals

Divide and simplify.

a) $\sqrt{30} \div \sqrt{3}$ **b)** $(5\sqrt{2}) \div (2\sqrt{5})$ **c)** $(15\sqrt{6}) \div (3\sqrt{2})$

Solution

a) $\sqrt{30} \div \sqrt{3} = \dfrac{\sqrt{30}}{\sqrt{3}} = \sqrt{10}$

b) $(5\sqrt{2}) \div (2\sqrt{5}) = \dfrac{5\sqrt{2}}{2\sqrt{5}} = \dfrac{5\sqrt{2} \cdot \sqrt{5}}{2\sqrt{5} \cdot \sqrt{5}}$ Rationalize the denominator.

$= \dfrac{5\sqrt{10}}{2 \cdot 5}$ Product rule for radicals

$= \dfrac{\sqrt{10}}{2}$ Reduce.

Note that $\sqrt{10} \div 2 \neq \sqrt{5}$.

c) $(15\sqrt{6}) \div (3\sqrt{2}) = \dfrac{15\sqrt{6}}{3\sqrt{2}} = 5\sqrt{3}$ $\sqrt{6} \div \sqrt{2} = \sqrt{3}$

Now do Exercises 63–70

CAUTION You can use the quotient rule to divide roots of the same index only. For example,

$$\frac{\sqrt{14}}{\sqrt{2}} = \sqrt{7} \quad \text{but} \quad \frac{\sqrt{14}}{2} \neq \sqrt{7}.$$

In Example 7, we simplify expressions with radicals in the numerator and whole numbers in the denominator.

EXAMPLE 7

Simplifying radical expressions

Simplify.

a) $\dfrac{4 - \sqrt{20}}{4}$

b) $\dfrac{-6 + \sqrt{27}}{3}$

‹ Helpful Hint ›

The expressions in Example 7 are the types of expression that you must simplify when you learn the quadratic formula in Chapter 9.

Solution

a) $\dfrac{4 - \sqrt{20}}{4} = \dfrac{4 - 2\sqrt{5}}{4}$ $\quad \sqrt{20} = \sqrt{4} \cdot \sqrt{5} = 2\sqrt{5}$

$= \dfrac{\cancel{2}(2 - \sqrt{5})}{\cancel{2} \cdot 2}$ $\quad$ Factor out the GCF, 2.

$= \dfrac{2 - \sqrt{5}}{2}$ $\quad$ Reduce.

b) $\dfrac{-6 + \sqrt{27}}{3} = \dfrac{-6 + 3\sqrt{3}}{3} = \dfrac{\cancel{3}(-2 + \sqrt{3})}{\cancel{3}} = -2 + \sqrt{3}$

Now do Exercises 71–80

CAUTION In the expression $\frac{2 - \sqrt{5}}{2}$ you cannot divide out the remaining 2's because 2 is not a *factor* of the numerator.

In Example 5(b) we used the rule for the product of a sum and a difference to get $(\sqrt{5} - 2)(\sqrt{5} + 2) = 1$. If we apply the same rule to other products of this type, we also get a rational number as the result. For example,

$$(\sqrt{7} + \sqrt{2})(\sqrt{7} - \sqrt{2}) = 7 - 2 = 5.$$

Expressions such as $\sqrt{5} + 2$ and $\sqrt{5} - 2$ are called **conjugates** of each other. The conjugate of $\sqrt{7} + \sqrt{2}$ is $\sqrt{7} - \sqrt{2}$. We can use conjugates to simplify a radical expression that has a sum or a difference in its denominator.

EXAMPLE 8

Rationalizing the denominator using conjugates

Simplify each expression.

a) $\dfrac{\sqrt{3}}{\sqrt{7} - \sqrt{2}}$

b) $\dfrac{4}{6 + \sqrt{2}}$

Solution

a) $\dfrac{\sqrt{3}}{\sqrt{7} - \sqrt{2}} = \dfrac{\sqrt{3}(\sqrt{7} + \sqrt{2})}{(\sqrt{7} - \sqrt{2})(\sqrt{7} + \sqrt{2})}$ Multiply by $\sqrt{7} + \sqrt{2}$, the conjugate of $\sqrt{7} - \sqrt{2}$.

$= \dfrac{\sqrt{21} + \sqrt{6}}{7 - 2}$

$= \dfrac{\sqrt{21} + \sqrt{6}}{5}$

b) $\dfrac{4}{6 + \sqrt{2}} = \dfrac{4(6 - \sqrt{2})}{(6 + \sqrt{2})(6 - \sqrt{2})}$ Multiply by $6 - \sqrt{2}$, the conjugate of $6 + \sqrt{2}$.

$= \dfrac{24 - 4\sqrt{2}}{36 - 2}$

$= \dfrac{24 - 4\sqrt{2}}{34}$

$= \dfrac{\cancel{2}(12 - 2\sqrt{2})}{\cancel{2} \cdot 17} = \dfrac{12 - 2\sqrt{2}}{17}$

Now do Exercises 81–88

‹ Helpful Hint ›

The word *conjugate* is used in many contexts in mathematics. According to the dictionary, conjugate means joined together, especially as in a pair.

Warm-Ups ▼

True or false? Explain your answer.

1. $\sqrt{9} + \sqrt{16} = \sqrt{25}$ False
2. $\dfrac{5}{\sqrt{5}} = \sqrt{5}$ True
3. $\sqrt{10} \div 2 = \sqrt{5}$ False
4. $3\sqrt{2} \cdot 3\sqrt{2} = 9\sqrt{2}$ False
5. $3\sqrt{5} \cdot 3\sqrt{2} = 9\sqrt{10}$ True
6. $\sqrt{5} + 3\sqrt{5} = 4\sqrt{10}$ False
7. $\dfrac{\sqrt{15}}{3} = \sqrt{5}$ False
8. $\sqrt{2} \div \sqrt{6} = \sqrt{3}$ False
9. $\dfrac{\sqrt{27}}{\sqrt{3}} = 3$ True
10. $(\sqrt{3} - 1)(\sqrt{3} + 1) = 2$ True

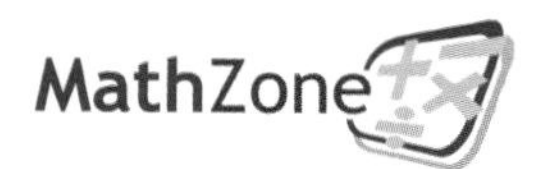

Boost your grade at mathzone.com!
> Practice Problems
> NetTutor
> Self-Tests
> e-Professors
> Videos

‹ Study Tips ›

- When you take notes, leave space. Go back later and fill in details and make corrections.
- You can even leave enough space to work another problem of the same type in your notes.

Reading and Writing *After reading this section, write out the answers to these questions. Use complete sentences.*

1. What are like radicals? Like radicals have the same index and same radicand.
2. How do we combine like radicals? We combine like radicals just like we combine like terms.
3. What operations can be performed with radicals? Radicals can be added, subtracted, multiplied, and divided.
4. What method can we use to multiply a sum of two square roots by a sum of two square roots? We use the FOIL method for multiplying sums of radicals.
5. What radical expressions are conjugates of each other? Radical expressions such as $\sqrt{a}+\sqrt{b}$ and $\sqrt{a}-\sqrt{b}$ are conjugates.
6. How do you rationalize a denominator that contains a sum of two radicals? Rationalizing a denominator that contains a sum can be done by multiplying the numerator and denominator by the conjugate of the denominator.

Assume that all variables in these exercises represent only positive real numbers.

‹1› Adding and Subtracting Radicals

Simplify each expression by combining like radicals. See Example 1.

7. $4\sqrt{5}+3\sqrt{5}$ $7\sqrt{5}$
8. $\sqrt{2}+\sqrt{2}$ $2\sqrt{2}$
9. $\sqrt[3]{2}+\sqrt[3]{2}$ $2\sqrt[3]{2}$
10. $4\sqrt[3]{6}-7\sqrt[3]{6}$ $-3\sqrt[3]{6}$
11. $3u\sqrt{11}+5u\sqrt{11}$ $8u\sqrt{11}$
12. $9m\sqrt{5}-12m\sqrt{5}$ $-3m\sqrt{5}$
13. $\sqrt{2}+\sqrt{3}-5\sqrt{2}+3\sqrt{3}$ $4\sqrt{3}-4\sqrt{2}$ (VIDEO)
14. $8\sqrt{6}-\sqrt{2}-3\sqrt{6}+5\sqrt{2}$ $5\sqrt{6}+4\sqrt{2}$
15. $3\sqrt{y}-\sqrt{x}-4\sqrt{y}-3\sqrt{x}$ $-4\sqrt{x}-\sqrt{y}$
16. $5\sqrt{7}-\sqrt{a}+3\sqrt{7}-5\sqrt{a}$ $8\sqrt{7}-6\sqrt{a}$
17. $3x\sqrt{y}-\sqrt{a}+2x\sqrt{y}+3\sqrt{a}$ $5x\sqrt{y}+2\sqrt{a}$
18. $a\sqrt{b}+5a\sqrt{b}-2\sqrt{a}+3\sqrt{a}$ $6a\sqrt{b}+\sqrt{a}$

Simplify each expression. See Example 2.

19. $\sqrt{24}+\sqrt{54}$ $5\sqrt{6}$
20. $\sqrt{12}+\sqrt{27}$ $5\sqrt{3}$
21. $2\sqrt{27}-4\sqrt{75}$ $-14\sqrt{3}$
22. $\sqrt{2}-\sqrt{18}$ $-2\sqrt{2}$
23. $\sqrt{50}-\sqrt{8}$ $3\sqrt{2}$
24. $\sqrt{80}-\sqrt{20}$ $2\sqrt{5}$
25. $\sqrt{3a}-\sqrt{12a}$ $-\sqrt{3a}$
26. $\sqrt{5w}-\sqrt{45w}$ $-2\sqrt{5w}$
27. $\sqrt{x^3}+x\sqrt{4x}$ $3x\sqrt{x}$
28. $\sqrt{27x^3}+5x\sqrt{12x}$ $13x\sqrt{3x}$
29. $\dfrac{1}{\sqrt{3}}+\dfrac{\sqrt{2}}{\sqrt{6}}$ $\dfrac{2\sqrt{3}}{3}$
30. $\dfrac{3}{\sqrt{5}}+\dfrac{\sqrt{2}}{\sqrt{10}}$ $\dfrac{4\sqrt{5}}{5}$ (VIDEO)
31. $\dfrac{1}{\sqrt{3}}+\sqrt{12}$ $\dfrac{7\sqrt{3}}{3}$
32. $\dfrac{1}{\sqrt{2}}+3\sqrt{8}$ $\dfrac{13\sqrt{2}}{2}$

‹2› Multiplying Radicals

Multiply and simplify. See Example 3.

33. $\sqrt{7}\cdot\sqrt{11}$ $\sqrt{77}$
34. $\sqrt{3}\cdot\sqrt{13}$ $\sqrt{39}$
35. $2\sqrt{6}\cdot 3\sqrt{6}$ 36
36. $4\sqrt{2}\cdot 3\sqrt{2}$ 24
37. $-3\sqrt{5}\cdot 4\sqrt{2}$ $-12\sqrt{10}$
38. $-8\sqrt{3}\cdot 3\sqrt{2}$ $-24\sqrt{6}$
39. $\sqrt{2a^3}\cdot\sqrt{6a^5}$ $2a^4\sqrt{3}$
40. $\sqrt{3w^7}\cdot\sqrt{w^9}$ $w^8\sqrt{3}$
41. $\sqrt[3]{9}\cdot\sqrt[3]{3}$ 3
42. $\sqrt[3]{-25}\cdot\sqrt[3]{5}$ -5
43. $\sqrt[3]{-4m^2}\cdot\sqrt[3]{2m}$ $-2m$
44. $\sqrt[3]{100m^4}\cdot\sqrt[3]{10m^2}$ $10m^2$

Multiply and simplify. See Example 4.

45. $\sqrt{2}(\sqrt{2}+\sqrt{3})$ $2+\sqrt{6}$
46. $\sqrt{3}(\sqrt{3}-\sqrt{2})$ $3-\sqrt{6}$
47. $3\sqrt{2}(2\sqrt{6}+\sqrt{10})$ $12\sqrt{3}+6\sqrt{5}$
48. $2\sqrt{3}(\sqrt{6}+2\sqrt{15})$ $6\sqrt{2}+12\sqrt{5}$ (VIDEO)
49. $2\sqrt{5}(\sqrt{5}-3\sqrt{10})$ $10-30\sqrt{2}$
50. $\sqrt{6}(\sqrt{24}-6)$ $12-6\sqrt{6}$

Multiply and simplify. See Example 5.

51. $(\sqrt{5}-4)(\sqrt{5}+3)$ $-7-\sqrt{5}$
52. $(\sqrt{6}-2)(\sqrt{6}-3)$ $12-5\sqrt{6}$
53. $(\sqrt{3}-1)(\sqrt{3}+1)$ 2
54. $(\sqrt{6}+2)(\sqrt{6}-2)$ 2 (VIDEO)
55. $(\sqrt{5}-\sqrt{2})(\sqrt{5}+\sqrt{2})$ 3
56. $(\sqrt{3}-\sqrt{6})(\sqrt{3}+\sqrt{6})$ -3
57. $(2\sqrt{5}+1)(3\sqrt{5}-2)$ $28-\sqrt{5}$
58. $(2\sqrt{2}+3)(4\sqrt{2}+4)$ $28+20\sqrt{2}$
59. $(2\sqrt{3}-3\sqrt{5})(3\sqrt{3}+4\sqrt{5})$ $-42-\sqrt{15}$
60. $(4\sqrt{3}+3\sqrt{7})(2\sqrt{3}+4\sqrt{7})$ $108+22\sqrt{21}$
61. $(2\sqrt{3}+5)^2$ $37+20\sqrt{3}$
62. $(3\sqrt{2}+\sqrt{6})^2$ $24+12\sqrt{3}$

‹3› Dividing Radicals

Divide and simplify. See Example 6.

63. $\sqrt{10}\div\sqrt{5}$ $\sqrt{2}$
64. $\sqrt{14}\div\sqrt{2}$ $\sqrt{7}$
65. $\sqrt{5}\div\sqrt{3}$ $\dfrac{\sqrt{15}}{3}$
66. $\sqrt{3}\div\sqrt{2}$ $\dfrac{\sqrt{6}}{2}$

67. $(4\sqrt{5}) \div (3\sqrt{6})$ $\frac{2\sqrt{30}}{9}$

68. $(3\sqrt{7}) \div (4\sqrt{3})$ $\frac{\sqrt{21}}{4}$

69. $(5\sqrt{14}) \div (3\sqrt{2})$ $\frac{5\sqrt{7}}{3}$

70. $(4\sqrt{15}) \div (5\sqrt{2})$ $\frac{2\sqrt{30}}{5}$

Simplify each expression. See Example 7.

71. $\frac{2 + \sqrt{8}}{2}$ $1 + \sqrt{2}$

72. $\frac{3 + \sqrt{18}}{3}$ $1 + \sqrt{2}$

73. $\frac{-4 + \sqrt{20}}{2}$ $-2 + \sqrt{5}$

74. $\frac{-6 + \sqrt{45}}{3}$ $-2 + \sqrt{5}$

75. $\frac{4 - \sqrt{20}}{6}$ $\frac{2 - \sqrt{5}}{3}$

76. $\frac{-6 - \sqrt{27}}{6}$ $\frac{-2 - \sqrt{3}}{2}$

77. $\frac{-4 - \sqrt{24}}{-6}$ $\frac{2 + \sqrt{6}}{3}$

78. $\frac{-3 - \sqrt{27}}{-3}$ $1 + \sqrt{3}$

79. $\frac{3 + \sqrt{12}}{6}$ $\frac{3 + 2\sqrt{3}}{6}$

80. $\frac{3 + \sqrt{8}}{3}$ $\frac{3 + 2\sqrt{2}}{3}$

Simplify each expression. See Example 8.

81. $\frac{5}{\sqrt{3} - \sqrt{2}}$ $5\sqrt{3} + 5\sqrt{2}$

82. $\frac{3}{\sqrt{6} + \sqrt{2}}$ $\frac{3\sqrt{6} - 3\sqrt{2}}{4}$

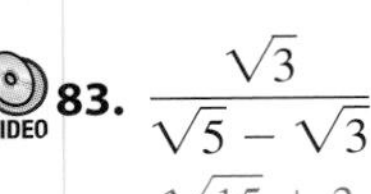

83. $\frac{\sqrt{3}}{\sqrt{5} - \sqrt{3}}$ $\frac{\sqrt{15} + 3}{2}$

84. $\frac{\sqrt{2}}{\sqrt{2} + \sqrt{5}}$ $\frac{-2 + \sqrt{10}}{3}$

85. $\frac{2 + \sqrt{3}}{5 - \sqrt{3}}$ $\frac{13 + 7\sqrt{3}}{22}$

86. $\frac{\sqrt{2} - \sqrt{3}}{\sqrt{3} - 1}$ $\frac{\sqrt{6} - 3 + \sqrt{2} - \sqrt{3}}{2}$

87. $\frac{\sqrt{7} - 5}{2\sqrt{7} + 1}$ $\frac{19 - 11\sqrt{7}}{27}$

88. $\frac{\sqrt{5} + 4}{3\sqrt{2} - \sqrt{5}}$ $\frac{3\sqrt{10} + 12\sqrt{2} + 5 + 4\sqrt{5}}{13}$

Miscellaneous

Simplify.

89. $\sqrt{5a} + \sqrt{20a}$ $3\sqrt{5a}$

90. $a\sqrt{6} \cdot a\sqrt{12}$ $6a^2\sqrt{2}$

91. $\sqrt{75} \div \sqrt{6}$ $\frac{5\sqrt{2}}{2}$

92. $\sqrt{24} - \sqrt{150}$ $-3\sqrt{6}$

93. $(5 + 3\sqrt{5})^2$ $70 + 30\sqrt{5}$

94. $(\sqrt{6} - \sqrt{5})(\sqrt{6} + \sqrt{5})$ 1

95. $\sqrt{5} + \frac{\sqrt{20}}{3}$ $\frac{5\sqrt{5}}{3}$

96. $\frac{5}{\sqrt{8} - \sqrt{3}}$ $2\sqrt{2} + \sqrt{3}$

Use a calculator to find the approximate value of each expression to three decimal places.

97. $\frac{2 + \sqrt{3}}{2}$ 1.866

98. $\frac{-2 + \sqrt{3}}{-6}$ 0.045

99. $\frac{-4 - \sqrt{6}}{5 - \sqrt{3}}$ −1.974

100. $\frac{-5 - \sqrt{2}}{\sqrt{3} + \sqrt{7}}$ −1.465

Applications

Solve each problem.

101. Find the exact area and perimeter of the given rectangle. 12 ft², $10\sqrt{2}$ ft

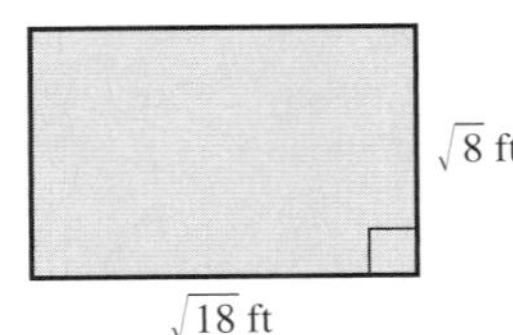

Figure for Exercise 101

102. Find the exact area and perimeter of the given triangle. 9, $5\sqrt{3} + \sqrt{39}$

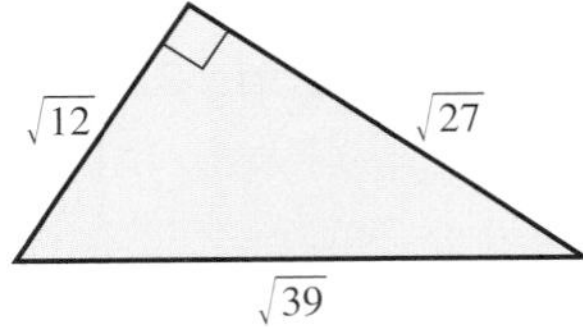

Figure for Exercise 102

103. Find the exact volume in cubic meters of the given rectangular box. 6 m³

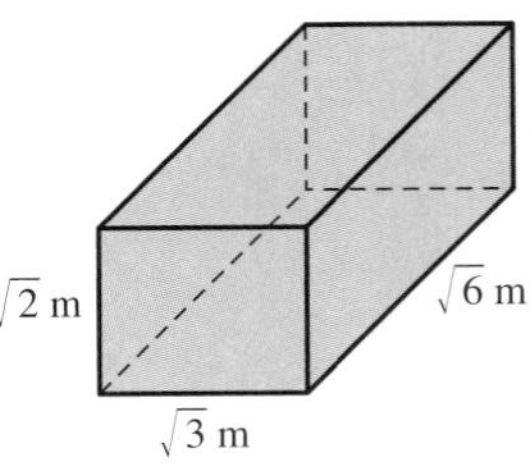

Figure for Exercise 103

104. Find the exact surface area of the box in Exercise 103. $2\sqrt{6} + 4\sqrt{3} + 6\sqrt{2}\,\text{m}^2$

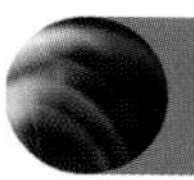

8.4 Solving Equations with Radicals and Exponents

In This Section

⟨ Teaching Tip ⟩

Have students solve $x^2 - 4 = 0$ by factoring and observe the two solutions. Then show the square root property. Students often forget that there are two solutions to $x^2 = 4$.

Equations involving radicals and exponents occur in many applications. In this section, you will learn to solve equations of this type, and you will see how these equations occur in applications.

⟨1⟩ The Square Root Property

An equation of the form $x^2 = k$ can have two solutions, one solution, or no solutions, depending on the value of k. For example,

$$x^2 = 4$$

has two solutions because $(2)^2 = 4$ and $(-2)^2 = 4$. So $x^2 = 4$ is equivalent to the compound equation

$$x = 2 \quad \text{or} \quad x = -2,$$

which is also written as $x = \pm 2$ and is read as "x equals positive or negative 2." The only solution to $x^2 = 0$ is 0. The equation

$$x^2 = -4$$

has no real solution because the square of every real number is nonnegative.

These examples illustrate the **square root property.**

Square Root Property (Solving $x^2 = k$)

For $k > 0$ the equation $x^2 = k$ is equivalent to the compound equation

$$x = \sqrt{k} \quad \text{or} \quad x = -\sqrt{k}. \qquad (\text{Also written } x = \pm\sqrt{k})$$

For $k = 0$ the equation $x^2 = k$ is equivalent to $x = 0$.
For $k < 0$ the equation $x^2 = k$ has no real solution.

CAUTION The expression $\sqrt{9}$ has a value of 3 only, but the equation $x^2 = 9$ has two solutions: 3 and -3.

EXAMPLE 1

Using the square root property

Solve each equation.

a) $x^2 = 12$ **b)** $2(x + 1)^2 - 18 = 0$ **c)** $x^2 = -9$ **d)** $(x - 16)^2 = 0$

Solution

a) $x^2 = 12$

$x = \pm\sqrt{12}$ Square root property

$x = \pm 2\sqrt{3}$

Check: $(2\sqrt{3})^2 = 4 \cdot 3 = 12$, and $(-2\sqrt{3})^2 = 4 \cdot 3 = 12$.

Note that $x^2 = 12$ is equivalent to $x = \pm\sqrt{12}$ because of the square root property. We are not "taking the square root of each side."

b) $2(x + 1)^2 - 18 = 0$

$$2(x + 1)^2 = 18 \quad \text{Add 18 to each side.}$$

$$(x + 1)^2 = 9 \quad \text{Divide each side by 2.}$$

$$x + 1 = \pm\sqrt{9} \quad \text{Square root property}$$

$$x + 1 = 3 \quad \text{or} \quad x + 1 = -3$$

$$x = 2 \quad \text{or} \quad x = -4$$

Check 2 and -4 in the original equation. Both -4 and 2 are solutions to the equation.

c) The equation $x^2 = -9$ has no real solution because no real number has a square that is negative.

d) $(x - 16)^2 = 0$

$$x - 16 = 0 \quad \text{Square root property}$$

$$x = 16$$

Check: $(16 - 16)^2 = 0$. The equation has only one solution, 16.

Now do Exercises 7–20

⟨2⟩ Obtaining Equivalent Equations

When solving equations, we use a sequence of equivalent equations with each one simpler than the last. To get an equivalent equation, we can

1. add the same number to each side,
2. subtract the same number from each side,
3. multiply each side by the same nonzero number, or
4. divide each side by the same nonzero number.

However, "doing the same thing to each side" is not the only way to obtain an equivalent equation. In Chapter 6 we used the zero factor property to obtain equivalent equations. For example, by the zero factor property the equation

$$(x - 3)(x + 2) = 0$$

is equivalent to the compound equation

$$x - 3 = 0 \quad \text{or} \quad x + 2 = 0.$$

In this section you just learned how to obtain equivalent equations by the square root property. This property tells us how to write an equation that is equivalent to the equation $x^2 = k$. Note that the square root property does not tell us to "take the square root of each side." Because a real number might have two, one, or no square roots, taking *the* square root of each side can lead to errors. To become proficient at solving equations, we must understand these methods. One of our main goals in algebra is to keep expanding our skills for solving equations.

⟨3⟩ Squaring Each Side of an Equation

Some equations involving radicals can be solved by squaring each side:

$$\sqrt{x} = 5$$

$$(\sqrt{x})^2 = 5^2 \quad \text{Square each side.}$$

$$x = 25$$

All three of these equations are equivalent. Because $\sqrt{25} = 5$ is correct, 25 satisfies the original equation.

However, squaring each side does not necessarily produce an equivalent equation. For example, consider the equation

$$x = 3.$$

Squaring each side, we get

$$x^2 = 9.$$

Both 3 and -3 satisfy $x^2 = 9$, but only 3 satisfies the original equation $x = 3$. So $x^2 = 9$ is not equivalent to $x = 3$. The extra solution to $x^2 = 9$ is called an **extraneous solution.**

These two examples illustrate the **squaring property of equality.**

Squaring Property of Equality

When we square each side of an equation, the solutions to the new equation include all of the solutions to the original equation. However, the new equation might have extraneous solutions.

This property means that *we may square each side of an equation, but we must check all of our answers to eliminate extraneous solutions.*

EXAMPLE 2

Using the squaring property of equality

Solve each equation.

a) $\sqrt{x^2 - 16} = 3$ **b)** $x = \sqrt{2x + 3}$

Solution

a)

$$\sqrt{x^2 - 16} = 3$$

$$(\sqrt{x^2 - 16})^2 = 3^2 \quad \text{Square each side.}$$

$$x^2 - 16 = 9$$

$$x^2 = 25$$

$$x = \pm 5 \quad \text{Square root property}$$

Check each solution:

$$\sqrt{5^2 - 16} = \sqrt{25 - 16} = \sqrt{9} = 3$$

$$\sqrt{(-5)^2 - 16} = \sqrt{25 - 16} = \sqrt{9} = 3$$

So both 5 and -5 are solutions to the equation.

b)

$$x = \sqrt{2x + 3}$$

$$x^2 = (\sqrt{2x + 3})^2 \quad \text{Square each side.}$$

$$x^2 = 2x + 3$$

$$x^2 - 2x - 3 = 0 \quad \text{Solve by factoring.}$$

$$(x - 3)(x + 1) = 0 \quad \text{Factor.}$$

$$x - 3 = 0 \quad \text{or} \quad x + 1 = 0 \quad \text{Zero factor property}$$

$$x = 3 \quad \text{or} \quad x = -1$$

Check in the original equation:

Check $x = 3$:	Check $x = -1$:
$3 = \sqrt{2 \cdot 3 + 3}$	$-1 = \sqrt{2(-1) + 3}$
$3 = \sqrt{9}$ Correct	$-1 = \sqrt{1}$ Incorrect

Because -1 does not satisfy the original equation, -1 is an extraneous solution. The only solution is 3.

Now do Exercises 21–30

The equations in Example 3 have radicals on both sides of the equation.

EXAMPLE 3

Radicals on both sides

Solve each equation.

a) $\sqrt{x - 3} = \sqrt{2x + 5}$ **b)** $\sqrt{x^2 - 4x} = \sqrt{2 - 3x}$

Solution

a)

$$\sqrt{x - 3} = \sqrt{2x + 5}$$
$$(\sqrt{x - 3})^2 = (\sqrt{2x + 5})^2 \quad \text{Square each side.}$$
$$x - 3 = 2x + 5 \quad \text{Simplify.}$$
$$x - 8 = 2x$$
$$-8 = x$$

Check $x = -8$ in the original equation:

$$\sqrt{-8 - 3} = \sqrt{2(-8) + 5}$$
$$\sqrt{-11} = \sqrt{-11}$$

Because $\sqrt{-11}$ is not a real number, -8 does not satisfy the equation and the equation has no solution.

b)

$$\sqrt{x^2 - 4x} = \sqrt{2 - 3x}$$
$$x^2 - 4x = 2 - 3x \quad \text{Square each side.}$$
$$x^2 - x - 2 = 0$$
$$(x - 2)(x + 1) = 0$$
$$x - 2 = 0 \quad \text{or} \quad x + 1 = 0 \quad \text{Zero factor property}$$
$$x = 2 \quad \text{or} \quad x = -1$$

Check each solution in the original equation:

Check $x = 2$:	Check $x = -1$:
$\sqrt{2^2 - 4 \cdot 2} = \sqrt{2 - 3 \cdot 2}$	$\sqrt{(-1)^2 - 4(-1)} = \sqrt{2 - 3(-1)}$
$\sqrt{-4} = \sqrt{-4}$	$\sqrt{5} = \sqrt{5}$

Because $\sqrt{-4}$ is not a real number, 2 is an extraneous solution. The only solution to the original equation is -1.

Now do Exercises 31–34

In Example 4, one of the sides of the equation is a binomial. When we square each side, we must be sure to square the binomial properly.

EXAMPLE 4

Isolating the radical

Solve the equation $x = \sqrt{-2 - 3x} - 2$

Solution

Isolate the radical before squaring each side:

$$x = \sqrt{-2 - 3x} - 2$$

$$x + 2 = \sqrt{-2 - 3x} \quad \text{Add 2 to each side.}$$

$$(x + 2)^2 = (\sqrt{-2 - 3x})^2 \quad \text{Square each side.}$$

$$x^2 + 4x + 4 = -2 - 3x \quad \text{Square the binomial on the left side.}$$

$$x^2 + 7x + 6 = 0$$

$$(x + 6)(x + 1) = 0 \quad \text{Factor.}$$

$$x + 6 = 0 \quad \text{or} \quad x + 1 = 0$$

$$x = -6 \quad \text{or} \quad x = -1$$

Check these solutions in the original equation:

Check $x = -6$:	Check $x = -1$:
$-6 = \sqrt{-2 - 3(-6)} - 2$	$-1 = \sqrt{-2 - 3(-1)} - 2$
$-6 = \sqrt{16} - 2$	$-1 = \sqrt{1} - 2$
$-6 = 2$ Incorrect	$-1 = -1$ Correct

The solution -6 does not check. The only solution to the original equation is -1.

Now do Exercises 35–46

‹ Teaching Tip ›

It is good to review squaring a binomial before this example. Point out that you are not squaring a binomial on the right side of this equation.

CAUTION After isolating the radical in Example 4 the left side is a binomial. Be sure to square the binomial correctly using the rule $(a + b)^2 = a^2 + 2ab + b^2$.

‹4› Solving for the Indicated Variable

In Example 5, we use the square root property to solve a formula for an indicated variable.

EXAMPLE 5

Solving for a variable

Solve the formula $A = \pi r^2$ for r.

Solution

$$A = \pi r^2$$

$$\frac{A}{\pi} = r^2 \quad \text{Divide each side by } \pi.$$

$$\pm\sqrt{\frac{A}{\pi}} = r \quad \text{Square root property}$$

The formula solved for r is

$$r = \pm\sqrt{\frac{A}{\pi}}.$$

‹ Teaching Tip ›

Example 5 illustrates that rationalizing the denominator is not always best. This formula would appear more complicated as

$$r = \frac{\sqrt{A\pi}}{\pi}$$

If r is the radius of a circle with area A, then r is positive and

$$r = \sqrt{\frac{A}{\pi}}.$$

Now do Exercises 47–54

⟨5⟩ Applications

Equations involving exponents occur in many applications. If the exact answer to a problem is an irrational number in radical notation, it is usually helpful to find a decimal approximation for the answer.

EXAMPLE 6

Finding the side of a square with a given diagonal

If the diagonal of a square window is 10 feet long, then what are the exact and approximate lengths of a side? Round the approximate answer to two decimal places.

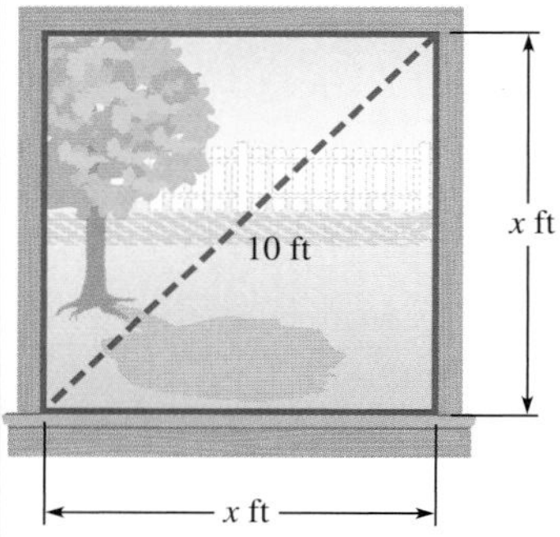

Figure 8.1

Solution

First make a sketch as in Fig. 8.1. Let x be the length of a side. The Pythagorean theorem tells us that the sum of the squares of the sides is equal to the diagonal squared:

$$x^2 + x^2 = 10^2$$
$$2x^2 = 100$$
$$x^2 = 50$$
$$x = \pm\sqrt{50}$$
$$= \pm 5\sqrt{2}$$

Because the length of a side must be positive, we disregard the negative solution. The exact length of a side is $5\sqrt{2}$ feet. Use a calculator to get $5\sqrt{2} \approx 7.07$. The symbol $\approx$ means "is approximately equal to." The approximate length of a side is 7.07 feet.

Now do Exercises 87–98

Warm-Ups ▼

True or false? Explain your answer.

1. The equation $x^2 = 9$ is equivalent to the equation $x = 3$. False
2. The equation $x^2 = -16$ has no real solution. True
3. The equation $a^2 = 0$ has no solution. False
4. Both $-\sqrt{5}$ and $\sqrt{5}$ are solutions to $x^2 + 5 = 0$. False
5. The equation $-x^2 = 9$ has no real solution. True
6. To solve $\sqrt{x + 4} = \sqrt{2x - 9}$, first take the square root of each side. False
7. All extraneous solutions give us a denominator of zero. False
8. Squaring both sides of $\sqrt{x} = -1$ will produce an extraneous solution. True
9. The equation $x^2 - 3 = 0$ is equivalent to $x = \pm\sqrt{3}$. True
10. The equation $-2 = \sqrt{6x^2 - x - 8}$ has no solution. True

8.4 Exercises

Study Tips

- Stay alert for the entire class period. The first 20 minutes are the easiest, and the last 20 minutes the hardest.
- Think of how much time you will have to spend outside of class figuring out what happened during the last 20 minutes in which you were daydreaming.

Reading and Writing *After reading this section, write out the answers to these questions. Use complete sentences.*

1. What is the square root property? The square root property says that $x^2 = k$ for $k > 0$ is equivalent to $x = \pm\sqrt{k}$.

2. When do we take the square root of each side of an equation? We do not take the square root of each side of an equation.

3. What new techniques were introduced in this section for solving equations? The square root property and squaring each side are two new techniques used for solving equations.

4. Is there any way to obtain an equivalent equation other than doing the same thing to each side? The square root property and the zero factor property produce equivalent equations without doing the same thing to each side.

5. Which property for solving equations can give extraneous roots? Squaring each side can produce extraneous roots.

6. Which property of equality does not always give you an equivalent equation? Squaring each side does not always give equivalent equations.

⟨1⟩ The Square Root Property

Solve each equation. See Example 1.

7. $x^2 = 16$ $\quad -4, 4$

8. $x^2 = 49$ $\quad -7, 7$

9. $x^2 - 40 = 0$ $\quad -2\sqrt{10}, 2\sqrt{10}$

VIDEO **10.** $x^2 - 24 = 0$ $\quad -2\sqrt{6}, 2\sqrt{6}$

11. $3x^2 = 2$ $\quad -\frac{\sqrt{6}}{3}, \frac{\sqrt{6}}{3}$

12. $2x^2 = 3$ $\quad -\frac{\sqrt{6}}{2}, \frac{\sqrt{6}}{2}$

13. $9x^2 = -4$ $\quad$ No solution

14. $25x^2 + 1 = 0$ $\quad$ No solution

15. $(x - 1)^2 = 4$ $\quad -1, 3$

16. $(x + 3)^2 = 9$ $\quad -6, 0$

17. $2(x - 5)^2 + 1 = 7$ $\quad 5 - \sqrt{3}, 5 + \sqrt{3}$

18. $3(x - 6)^2 - 4 = 11$ $\quad 6 - \sqrt{5}, 6 + \sqrt{5}$

19. $(x + 19)^2 = 0$ $\quad -19$

20. $5x^2 + 5 = 5$ $\quad 0$

⟨3⟩ Squaring Each Side of an Equation

Solve each equation. See Examples 2 and 3.

21. $\sqrt{x - 9} = 9$ $\quad 90$

22. $\sqrt{x + 3} = 4$ $\quad 13$

23. $\sqrt{2x - 3} = -4$ $\quad$ No solution

24. $\sqrt{3x - 5} = -9$ $\quad$ No solution

25. $4 = \sqrt{x^2 - 9}$ $\quad -5, 5$

26. $1 = \sqrt{x^2 - 1}$ $\quad -\sqrt{2}, \sqrt{2}$

27. $x = \sqrt{18 - 3x}$ $\quad 3$

VIDEO **28.** $x = \sqrt{6x + 27}$ $\quad 9$

29. $x = \sqrt{x}$ $\quad 0, 1$

30. $x = \sqrt{2x}$ $\quad 0, 2$

31. $\sqrt{x + 1} = \sqrt{2x - 5}$ $\quad 6$

32. $\sqrt{1 - 3x} = \sqrt{x + 5}$ $\quad -1$

33. $\sqrt{1 - x} = \sqrt{2x - 14}$ $\quad$ No solution

34. $\sqrt{2x - 3} = \sqrt{x - 5}$ $\quad$ No solution

Solve each equation. See Example 4.

35. $x = \sqrt{6 - x}$ $\quad 2$

36. $x = \sqrt{x + 20}$ $\quad 5$

37. $3\sqrt{2x - 1} - 3 = 12$ $\quad 13$

38. $4\sqrt{x + 5} - 3 = 9$ $\quad 4$

39. $x = 3 + \sqrt{2x - 6}$ $\quad 3, 5$

40. $x = 1 + \sqrt{3x - 5}$ $\quad 2, 3$

41. $1 = \sqrt{x + 13} - x$ $\quad 3$

42. $1 = \sqrt{22 - 2x} - x$ $\quad 3$

43. $\sqrt{10x - 44} + 2 = x$ $\quad 6, 8$

44. $\sqrt{8x - 7} - 1 = x$ $\quad 2, 4$

45. $3\sqrt{x - 4} + 2 = 5$ $\quad 5$

46. $5\sqrt{x - 7} - 4 = 6$ $\quad 11$

⟨4⟩ Solving for the Indicated Variable

Solve each formula for the indicated variable. See Example 5.

47. $V = \pi r^2 h$ for r $\quad r = \pm\sqrt{\frac{V}{\pi h}}$

48. $V = \frac{4}{3}\pi r^2 h$ for r $\quad r = \pm\sqrt{\frac{3V}{4\pi h}}$

49. $a^2 + b^2 = c^2$ for b $\quad b = \pm\sqrt{c^2 - a^2}$

50. $y = ax^2 + c$ for x $\quad x = \pm\sqrt{\frac{y - c}{a}}$

51. $b^2 - 4ac = 0$ for b $\quad b = \pm 2\sqrt{ac}$

52. $s = \frac{1}{2}gt^2 + v$ for t $\quad t = \pm\sqrt{\frac{2s - 2v}{g}}$

53. $v = \sqrt{2pt}$ for t $\quad t = \frac{v^2}{2p}$

54. $y = \sqrt{2x}$ for x $\quad x = \frac{y^2}{2}$

Miscellaneous

Solve each equation.

55. $x^2 = \frac{1}{4}$ $\quad -\frac{1}{2}, \frac{1}{2}$

56. $x^2 = \frac{1}{9}$ $\quad -\frac{1}{3}, \frac{1}{3}$

57. $x^2 + \frac{1}{4} = 0$ $\quad$ No solution

58. $x^2 + \frac{1}{9} = 0$ $\quad$ No solution

59. $\sqrt{x} = \frac{1}{9}$ $\quad \frac{1}{81}$

60. $\sqrt{x} = \frac{1}{4}$ $\quad \frac{1}{16}$

61. $\sqrt{x^2 - 15} = 7$ $\quad -8, 8$

62. $\sqrt{2x - 1} = 3$ $\quad 5$

63. $\sqrt{x} = 2x$ $\quad 0, \frac{1}{4}$

64. $\sqrt{2x} = 3x$ $\quad 0, \frac{2}{9}$

65. $(x + 1)^2 = 4$ $-3, 1$

66. $(x + 2)^2 = 16$ $-6, 2$

67. $3x^2 - 6 = 0$
$-\sqrt{2}, \sqrt{2}$

VIDEO **68.** $5x^2 + 3 = 0$
No solution

69. $\sqrt{2x - 3} = \sqrt{3x + 1}$
No solution

70. $\sqrt{2x - 4} = \sqrt{x - 9}$
No solution

71. $(2x - 1)^2 = 8$
$\frac{1 + 2\sqrt{2}}{2}, \frac{1 - 2\sqrt{2}}{2}$

72. $(3x - 2)^2 = 18$
$\frac{2 - 3\sqrt{2}}{3}, \frac{2 + 3\sqrt{2}}{3}$

73. $\sqrt{2x - 9} = 0$ $\frac{9}{2}$

74. $\sqrt{5 - 3x} = 0$ $\frac{5}{3}$

75. $x + 1 = \sqrt{2x + 10}$ 3

76. $x - 3 = \sqrt{2x + 18}$ 9

77. $3(x + 1)^2 - 27 = 0$
$-4, 2$

78. $2(x - 3)^2 - 50 = 0$
$-2, 8$

79. $(2x - 5)^2 = 0$ $\frac{5}{2}$

80. $(3x - 1)^2 = 0$ $\frac{1}{3}$

Use a calculator to find approximate solutions to each equation. Round your answers to three decimal places.

81. $x^2 = 3.25$
$-1.803, 1.803$

82. $(x + 1)^2 = 20.3$
$-5.506, 3.506$

83. $\sqrt{x + 2} = 1.73$
0.993

84. $\sqrt{2.3x - 1.4} = 3.3$
5.343

85. $1.3(x - 2.4)^2 = 5.4$
$0.362, 4.438$

86. $-2.4x^2 = -9.55$
$-1.995, 1.995$

‹5› Applications

Find the exact answer to each problem. If the answer is irrational, then find an approximation to three decimal places. See Example 6.

87. ***Side of a square.*** Find the length of the side of a square whose area is 18 square feet. $3\sqrt{2}$ or 4.243 ft

88. ***Side of a field.*** Find the length of the side of a square wheat field whose area is 75 square miles. $5\sqrt{3}$ or 8.660 mi

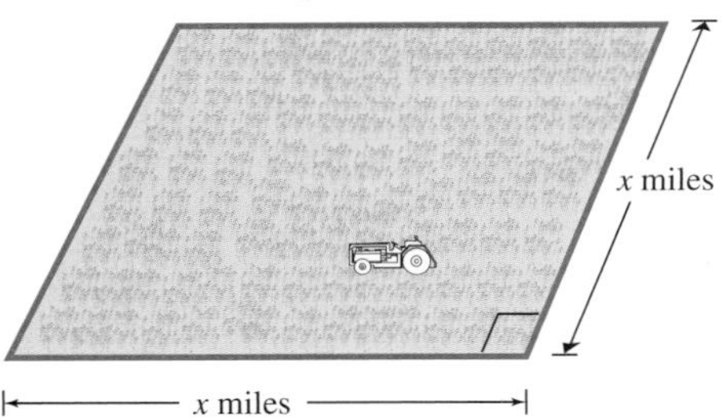

Figure for Exercise 88

VIDEO **89.** ***Side of a table.*** Find the length of the side of a square coffee table whose diagonal is 6 feet. $3\sqrt{2}$ or 4.243 ft

90. ***Side of a square.*** Find the length of the side of a square whose diagonal measures 1 yard. $\frac{\sqrt{2}}{2}$ or 0.707 yd

91. ***Diagonal of a tile.*** Find the length of the diagonal of a square floor tile whose sides measure 1 foot each. $\sqrt{2}$ or 1.414 ft

92. ***Diagonal of a sandbox.*** The sandbox at Totland is shaped like a square with an area of 20 square meters. Find the length of the diagonal of the square. $2\sqrt{10}$ or 6.325 m

93. ***Diagonal of a tub.*** Find the length of the diagonal of a rectangular bathtub with sides of 3 feet and 4 feet. 5 ft

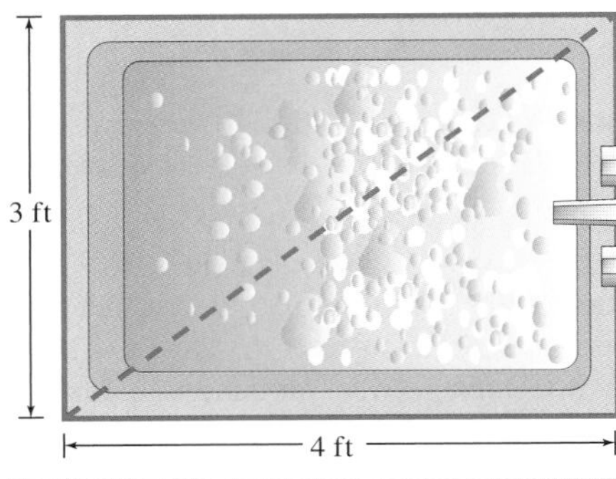

Figure for Exercise 93

94. ***Diagonal of a rectangle.*** What is the length of the diagonal of a rectangular office whose sides are 6 feet and 8 feet? 10 ft

95. ***Falling bodies.*** If we neglect air resistance, then the number of feet that a body falls from rest during t seconds is given by $s = 16t^2$. How long does it take a pine cone to fall from the top of a 100-foot pine tree? 2.5 sec

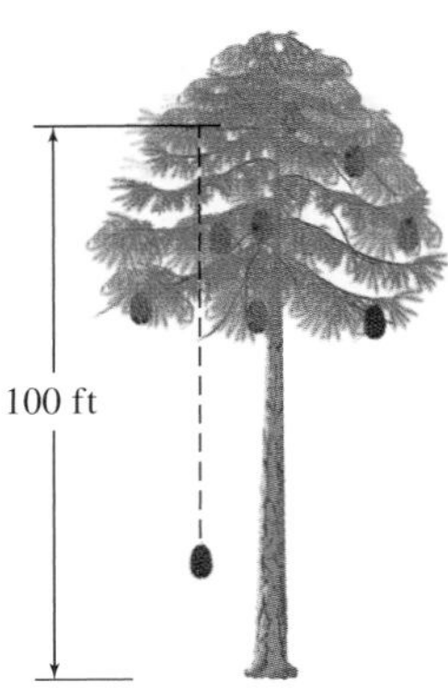

Figure for Exercise 95

96. ***America's favorite pastime.*** A baseball diamond is actually a square, 90 feet on each side. See the figure on the next page. How far is it from home plate to second base? $90\sqrt{2}$ or 127.279 ft

97. ***Length of a guy wire.*** A guy wire from the top of a 200-foot tower is to be attached to a point on the ground whose distance from the base of the tower is $\frac{2}{3}$ of the height of the tower. Find the length of the guy wire.
$\frac{200\sqrt{13}}{3}$ or 240.370 ft

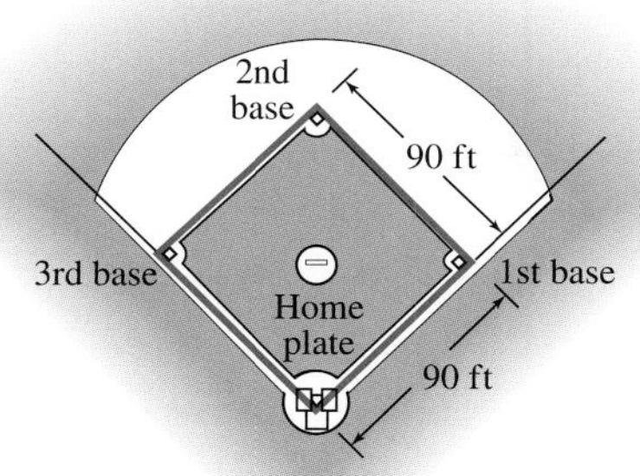

Figure for Exercise 96

98. ***America's favorite pastime.*** The size of a rectangular television screen is commonly given by the manufacturer as the length of the diagonal of the rectangle. If a television screen measures 10 inches wide and 8 inches high, then what is the exact length of the diagonal of the screen? What is the approximate size of this television screen to the nearest inch? $2\sqrt{41}$ or 13 in.

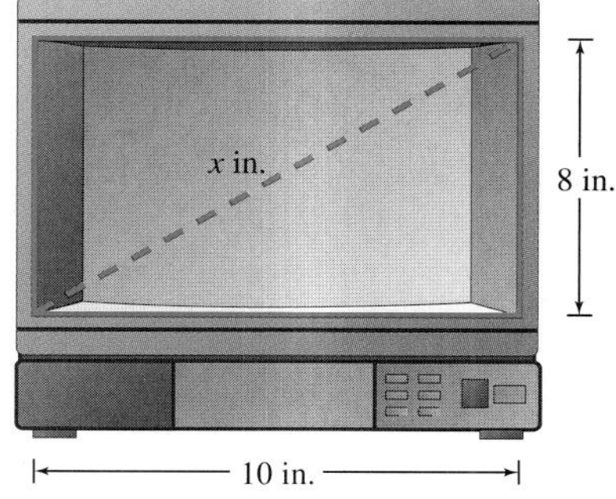

Figure for Exercise 98

8.5 Fractional Exponents

In This Section

- ⟨1⟩ Fractional Exponents
- ⟨2⟩ Using the Rules

You have learned how to use exponents to express powers of numbers and radicals to express roots. In this section, you will see that roots can be expressed with exponents also. The advantage of using exponents to express roots is that the rules of exponents can be applied to the expressions.

⟨ Calculator Close-Up ⟩

You can find the fifth root of 2 using radical notation or exponent notation. Note that the fractional exponent 1/5 must be in parentheses. If you use the decimal equivalent 0.2, then no parentheses are needed

```
5×√(2)
          1.148698355
2^(1/5)
          1.148698355
2^.2
          1.148698355
```

⟨1⟩ Fractional Exponents

The nth root of a number can be expressed using radical notation or the exponent $1/n$. For example, $5^{1/2} = \sqrt{5}$, $(-2)^{1/3} = \sqrt[3]{-2}$, and $6^{1/4} = \sqrt[4]{6}$. An expression such as $(-4)^{1/2}$ is undefined because $\sqrt{-4}$ is not a real number.

Definition of $a^{1/n}$

If n is any positive integer, then

$$a^{1/n} = \sqrt[n]{a},$$

provided that $\sqrt[n]{a}$ is a real number.

EXAMPLE 1

Radicals or exponents

Write each radical expression using exponent notation and each exponential expression using radical notation.

a) $\sqrt[3]{35}$ **b)** $\sqrt[4]{xy}$ **c)** $\sqrt{-x}$ **d)** $5^{1/2}$ **e)** $a^{1/5}$ **f)** $-5^{1/3}$

Solution

a) $\sqrt[3]{35} = 35^{1/3}$ b) $\sqrt[4]{xy} = (xy)^{1/4}$ c) $\sqrt{-x} = (-x)^{1/2}$

d) $5^{1/2} = \sqrt{5}$ e) $a^{1/5} = \sqrt[5]{a}$ f) $-5^{1/3} = -\sqrt[3]{5}$

Now do Exercises 7–18

In Example 2, we evaluate some exponential expressions.

EXAMPLE 2

Finding roots

Evaluate each expression.

a) $4^{1/2}$ b) $(-8)^{1/3}$ c) $81^{1/4}$ d) $(-9)^{1/2}$ e) $-9^{1/2}$

Solution

a) $4^{1/2} = \sqrt{4} = 2$ b) $(-8)^{1/3} = \sqrt[3]{-8} = -2$ c) $81^{1/4} = \sqrt[4]{81} = 3$

d) Because $(-9)^{1/2}$ or $\sqrt{-9}$ is an even root of a negative number, it is not a real number.

e) Because the exponent $1/2$ is applied to 9 only, $-9^{1/2} = -\sqrt{9} = -3$.

Now do Exercises 19–32

‹ Teaching Tip ›

Again have students list the perfect squares, perfect cubes, and so on.

We now extend the definition of the exponent $1/n$ to include any fraction or rational number as an exponent. The numerator of the rational number indicates the power, and the denominator indicates the root. For example, the expression

$$8^{2/3}$$

(2 → Power; 3 → Root)

represents the square of the cube root of 8. So we have

$$8^{2/3} = (8^{1/3})^2 = (2)^2 = 4.$$

Note that you can evaluate $8^{2/3}$ by finding the power first and then the root. In symbols, $8^{2/3} = (8^2)^{1/3} = 64^{1/3} = 4$. Since it is usually simpler to find the root first and then the power, that is how we define $a^{m/n}$.

‹ Helpful Hint ›

Note that in $a^{m/n}$ we do not require m/n to be reduced. As long as the nth root of a is real, then the value of $a^{m/n}$ is the same whether or not m/n is in lowest terms.

Definition of $a^{m/n}$

If m and n are positive integers, then

$$a^{m/n} = (a^{1/n})^m,$$

provided that $a^{1/n}$ is a real number.

We define negative rational exponents just like negative integral exponents.

Definition of $a^{-m/n}$

If m and n are positive integers and $a \neq 0$, then

$$a^{-m/n} = \frac{1}{a^{m/n}},$$

provided that $a^{1/n}$ is a real number.

EXAMPLE 3

Radicals or exponents

Write each radical expression using exponent notation and each exponential expression using radical notation.

a) $\sqrt[3]{x^2}$ **b)** $\dfrac{1}{\sqrt[4]{m^3}}$ **c)** $5^{2/3}$ **d)** $a^{-2/5}$

Solution

a) $\sqrt[3]{x^2} = x^{2/3}$ **b)** $\dfrac{1}{\sqrt[4]{m^3}} = \dfrac{1}{m^{3/4}} = m^{-3/4}$ **c)** $5^{2/3} = \sqrt[3]{5^2}$ **d)** $a^{-2/5} = \dfrac{1}{\sqrt[5]{a^2}}$

Now do Exercises 33–44

To evaluate an expression with a negative rational exponent, remember that the denominator indicates root, the numerator indicates power, and the negative sign indicates reciprocal:

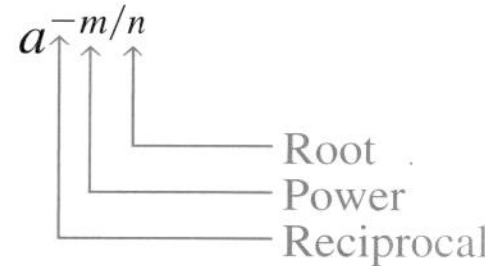

The root, power, and reciprocal can be evaluated in any order. However, to evaluate $a^{-m/n}$ it is usually simplest to use the following strategy.

Strategy for Evaluating $a^{-m/n}$

1. Find the nth root of a.
2. Raise your result to the mth power.
3. Find the reciprocal.

For example, to evaluate $8^{-2/3}$ we find the cube root of 8 (which is 2), square 2 to get 4, then find the reciprocal of 4 to get $\frac{1}{4}$. In print, $8^{-2/3}$ could be written for evaluation as $((8^{1/3})^2)^{-1}$ or $\frac{1}{(8^{1/3})^2}$. We prefer the latter because it looks a little simpler.

EXAMPLE 4

Rational exponents

Evaluate each expression.

a) $27^{2/3}$ **b)** $4^{-3/2}$ **c)** $81^{-3/4}$ **d)** $(-8)^{-5/3}$ **e)** $-4^{-3/2}$

Solution

a) Because the exponent is $2/3$, we find the cube root of 27, which is 3, and then square it to get 9. In symbols,

$$27^{2/3} = (27^{1/3})^2 = 3^2 = 9.$$

b) Because the exponent is $-3/2$, we find the principal square root of 4, which is 2, cube it to get 8, and then find the reciprocal to get $\frac{1}{8}$. In symbols,

$$4^{-3/2} = \frac{1}{(4^{1/2})^3} = \frac{1}{2^3} = \frac{1}{8}.$$

‹ Calculator Close-Up ›

A negative fractional exponent indicates a reciprocal, a root, and a power. To find $4^{-3/2}$ you can find the reciprocal first, the square root first, or the third power first as shown here.

```
(1/4)^(3/2)
                .125
(√(4))^-3
                .125
(4³)^(-1/2)
                .125
```

c) Because the exponent is $-3/4$, we find the principal fourth root of 81, which is 3, cube it to get 27, and then find the reciprocal to get $\frac{1}{27}$. In symbols,

$$81^{-3/4} = \frac{1}{(81^{1/4})^3} = \frac{1}{3^3} = \frac{1}{27}.$$

d) $(-8)^{-5/3} = \dfrac{1}{((-8)^{1/3})^5} = \dfrac{1}{(-2)^5} = \dfrac{1}{-32} = -\dfrac{1}{32}$

e) Because the exponent $-3/2$ is applied to 4 only,

$$-4^{-3/2} = -\frac{1}{(\sqrt{4})^3} = -\frac{1}{8}.$$

Now do Exercises 45–62

CAUTION An expression with a negative base and a negative exponent can have a positive or a negative value. For example,

$$(-8)^{-5/3} = -\frac{1}{32} \quad \text{and} \quad (-8)^{-2/3} = \frac{1}{4}.$$

‹2› Using the Rules

As we mentioned earlier, the advantage of using exponents to express roots is that the rules for integral exponents from Chapter 5 can also be used for rational exponents. For convenience we restate those rules here.

Rules for Rational Exponents

The following rules hold for nonzero real numbers a and b and any rational numbers r and s.

1. $a^r \cdot a^s = a^{r+s}$ Product rule for exponents
2. $\dfrac{a^r}{a^s} = a^{r-s}$ Quotient rule for exponents
3. $(a^r)^s = a^{rs}$ Power rule for exponents
4. $(ab)^r = a^r \cdot b^r$ Power of a product rule
5. $\left(\dfrac{a}{b}\right)^r = \dfrac{a^r}{b^r}$ Power of a quotient rule

We use these rules to simplify expressions with rational exponents in Example 5.

EXAMPLE 5

Using the rules of exponents

Simplify each expression. Write answers with positive exponents. Assume that all variables represent positive real numbers.

a) $2^{1/2} \cdot 2^{3/2}$ **b)** $\dfrac{x}{x^{2/3}}$ **c)** $(b^{1/2})^{1/3}$ **d)** $(x^4y^{-6})^{1/2}$ **e)** $\left(\dfrac{x^6}{y^3}\right)^{-2/3}$

Solution

a) $2^{1/2} \cdot 2^{3/2} = 2^{1/2+3/2}$ Product rule
$= 2^2$ $\frac{1}{2} + \frac{3}{2} = \frac{4}{2} = 2$
$= 4$

b) $\dfrac{x}{x^{2/3}} = x^{1-2/3}$ Quotient rule
$= x^{1/3}$ $1 - \frac{2}{3} = \frac{3}{3} - \frac{2}{3} = \frac{1}{3}$

c) $(b^{1/2})^{1/3} = b^{(1/2)\cdot(1/3)}$ Power rule
$= b^{1/6}$ $\frac{1}{2} \cdot \frac{1}{3} = \frac{1}{6}$

‹ Helpful Hint ›

Look what happens when we apply legitimate rules to an illegitimate expression:

$$(-1)^{2/2} = (-1)^1 = -1$$

and

$$(-1)^{2/2} = ((-1)^2)^{1/2} = 1^{1/2} = 1$$

So we conclude that $1 = -1$! However, $(-1)^{2/2}$ is not a legal expression because there is no real square root of -1.

d) $(x^4y^{-6})^{1/2} = (x^4)^{1/2}(y^{-6})^{1/2}$ Power of a product rule

$= x^2y^{-3}$ Power rule

$= \dfrac{x^2}{y^3}$ Definition of negative exponent

e) $\left(\dfrac{x^6}{y^3}\right)^{-2/3} = \left(\dfrac{y^3}{x^6}\right)^{2/3}$ Negative exponent rule

$= \dfrac{(y^3)^{2/3}}{(x^6)^{2/3}}$ Power of a quotient rule

$= \dfrac{y^2}{x^4}$ Power rule

Now do Exercises 63–78

Warm-Ups

True or false? Explain your answer.

1. $9^{1/3} = \sqrt[3]{9}$ True
2. $8^{5/3} = \sqrt[5]{8^3}$ False
3. $(-16)^{1/2} = -16^{1/2}$ False
4. $9^{-3/2} = \dfrac{1}{27}$ True
5. $6^{-1/2} = \dfrac{\sqrt{6}}{6}$ True
6. $\dfrac{2}{2^{1/2}} = 2^{1/2}$ True
7. $2^{1/2} \cdot 2^{1/2} = 4^{1/2}$ True
8. $16^{-1/4} = -2$ False
9. $6^{1/6} \cdot 6^{1/6} = 6^{1/3}$ True
10. $(2^8)^{3/4} = 2^6$ True

8.5 Exercises

‹ Study Tips ›

- When your mind starts to wander, don't give in to it.
- Recognize when you are losing it and force yourself to stay alert.

Reading and Writing *After reading this section, write out the answers to these questions. Use complete sentences.*

1. How do we indicate an nth root using exponents? The nth root of a is $a^{1/n}$.
2. How do we indicate the mth power of the nth root using exponents? The mth power of the nth root of a is $a^{m/n}$.
3. What is the meaning of a negative rational exponent? The expression $a^{-m/n}$ means $\dfrac{1}{a^{m/n}}$.
4. Which rules of exponents hold for rational exponents? All of the rules of exponents hold for rational exponents.
5. In what order must you perform the operations indicated by a negative rational exponent? The operations can be performed in any order, but the easiest is usually root, power, and then reciprocal.
6. When is $a^{-m/n}$ a real number? The expression $a^{-m/n}$ is a real number except when n is even and a is negative, or when $a = 0$.

Assume all variables represent positive numbers.

⟨1⟩ Fractional Exponents

Write each radical expression using exponent notation and each exponential expression using radical notation. See Example 1.

7. $\sqrt[4]{7}$ $7^{1/4}$ **8.** $\sqrt[3]{cbs}$ $(cbs)^{1/3}$ **9.** $9^{1/5}$ $\sqrt[5]{9}$
10. $3^{1/2}$ $\sqrt{3}$ **11.** $\sqrt{5x}$ $(5x)^{1/2}$ **12.** $\sqrt{3y}$ $(3y)^{1/2}$
13. $(-a)^{1/2}$ $\sqrt{-a}$ **14.** $(-b)^{1/5}$ $\sqrt[5]{-b}$ **15.** $-\sqrt{x}$ $-x^{1/2}$
16. $-\sqrt[3]{5}$ $-5^{1/3}$ **17.** $-6^{1/4}$ $-\sqrt[4]{6}$ **18.** $-a^{1/2}$ $-\sqrt{a}$

Evaluate each expression. See Example 2.

19. $25^{1/2}$ 5 **20.** $16^{1/2}$ 4 **21.** $125^{1/3}$ 5
22. $16^{1/4}$ 2 **23.** $(-125)^{1/3}$ −5 **24.** $(-32)^{1/5}$ −2
25. $(-8)^{1/3}$ −2 **26.** $(-27)^{1/3}$ −3 **27.** $(-4)^{1/2}$ Not a real number
28. $(-16)^{1/4}$ Not a real number **29.** $-4^{1/2}$ −2
30. $-16^{1/4}$ −2 **31.** $-64^{1/3}$ −4 **32.** $-36^{1/2}$ −6

Write each radical expression using exponent notation and each exponential expression using radical notation. See Example 3.

33. $\sqrt[3]{w^7}$ $w^{7/3}$ **34.** $\sqrt{a^5}$ $a^{5/2}$ **35.** $\dfrac{1}{\sqrt[3]{2^{10}}}$ $2^{-10/3}$

36. $\sqrt[3]{\dfrac{1}{a^2}}$ $a^{-2/3}$ **37.** $w^{-3/4}$ $\dfrac{1}{\sqrt[4]{w^3}}$ **38.** $6^{-5/3}$ $\dfrac{1}{\sqrt[3]{6^5}}$

39. $(ab)^{3/2}$ $\sqrt{(ab)^3}$ **40.** $(3m)^{-1/5}$ $\dfrac{1}{\sqrt[5]{3m}}$ **41.** $-\sqrt[4]{t^3}$ $-t^{3/4}$

42. $-\sqrt{p^3}$ $-p^{3/2}$ **43.** $-a^{-3/2}$ $-\dfrac{1}{\sqrt{a^3}}$ **44.** $-w^{-3/4}$ $-\dfrac{1}{\sqrt[4]{w^3}}$

Evaluate each expression.

See Example 4.

See the Strategy for Evaluating $a^{-m/n}$ box on page 527.

45. $125^{2/3}$ 25 **46.** $1000^{2/3}$ 100 **47.** $25^{3/2}$ 125
48. $16^{3/2}$ 64 **49.** $27^{-4/3}$ $\frac{1}{81}$ **50.** $16^{-3/4}$ $\frac{1}{8}$
51. $4^{-3/2}$ $\frac{1}{8}$ **52.** $25^{-3/2}$ $\frac{1}{125}$ **53.** $(-27)^{-1/3}$ $-\frac{1}{3}$
54. $(-8)^{-4/3}$ $\frac{1}{16}$ **55.** $(-16)^{-1/4}$ Not a real number **56.** $(-100)^{-3/2}$ Not a real number
57. $-16^{3/4}$ −8 **58.** $-8^{2/3}$ −4 **59.** $-8^{-2/3}$ $-\frac{1}{4}$
60. $-27^{-2/3}$ $-\frac{1}{9}$ **61.** $(-4)^{3/2}$ Not a real number **62.** $(-81)^{3/4}$ Not a real number

⟨2⟩ Using the Rules

Simplify each expression. Write answers with positive exponents only. See Example 5.

63. $x^{1/4}x^{1/4}$ $x^{1/2}$ **64.** $y^{1/3}y^{2/3}$ y **65.** $n^{1/2}n^{-1/3}$ $n^{1/6}$

66. $w^{-1/4}w^{3/5}$ $w^{7/20}$ **67.** $\dfrac{x^2}{x^{1/2}}$ $x^{3/2}$ **68.** $\dfrac{a^{1/2}}{a^{1/3}}$ $a^{1/6}$

69. $\dfrac{8t^{1/2}}{4t^{1/4}}$ $2t^{1/4}$ **70.** $\dfrac{6w^{1/4}}{3w^{1/3}}$ $\dfrac{2}{w^{1/12}}$ **71.** $(x^6)^{1/3}$ x^2

72. $(y^{-4})^{1/2}$ $\dfrac{1}{y^2}$ **73.** $(5^{-1/4})^{-1/2}$ $5^{1/8}$ **74.** $(7^{-3/4})^6$ $\dfrac{1}{7^{9/2}}$

75. $(x^2y^6)^{1/2}$ xy^3 **76.** $(t^3w^6)^{1/3}$ tw^2 **77.** $(9x^{-2}y^8)^{-1/2}$ $\dfrac{x}{3y^4}$

78. $(4w^{-2}t^{-4})^{-1/2}$ $\dfrac{wt^2}{2}$

Evaluate each expression.

79. $16^{-1/2} + 2^{-1}$ $\frac{3}{4}$ **80.** $4^{-1/2} - 8^{-2/3}$ $\frac{1}{4}$ **81.** $27^{-1/6} \cdot 27^{-1/2}$ $\frac{1}{9}$

82. $32^{-1/10} \cdot 32^{-1/10}$ $\frac{1}{2}$ **83.** $\dfrac{81^{5/6}}{81^{1/12}}$ 27 **84.** $\dfrac{25^{-3/4}}{25^{3/4}}$ $\frac{1}{125}$

85. $(3^{-4} \cdot 6^8)^{-1/4}$ $\frac{1}{12}$ **86.** $(-2^{-9} \cdot 3^6)^{-1/3}$ $-\frac{8}{9}$

Applications

Solve each problem.

87. ***Yacht dimensions.*** Since 1988, a yacht competing for the America's Cup must satisfy the inequality

$$L + 1.25S^{1/2} - 9.8D^{1/3} \le 16.296,$$

where L is the boat's length in meters, S is the sail area in square meters, and D is the displacement in cubic meters (www.americascupnews.com). Does a boat with a

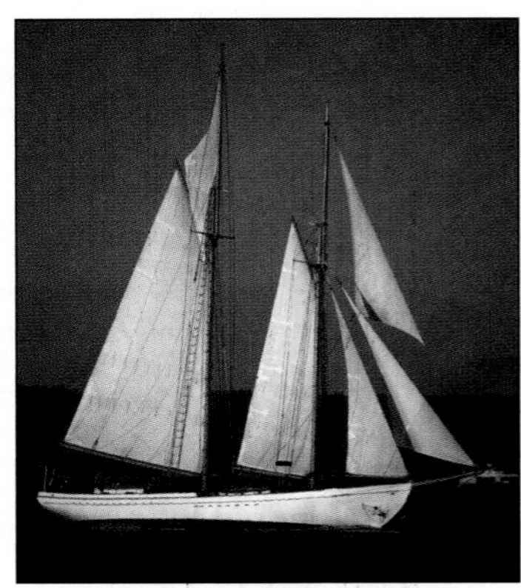

Photo for Exercise 87

displacement of 21.8 m^3, a sail area of 305.4 m^2, and a length of 21.5 m satisfy the inequality? If the length and displacement are not changed, then what is the maximum number of square meters of sail that could be added and still have the boat satisfy the inequality? Yes, 9.2 m^2

88. ***Surface area.*** If A is the surface area of a cube and V is its volume, then

$$A = 6V^{2/3}.$$

Find the surface area of a cube that has a volume of 27 cubic centimeters. What is the surface area of a cube whose sides measure 5 centimeters each? 54 cm^2, 150 cm^2

89. ***Average annual return.*** The average annual return on an investment, r, is given by the formula

$$r = \left(\frac{S}{P}\right)^{1/n} - 1$$

where P is the original investment and S is the value of the investment after n years. An investment of \$10,000 in 1994 in T. Rowe Price's Equity Income Fund amounted to \$30,468 in 2004 (www.troweprice.com). What was the average annual return to the nearest tenth of a percent? 11.8%

90. ***Population growth.*** The U.S. population grew from 248.7 million in 1990 to 300.1 million in 2006 (U.S. Census Bureau, www.census.gov). Use the formula from Exercise 89 to find the average annual rate of growth to the nearest tenth of a percent. 1.2%

91. ***Sail area-displacement ratio.*** The sail area-displacement ratio r for a boat with sail area A (in square feet) and displacement d (in pounds) is given by

$$r = A(d/64)^{-2/3}.$$

The Tartan 4100 has a sail area of 810 ft^2 and a displacement of 23,245 pounds.

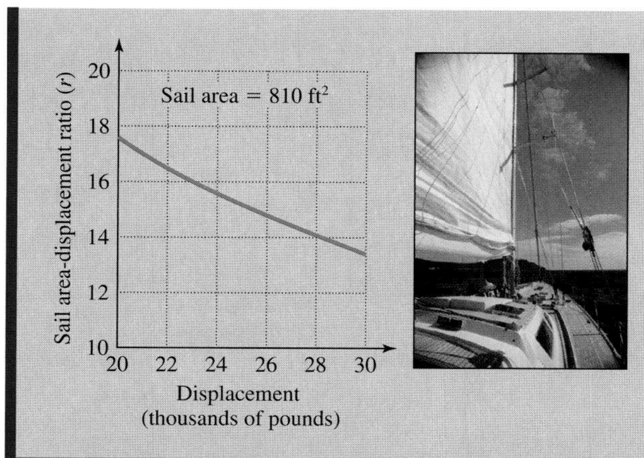

Figure for Exercise 91

a) Find r for this boat. 15.9

b) Use the accompanying graph to determine whether the ratio is increasing or decreasing as the displacement increases, with sail area fixed at 810 ft^2. Decreasing

c) Estimate the displacement for $r = 14$ using the accompanying graph. 28,000 pounds

92. ***Piano tuning.*** The note middle C on a piano is tuned so that the string vibrates at 262 cycles per second, or 262 Hz (Hertz). The C note that is one octave higher is tuned to 524 Hz. Tuning for the 11 notes in between using the method of *equal temperament* is $262 \cdot 2^{n/12}$, where n takes the values 1 through 11. Find the tuning rounded to the nearest whole Hertz for those 11 notes.
278, 294, 312, 330, 350, 371, 393, 416, 441, 467, 495 Hz

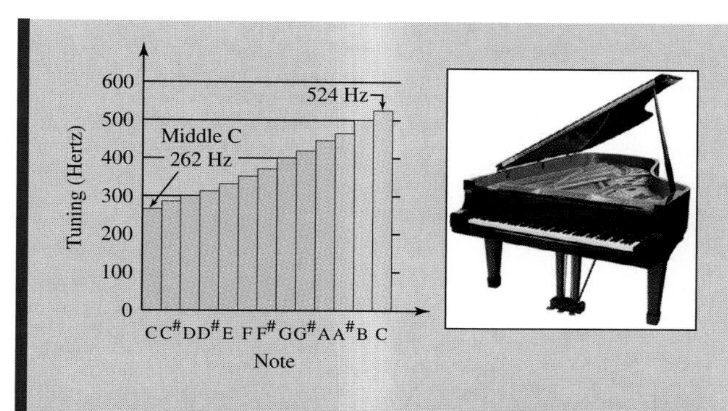

Figure for Exercise 92

Getting More Involved

93. ***Discussion***

If $a^{-m/n} < 0$, then what can you conclude about the values of a, m, and n? $a < 0$ and m and n are odd

94. ***Discussion***

If $a^{-m/n}$ is not a real number, then what can you conclude about the values of a, m, and n?
$a < 0$ and n even, or $a = 0$

95. ***Exploration***

Arrange the following expressions in order from smallest to largest. Use a calculator if you need it.

$$3^0,\ 3^{-8/9},\ 3^{8/9},\ 3^{-2/3},\ 3^{-1/2},\ 3^{2/3},\ 3^{1/2}$$

Now arrange the following expressions in order from smallest to largest. Do not use a calculator.

$$7^{-3/4},\ 7^0,\ 7^{1/3},\ 7^{-1/3},\ 7^{3/4},\ 7^{9/10},\ 7^{-9/10}$$

Use a calculator to check both arrangements. If $5^m < 5^n$, what can you say about m and n? $3^{-8/9} < 3^{-2/3} < 3^{-1/2} < 3^0 < 3^{1/2} < 3^{2/3} < 3^{8/9}$, $7^{-9/10} < 7^{-3/4} < 7^{-1/3} < 7^0 < 7^{1/3} < 7^{3/4} < 7^{9/10}$, $m < n$

Chapter 8 Wrap-Up

Summary

Powers and Roots		**Examples**
nth roots	If $a = b^n$ for a positive integer n, then b is an nth root of a.	2 and -2 are fourth roots of 16.
Principal root	The positive even root of a positive number	The principal fourth root of 16 is 2.
Radical notation	If n is a positive even integer and a is positive, then the symbol $\sqrt[n]{a}$ denotes the principal nth root of a. If n is a positive odd integer, then the symbol $\sqrt[n]{a}$ denotes the nth root of a. If n is any positive integer, then $\sqrt[n]{0} = 0$.	$\sqrt[4]{16} = 2$ $\sqrt[4]{16} \neq -2$ $\sqrt[3]{-8} = -2$, $\sqrt[3]{8} = 2$ $\sqrt[5]{0} = 0$, $\sqrt[6]{0} = 0$
Definition of $a^{1/n}$	If n is any positive integer, then $a^{1/n} = \sqrt[n]{a}$ provided that $\sqrt[n]{a}$ is a real number.	$8^{1/3} = \sqrt[3]{8} = 2$ $(-4)^{1/2}$ is not real.
Definition of $a^{m/n}$	If m and n are positive integers, then $a^{m/n} = (a^{1/n})^m$, provided that $a^{1/n}$ is a real number.	$8^{2/3} = (8^{1/3})^2 = 2^2 = 4$ $(-16)^{3/4}$ is not real.
Definition of $a^{-m/n}$	If m and n are positive integers and $a \neq 0$, then $a^{-m/n} = \frac{1}{a^{m/n}}$, provided that $a^{1/n}$ is a real number.	$8^{-2/3} = \frac{1}{8^{2/3}} = \frac{1}{4}$

Rules of Exponents — **Examples**

The following rules hold for any rational numbers m and n and nonzero real numbers a and b, provided that all expressions represent real numbers.

Rule		Examples
Zero exponent	$a^0 = 1$	$8^0 = 1$, $(3x - y)^0 = 1$
Product rule	$a^m a^n = a^{m+n}$	$3^3 \cdot 3^4 = 3^7$, $x^5 x^{-2} = x^3$
Quotient rule	$\frac{a^m}{a^n} = a^{m-n}$	$\frac{3^5}{3^7} = 3^{-2}$, $\frac{x}{x^{1/4}} = x^{3/4}$
Power rule	$(a^m)^n = a^{mn}$	$(2^2)^3 = 2^6$ $(w^{3/4})^4 = w^3$
Power of a product rule	$(ab)^n = a^n b^n$	$(2t)^{1/2} = 2^{1/2}t^{1/2}$
Power of a quotient rule	$\left(\frac{a}{b}\right)^n = \frac{a^n}{b^n}$	$\left(\frac{x}{3}\right)^{-3} = \frac{x^{-3}}{3^{-3}}$

Rules for Radicals		**Examples**
The following rules hold, provided that all roots are real numbers and n is a positive integer.		
Product rule for radicals	$\sqrt[n]{ab} = \sqrt[n]{a} \cdot \sqrt[n]{b}$	$\sqrt{2} \cdot \sqrt{3} = \sqrt{6}$ $\sqrt{9y} = 3\sqrt{y}$
Quotient rule for radicals	$\sqrt[n]{\frac{a}{b}} = \frac{\sqrt[n]{a}}{\sqrt[n]{b}}$	$\sqrt{\frac{5}{4}} = \frac{\sqrt{5}}{2}$ $\frac{\sqrt{6}}{\sqrt{2}} = \sqrt{\frac{6}{2}} = \sqrt{3}$
Simplified form for square roots	A square root expression is in simplified form if it has 1. *no* perfect square factors inside the radical,	$\sqrt{12} = \sqrt{4 \cdot 3} = 2\sqrt{3}$
	2. *no* fractions inside the radical, and	$\sqrt{\frac{5}{2}} = \frac{\sqrt{5}}{\sqrt{2}}$
	3. *no* radicals in the denominator.	$\frac{\sqrt{5}}{\sqrt{2}} = \frac{\sqrt{5} \cdot \sqrt{2}}{\sqrt{2} \cdot \sqrt{2}} = \frac{\sqrt{10}}{2}$

Solving Equations Involving Squares and Square Roots		**Examples**
Square root property (solving $x^2 = k$)	If $k > 0$, the equation $x^2 = k$ is equivalent to $x = \sqrt{k}$ or $x = -\sqrt{k}$ (also written $x = \pm\sqrt{k}$).	$x^2 = 6$ $x = \pm\sqrt{6}$
	If $k = 0$, the equation $x^2 = k$ is equivalent to $x = 0$.	$t^2 = 0$ $t = 0$
	If $k < 0$, the equation $x^2 = k$ has no real solution.	$x^2 = -8$, no solution
Squaring property of equality	Squaring each side of an equation may introduce extraneous solutions. We must check all of our answers.	$\sqrt{x} = -3$ $(\sqrt{x})^2 = (-3)^2$ $x = 9$ Extraneous solution

Enriching Your Mathematical Word Power

For each mathematical term, choose the correct meaning.

1. *n*th root of *a*
a. a square root
b. the root of a^n
c. a number b such that $a^n = b$
d. a number b such that $b^n = a$ d

2. square of *a*
a. a number b such that $b^2 = a$
b. a^2
c. $|a|$
d. $\sqrt{a}$ b

3. cube root of *a*
a. a^3
b. a number b such that $b^3 = a$
c. $a/3$
d. a number b such that $b = a^3$ b

4. principal root
a. the main root
b. the positive even root of a positive number
c. the positive odd root of a negative number
d. the negative odd root of a negative number b

5. odd root of a
a. the number b such that $b^n = a$ where a is an odd number
b. the opposite of the even root of a
c. the nth root of a
d. the number b such that $b^n = a$ where n is an odd number d

6. index of a radical
a. the number n in $n\sqrt{a}$
b. the number n in $\sqrt[n]{a}$
c. the number n in a^n
d. the number n in $\sqrt{a^n}$ b

7. like radicals
a. radicals with the same index
b. radicals with the same radicand
c. radicals with the same radicand and the same index
d. radicals with even indices c

8. rational exponent
a. an exponent that produces a rational number
b. an integral exponent
c. an exponent that is a real number
d. an exponent that is a rational number d

Review Exercises

8.1 Roots, Radicals, and Rules

Find each root. All variables represent positive real numbers.

1. $\sqrt[5]{32}$ 2
2. $\sqrt[3]{-27}$ -3
3. $\sqrt[3]{1000}$ 10
4. $\sqrt{100}$ 10
5. $\sqrt{x^{12}}$ x^6
6. $\sqrt{a^{10}}$ a^5
7. $\sqrt[3]{x^6}$ x^2
8. $\sqrt[3]{a^9}$ a^3
9. $\sqrt{4x^2}$ $2x$
10. $\sqrt{9y^4}$ $3y^2$
11. $\sqrt[3]{125x^6}$ $5x^2$
12. $\sqrt[3]{8y^{12}}$ $2y^4$
13. $\sqrt{\dfrac{4x^{16}}{y^{14}}}$ $\dfrac{2x^8}{y^7}$
14. $\sqrt{\dfrac{9y^8}{t^{10}}}$ $\dfrac{3y^4}{t^5}$
15. $\sqrt{\dfrac{w^2}{16}}$ $\dfrac{w}{4}$
16. $\sqrt{\dfrac{a^4}{25}}$ $\dfrac{a^2}{5}$

8.2 Simplifying Square Roots

Write each expression in simplified form. All variables represent positive real numbers.

17. $\sqrt{72}$ $6\sqrt{2}$
18. $\sqrt{48}$ $4\sqrt{3}$
19. $\dfrac{1}{\sqrt{3}}$ $\dfrac{\sqrt{3}}{3}$
20. $\dfrac{2}{\sqrt{5}}$ $\dfrac{2\sqrt{5}}{5}$
21. $\sqrt{\dfrac{3}{5}}$ $\dfrac{\sqrt{15}}{5}$
22. $\sqrt{\dfrac{5}{6}}$ $\dfrac{\sqrt{30}}{6}$
23. $\dfrac{\sqrt{33}}{\sqrt{3}}$ $\sqrt{11}$
24. $\dfrac{\sqrt{50}}{\sqrt{5}}$ $\sqrt{10}$
25. $\dfrac{\sqrt{3}}{\sqrt{8}}$ $\dfrac{\sqrt{6}}{4}$
26. $\dfrac{\sqrt{2}}{\sqrt{18}}$ $\dfrac{1}{3}$
27. $\sqrt{y^6}$ y^3
28. $\sqrt{z^{10}}$ z^5
29. $\sqrt{24t^9}$ $2t^4\sqrt{6t}$
30. $\sqrt{8p^7}$ $2p^3\sqrt{2p}$
31. $\sqrt{12m^5t^3}$ $2m^2t\sqrt{3mt}$
32. $\sqrt{18p^3q^7}$ $3pq^3\sqrt{2pq}$
33. $\dfrac{\sqrt{2}}{\sqrt{x}}$ $\dfrac{\sqrt{2x}}{x}$
34. $\dfrac{\sqrt{5}}{\sqrt{y}}$ $\dfrac{\sqrt{5y}}{y}$
35. $\sqrt{\dfrac{3a^5}{2s}}$ $\dfrac{a^2\sqrt{6as}}{2s}$
36. $\sqrt{\dfrac{5x^7}{3w}}$ $\dfrac{x^3\sqrt{15xw}}{3w}$

8.3 Operations with Radicals

Perform each computation and simplify.

37. $2\sqrt{7} + 8\sqrt{7}$ $10\sqrt{7}$
38. $3\sqrt{6} - 5\sqrt{6}$ $-2\sqrt{6}$
39. $\sqrt{12} - \sqrt{27}$ $-\sqrt{3}$
40. $\sqrt{18} + \sqrt{50}$ $8\sqrt{2}$
41. $2\sqrt{3} \cdot 5\sqrt{3}$ 30
42. $-3\sqrt{6} \cdot 2\sqrt{6}$ -36
43. $-3\sqrt{6} \cdot 5\sqrt{3}$ $-45\sqrt{2}$
44. $4\sqrt{12} \cdot 6\sqrt{8}$ $96\sqrt{6}$
45. $-3\sqrt{3}(5 + \sqrt{3})$ $-15\sqrt{3} - 9$
46. $4\sqrt{2}(6 + \sqrt{8})$ $24\sqrt{2} + 16$
47. $-\sqrt{3}(\sqrt{6} - \sqrt{15})$ $-3\sqrt{2} + 3\sqrt{5}$
48. $-\sqrt{2}(\sqrt{6} - \sqrt{2})$ $2 - 2\sqrt{3}$
49. $(\sqrt{3} - 5)(\sqrt{3} + 5)$ -22
50. $(\sqrt{2} + \sqrt{7})(\sqrt{2} - \sqrt{7})$ -5
51. $(2\sqrt{5} - \sqrt{6})^2$ $26 - 4\sqrt{30}$
52. $(3\sqrt{2} + \sqrt{6})^2$ $24 + 12\sqrt{3}$
53. $(4 - 3\sqrt{6})(5 - \sqrt{6})$ $38 - 19\sqrt{6}$
54. $(\sqrt{3} - 2\sqrt{5})(\sqrt{3} + 4\sqrt{5})$ $-37 + 2\sqrt{15}$
55. $3\sqrt{5} \div (6\sqrt{2})$ $\dfrac{\sqrt{10}}{4}$
56. $6\sqrt{5} \div (4\sqrt{3})$ $\dfrac{\sqrt{15}}{2}$
57. $\dfrac{2 - \sqrt{20}}{10}$ $\dfrac{1 - \sqrt{5}}{5}$
58. $\dfrac{6 - \sqrt{12}}{-2}$ $-3 + \sqrt{3}$
59. $\dfrac{3}{1 - \sqrt{5}}$ $-\dfrac{3 + 3\sqrt{5}}{4}$
60. $\dfrac{\sqrt{2}}{\sqrt{6} + \sqrt{3}}$ $\dfrac{2\sqrt{3} - \sqrt{6}}{3}$

8.4 Solving Equations with Radicals and Exponents

Solve each equation.

61. $x^2 = 400$ $-20, 20$

62. $x^2 = 121$ $-11, 11$

63. $7x^2 = 3$ $-\frac{\sqrt{21}}{7}, \frac{\sqrt{21}}{7}$

64. $3x^2 - 7 = 0$ $-\frac{\sqrt{21}}{3}, \frac{\sqrt{21}}{3}$

65. $(x - 4)^2 - 18 = 0$ $4 - 3\sqrt{2}, 4 + 3\sqrt{2}$

66. $2(x + 1)^2 - 40 = 0$ $-1 - 2\sqrt{5}, -1 + 2\sqrt{5}$

67. $\sqrt{x} = 9$ 81

68. $\sqrt{x} - 20 = 0$ 400

69. $x = \sqrt{36 - 5x}$ 4

70. $x = \sqrt{2 - x}$ 1

71. $x + 2 = \sqrt{52 + 2x}$ 6

72. $x - 4 = \sqrt{x - 4}$ 4, 5

Solve each formula for t.

73. $t^2 - 8sw = 0$ $t = \pm 2\sqrt{2sw}$

74. $(t + b)^2 = b^2 - 4ac$ $t = -b \pm \sqrt{b^2 - 4ac}$

75. $3a = \sqrt{bt}$ $t = \frac{9a^2}{b}$

76. $a - \sqrt{t} = w$ $t = (a - w)^2$

8.5 Fractional Exponents

Simplify each expression. Answers with exponents should have positive exponents only.

77. $25^{-3/2}$ $\frac{1}{125}$

78. $9^{-5/2}$ $\frac{1}{243}$

79. $25^{1/2}$ 5

80. $9^{3/2}$ 27

81. $64^{-1/2}$ $\frac{1}{8}$

82. $125^{-2/3}$ $\frac{1}{25}$

83. $-25^{-3/2}$ $-\frac{1}{125}$

84. $-9^{-3/2}$ $-\frac{1}{27}$

85. $(-25)^{-3/2}$ Not a real number

86. $(-9)^{-3/4}$ Not a real number

87. $(-8)^{-1/3}$ $-\frac{1}{2}$

88. $(-27)^{-4/3}$ $\frac{1}{81}$

89. $x^{-3/5}x^{-2/5}$ $\frac{1}{x}$

90. $t^{-1/3}t^{1/2}$ $t^{1/6}$

91. $(-8x^{-6})^{-1/3}$ $-\frac{1}{2}x^2$

92. $(-27x^{-9})^{-2/3}$ $\frac{1}{9}x^6$

93. $w^{-3/2} \div w^{-7/2}$ w^2

94. $m^{1/3} \div m^{-1/4}$ $m^{7/12}$

95. $\left(\frac{9t^{-6}}{s^{-4}}\right)^{-1/2}$ $\frac{t^3}{3s^2}$

96. $\left(\frac{8y^{-3}}{x^6}\right)^{-2/3}$ $\frac{x^4y^2}{4}$

97. $\left(\frac{8x^{-12}}{y^{30}}\right)^{2/3}$ $\frac{4}{x^8y^{20}}$

98. $\left(\frac{16y^{-3/4}}{t^{1/2}}\right)^{-2}$ $\frac{y^{3/2}t}{256}$

Applications

Solve each problem.

99. ***Depreciation of a Lumina.*** If the cost of a piece of equipment was C dollars and it is sold for S dollars after n years, then the annual depreciation rate is given by

$$r = 1 - \left(\frac{S}{C}\right)^{1/n}.$$

A 1994 Chevrolet Lumina that sold new for \$15,446 sells for \$1789 in 2006 (www.edmunds.com).

a) Find the depreciation rate for this car to the nearest tenth of a percent.

b) Use the accompanying graph to determine whether this car depreciated more during the first two years or the last two years shown.

a) 16.4% **b)** First two years

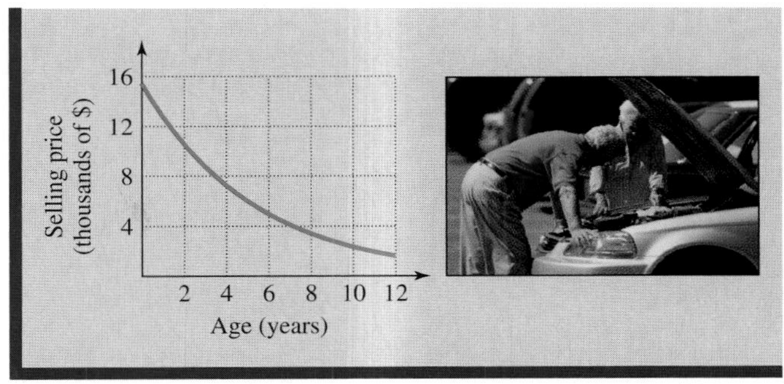

Figure for Exercise 99

100. ***Depreciation of a Thunderbird.*** A 1996 Ford Thunderbird that sold new for \$16,892 sells for \$2583 in 2006 (www.edmunds.com). Use the formula from the previous exercise to find the depreciation rate to the nearest tenth of a percent. 17.1%

101. ***Radius of a drop.*** The amount of water in a large raindrop is 0.25 cm^3. Use the formula

$$r = \left(\frac{3V}{4\pi}\right)^{1/3}$$

to find the radius of the spherical drop to the nearest tenth of a centimeter. 0.4 cm

102. ***Radius of a circle.*** Solve the formula $A = \pi r^2$ for r.

$r = \sqrt{\frac{A}{\pi}}$

103. ***Waffle cones.*** A large waffle cone has a height of 6 in. and a radius of 2 in. as shown in the accompanying figure. Find the exact amount of waffle in a cone this size. The formula $A = \pi r\sqrt{r^2 + h^2}$ gives the lateral surface area of a right circular cone with radius r and height h. Be sure to

simplify the radical. Use a calculator to find the answer to the nearest square inch.
$4\pi\sqrt{10}$ or 40 in.^{2}

Figure for Exercise 103

104. ***Salting the roads.*** A city manager wants to find the amount of canvas required to cover a conical salt pile that is stored for the winter. The height of the pile is 10 yards, and the diameter of the base is 24 yards. Use the formula in Exercise 103 to find the exact number of square yards of canvas needed. Simplify the radical. Use a calculator to find the answer to the nearest square yard.
$24\pi\sqrt{61}$ or 589 yd^2

105. ***Wide screen TV.*** The screen on a new Panasonic widescreen flat panel television measures 10.8 in. by 19.2 in. Find the diagonal measure of the screen to the nearest inch.
22 in.

106. ***Wider screen TV.*** The diagonal measure of the screen on a flat panel Samsung television is 40 in. The aspect ratio (ratio of the length to the width) of the screen is 16 to 9. Find the length and width to the nearest tenth of an inch.
34.9 in. by 19.6 in.

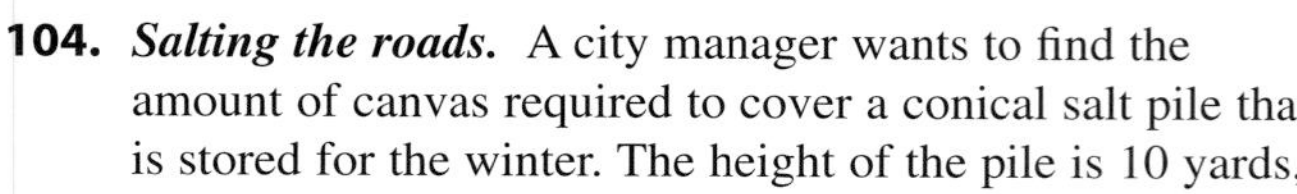

Chapter 8 Test

Simplify each expression.

1. $\sqrt{36}$ 6

2. $\sqrt{144}$ 12

3. $\sqrt[3]{-27}$ -3

4. $\sqrt[5]{32}$ 2

5. $16^{1/4}$ 2

6. $\sqrt{24}$ $2\sqrt{6}$

7. $\sqrt{\dfrac{3}{8}}$ $\dfrac{\sqrt{6}}{4}$

8. $(-4)^{3/2}$ Not a real number

9. $27^{4/3}$ 81

10. $(-27)^{-1/3}$ $-\dfrac{1}{3}$

11. $-8^{4/3}$ -16

12. $\sqrt{8} + \sqrt{2}$ $3\sqrt{2}$

13. $(2 + \sqrt{3})^2$ $7 + 4\sqrt{3}$

14. $(3\sqrt{2} - \sqrt{7})(3\sqrt{2} + \sqrt{7})$ 11

15. $\sqrt{21} \div \sqrt{3}$
$\sqrt{7}$

16. $\sqrt{20} \div \sqrt{3}$
$\dfrac{2\sqrt{15}}{3}$

17. $\dfrac{2 + \sqrt{8}}{2}$
$1 + \sqrt{2}$

18. $\sqrt{3}(\sqrt{6} - \sqrt{3})$
$3\sqrt{2} - 3$

Simplify. Assume that all variables represent positive real numbers, and write answers with positive exponents only.

19. $y^{1/2} \cdot y^{1/4}$ $y^{3/4}$

20. $\dfrac{6x}{2x^{1/3}}$ $3x^{2/3}$

21. $(x^3y^9)^{1/3}$ xy^3

22. $\left(\dfrac{125w^3}{u^{-12}}\right)^{-1/3}$ $\dfrac{1}{5u^4w}$

23. $\sqrt{\dfrac{3}{t}}$ $\dfrac{\sqrt{3t}}{t}$

24. $\sqrt{4y^6}$ $2y^3$

25. $\sqrt[3]{8y^{12}}$ $2y^4$

26. $\sqrt{18t^7}$ $3t^3\sqrt{2t}$

Solve each equation.

27. $(x + 3)^2 = 36$ $-9, 3$

28. $\sqrt{x + 7} = 5$ 18

29. $5x^2 = 2$
$-\dfrac{\sqrt{10}}{5}, \dfrac{\sqrt{10}}{5}$

30. $(3x - 4)^2 = 0$
$\dfrac{4}{3}$

31. $x - 3 = \sqrt{5x + 9}$ 11

Solve the equation for the specified variable.

32. $S = \pi r^2 h$ for r
$r = \pm\sqrt{\dfrac{S}{\pi h}}$

33. $a^2 + b^2 = c^2$ for b
$b = \pm\sqrt{c^2 - a^2}$

Show a complete solution to each problem.

34. Find the exact length of the side of a square whose diagonal is 5 meters.
$\dfrac{5\sqrt{2}}{2}$ meters

35. To utilize a center-pivot irrigation system, a farmer planted his crop in a circular field of 100,000 square meters. Find the radius of the circular field to the nearest tenth of a meter. 178.4 meters

Making Connections | A Review of Chapters 1–8

Find the solution set to each equation or inequality. For the inequalities, also sketch the graph of the inequality and state the solution set using interval notation.

1. $2x + 3 = 0$ $\left\{-\frac{3}{2}\right\}$

2. $2x = 3$ $\left\{\frac{3}{2}\right\}$

3. $2x + 3 > 0$ $\left(-\frac{3}{2}, \infty\right)$

4. $-2x + 3 > 0$ $\left(-\infty, \frac{3}{2}\right)$

5. $2(x + 3) = 0$ $\{-3\}$

6. $2x^2 = 3$ $\left\{-\frac{\sqrt{6}}{2}, \frac{\sqrt{6}}{2}\right\}$

7. $\frac{x}{3} = \frac{2}{x}$ $\{-\sqrt{6}, \sqrt{6}\}$

8. $\frac{x-1}{x} = \frac{x}{x-2}$ $\left\{\frac{2}{3}\right\}$

9. $(2x + 3)^2 = 0$ $\left\{-\frac{3}{2}\right\}$

10. $(2x + 3)(x - 3) = 0$ $\left\{-\frac{3}{2}, 3\right\}$

11. $2x^2 + 3 = 0$ No solution, $\emptyset$

12. $(2x + 3)^2 = 1$ $\{-2, -1\}$

13. $(2x + 3)^2 = -1$ No solution, $\emptyset$

14. $\sqrt{2x^2 - 14} = x - 1$ $\{3\}$

Let $a = 2$, $b = -3$, and $c = -9$. Find the value of each algebraic expression.

15. b^2 9

16. $-4ac$ 72

17. $b^2 - 4ac$ 81

18. $\sqrt{b^2 - 4ac}$ 9

19. $-b + \sqrt{b^2 - 4ac}$ 12

20. $-b - \sqrt{b^2 - 4ac}$ -6

21. $\frac{-b + \sqrt{b^2 - 4ac}}{2a}$ 3

22. $\frac{-b - \sqrt{b^2 - 4ac}}{2a}$ $-\frac{3}{2}$

Factor each trinomial completely.

23. $x^2 - 6x + 9$ $(x - 3)^2$

24. $x^2 + 10x + 25$ $(x + 5)^2$

25. $x^2 + 12x + 36$ $(x + 6)^2$

26. $x^2 - 20x + 100$ $(x - 10)^2$

27. $2x^2 - 8x + 8$ $2(x - 2)^2$

28. $3x^2 + 6x + 3$ $3(x + 1)^2$

Perform the indicated operation.

29. $(3 + 2x) - (6 - 5x)$ $7x - 3$

30. $(5 + 3t)(4 - 5t)$ $-15t^2 - 13t + 20$

31. $(8 - 6j)(3 + 4j)$ $-24j^2 + 14j + 24$

32. $(1 - u) + (5 + 7u)$ $6u + 6$

33. $(3 - 4v) - (2 - 5v)$ $v + 1$

34. $(2 + t)^2$ $t^2 + 4t + 4$

35. $(t - 7)(t + 7)$ $t^2 - 49$

36. $(3 - 2n)(3 + 2n)$ $-4n^2 + 9$

37. $(1 - m)^2$ $m^2 - 2m + 1$

38. $(-4 - 6t) - (-3 - 8t)$ $2t - 1$

39. $(1 + r)(3 - 4r)$ $-4r^2 - r + 3$

40. $(2 - 6y)(1 + 3y)$ $-18y^2 + 2$

41. $(1 - 2j) + (-6 + 5j)$ $3j - 5$

42. $(-2 - j) + (4 - 5j)$ $-6j + 2$

43. $\frac{4 - 6x}{2}$ $2 - 3x$

44. $\frac{-3 - 9p}{3}$ $-1 - 3p$

45. $\frac{8 - 12q}{-4}$ $-2 + 3q$

46. $\frac{20 - 5z}{-5}$ $-4 + z$

Solve the problem.

47. ***Oxygen uptake.*** In studying the oxygen uptake rate for marathon runners, Costill and Fox calculate the power expended P in kilocalories per minute using the formula $P = M(av - b)$, where M is the mass of the runner in kilograms and v is the speed in meters per minute (*Medicine and Science in Sports,* Vol. 1). The constants a and b have values $a = 1.02 \times 10^{-3}$ and $b = 2.62 \times 10^{-2}$.

a) Find P for a 60-kg runner who is running at 300 m/min. 16.788 kilocalories per minute

b) Find the velocity of a 55-kg runner who is expending 14 kcal/min. 275.24 m/min

c) Judging from the accompanying graph of velocity and power expenditure for a 55-kg runner, is power expenditure increasing or decreasing as the velocity increases? Increasing

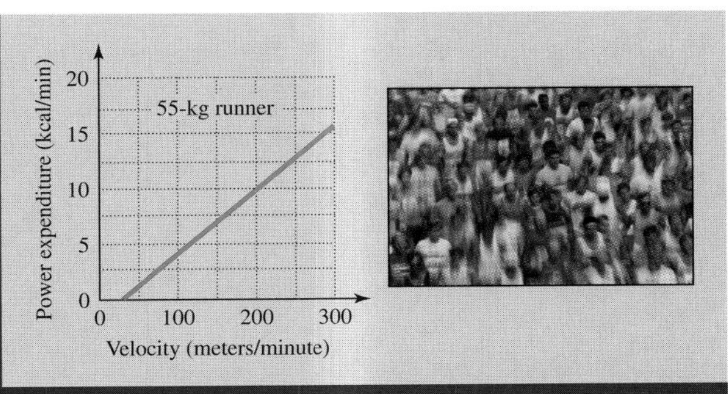

Figure for Exercise 47

Critical Thinking | For Individual or Group Work | Chapter 8

These exercises can be solved by a variety of techniques, which may or may not require algebra. So be creative and think critically. Explain all answers. Answers are in the Instructor's Edition of this text.

1. ***Summing angles.*** Find the sum of the measures of the angles at the points of the irregular five-pointed star shown in the accompanying figure. That is, find

$$m\angle A + m\angle B + m\angle C + m\angle D + m\angle E.$$

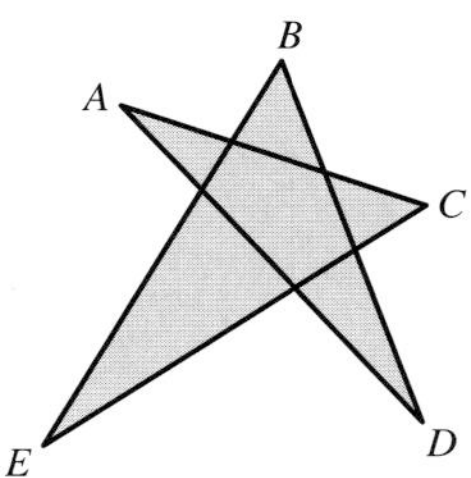

Figure for Exercise 1

2. ***Cheese head.*** A Green Bay Packer fan has a cubic block of cheese that measures 4 inches on each side. He has a knife that can cut through anything and wants to cut the cheese block into 64 cubes that are 1 inch on each side. If he can rearrange the pieces before each cut, then what is the minimum number of cuts that will accomplish this task?

3. ***Wage earners.*** Alice and Beth together have the same hourly wage as Carl. Carl and Don together have the same hourly wage as Eustis. Eustis and Alice together have the same hourly wage as Frank. If Beth's, Don's, and Frank's hourly wages total $100 and Alice makes $8 per hour, then what is Frank's hourly wage?

4. ***Factoring fever.*** Express $2^{24} - 1$ as a product of prime numbers without using a calculator.

5. ***Average joggers.*** Two friends jog from their apartment down to the beach at an average speed of 6 miles per hour. They jog back to the apartment at an average of 4 miles per hour. What was the average speed for the entire trip?

6. ***Three pairs.*** Find three integral solutions to

$$180x - y^3 = 0.$$

7. ***Perfect squares.*** For what integral values of n will the value of

$$\frac{n}{20 - n}$$

be a perfect square?

8. ***Waiting for water.*** A hot water pipe is 1/2 in. in diameter and the shower head is located 70 feet from the hot water tank. If the water runs at 3 gallons per minute, then how long (to the nearest second) does it take for the hot water in the tank to reach the shower head?

Photo for Exercise 8

1. 180° **2.** Six cuts **3.** $58 per hour **4.** $3^2 \cdot 5 \cdot 7 \cdot 13 \cdot 17 \cdot 241$ **5.** 4.8 miles per hour **6.** (0, 0), (150, 30), (−150, −30) **7.** 0, 10, 16, 18 **8.** 14 sec

Chapter 9

Quadratic Equations, Parabolas, and Functions

Throughout time, humans have been building bridges over waterways. Primitive people threw logs across streams or attached ropes to branches to cross the waters. Later, the Romans built stone structures to span rivers and chasms. Throughout the centuries, bridges have been made of wood and stone and later from cast iron, concrete, and steel. Today's bridges are among the most beautiful and complex creations of modern engineering. Whether the bridge spans a small creek or a 4-mile-wide stretch of water, mathematics is a part of its very foundation.

The function of a bridge, the length it must span, and the load it must carry often determine the type of bridge that is built. Some common types designed by civil engineers are cantilevered, arch, cable-stayed, and suspension bridges. The military is known for building trestle bridges and floating or pontoon bridges.

New technology has enabled engineers to build bridges that are stronger, lighter, and less expensive than in the past, as well as being esthetically pleasing. Currently, some engineers are working on making bridges earthquake resistant. Another idea that is being explored is incorporating carbon fibers in cement to warn of small cracks through electronic signals.

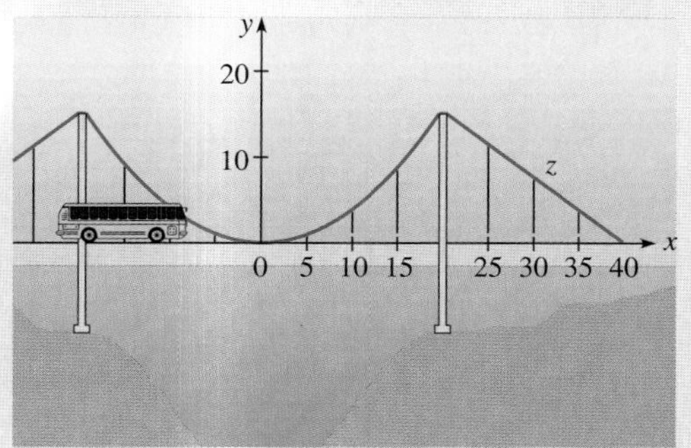

In Exercise 47 of Section 9.6 you will see how quadratic equations are used in designing suspension bridges.

9.1 The Square Root Property and Factoring

In This Section

We solved some quadratic equations in Chapters 6 and 7 by factoring. In Chapter 8, we solved some quadratic equations using the square root property. In this section we will review the types that you have already learned to solve. In Section 9.2, you will learn a method by which you can solve any quadratic equation.

⟨1⟩ Quadratic Equations

We saw the definition of a quadratic equation in Chapter 6, but we will repeat it here.

Quadratic Equation

A **quadratic equation** is an equation of the form

$$ax^2 + bx + c = 0,$$

where a, b, and c are real numbers with $a \neq 0$.

Equations that can be written in the form of the definition may also be called quadratic equations. In Chapters 6, 7, and 8 we solved quadratic equations such as

$$x^2 = 10, \qquad 5(x - 2)^2 = 20, \qquad \text{and} \qquad x^2 - 5x = -6.$$

⟨2⟩ Using the Square Root Property

If $b = 0$ in $ax^2 + bx + c = 0$, then the quadratic equation can be solved by using the square root property.

EXAMPLE 1

Using the square root property

Solve the equations.

a) $x^2 - 9 = 0$

b) $2x^2 - 3 = 0$

c) $-3(x + 1)^2 = -6$

⟨ Teaching Tip ⟩

Since we need the square root property in completing the square, it is good to review it here.

Solution

a) Solve the equation for x^2, and then use the square root property:

$$x^2 - 9 = 0$$

$$x^2 = 9 \qquad \text{Add 9 to each side.}$$

$$x = \pm 3 \qquad \text{Square root property}$$

Check 3 and -3 in the original equation. Both 3 and -3 are solutions to $x^2 - 9 = 0$.

b) $2x^2 - 3 = 0$

$$2x^2 = 3$$

$$x^2 = \frac{3}{2}$$

$$x = \pm\sqrt{\frac{3}{2}} \quad \text{Square root property}$$

$$x = \pm\frac{\sqrt{3}\cdot\sqrt{2}}{\sqrt{2}\cdot\sqrt{2}} \quad \text{Rationalize the denominator.}$$

$$x = \pm\frac{\sqrt{6}}{2}$$

Check. The solutions to $2x^2 - 3 = 0$ are $\frac{\sqrt{6}}{2}$ and $-\frac{\sqrt{6}}{2}$.

c) If we expand $(x + 1)^2$ into $x^2 + 2x + 1$, we get a term involving x, and b is not zero as it is in parts (a) and (b). Instead of expanding $(x + 1)^2$, we isolate it and then apply the square root property:

$$-3(x + 1)^2 = -6$$

$$(x + 1)^2 = 2 \quad \text{Divide each side by } -3.$$

$$x + 1 = \pm\sqrt{2} \quad \text{Square root property}$$

$$x = -1 \pm \sqrt{2} \quad \text{Subtract 1 from each side.}$$

Check $x = -1 \pm \sqrt{2}$ in the original equation:

$$-3(-1 \pm \sqrt{2} + 1)^2 = -3(\pm\sqrt{2})^2 = -3(2) = -6$$

The solutions are $-1 + \sqrt{2}$ and $-1 - \sqrt{2}$.

Now do Exercises 7–12

EXAMPLE 2

A quadratic equation with no real solution

Solve $x^2 + 12 = 0$.

Solution

The equation $x^2 + 12 = 0$ is equivalent to $x^2 = -12$. Because the square of any real number is nonnegative, this equation has no real solution.

Now do Exercises 13–32

⟨3⟩ Solving Equations by Factoring

In Chapter 6, you learned to factor trinomials and to use factoring to solve some quadratic equations. Recall that quadratic equations are solved by factoring as follows.

Strategy for Solving Quadratic Equations by Factoring

1. Write the equation with 0 on one side of the equal sign.
2. Factor the other side.
3. Use the zero factor property. (Set each factor equal to 0.)
4. Solve the two linear equations.
5. Check the answers in the original quadratic equation.

EXAMPLE 3

Solving a quadratic equation by factoring

Solve by factoring.

a) $x^2 + 2x = 8$

b) $3x^2 + 13x - 10 = 0$

c) $\frac{1}{6}x^2 - \frac{1}{2}x = 3$

Solution

a)

$$x^2 + 2x = 8$$

$$x^2 + 2x - 8 = 0 \quad \text{Get 0 on the right-hand side.}$$

$$(x + 4)(x - 2) = 0 \quad \text{Factor.}$$

$$x + 4 = 0 \quad \text{or} \quad x - 2 = 0 \quad \text{Zero factor property}$$

$$x = -4 \quad \text{or} \quad x = 2 \quad \text{Solve the linear equations.}$$

Check in the original equation:

$$(-4)^2 + 2(-4) = 16 - 8 = 8$$

$$2^2 + 2 \cdot 2 = 4 + 4 = 8$$

Both -4 and 2 are solutions to the equation.

b)

$$3x^2 + 13x - 10 = 0$$

$$(3x - 2)(x + 5) = 0 \quad \text{Factor.}$$

$$3x - 2 = 0 \quad \text{or} \quad x + 5 = 0 \quad \text{Zero factor property}$$

$$3x = 2 \quad \text{or} \quad x = -5$$

$$x = \frac{2}{3} \quad \text{or} \quad x = -5$$

Check in the original equation. Both -5 and $\frac{2}{3}$ are solutions to the equation.

c)

$$\frac{1}{6}x^2 - \frac{1}{2}x = 3$$

$$x^2 - 3x = 18 \quad \text{Multiply each side by 6.}$$

$$x^2 - 3x - 18 = 0 \quad \text{Get 0 on the right-hand side.}$$

$$(x - 6)(x + 3) = 0 \quad \text{Factor.}$$

$$x - 6 = 0 \quad \text{or} \quad x + 3 = 0 \quad \text{Zero factor property}$$

$$x = 6 \quad \text{or} \quad x = -3$$

Check in the original equation. The solutions are -3 and 6.

Now do Exercises 33–54

‹ Helpful Hint ›

After you have factored the quadratic polynomial, use FOIL to check that you have factored correctly before proceeding to the next step.

‹ Teaching Tip ›

We learned to solve equations by factoring in Chapter 6. So it is good to review it here and see all of the methods for solving quadratics in one place.

CAUTION You can set each factor equal to zero only when the product of the factors is zero. Note that $x^2 - 3x = 18$ is equivalent to $x(x - 3) = 18$, but you can make no conclusion about two factors that have a product of 18.

Warm-Ups 

True or false? Explain your answer.

1. Both -4 and 4 satisfy the equation $x^2 - 16 = 0$. True
2. The equation $(x - 3)^2 = 8$ is equivalent to $x - 3 = 2\sqrt{2}$. False
3. Every quadratic equation can be solved by factoring. False
4. Both -5 and 4 are solutions to $(x - 4)(x + 5) = 0$. True
5. The quadratic equation $x^2 = -3$ has no real solutions. True
6. The equation $x^2 = 0$ has no real solutions. False
7. The equation $(2x + 3)(4x - 5) = 0$ is equivalent to $x = \frac{3}{2}$ or $x = \frac{5}{4}$. False
8. The only solution to the equation $(x + 2)^2 = 0$ is -2. True
9. $(x - 3)(x - 5) = 4$ is equivalent to $x - 3 = 2$ or $x - 5 = 2$. False
10. All quadratic equations have two distinct solutions. False

Boost your grade at mathzone.com!
- Practice Problems
- NetTutor
- Self-Tests
- e-Professors
- Videos

9.1 Exercises

‹ Study Tips ›

- Many schools have study skills centers that offer courses, workshops, and individual help on how to study.
- A search for "study skill" on the World Wide Web will turn up an endless amount of useful information.

Reading and Writing *After reading this section, write out the answers to these questions. Use complete sentences.*

1. What is a quadratic equation? A quadratic equation is an equation of the form $ax^2 + bx + c = 0$, where $a \neq 0$.
2. What property do we use to solve quadratic equations in which $b = 0$? If $b = 0$, a quadratic equation can be solved by the square root property.
3. How can a quadratic equation in which $b = 0$ fail to have a real solution? If $b = 0$, we can get the square root of a negative number and no real solution.
4. What method is discussed for solving quadratic equations in which $b \neq 0$? If $b \neq 0$, some quadratics can be solved by factoring.
5. When do you need to solve linear equations to find the solutions to a quadratic equation? After applying the zero factor property we will have linear equations to solve.
6. What is the first step for solving a quadratic equation by factoring if the coefficients are fractions? Multiply each side by the LCD to get integral coefficients.

‹2› Using the Square Root Property

Solve each equation. See Examples 1 and 2.

7. $x^2 = 64$ $-8, 8$
8. $x^2 = 49$ $-7, 7$
9. $x^2 = \frac{9}{4}$ $-\frac{3}{2}, \frac{3}{2}$
10. $x^2 = \frac{25}{81}$ $-\frac{5}{9}, \frac{5}{9}$
11. $x^2 - 36 = 0$ $-6, 6$
12. $x^2 - 81 = 0$ $-9, 9$
13. $x^2 + 10 = 0$ No real solution
14. $x^2 + 4 = 0$ No real solution
15. $5x^2 = 50$ $-\sqrt{10}, \sqrt{10}$
16. (VIDEO) $7x^2 = 14$ $-\sqrt{2}, \sqrt{2}$
17. $3t^2 - 5 = 0$ $-\frac{\sqrt{15}}{3}, \frac{\sqrt{15}}{3}$
18. $5y^2 - 7 = 0$ $-\frac{\sqrt{35}}{5}, \frac{\sqrt{35}}{5}$

19. $-3y^2 + 8 = 0$ $-\frac{2\sqrt{6}}{3}, \frac{2\sqrt{6}}{3}$

20. $-5w^2 + 12 = 0$ $-\frac{2\sqrt{15}}{5}, \frac{2\sqrt{15}}{5}$

21. $(x - 3)^2 = 4$ $1, 5$

VIDEO **22.** $(x + 5)^2 = 9$ $-8, -2$

23. $(y - 2)^2 = 18$ $2 - 3\sqrt{2}, 2 + 3\sqrt{2}$

24. $(m - 5)^2 = 20$ $5 - 2\sqrt{5}, 5 + 2\sqrt{5}$

25. $2(x + 1)^2 = \frac{1}{2}$ $-\frac{3}{2}, -\frac{1}{2}$

26. $-3(x - 1)^2 = -\frac{3}{4}$ $\frac{3}{2}, \frac{1}{2}$

VIDEO **27.** $(x - 1)^2 = \frac{1}{2}$ $\frac{2 - \sqrt{2}}{2}, \frac{2 + \sqrt{2}}{2}$

28. $(y + 2)^2 = \frac{1}{2}$ $\frac{-4 - \sqrt{2}}{2}, \frac{-4 + \sqrt{2}}{2}$

29. $\left(x + \frac{1}{2}\right)^2 = \frac{1}{2}$ $\frac{-1 - \sqrt{2}}{2}, \frac{-1 + \sqrt{2}}{2}$

30. $\left(x - \frac{1}{2}\right)^2 = \frac{3}{2}$ $\frac{1 - \sqrt{6}}{2}, \frac{1 + \sqrt{6}}{2}$

31. $(x - 11)^2 = 0$ 11

32. $(x + 45)^2 = 0$ -45

‹3› Solving Equations by Factoring

Solve by factoring.

See Example 3.

See the Strategy for Solving Quadratic Equations by Factoring box on page 541.

33. $x^2 + 3x + 2 = 0$ $-2, -1$

34. $x^2 + 6x + 5 = 0$ $-5, -1$

35. $x^2 - x - 30 = 0$ $-5, 6$

36. $x^2 + x - 20 = 0$ $-5, 4$

37. $x^2 - 2x - 15 = 0$ $-3, 5$

38. $x^2 - x - 12 = 0$ $-3, 4$

39. $x^2 + 6x + 9 = 0$ -3

40. $x^2 + 10x + 25 = 0$ -5

41. $4x^2 - 4x = 8$ $-1, 2$

VIDEO **42.** $3x^2 + 3x = 90$ $-6, 5$

43. $3x^2 - 6x = 0$ $0, 2$

44. $-5x^2 + 10x = 0$ $0, 2$

45. $-4t^2 + 6t = 0$ $0, \frac{3}{2}$

46. $-6w^2 + 15w = 0$ $0, \frac{5}{2}$

47. $2x^2 + 11x - 21 = 0$ $-7, \frac{3}{2}$

48. $2x^2 - 5x + 2 = 0$ $2, \frac{1}{2}$

49. $x^2 - 10x + 25 = 0$ 5

50. $x^2 - 4x + 4 = 0$ 2

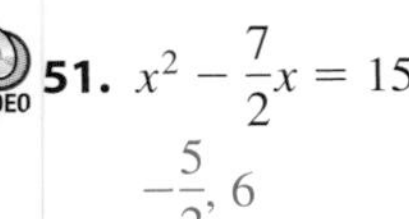

VIDEO **51.** $x^2 - \frac{7}{2}x = 15$ $-\frac{5}{2}, 6$

52. $3x^2 - \frac{2}{5}x = \frac{1}{5}$ $-\frac{1}{5}, \frac{1}{3}$

53. $\frac{1}{10}a^2 - a + \frac{12}{5} = 0$ $4, 6$

54. $\frac{2}{9}w^2 + \frac{5}{3}w - 3 = 0$ $-9, \frac{3}{2}$

Miscellaneous

Solve each equation.

55. $2x^2 - \frac{1}{2} = 0$ $-\frac{1}{2}, \frac{1}{2}$

56. $3x^2 - \frac{1}{3} = 0$ $-\frac{1}{3}, \frac{1}{3}$

57. $(x + 1)^2 = 25$ $-6, 4$

58. $(x - 3)^2 = 1$ $2, 4$

59. $(x + 1)^2 = 1$ $-2, 0$

60. $(2x + 3)^2 = 9$ $-3, 0$

61. $x^2 + 2x - 24 = 0$ $-6, 4$

62. $x^2 - 5x - 50 = 0$ $-5, 10$

63. $4x^2 + 36x + 81 = 0$ $-\frac{9}{2}$

64. $9x^2 - 30x + 25 = 0$ $\frac{5}{3}$

65. $x^2 - 2x = 2(3 - x)$ $-\sqrt{6}, \sqrt{6}$

66. $x^2 + 2x = \frac{1 + 4x}{2}$ $-\frac{\sqrt{2}}{2}, \frac{\sqrt{2}}{2}$

67. $x = \frac{27}{12 - x}$ $3, 9$

68. $x = \frac{6}{x + 1}$ $-3, 2$

69. $\sqrt{3x - 8} = x - 2$ $3, 4$

70. $\sqrt{3x - 14} = x - 4$ $5, 6$

Applications

Solve each problem.

71. ***Side of a square.*** If the diagonal of a square is 5 meters, then what is the length of a side? $\frac{5\sqrt{2}}{2}$ meters

72. ***Diagonal of a square.*** If the side of a square is 5 meters, then what is the length of the diagonal? $5\sqrt{2}$ meters

73. ***Howard's journey.*** Howard walked eight blocks east and then four blocks north to reach the public library. How far was he then from where he started? $4\sqrt{5}$ blocks

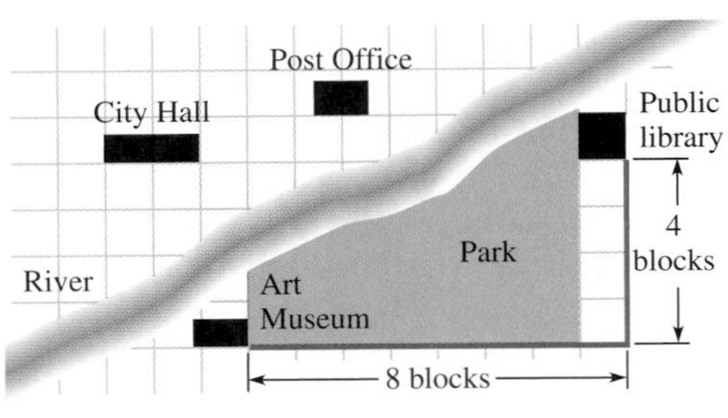

Figure for Exercise 73

74. ***Side and diagonal.*** Each side of a square has length s, and its diagonal has length d. Write a formula for s in terms of d. $s = \frac{d\sqrt{2}}{2}$

75. ***Designing a bridge.*** Find the length d of the diagonal brace shown in the accompanying diagram. $2\sqrt{61}$ feet

76. ***Designing a bridge.*** Find the length labeled w in the accompanying diagram. 9 feet

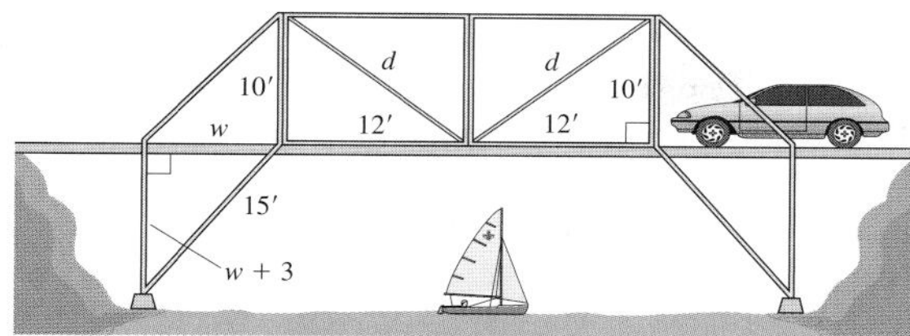

Figure for Exercises 75 and 76

77. ***Two years of interest.*** Tasha deposited \$500 into an account that paid interest compounded annually. At the end of two years she had \$565. Solve the equation $565 = 500(1 + r)^2$ to find the annual rate r to the nearest tenth of a percent. 6.3%

78. ***Rate of increase.*** The price of a new 2005 Dodge Viper convertible was \$80,995 and a new 2007 Viper convertible was \$81,895 (www.edmunds.com). Find the average annual rate of increase (to the nearest tenth of a percent) for that time period by solving the equation

$$81{,}895 = 80{,}955(1 + r)^2. \quad 0.6\%$$

79. ***Projectile motion.*** If a ball is projected vertically upward with initial velocity v_0 ft/sec from an initial height of s_0 feet, then its height in feet t seconds after it is projected is given by

$$h(t) = -16t^2 + v_0t + s_0.$$

Suppose that a baseball is projected vertically upward at 80 ft/sec from a height of 6 feet.

a) Find $h(4)$. 70 feet

b) For what values of t is the baseball 102 feet above the ground? 2 sec and 3 sec

c) For what value of t is the baseball back at a height of 6 feet? 5 sec

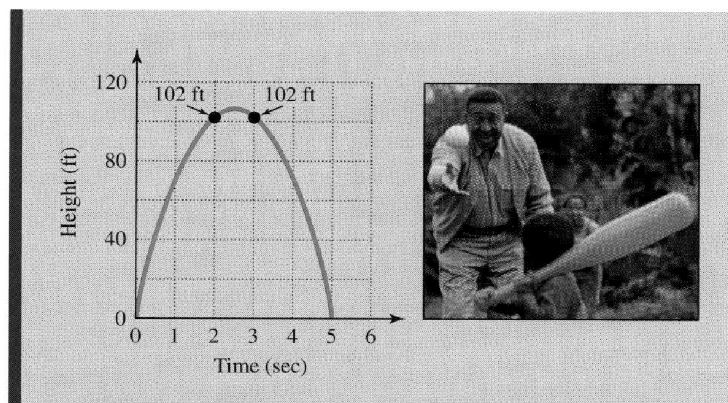

Figure for Exercise 79

80. ***Diving time.*** A springboard diver can perform complicated maneuvers in a short period of time. If a diver springs vertically into the air at 24 ft/sec from a board that is 16 feet above the water, then in how many seconds will she hit the water? Use the formula from Exercise 79. 2 sec

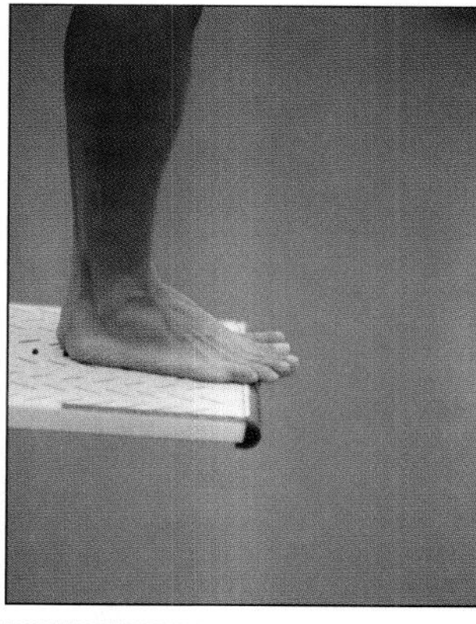

Photo for Exercise 80

81. ***Sum of integers.*** The formula $S = \frac{n^2 + n}{2}$ gives the sum of the first n positive integers. For what value of n is this sum equal to 45? 9

82. ***Serious reading.*** Kristy's New Year's resolution is to read one page of *Training Your Boa to Squeeze* on January 1, two pages on January 2, three pages on January 3, and so on. On what date will she finish the 136-page book? See Exercise 81. January 16

Getting More Involved

83. *Writing*

One of the following equations has no real solutions. Find it by inspecting all of the equations (without solving). Explain your answer.

a) $x^2 - 99 = 0$

b) $2(v + 77)^2 = 0$

c) $3(y - 22)^2 + 11 = 0$

d) $5(w - 8)^2 - 9 = 0$ c

84. *Cooperative learning*

For each of three soccer teams A, B, and C to play the other two teams once, it takes three games (AB, AC, and BC). Work in groups to answer the following questions.

a) How many games are required for each team of a four-team league to play every other team once? 6

b) How many games are required in a five-team soccer league? 10

c) Find an expression of the form $an^2 + bn + c$ that gives the number of games required in a soccer league of n teams. $\frac{1}{2}n^2 - \frac{1}{2}n$

d) The Urban Soccer League has fields available for a 120-game season. If the organizers want each team to play every other team once, then how many teams should be in the league? 16

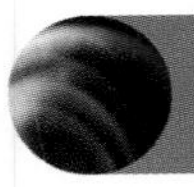

9.2 Completing the Square

In This Section

The quadratic equations in Section 9.1 were solved by factoring or the square root property, but some quadratic equations cannot be solved by either of those methods. In this section, you will learn a method that works on *any* quadratic equation.

⟨1⟩ Perfect Square Trinomials

The new method for solving any quadratic equation depends on perfect square trinomials. Recall that a perfect square trinomial is the square of a binomial. Just as we recognize the numbers

$$1, \quad 4, \quad 9, \quad 16, \quad 25, \quad 36, \quad \ldots$$

as being the squares of the positive integers, we can recognize a perfect square trinomial. The following is a list of some perfect square trinomials with a leading coefficient of 1:

$$x^2 + 2x + 1 = (x + 1)^2 \qquad x^2 - 2x + 1 = (x - 1)^2$$
$$x^2 + 4x + 4 = (x + 2)^2 \qquad x^2 - 4x + 4 = (x - 2)^2$$
$$x^2 + 6x + 9 = (x + 3)^2 \qquad x^2 - 6x + 9 = (x - 3)^2$$
$$x^2 + 8x + 16 = (x + 4)^2 \qquad x^2 - 8x + 16 = (x - 4)^2$$

⟨ Teaching Tip ⟩

Have students each make their own list of perfect square trinomials through $(x \pm 12)^2$.

To solve quadratic equations using perfect square trinomials, we must be able to determine the last term of a perfect square trinomial when given the first two terms. This process is called **completing the square.** For example, the perfect square trinomial whose first two terms are $x^2 + 6x$ is $x^2 + 6x + 9$.

If the coefficient of x^2 is 1, there is a simple rule for finding the last term in a perfect square trinomial.

Finding the Last Term

The last term of a perfect square trinomial is the square of one-half of the coefficient of the middle term. In symbols, the perfect square trinomial whose first two terms are $x^2 + bx$ is $x^2 + bx + \left(\frac{b}{2}\right)^2$.

EXAMPLE 1

Completing the square

Find the perfect square trinomial whose first two terms are given, and factor the trinomial.

a) $x^2 + 10x$ **b)** $x^2 - 20x$ **c)** $x^2 + 3x$ **d)** $x^2 - x$

Solution

a) One-half of 10 is 5, and 5 squared is 25. So the perfect square trinomial is $x^2 + 10x + 25$. Factor as follows:

$$x^2 + 10x + 25 = (x + 5)^2$$

Helpful Hint

Review the rule for squaring a binomial: square the first term, find twice the product of the two terms, then square the last term. If you are still using FOIL to find the square of a binomial, it is time to learn a more efficient rule.

b) One-half of -20 is -10, and -10 squared is 100. So the perfect square trinomial is $x^2 - 20x + 100$. Factor as follows:

$$x^2 - 20x + 100 = (x - 10)^2$$

c) One-half of 3 is $\frac{3}{2}$, and $\frac{3}{2}$ squared is $\frac{9}{4}$. So the perfect square trinomial is $x^2 + 3x + \frac{9}{4}$. Factor as follows:

$$x^2 + 3x + \frac{9}{4} = \left(x + \frac{3}{2}\right)^2$$

d) One-half of -1 is $-\frac{1}{2}$, and $\left(-\frac{1}{2}\right)^2 = \frac{1}{4}$. So the perfect square is $x^2 - x + \frac{1}{4}$. Factor as follows:

$$x^2 - x + \frac{1}{4} = \left(x - \frac{1}{2}\right)^2$$

Now do Exercises 5–32

⟨2⟩ Solving a Quadratic Equation by Completing the Square

To complete the squares in Example 1, we simply found the missing last terms. In Examples 2, 3, and 4 we use that process along with the square root property to solve equations of the form $ax^2 + bx + c = 0$. When we use completing the square to solve an equation, we add the appropriate last term to both sides of the equation to obtain an equivalent equation. We first consider an equation in which the coefficient of x^2 is 1.

EXAMPLE 2

Solving by completing the square ($a = 1$)

Solve $x^2 + 6x - 7 = 0$ by completing the square.

Solution

Add 7 to each side of the equation to isolate $x^2 + 6x$:

$$x^2 + 6x = 7$$

Now complete the square for $x^2 + 6x$. One-half of 6 is 3, and $3^2 = 9$.

$$\begin{aligned} x^2 + 6x + 9 &= 7 + 9 && \text{Add 9 to each side.} \\ (x + 3)^2 &= 16 && \text{Factor the left side, and simplify the right side.} \\ x + 3 &= \pm 4 && \text{Square root property} \\ x &= -3 \pm 4 \\ x = -3 + 4 \quad &\text{or} \quad x = -3 - 4 \\ x = 1 \quad &\text{or} \quad x = -7 \end{aligned}$$

Check these answers in the original equation. The solutions are -7 and 1.

Now do Exercises 33–38

Helpful Hint

Always check that you have completed the square correctly by squaring the binomial. In this case $(x + 3)^2 = x^2 + 6x + 9$ is correct.

All of the perfect square trinomials in Examples 1 and 2 have 1 as the leading coefficient. If the leading coefficient is not 1, then we must divide each side of the equation by the leading coefficient to get an equation with a leading coefficient of 1.

The steps to follow in solving a quadratic equation by completing the square are summarized as follows.

Strategy for Solving a Quadratic Equation by Completing the Square

1. The coefficient of x^2 must be 1.
2. Write the equation with only the x^2-terms and the x-terms on the left-hand side.
3. Complete the square on the left-hand side by adding the square of $\frac{1}{2}$ the coefficient of x to both sides of the equation.
4. Factor the perfect square trinomial as the square of a binomial.
5. Apply the square root property.
6. Solve for x and simplify the answer.
7. Check in the original equation.

In Example 3, we solve a quadratic equation in which the coefficient of x^2 is not 1.

EXAMPLE 3

Solving by completing the square ($a \neq 1$)

Solve $2x^2 - 5x - 3 = 0$ by completing the square.

Solution

Our perfect square trinomial must begin with x^2 and not $2x^2$:

$$\frac{2x^2 - 5x - 3}{2} = \frac{0}{2} \quad \text{Divide each side by 2 to get 1 for the coefficient of } x^2.$$

$$x^2 - \frac{5}{2}x - \frac{3}{2} = 0 \quad \text{Simplify.}$$

$$x^2 - \frac{5}{2}x = \frac{3}{2} \quad \text{Write only the } x^2\text{- and } x\text{-terms on the left-hand side.}$$

$$x^2 - \frac{5}{2}x + \frac{25}{16} = \frac{3}{2} + \frac{25}{16} \quad \text{Complete the square: } \frac{1}{2}\left(-\frac{5}{2}\right) = -\frac{5}{4}, \left(-\frac{5}{4}\right)^2 = \frac{25}{16}$$

$$\left(x - \frac{5}{4}\right)^2 = \frac{49}{16} \quad \text{Factor the left-hand side.}$$

$$x - \frac{5}{4} = \pm\frac{7}{4} \quad \text{Square root property}$$

$$x = \frac{5}{4} \pm \frac{7}{4}$$

$$x = \frac{5}{4} + \frac{7}{4} \quad \text{or} \quad x = \frac{5}{4} - \frac{7}{4}$$

$$x = \frac{12}{4} \quad \text{or} \quad x = -\frac{2}{4}$$

$$x = 3 \quad \text{or} \quad x = -\frac{1}{2}$$

Check these answers in the original equation. The solutions to the equation are $-\frac{1}{2}$ and 3.

Now do Exercises 39–44

‹ Teaching Tip ›

Students often have trouble with fractions in completing the square. However, this is an excellent opportunity to review the operations with fractions.

The equations in Examples 2 and 3 could have been solved by factoring. The quadratic equation in Example 4 cannot be solved by factoring, but it can be solved by completing the square. In fact, every quadratic equation can be solved by completing the square.

EXAMPLE 4

A quadratic equation with irrational solutions

Solve $x^2 + 4x - 3 = 0$ by completing the square.

Solution

$$x^2 + 4x - 3 = 0 \qquad \text{Original equation}$$

$$x^2 + 4x \quad = 3 \qquad \text{Add 3 to each side to isolate the } x^2\text{- and } x\text{-terms.}$$

$$x^2 + 4x + 4 = 3 + 4 \qquad \text{Complete the square by adding 4 to both sides.}$$

$$(x + 2)^2 = 7 \qquad \text{Factor the left-hand side.}$$

$$x + 2 = \pm\sqrt{7} \qquad \text{Square root property}$$

$$x = -2 \pm \sqrt{7}$$

$$x = -2 + \sqrt{7} \quad \text{or} \quad x = -2 - \sqrt{7}$$

Checking answers involving radicals can be done by using the operations with radicals that you learned in Chapter 8. Replace x with $-2 + \sqrt{7}$ in $x^2 + 4x - 3$:

$$(-2 + \sqrt{7})^2 + 4(-2 + \sqrt{7}) - 3 = 4 - 4\sqrt{7} + 7 - 8 + 4\sqrt{7} - 3$$
$$= 0$$

You should check $-2 - \sqrt{7}$. Both $-2 + \sqrt{7}$ and $-2 - \sqrt{7}$ satisfy the equation.

Now do Exercises 45–58

‹ Calculator Close-Up ›

A good way to check an irrational solution with a calculator is to use the answer key (ANS). The value of ANS is the last value calculated by the calculator.

```
-2-√(7)
         -4.645751311
Ans²+4Ans-3
                    0
```

‹3› Applications

In Example 5, we use completing the square to solve a geometric problem.

EXAMPLE 5

A geometric problem

The sum of the lengths of the two legs of a right triangle is 8 feet. If the area of the right triangle is 5 square feet, then what are the lengths of the legs?

Solution

If x represents the length of one leg, then $8 - x$ represents the length of the other. See Fig. 9.1. The area of a triangle is given by the formula $A = \frac{1}{2}bh$. Let $A = 5$, $b = x$, and $h = 8 - x$ in this formula:

$$5 = \frac{1}{2}x(8 - x)$$

$$2 \cdot 5 = 2 \cdot \frac{1}{2}x(8 - x) \qquad \text{Multiply each side by 2.}$$

$$10 = 8x - x^2$$

$$x^2 - 8x + 10 = 0$$

$$x^2 - 8x \quad = -10 \qquad \text{Subtract 10 from each side to isolate the } x^2\text{- and } x\text{-terms.}$$

$$x^2 - 8x + 16 = -10 + 16 \qquad \text{Complete the square: } \tfrac{1}{2}(-8) = -4,\ (-4)^2 = 16$$

$$(x - 4)^2 = 6 \qquad \text{Factor.}$$

$$x - 4 = \pm\sqrt{6}$$

$$x - 4 = \sqrt{6} \quad \text{or} \quad x - 4 = -\sqrt{6}$$

$$x = 4 + \sqrt{6} \quad \text{or} \quad x = 4 - \sqrt{6}$$

If $x = 4 + \sqrt{6}$, then

$$8 - x = 8 - (4 + \sqrt{6}) = 4 - \sqrt{6}.$$

x

8 − x

Figure 9.1

‹ Teaching Tip ›

Students do not like to check answers involving roots, but this is an excellent opportunity to review the operations that were covered in Chapter 8.

If $x = 4 - \sqrt{6}$, then

$$8 - x = 8 - (4 - \sqrt{6}) = 4 + \sqrt{6}.$$

There is only one pair of possible lengths for the legs: $4 + \sqrt{6}$ ft and $4 - \sqrt{6}$ ft. Check that the area is 5 square feet:

$$A = \frac{1}{2}(4 + \sqrt{6})(4 - \sqrt{6}) = \frac{1}{2}(16 - 6) = \frac{1}{2}(10) = 5$$

Now do Exercises 79–84

Warm-Ups

True or false? Explain your answer.

1. Completing the square is used for finding the area of a square. False
2. The polynomial $x^2 + \frac{2}{3}x + \frac{4}{9}$ is a perfect square trinomial. False
3. Every quadratic equation can be solved by factoring. False
4. The polynomial $x^2 - x + 1$ is a perfect square trinomial. False
5. Every quadratic equation can be solved by completing the square. True
6. The solutions to the equation $x - 2 = \pm\sqrt{3}$ are $2 + \sqrt{3}$ and $2 - \sqrt{3}$. True
7. There are no real numbers that satisfy $(x + 7)^2 = -5$. True
8. To solve $x^2 - 5x = 4$ by completing the square, we can add $\frac{25}{4}$ to each side. True
9. One-half of four-fifths is two-fifths. True
10. One-half of three-fourths is three-eighths. True

9.2 Exercises

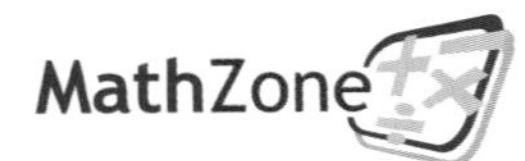

‹ Study Tips ›

- If you are having the kind of success in school that you desire, congratulations.
- If you are not having the success you want, do something about it. What you do now will affect the rest of your life.

Reading and Writing *After reading this section, write out the answers to these questions. Use complete sentences.*

1. Can every quadratic equation be solved by factoring or the square root property? Not every quadratic can be solved by factoring or the square root property.
2. What method can be used to solve any quadratic equation? Any quadratic can be solved by completing the square.
3. How do we find the last term in a perfect square trinomial when we know the first two terms? The last term is the square of one-half of the coefficient of the middle term.
4. What is the first step for solving a quadratic equation by completing the square when $a \neq 1$? If $a \neq 1$, divide each side by a.

‹1› Perfect Square Trinomials

Find the perfect square trinomial whose first two terms are given, then factor the trinomial. See Example 1.

5. $x^2 + 6x$ $\quad x^2 + 6x + 9 = (x + 3)^2$
6. $x^2 - 4x$ $\quad x^2 - 4x + 4 = (x - 2)^2$

7. $x^2 + 14x$ $x^2 + 14x + 49 = (x + 7)^2$

8. $x^2 + 16x$ $x^2 + 16x + 64 = (x + 8)^2$

9. $x^2 - 16x$ $x^2 - 16x + 64 = (x - 8)^2$

VIDEO **10.** $x^2 - 14x$ $x^2 - 14x + 49 = (x - 7)^2$

11. $t^2 - 18t$ $t^2 - 18t + 81 = (t - 9)^2$

12. $w^2 + 18w$ $w^2 + 18w + 81 = (w + 9)^2$

13. $m^2 + 3m$ $m^2 + 3m + \frac{9}{4} = \left(m + \frac{3}{2}\right)^2$

14. $n^2 - 5n$ $n^2 - 5n + \frac{25}{4} = \left(n - \frac{5}{2}\right)^2$

15. $z^2 + z$ $z^2 + z + \frac{1}{4} = \left(z + \frac{1}{2}\right)^2$

16. $v^2 - v$ $v^2 - v + \frac{1}{4} = \left(v - \frac{1}{2}\right)^2$

17. $x^2 - \frac{1}{2}x$ $x^2 - \frac{1}{2}x + \frac{1}{16} = \left(x - \frac{1}{4}\right)^2$

18. $y^2 + \frac{1}{3}y$ $y^2 + \frac{1}{3}y + \frac{1}{36} = \left(y + \frac{1}{6}\right)^2$

19. $y^2 + \frac{1}{4}y$ $y^2 + \frac{1}{4}y + \frac{1}{64} = \left(y + \frac{1}{8}\right)^2$

20. $z^2 - \frac{4}{3}z$ $z^2 - \frac{4}{3}z + \frac{4}{9} = \left(z - \frac{2}{3}\right)^2$

Factor each perfect square trinomial as the square of a binomial.

21. $x^2 + 10x + 25$ $(x + 5)^2$

22. $x^2 - 6x + 9$ $(x - 3)^2$

23. $m^2 - 2m + 1$ $(m - 1)^2$

24. $n^2 + 4n + 4$ $(n + 2)^2$

25. $w^2 - 12w + 36$ $(w - 6)^2$

26. $z^2 + 18z + 81$ $(z + 9)^2$

27. $x^2 + x + \frac{1}{4}$ $\left(x + \frac{1}{2}\right)^2$

28. $y^2 - y + \frac{1}{4}$ $\left(y - \frac{1}{2}\right)^2$

29. $t^2 + \frac{1}{3}t + \frac{1}{36}$ $\left(t + \frac{1}{6}\right)^2$

VIDEO **30.** $v^2 - \frac{2}{3}v + \frac{1}{9}$ $\left(v - \frac{1}{3}\right)^2$

31. $x^2 + \frac{2}{5}x + \frac{1}{25}$ $\left(x + \frac{1}{5}\right)^2$

32. $y^2 - \frac{1}{4}y + \frac{1}{64}$ $\left(y - \frac{1}{8}\right)^2$

⟨2⟩ Solving a Quadratic Equation by Completing the Square

Solve by completing the square.

See Examples 2 and 3.

See the Strategy for Solving Quadraic Equations by Completing the Square box on page 548.

33. $x^2 + 2x - 15 = 0$ $-5, 3$

34. $x^2 + 2x - 24 = 0$ $-6, 4$

35. $x^2 - 4x - 21 = 0$ $-3, 7$

VIDEO **36.** $x^2 - 4x - 12 = 0$ $-2, 6$

37. $x^2 + 6x + 9 = 0$ -3

38. $x^2 - 10x + 25 = 0$ 5

39. $2t^2 - 3t + 1 = 0$ $\frac{1}{2}, 1$

40. $2t^2 - 3t - 2 = 0$ $-\frac{1}{2}, 2$

VIDEO **41.** $2w^2 - 7w + 6 = 0$ $\frac{3}{2}, 2$

42. $4t^2 + 5t - 6 = 0$ $\frac{3}{4}, -2$

43. $3x^2 + 2x - 1 = 0$ $-1, \frac{1}{3}$

44. $3x^2 - 8x - 3 = 0$ $-\frac{1}{3}, 3$

Solve each quadratic equation by completing the square. See Example 4.

45. $x^2 + 2x - 6 = 0$
$-1 - \sqrt{7}, -1 + \sqrt{7}$

46. $x^2 + 4x - 4 = 0$
$-2 - 2\sqrt{2}, -2 + 2\sqrt{2}$

47. $x^2 + 6x + 1 = 0$
$-3 - 2\sqrt{2}, -3 + 2\sqrt{2}$

VIDEO **48.** $x^2 - 6x - 3 = 0$
$3 - 2\sqrt{3}, 3 + 2\sqrt{3}$

49. $y^2 - y - 3 = 0$
$\frac{1 - \sqrt{13}}{2}, \frac{1 + \sqrt{13}}{2}$

50. $t^2 + t - 1 = 0$
$\frac{-1 - \sqrt{5}}{2}, \frac{-1 + \sqrt{5}}{2}$

51. $v^2 + 3v - 3 = 0$
$\frac{-3 - \sqrt{21}}{2}, \frac{-3 + \sqrt{21}}{2}$

52. $u^2 - 3u + 1 = 0$
$\frac{3 - \sqrt{5}}{2}, \frac{3 + \sqrt{5}}{2}$

53. $2m^2 - m - 4 = 0$
$\frac{1 - \sqrt{33}}{4}, \frac{1 + \sqrt{33}}{4}$

54. $4q^2 + 2q - 1 = 0$
$\frac{-1 - \sqrt{5}}{4}, \frac{-1 + \sqrt{5}}{4}$

55. $2x^2 + 6x - 3 = 0$
$\frac{-3 - \sqrt{15}}{2}, \frac{-3 + \sqrt{15}}{2}$

56. $2x^2 - 10x - 1 = 0$
$\frac{5 - 3\sqrt{3}}{2}, \frac{5 + 3\sqrt{3}}{2}$

57. $4x^2 - 6x + 1 = 0$
$\frac{3 - \sqrt{5}}{4}, \frac{3 + \sqrt{5}}{4}$

58. $2x^2 - 2x - 5 = 0$
$\frac{1 - \sqrt{11}}{2}, \frac{1 + \sqrt{11}}{2}$

Miscellaneous

Solve each equation by whichever method is appropriate.

59. $(x - 5)^2 = 7$
$5 - \sqrt{7}, 5 + \sqrt{7}$

60. $x^2 + x = 12$
$-4, 3$

61. $3n^2 - 5 = 0$
$-\frac{\sqrt{15}}{3}, \frac{\sqrt{15}}{3}$

62. $2m^2 + 16 = 0$
No real solution

63. $4x^2 + 8x - 1 = 0$
$\frac{-2 - \sqrt{5}}{2}, \frac{-2 + \sqrt{5}}{2}$

64. $2x^2 - 3x - 1 = 0$
$\frac{3 - \sqrt{17}}{4}, \frac{3 + \sqrt{17}}{4}$

65. $3x^2 + 1 = 0$
No real solution

66. $x^2 + 6x + 7 = 0$
$-3 - \sqrt{2}, -3 + \sqrt{2}$

67. $x^2 + 5 = 8x - 3$
$4 - 2\sqrt{2}, 4 + 2\sqrt{2}$

68. $2x^2 + 3x = 42 - 2x$
$-6, \frac{7}{2}$

69. $(2x - 7)^2 = 0$ $\frac{7}{2}$

70. $x^2 - 7 = 0$ $-\sqrt{7}, \sqrt{7}$

71. $y^2 + 6y = 11$
$-3 - 2\sqrt{5}, -3 + 2\sqrt{5}$

72. $y^2 + 6y = 0$
$-6, 0$

73. $\frac{1}{4}w^2 + \frac{1}{2} = w$
$2 - \sqrt{2}, 2 + \sqrt{2}$

74. $\frac{1}{2}z^2 + \frac{1}{2} = 2z$
$2 - \sqrt{3}, 2 + \sqrt{3}$

75. $t^2 + 0.2t = 0.24$
$-0.6, 0.4$

76. $p^2 - 0.9p + 0.18 = 0$
$0.3, 0.6$

77. $4x^2 + 4x - 7 = 0$
$\frac{-1 - 2\sqrt{2}}{2}, \frac{-1 + 2\sqrt{2}}{2}$

78. $2x^2 - 8x + 5 = 0$
$\frac{4 - \sqrt{6}}{2}, \frac{4 + \sqrt{6}}{2}$

⟨3⟩ Applications

Use a quadratic equation and completing the square to solve each problem. See Example 5.

79. ***Area of a triangle.*** The sum of the measures of the base and height of a triangle is 10 inches. If the area of the triangle is 11 square inches, then what are the measures of the base and height?
$5 - \sqrt{3}$ in. and $5 + \sqrt{3}$ in.

80. ***Dimensions of a rectangle.*** A rectangle has a perimeter of 12 inches and an area of 6 square inches. What are the length and width of the rectangle?
Length $3 + \sqrt{3}$ in., width $3 - \sqrt{3}$ in.

81. ***Missing numbers.*** The sum of two numbers is 12, and their product is 34. What are the numbers?
$6 - \sqrt{2}$ and $6 + \sqrt{2}$

82. ***More missing numbers.*** The sum of two numbers is 8, and their product is 11. What are the numbers?
$4 - \sqrt{5}$ and $4 + \sqrt{5}$

83. ***Saving candles.*** Joan has saved the candles from her birthday cake for every year of her life. If Joan has 78 candles, then how old is Joan? (See Exercise 81 of Section 9.1.)
12 years old

84. ***Raffle tickets.*** The Booster Club is selling chances to win a Corvette. If the tickets are x dollars each, then the members will sell $5000 - 200x$ tickets. So the total revenue in dollars is given by

$$R(x) = x(5000 - 200x).$$

a) Find $R(8)$.
b) For what ticket price is the revenue \$30,000?
c) Use the accompanying graph to estimate the ticket price that will produce the maximum revenue.
a) \$27,200 **b)** \$10 and \$15 **c)** \$12.50

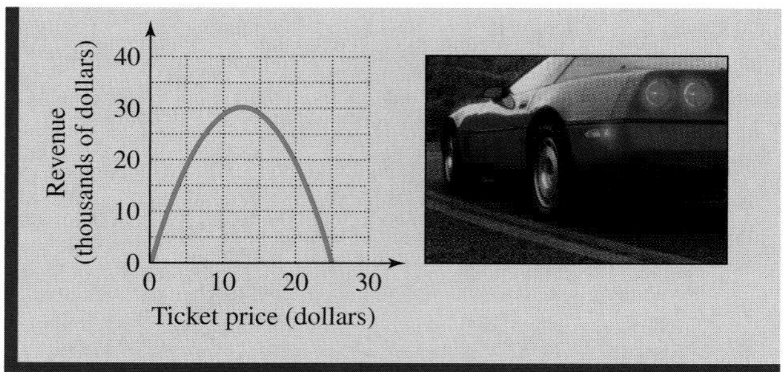

Figure for Exercise 84

Getting More Involved

85. ***Exploration***

a) Find the product $[x - (5 + \sqrt{3})][x - (5 - \sqrt{3})]$.
b) Use completing the square to solve the quadratic equation formed by setting the answer to part (a) equal to zero.
c) Write a quadratic equation (in the form $ax^2 + bx + c = 0$) that has solutions $\frac{3 + \sqrt{2}}{2}$ and $\frac{3 - \sqrt{2}}{2}$.
d) Explain how to find a quadratic equation in the form $ax^2 + bx + c = 0$ for any two given solutions.
a) $x^2 - 10x + 22$ **b)** $5 \pm \sqrt{3}$
c) $x^2 - 3x + \frac{7}{4} = 0$

9.3 The Quadratic Formula

In This Section

⟨1⟩ The Quadratic Formula
⟨2⟩ The Discriminant
⟨3⟩ Which Method to Use

In Section 9.2, you learned that every quadratic equation can be solved by completing the square. In this section, we use completing the square to get a formula, the quadratic formula, for solving any quadratic equation.

⟨1⟩ The Quadratic Formula

To develop a formula for solving any quadratic equation, we start with the general quadratic equation

$$ax^2 + bx + c = 0$$

Teaching Tip

Do not spend too much time on the proof of the quadratic formula. If the details are too complicated, just point out that it is simply completing the square with letters.

and solve it by completing the square. Assume that a is positive for now, and divide each side by a:

$$\frac{ax^2 + bx + c}{a} = \frac{0}{a} \quad \text{Divide by } a \text{ to get 1 for the coefficient of } x^2.$$

$$x^2 + \frac{b}{a}x + \frac{c}{a} = 0 \quad \text{Simplify.}$$

$$x^2 + \frac{b}{a}x = -\frac{c}{a} \quad \text{Isolate the } x^2\text{- and } x\text{-terms.}$$

Now complete the square on the left. One-half of $\frac{b}{a}$ is $\frac{b}{2a}$, and $\left(\frac{b}{2a}\right)^2 = \frac{b^2}{4a^2}$.

$$x^2 + \frac{b}{a}x + \frac{b^2}{4a^2} = \frac{b^2}{4a^2} - \frac{c}{a} \quad \text{Add } \frac{b^2}{4a^2} \text{ to each side.}$$

$$\left(x + \frac{b}{2a}\right)^2 = \frac{b^2}{4a^2} - \frac{4ac}{4a^2} \quad \text{Factor on the left-hand side, and get a common denominator on the right-hand side.}$$

$$\left(x + \frac{b}{2a}\right)^2 = \frac{b^2 - 4ac}{4a^2}$$

$$x + \frac{b}{2a} = \pm\sqrt{\frac{b^2 - 4ac}{4a^2}} \quad \text{Square root property}$$

$$x = -\frac{b}{2a} \pm \frac{\sqrt{b^2 - 4ac}}{2a} \quad \text{Because } a > 0,\ \sqrt{4a^2} = 2a.$$

$$x = \frac{-b \pm \sqrt{b^2 - 4ac}}{2a} \quad \text{Combine the two expressions.}$$

The last equation is a formula for finding x in terms of a, b, and c. It is called the **quadratic formula.** This formula is usually used instead of completing the square to solve a quadratic equation that cannot be factored.

In developing the formula, we assumed $a > 0$ so that $\sqrt{4a^2} = 2a$. If $a < 0$, then $\sqrt{4a^2} = -2a$ and we get $x = \frac{-b}{2a} \pm \frac{\sqrt{b^2 - 4ac}}{-2a}$. But the negative sign can be deleted from $-2a$. To see why, evaluate $\pm\frac{6}{-2}$ and $\pm\frac{6}{2}$. So the quadratic formula is valid whether a is positive or negative.

The Quadratic Formula

The solutions to $ax^2 + bx + c = 0$, where $a \neq 0$, are given by

$$x = \frac{-b \pm \sqrt{b^2 - 4ac}}{2a}.$$

EXAMPLE 1

Equations with rational solutions

Use the quadratic formula to solve each equation.

a) $x^2 + 2x - 3 = 0$ **b)** $4x^2 = -9 + 12x$

‹ Teaching Tip ›

Remind students to double check the signs on a, b, and c before putting them into the quadratic formula.

Solution

a) To use the formula, we first identify a, b, and c. For the equation

$$\underset{a}{\underset{\uparrow}{1}}x^2 + \underset{b}{\underset{\uparrow}{2}}x - \underset{c}{\underset{\uparrow}{3}} = 0,$$

$a = 1$, $b = 2$, and $c = -3$. Now use these values in the quadratic formula:

$$x = \frac{-b \pm \sqrt{b^2 - 4ac}}{2a}$$

$$x = \frac{-2 \pm \sqrt{2^2 - 4(1)(-3)}}{2(1)} \qquad 2^2 - 4(1)(-3) = 4 + 12 = 16$$

$$x = \frac{-2 \pm \sqrt{16}}{2}$$

$$x = \frac{-2 \pm 4}{2}$$

$$x = \frac{-2 + 4}{2} \quad \text{or} \quad x = \frac{-2 - 4}{2}$$

$$x = 1 \quad \text{or} \quad x = -3$$

Check these answers in the original equation. The solutions are -3 and 1.

b) Write the equation in the form $ax^2 + bx + c = 0$ to identify a, b, and c:

$$4x^2 = -9 + 12x$$

$$4x^2 - 12x + 9 = 0$$

Now $a = 4$, $b = -12$, and $c = 9$. Use these values in the formula:

$$x = \frac{-(-12) \pm \sqrt{(-12)^2 - 4(4)(9)}}{2(4)}$$

$$x = \frac{12 \pm \sqrt{0}}{8} = \frac{12}{8} = \frac{3}{2}$$

Check. The only solution to the equation is $\frac{3}{2}$.

Now do Exercises 7–14

The equations in Example 1 could have been solved by factoring. (Try it.) The quadratic equation in Example 2 has an irrational solution and cannot be solved by factoring.

EXAMPLE 2

An equation with an irrational solution

Solve $3x^2 - 6x + 1 = 0$.

Solution

For this equation, $a = 3$, $b = -6$, and $c = 1$:

$$x = \frac{-(-6) \pm \sqrt{(-6)^2 - 4(3)(1)}}{2(3)} = \frac{6 \pm \sqrt{24}}{6}$$

$$= \frac{6 \pm 2\sqrt{6}}{6} \qquad \sqrt{24} = \sqrt{4}\sqrt{6} = 2\sqrt{6}$$

$$= \frac{2(3 \pm \sqrt{6})}{2(3)} \qquad \text{Numerator and denominator have 2 as a common factor.}$$

$$= \frac{3 \pm \sqrt{6}}{3}$$

The two solutions are the irrational numbers $\frac{3 + \sqrt{6}}{3}$ and $\frac{3 - \sqrt{6}}{3}$.

Now do Exercises 15–20

‹ Calculator Close-Up ›

Check irrational solutions using the answer key as shown here.

```
(3+√(6))/3
       1.816496581
3Ans²-6Ans+1
                 0
```

We have seen quadratic equations such as $x^2 = -9$ that do not have any real number solutions. In general, you can conclude that a quadratic equation has no real number solutions if you get a square root of a negative number in the quadratic formula.

EXAMPLE 3

A quadratic equation with no real number solutions

Solve $5x^2 - x + 1 = 0$.

Solution

For this equation we have $a = 5$, $b = -1$, and $c = 1$:

$$x = \frac{1 \pm \sqrt{(-1)^2 - 4(5)(1)}}{2(5)} \qquad b = -1, -b = 1$$

$$x = \frac{1 \pm \sqrt{-19}}{10}$$

The equation has no real solutions because $\sqrt{-19}$ is not real.

Now do Exercises 21–30

‹2› The Discriminant

We have seen in Examples 1–3 that a quadratic equation can have 2, 1, or 0 real solutions. What causes this behavior? If you look back at these examples, you will see that it is the radical part of the quadratic formula. If $b^2 - 4ac$ is positive, there are two real solutions [Examples 1(a) and 2]. If $b^2 - 4ac$ is 0, there is only one solution [Example 1(b)]. If $b^2 - 4ac$ is negative there are no real solutions (Example 3). Table 9.1 summarizes these facts.

‹ Helpful Hint ›

In Section 9.5, we will see that there are two imaginary solutions when $b^2 - 4ac$ is negative.

Table 9.1

Value of $b^2 - 4ac$	Number of Real Solutions to $ax^2 + bx + c = 0$
Positive	2
Zero	1
Negative	0

The expression $b^2 - 4ac$ is called the **discriminant** because its value determines the number of real solutions to a quadratic equation.

EXAMPLE 4

The number of real solutions

Find the value of the discriminant, and determine the number of real solutions to each equation.

a) $3x^2 - 5x + 1 = 0$ **b)** $x^2 + 6x + 9 = 0$ **c)** $2x^2 + 1 = x$

Solution

a) For the equation $3x^2 - 5x + 1 = 0$ we have $a = 3$, $b = -5$, and $c = 1$. Now find the value of the discriminant:

$$b^2 - 4ac = (-5)^2 - 4(3)(1) = 25 - 12 = 13$$

Because the discriminant is positive, there are two real solutions to this quadratic equation.

b) For the equation $x^2 + 6x + 9 = 0$, we have $a = 1$, $b = 6$, and $c = 9$:

$$b^2 - 4ac = 6^2 - 4(1)(9) = 36 - 36 = 0$$

Since the discriminant is zero, there is only one real solution to the equation.

c) We must first rewrite the equation:

$$2x^2 + 1 = x$$

$$2x^2 - x + 1 = 0 \quad \text{Subtract } x \text{ from each side.}$$

Now $a = 2$, $b = -1$, and $c = 1$.

$$b^2 - 4ac = (-1)^2 - 4(2)(1) = 1 - 8 = -7$$

Because the discriminant is negative, the equation has no real number solutions.

Now do Exercises 31–42

‹ Teaching Tip ›

Students should know all of the methods for solving quadratic equations. They might need a lot of practice in deciding what method to use.

‹3› Which Method to Use

If the quadratic equation is simple enough, we can solve it by factoring or by the square root property. These methods should be considered first. *All quadratic equations can be solved by the quadratic formula.* Remember that the quadratic formula is just a shortcut to completing the square and is usually easier to use. However, you should learn completing the square because it is used elsewhere in algebra. The available methods are summarized as follows.

‹ Helpful Hint ›

If our only intent is to get the answer, then we would probably use a calculator that is programmed with the quadratic formula. However, by learning different methods we gain insight into the problem and get valuable practice with algebra. So be sure you learn all of the methods.

Summary of Methods for Solving $ax^2 + bx + c = 0$

Method	Comments	Examples
Square root property	Use when $b = 0$.	If $x^2 = 7$, then $x = \pm\sqrt{7}$. If $(x - 2)^2 = 9$, then $x - 2 = \pm 3$.
Factoring	Use when the polynomial can be factored.	$x^2 + 5x + 6 = 0$ $(x + 2)(x + 3) = 0$
Quadratic formula	Use when the first two methods do not apply.	$x^2 + 2x - 6 = 0$ $x = \dfrac{-2 \pm \sqrt{2^2 - 4 \cdot 1 \cdot (-6)}}{2 \cdot 1}$
Completing the square	Use only when this method is specified.	$x^2 + 4x - 9 = 0$ $x^2 + 4x + 4 = 9 + 4$ $(x + 2)^2 = 13$

Warm-Ups 

True or false? Explain your answer.

1. Completing the square is used to develop the quadratic formula. True
2. For the equation $x^2 - x + 1 = 0$, we have $a = 1$, $b = -x$, and $c = 1$. False
3. For the equation $x^2 - 3 = 5x$, we have $a = 1$, $b = -3$, and $c = 5$. False
4. The quadratic formula can be expressed as $x = -b \pm \frac{\sqrt{b^2 - 4ac}}{2a}$. False
5. The quadratic equation $2x^2 - 6x = 0$ has two real solutions. True
6. All quadratic equations have two distinct real solutions. False
7. Some quadratic equations cannot be solved by the quadratic formula. False
8. We could solve $2x^2 - 6x = 0$ by factoring, completing the square, or the quadratic formula. True
9. The equation $x^2 = x$ is equivalent to $\left(x - \frac{1}{2}\right)^2 = \frac{1}{4}$. True
10. The only solution to $x^2 + 6x + 9 = 0$ is -3. True

9.3 Exercises

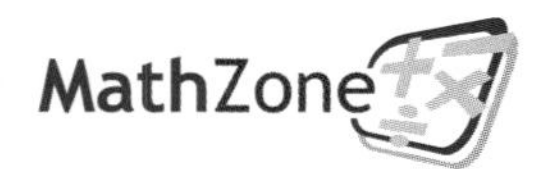

‹ Study Tips ›

- Be sure to ask your instructor what to expect on the final exam. Will it be the same format as other tests?
- If there are any sample final exams available, use them as a guide for your studying.

Reading and Writing *After reading this section, write out the answers to these questions. Use complete sentences.*

1. What method presented here can be used to solve any quadratic equation?
   The quadratic formula solves any quadratic equation.
2. What is the quadratic formula?
   The quadratic formula is $x = \frac{-b \pm \sqrt{b^2 - 4ac}}{2a}$.
3. What is the quadratic formula used for?
   The quadratic formula is used to solve $ax^2 + bx + c = 0$ where $a \neq 0$.
4. What is the discriminant? The discriminant is $b^2 - 4ac$.
5. How can you determine whether there are no real solutions to a quadratic equation?
   If $b^2 - 4ac < 0$, then there are no real solutions.
6. What methods have we studied for solving quadratic equations? We have solved quadratic equations by factoring, the square root property, completing the square, and the quadratic formula.

‹1› The Quadratic Formula

Solve by the quadratic formula. See Examples 1–3.

7. $x^2 + 2x - 15 = 0$
$-5, 3$

8. (VIDEO) $x^2 - 3x - 18 = 0$
$6, -3$

9. $x^2 + 10x + 25 = 0$ -5

10. $x^2 - 12x + 36 = 0$ 6

11. $2x^2 + x - 6 = 0$
$-2, \frac{3}{2}$

12. $2x^2 + x - 15 = 0$
$-3, \frac{5}{2}$

13. $4x^2 + 4x - 3 = 0$
$-\frac{3}{2}, \frac{1}{2}$

14. $4x^2 + 8x + 3 = 0$
$-\frac{3}{2}, -\frac{1}{2}$

15. $x^2 - 6x + 4 = 0$
$3 - \sqrt{5}, 3 + \sqrt{5}$

16. $x^2 - 10x + 19 = 0$
$5 - \sqrt{6}, 5 + \sqrt{6}$

17. $2y^2 - 6y + 3 = 0$
$\frac{3 - \sqrt{3}}{2}, \frac{3 + \sqrt{3}}{2}$

18. (VIDEO) $3y^2 + 6y + 2 = 0$
$\frac{-3 - \sqrt{3}}{3}, \frac{-3 + \sqrt{3}}{3}$

19. $2t^2 + 4t = -1$ $\frac{-2-\sqrt{2}}{2}, \frac{-2+\sqrt{2}}{2}$

20. $w^2 + 2 = 4w$ $2-\sqrt{2}, 2+\sqrt{2}$

VIDEO **21.** $2x^2 - 2x + 3 = 0$ No real solution

22. $-2x^2 + 3x - 9 = 0$ No real solution

23. $8x^2 = 4x$ $0, \frac{1}{2}$

24. $9y^2 + 3y = -6y$ $-1, 0$

25. $5w^2 - 3 = 0$ $-\frac{\sqrt{15}}{5}, \frac{\sqrt{15}}{5}$

26. $4 - 7z^2 = 0$ $-\frac{2\sqrt{7}}{7}, \frac{2\sqrt{7}}{7}$

27. $\frac{1}{2}h^2 + 7h + \frac{1}{2} = 0$ $-7+4\sqrt{3}, -7-4\sqrt{3}$

28. $\frac{1}{4}z^2 - 6z + 3 = 0$ $12-2\sqrt{33}, 12+2\sqrt{33}$

29. $w^2 - 2w + 6 = 0$ No real solution

30. $3z^2 + 8z + 8 = 0$ No real solution

‹2› The Discriminant

Find the value of the discriminant, and state how many real solutions there are to each quadratic equation. See Example 4.

31. $4x^2 - 4x + 1 = 0$ 0, one

32. $9x^2 + 6x + 1 = 0$ 0, one

33. $6x^2 - 7x + 4 = 0$ -47, none

34. $-3x^2 + 5x - 7 = 0$ -59, none

35. $-5t^2 - t + 9 = 0$ 181, two

36. $-2w^2 - 6w + 5 = 0$ 76, two

37. $4x^2 - 12x + 9 = 0$ 0, one

38. $9x^2 + 12x + 4 = 0$ 0, one

39. $x^2 + x + 4 = 0$ -15, none

40. $y^2 - y + 2 = 0$ -7, none

41. $x - 5 = 3x^2$ -59, none

42. $4 - 3x = x^2$ 25, two

‹3› Which Method to Use

Solve by the method of your choice.

See the Summary of Methods for Solving $ax^2 + bx + c = 0$ box on page 556.

43. $x^2 + \frac{3}{2}x = 1$ $-2, \frac{1}{2}$

VIDEO **44.** $x^2 - \frac{7}{2}x = 2$ $-\frac{1}{2}, 4$

45. $(x-1)^2 + (x-2)^2 = 5$ 0, 3

46. $x^2 + (x-3)^2 = 29$ $-2, 5$

47. $\frac{1}{x} + \frac{1}{x+2} = \frac{5}{12}$ $-\frac{6}{5}, 4$

48. $\frac{1}{x} + \frac{1}{x+1} = \frac{5}{6}$ $-\frac{3}{5}, 2$

49. $x^2 + 6x + 8 = 0$ $-4, -2$

50. $2x^2 - 5x - 3 = 0$ $-\frac{1}{2}, 3$

51. $x^2 - 9x = 0$ 0, 9

52. $x^2 - 9 = 0$ $-3, 3$

53. $(x+5)^2 = 9$ $-8, -2$

54. $(3x-1)^2 = 0$ $\frac{1}{3}$

55. $x(x-3) = 2 - 3(x+4)$ No real solution

56. $(x-1)(x+4) = (2x-4)^2$ $\frac{4}{3}, 5$

57. $\frac{x}{3} = \frac{x+2}{x}$ $\frac{3-\sqrt{33}}{2}, \frac{3+\sqrt{33}}{2}$

58. $\frac{x-2}{x} = \frac{5}{x+2}$ $\frac{5-\sqrt{41}}{2}, \frac{5+\sqrt{41}}{2}$

59. $2x^2 - 3x = 0$ $0, \frac{3}{2}$

60. $x^2 = 5$ $-\sqrt{5}, \sqrt{5}$

Use a calculator to find the approximate solutions to each quadratic equation. Round answers to two decimal places.

61. $x^2 - 3x - 3 = 0$ $-0.79, 3.79$

62. $x^2 - 2x - 2 = 0$ $-0.73, 2.73$

63. $x^2 - x - 3.2 = 0$ $-1.36, 2.36$

64. $x^2 - 4.3x + 3 = 0$ 0.88, 3.42

65. $5.29x^2 - 3.22x + 0.49 = 0$ 0.30

66. $2.6x^2 + 3.1x - 5 = 0$ $-2.11, 0.91$

Applications

Use a calculator to solve each problem.

67. ***Concert revenue.*** A promoter uses the formula

$$R(x) = -500x^2 + 20{,}000x$$

to predict the concert revenue in dollars when the price of a ticket is x dollars.

a) Find $R(10)$. \$150,000

b) What ticket price would produce zero revenue? \$0 and \$40

c) What is the ticket price if the revenue is \$196,875? \$17.50 or \$22.50

d) Examine the accompanying graph to determine the ticket price that produces the maximum revenue. \$20

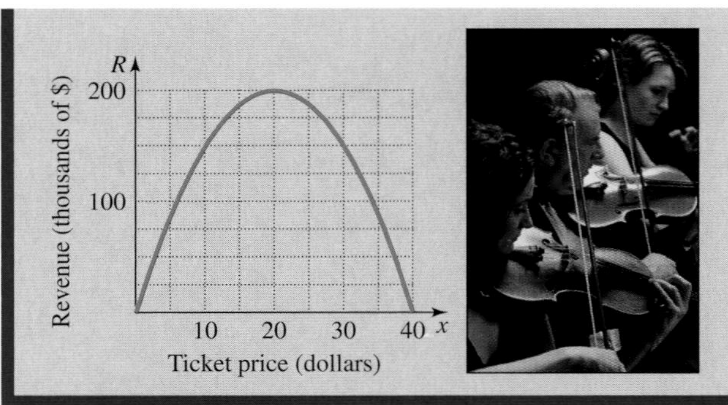

Figure for Exercise 67

68. ***Raffle tickets.*** The formula $R(x) = -200x^2 + 5000x$ was used (in factored form) in Exercise 84 of Section 9.2 to predict the revenue when raffle tickets are sold for x dollars each. For what ticket price is the revenue \$25,000? \$6.91 and \$18.09

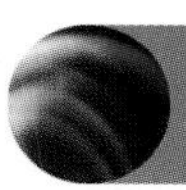

9.4 Applications of Quadratic Equations

In This Section

In this section we will solve problems that involve quadratic equations.

⟨1⟩ Geometric Applications

Quadratic equations can be used to solve problems involving area.

EXAMPLE 1

Dimensions of a rectangle

The length of a rectangular flower bed is 2 feet longer than the width. If the area is 6 square feet, then what are the exact length and width? Also find the approximate dimensions of the rectangle to the nearest tenth of a foot.

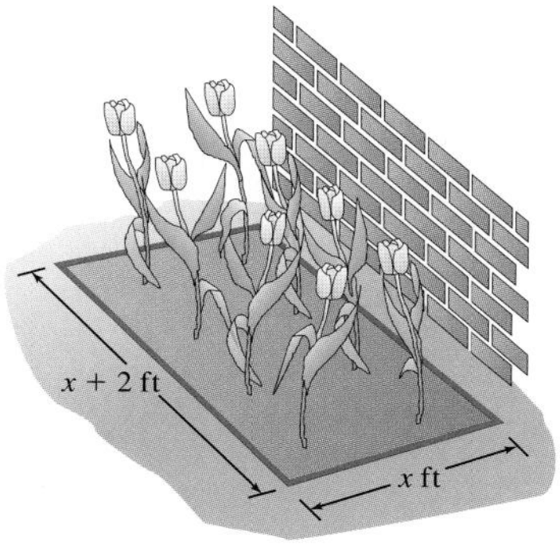

Figure 9.2

Solution

Let x represent the width, and $x + 2$ represent the length as shown in Fig. 9.2. Write an equation using the formula for the area of a rectangle, $A = LW$:

$$x(x + 2) = 6 \quad \text{The area is 6 square feet.}$$
$$x^2 + 2x - 6 = 0$$

We use the quadratic formula to solve the equation:

$$x = \frac{-2 \pm \sqrt{2^2 - 4(1)(-6)}}{2(1)} = \frac{-2 \pm \sqrt{28}}{2}$$
$$= \frac{-2 \pm 2\sqrt{7}}{2} = \frac{2(-1 \pm \sqrt{7})}{2} = -1 \pm \sqrt{7}$$

Because $-1 - \sqrt{7}$ is negative, it cannot be the width of a rectangle. If

$$x = -1 + \sqrt{7},$$

then

$$x + 2 = -1 + \sqrt{7} + 2 = 1 + \sqrt{7}.$$

So the exact width is $-1 + \sqrt{7}$ feet, and the exact length is $1 + \sqrt{7}$ feet. We can check that these dimensions give an area of 6 square feet as follows:

$$LW = (1 + \sqrt{7})(-1 + \sqrt{7}) = -1 - \sqrt{7} + \sqrt{7} + 7 = 6$$

Use a calculator to find the approximate dimensions of 1.6 and 3.6 feet.

Now do Exercises 1–8

⟨2⟩ Work Problems

The work problems in this section are similar to the work problems that you solved in Chapter 6. However, you will need the quadratic formula to solve the work problems presented in this section.

EXAMPLE 2

Working together

Amy can mow the lawn by herself in 2 hours less time than Bob takes to mow the lawn by himself. When they work together, it takes them only 6 hours to mow the lawn. How long would it take each of them to mow the lawn working alone? Find the exact and approximate answers.

Helpful Hint

To get familiar with Example 2, guess that Amy's time alone is 12 hours and Bob's time alone is 14 hours. In 6 hours of working together, Amy mows 6/12 of the lawn and Bob mows 6/14 of the lawn. Now

$$\frac{6}{12} + \frac{6}{14} = \frac{13}{14}.$$

In 6 hours they would finish only 13/14 of the lawn. So these times are not correct, but they are close.

Teaching Tip

Word problems in this section require the quadratic formula. So a calculator will be needed to obtain approximate answers and check. Approximate answers will not check exactly.

Solution

If x is the number of hours it takes Amy by herself to mow the lawn, then Amy mows at the rate of $\frac{1}{x}$ of the lawn per hour. If $x + 2$ is the number of hours it takes Bob to mow the lawn by himself, then Bob mows at the rate of $\frac{1}{x+2}$ of the lawn per hour. Make a table using the fact that the product of the rate and the time gives the amount of work completed (or the fraction of the lawn mowed).

	Rate	Time	Amount of Work
Amy	$\frac{1}{x}\frac{\text{lawn}}{\text{hr}}$	6 hr	$\frac{6}{x}$ lawn
Bob	$\frac{1}{x+2}\frac{\text{lawn}}{\text{hr}}$	6 hr	$\frac{6}{x+2}$ lawn

From the table, the amount of work done by Amy is $\frac{6}{x}$ lawn and the amount of work done by Bob is $\frac{6}{x+2}$ lawn. Since the *total* amount of work done is 1 lawn, we can write and solve the following equation:

$$\frac{6}{x} + \frac{6}{x+2} = 1$$

$$x(x+2)\frac{6}{x} + x(x+2)\frac{6}{x+2} = x(x+2)1 \quad \text{Multiply by the LCD.}$$

$$6x + 12 + 6x = x^2 + 2x$$

$$12x + 12 = x^2 + 2x$$

$$-x^2 + 10x + 12 = 0$$

$$x^2 - 10x - 12 = 0 \quad \text{Multiply each side by } -1.$$

Use the quadratic formula with $a = 1$, $b = -10$, and $c = -12$:

$$x = \frac{10 \pm \sqrt{(-10)^2 - 4(1)(-12)}}{2(1)}$$

$$x = \frac{10 \pm \sqrt{148}}{2} = \frac{10 \pm 2\sqrt{37}}{2} = 5 \pm \sqrt{37}$$

Use a calculator to find that

$$x = 5 - \sqrt{37} \approx -1.08 \qquad \text{and} \qquad x = 5 + \sqrt{37} \approx 11.08.$$

Because x must be positive, Amy's time alone is $5 + \sqrt{37}$, or approximately 11.1 hours. Because Bob's time alone is 2 hours more than Amy's, Bob's time is $7 + \sqrt{37}$ or approximately 13.1 hours.

Now do Exercises 9–12

⟨3⟩ Vertical Motion

If an object is projected vertically upward or downward with an initial velocity of v_0 feet per second from an altitude of s_0 feet, then its altitude s in feet after t seconds is given by the formula

$$s = -16t^2 + v_0t + s_0.$$

We use this formula in Example 3.

EXAMPLE 3

Vertical motion

A soccer ball bounces straight up into the air off the head of a soccer player from an altitude of 6 feet with an initial velocity of 40 feet per second. How long does it take the ball to reach the earth? Find the exact answer and an approximate answer.

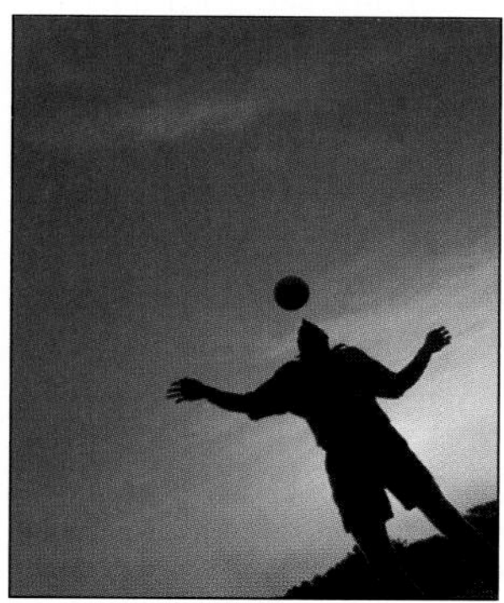

Solution

The time that it takes the ball to reach the earth is the value of t for which s has a value of 0 in the formula $s = -16t^2 + v_0t + s_0$. To find t, we use $s = 0$, $v_0 = 40$, and $s_0 = 6$:

$$0 = -16t^2 + 40t + 6$$

$$16t^2 - 40t - 6 = 0$$

$$8t^2 - 20t - 3 = 0 \quad \text{Divide each side by 2.}$$

$$t = \frac{20 \pm \sqrt{(-20)^2 - 4(8)(-3)}}{2(8)}$$

$$= \frac{20 \pm \sqrt{496}}{16} = \frac{20 \pm 4\sqrt{31}}{16}$$

$$= \frac{5 \pm \sqrt{31}}{4}$$

Because the time must be positive, we have

$$t = \frac{5 + \sqrt{31}}{4} \approx 2.64 \text{ seconds.}$$

It takes the ball $\frac{5 + \sqrt{31}}{4}$ or 2.64 seconds to reach the earth.

Now do Exercises 13–16

‹ Helpful Hint ›

There is a big difference between Example 3 and Examples 1 and 2. In Example 3 we use a well-known formula that gives the position of a ball at any time and we solve for t. In Examples 1 and 2 we had to decide how two unknown quantities were related and write an equation expressing the relationship.

Warm-Ups

True or false? Explain your answer.

1. Two numbers that have a sum of 10 are represented by x and $x + 10$. False
2. The area of a right triangle is one-half the product of the lengths of the legs. True
3. If the speed of a boat in still water is x mph and the current is 5 mph, then the speed of the boat with the current is $5x$ mph. False
4. If Boudreaux eats a 50-pound bag of crawfish in x hours, then his eating rate is $\frac{50}{x}$ bag/hr. False
5. If the Concorde flew 1800 miles in $x + 2$ hours, then its average speed was $\frac{1800}{x + 2}$ mph. True
6. The quantity $\frac{7 - \sqrt{50}}{2}$ is negative. True
7. The quantity $(-5 + \sqrt{27})$ is positive. True
8. If the length of one side of a square is $x + 9$ meters, then the area of the square is $x^2 + 81$ square meters. False
9. If Julia mows an entire lawn in x hours, then her mowing rate is $\frac{1}{x}$ lawn/hr. True
10. If John's boat goes 20 miles per hour in still water, then against a 5-mph current it will go 15 miles per hour. True

9.4 Exercises

Boost your grade at mathzone.com!

- Practice Problems
- NetTutor
- Self-Tests
- e-Professors
- Videos

‹ Study Tips ›

- Don't worry about the final exam. If you have been studying all semester, there is nothing to worry about.
- Most students perform about the same on the final as they have all semester. A few get all fired up and outperform, and a few get lazy and underperform.

‹1› Geometric Applications

Find the exact solution to each problem. See Example 1.

1. ***Length and width.*** The length of a rectangle is 2 meters longer than the width. If the area is 10 square meters, then what are the length and width?
Width $-1 + \sqrt{11}$ meters, length $1 + \sqrt{11}$ meters

2. ***Unequal legs.*** One leg of a right triangle is 4 centimeters longer than the other leg. If the area of the triangle is 8 square centimeters, then what are the lengths of the legs?
$-2 + 2\sqrt{5}$ cm and $2 + 2\sqrt{5}$ cm

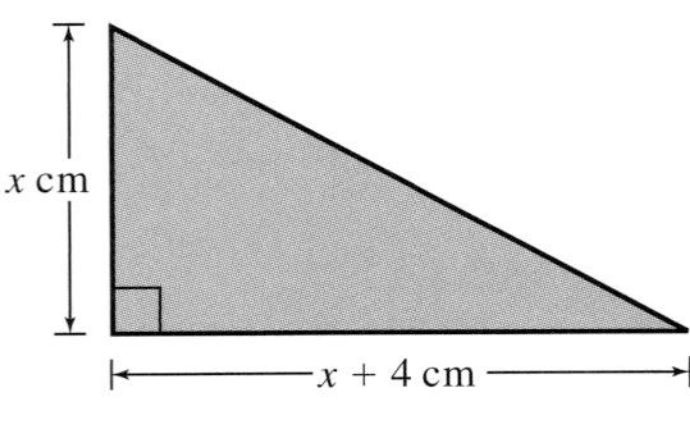

Figure for Exercise 2

3. ***Bracing a gate.*** If the diagonal brace of the square gate shown in the figure is 8 feet long, then what is the length of a side of the square gate?
$4\sqrt{2}$ feet

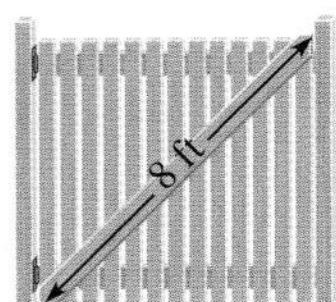

Figure for Exercise 3

4. ***Dimensions of a rectangle.*** If one side of a rectangle is 2 meters shorter than the other side and the diagonal is 10 meters long, then what are the dimensions of the rectangle? 6 meters by 8 meters

5. ***Area of a parallelogram.*** The base of a parallelogram is 6 inches longer than its height. If the area of the parallelogram is 10 square inches, then what are the base and height?
Height $-3 + \sqrt{19}$ inches, base $3 + \sqrt{19}$ inches

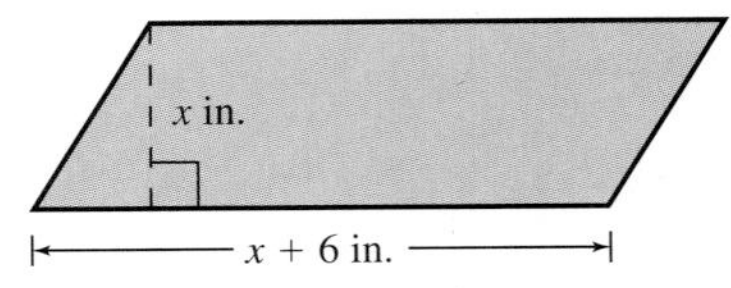

Figure for Exercise 5

VIDEO

6. ***Another Parallelogram.*** The sum of the base and height of a parallelogram is 8. If the base is longer than the height and the area is 4, then what are the base and height?
$4 + 2\sqrt{3}$ and $4 - 2\sqrt{3}$

7. ***Rectangular frame.*** The area of a rectangular painting is 76 square inches and its perimeter is 36 inches. What are the length and width? Length $9 + \sqrt{5}$ in., width $9 - \sqrt{5}$ in.

8. ***Rectangular cardboard.*** The area of a rectangular piece of cardboard is 47 square inches and its perimeter is 28 inches. What are the length and width?
Length $7 + \sqrt{2}$ in., width $7 - \sqrt{2}$ in.

‹2› Work Problems

Solve each problem. Give the exact answer and an approximate answer rounded to two decimal places. See Example 2.

9. ***In the berries.*** On Monday, Alberta picked the strawberry patch, and Ernie sold the berries. On Tuesday, Ernie picked and Alberta sold, but it took him 2 hours longer to get the berries picked than it took Alberta. On Wednesday they worked together and got all of the berries picked in 2 hours. How long did it take Ernie to pick the berries by himself? $3 + \sqrt{5}$ or 5.24 hours

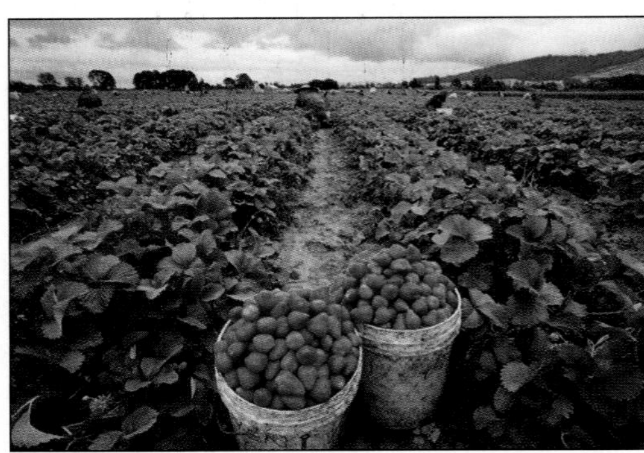

Photo for Exercise 9

10. ***Meter readers.*** Claude and Melvin read the water meters for the city of Ponchatoula. When Claude reads all of the meters by himself, it takes him a full day longer than it takes Melvin to read all of the meters by himself. If they can get the job done working together in 2 days, then how long does it take Claude by himself? $\frac{5+\sqrt{17}}{2}$ or 4.56 days

11. ***Hanging wallpaper.*** Working alone, Tasha can hang all of the paper in the McLendons' new house in 8 hours less time than it takes Tena working alone. Working together, they completed the job in 20 hours. How long would it take Tasha working alone? $16 + 4\sqrt{26}$ or 36.40 hours

12. ***Laying bricks.*** Chau's team of bricklayers can lay all of the bricks in the McLendons' new house in 3 working days less than Hong's team. To speed things up, the McLendons hire both teams and get the job done in 10 working days. How many working days do the McLendons save by using both teams rather than just the faster team? $\frac{-3+\sqrt{409}}{2}$ or 8.61 days

‹3› Vertical Motion

Solve each problem. Give the exact answer and an approximate answer rounded to two decimal places. See Example 3.

13. ***Hang time.*** A punter kicks a football straight up from a height of 4 feet with an initial velocity of 60 feet per second. How long will it take the ball to reach the earth? $\frac{15+\sqrt{241}}{8}$ or 3.82 seconds

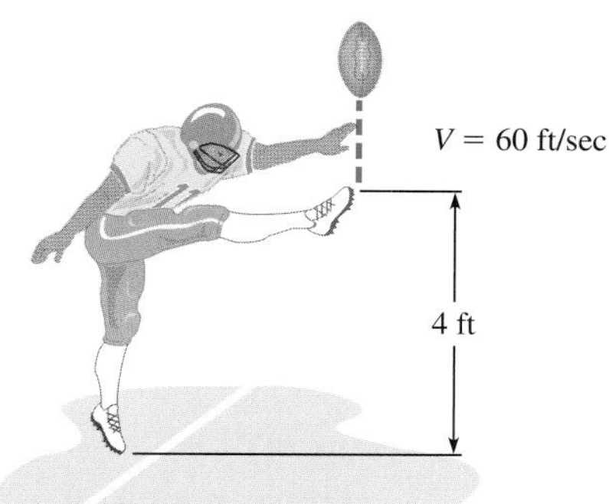

Figure for Exercise 13

14. ***Hunting accident.*** Dwight accidentally fired his rifle straight into the air while sitting in his deer stand 30 feet off the ground. If the bullet left the barrel with a velocity of 200 feet per second, then how long did it take the bullet to fall to the earth? $\frac{25+\sqrt{655}}{4}$ or 12.65 seconds

VIDEO **15.** ***Going up.*** A ball is tossed vertically into the air at 20 feet per second from a height of 5 feet. How long (to the nearest tenth of a second) will it take the ball to reach the ground? 1.5 seconds

16. ***Going down.*** A comedian throws a watermelon downward at 30 feet per second from a height of 200 feet. How long (to the nearest tenth of a second) will it take the watermelon to reach the ground? (The initial velocity of the watermelon is negative.) $\frac{-15+5\sqrt{137}}{16}$ or 2.7 seconds

Miscellaneous

Solve each problem. Give the exact answer and an approximate answer rounded to two decimal places.

17. ***Gone fishing.*** Nancy traveled 6 miles upstream to do some fly fishing. It took her 20 minutes longer to get there than to return. If the current in the river is 2 miles per hour, then how fast will her boat go in still water? $2\sqrt{19}$ or 8.72 mph

18. ***Commuting to work.*** Gladys and Bonita commute to work daily. Bonita drives 40 miles and averages 9 miles per hour more than Gladys. Gladys drives 50 miles, and she is on the road one-half hour longer than Bonita. How fast does each of them drive? Gladys 36 mph, Bonita 45 mph

19. ***Expanding garden.*** Olin's garden is 5 feet wide and 8 feet long. He bought enough okra seed to plant 100 square feet in okra. If he wants to increase the width and the length by the same amount to plant all of his okra, then what should the increase be? $\frac{-13+\sqrt{409}}{2}$ or 3.61 feet

20. ***Spring flowers.*** Lillian has a 5-foot-square bed of tulips. She plans to surround this bed with a crocus bed of uniform width. If she has enough crocus bulbs to plant 100 square feet of crocus, then how wide should the crocus bed be? $\frac{-5+5\sqrt{5}}{2}$ or 3.09 feet

Photo for Exercise 20

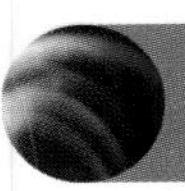

9.5 Complex Numbers

In This Section

In this chapter, we have seen quadratic equations that have no solution in the set of real numbers. In this section, you will learn that the set of real numbers is contained in the set of complex numbers. *Quadratic equations that have no real number solutions have solutions that are complex numbers.*

⟨1⟩ Complex Numbers

If we try to solve the equation $x^2 + 1 = 0$ by the square root property, we get

$$x^2 = -1 \qquad \text{or} \qquad x = \pm\sqrt{-1}.$$

Because $\sqrt{-1}$ has no meaning in the real number system, the equation has no real solution. However, there is an extension of the real number system, called the *complex numbers,* in which $x^2 = -1$ has two solutions.

The complex numbers are formed by adding the **imaginary unit** i to the real number system. We make the definitions that

$$i = \sqrt{-1} \qquad \text{and} \qquad i^2 = -1.$$

In the complex number system, $x^2 = -1$ has two solutions: i and $-i$.

The set of complex numbers is defined as follows.

⟨ Teaching Tip ⟩

If $a = 0$ and $b \neq 0$ in $a + bi$, then the number is called *pure imaginary*. That term was omitted here to keep the situation simpler.

Complex Numbers

The set of complex numbers is the set of all numbers of the form

$$a + bi,$$

where a and b are real numbers, $i = \sqrt{-1}$, and $i^2 = -1$.

In the complex number $a + bi$, a is called the **real part** and b is called the **imaginary part.** If $b \neq 0$, the number $a + bi$ is called an **imaginary number.**

In dealing with complex numbers, we treat $a + bi$ as if it were a binomial with variable i. Thus we would write $2 + (-3)i$ as $2 - 3i$. We agree that $2 + i3$, $3i + 2$, and $i3 + 2$ are just different ways of writing $2 + 3i$. Some examples of complex numbers are

$$2 + 3i, \quad -2 - 5i, \quad 0 + 4i, \quad 9 + 0i, \quad \text{and} \quad 0 + 0i.$$

For simplicity we will write only $4i$ for $0 + 4i$. The complex number $9 + 0i$ is the real number 9, and $0 + 0i$ is the real number 0. Any complex number with $b = 0$ is a real number. The diagram in Fig. 9.3 shows the relationships between the complex numbers, the real numbers, and the imaginary numbers.

⟨ Helpful Hint ⟩

All numbers are ideas. They exist only in our minds. So in a sense we "imagine" all numbers. However, the imaginary numbers are a bit harder to imagine than the real numbers and so only they are called imaginary.

Complex numbers

Real numbers	Imaginary numbers
$-3, \pi, \frac{5}{2}, 0, -9, \sqrt{2}$	$i, 2 + 3i, \sqrt{-5}, -3 - 8i$

Figure 9.3

⟨2⟩ Operations with Complex Numbers

Addition and subtraction of complex numbers are performed as if the complex numbers were binomials with i being a variable.

EXAMPLE 1

Adding and subtracting complex numbers

Perform the indicated operations.

a) $(2 + 3i) + (4 + 5i)$
b) $(2 - 3i) + (-1 - i)$
c) $(3 + 4i) - (1 + 7i)$
d) $(2 - 3i) - (-2 - 5i)$

Solution

a) $(2 + 3i) + (4 + 5i) = 6 + 8i$

b) $(2 - 3i) + (-1 - i) = 1 - 4i$

c) $(3 + 4i) - (1 + 7i) = 3 + 4i - 1 - 7i$
$= 2 - 3i$

d) $(2 - 3i) - (-2 - 5i) = 2 - 3i + 2 + 5i$
$= 4 + 2i$

Now do Exercises 7–18

For completeness we state a formal definition of addition and subtraction as follows. However, it is not necessary to use or memorize this definition. Just perform addition and subtraction as in Example 1.

Addition and Subtraction of Complex Numbers

$$(a + bi) + (c + di) = (a + c) + (b + d)i$$
$$(a + bi) - (c + di) = (a - c) + (b - d)i$$

Multiplication of complex numbers is performed just like multiplication of polynomials. Since $i^2 = -1$, we replace i^2 with -1 whenever it occurs.

EXAMPLE 2

Multiplying complex numbers

Perform the indicated operations.

a) $2i(1 - 3i)$
b) $(-2 - 5i)(6 - 7i)$
c) $(5i)^2$
d) $(-5i)^2$
e) $(3 - 2i)(3 + 2i)$

Solution

a) $2i(1 - 3i) = 2i - 6i^2$ Distributive property
$= 2i - 6(-1)$ $i^2 = -1$
$= 6 + 2i$

‹ Calculator Close-Up ›

Many calculators can perform operations with complex numbers.

```
2i(1-3i)
                6+2i
(-2-5i)(6-7i)
              -47-16i
(5i)²
                 -25
```

b) Use FOIL to multiply these complex numbers:

$$\begin{aligned}(-2 - 5i)(6 - 7i) &= -12 + 14i - 30i + 35i^2 \\ &= -12 - 16i + 35(-1) \quad i^2 = -1 \\ &= -12 - 16i - 35 \\ &= -47 - 16i\end{aligned}$$

c) $(5i)^2 = 25i^2 = 25(-1) = -25$

d) $(-5i)^2 = (-5)^2i^2 = 25(-1) = -25$

e) $(3 - 2i)(3 + 2i) = 9 - 4i^2$

$$\begin{aligned}&= 9 - 4(-1) \\ &= 9 + 4 \\ &= 13\end{aligned}$$

Now do Exercises 19–32

For completeness we state the formal definition of multiplication as follows. However, it is not necessary to use or memorize this definition. Just perform multiplication as in Example 2.

Multiplication of Complex Numbers

$$(a + bi)(c + di) = (ac - bd) + (ad + bc)i$$

Notice that the product of the imaginary numbers $3 - 2i$ and $3 + 2i$ in Example 2(e) is a real number. We call $3 - 2i$ and $3 + 2i$ *complex conjugates* of each other.

Complex Conjugates

The complex numbers $a + bi$ and $a - bi$ are called **complex conjugates** of each other. Their product is the real number $a^2 + b^2$.

EXAMPLE 3

Complex conjugates

Find the product of the given complex number and its conjugate.

a) $4 - 3i$ **b)** $-2 + 5i$ **c)** $-i$

‹ Helpful Hint ›

The last time we used "conjugate" was to refer to expressions such as $1 + \sqrt{3}$ and $1 - \sqrt{3}$ as conjugates. Note that we use the rule for the product of a sum and a difference to multiply the radical conjugates or the complex conjugates.

Solution

a) The complex conjugate of $4 - 3i$ is $4 + 3i$:

$$(4 - 3i)(4 + 3i) = 16 - 9i^2 = 16 + 9 = 25$$

b) The conjugate of $-2 + 5i$ is $-2 - 5i$:

$$(-2 + 5i)(-2 - 5i) = (-2)^2 + 5^2 = 4 + 25 = 29$$

c) The conjugate of $-i$ is i:

$$(-i)(i) = -i^2 = -(-1) = 1$$

Now do Exercises 33–40

To divide a complex number by a real number, we divide each part by the real number. For example,

$$\frac{4 - 6i}{2} = 2 - 3i.$$

We use the idea of complex conjugates to divide by a complex number. The process is similar to rationalizing the denominator.

Dividing by a Complex Number

To divide by a complex number, multiply the numerator and denominator of the quotient by the complex conjugate of the denominator.

EXAMPLE 4

Dividing complex numbers

Perform the indicated operations.

a) $\dfrac{2}{3 - 4i}$ **b)** $\dfrac{6}{2 + i}$ **c)** $\dfrac{3 - 2i}{i}$

‹ Teaching Tip ›

Emphasize that dividing complex numbers is similar to rationalizing the denominator with roots. This again illustrates that the numerator and denominator of a fraction can be multiplied by the same nonzero number.

Solution

a) Multiply the numerator and denominator by $3 + 4i$, the conjugate of $3 - 4i$:

$$\begin{aligned}\frac{2}{3 - 4i} &= \frac{2(3 + 4i)}{(3 - 4i)(3 + 4i)} \\ &= \frac{6 + 8i}{9 - 16i^2} \\ &= \frac{6 + 8i}{25} \qquad 9 - 16i^2 = 9 - 16(-1) = 25 \\ &= \frac{6}{25} + \frac{8}{25}i\end{aligned}$$

b) Multiply the numerator and denominator by $2 - i$, the conjugate of $2 + i$:

$$\begin{aligned}\frac{6}{2 + i} &= \frac{6(2 - i)}{(2 + i)(2 - i)} \\ &= \frac{12 - 6i}{4 - i^2} \\ &= \frac{12 - 6i}{5} \qquad 4 - i^2 = 4 - (-1) = 5 \\ &= \frac{12}{5} - \frac{6}{5}i\end{aligned}$$

c) Multiply the numerator and denominator by $-i$, the conjugate of i:

$$\frac{3 - 2i}{i} = \frac{(3 - 2i)(-i)}{i(-i)} = \frac{-3i + 2i^2}{-i^2} = \frac{-3i - 2}{1} = -2 - 3i$$

Now do Exercises 41–52

‹3› Square Roots of Negative Numbers

In Example 2, we saw that both

$$(5i)^2 = -25 \qquad \text{and} \qquad (-5i)^2 = -25.$$

Because the square of each of these complex numbers is -25, both $5i$ and $-5i$ are square roots of -25. When we use the radical notation, we write

$$\sqrt{-25} = 5i.$$

The square root of a negative number is not a real number; it is a complex number.

Square Root of a Negative Number

For any positive number b,

$$\sqrt{-b} = i\sqrt{b}.$$

For example, $\sqrt{-9} = i\sqrt{9} = 3i$ and $\sqrt{-7} = i\sqrt{7}$. Note that the expression $\sqrt{7}i$ could easily be mistaken for the expression $\sqrt{7i}$, where i is under the radical. For this reason, when the coefficient of i contains a radical, we write i preceding the radical.

EXAMPLE 5

Square roots of negative numbers

Write each expression in the form $a + bi$, where a and b are real numbers.

a) $2 + \sqrt{-4}$ **b)** $\dfrac{2 + \sqrt{-12}}{2}$ **c)** $\dfrac{-2 - \sqrt{-18}}{3}$

Solution

a) $2 + \sqrt{-4} = 2 + i\sqrt{4}$

$= 2 + 2i$

b) $\dfrac{2 + \sqrt{-12}}{2} = \dfrac{2 + i\sqrt{12}}{2}$

$= \dfrac{2 + 2i\sqrt{3}}{2}$ $\quad \sqrt{12} = \sqrt{4} \cdot \sqrt{3} = 2\sqrt{3}$

$= 1 + i\sqrt{3}$

c) $\dfrac{-2 - \sqrt{-18}}{3} = \dfrac{-2 - i\sqrt{18}}{3}$

$= \dfrac{-2 - 3i\sqrt{2}}{3}$ $\quad \sqrt{18} = \sqrt{9}\sqrt{2} = 3\sqrt{2}$

$= -\dfrac{2}{3} - i\sqrt{2}$

Now do Exercises 53–64

Note that we must rewrite square roots of negative numbers with i before performing operations. A common mistake is to use the product rule for radicals with negative numbers:

$$\sqrt{-4} \cdot \sqrt{-9} = \sqrt{36} = 6 \qquad \text{Incorrect}$$

If we rewrite the radicals with i, we get the correct result:

$$\sqrt{-4} \cdot \sqrt{-9} = 2i \cdot 3i = 6i^2 = 6(-1) = -6 \qquad \text{Correct}$$

‹ Helpful Hint ›

The fundamental theorem of algebra says that an *n*th degree polynomial equation has exactly *n* solutions in the system of complex numbers. They don't all have to be different. For example, a quadratic equation such as $x^2 + 6x + 9 = 0$ has two solutions, both of which are -3.

‹4› Complex Solutions to Quadratic Equations

The equation $x^2 = -4$ has no real number solutions, but it has two complex solutions, which can be found as follows:

$$x^2 = -4$$
$$x = \pm\sqrt{-4} = \pm i\sqrt{4} = \pm 2i$$

Check:

$$(2i)^2 = 4i^2 = 4(-1) = -4$$
$$(-2i)^2 = 4i^2 = -4$$

Both $2i$ and $-2i$ are solutions to the equation.

The number of solutions to the general quadratic equation $ax^2 + bx + c = 0$, where a, b, and c are real numbers, depends on which number system you are using. If $b^2 - 4ac > 0$, the equation has two real solutions. Since the real numbers are contained in the complex numbers, the two real solutions are also complex solutions. If $b^2 - 4ac = 0$, the equation has one real solution, which is also a complex solution. If $b^2 - 4ac < 0$, the equation has no real solutions, but it does have two complex solutions. See Table 9.2.

Table 9.2

Value of $b^2 - 4ac$	Number of Real Solutions	Number of Complex Solutions
Positive	2	2
Zero	1	1
Negative	0	2

In the complex number system, all quadratic equations have solutions and we can use the quadratic formula to find them, as shown in Example 6.

EXAMPLE 6

Quadratics with imaginary solutions

Find the complex solutions to the quadratic equations.

a) $x^2 - 2x + 5 = 0$

b) $2x^2 + 3x + 5 = 0$

‹ Teaching Tip ›

Students do not like to check imaginary solutions to equations. But checking will review many rules that were studied in this text.

Solution

a) To solve $x^2 - 2x + 5 = 0$, use $a = 1$, $b = -2$, and $c = 5$ in the quadratic formula:

$$x = \frac{2 \pm \sqrt{(-2)^2 - 4(1)(5)}}{2(1)}$$
$$= \frac{2 \pm \sqrt{-16}}{2} = \frac{2 \pm 4i}{2} = 1 \pm 2i$$

We can use the operations with complex numbers to check these solutions:

$$(1 + 2i)^2 - 2(1 + 2i) + 5 = 1 + 4i + 4i^2 - 2 - 4i + 5$$
$$= 1 + 4i - 4 - 2 - 4i + 5 = 0$$

You should verify that $1 - 2i$ also satisfies the equation. The solutions are $1 - 2i$ and $1 + 2i$.

‹ Calculator Close-Up ›

The answers in Example 6(b) can be checked with a calculator as shown here.

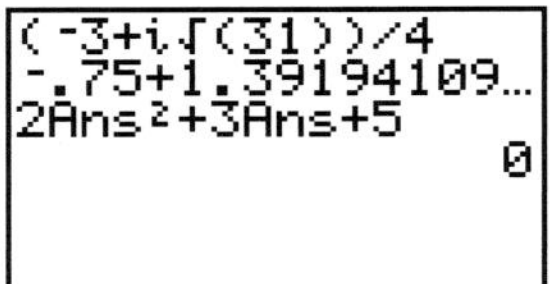

b) To solve $2x^2 + 3x + 5 = 0$, use $a = 2$, $b = 3$, and $c = 5$ in the quadratic formula:

$$x = \frac{-3 \pm \sqrt{3^2 - 4(2)(5)}}{2(2)}$$

$$= \frac{-3 \pm \sqrt{-31}}{4} = \frac{-3 \pm i\sqrt{31}}{4}$$

Check these answers. The solutions are $\frac{-3 + i\sqrt{31}}{4}$ and $\frac{-3 - i\sqrt{31}}{4}$.

Now do Exercises 65–86

The following box summarizes the basic facts about complex numbers.

Complex Numbers

1. $i = \sqrt{-1}$ and $i^2 = -1$.
2. A complex number has the form $a + bi$, where a and b are real numbers.
3. The complex number $a + 0i$ is the real number a.
4. If b is a positive real number, then $\sqrt{-b} = i\sqrt{b}$.
5. The complex conjugate of $a + bi$ is $a - bi$.
6. Add, subtract, and multiply complex numbers as if they were binomials with variable i. Replace i^2 with -1 whenever it occurs.
7. Divide complex numbers by multiplying the numerator and denominator by the conjugate of the denominator.
8. In the complex number system, all quadratic equations have solutions.

Warm-Ups ▼

True or false? Explain your answer.

1. $(3 + i) + (2 - 4i) = 5 - 3i$ True
2. $(4 - 2i)(3 - 5i) = 2 - 26i$ True
3. $(4 - i)(4 + i) = 17$ True
4. $i^4 = 1$ True
5. $\sqrt{-5} = 5i$ False
6. $\sqrt{-36} = \pm 6i$ False
7. The complex conjugate of $-2 + 3i$ is $2 - 3i$. False
8. Zero is the only real number that is also a complex number. False
9. Both $2i$ and $-2i$ are solutions to the equation $x^2 = 4$. False
10. Every quadratic equation has at least one complex solution. True

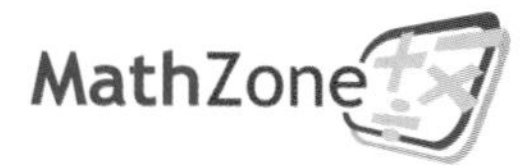

‹ Study Tips ›

- Study for the final exam by reworking all of your old test questions.
- It might have been a couple of months since you last worked a certain type of problem. Don't assume that you can do it correctly now just because you did it correctly a long time ago.

Reading and Writing *After reading this section, write out the answers to these questions. Use complete sentences.*

1. What is a complex number?
A complex number is a number of the form $a + bi$, where a and b are real and $i = \sqrt{-1}$.

2. What is the relationship between the complex numbers, the real numbers, and the imaginary numbers?
The real numbers together with the imaginary numbers make up the set of complex numbers.

3. How do you add or subtract complex numbers?
Complex numbers are added or subtracted like binomials in which i is the variable.

4. What is a complex conjugate?
The complex conjugate of $a + bi$ is $a - bi$.

5. What is the square root of a negative number in the complex number system? If $b > 0$, then $\sqrt{-b} = i\sqrt{b}$.

6. How many solutions do quadratic equations have in the complex number system?
In the complex number system all quadratic equations have at least one solution.

‹2› Operations with Complex Numbers

Perform the indicated operations. See Example 1.

7. $(3 + 5i) + (2 + 4i)$ $5 + 9i$

8. $(8 + 3i) + (1 + 2i)$ $9 + 5i$

9. $(-1 + i) + (2 - i)$ 1

VIDEO **10.** $(-2 - i) + (-3 + 5i)$ $-5 + 4i$

11. $(4 - 5i) - (2 + 3i)$ $2 - 8i$

12. $(3 - 2i) - (7 + 6i)$ $-4 - 8i$

13. $(-3 - 5i) - (-2 - i)$ $-1 - 4i$

14. $(-4 - 8i) - (-2 - 3i)$ $-2 - 5i$

15. $(8 - 3i) - (9 - 3i)$ -1

16. $(5 + 6i) - (-3 + 6i)$ 8

17. $\left(\frac{1}{2} + i\right) + \left(\frac{1}{4} - \frac{1}{2}i\right)$ $\frac{3}{4} + \frac{1}{2}i$

18. $\left(\frac{2}{3} - i\right) - \left(\frac{1}{4} - \frac{1}{2}i\right)$ $\frac{5}{12} - \frac{1}{2}i$

Perform the indicated operations. See Example 2.

19. $3(2 - 3i)$ $6 - 9i$

20. $-4(3 - 2i)$ $-12 + 8i$

21. $(6i)^2$ -36

22. $(3i)^2$ -9

23. $(-6i)^2$ -36

24. $(-3i)^2$ -9

VIDEO **25.** $(2 + 3i)(3 - 5i)$ $21 - i$

26. $(4 - i)(3 - 6i)$ $6 - 27i$

27. $(5 - 2i)^2$ $21 - 20i$

28. $(3 + 4i)^2$ $-7 + 24i$

29. $(4 - 3i)(4 + 3i)$ 25

30. $(-3 + 5i)(-3 - 5i)$ 34

31. $(1 - i)(1 + i)$ 2

32. $(3 - i)(3 + i)$ 10

Find the product of the given complex number and its conjugate. See Example 3.

33. $2 + 5i$ 29

34. $3 + 4i$ 25

35. $4 - 6i$ 52

36. $2 - 7i$ 53

37. $-3 + 2i$ 13

38. $-4 - i$ 17

39. i 1

40. $-2i$ 4

Perform the indicated operations. See Example 4.

41. $(2 - 6i) \div 2$ $1 - 3i$

42. $(-3 + 6i) \div (-3)$ $1 - 2i$

43. $\frac{-2 + 8i}{2}$ $-1 + 4i$

44. $\frac{6 - 9i}{-3}$ $-2 + 3i$

45. $\frac{4 + 6i}{-2i}$ $-3 + 2i$

46. $\frac{3 - 8i}{i}$ $-8 - 3i$

VIDEO **47.** $\frac{4i}{3 + 2i}$ $\frac{8}{13} + \frac{12}{13}i$

48. $\frac{5}{4 - 5i}$ $\frac{20}{41} + \frac{25}{41}i$

49. $\frac{2 + i}{2 - i}$ $\frac{3}{5} + \frac{4}{5}i$

50. $\frac{i - 5}{5 - i}$ -1

51. $\frac{4 - 12i}{3 + i}$ $-4i$

52. $\frac{-4 + 10i}{5 - i}$ $-\frac{15}{13} + \frac{23}{13}i$

‹3› Square Roots of Negative Numbers

Write each expression in the form $a + bi$, where a and b are real numbers. See Example 5.

53. $5 + \sqrt{-9}$ $5 + 3i$

54. $6 + \sqrt{-16}$ $6 + 4i$

55. $-3 - \sqrt{-7}$ $-3 - i\sqrt{7}$

56. $2 - \sqrt{-3}$ $2 - i\sqrt{3}$

57. $\frac{-2 + \sqrt{-12}}{2}$ $-1 + i\sqrt{3}$

VIDEO **58.** $\frac{-6 + \sqrt{-18}}{3}$ $-2 + i\sqrt{2}$

59. $\frac{-8 - \sqrt{-20}}{-4}$ $2 + \frac{1}{2}i\sqrt{5}$

60. $\frac{6 + \sqrt{-24}}{-2}$ $-3 - i\sqrt{6}$

61. $\frac{-4 + \sqrt{-28}}{6}$ $-\frac{2}{3} + \frac{1}{3}i\sqrt{7}$

62. $\frac{6 - \sqrt{-45}}{6}$ $1 - \frac{1}{2}i\sqrt{5}$

63. $\frac{-2 + \sqrt{-100}}{-10}$ $\frac{1}{5} - i$

64. $\frac{-3 + \sqrt{-81}}{-9}$ $\frac{1}{3} - i$

⟨4⟩ Complex Solutions to Quadratic Equations

Find the complex solutions to each quadratic equation. See Example 6.

65. $x^2 = -36$ $\quad -6i, 6i$

66. $x^2 = -100$ $\quad -10i, 10i$

67. $x^2 + 81 = 0$ $\quad -9i, 9i$

68. $x^2 + 100 = 0$ $\quad -10i, 10i$

69. $x^2 - 49 = 0$ $\quad -7, 7$

70. $x^2 - 1 = 0$ $\quad -1, 1$

71. $x^2 + 5 = 0$ $\quad -i\sqrt{5}, i\sqrt{5}$

72. $x^2 + 6 = 0$ $\quad -i\sqrt{6}, i\sqrt{6}$

73. $3y^2 + 2 = 0$
$-i\dfrac{\sqrt{6}}{3}, i\dfrac{\sqrt{6}}{3}$

74. $5y^2 + 3 = 0$
$-i\dfrac{\sqrt{15}}{5}, i\dfrac{\sqrt{15}}{5}$

75. $x^2 - 4x + 5 = 0$
$2 - i, 2 + i$

76. $x^2 - 6x + 10 = 0$
$3 - i, 3 + i$

77. $y^2 + 13 = 6y$
$3 - 2i, 3 + 2i$

VIDEO **78.** $y^2 + 29 = 4y$
$2 - 5i, 2 + 5i$

79. $x^2 - 4x + 7 = 0$
$2 - i\sqrt{3}, 2 + i\sqrt{3}$

80. $x^2 - 10x + 27 = 0$
$5 - i\sqrt{2}, 5 + i\sqrt{2}$

81. $9y^2 - 12y + 5 = 0$
$\dfrac{2 - i}{3}, \dfrac{2 + i}{3}$

82. $2y^2 - 2y + 1 = 0$
$\dfrac{1}{2} - \dfrac{1}{2}i, \dfrac{1}{2} + \dfrac{1}{2}i$

83. $x^2 - x + 1 = 0$
$\dfrac{1 - i\sqrt{3}}{2}, \dfrac{1 + i\sqrt{3}}{2}$

84. $4x^2 - 20x + 27 = 0$
$\dfrac{5}{2} - \dfrac{1}{2}i\sqrt{2}, \dfrac{5}{2} + \dfrac{1}{2}i\sqrt{2}$

85. $-4x^2 + 8x - 9 = 0$
$\dfrac{2 - i\sqrt{5}}{2}, \dfrac{2 + i\sqrt{5}}{2}$

86. $-9x^2 + 12x - 10 = 0$
$\dfrac{2}{3} - \dfrac{1}{3}i\sqrt{6}, \dfrac{2}{3} + \dfrac{1}{3}i\sqrt{6}$

Miscellaneous

Solve each problem.

87. Evaluate $(2 - 3i)^2 + 4(2 - 3i) - 9$. $\quad -6 - 24i$

88. Evaluate $(3 + 5i)^2 - 2(3 + 5i) + 5$. $\quad -17 + 20i$

89. What is the value of $x^2 - 8x + 17$ if $x = 4 - i$? $\quad 0$

90. What is the value of $x^2 - 6x + 34$ if $x = 3 + 5i$? $\quad 0$

91. Find the product $[x - (6 - i)][x - (6 + i)]$.
$x^2 - 12x + 37$

92. Find the product $[x - (3 + 7i)][x - (3 - 7i)]$.
$x^2 - 6x + 58$

93. Write a quadratic equation that has $3i$ and $-3i$ as its solutions. $\quad x^2 + 9 = 0$

94. Write a quadratic equation that has $2 + 5i$ and $2 - 5i$ as its solutions. $\quad x^2 - 4x + 29 = 0$

Getting More Involved

95. ***Discussion***

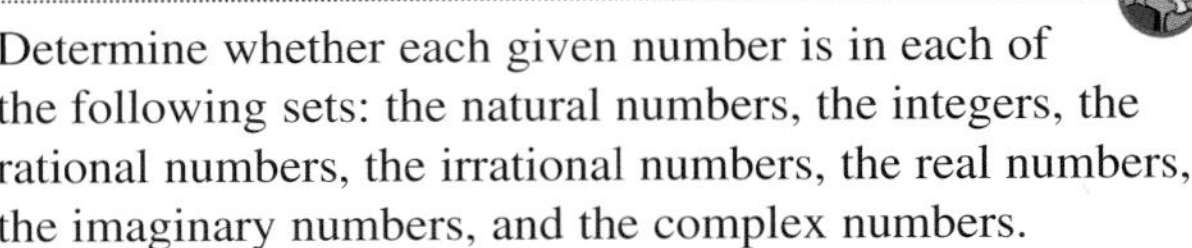

Determine whether each given number is in each of the following sets: the natural numbers, the integers, the rational numbers, the irrational numbers, the real numbers, the imaginary numbers, and the complex numbers.

a) 54 **b)** $-\dfrac{3}{8}$ **c)** $3\sqrt{5}$ **d)** $6i$ **e)** $\pi + i\sqrt{5}$

Natural: 54, integers: 54, rational: 54, $-3/8$, irrational: $3\sqrt{5}$, real: 54, $-3/8$, $3\sqrt{5}$, imaginary: $6i$, $\pi + i\sqrt{5}$, complex: all

96. ***Discussion***

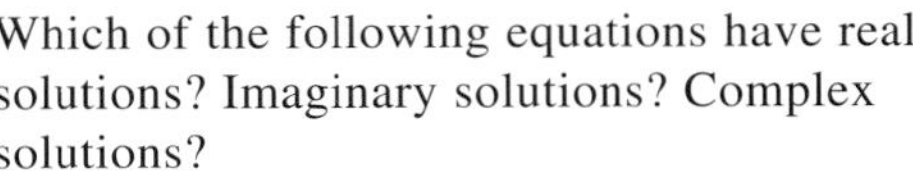

Which of the following equations have real solutions? Imaginary solutions? Complex solutions?

a) $3x^2 - 2x + 9 = 0$

b) $5x^2 - 2x - 10 = 0$

c) $\dfrac{1}{2}x^2 - x + 3 = 0$

d) $7w^2 + 12 = 0$

Real: b, imaginary: a, c, d, complex: all

9.6 Graphing Parabolas

In This Section

The graph of any equation of the form $y = mx + b$ is a straight line. In this section, we will see that all equations of the form $y = ax^2 + bx + c$ have graphs that are in the shape of a *parabola*.

⟨1⟩ Finding Ordered Pairs

It is straightforward to calculate y when given x for an equation of the form $y = ax^2 + bx + c$. However, if we are given y and want to find x, then we must use methods for solving quadratic equations.

EXAMPLE 1

Finding ordered pairs

Complete each ordered pair so that it satisfies the given equation. For part (a) the pairs are of the form (x, y) and for part (b) they are of the form (t, s).

a) $y = x^2 - x - 6$; $(2, \quad)$, $(\quad, 0)$

b) $s = -16t^2 + 48t + 84$; $(0, \quad)$, $(\quad, 20)$

Solution

a) If $x = 2$, then $y = 2^2 - 2 - 6 = -4$. So the ordered pair is $(2, -4)$. To find x when $y = 0$, replace y by 0 and solve the resulting quadratic equation:

$$x^2 - x - 6 = 0$$
$$(x - 3)(x + 2) = 0$$
$$x - 3 = 0 \quad \text{or} \quad x + 2 = 0$$
$$x = 3 \quad \text{or} \quad x = -2$$

The ordered pairs are $(-2, 0)$ and $(3, 0)$.

b) If $t = 0$, then $s = -16 \cdot 0^2 + 48 \cdot 0 + 84 = 84$. The ordered pair is $(0, 84)$. To find t when $s = 20$, replace s by 20 and solve the equation for t:

$$-16t^2 + 48t + 84 = 20$$
$$-16t^2 + 48t + 64 = 0 \qquad \text{Subtract 20 from each side.}$$
$$t^2 - 3t - 4 = 0 \qquad \text{Divide each side by } -16.$$
$$(t - 4)(t + 1) = 0 \qquad \text{Factor.}$$
$$t - 4 = 0 \quad \text{or} \quad t + 1 = 0 \qquad \text{Zero factor property}$$
$$t = 4 \quad \text{or} \quad t = -1$$

The ordered pairs are $(-1, 20)$ and $(4, 20)$.

Now do Exercises 7–12

CAUTION In ordered pairs, the independent variable is usually written first and the dependent variable second. In Example 1(b), the dependent variable is s because s depends on or is determined from t by the formula $s = -16t^2 + 48t + 84$. So the ordered pairs are of the form (t, s) rather than in alphabetical order (s, t).

⟨2⟩ Graphing Parabolas

The graph of any equation of the form $y = ax^2 + bx + c$ (with $a \neq 0$) is called a **parabola.** To graph a parabola we simply plot points as we did when we first graphed lines in Section 3.1. Note that any real number may be used in place of x in the equation $y = ax^2 + bx + c$.

EXAMPLE 2

The simplest parabola

Graph $y = x^2$.

Solution

Arbitrarily select some values for the independent variable x and calculate the corresponding values for the dependent variable y:

If $x = -2$, then $y = (-2)^2 = 4$.

If $x = -1$, then $y = (-1)^2 = 1$.

‹ Calculator Close-Up ›

This close-up view of $y = x^2$ shows how rounded the curve is at the bottom. When drawing a parabola by hand, be sure to draw it smoothly.

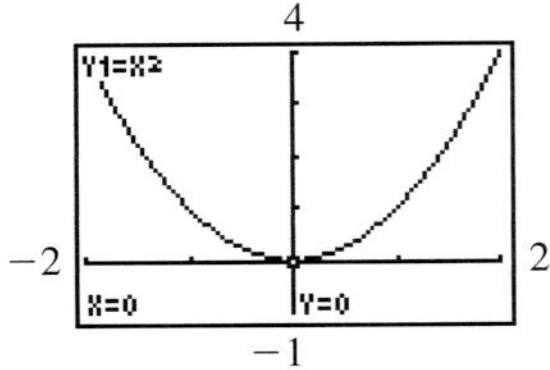

If $x = 0$, then $y = 0^2 = 0$.
If $x = 1$, then $y = 1^2 = 1$.
If $x = 2$, then $y = 2^2 = 4$.

These values are displayed in the following table:

x	−2	−1	0	1	2
$y = x^2$	4	1	0	1	4

From the table we get the points $(-2, 4)$, $(-1, 1)$, $(0, 0)$, $(1, 1)$, and $(2, 4)$. Plot these points and draw a parabola through them, as shown in Fig. 9.4. Note that the x-coordinates can be any real numbers, but there are no negative y-coordinates. So $y \geq 0$ in every point on the graph.

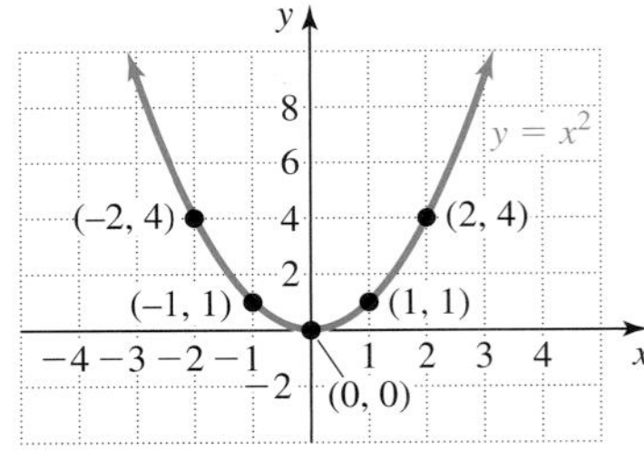

Figure 9.4

Now do Exercises 13–16

The parabola in Fig. 9.4 is said to **open upward.** In Example 3, we see a parabola that **opens downward.** If $a > 0$ in the equation $y = ax^2 + bx + c$, then the parabola opens upward. If $a < 0$, then the parabola opens downward.

EXAMPLE 3

A parabola that opens downward

Graph $y = 4 - x^2$.

‹ Teaching Tip ›

Mention to students that tables can be made horizontally or vertically. Students often prefer to make vertical tables.

Solution

Find some ordered pairs as follows:

x	−2	−1	0	1	2
$y = 4 - x^2$	0	3	4	3	0

Plot $(-2, 0)$, $(-1, 3)$, $(0, 4)$, $(1, 3)$, and $(2, 0)$, as shown in Fig. 9.5, and sketch a parabola through the points. Note that the largest y-coordinate on this graph is 4. So $y \leq 4$ in every ordered pair on the graph.

Now do Exercises 17–22

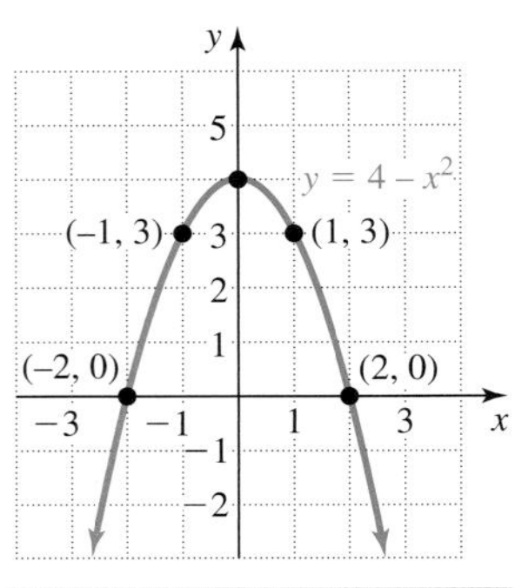

Figure 9.5

Notice the symmetry in the parabolas in Figs. 9.4 and 9.5. The points on a parabola occur in corresponding pairs. In Fig. 9.5 we have $(1, 3)$ and $(-1, 3)$, $(2, 0)$ and $(-2, 0)$. If you were to fold the graph along the y-axis, the two sides of the parabola would match up. The only point that does not occur as a pair is the highest or lowest point.

⟨3⟩ The Vertex and Intercepts

The lowest point on a parabola that opens upward or the highest point on a parabola that opens downward is called the **vertex.** The y-coordinate of the vertex is the **minimum** y-value on the graph if the parabola opens upward, or it is the **maximum** y-value if the parabola opens downward. For $y = x^2$, the vertex is (0, 0) and 0 is the minimum y-value on the graph. For $y = 4 - x^2$, the vertex is (0, 4) and 4 is the maximum y-value on the graph.

Because the vertex is the highest or lowest point on a parabola, it is an important feature of the parabola. Notice in Fig. 9.5 that the vertex is halfway between the x-intercepts. To find the x-intercepts for $y = ax^2 + bx + c$ we must solve $ax^2 + bx + c = 0$. Of course, the solution to this equation is given by the quadratic formula. So the x-coordinates of the x-intercepts are

$$\frac{-b + \sqrt{b^2 - 4ac}}{2a} \quad \text{and} \quad \frac{-b - \sqrt{b^2 - 4ac}}{2a}.$$

Adding these expressions and dividing by 2 yields the following formula.

Vertex of a Parabola

The x-coordinate of the vertex of $y = ax^2 + bx + c$ is $\frac{-b}{2a}$, provided that $a \neq 0$.

⟨ Helpful Hint ⟩

To draw a parabola or any curve by hand, use your hand like a compass. The two halves of a parabola should be drawn in two steps. Position your paper so that your hand is approximately at the "center" of the arc you are trying to draw.

You can remember $\frac{-b}{2a}$ by observing that it is part of the quadratic formula:

$$x = \frac{-b \pm \sqrt{b^2 - 4ac}}{2a}$$

In Examples 2 and 3, we drew the graph by selecting five x-values and calculating y. But how did we know what to select for x? The best way to graph a parabola is to find the vertex first, then select two x-coordinates to the left of the vertex and two to the right of the vertex. This way you will always get a graph that shows the typical parabolic shape.

EXAMPLE 4

Using the vertex in graphing a parabola

Graph $y = -x^2 - x + 2$.

Solution

First find the x-coordinate of the vertex:

$$x = \frac{-b}{2a} = \frac{-(-1)}{2(-1)} = \frac{1}{-2} = -\frac{1}{2}$$

Now find y for $x = -\frac{1}{2}$:

$$y = -\left(-\frac{1}{2}\right)^2 - \left(-\frac{1}{2}\right) + 2 = -\frac{1}{4} + \frac{1}{2} + 2 = \frac{9}{4}$$

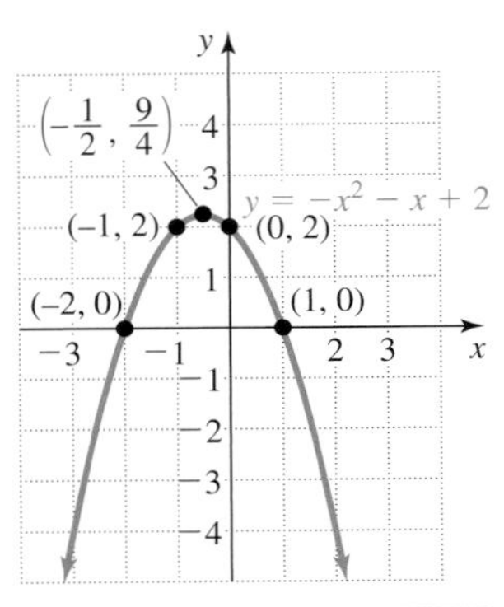

Figure 9.6

The vertex is $\left(-\frac{1}{2}, \frac{9}{4}\right)$. Now find a few points on either side of the vertex:

x	-2	-1	$-\frac{1}{2}$	0	1
$y = -x^2 - x + 2$	0	2	$\frac{9}{4}$	2	0

Sketch a parabola through these points as in Fig. 9.6.

Now do Exercises 23–28

The y-intercept is the point where the parabola crosses the y-axis. Its first coordinate is 0. The x-intercepts are the points where the parabola crosses the x-axis. Their second coordinates are 0. There is always one y-intercept, but there could be 2, 1, or 0 x-intercepts.

EXAMPLE 5

Using the intercepts in graphing a parabola

Find the vertex and intercepts, and sketch the graph of each equation.

a) $y = x^2 - 2x - 8$

b) $s = -16t^2 + 64t$

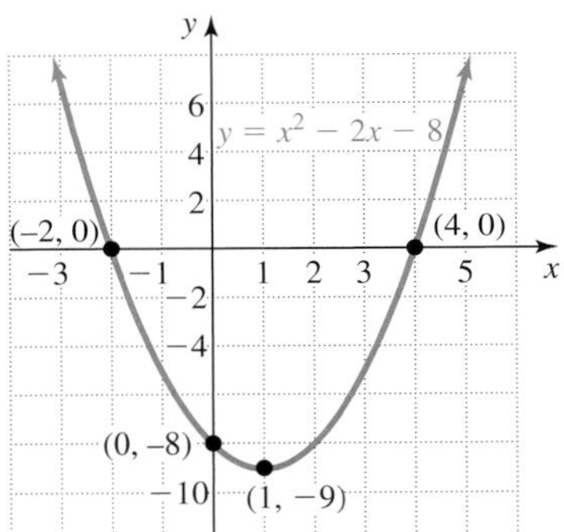

Figure 9.7

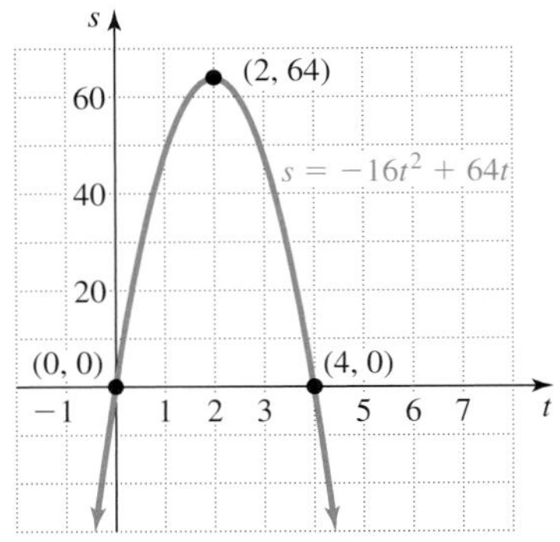

Figure 9.8

Solution

a) Use $x = \frac{-b}{2a}$ to get $x = 1$ as the x-coordinate of the vertex. If $x = 1$, then

$$\begin{aligned} y &= 1^2 - 2 \cdot 1 - 8 \\ &= -9. \end{aligned}$$

So the vertex is $(1, -9)$. If $x = 0$, then

$$\begin{aligned} y &= 0^2 - 2 \cdot 0 - 8 \\ &= -8. \end{aligned}$$

The y-intercept is $(0, -8)$. To find the x-intercepts, replace y by 0:

$$\begin{aligned} x^2 - 2x - 8 &= 0 \\ (x - 4)(x + 2) &= 0 \\ x - 4 = 0 \quad &\text{or} \quad x + 2 = 0 \\ x = 4 \quad &\text{or} \quad x = -2 \end{aligned}$$

The x-intercepts are $(-2, 0)$ and $(4, 0)$. The graph is shown in Fig. 9.7.

b) Because s is expressed in terms of t, the first coordinate is t. Use $t = \frac{-b}{2a}$ to get

$$t = \frac{-64}{2(-16)} = 2.$$

If $t = 2$, then

$$\begin{aligned} s &= -16 \cdot 2^2 + 64 \cdot 2 \\ &= 64. \end{aligned}$$

So the vertex is $(2, 64)$. If $t = 0$, then

$$\begin{aligned} s &= -16 \cdot 0^2 + 64 \cdot 0 \\ &= 0. \end{aligned}$$

So the s-intercept is (0, 0). To find the t-intercepts, replace s by 0:

$$-16t^2 + 64t = 0$$
$$-16t(t - 4) = 0$$
$$-16t = 0 \quad \text{or} \quad t - 4 = 0$$
$$t = 0 \quad \text{or} \quad t = 4$$

The t-intercepts are (0, 0) and (4, 0). The graph is shown in Fig. 9.8.

Now do Exercises 29–32

‹ Calculator Close-Up ›

You can find the vertex of $y = x^2 - 2x - 8$ with a calculator by using either the maximum or minimum feature. First graph the parabola as shown.

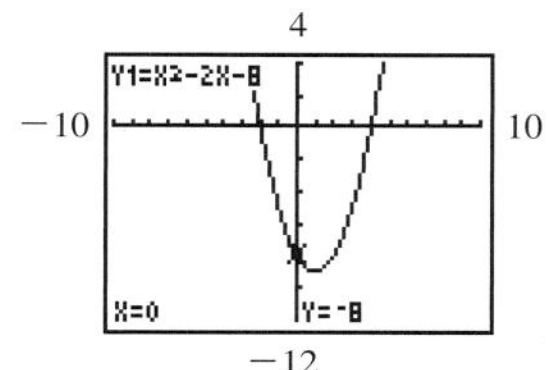

Because this parabola opens upward, the y-coordinate of the vertex is the minimum y-coordinate on the graph. Press CALC and choose minimum.

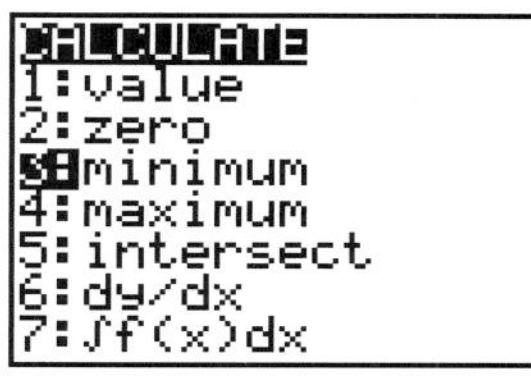

The calculator will ask for a left bound, a right bound, and a guess. For the left bound choose a point to the left of the vertex by moving the cursor to the point and pressing ENTER. For the right bound choose a point to the right of the vertex. For the guess choose a point close to the vertex.

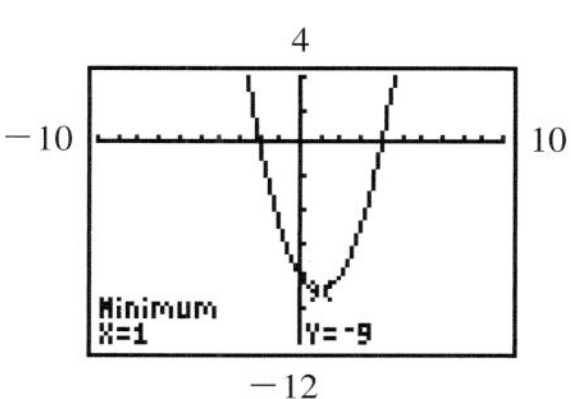

‹4› Applications

In applications, we are often interested in finding the maximum or minimum value of a variable. If a parabola opens downward, then the maximum value of the dependent variable is the second coordinate of the vertex. If a parabola opens upward, then the minimum value of the dependent variable is the second coordinate of the vertex.

EXAMPLE 6

Finding the maximum height

A ball is tossed upward with a velocity of 64 feet per second from a height of 5 feet. What is the maximum height reached by the ball?

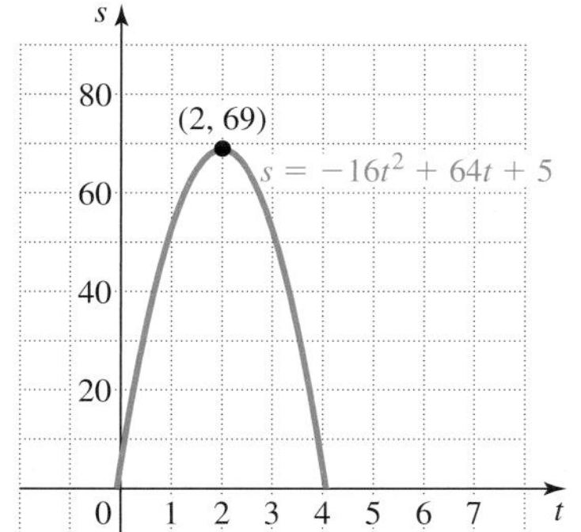

Figure 9.9

Solution

The height s of the ball for any time t is given by $s = -16t^2 + 64t + 5$. Because the maximum height occurs at the vertex of the parabola, we use $t = \frac{-b}{2a}$ to find the vertex:

$$t = \frac{-64}{2(-16)} = 2$$

Now use $t = 2$ to find the second coordinate of the vertex:

$$s = -16(2)^2 + 64(2) + 5 = 69$$

The maximum height reached by the ball is 69 feet. See Fig. 9.9.

Now do Exercises 41–47

Warm-Ups 

True or false? Explain your answer.

1. The ordered pair $(-2, -1)$ satisfies $y = x^2 - 5$. True
2. The y-intercept for $y = x^2 - 3x + 9$ is $(9, 0)$. False
3. The x-intercepts for $y = x^2 - 5$ are $(\sqrt{5}, 0)$ and $(-\sqrt{5}, 0)$. True
4. The graph of $y = x^2 - 12$ opens upward. True
5. The graph of $y = 4 + x^2$ opens downward. False
6. The vertex of $y = x^2 + 2x$ is $(-1, -1)$. True
7. The parabola $y = x^2 + 1$ has no x-intercepts. True
8. The y-intercept for $y = ax^2 + bx + c$ is $(0, c)$. True
9. If $w = -2v^2 + 9$, then the maximum value of w is 9. True
10. If $y = 3x^2 - 7x + 9$, then the maximum value of y occurs when $x = \frac{7}{6}$. False

9.6 Exercises

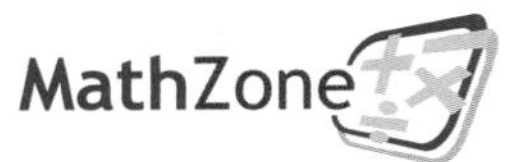

Boost your grade at mathzone.com!
- Practice Problems
- NetTutor
- Self-Tests
- e-Professors
- Videos

‹ Study Tips ›

- Don't sell this book back to the bookstore.
- If you need to reference this material in the future, it is much easier to use a familiar book.

Reading and Writing *After reading this section, write out the answers to these questions. Use complete sentences.*

1. What type of equation has a straight line as its graph?
   The graph of $y = mx + b$ is a straight line.
2. What type of equation has a parabola as its graph?
   The graph of $y = ax^2 + bx + c$ with $a \neq 0$ is a parabola.
3. When does a parabola open upward?
   The graph of $y = ax^2 + bx + c$ opens upward if $a > 0$.
4. What is the vertex of a parabola?
   The vertex is the highest point on a parabola that opens downward or the lowest point on a parabola that opens upward.
5. What is the first coordinate of the vertex for the parabola $y = ax^2 + bx + c$?
   The x-coordinate of the vertex is $-b/(2a)$.
6. How do you find the second coordinate of the vertex?
   Use $x = -b/(2a)$ to find x and then use the original equation to find y.

‹1› Finding Ordered Pairs

Complete each ordered pair so that it satisfies the given equation. See Example 1.

7. $y = x^2 - 1$ $(2, \quad), (\quad, 0)$
   $(2, 3), (-1, 0), (1, 0)$
8. $y = x^2 + 2$ $(0, \quad), (\quad, 3)$
   $(0, 2), (-1, 3), (1, 3)$
9. $y = x^2 - x - 12$ $(3, \quad), (\quad, 0)$
   $(3, -6), (4, 0), (-3, 0)$
10. $y = -\frac{1}{2}x^2 - x + 1$ $(0, \quad), (\quad, -3)$
    $(0, 1), (-4, -3), (2, -3)$
11. $s = -16t^2 + 32t$ $(4, \quad), (\quad, 0)$
    $(4, -128), (0, 0), (2, 0)$
12. $a = b^2 + 4b + 5$ $(-2, \quad), (\quad, 2)$
    $(-2, 1), (-1, 2), (-3, 2)$

⟨2⟩ Graphing Parabolas

Graph each equation. See Examples 2 and 3.

13. $y = x^2 + 2$

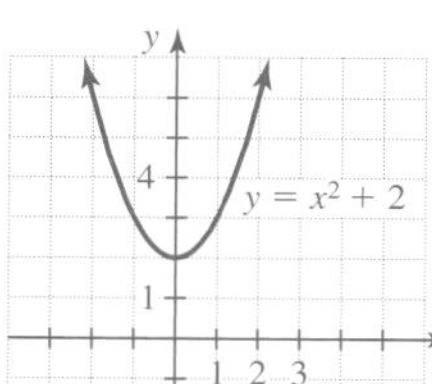

14. $y = x^2 - 4$

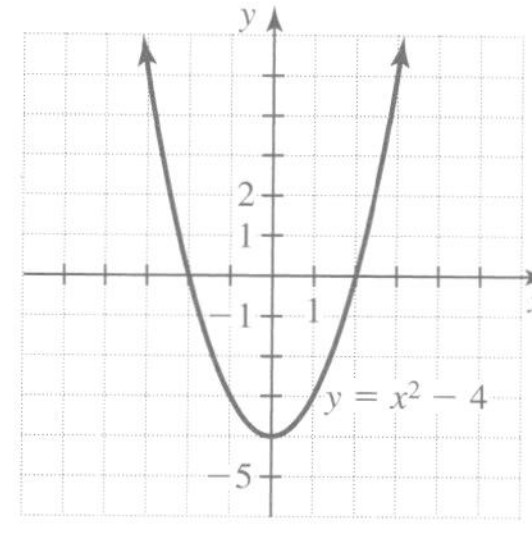

15. $y = \frac{1}{2}x^2 - 4$

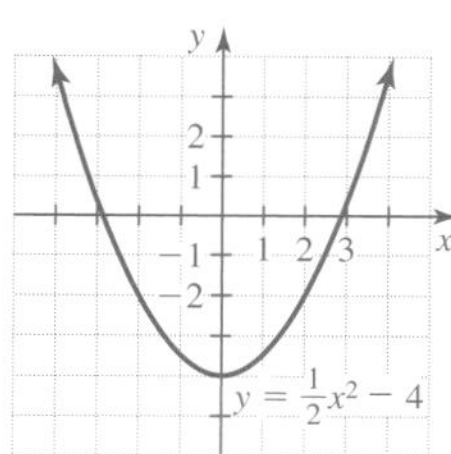

16. $y = \frac{1}{3}x^2 - 6$

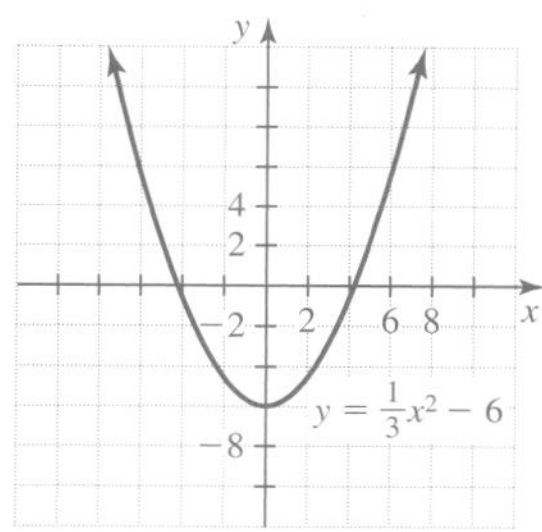

17. $y = -2x^2 + 5$

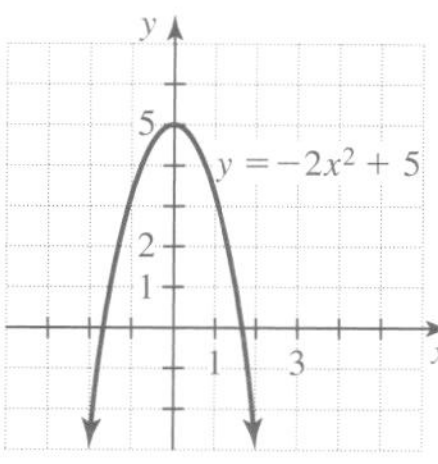

18. $y = -x^2 - 1$

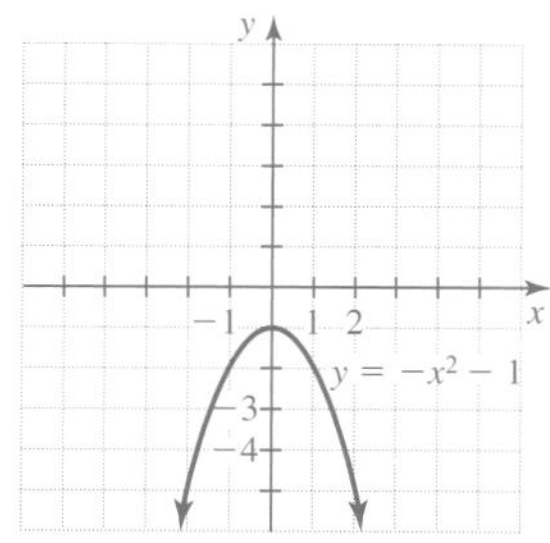

19. $y = -\frac{1}{3}x^2 + 5$

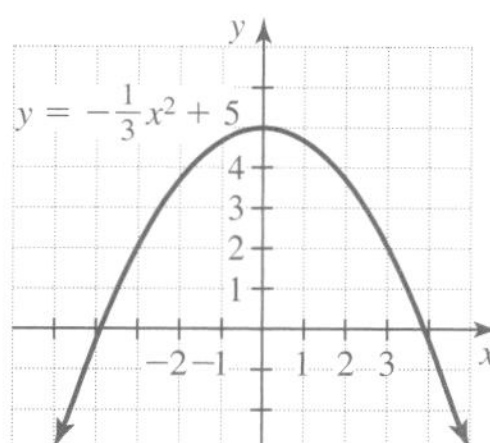

20. $y = -\frac{1}{2}x^2 + 3$

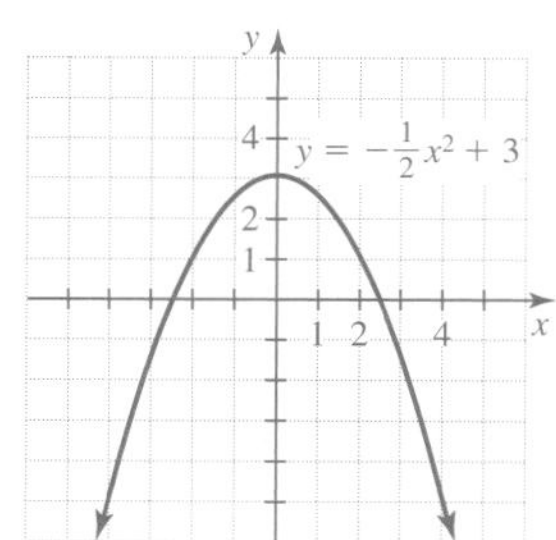

21. $y = (x - 2)^2$

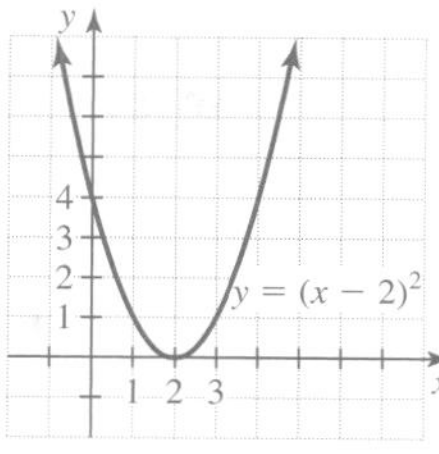

22. $y = (x + 3)^2$

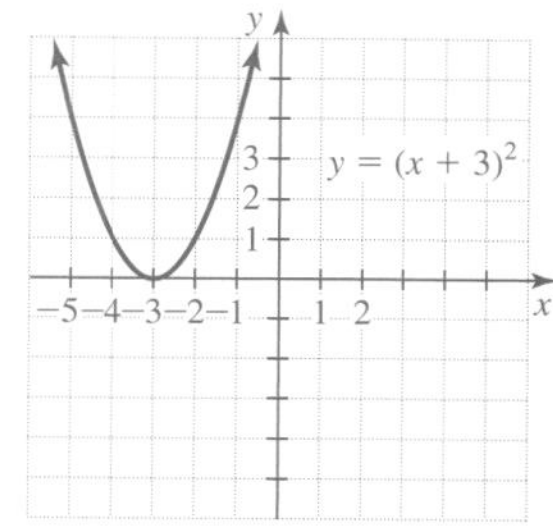

⟨3⟩ The Vertex and Intercepts

Find the vertex and intercepts for each parabola. Then sketch the graph. See Examples 4 and 5.

23. $y = x^2 - x - 2$
Vertex $\left(\frac{1}{2}, -\frac{9}{4}\right)$, intercepts $(0, -2)$, $(-1, 0)$, $(2, 0)$

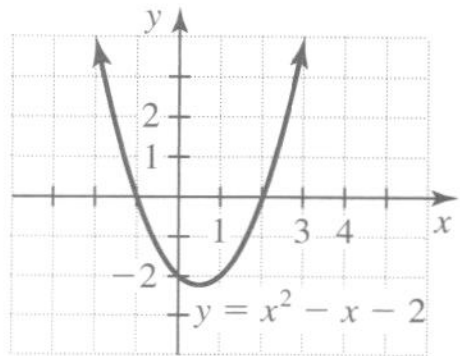

24. $y = x^2 + 2x - 3$
Vertex $(-1, -4)$, intercepts $(0, -3)$, $(-3, 0)$, $(1, 0)$

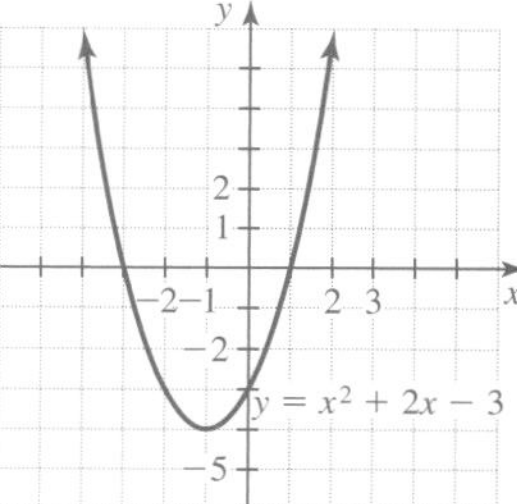

25. $y = x^2 + 2x - 8$
Vertex $(-1, -9)$, intercepts $(0, -8)$, $(-4, 0)$, $(2, 0)$

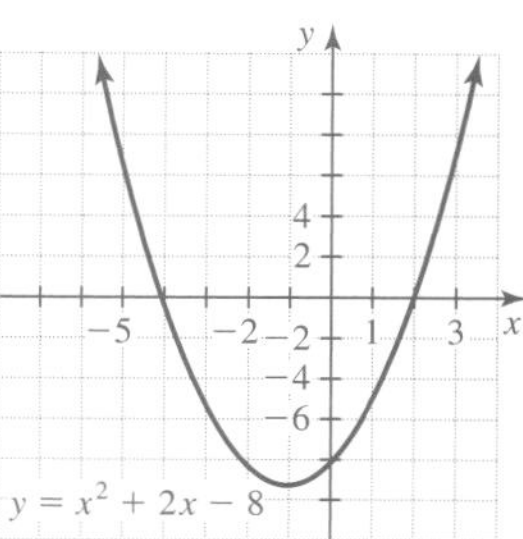

26. $y = x^2 + x - 6$
Vertex $\left(-\frac{1}{2}, -\frac{25}{4}\right)$, intercepts $(0, -6)$, $(-3, 0)$, $(2, 0)$

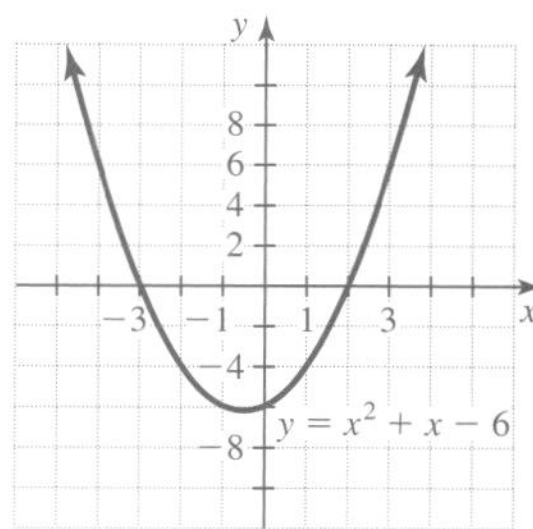

VIDEO **27.** $y = -x^2 - 4x - 3$
Vertex $(-2, 1)$, intercepts $(0, -3)$, $(-1, 0)$, $(-3, 0)$

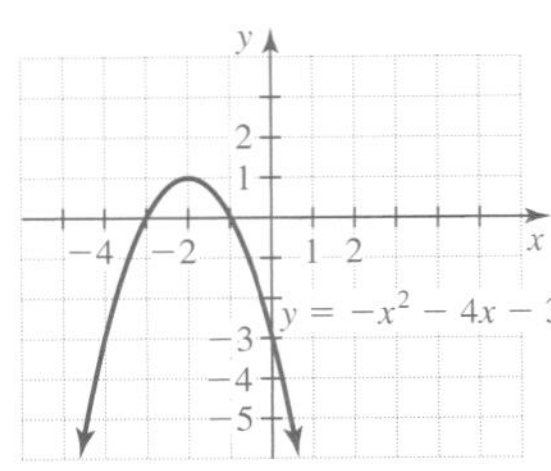

28. $y = -x^2 - 5x - 4$
Vertex $\left(-\frac{5}{2}, \frac{9}{4}\right)$, intercepts $(0, -4)$, $(-1, 0)$, $(-4, 0)$

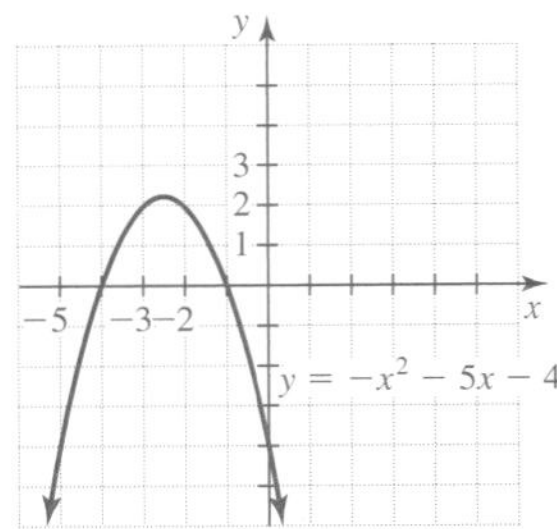

29. $y = -x^2 + 3x + 4$
Vertex $\left(\frac{3}{2}, \frac{25}{4}\right)$, intercepts $(0, 4)$, $(4, 0)$, $(-1, 0)$

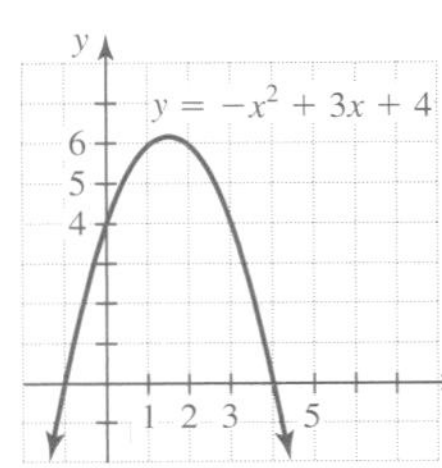

30. $y = -x^2 - 2x + 8$
Vertex $(-1, 9)$, intercepts $(0, 8)$, $(-4, 0)$, $(2, 0)$

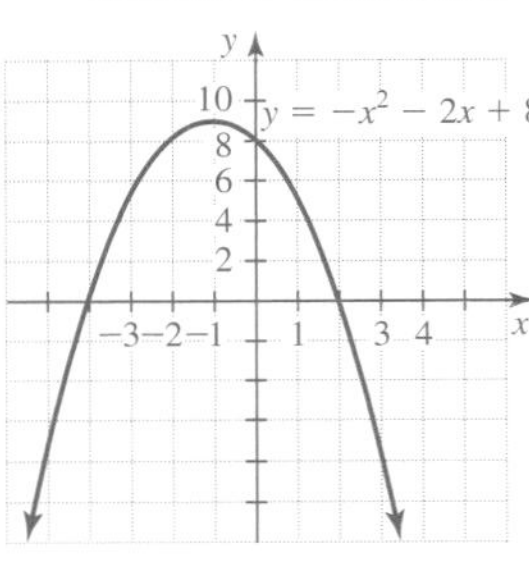

31. $a = b^2 - 6b - 16$
Vertex $(3, -25)$, intercepts $(0, -16)$, $(8, 0)$, $(-2, 0)$

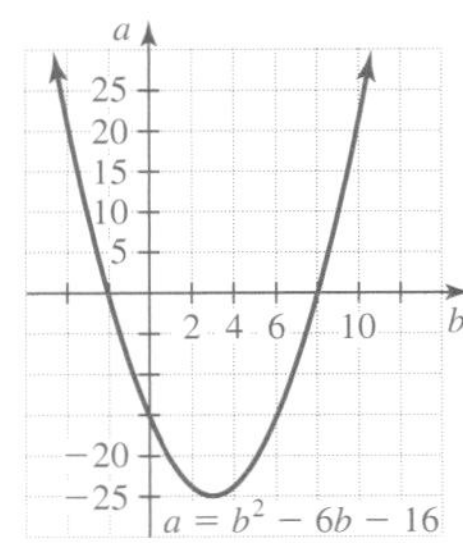

32. $v = -u^2 - 8u + 9$
Vertex $(-4, 25)$, intercepts $(0, 9)$, $(-9, 0)$, $(1, 0)$

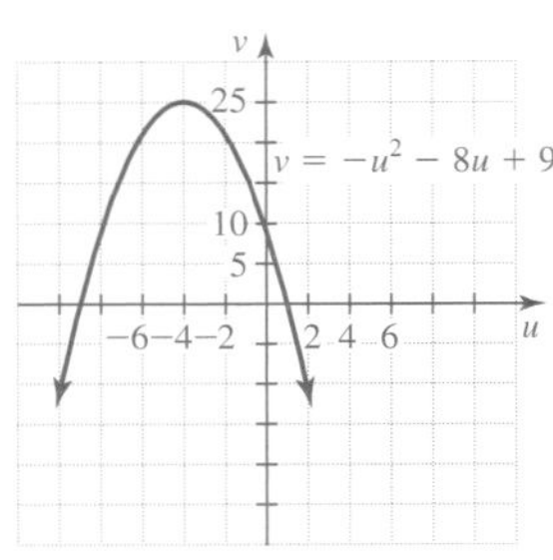

Find the maximum or minimum value for y for each equation.

33. $y = x^2 - 8$
Minimum -8

34. $y = 33 - x^2$
Maximum 33

35. $y = -3x^2 + 14$
Maximum 14

36. $y = 6 + 5x^2$
Minimum 6

37. $y = x^2 + 2x + 3$
Minimum 2

VIDEO **38.** $y = x^2 - 2x + 5$
Minimum 4

39. $y = -2x^2 - 4x$
Maximum 2

40. $y = -3x^2 + 24x$
Maximum 48

⟨4⟩ Applications

Solve each problem. See Example 6.

41. ***Maximum height.*** If a baseball is projected vertically upward from ground level with an initial velocity of 64 feet per second, then $s = -16t^2 + 64t$ gives its height in feet s in terms of time in seconds t. Graph this equation for $0 \le t \le 4$. What is the maximum height reached by the ball?
Maximum 64 feet

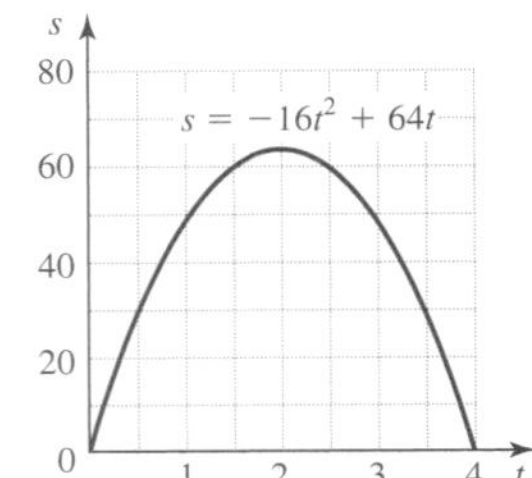

42. ***Maximum height.*** If a soccer ball is kicked straight up with an initial velocity of 32 feet per second, then $s = -16t^2 + 32t$ gives its height in feet s in terms of time in seconds t. Graph this equation for $0 \le t \le 2$. What is the maximum height reached by this ball?
Maximum 16 feet

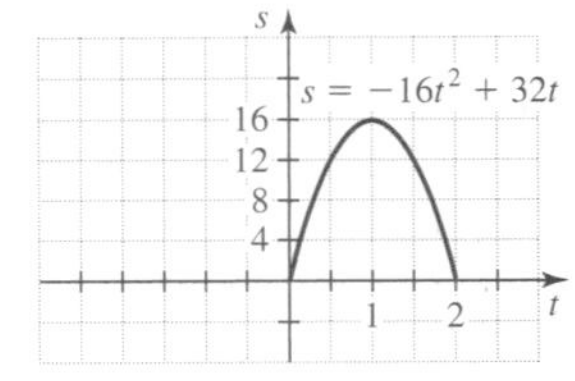

43. ***Maximum area.*** Jason plans to fence a rectangular area with 100 meters of fencing. He has written the formula $A = w(50 - w)$ to express the area in square meters A in terms of the width in meters w. What is the maximum possible area that he can enclose with his fencing?
625 square meters

44. ***Minimizing cost.*** A company uses the formula $C = 0.02x^2 - 3.4x + 150$ to model the unit cost in dollars C for producing x stabilizer bars. For what number of bars is the unit cost at its minimum? What is the unit cost at that level of production? 85, \$5.50

45. ***Air pollution.*** The formula $A = -2t^2 + 32t + 12$ gives the amount of nitrogen dioxide A in parts per million (ppm) that was present in the air in the city of Homer on June 14, where t is the number of hours after 6:00 A.M. Use this

Photo for Exercise 43

equation to find the time at which the nitrogen dioxide level was at its maximum. 2 P.M.

46. ***Stabilization ratio.*** The stabilization ratio (births/deaths) for South and Central America can be modeled by the equation

$$y = -0.0012x^2 + 0.074x + 2.69,$$

where y is the number of births divided by the number of deaths in the year $1950 + x$ (World Resources Institute, www.wri.org).

a) Use the accompanying graph to estimate the year in which the stabilization ratio was at its maximum.
b) Use the equation to find the year in which the stabilization ratio was at its maximum.
c) What is the maximum stabilization ratio from part (b)?
d) What is the significance of a stabilization ratio of 1?
a) 1980 **b)** 1981 **c)** 3.83 **d)** Stable population

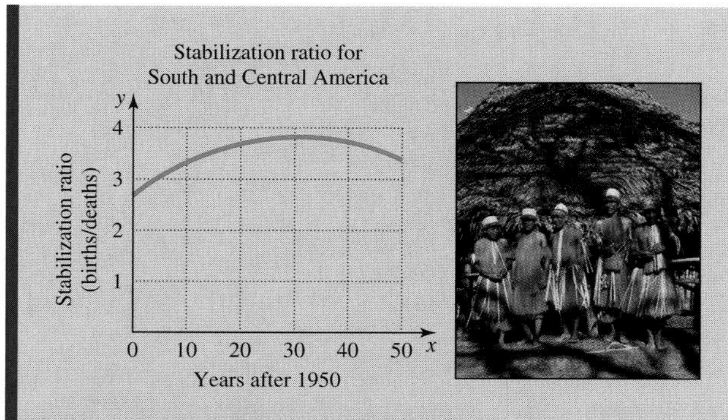

Figure for Exercise 46

47. ***Suspension bridge.*** The cable of the suspension bridge shown in the accompanying figure hangs in the shape of a parabola with equation $y = 0.0375x^2$, where x and y are in meters. What is the height of each tower above the roadway? What is the length z for the cable bracing the tower? 15 meters, 25 meters

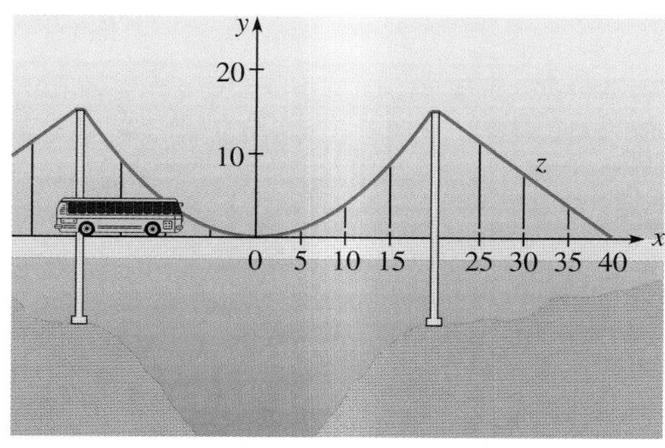

Figure for Exercise 47

Getting More Involved

48. ***Exploration***

a) Write $y = 3(x - 2)^2 + 6$ in the form $y = ax^2 + bx + c$, and find the vertex of the parabola using the formula $x = \frac{-b}{2a}$.
b) Repeat part (a) with $y = -4(x - 5)^2 - 9$ and $y = 3(x + 2)^2 - 6$.
c) What is the vertex for a parabola that is written in the form $y = a(x - h)^2 + k$? Explain your answer.
a) $y = 3x^2 - 12x + 18$, $(2, 6)$
b) $y = -4x^2 + 40x - 109$, $(5, -9)$, $y = 3x^2 + 12x + 6$, $(-2, -6)$ **c)** (h, k)

Graphing Calculator Exercises

49. Graph $y = x^2$, $y = \frac{1}{2}x^2$, and $y = 2x^2$ on the same coordinate system. What can you say about the graph of $y = ax^2$ for $a > 0$?
The graph of $y = ax^2$ gets narrower as a gets larger.

50. Graph $y = x^2$, $y = (x - 3)^2$, and $y = (x + 3)^2$ on the same coordinate system. How does the graph of $y = (x - h)^2$ compare to the graph of $y = x^2$?
The graph of $y = (x - h)^2$ lies h units to the right of $y = x^2$ if $h > 0$ and $-h$ units to the left of $y = x^2$ if $h < 0$.

51. The equation $x = y^2$ is equivalent to $y = \pm\sqrt{x}$. Graph both $y = \sqrt{x}$ and $y = -\sqrt{x}$ on a graphing calculator. How does the graph of $x = y^2$ compare to the graph of $y = x^2$?
The graph of $y = x^2$ has the same shape as $x = y^2$.

52. Graph each of the following equations by solving for y.

a) $x = y^2 - 1$
$y = \pm\sqrt{x + 1}$

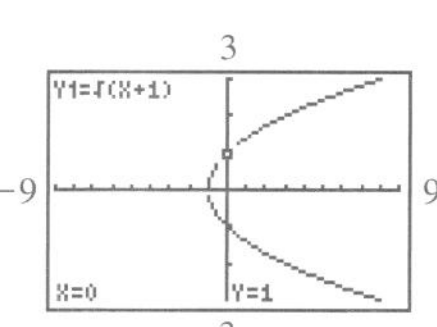

b) $x = -y^2$
$y = \pm\sqrt{-x}$

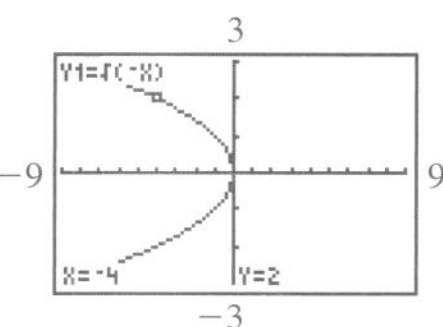

c) $x^2 + y^2 = 4$

$y = \pm\sqrt{4 - x^2}$

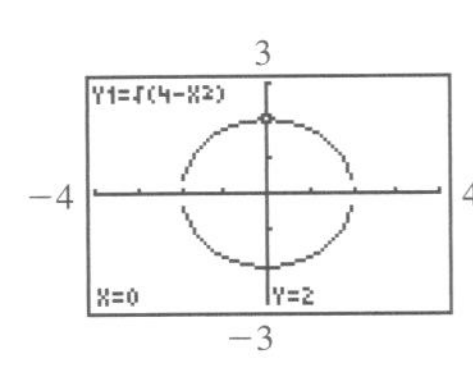

53. Determine the approximate vertex and x-intercepts for each parabola.

a) $y = 3.2x^2 - 5.4x + 1.6$

b) $y = -1.09x^2 + 13x + 7.5$

a) Vertex $(0.84, -0.68)$, x-intercepts $(1.30, 0)$, $(0.38, 0)$
b) Vertex $(5.96, 46.26)$, x-intercepts $(12.48, 0)$, $(-0.55, 0)$

9.7 Introduction to Functions

In This Section

- ⟨1⟩ Functions Expressed by Formulas
- ⟨2⟩ Functions Expressed by Tables
- ⟨3⟩ Functions Expressed by Ordered Pairs
- ⟨4⟩ Graphs of Functions
- ⟨5⟩ Domain and Range
- ⟨6⟩ Function Notation

Even though we have not yet defined the term *function*, we have used functions throughout this text. In Chapter 5, we used function notation $P(x)$ to name and evaluate polynomials. In this section, we will study the concept of functions and see that they have been with us from the beginning.

⟨1⟩ Functions Expressed by Formulas

If you get a speeding ticket, then your speed determines the cost of the ticket. You may not know exactly how the judge determines the cost, but the judge is using some rule to determine a cost from knowing your speed. The cost of the ticket is a function of your speed.

Function (as a Rule)

A function is a rule by which any allowable value of one variable (the **independent variable**) determines a *unique* value of a second variable (the **dependent variable**).

⟨ Helpful Hint ⟩

According to the dictionary, "determine" means to settle conclusively. If the value of the dependent variable is inconclusive or there is more than one, then the rule is not a function.

One way to express a function is to use a formula. For example, the formula

$$A = \pi r^2$$

gives the area of a circle as a function of its radius. The formula gives us a rule for finding a *unique* area for any given radius. A is the dependent variable, and r is the independent variable. The formula

$$s = -16t^2 + v_0 t + s_0$$

expresses altitude s of a projectile as a function of time t, where v_0 is the initial velocity and s_0 is the initial altitude. In this case s is the dependent variable, and t is the independent variable.

Since a formula can be used as a rule for obtaining the value of the dependent variable from the value of the independent variable, we say that the formula is a function. Formulas describe or **model** relationships between variables. In Example 1, we find a function in a real situation.

EXAMPLE 1 **Writing a formula for a function**

A carpet layer charges \$25 plus \$4 per square yard for installing carpet. Write the total charge C as a function of the number n of square yards of carpet installed.

Solution

At \$4 per square yard, n square yards installed cost $4n$ dollars. If we include the \$25 charge, then the total cost is $4n + 25$ dollars. Thus the equation

$$C = 4n + 25$$

expresses C as a function of n.

Now do Exercises 7–10

Any formula that has the form $y = mx + b$ is a **linear function.** So in Example 1, the charge is a linear function of the number of square yards installed and we say that $C = 4n + 25$ is a linear function.

EXAMPLE 2

A function in geometry

Express the area of a circle as a function of its diameter.

Solution

The area of a circle is given by $A = \pi r^2$. Because the radius of a circle is one-half of the diameter, we have $r = \frac{d}{2}$. Now replace r by $\frac{d}{2}$ in the formula $A = \pi r^2$:

$$A = \pi\left(\frac{d}{2}\right)^2$$

$$= \frac{\pi}{4}d^2$$

So $A = \frac{\pi}{4}d^2$ expresses the area of a circle as a function of its diameter.

Now do Exercises 11–16

Any formula that has the form $y = ax^2 + bx + c$ (with $a \neq 0$) is a **quadratic function.** So in Example 2, the area is a quadratic function of the diameter and we say that $A = \frac{\pi}{4}d^2$ is a quadratic function.

⟨2⟩ Functions Expressed by Tables

Another way to express a function is with a table. For example, Table 9.3 can be used to determine the cost at United Freight Service for shipping a package that weighs under 100 pounds. For any *allowable* weight, the table gives us a rule for finding the unique shipping cost. The weight is the independent variable, and the cost is the dependent variable.

Now consider Table 9.4. It does not look much different from Table 9.3, but there is an important difference. The cost for shipping a 12-pound package according to Table 9.4 is either \$4.60 or \$12.75. Either the table has an error or perhaps \$4.60 and

‹ Teaching Tip ›

The definition of function is difficult for students to understand. They need to see many examples.

Table 9.3

Weight in Pounds	Cost
0 to 10	\$4.60
11 to 30	\$12.75
31 to 79	\$32.90
80 to 99	\$55.82

Table 9.4

Weight in Pounds	Cost
0 to 15	\$4.60
10 to 30	\$12.75
31 to 79	\$32.90
80 to 99	\$55.82

\$12.75 are costs for shipping to different destinations. In any case the weight does not determine a unique cost. So Table 9.4 does not express the cost as a function of the weight.

EXAMPLE 3

Functions defined by tables

Which of the following tables expresses y as a function of x?

a)

x	y
1	3
2	6
3	9
4	12
5	15

b)

x	y
1	1
−1	1
2	2
−2	2
3	3
−3	3

c)

x	y
1988	27,000
1989	27,000
1990	28,500
1991	29,000
1992	30,000
1993	30,750

d)

x	y
23	48
35	27
19	28
23	37
41	56
22	34

Solution

In Tables a), b), and c), every value of x corresponds to only one value of y. Tables a), b), and c) each express y as a function of x. Notice that different values of x may correspond to the same value of y. In Table d), we have the value of 23 for x corresponding to two different values of y, 48 and 37. So Table d) does not express y as a function of x.

Now do Exercises 17–24

‹ Helpful Hint ›

In a function, every value for the independent variable determines conclusively a corresponding value for the dependent variable. If there is more than one possible value for the dependent variable, then the set of ordered pairs is not a function.

‹3› Functions Expressed by Ordered Pairs

A computer at your grocery store determines the price of each item by searching a long list of ordered pairs in which the first coordinate is the universal product code and the second coordinate is the price of the item with that code. For each product code there is a unique price. This process certainly satisfies the rule definition of a function. Since the set of ordered pairs is the essential part of this rule we say that the set of ordered pairs is a function.

Function (as a Set of Ordered Pairs)

A function is a set of ordered pairs of real numbers such that no two ordered pairs have the same first coordinates and different second coordinates.

Note the importance of the phrase "no two ordered pairs have the same first coordinates and different second coordinates." Imagine the problems at the grocery store if the computer gave two different prices for the same universal product code. Note also that the product code is an identification number and it cannot be used in calculations. So the computer can use a function defined by a formula to determine the amount of tax, but it cannot use a formula to determine the price from the product code.

EXAMPLE 4

Functions expressed by a set of ordered pairs

Determine whether each set of ordered pairs is a function.

a) $\{(1, 2), (1, 5), (-4, 6)\}$ **b)** $\{(-1, 3), (0, 3), (6, 3), (-3, 2)\}$

‹ Teaching Tip ›

When an equation is given that produces ordered pairs, it must be made clear which variable corresponds to the first coordinate. Asking whether $b^2 = w$ is a function is not a clear question. The set $\{(b, w) \mid b^2 = w\}$ is a function; $\{(w, b) \mid b^2 = w\}$ is not.

Solution

a) This set of ordered pairs is not a function because (1, 2) and (1, 5) have the same first coordinates but different second coordinates.

b) This set of ordered pairs is a function. Note that the same second coordinate with different first coordinates is permitted in a function.

Now do Exercises 25–32

If there are infinitely many ordered pairs in a function, then we can use set-builder notation from Chapter 1 along with an equation to express the function. For example,

$$\{(x, y) \mid y = x^2\}$$

is the set of ordered pairs in which the y-coordinate is the square of the x-coordinate. Ordered pairs such as (0, 0), (2, 4), and (−2, 4) belong to this set. This set is a function because every value of x determines only one value of y.

EXAMPLE 5

Functions expressed by set-builder notation

Determine whether each set of ordered pairs is a function.

a) $\{(x, y) \mid y = 3x^2 - 2x + 1\}$ **b)** $\{(x, y) \mid y^2 = x\}$ **c)** $\{(x, y) \mid x + y = 6\}$

‹ Helpful Hint ›

Real-life variables are generally not as simple as the ones we consider. A student's college GPA is not a function of age, because many students with the same age have different GPAs. However, GPA is probably a function of a large number of variables: age, IQ, high school GPA, number of working hours, mother's IQ, and so on.

Solution

a) This set is a function because each value we select for x determines only one value for y.

b) If $x = 9$, then we have $y^2 = 9$. Because both 3 and −3 satisfy $y^2 = 9$, both (9, 3) and (9, −3) belong to this set. So the set is not a function.

c) If we solve $x + y = 6$ for y, we get $y = -x + 6$. Because each value of x determines only one value for y, this set is a function. In fact, this set is a linear function.

Now do Exercises 33–40

We often omit the set notation when discussing functions. For example, the equation

$$y = 3x^2 - 2x + 1$$

expresses y as a function of x because the set of ordered pairs determined by the equation is a function. However, the equation

$$y^2 = x$$

does not express y as a function of x because ordered pairs such as (9, 3) and (9, −3) satisfy the equation.

EXAMPLE 6

Functions expressed by equations

Determine whether each equation expresses y as a function of x.

a) $y = |x|$ **b)** $y = x^3$ **c)** $x = |y|$

‹ Helpful Hint ›

To determine whether an equation expresses y as a function of x, always select a number for x (the independent variable) and then see if there is more than one corresponding value for y (the dependent variable). If there is more than one corresponding y-value, then y is not a function of x.

Solution

a) Because every number has a unique absolute value, $y = |x|$ is a function.

b) Because every number has a unique cube, $y = x^3$ is a function.

c) The equation $x = |y|$ does not express y as a function of x because both (4, −4) and (4, 4) satisfy this equation. These ordered pairs have the same first coordinate but different second coordinates.

Now do Exercises 41–48

Calculator Close-Up

Most calculators graph only functions. If you enter an equation using the Y= key and the calculator accepts it and draws a graph, the equation defines y as a function of x.

⟨4⟩ Graphs of Functions

Every function determines a set of ordered pairs, and any set of ordered pairs has a graph in the rectangular coordinate system. For example, the set of ordered pairs determined by the linear function $y = 2x - 1$ is shown in Fig. 9.10.

Every graph illustrates a set of ordered pairs, but not every graph is a graph of a function. For example, the circle in Fig. 9.11 is not a graph of a function because the ordered pairs $(0, 4)$ and $(0, -4)$ are both on the graph, and these two ordered pairs have the same first coordinate and different second coordinates. Whether a graph has such ordered pairs can be determined by a simple visual test called the **vertical-line test.**

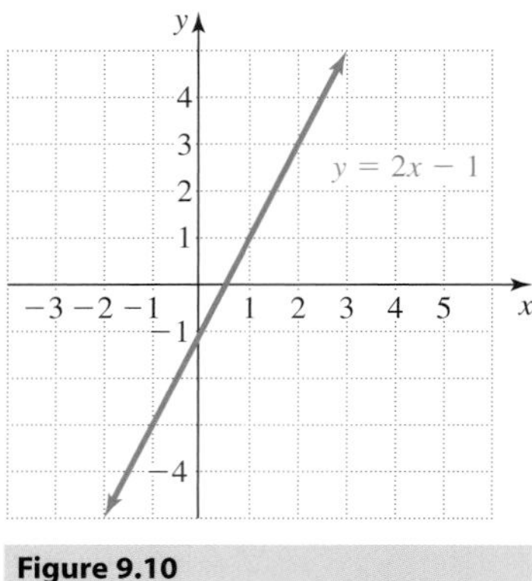

Figure 9.10

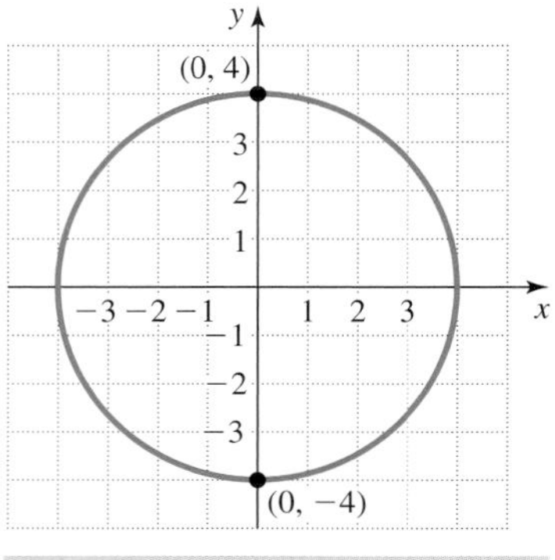

Figure 9.11

Vertical-Line Test

If it is possible to draw a vertical line that crosses a graph two or more times, then the graph is not the graph of a function (y is not a function of x).

For the vertical-line test to make sense, the graph must be drawn with the x-axis horizontal and the y-axis vertical. If other letters are used to name the axes, then the vertical-line test will determine whether the variable on the vertical axis is a function of the variable on the horizontal axis.

If there is a vertical line that crosses a graph twice (or more), then we have two points (or more) with the same x-coordinate and different y-coordinates, and so the graph is not the graph of a function. If you mentally consider every possible vertical line and none of them cross the graph more than once, then you can conclude that the graph is the graph of a function.

EXAMPLE 7

Using the vertical-line test

Which of the following graphs are graphs of functions?

a) **b)** **c)**

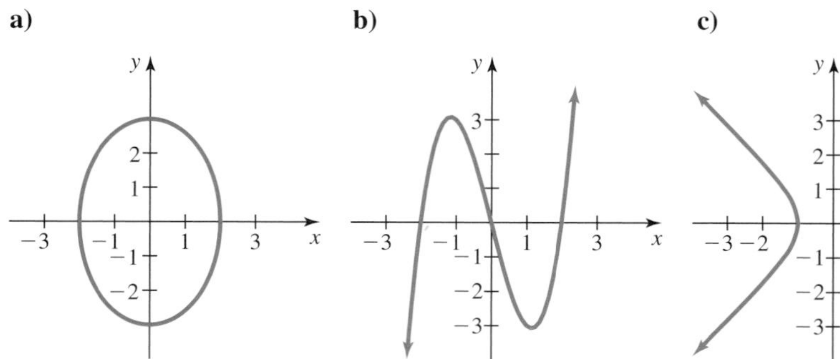

Helpful Hint

Note that the vertical-line test works in theory, but it is certainly limited by the accuracy of the graph. Pictures are often deceptive. However, in spite of its limitations, the vertical-line test gives us a visual idea of what the graph of a function looks like.

Solution

Neither a) nor c) is the graph of a function, since we can draw vertical lines that cross these graphs twice. Graph b) is the graph of a function, since no vertical line crosses it twice.

Now do Exercises 49–54

⟨5⟩ Domain and Range

A function is a set of ordered pairs. The set of all first coordinates of the ordered pairs is the **domain** of the function and the set of all second coordinates of the ordered pairs is the **range** of the function. In Example 8, we identify the domain and range for functions that are given as sets of ordered pairs.

EXAMPLE 8

Domain and range

Determine the domain and range of each function.

a) $\{(3, -1), (2, 5), (1, -4)\}$ **b)** $\{(2, 3), (4, 3), (6, 3), (8, 3)\}$

Solution

a) The domain is the set of numbers that occur as first coordinates, $\{1, 2, 3\}$. The range is the set of second coordinates, $\{-4, -1, 5\}$.

b) The domain is $\{2, 4, 6, 8\}$. Since 3 is the only number used as the second coordinate, the range is $\{3\}$.

Now do Exercises 55–58

If a function is defined by an equation, then the domain consists of those real numbers that can be used for the independent variable in the equation. For example, in $y = 3x$ we can use any real number for x. In $y = \frac{1}{x}$ we can use any nonzero real number for x. The domain is often the set of all real numbers, which is abbreviated as R.

The graph of a function is a picture of all ordered pairs of the function. So if a function is defined by an equation, it is usually helpful to graph the function and then use the graph as an aid in determining the domain and range.

EXAMPLE 9

Finding domain and range from a graph

Graph each function and then determine its domain and range.

a) $y = 2x - 1$ **b)** $y = 2x^2 - 8x + 5$ **c)** $y = -x^2 - 6x$

Solution

a) The graph of $y = 2x - 1$ is a line with y-intercept $(0, -1)$ and slope 2 as shown in Fig. 9.12. Any real number can be used for x in $y = 2x - 1$. So the domain is the set of real numbers, R. From the graph we can see that the line extends infinitely upward and downward. So the range is also R.

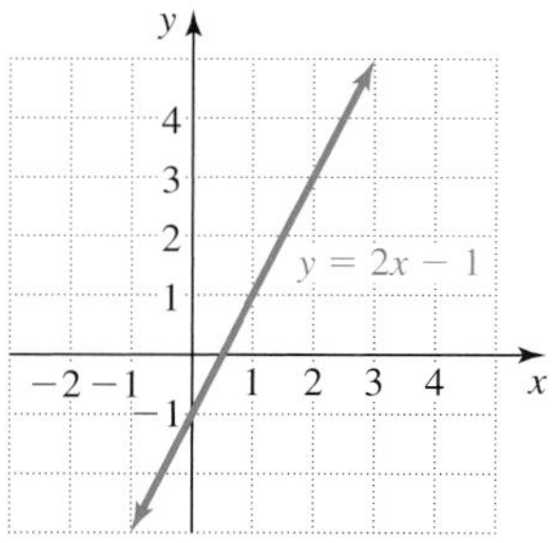

y
4
3
2
1
−2 −1 1 2 3 4 x
−1
y = 2x − 1

Figure 9.12

b) To graph the parabola $y = 2x^2 - 8x + 5$, first find the vertex:

$$x = \frac{-b}{2a} = \frac{8}{4} = 2 \qquad y = 2(2)^2 - 8(2) + 5 = -3$$

The vertex is $(2, -3)$. The parabola also goes through $(1, -1)$ and $(3, -1)$ as shown in Fig. 9.13 on the next page. Since any number can be used for x in

$y = 2x^2 - 8x + 5$, the domain is R. Since the parabola opens upward, the smallest y-coordinate on the graph is -3. So the range is the set of real numbers that are greater than or equal to -3, which is written in set-builder notation as $\{y \mid y \geq -3\}$ or in interval notation as $[-3, \infty)$.

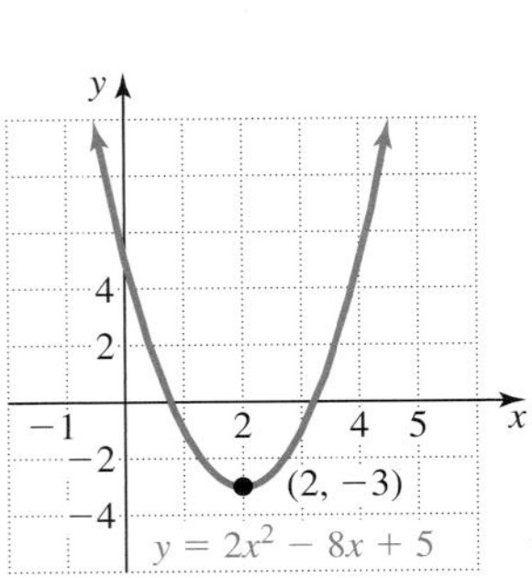

Figure 9.13

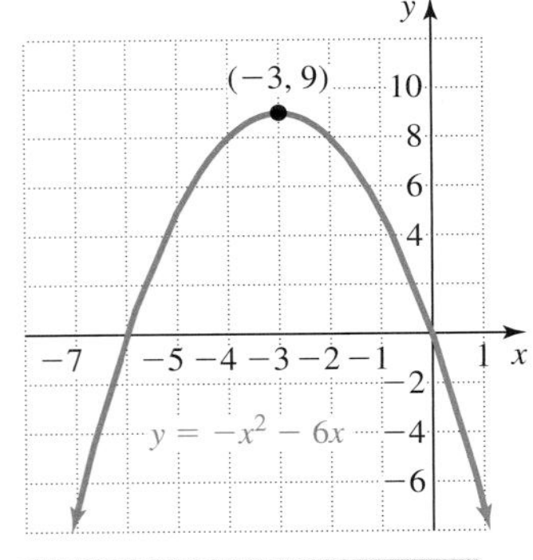

Figure 9.14

c) To graph the parabola $y = -x^2 - 6x$, first find the vertex:

$$x = \frac{-b}{2a} = \frac{6}{-2} = -3 \qquad y = -(-3)^2 - 6(-3) = 9$$

The vertex is $(-3, 9)$. The parabola also goes through $(-2, 8)$ and $(-4, 8)$ as shown in Fig. 9.14. Since any real number can be used in place of x in $y = -x^2 - 6x$, the domain is R. Since the parabola opens downward, the largest y-coordinate on the graph is 9. So the range is the set of real numbers that are less than or equal to 9, which is written in set notation as $\{y \mid y \leq 9\}$ or in interval notation as $(-\infty, 9]$.

Now do Exercises 59–66

‹6› Function Notation

When the variable y is a function of x, we may use the notation $f(x)$ to represent y. This **function notation** was first used in Section 5.3 with polynomial functions.

The symbol $f(x)$ is read as "f of x." So if x is the independent variable, we may use y or $f(x)$ to represent the dependent variable. For example, the function

$$y = 2x + 3$$

can also be written as

$$f(x) = 2x + 3.$$

We use y and $f(x)$ interchangeably. We think of f as the name of the function. We may use letters other than f. For example, the function $g(x) = 2x + 3$ is the same function as $f(x) = 2x + 3$.

The expression $f(x)$ represents the second coordinate when the first coordinate is x; it does not mean f times x. For example, if we replace x by 4 in $f(x) = 2x + 3$, we get

$$f(4) = 2 \cdot 4 + 3 = 11.$$

So if the first coordinate is 4, then the second coordinate is $f(4)$, or 11. The ordered pair (4, 11) belongs to the function f. This statement means that the function f pairs 4 with 11. We can use the diagram in Fig. 9.15 to picture this situation.

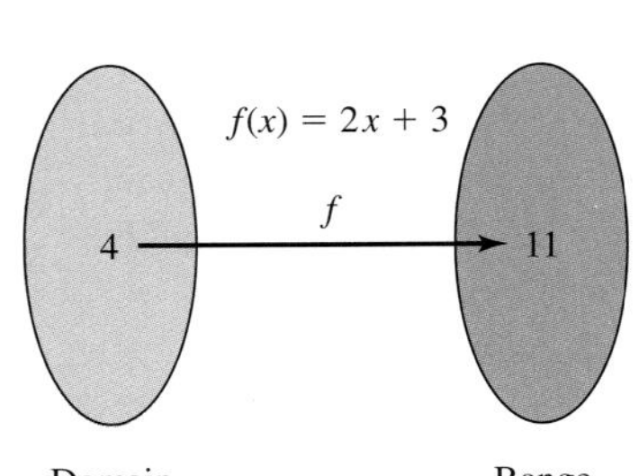

Figure 9.15

EXAMPLE 10

Using function notation

Suppose $f(x) = x^2 - 1$ and $g(x) = -3x + 2$. Find the following:

a) $f(-2)$ **b)** $f(-1)$ **c)** $g(0)$ **d)** $g(6)$

Solution

a) Replace x by -2 in the formula $f(x) = x^2 - 1$:

$$\begin{aligned} f(-2) &= (-2)^2 - 1 \\ &= 4 - 1 \\ &= 3 \end{aligned}$$

So $f(-2) = 3$.

b) Replace x by -1 in the formula $f(x) = x^2 - 1$:

$$\begin{aligned} f(-1) &= (-1)^2 - 1 \\ &= 1 - 1 \\ &= 0 \end{aligned}$$

So $f(-1) = 0$.

c) Replace x by 0 in the formula $g(x) = -3x + 2$:

$$g(0) = -3 \cdot 0 + 2 = 2$$

So $g(0) = 2$.

d) Replace x by 6 in $g(x) = -3x + 2$ to get $g(6) = -16$.

Now do Exercises 67–78

CAUTION The notation $f(x)$ does not mean f times x.

EXAMPLE 11

Using function notation in an application

The formula $C(n) = 0.10n + 4.95$ gives the monthly cost in dollars for n minutes of long-distance calls. Find $C(40)$ and $C(100)$.

Solution

Replace n with 40 in the formula:

$$\begin{aligned} C(n) &= 0.10n + 4.95 \\ C(40) &= 0.10(40) + 4.95 \\ &= 8.95 \end{aligned}$$

So $C(40) = 8.95$. The cost for 40 minutes of calls is \$8.95. Now

$$C(100) = 0.10(100) + 4.95 = 14.95.$$

So $C(100) = 14.95$. The cost of 100 minutes of calls is \$14.95.

Now do Exercises 93–98

CAUTION $C(n)$ is not C times n. In the context of functions, $C(n)$ represents the value of C corresponding to a value of n.

‹ Calculator Close-Up ›

A graphing calculator can be used to evaluate a formula in the same manner as in Example 11. To evaluate

$$C = 0.10n + 4.95$$

enter the formula into your calculator as $y_1 = 0.10x + 4.95$ using the Y = key:

```
Plot1 Plot2 Plot3
\Y1■.10X+4.95
\Y2=
\Y3=
\Y4=
\Y5=
\Y6=
\Y7=
```

To find the cost of 40 minutes of calls, enter $y_1(40)$ on the home screen and press ENTER:

```
Y1(40)
                8.95
Y1(100)
               14.95
```

Warm-Ups ▼

True or false? Explain your answer.

1. Any set of ordered pairs is a function. False
2. The area of a square is a function of the length of a side. True
3. The set $\{(-1, 3), (-3, 1), (-1, -3)\}$ is a function. False
4. The set $\{(1, 5), (3, 5), (7, 5)\}$ is a function. True
5. The domain of $\{(1, 2), (3, 4)\}$, is $\{1, 3\}$. True
6. The domain of $y = x^2$ is R. True
7. The range of $y = x^2$ is $\{y \mid y \geq 0\}$. True
8. The set $\{(x, y) \mid x = 2y\}$ is a function. True
9. The set $\{(x, y) \mid x = y^2\}$ is a function. False
10. If $f(x) = x^2 - 5$, then $f(-2) = -1$. True

9.7 Exercises

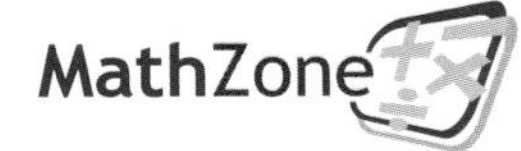

Boost your grade at mathzone.com!
> Practice Problems
> NetTutor
> Self-Tests
> e-Professors
> Videos

‹ Study Tips ›

- Everyone learns and studies differently. So all of these *Study Tips* will not apply to everyone.
- If you find something in these tips that applies to you or helps you, then that is good.

Reading and Writing *After reading this section, write out the answers to these questions. Use complete sentences.*

1. What is a function?
A function is a set of ordered pairs in which no two have the same first coordinate and different second coordinates.
2. What are the different ways to express functions?
Functions can be expressed by means of a verbal rule, a formula, a table, a list, or a graph.
3. What do all descriptions of functions have in common?
All descriptions of functions involve ordered pairs that satisfy the definition.
4. How can you tell at a glance if a graph is a graph of a function? A graph is the graph of a function if no vertical line crosses the graph more than once.
5. What is the domain of a function? The domain is the set of all first coordinates of the ordered pairs.
6. What is function notation? In function notation x represents the first coordinate and $f(x)$ represents the second coordinate.

〈1〉 Functions Expressed by Formulas

Write a formula that describes the function for each of the following. See Examples 1 and 2.

7. A small pizza costs \$5.00 plus 50 cents for each topping. Express the total cost C as a function of the number of toppings t. $C = 0.50t + 5$

8. A developer prices condominiums in Florida at \$20,000 plus \$40 per square foot of living area. Express the cost C as a function of the number of square feet of living area s. $C = 40s + 20{,}000$

9. The sales tax rate on groceries in Mayberry is 9%. Express the total cost T (including tax) as a function of the total price of the groceries S. $T = 1.09S$

10. With a GM MasterCard, 5% of the amount charged is credited toward a rebate on the purchase of a new car. Express the rebate R as a function of the amount charged A. $R = 0.05A$

11. Express the circumference of a circle as a function of its radius. $C = 2\pi r$

12. Express the circumference of a circle as a function of its diameter. $C = \pi d$

13. Express the perimeter P of a square as a function of the length s of a side. $P = 4s$

14. Express the perimeter P of a rectangle with width 10 ft as a function of its length L. $P = 2L + 20$

15. Express the area A of a triangle with a base of 10 m as a function of its height h. $A = 5h$

16. Express the area A of a trapezoid with bases 12 cm and 10 cm as a function of its height h. $A = 11h$

〈2〉 Functions Expressed by Tables

Determine whether each table expresses the second variable as a function of the first variable. See Example 3.

17. Yes

x	y
1	1
4	2
9	3
16	4
25	5
36	6
49	8

18. Yes

x	y
2	4
3	9
4	16
5	25
8	36
9	49
10	100

19. Yes

t	v
2	2
−2	2
3	3
−3	3
4	4
−4	4
5	5

20. Yes

s	W
5	17
6	17
−1	17
−2	17
−3	17
7	17
8	17

VIDEO **21.** No

a	P
2	2
2	−2
3	3
3	−3
4	4
4	−4
5	5

22. No

n	r
17	5
17	6
17	−1
17	−2
17	−3
17	−4
17	−5

23. Yes

b	q
1970	0.14
1972	0.18
1974	0.18
1976	0.22
1978	0.25
1980	0.28

24. Yes

c	h
345	0.3
350	0.4
355	0.5
360	0.6
365	0.7
370	0.8
380	0.9

〈3〉 Functions Expressed by Ordered Pairs

Determine whether each set of ordered pairs is a function. See Example 4.

25. $\{(1, 2), (2, 3), (3, 4)\}$ Yes

26. $\{(1, -3), (1, 3), (2, 12)\}$ No

27. $\{(-1, 4), (2, 4), (3, 4)\}$ Yes

28. $\{(1, 7), (7, 1)\}$ Yes

29. $\{(0, -1), (0, 1)\}$ No

30. $\{(1, 7), (-2, 7), (3, 7), (4, 7)\}$ Yes

31. $\{(50, 50)\}$ Yes

32. $\{(0, 0)\}$ Yes

Determine whether each set is a function. See Example 5.

33. $\{(x, y) \mid y = x - 3\}$ Yes

34. $\{(x, y) \mid y = x^2 - 2x - 1\}$ Yes

35. $\{(x, y) \mid x = |y|\}$ No

36. $\{(x, y) \mid x = y^2 + 1\}$ No

37. $\{(x, y) \mid x = y + 1\}$ Yes

38. $\left\{(x, y) \middle| y = \frac{1}{x}\right\}$ Yes

39. $\{(x, y) \mid x = y^2 - 1\}$ No

40. $\{(x, y) \mid x = 3y\}$ Yes

Determine whether each equation expresses y as a function of x. See Example 6.

41. $x = 4y$ Yes

42. $x = -3y$ Yes

VIDEO **43.** $y = \frac{2}{x}$ Yes

44. $y = \frac{x}{2}$ Yes

45. $y = x^3 - 1$ Yes

46. $y = |x - 1|$ Yes

47. $x^2 + y^2 = 25$ No

48. $x^2 - y^2 = 9$ No

⟨4⟩ Graphs of Functions

For each graph determine whether y is a function of x. See Example 7.

49. Yes

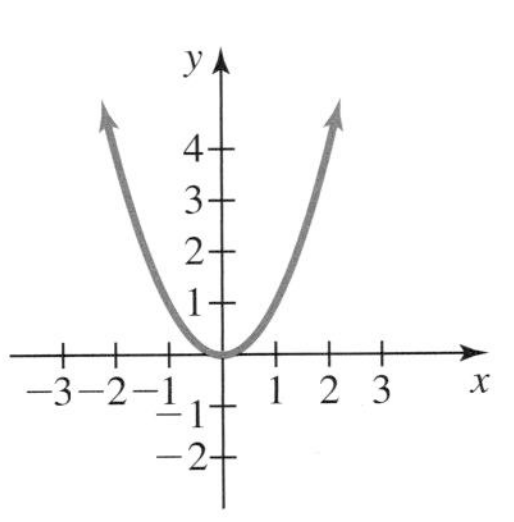

50. Yes

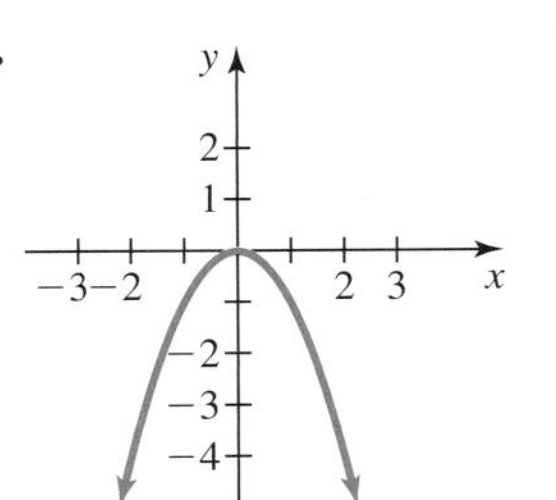

51. No

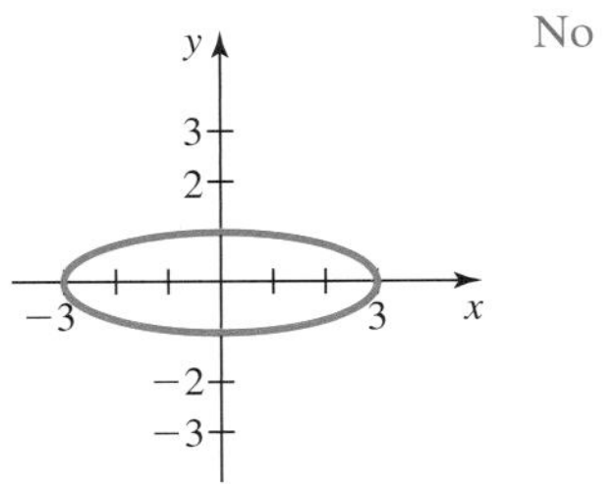

52. No

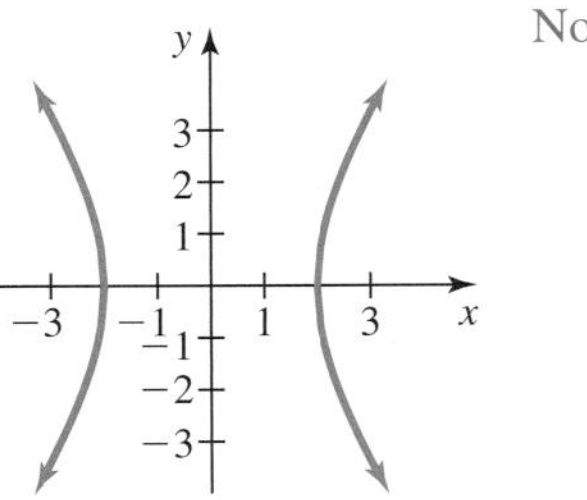

53. No

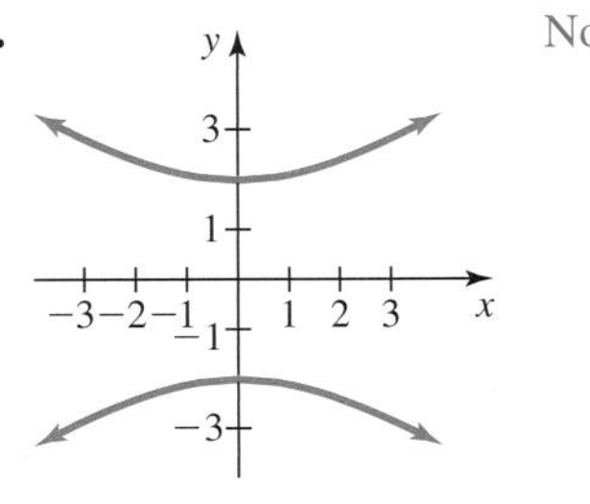

54. Yes

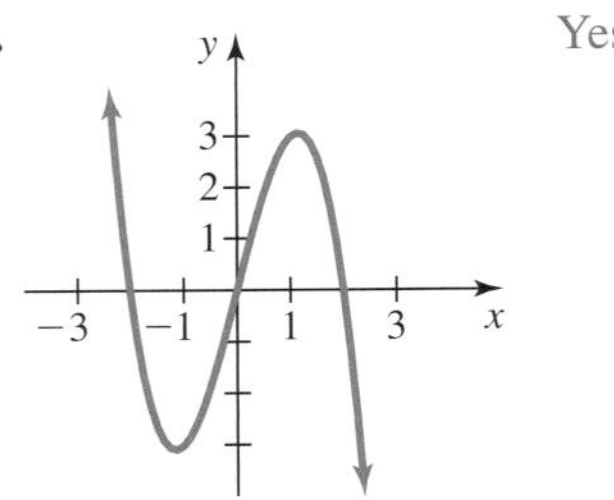

⟨5⟩ Domain and Range

Determine the domain and range of each function. See Example 8.

55. $\{(3, 3), (2, 5), (1, 7)\}$ $\{1, 2, 3\}, \{3, 5, 7\}$

56. $\{(-1, 4), (3, 5)\}$ $\{-1, 3\}, \{4, 5\}$

VIDEO **57.** $\{(0, 1), (2, 1), (4, 1)\}$ $\{0, 2, 4\}, \{1\}$

58. $\{(4, -2), (5, -2), (7, -2), (8, -2)\}$ $\{4, 5, 7, 8\}, \{-2\}$

Graph each function and identify the domain and range. See Example 9.

59. $y = 2x - 6$

R (real numbers), R

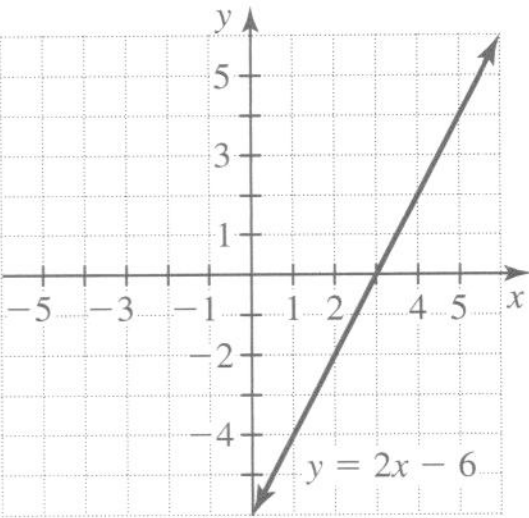

60. $y = 3x + 2$

R, R

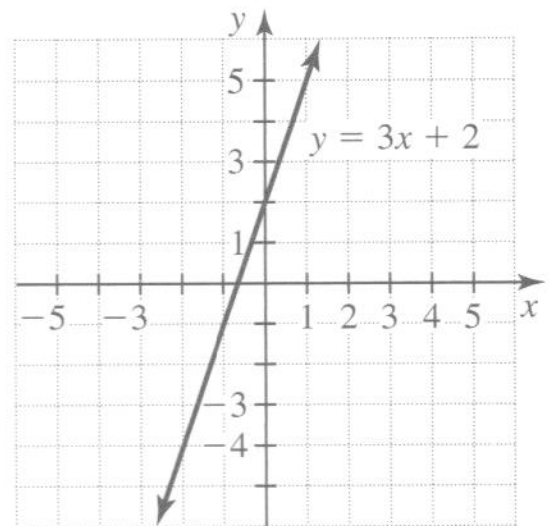

61. $y = -x$

R, R

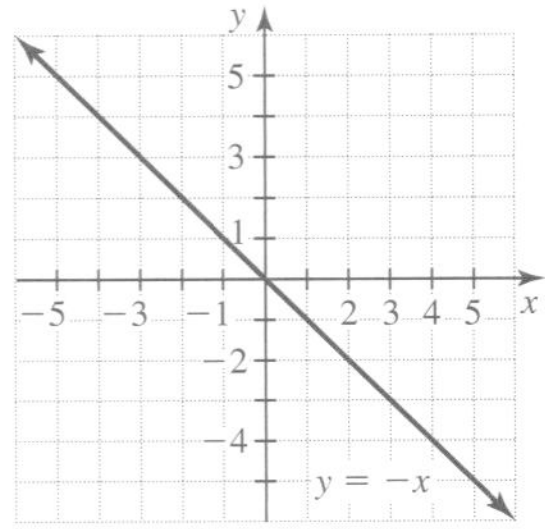

62. $y = 5 - x$
R, R

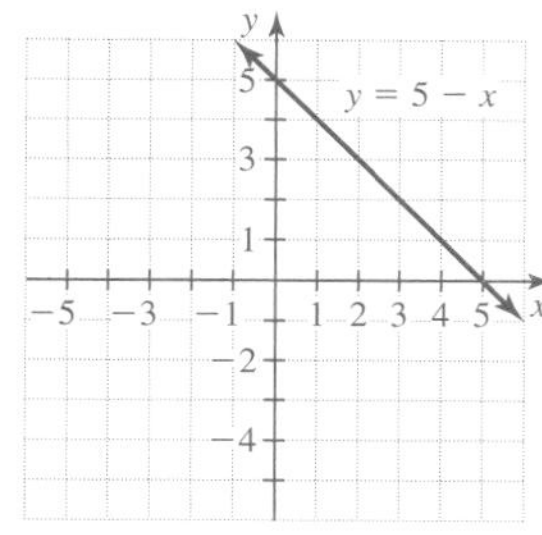

63. $y = x^2 - 4x + 2$
R, $\{y \mid y \geq -2\}$ or $[-2, \infty)$

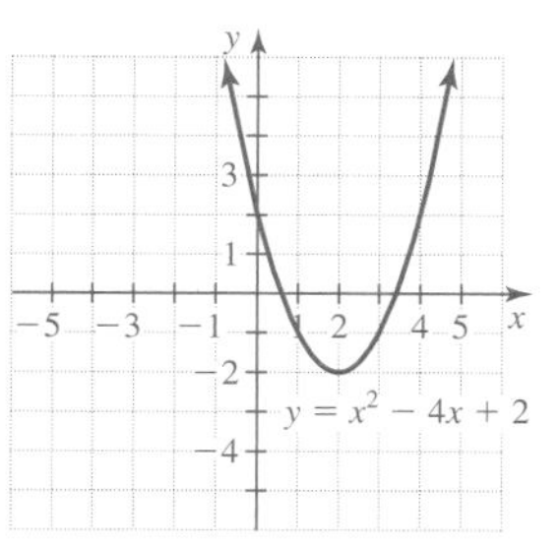

64. $y = x^2 + 6x + 5$
R, $\{y \mid y \geq -4\}$ or $[-4, \infty)$

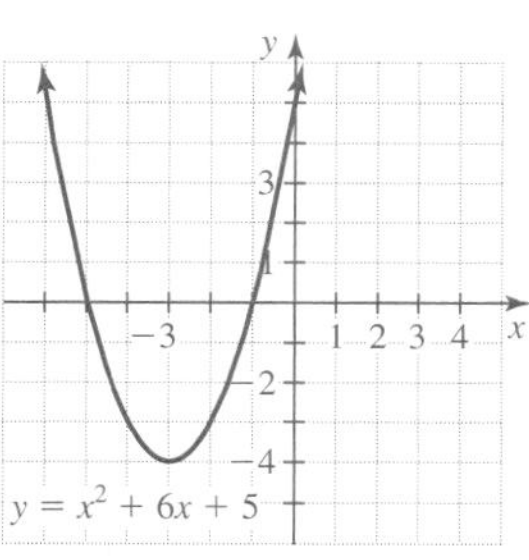

65. $y = -2x^2 - 4x + 5$
R, $\{y \mid y \leq 7\}$ or $(-\infty, 7]$

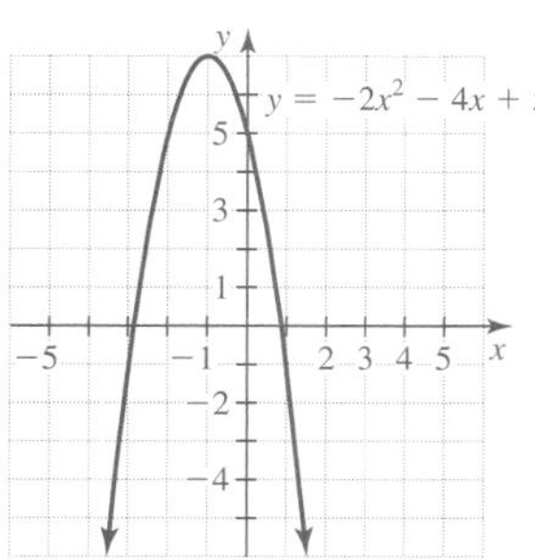

66. $y = -4x^2 + 8x$
R, $\{y \mid y \leq 4\}$ or $(-\infty, 4]$

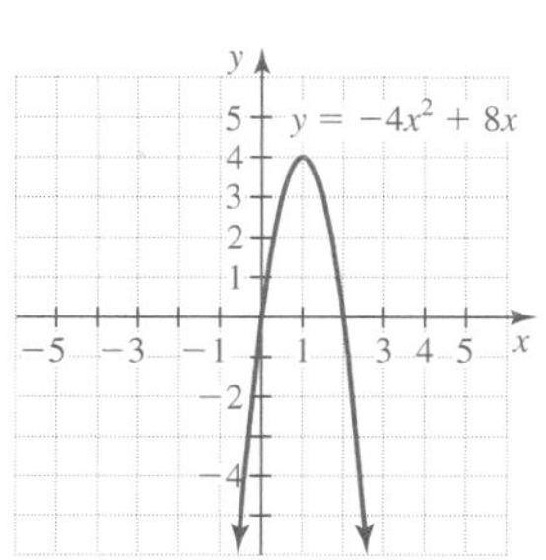

‹6› Function Notation

Let $f(x) = 2x - 1$, $g(x) = x^2 - 3$, and $h(x) = |x - 1|$. Find the following. See Example 10.

67. $f(0)$ -1

68. $f(-1)$ -3

69. $f\left(\frac{1}{2}\right)$ 0

70. $f\left(\frac{3}{4}\right)$ $\frac{1}{2}$

71. $g(4)$ 13

VIDEO **72.** $g(-4)$ 13

73. $g(0.5)$ -2.75

74. $g(-1.5)$ -0.75

75. $h(3)$ 2

76. $h(-1)$ 2

77. $h(0)$ 1

78. $h(1)$ 0

Let $f(x) = \frac{2}{3}x - 4$, $g(x) = \sqrt{8 - x}$, and $h(x) = \sqrt[3]{x}$. Find the following.

79. $f(-3)$ -6

80. $f(3)$ -2

81. $f(6)$ 0

82. $g(-1)$ 3

83. $g(0)$ $2\sqrt{2}$

84. $g(-8)$ 4

85. $g(7)$ 1

86. $h(0)$ 0

87. $h(-1)$ -1

88. $h(8)$ 2

Let $f(x) = x^3 - x^2$ and $g(x) = x^2 - 4.2x + 2.76$. Find the following. Round each answer to three decimal places.

89. $f(5.68)$ 150.988

90. $g(-2.7)$ 21.39

91. $g(3.5)$ 0.31

92. $f(67.2)$ 298,948.608

Solve each problem. See Example 11.

93. ***Velocity and time.*** If a ball is thrown straight upward into the air with a velocity of 100 ft/sec, then its velocity t seconds later is given by

$$v(t) = -32t + 100.$$

a) Find $v(0)$, $v(1)$, and $v(2)$. 100 ft/sec, 68 ft/sec, 36 ft/sec

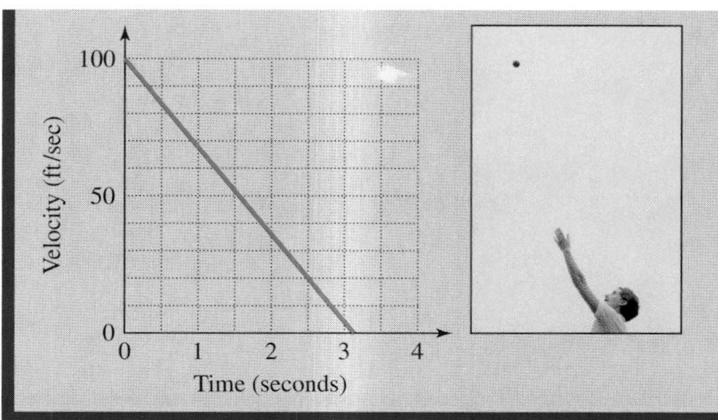

Figure for Exercise 93

b) Judging from the accompanying graph, is the velocity increasing or decreasing as the time increases?
Decreasing

c) Find $v(4)$ and explain your answer.
-28 ft/sec; The ball has negative velocity as it is coming down.

94. ***Cost and toppings.*** The cost c in dollars for a pizza with n toppings is given by

$$c(n) = 0.75n + 6.99.$$

a) Find $c(2)$, $c(4)$, and $c(5)$.
\$8.49, \$9.99, \$10.74

b) Is the cost increasing or decreasing as the number of toppings increases?
Increasing

95. ***Threshold weight.*** The threshold weight for an individual is the weight beyond which the risk of death increases significantly. For middle-aged males the function $W(h) = 0.000534h^3$ expresses the threshold weight in pounds as a function of the height h in inches. Find $W(70)$. Find the threshold weight for a 6′2″ middle-aged male.
183 pounds, 216 pounds

96. ***Pole vaulting.*** The height a pole vaulter attains is a function of the vaulter's velocity on the runway. The function

$$h(v) = \frac{1}{64}v^2$$

gives the height in feet as a function of the velocity v in feet per second.

a) Find $h(35)$ to the nearest tenth of an inch.
19 ft 1.7 in.

b) Who gains more height from an increase of 1 ft/sec in velocity: a fast runner or a slow runner?
Fast runner

Figure for Exercise 96

97. ***Credit card fees.*** A certain credit card company gets 4% of each charge, and the retailer receives the rest. At the end of a billing period the retailer receives a statement showing only the retailer's portion of each transaction. Express the original amount charged C as a function of the retailer's portion r.
$C(r) = \frac{r}{0.96}$

98. ***More credit card fees.*** Suppose that the amount charged on the credit card in the previous exercise includes 8% sales tax. The credit card company does not get any of the sales tax. In this case the retailer's portion of each transaction includes sales tax on the original cost of the goods. Express the original amount charged C as a function of the retailer's portion r.
$C(r) = \frac{27}{26}r$

Getting More Involved

Discussion

In each situation determine whether a is a function of b, b is a function of a, or neither. Answers may vary depending on interpretations.

99. a = the price per gallon of regular unleaded.
b = the number of gallons that you get for \$10.
Both

100. a = the universal product code of an item at Sears.
b = the price of that item.
b is a function of a

101. a = a student's score on the last test in this class.
b = the number of hours he/she spent studying.
Neither

102. a = a student's score on the last test in this class.
b = the IQ of the student's mother.
Neither

103. a = the weight of a package shipped by UPS.
b = the cost of shipping that package.
Neither

104. a = the Celsius temperature at any time.
b = the Fahrenheit temperature at the same time.
Both

105. a = the weight of a letter.
b = the cost of mailing the letter within the U.S.
b is a function of a

106. a = the cost of a gallon of milk.
b = the amount of sales tax on that gallon.
b is a function of a

Math *at Work* Body Surface Area

Body surface area (BSA) is difficult to determine but is essential for cancer chemotherapy dosage calculations. A recent study of 2819 chemotherapy orders found that 93 of them contained at least one error in the dose. Three of the errors were classified as potentially lethal. In chemotherapy the difference between an underdose and an overdose is small and the consequences of error can be fatal.

In 1916 Du Bois and Du Bois examined nine individuals of varying age, shape, and size. They measured their BSA directly using molds. From these measurements they derived the formula BSA $= 0.20247\,(h/100)^{0.725}\,w^{0.425}$ using height h (cm) and weight w (kg). The Du Bois formula was challenged in the 1970s by Gehan and George, who directly measured the skin-surface area of 401 individuals. They found that the Du Bois formula significantly overestimated BSA in about 15% of their cases. However, the Du Bois formula prevailed and is still a widely used method for finding BSA. More recently, Mosteller produced the formula BSA $= \sqrt{\dfrac{hw}{3600}}$, which is easier to remember and use. The Mosteller formula is now being promoted as the new standard for determining BSA.

To maintain consistency in chemotherapy a systematic approach to dosage calculations is needed. All BSA calculations should be based on the same formula. Current heights and weights should be used in BSA calculations and all dosage calculations should be checked. Verifying BSA and dose are needed to ensure optimal treatment and to prevent chemotherapy underdosing or overdosing.

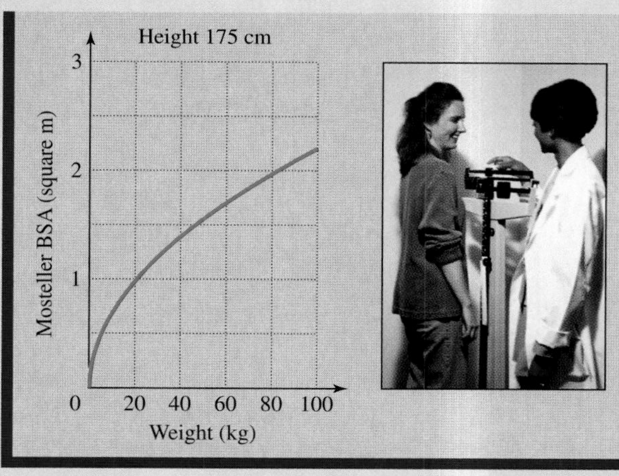

9.8 Combining Functions

In This Section

- ⟨1⟩ Basic Operations with Functions
- ⟨2⟩ Composition

In this section, you will learn how to combine functions to obtain new functions.

⟨1⟩ Basic Operations with Functions

An entrepreneur plans to rent a stand at a farmers market for \$25 per day to sell strawberries. If she buys x flats of berries for \$5 per flat and sells them for \$9 per flat, then her daily cost in dollars can be written as a function of x:

$$C(x) = 5x + 25$$

Assuming she sells as many flats as she buys, her revenue in dollars is also a function of x:

$$R(x) = 9x$$

Because profit is revenue minus cost, we can find a function for the profit by subtracting the functions for cost and revenue:

$$\begin{aligned} P(x) &= R(x) - C(x) \\ &= 9x - (5x + 25) \\ &= 4x - 25 \end{aligned}$$

The function $P(x) = 4x - 25$ expresses the daily profit as a function of x. Since $P(6) = -1$ and $P(7) = 3$, the profit is negative if 6 or fewer flats are sold and positive if 7 or more flats are sold.

In the example of the entrepreneur, we subtracted two functions to find a new function. In other cases, we may use addition, multiplication, or division to combine two functions. For any two given functions we can define the sum, difference, product, and quotient functions as follows.

‹ Teaching Tip ›

Performing operations with functions relates this topic to many of the topics studied earlier in this text.

Sum, Difference, Product, and Quotient Functions

Given two functions f and g, the functions $f + g$, $f - g$, $f \cdot g$, and $\frac{f}{g}$ are defined as follows:

Sum function:	$(f + g)(x) = f(x) + g(x)$	
Difference function:	$(f - g)(x) = f(x) - g(x)$	
Product function:	$(f \cdot g)(x) = f(x) \cdot g(x)$	
Quotient function:	$\left(\frac{f}{g}\right)(x) = \frac{f(x)}{g(x)}$	provided that $g(x) \neq 0$

The domain of the function $f + g$, $f - g$, $f \cdot g$, or $\frac{f}{g}$ is the intersection of the domain of f and the domain of g. For the function $\frac{f}{g}$ we also rule out any values of x for which $g(x) = 0$.

EXAMPLE 1

Operations with functions

Let $f(x) = 4x - 12$ and $g(x) = x - 3$. Find the following.

a) $(f + g)(x)$ **b)** $(f - g)(x)$ **c)** $(f \cdot g)(x)$ **d)** $\left(\frac{f}{g}\right)(x)$

‹ Helpful Hint ›

Note that we use $f + g$, $f - g$, $f \cdot g$, and f/g to name these functions only because there is no application in mind here. We generally use a single letter to name functions after they are combined as we did when using P for the profit function rather than $R - C$.

Solution

a) $$\begin{aligned} (f + g)(x) &= f(x) + g(x) \\ &= 4x - 12 + x - 3 \\ &= 5x - 15 \end{aligned}$$

b) $$\begin{aligned} (f - g)(x) &= f(x) - g(x) \\ &= 4x - 12 - (x - 3) \\ &= 3x - 9 \end{aligned}$$

c) $$\begin{aligned} (f \cdot g)(x) &= f(x) \cdot g(x) \\ &= (4x - 12)(x - 3) \\ &= 4x^2 - 24x + 36 \end{aligned}$$

d) $$\begin{aligned} \left(\frac{f}{g}\right)(x) &= \frac{f(x)}{g(x)} = \frac{4x - 12}{x - 3} \\ &= \frac{4(x - 3)}{x - 3} = 4 \quad \text{for } x \neq 3. \end{aligned}$$

Now do Exercises 5–8

EXAMPLE 2

Evaluating a sum function

Let $f(x) = 4x - 12$ and $g(x) = x - 3$. Find $(f + g)(2)$.

Solution

In Example 1(a) we found a general formula for the function $f + g$, namely, $(f + g)(x) = 5x - 15$. If we replace x by 2, we get

$$\begin{aligned}(f + g)(2) &= 5(2) - 15\\ &= -5.\end{aligned}$$

We can also find $(f + g)(2)$ by evaluating each function separately and then adding the results. Because $f(2) = -4$ and $g(2) = -1$, we get

$$\begin{aligned}(f + g)(2) &= f(2) + g(2)\\ &= -4 + (-1)\\ &= -5.\end{aligned}$$

Now do Exercises 9–16

‹ Helpful Hint ›

The difference between the first four operations with functions and composition is like the difference between parallel and series in electrical connections. Components connected in parallel operate simultaneously and separately. If components are connected in series, then electricity must pass through the first component to get to the second component.

‹2› Composition

A salesperson's monthly salary is a function of the number of cars he sells: \$1000 plus \$50 for each car sold. If we let S be his salary and n be the number of cars sold, then S in dollars is a function of n:

$$S = 1000 + 50n$$

Each month the dealer contributes \$100 plus 5% of his salary to a profit-sharing plan. If P represents the amount put into profit sharing, then P (in dollars) is a function of S:

$$P = 100 + 0.05S$$

Now P is a function of S, and S is a function of n. Is P a function of n? The value of n certainly determines the value of P. In fact, we can write a formula for P in terms of n by substituting one formula into the other:

$$\begin{aligned}P &= 100 + 0.05S\\ &= 100 + 0.05(1000 + 50n) && \text{Substitute } S = 1000 + 50n.\\ &= 100 + 50 + 2.5n && \text{Distributive property}\\ &= 150 + 2.5n\end{aligned}$$

Now P is written as a function of n, bypassing S. We call this idea **composition of functions.**

EXAMPLE 3

The composition of two functions

Given that $y = x^2 - 2x + 3$ and $z = 2y - 5$, write z as a function of x.

Solution

Replace y in $z = 2y - 5$ by $x^2 - 2x + 3$:

$$\begin{aligned}z &= 2y - 5\\ &= 2(x^2 - 2x + 3) - 5 && \text{Replace } y \text{ by } x^2 - 2x + 3.\\ &= 2x^2 - 4x + 1\end{aligned}$$

The equation $z = 2x^2 - 4x + 1$ expresses z as a function of x.

Now do Exercises 17–26

The composition of two functions using function notation is defined as follows.

Composition of Functions

The **composition** of f and g is denoted $f \circ g$ and is defined by the equation

$$(f \circ g)(x) = f(g(x)),$$

provided that $g(x)$ is in the domain of f.

The notation $f \circ g$ is read as "the composition of f and g" or "f compose g." The notation $(f \circ g)(x)$ is read as "f of g of x." The diagram in Fig. 9.16 shows a function g pairing numbers in its domain with numbers in its range. If the range of g is contained in or equal to the domain of f, then f pairs the second coordinates of g with numbers in the range of f. The composition function $f \circ g$ is a rule for pairing numbers in the domain of g directly with numbers in the range of f, bypassing the middle set. The domain of the function $f \circ g$ is the domain of g (or a subset of it) and the range of $f \circ g$ is the range of f (or a subset of it).

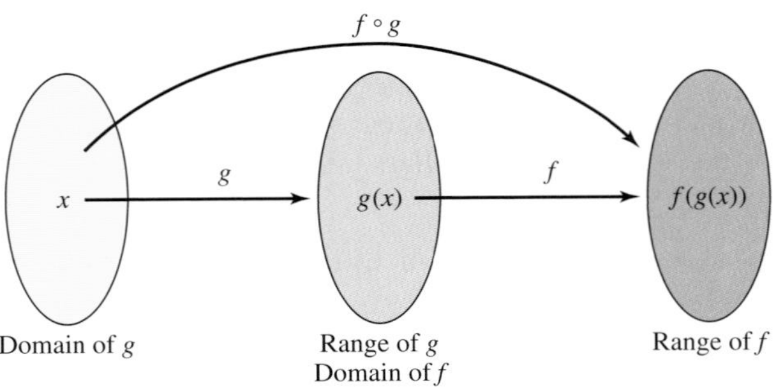

Figure 9.16

CAUTION The order in which functions are written is important in composition. For the function $f \circ g$ the function f is applied to $g(x)$. For the function $g \circ f$, the function g is applied to $f(x)$. The function closest to the variable x is applied first.

EXAMPLE 4

Composition of functions

Let $f(x) = 3x - 2$ and $g(x) = x^2 + 2x$. Find the following.

a) $(g \circ f)(2)$ **b)** $(f \circ g)(2)$ **c)** $(g \circ f)(x)$ **d)** $(f \circ g)(x)$

Solution

a) Because $(g \circ f)(2) = g(f(2))$, we first find $f(2)$:

$$f(2) = 3 \cdot 2 - 2 = 4$$

Because $f(2) = 4$, we have

$$(g \circ f)(2) = g(f(2)) = g(4) = 4^2 + 2 \cdot 4 = 24.$$

So $(g \circ f)(2) = 24$.

b) Because $(f \circ g)(2) = f(g(2))$, we first find $g(2)$:

$$g(2) = 2^2 + 2 \cdot 2 = 8$$

‹ Calculator Close-Up ›

Set $y_1 = 3x - 2$ and $y_2 = x^2 + 2x$. You can find the composition for Examples 4(a) and 4(b) by evaluating $y_2(y_1(2))$ and $y_1(y_2(2))$. Note that the order in which you evaluate the functions is critical.

```
Y2(Y1(2))
                24
Y1(Y2(2))
                22
```

Because $g(2) = 8$, we have

$$(f \circ g)(2) = f(g(2)) = f(8) = 3 \cdot 8 - 2 = 22.$$

Thus, $(f \circ g)(2) = 22$. In part (a) we found $(g \circ f)(2) = 24$. So composition of functions is not commutative.

c) $(g \circ f)(x) = g(f(x))$

$$= g(3x - 2)$$
$$= (3x - 2)^2 + 2(3x - 2)$$
$$= 9x^2 - 12x + 4 + 6x - 4 = 9x^2 - 6x$$

So $(g \circ f)(x) = 9x^2 - 6x$.

d) $(f \circ g)(x) = f(g(x))$

$$= f(x^2 + 2x)$$
$$= 3(x^2 + 2x) - 2 = 3x^2 + 6x - 2$$

So $(f \circ g)(x) = 3x^2 + 6x - 2$.

Now do Exercises 27–50

‹ Helpful Hint ›

A composition of functions can be viewed as two function machines where the output of the first is the input of the second.

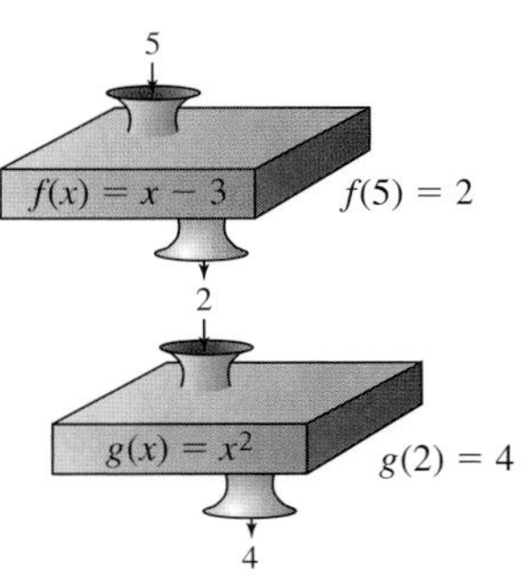

Notice that in Example 4(a) and (b), $(g \circ f)(2) \neq (f \circ g)(2)$. In Example 4(c) and (d) we see that $(g \circ f)(x)$ and $(f \circ g)(x)$ have different formulas defining them. In general, $f \circ g \neq g \circ f$.

It is often useful to view a complicated function as a composition of simpler functions. For example, the function $Q(x) = (x - 3)^2$ consists of two operations, subtracting 3 and squaring. So Q can be described as a composition of the functions $f(x) = x - 3$ and $g(x) = x^2$. To check this, we find $(g \circ f)(x)$:

$$(g \circ f)(x) = g(f(x))$$
$$= g(x - 3)$$
$$= (x - 3)^2$$

We can express the fact that Q is the same as the composition function $g \circ f$ by writing $Q = g \circ f$ or $Q(x) = (g \circ f)(x)$.

EXAMPLE 5

Expressing a function as a composition of simpler functions

Let $f(x) = x - 2$, $g(x) = 3x$, and $h(x) = \sqrt{x}$. Write each of the following functions as a composition, using f, g, and h.

a) $F(x) = \sqrt{x - 2}$ **b)** $H(x) = x - 4$ **c)** $K(x) = 3x - 6$

Solution

a) The function F consists of first subtracting 2 from x and then taking the square root of that result. So $F = h \circ f$. Check this result by finding $(h \circ f)(x)$:

$$(h \circ f)(x) = h(f(x)) = h(x - 2) = \sqrt{x - 2}$$

b) Subtracting 4 from x can be accomplished by subtracting 2 from x and then subtracting 2 from that result. So $H = f \circ f$. Check by finding $(f \circ f)(x)$:

$$(f \circ f)(x) = f(f(x)) = f(x - 2) = x - 2 - 2 = x - 4$$

c) Notice that $K(x) = 3(x - 2)$. The function K consists of subtracting 2 from x and then multiplying the result by 3. So $K = g \circ f$. Check by finding $(g \circ f)(x)$:

$$(g \circ f)(x) = g(f(x)) = g(x - 2) = 3(x - 2) = 3x - 6$$

Now do Exercises 51–60

CAUTION In Example 5(a) we have $F = h \circ f$ because in F we subtract 2 before taking the square root. If we had the function $G(x) = \sqrt{x} - 2$, we would take the square root before subtracting 2. So $G = f \circ h$. Notice how important the order of operations is here.

Warm-Ups ▼

True or false? Explain your answer.

1. If $f(x) = x - 2$ and $g(x) = x + 3$, then $(f - g)(x) = -5$. True
2. If $f(x) = x + 4$ and $g(x) = 3x$, then $\left(\frac{f}{g}\right)(2) = 1$. True
3. The functions $f \circ g$ and $g \circ f$ are always the same. False
4. If $f(x) = x^2$ and $g(x) = x + 2$, then $(f \circ g)(x) = x^2 + 2$. False
5. The functions $f \circ g$ and $f \cdot g$ are always the same. False
6. If $f(x) = \sqrt{x}$ and $g(x) = x - 9$, then $g(f(x)) = f(g(x))$ for every x. False
7. If $f(x) = 3x$ and $g(x) = \frac{x}{3}$, then $(f \circ g)(x) = x$. True
8. If $a = 3b^2 - 7b$, and $c = a^2 + 3a$, then c is a function of b. True
9. The function $F(x) = \sqrt{x - 5}$ is a composition of two functions. True
10. If $F(x) = (x - 1)^2$, $h(x) = x - 1$, and $g(x) = x^2$, then $F = g \circ h$. True

9.8 Exercises

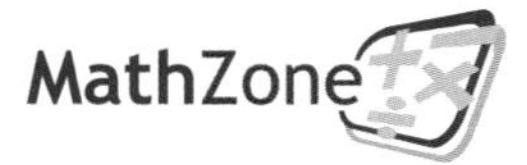

Boost your grade at mathzone.com!
- Practice Problems
- NetTutor
- Self-Tests
- e-Professors
- Videos

‹ Study Tips ›

- If you haven't been working with a group all semester, form a study group for the final exam.
- You might even ask your instructor to meet with your study group.

Reading and Writing *After reading this section, write out the answers to these questions. Use complete sentences.*

1. What are the basic operations with functions?
   The basic operations of functions are addition, subtraction, multiplication, and division.
2. How do we perform the basic operations with functions?
   We perform the operations with functions by adding, subtracting, multiplying, or dividing the expressions that define the functions.
3. What is the composition of two functions?
   In the composition function the second function is evaluated on the result of the first function.
4. How is the order of operations related to composition of functions?
   Since each operation is a function, the order of operations determines the order in which the functions are composed.

⟨1⟩ Basic Operations with Functions

Let $f(x) = 4x - 3$, *and* $g(x) = x^2 - 2x$. *Find the following. See Examples 1 and 2.*

5. $(f + g)(x)$ $x^2 + 2x - 3$

6. $(f - g)(x)$ $-x^2 + 6x - 3$

7. $(f \cdot g)(x)$ $4x^3 - 11x^2 + 6x$

8. $\left(\frac{f}{g}\right)(x)$ $\frac{4x - 3}{x(x - 2)}$ for $x \neq 0, 2$

9. $(f + g)(3)$ 12

10. $(f + g)(2)$ 5

11. $(f - g)(-3)$ -30

12. $(f - g)(-2)$ -19

13. $(f \cdot g)(-1)$ -21

14. $(f \cdot g)(-2)$ -88

15. $\left(\frac{f}{g}\right)(4)$ $\frac{13}{8}$

16. $\left(\frac{f}{g}\right)(-2)$ $-\frac{11}{8}$

⟨2⟩ Composition

For Exercises 17–26, use the two functions to write y as a function of x. See Example 3.

17. $y = 2a, a = 3x$ $y = 6x$

18. $y = a + 2, a = x + 3$ $y = x + 5$

19. $y = 3a - 2, a = 2x - 6$ $y = 6x - 20$

20. $y = 2c + 3, c = -3x + 4$ $y = -6x + 11$

21. $y = 2d + 1, d = \frac{x + 1}{2}$ $y = x + 2$

22. $y = -3d + 2, d = \frac{2 - x}{3}$ $y = x$

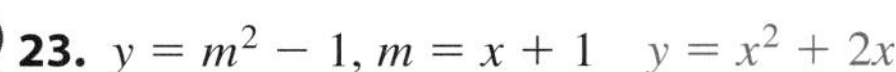

23. $y = m^2 - 1, m = x + 1$ $y = x^2 + 2x$

24. $y = n^2 - 3n + 1, n = x + 2$ $y = x^2 + x - 1$

25. $y = \frac{a - 3}{a + 2}, a = \frac{2x + 3}{1 - x}$ $y = x$ for $x \neq 1$

26. $y = \frac{w + 2}{w - 5}, w = \frac{5x + 2}{x - 1}$ $y = x$ for $x \neq 1$

Let $f(x) = 2x - 3$, $g(x) = x^2 + 3x$, *and* $h(x) = \frac{x + 3}{2}$. *Find the following. See Example 4.*

27. $(g \circ f)(1)$ -2

28. $(f \circ g)(-2)$ -7

29. $(f \circ g)(1)$ 5

30. $(g \circ f)(-2)$ 28

31. $(f \circ f)(4)$ 7

32. $(h \circ h)(3)$ 3

33. $(h \circ f)(5)$ 5

34. $(f \circ h)(0)$ 0

35. $(f \circ h)(5)$ 5

36. $(h \circ f)(0)$ 0

37. $(g \circ h)(-1)$ 4

38. $(h \circ g)(-1)$ $\frac{1}{2}$

39. $(f \circ g)(2.36)$ 22.2992

40. $(h \circ f)(23.761)$ 23.761

41. $(g \circ f)(x)$ $4x^2 - 6x$

42. $(g \circ h)(x)$ $\frac{x^2 + 12x + 27}{4}$

43. $(f \circ g)(x)$ $2x^2 + 6x - 3$

44. $(h \circ g)(x)$ $\frac{x^2 + 3x + 3}{2}$

45. $(h \circ f)(x)$ x

46. $(f \circ h)(x)$ x

47. $(f \circ f)(x)$ $4x - 9$

48. $(g \circ g)(x)$ $x^4 + 6x^3 + 12x^2 + 9x$

49. $(h \circ h)(x)$ $\frac{x + 9}{4}$

50. $(f \circ f \circ f)(x)$ $8x - 21$

Let $f(x) = \sqrt{x}$, $g(x) = x^2$, *and* $h(x) = x - 3$. *Write each of the following functions as a composition using f, g, or h. See Example 5.*

51. $F(x) = \sqrt{x - 3}$
$F = f \circ h$

52. $N(x) = \sqrt{x} - 3$
$N = h \circ f$

53. $G(x) = x^2 - 6x + 9$
$G = g \circ h$

54. $P(x) = x$ for $x \geq 0$
$P = f \circ g$

55. $H(x) = x^2 - 3$
$H = h \circ g$

56. $M(x) = x^{1/4}$
$M = f \circ f$

57. $J(x) = x - 6$
$J = h \circ h$

58. $R(x) = \sqrt{x^2 - 3}$
$R = f \circ h \circ g$

59. $K(x) = x^4$
$K = g \circ g$

60. $Q(x) = \sqrt{x^2 - 6x + 9}$
$Q = f \circ g \circ h$

Applications

Solve each problem.

61. ***Color monitor.*** A color monitor has a square viewing area that has a diagonal measure of 15 inches. Find the area of the viewing area in square inches (in.^{2}). Write a formula for the area of a square as a function of the length of its diagonal.
112.5 in.^{2}, $A = \frac{d^2}{2}$

62. ***Perimeter.*** Write a formula for the perimeter of a square as a function of its area.
$P = 4\sqrt{A}$

63. ***Profit function.*** A plastic bag manufacturer has determined that the company can sell as many bags as it can produce each month. If it produces x thousand bags in a month, the revenue is $R(x) = x^2 - 10x + 30$ dollars, and the cost is $C(x) = 2x^2 - 30x + 200$ dollars. Use the fact that profit is revenue minus cost to write the profit as a function of x.
$P(x) = -x^2 + 20x - 170$

64. ***Area of a sign.*** A sign is in the shape of a square with a semicircle of radius x adjoining one side and a semicircle of diameter x removed from the opposite side. If the sides of the square are length $2x$, then write the area of the sign as a function of x. See the figure on the next page.
$A = \frac{(32 + 3\pi)x^2}{8}$

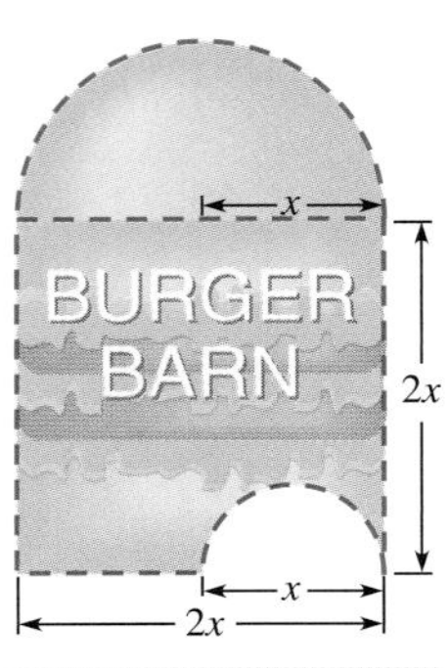

Figure for Exercise 64

65. ***Junk food expenditures.*** Suppose the average family spends 25% of its income on food, $F = 0.25I$, and 10% of each food dollar on junk food, $J = 0.10F$. Write J as a function of I. $J = 0.025I$

66. ***Area of an inscribed circle.*** A pipe of radius r must pass through a square hole of area M as shown in the figure. Write the cross-sectional area of the pipe A as a function of M.

$A = \pi\frac{M}{4}$

Figure for Exercise 66

67. ***Displacement-length ratio.*** To find the displacement-length ratio D for a sailboat, first find x, where $x = (L/100)^3$ and L is the length at the water line in feet. Next find D, where $D = (d/2240)/x$ and d is the displacement in pounds.

a) For the Pacific Seacraft 40, $L = 30$ ft 3 in. and $d = 24{,}665$ pounds. Find D.

b) For a boat with a displacement of 25,000 pounds, write D as a function of L.

c) The graph for the function in part (b) is shown in the accompanying figure. For a fixed displacement, does the displacement-length ratio increase or decrease as the length increases?

a) 397.8 **b)** $D = \frac{1.116 \times 10^7}{L^3}$ **c)** Decreases

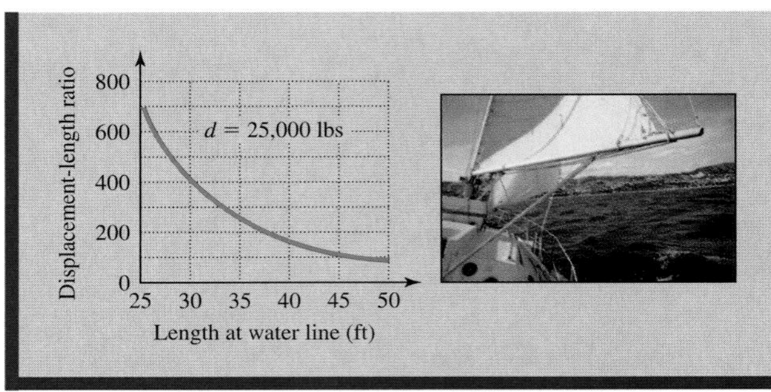

Figure for Exercise 67

68. ***Sail area-displacement ratio.*** To find the sail area-displacement ratio S, first find y, where $y = (d/64)^{2/3}$ and d is the displacement in pounds. Next find S, where $S = A/y$ and A is the sail area in square feet.

a) For the Pacific Seacraft 40, $A = 846$ square feet (ft^2) and $d = 24{,}665$ pounds. Find S.

b) For a boat with a sail area of 900 ft^2, write S as a function of d.

c) For a fixed sail area, does S increase or decrease as the displacement increases?

a) 15.97
b) $S = 14{,}400d^{-2/3}$
c) Decreases

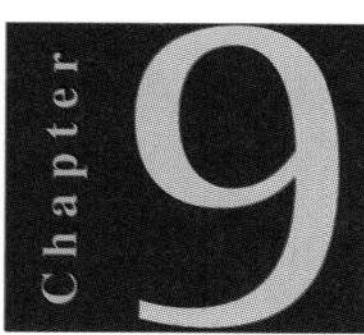

Wrap-Up

Summary

Quadratic Equations		Examples
Quadratic equation	An equation of the form $ax^2 + bx + c = 0$, where a, b, and c are real numbers with $a \neq 0$	$x^2 = 10$ $(x + 3)^2 = 8$ $x^2 + 5x - 7 = 0$
Methods for solving quadratic equations	Factoring	$x^2 + 5x + 6 = 0$ $(x + 3)(x + 2) = 0$
	Square root property	$(x - 3)^2 = 6$ $x - 3 = \pm\sqrt{6}$
	Completing the square (works on any quadratic): take one-half of middle term, square it, then add it to each side.	$x^2 + 6x = 7$ $x^2 + 6x + 9 = 7 + 9$ $(x + 3)^2 = 16$
	Quadratic formula (works on any quadratic): $x = \dfrac{-b \pm \sqrt{b^2 - 4ac}}{2a}$	$2x^2 - 3x - 6 = 0$ $x = \dfrac{3 \pm \sqrt{9 - 4(2)(-6)}}{2(2)}$
Number and types of solutions	Determined by the discriminant $b^2 - 4ac$ $b^2 - 4ac > 0$: two real solutions	$x^2 + 5x - 9 = 0$ has two real solutions because $5^2 - 4(1)(-9) > 0$.
	$b^2 - 4ac = 0$: one real solution	$x^2 + 6x + 9 = 0$ has one real solution because $6^2 - 4(1)(9) = 0$.
	$b^2 - 4ac < 0$: no real solutions (two complex solutions)	$x^2 + 3x + 10 = 0$ has no real solutions because $3^2 - 4(1)(10) < 0$.

Complex Numbers		Examples
Complex numbers	Numbers of the form $a + bi$, where a and b are real numbers, $i = \sqrt{-1}$, and $i^2 = -1$	$12, -3i, 5 + 4i, \sqrt{2} - i\sqrt{3}$
Imaginary numbers	Numbers of the form $a + bi$, where $b \neq 0$	$5i, 13 + i\sqrt{6}$
Square root of a negative number	If b is a positive real number, then $\sqrt{-b} = i\sqrt{b}$.	$\sqrt{-3} = i\sqrt{3}$ $\sqrt{-4} = i\sqrt{4} = 2i$

Complex conjugates	The complex numbers $a + bi$ and $a - bi$ are called complex conjugates of each other. Their product is a real number.	$(1 + 2i)(1 - 2i) = 1 + 4 = 5$
Complex number operations	Add, subtract, and multiply as if the complex numbers were binomials with variable i. Use the distributive property for multiplication. Remember that $i^2 = -1$. Divide complex numbers by multiplying the numerator and denominator by the conjugate of the denominator, then simplify.	$(2 + 3i) + (3 - 5i) = 5 - 2i$ $(2 - 5i) - (4 - 2i) = -2 - 3i$ $(3 - 4i)(2 + 5i) = 26 + 7i$ $\frac{4 - 6i}{5 + 2i} = \frac{(4 - 6i)(5 - 2i)}{(5 + 2i)(5 - 2i)}$
Parabolas		**Examples**
Opening	The parabola $y = ax^2 + bx + c$ opens upward if $a > 0$ or downward if $a < 0$.	$y = x^2 - 2x$ opens upward. $y = -x^2$ opens downward.
Vertex	The first coordinate of the vertex is $x = \frac{-b}{2a}$. The second coordinate of the vertex is the minimum value of y if $a > 0$ or the maximum value of y if $a < 0$.	$y = x^2 - 2x$ opens upward with vertex $(1, -1)$. Minimum y-value is -1.
Intercepts	The x-intercepts are found by solving $ax^2 + bx + c = 0$. The y-intercept is found by replacing x by 0 in $y = ax^2 + bx + c$.	$y = x^2 - 2x - 8$ has x-intercepts $(-2, 0)$ and $(4, 0)$ and y-intercept $(0, -8)$.
Functions		**Examples**
Definition of a function	A function is a rule by which any allowable value of one variable (the independent variable) determines a unique value of a second variable (the dependent variable).	$A = \pi r^2$
Equivalent definition of a function	A function is a set of ordered pairs such that no two ordered pairs have the same first coordinates and different second coordinates. To say that y is a function of x means that y is determined uniquely by x.	$\{(1, 0), (3, 8)\}$ $\{(x, y) \mid y = x^2\}$
Domain	The set of values of the independent variable, x	$y = x^2$ Domain: all real numbers, R
Range	The set of values of the dependent variable, y	$y = x^2$ Range: nonnegative real numbers, $\{y \mid y \geq 0\}$ or $[0, \infty)$
Linear function	If $y = mx + b$, we say that y is a linear function of x.	$F = \frac{9}{5}C + 32$

Quadratic function	A function of the form $y = ax^2 + bx + c$, where a, b, and c are real numbers and $a \neq 0$	$y = 3x^2 - 8x + 9$ $p = -3q^2 - 8q + 1$
Function notation	If x is the independent variable, then we use the notation $f(x)$ to represent the dependent variable.	$y = 2x + 3$ $f(x) = 2x + 3$
Combining Functions		**Examples**
Sum	$(f + g)(x) = f(x) + g(x)$	For $f(x) = x^2$ and $g(x) = x + 1$ $(f + g)(x) = x^2 + x + 1$
Difference	$(f - g)(x) = f(x) - g(x)$	$(f - g)(x) = x^2 - x - 1$
Product	$(f \cdot g)(x) = f(x) \cdot g(x)$	$(f \cdot g)(x) = x^3 + x^2$
Quotient	$\left(\frac{f}{g}\right)(x) = \frac{f(x)}{g(x)}$ for $g(x) \neq 0$	$\left(\frac{f}{g}\right)(x) = \frac{x^2}{x + 1}$ for $x \neq -1$
Composition	$(g \circ f)(x) = g(f(x))$ $(f \circ g)(x) = f(g(x))$	$(g \circ f)(x) = g(x^2) = x^2 + 1$ $(f \circ g)(x) = f(x + 1)$ $= x^2 + 2x + 1$

Enriching Your Mathematical Word Power

For each mathematical term, choose the correct meaning.

1. quadratic equation
a. $ax + b = c$ with $a \neq 0$
b. $ax^2 + bx + c = 0$ with $a \neq 0$
c. $ax + b = 0$ with $a \neq 0$
d. $a/x^2 + b/x = c$ with $x \neq 0$ b

2. perfect square trinomial
a. a trinomial of the form $a^2 + 2ab + b^2$
b. a trinomial of the form $a^2 + b^2$
c. a trinomial of the form $a^2 + ab + b^2$
d. a trinomial of the form $a^2 - 2ab - b^2$ a

3. completing the square
a. drawing a perfect square
b. evaluating $(a + b)^2$
c. drawing the fourth side when given three sides of a square
d. finding the third term of a perfect square trinomial d

4. quadratic formula
a. $x = \frac{-b \pm \sqrt{b^2 - 4ac}}{2}$
b. $x = -b \pm \frac{\sqrt{b^2 - 4ac}}{2a}$
c. $x = \frac{-b \pm \sqrt{b^2 - 4ac}}{2a}$
d. $x = \frac{b \pm \sqrt{b^2 - 4ac}}{2a}$ c

5. discriminant
a. the vertex of a parabola
b. the radicand in the quadratic formula
c. the leading coefficient in $ax^2 + bx + c$
d. to treat unfairly b

6. complex numbers
a. $a + bi$, where a and b are real
b. irrational numbers
c. imaginary numbers
d. $\sqrt{-1}$ a

7. imaginary unit
a. 1
b. -1
c. i
d. $\sqrt{1}$ c

8. imaginary numbers
a. $a + bi$, where a and b are real and $b \neq 0$
b. i
c. a complex number
d. a complex number in which the real part is 0 a

9. complex conjugates
a. i and $\sqrt{-1}$
b. $a + bi$ and $a - bi$
c. $(a + b)(a - b)$
d. i and -1 b

10. function
a. domain and range
b. a set of ordered pairs
c. a rule by which any allowable value of one variable determines a unique value of a second variable
d. a graph c

11. domain
a. the set of first coordinates of a function
b. the set of second coordinates of a function
c. the set of real numbers
d. the integers a

12. range
a. all of the possibilities
b. the coordinates of a function
c. the entire set of numbers
d. the set of second coordinates of a function d

13. quadratic function
a. $y = ax + b$ with $a \neq 0$
b. a parabola
c. $y = ax^2 + bx + c$ with $a \neq 0$
d. the quadratic formula c

14. composition of f and g
a. the function $f \circ g$ where $(f \circ g)(x) = f(g(x))$
b. the function $f \circ g$ where $(f \circ g)(x) = g(f(x))$
c. the function $f \cdot g$ where $(f \cdot g)(x) = f(x) \cdot g(x)$
d. a diagram showing f and g a

15. sum of f and g
a. the function $f \cdot g$ where $(f \cdot g)(x) = f(x) \cdot g(x)$
b. the function $f + g$ where $(f + g)(x) = f(x) + g(x)$
c. the function $f \circ g$ where $(f \circ g)(x) = g(f(x))$
d. the function obtained by adding the domains of f and g b

Review Exercises

9.1 The Square Root Property and Factoring

Solve each equation.

1. $x^2 - 9 = 0$
$-3, 3$

2. $x^2 - 1 = 0$
$-1, 1$

3. $x^2 - 9x = 0$
$0, 9$

4. $x^2 - x = 0$
$0, 1$

5. $x^2 - x = 2$
$-1, 2$

6. $x^2 - 9x = 10$
$-1, 10$

7. $(x - 9)^2 = 10$
$9 - \sqrt{10}, 9 + \sqrt{10}$

8. $(x + 5)^2 = 14$
$-5 - \sqrt{14}, -5 + \sqrt{14}$

9. $4x^2 - 12x + 9 = 0$
$\frac{3}{2}$

10. $9x^2 + 6x + 1 = 0$
$-\frac{1}{3}$

11. $t^2 - 9t + 20 = 0$
$4, 5$

12. $s^2 - 4s + 3 = 0$
$1, 3$

13. $\frac{x}{2} = \frac{7}{x + 5}$ $-7, 2$

14. $\sqrt{x + 4} = \frac{2x - 1}{3}$ 5

15. $\frac{1}{2}x^2 + \frac{7}{4}x = 1$
$-4, \frac{1}{2}$

16. $\frac{2}{3}x^2 - 1 = -\frac{1}{3}x$
$-\frac{3}{2}, 1$

9.2 Completing the Square

Solve each equation by completing the square.

17. $x^2 + 4x - 7 = 0$
$-2 - \sqrt{11}, -2 + \sqrt{11}$

18. $x^2 + 6x - 3 = 0$
$-3 - 2\sqrt{3}, -3 + 2\sqrt{3}$

19. $x^2 + 3x - 28 = 0$
$-7, 4$

20. $x^2 - x - 6 = 0$
$-2, 3$

21. $x^2 + 3x - 5 = 0$
$\frac{-3 - \sqrt{29}}{2}, \frac{-3 + \sqrt{29}}{2}$

22. $x^2 + \frac{4}{3}x - \frac{1}{3} = 0$
$\frac{-2 - \sqrt{7}}{3}, \frac{-2 + \sqrt{7}}{3}$

23. $2x^2 + 9x - 5 = 0$
$-5, \frac{1}{2}$

24. $2x^2 + 6x - 5 = 0$
$\frac{-3 - \sqrt{19}}{2}, \frac{-3 + \sqrt{19}}{2}$

9.3 The Quadratic Formula

Find the value of the discriminant, and tell how many real solutions each equation has.

25. $25t^2 - 10t + 1 = 0$
0, one

26. $3x^2 + 2 = 0$
-24, none

27. $-3w^2 + 4w - 5 = 0$
-44, none

28. $5x^2 - 7x = 0$
49, two

29. $-3v^2 + 4v = -5$
76, two

30. $49u^2 + 42u + 9 = 0$
0, one

Use the quadratic formula to solve each equation.

31. $6x^2 + x - 2 = 0$ $\quad -\frac{2}{3}, \frac{1}{2}$

32. $-6x^2 + 11x + 10 = 0$ $\quad -\frac{2}{3}, \frac{5}{2}$

33. $x^2 - x = 4$ $\quad \frac{1 - \sqrt{17}}{2}, \frac{1 + \sqrt{17}}{2}$

34. $y^2 - 2y = 4$ $\quad 1 - \sqrt{5}, 1 + \sqrt{5}$

35. $5x^2 - 6x - 1 = 0$ $\quad \frac{3 - \sqrt{14}}{5}, \frac{3 + \sqrt{14}}{5}$

36. $t^2 - 6t + 4 = 0$ $\quad 3 - \sqrt{5}, 3 + \sqrt{5}$

37. $3x^2 - 5x = 0$ $\quad 0, \frac{5}{3}$

38. $2w^2 - w = 15$ $\quad -\frac{5}{2}, 3$

9.4 Applications of Quadratic Equations

For each problem, find the exact and approximate answers. Round the decimal answers to three decimal places.

39. ***Bird watching.*** Chuck is standing 12 meters from a tree, watching a bird's nest that is 5 meters above eye level. Find the distance from Chuck's eyes to the nest. 13 meters

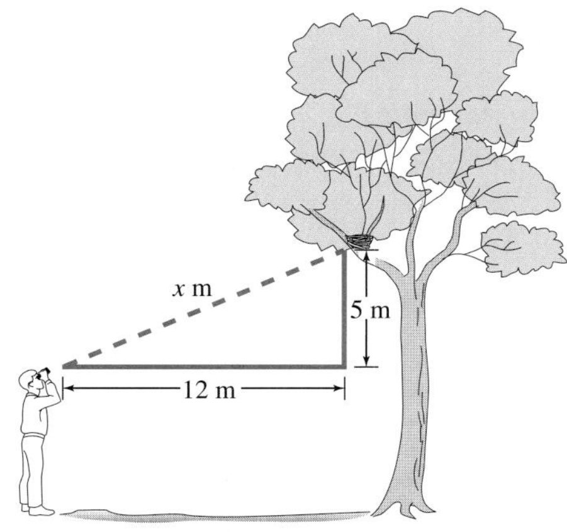

Figure for Exercise 39

40. ***Diagonal of a square.*** Find the diagonal of a square if the length of each side is 20 yards. $20\sqrt{2}$ or 28.284 yards

41. ***Lengthy legs.*** The hypotenuse of a right triangle measures 5 meters, and one leg is 2 meters longer than the other. Find the lengths of the legs.
$\frac{-2 + \sqrt{46}}{2}$ or 2.391 meters and $\frac{2 + \sqrt{46}}{2}$ or 4.391 meters

42. ***Width and height.*** The width of a rectangular bookcase is 3 feet shorter than the height. If the diagonal is 7 feet, then what are the dimensions of the bookcase?
Width $\frac{-3 + \sqrt{89}}{2}$ or 3.217 feet,
height $\frac{3 + \sqrt{89}}{2}$ or 6.217 feet

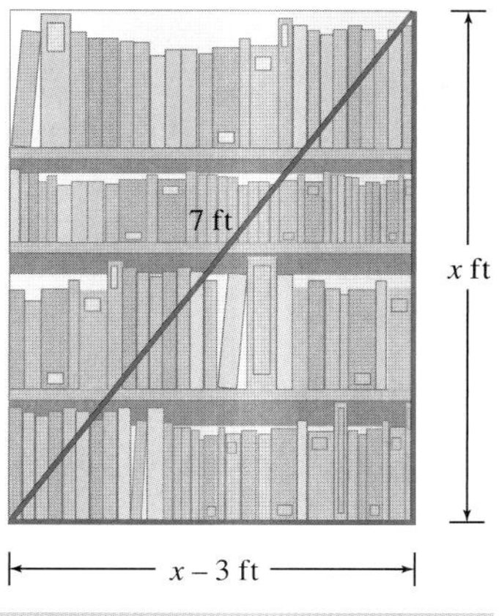

Figure for Exercise 42

43. ***Base and height.*** The base of a triangle is 4 inches longer than the height. If the area of the triangle is 20 square inches, then what are the lengths of the base and height?
Height $-2 + 2\sqrt{11}$ or 4.633 inches, base $2 + 2\sqrt{11}$ or 8.633 inches

44. ***Dimensions of a parallelogram.*** The base of a parallelogram is 1 meter longer than the height. If the area of the parallelogram is 8 square meters, then what are the lengths of the base and height?
Base $\frac{1 + \sqrt{33}}{2}$ or 3.372 meters,
height $\frac{-1 + \sqrt{33}}{2}$ or 2.372 meters

45. ***Unknown numbers.*** Find two positive real numbers whose sum is 6 and whose product is 7.
$3 + \sqrt{2}$ or 4.414 and $3 - \sqrt{2}$ or 1.586

46. ***Dimensions of a rectangle.*** The perimeter of a rectangle is 16 feet, and its area is 13 square feet. What are the dimensions of the rectangle?
Width $4 - \sqrt{3}$ or 2.268 feet, length $4 + \sqrt{3}$ or 5.732 feet

47. ***Printing time.*** The old printer took 2 hours longer than the new printer to print 100,000 mailing labels. With both printers working on the job, the 100,000 labels can be printed in 8 hours. How long would it take each printer working alone to do the job?

New printer $7 + \sqrt{65}$ or 15.062 hours, old printer $9 + \sqrt{65}$ or 17.062 hours

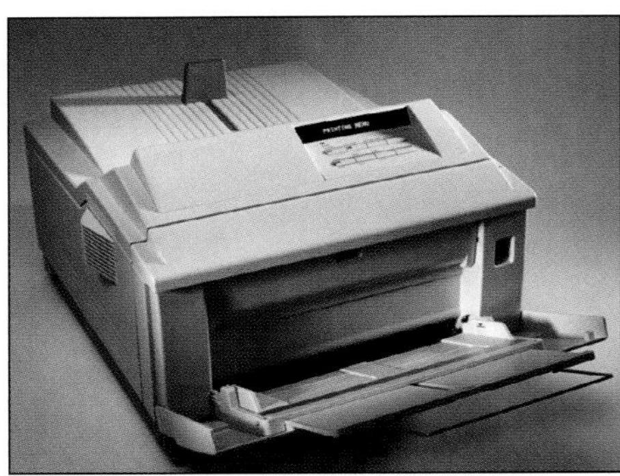

Photo for Exercise 47

48. ***Tilling the garden.*** When Blake uses his old tiller, it takes him 3 hours longer to till the garden than it takes Cassie using her new tiller. If Cassie will not let Blake use her new tiller and they can till the garden together in 6 hours, then how long would it take each one working alone?

Blake $\frac{15 + 3\sqrt{17}}{2}$ or 13.685 hours, Cassie $\frac{9 + 3\sqrt{17}}{2}$ or 10.685 hours.

Photo for Exercise 48

9.5 Complex Numbers

Perform the indicated operations. Write answers in the form $a + bi$.

49. $(2 + 3i) + (5 - 6i)$
$7 - 3i$

50. $(2 - 5i) + (-9 - 4i)$
$-7 - 9i$

51. $(-5 + 4i) - (-2 - 3i)$
$-3 + 7i$

52. $(1 - i) - (1 + i)$
$-2i$

53. $(2 - 9i)(3 + i)$
$15 - 25i$

54. $2i - 3(6 - 2i)$
$-18 + 8i$

55. $(3 + 8i)^2$
$-55 + 48i$

56. $(-5 - 2i)(-5 + 2i)$
29

57. $\dfrac{-2 - \sqrt{-8}}{2}$
$-1 - i\sqrt{2}$

58. $\dfrac{-6 + \sqrt{-54}}{-3}$
$2 - i\sqrt{6}$

59. $\dfrac{1 + 3i}{6 - i}$
$\frac{3}{37} + \frac{19}{37}i$

60. $\dfrac{3i}{8 + 3i}$
$\frac{9}{73} + \frac{24}{73}i$

61. $\dfrac{5 + i}{4 - i}$
$\frac{19}{17} + \frac{9}{17}i$

62. $\dfrac{3 + 2i}{i}$
$2 - 3i$

Find the complex solutions to the quadratic equations.

63. $x^2 + 121 = 0$
$-11i, 11i$

64. $x^2 + 120 = 0$
$-2i\sqrt{30}, 2i\sqrt{30}$

65. $x^2 - 16x + 65 = 0$
$8 - i, 8 + i$

66. $x^2 - 10x + 28 = 0$
$5 - i\sqrt{3}, 5 + i\sqrt{3}$

67. $2x^2 - 3x + 9 = 0$
$\frac{3 - 3i\sqrt{7}}{4}, \frac{3 + 3i\sqrt{7}}{4}$

68. $3x^2 - 6x + 4 = 0$
$\frac{3 - i\sqrt{3}}{3}, \frac{3 + i\sqrt{3}}{3}$

9.6 Graphing Parabolas

Find the vertex and intercepts for each parabola and sketch its graph.

69. $y = x^2 - 6x$
Vertex $(3, -9)$, intercepts $(0, 0)$, $(6, 0)$

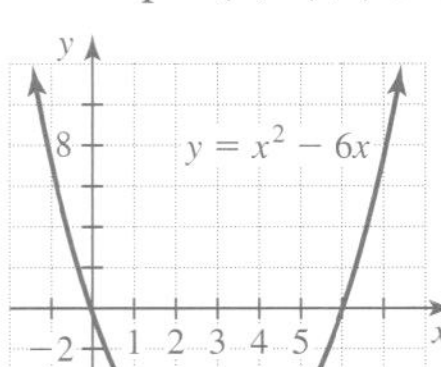

70. $y = x^2 + 4x$
Vertex $(-2, -4)$, intercepts $(0, 0)$, $(-4, 0)$

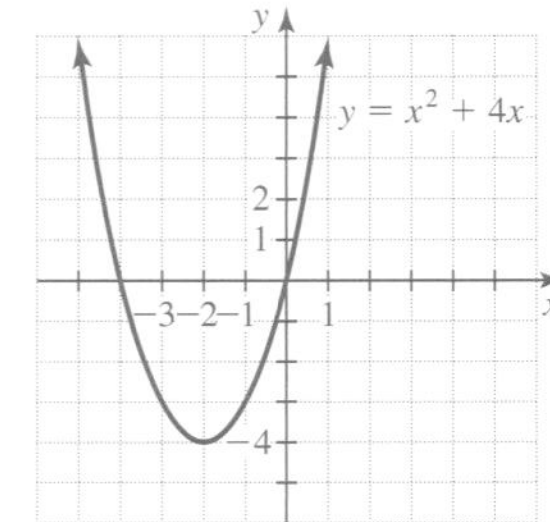

71. $y = x^2 - 4x - 12$
Vertex $(2, -16)$, intercepts $(0, -12)$, $(-2, 0)$, and $(6, 0)$

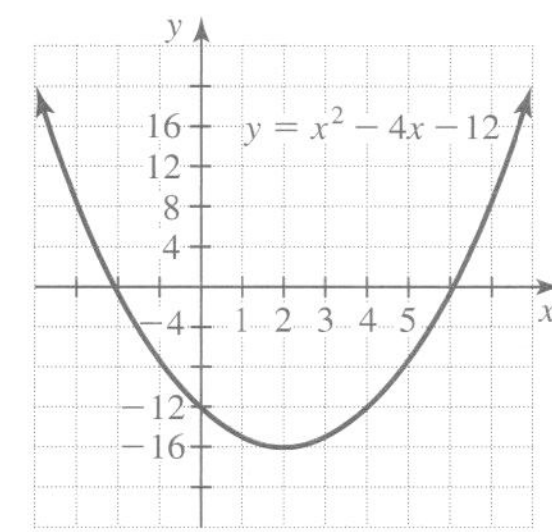

72. $y = x^2 + 2x - 24$
Vertex $(-1, -25)$, intercepts $(0, -24)$, $(-6, 0)$, $(4, 0)$

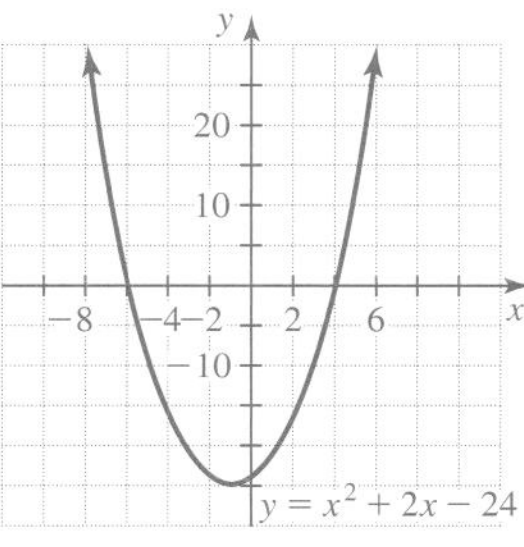

73. $y = -2x^2 + 8x$
Vertex $(2, 8)$, intercepts $(0, 0)$, $(4, 0)$

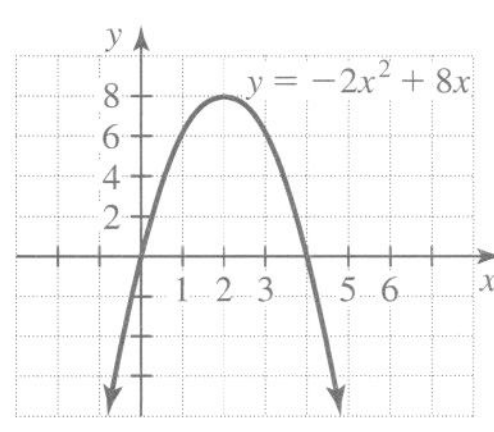

74. $y = -3x^2 + 6x$
Vertex $(1, 3)$, intercepts $(0, 0)$, $(2, 0)$

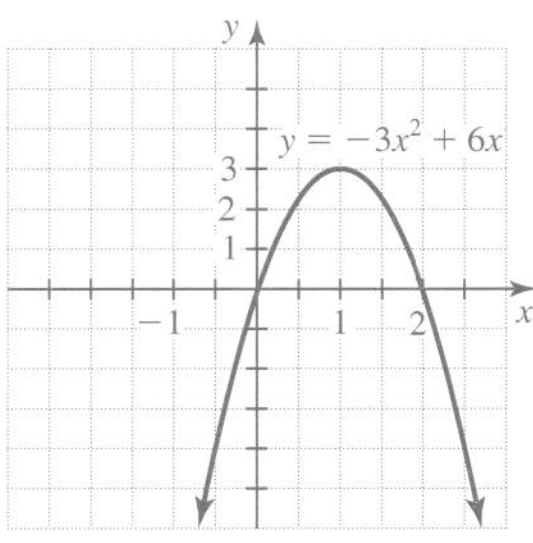

75. $y = -x^2 + 2x + 3$
Vertex $(1, 4)$, intercepts $(0, 3)$, $(-1, 0)$, $(3, 0)$

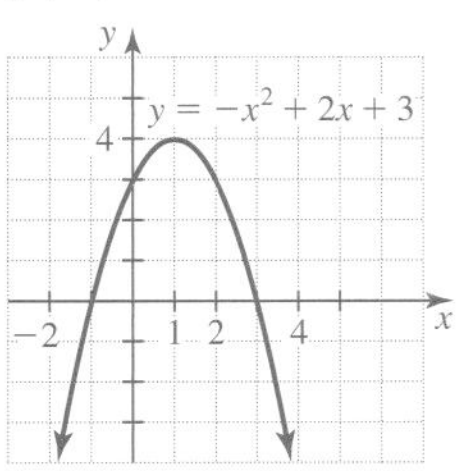

76. $y = -x^2 - 3x - 2$
Vertex $\left(-\frac{3}{2}, \frac{1}{4}\right)$, intercepts $(0, -2)$, $(-2, 0)$, $(-1, 0)$

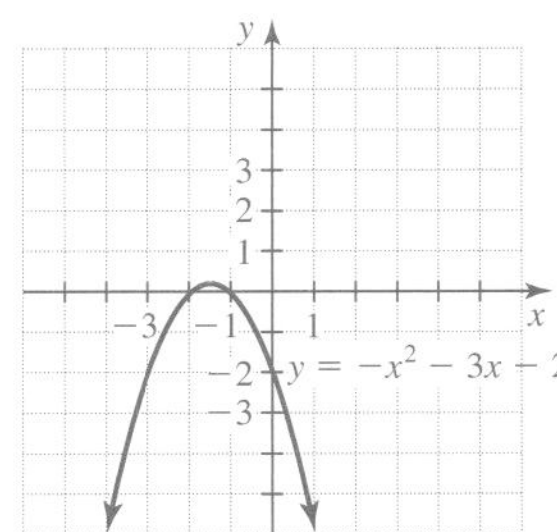

Solve each problem.

77. ***Minimizing cost.*** The unit cost in dollars for manufacturing n starters is given by $C = 0.004n^2 - 3.2n + 660$. What is the unit cost when 390 starters are manufactured? For what number of starters is the unit cost at a minimum?
\$20.40, 400

78. ***Maximizing profit.*** The total profit (in dollars) for sales of x rowing machines is given by $P = -0.2x^2 + 300x - 200$. What is the profit if 500 are sold? For what value of x will the profit be at a maximum?
\$99,800, 750

9.7 Introduction to Functions

Determine whether each set of ordered pairs is a function.

79. $\{(4, 3), (5, 3)\}$ Yes

80. $\{(0, 0), (0, 1), (0, 2)\}$ No

81. $\{(3, 4), (3, 5)\}$ No

82. $\{(1, 2), (2, 3), (3, 4)\}$ Yes

Determine whether each equation expresses y as a function of x.

83. $y = x^2 + 10$ Yes

84. $y = 2x - 7$ Yes

85. $x^2 + y^2 = 1$ No

86. $x^2 = y^2$ No

Determine the domain and range of each function.

87. $\{(1, 2), (2, 0), (3, 0)\}$ $\{1, 2, 3\}$, $\{0, 2\}$

88. $\{(2, 3), (4, 3), (6, 3)\}$ $\{2, 4, 6\}$, $\{3\}$

Find the domain and range of each quadratic function.

89. $y = x^2 + 4x + 1$ Domain R, range $\{y \mid y \geq -3\}$ or $[-3, \infty)$

90. $y = x^2 - 6x + 2$ Domain R, range $\{y \mid y \geq -7\}$ or $[-7, \infty)$

91. $y = -2x^2 - x + 4$ Domain R, range $\{y \mid y \leq 4.125\}$ or $(-\infty, 4.125]$

92. $y = -3x^2 + 2x + 7$ Domain R, range $\left\{y \mid y \leq \frac{22}{3}\right\}$ or $\left(-\infty, \frac{22}{3}\right]$

9.8 Combining Functions

Let $f(x) = \frac{1}{2}x + 1$, $g(x) = |5 - 2x|$, *and* $h(x) = \frac{1}{x - 1}$.
Find the following.

93. $f(1/2)$ 5/4

94. $f(-4/5)$ 3/5

95. $f(-8)$ -3

96. $g(5/2)$ 0

97. $g(-1/2)$ 6

98. $g(3)$ 1

99. $g(0)$ 5

100. $h(1/2)$ -2

101. $h(-1)$ $-1/2$

102. $h(5/4)$ 4

Let $f(x) = 3x + 5$, $g(x) = x^2 - 2x$, *and* $h(x) = \frac{x - 5}{3}$. *Find the following.*

103. $f(-3)$ -4

104. $h(-4)$ -3

105. $(h \circ f)(\sqrt{2})$ $\sqrt{2}$

106. $(f \circ h)(319)$ 319

107. $(g \circ f)(2)$ 99

108. $(g \circ f)(x)$ $9x^2 + 24x + 15$

109. $(f + g)(3)$ 17

110. $(f - g)(x)$ $-x^2 + 5x + 5$

111. $(f \cdot g)(x)$ $3x^3 - x^2 - 10x$

112. $\left(\frac{f}{g}\right)(1)$ -8

113. $(f \circ f)(0)$ 20

114. $(f \circ f)(x)$ $9x + 20$

Let $f(x) = |x|$, $g(x) = x + 2$, and $h(x) = x^2$. Write each of the following functions as a composition of functions, using f, g, or h.

115. $F(x) = |x + 2|$ $F = f \circ g$

116. $G(x) = |x| + 2$ $G = g \circ f$

117. $H(x) = x^2 + 2$ $H = g \circ h$

118. $K(x) = x^2 + 4x + 4$ $K = h \circ g$

119. $I(x) = x + 4$ $I = g \circ g$

120. $J(x) = x^4 + 2$ $J = g \circ h \circ h$

Chapter 9 Test

Calculate the value of $b^2 - 4ac$ and state how many real solutions each equation has.

1. $9x^2 - 12x + 4 = 0$ 0, one

2. $-2x^2 + 3x - 5 = 0$ -31, none

3. $-2x^2 + 5x - 1 = 0$ 17, two

Solve by using the quadratic formula.

4. $5x^2 + 2x - 3 = 0$ $-1, \frac{3}{5}$

5. $2x^2 - 4x - 3 = 0$ $\frac{2 - \sqrt{10}}{2}, \frac{2 + \sqrt{10}}{2}$

Solve by completing the square.

6. $x^2 + 4x - 21 = 0$ $-7, 3$

7. $x^2 + 3x - 5 = 0$ $\frac{-3 - \sqrt{29}}{2}, \frac{-3 + \sqrt{29}}{2}$

Solve by any method.

8. $x(x + 1) = 20$ $-5, 4$

9. $x^2 - 28x + 75 = 0$ $3, 25$

10. $\frac{x - 1}{3} = \frac{x + 1}{2x}$ $-\frac{1}{2}, 3$

Perform the indicated operations. Write answers in the form $a + bi$.

11. $(2 - 3i) + (8 + 6i)$ $10 + 3i$

12. $(-2 - 5i) - (4 - 12i)$ $-6 + 7i$

13. $(-6i)^2$ -36

14. $(3 - 5i)(4 + 6i)$ $42 - 2i$

15. $(8 - 2i)(8 + 2i)$ 68

16. $(4 - 6i) \div 2$ $2 - 3i$

17. $\frac{-2 + \sqrt{-12}}{2}$ $-1 + i\sqrt{3}$

18. $\frac{6 - \sqrt{-18}}{-3}$ $-2 + i\sqrt{2}$

19. $\frac{5i}{4 + 3i}$ $\frac{3}{5} + \frac{4}{5}i$

Find the complex solutions to the quadratic equations.

20. $x^2 + 6x + 12 = 0$ $-3 - i\sqrt{3}, -3 + i\sqrt{3}$

21. $-5x^2 + 6x - 5 = 0$ $\frac{3}{5} - \frac{4}{5}i, \frac{3}{5} + \frac{4}{5}i$

Graph each quadratic function. State the domain and range.

22. $y = 16 - x^2$

Domain R, range $\{y \mid y \le 16\}$ or $(-\infty, 16]$

23. $y = x^2 - 3x$

Domain R, range $\left\{y \mid y \ge -\frac{9}{4}\right\}$ or $\left[-\frac{9}{4}, \infty\right)$

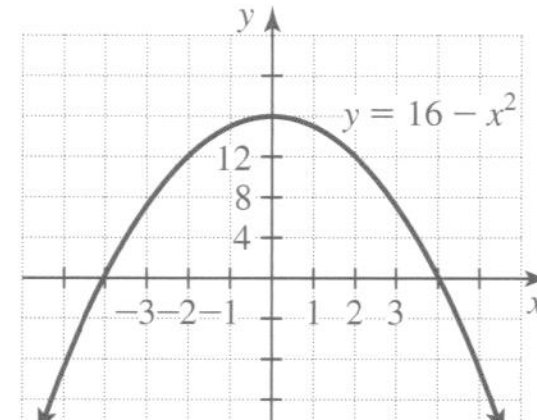

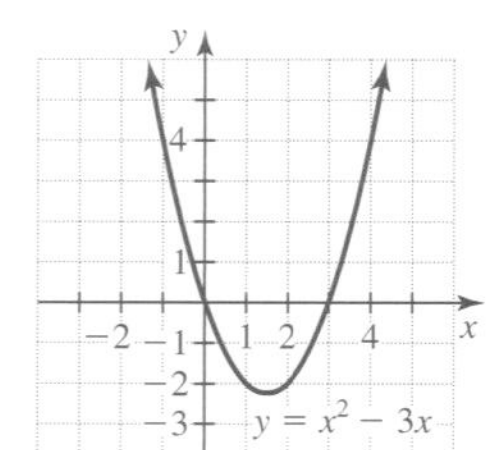

Let $f(x) = -2x + 5$ *and* $g(x) = x^2 + 4$. *Find the following.*

24. $f(-3)$
11

25. $(g \circ f)(-3)$
125

26. $(g + f)(x)$
$x^2 - 2x + 9$

27. $(f \cdot g)(1)$
15

28. $(f/g)(2)$
$\frac{1}{8}$

29. $(f \circ g)(x)$
$-2x^2 - 3$

30. $(g \circ f)(x)$
$4x^2 - 20x + 29$

Let $f(x) = x - 7$ *and* $g(x) = x^2$. *Write each of the following functions as a composition of functions using f and g.*

31. $H(x) = x^2 - 7$
$H = f \circ g$

32. $W(x) = x^2 - 14x + 49$
$W = g \circ f$

Solve each problem.

33. Find the x-intercepts for the parabola $y = x^2 - 6x + 5$.
(1, 0), (5, 0)

34. The height in feet for a ball thrown vertically upward at 48 feet per second is given by $s = -16t^2 + 48t$, where t is the time in seconds after the ball is tossed. What is the maximum height that the ball will reach?
36 feet

35. Find two positive numbers that have a sum of 10 and a product of 23. Give exact answers.
$5 - \sqrt{2}$ and $5 + \sqrt{2}$

*Making***Connections** | A Review of Chapters 1–9

Solve each equation.

1. $2x - 1 = 0$
$\frac{1}{2}$

2. $2(x - 1) = 0$
1

3. $2x^2 - 1 = 0$
$-\frac{\sqrt{2}}{2}, \frac{\sqrt{2}}{2}$

4. $(2x - 1)^2 = 8$
$\frac{1 - 2\sqrt{2}}{2}, \frac{1 + 2\sqrt{2}}{2}$

5. $2x^2 - 4x - 1 = 0$
$\frac{2 - \sqrt{6}}{2}, \frac{2 + \sqrt{6}}{2}$

6. $2x^2 - 4x = 0$
$0, 2$

7. $2x^2 + x = 1$
$-1, \frac{1}{2}$

8. $x - 2 = \sqrt{2x - 1}$
5

9. $\frac{1}{x} = \frac{x}{2x - 15}$
$1 - i\sqrt{14}, 1 + i\sqrt{14}$

10. $\frac{1}{x} - \frac{1}{x - 1} = -\frac{1}{2}$
$-1, 2$

Solve each equation for y.

11. $5x - 4y = 8$
$y = \frac{5}{4}x - 2$

12. $3x - y = 9$
$y = 3x - 9$

13. $\frac{y - 4}{x + 2} = \frac{2}{3}$
$y = \frac{2}{3}x + \frac{16}{3}$

14. $ay + b = 0$
$y = -\frac{b}{a}$

15. $ay^2 + by + c = 0$
$y = \frac{-b \pm \sqrt{b^2 - 4ac}}{2a}$

16. $y - 1 = -\frac{2}{3}(x - 9)$
$y = -\frac{2}{3}x + 7$

17. $\frac{2}{3}x + \frac{1}{2}y = \frac{1}{9}$
$y = -\frac{4}{3}x + \frac{2}{9}$

18. $x^2 + y^2 = a^2$
$y = \pm\sqrt{a^2 - x^2}$

Suppose that each side of a square has length s, the diagonal has length d, the area of the square is A, and its perimeter is P.

19. Write P in terms of s.
$P = 4s$

20. Write A in terms of s.
$A = s^2$

21. Write P in terms of d.
$P = 2d\sqrt{2}$

22. Write d in terms of A.
$d = \sqrt{2A}$

Solve each system of equations.

23. $3x - 2y = 12$
$2x + 5y = -11$
$(2, -3)$

24. $y = 3x + 1$
$3x - 0.6y = 3$
$(3, 10)$

Factor each polynomial completely.

25. $3y^3 - 363y$ $\quad 3y(y + 11)(y - 11)$

26. $2y^4 - 32$ $\quad 2(y + 2)(y - 2)(y^2 + 4)$

27. $yw + 2w - 4y - 8$ $\quad (y + 2)(w - 4)$

28. $y^3 - 27$ $\quad (y - 3)(y^2 + 3y + 9)$

29. $-3y^2 - 12y + 135$ $\quad -3(y - 5)(y + 9)$

30. $-24y^3 - 2y^2 + 12y$ $\quad -2y(3y - 2)(4y + 3)$

31. $4a^3 - 4a^2 + 12a$ $\quad 4a(a^2 - a + 3)$

32. $2a^3b^3 + 2ab^5$ $\quad 2ab^3(a^2 + b^2)$

Reduce each rational expression to lowest terms.

33. $\frac{18x^3}{42x^4}$
$\frac{3}{7x}$

34. $\frac{12x^8}{18x}$
$\frac{2x^7}{3}$

35. $\frac{2x + 8}{2x - 14}$
$\frac{x + 4}{x - 7}$

36. $\frac{x^2 - y^2}{x^2 - xy}$
$\frac{x + y}{x}$

37. $\frac{x^2 - x - 30}{x^2 - 5x - 6}$
$\frac{x + 5}{x + 1}$

38. $\frac{2x^2 + 9x + 4}{2x^2 - x - 1}$
$\frac{x + 4}{x - 1}$

Graph each function.

39. $y = x - 3$

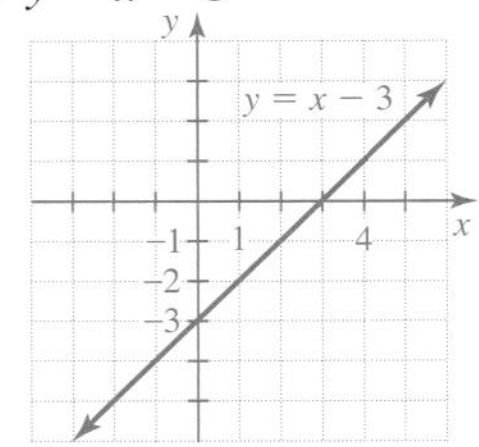

40. $y = 2 - x$

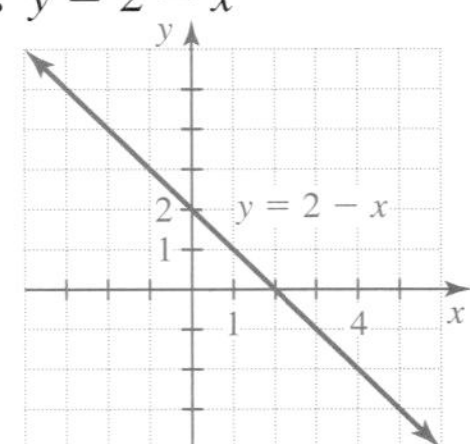

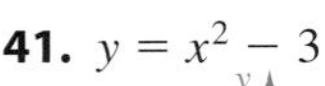
41. $y = x^2 - 3$

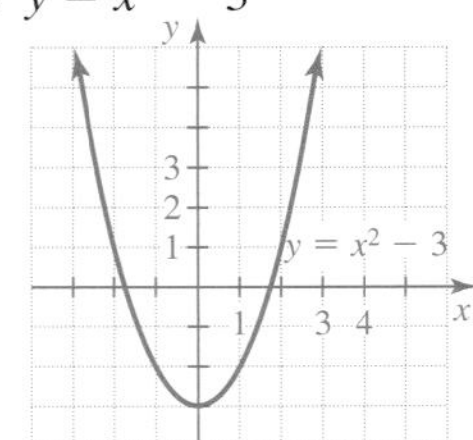

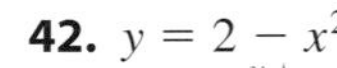
42. $y = 2 - x^2$

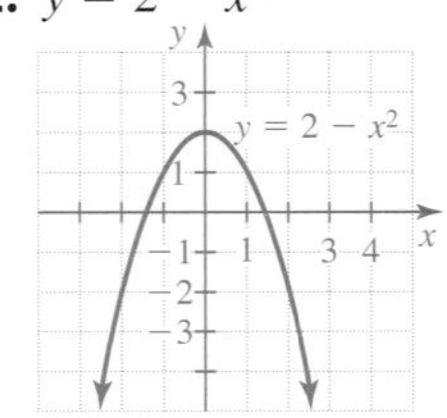

43. $y = \frac{2}{3}x - 4$

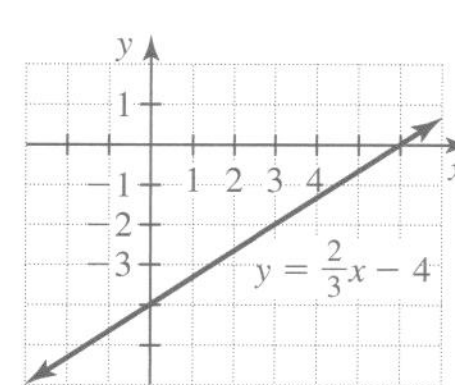

44. $y = -\frac{4}{3}x + 5$

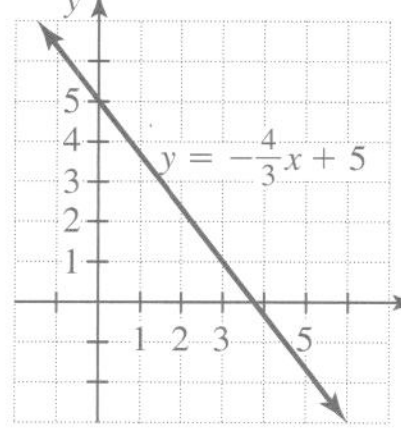

Solve the problem.

45. ***Maximizing revenue.*** For the last three years the Lakeland Air Show has raised the price of its tickets and has sold fewer and fewer tickets, as shown in the table.

Ticket price	\$10	\$12	\$16
Tickets sold	8000	7500	6500

a) Use this information to write the number of tickets sold s as a linear function of the ticket price p.
b) Has the revenue from ticket sales increased or decreased as the ticket price was raised?
c) Write the revenue R as a function of the ticket price p.
d) What ticket price would produce the maximum revenue?
a) $s = -250p + 10{,}500$ **b)** Increased
c) $R = -250p^2 + 10{,}500p$ **d)** \$21

Critical **Thinking** | For Individual or Group Work | Chapter 9

These exercises can be solved by a variety of techniques, which may or may not require algebra. So be creative and think critically. Explain all answers. Answers are in the Instructor's Edition of this text.

1. ***Adjacent squares.*** A small square of area a is adjacent to a larger square of area b as shown in the accompanying figure. Find the distance between the centers of the two squares.

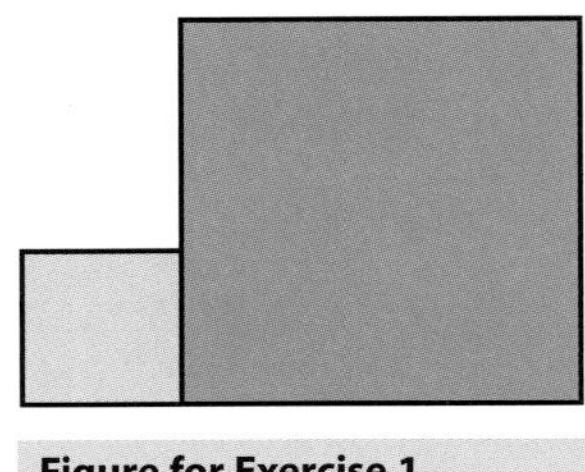

Figure for Exercise 1

2. ***Buried treasure.*** A pirate landed his boat on the northern most point of a circular island that had a diameter of 5 km. He walked 1 km due south and then walked due west until he reached the ocean. From there he walked 1 km due south and then walked due east until he reached the ocean. From there he walked 0.5 km due south and buried his treasure. As the crow flies, how far was it back to his boat?

3. ***Treadmill time.*** Angela starts running on a treadmill at 4 P.M. exactly. She quits running as soon as the minute hand and hour hand of the clock coincide. Find the amount of time she spent on the treadmill to the nearest tenth of a second.

4. ***Perfect square.*** Find the smallest positive integer n such that $882n$ is a perfect square.

5. ***Pipeline problem.*** One-sixth of a gas pipeline is under water, two-fifths of the pipeline is in wetlands, and 78 kilometers is on dry land. How long is the pipeline?

6. ***Joni's rope.*** Joni positions her rope on the ground in the shape of an equilateral triangle. She then positions her rope on the ground in the shape of a regular hexagon. For each figure she uses the entire length of her rope.

a) Which figure has the greater area?

b) What is the ratio of the area of the hexagon to the area of the triangle?

7. ***Intersecting circles.*** What is the maximum number of times that five circles with the same radius but different centers could intersect? Six circles? What is an expression that gives the maximum number of intersections with n circles? How could you actually position 100 circles to intersect the maximum number of times?

8. ***Replacing football.*** A college has a football field that is surrounded by a 400-meter track. The track consists of two 100-meter straight sections and two 100-meter semicircles (measured on the inside edge) as shown in the accompanying figure. There is talk of replacing the football field with a soccer field. Will a soccer field fit inside the track? A college soccer field must be between 115 and 120 yards long and between 70 and 80 yards wide.

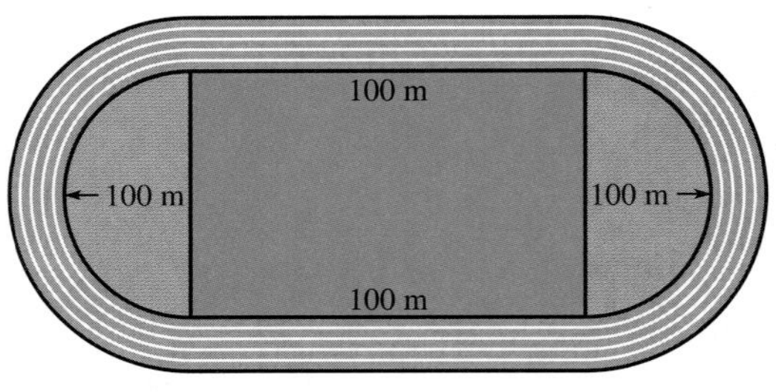

Figure for Exercise 8

1. $\sqrt{(a + b)/2}$ **2.** 3.5 km **3.** 21 minutes 49.1 seconds **4.** 2 **5.** 180 km **6. a)** Hexagon **b)** 3 to 2 **7.** 20, 30, $n(n - 1)$, One possibility is to draw a circle of radius 100 centered at each integer from 1 through 100 on a number line. **8.** No

Appendix A

Geometry Review Exercises

(Answers are at the end of the answer section in this text.)

1. Find the perimeter of a triangle whose sides are 3 in., 4 in., and 5 in. 12 in.
2. Find the area of a triangle whose base is 4 ft and height is 12 ft. 24 ft^2
3. If two angles of a triangle are 30° and 90°, then what is the third angle? 60°
4. If the area of a triangle is 36 ft^2 and the base is 12 ft, then what is the height? 6 ft
5. If the side opposite 30° in a 30-60-90 right triangle is 10 cm, then what is the length of the hypotenuse? 20 cm
6. Find the area of a trapezoid whose height is 12 cm and whose parallel sides are 4 cm and 20 cm. 144 cm^2
7. Find the area of the right triangle that has sides of 6 ft, 8 ft, and 10 ft. 24 ft^2
8. If a right triangle has sides of 5 ft, 12 ft, and 13 ft, then what is the length of the hypotenuse? 13 ft
9. If the hypotenuse of a right triangle is 50 cm and the length of one leg is 40 cm, then what is the length of the other leg? 30 cm
10. Is a triangle with sides of 5 ft, 10 ft, and 11 ft a right triangle? No
11. What is the area of a triangle with sides of 7 yd, 24 yd, and 25 yd? 84 yd^2
12. Find the perimeter of a parallelogram in which one side is 9 in. and another side is 6 in. 30 in.
13. Find the area of a parallelogram which has a base of 8 ft and a height of 4 ft. 32 ft^2
14. If one side of a rhombus is 5 km, then what is its perimeter. 20 km
15. Find the perimeter and area of a rectangle whose width is 18 in. and length is 2 ft. 7 ft, 3 ft^2
16. If the width of a rectangle is 8 yd and its perimeter is 60 yd, then what is its length? 22 yd
17. The radius of a circle is 4 ft. Find its area to the nearest tenth of a square foot. 50.3 ft^2
18. The diameter of a circle is 12 ft. Find its circumference to the nearest tenth of a foot. 37.7 ft
19. A right circular cone has radius 4 cm and height 9 cm. Find its volume to the nearest hundredth of a cubic centimeter. 150.80 cm^3
20. A right circular cone has a radius 12 ft and a height of 20 ft. Find its lateral surface area to the nearest hundredth of a square foot. 879.29 ft^2
21. A shoe box has a length of 12 in., a width of 6 in., and a height of 4 in. Find its volume and surface area. 288 $in.^3$, 288 $in.^2$
22. The volume of a rectangular solid is 120 cm^3. If the area of its bottom is 30 cm^2, then what is its height? 4 cm
23. What is the area and perimeter of a square in which one of the sides is 10 mi long? 100 mi^2, 40 mi
24. Find the perimeter of a square whose area is 25 km^2. 20 km
25. Find the area of a square whose perimeter is 26 cm. 42.25 cm^2
26. A sphere has a radius of 2 ft. Find its volume to the nearest thousandth of a cubic foot and its surface area to the nearest thousandth of a square foot. 33.510 ft^3, 50.265 ft^2
27. A can of soup (right circular cylinder) has a radius of 2 in. and a height of 6 in. Find its volume to the nearest tenth of a cubic inch and total surface area to the nearest tenth of a square inch. 75.4 $in.^3$, 100.5 $in.^2$
28. If one of two complementary angles is 34°, then what is the other angle? 56°
29. If the perimeter of an isosceles triangle is 29 cm and one of the equal sides is 12 cm, then what is the length of the shortest side of the triangle? 5 cm
30. A right triangle with sides of 6 in., 8 in., and 10 in. is similar to another right triangle that has a hypotenuse of 25 in. What are the lengths of the other two sides in the second triangle? 15 in. and 20 in.
31. If one of two supplementary angles is 31°, then what is the other angle? 149°
32. Find the perimeter of an equilateral triangle in which one of the sides is 4 km. 12 km
33. Find the length of a side of an equilateral triangle that has a perimeter of 30 yd. 10 yd

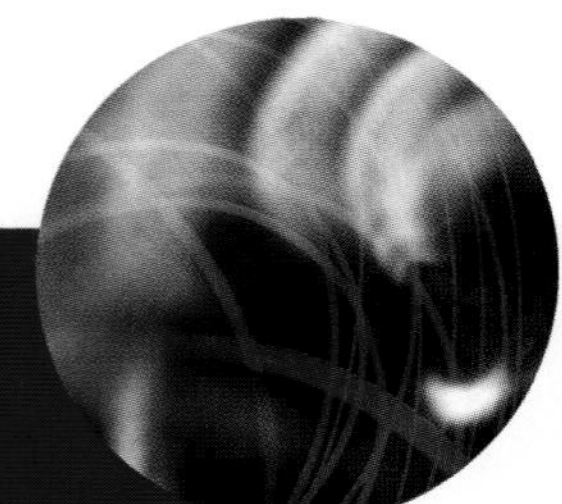

Appendix B

Sets

In This Section

Every subject has its own terminology, and **algebra** is no different. In this section, we will learn the basic terms and facts about sets.

⟨1⟩ Set Notation

A **set** is a collection of objects. At home you may have a set of dishes and a set of steak knives. In algebra we generally discuss sets of numbers. For example, we refer to the numbers 1, 2, 3, 4, 5, and so on as the set of **counting numbers** or **natural numbers.** Of course, these are the numbers that we use for counting.

The objects or numbers in a set are called the **elements** or **members** of the set. To describe sets with a convenient notation, we use braces, { }, and name the sets with capital letters. For example,

$$A = \{1, 2, 3\}$$

means that set A is the set whose members are the natural numbers 1, 2, and 3. The letter N is used to represent the entire set of natural numbers.

A set that has a fixed number of elements such as {1, 2, 3} is a **finite** set, whereas a set without a fixed number of elements such as the natural numbers is an **infinite** set. When listing the elements of a set, we use a series of three dots to indicate a continuing pattern. For example, the set of natural numbers is written as

$$N = \{1, 2, 3, \ldots\}.$$

The set of natural numbers *between* 4 and 40 can be written

$$\{5, 6, 7, 8, \ldots, 39\}.$$

Note that since the members of this set are *between* 4 and 40, it does not include 4 or 40.

Set-builder notation is another method of describing sets. In this notation we use a variable to represent the numbers in the set. A **variable** is a letter that is used to stand for some numbers. The set is then built from the variable and a description of the numbers that the variable represents. For example, the set

$$B = \{1, 2, 3, \ldots, 49\}$$

is written in set-builder notation as

$$B = \{x \mid x \text{ is a natural number less than } 50\}.$$

↑ ↑ ↑
The set of numbers such that — condition for membership

This notation is read as "B is the set of numbers x such that x is a natural number less than 50." Notice that the number 50 is not a member of set B.

The symbol $\in$ is used to indicate that a specific number is a member of a set, and $\notin$ indicates that a specific number is not a member of a set. For example, the statement $1 \in B$ is read as "1 is a member of B," "1 belongs to B," "1 is in B," or "1 is an element of B." The statement $0 \notin B$ is read as "0 is not a member of B," "0 does not belong to B," "0 is not in B," or "0 is not an element of B."

Two sets are **equal** if they contain exactly the same members. Otherwise, they are said to be not equal. To indicate equal sets, we use the symbol $=$. For sets that are not equal we use the symbol $\neq$. The elements in two equal sets do not need to be written in the same order. For example, $\{3, 4, 7\} = \{3, 4, 7\}$ and $\{2, 4, 1\} = \{1, 2, 4\}$, but $\{3, 5, 6\} \neq \{3, 5, 7\}$.

EXAMPLE 1

Set notation

Let $A = \{1, 2, 3, 5\}$ and $B = \{x \mid x \text{ is an even natural number less than } 10\}$. Determine whether each statement is true or false.

a) $3 \in A$ **b)** $5 \in B$ **c)** $4 \notin A$ **d)** $A = N$
e) $A = \{x \mid x \text{ is a natural number less than } 6\}$ **f)** $B = \{2, 4, 6, 8\}$

Solution

a) True, because 3 is a member of set A.
b) False, because 5 is not an even natural number.
c) True, because 4 is not a member of set A.
d) False, because A does not contain all of the natural numbers.
e) False, because 4 is a natural number less than 6, and $4 \notin A$.
f) True, because the even counting numbers less than 10 are 2, 4, 6, and 8.

‹2› Union and Intersection of Sets

Any two sets A and B can be combined to form a new set called their union that consists of all elements of A together with all elements of B.

Union of Sets

If A and B are sets, the **union** of A and B, denoted $A \cup B$, is the set of all elements that are either in A, in B, or in both. In symbols,

$$A \cup B = \{x \mid x \in A \text{ or } x \in B\}.$$

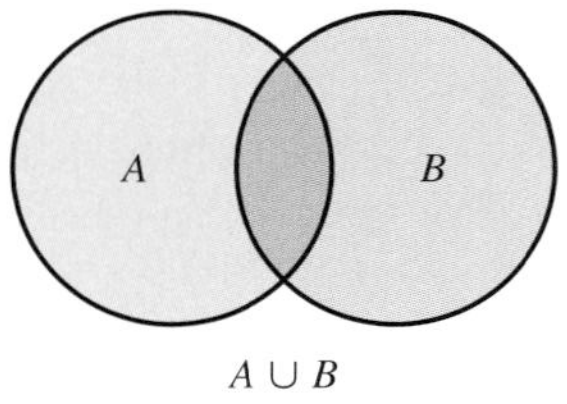

A B

$A \cup B$

Figure B.1

In mathematics the word "or" is always used in an inclusive manner (allowing the possibility of both alternatives). The diagram in Fig. B.1 can be used to illustrate $A \cup B$. Any point that lies within circle A, circle B, or both is in $A \cup B$. Diagrams (like Fig. B.1) that are used to illustrate sets are called **Venn diagrams.**

EXAMPLE 2

Union of sets

Let $A = \{0, 2, 3\}$, $B = \{2, 3, 7\}$, and $C = \{7, 8\}$. List the elements in each of these sets.

a) $A \cup B$ **b)** $A \cup C$

Solution

a) $A \cup B$ is the set of numbers that are in A, in B, or in both A and B.

$$A \cup B = \{0, 2, 3, 7\}$$

b) $A \cup C = \{0, 2, 3, 7, 8\}$

‹ Helpful Hint ›

To remember what "union" means think of a labor union, which is a group formed by joining together many individuals.

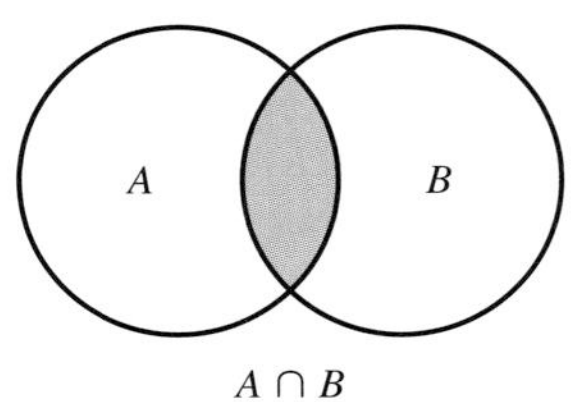

$A \cap B$

Figure B.2

‹ Helpful Hint ›

To remember the meaning of "intersection," think of the intersection of two roads. At the intersection you are on both roads.

Another way to form a new set from two known sets is by considering only those elements that the two sets have in common. The diagram shown in Fig. B.2 illustrates the intersection of two sets A and B.

Intersection of Sets

If A and B are sets, the **intersection** of A and B, denoted $A \cap B$, is the set of all elements that are in both A and B. In symbols,

$$A \cap B = \{x \mid x \in A \text{ and } x \in B\}.$$

It is possible for two sets to have no elements in common. A set with no members is called the **empty set** and is denoted by the symbol $\emptyset$. Note that $A \cup \emptyset = A$ and $A \cap \emptyset = \emptyset$ for any set A.

CAUTION The set $\{0\}$ is not the empty set. The set $\{0\}$ has one member, the number 0. Do not use the number 0 to represent the empty set.

EXAMPLE 3

Intersection of sets

Let $A = \{0, 2, 3\}$, $B = \{2, 3, 7\}$, and $C = \{7, 8\}$. List the elements in each of these sets.

a) $A \cap B$ **b)** $B \cap C$ **c)** $A \cap C$

Solution

a) $A \cap B$ is the set of all numbers that are in both A and B. So $A \cap B = \{2, 3\}$.

b) $B \cap C = \{7\}$ **c)** $A \cap C = \emptyset$

EXAMPLE 4

Membership and equality

Let $A = \{1, 2, 3, 5\}$, $B = \{2, 3, 7, 8\}$, and $C = \{6, 7, 8, 9\}$. Place one of the symbols $=$, $\neq$, $\in$, or $\notin$ in the blank to make each statement correct.

a) 5 _____ $A \cup B$ **b)** 5 _____ $A \cap B$

c) $A \cup B$ _____ $\{1, 2, 3, 5, 7, 8\}$ **d)** $A \cap B$ _____ $\{2\}$

Solution

a) $5 \in A \cup B$ because 5 is a member of A.

b) $5 \notin A \cap B$ because 5 must belong to *both* A and B to be a member of $A \cap B$.

c) $A \cup B = \{1, 2, 3, 5, 7, 8\}$ because the elements of A together with those of B are listed. Note that 2 and 3 are members of both sets but are listed only once.

d) $A \cap B \neq \{2\}$ because $A \cap B = \{2, 3\}$.

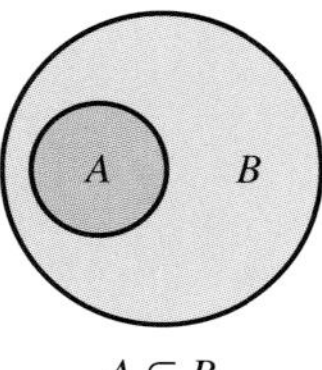

$A \subseteq B$

Figure B.3

‹3› Subsets

If every member of set A is also a member of set B, then we write $A \subseteq B$ and say that A is a **subset** of B. See Fig. B.3. For example,

$$\{2, 3\} \subseteq \{2, 3, 4\}$$

because $2 \in \{2, 3, 4\}$ and $3 \in \{2, 3, 4\}$. Note that the symbol for membership ($\in$) is used between a single element and a set, whereas the symbol for subset ($\subseteq$) is used between two sets. If A is not a subset of B, we write $A \not\subseteq B$.

CAUTION To claim that $A \not\subseteq B$, there *must* be an element of A that does *not* belong to B. For example,

$$\{1, 2\} \not\subseteq \{2, 3, 4\}$$

because 1 is a member of the first set but not of the second.

Is the empty set $\varnothing$ a subset of $\{2, 3, 4\}$? If we say that $\varnothing$ is *not* a subset of $\{2, 3, 4\}$, then there must be an element of $\varnothing$ that does not belong to $\{2, 3, 4\}$. But that cannot happen because $\varnothing$ is empty. So $\varnothing$ is a subset of $\{2, 3, 4\}$. In fact, by the same reasoning, *the empty set is a subset of every set.*

EXAMPLE 5

Subsets

Determine whether each statement is true or false.

a) $\{1, 2, 3\}$ is a subset of the set of natural numbers.
b) The set of natural numbers is not a subset of $\{1, 2, 3\}$.
c) $\{1, 2, 3\} \not\subseteq \{2, 4, 6, 8\}$
d) $\{2, 6\} \subseteq \{1, 2, 3, 4, 5\}$
e) $\varnothing \subseteq \{2, 4, 6\}$

‹ Helpful Hint ›

The symbols $\subseteq$ and $\subset$ are often used interchangeably. The symbol $\subseteq$ combines the subset symbol $\subset$ and the equal symbol $=$. We use it when sets are equal, $\{1, 2\} \subseteq \{1, 2\}$, and when they are not, $\{1\} \subseteq \{1, 2\}$. When sets are not equal, we could simply use $\subset$, as in $\{1\} \subset \{1, 2\}$.

Solution

a) True, because 1, 2, and 3 are natural numbers.
b) True, because 5, for example, is a natural number and $5 \notin \{1, 2, 3\}$.
c) True, because 1 is in the first set but not in the second.
d) False, because 6 is in the first set but not in the second.
e) True, because we cannot find anything in $\varnothing$ that fails to be in $\{2, 4, 6\}$.

‹4› Combining Three or More Sets

We know how to find the union and intersection of two sets. For three or more sets we use parentheses to indicate which pair of sets to combine first. In Example 6, notice that different results are obtained from different placements of the parentheses.

EXAMPLE 6

Operations with three sets

Let $A = \{1, 2, 3, 4\}$, $B = \{2, 5, 6, 8\}$, and $C = \{4, 5, 7\}$. List the elements of each of these sets.

a) $(A \cup B) \cap C$ **b)** $A \cup (B \cap C)$

Solution

a) The parentheses indicate that the union of A and B is to be found first and then the result, $A \cup B$, is to be intersected with C.

$$A \cup B = \{1, 2, 3, 4, 5, 6, 8\}$$

Now examine $A \cup B$ and C to find the elements that belong to both sets:

$$A \cup B = \{1, 2, 3, 4, 5, 6, 8\}$$
$$C = \{4, 5, 7\}$$

The only numbers that are members of $A \cup B$ and C are 4 and 5. Thus

$$(A \cup B) \cap C = \{4, 5\}.$$

b) In $A \cup (B \cap C)$, first find $B \cap C$:

$$B \cap C = \{5\}$$

Now $A \cup (B \cap C)$ consist of all members of A together with 5 from $B \cap C$:

$$A \cup (B \cap C) = \{1, 2, 3, 4, 5\}$$

Exercises

Boost your grade at mathzone.com!
- Practice Problems
- NetTutor
- Self-Tests
- e-Professors
- Videos

Reading and Writing *After reading this section, write out the answers to these questions. Use complete sentences.*

1. What is a set? A set is a collection of objects.

2. What is the difference between a finite set and an infinite set?
A finite set has a fixed number of elements and an infinite set does not.

3. What is a Venn diagram used for?
A Venn diagram is used to illustrate relationships between sets.

4. What is the difference between the intersection and the union of two sets?
The intersection of two sets consists of elements that are in both sets, whereas the union of two sets consists of elements that are in one, in the other, or in both sets.

5. What does it mean to say that set A is a subset of set B?
Every member of set A is also a member of set B.

6. Which set is a subset of every set?
The empty set is a subset of every set.

‹1› Set Notation

Using the sets A, B, C, and N, determine whether each statement is true or false. Explain. See Example 1.

$A = \{1, 3, 5, 7, 9\}$ $B = \{2, 4, 6, 8\}$
$C = \{1, 2, 3, 4, 5\}$ $N = \{1, 2, 3, \ldots\}$

7. $6 \in A$ False
8. $8 \in A$ False
9. $A \neq B$ True
10. $A = \{1, 3, 5, 7, \ldots\}$ False
11. $3 \in C$ True
12. $4 \notin B$ False
13. $A = \{1, 3, 7, 9\}$ False
14. $B \neq C$ True
15. $0 \in N$ False
16. $2.5 \in N$ False
17. $C = N$ False
18. $N = A$ False

‹2› Union and Intersection of Sets

Using the sets A, B, C, and N, list the elements in each set. If the set is empty write ∅. See Examples 2 and 3.

$A = \{1, 3, 5, 7, 9\}$ $B = \{2, 4, 6, 8\}$
$C = \{1, 2, 3, 4, 5\}$ $N = \{1, 2, 3, \ldots\}$

19. $A \cap B$ $\varnothing$
20. $A \cup B$ $\{1, 2, 3, 4, 5, 6, 7, 8, 9\}$
21. $A \cap C$ $\{1, 3, 5\}$
22. $A \cup C$ $\{1, 2, 3, 4, 5, 7, 9\}$
23. $B \cup C$ $\{1, 2, 3, 4, 5, 6, 8\}$
24. $B \cap C$ $\{2, 4\}$
25. $A \cup \varnothing$ A
26. $B \cup \varnothing$ B
27. $A \cap \varnothing$ $\varnothing$
28. $B \cap \varnothing$ $\varnothing$
29. $A \cap N$ A
30. $A \cup N$ N

Use one of the symbols ∈, ∉, =, ≠, ∪, or ∩ in each blank to make a true statement. See Example 4.

$A = \{1, 3, 5, 7, 9\}$ $B = \{2, 4, 6, 8\}$
$C = \{1, 2, 3, 4, 5\}$ $N = \{1, 2, 3, \ldots\}$

31. $A \cap B$ __=__ $\varnothing$
32. $A \cap C$ __≠__ $\varnothing$

33. $A \underline{\ \cup\ } B = \{1, 2, 3, 4, 5, 6, 7, 8, 9\}$

34. $A \underline{\ \cap\ } B = \varnothing$

35. $B \underline{\ \cap\ } C = \{2, 4\}$

36. $B \underline{\ \cup\ } C = \{1, 2, 3, 4, 5, 6, 8\}$

37. $3 \underline{\ \notin\ } A \cap B$ **38.** $3 \underline{\ \in\ } A \cap C$

39. $4 \underline{\ \in\ } B \cap C$ **40.** $8 \underline{\ \in\ } B \cup C$

⟨3⟩ Subsets

Determine whether each statement is true or false. Explain your answer. See Example 5.

$A = \{1, 3, 5, 7, 9\}$ $B = \{2, 4, 6, 8\}$
$C = \{1, 2, 3, 4, 5\}$ $N = \{1, 2, 3, \ldots\}$

41. $A \subseteq N$ True **42.** $B \subseteq N$ True

43. $\{2, 3\} \subseteq C$ True **44.** $C \subseteq A$ False

45. $B \not\subseteq C$ True **46.** $C \not\subseteq A$ True

47. $\varnothing \subseteq B$ True **48.** $\varnothing \subseteq C$ True

49. $A \subseteq \varnothing$ False **50.** $B \subseteq \varnothing$ False

51. $A \cap B \subseteq C$ True **52.** $B \cap C \subseteq \{2, 4, 6, 8\}$ True

⟨4⟩ Combining Three or More Sets

Using the sets D, E, and F, list the elements in each set. If the set is empty write ∅. See Example 6.

$D = \{3, 5, 7\}$ $E = \{2, 4, 6, 8\}$ $F = \{1, 2, 3, 4, 5\}$

53. $D \cup E$
$\{2, 3, 4, 5, 6, 7, 8\}$

54. $D \cap E$
$\varnothing$

55. $D \cap F$
$\{3, 5\}$

56. $D \cup F$
$\{1, 2, 3, 4, 5, 7\}$

57. $E \cup F$
$\{1, 2, 3, 4, 5, 6, 8\}$

58. $E \cap F$
$\{2, 4\}$

59. $(D \cup E) \cap F$
$\{2, 3, 4, 5\}$

60. $(D \cup F) \cap E$
$\{2, 4\}$

61. $D \cup (E \cap F)$
$\{2, 3, 4, 5, 7\}$

62. $D \cup (F \cap E)$
$\{2, 3, 4, 5, 7\}$

63. $(D \cap F) \cup (E \cap F)$
$\{2, 3, 4, 5\}$

64. $(D \cap E) \cup (F \cap E)$
$\{2, 4\}$

65. $(D \cup E) \cap (D \cup F)$
$\{2, 3, 4, 5, 7\}$

66. $(D \cup F) \cap (D \cup E)$
$\{2, 3, 4, 5, 7\}$

Miscellaneous

Use one of the symbols ∈, ⊆, =, ∪, or ∩ in each blank to make a true statement.

$D = \{3, 5, 7\}$ $E = \{2, 4, 6, 8\}$ $F = \{1, 2, 3, 4, 5\}$

67. $D \underline{\ \subseteq\ } \{x \mid x \text{ is an odd natural number}\}$

68. $E \underline{\ =\ } \{x \mid x \text{ is an even natural number smaller than } 9\}$

69. $3 \underline{\ \in\ } D$ **70.** $\{3\} \underline{\ \subseteq\ } D$

71. $D \underline{\ \cap\ } E = \varnothing$ **72.** $D \cap E \underline{\ \subseteq\ } D$

73. $D \cap F \underline{\ \subseteq\ } F$ **74.** $3 \notin E \underline{\ \cap\ } F$

75. $E \not\subseteq E \underline{\ \cap\ } F$ **76.** $E \subseteq E \underline{\ \cup\ } F$

77. $D \underline{\ \cup\ } F = F \cup D$ **78.** $E \underline{\ \cap\ } F = F \cap E$

List the elements in each set.

79. $\{x \mid x \text{ is an even natural number less than } 20\}$
$\{2, 4, 6, \ldots, 18\}$

80. $\{x \mid x \text{ is a natural number greater than } 6\}$
$\{7, 8, 9, \ldots\}$

81. $\{x \mid x \text{ is an odd natural number greater than } 11\}$
$\{13, 15, 17, \ldots\}$

82. $\{x \mid x \text{ is an odd natural number less than } 14\}$
$\{1, 3, 5, \ldots, 13\}$

83. $\{x \mid x \text{ is an even natural number between 4 and } 79\}$
$\{6, 8, 10, \ldots, 78\}$

84. $\{x \mid x \text{ is an odd natural number between 12 and } 57\}$
$\{13, 15, 17, \ldots, 55\}$

Write each set using set-builder notation. Answers may vary.

85. $\{3, 4, 5, 6\}$
$\{x \mid x \text{ is a natural number between 2 and } 7\}$

86. $\{1, 3, 5, 7\}$
$\{x \mid x \text{ is an odd natural number less than } 8\}$

87. $\{5, 7, 9, 11, \ldots\}$
$\{x \mid x \text{ is an odd natural number greater than } 4\}$

88. $\{4, 5, 6, 7, \ldots\}$
$\{x \mid x \text{ is a natural number greater than } 3\}$

89. $\{6, 8, 10, 12, \ldots, 82\}$
$\{x \mid x \text{ is an even natural number between 5 and } 83\}$

90. $\{9, 11, 13, 15, \ldots, 51\}$
$\{x \mid x \text{ is an odd natural number between 8 and } 52\}$

Determine whether each statement is true or false.

$A = \{1, 2, 3, 4\}$ $B = \{3, 4, 5\}$ $C = \{3, 4\}$

91. $A = \{x \mid x \text{ is a counting number}\}$ False

92. The set B has an infinite number of elements. False

93. The set of counting numbers less than 50 million is an infinite set. False

94. $1 \in A \cap B$ False **95.** $3 \in A \cup B$ True

96. $A \cap B = C$ True **97.** $C \subseteq B$ True

98. $A \subseteq B$ False **99.** $\varnothing \subseteq C$ True

100. $A \not\subseteq C$ True

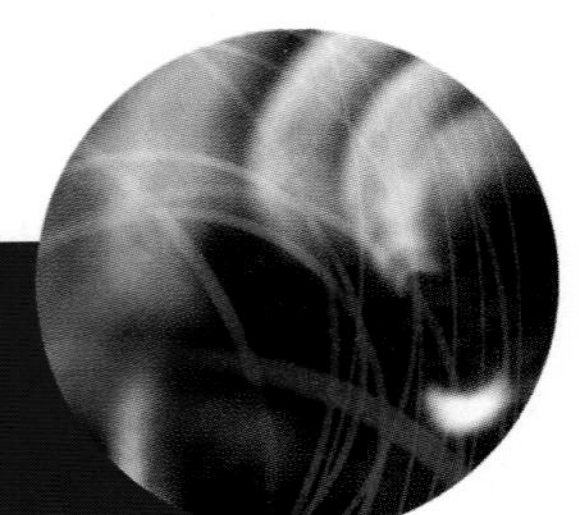

Appendix C

Final Exam Review

Note that this review does not cover every topic in this text. Use this review as a starting point for studying for your final exam. Check your tests, quizzes, and homework assignments to make sure that you have reviewed every topic covered in your course. The answers for all of these exercises can be found at the end of the answer section in this text.

Chapter 1

Evaluate each expression.

1. $\frac{3}{4} \cdot \frac{7}{9}$ $\frac{7}{12}$

2. $\frac{1}{4} + \frac{5}{6}$ $\frac{13}{12}$

3. $\frac{8}{9} \div 4$ $\frac{2}{9}$

4. $-4^2 - 3^3$ -43

5. $|3 - 2^2| - |7 - 19|$ -11

6. $\frac{-3 - 5}{-2 - (-1)}$ 8

Name the property that justifies each equation.

7. $3(x + 4) = 3x + 12$ Distributive property

8. $x \cdot 7 = 7x$ Commutative property of multiplication

9. $4 + (9 + y) = (4 + 9) + y$
Associative property of addition

10. $0 + 3 = 3$ Additive identity

Simplify each expression.

11. $5x - (3 - 8x)$ $13x - 3$

12. $x + 3 - 0.2(5x - 30)$ 9

13. $(-3x)(-5x)$ $15x^2$

14. $\frac{3x + 12}{-3}$ $-x - 4$

Chapter 2

Solve each equation and check your answer.

15. $11x - 2 = 3$ $\left\{\frac{5}{11}\right\}$

16. $4x - 5 = 12x + 11$ $\{-2\}$

17. $3(x - 6) = 3x - 6$ No solution, $\emptyset$

18. $x - 0.1x = 0.9x$ All real numbers

Solve each equation for y.

19. $5x - 3y = 9$ $y = \frac{5}{3}x - 3$

20. $ay + b = 0$ $y = -\frac{b}{a}$

21. $a = t - by$ $y = \frac{t - a}{b}$

22. $\frac{a}{2} + \frac{y}{3} = \frac{3a}{4}$ $y = \frac{3}{4}a$

Solve each problem. Show all details.

23. The sum of three consecutive integers is 102. What are the integers?
33, 34, 35

24. The perimeter of a rectangular painting is 100 inches. If the width is 4 inches less than the length, then what is the width?
23 in.

25. The area of a triangular piece of property is 44,000 square feet. If the base of the triangle is 400 feet, then what is the height?
220 ft

26. Ivan has 400 pounds of mixed nuts that contain no peanuts. How many pounds of peanuts should he put into the mixed nuts so that 20% of the mixture is peanuts?
100 pounds

Solve each inequality. Express the solution set in interval notation.

27. $3x - 4 \le 11$ $(-\infty, 5]$

28. $5 - 7w > 26$ $(-\infty, -3)$

29. $-1 < 2a - 9 \le 7$ $(4, 8]$

30. $5 < 6 - x < 6$ $(0, 1)$

Chapter 3

Graph each equation in the coordinate plane and identify all intercepts.

31. $y = \frac{2}{3}x - 2$ (0, −2), (3, 0)

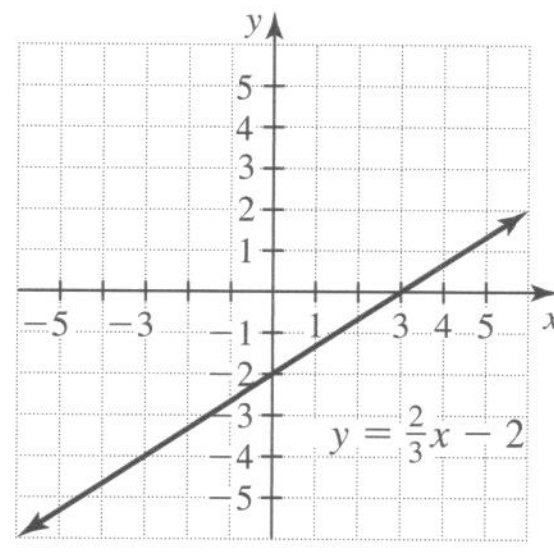

32. $3x - 5y = 150$ (0, −30), (50, 0)

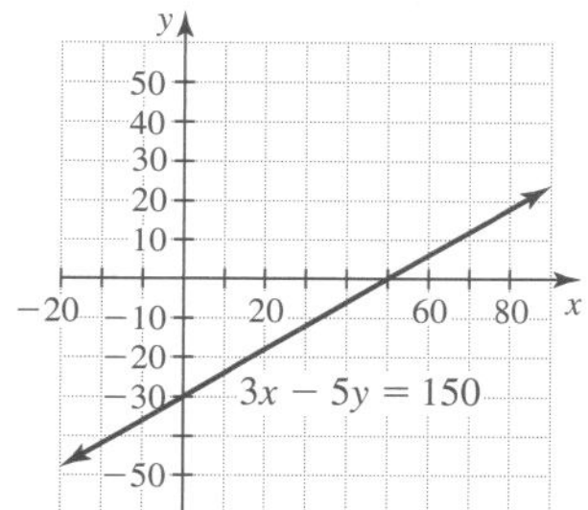

33. $y = 2$ (0, 2)

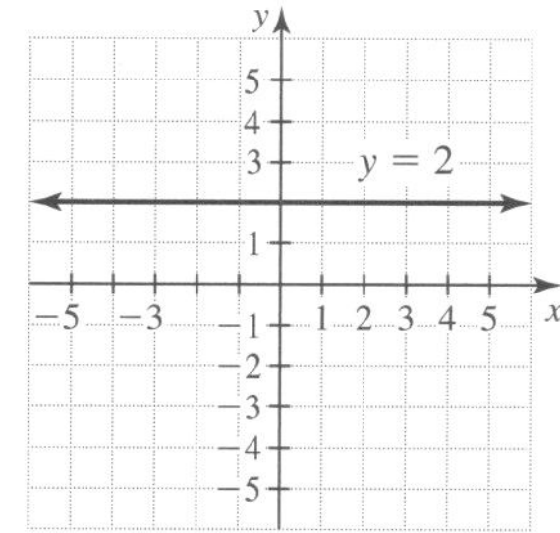

34. $x = 2$ (2, 0)

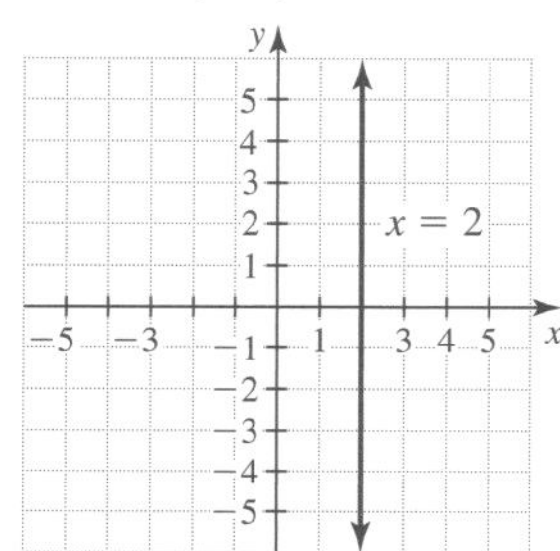

Find the slope of each line.

35. The line passing through the points (1, 2) and (3, 6) 2

36. The line $y = \frac{1}{2}x - 4$ $\frac{1}{2}$

37. The line parallel to $2x + 3y = 9$ $-\frac{2}{3}$

38. The line perpendicular to $y = -3x + 5$ $\frac{1}{3}$

Find the equation of each line in slope-intercept form when possible.

39. The line passing through the points (0, 3) and (2, 11)
$y = 4x + 3$

40. The line passing through the points (−2, 4) and (1, −2)
$y = -2x$

41. The line through (3, 5) that is parallel to $x = 4$ $x = 3$

42. The line through (0, 8) that is perpendicular to $y = \frac{1}{2}x$
$y = -2x + 8$

Chapter 4

Solve the system by graphing.

43. $x + y = 4$ (1, 3)
$y = 2x + 1$

44. $3x - 2y = 1$ (1, 1)
$4x + y = 5$

45. $x - y = 3$ (1, −2)
$y = -2$

Solve each system by substitution.

46. $y = 3x - 1$ (2, 5)
$6x + 5y = 37$

47. $x + y = 2$ (−4, 6)
$-5x - y = 14$

48. $3x - 11y = 27$ (−2, −3)
$6x + y = -15$

Solve each system by the addition method.

49. $3x + 5y = 33$ (1, 6)
$6x - 5y = -24$

50. $x - 3y = -1$ (−2, −1/3)
$5x + 6y = -12$

51. $4x - 3y = 14$ (1/2, −4)
$6x - 2y = 11$

Determine whether each system is independent, inconsistent, or dependent.

52. $y = 2x + 2$ Inconsistent
$y = 2x - 1$

53. $2x - 3y = 1$ Dependent
$8x - 12y = 4$

54. $y = 6x$ Independent
$y = -4x$

For each problem, write a system of equations in two variables. Use the method of your choice to solve each system.

55. Bob and Carl studied a total of 72 hours for the final. If Bob studied only one-third as many hours as Carl, then how many hours did each of them study?

Bob 18 hours and Carl 54 hours

56. Hamburger Haven sold 15 singles and 22 doubles to one customer for a total of \$51.75. The next customer bought 17 singles and 11 doubles for a total of \$37.75. The third customer purchased only 1 single and 2 doubles. How much did the third customer spend?

\$4.25

Graph the solution set to each inequality in the coordinate plane.

57. $3x - 4y > 12$

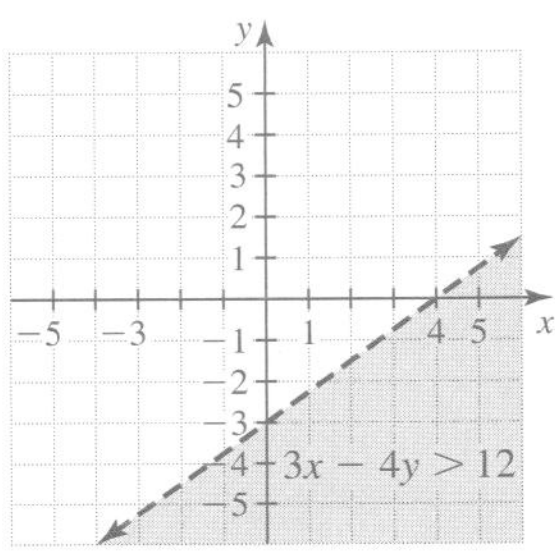

58. $y \leq 3x + 2$

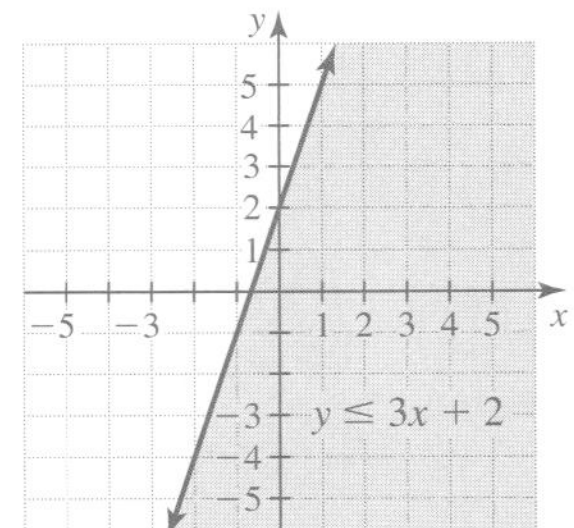

59. $x > -2$

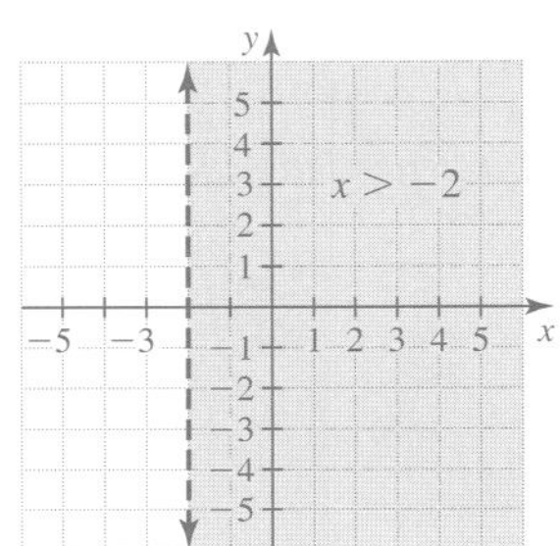

60. $y \leq 4$

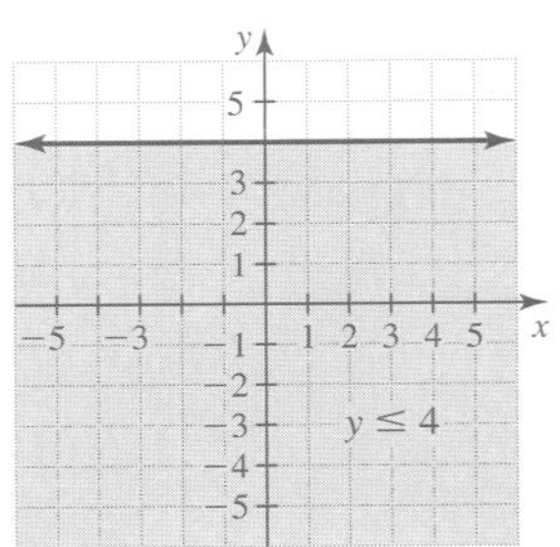

Chapter 5

Perform the indicated operations.

61. $(x^2 - 3x + 2) - (3x^2 + 9x - 4)$

$-2x^2 - 12x + 6$

62. $-3x^2(-2x^2 - 3)$

$6x^4 + 9x^2$

63. $(x + 7)(x - 9)$

$x^2 - 2x - 63$

64. $(x + 2)(x^2 - 2x + 4)$

$x^3 + 8$

65. $(4w^2 - 3)^2$

$16w^4 - 24w^2 + 9$

66. $(-8m^7) \div (2m^2)$

$-4m^5$

67. $(-9y^3 - 6y^2 + 3y) \div (3y)$

$-3y^2 - 2y + 1$

68. $(x^3 - 2x^2 - x - 6) \div (x - 3)$

$x^2 + x + 2$

Use the rules of exponents to simplify each expression. Write the answers without negative exponents.

69. $-8x^4 \cdot 4x^3$ $-32x^7$

70. $3x(5x^2)^3$ $375x^7$

71. $\dfrac{-6x^2y^3}{-2x^{-3}y^4}$ $\dfrac{3x^5}{y}$

72. $\left(\dfrac{2a^2}{a^{-3}}\right)^3$ $8a^{15}$

Perform each operation without a calculator. Write the answer in scientific notation.

73. $400{,}000 \cdot 600$ 2.4×10^8

74. $(9 \times 10^3)(2 \times 10^6)$ 1.8×10^{10}

75. $(2 \times 10^{-3})^4$ 1.6×10^{-11}

76. $\dfrac{2 \times 10^{-9}}{2000}$ 1×10^{-12}

Chapter 6

Factor each polynomial completely.

77. $24x^2y^3 + 18xy^5$ $6xy^3(4x + 3y^2)$

78. $x^2 + 2x + ax + 2a$ $(x + a)(x + 2)$

79. $4m^2 - 49$ $(2m - 7)(2m + 7)$

80. $x^2 - 3x - 54$ $(x - 9)(x + 6)$

81. $6t^2 - 11t - 10$ $(2t - 5)(3t + 2)$

82. $4w^2 - 36w + 81$ $(2w - 9)^2$

83. $2a^3 - 6a^2 - 108a$ $2a(a - 9)(a + 6)$

84. $w^4 - 16$ $(w^2 + 4)(w + 2)(w - 2)$

Solve each equation.

85. $x^2 = x$ $\{0, 1\}$

86. $2x^3 - 8x = 0$ $\{-2, 0, 2\}$

87. $a^2 + a - 6 = 0$ $\{-3, 2\}$

88. $(b - 2)(b + 3) = 24$ $\{-6, 5\}$

Write a complete solution to each problem.

89. The sum of two numbers is 10 and their product is 21. Find the numbers. 3 and 7

90. The length of a new television screen is 14 inches larger than the width and the diagonal is 26 inches. What are the length and width? Length 24 in., width 10 in.

Chapter 7

Solve each formula for y.

91. $\frac{3}{y} = \frac{5}{x}$ $y = \frac{3}{5}x$

92. $a = \frac{1}{2}y(w - c)$ $y = \frac{2a}{w - c}$

93. $\frac{y - 3}{x + 5} = -3$ $y = -3x - 12$

94. $\frac{3}{y} + \frac{1}{2} = \frac{1}{t}$ $y = \frac{6t}{2 - t}$

Perform the indicated operations. Write answers in lowest terms.

95. $\frac{5}{2} - \frac{3}{5}$ $\frac{19}{10}$

96. $\frac{1}{x} + \frac{1}{2x}$ $\frac{3}{2x}$

97. $\frac{5}{a - 7} - \frac{2}{7 - a}$ $\frac{7}{a - 7}$

98. $\frac{5}{x^2 - 1} - \frac{3}{x^2 + 2x + 1}$ $\frac{2x + 8}{(x - 1)(x + 1)^2}$

99. $\frac{12}{x^2 - 9} + \frac{2}{x + 3}$ $\frac{2}{x - 3}$

100. $\frac{a^2 - 25}{(a - 5)^2} \cdot \frac{2a - 10}{4a + 20}$ $\frac{1}{2}$

101. $\frac{a - 9}{4} \div \frac{81 - a^2}{18}$ $\frac{-9}{2(9 + a)}$

102. $\frac{3x^4y^3}{8x^3} \cdot \frac{10x^2y^8}{24xy^2}$ $\frac{5x^2y^9}{32}$

Simplify each complex fraction.

103. $\dfrac{\frac{1}{2} + \frac{2}{3}}{\frac{5}{6} - \frac{4}{9}}$ 3

104. $\dfrac{\frac{2}{x} - \frac{1}{x - 3}}{\frac{3}{x - 3} - \frac{7}{x}}$ $\frac{x - 6}{-4x + 21}$

Solve each equation.

105. $\frac{5}{x} = \frac{2}{3}$ $\left\{\frac{15}{2}\right\}$

106. $\frac{1}{w - 3} = \frac{2}{w + 5}$ $\{11\}$

107. $\frac{x}{x - 1} - \frac{4}{x} = \frac{1}{6}$ $\left\{\frac{8}{5}, 3\right\}$

108. $\frac{x}{3} - \frac{2}{3x} = \frac{1}{3}$ $\{2, -1\}$

Chapter 8

Simplify each expression.

109. $\sqrt{8}$ $2\sqrt{2}$

110. $\sqrt{225}$ 15

111. $\sqrt[3]{8}$ 2

112. $\sqrt{\frac{3}{8}}$ $\frac{\sqrt{6}}{4}$

113. $(\sqrt{3})^2$ 3

114. $\sqrt{18} + \sqrt{2}$ $4\sqrt{2}$

115. $(1 + \sqrt{3})^2$ $4 + 2\sqrt{3}$

116. $(\sqrt{6} - \sqrt{5})(\sqrt{6} + \sqrt{5})$ 1

117. $\sqrt{20} \div \sqrt{2}$ $\sqrt{10}$

118. $\sqrt{36} \div \sqrt{3}$ $2\sqrt{3}$

119. $\frac{2 + \sqrt{8}}{2}$ $1 + \sqrt{2}$

120. $\sqrt{2}(\sqrt{8} - \sqrt{3})$ $4 - \sqrt{6}$

121. $(2\sqrt{5} - 3)(\sqrt{5} + 7)$ $-11 + 11\sqrt{5}$

122. $\sqrt{\dfrac{18}{5}}$ $\dfrac{3\sqrt{10}}{5}$

123. $\dfrac{\sqrt{5}+6}{\sqrt{5}-1}$ $\dfrac{11+7\sqrt{5}}{4}$

Write each radical expression in simplified form. Assume that all variables represent nonnegative real numbers.

124. $\sqrt{x^6}$ x^3

125. $\sqrt[3]{x^6}$ x^2

126. $\sqrt{x^3}$ $x\sqrt{x}$

127. $\sqrt{18y^{10}}$ $3y^5\sqrt{2}$

128. $\sqrt[3]{125y^{18}}$ $5y^6$

129. $\sqrt{40t^{13}}$ $2t^6\sqrt{10t}$

130. $\sqrt{\dfrac{3x}{2y}}$ $\dfrac{\sqrt{6xy}}{2y}$

Solve each equation.

131. $x = \sqrt{2x+3}$ $\{3\}$

132. $(x-4)^2 = 12$ $\{4 \pm 2\sqrt{3}\}$

133. $2\sqrt{x} = 1$ $\left\{\dfrac{1}{4}\right\}$

Chapter 9

Solve by using the quadratic formula.

134. $x^2 + 2x - 5 = 0$ $\{-1 \pm \sqrt{6}\}$

135. $6x^2 - 5x + 1 = 0$ $\left\{\dfrac{1}{2}, \dfrac{1}{3}\right\}$

136. $9x^2 - 6x + 1 = 0$ $\left\{\dfrac{1}{3}\right\}$

Solve by completing the square.

137. $x^2 + 4x - 1 = 0$ $\{-2 \pm \sqrt{5}\}$

138. $x^2 + 3x - 1 = 0$ $\left\{\dfrac{-3 \pm \sqrt{13}}{2}\right\}$

139. $2x^2 - 4x - 3 = 0$ $\left\{\dfrac{2 \pm \sqrt{10}}{2}\right\}$

Graph each parabola.

140. $y = 4 - x^2$

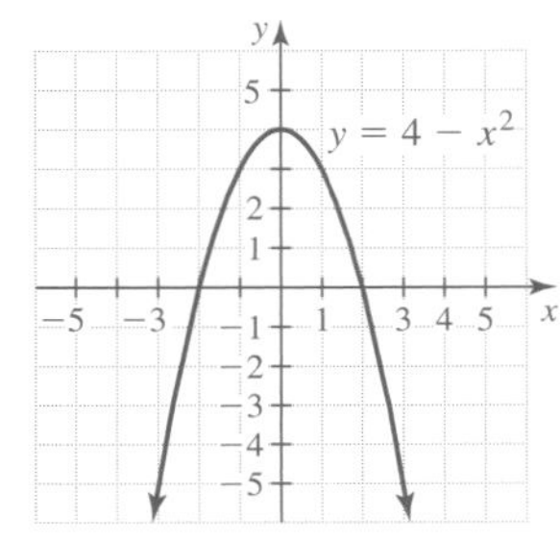

141. $y = x^2 - 5x$

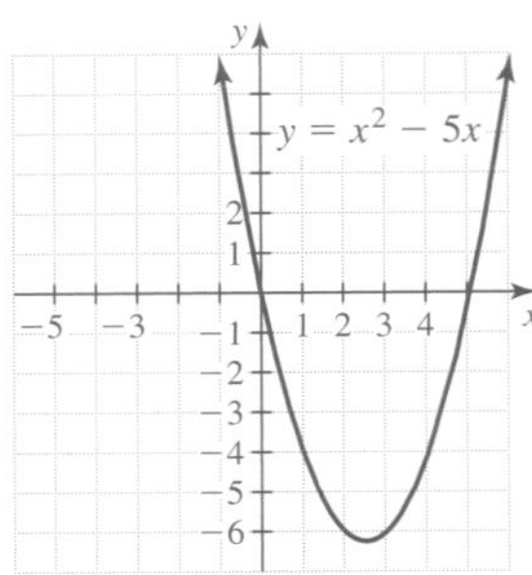

142. $y = -x^2 + 2x + 1$

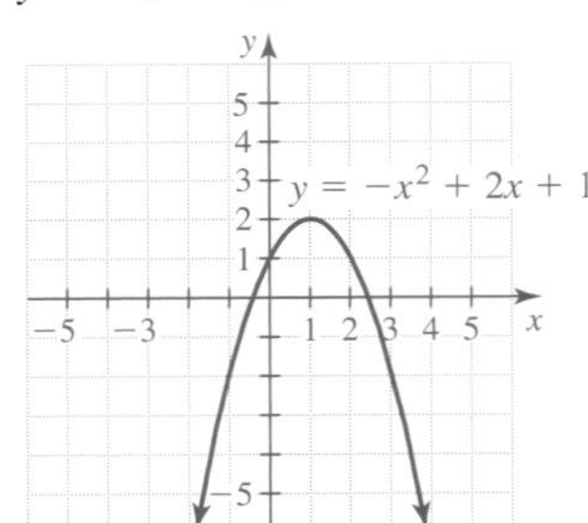

Solve each problem.

143. Find the intercepts and vertex for the parabola $y = x^2 - 6x + 8$. (2, 0), (4, 0), (0, 8), (3, −1)

144. Find the maximum value for y on the graph of $y = -x^2 + 4x - 3$. 1

145. Find the minimum value for y on the graph of $y = 6x^2 + 2x$.
$-\dfrac{1}{6}$

146. The height in feet for a ball thrown upward at 16 feet per second is given by $h = -16t^2 + 16t$, where t is the time in seconds after the ball is tossed. What is the maximum height reached by the ball?
4 feet

Let $f(x) = -2x - 1$, $g(x) = |3x - 1|$, and $h(x) = \frac{5}{x}$. Find the following.

147. $f(-1/2)$ 0

148. $f(-3)$ 5

149. $f(0)$ −1

150. $g(1/3)$ 0

151. $g(-5)$ 16

152. $g(0)$ 1

153. $h(0)$ Undefined

154. $h(1/2)$ 10

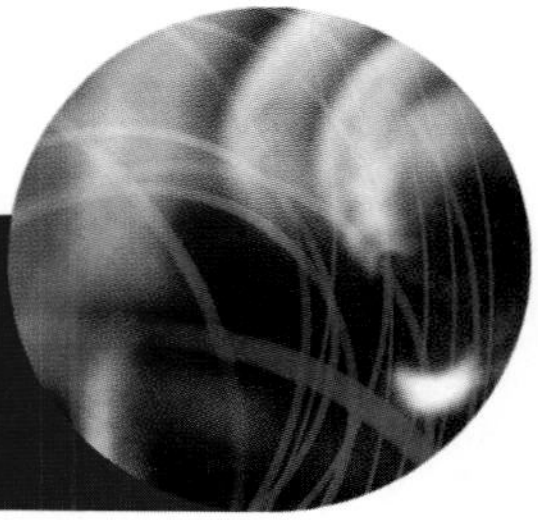

Answers to Selected Exercises

Chapter 1

Section 1.1 Warm-Ups T T F F T F T T F F

1. The integers are the numbers in the set $\{\ldots, -3, -2, -1, 0, 1, 2, 3, \ldots\}$.
3. A rational number is a ratio of integers and an irrational number is not.
5. The number a is larger than b if a lies to the right of b on the number line.
7. 6 **9.** 6 **11.** 0 **13.** -2 **15.** -12 **17.** -2.1
19. 1, 2, 3, 4, 5 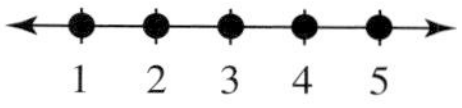
21. 0, 1, 2, 3, 4 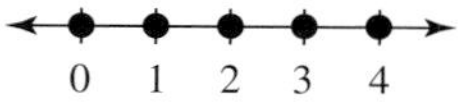
23. 0, 1, 2, 3, 4 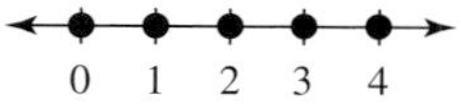
25. 1, 2, 3, 4, 5, . . . 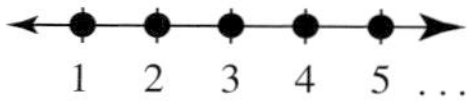
27. 1, 2, 3, 4, 5, . . . 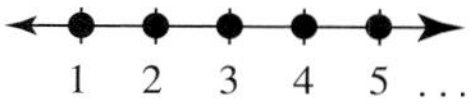
29. True **31.** False **33.** True **35.** True **37.** True **39.** False
41. $(0, 1)$ 
43. $[-2, 2]$ 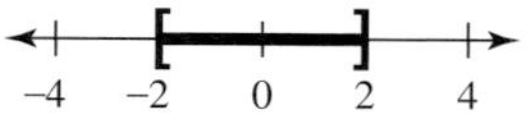
45. $(0, 5]$ 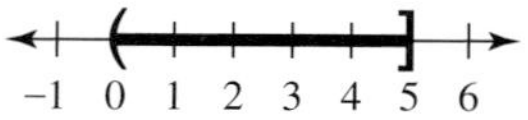
47. $(4, \infty)$ 
49. $(-\infty, -1]$ 
51. $[0, \infty)$
53. 6 **55.** 0 **57.** 7 **59.** 9 **61.** 45 **63.** $\frac{3}{4}$ **65.** 5.09
67. -16 **69.** $-\frac{5}{2}$ **71.** 2 **73.** 3 **75.** -9 **77.** 16
79. -4 **81.** -1.99 **83.** 74 **85.** 5.25 **87.** 40 **89.** $\frac{1}{2}$
91. -3 and 3 **93.** $-4, -3, 3, 4$ **95.** $-1, 0, 1$ **97.** $[3, 8]$
99. $(-30, -20]$ **101.** $[30, \infty)$ **103.** True **105.** True **107.** True
109. a) $\frac{7}{24}$ **b)** -3.115 **c)** 0.66669
d) Add them and divide the result by 2.
111. Real: all; irrational: π, $\sqrt{3}$; rational: all except π and $\sqrt{3}$; integer: -2, $\sqrt{9}$, 6, 0; whole: $\sqrt{9}$, 6, 0; counting: $\sqrt{9}$, 6

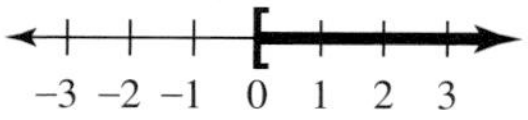

Section 1.2 Warm-Ups T T F T T T T T F T

1. If two fractions are identical when reduced to lowest terms, then they are equivalent fractions.
3. To reduce a fraction to lowest terms means to find an equivalent fraction that has no factor common to the numerator and denominator.
5. Convert a fraction to a decimal by dividing the denominator into the numerator.
7. $\frac{6}{8}$ **9.** $\frac{32}{12}$ **11.** $\frac{10}{2}$ **13.** $\frac{75}{100}$ **15.** $\frac{30}{100}$ **17.** $\frac{70}{42}$ **19.** $\frac{1}{2}$
21. $\frac{2}{3}$ **23.** 3 **25.** $\frac{1}{2}$ **27.** 2 **29.** $\frac{3}{8}$ **31.** $\frac{13}{21}$ **33.** $\frac{12}{13}$
35. $\frac{10}{27}$ **37.** 5 **39.** $\frac{7}{10}$ **41.** $\frac{7}{13}$ **43.** $\frac{3}{5}$ **45.** $\frac{1}{6}$
47. 1152 in. **49.** 22.88 km **51.** 5.31 in. **53.** 402.57 g
55. 58.67 ft/sec **57.** 548.53 km/hr **59.** 3
61. $\frac{1}{15}$ **63.** 4 **65.** $\frac{4}{5}$ **67.** $\frac{3}{40}$ **69.** $\frac{1}{2}$ **71.** $\frac{1}{3}$ **73.** $\frac{1}{4}$
75. $\frac{7}{12}$ **77.** $\frac{1}{12}$ **79.** $\frac{19}{24}$ **81.** $\frac{11}{72}$ **83.** $\frac{199}{48}$ **85.** 60%, 0.6
87. $\frac{9}{100}$, 0.09 **89.** 8%, $\frac{2}{25}$ **91.** 0.75, 75% **93.** $\frac{1}{50}$, 0.02
95. $\frac{1}{100}$, 1% **97.** 3 **99.** 1 **101.** $\frac{71}{96}$ **103.** $\frac{17}{120}$
105. $\frac{65}{16}$ **107.** $\frac{69}{4}$ **109.** $\frac{13}{12}$ **111.** $\frac{1}{8}$ **113.** $\frac{3}{8}$ **115.** $\frac{3}{16}$
117. $\frac{2}{3}$ **119.** $\frac{1}{2}$ **121.** $\frac{19}{96}$
123. a) 1.3 yd^3 **b)** $36\frac{11}{24}$ ft^3 or $1\frac{227}{648}$ yd^3
127. Each daughter gets 3 $km^2 \div 4$ or a $\frac{3}{4}$-km^2 piece of the farm. Divide the farm into 12 equal squares. Give each daughter an L-shaped piece consisting of 3 of those 12 squares.

Section 1.3 Warm-Ups T T T F F F T F T F

1. We studied addition and subtraction of signed numbers.
3. Two numbers are additive inverses of each other if their sum is zero.
5. To find the sum of two numbers with unlike signs, subtract their absolute values. The answer is given the sign of the number with the larger absolute value.
7. 13 **9.** -13 **11.** -8 **13.** -1.15 **15.** $-\frac{1}{2}$ **17.** 0 **19.** 0
21. 2 **23.** -6 **25.** 5.6 **27.** -2.9 **29.** $-\frac{1}{4}$ **31.** $8 + (-2)$
33. $4 + (-12)$ **35.** $-3 + 8$ **37.** $8.3 + (1.5)$ **39.** -4
41. -10 **43.** 11 **45.** -11 **47.** $-\frac{1}{4}$ **49.** $\frac{3}{4}$ **51.** 7

53. 0.93 **55.** 9.3 **57.** −5.03 **59.** 3 **61.** −9 **63.** −120
65. 78 **67.** −27 **69.** −7 **71.** −201 **73.** −322
75. −15.97 **77.** −2.92 **79.** −3.73 **81.** 3.7 **83.** $\frac{3}{20}$ **85.** $\frac{7}{24}$
87. 13 **89.** −10 **91.** 14 **93.** −4 **95.** −3 **97.** −3.49
99. −0.3422 **101.** −48.84 **103.** −8.85 **105.** −\$8.85
107. −7°C
109. When adding signed numbers, we add or subtract only positive numbers which are the absolute values of the original numbers. We then determine the appropriate sign for the answer.
111. The distance between x and y is given by either $|x - y|$ or $|y - x|$.

Section 1.4 Warm-Ups T F T F T T T F T F

1. We learned to multiply and divide signed numbers.
3. To find the product of signed numbers, multiply their absolute values and then affix a negative sign if the two original numbers have opposite signs.
5. To find the quotient of nonzero numbers divide their absolute values and then affix a negative sign if the two original numbers have opposite signs.
7. −27 **9.** 132 **11.** $-\frac{1}{3}$ **13.** −0.3 **15.** 144 **17.** 0
19. −1 **21.** 3 **23.** $-\frac{2}{3}$ **25.** $\frac{5}{6}$ **27.** 0 **29.** −80
31. 0.25 **33.** 0 **35.** Undefined **37.** Undefined **39.** 0
41. −100 **43.** 27 **45.** −3 **47.** −4 **49.** −30 **51.** 19
53. −0.18 **55.** 0.3 **57.** −6 **59.** 1.5 **61.** 22
63. $-\frac{1}{3}$ **65.** −164.25 **67.** 1529.41 **69.** −12
71. −8 **73.** −6 **75.** −1 **77.** 5 **79.** 16 **81.** −8
83. 0 **85.** 0 **87.** −3.9 **89.** −40 **91.** 0.4 **93.** 0.4
95. −0.2 **97.** −7.5 **99.** $-\frac{1}{30}$ **101.** $-\frac{1}{10}$ **103.** 7.562
105. 19.35 **107.** 0 **109.** Undefined **111.** −\$24,163/min

Section 1.5 Warm-Ups F F T F F F F T F T

1. An arithmetic expression is the result of writing numbers in a meaningful combination with the ordinary operations of arithmetic.
3. An exponential expression is an expression of the form a^n.
5. The order of operations tells us the order in which to perform operations when grouping symbols are omitted.
7. −4 **9.** 1 **11.** −8 **13.** −7 **15.** −16 **17.** −4
19. 4^4 **21.** $(-5)^4$ **23.** $(-y)^3$ **25.** $\left(\frac{3}{7}\right)^5$ **27.** $5 \cdot 5 \cdot 5$
29. $b \cdot b$ **31.** $\left(-\frac{1}{2}\right)\left(-\frac{1}{2}\right)\left(-\frac{1}{2}\right)\left(-\frac{1}{2}\right)\left(-\frac{1}{2}\right)$
33. 81 **35.** 0 **37.** 625 **39.** −216 **41.** 100,000
43. −0.001 **45.** $\frac{1}{8}$ **47.** $\frac{1}{4}$ **49.** −64 **51.** −4096
53. 27 **55.** −13 **57.** 50 **59.** 10 **61.** 36 **63.** 18
65. −19 **67.** −17 **69.** −44 **71.** 18 **73.** −78 **75.** 0
77. 27 **79.** 1 **81.** 8 **83.** 7 **85.** 11 **87.** 111 **89.** 21
91. −1 **93.** −11 **95.** 9 **97.** 16 **99.** 28 **101.** 121
103. −73 **105.** 25 **107.** 0 **109.** −2 **111.** 12 **113.** 82
115. −54 **117.** −79 **119.** −24 **121.** 41.92
123. 184.643547 **125.** 8.0548
127. a) \$1280 **b)** \$1275
129. a) 347.5 million **b)** 2033
131. $(-5)^3 = -(5^3) = -5^3 = -1 \cdot 5^3$ and $-(-5)^3 = 5^3$

Section 1.6 Warm-Ups T F T F T F F F T F

1. An algebraic expression is the result of combining numbers and variables with the operations of arithmetic in some meaningful way.
3. An algebraic expression is named according to the last operation to be performed.
5. An equation is a sentence that expresses equality between two algebraic expressions.
7. Difference **9.** Cube **11.** Sum **13.** Difference
15. Product **17.** Square **19.** The difference of x^2 and a^2
21. The square of $x - a$ **23.** The quotient of $x - 4$ and 2
25. The difference of $\frac{x}{2}$ and 4 **27.** The cube of ab
29. $8 + y$ **31.** $5xz$ **33.** $8 - 7x$ **35.** $\frac{6}{x + 4}$
37. $(a + b)^2$ **39.** $x^3 + y^2$ **41.** $5m^2$ **43.** $(s + t)^2$
45. 3 **47.** 3 **49.** 16 **51.** −9 **53.** −3 **55.** −8
57. $-\frac{2}{3}$ **59.** 4 **61.** −1 **63.** 1 **65.** −4 **67.** 0
69. Yes **71.** No **73.** Yes **75.** Yes **77.** Yes
79. No **81.** No **83.** $5x + 3x = 8x$ **85.** $3(x + 2) = 12$
87. $\frac{x}{3} = 5x$ **89.** $(a + b)^2 = 9$
91. −7, −5, −3, −1, 1
93. 4, 8, 16; $\frac{1}{4}, \frac{1}{8}, \frac{1}{16}$; 100, 1000, 10,000; 0.01, 0.001, 0.0001
95. 14.65 **97.** 37.12 **99.** 169.3 cm, 41 cm
101. 4, 5, 14, 16.5 **103.** 920 feet
105. For the square of the sum consider $(2 + 3)^2 = 5^2 = 25$. For the sum of the squares consider $2^2 + 3^2 = 4 + 9 = 13$. So $(2 + 3)^2 \neq 2^2 + 3^2$.

Section 1.7 Warm-Ups F F T F T T T T T T

1. The commutative property says that $a + b = b + a$ and the associative property says that $(a + b) + c = a + (b + c)$.
3. Factoring is the process of writing an expression or number as a product.
5. The properties help us to understand the operations and how they are related to each other.
7. $r + 9$ **9.** $3(x + 2)$ **11.** $-5x + 4$ **13.** $6x$
15. $-2(x - 4)$ **17.** $4 - 8y$ **19.** $4w^2$ **21.** $3a^2b$ **23.** $9x^3z$
25. −3 **27.** −10 **29.** −21 **31.** 0.6
33. $3x - 15$ **35.** $2a + at$ **37.** $-3w + 18$ **39.** $-20 + 4y$
41. $-a + 7$ **43.** $-t - 4$ **45.** $2(m + 6)$ **47.** $4(x - 1)$
49. $4(y - 4)$ **51.** $4(a + 2)$ **53.** $x(1 + y)$ **55.** $2(3a - b)$
57. 2 **59.** $-\frac{1}{5}$ **61.** $\frac{1}{7}$ **63.** 1 **65.** −4 **67.** $\frac{2}{5}$
69. Commutative property of multiplication
71. Distributive property
73. Associative property of multiplication
75. Additive inverse property
77. Commutative property of multiplication
79. Multiplicative identity property
81. Distributive property
83. Additive inverse property
85. Multiplication property of 0
87. Distributive property
89. $y + a$ **91.** $(5a)w$ **93.** $\frac{1}{2}(x + 1)$ **95.** $3(2x + 5)$
97. 1 **99.** 0 **101.** $\frac{100}{33}$
103. The perimeter is twice the sum of the length and width.
105. a) Commutative **b)** Not commutative

Section 1.8 Warm-Ups T F T T F F F F F T

1. Like terms are terms with the same variables and exponents.
3. We can add or subtract like terms.
5. If a negative sign precedes a set of parentheses, then signs for all terms in the parentheses are changed when the parentheses are removed.
7. 7000 **9.** 1 **11.** 356 **13.** 350 **15.** 36 **17.** 36,000
19. 0 **21.** 98 **23.** $11w$ **25.** $3x$ **27.** $5x$ **29.** $-a$
31. $-2a$ **33.** $10 - 6t$ **35.** $8x^2$ **37.** $-4x + 2x^2$
39. $-7mw^2$ **41.** $\frac{5}{6}a$ **43.** $12h$ **45.** $-18b$ **47.** $-9m^2$
49. $12d^2$ **51.** y^2 **53.** $-15ab$ **55.** $-6a - 3ab$
57. $-k + k^2$ **59.** y **61.** $-3y$ **63.** y **65.** $2y^2$ **67.** $2a - 1$
69. $3x - 2$ **71.** $2x - 1$ **73.** $6c - 13$ **75.** $-7b + 1$
77. $2w - 4$ **79.** $-2x + 1$ **81.** $8 - y$ **83.** $m - 6$
85. $w - 5$ **87.** $8x + 15$ **89.** $5x - 1$ **91.** $-2a - 1$
93. $5a - 2$ **95.** $6x^2 + x - 15$ **97.** $-2b^2 - 7b + 4$
99. $3m - 18$ **101.** $-3x - 7$ **103.** $0.95x - 0.5$
105. $4x - 4$ **107.** $2y + 4$ **109.** $2y + m - 1$ **111.** 3
113. $\frac{7}{6}a + \frac{13}{6}$ **115.** $0.15x - 0.4$ **117.** $-14k + 23$
119. 45 **121.** $4x + 80$, 200 feet **123. a)** $0.25x - 6885$ **b)** \$13,115 **c)** \$46,000 **d)** \$303,000
125. a) $4(2 + x) = 8 + 4x$ **b)** $4(2x) = (4 \cdot 2)x = 8x$
c) $\frac{4 + x}{2} = \frac{1}{2}(4 + x) = 2 + \frac{1}{2}x$
d) $5 - (x - 3) = 5 - x + 3 = 8 - x$

Enriching Your Mathematical Word Power

1. c **2.** b **3.** a **4.** d **5.** b **6.** d **7.** a **8.** d
9. c **10.** a

Review Exercises

1. 0, 1, 2, 10 **3.** −2, 0, 1, 2, 10 **5.** $-\sqrt{5}, \pi$
7. True **9.** False **11.** False **13.** True
15. −3 −2 −1 0 1 2 3 **17.** −2 −1 0 1 2 3 4 5
19. [4, 6] **21.** [−30, ∞) **23.** $\frac{17}{24}$ **25.** 6 **27.** $\frac{3}{7}$ **29.** $\frac{14}{3}$
31. $\frac{13}{12}$ **33.** 2 **35.** −13 **37.** −7 **39.** −7 **41.** 11.95
43. −0.05 **45.** $-\frac{1}{6}$ **47.** $-\frac{11}{15}$ **49.** −15 **51.** 4 **53.** 5
55. $\frac{1}{6}$ **57.** −0.3 **59.** −0.24 **61.** 1 **63.** 66 **65.** 49
67. 41 **69.** 1 **71.** 50 **73.** −135 **75.** −2 **77.** −16
79. 16 **81.** 5 **83.** 9 **85.** 7 **87.** $-\frac{1}{3}$ **89.** 1 **91.** −9
93. Yes **95.** No **97.** Yes **99.** No
101. Distributive property
103. Multiplicative inverse property
105. Additive identity property
107. Associative property of addition
109. Commutative property of multiplication
111. Additive inverse property
113. Multiplicative identity property
115. $-a + 12$ **117.** $6a^2 - 6a$ **119.** $-12t + 39$
121. $-0.9a - 0.57$ **123.** $-0.05x - 4$ **125.** $27x^2 + 6x + 5$
127. $-2a$ **129.** $x^2 + 4x - 3$ **131.** 0 **133.** 8 **135.** −21
137. $\frac{1}{2}$ **139.** −0.5 **141.** −1 **143.** $x + 2$ **145.** $4 + 2x$
147. $2x$ **149.** $-4x + 8$ **151.** $6x$ **153.** x **155.** $8x$
157. $-x^2 + 6x - 8$ **159.** $\frac{1}{4}x - \frac{3}{2}$ **161.** 3, 2, 1, 0, −1
163. 25, 125, 625; 16, −64, 256
165. a) $0.35x - 20{,}139.5$ **b)** Approximately \$150,000 **c)** \$8,968,115

Chapter 1 Test

1. 0, 8 **2.** −3, 0, 8 **3.** $-3, -\frac{1}{4}, 0, 8$ **4.** $-\sqrt{3}, \sqrt{5}, \pi$
5. −21 **6.** −4 **7.** 9 **8.** −7 **9.** −0.95 **10.** −56
11. 978 **12.** 13 **13.** −1 **14.** 0 **15.** 9740 **16.** $-\frac{7}{24}$
17. −20 **18.** $-\frac{1}{6}$ **19.** −39
20. −1 0 1 2 3 4 5 **21.** −1 0 1 2 3 4 5
22. (2, ∞) **23.** [3, 9) **24.** Distributive property
25. Commutative property of multiplication
26. Associative property of addition
27. Additive inverse property **28.** Multiplicative identity property
29. Multiplication property of 0 **30.** $3(x + 10)$ **31.** $7(w - 1)$
32. $6x + 6$ **33.** $4x - 2$ **34.** $7x - 3$ **35.** $0.9x + 7.5$
36. $14a^2 + 5a$ **37.** $x + 2$ **38.** $4t$ **39.** $54x^2y^2$
40. $\frac{3}{4}x + \frac{3}{2}$ **41.** 41 **42.** 5 **43.** −12 **44.** No **45.** Yes
46. Yes **47.** $3.66R - 0.06A + 82.205$, 168.905 cm

Chapter 2

Section 2.1 Warm-Ups T T F T F T T T T T

1. The addition property of equality says that adding the same number to each side of an equation does not change the solution to the equation.
3. The multiplication property of equality says that multiplying both sides of an equation by the same nonzero number does not change the solution to the equation.
5. Replace the variable in the equation with your solution. If the resulting statement is correct, then the solution is correct.
7. {1} **9.** {9} **11.** {1} **13.** $\left\{\frac{2}{3}\right\}$ **15.** {−9} **17.** {−19}
19. $\left\{\frac{1}{4}\right\}$ **21.** {0} **23.** {5.95} **25.** {−5} **27.** {−4} **29.** {3}
31. $\left\{\frac{1}{4}\right\}$ **33.** {−8} **35.** {1.8} **37.** $\left\{\frac{2}{3}\right\}$ **39.** $\left\{\frac{1}{2}\right\}$ **41.** {−5}
43. {5} **45.** {1.25} **47.** $\left\{\frac{1}{4}\right\}$ **49.** $\left\{\frac{3}{20}\right\}$ **51.** {−2} **53.** {120}
55. $\left\{\frac{5}{9}\right\}$ **57.** $\left\{-\frac{1}{2}\right\}$ **59.** {−8} **61.** $\left\{\frac{1}{3}\right\}$ **63.** {−3.4} **65.** {99}
67. {−7} **69.** {9} **71.** {8} **73.** {5} **75.** {−5} **77.** {−8}
79. {2} **81.** $\left\{\frac{1}{6}\right\}$ **83.** $\left\{-\frac{1}{3}\right\}$ **85.** {44} **87.** $\left\{\frac{3}{4}\right\}$ **89.** {7}
91. {−14} **93.** $\left\{\frac{3}{8}\right\}$
95. a) $\frac{4}{5}x = 48.5$, 60.6 births per 1000 females **b)** 54 births per 1000 females
97. 2877 stocks **99.** 3000 students

Section 2.2 Warm-Ups T T T F T F T T T T

1. We can solve $ax + b = 0$ with the addition property and the multiplication property of equality.
3. Use the multiplication property of equality to solve $-x = 8$.

5. {2} **7.** {−2} **9.** $\left\{\frac{2}{3}\right\}$ **11.** {6} **13.** {12} **15.** $\left\{\frac{1}{2}\right\}$
17. $\left\{-\frac{1}{6}\right\}$ **19.** {4} **21.** $\left\{\frac{5}{6}\right\}$ **23.** {4} **25.** {−5} **27.** {34}
29. {9} **31.** {1.2} **33.** {3} **35.** {4} **37.** {−3} **39.** $\left\{\frac{1}{2}\right\}$
41. {30} **43.** {6} **45.** {−2} **47.** {18} **49.** {0} **51.** $\left\{\frac{1}{6}\right\}$
53. {−2} **55.** $\left\{\frac{7}{3}\right\}$ **57.** {1} **59.** {−6} **61.** {−12} **63.** {−4}
65. {−13} **67.** {1.7} **69.** {2} **71.** {4.6} **73.** {8} **75.** {34}
77. {6} **79.** {0} **81.** {−10} **83.** {18} **85.** {−20} **87.** {−3}
89. {−4.3} **91.** 17 hr **93.** 20°C **95.** 9 ft **97.** $14,550

Section 2.3 Warm-Ups T T F F F T T F T T

1. If an equation involves fractions we usually multiply each side by the LCD of all of the fractions.
3. An identity is an equation that is satisfied by all numbers for which both sides are defined.
5. An inconsistent equation has no solutions.

7. $\left\{\frac{6}{5}\right\}$ **9.** $\left\{\frac{2}{9}\right\}$ **11.** {7} **13.** {24} **15.** {16} **17.** {−12}
19. {60} **21.** {24} **23.** $\left\{-\frac{4}{3}\right\}$ **25.** {90} **27.** {6} **29.** {−2}
31. {80} **33.** {60} **35.** {200} **37.** {800} **39.** $\left\{\frac{9}{2}\right\}$ **41.** {3}
43. {25} **45.** {−2} **47.** {−3} **49.** {5} **51.** {−10} **53.** {2}
55. All real numbers, identity **57.** ∅, inconsistent
59. {0}, conditional **61.** ∅, inconsistent **63.** ∅, inconsistent
65. {1}, conditional **67.** ∅, inconsistent
69. All real numbers, identity **71.** All nonzero real numbers, identity
73. All real numbers, identity **75.** {−4} **77.** *R* **79.** *R* **81.** {100}
83. $\left\{-\frac{3}{2}\right\}$ **85.** {30} **87.** {6} **89.** {0.5} **91.** {19,608}
93. $128,000 **95. a)** $240,000 **b)** $244,089

Section 2.4 Warm-Ups F F F F F T T T F T

1. A formula is an equation with two or more variables.
3. To solve for a variable means to find an equivalent equation in which the variable is isolated.
5. To find the value of a variable in a formula, we can solve for the variable and then insert values for the other variables, or insert values for the other variables and then solve for the variable.

7. $R = \frac{D}{T}$ **9.** $D = \frac{C}{\pi}$ **11.** $P = \frac{I}{rt}$ **13.** $C = \frac{5}{9}(F - 32)$
15. $h = \frac{2A}{b}$ **17.** $L = \frac{P - 2W}{2}$ **19.** $a = 2A - b$
21. $r = \frac{S - P}{Pt}$ **23.** $a = \frac{2A - bh}{h}$ **25.** $x = \frac{b - a}{2}$ **27.** $x = -7a$
29. $x = 12 - a$ **31.** $x = 7ab$ **33.** $y = -x - 9$ **35.** $y = -x + 6$
37. $y = 2x - 2$ **39.** $y = 3x + 4$ **41.** $y = -\frac{1}{2}x + 2$ **43.** $y = x - \frac{1}{2}$
45. $y = 3x - 14$ **47.** $y = \frac{1}{2}x$ **49.** $y = \frac{3}{2}x + 6$ **51.** $y = \frac{3}{2}x + \frac{13}{2}$
53. $y = -\frac{1}{4}x + \frac{5}{8}$ **55.** 2 **57.** 7 **59.** $-\frac{9}{5}$ **61.** 1 **63.** 1.33
65. 60, 30, 0, −30, −60 **67.** 14, 23, 32, 104, 212 **69.** 40, 20, 10, 5, 4
71. 1, 3, 6, 10, 15 **73.** 4%, $4\frac{2}{3}$%, $5\frac{1}{3}$% **75.** 4 years
77. 14 yards, $9\frac{1}{3}$ yards, 7 yards **79.** 225 feet **81.** $60,500
83. $300 **85.** 20% **87.** 160 feet **89.** 24 cubic feet **91.** 4 inches
93. 8 feet **95.** 12 inches **97.** 640 milligrams, age 13
99. 3.75 milliliters **101.** $L = F\sqrt{S} - 2D + 5.688$

Section 2.5 Warm-Ups T T T F T F F F T F

1. To express addition we use words such as plus, sum, increased by, and more than.
3. Complementary angles have degree measures with a sum of 90°.
5. Distance is the product of rate and time.

7. $x + 3$ **9.** $x - 3$ **11.** $5x$ **13.** $0.1x$ **15.** $\frac{x}{3}$ **17.** $\frac{1}{3}x$
19. x and $x + 15$ **21.** x and $6 - x$
23. x and $x + 3$ **25.** x and $0.05x$ **27.** x and $1.30x$
29. x and $90 - x$ **31.** x and $120 - x$
33. n and $n + 2$, where n is an even integer
35. x and $x + 1$, where x is an integer
37. x, $x + 2$, and $x + 4$, where x is an odd integer
39. x, $x + 2$, $x + 4$, and $x + 6$, where x is an even integer
41. $3x$ miles **43.** $0.25q$ dollars **45.** $\frac{x}{20}$ hour
47. $\frac{x - 100}{12}$ meters per second **49.** $5x$ square meters
51. $2w + 2(w + 3)$ inches **53.** $150 - x$ feet **55.** $2x + 1$ feet
57. $x(x + 5)$ square meters **59.** $0.18(x + 1000)$
61. $\frac{16.50}{x}$ dollars per pound **63.** $90 - x$ degrees
65. x is the smaller number, $x(x + 5) = 8$
67. x is the selling price, $x - 0.07x = 84{,}532$
69. x is the percent, $500x = 100$
71. x is the number of nickels, $0.05x + 0.10(x + 2) = 3.80$
73. x is the number, $x + 5 = 13$
75. x is the smallest integer, $x + (x + 1) + (x + 2) = 42$
77. x is the smaller integer, $x(x + 1) = 182$
79. x is Harriet's income, $0.12x = 3000$
81. x is the number, $0.05x = 13$
83. x is the width, $x(x + 5) = 126$
85. n is the number of nickels, $5n + 10(n - 1) = 95$
87. x is the measure of the larger angle, $x + x - 38 = 180$
89. a) $r + 0.6(220 - (30 + r)) = 144$, where r is the resting heart rate **b)** Target heart rate increases as resting heart rate increases.
91. $6 + x$ **93.** $m + 9$ **95.** $11t$ **97.** $5(x - 2)$ **99.** $m - 3m$
101. $\frac{h + 8}{h}$ **103.** $\frac{5}{y - 9}$ **105.** $\frac{w - 8}{2w}$ **107.** $-3v - 9$
109. $x - \frac{x}{7}$ **111.** $m^2 - (m + 7)$ **113.** $x + (9x - 8)$ **115.** $13n - 9$
117. $6 + \frac{1}{3}(x + 2)$ **119.** $\frac{x}{2} + x$ **121.** $x(x + 3) = 24$
123. $w(w - 4) = 24$

Section 2.6 Warm-Ups F T T F F T T T F T

1. In this section we studied number, geometric, and uniform motion problems.
3. Uniform motion is motion at a constant rate of speed.
5. Complementary angles are angles whose degree measures have a sum of 90°.

7. 39, 40 **9.** 46, 47, 48 **11.** 75, 77 **13.** 47, 48, 49, 50
15. Length 50 meters, width 25 meters
17. Width 42 inches, length 46 inches
19. 13 inches **21.** 35°

23. 65 miles per hour **25.** 55 miles per hour **27.** 4 hours, 2048 miles
29. Length 20 inches, width 12 inches **31.** 5 ft, 5 ft, 3 ft
33. 20°, 40°, 120° **35.** 20°, 80°, 80° **37.** Raiders 32, Vikings 14
39. 3 hours, 106 miles **41.** Crawford 1906, Wayne 1907, Stewart 1908
43. 7 ft, 7 ft, 16 ft

Section 2.7 Warm-Ups T F T F T T F T F T

1. We studied discount, investment, and mixture problems in this section.
3. The product of the rate and the original price gives the amount of discount. The original price minus the discount is the sale price.
5. A table helps us to organize the information given in a problem.
7. \$320 **9.** \$400 **11.** \$125,000 **13.** \$30.24
15. 100 Fund \$10,000, 101 Fund \$13,000
17. Fidelity \$14,000, Price \$11,000
19. 30 gallons **21.** 20 liters of 5% alcohol, 10 liters of 20% alcohol
23. 55,700 voters **25.** \$15,000 **27.** 75% **29.** 600 students
31. 42 private rooms, 30 semiprivate rooms **33.** 12 pounds
35. 4 nickels, 6 dimes **37.** 800 gallons **39.** $\frac{2}{3}$ gallon
41. Shorts \$12, tops \$6

Section 2.8 Warm-Ups T T F T F T F F T F

1. The inequality symbols are $<$, $\le$, $>$, and $\ge$.
3. For $\le$ and $\ge$ use a bracket and for $<$ and $>$ use a parenthesis.
5. The compound inequality $a < b < c$ means $b > a$ and $b < c$, or b is between a and c.
7. False **9.** True **11.** True **13.** False **15.** True **17.** True
19. True **21.** True

23. $(-\infty, 3]$

25. $(-2, \infty)$

27. $(-\infty, -1)$

29. $[-2, \infty)$

31. $\left[\frac{1}{2}, \infty\right)$

33. $(-\infty, 5.3]$

35. $(-3, 1)$

37. $[3, 7]$

39. $[-5, 0)$

41. $(40, 100]$

43. $x > 3$, $(3, \infty)$ **45.** $x \le 2$, $(-\infty, 2]$ **47.** $0 < x < 2$, $(0, 2)$

49. $-5 < x \le 7$, $(-5, 7]$ **51.** $x > -4$, $(-4, \infty)$
53. Yes **55.** No **57.** No **59.** Yes **61.** Yes **63.** Yes
65. No **67.** Yes **69.** No **71.** 0, 5.1 **73.** 5.1 **75.** 5.1
77. −5.1, 0, 5.1 **79.** $0.08p > 1500$ **81.** $p + 2p + p + 0.25 < 2.00$
83. $\frac{44 + 72 + s}{3} \ge 60$ **85.** $396 < 8R < 453$ **87.** $60 < 90 - x < 70$
89. **a)** $45 + 2(30) + 2h \le 130$ **b)** Approximately 12 in.
91. 79, moderate effort on level ground

Section 2.9 Warm-Ups T F F T F T F T T F

1. Equivalent inequalities are inequalities that have the same solutions.
3. According to the multiplication property of inequality, the inequality symbol is reversed when multiplying (or dividing) by a negative number and not reversed when multiplying (or dividing) by a positive number.
5. We solve compound inequalities using the properties of inequality as we do for simple inequalities.
7. $>$ **9.** $\ge$ **11.** $>$ **13.** $>$ **15.** $\le$

17. $(-3, \infty)$ **19.** $(-2, \infty)$

21. $(-\infty, 4)$ **23.** $\left[-\frac{1}{2}, \infty\right)$

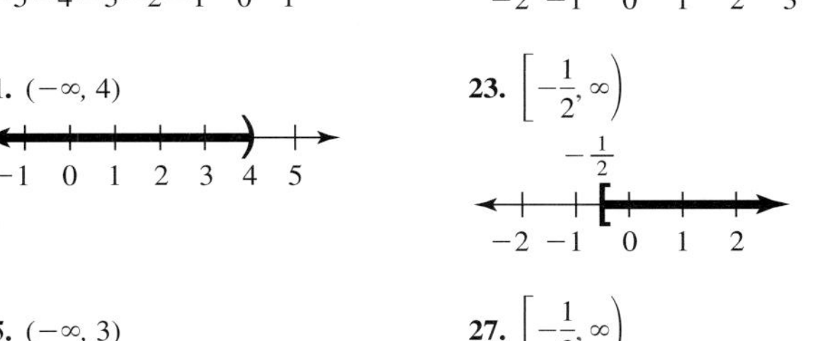

25. $(-\infty, 3)$ **27.** $\left[-\frac{1}{3}, \infty\right)$

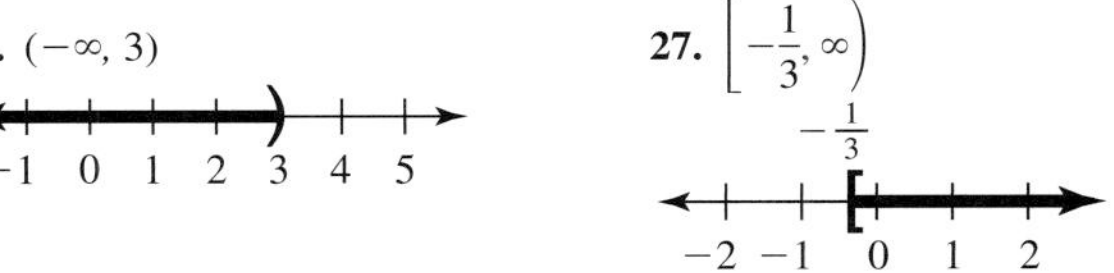

29. $(-3, \infty)$ **31.** $(-\infty, 13)$

33. $(-\infty, 24]$ **35.** $\left(-\infty, \frac{7}{2}\right]$

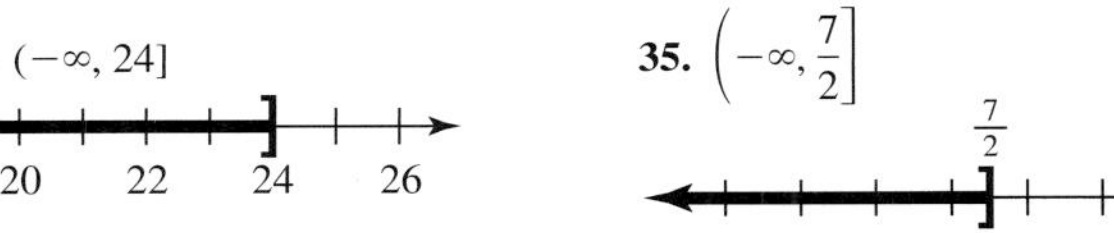

37. $(-1.5, \infty)$ **39.** $(-\infty, -11)$

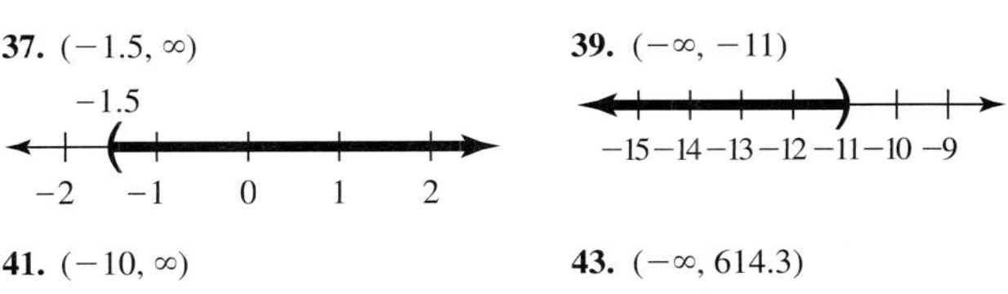

41. $(-10, \infty)$ **43.** $(-\infty, 614.3)$

45. $(8, 10)$ **47.** $\left(1, \frac{9}{2}\right)$

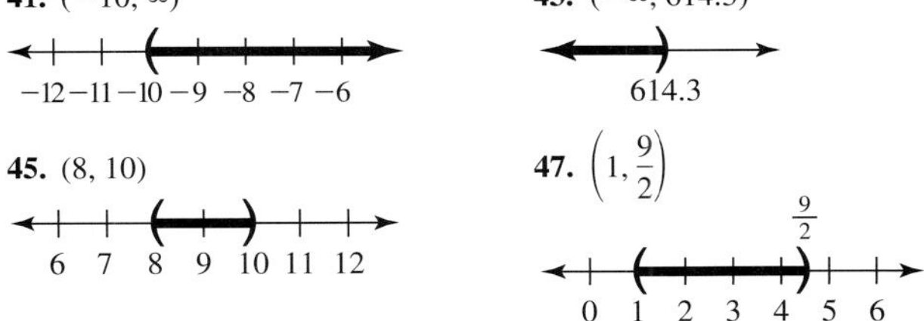

49. $[-2, 9]$

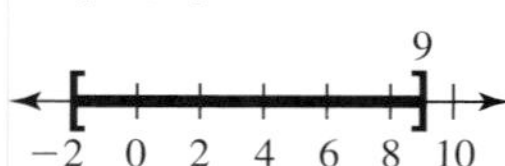

51. $[-5, 3)$

53. $(12, 30)$

55. $\left(-\frac{1}{2}, \frac{3}{2}\right]$

57. $(102.1, 108.3)$

59. $(-\infty, 6]$

61. $(-\infty, 0)$

63. $(2, 3)$

65. At least 28 meters **67.** Less than \$9358 **69.** At most \$550
71. At least 64 **73.** Between 81 and 94.5 inclusive
75. Between 49.5 and 56.625 miles per hour
77. Between 55° and 85°
79. a) Between 27 and 35 teeth inclusive **b)** Between 23.02 in. and 24.79 in. **c)** At least 14 teeth

Enriching Your Mathematical Word Power

1. b **2.** d **3.** c **4.** c **5.** d **6.** d **7.** a **8.** b **9.** c
10. d

Review Exercises

1. $\{35\}$ **3.** $\{-6\}$ **5.** $\{-7\}$ **7.** $\{13\}$ **9.** $\{7\}$ **11.** $\{2\}$ **13.** $\{7\}$
15. $\{0\}$ **17.** $\{-8\}$ **19.** $\varnothing$, inconsistent
21. All real numbers, identity **23.** All nonzero real numbers, identity
25. $\{24\}$, conditional **27.** $\{80\}$, conditional **29.** $\{1000\}$, conditional
31. $\left\{\frac{1}{4}\right\}$ **33.** $\left\{\frac{21}{8}\right\}$ **35.** $\left\{-\frac{4}{5}\right\}$ **37.** $\{4\}$ **39.** $\{24\}$ **41.** $\{-100\}$
43. $x = -\frac{b}{a}$ **45.** $x = \frac{b+2}{a}$ **47.** $x = \frac{V}{LW}$ **49.** $x = -\frac{b}{3}$
51. $y = -\frac{5}{2}x + 3$ **53.** $y = -\frac{1}{2}x + 4$ **55.** $y = -2x + 16$
57. -13 **59.** $-\frac{2}{5}$ **61.** 17 **63.** 15, 10, 5, 0, −5
65. −3, −1, 1, 3 **67.** $x + 9$, where x is the number
69. x and $x + 8$, where x is the smaller number
71. $0.65x$, where x is the number
73. $x(x + 5) = 98$, where x is the width
75. $2x = 3(x - 10)$, where x is Jim's rate
77. $x + x + 2 + x + 4 = 90$, where x is the smallest of the three even integers
79. $t + 2t + t - 10 = 180$, where t is the degree measure of an angle
81. 77, 79, 81 **83.** Betty 45 mph, Lawanda 60 mph
85. Wanda \$36,000, husband \$30,000 **87.** No **89.** No
91. $x > 1$, $(1, \infty)$ **93.** $x \geq 2$, $[2, \infty)$ **95.** $-3 \leq x < 3$, $[-3, 3)$
97. $x < -1$, $(-\infty, -1)$
99. $(-1, \infty)$

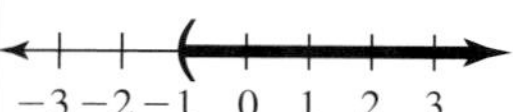

101. $(-\infty, 3)$

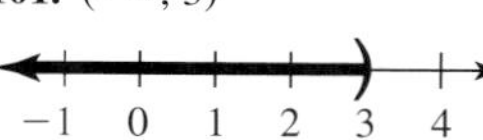

103. $(-\infty, -4]$

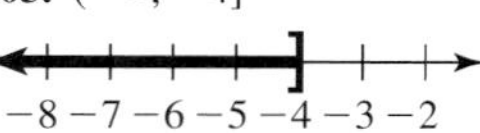

105. $(-4, \infty)$

107. $(-1, 5)$

109. $\left(-2, \frac{1}{2}\right]$

111. $[0, 3]$

113. $(0, 1)$

115. \$2800 **117.** \$8500 **119.** \$537.50 **121.** 400 movies
123. 31° **125.** Less than 6 feet

Chapter 2 Test

1. $\{-7\}$ **2.** $\{2\}$ **3.** $\{-9\}$ **4.** $\{700\}$ **5.** $\{1\}$ **6.** $\left\{\frac{7}{6}\right\}$ **7.** $\{2\}$
8. $\varnothing$ **9.** All real numbers **10.** $y = \frac{2}{3}x - 3$ **11.** $a = \frac{m + w}{P}$
12. $-3 < x \leq 2$, $(-3, 2]$ **13.** $x > 1$, $(1, \infty)$
14. $(19, \infty)$ **15.** $(-7, -1)$
16. $(1, 3)$ **17.** $(-6, \infty)$
18. 14 meters **19.** 9 in. **20.** 150 liters **21.** At most \$2000
22. 30°, 60°, 90°

Making Connections Chapters 1–2

1. $8x$ **2.** $15x^2$ **3.** $2x + 1$ **4.** $4x - 7$ **5.** $-2x + 13$
6. 60 **7.** 72 **8.** −10 **9.** $-2x^3$ **10.** −1 **11.** $\frac{2}{3}$
12. $\frac{1}{6}$ **13.** $\frac{1}{9}$ **14.** $\frac{5}{9}$ **15.** 13 **16.** 8 **17.** $2x + 1$
18. $10x - 9$ **19.** $\left\{\frac{2}{3}\right\}$ **20.** $\left\{\frac{1}{6}\right\}$ **21.** $\left(\frac{2}{3}, \infty\right)$ **22.** $\left(-\infty, \frac{1}{6}\right]$
23. $\left\{\frac{1}{9}\right\}$ **24.** $\left\{\frac{5}{9}\right\}$ **25.** $\left[-\frac{1}{9}, \infty\right)$ **26.** $\left(-\infty, -\frac{5}{9}\right)$ **27.** $\left\{\frac{3}{10}\right\}$
28. $\left\{\frac{16}{5}\right\}$ **29.** $\left\{\frac{1}{2}\right\}$ **30.** $\left\{\frac{7}{5}\right\}$ **31.** $\{1\}$ **32.** All real numbers
33. $\{0\}$ **34.** $\{1\}$ **35.** $(0, \infty)$ **36.** $\varnothing$ **37.** $\{2\}$ **38.** $\{2\}$
39. $\left\{\frac{13}{2}\right\}$ **40.** $\{200\}$ **41. a)** \$13,600 **b)** \$10,000 **c)** \$12,000

Chapter 3

Section 3.1 Warm-Ups F F F F T T T F F T
1. An ordered pair is a pair of numbers in which there is a first number and a second number, usually written as (a, b).
3. The origin is the point of intersection of the x-axis and y-axis.
5. A linear equation in two variables is an equation of the form $Ax + By = C$, where A and B are not both zero.
7. (0, 9), (5, 24), (2, 15) **9.** (0, −7), $\left(\frac{1}{3}, -8\right)$, $\left(-\frac{2}{3}, -5\right)$
11. (0, 54.3), (10, 66.3), (0.5, 54.9) **13.** (3, 0), (0, −2), (12, 6)
15. (5, −3), (5, 5), (5, 0) **17.** (−2, 9), (0, 5), (2, 1), (4, −3), (6, −7)

19. (−6, 0), (−3, 1), (0, 2), (3, 3)

21. (−30, −200), (−20, 0), (−10, 200), (0, 400), (10, 600)

23–37 odd

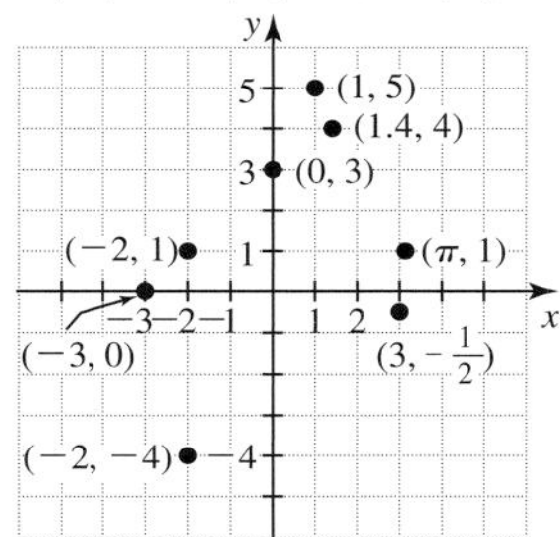

39. Quadrant II **41.** x-axis **43.** Quadrant III

45. Quadrant I **47.** Quadrant II **49.** y-axis

51.

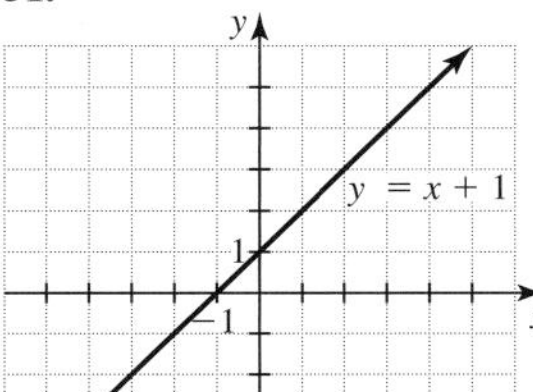

53.

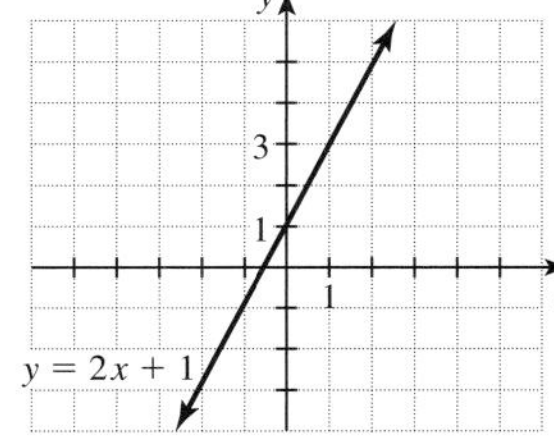

55.

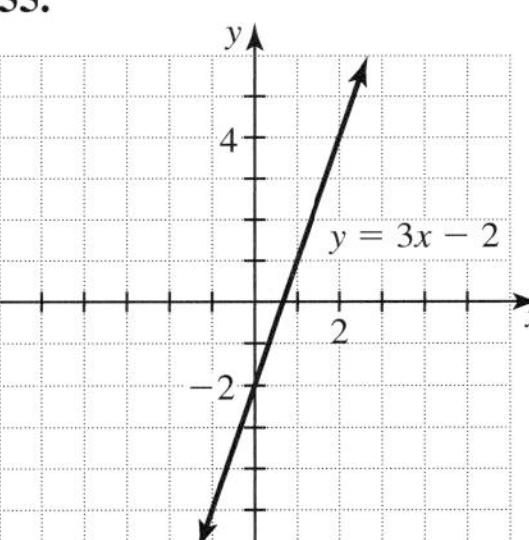

57.

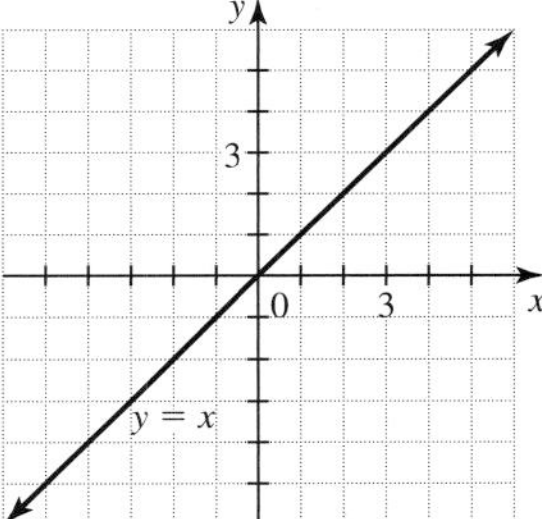

59.

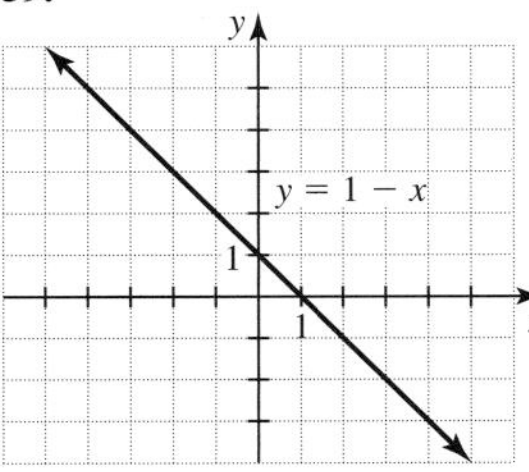

61.

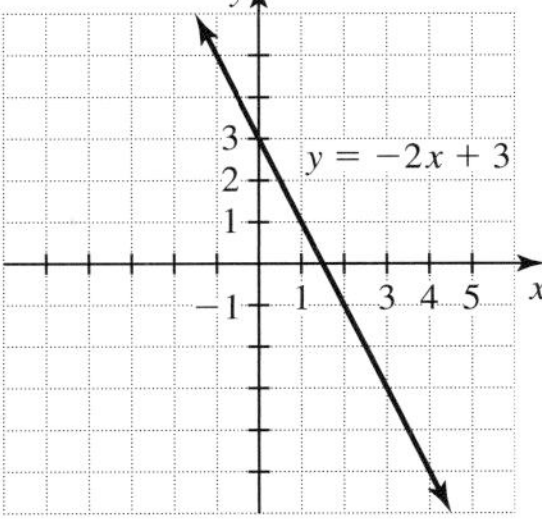

63.

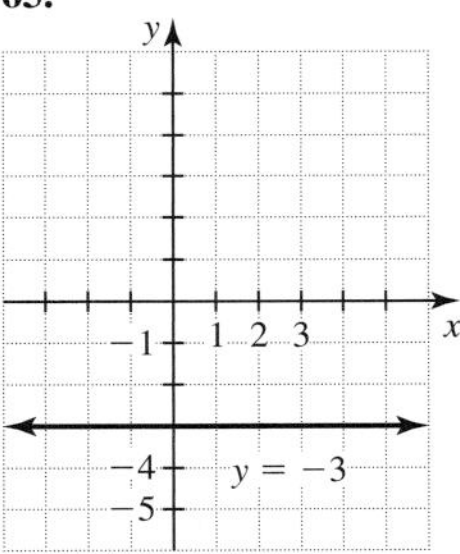

65.

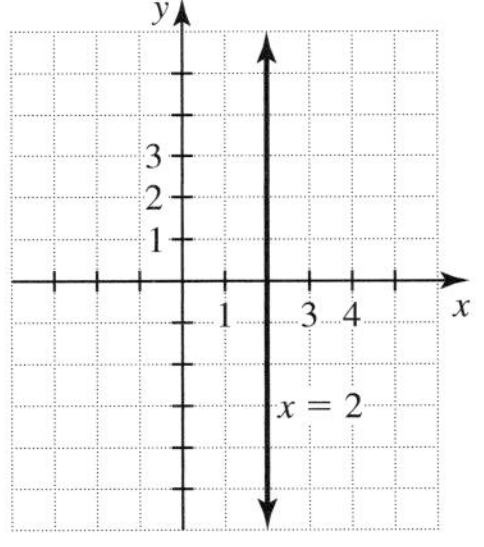

67.

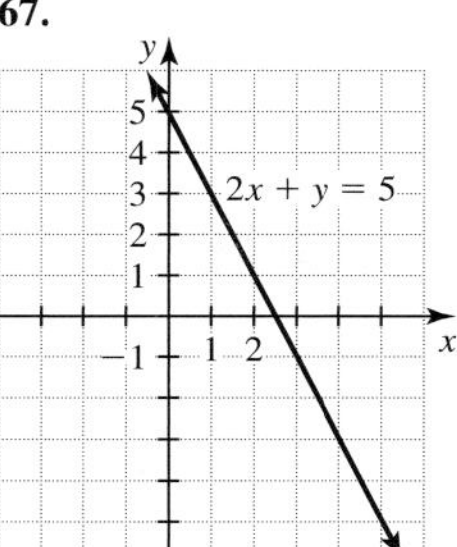

69.

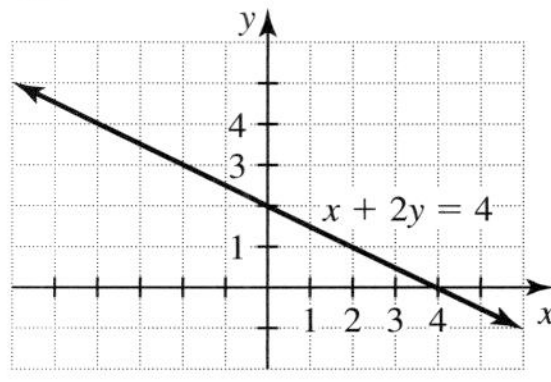

71.

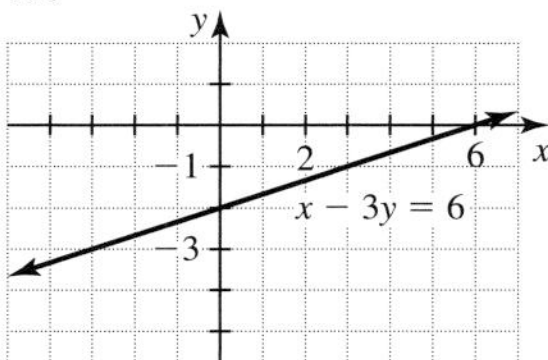

73.

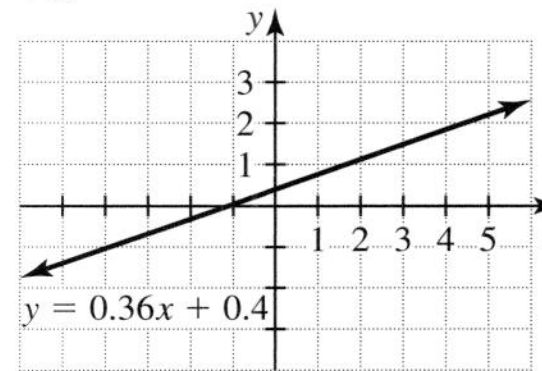

75.

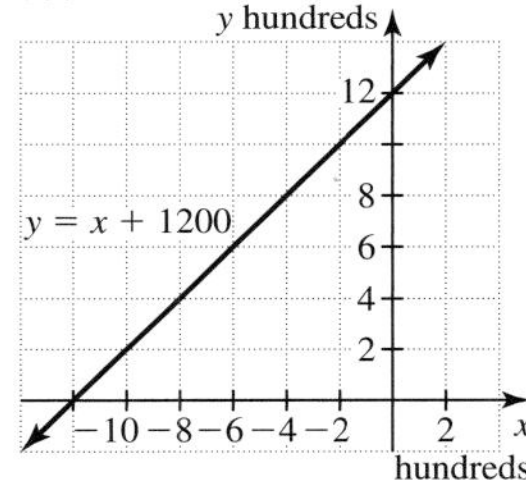

77.

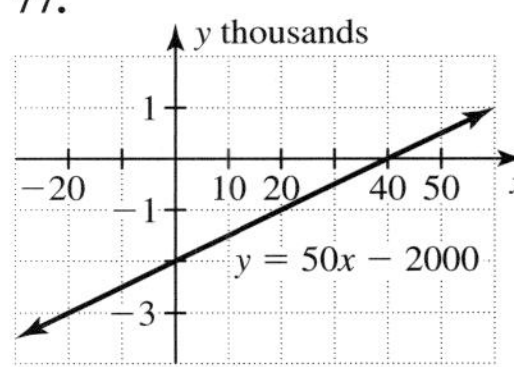

79.

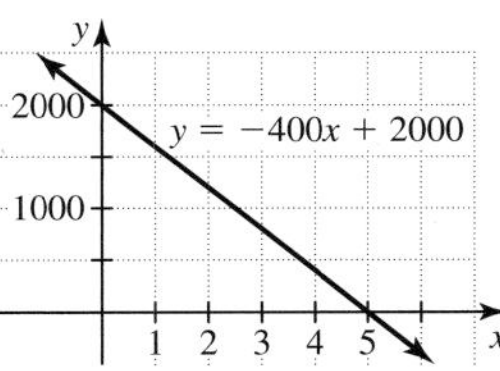

81. (2, 0), (0, 3)

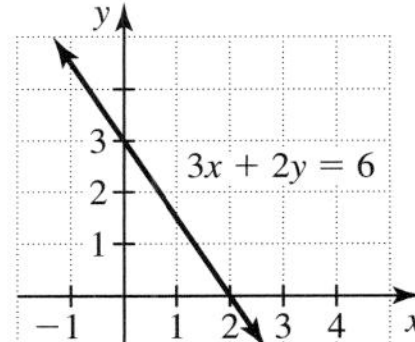

83. (4, 0), (0, −1)

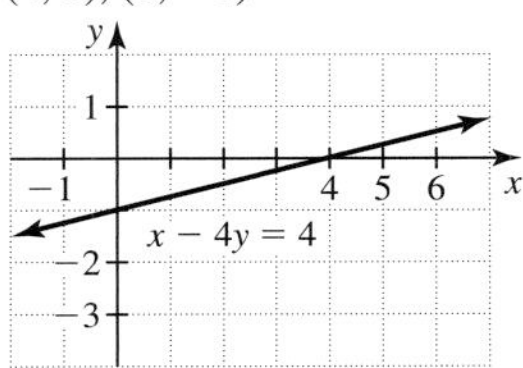

85. (12, 0), (0, −9)

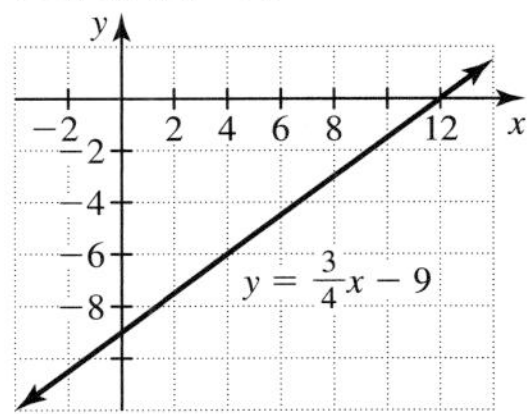

87. (2, 0), (0, 4)

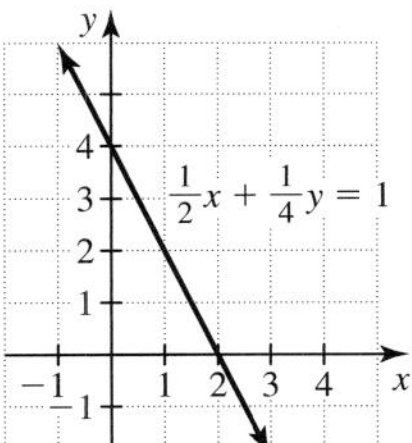

89. 75%, 67, 68 and up

91. a) \$97.3 billion **b)** 2016

c)

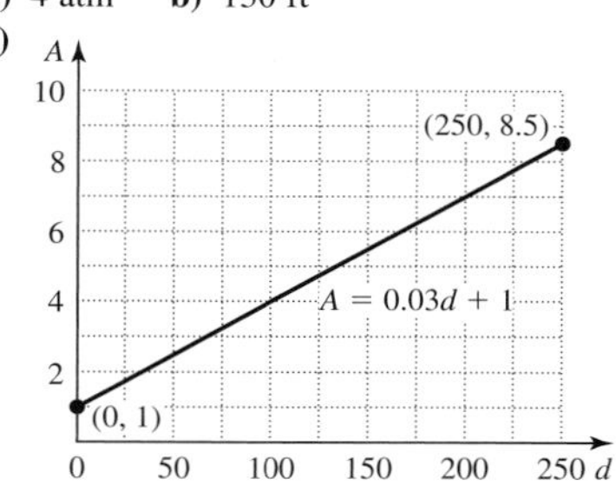

93. a) 4 atm **b)** 130 ft

c)

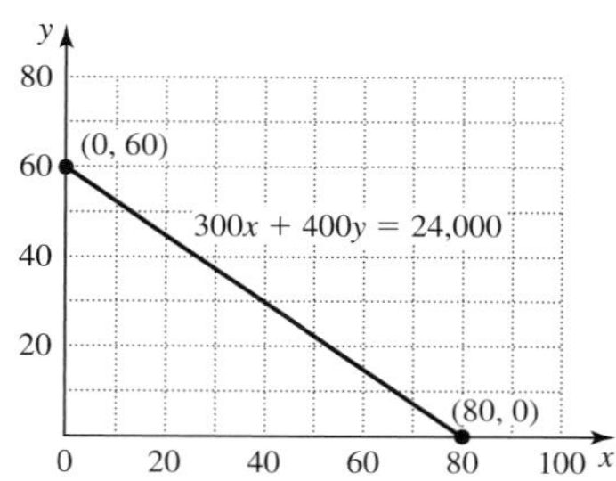

95. x = the number of radio ads, y = the number of TV ads, 21 solutions

y

80

(0, 60)

60

300x + 400y = 24,000

40

20

(80, 0)

0 20 40 60 80 100 x

97.

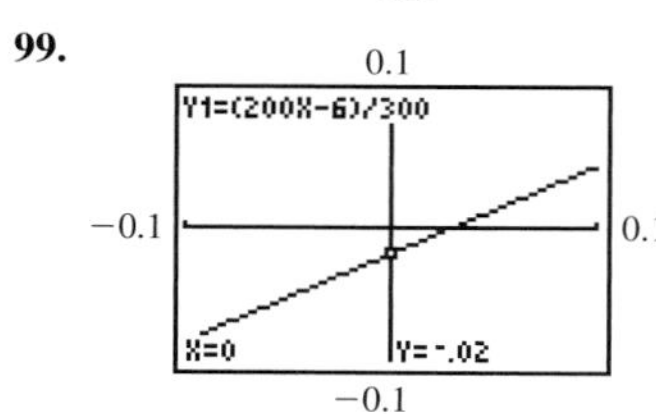

99.

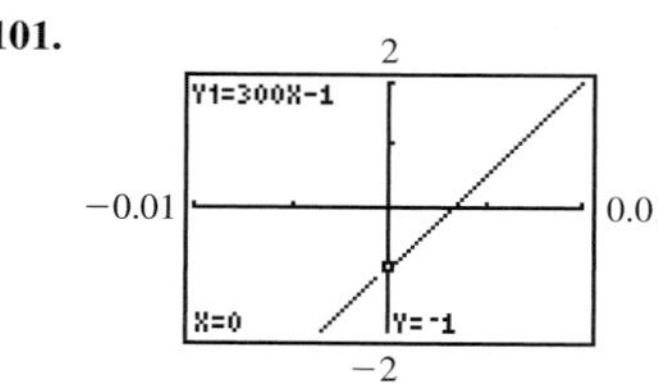

101.

2

Y1=300X-1

−0.01

0.01

X=0

Y=-1

−2

Section 3.2 Warm-Ups T T F T F F F F T T

1. The slope of a line is the ratio of its rise and run.

3. Slope is undefined for vertical lines.

5. Lines with positive slope are rising as you go from left to right, while lines with negative slope are falling as you go from left to right.

7. $-\frac{2}{3}$ **9.** $\frac{2}{3}$ **11.** $\frac{3}{2}$ **13.** 0 **15.** $\frac{2}{5}$ **17.** Undefined **19.** 2

21. $\frac{5}{4}$ **23.** $-\frac{5}{3}$ **25.** $\frac{5}{7}$ **27.** $-\frac{4}{3}$ **29.** -1 **31.** 1

33. Undefined **35.** 0 **37.** 3

39.

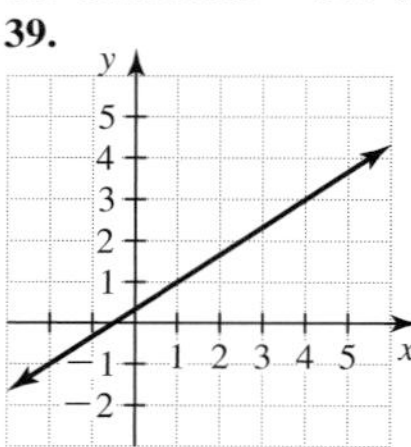

41.

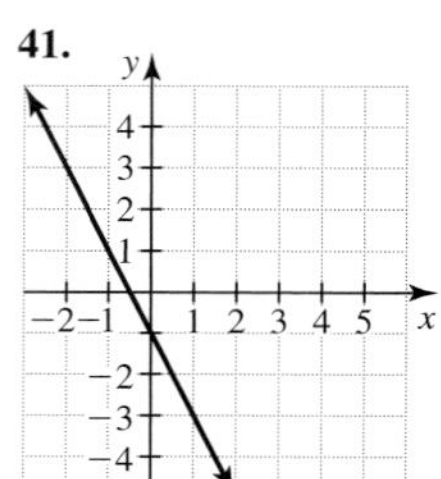

43.

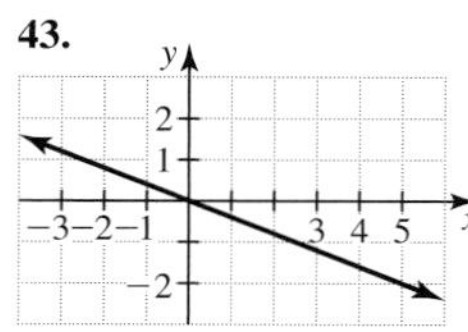

45.

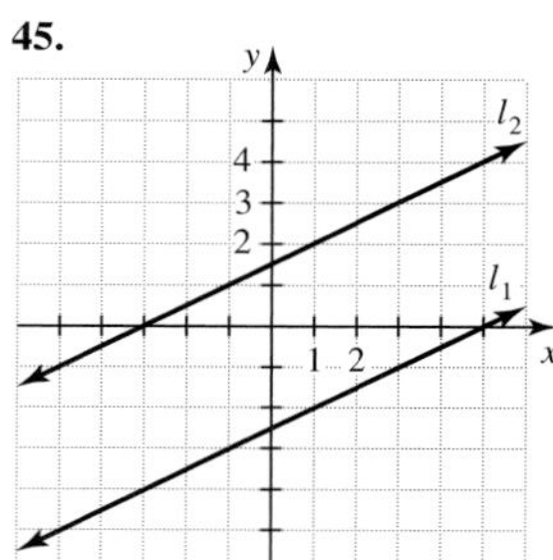

47.

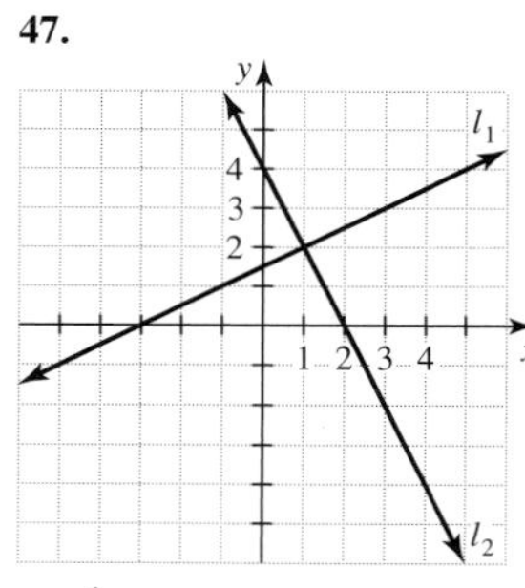

49. $-\frac{4}{3}$

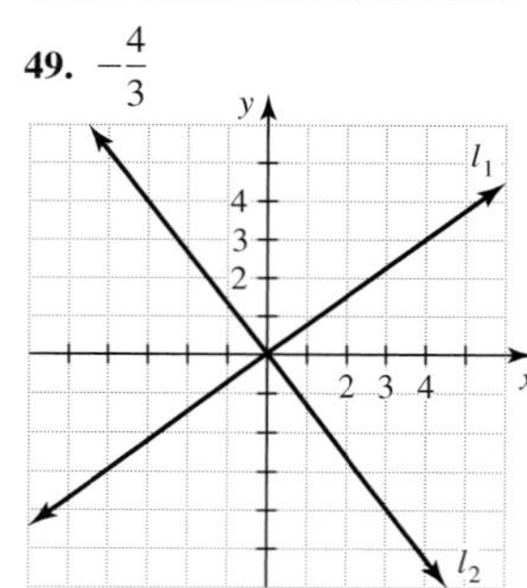

51. $\frac{1}{2}$

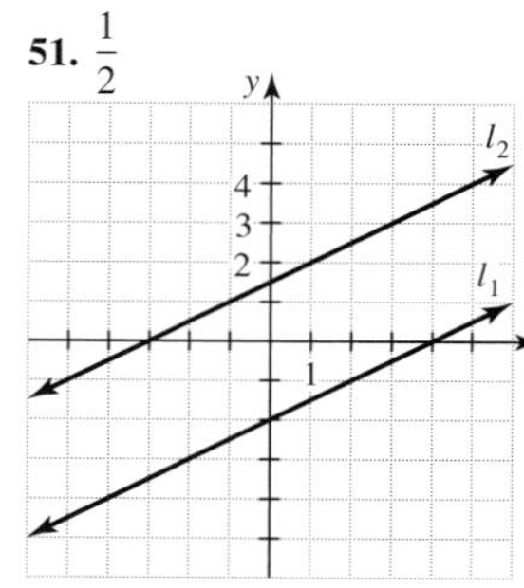

53. 1

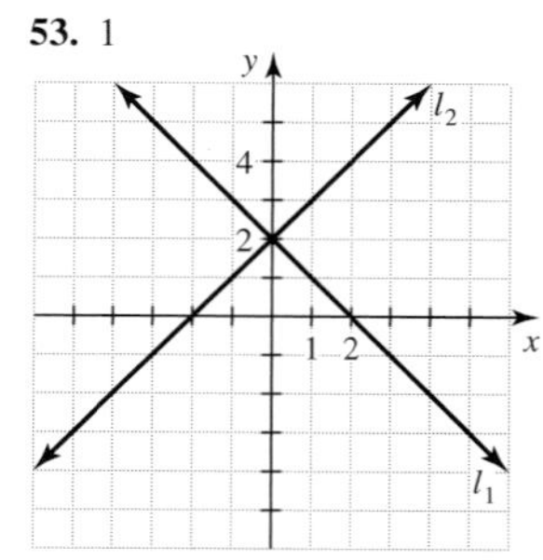

55. Parallel **57.** Neither **59.** Parallel **61.** Perpendicular

63. a) Slope 0.1875; Cost is increasing about \$187,500 per year. **b)** \$2.05 million; yes **c)** \$3.55 million

65. 1 slope; The percentage increases 1% per year.

67. (2000, 28,100), (2003, 29,300), (2012, 32,900), (2015, 34,100)

69. Yes **71.** No

Section 3.3 Warm-Ups T F T T T F F T T F

1. Slope-intercept form is $y = mx + b$.
3. The standard form is $Ax + By = C$.
5. The slope-intercept form allows us to write the equation from the y-intercept and the slope.
7. $y = \frac{3}{2}x + 1$ **9.** $y = -2x + 2$ **11.** $y = x - 2$ **13.** $y = -x$
15. $y = -1$ **17.** $x = -2$ **19.** 3, (0, −9) **21.** $-\frac{1}{2}$, (0, 3)
23. 0, (0, 4) **25.** 1, (0, 0) **27.** −3, (0, 0) **29.** −1, (0, 5)
31. $\frac{1}{2}$, (0, −2) **33.** $\frac{2}{5}$, (0, −2) **35.** 2, (0, 3)
37. Undefined slope, no y-intercept **39.** $x + y = 2$ **41.** $x - 2y = -6$
43. $9x - 6y = 2$ **45.** $6x + 10y = 7$ **47.** $x = -10$ **49.** $3y = 10$
51. $5x - 6y = 0$ **53.** $x - 50y = -25$

55.

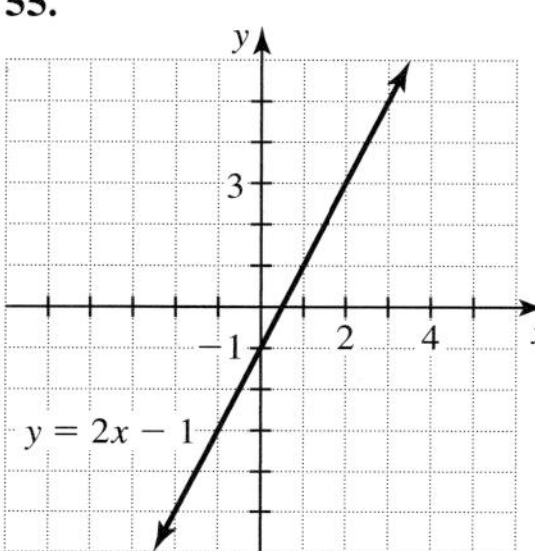

57.

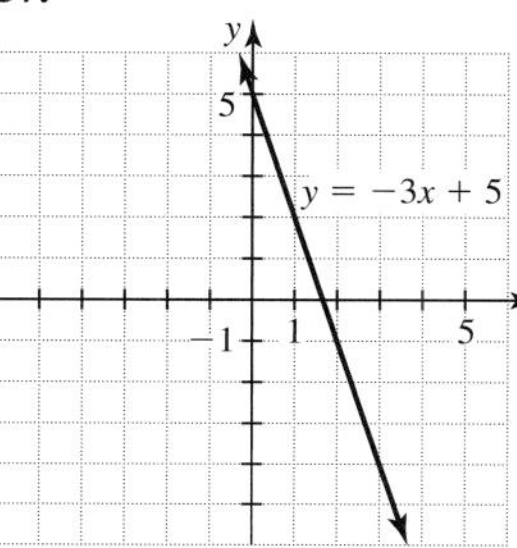

59.

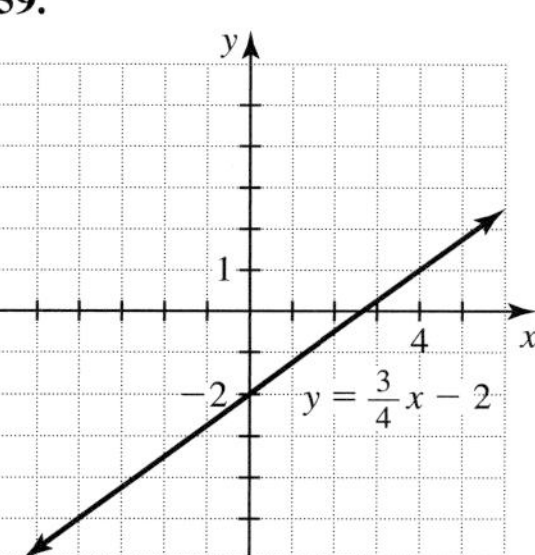

61.

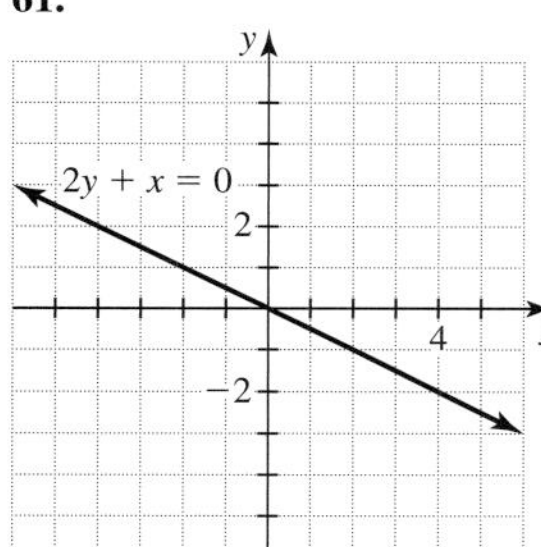

63.

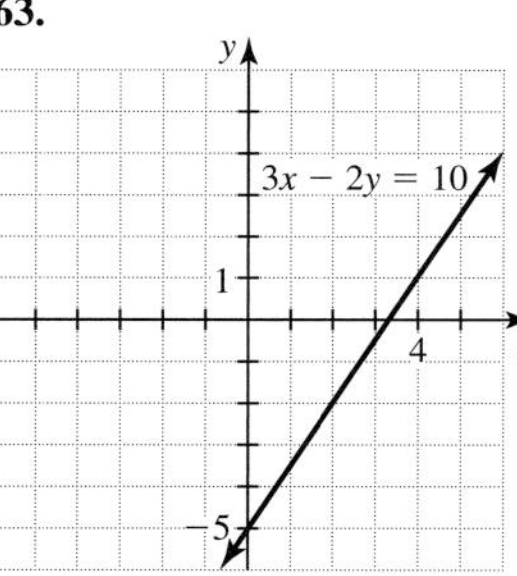

65.

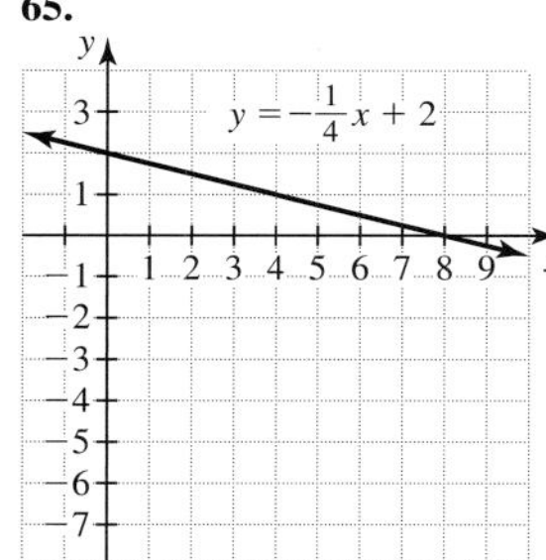

67.

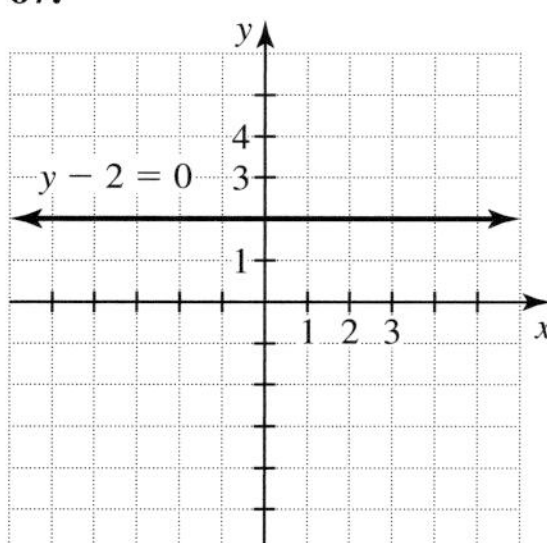

69. Parallel **71.** Neither

73. Parallel **75.** Perpendicular **77.** $y = \frac{1}{2}x - 4$ **79.** $y = 2x + 3$
81. $y = -\frac{1}{3}x + 6$ **83.** $y = -2x + 3$ **85.** $y = 3$
87. $y = -\frac{3}{2}x + 4$ **89.** $y = -\frac{4}{5}x + 4$
91. a) \$80, \$130, \$180 **b)** 50, (0, 80) **c)** There is an \$80 fixed cost, plus \$50 per hour. **93.** \$1,150,000, \$1,150,200, \$200
95. a) A slope of 1 means that the percentage of workers receiving training is going up 1% per year. **b)** $y = x + 5$ where x is the number of years since 1982 **c)** The y-intercept (0, 5) means that 5% of the workers received training in 1982. **d)** 33%
97. a) x = the number of packs of pansies, y = the number of packs of snapdragons
b)

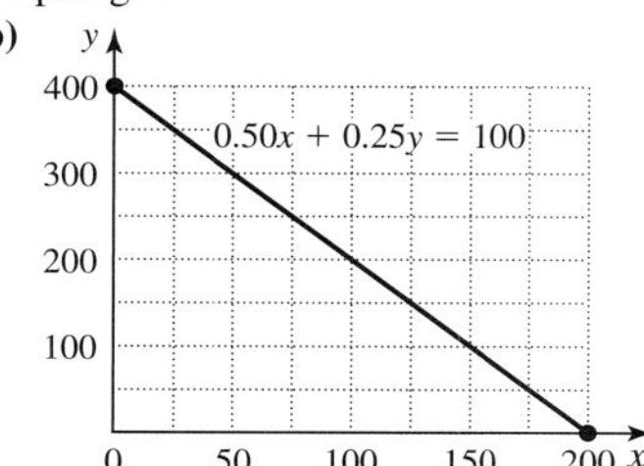

c) $y = -2x + 400$
d) −2
e) If the number of packs of pansies goes up by 1, then the number of packs of snapdragons goes down by 2.

99. (2, 0), (0, 3) **101.** $\frac{x}{9} + \frac{y}{5} = 1$

103.

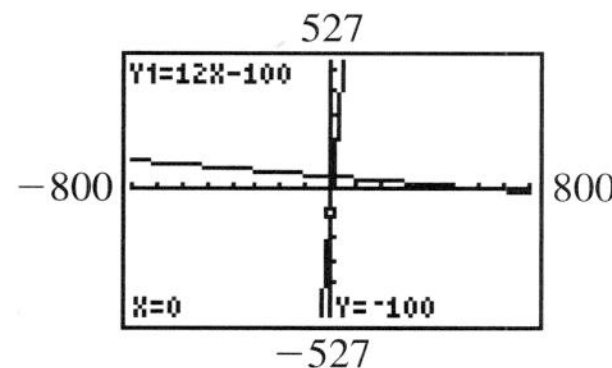

Section 3.4 Warm-Ups F F T T F T T T T T

1. Point-slope form is $y - y_1 = m(x - x_1)$.
3. If you know two points on a line, find the slope. Then use it along with either point in point-slope form to write the equation of the line.
5. Nonvertical parallel lines have equal slopes. **7.** $y = -x + 1$
9. $y = 5x + 11$ **11.** $y = \frac{3}{4}x - 20$ **13.** $y = \frac{2}{3}x + \frac{1}{3}$ **15.** $y = 3x - 1$
17. $y = \frac{1}{2}x + 3$ **19.** $y = \frac{1}{3}x + \frac{7}{3}$ **21.** $y = -\frac{1}{2}x + 4$
23. $y = -6x - 13$ **25.** $2x - y = 7$ **27.** $x - 2y = 6$
29. $2x - 3y = 2$ **31.** $2x - y = -1$ **33.** $x - y = 0$
35. $3x - 2y = -1$ **37.** $3x + 5y = -11$ **39.** $x - y = -2$
41. $x = 2$ **43.** $y = 9$ **45.** $y = -x + 4$ **47.** $y = \frac{5}{3}x - 1$
49. $y = x + 3$ **51.** $y = -\frac{1}{3}x + 5$ **53.** $y = -\frac{2}{3}x + \frac{5}{3}$
55. $y = -2x - 5$ **57.** $y = \frac{1}{3}x + \frac{7}{3}$ **59.** $y = 2x - 1$ **61.** $y = 2$
63. $y = \frac{2}{3}x$ **65.** $y = -x$ **67.** $y = 50$ **69.** $y = -\frac{3}{5}x - 4$
71. e **73.** f **75.** h **77.** g
79. a) Slope 0.9 means that the number of ATM transactions is increasing by 0.9 billion per year. **b)** $y = 0.9x + 10.6$ **c)** 23.2 billion

81. a) $y = 1.5x + 53.8$ **b)** $x =$ years since 1990, $y =$ GDP in thousands of dollars **c)** \$83,800
d)

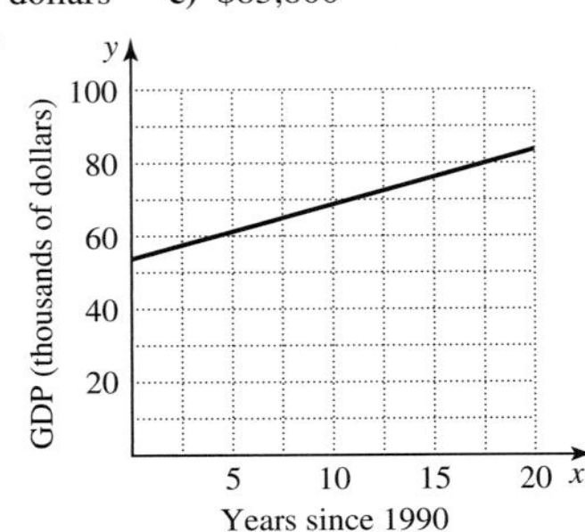

83. $C = 20n + 30$, \$170 **85.** $S = 3L - \frac{41}{4}$, 8.5

87. $v = 32t + 10$, 122 ft/sec

89. a) $w = -\frac{1}{120}t + \frac{3}{2}$ **b)** $\frac{5}{6}$ inch **c)** 60°F

91. $A = 0.6w$, 3.6 in. **93. a)** $a = 0.08c$ **b)** 0.24 **c)** 6.25 mg/ml

95. 2, 3, $-\frac{2}{3}$; 4, -5, $\frac{4}{5}$; $\frac{1}{2}$, 3, $-\frac{1}{6}$; 2, $-\frac{1}{3}$, 6

97. a)

500
Y1=20X-300
−20 20
X=0 Y=-300
−500

b)

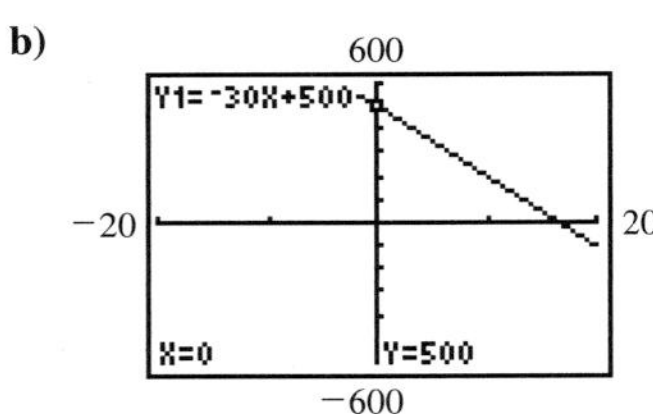

c)

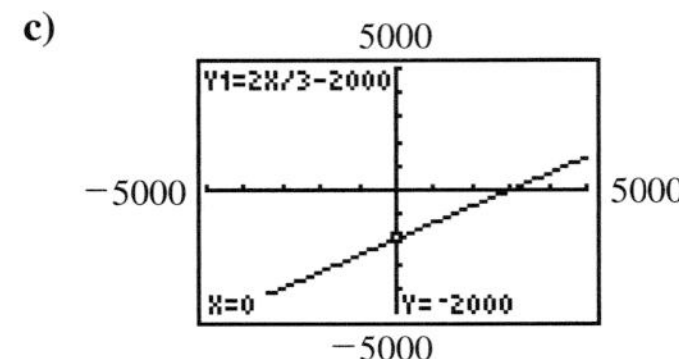

99. $-1 \le x \le 1$, $-1 \le y \le 1$

Section 3.5 Warm-Ups T F T F F T T T F F

1. If y varies directly as x, then there is a constant k such that $y = kx$.
3. If y is inversely proportional to x, then there is a constant k such that $y = \frac{k}{x}$.
5. $T = kh$ **7.** $y = \frac{k}{r}$ **9.** $R = kts$ **11.** $i = kb$ **13.** $A = kym$
15. $y = \frac{5}{3}x$ **17.** $A = \frac{6}{B}$ **19.** $m = \frac{198}{p}$ **21.** $A = 2tu$ **23.** $T = \frac{9}{2}u$
25. 25 **27.** 1 **29.** 105
31. 100.3 pounds **33.** 50 minutes **35.** \$17.40 **37.** 80 mph
39. 3 days **41.** 1600, 12, 12
43. $\left(\frac{1}{2}, 600\right)$, (1, 300), (30, 10), $\left(900, \frac{1}{3}\right)$, Inversely
45. $\left(\frac{1}{3}, \frac{1}{4}\right)$, (8, 6), (12, 9), (20, 15), Directly **47.** Directly, $y = 3.5x$
49. Inversely, $y = \frac{20}{x}$ **51.** (1, 65), (2, 130), (3, 195), (4, 260)
53. (20, 20), (40, 10), (50, 8), (200, 2) **55.** k, (0, 0), no, $y = kx$

Enriching Your Mathematical Word Power
1. d **2.** a **3.** b **4.** c **5.** b **6.** a **7.** c **8.** c **9.** d
10. b **11.** c **12.** d

Review Exercises
1. Quadrant II **3.** x-axis **5.** y-axis **7.** Quadrant IV
9. $(0, -5)$, $(-3, -14)$, $(4, 7)$
11. $\left(0, -\frac{8}{3}\right)$, $\left(3, -\frac{2}{3}\right)$, $\left(-6, -\frac{20}{3}\right)$
13.

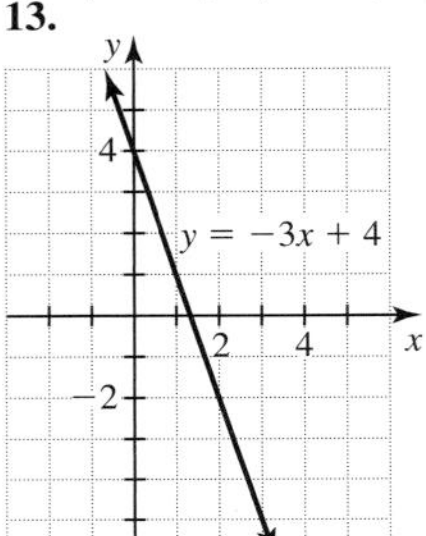

15.

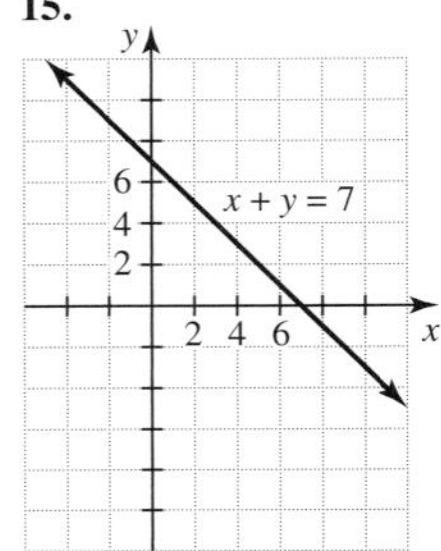

17. 1 **19.** $\frac{3}{2}$ **21.** $\frac{3}{7}$ **23.** 3, $(0, -18)$ **25.** 2, $(0, -3)$
27. 2, $(0, -4)$
29.

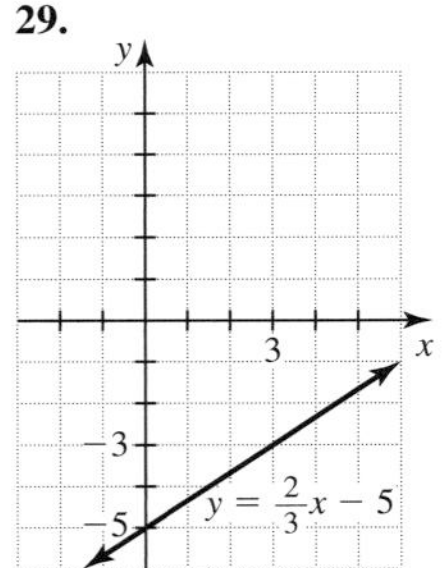

31.

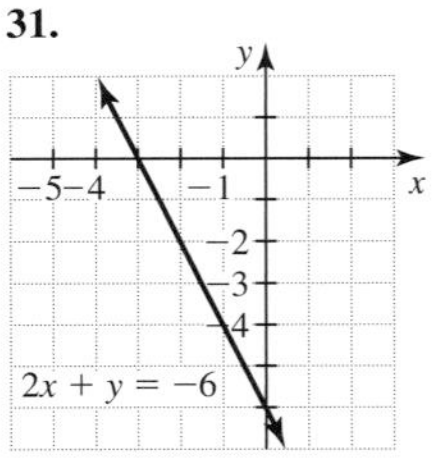

33.

y
−1 3 x
−2
y = −4 −3
−5

35. $x - 3y = -12$ **37.** $x + 2y = 0$ **39.** $y = 5$ **41.** $y = \frac{2}{3}x + 7$
43. $y = \frac{3}{7}x - 2$ **45.** $y = -\frac{3}{4}x + \frac{17}{4}$ **47.** $y = -2x - 1$

49. $y = \frac{6}{5}x + \frac{17}{5}$ **51.** $y = 3x - 14$ **53.** $C = 32n + 49$, \$177
55. a) $q = 1 - p$ **b)** 1 **57.** $y = 0.1x + 0.6$ **59.** 132 **61.** 2
63. 60 **65. a)** $C = 0.75T$ **b)** \$15 **c)** Increasing
67. $y = x - 1$ **69.** $y = -\frac{1}{2}x + 4$ **71.** $y = 4x - 5$ **73.** $y = \frac{3}{2}x - 36$
75. (1, 0), (0, 1) **77.** (4, 0), (0, 3) **79.** $\left(\frac{1}{2}, 0\right)$, (0, −2)
81. (4, 0), (0, 18) **83.** $y = \frac{1}{2}x - 3$ **85.** $y = 3$ **87.** $y = 3x + 9$
89. $y = -\frac{1}{3}x + \frac{4}{3}$ **91.** $y = -4x + 2$ **93.** $y = 3x - 1$

Chapter 3 Test

1. Quadrant II **2.** x-axis **3.** Quadrant IV **4.** y-axis
5. 1 **6.** $-\frac{5}{6}$ **7.** 3 **8.** 0 **9.** Undefined **10.** $\frac{2}{3}$
11. $y = -\frac{1}{2}x + 3$ **12.** $y = \frac{3}{7}x - \frac{11}{7}$ **13.** $x - 3y = 11$
14. $5x + 3y = 27$

15.

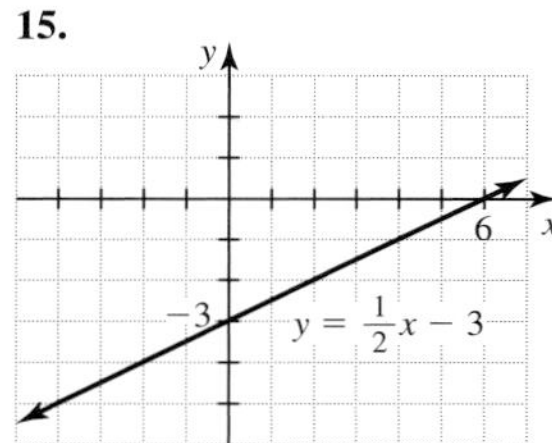

16.

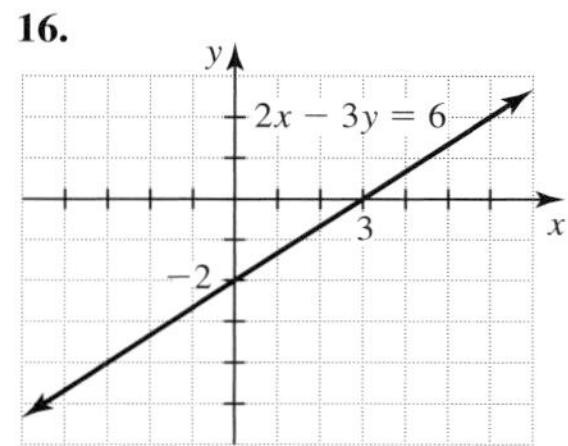

17.

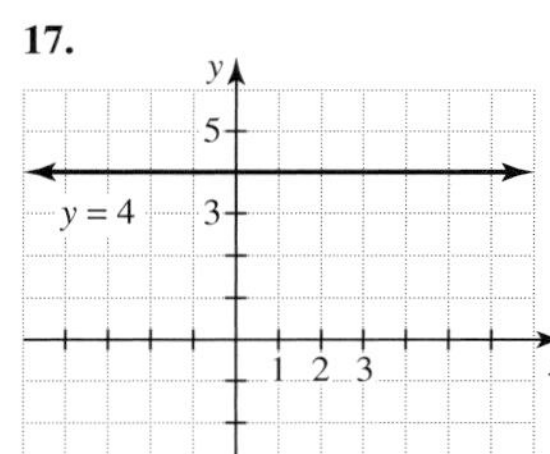

18.

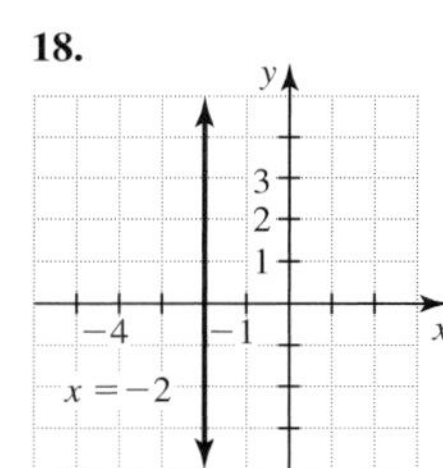

19. $S = 0.75n + 2.50$ **20. a)** $P = 3v + 20$ **b)** 80 cents
21. a) 800 **b)** (0, 1000), (50, 0); At \$0 per ticket 1000 tickets will be sold and at \$50 per ticket zero tickets will be sold.
c) −20 tickets/dollar; For every \$1 increase in price, 20 fewer tickets will be sold.

22. a) $P = kw$ **b)** \$2.80
23. a) $n = \frac{k}{A}$ **b)** 18.75 days **c)** Decreases
24. a) $C = kLW$ **b)** \$770

Making Connections Chapters 1–3

1. −1 **2.** −34 **3.** 1 **4.** 72 **5.** −4
6. −28 **7.** $-\frac{7}{2}$ **8.** 0.4 **9.** $\frac{1}{10}$ **10.** 15 **11.** $13x$
12. $3x - 36$ **13.** $\left\{\frac{5}{2}\right\}$ **14.** $\left\{\frac{7}{3}\right\}$ **15.** $\frac{1}{6}$ **16.** $\frac{5}{12}$
17. {2} **18.** {−4} **19.** $2x - 4$ **20.** $x + 2$
21. {5} **22.** {3} **23.** ∅ **24.** All real numbers
25. (4.5, ∞) **26.** $\left(-\frac{2}{3}, \infty\right)$ **27.** [10, ∞) **28.** [20, ∞)
29. $\left[-\frac{1}{2}, \frac{5}{2}\right)$ **30.** $\left[0, \frac{2}{3}\right)$ **31.** $y = \frac{t - 2}{3\pi}$ **32.** $y = mx + b$
33. $y = x - 4$ **34.** $y = 6$ **35.** $y = \frac{4}{5}$ **36.** $y = 200$
37. a) $\frac{2}{15}$ **b)** $\frac{1}{5}$ **c)** About 13% per year
d) \$276,000 saved, \$12,000 per year

Chapter 4

Section 4.1 Warm-Ups T F F F T T T T T F
1. A system of equations is a pair of equations.
3. In this section systems of equations were solved by graphing.
5. A dependent system is one that has infinitely many solutions.
7. (3, −2) **9.** All three **11.** None **13.** (−2, 3) **15.** (2, 4)
17. (1, 2) **19.** (0, −5) **21.** (−2, 3) **23.** (0, 0) **25.** (2, 3)
27. (3, 1) **29.** (−2, 3) **31.** (2, 7) **33.** (10, 12) **35.** (−10, 22)
37. (0.5, −0.3) **39.** $\{(x, y) \mid x - y = 3\}$ **41.** $\{(x, y) \mid x - 2y = 8\}$
43. No solution **45.** No solution **47.** Inconsistent **49.** Dependent
51. Independent **53.** Inconsistent **55.** Inconsistent
57. Independent **59.** Inconsistent **61.** (1, −2), independent
63. No solution, inconsistent **65.** (−3, 1), independent
67. $\{(x, y) \mid x - y = 1\}$, dependent **69.** (−4, −3), independent
71. a) (5, 20)
b) For 5 toppings the cost is \$20 at both restaurants.
73. a) 800, 500; 1050, 850; 1300, 1200; 1800, 1900
b)

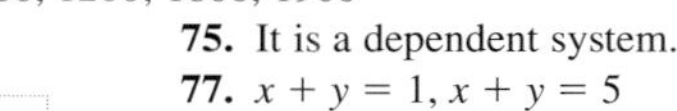
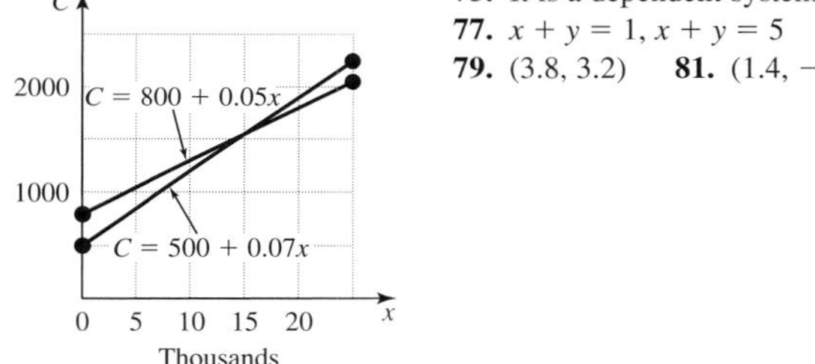

c) 15,000 **d)** Panasonic

75. It is a dependent system.
77. $x + y = 1$, $x + y = 5$
79. (3.8, 3.2) **81.** (1.4, −0.1)

Section 4.2 Warm-Ups T T T T T T F T T T
1. In this section we used the substitution method.
3. A dependent system is one that has infinitely many solutions.
5. Using substitution on a dependent system results in an equation that is always true. **7.** (3, 5) **9.** (4, 7) **11.** (2, 5) **13.** (2, 3)
15. (−2, 9) **17.** (−5, 5) **19.** $\left(\frac{1}{3}, \frac{2}{3}\right)$ **21.** $\left(\frac{1}{2}, \frac{1}{3}\right)$
23. $\{(x, y) \mid 3x - y = 5\}$, dependent **25.** $\left(3, \frac{5}{2}\right)$, independent
27. No solution, inconsistent **29.** No solution, inconsistent
31. $\left(\frac{11}{5}, \frac{3}{25}\right)$, independent **33.** (3, 2) **35.** (3, 1) **37.** No solution
39. Inconsistent **41.** Dependent **43.** Independent **45.** Inconsistent
47. Length 28 ft, width 14 ft **49.** \$12,000 at 10%, \$8000 at 5%
51. *Titanic* \$601 million, *Star Wars* \$461 million
53. Lawn \$12, sidewalk \$7
55. Left rear 288 pounds, left front 287 pounds, no
57. \$2.40 per pound
59. a) 69.2 years, 76.8 years

b)

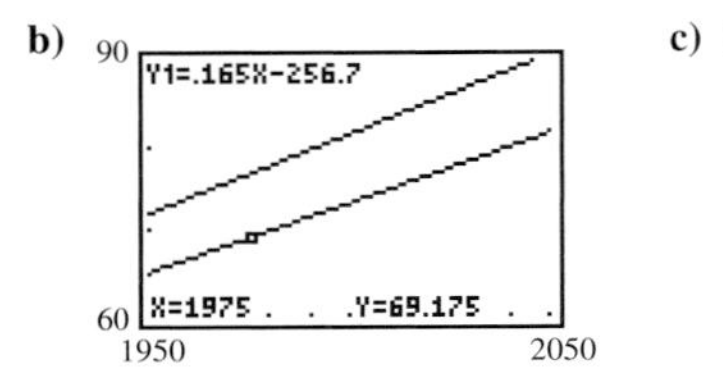

c) No **d)** 1614

Section 4.3 Warm-Ups F T T T T F F F F T

1. In this section we learned to solve systems by the addition method.
3. In addition and substitution we eliminate a variable and solve for the remaining variable.
5. Eliminate the variable that is easiest to eliminate.
7. (4, 1) **9.** (3, −1) **11.** (−3, 5) **13.** (−4, 3)
15. (10, −2) **17.** (8, 31) **19.** (−2, −3)
21. (−1, 4) **23.** (−1, 2) **25.** (3, −1) **27.** (1, 2)
29. (12, 6) **31.** (24, 16) **33.** No solution, inconsistent
35. $\{(x, y) \mid x + y = 5\}$, dependent **37.** $\{(x, y) \mid 2x = y + 3\}$, dependent
39. $\{(x, y) \mid x + 3y = 3\}$, dependent **41.** No solution, inconsistent
43. (12, 18), independent **45.** (40, 60), independent
47. (0.1, 0.1), independent **49.** (1.5, −2.8) **51.** (4, 3)
53. (4, 1) **55.** No solution **57.** 150 cars, 100 trucks
59. 24 dimes, 16 nickels **61.** 24 dimes, 7 quarters
63. 6 adults, 24 children **65.** Coffee \$0.45, doughnut \$0.35
67. 300 men, 360 women **69.** 180 hours regular time, 30 hours overtime
71. \$3000 at 7%, \$5000 at 10% **73.** \$12,000 in stocks, \$9000 in bonds
75. \$1800 at 15%, \$3000 at 9%
77. 200 pounds of 20% synthetic, 600 pounds of 40% synthetic
79. 40 ounces of 10%, 80 ounces of 22%
81. 64 ounces of \$4.40 metal, 36 ounces of \$2.40 metal
83. 60 pounds of \$4.20 hamburger, 40 pounds of \$3.10 hamburger

Section 4.4 Warm-Ups T T T F F F T F T F

1. A linear inequality has the same form as a linear equation except that an inequality symbol is used.
3. If the inequality symbol includes equality, then the boundary line is solid; otherwise it is dashed.
5. In the test-point method we test a point to see which side of the boundary line satisfies the inequality.
7. (3, −1) **9.** (−3, −9) **11.** (3, 0), (1, 3) **13.** (2, 3), (0, 5)

15.

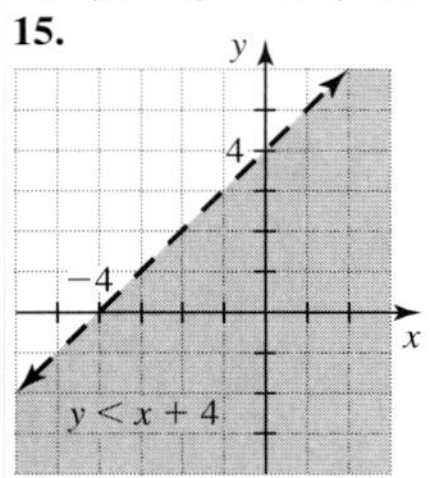

17.

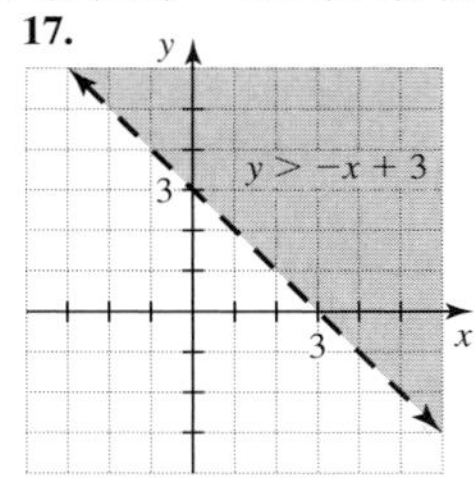

19.

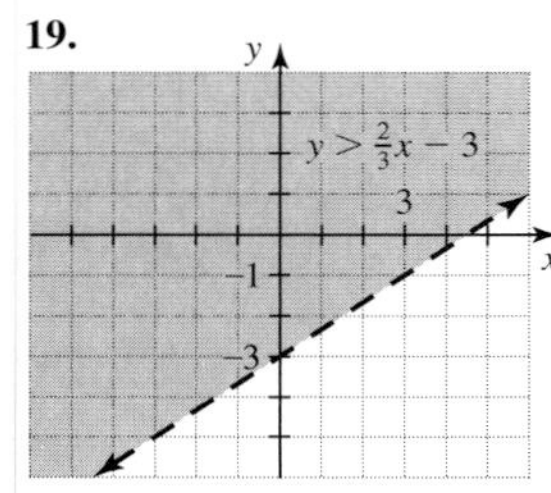

21.

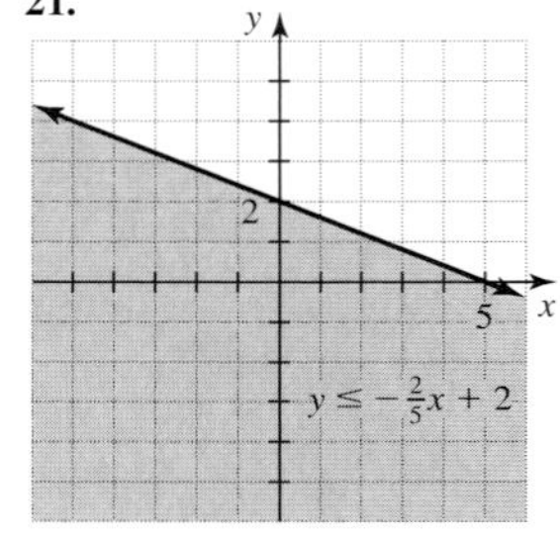

23.

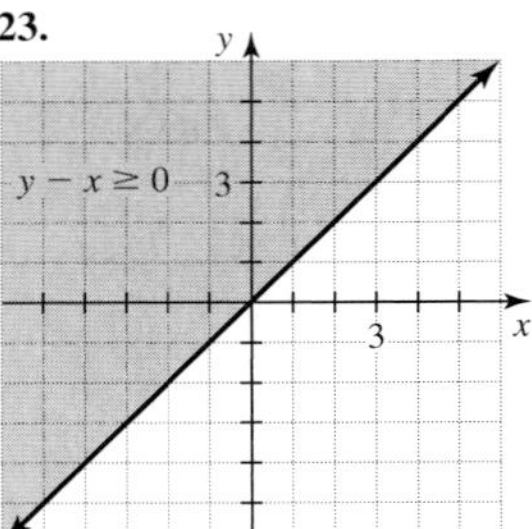

25.

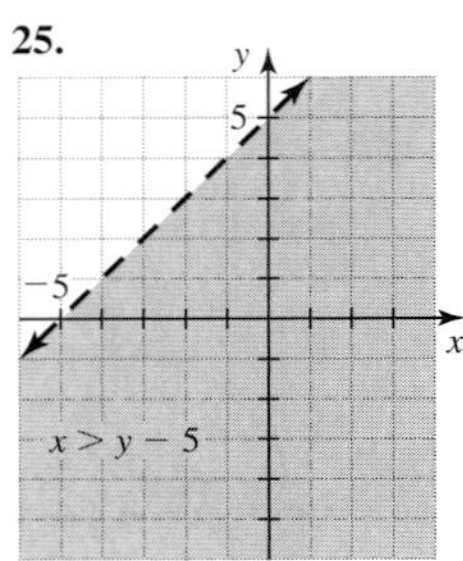

27.

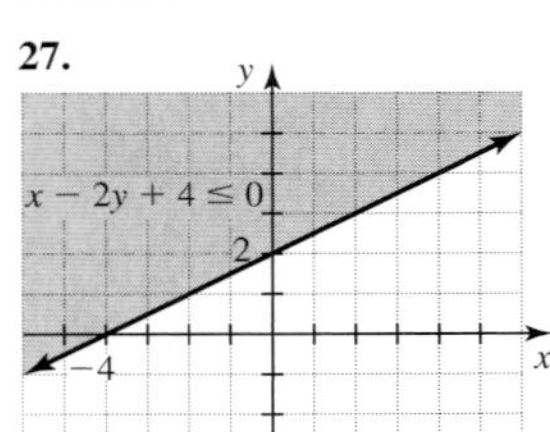

29.

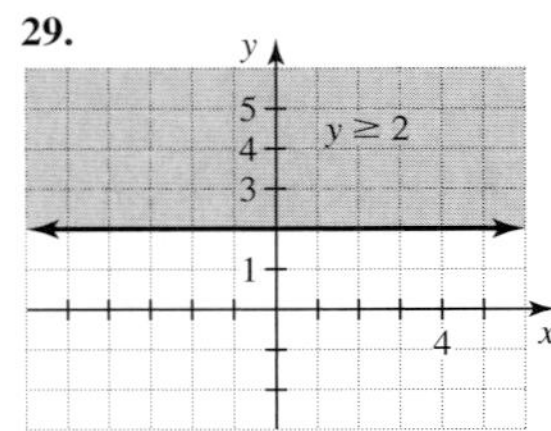

31.

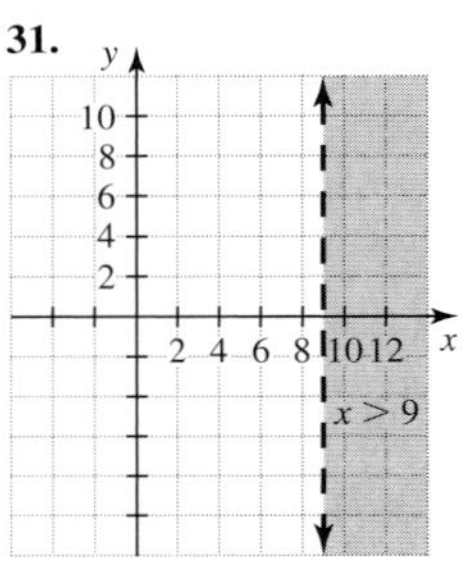

33.

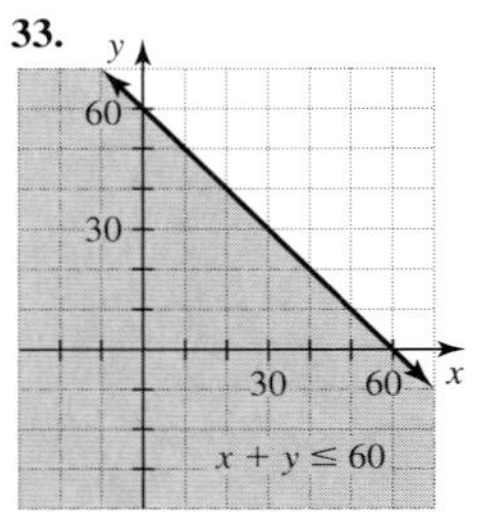

35.

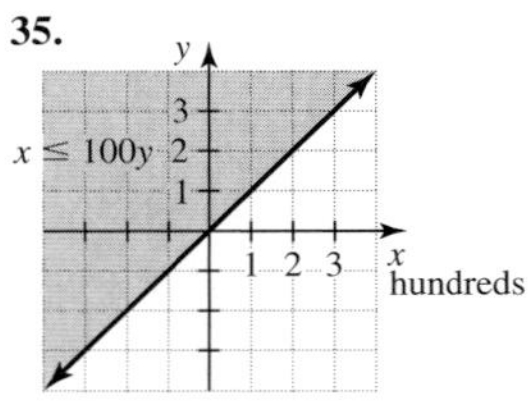

37.

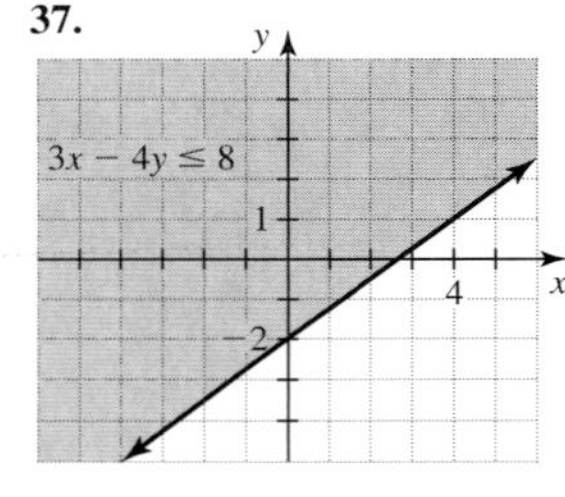

39.

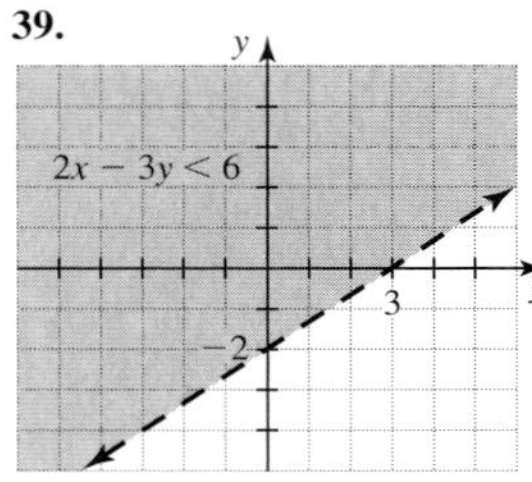

41.

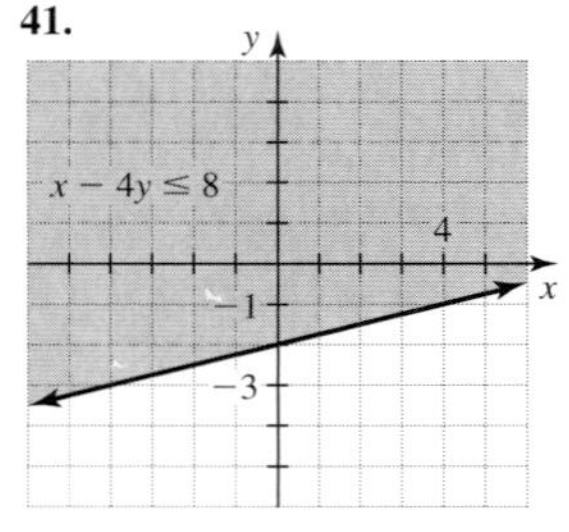

43.

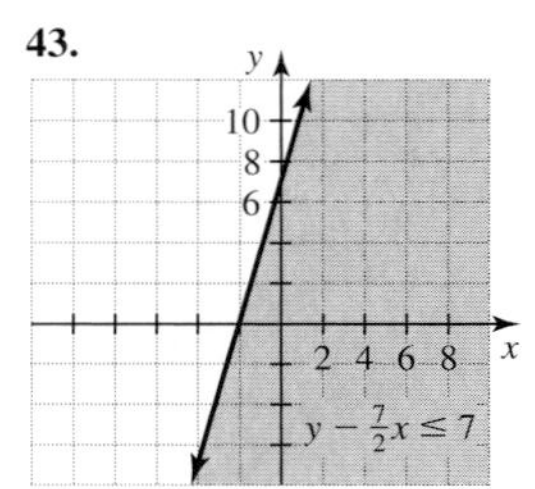

45.

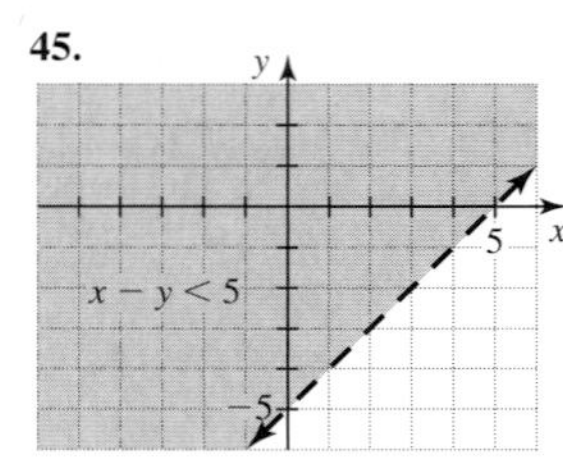

47.

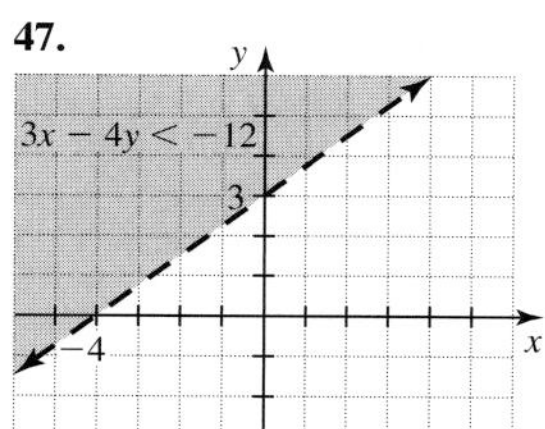
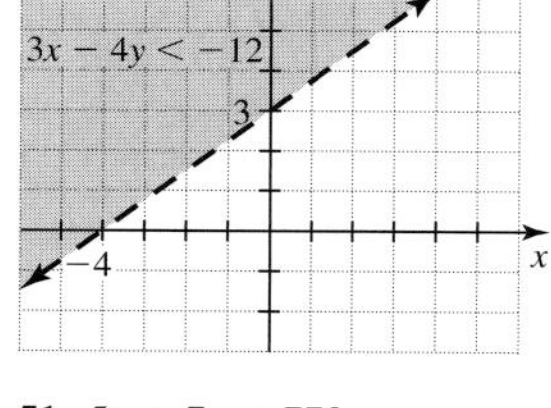

49.

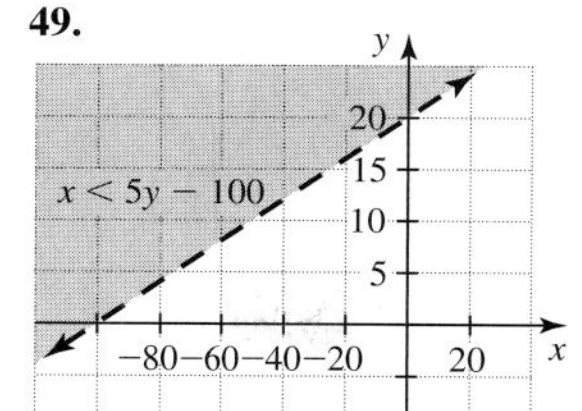

51. $5x + 7y \le 770$

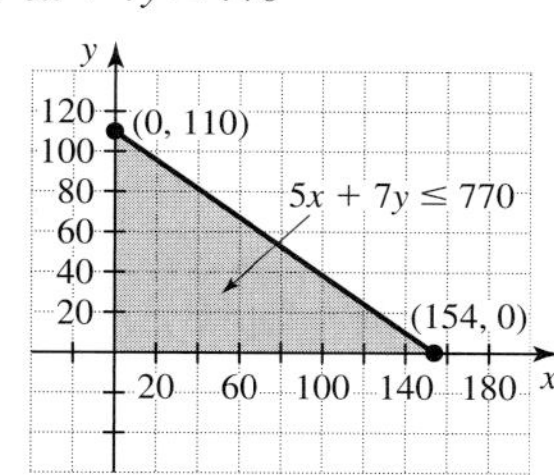

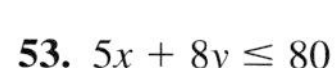

53. $5x + 8y \le 80$

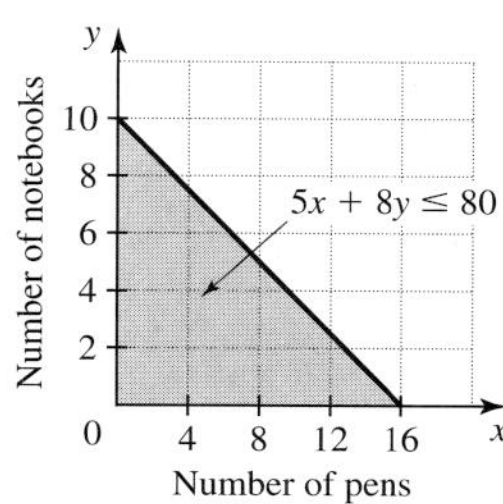

Section 4.5 Warm-Ups F T T T F F T F T T

1. A system of linear inequalities in two variables is a pair of linear inequalities in two variables.
3. The solution set to a system of inequalities is usually described with a graph.
5. To use the test-point method, select a point in each region determined by the graphs of the boundary lines.

7. (9, −5) **9.** (1, 3) **11.** (4, 3) **13.** (3, 6)

15.

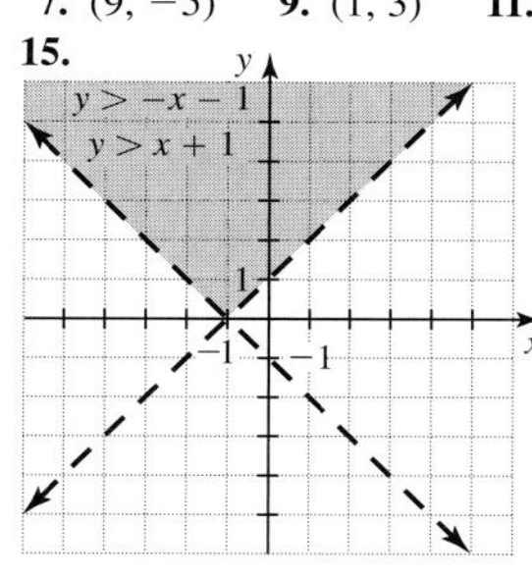

17.

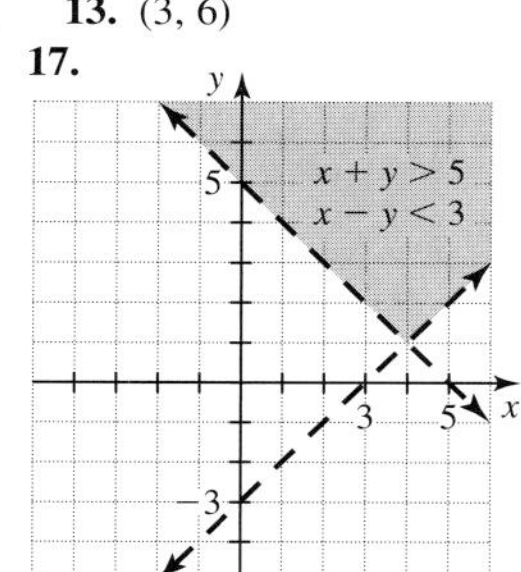

19.

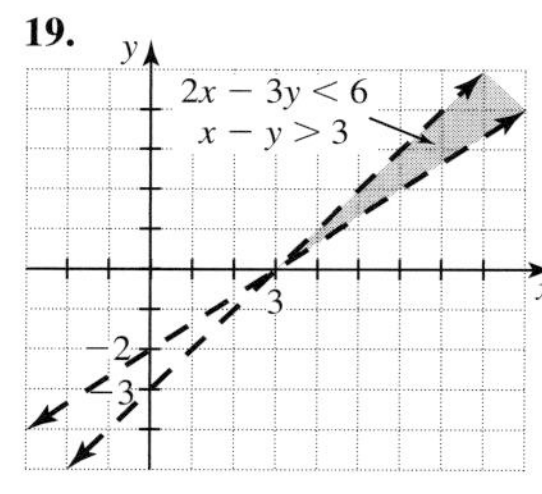

21.

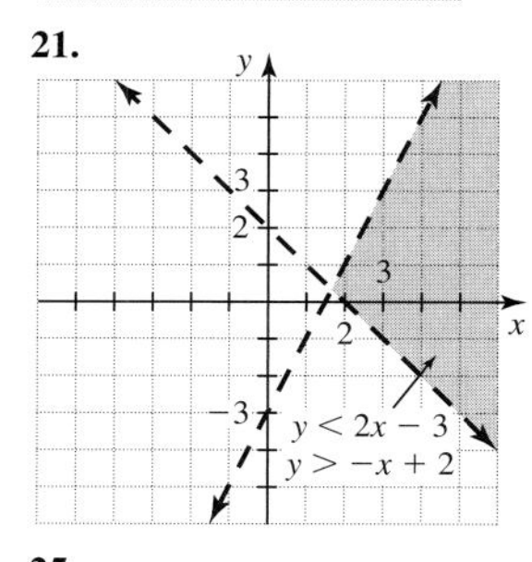

23.

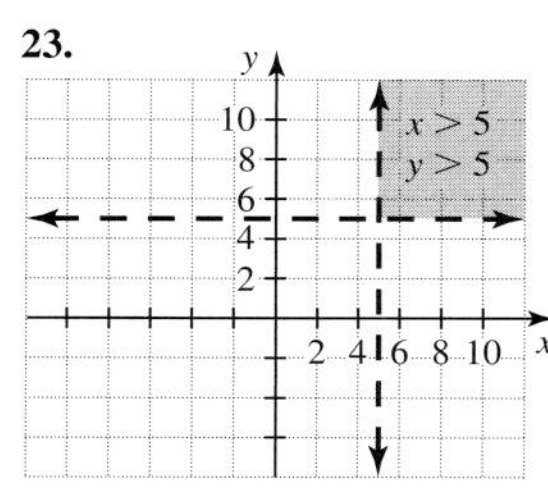

25.

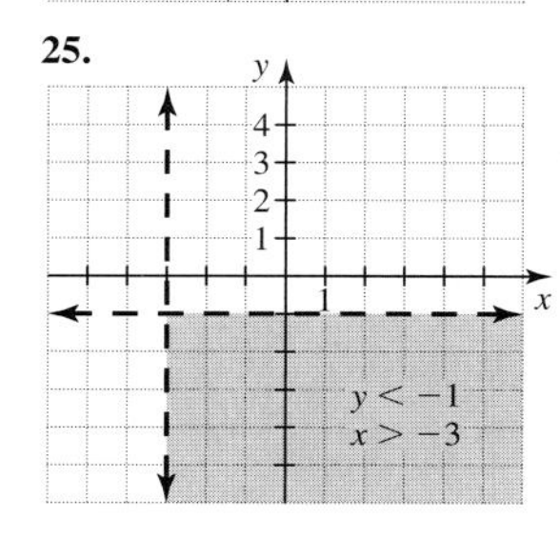

27.

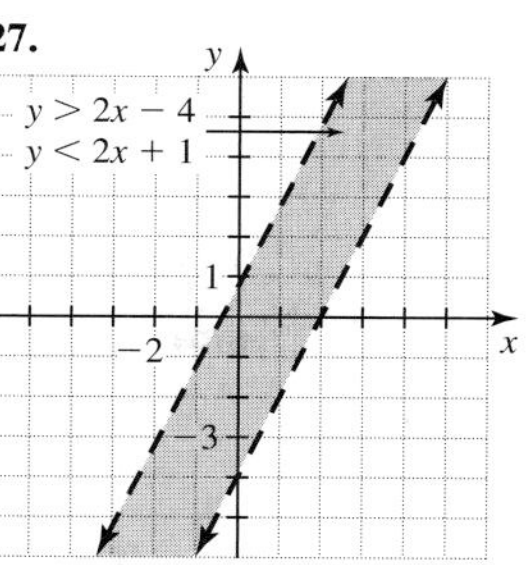

29.

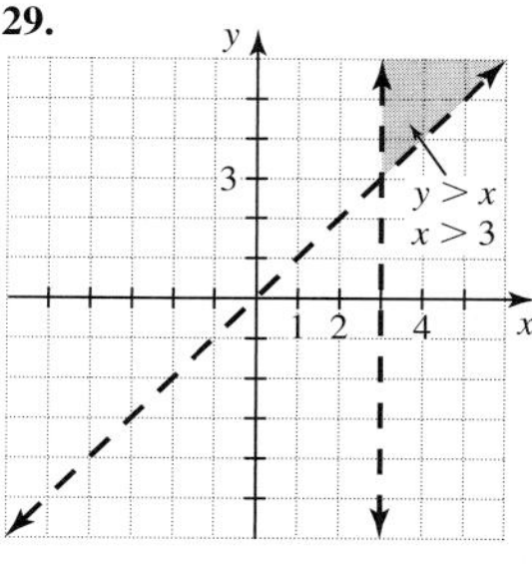

31.

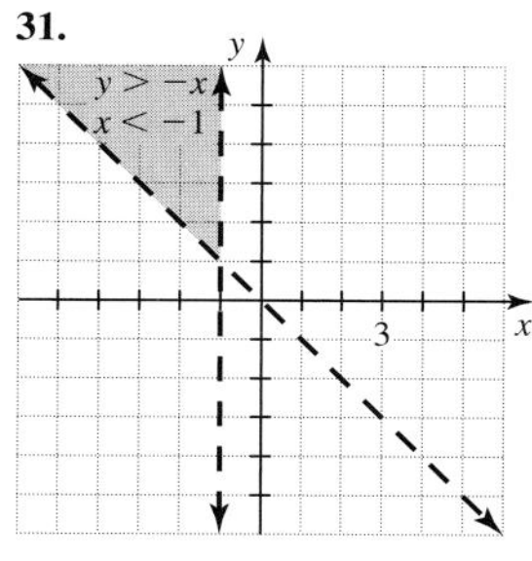

33.

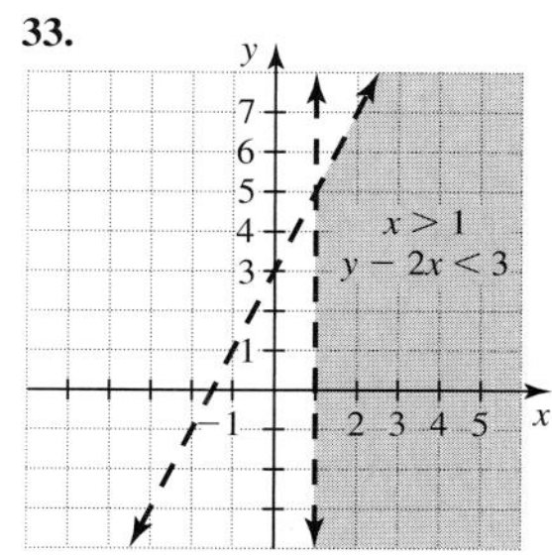

35.

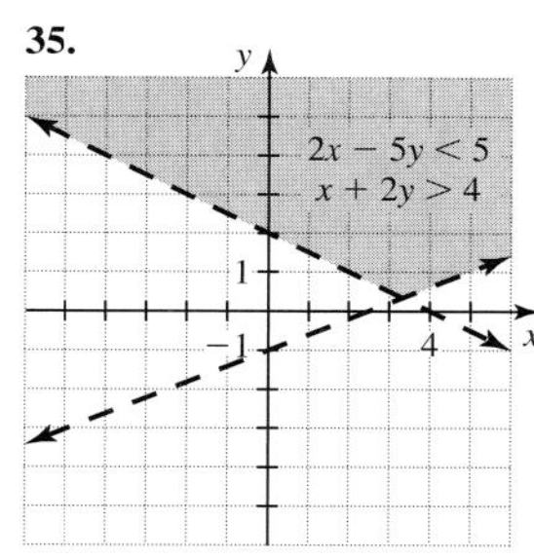

37.

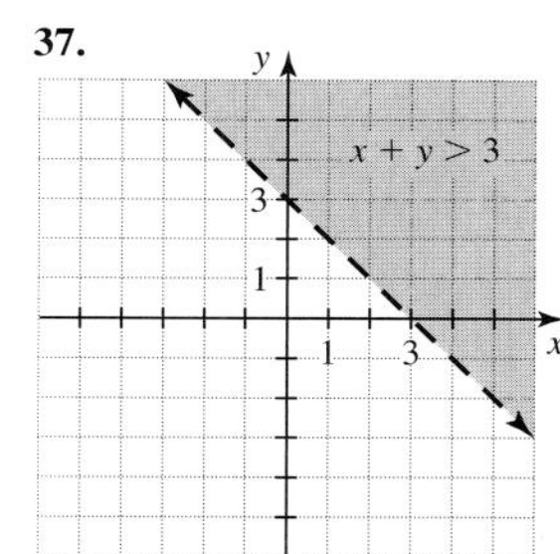

39.

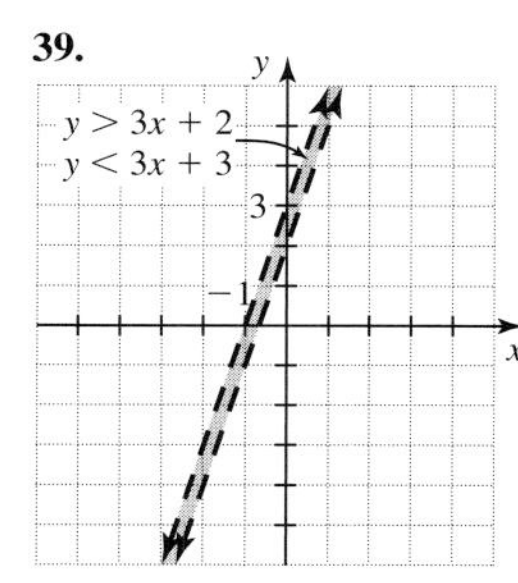

41.

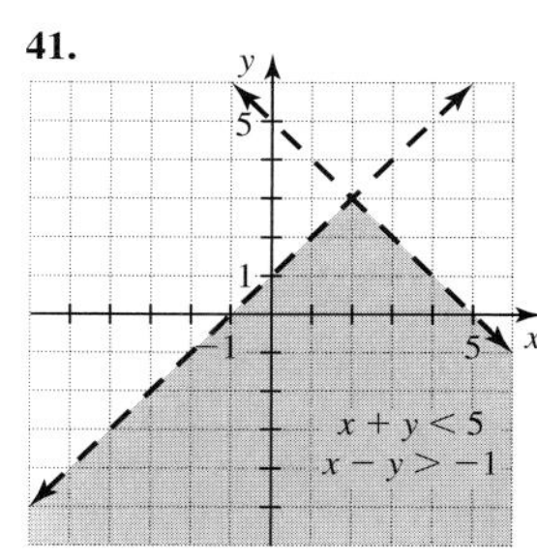

43.

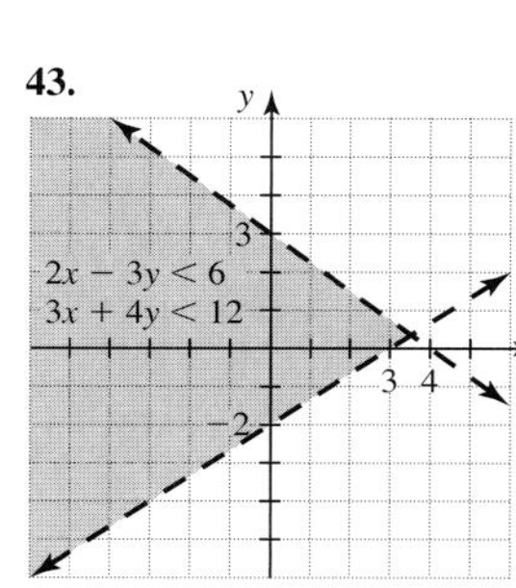

45.

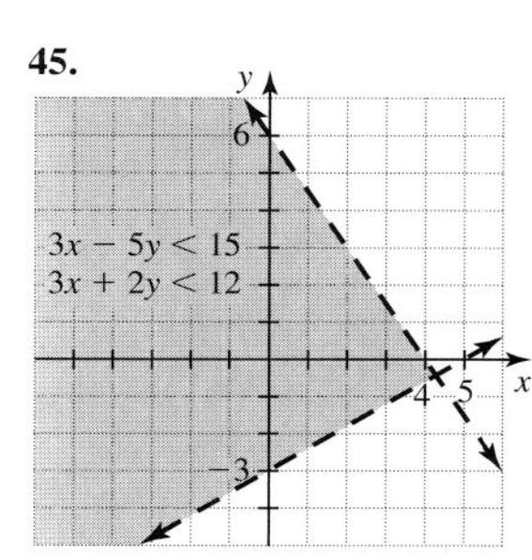

47. ∅ **49.** Not the empty set **51.** ∅ **53.** ∅
55. Not the empty set **57.** Quadrant III **59.** Quadrant II

61.

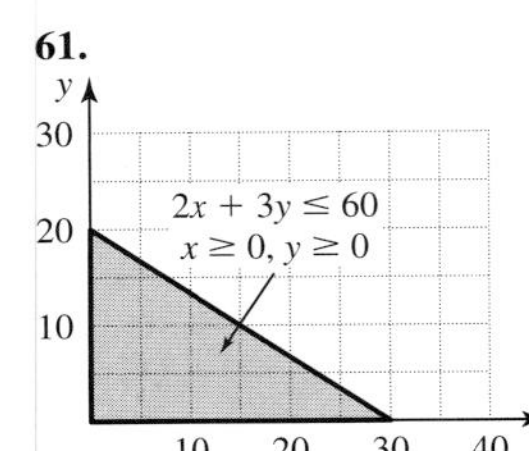

63.

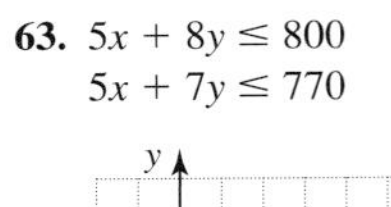

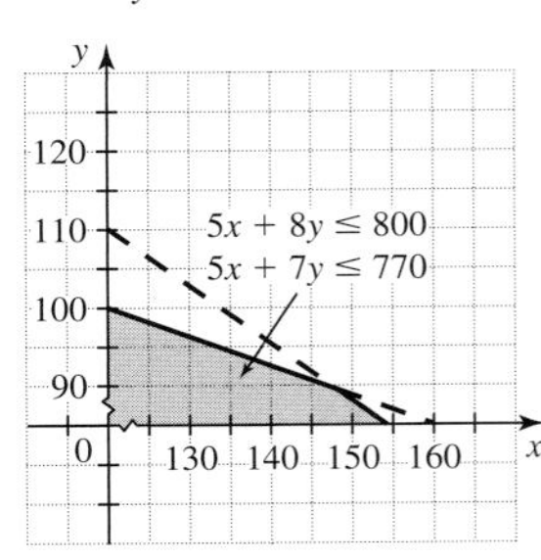

Enriching Your Mathematical Word Power

1. c **2.** a **3.** a **4.** d **5.** b **6.** c **7.** d
8. b **9.** a **10.** b

Review Exercises

1. (1, 3) **3.** (−1, 1)
5. (2, 6) **7.** (−8, −3)
9. (3, −1), independent
11. $\{(x, y) \mid x - 2y = 4\}$, dependent
13. (1, −2), independent
15. (0, 0), independent
17. $\{(x, y) \mid x - y = 6\}$, dependent
19. No solution, inconsistent

21.

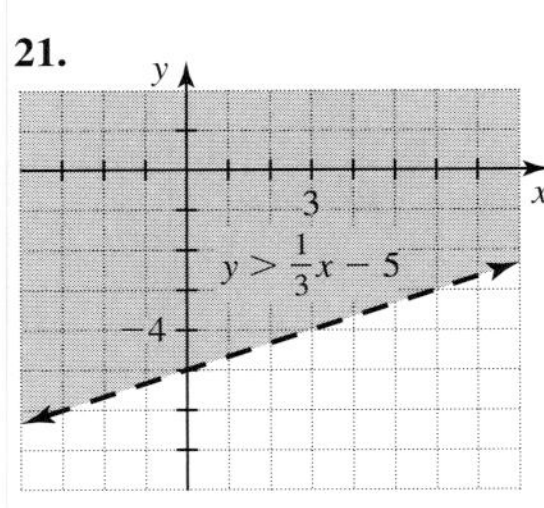

23.

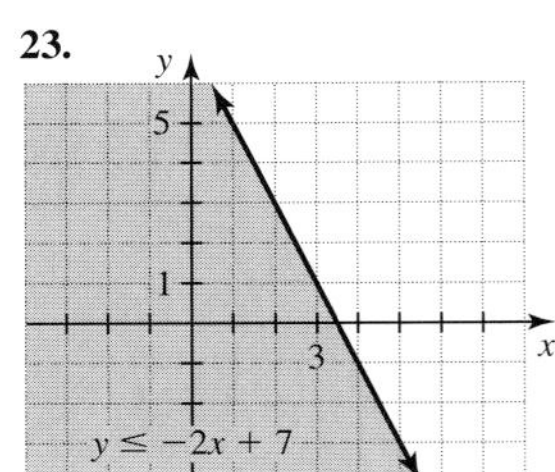

25.

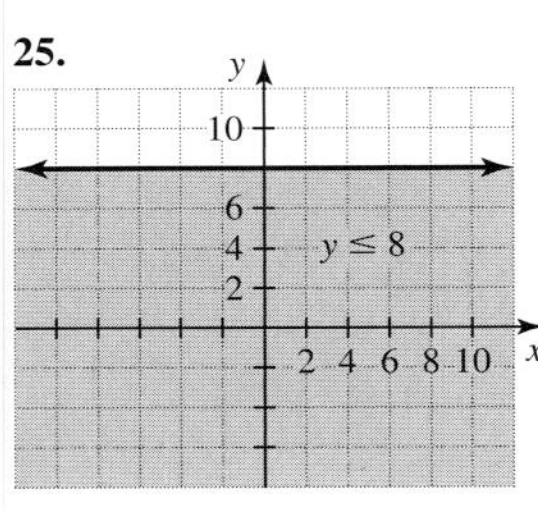

27.

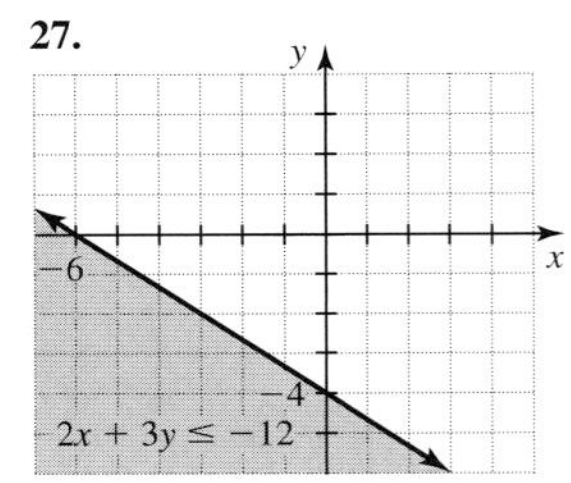

29.

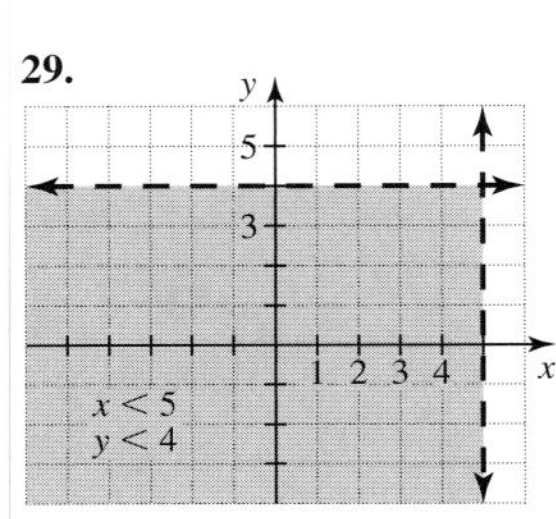

31.

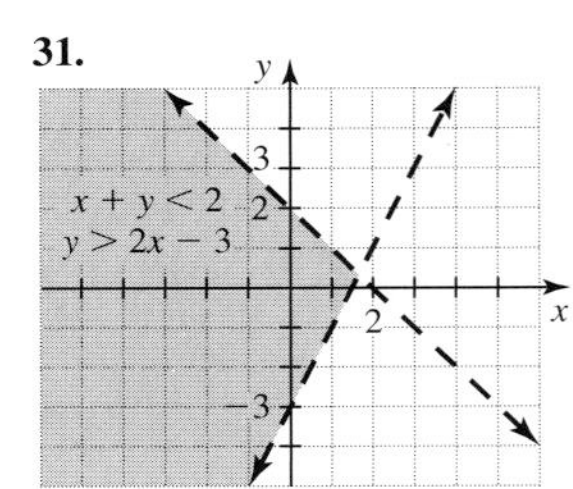

33.

$y > 5x - 7$
$y < 5x + 1$

35.

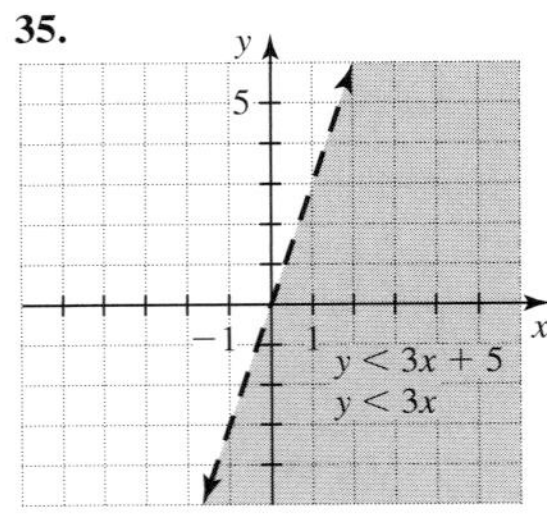

37. (23, 14) **39.** (−2, −6) **41.** (7, 9)
43. (1, 4) **45.** Apple \$0.45, orange \$0.35 **47.** 32 fives, 22 tens
49. 4 servings green beans, 3 servings chicken soup

Chapter 4 Test

1. (−1, 3) **2.** (2, 1) **3.** (3, −1) **4.** (2, 3) **5.** (4, 1)
6. Inconsistent **7.** Dependent
8. Independent

9.

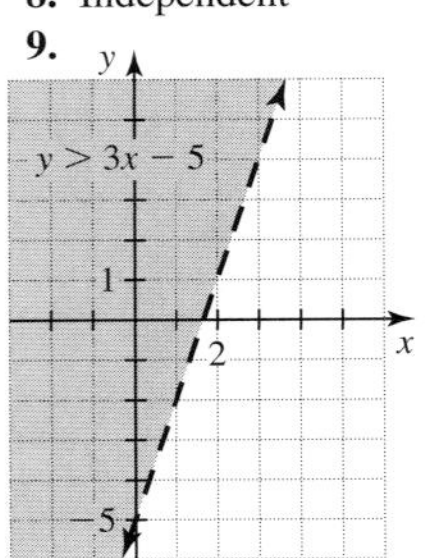

10.

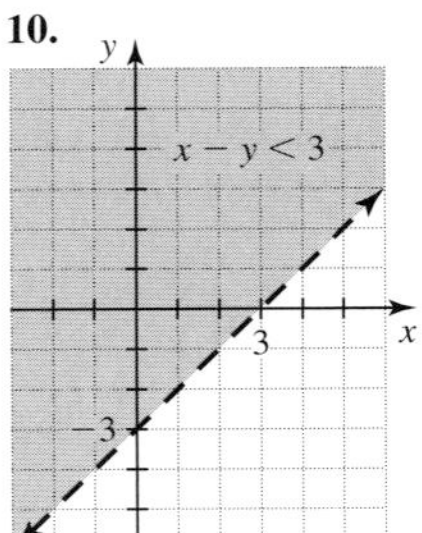

11.

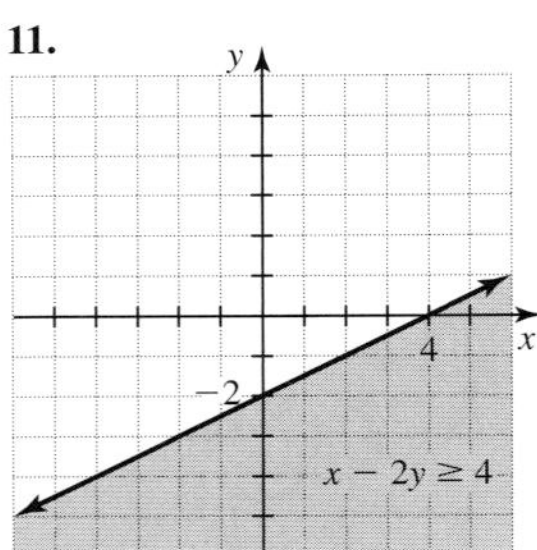

12.

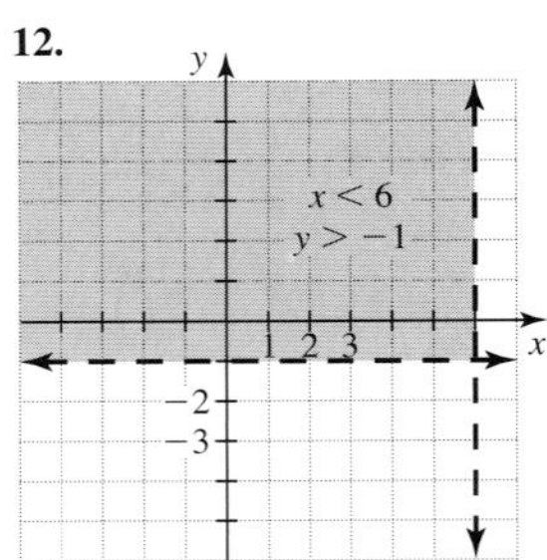

13.

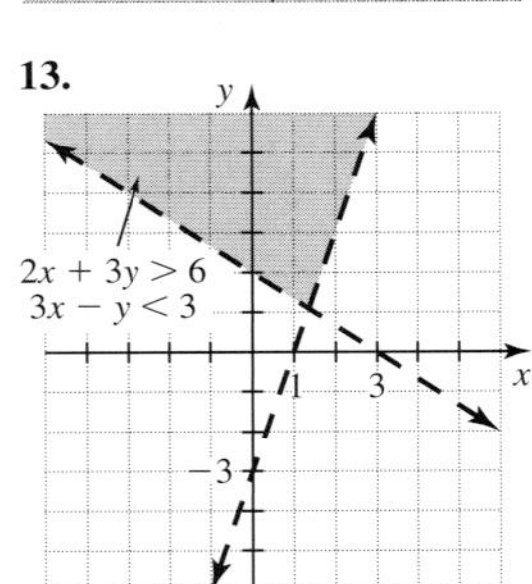

14.

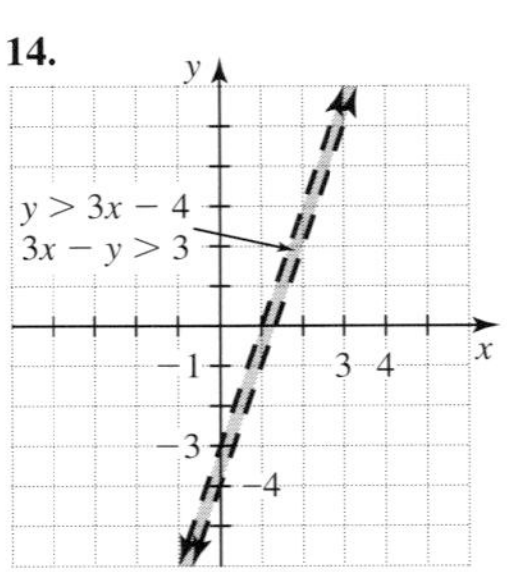

15. Kathy 36 hours, Chris 18 hours **16.** \$48

Making Connections A Review of Chapters 1–4

1. {7} **2.** $\left\{\frac{5}{3}\right\}$ **3.** {12} **4.** {1000} **5.** ∅ **6.** All real numbers
7. $(4, \infty)$ 2 3 4 5 6 7 8

8. $\left[\frac{1}{2}, 5\right]$
9. $[1, \infty)$

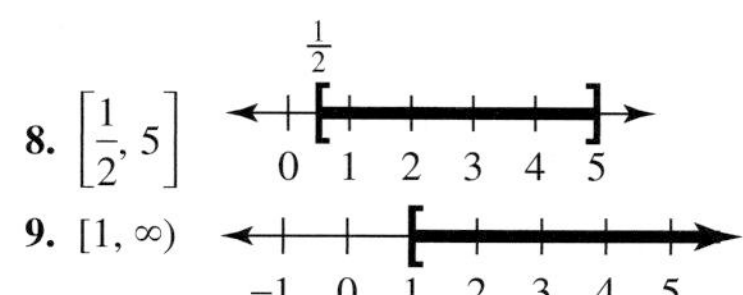

10.

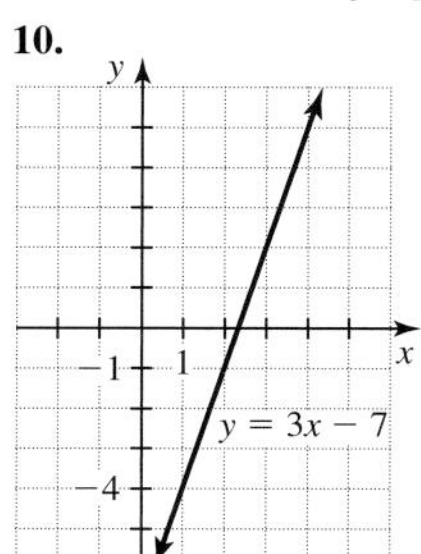

11.

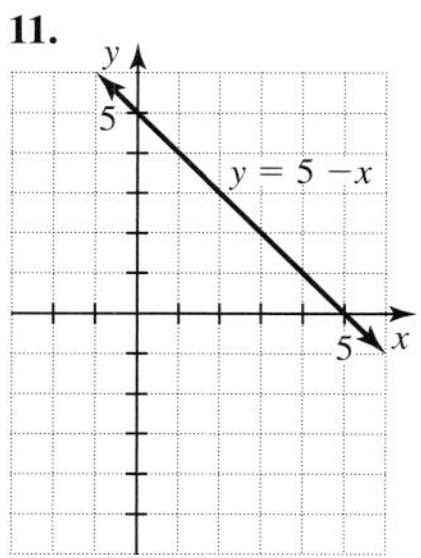

12.

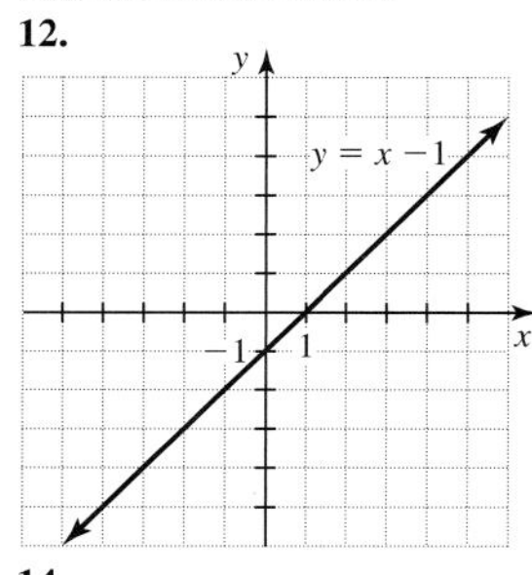

13.

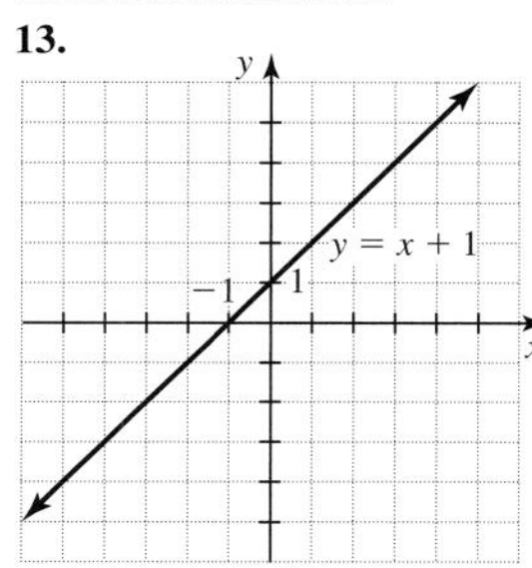

14.

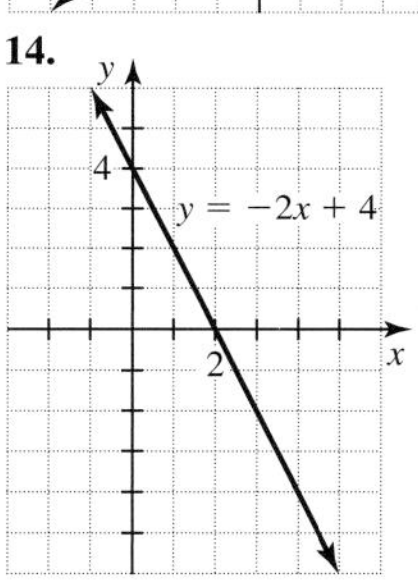

15.

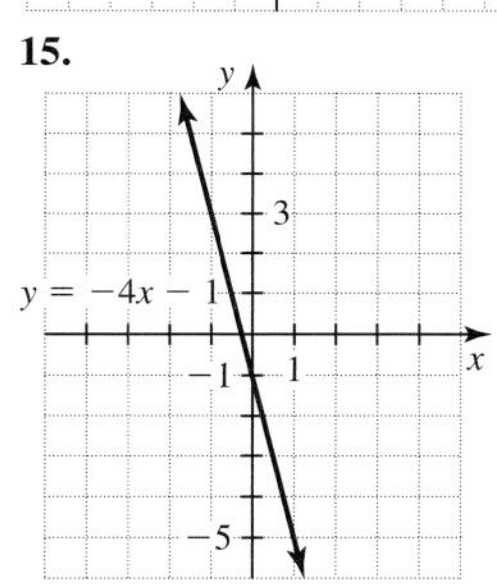

16.

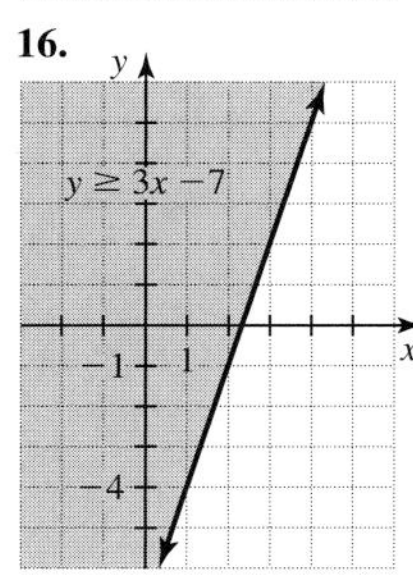

17.

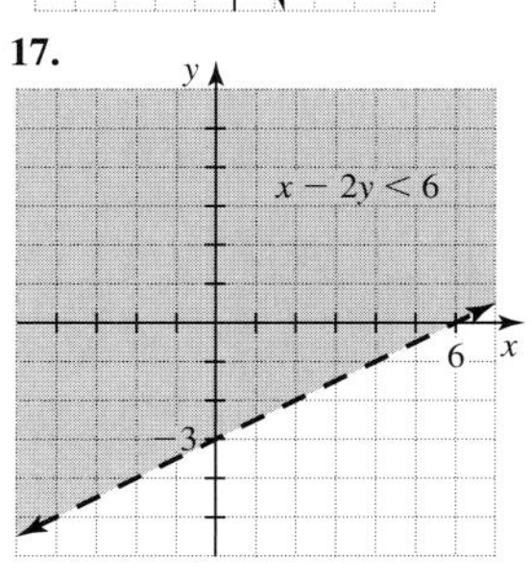

18.

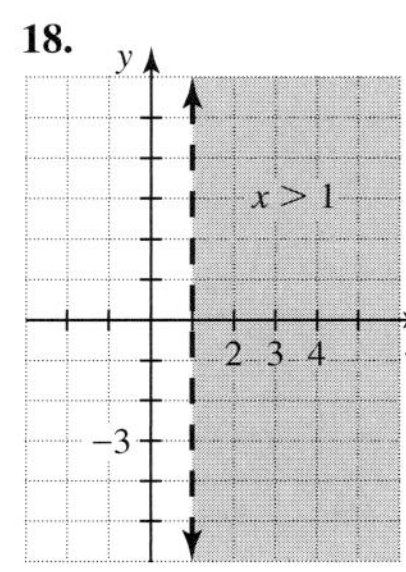

19. $y = 6x + 36$
20. $y = -7x + 95$
21. $-13x + 10$
22. $x + 12$
23. $2a$
24. $5b - 6$
25. $-4c + 17$
26. $-6d + 34$
27. $3m - 14$
28. $-2n + 18$
29. 2

30. −3 **31.** −2 **32.** 3 **33.** 0 **34.** 1
35. −1 **36.** 1 **37.** 18 **38.** 10

39. a) $p = -\frac{9}{10}x + 25$
b) $p = \frac{9}{10}x + 10$
c) $8\frac{1}{3}$ years after 1990 or 1998

Chapter 5

Section 5.1 Warm-Ups T T F T T F F F T T

1. The product rule for exponents says that $a^m \cdot a^n = a^{m+n}$.
3. The power of a power rule says that $(a^m)^n = a^{mn}$.
5. The power of a quotient rule says that $\left(\frac{a}{b}\right)^n = \frac{a^n}{b^n}$.

7. $27x^5$ **9.** $14a^{11}$ **11.** $-30x^4$ **13.** $27x^{17}$ **15.** $-54s^2t^2$
17. $24t^7w^8$ **19.** 1 **21.** 1 **23.** −3 **25.** 1 **27.** x^3 **29.** m^{12}
31. u^3 **33.** 1 **35.** $-3a^2$ **37.** $-4st^8$ **39.** $2x^6$ **41.** x^6
43. $2x^{12}$ **45.** t **47.** 1 **49.** $-\frac{1}{2}$ **51.** x^3y^6 **53.** $-8t^{15}$
55. $-8x^6y^{15}$ **57.** $a^8b^{10}c^{12}$ **59.** $\frac{x^3}{8}$ **61.** $\frac{a^{12}}{64}$ **63.** $\frac{16a^8}{b^{12}}$
65. $-\frac{x^6y^3}{8}$ **67.** 200 **69.** 1,000,000 **71.** 64 **73.** x^7
75. x^5 **77.** 1 **79.** a^{32} **81.** $a^{12}b^6$ **83.** x^3 **85.** $\frac{a^9}{b^{12}}$
87. $36a^{10}b^8$ **89.** \$33,502.39 **91.** \$86,357.00
93. Product rule for exponents, $P(1 + r)^{15}$

Section 5.2 Warm-Ups T F F T T F F T T F

1. A negative exponent means "reciprocal," as in $a^{-n} = \frac{1}{a^n}$.
3. The product rule is valid for any integral exponents.
5. Convert from standard notation by counting the number of places the decimal point must move so that there is one nonzero digit to the left of the decimal point.

7. $\frac{1}{3}$ **9.** $\frac{1}{16}$ **11.** $-\frac{1}{16}$ **13.** $-\frac{1}{27}$ **15.** 4 **17.** $\frac{1}{3}$ **19.** 1250
21. $\frac{3b^9}{a^3}$ **23.** b^7 **25.** $\frac{8}{125}$ **27.** x^4 **29.** $\frac{1}{x^3}$ **31.** $\frac{1}{y^8}$ **33.** $-\frac{16}{x^4}$
35. $\frac{1}{b^6}$ **37.** $-\frac{3}{a^2}$ **39.** $\frac{1}{u^8}$ **41.** $-4t^2$ **43.** $\frac{1}{y^{12}}$ **45.** $2x^7$ **47.** b
49. $\frac{1}{16x^4}$ **51.** $\frac{y^6}{x^3}$ **53.** $\frac{81}{x^8}$ **55.** $\frac{16n^8}{m^{12}}$ **57.** $\frac{8b^6}{a^3}$ **59.** \$13,940.65
61. \$171,928.70 **63.** \$10,727.41 **65.** 9,860,000,000 **67.** 0.00137
69. 0.000001 **71.** 600,000 **73.** 9×10^3 **75.** 7.8×10^{-4}
77. 8.5×10^{-6} **79.** 5.25×10^{11} **81.** 6×10^{-10} **83.** 2×10^{-38}
85. 5×10^{27} **87.** 9×10^{24} **89.** 1.25×10^{14} **91.** 2.5×10^{-33}
93. 8.6×10^9 **95.** 2.1×10^2 **97.** 2.7×10^{-23} **99.** 3×10^{15}
101. 9.135×10^2 **103.** 5.715×10^{-4} **105.** 4.426×10^7
107. 1.577×10^{182} **109.** 4.910×10^{11} feet
111. 4.65×10^{-28} hours **113.** 9.040×10^8 feet
115. a) $w < 0$ **b)** m is odd **c)** $w < 0$ and m odd

Section 5.3 Warm-Ups F F T T F T F T T F

1. A term is a single number or the product of a number and one or more variables raised to powers.
3. The degree of a polynomial in one variable is the highest power of the variable in the polynomial.

5. Polynomials are added by adding the like terms.
7. $-3, 7$ **9.** $0, 6$ **11.** $\frac{1}{3}, \frac{7}{2}$ **13.** Monomial, 0
15. Monomial, 3 **17.** Binomial, 1 **19.** Trinomial, 10
21. Binomial, 6 **23.** Trinomial, 3 **25.** 10 **27.** 6 **29.** $\frac{5}{8}$
31. -85 **33.** 5 **35.** 71 **37.** -4.97665 **39.** $4x - 8$
41. $2q$ **43.** $x^2 + 3x - 2$ **45.** $x^3 + 9x - 7$ **47.** $3a^2 - 7a - 4$
49. $-3w^2 - 8w + 5$ **51.** $9.66x^2 - 1.93x - 1.49$
53. $-4x + 6$ **55.** -5 **57.** $-z^2 + 2z$ **59.** $w^5 + w^4 - w^3 - w^2$
61. $2t + 13$ **63.** $-8y + 7$ **65.** $-22.85x - 423.2$
67. $4a + 2$ **69.** $-2x + 4$ **71.** $2a$ **73.** $-5m + 7$
75. $4x^2 + 1$ **77.** $a^3 - 9a^2 + 2a + 7$ **79.** $-3x + 9$
81. $2y^3 + 4y^2 - 3y - 14$ **83.** $-3m + 3$ **85.** $-11y - 3$
87. $2x^2 - 6x + 12$ **89.** $-5z^4 - 8z^3 + 3z^2 + 7$
91. a) $P(x) = 280x - 800$ **b)** \$13,200
93. $P(x) = 6x + 3$, $P(4) = 27$ meters
95. $D(x) = 5x + 30$, 255 miles **97.** 800 feet, 800 feet
99. $T(x) = 0.17x + 74.47$ dollars, \$244.47 **101.** Yes, yes, yes
103. The highest power of x is 3.

Section 5.4 Warm-Ups F F T F T T T T T F
1. The product rule for exponents says that $a^m \cdot a^n = a^{m+n}$.
3. To multiply a monomial and a polynomial we use the distributive property.
5. To multiply any two polynomials we multiply each term of the first polynomial by every term of the second polynomial.
7. $27x^5$ **9.** $14a^{11}$ **11.** $-30x^4$ **13.** $27x^{17}$ **15.** $-54s^2t^2$
17. $24t^7w^8$ **19.** $25y^2$ **21.** $4x^6$ **23.** $x^2 + xy^2$ **25.** $4y^7 - 8y^3$
27. $-18y^2 + 12y$ **29.** $-3y^3 + 15y^2 - 18y$ **31.** $-xy^2 + x^3$
33. $15a^4b^3 - 5a^5b^2 - 10a^6b$ **35.** $-2t^5v^3 + 3t^3v^2 + 2t^2v^2$
37. $x^2 + 3x + 2$ **39.** $x^2 + 2x - 15$ **41.** $t^2 - 13t + 36$
43. $x^3 + 3x^2 + 4x + 2$ **45.** $6y^3 + y^2 + 7y + 6$
47. $2y^8 - 3y^6z - 5y^4z^2 + 3y^2z^3$ **49.** $u - 3t$ **51.** $-3x - y$
53. $3a^2 + a - 6$ **55.** $-3w^2 - w + 6$ **57.** $-6x^2 + 27x$
59. $-6x^2 + 27x + 2$ **61.** $-x - 7$ **63.** $36x^{12}$ **65.** $-6a^3b^{10}$
67. $25x^2 + 60x + 36$ **69.** $25x^2 - 36$ **71.** $6x^7 - 8x^4$
73. $m^3 - 1$ **75.** $3x^3 - 5x^2 - 25x + 18$
77. $A(x) = x^3 + 4x$, 140 square feet
79. $A(x) = x^2 + \frac{1}{2}x$, $A(5) = 27.5$ square feet
81. $x^2 + 5x$ or $x^2 - 5x$ **83.** $8.05x^2 + 15.93x + 6.12$ square meters
85. a) 30,000 **b)** \$300,000 **c)** $R(p) = 40{,}000p - 1000p^2$
d) \$400,000, \$300,000, \$175,000

Section 5.5 Warm-Ups F T T T T F T F F T
1. We use the distributive property to find the product of two binomials.
3. The purpose of FOIL is to provide a faster method for finding the product of two binomials.
5. $x^2 + 6x + 8$ **7.** $a^2 + 5a + 4$ **9.** $x^2 + 19x + 90$
11. $2x^2 + 7x + 3$ **13.** $a^2 - a - 6$ **15.** $2x^2 - 5x + 2$
17. $2a^2 - a - 3$ **19.** $w^2 - 60w + 500$ **21.** $y^2 + 5y - ay - 5a$
23. $5w + 5m - w^2 - mw$ **25.** $10m^2 - 9mt - 9t^2$
27. $45a^2 + 53ab + 14b^2$ **29.** $x^4 - 3x^2 - 10$ **31.** $h^6 + 10h^3 + 25$
33. $3b^6 + 14b^3 + 8$ **35.** $y^3 - 2y^2 - 3y + 6$ **37.** $6m^6 + 7m^3n^2 - 3n^4$
39. $12u^4v^2 + 10u^2v - 12$ **41.** $w^2 + 3w + 2$ **43.** $b^2 + 9b + 20$
45. $x^2 + 6x - 27$ **47.** $a^2 + 10a + 25$ **49.** $4x^2 - 4x + 1$
51. $z^2 - 100$ **53.** $a^2 + 2ab + b^2$ **55.** $a^2 - 3a + 2$
57. $2x^2 + 5x - 3$ **59.** $5t^2 - 7t + 2$ **61.** $h^2 - 16h + 63$
63. $h^2 + 14hw + 49w^2$ **65.** $4h^4 - 4h^2 + 1$ **67.** $a^3 + 4a^2 - 7a - 10$
69. $h^3 + 9h^2 + 26h + 24$ **71.** $x^3 - 2x^2 - 64x + 128$
73. $x^3 + 8x^2 - \frac{1}{4}x - 2$ **75.** $x^2 + 15x + 50$ **77.** $x^2 + x + \frac{1}{4}$
79. $8x^2 + 2x + \frac{1}{8}$ **81.** $8a^2 + a - \frac{1}{4}$ **83.** $\frac{1}{8}x^2 + \frac{1}{6}x - \frac{1}{6}$
85. $a^3 + 7a^2 + 12a$ **87.** $x^5 + 13x^4 + 42x^3$
89. $-12x^6 - 26x^5 + 10x^4$ **91.** $x^3 + 3x^2 - x - 3$
93. $9x^3 + 45x^2 - 4x - 20$ **95.** $2x + 10$
97. $A(x) = 2x^2 + 5x - 3$, 49 square feet
99. $A(x) = 4x^2 - 6x + 2$, 72 square feet
101. 12 ft², $3h$ ft², $4h$ ft²; h^2 ft², $h^2 + 7h + 12$ ft²; $(h + 3)(h + 4) = h^2 + 7h + 12$

Section 5.6 Warm-Ups F T T T F T T T F F
1. The special products are $(a + b)^2$, $(a - b)^2$, and $(a + b)(a - b)$.
3. It is faster to do by the new rule than with FOIL.
5. $(a + b)(a - b) = a^2 - b^2$ **7.** $x^2 + 2x + 1$ **9.** $y^2 + 8y + 16$
11. $m^2 + 12m + 36$ **13.** $a^2 + 18a + 81$ **15.** $9x^2 + 48x + 64$
17. $s^2 + 2st + t^2$ **19.** $4x^2 + 4xy + y^2$ **21.** $4t^2 + 12ht + 9h^2$
23. $p^2 - 4p + 4$ **25.** $a^2 - 6a + 9$ **27.** $t^2 - 2t + 1$
29. $9t^2 - 12t + 4$ **31.** $s^2 - 2st + t^2$ **33.** $9a^2 - 6ab + b^2$
35. $9z^2 - 30yz + 25y^2$ **37.** $a^2 - 25$ **39.** $y^2 - 1$
41. $9x^2 - 64$ **43.** $r^2 - s^2$ **45.** $64y^2 - 9a^2$ **47.** $25x^4 - 4$
49. $x^3 + 3x^2 + 3x + 1$ **51.** $8a^3 - 36a^2 + 54a - 27$
53. $a^4 - 12a^3 + 54a^2 - 108a + 81$ **55.** $a^4 + 4a^3b + 6a^2b^2 + 4ab^3 + b^4$
57. $a^2 - 400$ **59.** $x^2 + 15x + 56$ **61.** $16x^2 - 1$
63. $81y^2 - 18y + 1$ **65.** $6t^2 - 7t - 20$ **67.** $4t^2 - 20t + 25$
69. $4t^2 - 25$ **71.** $x^4 - 1$ **73.** $4y^6 - 36y^3 + 81$
75. $4x^6 + 12x^3y^2 + 9y^4$ **77.** $\frac{1}{4}x^2 + \frac{1}{3}x + \frac{1}{9}$
79. $0.04x^2 - 0.04x + 0.01$ **81.** $a^3 + 3a^2b + 3ab^2 + b^3$
83. $2.25x^2 + 11.4x + 14.44$ **85.** $12.25t^2 - 6.25$
87. $A(x) = x^2 + 6x + 9$
89. a) $A(x) = x^2 - 25$ **b)** 25 square feet
91. $A(b) = 3.14b^2 + 6.28b + 3.14$
93. $v = k(R^2 - r^2)$ **95.** $P + 2Pr + Pr^2$, \$242 **97.** \$20,230.06
99. The first is an identity and the second is a conditional equation.

Section 5.7 Warm-Ups F F T F T F T T T T
1. The quotient rule is used for dividing monomials.
3. When dividing a polynomial by a monomial, the quotient should have the same number of terms as the polynomial.
5. The long division process stops when the degree of the remainder is less than the degree of the divisor.
7. x^6 **9.** w^9 **11.** a^9 **13.** $3a^5$ **15.** a^6 **17.** $-4x^4$ **19.** $-y$
21. $-3x$ **23.** $-3x^3$ **25.** $x - 2$ **27.** $x^3 + 3x^2 - x$
29. $4xy - 2x + y$ **31.** $y^2 - 3xy$ **33.** $2, -1$ **35.** $x + 5, 16$
37. $x + 2, 7$ **39.** $2, -10$ **41.** $a^2 + 2a + 8, 13$ **43.** $x - 4, 4$
45. $h^2 + 3h + 9, 0$ **47.** $2x - 3, 1$ **49.** $x^2 + 1, -1$
51. $3 + \frac{15}{x - 5}$ **53.** $-1 + \frac{3}{x + 3}$ **55.** $1 - \frac{1}{x}$ **57.** $3 + \frac{1}{x}$
59. $x - 1 + \frac{1}{x + 1}$ **61.** $x - 2 + \frac{8}{x + 2}$ **63.** $x^2 + 2x + 4 + \frac{8}{x - 2}$
65. $x^2 + \frac{3}{x}$ **67.** $-3a$ **69.** $4w^5t^4$ **71.** $-a + 4$ **73.** $x - 3$
75. $-6x^2 + 2x - 3$ **77.** $t + 4$ **79.** $2w + 1$ **81.** $4x^2 - 6x + 9$
83. $t^2 - t + 3$ **85.** $v^2 - 2v + 1$ **87.** $x - 5$ meters
89. $x^8 + x^7 + x^6 + x^5 + x^4 + x^3 + x^2 + x + 1$
91. $10x \div 5x$ is not equivalent to the other two.

Enriching Your Mathematical Word Power

1. a **2.** c **3.** a **4.** d **5.** b **6.** c **7.** d **8.** b **9.** a **10.** b **11.** c **12.** a

Review Exercises

1. 0 **3.** $-6a^7$ **5.** $-5c^6$ **7.** b^{30} **9.** $-8x^9y^6$ **11.** $\frac{8a^3}{b^6}$ **13.** $\frac{8x^6y^{15}}{z^{18}}$ **15.** $\frac{1}{8}$ **17.** 7 **19.** $\frac{1}{x^3}$ **21.** a^4 **23.** $\frac{1}{x^{12}}$ **25.** $\frac{x^9}{8}$ **27.** $\frac{9}{a^2b^6}$ **29.** 8,360,000 **31.** 0.00057 **33.** 8.07×10^6 **35.** 7.09×10^{-4} **37.** 1×10^{15} **39.** 2×10^1 **41.** 1×10^2 **43.** $5w - 2$ **45.** $-6x + 4$ **47.** $2w^2 - 7w - 4$ **49.** $-2m^2 + 3m - 1$ **51.** 0 **53.** 5 **55.** $-50x^{11}$ **57.** $121a^{14}$ **59.** $-4x + 15$ **61.** $3x^2 - 10x + 12$ **63.** $15m^5 - 3m^3 + 6m^2$ **65.** $x^3 - 7x^2 + 20x - 50$ **67.** $3x^3 - 8x^2 + 16x - 8$ **69.** $q^2 + 2q - 48$ **71.** $2t^2 - 21t + 27$ **73.** $20y^2 - 7y - 6$ **75.** $6x^4 + 13x^2 + 5$ **77.** $z^2 - 49$ **79.** $y^2 + 14y + 49$ **81.** $w^2 - 6w + 9$ **83.** $x^4 - 9$ **85.** $9a^2 + 6a + 1$ **87.** $16 - 8y + y^2$ **89.** $-5x^2$ **91.** $-2a^2b^2$ **93.** $-x + 3$ **95.** $-3x^2 + 2x - 1$ **97.** -1 **99.** $m^3 + 2m^2 + 4m + 8$ **101.** $m^2 - 3m + 6, 0$ **103.** $b - 5, 15$ **105.** $2x - 1, -8$ **107.** $x^2 + 2x - 9, 1$ **109.** $2 + \frac{6}{x - 3}$ **111.** $-2 + \frac{2}{1 - x}$ **113.** $x - 1 + \frac{-2}{x + 1}$ **115.** $x - 1 + \frac{1}{x + 1}$ **117.** $x^2 + 10x + 21$ **119.** $t^2 - 7ty + 12y^2$ **121.** 2 **123.** $-27h^3t^{18}$ **125.** $2w^2 - 9w - 18$ **127.** $9u^2 - 25v^2$ **129.** $9h^2 + 30h + 25$ **131.** $x^3 + 9x^2 + 27x + 27$ **133.** $14s^5t^6$ **135.** $\frac{k^8}{16}$ **137.** $x^2 - 9x - 5$ **139.** $5x^2 - x - 12$ **141.** $x^3 - x^2 - 19x + 4$ **143.** $x + 6$ **145.** $P(w) = 4w + 88$, $A(w) = w^2 + 44w$, $P(50) = 288$ ft, $A(50) = 4700$ ft^2 **147.** $R(p) = -15p^2 + 600p$, \$5040, \$20 **149.** \$19,126.18 **151.** \$21,252.76

Chapter 5 Test

1. $-35x^8$ **2.** $12x^5y^9$ **3.** $-2ab^4$ **4.** $15x^5$ **5.** $\frac{-32a^5}{b^{10}}$ **6.** $\frac{3a^4}{b^2}$ **7.** $\frac{3}{t^{16}}$ **8.** $\frac{1}{w^2}$ **9.** $\frac{s^6}{9t^4}$ **10.** $\frac{-8y^3}{x^{18}}$ **11.** 5.433×10^6 **12.** 6.5×10^{-6} **13.** 4.8×10^{-1} **14.** 8.1×10^{-27} **15.** $7x^3 + 4x^2 + 2x - 11$ **16.** $-x^2 - 9x + 2$ **17.** $-2y^2 + 3y$ **18.** -1 **19.** $x^2 + x - 1$ **20.** $15x^5 - 21x^4 + 12x^3 - 3x^2$ **21.** $x^2 + 3x - 10$ **22.** $6a^2 + a - 35$ **23.** $a^2 - 14a + 49$ **24.** $16x^2 + 24xy + 9y^2$ **25.** $b^2 - 9$ **26.** $9t^4 - 49$ **27.** $4x^4 + 5x^2 - 6$ **28.** $x^3 - 3x^2 - 10x + 24$ **29.** $2 + \frac{6}{x - 3}$ **30.** $x - 5 + \frac{15}{x + 2}$ **31.** 13 **32.** 2, -4 **33.** $x - 2$, 3 **34.** $-2x^2 + x + 15$ **35.** $A(x) = x^2 + 4x$, $P(x) = 4x + 8$, $A(4) = 32$ ft^2, $P(4) = 24$ ft **36.** $R(q) = -150q^2 + 3000q$, \$14,400 **37.** \$306,209.52

Making Connections A Review of Chapters 1–5

1. 8 **2.** 32 **3.** 41 **4.** -2 **5.** 32 **6.** 32 **7.** -144 **8.** 144 **9.** $\frac{5}{8}$ **10.** $\frac{1}{9}$ **11.** 64 **12.** 34 **13.** $\frac{5}{6}$ **14.** $\frac{5}{36}$ **15.** 899 **16.** -1 **17.** $x^2 + 8x + 15$ **18.** $4x + 15$ **19.** $-15t^5v^7$ **20.** $5tv$ **21.** $x^2 + 9x + 20$ **22.** $x^2 + 7x + 10$ **23.** $x + 3$ **24.** $x^3 + 13x^2 + 55x + 75$ **25.** $3y - 4$ **26.** $6y^2 - 4y + 1$ **27.** $\left\{-\frac{1}{2}\right\}$ **28.** $\{7\}$ **29.** $\left\{\frac{14}{3}\right\}$ **30.** $\left\{\frac{7}{4}\right\}$ **31.** $\{0\}$ **32.** All real numbers **33.** $\left(-\frac{1}{2}, 0\right)$ **34.** $(0, -7)$ **35.** 2 **36.** $\frac{2}{3}$ **37.** $\frac{14}{3}$ **38.** $-\frac{1}{2}$ **39.** $\frac{2.25n + 100{,}000}{n}$; \$102.25, \$3.25, \$2.35; It averages out to 10 cents per disk.

Chapter 6

Section 6.1 Warm-Ups F F F T T T T F F T

1. To factor means to write as a product. **3.** You can find the prime factorization by dividing by prime factors until the result is prime. **5.** The GCF for two monomials consists of the GCF of their coefficients and every variable that they have in common raised to the lowest power that appears on the variable. **7.** $2 \cdot 3^2$ **9.** $2^2 \cdot 13$ **11.** $2 \cdot 7^2$ **13.** $2^3 \cdot 3^3$ **15.** $2^2 \cdot 5 \cdot 23$ **17.** $2^2 \cdot 3 \cdot 7 \cdot 11$ **19.** 4 **21.** 12 **23.** 8 **25.** 4 **27.** 1 **29.** $2x$ **31.** $2x$ **33.** xy **35.** $12ab$ **37.** 1 **39.** $6ab$ **41.** $3x$ **43.** $3t$ **45.** $9y^3$ **47.** u^3v^2 **49.** $-7n^3$ **51.** $11xy^2z$ **53.** $2(w + 2t)$ **55.** $6(2x - 3y)$ **57.** $x(x^2 - 6)$ **59.** $5a(x + y)$ **61.** $h^3(h^2 + 1)$ **63.** $2k^3m^4(-k^4 + 2m^2)$ **65.** $2x(x^2 - 3x + 4)$ **67.** $6x^2t(2x^2 + 5x - 4t)$ **69.** $(x - 3)(a + b)$ **71.** $(x - 5)(x - 1)$ **73.** $(m + 1)(m + 9)$ **75.** $(a + b)(y + 1)^2$ **77.** $8(x - y), -8(-x + y)$ **79.** $4x(-1 + 2x), -4x(1 - 2x)$ **81.** $1(x - 5), -1(-x + 5)$ **83.** $1(4 - 7a), -1(-4 + 7a)$ **85.** $8a^2(-3a + 2), -8a^2(3a - 2)$ **87.** $6x(-2x - 3), -6x(2x + 3)$ **89.** $2x(-x^2 - 3x + 7), -2x(x^2 + 3x - 7)$ **91.** $2ab(2a^2 - 3ab - 2b^2), -2ab(-2a^2 + 3ab + 2b^2)$ **93.** $x + 2$ hours **95. a)** $S = 2\pi r(r + h)$ **b)** $S = 2\pi r^2 + 10\pi r$ **c)** 3 in. **97.** The GCF is an algebraic expression.

Section 6.2 Warm-Ups F T F F T T F F T T

1. A perfect square is the square of an integer or an algebraic expression. **3.** A perfect square trinomial is of the form $a^2 + 2ab + b^2$ or $a^2 - 2ab + b^2$. **5.** A polynomial is factored completely when it is a product of prime polynomials. **7.** $(a - 2)(a + 2)$ **9.** $(x - 7)(x + 7)$ **11.** $(a + 11)(a - 11)$ **13.** $(y + 3x)(y - 3x)$ **15.** $(5a + 7b)(5a - 7b)$ **17.** $(11m + 1)(11m - 1)$ **19.** $(3w - 5c)(3w + 5c)$ **21.** Perfect square trinomial **23.** Neither **25.** Perfect square trinomial **27.** Neither **29.** Difference of two squares **31.** Perfect square trinomial **33.** $(x + 1)^2$ **35.** $(a + 3)^2$ **37.** $(x + 6)^2$ **39.** $(a - 2)^2$ **41.** $(2w + 1)^2$ **43.** $(4x - 1)^2$ **45.** $(2t + 5)^2$ **47.** $(3w + 7)^2$ **49.** $(n + t)^2$ **51.** $5(x - 5)(x + 5)$ **53.** $-2(x - 3)(x + 3)$ **55.** $a(a - b)(a + b)$ **57.** $3(x + 1)^2$ **59.** $-5(y - 5)^2$ **61.** $x(x - y)^2$ **63.** $-3(x - y)(x + y)$ **65.** $2a(x - 7)(x + 7)$ **67.** $3a(b - 3)^2$ **69.** $-4m(m - 3n)^2$ **71.** $(b + c)(x + y)$ **73.** $(x - 2)(x + 2)(x + 1)$ **75.** $(3 - x)(a - b)$ **77.** $(a^2 + 1)(a + 3)$ **79.** $(a + 3)(x + y)$ **81.** $(c - 3)(ab + 1)$ **83.** $(a + b)(x - 1)(x + 1)$ **85.** $(y + b)(y + 1)$ **87.** $6ay(a + 2y)^2$ **89.** $6ay(2a - y)(2a + y)$ **91.** $2a^2y(ay - 3)$ **93.** $(b - 4w)(a + 2w)$ **95.** $(a - b)(1 - b)$ **97.** $(2x - 1)^2(2x + 1)$ **99. a)** $h(t) = -16(t - 20)(t + 20)$ **b)** 6336 feet **101. a)** $V(x) = x(x - 3)^2$ **b)** $x - 3$ inches

Section 6.3 Warm-Ups T T F F T F T F F F

1. We factored $ax^2 + bx + c$ with $a = 1$.
3. If there are no two integers that have a product of c and a sum of b, then $x^2 + bx + c$ is prime.
5. A polynomial is factored completely when all of the factors are prime polynomials.
7. $(x + 3)(x + 1)$ **9.** $(x + 3)(x + 6)$ **11.** $(a + 2)(a + 5)$
13. $(a - 3)(a - 4)$ **15.** $(b - 6)(b + 1)$ **17.** $(x - 2)(x + 5)$
19. $(x + 8)(x - 3)$ **21.** $(y + 2)(y + 5)$ **23.** $(a - 2)(a - 4)$
25. $(m - 8)(m - 2)$ **27.** $(w + 10)(w - 1)$ **29.** $(w - 4)(w + 2)$
31. Prime **33.** $(m + 16)(m - 1)$ **35.** Prime **37.** $(z - 5)(z + 5)$
39. Prime **41.** $(m + 2)(m + 10)$ **43.** Prime **45.** $(m - 18)(m + 1)$
47. Prime **49.** $(t + 8)(t - 3)$ **51.** $(t - 6)(t + 4)$
53. $(t - 20)(t + 10)$ **55.** $(x - 15)(x + 10)$ **57.** $(y + 3)(y + 10)$
59. $(x + 3a)(x + 2a)$ **61.** $(x - 6y)(x + 2y)$ **63.** $(x - 12y)(x - y)$
65. Prime **67.** $5x(x^2 + 1)$ **69.** $w(w - 8)$ **71.** $2(w - 9)(w + 9)$
73. $-2(b^2 + 49)$ **75.** $(x + 3)(x - 3)(x - 2)$ **77.** Prime
79. $x^2(w^2 + 9)$ **81.** $(w - 9)^2$ **83.** $6(w - 3)(w + 1)$
85. $3(y^2 + 25)$ **87.** $(a + c)(x + y)$ **89.** $-2(x + 2)(x + 3)$
91. $2x^2(4 - x)(4 + x)$ **93.** $3(w + 3)(w + 6)$ **95.** $w(w^2 + 18w + 36)$
97. $(3y + 1)^2$ **99.** $8v(w + 2)^2$ **101.** $6xy(x + 3y)(x + 2y)$
103. $(3w + 5)(w + 1)$ **105.** $-3y(y - 1)^2$ **107.** $(a + 3)(a^2 + b)$
109. a) 80 square feet **b)** $x + 4$ feet **111.** 3 feet and 5 feet **113.** d

Section 6.4 Warm-Ups T F T F T F F F F T

1. We factored $ax^2 + bx + c$ with $a \neq 1$.
3. If there are no two integers whose product is ac and whose sum is b, then $ax^2 + bx + c$ is prime.
5. 3 and 4 **7.** -2 and -15 **9.** -6 and 2 **11.** 3 and 4
13. -2 and -9 **15.** -3 and 4 **17.** $(2x + 1)(x + 1)$
19. $(2x + 1)(x + 4)$ **21.** $(3t + 1)(t + 2)$ **23.** $(2x - 1)(x + 3)$
25. $(3x - 1)(2x + 3)$ **27.** Prime **29.** $(2x - 3)(x - 2)$
31. $(5b - 3)(b - 2)$ **33.** $(4y + 1)(y - 3)$ **35.** Prime
37. $(4x + 1)(2x - 1)$ **39.** $(3t - 1)(3t - 2)$ **41.** $(5x + 1)(3x + 2)$
43. $(2a + 3b)(2a + 5b)$ **45.** $(3m - 5n)(2m + n)$
47. $(x - y)(3x - 5y)$ **49.** $(5a + 1)(a + 1)$ **51.** $(2x + 1)(3x + 1)$
53. $(5a + 1)(a + 2)$ **55.** $(2w + 3)(2w + 1)$ **57.** $(5x - 2)(3x + 1)$
59. $(4x - 1)(2x - 1)$ **61.** $(15x - 1)(x - 2)$ **63.** Prime
65. $2(x^2 + 9x - 45)$ **67.** $(3x - 5)(x + 2)$ **69.** $(5x + y)(2x - y)$
71. $(6a - b)(7a - b)$ **73.** $3x + 1$ **75.** $x + 2$ **77.** $2a - 5$
79. $w(9w - 1)(9w + 1)$ **81.** $2(2w - 5)(w + 3)$ **83.** $3(2x + 3)^2$
85. $(3w + 5)(2w - 7)$ **87.** $3z(x - 3)(x + 2)$ **89.** $3x(3x^2 - 7x + 6)$
91. $(a + 5b)(a - 3b)$ **93.** $y^2(2x^2 + x + 3)$ **95.** $-t(3t + 2)(2t - 1)$
97. $2t^2(3t - 2)(2t + 1)$ **99.** $y(2x - y)(2x - 3y)$
101. $-1(w - 1)(4w - 3)$ **103.** $-2a(2a - 3b)(3a - b)$
105. a) 24, 48, 40, 0 feet **b)** $h(t) = -8(2t + 1)(t - 3)$ **c)** 0 feet
107. a) ± 4 **b)** $\pm 8, \pm 16$ **c)** $\pm 1, \pm 7, \pm 13, \pm 29$

Section 6.5 Warm-Ups F F T T F T F T T F

1. If there is no remainder, then the dividend factors as the divisor times the quotient.
3. If you divide $a^3 + b^3$ by $a + b$ there will be no remainder.
5. $a^3 + b^3 = (a + b)(a^2 - ab + b^2)$
7. $(x + 1)(x + 2)(x + 3)$ **9.** $(x + 4)(x - 3)(x + 2)$
11. $(x - 1)(x + 3)(x + 2)$ **13.** $(x - 2)(x^2 + 2x + 4)$
15. $(x + 5)(x^2 - x + 2)$ **17.** $(x + 1)(x^2 + x + 1)$
19. $(m - 1)(m^2 + m + 1)$ **21.** $(x + 2)(x^2 - 2x + 4)$
23. $(a + 5)(a^2 - 5a + 25)$ **25.** $(c - 7)(c^2 + 7c + 49)$
27. $(2w + 1)(4w^2 - 2w + 1)$ **29.** $(2t - 3)(4t^2 + 6t + 9)$
31. $(x - y)(x^2 + xy + y^2)$ **33.** $(2t + y)(4t^2 - 2ty + y^2)$
35. $(x - y)(x + y)(x^2 + y^2)$ **37.** $(x - 1)(x + 1)(x^2 + 1)$
39. $(2b - 1)(2b + 1)(4b^2 + 1)$ **41.** $(a - 3b)(a + 3b)(a^2 + 9b^2)$
43. $2(x - 3)(x + 3)$ **45.** Prime **47.** $4(x + 5)(x - 3)$
49. $x(x + 2)^2$ **51.** $5am(x^2 + 4)$ **53.** Prime **55.** $(3x + 1)^2$
57. Prime **59.** $(w - z)(w + z)(w^2 + z^2)$ **61.** $y(3x + 2)(2x - 1)$
63. Prime **65.** $3(4a - 1)^2$ **67.** $2(4m + 1)(2m - 1)$
69. $(s - 2t)(s + 2t)(s^2 + 4t^2)$ **71.** $(3a + 4)^2$ **73.** $2(3x - 1)(4x - 3)$
75. $3(m^2 + 9)$ **77.** $3a(a - 9)$ **79.** $2(2 - x)(2 + x)$ **81.** Prime
83. $x(6x^2 - 5x + 12)$ **85.** $ab(a - 2)(a + 2)$ **87.** $(x - 2)(x + 2)^2$
89. $-7mn(m^2 + 4n^2)$ **91.** $2(x + 2)(x^2 - 2x + 4)$
93. $2w(w - 2)(w^2 + 2w + 4)$ **95.** $3w(a - 3)^2$
97. $5(x - 10)(x + 10)$ **99.** $(2 - w)(m + n)$
101. $3x(x + 1)(x^2 - x + 1)$ **103.** $4(w^2 + w - 1)$
105. $a^2(a + 10)(a - 3)$ **107.** $aw(2w - 3)^2$ **109.** $(t + 3)^2$
111. a) 240 cubic centimeters **b)** Length $x + 5$ cm, width $x + 3$ cm **c)** 240 cubic centimeters
113. $(-1 + 1)^3 = (-1)^3 + 1^3$, $(1 + 2)^3 \neq 1^3 + 2^3$ **115.** $3(w + 5)^2$
117. $(9 + b)(9 - b)$ **119.** $w(w - 8)$ **121.** $3(x - 5)(x + 7)$
123. $(x - 5)(a + 4)$ **125.** $(3x - 4)(4x + 3)$ **127.** $-3(3x - 1)(x + 2)$
129. $(w - 3)(w^2 + 3w + 9)$ **131.** $(y + 1)(y^2 + 1)$
133. $(m + 3)(m - 3)(m^2 + 9)$ **135.** $(a + 2b)(a - 4b)$
137. $my(m + 3y)^2$ **139.** $x^2(x^2 + 2x + 4)$
141. $y^3(y + 1)(y - 1)(y^2 + 1)$ **143.** $(x - 6)(x - 12)$
145. $-a(2a + 1)(3a - 4)$ **147.** $x(x - 2)(x^2 + 2x + 4)$
149. $(4t - 3x)^2$

Section 6.6 Warm-Ups F F T T T F T T T F

1. A quadratic equation has the form $ax^2 + bx + c = 0$ with $a \neq 0$.
3. The zero factor property says that if $ab = 0$ then $a = 0$ or $b = 0$.
5. Dividing each side by a variable is not usually done because the variable might have a value of zero.
7. $-4, -5$ **9.** $-\frac{5}{2}, \frac{4}{3}$ **11.** $-2, -1$ **13.** 2, 7 **15.** $-4, 6$
17. $-1, \frac{1}{2}$ **19.** 0, 1 **21.** $0, -7$ **23.** $-5, 4$ **25.** $\frac{1}{2}, -3$
27. $0, -8$ **29.** $-\frac{9}{2}, 2$ **31.** $\frac{2}{3}, -4$ **33.** 5 **35.** $\frac{3}{2}$ **37.** $0, -3, 3$
39. $-4, -2, 2$ **41.** $-1, 1, 3$ **43.** $-\frac{1}{2}, 0, \frac{2}{3}$ **45.** $-1, 6$
47. $-9, 3$ **49.** $-10, 2$ **51.** $-4, \frac{5}{3}$ **53.** $-4, 4$ **55.** $-\frac{3}{2}, \frac{3}{2}$
57. $0, -1, 1$ **59.** $-3, -2$ **61.** $-\frac{3}{2}, -4$ **63.** $-6, 4$ **65.** $-1, 3$
67. $-4, 2$ **69.** $-5, -3, 5$ **71.** Length 12 ft, width 5 ft
73. Width 5 ft, length 12 ft **75.** 2 and 3, or -3 and -2 **77.** 5 and 6
79. $-8, -6, -4$, or 4, 6, 8 **81.** -2 and -1, or 3 and 4
83. -7 and -2, or 2 and 7 **85.** Length 12 feet, width 6 feet
87. 9 meters and 12 meters
89. a) 25 sec **b)** last 5 sec **c)** increasing
91. a) 680 feet **b)** 608 feet **c)** 6 sec
93. Base 6 in., height 13 in. **95.** 20 ft by 20 ft **97.** 80 ft
99. 3 yd by 3 yd, 6 yd by 6 yd **101.** 12 mi **103.** 25%

Enriching Your Mathematical Word Power

1. a **2.** d **3.** c **4.** a **5.** c **6.** b **7.** c **8.** a
9. d **10.** c

Review Exercises

1. $2^4 \cdot 3^2$ **3.** $2 \cdot 29$ **5.** $2 \cdot 3 \cdot 5^2$ **7.** 18 **9.** $4x$ **11.** $x + 2$
13. $-a + 10$ **15.** $a(2 - a)$ **17.** $3x^2y(2y - 3x^3)$
19. $3y(x^2 - 4x - 3y)$ **21.** $(y - 20)(y + 20)$ **23.** $(w - 4)^2$
25. $(2y + 5)^2$ **27.** $(r - 2)^2$ **29.** $2t(2t - 3)^2$ **31.** $(x + 6y)^2$

33. $(x - y)(x + 5)$ **35.** $(b + 8)(b - 3)$ **37.** $(r - 10)(r + 6)$
39. $(y - 11)(y + 5)$ **41.** $(u + 20)(u + 6)$ **43.** $3t^2(t + 4)$
45. $5w(w^2 + 5w + 5)$ **47.** $ab(2a + b)(a + b)$
49. $x(3x - y)(3x + y)$ **51.** $(7t - 3)(2t + 1)$ **53.** $(3x + 1)(2x - 7)$
55. $(3p + 4)(2p - 1)$ **57.** $-2p(5p + 2)(3p - 2)$
59. $(6x + y)(x - 5y)$ **61.** $2(4x + y)^2$ **63.** $5x(x^2 + 8)$
65. $(3x - 1)(3x + 2)$ **67.** Prime **69.** $(x + 2)(x - 1)(x + 1)$
71. $xy(x - 16y)$ **73.** Prime **75.** $(a + 1)^2$ **77.** $(x^2 + 1)(x - 1)$
79. $(a + 2)(a + b)$ **81.** $-2(x - 6)(x - 2)$
83. $(m - 10)(m^2 + 10m + 100)$ **85.** $(p - q)(p + q)(p^2 + q^2)$
87. $(x + 2)(x^2 - 2x + 5)$ **89.** $(x + 4)(x + 5)(x - 3)$
91. 0, 5 **93.** 0, 5 **95.** $-\frac{1}{2}, 5$ **97.** $-4, -3, 3$ **99.** $-2, -1$
101. $-\frac{1}{2}, \frac{1}{4}$ **103.** $\frac{1}{5}, \frac{1}{2}$ **105.** 5, 11 **107.** 6 in. by 8 in.
109. $v = k(R - r)(R + r)$ **111.** 6 ft

Chapter 6 Test

1. $2 \cdot 3 \cdot 11$ **2.** $2^4 \cdot 3 \cdot 7$ **3.** 16 **4.** 6 **5.** $3y^2$ **6.** $6ab$
7. $5x(x - 2)$ **8.** $6y^2(x^2 + 2x + 2)$ **9.** $3ab(a - b)(a + b)$
10. $(a + 6)(a - 4)$ **11.** $(2b - 7)^2$ **12.** $3m(m^2 + 9)$
13. $(a + b)(x - y)$ **14.** $(a - 5)(x - 2)$ **15.** $(3b - 5)(2b + 1)$
16. $(m + 2n)^2$ **17.** $(2a - 3)(a - 5)$ **18.** $z(z + 3)(z + 6)$
19. $(x + 5)(x^2 - 5x + 25)$ **20.** $a(a - b)(a^2 + ab + b^2)$
21. $(x - 1)(x - 2)(x - 3)$ **22.** -3 **23.** $\frac{3}{2}, -4$ **24.** $0, -2, 2$
25. $-2, \frac{5}{6}$ **26.** 2, 4 **27.** $\frac{2}{3}, 5$ **28.** Length 12 ft, width 9 ft
29. -4 and 8 **30.** **a)** 48 feet **b)** 2 seconds

Making Connections A Review of Chapters 1–6

1. -1 **2.** 2 **3.** -3 **4.** 57 **5.** 16 **6.** 7 **7.** $2x^2$ **8.** $3x$
9. $3 + x$ **10.** $6x$ **11.** $24yz$ **12.** $6y + 8z$ **13.** $4z - 1$
14. $x - 7$ **15.** t^6 **16.** t^{10} **17.** $\frac{1}{t^6}$ **18.** t^{16} **19.** $4t^6$ **20.** $\frac{1}{3y^7}$
21. $\frac{2x^2}{5}$ **22.** $\frac{2}{3}$ **23.** $-\frac{8y^6}{x^9}$ **24.** $9x^4y^6$ **25.** -5 **26.** -28
27. $(-\infty, -9)$

$-13\ -12\ -11\ -10\ -9\ -8\ -7$

28. $[3, \infty)$

1 2 3 4 5 6 7

29. $(12, \infty)$

10 11 12 13 14 15 16

30. $(-\infty, 600)$

0 200 400 600 800

31. $\left\{\frac{3}{2}\right\}$ **32.** $\left\{-\frac{1}{2}\right\}$ **33.** $\{3, -5\}$ **34.** $\left\{\frac{3}{2}, -\frac{1}{2}\right\}$ **35.** $\{0, 3\}$
36. $\{0, 1\}$ **37.** R **38.** No solution or $\varnothing$ **39.** $\{10\}$
40. $\{40\}$ **41.** $\{-3, 3\}$ **42.** $\left\{-5, \frac{3}{2}\right\}$
43. Length 21 ft, width 13.5 ft

Chapter 7

Section 7.1 Warm-Ups F T T F F T T F F T

1. A rational number is a ratio of two integers with the denominator not 0.
3. A rational number is reduced to lowest terms by dividing the numerator and denominator by the GCF.
5. The quotient rule is used in reducing ratios of monomials.

7. -3 **9.** 5 **11.** $-0.6, 9, 401, -199$ **13.** -1
15. $\frac{5}{3}$ **17.** 4, -4 **19.** Any number can be used.
21. All real numbers except 2 **23.** All real numbers except -3 and -2
25. R **27.** All real numbers except 0 **29.** $\frac{2}{9}$ **31.** $\frac{7}{15}$
33. $\frac{2a}{5}$ **35.** $\frac{13}{5w}$ **37.** $\frac{3x + 1}{3}$ **39.** $\frac{2}{3}$ **41.** $\frac{b - 3}{2b - 5}$
43. $w - 7$ **45.** $\frac{a - 1}{a + 1}$ **47.** $\frac{x + 1}{2(x - 1)}$ **49.** $\frac{x + 3}{7}$
51. $\frac{a^2 - 2a + 4}{2}$ **53.** x^3 **55.** $\frac{1}{z^5}$ **57.** $-2x^2$
59. $\frac{-3m^3n^2}{2}$ **61.** $\frac{-3}{4c^3}$ **63.** $\frac{5c}{3a^4b^{16}}$ **65.** $\frac{35}{44}$ **67.** $\frac{11}{8}$
69. $\frac{21}{10x^4}$ **71.** $\frac{33a^4}{16}$ **73.** -1 **75.** $-h - t$ **77.** $\frac{-2}{3h + g}$
79. $\frac{-x - 2}{x + 3}$ **81.** -1 **83.** $\frac{-2y}{3}$ **85.** $\frac{x + 2}{2 - x}$ **87.** $\frac{-6}{a + 3}$
89. $\frac{-a^2 - ab - b^2}{2b}$ **91.** $\frac{x^4}{2}$ **93.** $\frac{x + 2}{2x}$ **95.** -1 **97.** $\frac{-2}{c + 2}$
99. $\frac{x + 2}{x - 2}$ **101.** $\frac{-2}{x + 3}$ **103.** q^2 **105.** $\frac{u + 2}{u - 8}$
107. $\frac{a^2 + 2a + 4}{2}$ **109.** $y + 2$ **111.** $\frac{2 - a}{x(x - w)}$
113. $\frac{300}{x + 10}$ hr **115.** $\frac{4.50}{x + 4}$ dollars/lb **117.** $\frac{1}{x}$ pool/hr
119. **a)** \$0.75 **b)** \$0.75, \$0.63, \$0.615 **c)** Approaches \$0.60

Section 7.2 Warm-Ups T T T F T F F T T T

1. Rational numbers are multiplied by multiplying their numerators and their denominators.
3. Reducing can be done before multiplying rational numbers or expressions.

5. $\frac{5}{9}$ **7.** $\frac{7}{9}$ **9.** $\frac{18}{5}$ **11.** $\frac{42}{5}$ **13.** $\frac{5}{6}$ **15.** $\frac{5x}{2}$ **17.** $\frac{a}{44}$
19. $\frac{-x^5}{a^3}$ **21.** $\frac{18t^8y^7}{w^4}$ **23.** $\frac{5}{7}$ **25.** $\frac{2a}{a - b}$ **27.** $3x - 9$
29. $\frac{8a + 8}{5(a^2 + 1)}$ **31.** $\frac{1}{2}$ **33.** 30 **35.** $\frac{2}{3}$ **37.** $\frac{10}{9}$ **39.** $\frac{x}{2}$
41. $\frac{7x}{2}$ **43.** $\frac{2m^2}{3n^6}$ **45.** -3 **47.** $\frac{2}{x + 2}$ **49.** $\frac{1}{4(t - 5)}$
51. $x^2 - 1$ **53.** $2x - 4y$ **55.** $\frac{x + 2}{2}$ **57.** $\frac{x^2 + 9}{15}$ **59.** $9x + 9y$
61. -3 **63.** $\frac{a + b}{a}$ **65.** $\frac{2b}{a}$ **67.** $\frac{y}{x}$ **69.** $\frac{-a^6b^8}{2}$ **71.** $\frac{1}{9m^3n}$
73. $\frac{x^2 + 5x}{3x - 1}$ **75.** $\frac{a^3 + 8}{2(a - 2)}$ **77.** 1 **79.** $\frac{m^2 + 6m + 9}{(m - 3)(m + k)}$
81. **a)** $\frac{26.2}{x}$ mph **b)** $\frac{13.1}{x}$ miles **83.** **a)** $\frac{1}{x}$ tank/min **b)** $\frac{2}{x}$ tank
85. 5 square meters **87.** **a)** $\frac{1}{8}$ **b)** $\frac{4}{3}$ **c)** $\frac{2x}{3}$ **d)** $\frac{3x}{4}$

Section 7.3 Warm-Ups F F T T F F F F T T

1. We can build up a denominator by multiplying the numerator and denominator of a fraction by the same nonzero number.
3. For fractions, the LCD is the smallest number that is a multiple of all of the denominators.

5. $\frac{9}{27}$ **7.** $\frac{12}{16}$ **9.** $\frac{7}{7}$ **11.** $\frac{12}{6}$ **13.** $\frac{5a}{ax}$ **15.** $\frac{14x}{2x}$ **17.** $\frac{15t}{3bt}$

19. $\frac{-36z^2}{8awz}$ **21.** $\frac{10a^2}{15a^3}$ **23.** $\frac{8xy^3}{10x^2y^5}$ **25.** $\frac{10}{2x+6}$ **27.** $\frac{-20}{-8x-8}$

29. $\frac{-32ab}{20b^2-20b^3}$ **31.** $\frac{3x-6}{x^2-4}$ **33.** $\frac{3x^2+3x}{x^2+2x+1}$ **35.** $\frac{y^2-y-30}{y^2+y-20}$

37. 48 **39.** 180 **41.** $30a^2$ **43.** $12a^4b^6$ **45.** $(x-4)(x+4)^2$

47. $x(x+2)(x-2)$ **49.** $2x(x-4)(x+4)$ **51.** $\frac{4}{24}, \frac{9}{24}$

53. $\frac{3}{6x}, \frac{5}{6x}$ **55.** $\frac{4b}{6ab}, \frac{3a}{6ab}$ **57.** $\frac{9b}{252ab}, \frac{20a}{252ab}$ **59.** $\frac{2x^3}{6x^5}, \frac{9}{6x^5}$

61. $\frac{4x^4}{36x^3y^5z}, \frac{3y^6z}{36x^3y^5z}, \frac{6xy^4z}{36x^3y^5z}$ **63.** $\frac{2x^2+4x}{(x-3)(x+2)}, \frac{5x^2-15x}{(x-3)(x+2)}$

65. $\frac{4}{a-6}, \frac{-5}{a-6}$ **67.** $\frac{x^2-3x}{(x-3)^2(x+3)}, \frac{5x^2+15x}{(x-3)^2(x+3)}$

69. $\frac{w^2+3w+2}{(w-5)(w+3)(w+1)}, \frac{-2w^2-6w}{(w-5)(w+3)(w+1)}$

71. $\frac{-5x-10}{6(x-2)(x+2)}, \frac{6x}{6(x-2)(x+2)}, \frac{9x-18}{6(x-2)(x+2)}$

73. $\frac{2q+8}{(2q+1)(q-3)(q+4)}, \frac{3q-9}{(2q+1)(q-3)(q+4)}, \frac{8q+4}{(2q+1)(q-3)(q+4)}$

75. Identical denominators are needed for addition and subtraction.

Section 7.4 Warm-Ups F T T T T F T F T F

1. We can add rational numbers with identical denominators as follows: $\frac{a}{c} + \frac{b}{c} = \frac{a+b}{c}$.

3. The LCD is the smallest number that is a multiple of all denominators.

5. $\frac{1}{5}$ **7.** $\frac{3}{4}$ **9.** $-\frac{2}{3}$ **11.** $-\frac{3}{4}$ **13.** $\frac{5}{9}$ **15.** $\frac{23}{15}$ **17.** $\frac{103}{144}$

19. $-\frac{31}{40}$ **21.** $\frac{5}{24}$ **23.** $\frac{1}{x}$ **25.** $\frac{5}{w}$ **27.** 3 **29.** -2 **31.** $\frac{3}{h}$

33. $\frac{x-4}{x+2}$ **35.** $\frac{3}{2a}$ **37.** $\frac{5x}{6}$ **39.** $\frac{6m}{5}$ **41.** $\frac{2x+y}{xy}$ **43.** $\frac{17}{10a}$

45. $\frac{w}{36}$ **47.** $\frac{b^2-4ac}{4a}$ **49.** $\frac{2w+3z}{w^2z^2}$ **51.** $\frac{2x+2}{x(x+2)}$

53. $\frac{-x-3}{x(x+1)}$ **55.** $\frac{3a+b}{(a-b)(a+b)}$ **57.** $\frac{15-4x}{5x(x+1)}$

59. $\frac{a^2+5a}{(a-3)(a+3)}$ **61.** 0 **63.** $\frac{7}{2(a-1)}$

65. $\frac{-2x+1}{(x-5)(x+2)(x-2)}$ **67.** $\frac{7x+17}{(x+2)(x-1)(x+3)}$

69. $\frac{bc+ac+ab}{abc}$ **71.** $\frac{2x^2-x-4}{x(x-1)(x+2)}$ **73.** $\frac{a+51}{6a(a-3)}$

75. a) F **b)** A **c)** E **d)** B **e)** D **f)** C **77.** $\frac{p+6}{p(p+4)}$

79. $\frac{6}{(a+1)(a+3)}$ **81.** $\frac{1}{(b+1)(b+2)}$ **83.** $\frac{-1}{2(t+2)}$

85. $\frac{11}{x}$ feet **87.** $\frac{120}{x}$ hr, $\frac{195}{x+5}$ hr, $\frac{315x+600}{x(x+5)}$ hours, 5 hours

89. $\frac{4x+6}{x(x+3)}$ job, $\frac{5}{9}$ job

Section 7.5 Warm-Ups F T F F F F F T T T

1. A complex fraction is a fraction that has fractions in its numerator, denominator, or both.

3. $\frac{3}{5}$ **5.** $-\frac{10}{3}$ **7.** $\frac{22}{7}$ **9.** $\frac{2}{3}$ **11.** $\frac{14}{17}$ **13.** $\frac{45}{23}$ **15.** $\frac{10}{3}$

17. $\frac{10}{9}$ **19.** 13 **21.** -3 **23.** $\frac{1}{2}$ **25.** $\frac{3a+b}{a-3b}$ **27.** $\frac{5a-3}{3a+1}$

29. $\frac{x^2-4x}{2(3x^2-1)}$ **31.** $\frac{10b}{3b^2-4}$ **33.** $\frac{1}{3}$ **35.** $\frac{y-2}{3y+4}$

37. $\frac{x^2-2x+4}{x^2-3x-1}$ **39.** $\frac{5x-14}{2x-7}$ **41.** $\frac{a-6}{3a-1}$ **43.** $\frac{-3m+12}{4m-3}$

45. $\frac{-w+5}{9w+1}$ **47.** -1 **49.** $\frac{a+2}{a+4}$ **51.** $\frac{3}{2x-1}$ **53.** $\frac{x-2}{x+3}$

55. $\frac{6x-27}{2(2x-3)}$ **57.** $\frac{2x^2}{3y}$ **59.** $\frac{a^2+7a+6}{a+3}$ **61.** $1-x$

63. $\frac{32}{95}, \frac{11}{35}$ **65. a)** Neither **b)** $\frac{8}{13}, \frac{13}{21}$ **c)** Converging to 0.61803

Section 7.6 Warm-Ups F F F F F T T T T T

1. The first step is usually to multiply each side by the LCD.

3. An extraneous solution is a number that appears to be a solution when we solve an equation, but it does not check in the original equation.

5. -4 **7.** 12 **9.** 30 **11.** 5 **13.** 2 **15.** 4 **17.** $\frac{2}{5}$ **19.** $\frac{3}{7}$

21. 4 **23.** 4 **25.** 3 **27.** 2 **29.** $-5, 2$ **31.** $-3, 2$ **33.** 2, 3

35. $-3, 3$ **37.** 2 **39.** No solution **41.** No solution **43.** 3

45. 10 **47.** 0 **49.** $-5, 5$ **51.** 3, 5 **53.** 1 **55.** 3

57. 0 **59.** 4 **61.** -20 **63.** 3 **65.** 3 **67.** $54\frac{6}{11}$ mm

Section 7.7 Warm-Ups T F F T T T F F F T

1. A ratio is a comparison of two numbers.

3. Equivalent ratios are ratios that are equivalent as fractions.

5. In the proportion $\frac{a}{b} = \frac{c}{d}$ the means are b and c and the extremes are a and d.

7. $\frac{2}{3}$ **9.** $\frac{4}{3}$ **11.** $\frac{5}{7}$ **13.** $\frac{8}{15}$ **15.** $\frac{7}{2}$ **17.** $\frac{9}{14}$ **19.** $\frac{5}{2}$

21. $\frac{15}{1}$ **23.** 3 to 2 **25.** 9 to 16 **27.** 31 to 1 **29.** 2 to 3 **31.** 6

33. $-\frac{2}{5}$ **35.** $-\frac{27}{5}$ **37.** 7 **39.** 5 **41.** $-\frac{3}{4}$ **43.** $\frac{5}{4}$ **45.** 108

47. 176,000 **49.** Lions 85, Tigers 51

51. 40 luxury cars, 60 sports cars **53.** 84 in. **55.** 15 min

57. $\frac{1610}{3}$ or 536.7 mi **59.** 3920 lb, 2000 lb **61.** 6000

63. a) 3 to 17 **b)** $\frac{201}{14}$ or 14.4 lb **65.** 4074

Section 7.8 Warm-Ups T T F T T F F T F T

1. $y = 3x + 1$ **3.** $y = 2x - 5$ **5.** $y = -\frac{1}{2}x - 2$

7. $y = mx - mb - a$ **9.** $y = -\frac{1}{3}x - \frac{1}{3}$ **11.** $C = \frac{B}{A}$

13. $p = \frac{a}{1 + am}$ **15.** $m_1 = \frac{r^2F}{km_2}$ **17.** $a = \frac{bf}{b-f}$ **19.** $r = \frac{S-a}{S}$

21. $P_2 = \frac{P_1V_1T_2}{T_1V_2}$ **23.** $h = \frac{3V}{4\pi r^2}$ **25.** $\frac{5}{12}$ **27.** $-\frac{6}{23}$ **29.** $\frac{128}{3}$

31. -6 **33.** $\frac{6}{5}$ **35.** Marcie 4 mph, Frank 3 mph

37. Bob 25 mph, Pat 20 mph **39.** 5 mph **41.** 6 hours

43. 40 minutes **45.** 1 hour 36 minutes
47. Master 2 hours, apprentice 6 hours
49. Bananas 8 pounds, apples 10 pounds **51.** 140 mph
53. 10 mph **55.** Ben 15 mph, Jerry 7.5 mph **57.** 1800 miles
59. 4 hours **61.** 1.2 hours or 1 hour 12 minutes **63.** 24 minutes

Enriching Your Mathematical Word Power

1. b **2.** a **3.** a **4.** d **5.** a **6.** b **7.** d **8.** a
9. c **10.** d

Review Exercises

1. All real numbers except 4
3. All real numbers except -1 and 5 **5.** $\frac{6}{7}$ **7.** $\frac{c^2}{4a^2}$
9. $\frac{2w-3}{3w-4}$ **11.** $-\frac{x+1}{3}$ **13.** $\frac{1}{2}k$ **15.** $\frac{2x}{3y}$
17. a^2-a-6 **19.** $\frac{1}{2}$ **21.** 108 **23.** $24a^7b^3$ **25.** $12x(x-1)$
27. $(x+1)(x-2)(x+2)$ **29.** $\frac{15}{36}$ **31.** $\frac{10x}{15x^2y}$ **33.** $\frac{-10}{12-2y}$
35. $\frac{x^2+x}{x^2-1}$ **37.** $\frac{29}{63}$ **39.** $\frac{3x-4}{x}$ **41.** $\frac{2a-b}{a^2b^2}$
43. $\frac{27a^2-8a-15}{(2a-3)(3a-2)}$ **45.** $\frac{3}{a-8}$ **47.** $\frac{3x+8}{2(x+2)(x-2)}$
49. $-\frac{3}{14}$ **51.** $\frac{6b+4a}{3(a-6b)}$ **53.** $\frac{-2x+9}{3x-1}$ **55.** $\frac{x^2+x-2}{-4x+13}$
57. $-\frac{15}{2}$ **59.** 9 **61.** -3 **63.** $\frac{21}{2}$ **65.** 5 **67.** 8
69. 56 cups water, 28 cups rice **71.** $y=mx+b$ **73.** $m=\frac{1}{F-v}$
75. $y=4x-13$ **77.** 200 hours **79.** Bert 60 cars, Ernie 50 cars
81. 27.83 million tons **83.** 10 **85.** -2 **87.** $3x$ **89.** $2m$
91. $\frac{1}{6}$ **93.** $a+1$ **95.** $\frac{5-a}{5a}$ **97.** $a-2$ **99.** $b-a$ **101.** $\frac{1}{10a}$
103. $\frac{3}{2x}$ **105.** $\frac{4+y}{6xy}$ **107.** $\frac{8}{a-5}$ **109.** $-1, 2$ **111.** $-\frac{5}{3}$
113. 6 **115.** $\frac{1}{2}$ **117.** $\frac{3x+7}{(x-5)(x+5)(x+1)}$
119. $\frac{-5a}{(a-3)(a+3)(a+2)}$ **121.** $\frac{2}{5}$

Chapter 7 Test

1. $-1, 1$ **2.** $\frac{2}{3}$ **3.** 0 **4.** $-\frac{14}{45}$ **5.** $\frac{1+3y}{y}$ **6.** $\frac{4}{a-2}$
7. $\frac{-x+4}{(x+2)(x-2)(x-1)}$ **8.** $\frac{2}{3}$ **9.** $\frac{-2}{a+b}$ **10.** $\frac{a^3}{18b^4}$ **11.** $-\frac{4}{3}$
12. $\frac{-3x+4}{2(x-3)}$ **13.** $\frac{15}{7}$ **14.** 2, 3 **15.** 12 **16.** $y=-\frac{1}{5}x+\frac{13}{5}$
17. $c=\frac{3M-bd}{b}$ **18.** 29 **19.** 7.2 minutes
20. Brenda 15 mph and Randy 20 mph, or Brenda 10 mph and Randy 15 mph
21. $72 billion

Making Connections A Review of Chapters 1–7

1. $\frac{7}{3}$ **2.** $-\frac{10}{3}$ **3.** -2 **4.** No solution **5.** 0 **6.** $-4, -2$
7. $-1, 0, 1$ **8.** $-\frac{15}{2}$ **9.** $-6, 6$ **10.** $-2, 4$ **11.** 5 **12.** 3
13. $y=\frac{c-2x}{3}$ **14.** $y=\frac{1}{2}x+\frac{1}{2}$ **15.** $y=\frac{c}{2-a}$ **16.** $y=\frac{AB}{C}$
17. $y=3B-3A$ **18.** $y=\frac{6A}{5}$ **19.** $y=\frac{8}{3-5a}$
20. $y=0$ or $y=B$ **21.** $y=\frac{2A-hb}{h}$ **22.** $y=-\frac{b}{2}$ **23.** 64
24. 16 **25.** 49 **26.** 121 **27.** $-2x-2$ **28.** $2a^2-11a+15$
29. x^4 **30.** $\frac{2x+1}{5}$ **31.** $\frac{1}{2x}$ **32.** $\frac{x+2}{2x}$ **33.** $\frac{x}{2}$ **34.** $\frac{x-2}{2x}$
35. $-\frac{7}{5}$ **36.** $\frac{3a}{4}$ **37.** x^2-64 **38.** $3x^3-21x$ **39.** $10a^{14}$
40. x^{10} **41.** $k^2-12k+36$ **42.** $j^2+10j+25$ **43.** -1
44. $3x^2-4x$ **45. a)** $P=\frac{r+2}{(1+r)^2}$ **b)** $1.81 **c)** $7.72

Chapter 8

Section 8.1 Warm-Ups T F T F T T F F T T
1. If $b^n=a$, then b is an nth root of a.
3. If $b^n=a$, then b is an even root provided n is even or an odd root provided n is odd.
5. The product rule for radicals says that $\sqrt[n]{a}\cdot\sqrt[n]{b}=\sqrt[n]{ab}$ provided all of these roots are real.
7. -5 and 5 **9.** 3 **11.** -3 and 3 **13.** -2 **15.** $\sqrt{8}$
17. $\sqrt[3]{-7}$ **19.** $\sqrt[4]{5}$ **21.** $\sqrt[6]{3}$ **23.** 6 **25.** 2 **27.** 10
29. Not a real number **31.** 0 **33.** -1 **35.** 1
37. Not a real number **39.** 2 **41.** -2 **43.** -10
45. Not a real number **47.** 5 **49.** 6 **51.** 3 **53.** 10 **55.** 3
57. m **59.** y^3 **61.** y^5 **63.** m **65.** 27 **67.** 32 **69.** 125
71. 10^{10} **73.** $3\sqrt{y}$ **75.** $2a$ **77.** x^2y **79.** $m^6\sqrt{5}$ **81.** $2\sqrt[3]{y}$
83. $-3w$ **85.** $2\sqrt[4]{s}$ **87.** $-5a^3y^2$ **89.** $\frac{\sqrt{t}}{2}$ **91.** $\frac{25}{4}$ **93.** $\frac{\sqrt[3]{t}}{2}$
95. $\frac{-2x^2}{y}$ **97.** $\frac{2a^3}{3}$ **99.** $\frac{\sqrt[4]{y}}{2}$ **101.** 3.968 **103.** -1.610
105. 6.001 **107.** 0.769 **109. a)** $3\sqrt{2}, 2$ **b)** 7.1 inches
111. 46 **113. a)** 228 mi **b)** 7000 ft
115. a) No **b)** Yes **c)** No **d)** Yes

Section 8.2 Warm-Ups T F T F T F T F F F
1. We use the product rule to factor out a perfect square from inside a square root.
3. To rationalize a denominator means to rewrite the expression so that the denominator is a rational number.
5. To simplify square roots containing variables use the same techniques as we use on square roots of numbers.
7. $2\sqrt{2}$ **9.** $2\sqrt{6}$ **11.** $2\sqrt{7}$ **13.** $3\sqrt{10}$ **15.** $10\sqrt{5}$
17. $5\sqrt{6}$ **19.** $\frac{\sqrt{5}}{5}$ **21.** $\frac{3\sqrt{2}}{2}$ **23.** $\frac{\sqrt{6}}{2}$ **25.** $\frac{-3\sqrt{10}}{10}$
27. $\frac{-10\sqrt{17}}{17}$ **29.** $\frac{\sqrt{77}}{7}$ **31.** $3\sqrt{7}$ **33.** $\frac{3\sqrt{2}}{2}$ **35.** $\frac{\sqrt{6}}{2}$
37. $\frac{\sqrt{10}}{4}$ **39.** $\frac{\sqrt{15}}{5}$ **41.** 5 **43.** $\frac{\sqrt{6}}{2}$ **45.** a^4 **47.** $a^4\sqrt{a}$
49. $2a^3\sqrt{2}$ **51.** $2a^2b^4\sqrt{5b}$ **53.** $3xy\sqrt{3xy}$ **55.** $3ab^4c\sqrt{3a}$
57. $\frac{\sqrt{x}}{x}$ **59.** $\frac{\sqrt{6a}}{3a}$ **61.** $\frac{\sqrt{5y}}{5y}$ **63.** $\frac{\sqrt{6xy}}{2y}$ **65.** $\frac{\sqrt{6xy}}{3x}$
67. $\frac{2x\sqrt{2xy}}{y}$ **69.** $2\sqrt{2a}$ **71.** w^2 **73.** $z^2\sqrt{z}$ **75.** $\frac{\sqrt{3p}}{3}$

77. $\frac{\sqrt{ab}}{a}$ **79.** $b\sqrt{a}$ **81.** $4x\sqrt{5x}$ **83.** $3y^4x^7\sqrt{yx}$ **85.** $4x^3\sqrt{5x}$
87. $\frac{-11\sqrt{6pq}}{3q}$ **89.** $a^3b^8c\sqrt{ac}$ **91.** $\frac{\sqrt{6y}}{3x^9y^4}$ **93.** 0 **95.** 0
97. a) $E = \frac{\sqrt{2AIS}}{I}$ **b)** 51.2

Section 8.3 Warm-Ups F T F F T F F F T T
1. Like radicals have the same index and same radicand.
3. Radicals can be added, subtracted, multiplied, and divided.
5. Radical expressions such as $\sqrt{a} + \sqrt{b}$ and $\sqrt{a} - \sqrt{b}$ are conjugates.
7. $7\sqrt{5}$ **9.** $2\sqrt[3]{2}$ **11.** $8u\sqrt{11}$ **13.** $4\sqrt{3} - 4\sqrt{2}$
15. $-4\sqrt{x} - \sqrt{y}$ **17.** $5x\sqrt{y} + 2\sqrt{a}$ **19.** $5\sqrt{6}$ **21.** $-14\sqrt{3}$
23. $3\sqrt{2}$ **25.** $-\sqrt{3a}$ **27.** $3x\sqrt{x}$ **29.** $\frac{2\sqrt{3}}{3}$ **31.** $\frac{7\sqrt{3}}{3}$
33. $\sqrt{77}$ **35.** 36 **37.** $-12\sqrt{10}$ **39.** $2a^4\sqrt{3}$ **41.** 3 **43.** $-2m$
45. $2 + \sqrt{6}$ **47.** $12\sqrt{3} + 6\sqrt{5}$ **49.** $10 - 30\sqrt{2}$ **51.** $-7 - \sqrt{5}$
53. 2 **55.** 3 **57.** $28 - \sqrt{5}$ **59.** $-42 - \sqrt{15}$ **61.** $37 + 20\sqrt{3}$
63. $\sqrt{2}$ **65.** $\frac{\sqrt{15}}{3}$ **67.** $\frac{2\sqrt{30}}{9}$ **69.** $\frac{5\sqrt{7}}{3}$ **71.** $1 + \sqrt{2}$
73. $-2 + \sqrt{5}$ **75.** $\frac{2 - \sqrt{5}}{3}$ **77.** $\frac{2 + \sqrt{6}}{3}$ **79.** $\frac{3 + 2\sqrt{3}}{6}$
81. $5\sqrt{3} + 5\sqrt{2}$ **83.** $\frac{\sqrt{15} + 3}{2}$ **85.** $\frac{13 + 7\sqrt{3}}{22}$
87. $\frac{19 - 11\sqrt{7}}{27}$ **89.** $3\sqrt{5a}$ **91.** $\frac{5\sqrt{2}}{2}$ **93.** $70 + 30\sqrt{5}$
95. $\frac{5\sqrt{5}}{3}$ **97.** 1.866 **99.** -1.974 **101.** 12 ft^2, $10\sqrt{2}$ ft
103. 6 m^3

Section 8.4 Warm-Ups F T F F T F F T T T
1. The square root property says that $x^2 = k$ for $k > 0$ is equivalent to $x = \pm\sqrt{k}$.
3. The square root property and squaring each side are two new techniques used for solving equations.
5. Squaring each side can produce extraneous roots.
7. $-4, 4$ **9.** $-2\sqrt{10}, 2\sqrt{10}$ **11.** $-\frac{\sqrt{6}}{3}, \frac{\sqrt{6}}{3}$
13. No solution **15.** $-1, 3$ **17.** $5 - \sqrt{3}, 5 + \sqrt{3}$ **19.** -19
21. 90 **23.** No solution **25.** $-5, 5$ **27.** 3 **29.** 0, 1
31. 6 **33.** No solution **35.** 2 **37.** 13 **39.** 3, 5
41. 3 **43.** 6, 8 **45.** 5 **47.** $r = \pm\sqrt{\frac{V}{\pi h}}$ **49.** $b = \pm\sqrt{c^2 - a^2}$
51. $b = \pm 2\sqrt{ac}$ **53.** $t = \frac{v^2}{2p}$ **55.** $-\frac{1}{2}, \frac{1}{2}$ **57.** No solution
59. $\frac{1}{81}$ **61.** $-8, 8$ **63.** $0, \frac{1}{4}$ **65.** $-3, 1$ **67.** $-\sqrt{2}, \sqrt{2}$
69. No solution **71.** $\frac{1 + 2\sqrt{2}}{2}, \frac{1 - 2\sqrt{2}}{2}$ **73.** $\frac{9}{2}$ **75.** 3
77. $-4, 2$ **79.** $\frac{5}{2}$ **81.** $-1.803, 1.803$ **83.** 0.993
85. 0.362, 4.438 **87.** $3\sqrt{2}$ or 4.243 ft **89.** $3\sqrt{2}$ or 4.243 ft
91. $\sqrt{2}$ or 1.414 ft **93.** 5 ft **95.** 2.5 sec
97. $\frac{200\sqrt{13}}{3}$ or 240.370 ft

Section 8.5 Warm-Ups T F F T T T T F T T
1. The nth root of a is $a^{1/n}$.
3. The expression $a^{-m/n}$ means $\frac{1}{a^{m/n}}$.
5. The operations can be performed in any order, but the easiest is usually root, power, and then reciprocal.
7. $7^{1/4}$ **9.** $\sqrt[5]{9}$ **11.** $(5x)^{1/2}$ **13.** $\sqrt{-a}$ **15.** $-x^{1/2}$ **17.** $-\sqrt[4]{6}$
19. 5 **21.** 5 **23.** -5 **25.** -2 **27.** Not a real number **29.** -2
31. -4 **33.** $w^{7/3}$ **35.** $2^{-10/3}$ **37.** $\frac{1}{\sqrt[4]{w^3}}$ **39.** $\sqrt{(ab)^3}$
41. $-t^{3/4}$ **43.** $-\frac{1}{\sqrt{a^3}}$ **45.** 25 **47.** 125 **49.** $\frac{1}{81}$ **51.** $\frac{1}{8}$
53. $-\frac{1}{3}$ **55.** Not a real number **57.** -8 **59.** $-\frac{1}{4}$
61. Not a real number **63.** $x^{1/2}$ **65.** $n^{1/6}$ **67.** $x^{3/2}$ **69.** $2t^{1/4}$
71. x^2 **73.** $5^{1/8}$ **75.** xy^3 **77.** $\frac{x}{3y^4}$ **79.** $\frac{3}{4}$ **81.** $\frac{1}{9}$ **83.** 27
85. $\frac{1}{12}$ **87.** Yes, 9.2 m^2 **89.** 11.8%
91. a) 15.9 **b)** Decreasing **c)** 28,000 pounds
93. $a < 0$ and m and n are odd
95. $3^{-8/9} < 3^{-2/3} < 3^{-1/2} < 3^0 < 3^{1/2} < 3^{2/3} < 3^{8/9}$, $7^{-9/10} < 7^{-3/4} < 7^{-1/3} < 7^0 < 7^{1/3} < 7^{3/4} < 7^{9/10}$, $m < n$

Enriching Your Mathematical Word Power
1. d **2.** b **3.** b **4.** b **5.** d **6.** b **7.** c **8.** d

Review Exercises
1. 2 **3.** 10 **5.** x^6 **7.** x^2 **9.** $2x$ **11.** $5x^2$ **13.** $\frac{2x^8}{y^7}$ **15.** $\frac{w}{4}$
17. $6\sqrt{2}$ **19.** $\frac{\sqrt{3}}{3}$ **21.** $\frac{\sqrt{15}}{5}$ **23.** $\sqrt{11}$ **25.** $\frac{\sqrt{6}}{4}$ **27.** y^3
29. $2t^4\sqrt{6t}$ **31.** $2m^2t\sqrt{3mt}$ **33.** $\frac{\sqrt{2x}}{x}$ **35.** $\frac{a^2\sqrt{6as}}{2s}$ **37.** $10\sqrt{7}$
39. $-\sqrt{3}$ **41.** 30 **43.** $-45\sqrt{2}$ **45.** $-15\sqrt{3} - 9$
47. $-3\sqrt{2} + 3\sqrt{5}$ **49.** -22 **51.** $26 - 4\sqrt{30}$ **53.** $38 - 19\sqrt{6}$
55. $\frac{\sqrt{10}}{4}$ **57.** $\frac{1 - \sqrt{5}}{5}$ **59.** $-\frac{3 + 3\sqrt{5}}{4}$ **61.** $-20, 20$
63. $-\frac{\sqrt{21}}{7}, \frac{\sqrt{21}}{7}$ **65.** $4 - 3\sqrt{2}, 4 + 3\sqrt{2}$ **67.** 81 **69.** 4
71. 6 **73.** $t = \pm 2\sqrt{2sw}$ **75.** $t = \frac{9a^2}{b}$ **77.** $\frac{1}{125}$ **79.** 5
81. $\frac{1}{8}$ **83.** $-\frac{1}{125}$ **85.** Not a real number **87.** $-\frac{1}{2}$ **89.** $\frac{1}{x}$
91. $-\frac{1}{2}x^2$ **93.** w^2 **95.** $\frac{t^3}{3s^2}$ **97.** $\frac{4}{x^8y^{20}}$
99. a) 16.4% **b)** First two years
101. 0.4 cm **103.** $4\pi\sqrt{10}$ or 40 in.^{2} **105.** 22 in.

Chapter 8 Test
1. 6 **2.** 12 **3.** -3 **4.** 2 **5.** 2 **6.** $2\sqrt{6}$ **7.** $\frac{\sqrt{6}}{4}$
8. Not a real number **9.** 81 **10.** $-\frac{1}{3}$ **11.** -16 **12.** $3\sqrt{2}$
13. $7 + 4\sqrt{3}$ **14.** 11 **15.** $\sqrt{7}$ **16.** $\frac{2\sqrt{15}}{3}$ **17.** $1 + \sqrt{2}$
18. $3\sqrt{2} - 3$ **19.** $y^{3/4}$ **20.** $3x^{2/3}$ **21.** xy^3 **22.** $\frac{1}{5u^4w}$
23. $\frac{\sqrt{3t}}{t}$ **24.** $2y^3$ **25.** $2y^4$ **26.** $3t^3\sqrt{2t}$ **27.** $-9, 3$ **28.** 18
29. $-\frac{\sqrt{10}}{5}, \frac{\sqrt{10}}{5}$ **30.** $\frac{4}{3}$ **31.** 11 **32.** $r = \pm\sqrt{\frac{S}{\pi h}}$
33. $b = \pm\sqrt{c^2 - a^2}$ **34.** $\frac{5\sqrt{2}}{2}$ meters **35.** 178.4 meters

Making Connections A Review of Chapters 1–8

1. $\left\{-\frac{3}{2}\right\}$ **2.** $\left\{\frac{3}{2}\right\}$

3. $\left(-\frac{3}{2}, \infty\right)$

4. $\left(-\infty, \frac{3}{2}\right)$

5. $\{-3\}$ **6.** $\left\{-\frac{\sqrt{6}}{2}, \frac{\sqrt{6}}{2}\right\}$ **7.** $\{-\sqrt{6}, \sqrt{6}\}$ **8.** $\left\{\frac{2}{3}\right\}$ **9.** $\left\{-\frac{3}{2}\right\}$

10. $\left\{-\frac{3}{2}, 3\right\}$ **11.** No solution, $\varnothing$ **12.** $\{-2, -1\}$

13. No solution, $\varnothing$ **14.** $\{3\}$ **15.** 9 **16.** 72 **17.** 81 **18.** 9

19. 12 **20.** -6 **21.** 3 **22.** $-\frac{3}{2}$ **23.** $(x-3)^2$ **24.** $(x+5)^2$

25. $(x+6)^2$ **26.** $(x-10)^2$ **27.** $2(x-2)^2$ **28.** $3(x+1)^2$

29. $7x - 3$ **30.** $-15t^2 - 13t + 20$ **31.** $-24j^2 + 14j + 24$

32. $6u + 6$ **33.** $v + 1$ **34.** $t^2 + 4t + 4$ **35.** $t^2 - 49$

36. $-4n^2 + 9$ **37.** $m^2 - 2m + 1$ **38.** $2t - 1$ **39.** $-4r^2 - r + 3$

40. $-18y^2 + 2$ **41.** $3j - 5$ **42.** $-6j + 2$ **43.** $2 - 3x$

44. $-1 - 3p$ **45.** $-2 + 3q$ **46.** $-4 + z$

47. a) 16.788 kilocalories per minute **b)** 275.24 m/min **c)** Increasing

Chapter 9

Section 9.1 Warm-Ups T F F T T F F T F F

1. A quadratic equation is an equation of the form $ax^2 + bx + c = 0$, where $a \neq 0$.

3. If $b = 0$, we can get the square root of a negative number and no real solution.

5. After applying the zero factor property we will have linear equations to solve.

7. $-8, 8$ **9.** $-\frac{3}{2}, \frac{3}{2}$ **11.** $-6, 6$ **13.** No real solution

15. $-\sqrt{10}, \sqrt{10}$ **17.** $-\frac{\sqrt{15}}{3}, \frac{\sqrt{15}}{3}$ **19.** $-\frac{2\sqrt{6}}{3}, \frac{2\sqrt{6}}{3}$ **21.** 1, 5

23. $2 - 3\sqrt{2}, 2 + 3\sqrt{2}$ **25.** $-\frac{3}{2}, -\frac{1}{2}$ **27.** $\frac{2-\sqrt{2}}{2}, \frac{2+\sqrt{2}}{2}$

29. $\frac{-1-\sqrt{2}}{2}, \frac{-1+\sqrt{2}}{2}$ **31.** 11 **33.** $-2, -1$ **35.** $-5, 6$

37. $-3, 5$ **39.** -3 **41.** $-1, 2$ **43.** 0, 2 **45.** $0, \frac{3}{2}$ **47.** $-7, \frac{3}{2}$

49. 5 **51.** $-\frac{5}{2}, 6$ **53.** 4, 6 **55.** $-\frac{1}{2}, \frac{1}{2}$ **57.** $-6, 4$ **59.** $-2, 0$

61. $-6, 4$ **63.** $-\frac{9}{2}$ **65.** $-\sqrt{6}, \sqrt{6}$ **67.** 3, 9 **69.** 3, 4

71. $\frac{5\sqrt{2}}{2}$ meters **73.** $4\sqrt{5}$ blocks **75.** $2\sqrt{61}$ feet

77. 6.3% **79. a)** 70 feet **b)** 2 sec and 3 sec **c)** 5 sec

81. 9 **83.** c

Section 9.2 Warm-Ups F F F F T T T T T T

1. Not every quadratic can be solved by factoring or the square root property.

3. The last term is the square of one-half of the coefficient of the middle term.

5. $x^2 + 6x + 9 = (x+3)^2$ **7.** $x^2 + 14x + 49 = (x+7)^2$

9. $x^2 - 16x + 64 = (x-8)^2$ **11.** $t^2 - 18t + 81 = (t-9)^2$

13. $m^2 + 3m + \frac{9}{4} = \left(m + \frac{3}{2}\right)^2$ **15.** $z^2 + z + \frac{1}{4} = \left(z + \frac{1}{2}\right)^2$

17. $x^2 - \frac{1}{2}x + \frac{1}{16} = \left(x - \frac{1}{4}\right)^2$ **19.** $y^2 + \frac{1}{4}y + \frac{1}{64} = \left(y + \frac{1}{8}\right)^2$

21. $(x+5)^2$ **23.** $(m-1)^2$ **25.** $(w-6)^2$ **27.** $\left(x + \frac{1}{2}\right)^2$

29. $\left(t + \frac{1}{6}\right)^2$ **31.** $\left(x + \frac{1}{5}\right)^2$ **33.** $-5, 3$ **35.** $-3, 7$ **37.** -3

39. $\frac{1}{2}, 1$ **41.** $\frac{3}{2}, 2$ **43.** $-1, \frac{1}{3}$ **45.** $-1 - \sqrt{7}, -1 + \sqrt{7}$

47. $-3 - 2\sqrt{2}, -3 + 2\sqrt{2}$ **49.** $\frac{1-\sqrt{13}}{2}, \frac{1+\sqrt{13}}{2}$

51. $\frac{-3-\sqrt{21}}{2}, \frac{-3+\sqrt{21}}{2}$ **53.** $\frac{1-\sqrt{33}}{4}, \frac{1+\sqrt{33}}{4}$

55. $\frac{-3-\sqrt{15}}{2}, \frac{-3+\sqrt{15}}{2}$ **57.** $\frac{3-\sqrt{5}}{4}, \frac{3+\sqrt{5}}{4}$

59. $5 - \sqrt{7}, 5 + \sqrt{7}$ **61.** $-\frac{\sqrt{15}}{3}, \frac{\sqrt{15}}{3}$ **63.** $\frac{-2-\sqrt{5}}{2}, \frac{-2+\sqrt{5}}{2}$

65. No real solution **67.** $4 - 2\sqrt{2}, 4 + 2\sqrt{2}$ **69.** $\frac{7}{2}$

71. $-3 - 2\sqrt{5}, -3 + 2\sqrt{5}$ **73.** $2 - \sqrt{2}, 2 + \sqrt{2}$ **75.** $-0.6, 0.4$

77. $\frac{-1-2\sqrt{2}}{2}, \frac{-1+2\sqrt{2}}{2}$ **79.** $5 - \sqrt{3}$ in. and $5 + \sqrt{3}$ in.

81. $6 - \sqrt{2}$ and $6 + \sqrt{2}$ **83.** 12 years old

85. a) $x^2 - 10x + 22$ **b)** $5 \pm \sqrt{3}$ **c)** $x^2 - 3x + \frac{7}{4} = 0$

Section 9.3 Warm-Ups T F F F T F F T T T

1. The quadratic formula solves any quadratic equation.

3. The quadratic formula is used to solve $ax^2 + bx + c = 0$ where $a \neq 0$.

5. If $b^2 - 4ac < 0$, then there are no real solutions.

7. $-5, 3$ **9.** -5 **11.** $-2, \frac{3}{2}$ **13.** $-\frac{3}{2}, \frac{1}{2}$ **15.** $3 - \sqrt{5}, 3 + \sqrt{5}$

17. $\frac{3-\sqrt{3}}{2}, \frac{3+\sqrt{3}}{2}$ **19.** $\frac{-2-\sqrt{2}}{2}, \frac{-2+\sqrt{2}}{2}$ **21.** No real solution

23. $0, \frac{1}{2}$ **25.** $-\frac{\sqrt{15}}{5}, \frac{\sqrt{15}}{5}$ **27.** $-7 + 4\sqrt{3}, -7 - 4\sqrt{3}$

29. No real solution **31.** 0, one **33.** -47, none **35.** 181, two

37. 0, one **39.** -15, none **41.** -59, none **43.** $-2, \frac{1}{2}$ **45.** 0, 3

47. $-\frac{6}{5}, 4$ **49.** $-4, -2$ **51.** 0, 9 **53.** $-8, -2$ **55.** No real solution

57. $\frac{3-\sqrt{33}}{2}, \frac{3+\sqrt{33}}{2}$ **59.** $0, \frac{3}{2}$ **61.** $-0.79, 3.79$

63. $-1.36, 2.36$ **65.** 0.30

67. a) \$150,000 **b)** \$0 and \$40 **c)** \$17.50 or \$22.50 **d)** \$20

Section 9.4 Warm-Ups F T F F T T T F T T

1. Width $-1 + \sqrt{11}$ meters, length $1 + \sqrt{11}$ meters

3. $4\sqrt{2}$ feet **5.** Height $-3 + \sqrt{19}$ inches, base $3 + \sqrt{19}$ inches

7. Length $9 + \sqrt{5}$ in., width $9 - \sqrt{5}$ in. **9.** $3 + \sqrt{5}$ or 5.24 hours
11. $16 + 4\sqrt{26}$ or 36.40 hours **13.** $\frac{15 + \sqrt{241}}{8}$ or 3.82 seconds
15. 1.5 seconds **17.** $2\sqrt{19}$ or 8.72 mph
19. $\frac{-13 + \sqrt{409}}{2}$ or 3.61 feet

Section 9.5 Warm-Ups T T T T F F F F F T

1. A complex number is a number of the form $a + bi$, where a and b are real and $i = \sqrt{-1}$.
3. Complex numbers are added or subtracted like binomials in which i is the variable.
5. If $b > 0$, then $\sqrt{-b} = i\sqrt{b}$. **7.** $5 + 9i$ **9.** 1 **11.** $2 - 8i$
13. $-1 - 4i$ **15.** -1 **17.** $\frac{3}{4} + \frac{1}{2}i$ **19.** $6 - 9i$ **21.** -36
23. -36 **25.** $21 - i$ **27.** $21 - 20i$ **29.** 25 **31.** 2 **33.** 29
35. 52 **37.** 13 **39.** 1 **41.** $1 - 3i$ **43.** $-1 + 4i$ **45.** $-3 + 2i$
47. $\frac{8}{13} + \frac{12}{13}i$ **49.** $\frac{3}{5} + \frac{4}{5}i$ **51.** $-4i$ **53.** $5 + 3i$ **55.** $-3 - i\sqrt{7}$
57. $-1 + i\sqrt{3}$ **59.** $2 + \frac{1}{2}i\sqrt{5}$ **61.** $-\frac{2}{3} + \frac{1}{3}i\sqrt{7}$ **63.** $\frac{1}{5} - i$
65. $-6i, 6i$ **67.** $-9i, 9i$ **69.** $-7, 7$ **71.** $-i\sqrt{5}, i\sqrt{5}$
73. $-i\frac{\sqrt{6}}{3}, i\frac{\sqrt{6}}{3}$ **75.** $2 - i, 2 + i$ **77.** $3 - 2i, 3 + 2i$
79. $2 - i\sqrt{3}, 2 + i\sqrt{3}$ **81.** $\frac{2 - i}{3}, \frac{2 + i}{3}$ **83.** $\frac{1 - i\sqrt{3}}{2}, \frac{1 + i\sqrt{3}}{2}$
85. $\frac{2 - i\sqrt{5}}{2}, \frac{2 + i\sqrt{5}}{2}$ **87.** $-6 - 24i$ **89.** 0 **91.** $x^2 - 12x + 37$
93. $x^2 + 9 = 0$
95. Natural: 54, integers: 54, rational: 54, $-3/8$, irrational: $3\sqrt{5}$, real: 54, $-3/8$, $3\sqrt{5}$, imaginary: $6i$, $\pi + i\sqrt{5}$, complex: all

Section 9.6 Warm-Ups T F T T F T T T T F

1. The graph of $y = mx + b$ is a straight line.
3. The graph of $y = ax^2 + bx + c$ opens upward if $a > 0$.
5. The x-coordinate of the vertex is $-b/(2a)$. **7.** (2, 3), $(-1, 0)$, (1, 0)
9. $(3, -6)$, (4, 0), $(-3, 0)$ **11.** $(4, -128)$, (0, 0), (2, 0)

13.

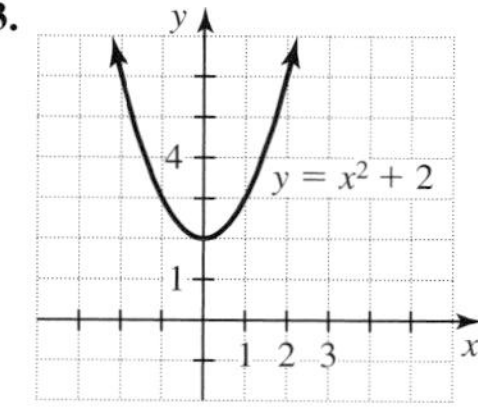

15.

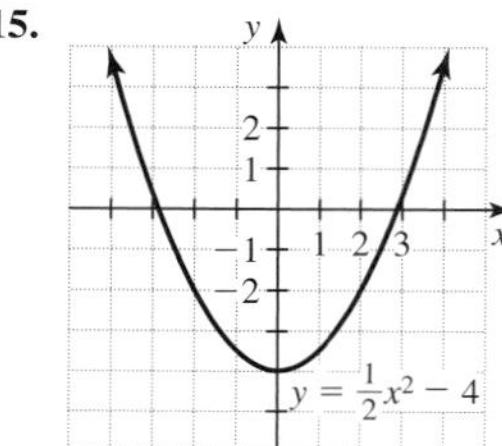

17.

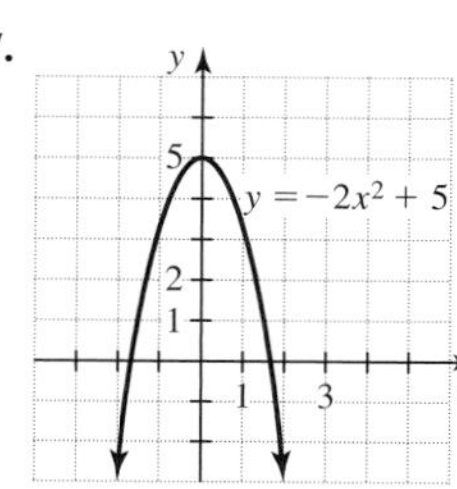

19.

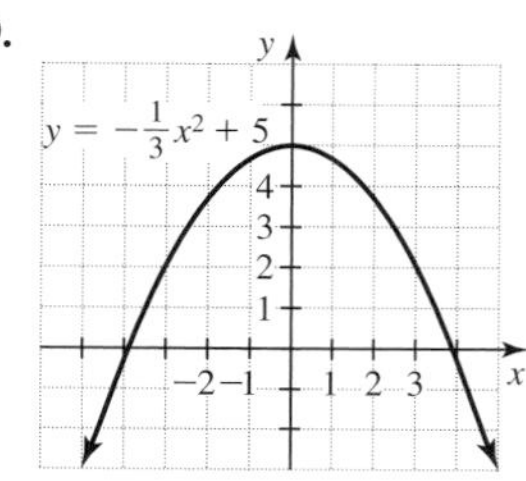

21.

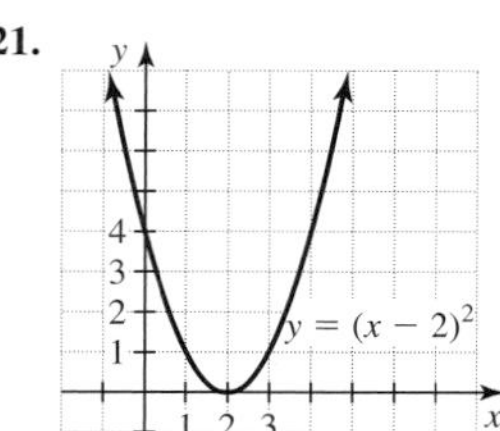

23. Vertex $\left(\frac{1}{2}, -\frac{9}{4}\right)$, intercepts $(0, -2)$, $(-1, 0)$, (2, 0)

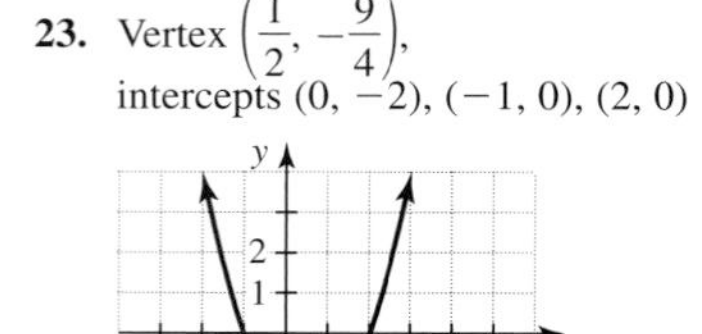

25. Vertex $(-1, -9)$, intercepts $(0, -8)$, $(-4, 0)$, (2, 0)

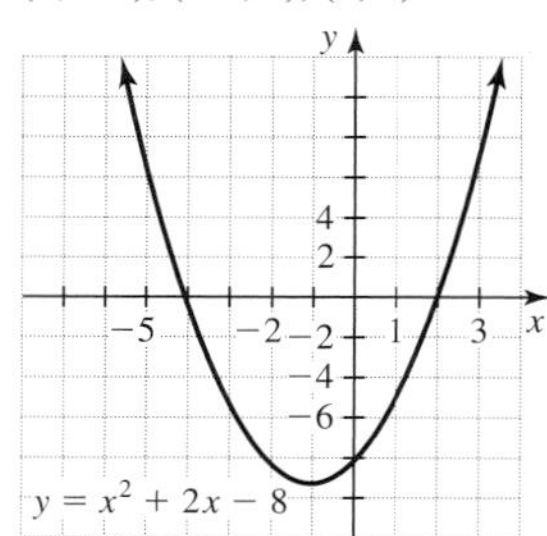

27. Vertex $(-2, 1)$, intercepts $(0, -3)$, $(-1, 0)$, $(-3, 0)$

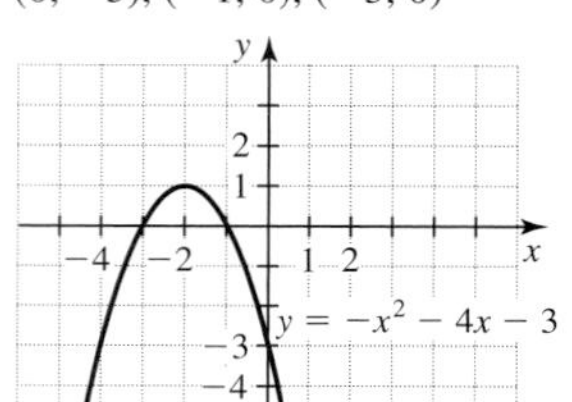

29. Vertex $\left(\frac{3}{2}, \frac{25}{4}\right)$, intercepts (0, 4), (4, 0), $(-1, 0)$

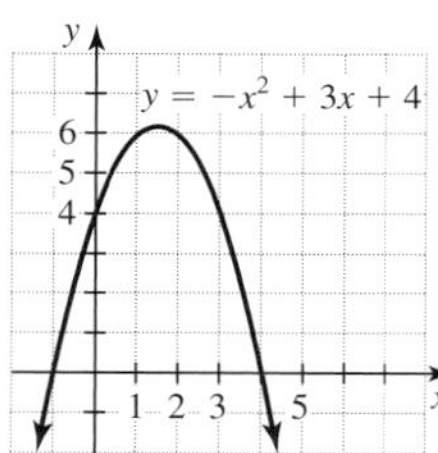

31. Vertex $(3, -25)$, intercepts $(0, -16)$, (8, 0), $(-2, 0)$

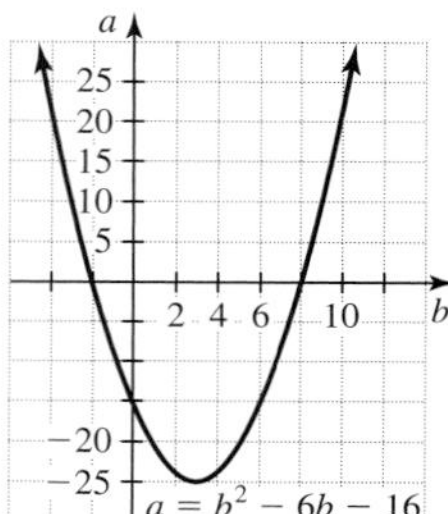

33. Minimum -8 **35.** Maximum 14 **37.** Minimum 2
39. Maximum 2
41. Maximum 64 feet

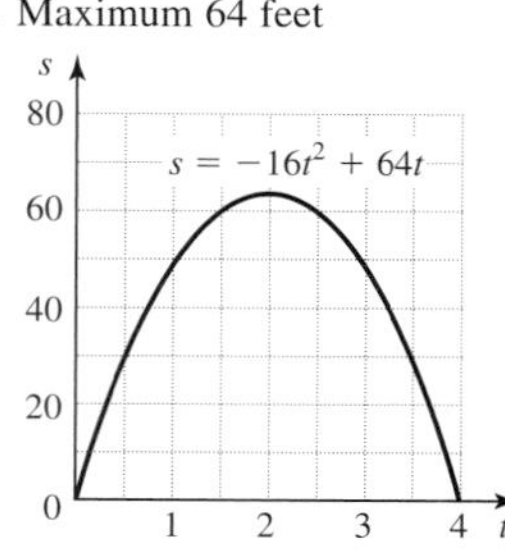

43. 625 square meters **45.** 2 P.M.
47. 15 meters, 25 meters
49. The graph of $y = ax^2$ gets narrower as a gets larger.
51. The graph of $y = x^2$ has the same shape as $x = y^2$.
53. **a)** Vertex $(0.84, -0.68)$, x-intercepts (1.30, 0), (0.38, 0)
b) Vertex (5.96, 46.26), x-intercepts (12.48, 0), $(-0.55, 0)$

Section 9.7 Warm-Ups F T F T T T T T F T

1. A function is a set of ordered pairs in which no two have the same first coordinate and different second coordinates.
3. All descriptions of functions involve ordered pairs that satisfy the definition.
5. The domain is the set of all first coordinates of the ordered pairs.
7. $C = 0.50t + 5$ **9.** $T = 1.09S$ **11.** $C = 2\pi r$ **13.** $P = 4s$
15. $A = 5h$ **17.** Yes **19.** Yes **21.** No **23.** Yes **25.** Yes

27. Yes **29.** No **31.** Yes **33.** Yes **35.** No **37.** Yes
39. No **41.** Yes **43.** Yes **45.** Yes **47.** No **49.** Yes
51. No **53.** No **55.** {1, 2, 3}, {3, 5, 7} **57.** {0, 2, 4}, {1}
59. R (real numbers), R **61.** R, R

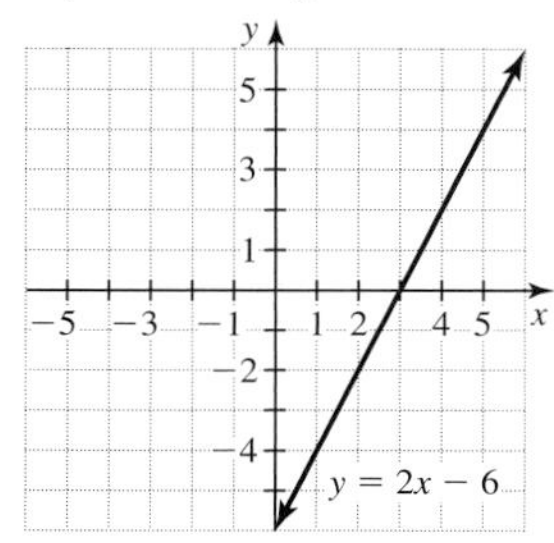

y = −x

63. R, $\{y \mid y \geq -2\}$ or $[-2, \infty)$ **65.** R, $\{y \mid y \leq 7\}$ or $(-\infty, 7]$

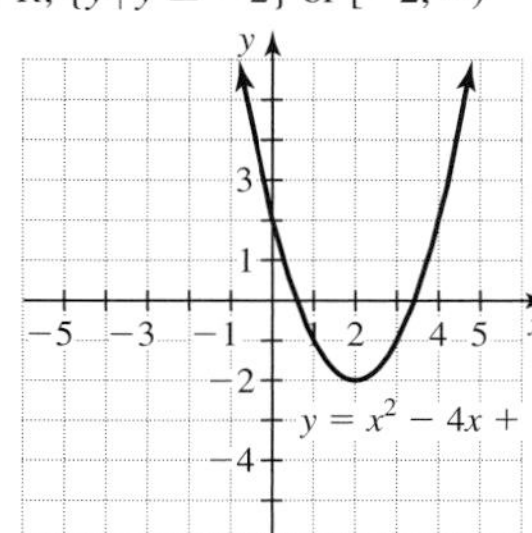

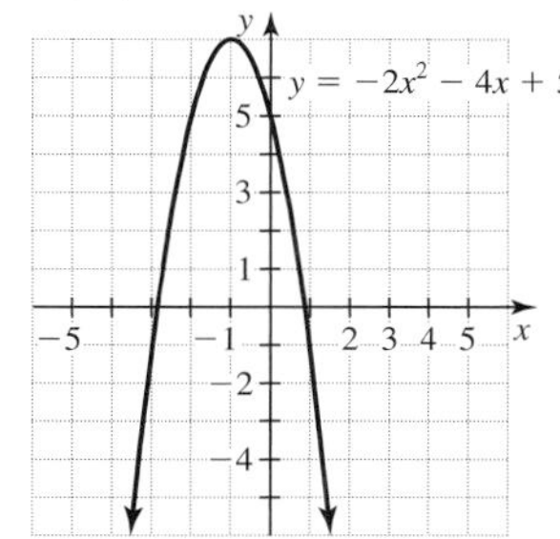

67. −1 **69.** 0 **71.** 13 **73.** −2.75 **75.** 2 **77.** 1 **79.** −6
81. 0 **83.** $2\sqrt{2}$ **85.** 1 **87.** −1 **89.** 150.988 **91.** 0.31
93. a) 100 ft/sec, 68 ft/sec, 36 ft/sec **b)** Decreasing
c) −28 ft/sec; The ball has negative velocity as it is coming down.
95. 183 pounds, 216 pounds **97.** $C(r) = \frac{r}{0.96}$ **99.** Both
101. Neither **103.** Neither **105.** b is a function of a

Section 9.8 Warm-Ups T T F F F F T T T T
1. The basic operations of functions are addition, subtraction, multiplication, and division.
3. In the composition function the second function is evaluated on the result of the first function.
5. $x^2 + 2x - 3$ **7.** $4x^3 - 11x^2 + 6x$ **9.** 12 **11.** −30 **13.** −21
15. $\frac{13}{8}$ **17.** $y = 6x$ **19.** $y = 6x - 20$ **21.** $y = x + 2$
23. $y = x^2 + 2x$ **25.** $y = x$ for $x \neq 1$ **27.** −2 **29.** 5 **31.** 7
33. 5 **35.** 5 **37.** 4 **39.** 22.2992 **41.** $4x^2 - 6x$ **43.** $2x^2 + 6x - 3$
45. x **47.** $4x - 9$ **49.** $\frac{x+9}{4}$ **51.** $F = f \circ h$ **53.** $G = g \circ h$
55. $H = h \circ g$ **57.** $J = h \circ h$ **59.** $K = g \circ g$ **61.** 112.5 in.², $A = \frac{d^2}{2}$
63. $P(x) = -x^2 + 20x - 170$ **65.** $J = 0.025I$
67. a) 397.8 **b)** $D = \frac{1.116 \times 10^7}{L^3}$ **c)** Decreases

Enriching Your Mathematical Word Power
1. b **2.** a **3.** d **4.** c **5.** b **6.** a **7.** c **8.** a **9.** b
10. c **11.** a **12.** d **13.** c **14.** a **15.** b

Review Exercises
1. −3, 3 **3.** 0, 9 **5.** −1, 2 **7.** $9 - \sqrt{10}, 9 + \sqrt{10}$ **9.** $\frac{3}{2}$
11. 4, 5 **13.** −7, 2 **15.** $-4, \frac{1}{2}$ **17.** $-2 - \sqrt{11}, -2 + \sqrt{11}$
19. −7, 4 **21.** $\frac{-3 - \sqrt{29}}{2}, \frac{-3 + \sqrt{29}}{2}$ **23.** $-5, \frac{1}{2}$ **25.** 0, one
27. −44, none **29.** 76, two **31.** $-\frac{2}{3}, \frac{1}{2}$
33. $\frac{1 - \sqrt{17}}{2}, \frac{1 + \sqrt{17}}{2}$ **35.** $\frac{3 - \sqrt{14}}{5}, \frac{3 + \sqrt{14}}{5}$
37. $0, \frac{5}{3}$ **39.** 13 meters
41. $\frac{-2 + \sqrt{46}}{2}$ or 2.391 meters and $\frac{2 + \sqrt{46}}{2}$ or 4.391 meters
43. Height $-2 + 2\sqrt{11}$ or 4.633 inches, base $2 + 2\sqrt{11}$ or 8.633 inches
45. $3 + \sqrt{2}$ or 4.414 and $3 - \sqrt{2}$ or 1.586
47. New printer $7 + \sqrt{65}$ or 15.062 hours, old printer $9 + \sqrt{65}$ or 17.062 hours
49. $7 - 3i$ **51.** $-3 + 7i$ **53.** $15 - 25i$ **55.** $-55 + 48i$
57. $-1 - i\sqrt{2}$ **59.** $\frac{3}{37} + \frac{19}{37}i$ **61.** $\frac{19}{17} + \frac{9}{17}i$ **63.** $-11i, 11i$
65. $8 - i, 8 + i$ **67.** $\frac{3 - 3i\sqrt{7}}{4}, \frac{3 + 3i\sqrt{7}}{4}$

69. Vertex (3, −9), intercepts (0, 0), (6, 0)

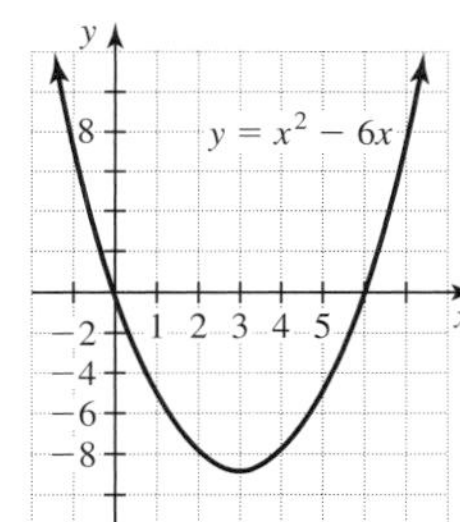

71. Vertex (2, −16), intercepts (0, −12), (−2, 0), and (6, 0)

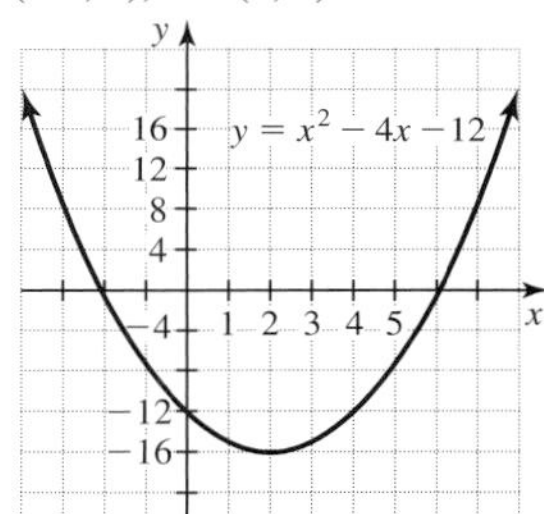

73. Vertex (2, 8), intercepts (0, 0), (4, 0)

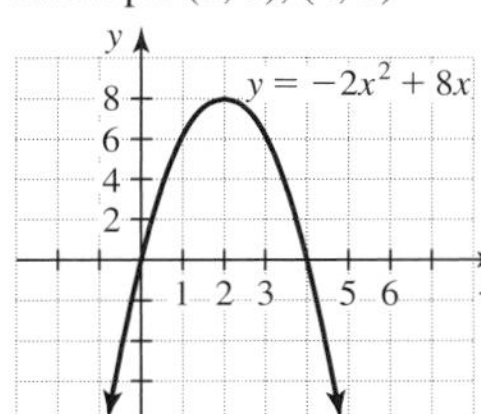

75. Vertex (1, 4), intercepts (0, 3), (−1, 0), (3, 0)

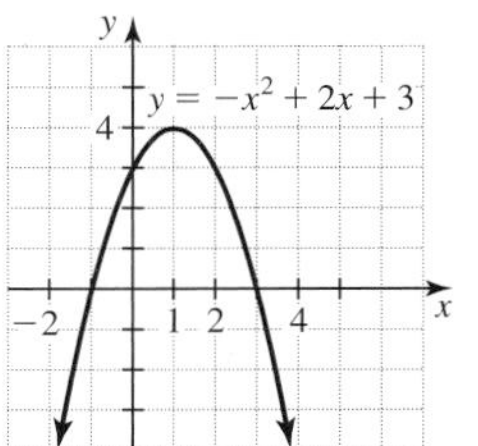

77. $20.40, 400 **79.** Yes **81.** No **83.** Yes **85.** No
87. {1, 2, 3}, {0, 2} **89.** Domain R, range $\{y \mid y \geq -3\}$ or $[-3, \infty)$
91. Domain R, range $\{y \mid y \leq 4.125\}$ or $(-\infty, 4.125]$ **93.** 5/4
95. −3 **97.** 6 **99.** 5 **101.** −1/2 **103.** −4 **105.** $\sqrt{2}$
107. 99 **109.** 17 **111.** $3x^3 - x^2 - 10x$ **113.** 20 **115.** $F = f \circ g$
117. $H = g \circ h$ **119.** $I = g \circ g$

Chapter 9 Test

1. 0, one **2.** −31, none **3.** 17, two **4.** $-1, \frac{3}{5}$

5. $\frac{2-\sqrt{10}}{2}, \frac{2+\sqrt{10}}{2}$ **6.** −7, 3 **7.** $\frac{-3-\sqrt{29}}{2}, \frac{-3+\sqrt{29}}{2}$

8. −5, 4 **9.** 3, 25 **10.** $-\frac{1}{2}, 3$ **11.** $10 + 3i$ **12.** $-6 + 7i$

13. −36 **14.** $42 - 2i$ **15.** 68 **16.** $2 - 3i$ **17.** $-1 + i\sqrt{3}$

18. $-2 + i\sqrt{2}$ **19.** $\frac{3}{5} + \frac{4}{5}i$ **20.** $-3 - i\sqrt{3}, -3 + i\sqrt{3}$

21. $\frac{3}{5} - \frac{4}{5}i, \frac{3}{5} + \frac{4}{5}i$

22. Domain R, range $\{y \mid y \le 16\}$ or $(-\infty, 16]$

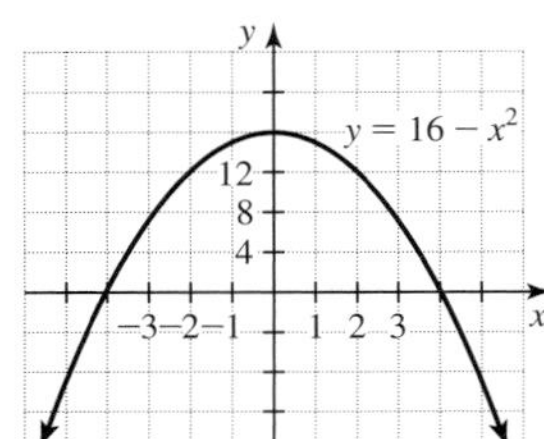

23. Domain R, range $\left\{y \mid y \ge -\frac{9}{4}\right\}$ or $\left[-\frac{9}{4}, \infty\right)$

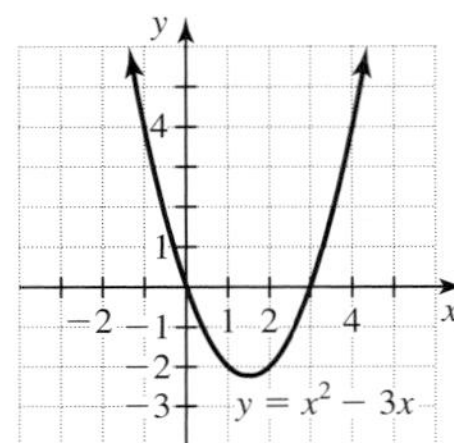

24. 11 **25.** 125 **26.** $x^2 - 2x + 9$ **27.** 15 **28.** $\frac{1}{8}$

29. $-2x^2 - 3$ **30.** $4x^2 - 20x + 29$ **31.** $H = f \circ g$ **32.** $W = g \circ f$

33. (1, 0), (5, 0) **34.** 36 feet **35.** $5 - \sqrt{2}$ and $5 + \sqrt{2}$

Making Connections A Review of Chapters 1–9

1. $\frac{1}{2}$ **2.** 1 **3.** $-\frac{\sqrt{2}}{2}, \frac{\sqrt{2}}{2}$ **4.** $\frac{1-2\sqrt{2}}{2}, \frac{1+2\sqrt{2}}{2}$

5. $\frac{2-\sqrt{6}}{2}, \frac{2+\sqrt{6}}{2}$ **6.** 0, 2 **7.** $-1, \frac{1}{2}$ **8.** 5

9. $1 - i\sqrt{14}, 1 + i\sqrt{14}$ **10.** −1, 2 **11.** $y = \frac{5}{4}x - 2$

12. $y = 3x - 9$ **13.** $y = \frac{2}{3}x + \frac{16}{3}$ **14.** $y = -\frac{b}{a}$

15. $y = \frac{-b \pm \sqrt{b^2 - 4ac}}{2a}$ **16.** $y = -\frac{2}{3}x + 7$ **17.** $y = -\frac{4}{3}x + \frac{2}{9}$

18. $y = \pm\sqrt{a^2 - x^2}$ **19.** $P = 4s$ **20.** $A = s^2$ **21.** $P = 2d\sqrt{2}$

22. $d = \sqrt{2A}$ **23.** (2, −3) **24.** (3, 10) **25.** $3y(y + 11)(y - 11)$

26. $2(y + 2)(y - 2)(y^2 + 4)$ **27.** $(y + 2)(w - 4)$

28. $(y - 3)(y^2 + 3y + 9)$ **29.** $-3(y - 5)(y + 9)$

30. $-2y(3y - 2)(4y + 3)$ **31.** $4a(a^2 - a + 3)$

32. $2ab^3(a^2 + b^2)$ **33.** $\frac{3}{7x}$ **34.** $\frac{2x^7}{3}$ **35.** $\frac{x+4}{x-7}$ **36.** $\frac{x+y}{x}$

37. $\frac{x+5}{x+1}$ **38.** $\frac{x+4}{x-1}$

39.

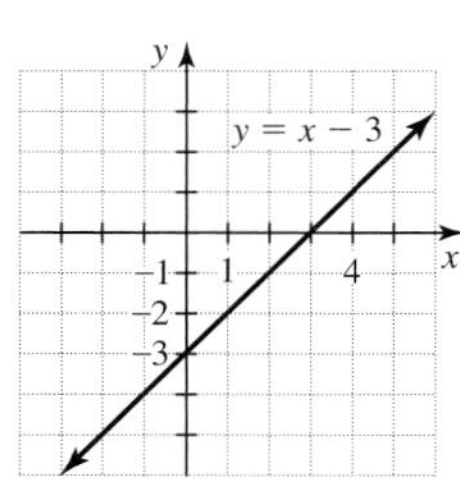

40.

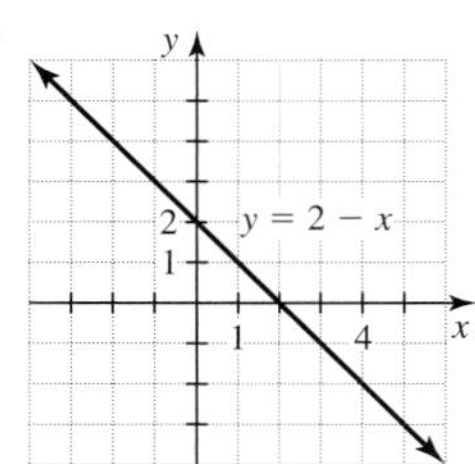

41.

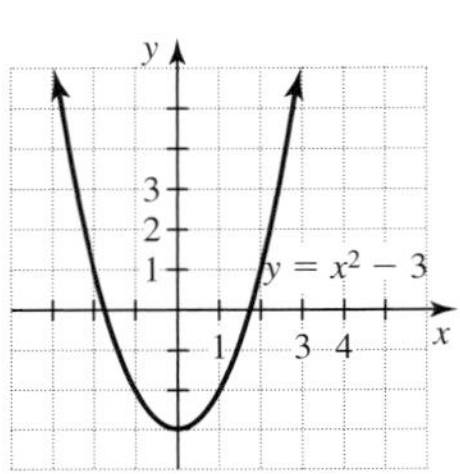

42.

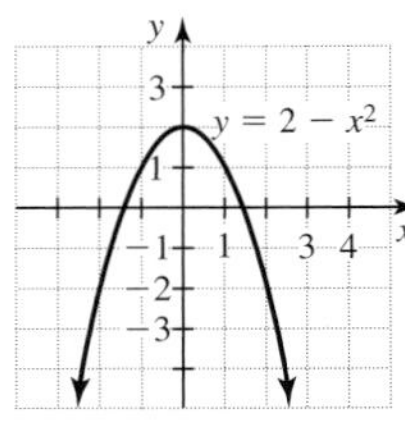

43.

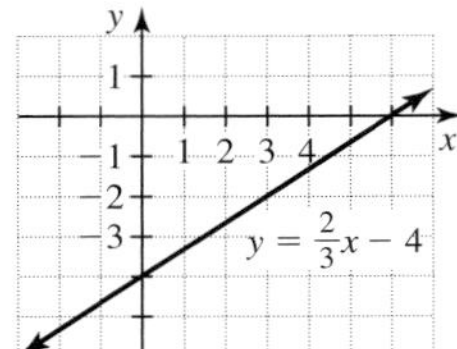

44.

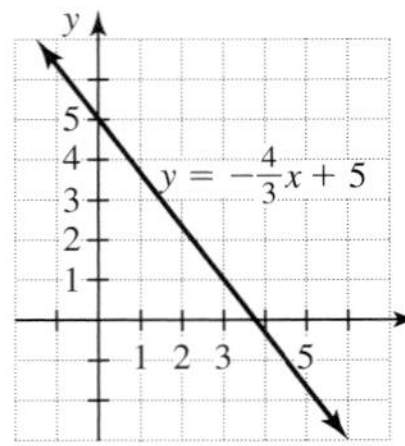

45. a) $s = -250p + 10{,}500$ **b)** Increased **c)** $R = -250p^2 + 10{,}500p$ **d)** \$21

Appendix A

Geometry Review Exercises

1. 12 in. **2.** 24 ft^2 **3.** 60° **4.** 6 ft **5.** 20 cm **6.** 144 cm^2
7. 24 ft^2 **8.** 13 ft **9.** 30 cm **10.** No **11.** 84 yd^2 **12.** 30 in.
13. 32 ft^2 **14.** 20 km **15.** 7 ft, 3 ft^2 **16.** 22 yd **17.** 50.3 ft^2
18. 37.7 ft **19.** 150.80 cm^3 **20.** 879.29 ft^2 **21.** 288 in.^{3}, 288 in.^{2}
22. 4 cm **23.** 100 mi^2, 40 mi **24.** 20 km **25.** 42.25 cm^2
26. 33.510 ft^3, 50.265 ft^2 **27.** 75.4 in.^{3}, 100.5 in.^{2} **28.** 56°
29. 5 cm **30.** 15 in. and 20 in. **31.** 149° **32.** 12 km
33. 10 yd

Appendix B

Sets

1. A set is a collection of objects.
2. A finite set has a fixed number of elements and an infinite set does not.
3. A Venn diagram is used to illustrate relationships between sets.
4. The intersection of two sets consists of elements that are in both sets, whereas the union of two sets consists of elements that are in one, in the other, or in both sets.
5. Every member of set A is also a member of set B.
6. The empty set is a subset of every set.
7. False **8.** False **9.** True **10.** False **11.** True **12.** False
13. False **14.** True **15.** False **16.** False **17.** False
18. False **19.** $\varnothing$ **20.** {1, 2, 3, 4, 5, 6, 7, 8, 9} **21.** {1, 3, 5}
22. {1, 2, 3, 4, 5, 7, 9} **23.** {1, 2, 3, 4, 5, 6, 8} **24.** {2, 4} **25.** A
26. B **27.** $\varnothing$ **28.** $\varnothing$ **29.** A **30.** N **31.** = **32.** $\ne$
33. $\cup$ **34.** $\cap$ **35.** $\cap$ **36.** $\cup$ **37.** $\notin$ **38.** $\in$ **39.** $\in$
40. $\in$ **41.** True **42.** True **43.** True **44.** False **45.** True
46. True **47.** True **48.** True **49.** False **50.** False
51. True **52.** True **53.** {2, 3, 4, 5, 6, 7, 8} **54.** $\varnothing$ **55.** {3, 5}
56. {1, 2, 3, 4, 5, 7} **57.** {1, 2, 3, 4, 5, 6, 8} **58.** {2, 4}
59. {2, 3, 4, 5} **60.** {2, 4} **61.** {2, 3, 4, 5, 7} **62.** {2, 3, 4, 5, 7}
63. {2, 3, 4, 5} **64.** {2, 4} **65.** {2, 3, 4, 5, 7} **66.** {2, 3, 4, 5, 7}
67. $\subseteq$ **68.** = **69.** $\in$ **70.** $\subseteq$ **71.** $\cap$ **72.** $\subseteq$ **73.** $\subseteq$
74. $\cap$ **75.** $\cap$ **76.** $\cup$ **77.** $\cup$ **78.** $\cap$ **79.** {2, 4, 6, . . . , 18}
80. {7, 8, 9, . . .} **81.** {13, 15, 17, . . .} **82.** {1, 3, 5, . . . , 13}

83. {6, 8, 10, . . . , 78} **84.** {13, 15, 17, . . . , 55}
85. $\{x \mid x$ is a natural number between 2 and 7}
86. $\{x \mid x$ is an odd natural number less than 8}
87. $\{x \mid x$ is an odd natural number greater than 4}
88. $\{x \mid x$ is a natural number greater than 3}
89. $\{x \mid x$ is an even natural number between 5 and 83}
90. $\{x \mid x$ is an odd natural number between 8 and 52}
91. False **92.** False **93.** False **94.** False
95. True **96.** True **97.** True **98.** False **99.** True
100. True

Appendix C

Final Exam Review

1. $\frac{7}{12}$ **2.** $\frac{13}{12}$ **3.** $\frac{2}{9}$ **4.** -43 **5.** -11 **6.** 8
7. Distributive property **8.** Commutative property of multiplication
9. Associative property of addition **10.** Additive identity
11. $13x - 3$ **12.** 9 **13.** $15x^2$ **14.** $-x - 4$ **15.** $\left\{\frac{5}{11}\right\}$
16. $\{-2\}$ **17.** No solution, $\varnothing$ **18.** All real numbers
19. $y = \frac{5}{3}x - 3$ **20.** $y = -\frac{b}{a}$ **21.** $y = \frac{t - a}{b}$ **22.** $y = \frac{3}{4}a$
23. 33, 34, 35 **24.** 23 in. **25.** 220 ft **26.** 100 pounds
27. $(-\infty, 5]$ **28.** $(-\infty, -3)$ **29.** $(4, 8]$ **30.** $(0, 1)$
31. $(0, -2)$, $(3, 0)$ **32.** $(0, -30)$, $(50, 0)$

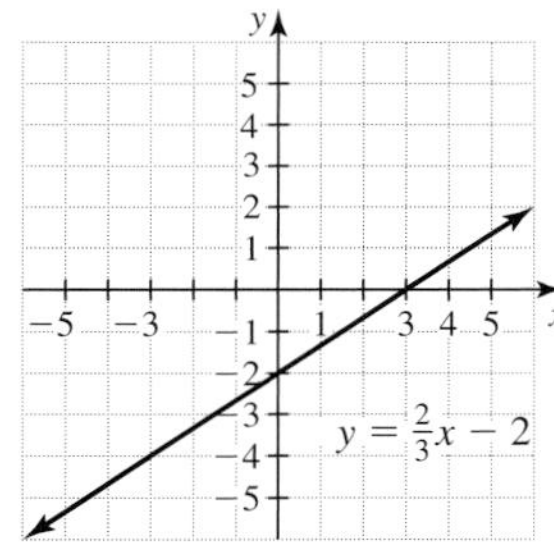

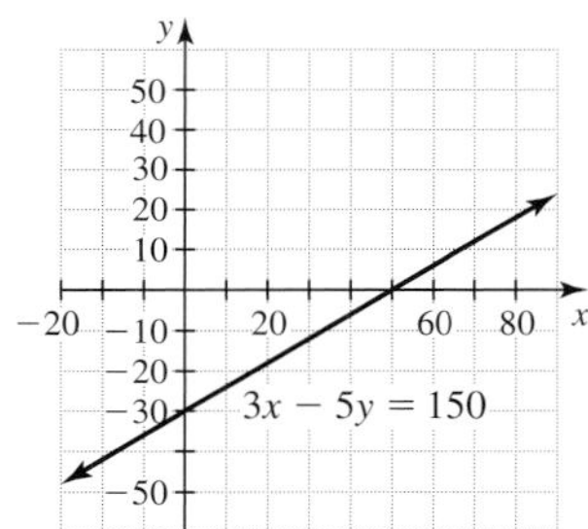

33. (0, 2) **34.** (2, 0)

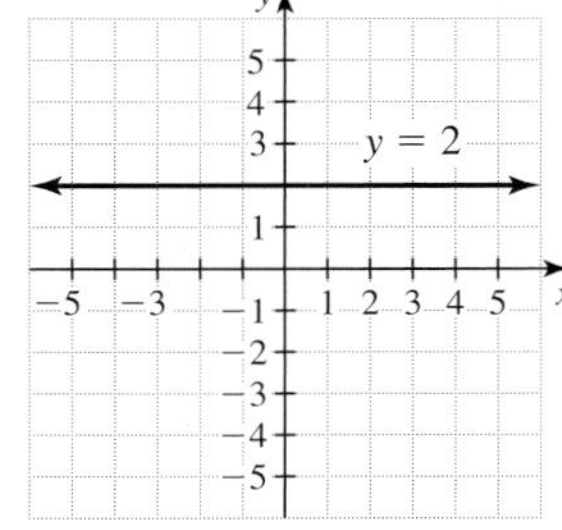

35. 2 **36.** $\frac{1}{2}$ **37.** $-\frac{2}{3}$ **38.** $\frac{1}{3}$ **39.** $y = 4x + 3$ **40.** $y = -2x$
41. $x = 3$ **42.** $y = -2x + 8$ **43.** (1, 3) **44.** (1, 1) **45.** (1, −2)
46. (2, 5) **47.** (−4, 6) **48.** (−2, −3) **49.** (1, 6)
50. (−2, −1/3) **51.** (1/2, −4) **52.** Inconsistent
53. Dependent **54.** Independent
55. Bob 18 hours and Carl 54 hours **56.** \$4.25

57.

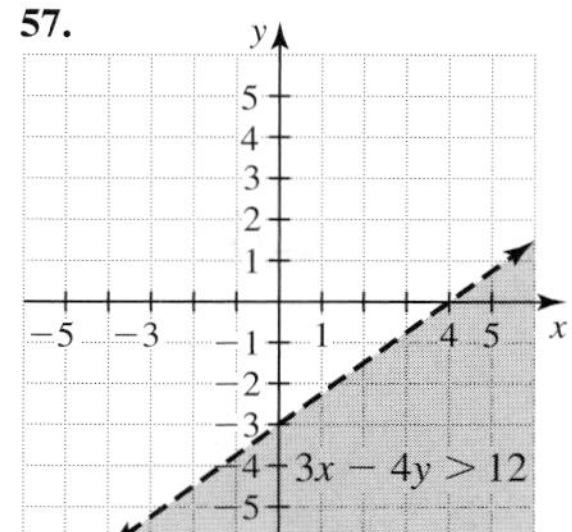

58.

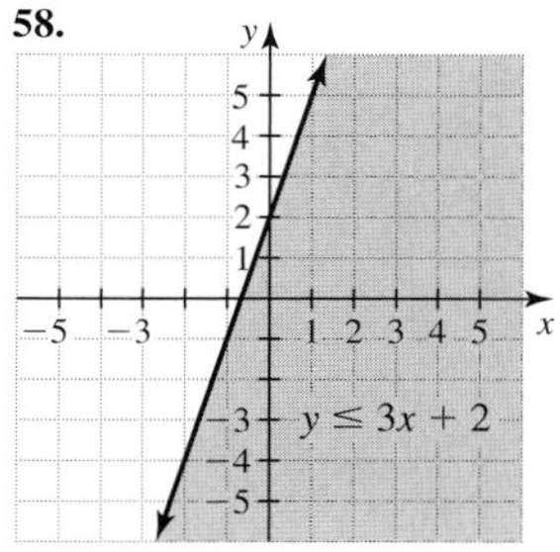

59.

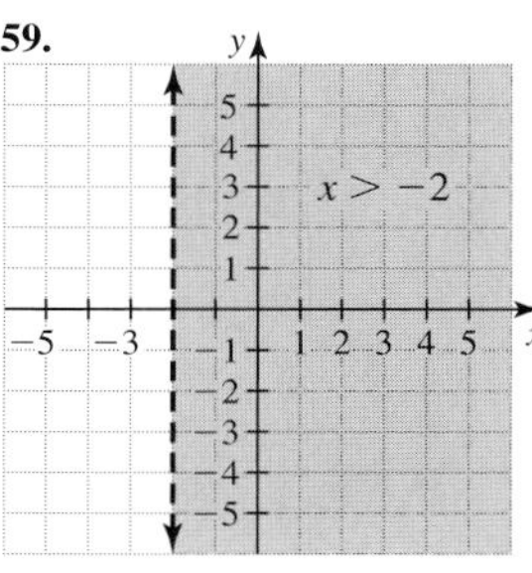

60.

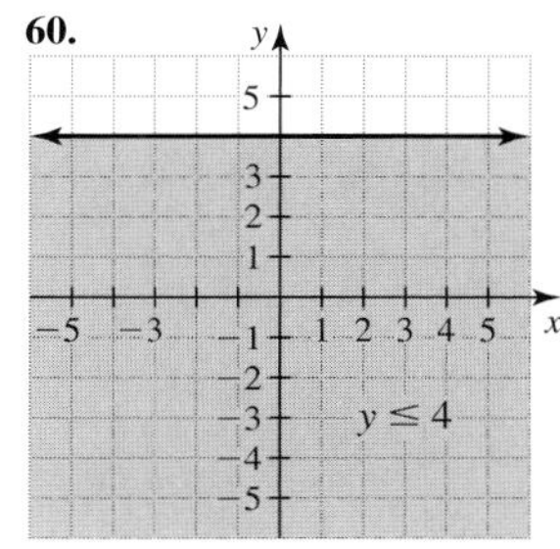

61. $-2x^2 - 12x + 6$ **62.** $6x^4 + 9x^2$ **63.** $x^2 - 2x - 63$
64. $x^3 + 8$ **65.** $16w^4 - 24w^2 + 9$ **66.** $-4m^5$ **67.** $-3y^2 - 2y + 1$
68. $x^2 + x + 2$ **69.** $-32x^7$ **70.** $375x^7$ **71.** $\frac{3x^5}{y}$ **72.** $8a^{15}$
73. 2.4×10^8 **74.** 1.8×10^{10} **75.** 1.6×10^{-11} **76.** 1×10^{-12}
77. $6xy^3(4x + 3y^2)$ **78.** $(x + a)(x + 2)$ **79.** $(2m - 7)(2m + 7)$
80. $(x - 9)(x + 6)$ **81.** $(2t - 5)(3t + 2)$ **82.** $(2w - 9)^2$
83. $2a(a - 9)(a + 6)$ **84.** $(w^2 + 4)(w + 2)(w - 2)$ **85.** $\{0, 1\}$
86. $\{-2, 0, 2\}$ **87.** $\{-3, 2\}$ **88.** $\{-6, 5\}$ **89.** 3 and 7
90. Length 24 in., width 10 in. **91.** $y = \frac{3}{5}x$ **92.** $y = \frac{2a}{w - c}$
93. $y = -3x - 12$ **94.** $y = \frac{6t}{2 - t}$ **95.** $\frac{19}{10}$ **96.** $\frac{3}{2x}$ **97.** $\frac{7}{a - 7}$
98. $\frac{2x + 8}{(x - 1)(x + 1)^2}$ **99.** $\frac{2}{x - 3}$ **100.** $\frac{1}{2}$ **101.** $\frac{-9}{2(9 + a)}$
102. $\frac{5x^2y^9}{32}$ **103.** 3 **104.** $\frac{x - 6}{-4x + 21}$ **105.** $\left\{\frac{15}{2}\right\}$ **106.** $\{11\}$
107. $\left\{\frac{8}{5}, 3\right\}$ **108.** $\{2, -1\}$ **109.** $2\sqrt{2}$ **110.** 15 **111.** 2
112. $\frac{\sqrt{6}}{4}$ **113.** 3 **114.** $4\sqrt{2}$ **115.** $4 + 2\sqrt{3}$ **116.** 1 **117.** $\sqrt{10}$
118. $2\sqrt{3}$ **119.** $1 + \sqrt{2}$ **120.** $4 - \sqrt{6}$ **121.** $-11 + 11\sqrt{5}$
122. $\frac{3\sqrt{10}}{5}$ **123.** $\frac{11 + 7\sqrt{5}}{4}$ **124.** x^3 **125.** x^2 **126.** $x\sqrt{x}$
127. $3y^5\sqrt{2}$ **128.** $5y^6$ **129.** $2t^6\sqrt{10t}$ **130.** $\frac{\sqrt{6xy}}{2y}$ **131.** $\{3\}$
132. $\{4 \pm 2\sqrt{3}\}$ **133.** $\left\{\frac{1}{4}\right\}$ **134.** $\{-1 \pm \sqrt{6}\}$ **135.** $\left\{\frac{1}{2}, \frac{1}{3}\right\}$
136. $\left\{\frac{1}{3}\right\}$ **137.** $\{-2 \pm \sqrt{5}\}$ **138.** $\left\{\frac{-3 \pm \sqrt{13}}{2}\right\}$ **139.** $\left\{\frac{2 \pm \sqrt{10}}{2}\right\}$

140.

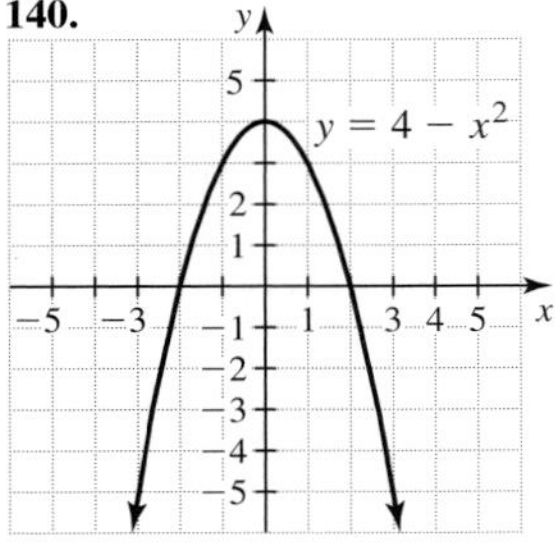

141.

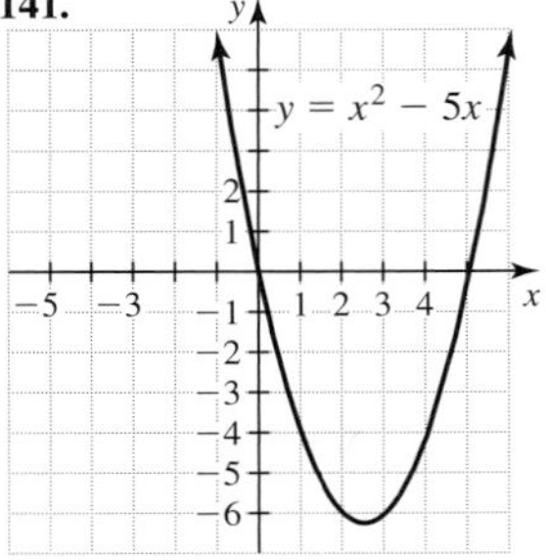

142.

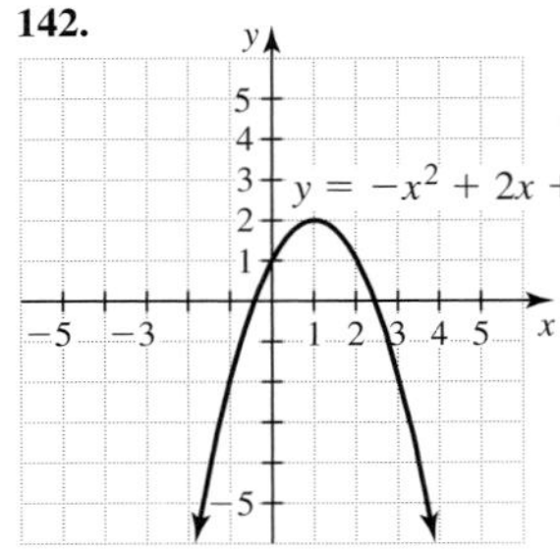

143. (2, 0), (4, 0), (0, 8), (3, −1)

144. 1 **145.** $-\frac{1}{6}$ **146.** 4 feet

147. 0 **148.** 5 **149.** −1

150. 0 **151.** 16 **152.** 1

153. Undefined **154.** 10

Index

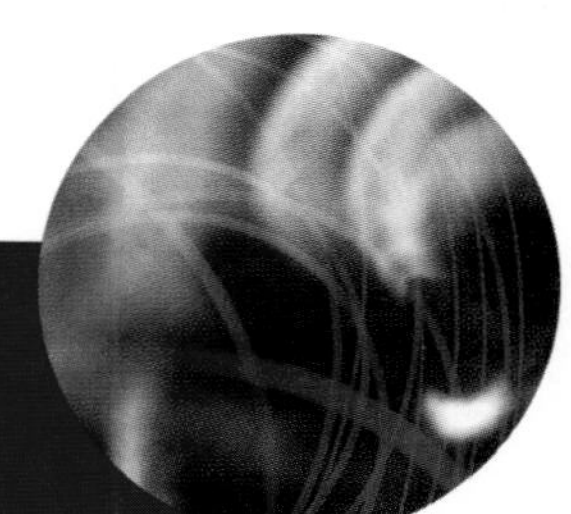

D

E

F

G

H

I

J

L

M

Q

R

S

T

U

V

W

X

Y

Z